Law and Religion in the Early Modern Period
Recht und Religion in der Frühen Neuzeit

Law and Religion in the Early Modern Period
Recht und Religion in der Frühen Neuzeit

VOL. 1

Paolo Astorri

Lutheran Theology and Contract Law in Early Modern Germany

(ca. 1520-1720)

Ferdinand Schöningh

The author: Paolo Astorri is currently Research Associate at the KU Leuven Faculty of Law

Cover illustration:
Lucas Cranach the Elder, *Christus treibt die Wucherer aus dem Tempel*, in *Passional Christi und Antichristi*, Wittenberg, 1521, 12 Bildpaar.

Bibliografische Information der Deutschen Nationalbibliothek

Die Deutsche Nationalbibliothek verzeichnet diese Publikation in der Deutschen Nationalbibliografie; detaillierte bibliografische Daten sind im Internet über http://dnb.d-nb.de abrufbar.

Internet: www.schoeningh.de

Einbandgestaltung: Nora Krull, Bielefeld
Herstellung: Brill Deutschland GmbH, Paderborn

ISBN 978-3-506-70150-3 (hardback)
ISBN 978-3-657-70150-6 (e-book)

To Patrizia and Mattia

Contents

PART II

A Biblical Framework for Contract Law: Basic Elements

PART III
Selected Issues from Particular Types of Contract

Acknowledgments

This book is the fruit of a doctoral dissertation defended at the Catholic University of Leuven (KU Leuven) in June 2018. Some years ago, I had the chance to read the two volumes of H.J. Berman's *Law and Revolution*. Berman wrote his books with a passion and charisma that I had never seen before. I was fascinated by his vision of integrative jurisprudence and by his vocation to restore the memory of the religious foundations of the Western legal tradition. Berman's words inspired my interest in the relationship between the Lutheran Reformation and contract law, which became the subject of this present work.

The realization of this work has been possible through the funding provided by the Faculty of Law at KU Leuven, by the *LOEWE-Schwerpunkt 'Außergerichtliche und gerichtliche Konfliktlösung'* at the Johann Wolfgang Goethe-University and at the Max Planck Institute for European Legal History (Frankfurt am Main) and by the Faculty of Law at the University of Roma Tre. I would like to express my gratitude to these institutions for their generous grants.

Because of this financial support I was able to access the collections of many inspiring libraries across Europe: the Bodleian Library at Oxford University, the library of the Max Planck Institute for European Legal History and the library of the J.W. Goethe University in Frankfurt am Main, the Staatsbibliothek in Berlin, the Biblioteca Nazionale and the Biblioteca Casanatense in Rome, the Forschungsbibliothek in Gotha, the Stadtbibliothek Stuttgart and the KU Leuven Library. I would like to thank all the librarians and curators for their precious help and collaboration. In particular, special thanks go to Mrs. Sigrid Amedick, director of the library of the Max Planck Institute in Frankfurt am Main, for the acquisition of several books necessary for this research.

On the long road of my doctorate many extraordinary people have supported me. In particular, my deepest gratitude goes to my supervisor and friend Professor Wim Decock. He has been the best supervisor I could have ever hoped for. His endless encouragement, constant guidance and true example of research have been essential for the completion of this project. I also owe an enormous debt to my co-supervisor, Professor Emanuele Conte. Since the beginning he believed in this project and directed me with his instruction. I have always admired his intellectual vigour and great willingness to help.

I am profoundly grateful to Professor Laurent Waelkens who always supported me (in every sense of the word) and to Professor John Witte Jr. who collaborated with this project with great enthusiasm. Their presence has been a precious gift and a profound source of motivation for improving my work.

I also would like to thank Professor Alain Wijffels, who provided me with his wise counsels and criticisms. In addition to these professors, I am also indebted to several excellent scholars who on different occasions gave me important advice. In particular, I would like to thank Professors Peter Collin, Thomas Duve, Paolo Prodi, Mathias Schmoeckel, Michael Stolleis and Christoph Strohm.

My warmest thanks go to all my colleagues at the research unit for Roman law and legal history at the KU Leuven who in various ways have enriched my life. These include Professors Randall Lesaffer and Stephan Dusil, Doctors Paolo Angelini, Dante Fedele and Inge van Hulle, Wouter Druwé, Viktorija Jakjimovska, Sebastian Krafzik, Joost Possemiers, Katrin Vanheule, Philippine Van den Brande, Cato van Paddenburgh, Gebreyesus Yimer and Jo Alaerts.

I would also like to express my gratitude to all the members of the Max Planck Institute for European Legal History and the research unit for legal history at Roma Tre University where I had the opportunity to spend very pleasant moments. In particular, I wish to thank Professor Sara Menzinger, and Doctors Monica Chiantini, Silvia di Paolo, Stefania Gialdroni and Flavia Mancini, David Harbecke and Oscar Hernandez.

I owe very special thanks to Carrie Schumacher for the proofreading of the English text, to Professor Luk Draye for the help with the translations of the Old German texts, and to Doctor Marieke Dhont for her assistance with the Hebrew terms.

I also must thank my family and friends. I have shared with them joyful and difficult moments, and they never left me without support. This thesis is dedicated to my wife Patrizia and my son Mattia who patiently endured too many days and nights of work. My last and most precious words are for Mary, mother of Jesus Christ and to my friend Jesus Christ, who made the impossible possible. From the depths of my heart, thank you.

Paolo Astorri
Leuven, 27.12.2018

Introduction

1 A Lutheran Doctrine of Contract?

In his *Commentaria moralia in evangelicam historiam* (1644), the Jesuit theologian Diego de Baeza (1582-1647) noticed:

> *In England, the Netherlands and Germany, the Lutherans are very rich merchants, but it is impossible to find anyone who investigates and discusses about the righteousness of contracts and restitution: neither a master, nor a plebeian. I heard from our wise father acting in Germany that no Lutheran man has ever asked about the righteousness of any actions. Among that plague* (i.e. the Lutheran Church) *there is neither a master who cares to teach the doctrine of morality, nor anyone who is engaged in preventing illegal actions.*[1]

The Lutheran merchants were very rich, but according to de Baeza no moral and juridical regulation of contracts existed within the Lutheran confession. This provoking claim did not remain without effect. Some decades later, the Lutheran professor of theology in Strasbourg, Johann Joachim Zentgrav (1643-1707), replied pungently to De Baeza. In his *Summa juris divini* (1699), he complained: "*how shameless is to pretend that among the Lutherans it cannot be found a master who cares about moral doctrine?*".[2] To Zentgrav, the Jesuit critic either was wrongly informed on the Lutherans or he entirely ignored the writings of Martin Luther (1483-1546), Philip Melanchthon (1497-1560), Martin Chemnitz (1522-1586), David Chytraeus (1530-1600), Friedrich Balduin (1574-1627), Caspar Rasmussen Brochmand (1585-1652) and others, which were collected by Felix Bidenbach (1564-1612) and Georg Dedekenn (1564-1628).[3] In

1 D. De Baeza, *Commentaria moralia in evangelicam historiam*, vol. 4, Lugduni, 1631, 865: "*In Anglia et Hollandia et Germania Lutherani sunt mercatores ditissimi, sed qui quaerat et disputet de contractibus licitis et restitutione facienda nec ullus invenitur, nec magister, nec plebeius. Audivi a Sapientissimo patre nostro in Germania agente, nullum umquam Lutheratum hominem quaesivisse de licito alicuius actionis. Nullus est apud has pestes magister, qui de moralibus curet doctrinam, nec qui de cavendis illicitis sit sollecitus*".

2 J.J. Zentgrav, *Summa juris divini, sive isagogica institutio doctrinae de iustitia et iure* [...], Argentorati, 1699, praefatio: "*Qua fronte dicitur NULLUM inveniri magistrum qui de moralibus curet doctrina?*" The passage is also quoted by J.F. Buddeus, *Isagoge historico-theologica ad theologiam universam*, v. 1, Lipsiae, 1730, 638.

3 J.J. Zentgrav, *Summa juris divini*, praefatio: "Verum vel ex his patet, quam male iniquus hic censor de Lutheranis informatus fuerit, qui nisi ignorasset, quid *Lutherus* ipse, *Melanchthon, Chemnitius, Chytraeus, Balduinus, Brochmannus* et alii a *Bidembachio et Dedekenno collecti scripserint* ...".

 | DOI:10.30965/9783657701506_002

other words, a Lutheran doctrine of contract law existed. It was expounded in the works of several theologians and subsequently gathered by others in systematic collections.[4] Therefore, either the Jesuit ignored these works or he was incorrectly informed.

The polemic between De Baeza and Zentgrav brings out the contribution of several Lutheran theologians who assiduously worked in the sphere of moral theology and especially of contract law. If one removes the ideological layer that covers the truth, the Lutheran analysis of contract law shines. Up to now, however, legal history has largely forgotten its existence. The works of the Protestant reformers have been copiously investigated by historians of economics and Church historians. Although the famous thesis of Max Weber was de facto refuted,[5] it nonetheless stimulated many studies on the impact of the Reformation on the theory of just price, interest and usury. In a nutshell these works have concluded that a new a theory of interest was built, reflecting the fundamental theological assumptions of the Protestant Reformers. This theory was originated principally by John Calvin (1509-1564) and Charles Du Moulin (1500-1566), and despite the theoretical differences with the scholastic theory, in practice it reached the same effects.[6]

In recent years, legal historians' attention has also been piqued about the contribution of the main reformers to ideas of interest and usury. Following

4 On these genres of books see I/2.

5 J.T. Gilchrist, *The Church and Economic Activity in the Middle Ages*, New York, Macmillan, 1969, 122-39; J.F. Mc Govern, *The Rise of New Economic Attitudes in Canon and Civil Law, A.D. 1200-1500*, in *The Jurist*, 32 (1972), 44-55. For a survey of the uncountable discussions, see W.H. Swatos, Jr., L. Kaelber, *The Protestant Ethic Turns 100: Essays on The Centenary of The Weber Thesis*, (first ed. 2005), Abingdon, Oxon, Routledge, 2016.

6 R.H. Tawney, *Religion and the Rise of Capitalism: A Historical Study*, first ed. London, Murray, 1933, 84-103; H.G. Assel, *Das kanonische Zinsverbot und der "Geist" des Frühkapitalismus in der Wirtschaftsethik bei Eck und Luther*, diss., Erlagen, 1948; E. Ramp, *Das Zinsproblem. Eine historische Untersuchung*, Zürich, Zwingli Verlag, 1949, 21-59; B.J. Nelson, *The Idea of Usury. From Tribal Brotherhood to Universal Otherhood*, Princeton, Princeton University Press, 1949; H. Barge, *Luther und der Frühkapitalismus*, Gütersloh, C. Bertelsmann Verlag, 1951; H. Kahlert, *Luther und Melanchthons Stellung zu den Wirtschaftsfragen ihrer Zeit*, in *Luther: Mitteilungen der Luthergesellschaft*, H. 3, 1956, 122-33; J.T. Noonan, Jr., *The Scholastic Analysis of Usury*, Cambridge Mass., Harvard University Press, 1957; T.F. Divine, S.J., *Interest. An Historical & Analytical Study in Economics & Modern Ethics*, Milwaukee, The Marquette University Press, 1959; H.J. Prien, *Luthers Wirtschaftsethik*, Göttingen, Vandenhoeck & Ruprecht, 1992; E. Kerridge, *Usury, Interest, and the Reformation*, Aldershot, Ashgate, 2002; D.W. Jones, *Reforming the Morality of Usury: A Study of Differences that Separated the Protestant Reformers*, Lanham, University Press of America, 2004; A. del Vigo Gutiérrez, *Economía y ética en el siglo XVI. Estudio comparativo entre los Padres de la Reforma y la Teología española*, Madrid, Biblioteca de autores cristianos, 2006; O. Langholm, *Martin Luther's Doctrine on Trade and Price in Its Literary Context*, in *History of Political Economy*, 41:1 (2009), 89-107.

the historians of economics, Berman has argued that the doctrines on the just price, interest and usury propelled by Lutheran philosophers and jurists were substantially the same of the Roman Catholic and Calvinist theologians.[7] Schmoeckel has examined and confronted the economic teachings of Luther, Calvin and Martín de Azpilcueta (1491-1586).[8] Among many other aspects, he has observed the influence of the Reformation theology on Luther's and Calvin's visions of legal and economic life.[9]

These studies have highlighted the interest theory of the founders of the Reformation, but their disciples, the theologians who supported them, also dealt with this topic. Only a few studies have investigated this point: Elert's, Nelson's, Prodi's and Savelli's studies are among those that have described the teachings on usury and interest offered not only by Luther, Melanchthon and Calvin, but also by Martin Bucer (1491-1551), Chemnitz, Balduin and others.[10] In particular, Elert has illustrated the engagement of the Lutheran moralists with financial issues.[11] Nelson has opined that the Lutherans followed the English writers (who in turn relied on the Calvinists) in adopting the new approaches towards usury and interest.[12] Prodi has looked at the theories on just price and the seventh commandment.[13] To him the Reformation thought stressed the responsibility of the single Christians who had to follow certain moral principles. Yet these principles were not developed in a concise, standardized system of norms. The political authority remained therefore essential for the regulation of the market.[14] Finally, Savelli has remarked upon the link between Du Moulin and the works of Melanchthon and Johann Aepinus (1499-1553).[15]

7 H.J. Berman, *Law and Revolution II. The Impact of the Protestant Reformations on the Western Legal Tradition*, Cambridge Mass., London, Harvard University Press, 2003, 161.

8 M. Schmoeckel, *Das Recht des Reformation. Die epistemologische Revolution der Wissenschaft und die Spaltung der Rechtsordnung in der Frühen Neuzeit*, Tübingen, Mohr Siebeck, 2014, 249-55; M. Schmoeckel, *Das kanonische Zinsverbot und die Konfessionalisierung*, in W. Decock, J.J. Ballor, M. Germann, L. Waelkens (eds.), *Law and Religion, The Legal Teachings of the Protestant and Catholic Reformations*, Göttingen, Vandenhoeck & Ruprecht, 2014, 186-212.

9 M. Schmoeckel, *Das Recht*, 249-52; M. Schmoeckel, *Das kanonische Zinsverbot*, 206-7.

10 W. Elert, *Morphologie des Luthertums*, vol. II, München, C.H. Bech, 1953, 466-92.

11 W. Elert, *Morphologie des Luthertums*, 486-92.

12 B.J. Nelson, *The Idea of Usury*, 89.

13 P. Prodi, *Settimo non rubare. Furto e mercato nella storia dell'Occidente*, Bologna, Il Mulino, 2009, 210-19.

14 P. Prodi, *Settimo non rubare*, 216.

15 R. Savelli, *Diritto romano e teologia riformata: Du Moulin di fronte al problema dell'interesse del denaro*, in *Materiali per una storia della cultura giuridica*, XXIII (1993), 291-324. This article was also published in Spanish: R. Savelli, *Derecho romano y teología reformada,*

Contract law was not only about the analysis of credit instruments, just price, interest and usury. Starting from the principle that agreements must be kept (*pacta sunt servanda*), a general theory of contract law was forged by canon lawyers and moral theologians of the early modern period. The excellent book by Wim Decock[16] has shown that the work of these authors was largely influential and entailed a profound transformation of the *ius commune*. Before him, a number of erudite scholars (like James Gordley) have also explored the relation between Roman Catholic theology and contract law.[17] At the same time, other works have emphasized the contribution of the natural lawyers for the development of the modern contract doctrine.[18]

Such attention has not been given to Lutheran moral theology. The theme of law and religion has increasingly gained importance.[19] Studies made by Witte Jr., Berman, von Friedeburg, Mäkinen, Strohm, Schmoeckel and Heckel have praised the contribution of the Reformation for the development of the legal science.[20] Nonetheless, little concern has been shown for the Lutheran

---

Du Moulin frente al problema del interés del dinero, in C. Petit (ed.), *Del 'Ius mercatorum' al derecho mercantil*, Madrid, Marcial Pons, 1997, 257-90.

16 W. Decock, *Theologians and Contract Law: The Moral Transformation of the Ius Commune*, Leiden, Boston, Martinus Nijhoff, 2013.

17 See bibliography in W. Decock, *Theologians and Contract Law*, 2.

18 See for instance M. Diesselhorst, *Die Lehre des Hugo Grotius vom Versprechen*, Köln, Graz, 1962; P. Cappellini, *Sulla formazione del moderno concetto di 'dottrina generale del diritto'*, (a proposito di M. Lipp, Die Bedeutung des Naturrechts für die Ausbildung der allgemeinen Lehren des Deutschen Privatrechts, Schriften zur Rechtstheorie, Heft. 88, Berlin, 1980), in *Quaderni fiorentini*, 10 (1981), 323-54; K.P. Nanz, *Die Entstehung des allgemeinen Vertragbegriffs im 16 bis 18 Jahrundert*, München, Schweitzer, 1985, 85-113; J. Gordley, *The Philosophical Origins of Modern Contract Doctrine*, Oxford, Oxford University Press, 1991; A. Somma, *Autonomia privata e struttura del consenso contrattuale*, Milano, Giuffrè, 2000. A gaze on the Protestant Althusius is in E. Reibstein, *Johannes Althusius als Fortsetzer der Schule von Salamanca. Untersuchungen zur Ideengeschichte des Rechtsstaates und zur altprotestantischen Naturrechtslehre*, Karlsruhe, Müller, 1955.

19 The classic example is the work of H.J. Berman, *Law and Revolution. The Formation of the Western Legal Tradition*, Cambridge Mass., London, Harvard University Press, 1983. See also K.W. Nörr, *Recht und Religion: über drei Schnittstellen im Recht der mittelalterlichen Kirche*, in *Zeitschrift der Savigny-Stiftung für Rechtsgeschichte*, Kan. Ab., vol. 79, 1, 1993, 1-15. On Martin Luther and the law see the pioneristic works of H.W. Beyer, *Luther und das Recht*, first ed. 1935, reprint, Nikosia, Verone, 2017; J. Heckel, *Lex charitatis. Eine juristische Untersuchung über das Recht in der Theologie Martin Luthers*, München, Bayerische Akademie der Wissenschaften, 1953.

20 J. Witte Jr., *Law and Protestantism: The Legal Teachings of the Lutheran Reformation*, Cambridge, Cambridge University Press, 2002; C. Strohm (ed.), *Martin Bucer und das Recht. Beiträge zum internationalen Symposium vom 1. bis 3 März 2001 in der Johannes a Lasco Bibliothek Emden*, Genève, Droz, 2002; H.J. Berman, *Law and Revolution II*, passim; V. Mäkinen (ed.), *Lutheran Reformation and the Law*, Leiden, Brill, 2006; C. Strohm,

theologians and the theory of contract law. Berman has noticed that Gordley did not consider the works of the Lutheran jurists on the theoretical elaboration of contract law.[21] Besides, he has sustained the need to study the connection between the jurisprudence of the reformers and their religious convictions.[22] Schmoeckel has recently pointed out the contribution of Melanchthon for the development of modern contract doctrine.[23]

On the whole, this quick roundup of information provided us with the idea to research the relationship between Lutheranism and contract law. The famous claim of the Italian Protestant jurist Alberico Gentili (1552-1608), *Silete theologi in munere alieno*,[24] resonated, among others, in the words of the Lutheran Johann Gerhard (1582-1637).[25] But it could not have been immediately effective, or at least its extent may have been reduced. Some traces hint at the existence of a Lutheran analysis of contract law, to which not only Luther and Melanchthon contributed, but also their supporters played a role. This point has not yet been investigated: a hole needs to be filled.

Calvinismus und Recht. Weltanschaulich-konfessionelle Aspekte im Werk reformierter Juristen in der Frühen Neuzeit, Tübingen, Mohr Siebeck, 2008; G. Essen, N. Jansen (eds.), *Dogmatisierungsprozesse in Recht und Religion*, Tübingen, Mohr Siebeck, 2011; N. Jansen, D. Kästle (eds.), *Kommentare in Recht und Religion*, Tübingen, Mohr Siebeck, 2014; M. Schmoeckel, *Das Recht*, passim; W. Decock, J.J. Ballor, M. Germann, L. Waelkens, (ed.), *Law and Religion*, passim; R. von Friedeburg, *Luther's Legacy: The Thirty Years' War and the Modern Notion of 'State' in the Empire, 1530s–1790s*, Cambridge, Cambridge University Press, 2015; C. Strohm, *Religion und Recht in der Frühen Neuzeit*, in *Zeitschrift für Rechtsgeschichte*, Kan. Abt. 102 (2016), 283-316; M. Schmoeckel, *Zur Bedeutung der Reformation*, in *Zeitschrift der Savigny-Stiftung für Rechtsgeschichte*, Kan. Abt. 102 (2016), 317-358; M. Heckel, *Martin Luthers Reformation und das Recht: Die Entwicklung der Theologie Luthers und ihre Auswirkung auf das Recht unter den Rahmenbedingungen der Reichsreform und der Territorialstaatsbildung im Kampf mit Rom und den »Schwärmern«*, Tübingen, Mohr Siebeck, 2016; C. Strohm (ed.), *Reformation und Recht. Ein Beitrag zur Kontroverse um die Kulturwirkungen der Reformation*, Tübingen, Mohr Siebeck, 2017. For a vaster perspective (not only including legal history, but also other disciplines) see M.W. McConnell, R.F. Cochran, Jr., A.C. Carmella (eds.), *Christian Perspectives on Legal Thought*, New Haven & London, Yale University Press, 2001.

21 H.J. Berman, *Law and Revolution II*, 401 fn. 2.

22 H.J. Berman, *Law and Revolution II*, 158.

23 M. Schmoeckel, *Melanchthons Konzeption der Verträge. Archäologie der Privatautonomie*, in *Zeitschrift der Savigny-Stiftung für Rechtsgeschichte*, Kan. Abt., vol. 104 (2018), 304-45.

24 Literature is abundant on this topic. See the recent work of G. Minnucci, Silete theologi in munere alieno. *Alberico Gentili tra diritto, teologia e religione*, Milano, Monduzzi, 2016.

25 E. Uhl, *Die Sozialethik Johann Gerhards*, München, Kaiser, 1932, 102 cit. in P. Prodi, *Settimo non rubare*, 216. Gerhard did not refer to Gentili, but stated that the preachers should not be allowed to express judgements over contracts, especially against the judgement of the public laws.

2 Research Hypothesis

The basic assumption at the origins of this book is that the Lutheran theologians (not only Luther and Melanchthon, but also their followers) developed a contract law doctrine. Luther's and Melanchthon's ideas circulated and should not only be analysed in an isolated way, but also through the spectrum of the people who read and interpreted them. Luther and Melanchthon drew fundamental premises that were cultivated and expanded by the theologians who supported them throughout the early modern era. The starting point for the theologians' involvement with contract law was the need to address current problems, like the necessity to counter the claims of the Anabaptists who refuted property and business, or the lawfulness of an imperial ordinance that allowed a particular financial operation suspected of violating the interest law. As the theologians strove to defend the lawfulness of property, business and contracts, they mapped out a set of general principles against commercial fraud and dictated norms to regulate the standard economic transactions. In addition, they attempted to resolve the problems of a consensualistic theory of contract law. They elaborated on the principle *pacta sunt servanda* and provided it with a solid body of rules for establishing the validity of the bond.

The contribution of the Lutheran theologians should not be viewed as though locked in a glass case, but as an analysis of a complex dynamics of relations. First of all, the reader should bear in mind the nexus between the Lutheran theologians and their Roman Catholic colleagues. Canon lawyers and scholastic theologians of the Middle Ages and the Early Modern Era were the indisputable protagonists of the *forum internum* or court of conscience. They realized a synthesis between Roman law and moral teachings that resulted in a sophisticated contract law doctrine. The Lutherans could not ignore the Roman Catholics' works. Despite the apparent hostility, they used canon law and scholastic moral teachings.[26] Thus, it would be a mistake to isolate

26 In addition to the works cited earlier on the relation between law and the Reformation, see R. Schäfer, *Die Geltung des kanonischen Recht in der evangelischen Kirche von Luther bis zum Gegenwart*, in *Zeitschrift der Savigny-Stiftung für Rechtsgeschichte*, Kan. Abt., vol. 36 (1915), 181-202; H. Liermann, *Das kanonische Recht als Gegenstand des gelehrten Unterrichts an den protestantischen Universitäten in den ersten Jahrunderten nach der Reformation*, in *Studia Gratiana*, vol. 3, Bologna 1955, 541-66 (547); U. Wolter, *Ius canonicum in iure civili*, Bohlau, Köln, 1975, 55-153; R. Helmholz (ed.), *Canon law in Protestant Lands*, Berlin, Duncker & Humblot, 1992; J. Witte Jr., *Canon law in Lutheran Germany: A Surprising Case of Legal Transplantation*, in M. Hoeflich (ed.), *Lex et Romanitas: Essays for Alan Watson*, Berkeley, 2000, 181-224. About the use of Gratian's *Decretum* see M. Reulos, *Le Décret de Gratien chez les humanistes, les gallicans et les réformés français du XVI siècle*, in *Studia Gratiana*, 2 (1954), 677-96; J. Heckel, *Das Decretum Gratiani und das evangelische*

Protestant moral theology as an independent phenomenon. Aspects of continuity and discontinuity can only be revealed by studying and confronting Roman Catholic and Lutheran theologians.[27]

A second aspect to ponder is the relation between the fathers of the Reformation, Luther and Melanchthon, and their followers. Were the Lutheran theologians always faithful to their masters?[28] As we are going to see, contrasts between religious confessions pertained less to certain moral-legal problems than to dogmatics. Opinions circulated between Catholics, Reformed, Lutherans and the natural lawyers. Contexts and problems changed over time, making it difficult to remain faithful to Luther's and Melanchthon's resolutions. The balance between these non-Lutheran sources and the fundamental authoritative statements of the Reformation is a sensitive point that needs to be addressed.

Finally, a crucial issue to tackle is the Lutheran theologians' relationship with the jurists. Was there any decisive interaction between *forum internum* and *forum externum*? On the one hand, this question aims to verify whether the religious convictions of the jurists were also influential in their writings. On the other hand, it wants to establish whether concepts, methods and solutions migrated from the theologians to the jurists and vice versa. The interplay between theological and juridical sources is not only a key to evaluate the impact of the Lutheran theology on contract law, but also to understand the importance of the legal science for moral theology.

Kirchenrecht, in *Studia Gratiana*, 3 (1955), 483-538; A. Pincherle, *Graziano e Lutero*, in *Studia Gratiana*, 3 (1955), 451-82; E. Schrage, *Luther und das Kirchenrecht*, in P. Maffei, G.M. Varanini (eds.), Honos alit artes *Studi per il settantesimo compleanno di Mario Ascheri. La formazione del diritto comune. Giuristi e diritti in Europa (secoli XII-XVIII)*, Firenze, Firenze University Press, 2014, 407-17; K. Pennington, *Protestant Ecclesiastical Law and the Ius Commune*, in *Rivista internazionale di diritto comune*, 26 (2015), 9-36; H. de Wall, *Von der Kanonistik zum evangelischen Kirchenrecht – Traditionen und Diskontinuitäten*, in *Zeitschrift der Savigny-Stiftung für Rechtgeschichte*, Kan. Ab., vol. 134 (2017), 262-76. On the use of canon law and scholastic moral teachings, see T. Rester, *Roman Canon Law in Protestant Reformed Theologians as Both Touchstone and Foil*, in W. Decock, J.J. Ballor, M. Germann, L. Waelkens (eds.), *Law and Religion*, 174-85; P. Astorri, *Il diritto canonico nella prima teologia pratica protestante: la formazione dei ministri ecclesiastici secondo Hyperius, Zepper e Voetius*, in *Glossae* 13 (2016), 5-29.

27 Concerning Protestant orthodoxy, this aspect has been noted by R.A. Muller, *Post-Reformation Reformed Dogmatics*, vol. I, Grand Rapids MI, Baker Academic, 2006, 27-46; regarding the study of the Holy Scripture, see R.A. Muller, *Post-Reformation Reformed Dogmatics*, vol. II, 24 and 30. This is also one of the main recommendations in W. Decock, C. Birr, *Recht und Moral in der Scholastik der frühen Neuzeit 1500-1700*, Berlin, Boston, De Gruyter, 2016, VII-VIII.

28 R.A. Muller, *Post-Reformation*, I, 44.

3 Selection of Sources

Before we can go on, a couple of notes on the limits of this research are necessary. The starting points for identifying the sources used were the histories of Lutheran moral theology.[29] These studies principally catalogued various types of ethical writings, such as collections of theological counsels, collections of cases of conscience, and manuals of moral theology. However, the first book of Lutheran casuistry was only published in 1628 and the first manual of moral theology in 1634. Casuistry and moral theology were just the peak of

29 G.T. Meier, *Introductio in universum theologiae moralis, cum dogmaticae, tum pragmaticae, studium, aua, quœ propria, quae aliena sunt theologiae morali, unde illa & in quantum possint debeantque accipi,* [...] *exhibetur*, Francofurti, Lipsiae, Helmstadii, 1671; M. Lippenius, *Bibliotheca realis theologica omnivm materivm, rerum et titulorum*, Tomus 2, Francofurti ad Moenum, 1685; J.M. Lang, *Dissertatio prooemialis de origine et progressv theologiae moralis systematicae*, in J.K. Dürr, *Compendium theologiae moralis*, Altdorfi Noricorum, 1698; J.F. Mayer, *Bibliotheca scriptorum theologiae moralis et conscientiariae*, in A. Strauch, *Theologia moralis*, Gryphiswaldiae, 1708; J.F. Buddeus, *Historia critica theologiae dogmaticae et moralis*, Francofurti ad Moenum, 1724; C.M. Pfaff, *Introductio in historiam theologiae literariam notis amplissimis: quae novum opus conficiunt, illustrata*, vol. I, Tubingae, 1724; J.F. Buddeus, *Isagoge historico-theologica ad theologiam universam*, Lipsiae, 1730; J.F. Reimmann, *Catalogus bibliothecae theologicae, systematico-criticus, in quo libri theologici in bibliotheca Reimanniana extantes* [...] *enumerantur: et quid in unoquoque sit peculiare vel vulgare, quae laudes et labes* [...] *at non intemperanter tamen* [...] *indicatur*, Hildesiae, 1731; G. Stolle, *Anleitung zur Historie der theologischen Gelahrheit*, Jena, 1739; J.G. Walch, *Bibliotheca theologica selecta litterariis adnotationibus instructa*, vol. 2, Jenae, 1758; C.T. Lilienthal, *Bibliotheca lilienthaliana sive apparatus librorum*, Regiomonti, 1782; J. von Horn, *Narratio pragmatica conversionum, quas theologia moralis seculo XVIII experta est apud lutheranos, reformatos, catholicos atque sectas christianas minores*, Goettinga, 1802; C.F. Stäudlin, *Geschichte der christlichen Moral seit dem Wiederaufleben der Wissenschaften*, Göttingen, 1808; W. Wette, M. de Leberecht, *Lehrbuch der christlichen Sittenlehre und der Geschichte derselben*, Berlin, 1833; A.F.L. Pelt, *Theologische Encyklopädie als System: im Zusammenhange mit der Geschichte der theologischen Wissenschaft und ihrer einzelnen Zweige entwickelt*, Hamburg, 1843, 513ff. and 553ff.; A. Wuttke, *Handbuch der christlichen Sittenlehre*, vol. 1, Berlin, 1861; L. Pelt, *Die christliche Ethik in der lutherischen Kirche vor Calixt*, in J. C. L. Gieseler, *Theologische Studien und Kritiken: Beitr. zur Theologie u. Religionswissenschaft* (ThStKr 21), Hamburg, 1848, 271-319; W. Gass, *Geschichte der christlichen Ethik*, vol. 2/1, Berlin, 1881; C. E. Luthardt, *Geschichte der christlichen Ethik, Zweite Hälfte: Geschichte der christlichen Ethik seit der Reformation*, Leipzig, 1893; O. Dittrich, *Geschichte der Ethik: Die Systeme der Moral vom Altertum bis zur Gegenwart, vol. 4, Von der Kirchenreformation bis zum Ausgang des Mittelalters: 1. Die Reformatoren und der lutherisch-kirchliche Protestantismus*, Leipzig, 1932; C. Frey, *Die Ethik des Protestantismus von der Reformation bis zur Gegenwart*, first ed. 1989, Gütersloh, Gütersloher Verlaghaus, 1994; H.D. Kittsteiner, *Die Entstehung des modernen Gewissen*, Frankfurt am Main, Leipzig, Insel Verlag, 1991; B.T.G. Mayes, *Counsel and Conscience. Lutheran Casuistry and Moral Reasoning after the Reformation*, Göttingen, Vandenhoeck & Ruprecht, 2011.

the process initiated previously in other literary genres. Before them, instructions for Christian morality were framed in the catechisms, sermons, theological treatises and biblical commentaries that rose at the beginning of the Reformation. The analysis of these works played also a considerable role in giving a full picture of the Lutheran theologians who tackled contract law issues.

The selected sources are printed texts written in sixteenth-seventeenth century Latin and German. The list is not exhaustive. Rather it aims to give an overview of the large variety of works that encompassed discussions on contract law. Generally, Church historians call the theologians who worked in the period after the Formula of Concord, 'Lutheran orthodoxy', with different ideological and temporal ramifications.[30] We do not ignore the fact that various factions existed within Lutheranism, but these seem to have little relevance to the development of contract law. Furthemore, we do not only consider the period after the Formula of Concord, but also theologians of the first generation, contemporaries of Luther. For these reasons, the simple adjective 'Lutheran' appeared to be sufficient to identify our theologians. The term 'Lutheran orthodoxy' will be used from time to time to mean the theologians after the Formula of Concord (1577) in general.

Another point that needs to be spotlighted is that not only Roman Catholic and Lutheran authors, but also Anglican, Puritan, Calvinist and more in general Reformed writers were engaged with casuistry and moral theology. They operated not only in Germany, but in France, England, the Netherlands, Denmark, Norway, Sweden and other countries. Including also these authors in this research would have resulted in an overwhelming enterprise, so we opted to concentrate only on the writings produced by German Lutheran authors. This is certainly a limitation of this research, as the relations between the Lutherans and the Reformed authors should be the subject of investigation. From time to time references to Reformed authors will appear, even though a complete examination would require another study.

Finally, the production of Lutheran morality was a process that crossed a large span of time: from the beginning of the Reformation through the whole eighteenth century. In a particular way, an explosion of moral theological works occurred from the second half of the seventeenth century till the beginning of the eighteenth century, because moral theology became an academic

30 See R. Keller, *Orthodoxie, altprotestantische*, in *Evangelisches Lexikon für Theologie und Gemeinde*, 3, 1994, 1492-4; R. Kolb, *Lutheran Theology in Seventeenth Century Germany*, in *Lutheran Quarterly*, Vol. XX (2006), 429-56. For a survey of the debate see M.J. Halvorson, *Heinrich Heshusius and Confessional Polemic in Early Lutheran Orthodoxy*, London, New York, Routledge, 2010, 18-20.

discipline and moved away from secular natural law. To follow this trend, yet avoid an excessive temporal framework, this research investigates the period between 1520 and 1720. Works concerning the second half of the eighteenth century were in the end excluded from the selection or are only sporadically considered.

4 Method

The knowledge of the past is a complex process that results from the filter of the historians' accounts.[31] The elements we sketched out so far should have already made clear that the approach we undertake considers law as an ensemble of societal relations.[32] This does not mean forgetting legal terminology, but catching the legal lines of a vaster panorama.[33] Contemporary legal history looks at norms and their interpretation, but also at outcomes of judgments and various procedures of conflict resolution.[34] They are more relevant than the enforcement of norms.[35] In this way, theological roots of the modern legal

31 See the reflections in K. Jenkins, *Re-thinking History*, first ed. 1991, London, Routledge, 2003.

32 E. Conte, *Per una storia del diritto medievale nel XXI secolo*, in *Eadem Utraque Europa*, Año 4, n. 7, Diciembre 2008, 57-87 (85); E. Conte, *Diritto comune. Storia e storiografia di un sistema dinamico*, Bologna, Il Mulino, 2009, 40-2.

33 P. Grossi, *Sulla 'natura' del contratto (qualche nota sul 'mestiere' di storico del diritto, a proposito di un recente corso di lezioni)*, in *Quaderni fiorentini* 15 (1986), 593-619; See also H.J. Berman, *Toward an Integrative Jurisprudence: Politics, Morality, History*, in *California Law Review*, vol. 76, July 1988, n. 4, 779-801. Berman suggested considering together the contribution of legal positivism, natural law theory and historicism.

34 D. Ibbetson, *Comparative Legal History: A Methodology*, in A. Musson, C. Stebbings (eds.), *Making Legal History: Approaches and Methodologies*, Cambridge, Cambridge University Press, 2012, 131-45. For conflict resolution see K. Härter, *Konfliktregulierung im Umfeld frühneuzeitlicher Strafgerichte. Das Konzept der Infrajustiz in der historischen Kriminalitätsforschung*, in *Kritische Vierteljahresschrift für Gesetzgebung und Rechtsprechung* 95, 2012, 130-44; R. Frassek, *Konflikte und Konfliktlösungen im frühen evangelischen Eherecht im sächsischen Raum*, in S. Schellenberger, A. Thieme, D. Welich (eds.), *Eine STARKE FRAUEN geschichte*. 500 Jahre Reformation. Markkleeberg 2014, 83-90; P. Collin (ed.), *Justice without the State. Judicial Self-Regulation in the Past and Present*, Frankfurt am Main, Klostermann, 2016.

35 L. Benton, R.J. Ross, *Empires and Legal Pluralism: Jurisdiction, Sovereignty, and Political Imagination in the Early Modern World*, in L. Benton, R.J. Ross (eds.), *Legal Pluralism and Empires*, 1-20 (6); S. Cummins, L. Kounine (eds.), *Cultures of Conflict Resolution in Early Modern Europe*, London, Routledge, 2016.

traditions have been the subject of increasing investigation.[36] And the interaction between multiple normative orders has become a salient feature of the legal historiography of the early modern era.[37] 'Multinormativity' and 'legal pluralism' seem to be key concepts for understanding dialogues between different legal spheres.[38] They also apply to religious legal systems,[39] and particularly to moral theology.[40]

A positivistic gaze would never see the contract law doctrine constructed by the Lutheran theologians.[41] A scholastic eye would also never find it, as Lutheran moral theology was essentially different from the scholastic. Not only were the Roman Catholic theologians educated in Roman law and canon law, but they also synthesized law and moral theology in their treatises. Instead, the Lutheran analysis of contract law mirrored the new articulation of law and morality that originated with the Reformation. In substance, the theologians proclaim the Gospel, while the jurists design and enforce the law. Their duties are distinct, but inseparable. This book is thus not directed towards law in an isolated perspective, rather it aims to catch the appraisal of the relation between law and theology. The underlying idea is that the knowledge of the Lutheran contribution to contract law depends upon the study of a combination of sources both theological and legal.

---

36 M. Schmoeckel, *Rechtsgeschichte im 21 Jahrhundert, Ein Diskussionsbeitrag zur Standortbestimmung*, in *Forum Historiae Iuris* (2000), http://www.forhistiur.de/2000-05-schmoeckel/ (accessed 22.12.2017); J.Q. Whitman, *The Origins of Reasonable Doubt: Theological Roots of the Criminal Trial*, New Haven and London, Yale University Press, 2008.

37 T. Duve, *Global Legal History – A Methodological Approach* in *Oxford Handbooks Online – Law*, Jan. 2017, DOI: 10.1093/oxfordhb/9780199935352.013.25 (Accessed 7.12.17).

38 R.J. Ross, *Puritan Godly Discipline in Comparative Perspective. Legal Pluralism and the Sources of 'Intensity'*, in *American Historical Review*, 113 (2008), 975-1002; L. Benton, R.J. Ross (eds.), *Legal Pluralism and Empires, 1500-1850*, New York, London, New York University Press, 2013; T. Duve, *Was ist ›Multinormativität‹ ? – Einführende Bemerkungen*, in *Rechtsgeschichte, Legal History*, 25/2017, 88-101; W. Decock, *Collaborative Legal Pluralism. Confessors as Law Enforcers in Mercado's Advice on Economic Governance (1571)*, in *Rechtsgeschichte Legal History*, 25 (2017), 103-14.

39 J. E. David, *Gesetzreligion und Rechtspluralismus*, in S. Grundmann, J. Thiessen (eds.), *Religiöse Werte im Recht*, Tübingen, Mohr Siebeck, 2017, 19-42.

40 T. Duve, *Global Legal History*. A, 1, b.

41 On the necessity to overcome a positivistic approach to law see the reflections of A. Falzea, *Complessità giuridica*, in P. Sirena (ed.), *Oltre il positivismo giuridico. Scritti in onore di Angelo Falzea*, Napoli, ESI, 2011, 3-36. For a more detailed analysis see A. Falzea, *Introduzione alle scienze giuridiche*, Milano, Giuffrè, 2008. See also E. W. Böckenförde, *Der Staat als sittlicher Staat, Der sakularisierte Staat: sein Charakter, seine Rechtfertigung und seine Probleme im 21. Jahrhundert*, München, Von Siemens Stiftung, 2007, 24-35.

After these general premises, we need to present a caveat regarding the translation of certain words. Sixteenth-seventeenth century contract law employed technical terms that might result difficult for the modern reader to understand. Specifically, the word *usura* can both be translated with *usury* or *interest*. Primarily with regard to the Middle Ages, a vast secondary literature translated *usura* as 'usury'. Usury was a sin consisting in lending for profit. However, in our opinion, this choice is not completely fitting for the early modern era. Many Lutheran theologians and jurists distinguished between an unlawful *usura* and a lawful *usura*. They realised that it is not lending at profit that is forbidden, but lending at an excessive profit, damaging the neighbour. Therefore, an appropriate translation of *usura* appeared to be *interest* and not *usury*. Of course, *usura* can also be translated as usury to individuate the sin of usury. Besides, *interest* has not to be meant in a strict sense, as money paid for the use of money lent, but more in general as whatever profit (money or in kind) results from a lending operation. In this way, however, we believe that the features of the Lutheran theory of *usura* can be better understood.

This discourse is also applicable to the German translation of the word *usura: Wucher.*[42] *Wucher* does not have a current meaning, but it can be translated as 'interest'. Instead, *Zins*, the current word for interest, had another meaning: *census* or annuity, identifying both the pecuniary payment and a specific financial operation. In this sense, it is relevant that Luther changed the translation of *usura* in his translation of the Bible: from *Wucher* (usury) to *Zinsen* (interest or *census*). Finally, for the translation of the word *interesse*, we used the term 'compensation for loss'. Not only does the literal translation 'interest' not correspond to the actual meaning, but it also would create confusion with the translation of *usura*.

5 Structure

In the attempt to answer the research questions, this book has been framed in four parts, each one divided into two or three chapters. The first part is dedicated to moral theology and law in general and comprises two chapters. Chapter one illustrates the creation of the tribunal for the soul and the salient features of the Roman Catholic moral theology, while chapter two focuses on

42 See J. Grimm, W. Grimm, *Deutsches Wörterbuch*, Leipzig, 1956, http://woerterbuchnetz.de/cgi-bin/WBNetz/wbgui_py?sigle=DWB (accessed 22.12.2017); H. Speer, A. Deutsch (eds.), *Deutsches Rechtswörterbuch*, http://drw-www.adw.uni-heidelberg.de/drw/info/index.html (accessed 22.12.2017).

the Lutheran theologians, their prominent biographical details and their attitudes towards contract law and theology. It also portrays the different literary genres and the contexts in which these books were produced. Hence, the purpose of this chapter is to give the basic coordinates of the connections and disconnections between the Roman Catholic and the Lutheran confessions.

Parts two and three examine the contract doctrine proposed by the Lutheran theologians. To dilute the tension between the original articulation of contract law proposed by the Lutheran theologians and the contemporary view on contract law, part two is dedicated to general elements and part three to specific contracts. Part second presents three chapters. Chapter one investigates the basic concepts utilized by the theologians to identify 'contract law'. Because they were discussed within the framework of the seventh and eighth commandments of the Decalogue, chapter two looks at the seventh commandment as a source for basic rules for the regulation of contracts in general. Chapter three then deals with principles and norms related to observance of agreements, which were associated with the eighth commandment.

Part three delves into specific contracts and is divided into two chapters. Chapter one is dedicated to the main commercial transactions: sale and lease. It also takes into consideration the doctrine of restitution. It reveals both the elaboration of innovative solutions and the recycling of scholastic teachings, in the framework of the Lutheran theology. The gap between the Roman Catholic and the Lutheran theologians is more prominent when looking at financial law. Loans and other financial operations presented tricky problems for which the Lutherans offered an innovative view.

Finally, part four enquires into the interaction between theologians and jurists. This interaction is observed in two distinct ways. Chapter one shows a rather practical design and analyses a dispute on an alleged breach of interest law in the city of Regensburg. This dispute was settled by the intervention of both theologians and jurists. It therefore provides a unique occasion to study and compare their methods, languages and solutions. Chapter two grapples with the jurists' opinions on the matter of interest-taking. In particular, it highlights the jurists' adherence to the theological underpinnings and their contributions to the new theory of interest.

PART I

Christian Spirituality and Law: Developments and Sources

CHAPTER 1

Care for the Souls before the Reformation and in the Early Modern Roman Catholic World

1.0 Introduction

In his *Introductio in universum theologiae moralis* (1671), Gebhard Theodor Meier (1633-1693), Lutheran theologian of Helmstedt, classified the authors who worked in the art of moral theology into three classes: writers from the first century till the age of Peter Lombard (c. 1096-1160); writers from Peter Lombard till the Reformation; writers from the Reformation till his day (1671).[1] A similar approach was followed by Johann Peter Lang (1664-1731), in his *Dissertatio de origine et progressu theologiae moralis systematicae* (1678). He began from the oriental Church Fathers, and then went through medieval theologians and canonists like Lombard, Peter Abelard (1079-1142), Henry of Segusio (Hostiensis, 1200-1271), Raymond de Peñafort (1175-1275) and others.[2] The style of these Lutheran theologians is rather polemic, as they narrate the history of moral theology to bring out the errors of the papacy. Still, these theologians acknowledged the necessity to investigate the roots of moral theology. They were aware that a long, well-established tradition preexisted their works and looked to past experience to better delimit the borders of the 'Lutheran' moral theology.

As with Meier and Lang, we cannot delve immediately into the writings of the Lutheran theologians, for we need to recall briefly the way the Roman Catholic theologians viewed the morality of contract law. They studied it within the framework of the sacrament of penance, which understanding was far different from today. Christian spiritual life was brindled by a body of norms that dictated its discipline. The enforcement of these rules was entrusted to priest-judges empowered with the authority to grant access to heaven or hell. This judgment took place in the conscience and in the confessional, configured as a tribunal for the soul.

The purpose of this chapter is then to pinpoint the origins and essential features of this tribunal till the sixteenth century. The Reformation arose as a reaction against a certain type of theology. And it is by displaying the roots of

1 G.T. Meier, *Introductio in universum theologiae moralis*, cap. IX.

2 J.M. Lang, *Dissertatio prooemialis*, passim.

 | DOI:10.30965/9783657701506_003

this theology that we lay the essential brick for the contextualization of our sources. We only need to sketch out the basic elements to grasp the difference from the Lutheran theological attitude. For this reason, the narrative style will be succinct and rather stylized.

1.1 The First Christian Communities

1.1.1 *Christian Life in the World*

In His teachings, Christ did not only invite His disciples to keep the commandments,[3] but also asked them to cultivate a spiritual and interior life:

> *Ye have heard that it was said of them of old time, Thou shalt not kill; and whosoever shall kill shall be in danger of the judgment. But I say unto you, That whosoever is angry with his brother without a cause shall be in danger of the judgment*[4]. *Ye have heard that it was said by them of old time, Thou shalt not commit adultery. But I say unto you, That whosoever looketh on a woman to lust after her hath committed adultery with her already in his heart.*[5]

These rules, together with others on divorce, oaths and aggressions, demanded an interior conversion. Christ called to internal purity. Not only did He request 'external actions', but He also claimed the renewal of heart as the source of the spiritual life.[6]

The message of Christ was not universally understood. As the Gospel says, the 'world',[7] as the realm of secular and materialistic, did not acknowledge Christ[8] and for this reason He and His followers were hated and persecuted.[9] Christ was not 'of the world', but he was 'in the world'. This paradox generated two problems. First, Christ's moral teachings had to be explained. For example,

3 Matt. 5,17.

4 Matt. 5,21-2.

5 Matt. 5,27-8.

6 In the Holy Bible, the heart is conceived as the centre of the spiritual life: Psalms 11,2; 78,72; Luke 8,15; Matthew 5,8 and sometimes it indicates also conscience: Rm 2,15. See *Heart*, in D.N. Freedman (ed.), *The Eerdmans Bible Dictionary*, Grand Rapids, Eerdmans, 1987, 471.

7 The word has multiple meanings. In this context, it means the realm of secular and materialistic, the domain of Satan. See *World* in D.N. Freedman (ed.), *The Eerdmans Bible Dictionary*, 1996, 1065-7. The theme of the Christian religion in the world was at the origins of the medieval problem of Church and state, see A. Black, *Political Thought in Europe 1250-1450*, Cambridge, Cambridge University Press, 1992, 42.

8 John 3,1-2; 1 John 4,1-5.

9 John 15,18-22; 1 John 2,15.

Christ clarified the correct interpretation of the rule of Sabbath for the Jews.[10] This new interpretation is anything but the concrete application of Christ's moral teachings to a single case. Second, if the world proposed another way of living, the Christian faithful could be seduced to live according to the world. The pressure of the world was always present, along with the risk of sinning.[11] Therefore, Christ, intending to avoid losing any believer,[12] taught a procedure for fraternal correction.[13]

1.1.2 *The Jurisdiction of the Church*

After the death and resurrection of Christ, the primitive Church proclaimed Christ's teachings[14] and faced Christ's same problems. Apostles, then bishops and councils dictated rules apt to guide the Christians 'in the world'.[15] For example, the Council of Illiberris (held in Spain, probably around A.D. 306), established norms against idolatry and adultery. The Christian who committed idolatry or a capital sin was forbidden to receive the Lord's Supper, even before death.[16] Many important rules about contract law were also issued in this period. The Council of Nicaea (325) asked clerics to perform gratuitous loans only, forbidding the practice of usury.[17] The Council of Carthage (348) established the binding nature of a simple agreement between two bishops, because peace must be maintained and the agreements observed.[18]

In parallel, concerning the leadership of bishops, a jurisdiction for the correction for sinners was gradually erected. After the baptism, the faithful who did not respect the Christian moral teachings was punished with the prohibition to participate in the Eucharist.[19] He could obtain reconciliation only after

10 Matt. 2,27; M. Honecker, *Einführung in die theologische Ethik: Grundlagen und Grundbegriffe*, Berlin, New York, De Gruyter, 1990, 171-2. The early Christians were Jews already immersed in the culture of biblical literature. F. Young, *The Interpretation of Scripture*, in G.R. Evans (ed.), *The First Christian Theologians*, Oxford, Blackwell, 2004, 24-38.

11 Luke 16,13.

12 Matt. 18,12-4.

13 Matt. 18,15-7.

14 Matt. 28,18 ff.

15 A.R. Jonsen, S. Edelston Toulmin, *The Abuse of Casuistry: A History of Moral Reasoning*, Berkeley, University of California Press, 1988, 93-4.

16 O.D. Watkins, *A History of Penance*, Vol. 1-2, New York, Burt Franklin, 1961, 277-9.

17 C.H. Turner, *Ecclesiae occidentalis monumenta iuris antiquissima*, 1, Oxford, 1899, 270.

18 X 1,35,1.

19 H.C. Lea, *A History of Auricular Confession and Indulgences in the Latin Church*, vol. 1, Philadelphia, 1896, 5-7.

remorse and penance. Penance was public, solemn and not repeatable.[20] Only the most severe offences, like homicide, idolatry and adultery, were punished. Moreover, penance and reconciliation did not regard the relationship between the sinner and God, but the violation was only considered to be an offence against the community.[21]

1.1.3 *Monasticism and the Reform of Spiritual Life*

Bishops and councils punished violations of the divine law externally, leaving to the individual believer the purification of heart before God. Furthermore, because of the impossibility of repetition, most of the believers had penance only before death.[22] This situation started to change with the emergence of monasticism.[23] Greek Fathers,[24] like Origen (185-254), Basil (329-379) and Gregory of Nyssa (335-395), described monasticism as a way of purification and assimilation to God, by the separation from the world and elimination of vices through virtues. If the monk strives to reach perfection with an ascetic and mystic walk,[25] he can attempt the return to paradise on earth.[26] The

20 H.C. Lea, *A History*, 20-49. See also R. Meens, *Penance in medieval Europe: 600-1200*, Cambridge, Cambridge University Press, 2014, 12-37.

21 H.C. Lea, *A History*, 8-9; Some references also in J. Bossy, *The Social History of Confession in the Age of the Reformation*, in *Transaction of the Royal Historical Society*, V. 25, December 1975, 21-38.

22 H.C. Lea, *A history*, 34-7; T.N. Tentler, *Sin and Confession in the Eve of the Reformation*, Princeton, Princeton University Press, 1977, 6-9.

23 Literature on monasticism is immense. We just mention some titles: C.H. Lawrence, *Medieval Monasticism*, New York, Longman Inc., 1984; J.E. Goehring, *Ascetics, Society, and the Desert. Studies in Early Egyptian Monasticism*, Harrisburg, Trinity Press International, 1999. M. Dunn, *The Emergence of Monasticism: from the Desert Fathers to the Early Middle Ages*, Oxford, Blackwell, 2003; W. Harmless S.J., *Desert Christians. An Introduction to the Literature of Early Monasticism*, Oxford, Oxford University Press, 2004; G. Agamben, A. Kotsko (trans.), *The Highest Poverty. Monastic Rules and Form-of-Life*, Stanford, Stanford University Press, 2013.

24 H.R. Drobner, *The Fathers of the Church. A Comprehensive Introduction*, Peabody, Hendrickson Publishers, 2007; M. Fiedrowicz, *Handbuch der Patristik. Quellentexte zur Theologie der Kirchenväter*, Freiburg im Breisgau, Herder, 2010.

25 On the character of the ascesis see: V.L. Wimbush, R. Valantasis (eds.), *Asceticism*, New York, Oxford University Press, 1995; L.R. Vaage, V.L. Wimbush (eds.), *Asceticism and the New Testament*, London and New York, Routledge, 1999.

26 G.B. Ladner, *The Idea of Reform: its Impact on Christian Thought and Action in the Age of the Fathers*, Cambridge (Mass), Harvard University Press, 1967, 63-132. For a critical review see: P.H. Stump, *The Influence of G. Ladner's The Idea of Reform*, in T.M. Izbicki, C.M. Bellitto (eds.), *Reform and Renewal in the Middle Ages and the Renaissance: Studies in Honor of Louis Pascoe, S.J.*, Leiden, Brill, 2000. He concludes that Ladner's book still remains the definitive study on reform's ideas.

Latin Fathers conceived this ascetic road in a different way. Tertullian (155-230), Cyprian (210-258), Ambrose (339-397) and others did not believe in the possibility to return to paradise. Rather, they opined that the intervention of Christ involved a plan of redemption, which does not mean *restoration* but *improvement*.[27] The monk is called to establish a relationship of love with the neighbour through activities like the care of strangers in hospices and of the sick, and intercession for the poor and oppressed, practices which will become much more commonplace in the Middle Ages.[28]

In both eastern and western Christianity, monasticism brought a new form of Christian inner life dedicated to individual work for spiritual perfection. Furthermore, it led to a new form of Christian education through a particular classification of sins and a new system of penance. Drawing upon Evagrius Ponticus, John Cassian (365-435) ordered sins in a rigid scheme of eight evils related to the ascetic road: from carnal sins (like gluttony or lechery) to spiritual sins (like pride or vainglory).[29] A spiritual director helped the monk in the struggle, and expected the monk to reveal his secret sins to him. The spiritual director was not a priest, but imposed acts of penance for the correction of monks. Progressively spiritual correction became to be exercised by monasteries for the benefit of laymen as well.[30]

1.2 From Augustine to Charlemagne

1.2.1 *Pilgrims towards Heaven*

The Christian inner life experienced a significant modification due to the theology of Augustine (354-430). On several occasions Jesus Christ announced the kingdom of God.[31] The Latin and Greek Fathers understood the biblical concept of the *Kingdom of God* as the paradise, the heavenly Jerusalem[32] that will descend to earth on the day of the last judgment,[33] and that is possible

27 G.B. Ladner, *The Idea of Reform*, 133-152.

28 See L.J.R. Mills, *Angelic Monks and Earthly Men. Monasticism and its Meaning to Medieval Society*, Woodbridge, The Boydell Press, 1992, 53-61; A.T. Crislip, *From Monastery to Hospital. Christian Monasticism & the Transformation of Health Care in Late Antiquity*, Ann Arbor, The University of Michigan Press, 2005.

29 C. Casagrande, S. Vecchio, *I sette vizi capitali: storia dei peccati nel Medioevo*, Torino, Einaudi, 2000, 182-3.

30 K. Holl, *Enthusiasmus und Bußgewalt beim griechischen Mönchtum*, (First ed. Leipzig 1898), Hildesheim, Olms, 1969, 262ff; G.B. Ladner, *The Idea of Reform*, 311.

31 John 18,36; Mark 9,1; Matt. 12; 28.

32 Hebr. 12,22ff.; Ap. 1,21ff.

33 G.B. Ladner, *The Idea of Reform*, 245-7.

to participate in the Kingdom in this life only through a process of ascesis. Because God became flesh but remained God, every man participating in Christ can reestablish the original resemblance with God. The faithful comes to an original perfection state as Adam before the Fall.[34] However, in his *De civitate Dei*, Augustine differentiated the kingdom of God from the city of God.[35] He distinguished between a terrestrial stage and a heavenly stage, which last step only is the kingdom of God. In this way, he separated life in heaven from life on earth.[36] Life on earth is then refigured as a pilgrimage where man walks towards heaven by contemplative and active works. The entire Christian community (not only monks) is called to take part in this pilgrimage. The monastic ideal of spiritual perfection should be extended to both clergy and lay people. Every Christian should be educated through the program presented in Augustine's *De doctrina christiana*.[37]

Opposite of the city of God, Augustine placed the city of the world. In the city of the world, people live in a perversion of soul originated by the rejection of the authority of God.[38] On the day of the final judgment, members of the city of the world will be condemned to eternal punishment, while members of the city of God will obtain the access to heaven.[39] Besides eternal punishment, however, Augustine made an essential addition: temporary punishments.[40] These can be performed during life but also after death. There are men that are damned, indeed, but men that could be saved through a purging fire. The fire of purgatory is a fire of expiation that in the end will lead men to heaven. It is for men that refused to do penance and for those who did not finish it on earth.[41] In this context, Augustine laid down the foundation for the doctrine of restitution. If a stolen thing is not returned, the sin cannot be forgiven.[42]

---

34 G.B. Ladner, *The Idea of Reform*, 117-8.

35 Bibliography on Augustine is practically boundless. See, among the recent literature: M. Hollingworth, *Saint Augustine of Hippo: An Intellectual Biography*, London, Bloomsbury, 2013; M.W. Levering, *The Theology of Augustine: An Introductory Guide to his Most Important Works*, Grand Rapids Baker Academic, 2013; On the *De civitate Dei*, see: G. O'Daly, *Augustine's City of God. A Reader's Guide*, Clarendon Press, Oxford, 1999; J. Wetzel (ed.), *Augustine's City of God. A critical guide*, Cambridge, Cambridge University Press, 2012. For the bibliography on *De civitate Dei* see: D.F. Donnelly, M.A. Sherman, *Augustine's* De civitate Dei. *An Annotated Bibliography of Modern Criticism, 1960-1990*, New York, Berlin, Bern, Frankfurt am Main, Paris, Wien, Peter Lang, 1991.

36 G.B. Ladner, *The Idea of Reform*, 267-8.

37 G.B. Ladner, *The Idea of Reform*, 350-77.

38 Augustinus Hipponensis, *De civitate Dei*, XIV, 1.

39 Augustinus Hipponensis, *De civitate Dei*, XXI-XXII.

40 Augustinus Hipponensis, *De civitate Dei*, XXI, 13.

41 J. Le Goff, *La Nascita del Purgatorio*, Torino, Einaudi, 1982, 80-6.

42 See III/1.

Augustine brought about a structural change in the idea of Christian spiritual life. All the believers are called to an active life and to perform penance for their sins in order to attain salvation. The violation of Christ's moral law, internal or external, implies not only repentance but also acts of penance to obtain salvation. Remission of sins is connected with penance. Public, non-repeatable penance administered by bishops continued to remain in effect. Monastic, repeatable, private penance nevertheless had a basis for development.[43]

1.2.2 *From Penitentials to Capitulars*

Monastic sources[44] constituted the background for the penitential books (*libri poenitentiales*)[45] developed in Ireland from the sixth-seventh centuries on.

---

43 Augustine never officially recognized private penance. R.C. Mortimer, *The Origins of Private Penance in the Western Church*, Oxford, Clarendon Press, 1939, 110; *Correption* in A. Fitzgerald, J.C. Cavadini, *Augustine Through the Ages: An Encyclopedia*, Grand Rapids, MI, Eerdmans Publishing Co., 1999, 242-44. For the previous debate see: B. Poschmann, *Kirchenbusse und correptio secreta bei Augustinus*, Braunsberg, Druck der Ermländischen Zeitungs- u. Verlagsdruckerei, 1923; B. Poschmann, *Die abendländische Kirchenbusse im Ausgang des christlichen Altertums*, Verlag Josef München, Kösel & Friedrich Pustet, 1928; K. Adam, *Die geheime Kirchenbusse nach dem heiligen Augustin. Ein Auseinandersetzung mit B. Poschmann*, Kempten, Kösel & Pustet, 1921.

44 On the reception of Augustine in Ireland, Britain and England see: D. Lambert, *The Making of Authority. Patterns of Augustine's reception, 430-c.700*, in K. Pollmann (ed.), *The Oxford Guide to the Historical Reception of Augustine*, Oxford, Oxford University Press, 2013, v. 1, 15-23 (21-2).

45 A.J. Frantzen, *The Literature of Penance in Anglo-Saxon England*, New Brunswick, New Jersey, Rutgers University Press, 1983, 25. On penitential books, literature is immense. See: F.W.H Wasserschleben, *Die Bussordnungen der abendlaendischen Kirche*, (First ed. Halle 1851), Graz, Akademische Druck- U. Verlagsanstalt, 1958; H.J. Schmitz, *Die Bussbücher und die Bussdisciplin der Kirche*, vol. I-II, (First ed. 1883-98 Mainz) Graz, Akademische Druck, U. Verlagsanstalt, 1958; T.P. Oakley, *English Penitential Discipline and Anglo-Saxon Law in their Joint Influence*, New York, Columbia University, Longmans, Green & Co, 1923; T.P. Oakley, *The Cooperation of Medieval Penance and Secular Law*, in *Speculum*, VII, (1932), 515-24; B. Poschmann, *Die abendländische Kirchenbuße im frühen Mittelalter*, Breslau, Müller & Seiffert, 1930; J.T. Mc Neill, H.M. Gamer, *Medieval Handbooks of Penance. A Translation of the Principal Libri Poenitentiales and Selections from Related Documents*, (First ed. New York 1938), New York, Columbia University Press, 1979; B. Poschmann, *Busse und Letzte Olung*, Freiburg, Verlag Herder, 1951; R. Pierce, *The 'Frankish' Penitentials*, in *Studies in Church History*, 11(1975), 31-39; C. Vogel, *Les <<Libri Paenitentiales>>*, Typologie des Sources du moyen Age Occidental, Fasc. 27, Turnhout, Brepols, 1978; M.G. Muzzarelli (ed.), *Una componente della mentalità occidentale: i Penitenziali nell'alto medioevo*, Bologna, Pàtron Editore, 1980; P.J. Payer, *The Humanism of the Penitentials and the Continuity of the Penitential Tradition*, in *Mediaeval Studies*, vol. XLVI, 1984, Toronto, Pontifical Institute of Mediaeval Studies, 340-54; R. Kottje, *Busspraxis und Bussritus*, in *Segni e riti nella Chiesa altomedioevale occidentale, Settimane di studio del Centro Italiano di Studi sull'Alto Medioevo*, 33, Centro Italiano di Studi sull'alto Medioevo, 1987, 369-95;

These lists of tariff-providing penances for sins were prepared for helping confessors, priests and bishops in their duties. The conversion of the Germanic peoples to Christianity involved sensitive modifications in the Christian spiritual life.[46] Confession of sins was intended as voluntary and repeatable, not only for monks as it was before, but also for clergy and lay people.[47] Penitential books catalogued sins according to the seven deadly sins. At the same time, however, the Church adopted part of the secular law, in order to ensure that barbaric rulers likewise adopted a religious component, before exercised by pagan religion.[48] As far as contract law is concerned, penitentials contained norms about usury or the payment of debts with the corresponding penance. For example, the *Excerpts from a book of David* (c. 500-525), 13 states: "*He who receives usury shall give up those things that he has received*"; St. Hubert's Penitential (c. 850), 22 says:

> *if anyone exacts usury from anybody, he shall do penance for three years. If he is a cleric, he shall not proceed to holy orders; if a deacon or a presbyter, he shall be deprived of his own rank.*

R.E. Reynolds, *Rites of Separation and Reconciliation in the Early Middle Ages*, in *Segni e riti nella Chiesa altomedioevale occidentale, Settimane di studio del Centro Italiano di Studi sull'Alto Medioevo*, 33, Centro Italiano di Studi sull'alto Medioevo, 1987, 405-33; C. Vogel, *Le pécheur et la penitence au moyen-age*, Paris, Cerf, 2007; R. Meens, *Penance in medieval Europe*, passim; R. Meens, *Penitential Varieties*, in J. Arnold (ed.), *The Oxford Handbook of Medieval Christianity*, Oxford, Oxford University Press, 2014, 254-70.

46 See J.C. Russell, *The Germanization of Early Medieval Christianity: A Sociohistorical Approach to Religious Transformation*, Oxford, Oxford University Press, 1994; C.M. Cusack, *Conversion Among the Germanic People*, Midsomer Norton, Bookcraft, 1998. Irish society was a non-urbanized and rural society that before was not part of the Roman Empire. M. Dunn, *The emergence of monasticism*, 142. See also R. Fletcher, M. Ni Mhaonaigh (eds.), *The Introduction of Christianity into the Early Medieval Insular World: Converting the Isles I*, Turnhout, Brepols, 2016.

47 We do not know exactly to which lay people these rules were directed and whether the confession of lay people was frequent. For a more detailed look on the problem see: R. Meens, *Penance in Medieval Europe*, 48-9. Subjects of the provisions were indeed all the components of Christian society. A.J. Frantzen, *The Literature of Penance*, 37.

48 A.J. Frantzen, *The Literature of Penance*, 44. T.P. Oaxley, *English Penitential Discipline and Anglo-Saxon law in their Joint Influence*, New York, Columbia University Press, 167; T.P. Oaxley, *Les commutations et les redemptions dans les pénitentiels du continent*, in: *Revue historique de droit francais et ètranger*, (4 Ser. 18), 1939, 39-57; M. Dunn, *The Emergence of Monasticism*, 140-2; R. Meens, *Penance in Medieval Europe*, 70.

Canons of a synod of Patrick, Auxilius and Iserninus, n. 20, 78 affirm: "*A Christian who defrauds anyone with respect to a debt in the manner of the pagans, shall be excommunicated until he pays the debt*".[49]

Penitential books were criticised for their rigidity and the possibility to commute the penance, but persisted throughout the Carolingian reform.[50] The tariff system passed in the capitulars and then was imposed by episcopal judges as obligatory punishments. Indeed, the competencies over penance and confession previously exercised by monasteries were transferred to bishops, who became the official delegates of the empire, provided also with civil powers. On the one hand, bishops exercised public justice founded on inquiry or voluntary public confession. On the other hand, they inflicted sanctions after voluntary and secret confession.[51]

The kingdom of Charlemagne[52] unified secular and spiritual competencies.[53] Kings and their collaborators were answering to God for the care of their people. They were tasked with keeping moral and social order. At the same time, the education system was developed by monks. Augustine's *De doctrina christiana* became the ground for the study of the Bible and for the emergence of theological schools,[54] while Alcuin of York favoured the moral construction of Charlemagne's Christian kingship.[55] After all, it is not by chance that Charlemagne's favorite book was Augustine's *De civitate Dei*.[56]

---

49 Quotations are from J.T. Mc Neill, H.M. Gamer, *Medieval Handbooks of Penance*, New York, Columbia University Press, 1979.

50 R. Meens, *Penance in medieval Europe*, 101-139.

51 E. Brambilla, *La giustizia intollerante: inquisizione e tribunali confessionali in Europa (secoli IV-XVIII)*, Roma, Carocci, 2006, 35-40. For an account of this process see also L. Waelkens, *Amne Adverso. Roman Legal Heritage in European Culture*, Leuven, Leuven University Press, 2015, 92-94.

52 In describing the activity of ruling, Carolingian writers used the word 'kingdom' (*regnum*) instead of the other well-known word 'republic' (*res publica*). See M. Innes, *Charlemagne's Government*, in J. Story (ed.), *Charlemagne: Empire and Society*, Manchester and New York, Manchester University Press, 2005, 71-89.

53 M. Innes, *Charlemagne's Government*, in J. Story (ed.), *Charlemagne: Empire and Society*, 71-89.

54 B. Smalley, *The Study of the Bible in the Middle Ages*, Oxford, Blackwell, 1952, 37.

55 Alcuin of York based the construction of Charlemagne as the model of Christian ruler on the theoretical fingerprints of Augustine. See L. Wallach, *Alcuin and Charlemagne: Studies in Carolingian History and Literature*, Ithaca, NY, Cornell University Press, 1959, 48-72. See also D.D. Allman, *Sin and the Construction of Carolingian Kingship*, in Richard Newhauser (ed.), *The Seven Deadly Sins. From Communities to Individuals*, Leiden, Boston, Brill, 2007, 38-40.

56 P.E. Dutton (ed. and trans.), *Charlemagne's Courtier. The Complete Einhard*, Peterborough, Broadview Press, 1998, n. 24. See also M. De Jong, *Charlemagne's Church* and R. McKitterick, *The Carolingian Renaissance of Culture and Learning*, in J. Story (ed.), *Charlemagne:*

1.3 The Jurisdiction of the Souls

1.3.1 *The Judgment of God*

The Church Fathers never formulated a systematic theory of divine justice, even though Augustine sketched its edges.[57] At the beginning of the millennium, two of the greatest Christian thinkers, Anselm of Canterbury (1033/1034-1109) and Peter Abelard (1079-1142), put forward two different doctrines on the atonement.[58] Drawing upon Augustine,[59] in his *Cur Deus homo*[60] Anselm characterized the relation between man and God in terms of retributive justice. The justice of God implies that God's punishment corresponds to man's sin, which is portrayed as a debt unpaid. Man is indebted to God for his very creation. Because God created man, man must submit with all his will to God in order to pay the debt. If man does not obey God, he does not pay the debt and thus commits a sin.[61] When Adam committed the original sin, God was dishonored and pretended satisfaction. Because Adam's sin was transmitted to the human race, every man is guilty. But God sent 'the God-Man', Jesus Christ, who paid the price of the original sin and reconciled man with God.[62] In this way, the original sin is forgiven by baptism. The actual sins, however, the sins committed every day, need to be forgiven. Man must be punished, as he has to pay the price not paid.[63] God determines the payment, and there is no possibility to

---

Empire and Society, Manchester and New York, Manchester University Press, 2005, 103-35, 151-66. T.K. Sidey, *The Government of Charlemagne as Influenced by Augustine's "City of God"*, in *The Classical Journal*, vol. 14, n. 2 (Nov. 1918), 119-127. He maintains that there is no direct evidence of Augustine's influence on Charlemagne's government.

57 A. Vidu, *Atonement, Law, and Justice: The Cross in Historical and Cultural Contexts*, Grand Rapids, Baker Academic, 2014, 45-88; For the distinction between Augustine and Anselm see: H.J. Berman, *Law and Revolution*, 175 fn. 20. For a general image of the Church at the threshold of the millennium see J. Howe, *Before the Gregorian Reform: The Latin Church at the Turn of the First Millennium*, Ithaca and London, Cornell University Press, 2016.

58 Bibliography is vast on this point. A useful guide is J. Johnson, *Patristic and Medieval Atonement Theory. A Guide to Research*, Lanham, Rowman & Littlefield, 2016.

59 G.R. Evans, *Law and Theology in the Middle Ages*, New York, Routledge, 2002, 8-9.

60 For a critical review of the literature on *Cur Deus Homo* see: N. Albanesi, *Cur deus homo: la logica della redenzione: studio sulla teoria della soddisfazione di S. Anselmo arcivescovo di Canterbury*, Roma, Pontificia Università Gregoriana, 2002, 13-80. On Anselm see, among the recent literature: B. Davies, B. Leftow (eds.), *The Cambridge Companion to Anselm*, Cambridge, Cambridge University Press, 2006; R.P. Hofmeister (ed.), *Anselm of Canterbury (1033-1109) – Philosophical Theology and Ethics*, Turnhout, Brepols, 2011; G.E.M. Gasper, I. Logan (eds.), *Saint Anselm of Canterbury and his legacy*, Toronto, Pontifical Institute of Mediaeval Studies, 2012.

61 Anselmus Cantauriensis, *Cur Deus homo*, in PL 158, I, 11, 376.

62 Anselmus Cantauriensis, *Cur Deus homo*, in PL 158, II, 19, 425-8.

63 H.J. Berman, *Law and Revolution*, 182-3.

be forgiven by mercy, because this would be contrary to justice.[64] Satisfaction may require restitution of property stolen or the payment of economic debts unpaid.[65]

Peter Abelard described the justice of God in a different way, attempting to separate the justice of God from the justice of the Church.[66] According to Abelard, God justifies man by His charity. The sin of Adam was transmitted to his descendants, but not his guilt as well.[67] Therefore, there is no legal debt that needs to be repaid from the original sin. Only the punitive effect of the sin of Adam must be absolved.[68] Man is justified by loving God, without the need to expiate the guilt.[69] Charity overcomes the punitive effect of sin and leads to heaven.[70] The crucifixion of Christ serves to inspire charity in believers.[71]

To Abelard, consent presents crucial importance. Sin is not a debt, but it has an interior character. Sin is the acquiescence to the desire of concupiscence. It is an evil will (*peccatum in mala voluntate consistat*)[72] expressed through consent. It is only the consent, even without execution. Venial sins are caused by negligence, ignorance or inadvertence. They are forgiven with daily confession, and not excommunication. Mortal sins, instead, are evil instantiations of deliberated consent. In addition, mortal sins concern grave matters, like

---

64 Anselmus Cantauriensis, *Cur Deus Homo*, in PL 158, I, 12, 377. G. Plasger, *Die Not-wendigkeit der Gerechtigkeit: eine Interpretation zu Cur Deus homo von Anselm von Canterbury*, Münster Aschendorff, 1993, 85-98; 98-106; 106-26. N. Albanesi, *Cur deus homo*, 76. The justice of God is then submitted to the right ordering of the universe. For the discussion of this concept see G. Sohngen, *Grundfragen einer Rechtstheologie*, München, Pustet, 1962, 48-50; H.J. Berman, *Law and Revolution*, 180.

65 N.E. Lombardo, *The Father's Will: Christ's Crucifixion and the Goodness of God*, Oxford, Oxford University Press, 2013, 160 nt. 37. The idea of satisfaction could be derived from the penitential practice.

66 See the brilliant reflections of P. Prodi, *Una storia della giustizia: del pluralismo dei fori al moderno dualismo tra coscienza e diritto*, Bologna, Il Mulino, 2000, 54-7.

67 P. Abelardus, *Commentary on the Romans*, II 5:19. For the Latin critical edition see: Peter Abelard, *Opera theologica*, v. 1, Turnhout, Brepols, 1969; N.E. Lombardo, *The Father's Will: Christ's Crucifixion*, 172-74. On Peter Abelard see, among the recent literature: J. Marenborn, *The Philosophy of Peter Abelard*, Cambridge, Cambridge University Press, 1997; G. Allegro, *Teologia e metodo in Pietro Abelardo*, Palermo, Officina di studi medievali, 2010.

68 R.E. Weingart, *The Logic of Divine Love: A Critical Analysis of the Soteriology of Peter Abelard*, Oxford, Clarendon Press, 1970, 44-6; N.E. Lombardo, *The Father's Will: Christ's Crucifixion*, 173.

69 P. Abelardus, *Commentary on the Romans*, III 8:18.

70 N.E. Lombardo, *The Father's Will: Christ's Crucifixion*, 174.

71 P. Abelardus, *Commentary on the Romans*, III 8:4.

72 D.E. Luscombe, *Peter Abelard's Ethics*, 6.

homicide or adultery, and as such require penance.[73] The charity of God stimulates a desire for penance within Christians. Penance, for Abelard, begins with the sorrow of mind (*dolor animi*) over what it has done wrong. Charity leads to a fruitful repentance and reconciliation with God,[74] but the believer must confess his sins to a priest in order to get satisfaction. God, indeed, forgives only the eternal punishment and not the temporal one. The penitent must perform the temporal penance imposed by priests.[75]

Although different in their main statements, these theories were complementary. Anselm stressed the retributive character of God's justice and the necessity of penance. Conversely, Abelard focused on the inner repentance, the intention and self-examination for the remittance of sins. Notwithstanding they intended its role differently,[76] both insisted on the practice of individual confession and penance.[77]

1.3.2 *Theology of Penance*

In the context of the moral crisis that accompanied the Gregorian Reform, repression of sins became a dominant theme.[78] Following the theories of atonement, priests were described as judges with the power to inflict acts of penance. According to Peter Lombard, the task of priests consists in exercising

---

73 R. Blomme, *La doctrine du péché dans les écoles théologiques de la première moitié du XIIe siècle*, Louvain, Publications universitaires de Louvain, 1958, 123-4. In general on Abelard's doctrine on sin: 113-217.

74 D.E. Luscombe, *Peter Abelard's Ethics*, 88-9.

75 D.E. Luscombe, *Peter Abelard's Ethics*, 88.

76 On the question of the confession for the remittance of sins see: P. Anciaux, *La théologie du sacrement de pénitence au XIIe siècle*, 164-274 and 392-490.

77 C. Morris, *The Discovery of the Individual. 1050-1200*, London, SPCK, 1972, 70-75; W. Pohl, *Introduction: ego trouble?*, in R. Corradini, M. Gillis, R. McKitterick, I. van Renswoude (eds.), *Ego Trouble. Authors and their Identities in the Early Middle Ages*, Vienna, Austrian Academy of Sciences, 2010, 9-21.

78 There is a very large literature on the Gregorian reform. I quote just some titles: A. Fliche, *La Réforme Grégorienne*, Louvain, Spicilegium sacrum Lovaniense, 1924-1937; O. Capitani, *L'Italia medievale nei secoli di trapasso: La riforma della Chiesa (1012-1122)*, Bologna, Pàtron, 1984; R.I. Moore, *The First European Revolution, c. 970-1215*, Oxford, Blackwell, 2000. On the legal aspects of the reform see: H.J. Berman, *Law and Revolution*, 85-119; K. Pennington, *Popes and Bishops. The Papal Monarchy in the Twelfth and Thirteenth Centuries*, Philadelphia PA, University of Pennsylvania Press, 1984; K. Pennington, *The Prince and the Law, 1200-1600: Sovereignty and Rights in the Western Legal Tradition*, Berkeley CA, University of California Press, 1993; C. Fantappiè, *Introduzione storica al diritto canonico*, Bologna, Il Mulino, 2003, 79-90; L. Waelkens, *"Libertas ecclesiae" herbekeken*, in J. Ockeley, J. Janssen, F. Gotzen, L. Verbesselt, V. Boulpaep, (eds.), *Recht in Geschiedenis. Een bundel bijdragen over rechtsgeschiedenis van de Middeleeuwen tot de hedendaagse tijd aangeboden aan Prof. dr. Fernand Vanhemelryck*, Leuven, Davidsfond, 2005, 497-504.

justice over the sinners (*opus enim justitiae exercent in peccatores*). They have to impose a just penance,[79] absolve with mercy, or excommunicate for the grave sins.[80] Priests possess the spiritual keys, namely the power of binding and loosing; they admit and exclude from the Church on both earth and heaven.[81] To Gratian[82] the confessor is a spiritual judge (*spiritualis iudex*), an inquisitor and an investigator that must be able to discover, with subtle, astute and skillful interrogations what is neglected and what the penitent wants to conceal.[83]

Confession and penance's new features required, in turn, the development of instruments for the education of confessors and penitents. Penitential literature already extant dedicated scarce space to inner intentions. It was not precise enough for the more sophisticated needs of the new theology, which postulated indeed a detailed evaluation of guilt and a more accurate imposition of penance than penitential books could offer. Moreover, the renaissance of canon law and Roman law provided theologians with methods and sources that were previously unavailable.[84] The link between theology and canon

---

79 P. Lombardus, *Liber sententiarum*, in PL192 Lib. IV Dist XVIII, 7, 888. This book was still an essential text at the beginning of the sixteenth century. See L. Vereecke, *Storia della teologia morale moderna*, III, Roma, 1979-1980, 124; P. Hurtubise, *La casuistique das tous ses états: De Martin Azpilcueta à Alphonse de Liguori*, Ottawa, Novalis, 2005, 207. For more bibliography on Peter Lombard's *Liber sententiarum* see G.R. Evans, *Mediaeval Commentaries on the sentences of Peter Lombard*, vol. 1, 2001; P.W. Rosemann (ed.), *Mediaeval Commentaries on the sentences of Peter Lombard*, vols 2 and 3, Leiden, Brill, 2009 and 2015.

80 P. Lombardus, *Liber sententiarum*, in PL192, Lib. IV, Dist XVIII, 7, 888.

81 P. Lombardus, *Liber sententiarum*, in PL192, Lib. IV, Dist XVIII, 5, 887-8.

82 He dedicated one part of his *Decretum* to penance: *De poenitentia*. C.33, q.3.3. Probably other authors integrated it. See S. Kuttner, *Research in Gratian: Acta and Agenda*, in P. Linehan (ed.), *Proceedings of the Seventh International Congress of Medieval Canon Law*, Vatican City, Biblioteca Apostolica Vaticana, 3-36, Repr. in S. Kuttner, *Studies in the History of Medieval Canon Law*, Aldershot, Variorum, 1990; J. Rambaud-Buhot, *Le leges de l'ancien droit: Gratien*, in G. Le Bras, C. Lefebvre, J. Rambaud (eds.), *L'Age classique 1140-1378*, vol. I, Paris, Sirey, 1965, 47-129. For a more recent analysis see: A. Winroth, *The Making of Gratian's Decretum*, Cambridge, Cambridge University Press, 2000. On this book see A.L. Larson, *Gratian's Tractatus de Poenitentia*, Washington D.C., The Catholic University of America Press, 2016; On Gratian's attitude towards penance see A.L. Larson, *Master of Penance: Gratian and the Development of Penitential Thought and Law in the Twelfth Century*, Washington D.C., The Catholic University of America Press, 2014; J.C. Wei, *Gratian the Theologian*, Washington D.C., The Catholic University of America Press, 2016.

83 C. 33, q.3, c.1: "*Caueat spiritualis iudex, ut, sicut non conmisit crimen nequiciae, ita non careat munere scientiae. Oportet, ut sciat cognoscere quicquid debet iudicare. Iudiciaria enim potestas hoc expostulat, ut quod debet iudicare discernat. Diligens igitur inquisitor subtilis inuestigator sapienter et quasi astute interroget a peccatore quod forsitan ignoret, uel uerecundia uelit occultare*".

84 W. Trusen, *Zur bedeutung des geistlichen Forum internum und externum für die spätmittelalterliche Gesellschaft*, in *Zeitschrift der Savigny-Stiftung für Rechtsgeschichte*, Kan. Ab.,

law was the development of a branch of theology finalized in the sacrament of penance. Peter the Chanter (d. 1197) and his disciples Robert of Courçon (1160/1170-1219), Robert of Flamborough (1135/80-1219/33), Peter of Poitiers (of Saint Victor, 1130-1215), and Thomas of Chobham (1160-1233/1236) drew the framework of this new discipline.[85]

In his *Summa de sacramentis*, Peter the Chanter brings into focus individual and practical questions in order to help confessors.[86] In particular, he insists on the role of circumstances of moral acts, which can interfere positively or negatively on the consideration of the sin and in the determination of the acts of penance. The Parisian theologians used these circumstances to classify the social group of the sinner and from there, the consequences on the penance. Distinctions were created between clergy: prelates, priests, monks, nuns; and among lay people: knights, merchants and farmers.[87] Confessors were instructed to ask specifically about the penitent's occupation. Involvement in certain professions could produce sins or present more sinful opportunities, relative to other jobs.[88]

The school of Paris also worked to develop an ordered system of sins.[89] Peter Lombard had already provided sins with a detailed classification: sins of thinking, sins of conversation, sins of works, sins of action and omission,

vol. 76 (1990), 254-85; W. Trusen, *Forum internum und gelehrtes Recht im Spätmittelalter. Summae confessorum und Traktate als Wegbereiter der Rezeption*, in *Zeitschrift der Savigny-Stiftung für Rechtsgeschichte*. Kan. Ab., vol. 57 (1971), 83-126. They are also included in W. Trusen, *Gelehrtes Recht im Mittelalter und in der frühen Neuzeit*, Goldbach, Keip, 1997.

85 See the classic work of J.W. Baldwin, *Masters, Princes and Merchants. The social views of Peter the Chanter and his Circle*, vol. I, Princeton, Princeton University Press, 48.

86 P. Anciaux, *La théologie*, 86-9, 417, 427, 505, 121; J.W. Baldwin, *Masters*, 53. As a physician must know the symptoms and conditions of an illness, so a confessor must investigate the circumstances of a particular sin in order to apply correct penitential medicine. The analogy with the physician of the body was applied to Christ by the Church fathers. R. Arbesmann, *The concept of "Christus medicus" in St. Augustine*, in *Traditio* 10 (1954), 1-28; P. Biller, *Confession in the Middle Ages: Introduction*, in P. Biller, J.A. Minnis (eds.), *Handling Sin: Confession in the Middle Ages*, York, York Medieval Press, 1998, 8.

87 J.W. Baldwin, *Masters*, 55-8.

88 P. Biller, *Confession in the Middle Ages*, 16-8.

89 About classification of sins see: M.W. Bloomfield, *The Seven Deadly Sins: An Introduction to the History of a Religious Concept, with Special Reference to Medieval English Literature*, East Lansing, Michigan State College Press, 1952; C. Casagrande, S. Vecchio, *I sette vizi capitali*, passim; R. Newhauser, *In the Garden of Evil: The Vices and Culture in the Middle Ages*, Toronto, Pontifical institute of mediaeval studies, 2005; Richard Newhauser (ed.), *The Seven Deadly Sins. From Communities to Individuals*, Leiden, Boston, Brill, 2007; R. Rusconi, *L'ordine dei peccati. La confessione tra Medioevo ed età moderna*, Bologna, Il Mulino, 2010; R.G. Newhauser, S.J. Ridyard (eds.), *Sin in Medieval and Early Modern Culture: The Tradition of the Seven Deadly Sins*, York, Woodbridge, 2012.

sins against the neighbour, sins against oneself, sins against God. He also used the Decalogue and, drawing upon Gregory the Great, structure of the seven deadly sins.[90] Thomas of Chobham in his *Summa de commendatio virtutum et extirpatione vitiorum* treats the question of the daughters (*filiae*) of the vices. Stephen Langton, Robert of Flamborough and Thomas of Chobham followed him. In his *Liber Penitentialis*, Robert of Flamborough includes an extensive list of sub-sins.[91] They were adopted as a guide for confession.[92]

In these first books for penance, contract law issues are also tackled. For example, Robert of Courçon and Thomas of Chobham review the main economic transactions, searching for possible sins. Commerce is subjected to the prohibition of fraud and excess profit. Starting from Roman law precepts, merchants are obliged to keep a just price and are reproached for false measurements or other deceitful strategies.[93] Loans must be gratuitous, as interest-taking is forbidden by the precept of Luke 6,35 and other Old Testament passages. Not only did the external action matter, but also the internal evil thinking. Robert of Courçon, for instance, defines usury as "*an evil desire to increase one's capital without risk of loss and without labor*".[94]

1.3.3 *The* forum poenitentiale

With the development of a special genre of literature dedicated to penance, the juridification of Christian interior life became meaningful. The Fourth Lateran Council of 1215 made the decisive step, putting into effect the results of the theological debates. The council proclaimed the return of God at the end of the time to judge the living and the dead. All people shall resurrect

90 P. Lombardus, *Liber sententiarum*, in PL192, Lib. II, Dist XLIII, 6-7, 752-3. The seven deadly sins were described as a complete indication of evils C. Casagrande, S. Vecchio, *I sette vizi capitali*, 203-4.

91 S.E. Young, *Scholarly community*, 174-6, 200.

92 C. Casagrande, S. Vecchio, *I sette vizi capitali*, 196. See for example: R. of Flamborough, J.J.F. Firth (ed.), *Liber Poenitentialis*, Toronto, Pontifical Institute of Mediaeval Studies, 1971, 62. On the evolution in the consideration of the sins see in particular: J. Bossy, *Moral Arithmetic: Seven Sins into Ten Commandments*, in E. Leites (ed.), *Conscience and Casuistry in Early Modern Europe*, Cambridge, Cambridge University Press, 1988, 214-43; C. Casagrande, S. Vecchio, *La classificazione dei peccati tra settenario e decalogo (XIII-XV)*, in *Documenti e studi sulla tradizione filosofica medievale. Rivista della Società Internazionale per lo Studio del Medioevo Latino*, V, 1994, 331-95.

93 O. Langholm, *Economics in the Medieval Schools. Wealth, exchange, value, money and usury according to the Paris theological tradition 1200-1350*, Leiden, New York, Köln, Brill, 1992, 37-62; O. Langholm, *The Merchant in the Confessional. Trade and Price in the Pre-Reformation Penitential Handbooks, Studies in Medieval and Reformation Thought*, Leiden-Boston, Brill, 2003, 24, 27-30.

94 See O. Langholm, *Economics in the Medieval Schools*, 45 and 52.

and receive according to their merits eternal punishment or eternal glory. If man commits sins after having received baptism, he can be restored by penance.[95] The famous canon 21 (*Omnes utriusque sexus*) established confession as mandatory at least once a year to a parish priest, and the canon 11 requested that every metropolitan church provide a theologian to instruct priests in the Sacred Scriptures and the *cura animarum*.[96] From one side it maintained the necessity of confession and penance for the remittance of sins, from another side, the need to educate confessors.[97]

The Lateran council institutionalized the remission of sins through confession to a priest and the imposition of penance.[98] This meant acknowledging officially a change of perspective, not only from public to individual penance, but also from a direct relationship between the penitent and God, who forgives sins, to a mediated relation, where sins are forgiven only by priests through the imposition of penance.[99] The Lateran council aimed to build a rigid penitential law centred on the subjection of the Christian to his parish priest, to whom he has to confess his sins. This proposal was partially unsuccessful, as Christians were often left free to choose another confessor.[100] The jurisdiction over the souls was distributed between the pope, papal penitentiary, bishops

---

95 Canon 1 in G. Alberigo, G. Dossetti, P. Joannou, C. Leonardi, P. Prodi (eds.), *Conciliorum oecumenicorum decreta*, Bologna, Istituto per le scienze religiose, 1973, 230-231; See also the English translation in: N.P. Tanner (ed.), *Decrees of the Ecumenical Councils*, vol. 1, Washington, Georgetown University Press, 1990.

96 Canon 11 and 21 in G. Alberigo (ed.), *Conciliorum oecumenicorum decreta*, 240 and 245.

97 On the education of priests see: L.E. Boyle, *The Constitution* Cum ex eo' *of Boniface VIII: Education of Parochial Clergy*, in *Mediaeval Studies*, vol. 24 (1962), 263-302; L.E. Boyle, *Aspects of Clerical Education in Fourteenth-Century England*, in P.E. Szarmach, B.S. Levy, *The Fourteenth Century*, Proceedings of the State University of New York Conferences in Medieval Studies, 19-32 both are reprinted in L.E. Boyle, *Pastoral Care, Clerical Education and Canon Law, 1200-1400*, London, Aldershot, 1981; J. Goering, *The Changing Face of the Village Parish: The Thirteenth Century*, in J.A. Raftis (ed.), *Pathways to Mediaeval Paesants*, Toronto, Pontifical Institute of Mediaeval Studies, 1981; J. Goering, *William de Montibus (ca. 1140-1213): The School and The Literature of Pastoral Care*, Toronto, Pontifical Institute of Mediaeval Studies, 1992; J. Goering, *The Internal Forum*, 405-427.

98 For the practice of confession and penance see A. Carpin, *La confessione tra il XII e il XIII secolo: teologia e prassi nella legislazione canonica medievale*, Bologna, Edizioni Studio Domenicano, 2006; U. Bruchhold, *Deutschsprachige Beichten im 13. und 14. Jahrhundert: Editionen und Typologien zur Überlieferungs-, Text- und Gebrauchsgeschichte vor dem Hintergrund der älteren Tradition*, Berlin, De Gruyter, 2010.

99 J. Bossy, *The Social History of Confession in the Age of the Reformation*, in *Transaction of the Royal Historical Society*, v. 25, December 1975, 21-38, (22).

100 P. Prodi, *Una storia della giustizia*, 80-83.

and parish priests.[101] However, because of privileges, friars could also receive confessions with the approval of the pope or the local bishops.[102] Priests and friars were intended to be judges, able to decide the access to heaven and the membership in Christian society on earth. They were provided with new tools with juridical characteristics in order to determine precisely the extent of guilt and the just penance. The *forum poenitentiale*,[103] as it was called in order to distinguish from the *forum iudiciale*, was now equipped with all the elements to operate.[104]

1.3.4 *Dominicans' and Franciscans'* summae

The involvement of mendicant orders (Dominicans and Franciscans) in the practice of penance provided the penitential literature with new lifeblood. The mendicant orders' model of Christianity was founded on a rediscovered idea of the apostolic life, which united ascesis to the proclamation of the Gospel.[105] In order to convert heretics, Dominicans obtained the license to preach sermons and hear confessions.[106] Dominican convents started a program for the formation of confessors,[107] and specialized texts for the instruction of confessors

---

101 J. Goering, *The Internal Forum*, 381-90. On the papal penitentiary see J. Ickx, *Ipsa vero officii maioris Penitentiarii institutio non reperitur? La nascita di un tribunale della coscienza*, in M. Sodi, J. Ickx (eds.), *La penitenzieria apostolica e il sacramento della penitenza. Percorsi storici, giuridici, teologici e prospettive pastorali*, Libreria Editrice Vaticana, Città del Vaticano, 2009, 19-50.

102 W. Trusen, *Zur Bedeutung*, 259-61.

103 H. Maihold, *‚Himmel und Erde'. Die Abrenzung von* forum internum *und* forum externum *in der frühen Neuzeit*, in M. Germann, W. Decock (eds.), *Das Gewissen in den Rechtslehren der protestantischen und katholischen Reformationen. Conscience in the Legal Teachings of the Protestant and Catholic Reformations*, Leipzig, Evangelische Verlagsanstalt, 2017, 57-8.

104 On the concept of *forum internum* see: P. Capobianco, *De ambitu fori interni in iure ante codicem*, in *Apollinaris*, 8 (1935), 591-605; 9 (1936): 364-74; K. Mörsdorf, *Der Rechtscharakter der iuridisdictio fori interni*, in *Münchener theologische Zeitschrift*, 8 (1957), 161-73; B. Fries, *Forum in der Rechtssprache*, in *Münchener theologische Studien* 3, Kan. Ab. 17, München, Hueber, 1963; A. Mostaza Rodríguez, *Forum internum-Forum externum. En torno a la naturaleza juridica del fuero interno*, in *Revista española de derecho canonico*, 23 (1967), 253-331; 24 (1968), 339-64; W. Trusen, *Forum internum und gelehrtes Recht im Spätmittelalter*, 83-126; J. Goering, *The Internal Forum*, 380; G. Minnucci, *Foro della coscienza e foro esterno nel pensiero giuridico della prima età moderna*, in G. Dilcher, D. Quaglioni (eds.), *Gli inizi del diritto pubblico, vol. 3: verso la costruzione del diritto pubblico tra medioevo e modernità*, Bologna, Il Mulino, 2011, 55-81.

105 C.H. Lawrence, *The Friars. The Impact of the Mendicant Orders on Medieval Society*, London, I.B. Tauris (first ed. 1994), 2013, 1-25.

106 W. Trusen, *Forum internum*, 11-12.

107 See W.A. Hinnebusch, *The History of the Dominican Order. Intellectual and Cultural Life to 1500*, vol. II, Staten Island, Alba House, 1966, 231-80; M. Mulchaney, *First the Bow is Bent*

and penitents were realized.[108] The most well-known examples of this genre are the *Summa de casibus poenitentiae* of Raymond de Peñafort (1238) and the *Summa confessorum* of John of Freiburg (ca. 1298).

in Study ... Dominican Education before 1350, Toronto, Pontifical Institute of Mediaeval Studies, 1998, 193-203.

108 The first works were the *Summa de penitentia* of Paul of Hungary (1221) and the *Summa penitentiae fratrum Predicatorum "Cum ad Sacerdotem"* (early 1220s). On the latter: J. Goering and P.J. Payer, *The 'Summa penitentie Fratrum Predicatorum': A Thirteenth-Century Confessional Formulary*, in *Mediaeval Studies* 55 (1993), 1-50. Literature on *Summae* is enormous. See: A. Teetaert, *La confession aux laiques dans l'église latine depuis le VIIIe jusqu'au XIVe siècle*, Wetteren, De Meester, 1926; J. Arnould, *Le Manuel des Pèchès, ètude de littèrature reigieuse anglo-normande (XIIIme siècle)*, Librarie e. Droz, Paris, 1940; P. Michaud-Quantin, *Sommes de casuistique et manuels de confession au Moyen Âge (xiie-xvie siècles)*, Louvain, Nauwelaerts, 1962; T.N. Tentler, *Sin and Confession*, 28-56; L. Hödl, *Die Geschichte der scholastischen Literatur und der Theologie der Schlüsselgewalt*, 1 Teil, Münster, Aschendorffsche Verlagsbuchhandlung, 1960; P. Grossi, *Somme penitenziali, diritto canonico, diritto comune*, in *Annali della Facoltà giuridica di Macerata*, 1 (1966), 95-134; L.E. Boyle, *Summae confessorum*, in *Les genres Littéraires dans les sources théologiques et philosophiques médiévales. Définition, critique et exploitation, Actes du Colloque international de Louvain-la-Neuve 25-27 Mai 1981*, Publications de l'institut d'études médiévales, 2e série: Textes, études, congrès, vol. 5, Lovain-La-Neuve, Université catholique de Louvain, 1982; Groupe de la Bussiere, *Practiques de la Confession. Des Pères du désert à Vatican II*, Paris, Cerf, 1983, 227-37; J. Delumeau, *La péché e la peur. La culpabilisation en Occident (XIIIe-XVIIIe siècles)*, Paris, Fayard, 1983; J. Delumeau, *L'aveu et le perdon. Les difficultés de la confession XIIIe-XVIIIe siècle*, Paris, Fayard, 1990; E. Brambilla, *Alle origini del Sant'Uffizio. Penitenza, confessione e giustizia dal medioevo al XVI secolo*, Bologna, Il Mulino, 2000; R. Rusconi, *L'ordine dei peccati*, passim; O. Langholm, *The Merchant in the Confessional*, passim; M. Schmoeckel, *Beichtstuhljurisprudenz*, in *Handwörterbuch zur deutschen Rechtsgeschichte* (HRG), vol. I, 505-8, https://www.hrgdigital.de/HRG.beichtstuhljurisprudenz (accessed 21.02.2018); B. Roest, *Franciscan Literature of Religious Instruction*, 314-55; J. Goering, *The Internal Forum and The Literature of Penance and Confession*, in W. Hartmann, K. Pennington, *The History of Medieval Canon Law in the Classical Period, 1140-1234: from Gratian to the Decretals of Pope Gregory IX*, Washington D.C., The Catholic University of America Press, 2008, 379-428; J. Goering, *The Scholastic Turn (1100-1500): Penitential Theology and Law in the Schools*, in A. Firey (ed.), *A New History of Penance*, Leiden, Brill, 2008, 219-38; H.A. Kelly, *Penitential Theology and Law at the Turn of the Fifteenth Century*, in A. Firey (ed.), *A New History of Penance*, 239-318; A. Prosperi, *Tribunali della coscienza. Inquisitori, confessori, missionari*, new ed., Torino, Einaudi, 2009; P.J. Payer, *Sex and the New Medieval Literature of Confession, 1150-1300*, Toronto, Pontifical Institute of Mediaeval Studies, 2009.

The *Summa* of Raymond[109] shows many of the technicalities developed in Paris combined with an extensive use of legal sources.[110] It is divided into three parts according to the type of sins; the confessor is considered a judge with jurisdiction and must accurately interrogate the penitent to produce his verdict.[111] As the priest is provided with judiciary power (*iudiciaria potestas*), he may judge Christians, and for this task he needs to know sins in detail. Interrogations must pinpoint the sin and its circumstances;[112] circumstances are based on the list of the seven deadly sins proposed by Gregory the Great;[113] special attention must be paid to different categories of religious, clergy and lay people, marking subdivisions and sinful activities.[114] Raymond's *Summa* also includes a treatment of contract law. Raymond utilizes excerpts from the *Decretals* of Gregory IX concerning usury in business transactions (mainly sales contracts with anticipated or deferred payment). Usury is considered a sin only for the intention to defraud the buyer or the seller. Besides usury, Raymond looks at the lawfulness of commerce, individuating the precautions to avoid sins.[115]

---

109 On Raymund's summa see: A. Teetaert, *La doctrine pénitentielle de St. Raymond de Penyafort* in *Analecta sacra Tarraconensia*, 4 (1928), 121-82; A. Teetaert, *La Summa de Poenitentia de Saint Raimond de Penyafort*, in *Ephemerides Theologicae Lovaniensis*, 5 (1928), 49-72; A. Teetaert, *Summa de matrimonio s. Raymundi de Penyafort*, in *Jus pontificium*, 9 (1929), 54-61, 228-34, 312-22; A. Teetaert, *La <<Summa de poenitentia>> de saint Raymond de Penyafort*, in *Dictionaire de théologie catholique*, v. XIII, Letouzey et Ané, Paris 1937, 1806-23; S. Kuttner, *Zur Entstehungsgeschichte der <<Summa de casibus poenitentiae>> des hl. Raymund von Penyafort*, in *Zeitschrift der Savigny-Stiftung für Rechtsgeschichte*, Kan. Ab., 70 (1953), 419-34; P. Michaud-Quantin, *Sommes de casuistique* 34-43; J.D. Mann, *Unstudied Manuscripts of the Summa de Poenitentia of Raymynd de Pennaforte*, in *Manuscripta* 34 (1990), 45-9; R. Rusconi, *L'ordine dei peccati*, 143.

110 P. Michaud-Quantin, *Sommes*, 40; M. Mulchaney, *First the Bow is Bent in Study*, 537.

111 R. de Pennaforte, S.J. Ochoa, A. Diez (eds.), *Summa de paenitentia*, Roma, Commentarius pro religiosis, 1976, n. 30, 828: "*Oportet ut sciat cognoscere quidquid debet iudicare. Iudiciaria enim potestas hoc expostulat, ut quod debet iudicare, discernat. Diligens igitur inquisitor, subtilis investigator sapienter et quasi astute interroget a peccatore quod forsitan ignoret, vel verecundia velit occultare*".

112 R. de Pennaforte, *Summa de paenitentia*, n. 31, 828: "*Ad aliud, scilicet, de quibus sint faciendae interrogationes, iam patet ex praemissa, quia de peccatis et circumstantiis eorumdem. Circumstantias autem istas, quas* praecipue *debet sacerdos attendere, nota in his versiculis*: quis, quid, ubi, per quos, quoties, cur, quomodo, quilibet observet medicamina dando. [Quando]".

113 R. de Pennaforte, *Summa de paenitentia*, n. 33-4, 832-3.

114 R. de Pennaforte, *Summa de paenitentia*, n. 35, 834-5.

115 O. Langholm, *The Merchant in the Confessional*, 34-40.

The Franciscan idea of apostolic life was not only concerned with voluntary poverty, but also with penance.[116] Franciscan friars went through Europe preaching sermons on repentance and confession.[117] For this reason, their system of education also encompassed preparation for confessors.[118] From the thirteenth century on, new manuals for confessors were compiled. Peter Quesnel's *Directorium iuris in foro conscientiae et iudiciali* and the *Summa* of John of Erfurt were among the first. The teachings of these manuals were studied together with sermon handbooks, for they were complementary aspects of the friars' program of religious education.[119] The lawfulness and use of property and possession, the merchants' role, the sins of simony and usury, and the correct practice of sale and restitution were among the most-discussed topics by the Franciscan theologians.[120] Pier Giovanni Olivi's (c. 1248-1298) *Tractatus de contractibus* still remains a milestone of their literary production.[121]

116 See the chapter XX of Francis's *regula non bullata* 1221, in *Opuscola*, 276 and the *Earlier rule* in *ER 20, FAED 1*, 77-8; *Opuscola*, 394. M. Lambert, *Franciscan Poverty: The Doctrine of the Absolute Poverty of Christ and the Apostles in the Franciscan Order, 1210-1323*, London, S.P.C.K., 1961; D. Flood (ed.), *Poverty in the Middle Ages*, Werl, D. Coelde, 1975; D. Burr, *The Correctorium Controversy and the Origins of the* Usus Pauper *Controversy*, in *Speculum* 60 (1985), 331-42. L.D. Isabell, ofm, *The Practice and Meaning of Confession in the Primitive Franciscan Community According to the Writings of Saint Francis of Assisi and Thomas of Celano*, Diss., Assisi, Instituto Theologiae Spiritualis Pontificiae Universitatis Gregorianae, 1973; E. Foley, *Franciscan Liturgical Prayer*, in T.J. Johnson (ed.), *Franciscans at Prayer*, Leiden, Boston, Brill, 2007, 365-412, (391-2).

117 D.L. D'Avray, *The Preaching of the Friars. Sermons diffused from Paris before 1300*, Oxford, Clarendon Press, 1985, 51; R. Rusconi, *L'ordine dei peccati*, 107-20; N. Şenocak, *The Poor and the Perfect. The Rise of Learning in the Franciscan Order, 1209-1310*, Ithaca, Cornell University Press, 2012, 149-50.

118 B. Roest, *A History of Franciscan Education* (*c.1210-1517*), Köln, Leiden, Boston, Brill, 2000, 123-37; 314-19. B. Roest, *Franciscan Learning, Preaching and Mission, c. 1220-1650. Cum scientia sit donum Dei, armatura ad defendendam sanctam fidem catholicam ...*, Leiden, Boston, Brill, 2015.

119 D.L. D'Avray, *The Preaching of the Friars*, 51. See also J.G. Ziegler, *Die Ehelehre der Poenitentialsummen von 1200-1350*, Regensburg, Pustet, 1956.

120 K. Weinzierl, *Die Restitutionslehre der Frühscholastik*, München, Heuber, 1936; G. Todeschini, *I mercanti e il tempio. La società cristiana e il circolo virtuoso della ricchezza fra Medioevo ed età Moderna*, Bologna, Il Mulino, 2002, 47-87; 133-92; 349-92; J. Goering, *The Internal Forum*, 200.

121 See the critical edition of S. Piron, *Pierre de Jean Olivi, Traité de contrats*, Paris, Les Belles Lettres, 2012. See also S. Piron, *Marchands et confesseurs, Le Traité des contrats d'Olivi dans son contexte* (*Narbonne, fin XIII*^{e}*-début XIV*^{e} *siècle*), in *L'Argent au Moyen Age, XXVIII*^{e} *Congrès de la SHMESP* (*Clermont-Ferrand, 1997*), Paris 1998, 289-308. See also J. Toivanen, *Voluntarist Anthropology in Peter of John Olivi's De contractibus*, in *Franciscan Studies*, vol. 74, 2016, 41-65.

1.4 The Specialists of Conscience

1.4.1 *Aristotelian Morality*

Besides manuals for confessors, another type of text for Christian moral education developed. The diffusion of translations of Aristotle's works, especially the *Nicomachean Ethics*, led to reconsiderations of programs of studies to include moral philosophy in the arts curriculums, which were preparatory for many disciplines, included law and theology.[122] Commentaries on Aristotle's *Nicomachean Ethics* circulated around Europe, and mendicant orders were significantly involved in this process.[123] Moral philosophy was taught in their *studia*, and their spiritual organization was described in a precise order of virtues.[124] Moreover, the *Nicomachean Ethics* contained essential ideas about voluntary and involuntary acts (book III), the virtue of truthfulness (book IV) and the virtue of justice (book V), which became underpinnings for the contract law elaborated by the scholastic theologians.[125]

Aristotle also appeared in dogmatic treatises. The *Summa theologiae* (1265-1274) of Thomas Aquinas (1225-1274) aired a new view of Christian spirituality, insisting on human freedom, natural law and conscience, conceived as a tribunal.[126] Drawing upon Aristotle and patristic sources, Aquinas argued that, as man is made in God's image, he is free to judge and is responsible for his actions.[127] By the freedom of will, man is called to carry out choices that move

122 D.A. Lines, *Aristotle's Ethics in the Italian Renaissance (Ca. 1300-1650). The Universities and the Problem of Moral Education*, Leiden, Boston, Köln, Brill, 2002, 45-9, 65-108. On Aristotle's interpretation see: C.H. Lohr, *The Medieval Interpretation of Aristotle*, in N. Kretzmann, A. Kenny, J. Pinborg (eds.) *The Cambridge History of Later Medieval Philosophy: From the Rediscovery of Aristotle to the Disintegration of Scholasticism, 1100-1600*, Cambridge, Cambridge University Press, 1988, 80-98.

123 P. Marangon, *Il rapporto culturale tra Università e ordini mendicanti nella Padova del Duecento*, in *Il Santo*, II, 18, 129-132; D.A. Lines, *Aristotle's Ethics in the Italian Renaissance*, 84-86; 95-96; 171, 174, 226. For the Franciscans see: B.D. Kent, *Aristotle and the Franciscans: Gerald Odonis' Commentary on the Nicomachean Ethics*, Diss., New York, Columbia University, 1984.

124 K. Pansters, *Franciscan Virtue. Spiritual Growth and the Virtues in Franciscan Literature and Instruction of the Thirteenth Century*, Leiden, Boston, Brill, 2012, 170-192.

125 For an outlook on the scholastic theology see U.G. Leinsle, M.J. Miller (trans.), *Introduction to Scholastic Theology*, Washington D.C., The Catholic University of America Press, 2010.

126 Of course, these are only minimal aspects. For a more detailed introduction see F. Kerr, *Thomas Aquinas: A Very Short Introduction*, Oxford, Oxford University Press, 2009; S.L. Brock, *The Philosophy of Saint Thomas Aquinas: A Sketch*, Eugene, Oregon, Cascade Books, 2015.

127 T. Aquinas, *Summa theologiae*, Iae, IIae, q. 1. ì.

him away or towards God.[128] This does not preclude, Aquinas says, the potential that an external force (like spiritual grace) could stimulate the action.[129] Still, in the absence of compulsion or ignorance, man is essentially free.[130] Human actions are made in three stages through the interaction between acts of intellect and acts of will. The first two are internal, while the last one is external. The two interior stages determine the end and the means of an action, while the third concerns the execution.[131]

In Aristotelian fashion, Aquinas affirmed that every action is directed to an end,[132] with God as the ultimate end.[133] The end is determined by human reason. Indeed, within the practical intellect (precisely in the *synderesis*), there is knowledge of the natural law.[134] The natural law participates in the eternal law, which rules the world according to the Divine Reason of God, therefore illuminating man with the wisdom of God.[135] Natural law is distinguished from human law, which possesses only an imperfect participation in eternal law, and from the positive divine law, which has, instead, a higher level of participation.[136]

When they abide by the natural law, human laws are binding in the *forum conscientiae*.[137] Conscience is separated from the *synderesis*, which is an operative disposition (*habitus*) to do the good and refrain from the evil.[138] Conscience determines the rightness of an action,[139] for it is the application of knowledge to an action.[140] The act of choice by the will accepts or refuses the judgment of conscience, between the universal moral precept and the factual knowledge

128 R. Cessario, O.P., *Introduction to Moral Theology*, Washington D.C., The Catholic University of America Press, 2001, 101.

129 T. Aquinas, *Summa theologiae*, Iae, IIae, q. 16, a. 1, ad. 1. R. Cessario, O.P., *Introduction to Moral Theology*, 102-3.

130 T. Aquinas, *Summa theologiae*, Iae, IIae, q. 6.

131 T. Aquinas, *Summa theologiae*, Iae, IIae, q. 16-17 for the third stage. The first two are discussed separately in *Summa theologiae*, Ia Iae, q. 8 a. 2; q. 12, a. 4; q. 14, a. 2; q. 15, a. 3. M.G. Baylor, *Action and Person*, 43. A. Donagan, *Thomas Aquinas on Human Action*, in N. Kretzmann (ed.), *The Cambridge History of Later Medieval Philosophy from the Rediscovery of Aristotle to the Disintegration of Scholasticism, 1100-1600*, Cambridge, Cambridge University Press, 1982, 642-52.

132 T. Aquinas, *Summa theologiae*, Iae, IIae, q. 8, a. 1.

133 T. Aquinas, *Summa theologiae*, Iae, IIae, q. 3, a. 4.

134 T. Aquinas, *Summa theologiae*, Iae, IIae, q. 94, a. 1 and 2.

135 T. Aquinas, *Summa theologiae*, Iae, IIae, q. 91, a. 2.

136 T. Aquinas, *Summa theologiae*, Iae, IIae, q. 91.

137 T. Aquinas, *Summa theologiae*, Iae, IIae, q. 96, a. 4; H. Mainhold, *Die Abgrenzung*, 58-9.

138 T. Aquinas, *Summa theologiae*, Iae, IIae, q. 79, art. 12.

139 For a complete description see: M.G. Baylor, *Action and Person. Conscience in Late Scholasticism and the Young Luther*, Leiden, Brill, 1977, 29-69; T.C. Potts, *Conscience in Medieval Philosophy*, Cambridge, Cambridge University Press, 1980, 45-60.

140 T. Aquinas, *Summa theologiae*, Iae, q. 79.

provided by the senses.[141] The conscience is right (*conscientia recta*) when acts in accordance with natural law, while the conscience is wrong (*conscientia erronea*) when it rejects it.[142]

Aquinas's doctrine of human free will, natural law and conscience had a lasting impact on the early modern scholastics.[143] But it was criticized by Franciscan theologians early on. John Duns Scotus (d. 1308) and William of Ockham (1285-1349), for instance, emphasized more the freedom of the will, which does not have an innate habit for the good, but it is absolutely free to choose the evil, and stressed the role of conscience as a necessary requisite for good action.[144] The following debate[145] was also reflected in the manuals for confessors and in the writings of the early modern scholastics. For instance, the *Summa Astesana* (1317), written by the Franciscan Astesanus (d. 1330), presents discussions on voluntary and involuntary acts and on moral or immoral internal and external actions.[146] Following Ockham, Francisco Suarez (1548-1617) stressed man's freedom of will, which is capable of good or evil actions.[147] In contrast to Luther, Luis de Molina (1535-1600) maintained that by human free will, man can perform morally good actions, without the grace of the Holy Spirit.[148]

1.4.2 *Gerson and the Early Modern Scholastics*

As a normative vision of the conscience emerged, Christian spiritual life was trapped in an oscillating circle between divine law, natural law and human

141 T. Aquinas, *Summa theologiae*, Iae, IIae, q. 76, a. 1.

142 T. Aquinas, *Summa theologiae*, Iae, IIae, q. 19.

143 For this terminology see W. Decock, *Theologians and Contract Law*, 15-6; W. Decock, C. Birr, *Recht und Moral*, 12-3.

144 On Ockham see: *Commentary on the Sentences*, 3 Sent. q. 13 S. and q. 13 B. For a more detailed account see: M.G. Baylor, *Action and Person*, 83-5. On Duns Scotus see E. Gilson, *Johannes Duns Scotus. Einführung in die Grundlagen seiner Lehre*, Düsseldorf, 1959; M. Kaufmann, *Die Willensfreiheit, das moralisch Gute und das Ziel des Menschen bei Duns Scotus, Ockham and Molina*, in H. Busche (ed.), *Departure from Modern Europe. A Handbook of Early Modern Philosophy* (1400-1700), Hamburg, Felix Meiner, 2011, 167-79.

145 B. Kent, *Virtues of the Will. The Transformation of Ethics in the Late Thirteenth Century*, Washington, The Catholic University of America Press, 1995.

146 Astesanus, *Summa Astensis*, Romae, 1728. Book II, title I concerns voluntary and involuntary acts. Titles III and IV deal with good or bad internal and external actions. Title V is concerned with merits and demerits of human actions. From title VI the discussion concerns virtue and vices.

147 T.U. Mullaney, *Suarez on Human Freedom*, Baltimore, Carroll Press, 1950, 8-96.

148 M. Kaufmann, *Willensfreiheit und Gewissen bei Luis de Molina*, in M. Germann, W. Decock (eds.), *Das Gewissen*, 72-86 (79).

law.[149] Aquinas had stated that human laws can also bind conscience, but only if they are just.[150] Jean Gerson (1363-1429) went further and separated laws directed to the spiritual life from laws directed to the civil and political life. The violation of civil law only constitutes a sin if it also entails a violation of the divine law. The legislator, both of the state and of the church, cannot impose punishments in the jurisdiction of the soul.[151] The founder of the School of Salamanca,[152] Francisco Vitoria (1483/1486-1546), rejected Gerson's statements

149 On this topic see among the numerous publications: F. Todescan, *Lex, natura, beatitudo, Il problema della legge nella scolastica Spagnola del sec. XVI*, Padova, CEDAM, 1973; M. Villey, *La promotion de la loi et du droit subjectif dans la Seconde Scolastique*, in P. Grossi (ed.), *La seconda scolastica nella formazione del diritto privato moderno*, Milano, Giuffrè, 1973, 53-72; R. Tortajada, *La renaissance de la scolastique, la Réforme et les théories du droit naturel*, in A. Béraud, G. Faccarello (eds.), *Nouvelle histoire de la pensée économique Vol.1. Des scolastiques aux classiques*, Paris, La Découverte, 1993, 71-91; P. Landau, *Methoden des kanonischen Rechts in der Frühen Neuzeit zwischen Humanismus und Naturrecht*, in *Zeitschrift für neure Rechtsgeschichte*, 21 (1999), 7-28; F. Hafner, A. Loretan, C. Spenlé, *Naturrecht und Menschenrecht. Der Beitrag der Spanischen Spätscholastik zur Entwicklung der Menschenrechte*, in F. Grunert, K. Seelmann (eds.), *Die Ordnung der Praxis. Neue Studien zur Spanischen Spätscholastik*, Berlin, De Gruyter, 2001, 123-53; F. Todescan, *Il problema del diritto naturale fra Seconda scolastica e giusnaturalismo laico secentesco. Una introduzione bibliografica*, in F. Arici, F. Todescan (eds.), *Iustus ordo e ordine della natura, Sacra doctrina e saperi politici fra XVI e XVIII secolo*, Padova, CEDAM, 2007, 1-61; T. Pink, *Action, Will and Law in Late Scholasticism*, in J. Kraye, R. Saarinen (eds.), *Moral Philosophy on the Threshold of Modernity*, Dordrecht, Springer, 2007, 31-51; F. Rexroth, *Die scholastische Wissenschaft in den Meistererzählungen der europäischen Geschichte*, in K. Ridder, S. Patzold (eds.), *Die Aktualität der Vormoderne. Epochenentwürfe zwischen Alterität und Kontinuität*, Berlin, De Gruyter, 2013, 111-34.

150 T. Aquinas, *Summa theologiae*, Iae, IIae, q. 96.

151 J. Gerson, *De vita spirituali animae*, in P. Glorieux (ed.), *Ouvres complètes*, lectio II, cor. 2-3, 133-4; lectio IV, cor 4-5, 161 cit. in P. Prodi, *Una storia della giustizia*, 182-4.

152 In general on the school of Salamanca see J.A. Trentman, *Scholasticism in the Seventeenth Century*, in N. Kretzmann, A. Kenny, J. Pinborg (eds.), *The Cambridge History of Later Medieval Philosophy. From the Rediscovery of Aristotle to the Disintegration of Scholasticism 1100-1600*, Cambridge, Cambridge University Press, 1982, 818-37; U.G. Leinsle, *Die Scholastik der Neuzeit bis zur Aufklärung*, in E. Coreth, W.M. Neidl, G. Pfligersdorffer (eds.), *Christliche Philosophie im katholischen Denken des 19. und 20. Jahrhunderts*, vol. 2, Graz, Wien, Köln, Styria, 1988, 54-69; E. Rummel, *The Humanistic-Scholastic Debate in the Renaissance and Reformation*, Cambridge (MA), London, Harvard University Press, 1995; J. Belda Plans, *La escuela de Salamanca y la renovación de la teología en el siglo XVI*, Madrid, Biblioteca de autores cristianos, 2000; L. Honnefelder, H. Möhle, J., Söder, *Scholastik*, in *LThK*[3] 9 (2000), 199-202; M.W.F. Stone, *Scholastic Schools and Early Modern Philosophy*, in D. Rutherford (ed.), *The Cambridge Companion to Early Modern Philosophy*, Cambridge, Cambridge University Press, 2006, 299-327; J. Hankins, *Humanism, Scholasticism and Renaissance Philosophy*, in J. Hankins (ed.), *The Cambridge Companion to Renaissance Philosophy*, Cambridge, Cambridge University Press, 2007, 30-48; S. Orrego-Sanchez, *The 16th century school of Salamanca as a context of synthesis between the Middle Ages*

on the efficacy of law in conscience. He maintained that the sovereign has the power to promulgate laws that bind the faithful in conscience. Human law, indeed, also comes from God and therefore must be respected.[153]

The relation between the different types of laws, their differences and their impacts on the conscience became a crucial problem, one which was especially investigated by the commentaries on justice and right (*De iustitia et iure*) started by the Dominican Domingo Soto (1494-1560), a disciple of Vitoria.[154] The early modern scholastics acted as jurists exploring the impact of the law in conscience.[155] Criminal law, international law, fiscal law, property law and all the main areas of law received attention.[156] In particular, systematic treatises presented vast discussions about contract law. Aquinas and the medieval scholastics had provided the just price theory, the interest-taking prohibition and the doctrine of restitution, with new foundations within the framework of Aristotelian philosophy. These topics were deeply explored, together with the

---

and the Renaissance in theological and philosophical matters, in C. Burnett, J. Meirinhos, J. Hamesse (eds.), *Continuities and Disruptions between the Middle Ages and the Renaissance*, Louvain-la-Neuve, FIDEM, 2008, 113-38; M.A. Pena González, *La Escuela de Salamanca. De la Monarquía hispánica al Orbe católico*, Madrid, Biblioteca de Autores Cristianos, 2009; A. Pagden, *The School of Salamanca*, in G. Klosko (ed.), *The Oxford Handbook of the History of Political Philosophy*, Oxford, Oxford University Press, 2011, 246-57; D.D. Novotný, *Ens rationis from Suárez to Caramuel: A Study in Scholasticism of the Baroque Era*, New York, Fordham University Press, 2013.

153 D. Deckers, *Gerechtigkeit und Recht. Eine historisch-kritische Untersuchung der Gerechtigkeitslehre des Francisco de Vitoria (1483-1546)*, Freiburg, Wien, Universitätsverlag, 1991; P. Prodi, *Una storia della giustizia*, 203-4.

154 See a list in P.A. Folgado o.s.a., *Los Tratados De Legibus y De Iustitia et Iure* en los autores españoles del siglo XVI y primera mitad del XVII, in *La ciudad de dios, revista agustiniana*, v. CLXXII, 1959, 275-302. A more general list of the early modern scholastics' works on law and morality is now in W. Decock, C. Birr, *Recht und Moral*, 35-49.

155 P. Legendre, *L'inscription du droit canon dans la théologie: Remarques sur la Seconde Scolastique*, in *Proceedings of the V International Congress of Medieval Canon Law*, Città del Vaticano, Biblioteca Apostolica Vaticana, 1980, 443-54 (450).

156 See for instance, P. Grossi, *La proprietà nel sistema privatistico della seconda scolastica*, in P. Grossi (ed.), *La seconda scolastica nella formazione*, 117-222; H. Maihold, *Strafe für fremde Schuld? Die Systematisierung des Strafbegriffs in der Spanischen Spätscholastik und Naturrechtslehre*, Wien, Köln, Weimar, Böhlau, 2005; V. Lavenia, Fraus et Cautela *Théologie morale et fiscalité*, in S. Boarini (ed.), *La casuistique classique: genèse, formes, devenir*, Saint-Étienne, Publications de l'Université de Saint-Étienne, 2009, 43-57; F. Todescan, *Jus gentium medium est intra jus naturale et jus civile: la "double face" du droit des gens dans la scolastique espagnole du 16ème siècle*, in P.M. Dupuy, V. Chetail, *The Roots of International Law / Les fondements du droit international. Liber Amicorum Peter Haggenmacher*, Leiden, Boston, Brill, 2013, 121-80; H. Maihold, *God's Wrath and Charity Criminal Law in (Counter-) Reforming Discourse of Redemption and Retribution*, in W. Decock, J.J. Ballor, M. Germann, L. Waelkens, (eds.), *Law and Religion*, 149-73.

construction of a general theory based on the canon law principle of the binding effect of simple agreements.[157]

Another theme that was familiar to the scholastic theologians was the 'doubtful conscience'.[158] Moral choices are particularly dangerous when faced with the application of two apparently contrasting rules. To Aquinas, moral uncertainty should be avoided. Yet, as complete avoidance is not always possible, he suggested following the safer way (*in dubiis tutior pars eligenda est*).[159] With the increase of theological and juridical authorities, this rule became very important. Indeed, it was necessary to locate the right solution in a jungle of opinions. For instance, the *Enchiridion* of Martín de Azpilcueta, or Dr. Navarrus, published in 1549,[160] contains a detailed examination of different opinions, as in Azpilcueta's view it is not licit to follow an opinion only because of the majority's support.[161]

Jean Gerson clarified Aquinas's rule, stating that it was to apply only when there was equal weight between the reasons *pro* or *contra* a determinate choice. He also allowed Christians to make risky moral decisions with the support of

157 F. Gómez Camacho, *Economia y filosofia moral: la formacion del pensamiento economico europeo en la Escolastica espanola*, Madrid, Sintesis, 1998; A. Del Vigo Gutiérrez, *Economía y ética en el siglo XVI. Estudio comparativo entre los Padres de la Reforma y la teología española*, Biblioteca de autores christianos, Madrid, 2006; W. Decock, *Theologians and Contract Law*, passim.

158 See M.W.F. Stone, *Scrupolosity and Conscience. Probabilism in Early Modern Scholastic Ethics*, in H. Braun, E. Wallace (eds.), *Contexts of Conscience in Early Modern Europe, 1500-1700*, 1-16.

159 I. Kantola, *Probability and Moral Uncertainty in Late Medieval and Early Modern Times*, Helsinki, Luther –Agricola Society, 1994, 83-4.

160 First published as *Manual de Confessores et penitentes* in 1549, then it was translated in Castiglian in 1553 and finally in latin in 1573 as *Enchiridion sive manuale confessariorum et poenitentium*. See E. Dunoyer, *L'Enchiridion Confessariorium del Navarro*, Pamplona, Gurea, 1957. The book is divided in four parts: 1) the confession; 2) the Decalogue; 3) the sacraments; 4) the status of life. On Roman Catholic casuistry in the early modern era see: R.M. Wenley, *Casuistry*, in J. Hastings, (ed.), *Encyclopedia of Religion and Ethics*, Edinburgh, 1910, 239; K.E. Kirk, *Conscience and Its Problems. An Introduction to Casuistry*, (first ed. 1927), Cambridge, James & Co., 1999; A.R. Jonsen, S.E. Toulmin, *The Abuse of Casuistry*, 101-37; E. Leites (ed.), *Conscience and Casuistry*, passim; M. Turrini, *La coscienza e le leggi. Morale e diritto nei testi per la confessione della prima Età moderna*, Bologna, Il Mulino, 1991; V. Lavenia, *L'infamia e il perdono: tributi, pene e confessione nella teologia morale della prima età moderna*, Il Mulino, Bologna, 2004; P. Hurtubise, *La casuistique*, passim; W. Stark, *Casuistry*, in P.P., Wiener (ed.), *Dictionary of the History of the Ideas, New York, Scribner, 1973-1974* http://web.archive.org/web/20060618095059/http://etext.lib.virginia.edu/cgi-local/DHI/dhi.cgi?id=dv1-35 (accessed 24.11.17); N. Reinhardt, *Voices of Conscience. Royal Confessors and Political Counsel in Seventeenth Century Spain and France*, Oxford, Oxford University Press, 2016.

161 M. Turrini, *La coscienza e le leggi*, 153-5.

only a limited amount of information. The opinion considered as the most reasonable could be adopted without the necessity of knowing the whole moral discussion.[162] Gerson applied it to business behaviours: merchants must only consult theologians or lawyers for the tricky moral aspects of a negotiation. Two of the greatest Dominican moral theologians of the fifteenth century, Johannes Nider (1380-1438) and Antonino of Florence (1389-1459), followed Gerson's positions.[163] Bartolomé de Medina (1527-1580) used Gerson's works as basis for his discussion on probabilism,[164] which was then advocated by many Jesuits.[165]

1.4.3 *Jesuit Moral Theology*

The Jesuits were involved with confession and casuistry from the beginning of their order. Already the first constitutions of the order (1541) imposed the study of cases of conscience, particularly with regard to restitution.[166] Based on the experience of Ignatius of Loyola,[167] Jesuits insisted on the high frequency of confession. Ignatius showed an ascetic road focused on self-controlled interior

162 R. Schüßler, *Johan Gerson, Moral Certainty and the Renaissance of Ancient Scepticism*, in H.E. Braun, E. Vallance (eds.), *The Reinassance Conscience*, Oxford, Wiley-Blackwell, 2011, 11-28 (15-9).

163 I. Kantola, *Probability and Moral Uncertainty*, 112; R. Schüßler, *Johan Gerson, Moral Certainty and the Renaissance*, 14 n. 9.

164 I. Kantola, *Probability and Moral Uncertainty*, 124-30; For a different account of the origins of probabilism see F. O' Reilly, *Duda y opinion, La consciencia moral en Soto y Medina*, Pamplona, Universidad de Navarra, 2006, 81-90. For an accurate synthesis, see: Wim Decock, *Theologians and Contract Law*, 74-7.

165 G. Otte, *Der Probabilismus: eine Theorie auf der Grenze zwischen Theologie und Jurisprudenz*, in P. Grossi, (ed.), *La seconda scolastica nella formazione*, 283-302; J. Mahoney, *Probabilismus*, in *TRE*, vol. XXVII, 1997, 465-8; J. Franklin, *The Science of Conjecture: Evidence and Probability before Pascal*, Baltimore, The John Hopkins University Press, 2001; R. Schüßler, *Moral im Zweifel*, Bd. I: *Die scholastische Theorie des Entscheidens unter moralischer Unsicherheit*, 2003 and Bd. II: *Die Herausforderung des Probabilismus*, Paderborn, Mentis, 2006; R. Schüßler, *Moral self-ownership and 'ius possessionis' in late scholastics*, in V. Mäkinen, P. Korkman (eds.), *Transformations in Medieval and Early-Modern Rights Discourse*, Dordrecht, Springer, 2006, 149-72; D. Schwartz, *Probabilism Reconsidered: Deference to Experts, Types of Uncertainty, and Medicines*, in *Journal of the History of Ideas* 75 (2014), 373-93; S. Tutino, *Uncertainty in Post-Reformation Catholicism: A History of Probabilism*, Oxford, Oxford University Press, 2017.

166 J. De Blic, *Jésuites. Théologie morale*, in *Dictionnaire de théologie catholique*, vol. VIII, 1069-70; P. Hurtubise, *La casuistique*, 206.

167 Ignazio di Loyola, *Racconto di un pellegrino*, Roma, Città Nuova, 1988. G. Angelozzi, *I gesuiti e la confessione*, in *Lo Sguardo. Rivista di filosofia*, 10, 2012 (III) – *La rivoluzione interiore*, 39-53 (46-7). More in general see R.A. Maryks, *A Companion to Ignatius of Loyola. Life, Writings, Spirituality, Influence*, Leiden-Boston, Brill, 2014.

discipline and confession.[168] Through their spiritual exercises, the Jesuits helped Christians to understand the will of God in their life, so that they could effectively strive against sin and reach salvation. For this reason, they were not only involved with the usual confession but also with the general confession, which concerned the whole life. It required an acute self-examination and preparation, and also the annotation of sins. Moreover, unlike the other orders, Jesuits decided not to obtain any privilege of confession. They accepted people coming of their own free will, because of the conviction of being better served.[169] Jesuits qualified the confessor not only like a doctor and judge, but also as a consoler. Consolation, exalting the mercy of God in the face of the difficulties of the Christian life, turned out to be the salient characteristic of a Jesuit confessor.[170] Moreover, it became a central aspect discussed at the Council of Trent.[171]

The Jesuit model of confession required a specific formation. At the beginning the Jesuits adopted manuals for confessors like the *Aurea armilla* (1549) of Bartolomeo Fumi (Fumo, d. ca. 1555), the *Summula peccatorum* of Thomas de Vio (Cajetan, 1469-1534), the *Enchiridion* of Azpilcueta and the *Breve directorium ad confessarii ac confitentis munus rite obeundum* (1554) of Johannes de Polanco (1516-1577). These works were directed to priests, but were not designed for lessons. In the second part of the sixteenth century, the Roman seminary designed an advanced two-year program for the education of confessors (*cursus minor*), which was based on the systematic examination of cases of conscience and aimed at educating the confessor as a professional.[172] The new courses dedicated to the cases of conscience were based on Heinrich

168 G. Angelozzi, *I gesuiti e la confessione*, 47-8.

169 J.W. O'Malley, *The First Jesuits*, Cambridge (MA), London, Harvard University Press, 1993, 69-74.

170 J.W. O'Malley, *The First Jesuits*, 136-52; M. Maher, SJ, *Confession and Consolation: The Society of Jesus and its Promotion of the General Confession*, in K. Jackson Lualdi, A.T. Thayer (eds.), *Penitence in the Age of Reformations*, Aldershot, Ashgate, 2000, 184-200.

171 A. Prosperi, *La confessione e il foro della coscienza*, in P. Prodi, W. Reinhard (eds.), *Il concilio di Trento e il moderno*, Bologna, Il Mulino, 1996, 225-54. On penance in this period see M. Schmoeckel, *Der Entwurf eines Strafrechts der Gegenreformation. Prova, pena e penitenza nel sistema post-tridentino*, in M. Cavina (eds.), *Tiberio Deciani (1509-1582). Alle origini del pensiero giuridico moderno*, Udine, Forum, 2004, 207-34.

172 G. Angelozzi, *L'insegnamento dei casi di coscienza nella pratica educativa della Compagnia di Gesù*, in G. Brizzi (ed.), *La 'Ratio studiorum'. Modelli culturali e pratiche educative dei gesuiti in Italia tra Cinque e Seicento*, Roma, Bulzoni, 1981, 121-62; G. Angelozzi, *Interpretazioni della penitenza sacramentale in età moderna*, in *Religioni e società*, I (1986), n. 2, 73-87. See also L. Giard (ed.) *Les Jésuites à la Renaissance. Système éducatif et production du savoir*, Paris, PUF, 1995; C. Pavur (ed. and trans.), *The Ratio Studiorum: The Official Plan for Jesuit Education*, St. Louis, The Institute of Jesuit Sources, 2005.

Henriquez' (1536-1608) and Juan Azor's (1536-1603) first manuals of moral theology:[173] the *Theologiae moralis summa* (1591) and the *Institutiones morales* (1600).[174] The latter, in particular, shows a preeminent juridical structure. The first book includes an analysis of human actions, emotions and sins, and then the law, natural law, canon law and part of the Decalogue. The remaining part of the Decalogue is described in the second and third books. Among the juridical matters, questions about property law are located under the fifth commandment, marriage under the sixth, and contract law under the seventh.[175]

Jesuit confessors became skilled lawyers, capable of assisting believers in the most delicate affairs. They studied law and analyzed the position of the faithful in terms of rights and legal and moral obligations.[176] Another specific feature of the Jesuit moral theology was the doctrine of mental reservations. The theologians affirmed that in specific cases (e.g. threat to life), it was not a lie if someone asserted what he believed to be false, adding some further statements in his mind that made it true.[177] The Jesuit moral-legalistic approach received bitter criticism from other Roman Catholics and Protestant theologians.[178] For example, Meier, the Lutheran theologian we quoted at the beginning, condemned Jesuit moral theology as 'demagogic' and 'laxist'.[179] Still, Jesuit writings were well known and discussed by the most cultured jurists and natural lawyers of the day.[180]

---

173 On the history of moral theology see: J. Theiner, *Die Entwicklung der Moraltheologie zur eigenständigen Disziplin*, Regensburg, Pustet, 1970; L. Vereecke, *Storia della teologia morale*, passim; L. Vereecke, *De Guillaume D'Ockham à Saint Alphonse de Liguori: études d'histoire de la théologie morale moderne 1300-1787*, Roma, Collegium S. Alfonsi de Urbe, 1986. See also the interesting reflections in C. Bergfeld, *Katholische Moraltheologie und Naturrechtslehre*, in H. Coing (ed.), *Handbuch der Quellen und Literatur der neueren europäischen Privatrechtsgeschichte*, vol. II, first part, München, C.H. Beck, 1973, 999-1033.

174 J. Theiner, *Die Entwicklung der Moraltheologie*, 253-76.

175 J. Azor, *Institutiones morales*, Coloniae Agrippinae, 1612.

176 W. Decock, *From Law to Paradise: Confessional Catholicism and Legal Scholarship*, in *Legal History, Rechtsgeschichte*, 18/2011, 12-34.

177 A.R. Jonsen, S. Edelston Toulmin, *The Abuse of Casuistry*, 195-215; J. Somerville, *The 'New Art of Lying': Equivocation, Mental Reservation and Casuistry*, in E. Leites (ed.), *Conscience and Casuistry*, 159-84 (160); R.B. Miller, *Moral Sources, Ordinary Life and Truth Telling in Jeremy Taylor's Casuistry*, in J.F. Keenan, SJ, T.A. Shannon, *The Context of Casuistry*, Washington, Georgetown University Press, 1995, 131-58.

178 S. Knebel, *Wille, Würfel und Wahrscheinlichkeit, Das System der moralischen Notwendigkeit in der Jesuitenscholastik*, Hamburg, Meiner, 2000, 20-4; H. Callewier, *Anti-jezuïtisme in de Zuidelijke Nederlanden (1542-1773)*, in *Trajecta*, 16 (2007), 30-50; P.A. Fabre, C. Maire (eds.), *Les Antijésuites. Discours, figures et lieux de l'antijésuitisme à l'époque moderne*, Rennes, Presses universitaires de Rennes, 2010; W. Decock, *Theologians and Contract Law*, 16.

179 G.T. Meier, *Introductio in universum theologiae moralis*, Cap. XVIII, n. 5.

180 W. Decock, *From Law to Paradise*, 34.

1.5 Conclusion

In these introductory notes, we briefly outlined some patterns of the Roman Catholic theology for the *forum internum* up to the sixteenth century. In this period, Christian spiritual life was not only understood in the light of Scripture, but also through a variegated assortment of teachings like monasticism, penitential books, Aristotelian philosophy, Roman law and canon law. Christians were viewed as pilgrims walking towards heaven. They had to fight against sins in order to win their salvation. The severe justice of God stipulated punishment for any sins committed, and priests were charged with preparing Christians for the final judgment. They exercised jurisdiction over the souls of their parishioners and must know sins in detail, to assess the guilt and mete out acts of penance. These acts were necessary for eternal salvation, as they satisfied God's just wrath over the sins.

In their spiritual walk, Christians were called to obey the divine law and natural law. They were considered free to perform good or evil acts, rejecting or accepting natural law or the human laws that comply with it. For this reason, theologians were deeply involved with law. They needed legal formation in order to be erudite counselors and judges. Education programs of many orders included the study of cases of conscience and moral theology. Priests had a vast literature at their disposition: manuals for confessors and penitents, collections of cases of conscience, manuals of moral theology, systematic treatises. These writings were expressions of the values of the different religious orders. They also looked in a special way at contract law issues. Commerce and finance were regulated by the doctrines of usury, just price, restitution, oaths and promises. These teachings reflected the fundamental theological and legal vision of the Roman Catholic Church. It is precisely this vision that the Lutheran theologians will condemn, turning back to the purity of the Christian revelation as expressed in Scripture.

CHAPTER 2

The Engagement of the Lutheran Theologians with Contract Law: Principles and Literature

2.0 Introduction

In his work on the biography and literature of jurists and theologians (1842) Karl Friedrich Göschel (1781-1861) began the chapter dedicated to the evangelical jurists with two legendary names: Dr. Martin Luther and Dr. Philipp Melanchthon.[1] Göschel, not only a jurist, but also a scholar of art, history, theology and philosophy, described the legal contribution of the fathers of the Reformation. Luther and Melanchthon were indeed deeply engaged with the formulation of legal theories. These theories did not only concern the administration of the Church, but also other spheres of law – for instance, criminal law, public law and contract law. In the light of their theological principles, Luther and Melanchthon articulated a sophisticated analysis of contract law.

Following the example of Luther and Melanchthon, a number of theologians also dealt with contract law. These theologians were very often not educated in law, but only in theology. This is an important aspect to consider while examining their works. Languages, concepts and methods that previously, among the scholastic theologians, showed a pregnant legal character, now tend to migrate towards a more theological setting. Furthermore, the Lutheran theologians did not develop consistent and systematic treatises of contract law, as their Roman Catholic colleagues did. They rather approached contract law in a multiform variety of writings, often not only dedicated to contract law, but also including many other different topics.

The purpose of this chapter is then to offer an overview of the Lutheran theologians and provide the basic information that is necessary to understand their works. Their contributions regarding contract law will not be examined in detail now, but in the following parts. This chapter is framed in four paragraphs dedicated approximately to four different periods: the first and second halves of the sixteenth century, and the first and second halves of the seventeenth

1 K.F. Göschel, *Zerstreute Blätter aus den Hand- und Hülfsakten eines Juristen: wissenschaftliches und Geschichtliches aus der Theorie und Praxis oder aus der Lehre und dem Leben des Rechts, 3.Th./2, Zur theologisch-juristischen Biographie und Literatur*, Schleusingen, 1842, 204-9; 210-13.

 | DOI:10.30965/9783657701506_004

century. Each one includes a brief introduction of the context and then concentrates on the biographical profile of the theologians, and on the essential features of their theological and legal attitudes.

2.1 The Reformation of Contract Law

2.1.1 *Introduction*

"The time to be silent is gone, the time to speak has come" (Eccl. 3, 7).[2] With these famous words, Luther began his groundbreaking pamphlet *An den christlichen Adel deutscher Nation* (1520), by which he illustrated his program for the reformation of the Roman Catholic Church. Not only did Luther attack the Church, but he also pilloried the credit system, which he saw as a means invented by the devil to support the Papal Church and destroy the German nation.[3] He railed against bankers like the Fuggers and disputed with capitalist supporters like the scholastic Johann Eck (1486-1543) and with partisans of the evangelical communion like the Anabaptist Jacob Strauss (1480-1533). He published a number of popular treatises dedicated to the investigation of the lawfulness and right application of the chief financial transactions and their legal platforms.

The German financial economy centred on three main forms of credit. The most common one was the purchase of annuities (*census, rent, Zins*). This agreement presented many variants, among which the *Zinskauf* or *widerkaufflicher Zins*. In return for use of the capital, it assured returns of approximately 5% yearly.[4] It was widespread especially in commercial cities like Cologne and in the Hanseatic region, where it was used to get capital for various economic needs. The annuities could be sold to a third party, and markets dedicated to the annuities were not uncommon. Together with annuities, other popular forms of credit were the payment in advance to the entrepreneur for wares that will be later delivered, partnership and joint-stock company.[5]

2 M. Luther, *An den christlichen Adel deutscher Nation*, in WA 6, 404.

3 E.F. Rice Jr., A. Grafton, *The Foundation of Early Modern Europe, 1460-1559*, New York, Norton, 1994, 184. The authors notice that in Augsburg at the beginning of the Reformation Luther's attack to the Roman Catholic Church was inseparable to the criticism towards capitalism.

4 See III/2 for further details.

5 W.J. Wright, *The Nature of Early Capitalism*, 187-8.

Financial instruments were mainly used in the cities,[6] as the German economy[7] was primarily agrarian.[8] In the first half of the century, trade routes connected Cologne and the Hanseatic region with the most important European economic centres. In Augsburg and Nuremberg, merchant's firms or banking families, such as the Fugger and the Welser, were formidable sources of capital.[9] Mining activity, manufacturing and textile industries were also widespread. In particular, the Thuringian region was the home for an important mining industry and for woad production.[10]

The sixteenth century observed the emergence of German capitalism. Yet, economic conditions were not always positive. The first half of the century saw a monetary crisis between 1500-1525,[11] which resulted in the Peasants' War (1524-1526).[12] In addition, a growth of population and the rise of prices for foodstuffs (this age is indeed recorded as the 'price revolution'[13]) caused a decrease of overall wealth.[14] The second half of the century was characterized

6 See E. Isenmann, *Die deutsche Stadt im Mittelalter 1150-1550. Stadtgestalt, Recht, Verfassung, Stadtregiment, Kirche, Gesellschaft, Wirtschaft*, 2nd. ed., Köln, Weimar, Wien, Böhlau, 2014, 957-72.

7 On the socio-economic context of the Lutheran Reformation bibliography is abundant. Among the more recent works see F. Irsigler, *Luthers Herkunf und Umwelt-Wirtschaft und Gesellschaft der Zeit*, in G. Bott (ed.), *Martin Luther und die Reformation in Deutschland*, Frankfurt am Main, Insel, 1983, 17-40; H.J. Prien, *Luthers Wirtschaftsethik*, 31-48; A. Del Vigo Gutiérrez, *Economia y ética*, 138-61; H. Peuckert, *Martin Luther: a First Modern Economist*, in J. Backhaus (ed.), *The Reformation: As a Pre-condition for Modern Capitalism*, Münster, Lit, 2010, 13-64 (18-20); M. Luther, *On Commerce and Usury*, ed. with introduction and notes by Philipp Robinson Rössner, London and New York, Anthem, 2015, 1-100.

8 P. Robinson Rössner, *The Crisis of the Reformation*, in *Le crisi finanziarie. Gestione, implicazioni sociali e conseguenze nell'età preindustriale. The Financial Crises. Their Management, Their Social Implications and Their Consequences in Pre-Industrial Times. Selezione di ricerche, Selection of Essays*, Firenze, Firenze University Press, 2016, 19-48 (22-23).

9 H. Lutz, *Reformation und Gegenreformation*, München, Wien, Oldenburg, 1979, 11; W.J. Wright, *The Nature of Early Capitalism*, in B. Scribner, *Germany. A New Social and Economic History*, Vol. I, 1450-630, London, Arnold, 1996, 181-208 (182-3).

10 P. Robinson Rössner, *On commerce and Usury*, 50-62.

11 P. Robinson Rössner, *The Crisis of the Reformation*, 22-23.

12 P. Blicke, *Die Revolution von 1525*, Münich, Wien, Oldenbourg, 1975. On the juridical and theological characters of 'the revolution of the common man' see G.K. Hasselhoff, D. von Mayenburg (eds.), *Die Zwölf Artikel von 1525 und das 'Göttliche Recht' der Bauern – rechtshistorische und theologische Dimensionen*, Würzburg, Erzog, 2012.

13 J.H. Munro, *Price Revolution*, in *The New Palgrave Dictionary of Economics*, 2nd ed., vol. 6, Basingstoke, Palgrave Macmillan, 2008, 631-34.

14 M. Luther, *On Commerce and Usury*, ed. with introduction and notes by Philipp Robinson Rössner, 46-7.

by economic decline, with the notable exception of Hamburg.[15] Augsburg suffered the bankruptcy of at least 70 companies between 1556 and 1584.[16] In response to these economic failures, reforms of the bankruptcy law took place, which acted at a systematic level against merchants who were unable to pay their debts.[17]

Commerce and financial operations gave rise to complex moral and juridical issues that the Roman Catholic Church resolved through the fundamental principles of its contract doctrines: the just price theory and the interest prohibition. As seen before, Roman Catholic theologians and canonists were formidable experts in solving these problems. Luther began from the conclusions already spotted by the Catholics, but envisaged a new way of looking at contract law in the light of his theological principles. Since the beginning of the Reformation, a flight of theologians undertook this road and wrestled with issues concerning contract law and financial economy. Urbanus Rhegius (1489-1541), Philip Melanchthon (1497-1560), Johannes Brenz (1499-1570) and Johannes Aepinus (1499-1553) expanded Luther's ideas and devised contract doctrines including theoretical principles and practical solutions for the lawfulness and application of these financial agreements.

In the following paragraphs, we are first going to explore Luther's and Melanchthon's theological principles, which form the background not only of their writings about contract law, but also of their followers. Then, we will provide the basic coordinates of Luther and Melanchthon's first disciples, who developed significant contributions about contract law.

15 C.M. Cipolla, *Storia economica dell'Europa pre-industriale*, Il Mulino, (new. ed.) 2002, 354-355.

16 T.M. Safley, *Business Failure and Civil Scandal in Early Modern Europe*, in *The Business History Review*, vol. 83, n. 1, A Special Issue on Scandals and Panics (Spring, 2009), 35-60; M. Häberlein, *Merchants' Bankruptcies, Economic Development and Social Relations in German Cities During the Long 16th Century*, in T.M. Safley (ed.), *The History of Bankruptcy. Economic, Social and Cultural Implications in Early Modern Europe*, New York, Routledge, 2013, 19-33.

17 P. Fischer, *Bankruptcy in Early Modern German Territories*, in T.M. Safley, *The History of Bankruptcy*, 173-184. For instance, in Ausburg an Ordinance of Police (1537) established that debtors who could not pay debts in excess of 200 *Rhenische Gulden* should be imprisoned, and debtors for inferior amounts had to leave the city until the debts were paid. At the imperial level, the Imperial Police Ordinances (*Reichpolizeiordnungen*) of 1548 and 1577 distinguished between merchants who had failed because of unfortunate circumstances, and merchants who sought to mislead their creditors. See M. Weber, *Die Reichpolizeiordnungen von 1530, 1548 und 1577: Historische Einführung und Edition*, Frankfurt am Main, Klostermann, 2002, 198-9; 252-4.

2.1.2 *Luther: Theological and Legal Premises*

2.1.2.1 Justification and Moral Actions

Luther's theology cannot be examined in depth here.[18] However, we need to recall some of his basic assumptions that will help in understanding his (and his supporters') contract doctrine. The starting point of his whole theology is the doctrine of justification. Medieval theology conceived life as an ascesis towards God, a road of purification, where the sins not absolved by penance would lead to eternal damnation.[19] In opposition, Luther intended salvation as an act gratuitously granted by God. Because of original sin, man is incapable of doing anything to procure his salvation. God wants to encounter man and to save him through His Word, which operates in indissoluble unity with the Holy Spirit and gives man faith. Through faith man obtains justification: God does not impute sins but forgives them. God grants the Christians righteousness, externally, by the righteousness of Christ.[20]

Justification is the source of any moral actions of the Christian. Because of his sin, man cannot fully understand God's will without justification. Justified by faith, instead, man is free and eager to do works pleasing to God. Man is unable to love God; it is only God who loves him through the Spirit. Unlike Aquinas, for Luther the principle of charitable actions is not in the human will but only in the Holy Spirit.[21] Man receives God's love and transmits it to the neighbour.[22] The neighbour is not seen as an instrument to gain spiritual merits in the eyes of God. Rather, the Christian acts out of gratitude for the salvation already obtained and only aims to help the neighbour.[23] Every Christian

18 Among the most recent essays on this topic see B. Lohse, *Martin Luther's Theology: Its Historical and Systematic Development*, trans. R.A. Harrisville, Edinburgh, T &T Clarck, 1999; A. Beutel (ed.), *Luther Handbuch*, Tübingen, Mohr Siebeck, 2005; O. Bayer, *Martin Luthers Theologie*, 3ed., Tübingen, Mohr Siebeck, 2007; R. Kolb, I. Dingel, L. Batka (eds.), *The Oxford Handbook of Martin Luther's Theology*, Oxford, Oxford University Press, 2014.

19 See I/1.

20 M. Mattes, *Luther on Justification as Forensic and Effective*, in R. Kolb, I. Dingel, L. Batka (eds.), *The Oxford Handbook of Martin Luther's Theology*, Oxford, Oxford University Press, 2014, 264-73.

21 I. Singer, *The Nature of Love*, Vol. 1, *Plato to Luther*, Chicago, The University of Chicago Press, 2nd ed., 1984, 327-9.

22 Luther does not presuppose love for oneself, rather love is totally focused upon the neighbour. See A. Raunio, *Summe des christlichen Lebens: die Goldene Regel als Gesetz der Liebe in der Theologie Martin Luthers von 1510-1527*, Mainz, Von Zabern, 2001; A. Raunio, *Divine and Natural Law in Luther and Melanchthon*, in V. Mäkinen (ed.), *Lutheran Reformation and the Law*, 21-62 (34-5).

23 See the classic work by P. Althaus, *Die Ethik Martin Luthers*, Gütersloh, Gerd Mohn, 1965, 11-31; M.J. Suda, *Die Ethik Martin Luthers*, Göttingen, Vandenhoeck & Ruprecht, 2006, 79-95.

is called to perform his tasks in the world through the grace of faith and the love for the neighbour.[24] These basic ideas determine Luther's understanding of Christian moral and social activity.

2.1.2.2 The Law and the Gospel

For Luther, God's Word displays two distinct and intimately united forms:[25] the law and the Gospel.[26] The Gospel is by definition the promise of Christ, who frees man from the dread of the law, from sin and death; it brings grace, the remission of sins, justice and eternal life.[27] The law is included in the Decalogue and presents two different uses: the political use (*usus politicus*) and the theological use (*usus theologicus*). God ordered the *usus politicus* for restraining men's trespasses (*ad cohercendas transgressiones*).[28] In this way, He assures the conservation of the secular world by the work of the secular authority that is called to the punishment of crimes and the assurance of peace.[29] The law serves the Gospel: it prevents tumults and insurrections from impeding the announcement of the Gospel.[30]

God ordered the other use, the *usus theologicus*, for the revelation of sins and the salvation of the world. The law reveals one's sins and makes the Christian a

24 A. Pawlas, *Die lutherische Beruf- und Wirtschaftsethik. Eine Einführung*, Neukirchen-Vluyn, Neukirchener, 2000, 64-7.

25 Luther's theology has often been defined as a doctrine of distinctions. See A. Beutel, *Theologie als Unterscheidungslehre*, in A. Beutel (ed.), *Luther Handbuch*, 450-4.

26 On Luther's legal theory see H.J. Berman, J. Witte Jr., *The Transformation of Western Legal Philosophy in Lutheran Germany*, in *Southern California Law Review*, v. 62, September 1989, n. 6, 1575-611; E. Stöve, *Natürliches Recht und Heilige Schrift. Zu einem vergessen Aspekt in Martin Luthers Hermeneutik*, in I. Dingel, V. Leppin, C. Strohm (eds.), *Recht und Reformation. Festschrift für Gottfried Seebas*, Gütersloh, Gütersloher Verlagshaus, 2002, 11-26; H.J. Berman, *Law and Revolution*, 123-35; W.J. Wright, Mandatum Dei *and* lex naturae *in Luther's Lectures on Genesis*, in *Lutherjahrbuch*, 71 (2004), 233 ff.; M. Schmoeckel, *Das Recht*, 24-6; M. Heckel, *Martin Luthers Reformation und das Recht*, 341-447; J. Witte Jr., *'The Law Written on the Heart': Natural Law and Equity in Early Lutheran Thought*, in W. Decock, J.J. Ballor, M. Germann, L. Waelkens, (ed.), *Law and Religion*, 231-65; J. Witte Jr., *From Gospel to Law: The Lutheran Reformation and its Impact on Legal Culture* in T.A. Howard, M.A. Noll (eds.), *Protestantism After 500 Years*, Oxford, Oxford University Press, 2016, 52-74.

27 M. Luther, *Die erste Disputation gegen die Antinomer* (1537), in WA 39, I, 387, 2-4: "*Evangelium propria definitione est promissio de Christo, quae liberat a terroribus legis, a peccato et morte, adfert gratiam, remissionem peccatorum, iustitiam et vitam aeternam*".

28 M. Luther, *In epistolam S. Pauli ad Galatas commentarius* [1531] 1535, in WA 40, 479, 18.

29 M. Luther, *Die dritte Disputation gegen die Antinomer* (1538), in WA 39, I, 549.

30 M. Luther, *In epistolam S. Pauli ad Galatas commentarius* [1531] 1535, in WA 40, 480, 23-25: "*Haec civilis cohercio propter omnes res conservandas, maxime vero, ne tumultibus et seditionibus ferocium hominum cursus Evangelium impediatur*".

sinner desirous of finding justification.[31] The 'true and main task' of the law is that it reveals to man his sin, Luther writes: the blindness, misery, impiety, ignorance, hate, contempt of God, death, hell, judgment and meritorious wrath of God.[32] The law can also have a third, 'pedagogical' use, to teach good works. Though Luther never expounded this use systematically, it nonetheless provided the background for Melanchthon's teachings. The law, with its two uses, and the Gospel identify two forms of the single Word of God that acts in the world.

The distinction between the law and the Gospel lays the foundation of the two kingdoms doctrine.[33] According to Luther, every Christian is simultaneously citizen of a physical and temporal kingdom, the 'earthly kingdom', and of the spiritual kingdom, the heavenly kingdom, illuminated by the Word of God. He is born under the law and sin in the earthly kingdom. He is called to obey the secular authority and to follow its justice based on external force. However, through faith, the Christian is a citizen of the heavenly kingdom. Here he is renovated by grace, justified and bound by the Gospel. He is educated by the Scriptures and as a member of the Church joins the community of saints, imperfect in this world and perfect after death.

In the earthly kingdom, God is hidden. He appears in the forms of 'masks' (*larvae*). These sets of masks include the human reason, the works of the Christians in the secular institutions, and the three natural orders – the *ordo economicus, ordo politicus* and *ordo ecclesiasticus*.[34] The first order concerns marriage and family, by which the Christians are educated. The second order is the state, instituted to guarantee peace and regularity. The third is the Church, which has no temporal power, but is only called to proclaim the Gospel, to administer the sacraments and to discipline its members. All these orders impute

31 M. Luther, *Die Thesen zu den Disputationen gegen die Antinomer*, in WA 39, I, 344, 30; 397, 9-16.

32 M. Luther, *In epistolam S. Pauli ad Galatas commentarius* [1531] 1535, in WA 40, 481, 13-16: "*Itaque verum officium et principalis ac proprius usus legis est, quod revelat homini suum peccatum, caecitatem, miseriam, impietatem, ignorantiam, odium, contemptum Dei, mortem, infernum, iudicium et commeritam iram apud Dei*".

33 M. Luther, *Von Weltlicher Oberkeit*, in WA 11, 247-81; P. Althaus, *Die Ethik*, 116-59; M.J. Suda, *Die Ethik Martin Luthers*, 117-37; J. Witte, Jr., *Law and Protestantism*, 85-118; H.J. Berman, *Law and revolution*, 123-35; W.J. Wright, *Martin Luther's Understanding of God's Two Kingdoms: A Response to Skepticism*, Grand Rapids, Mi., Baker Academic, 2010, 110-46; M. Heckel, *Martin Luthers Reformation und das Recht*, 137-65. This topic also interested historians of political thought. See the classic study of Q. Skinner, *The Foundation of Modern Political Thought, vol. 2, The Age of the Reformation*, Cambridge, Cambridge University Press, 1978. For further references see: J.A. Carty, *God and Government: Martin Luther's Political Thought*, Montreal, McGill-Queen's University Press, 2017.

34 M. Luther, *Die Zirkulardisputation über das Recht des Widerstands gegen den Kaiser* (1539), in WA 39, II, 42.

God's law and authority in the earthly kingdom, but also transmit God's truth and knowledge.[35] They draw the framework of a specific character of Lutheran morality, which will constantly emphasize the duties and ends of these three orders.

2.1.2.3 Contract Law and the Love for Man's Neighbours

All the three orders are called to give voice to natural law. For Luther, natural law is universal, for all men, both Christians and pagans. It is instilled into human reason. Yet, since reason is corrupted by sin, the appreciation of natural law is to be reawakened in men. Only men justified by faith can recognize the true sense of the natural law. Natural law reveals to men the impossibility of fulfilling the commandments through their own strength, so that they can find salvation in faith.[36] At the same time, only the Christian, moved by the love of God, can fulfil natural law.[37]

The content of the natural law is the Decalogue (Ex. 2,17; Lev. 19,18), resumed in the love for the neighbour (Matt. 7,12 and 22,39; Luke 6,31; Rom. 13,9ff.; Gal. 5,14), and in the discourse of the mountain (Matt. 5,21-28; 22,37-39).[38] The natural law, writes Luther, requires that you shall do and permit to the other what you want that is permitted and done to you.[39] The natural law constitutes the foundation of Luther's perspective on contract law. Indeed, the magistrate is called to issue his law in accordance with natural law, as all the laws must be founded on natural law.[40]

In commenting on the seventh commandment, Luther formulates a set of theoretical principles concerning the lawfulness and right use of private property, commerce and lending.[41] In addition, given the pressure of the market, and the turbulent disputes with Johannes Eck (1486-1543) and Jakob Strauss

35 J. Witte, Jr., *Law and Protestantism*, 89-93.

36 M. Heckel, *Martin Luthers Reformation und das Recht*, 460-1.

37 P. Althaus, *Die Ethik*, 40-1.

38 See M. Heckel, *Martin Luthers Reformation und das Recht*, 441.

39 See for instance M. Luther, *Fastenpostille 1525, Epistel auf den 4 Sonntag nach Epiphanias Rom. 13, 8ff.*, in WA 17, 102, 8-12: "*Denn niemand ist, der nicht fulet und bekennen muesse, das es recht und war sy, da das natuerlich gesetz spricht: Was du dyr gethan und gelassen willt haben, das thue und las auch eym andern, das licht lebet und leucht ynn aller menschen vernunfft, und wenn sie es wollten ansehen, was durfften sie der bucher, lerer odder yrgent eyns gesetzs?*".

40 H.J. Berman, *Law and Revolution*, 74.

41 See P. Athaus, *Die Ethik*, 38. The contracts of sale and the various forms of lending are analysed in the detail in the two catechisms. On Luther's catechisms and their influence, see G. Bode, *Instruction of the Christian Faith by Lutherans after Luther*, in R. Kolb (ed.), *Lutheran Ecclesiastical Culture*, 159-204.

(1480-1533), Luther published four sermons specifically dedicated to the most common financial operations, the interest prohibition and commercial fraud.[42] Starting from the love for the neighbour, Luther offers solutions that emphasize the needs of the debtors and particularly the poor. We will explore these writings in the following chapters.

2.1.3 *Melanchthon: Theological and Legal Premises*

2.1.3.1 The Will, the Law and the Gospel

As with Luther, we focus only on certain aspects of Melanchthon's theology,[43] with no aim of comprehensiveness. Like Luther, Melanchthon distinguishes but connects the two realms – the law, creation, and reason with the Gospel, grace and salvation. According to him, because of sin, man only loves himself and is only capable of external actions. He cannot perform internal actions, namely actions of spirit and love.[44] The divine law, however, requires a 'perfect obedience', which is realized by external and internal actions.[45] Though the divine law requires perfect obedience, man cannot fulfil the law, because he is only capable of external actions. Thus, he can only be saved by the grace of the Holy Spirit through the Word of God.[46]

The Word of God is law and Gospel. Melanchthon claims that God designed not two but three uses of the law.[47] The first use (*usus*) is pedagogical or

42 M. Luther, *(Kleiner) Sermon von dem Wucher* (1519), in WA 6, 3-8; *Ein (Grosser) Sermon von dem Wucher* (1520), in WA 6, 36-60; M. Luther, *Von Kaufshandlung und Wucher* (1524), in WA 15, 293-313; M. Luther, *An die Pfarrherrn, wider den Wucher zu predigen* (1540), in WA 51, 331-424. Several translations exist. See for instance H.J. Hillerbrand, *On Business and Usury*, in H.J. Hillerbrand, *The Annotate Luther. Christian Life in the World*, vol. 5, Minneapolis, Fortress Press, 2017, 131-183; and *An die Pfarrherrn, wider den Wucher zu predigen* in P.D.W. Krey, P.D.S. Krey, *Luther's Spirituality*, New York, Mahwah, Paulist Press, 2007, 34-45.

43 Among the recent works on Melanchthon's theology see G. Frank (ed.), *Der Theologe Melanchthon*, Stuttgart, Thorbecke, 2000; G. Frank, F. Mundt (eds.), *Der Philosoph Melanchthon*, Berlin-Boston, De Gruyter, 2012; I. Dingel, R. Kolb, N. Kuropka, T.J. Wengert (eds), *Philip Melanchthon. Theologian in Classroom, Confession, and Controversy*, Göttingen, Vandenhoeck & Ruprecht, 2012; H. Scheible, *Melanchthon. Vermittler der Reformation. Eine Biographie*. München, C.H. Beck, 2016; G. Frank (ed.), *Philipp Melanchthon. Der Reformator zwischen Glauben und Wissen*, Berlin, Boston, De Gruyter, 2017.

44 P. Melanchthon, *Loci communes (prima eorum aetas)*, in CR XXI, 115. I also used the translations made by H.G. Pöhlmann, *Loci communes 1521*, Gütersloh, Gütersloher Verlaghaus, 1997; C. Preus, *Commonplaces, Loci communes 1521*, Saint Louis, Concordia Publishing House, 2014.

45 P. Melanchthon, *Loci communes (secunda eorum aetas)*, in CR XXI, 303-11.

46 G. Sauter, *Rechtfertigung IV*, in *TRE*, vol. XXVIII, 1997, 315-28 (320-2).

47 On Melanchthon's legal doctrine see: J. Witte Jr., *Law and Protestantism*, 121-39; H.J. Berman, *Law and Revolution*, 78-87; M. Schmoeckel, *Das Recht*, 26-34.

political (*paedagogicus seu politicus*). God ordered the law to restrain the behaviour of all men, so that crimes are not committed.[48] The second use of the law is to reveal man's sins. This accusation of sin paves the way for the work of the Holy Spirit and brings man to the consolation of the Gospel. The Gospel is a promise of salvation. This promise is free of conditions and only requires faith.[49] Justified by faith, man has also to follow the law.[50] For Melanchthon, God uses the law to teach men the good works He desires.[51] The nature of the divine law is that it requires perfect obedience, not only with external actions, but also with the fear and love (*dilectio*) of God. These internal actions cannot exist without faith,[52] which gives birth to the love of God and the neighbour.[53] In this vision the difference between justified and unjustified man emerges sharply. Even though God governs the world with law, and man is capable of performing external actions, faith nonetheless represents an essential element.

This aspect is further expressed in the fact that Melanchthon configures the relation between grace and human will in accordance with the three uses of the law.[54] Concerning the first use of the law, man has freedom of will. But this freedom is only capable of an external obedience of the law. Regarding the second use, the law requires not only external works but also the movement of the heart with the will. In this case, because of sin, man has no free will. Only the grace of the gratuitous remissions of sins through the Holy Spirit establishes the freedom of the will to seek the good. This freedom works concretely in the third use of the law. Thanks to the Holy Spirit, man knows God's will as a right reason (*recta ratio*).[55] The freedom of the will is bound with the Word of God and the Holy Spirit. Melanchthon rejects the unitarian vision of free will propelled by some scholastics,[56] arguing rather that man is only free when knows the will of God; this can only happen through justification.

48 P. Melanchthon, *Loci communes* (*tertia eorum aetas*), in CR XXI, 716-7. I also used the translation by J.A.O. Preus, *The Chief Theological Topics*, second english edition, Saint Louis, Concordia Publishing House, 2011.

49 P. Melanchthon, *Loci communes* (*prima eorum aetas*), in CR XXI, 191.

50 P. Melanchthon, *Loci communes* (*tertia eorum aetas*), in CR XXI, 717-9.

51 P. Melanchthon, *Loci communes* (*tertia eorum aetas*), in CR XXI, 719: "*Item, lex renatis ideo proponenda est, ut doceat certa opera, in quibus Deus vult nos exercere obedientiam*".

52 P. Melanchthon, *Loci communes* (*secunda eorum aetas*), in CR XXI, 308.

53 P. Melanchthon, *Loci communes* (*prima eorum aetas*), in CR XXI, 163: "*Ex his adparet, quomodo ex fide nascantur Amor Dei et amor proximi, quem caritatem vocant*".

54 W. Matz, *Der befreite Mensch. Die Willenslehre in der Theologie Philipp Melanchthons*, Göttingen, Vandenhoeck & Ruprecht, 2001, 182-8.

55 W. Matz, *Der befreite Mensch*, 55, 124, 224.

56 T. Irwin, *The Development of Ethics. A Historical and Critical Study, vol. I: From Socrates to the Reformation*, Oxford, Oxford University Press, 2007, 763-4. However, the author

2.1.3.2 Divine Law and Natural Law

Melanchthon distinguishes three types of law: divine law, natural law and human law. The divine law is included in the Decalogue and in the Gospel. It requires perfect obedience, not only with external actions but also with internal actions, with burning love.[57] Instead, human law only requires external performance.[58] Natural law is the natural knowledge (*notitia*) of God, the logical concepts, as the numbers and moral concepts, as the difference between the 'honourable' and the 'shameful'. This knowledge is however obscured by sin, and it must be awakened through the preaching of the Word of God. Thus, for Melanchthon natural law is repeated and explained in the moral laws included in the Decalogue. He applies the traditional (even used by Thomas Aquinas) distinction of the Mosaic law as ceremonial, judicial (*forenses*) and moral law.[59] The ceremonial and judicial laws were given by God only to the Jews to provide for their governance for a certain period of time. Instead, the moral laws listed in the Decalogue are still valid for Christians.[60]

---

underlines that Melanchthon and Luther's view does not necessarily oppose Aquinas's conception of free will.

57 P. Melanchthon, *Loci communes* (*tertia eorum aetas*), in CR XXI, 685: "*Lex Dei est doctrina a Deo tradita, praecipiens, quales nos esse et quae facere, quae omittere oportet, et requirens perfectam obedientiam erga Deum ac pronuntians irasci Deum et punire aeterna morte non praestantes perfectam obedientiam*"; See also P. Melanchthon, *Ethicae doctrinae elementorum libri duo*, in CR XVI, 227: "*Leges divinae sunt quae a Deo traditae sunt quocunque tempore et extant scriptae passim in Moyse et libris Evangelii*".

58 P. Melanchthon, *Loci communes* (*tertia eorum aetas*), in CR XXI, 686.

59 On this distinction see H.J. Berman, J. Witte Jr., *The Transformation of Western Legal Philosophy*, 1618-9.

60 P. Melanchthon, *Loci communes* (*tertia eorum aetas*), in CR XXI, 687-8. See also P. Melanchthon, *Ethicae doctrinae elementorum libri duo*, in CR XVI, 227-8. P. Melanchthon, *Compendiaria dialectices ratio* (1520), in CR XX, 748; P. Melanchthon, *De locis communibus ratio* (1526), in CR XX, 695. On Melanchthon's natural law see C. Bauer, *Die Naturrechtsvorstellungen des jüngeren Melanchthon*, in R. Nürnberger (ed.), *Festschfrift für Gerhard Ritter zum 60. Geburstag*, Tübingen, Mohr, 1950, 244-55; C. Bauer, *Melanchthons Naturrechtslehre*, in *ARG*, 42 (1951), 64-100; H.J. Berman, J. Witte Jr., *The Transformation of Western Legal Philosophy*, 1611-35; S. Kusukawa, *The Trasformation of Natural Philosophy: The Case of Philip Melanchthon*, Cambridge, Cambridge University Press, 1995, 27-210; R. von Friedeburg, *Widerstandsrecht und Konfessionskonflikt. Notwehr und gemeiner Mann im deutsch-britischen Vergleich 1530 bis 1669*, Berlin, Duncker & Humbolt, 1999, 57-8; C. Strohm, *Die Voraussetzungen reformatorischer Naturrechts- lehre in der humanistischen Jurisprudenz*, in *Zeitschrift der Savigny-Stiftung für Rechtsgeschichte*, Kan. Ab., 2000 (86), 398-413 (410-3); I. Deflers, *Lex und Ordo. Eine rechtshistorische Untersuchung der Rechtsauffassung Melanchthons*, Berlin, Duncker & Humbolt, 2005, 32-50; C. Strohm, *Zugänge zum Naturrecht bei Melanchthon*, in G. Frank (ed.), *Der Theologe Melanchthon*, 339-356; H.J. Berman, *Law and revolution II*, 144-56; M. Schmoeckel, *Erkenntnis durch ratio und conscientia: Die Begründung der modernen Wissenschflichkeit des Rechts durch*

Melanchthon entrusts the explanation of natural law to moral philosophy,[61] defined as the part of the divine law that concerns external actions.[62] Despite the fact that he leans on Aristotle's philosophy,[63] Melanchthon designs this discipline from a strictly theological perspective.[64] The aim of moral philosophy, he writes, is the recognition of God and obedience to Him.[65] God instilled in the human mind theoretical and practical knowledge of the image of His own mind. This image shines in the human mind and allows the recognition of God, which is man's final objective.[66] The human intellect is directed towards the knowledge of God and all things, as man has been created for their recognition.[67] Behind this idea lies the patristic conception of man's resemblance to God, cultivated in scholastic theology.[68] Yet in the light of the fundamental distinction between the law and the Gospel, Melanchthon stresses that the knowledge of the natural law is different from salvation, which only comes with the Gospel. In other words, with philosophy man can only reach a natural and worldly knowledge of God, for the revelation of God's will derives from the grace of faith.[69]

This view determines Melanchthon's doctrine of virtues. To Melanchthon, four reasons justify the study of the virtues. First, they are a testimony of God's existence. The distinction between the 'honourable' and the 'shameful' testifies that human nature does not originate from chance, but by some eternal inventing mind. Second, the virtues teach us the characteristics of God. God

Melanchthons Naturrechtslehre, in G.K. Hasselhoff, M. Meyer-Blanck, *Religion und Rationalität*, Würzburg, Ergon, 2008, 179-220; M. Svesson, *Phillip Melanchthon and the Reception of Aristotelian Natural Law Theory in the European Reformation*, in A. Néstor García Martínez, M., Šilar, J.M. Torralba, *Natural Law. Historical, Systematic and Juridical Approaches*, Newcastle upon Tyne, Cambridge Scholars Publishing, 2008, 109-26; I. Deflers, *Konfession und Jurisprudenz bei Melanchthon*, in C. Strohm, H. de Wall (eds.), *Konfessionalität und Jurisprudenz in der frühen Neuzeit*, Berlin, Duncker & Humbolt, 2009, 33-46; A. Raunio, *Divine and Natural Law in Luther and Melanchthon*, in V. Mäkinen (ed.), *Lutheran Reformation and the Law*, 21-62.

61 P. Melanchthon, *Ethicae doctrinae elementorum libri duo*, in CR XVI, 167.

62 P. Melanchthon, *Philosophiae moralis epitomes libri duo*, in CR XVI, 22.

63 On the use of Aristotle, see the classic work by P. Petersen, *Geschichte der Aristotelischen Philosophie im Protestantischen Deutschland*, Leipzig, 1921, 41-107.

64 G. Frank, *The Reason of Acting: Melanchthon's Concept of Practical Philosophy and the Question of the Unity and Consistency in His Philosophy*, in J. Kraye, R. Saarinen (eds.), *Moral Philosophy on the Threshold of Modernity*, 217-33 (230).

65 P. Melanchthon, *Philosophiae moralis epitomes libri duo*, in CR XVI, 28.

66 P. Melanchthon, *Philosophiae moralis epitomes libri duo*, in CR XVI, 28.

67 P. Melanchthon, *Liber de anima*, in CR XIII, 143. On Melanchthon's epistemology, see M. Schomoeckel, *Das Recht der Reformation*, 39-42.

68 See I/1.

69 G. Frank, *The Reason of Acting*, 220-1.

is wise, just, truthful, etc. Third, the virtues are testimony of God's judgment. They make man aware of his crimes against God. Fourth, they are the rule for man's external actions.[70] Melanchthon relies on Aristotle, but corrects him on two essential points. Every virtue is primarily directed to the recognition and obedience to God and only secondarily to accomplishing the specific content of the virtue.[71] Furthermore, this obedience results from the movement of the heart and will. As the heart is corrupted by sin, the virtue can only be fulfilled by the externally granted grace. Human will is free only concerning external actions. The internal movement of the actions requires the assistance of the Holy Spirit.[72] The fulfilment of the virtue is thus inseparable from faith. In short, Melanchthon differentiates from Aristotle both in relating all the virtues to the recognition of God[73] and in demanding the intervention of the external grace of the Holy Spirit for their satisfaction.[74]

2.1.3.3 Contract Law as Divine Institution

Natural law is the foundation and scope of the human law decreed by the magistrate. Melanchthon sees the magistrate as the guardian of both tables of the Decalogue. In this role, he is called to promulgate and enforce laws that comply with natural law. Human law has to specify the circumstances not defined by natural law.[75] On the other hand, these human laws have to be directed towards social utility and common good.[76] To Melanchthon, natural law founds a juridical order based on a body of institutions.[77] Drawing upon Cicero, Aristotle and Rom. 13, he maintains that natural law embraces a catalogue of institutions that constitute the political order (*ordo politicus*). These institutions are created and preserved by God. These institutions are the magistrate, marriage, property, contract law and penal law, which correspond to the first, fourth, five, six, seventh and eighth commandments of the Decalogue. The magistrate is a *Minister Dei* and has the task to regulate these disciplines in accordance with

---

70 P. Melanchthon, *Ethicae doctrinae elementorum libri duo*, in CR XVI, 166-7.

71 P. Melanchthon, *Philosophiae moralis epitomes libri duo*, in CR XVI, 30.

72 P. Melanchthon, *Ethicae doctrinae elementorum libri duo*, in CR XVI, 192.

73 G. Frank, *The Reason of Acting*, 231.

74 H. Ziebritzki, *Tugend und Affekt: Ansatz, Aufriß und Problematik von Melanchthons Tugendethik, dargestellt anhand der "Ethicae doctrinae elementa" von 1550*, in G. Frank (ed.), *Der Theologe Melanchthon*, Stuttgart, Thorbecke, 2000, 357-73 (370).

75 P. Melanchthon, *Ethicae doctrinae elementorum libri duo*, in CR XVI, 229: "*Ius positivum est decretum legitimae potestatis non pugnans cum iure naturae sed addens ad ius naturae circumstantiam aliquam probabili ratione, non necessario definitam*".

76 J. Witte Jr., *Law and Protestantism*, 129-40; H.J. Berman, *Law and Revolution II*, 81-7.

77 C. Bauer, *Melanchthons Naturrechtslehre*, 75; G. Weber, *Grundlagen und Normen politischer Ethik bei Melanchthon*, München, Kaiser, 1962, 31.

his supernatural responsibility. As a consequence, if men do not obey, they are committing a mortal sin (Rom. 13,5).[78]

The *ordo politicus* derives from the creation of God, but its divine origin can only be realized through the revelation accepted by faith.[79] Contract law is part of the *ordo politicus*, a divine institution founded on natural law. The *ordo politicus* guarantees the lawfulness of contract law and determines its constitution in the light of the Decalogue. The seventh and eighth commandments of the Decalogue contain general principles concerning the compliance with contractual equality and the validity of pacts and promises. In addition, Melanchthon formulates a more expanded analysis in his main works of moral philosophy: *Prolegomena in officia Ciceronis* (written in 1530, published in 1562), *Philosophiae moralis epitome* (1538), *Ethicae doctrinae elementa* (1550), and in his *Dissertatio de contractibus* (1545). Even though Melanchthon addresses the lawfulness and the correct application of the main credit instruments also in other writings (e.g. in the *Catechesis puerilis*, 1541), here he explores them in detail.

2.1.4 *The Contributions of the First Disciples*

2.1.4.1 Introduction

Without underestimating the importance of Luther and Melanchthon,[80] contemporary theologians, like Urbanus Rhegius (1489-1541), Johannes Aepinus (1499-1553), and Johannes Brenz (1499-1570), were also involved in the analysis of the crucial issues of contract law. Starting from Luther and Melanchthon's theology, these authors constructed solutions for the lawfulness and application of the most widely-used credit instruments that remained fundamental

78 P. Melanchthon, *Loci communes (tertia eorum aetas)*, in CR XXI, 1009: "*Evangelii doctrina adeo severe praecipit de obedientia, ut affirmet peccatum mortale esse, non obedire mandatis legitimi magistratus, si tamen non iubeant facere contra mandata Dei. Hanc regula expresse traditur Rom. 13. [vs. 5]: « necesse est obedire non solum propter iram, sed etiam propter conscientiam »*". On the role of the magistrate see J.M. Estes, *Peace, Order and the Glory of God. Secular Authority and the Church in the Thought of Luther and Melanchthon, 1518-1559*, Leiden, Boston, Brill, 2005.

79 R.B. Huschke, *Melanchthons Lehre vom Ordo Politicus. Ein Beitrag zum Verhältnis von Glauben und politischem Handeln bei Melanchthon*, Gütersloh, Gerd Mohn, 1968, 144-6. I. Deflers, *Lex und Ordo*, 174-81.

80 On the authoritative role that Luther and Melanchthon assumed on their followers see I. Dingel, *Ablehnung und Aneignung: Die Bewertung der Autorität Martin Luthers in den Auseinandersetzungen um die Konkordienformel*, in *Zeitschrift für Kirchengeschichte*, n. 105, 35-57 (38-43); I. Dingel, *Melanchthon and the Establishment of Confessional Norms*, in I. Dingel, R. Kolb, N. Kuropka, T.J. Wengert (eds), *Philip Melanchthon. Theologian in Classroom*, 161-80.

throughout the sixteenth and seventeenth centuries. The following paragraphs briefly describe these authors and their works on contract law.

2.1.4.2 Rhegius: The Student of Eck

Urbanus Rhegius (German: Rieger von Langenargen)[81] studied theology and liberal arts in Freiburg (1508-1512) where he lived at Ulrich Zasius' (1461-1535/1536) home. There, Rhegius was a student of Johannes Eck, Luther's celebrated adversary, and in order to follow him, he moved to Ingolstadt (1512-1518). He then continued his studies in Tübingen (1519) and finally in Basel, where he received his doctorate in 1520. Rhegius was appointed preacher at the Augsburg cathedral, but since he began supporting Luther, he soon had to leave that post. He preached in Hall and Tirol and in 1524 returned to Augsburg. Rhegius took part in the Diet of Worms, where he met the Duke Ernest of Lüneburg (1497-1546). The duke invited Rhegius to become superintendent of the duchy of Brunswich-Lüneburg, where he remained from 1531 to 1541.

Rhegius committed himself to the pastoral practice and administration of the Church. He authored the Church ordinances (*Kirchenordungen*) of Lüneburg (1531) and Hanover (1536), and published numerous sermons elucidating the Reformation theology and providing for spiritual care. He aimed to demonstrate the truth of the Reformation statements by showing their conformity with the Scriptures and the early Church Fathers, more than by producing a comprehensive doctrinal treatment of theology.[82] In a commentary on Psalm 15 (*Der xv. Psalm Davids, sampt einer Christlichen unterrichtung, von einem unchristlichen unerhörten wucher, ausgelegt durch D. Urbanum Regium*) published in 1536 (reprinted in 1537 and 1538), Rhegius addressed the issues of the *Zinskauf*, or the five percent contract, a special type of purchase of annuities. He faced obstacles concerning its lawfulness and application. The topic of contract law is also considered in Rhegius' *Loci theologici e patribus et scholasticis neotericisque collecti* (1541). As the name suggests, this work does not only examine the Scriptures in the light of the Church Fathers, but also uses the

81 On Rhegius' biography see M. Liebmann, *Urbanus Rhegius und die Anfänge der Reformation: Beiträge zu seinem Leben, seiner Lehre und seinem Wirken bis zum Augsburger Reichstag von 1530 mit einer Bibliographie seiner Schriften*, Münster, Aschendorff, 1980; D. Lamprecht, *Urbanus Rhegius: der vergessene Reformator der Lüneburger Heide; eine Erinnerung*, Hermannsburg, Missionsbuchhandlung, 1980; H. Zschoch, *Rhegius Urbanus*, in *BBKL*, vol. VIII, 1994, 122-34; H. Zschoch, *Reformatorische Existenz und konfessionelle Identität. Urbanus Rhegius als evangelischer Theologe in den Jahren 1520 bis 1530*, Tübingen, Mohr Siebeck, 1995; S. Hendrix, *Rhegius, Urbanus*, in *TRE*, vol. XXIX, 1998, 155-7; H. Zschoch, *Rhegius, Urbanus*, in *RPP*, vol. XI, 2012, 191.

82 S. Hendrix, *Urbanus Rhegius*, in C. Lindberg (ed.), *The Reformation Theologians. An Introduction to Theology in the Early Modern Period*, Malden, Blackwell, 2002, 118.

scholastics as sources, read through Luther's criticism. In the *locus* dedicated to riches and avarice, Rhegius formulates some principles concerning lending and commerce.

2.1.4.3 Brenz: The Magistrate as Servant of Conscience

Another author that was deeply involved with the analysis of the new financial instruments was Johannes Brenz. Brenz[83] graduated in theology in Heidelberg (M.A. 1518) and, after his conversion to Luther's positions in 1522, became preacher at St. Michael's Church in the imperial city of Schwäbisch Hall. In 1525-1526 Brenz formulated the *Kirchenordnung* of Schwäbisch Hall, and in 1527 he authored a catechism. After Luther's, this catechism was the most used throughout the sixteenth century. It was published countless times and translated into many languages.[84]

Brenz was fully immersed in politics. As adviser of the Margrave of Brandenburg, he collaborated to the Brandenburg-Nürenberg *Kirchenordnung*, attended the Colloquy of Marburg in 1529 and the Diet of Augsburg in 1530. On his recommendation, the 1535/36 marriage ordinance of Württemberg was written. In 1537-1538, Brenz taught at the University of Tübingen. After the defeat of the Schmalkald War, he fled to nearby Schwäbisch Hall, where he worked for Duke Ulrich of Württemberg and then for his son, the Duke Christoph. Tasked by the latter, Brenz composed the *Confessio Virtembergica*, a document based on the *Confessio Augustana*, to be presented at the Council of Trent.

In 1528-1530 Brenz was involved in controversies with the Anabaptists of Nürenberg. This conflict played a role in the development of his theology. He had to establish 'whether the magistrate violated conscience when it banished false teachers'. He answered that while the magistrate serves conscience, he does not rule it.[85] Drawing upon Luther's two kingdoms doctrine, he held that

---

83 On Brenz's biography see H. Hermelink, *Brenz, Johannes*, in *Neue Deutsche Biographie* 2 (1955), 598 f. (accessed 18.12.2018) http://www.deutsche-biographie.de/pnd118515128.html; F.W. Bautz, *Brenz, Johannes*, in *BBKL*, vol. I, 1990, 743-4; H. Ehmer, *Johannes Brenz (1499-1570)*, in C. Lindberg (ed.), *The Reformation Theologians. An Introduction to Theology in the Early Modern Period*, 124-39; J.M. Estes, *Christian Magistrate and Territorial Church. Johannes Brenz and the German Reformation*, Toronto, CRRS Publications, 2007.

84 C. Weismann, *Die Katechismen des Johannes Brenz*, 1, *Die Entstehung-, Text- und Wirkungsgeschichte*, Berlin, New York, De Gruyter, 1990; G. Bode, *Instruction of the Christian Faith by Lutherans after Luther*, in R. Kolb (ed.), *Lutheran Ecclesiastical Culture*, 159-204 (162); H. Ehmer, *Johannes Brenz*, 128, 138. On the catechism genre see A. Ohlemacher, *Lateinische Katechetik der frühen lutherischen Orthodoxie*, Göttingen, Vandenhoeck & Ruprecht, 2010.

85 J.M. Estes, *Christian Magistrate*, 79-80.

the civil authority is an ordinance of God aimed at preserving the common good and peace. The civil authority is responsible for the enforcement of the Ten Commandments.[86] Salvation does not only concern the single believers, but the whole community as guided by the ruler. Thus, the subjects must obey the civil authority, as rebellion against the rulers would be rebellion against God. When the imperial law complies with the dictates of Scripture, it is binding as a divine ordinance.[87]

Brenz' theology is reflected in his analysis of contract law, as we are going to see in the following chapters. His catechism, in commenting on the seventh and eighth commandments, includes fundamental principles and a brief analysis of the most commonly used financial agreements. In other writings – for instance, two homilies published in 1537-40[88] and a counsel published by Felix Bidenbach in 1608[89] – Brenz addresses in detail the issues of the lawfulness of the *Zinskauf* and the interest-taking prohibition.

2.1.4.4 Aepinus: The Superintendent of Hamburg

A native of Ziesar, Johannes Aepinus[90] (German: Hoeck) studied in Wittenberg[91] under the direction of Luther and Melanchthon. After his *Baccalaureatus* (1520) he came back home and was a schoolteacher. Because of this Lutheran instruction, he was imprisoned by order of the territorial prince Joachim I of Brandenburg (1484-1535), but fled and continued to teach in Greifwald and Stralsund. From 1524 till 1528, he was a rector of a private school in Stralsund and composed the local *Kirchenordung* (1525). In 1529 he was appointed as the first Lutheran pastor of the Church of St. Peter in Hamburg, and in 1533 he obtained a doctorate in theology at the University of Wittenberg.

---

86 J.M. Estes, *Christian Magistrate*, 95-6.

87 H. Ehmer, *Johannes Brenz*, 133-5.

88 J. Brenz, *In evangelii quod inscribitur secundum Lucam, duodecim priora capita homiliae centum et decem*, Francofurti, 1541, Homilia 61; J. Brenz, *In evangelii quod inscribitur, secundum Lucam, duodecim posteriora capita, homiliae octoginta*, Halae Svevorum, 1540, Luke 19, Homilia 29.

89 F. Bidenbach, *Consiliorum theologicorum decas I*, Franckfurt am Meyn, 1608, 20-2.

90 On Aepinus biography see T. Knolle, *Aepinus, Johannes*, in *Neue Deutsche Biographie* 1 (1953), 91 (accessed 05.04.2016), http://www.deutsche-biographie.de/pnd116296283.html; H. Düfel, *Aepinus, Johannes*, in *TRE*, vol. I, 1977, 535-44; S. Hendrix, *Urbanus Rhegius*, in C. Lindberg (ed.), *The Reformation Theologians*, 109-23; H. Scheible, *Aepinus, Johannes*, in *RPP*, vol. I, 2007, 73.

91 On the Wittenberg University, see A. Kohle, B. Kusche, *Die Wittenberger Theologische Fakultät in ihrer Anfangszeit-Beobachtungen zu Strukturen, Personal und Profil*, in H.J. Selderhuis, E.J. Waschke (eds.), *Reformation und Rationalität*, Göttingen, Vandenhoeck & Ruprecht, 2015, 27-42.

From 1532 till his death (1553), Aepinus was superintendent of Hamburg. During this long period, he was involved in the organization of the Church, collaborated with the city council, and wrote a new *Kirchenordnung* (1539). He also authored numerous writings against the Roman Catholic Church, and sermons and comments for the proclamation of the Reformation's ideas. In particular, he worked on an interpretation of the Psalms. Aepinus' teachings on contract doctrine are mainly expounded in his influential *Auszlegung vber den XV. Psalm Davids*, also published in Latin as *In psalmum XV commentarius*, in 1543. This work is principally dedicated to the analysis of the lawfulness and application of the most common credit instruments: the purchase of annuities in the form of *Zinskauf* and loans with the payment of moratory interest (*interesse*).

2.2 The Struggle for Confessional Identity

2.2.1 *Introduction*

The Augsburg Confession[92] (1530) set a fundamental step for the emergence of the Lutheran Church.[93] From 1531 to 1547, indeed, the intense activity of Protestant princes and magistrates implemented Luther's, Melanchthon's and other theologians' ideas.[94] The Augsburg Confession was not an isolated case, as other confessions of faith were formulated in the same period,[95] giving rise to what has been called 'the confessionalization of Europe'.[96] The three

92 For the editions see W.H. Neuser, *Bibliographie der Confessio Augustana und Apologie 1530-1580*, Leiden, Boston, Brill, 1987.

93 C. Lindberg, *The European Reformations*, Cambridge, Mass., Blackwell, 1996, 229-48.

94 T.A. Brady, *Emergence and Consolidation of Protestantism in the Holy Roman Empire to 1600*, in R. Po-chia Hsia (ed.), *The Cambridge History of Christianity, Reform and Expansion 1550-1660*, vol. 6, Cambridge, Cambridge University Press, 2007, 20-36. For a more detailed analysis see: S. Ehrenpreis, U. Lotz-Heumann, *Reformation und konfessionelles Zeitalter*, Darmstadt, Wissenschaftliche Buchgesellschaft, 2002; O. Mörke, *Die Reformation. Voraussetzungen und Durchsetzung*, München, Oldenbourg, 2005.

95 See the recent essays in C. Scott Dixon, D. Friest, M. Greengrass (eds), *Living with Religious Diversity in Early Modern Europe*, Aldershot, Burlington USA, Singapore, Sydney, Ashgate, 2009; T.M. Safley (ed.), *A Companion to Multiconfessionalism in the Early Modern World*, Leiden, Boston, Brill, 2011.

96 The theorical model of *confessionalisation* (*Konfessionsbildung*) was developed by W. Reinhardt and H. Schilling, meaning 'a significative process of integration between religion, politics, and society, which produces an extensive influence upon the public and private life of societies'. See H. Schilling, *Religion, Political Culture and The Emergence of Early Modern Society. Essays in German and Dutch History*, Leiden, New York, Köln, E.J. Brill, 1992, 209. This model has been the subject of large discussions but is anything but

greater Churches (Lutheranism, Calvinism and Roman Catholicism) stood together with a myriad of Protestant and non-Christian churches.[97] Theology played an important role for the construction of the confessional states.[98] The confessions of faith, as bodies of dogmatic principles, impacted the cultural and social system, and generated 'a process of identity formation and cultural differentiation'.[99] The maintenance of the system was then entrusted to 'specific institutions equipped with pervasive powers'.[100] Jurisprudence supported the relation between politics and religion, but also gradually encouraged processes of secularization.[101]

The fragmentation of Christendom ran in parallel with the internal division of the Lutherans. When Luther died in 1546, his followers branched into a number of factions. In brief, the Interimists, the Synergists and the Crypto-Calvinists, together called Philippists, aimed to replace Luther's theology with Melanchthon's. Instead, the Gnesio-Lutherans swore an oath of fidelity to Luther's teachings.[102] These factions were involved in a jungle of controversies that lacerated the nascent Lutheranism (the adiaphoristic controversy, the

---

death. For a summary see among the recent literature: T. Brockmann, D.J. Weiss, *Das Konfessionalisierungsparadigma. Leistungen, Probleme, Grenzen*, Münster, Aschendorff, 2013; P. Shore, *Theology and the Development of the European Confessional State*, in U.L. Lehner, R.A. Muller, A.G. Roeber (eds.), *The Oxford Handbook of Early Modern Theology, 1600-1800*, Oxford, Oxford University Press, 2016, 43-57 (43-5); J.M. Headley, H.J. Hillerbrand, A.J. Papalas (eds.), *Confessionalization in Europe, 1555-1700: Essays in Honor and Memory of Bodo Nischan*, 2nd ed., Abingdon, Oxon, New York, Routledge, 2016; C.A. Zwierlein *'Konfessionalisierung' europäisch, global als epistemischer Prozess. Zu den Folgen der Reformation und zur Methodendiskussion*, in C. Strohm (ed.), *Reformation und Recht*, 1-52.

97 C.A. Zwierlein, *'Konfessionaliseirung' europäisch*, 11-34.

98 P. Shore, *Theology and the Development*, 55.

99 H. Schilling, I.G. Tóth, *From Empire to Family Circles: Religious and Cultural Borderlines in the Age of Confessionalization*, in H. Schilling, I.G. Tóth (eds.), *Religion and Cultural Exchange in Europe, 1400-1700*, Cambridge, Cambridge University Press, 2006, 25-48 (29).

100 H. Schilling, I.G. Tóth, *From Empire to Family Circles*, 27: the visitations in Roman Catholic and Lutheran Churches, the Presbyterian Church discipline of the Calvinists, and the Inquisition.

101 M. Heckel, *Reichsrecht und 'Zweite Reformation': Theologisch-juristische Probleme der reformierten Konfessionalisierung*, in H. Schilling (ed.), *Die reformierte Konfessionalisierung in Deutschland – Das Problem der 'Zweite Reformation'*, Gütersloh, Gütersloher Verlagshaus, 1986, 379-386; M. Stolleis, *'Konfessionalisierung' oder 'Säkularisierung' bei der Entstehung des frühmodernen Staates*, in *Ius Commune*, 20 (1993), 1-23; M. Heckel, *Deutschland in konfessionellen Zeitalter*, 2nd. ed., Göttingen, Vandenhoeck & Ruprecht, 2001, 67-127; M. Stolleis, *Geschichte des öffentlichen Rechts in Deutschland. Erster Band 1600-1800*, 2nd ed., München, CH Beck, 2012, 154-211.

102 E. Koch, *Das konfessionelle Zeitalter*, 213-4.

majoristic controversy and the synergist controversy, just to mention some).[103] The *Formula of Concord* (1577), fruit of the intense work of a group of formidable theologians, and the subsequent Book of Concord (1580), including the essential doctrines of the Lutheran Reformation, brought peace and gave rise to the period usually called the Lutheran orthodoxy.[104]

Confessional differences had specific resonances in the sphere of culture and education.[105] Universities propelled the formation and implementation of the Reformation teachings in each territory. The relation between the Christian prince and his subjects was an essential aspect cultivated by the Lutheran theologians.[106] Princes embraced Luther's ideas for reforming universities. Marburg was reformed in 1527, Wittenberg in 1536, Tübingen in 1535-1538, Greifswald in 1539, Leipzig in 1539-1540. Heidelberg in 1558 and Rostock in 1563 had new statutes. Jena's University was founded in 1548.[107] Professors were forced to swear an oath of allegiance to the Formula of Concord, and it was practically impossible to teach without the approval of local political and religious authorities.[108]

In this climate of struggle for confessional identity, the legal and, more specifically, contract doctrines formulated by Luther, Melanchthon and the other theologians of the first generation were cultivated and expanded by their followers belonging to the different factions. They incorporated them in writings of various natures: ethical treatises, commonplaces (*loci communes*),

---

103 A brief summary is now in T. Kaufmann, *Erlöste und Verdammte. Eine Geschichte der Reformation*, München, C.H. Beck, 2nd ed., 2017, 302-7. For a profound analysis of the debate that led to the formulation of the *Formula* see I. Dingel, *Concordia controversa. Die öffentlichen Diskussionen um das lutherische Konkordienwerk am Ende des 16. Jahrhunderts*, Gütersloh, Gütersloher Verlaghaus, 1996.

104 Whether this period should be called 'ortodoxy' is the subject of discussion. See R. Kolb, *Lutheran Theology in Seventeenth Century Germany*, passim.

105 See C. Strohm, *Die produktive Kraft konfessioneller Konkurrenz für die Rechtsentwicklung*, in C. Strohm (ed.), *Reformation und Recht*, 131-72 (141-7).

106 On this point see the recent work of R. von Friedeburg, *Luther's Legacy: The Thirty Years' War and the Modern Notion of 'State' in the Empire*, passim.

107 E. Koch, *Das konfessionelle Zeitalter-Katholizismus, Luthertum, Calvinismus (1563-1675)*, Leipzig, Evangelische Verlagsanstalt, 2000, 218-21; T. Kaufmann, *Konfession und Kultur. Lutherischen Protestantismus in der zweiten Hälfte des Reformationsjahrhunderts*, Tübingen, Mohr Siebeck, 2006, 303-6; K.G. Appold, *Academic Life and Teaching in Post-Reformation Lutheranism*, in R. Kolb (ed.), *Lutheran Ecclesiastical Culture, 1550-1675*, Brill, Leiden-Boston, 2008, 79. On the reformed universities, see C. Strohm, *Calvinismus und Recht*, 39-53.

108 M. Steinmetz, *Die Konzeption der deutschen Universitäten im Zeitälter von Humanismus und Reformation*, in *Les universités européennes du XIV au XVIII siècle: Aspects et problèmes: Actes du Colloque International à l'occasion du VI Centenarie de L'universitè Jagellone de Craovie, 6-8 mai 1964*, Droz, Geneve, 1967, 119; K.G. Appold, *Academic Life*, 87.

catechetical books, biblical commentaries and sermons. The inclusion of this topic in differing genres is in a way indicative of the approach used by these authors and the audience toward which the works were geared. If sermons and catechetical books aimed at a more popular reading and were more disseminated, then commonplaces and ethical writings were primarily destined for academic teaching.[109] The main subject of the analysis remained however the same: general principles concerning charity, absence of frauds and commutative justice, and more extended analysis of the moral implications of most universal financial instruments.

2.2.2 *Ethical Treatises*

2.2.2.1 Introduction

Under the impulse of Melanchthon's ethical works, a number of theologians produced treatises of moral philosophy. These writings read classical authors like Aristotle and Cicero through the eyes of Melanchthon's philosophical approach. The Decalogue and the doctrine of the virtues were among the main topics addressed. Thus, sections dedicated to contract law can be found in the comments over the seventh and eighth commandment, as well in the description of the virtue of commutative justice and the virtue of truthfulness. We take three examples: David Chytraeus (1531-1600), Paul von Eitzen (1521-1598) and Victorin Strigel (1524-1569).

2.2.2.2 Chytraeus and the Reformation in Rostock

David Chytraeus[110] (German, Kochhafe), the last of the fathers of the Lutheran Church, was a pupil of Melanchthon. Born in Ingelfingen, he studied in Tübingen, Heidelberg and Wittenberg, where he lived at Melanchthon's house and attended Luther's lectures on Genesis. As Loesche wrote: "*he was no original genius, but owing to his disposition and power of work, he was a scholar of almost encyclopedic knowledge*".[111] At the end of his studies, Chytraeus started teaching in Rostock, where he also aided the formation of the nascent

109 See J.L. Flook, *The Book in Reformation Germany*, in J.F. Gilmont, K. Maag (trans.), *The Reformation and the Book*, first ed. 1990, Abigdon Oxon, New York, Routledge, 2016, 21-103.

110 On Chytraeus' biography see: E. Wolf, *Chytraeus, David*, in *Neue Deutsche Biographie* 3 (1957), 254: http://www.deutsche-biographie.de/ppn119009137.html (accessed 11.04.15); P.F. Barton, *Chyträus, David (1531-1600)*, in *TRE*, vol. VIII, 1981, 88-90; R. Keller, *Die Confessio Augustana im theologischen Wirken des Rostocker Professors David Chyträus (1530-1600)*, Göttingen, Vandenhoeck & Ruprecht, 1994; R. Keller, *David Chytraeus (1530-1600). Melanchthons Geist im Luthertum*, in H. Scheible (ed.), *Melanchthon in seinen Schülern*, Wiesbaden, Harrassowitz, 1997, 361-71.

111 G. Loesche, *Chytraeus, David*, in S. Macauley Jackson (ed.), *The New Scharzog Encyclopedia of Religious Knowledge*, vol. III, Grand Rapids, MI, Baker, 1952, 116.

university,[112] and where he was involved in several theological disputes. He defended the Formula of Concord and helped the diffusion of Lutheranism in Austria and the Scandinavian kingdoms.

In 1556 Chytraeus composed one of the most widespread commentaries on the Ten Commandments, the *Regulae vitae: virtutum descriptiones methodicae*.[113] This work combines Aristotelian philosophy with Luther's and Melanchthon's ideas. Chytraeus comments on the Ten Commandments by illustrating the virtues associated with them. The seventh commandment concerns both the 'just' possession of goods, commutative justice and liberality. The analysis of contract law (mostly principles) is treated in the light of commutative justice.[114] In his writings on the eighth commandment, instead, Chytraeus makes only a glancing reference to the binding nature of pacts and promises.[115] A short summary of these teachings is included in Chytraeus' *Catechesis* first published in 1554.

Chytraeus' contract doctrine is also presented in a detailed exposition of the Deuteronomy published in 1575. Chapter 24 is dedicated to contract law (*De contractibus*) and begins with the general principles of contract law. Following Melanchthon, he declares that the contract is a political ordinance to be used in faith, fear of God and good conscience. Christians have to practice justice and equality in it. Equality obligates all men to love and reciprocal respect. Then, Chytraeus reviews the specific Roman law contracts: *emptio venditio, locatio conductio, societas, mandatum, donatio, fiducia, mutuatio, commodatum, depositum, pignus, fideiussio*.[116] In the light of Scripture, he outlines the duties of the parties.

---

112 On the Rostock University see T. Kaufmann, *Universität und lutherische Konfessionalisierung. Die Rostocker Theologieprofessoren und ihr Beitrag zur theologischen Bildung und kirchlichen Gestaltung im Herzogtum Mecklenburg zwischen 1550 und 1675*, Gütersloh, Gütersloher Verlaghaus, 1997.

113 D. Chyträus, *Regulae vitae: virtutum descriptiones methodicae*, Wittenbergae, 1556. The book had many editions: Vitenbergae 1555, Vitenbergae 1556, Vitenbergae 1557, Leipzig 1558, Vitenbergae 1559, Vitenbergae 1560, Leipzig 1561, Vitenbergae 1562, Lipsiae 1563, Lipsiae 1566, Witenbergae 1567, Witenbergae 1570, Lipsiae 1570, Budissinae 1571, Witenbergae 1573, Witenbergae 1580, Witenbergae 1585, Francofurti ad Moenum 1582, Witenbergae 1587, Witenbergae 1589, Lipsiae 1593, Eisleben 1598, Argentinae 1601, Argentorati 1613, Hamburgi 1614.

114 D. Chytraeus, *Regulae vitae: Virtutum descriptiones methodicae*, septimi praecepti virtutes Wittenbergae, 1556.

115 D. Chytraeus, *Regulae vitae*, octavi praecepti virtutes.

116 D. Chytraeus, *In deuteronomium Mosis enarratio*, Witebergae, 1575, 450-64.

2.2.2.3 Von Eitzen: Rostock, Hamburg and Schleswig

Another disciple and friend of Melanchthon, Paul von Eitzen,[117] offered an analysis of contract law in his work of moral philosophy, *Ethica doctrina*, which first part was published in 1572 and the second part in 1573. Von Eitzen obtained his master's degree (1543) and doctorate (1556) in theology at the University of Wittenberg. In 1547 he was appointed professor of logic at the University of Rostock; in 1548 he was preacher and lecturer at the cathedral of Hamburg and then superintendent from 1555. In 1562 he was general superintendent of the Duchy of Holstein-Gottorf in Schleswig.

The *Ethica* is divided in nine books. The first book opens with a description of the law and its division.[118] There are human laws and divine laws, Von Eitzen claims. Divine laws are natural law and the Mosaic law. Natural law is divinely placed in the human creature. Yet, because of original sin, man is corrupted and the light of natural law is obscured. The result is that classic philosophers understood natural law as knowledge of the 'just' and the 'honest', infused in human reason. But the right content of natural law must be clarified: it coincides precisely with the Decalogue.[119]

As for Melanchthon, moral philosophy is dedicated to the study of the part of divine law that concerns external actions. It is necessary for four reasons: 1) all rational creatures must obey God; 2) to avoid punishments; 3) for the conservation of peace; and 4) the law is a 'schoolmaster' in Christ: even if the law does not remove sins, men can learn about the Son of God who has this power.[120] Again relying on Melanchthon, Von Eitzen clarifies that there is a fundamental distinction among the virtues. Philosophical virtues are caused by human mind following natural law, while Christian virtues are only caused by the Holy Spirit, which moves the human will according to the will of God.[121]

After some sentences on the three uses of the law, a great part of the work is dedicated to the explanation of the Decalogue. A long discussion concerns the

---

117 For the biography see: H. Schüssler, *von Eitzen, Paul*, in *Neue Deutsche Biographie* 4 (1959), 426 f.: http://www.deutsche-biographie.de/ppn129922706.html (accessed 16.04.15); F.W. Bautz: *Eitzen, Paul von*, in *BBKL*, vol. 1, 1990, 1483-1484; J. Schilling, *Paul von Eitzen – ein Kirchenvater Schleswig-Holsteins*, in M. Bejschowetz-Iserholt, R. Witt (eds.), *Kirchliches Leben in Schleswig-Holstein im 17. Jahrhundert. Vorträge zu einer Ausstellung im Landesarchiv Schleswig-Holstein*. Schleswig-Holsteinischen Landesarchivs 78, Schleswig, 2003, 41-58; H. Scheible, *Eitzen, Paul v.* in *RPP*, vol. IV, 2008, 387.

118 P. Von Eitzen, *Ethicae doctrinae libri novem, pars prima*, Slesvigae in isthmo cimbrico, 1585, liber I, caput II, 2.

119 P. Von Eitzen, *Ethicae doctrinae libri novem*, liber I, caput II, 2-5.

120 P. Von Eitzen, *Ethicae doctrinae libri novem*, liber I, caput VII.

121 P. Von Eitzen, *Ethicae doctrinae libri novem*, liber I, caput VII.

magistrate under the fourth commandment,[122] where Von Eitzen expounds the distinction between the role of the magistrate and the minister of the Church,[123] and between law and equity.[124] Marriage law is discussed in the sixth commandment, while contract doctrine finds its place in the seventh and eighth commandments. To substantiate his claims, Von Eitzen moulds statements of Cicero and Aristotle in with references to the Holy Scripture.

2.2.2.4 Strigel and the *doctrina dulcissima de contractibus*

Victorin Strigel[125] studied theology and philosophy at the University of Wittenberg. On Melanchthon's advice he undertook an academic career. He first became professor of ethics at the newly founded University of Jena and then rector and dean of the faculty of philosophy. In 1562 he moved to Leipzig, where he continued to teach ethics, but also history. Finally, he was dean of the philosophy faculty in Heidelberg (1568-1569). Strigel's *In epitomen philosophiae moralis Philippi Melanchthonis, Hypomnēmata* (1580) is, as the name suggests, a commentary on the work of Melanchthon. Moral philosophy, Strigel says, is useful for the jurist. It is from moral philosophy that all the honest and praiseworthy laws come and all the civil laws derive.[126] Contract law is treated as a species of particular justice. With elegant words, Strigel affirms that in ethics there is nothing more useful and erudite than the very sweet doctrine of contracts (*doctrina dulcissima de contractibus*).[127] At the beginning, Strigel explains that he will treat contracts *more scholastico et philosophico*.[128] Following a dialectic method, he first presents a definition of contract. Then he continues with the division, *causae* and *res*.

For Strigel, the contract doctrine has a triple meaning. First, a contract doctrine encourages a bond for society (*vinculum societatis*). Second, it is an example that remembers the love for the neighbour: by practicing justice and equality, men do not gain profit and advantage from the damage of the

122 P. Von Eitzen, *Ethicae doctrinae libri novem*, liber III, caput VI-XII, 137-60.

123 P. Von Eitzen, *Ethicae doctrinae libri novem*, liber III, caput IX, 147-9.

124 P. Von Eitzen, *Ethicae doctrinae libri novem*, liber III, caput IX, 160-5.

125 On Strigel's biography, see T. Pfundner, *Strigel, Victorin*, in *Neue Deutsche Biographie* 25 (2013), 555-6 (accessed 20.10.2017), https://www.deutsche-biographie.de/gnd124408494.html#ndbcontent; E. Koch, *Victorin Strigel (1524-1569). Von Jena nach Heidelberg*, in H. Scheible (ed.), *Melanchthon in seinen Schülern*, 391-404; E. Koch, *Strigel, Victorin[us]*, in *TRE*, vol. XXXII, 2001, 252-5; G. Collet, *Strigel, Victorinus*, in *RPP*, vol. XII, 304.

126 V. Strigel, *In epitomen philosophiae moralis Philippi Melanchthonis, Hypomnēmata*, Neapoli Nemetum, 1582, 2.

127 V. Strigel, *In epitomen philosophiae moralis*, 782.

128 On Protestant Scholasticism see the bibliography in W. Decock, C. Birr, *Recht und Moral*, 14-6.

neighbour. Third, the contract doctrine is a 'pedagogy' or schoolmaster for the knowledge of God. By observing the equality of goods and price, Christians can know that God is just and equal, in the way proposed in the law and the Gospel. On the one hand, with the law, God accuses all men. On the other hand, with the Gospel, he offers the grace and remission of sins.[129] God is 'just' for Strigel, in the sense that He accuses men with the law, but He forgives sins with the Gospel.

2.2.3 *Dogmatic Treatises*

2.2.3.1 Introduction

Melanchthon's *Loci* influenced generations of students throughout the whole sixteenth century and a good part of the seventeenth.[130] The method of the *Loci* consists in the identification and explanation of certain *commonplaces* of the Scriptures. The source is only Scripture, but for the description Melanchthon employs the Aristotelian logical and rhetorical scheme. The order of the *loci* follows the events of Scripture through the spectrum of Paul's Letters on which interpretation the *loci* were originally designed.[131] Strictly dependent on Melanchthon's *loci* are the dogmatic works of Martin Chemnitz (1522-1586), Niels Hemmingsen (1513-1600) and Johann Gerhard (1582-1637). They offer an analysis of contract law within the theological system of the *loci communes*.

2.2.3.2 Chemnitz: Conserving the Genuine Doctrine

Martin Chemnitz,[132] named 'the second Martin' for his importance, was for the great part a self-taught person. His father, a merchant and clothmaker in Treurenbrietzen, died when Chemnitz was ten years old. Chemnitz attended

129 V. Strigel, *In epitomen philosophiae moralis*, 784-5.

130 On Melanchthon's influence, see U. Sträter (ed.), *Melanchthonbild und Melanchthon-rezeption in der Lutherischen Orthodoxie und im Pietismus. Referate des dritten Wittenberger Symposiums zur Erforschung der Lutherischen Orthodoxie*, Wittenberg, Hans Luft, 1999.

131 K.G. Appold, *Abraham Calov's Doctrine of Vocatio in its Systematic Context*, Tübingen, Mohr Siebeck, 1998, 18-20.

132 On Martin Chemnitz's biography see: H. Hachfeld, *Martin Chemnitz nach seinem Leben und Wirken*, Leipzig, 1867; G. Noth, *Grundlinien der Theologie des Martin Chemnitz*, Erlagen, 1930; E. Wolf, *Chemnitz, Martin, evangelischer*, in *Neue Deutsche Biographie* 3 (1957), 201 (accessed 08.12.2015), http://www.deutsche-biographie.de/pnd118829157.html; T. Mahlmann, *Chemnitz, Martin*, in *TRE*, vol. VII, 1981, 714-21; W.A. Jünke (ed.), *Der zweite Martin der Lutherischen Kirche. Festschrift zum 400. Todestag von Martin Chemnitz*, Braunschweig, Ev.-luth. Stadtkirchenverband und Propstei Braunschweig, 1986; F.W. Bautz, *Chemnitz, Martin*, in *BBKL*, vol. I, 1990, 991-2; J.A.O. Preus, *The Second Martin: The Life and Theology of Martin Chemnitz*, St. Louis, Concordia Publishing House, 1994; T. Kaufmann, *Martin Chemnitz (1522-1586) Zur Wirkungsgeschichte der theologischen Loci*, in H. Scheible (ed.), *Melanchthon in seinen Schülern*, 183-254; R. Kolb, *Martin Chemnitz (1522-1586)*, in

school in Wittenberg (1536) and Magdeburg (1539-1542). He enrolled at the University of Frankfurt an der Oder (1544) and then at Wittenberg (1545), where he had the chance to listen Luther's lectures and to meet Melanchthon, who later became his friend. The spreading of the Schmalkald War forced Chemnitz to flee to Königsberg. There he was librarian for the Duke Albrecht of Prussia (1550-1553) and in this way he expanded his knowledge of the Church Fathers. In 1554 he returned to Wittenberg and was selected to give classes on Melanchthon's *Loci theologici*. In the same year he was also ordained priest and accepted the position of coaudiotor with Joachim Mörlin[133] (1514-1571) in the leadership of the Church of Braunschweig. Together with Mörlin, Chemnitz participated in a set of theological disputes, which also brought him into opposition with his mentor and friend Melanchthon.

Between 1565 and 1573 Chemnitz published a monumental critique of the Tridentine council: *Examen decretorum concilii Tridentini*, where he especially refused the vision on justification. In 1568 Chemnitz was appointed theological adviser of Duke Julius of Braunschweig-Wolfenbüttel and was tasked to introduce the Reformation in his land. To fulfil his duties, Chemnitz authored a textbook for the pastors on the basic teachings of the Reformation: *Die fürnemsten Heupstu[e]ck der Christlichen Lehre* (1569). The following years were significantly spent working for the unification of the splintered Lutheranism. Together with Jacob Andreae, David Chytraeus and other leading theologians, Chemnitz was summoned by the electoral prince August of Saxony (1526-1586) for a committee entrusted to solve the tensions among the different doctrinal factions. The result of this project was the *Formula of Concord* (1580), of which Chemnitz and Andreae were the most important contributors.

Chemnitz was the first Lutheran theologian to write an expansive dogmatics in the modern sense. His masterpiece, the *Loci theologici*, published five years after his death (vol. I-II, 1591; vol. III, 1592) by Polycarp Leyser (1552-1610) received over ten editions. To Chemnitz, theology must not be contaminated with scholastic or philosophical terminology. Crucial attention is given to the Scriptures and the Church Fathers, which in his opinion have greatly contributed to the Church. In addition, Chemnitz' method focuses on the distinction between the law and the Gospel, as for him the source of all errors lies in their confusion.[134]

C. Lindberg, *The Reformation*, 140-53; T. Mahlmann, *Chemnitz, Martin*, in *RPP*, vol. II, 2007, 509-10.

133 I. Mager, *Mörlin, Joachim*, in *BBKL*, vol. VI, 1993, 8-11.

134 R.D. Preus, *The Theology of Post-Reformation Lutheranism. A Study of Theological Prolegomena*, London, Concordia Publishing House, 1970, 92-8.

In second part of the *Loci*, at the *locus* dedicated to poverty (*de paupertate*), chapter V (*de contractibus*), Chemnitz grapples with the contract doctrine.[135] Chemnitz considers this chapter to be an explanation of the seventh commandment. Not only does he touch upon the most controversial themes, such as the interest-taking prohibition, the purchase of annuities, loans with moratory interest and partnership, but he also provides general principles valid for all the economic transactions. Among his sources, together with the Scriptures and Church Fathers, Luther and Melanchthon play a primary role, and Aepinus and Rhegius also are expressly cited.

Chemnitz' contract doctrine influenced in a special way Salomon Gessner (1559-1605),[136] professor of theology and court chaplain of the Castle Church in Wittenberg. Gessner studied in Wittenberg, where he obtained his doctorate in 1593. In his commentary on the Psalms (*Commentationes in psalmos Davidis*), published in 1605, he faces the most critical issues of contract law involving the lawfulness of the purchase of annuities and the *Zinskauf.* In substance he conformed to Chemnitz' line.[137]

2.2.3.3 Hemmingsen: *praeceptor universalis Daniae*

Niels Hemmingsen[138] was not a German, but a Danish theologian. He studied in Wittenberg (1537-1542) and was deeply influenced by his master Melanchthon. In 1543 Hemmingsen was made professor of Greek at the University of Copenhagen, of dialectics in 1545 and finally of theology in 1553, while in 1557 he received his doctorate in theology. Hemmingsen four times assumed the role of rector, and in 1572 he was vice chancellor. His literary production includes writings of exegesis, dogmatics, ethics and pastoral theology. These works were not only influential in his homeland, but also spread through Europe.

135 A translation of the *Loci theologici* was made by the Concordia Publishing House in 1989. However, the translation of the *locus De paupertate* (On poverty) is omitted.

136 A. Schimmelpfennig, *Geßner, Salomon*, in *Allgemeine Deutsche Biographie* 9 (1879), 121-2 (accessed 6.11.2017), https://www.deutsche-biographie.de/gnd117543640.html#adb content.

137 S. Gessner, *Commentationes in psalmos Davidis*, Witebergae, 1609, 143-8.

138 On Hemmingsen's biography see: D. Tamm, *Nolo falcem in alienam messem mittere. Der Dänische Teologe Niels Hemmingsen (1513-1600) aus juristischer Sicht*, in D. Tamm, *Med lov skal land bygges og andre rethistoriske afhandliger*, Kopenhagen, Danske Bylag, 1989, 175-84; M. Jakubowski-Tiessen, *Hemmingsen, Niels*, in *RPP*, Vol. VI, 2009, 52-3; E. Lund, *Hemmingsen, Niels*, in T.J. Wengert, M.A. Granquist, M.J. Haemig, R. Kolb, M.C. Mattes, J. Strom (eds.), *Dictionary of Luther and the Lutheran traditions*, Grand Rapids MI, Baker, 2017.

Concerning law, his *De lege naturae apodictica methodus*[139] (1562), made Hemmingsen famous as 'an important forerunner of the more recent founders of natural law'.[140] Starting from Paul's letter to the Romans, he aimed to investigate the force of natural law among the Gentiles and to demonstrate its correspondence with the Decalogue.[141] Hemmingsen's contract doctrine is, however, included in the *Enchiridion theologicum* (1557) and in chapter V of the commentary on the Epistle of James (*In epistolam divi Iacobi apostoli commentarius*, 1563). The *Enchiridion* was intended to be an introduction to Melanchthon's *Loci*. The book is divided in four orders, according to God's revelation: the first order concerns the kingdom of God; the second order includes common rules for life; the third order regards the regulation of the Church; the fourth order addresses political and economic life. In the fourth order, chapter II, dedicated to the magistrate, Hemmingsen wrestles with the interest-taking prohibition, while in the sixth chapter he formulates a set of general principles.

Hemmingsen's contract doctrine influenced Nikolaus Selnecker (1530-1592).[142] Selnecker was originally destined by his father, Melanchthon's friend, to study law. He studied instead theology in Wittenberg. From 1558 till 1565, Selnecker was appointed as court chaplain in Dresden. Then he served as professor in Jena (1565) and Leipzig (1568). In 1570 he was nominated general superintendent of Wolfenbüttel and Oldenburg, but in 1573-1574 we find him again teaching in Leipzig. From 1576 he was superintendent and pastor of St. Thomas Church. In 1590 Selnecker was appointed as superintendent in Hildesheim, but returned in Leipzig in 1592. Selnecker was one of the fathers of the Formula of Concord and published a massive number of theological writings (about 175).[143] His contract doctrine resembles closely Hemmingsen's and can be found in the first volume of his catechetical work *Paedagogia Christiana*

139 See now the recent translation by E.J. Hutchinson (trans. ed. intr.), K.D. Maas (intr.), *On the Law of Nature. A Demonstrative Method*, Grand Rapids, MI, CLP Academic, 2018.

140 F.J. Billeskov Janson, *From the Reformation to the Baroque*, in S. Hakon Rossel (ed.), *A History of Danish Literature*, Lincoln, University of Nebraska Press, 1993, 78.

141 E. Hutchinson, K. Maas, *Niels Hemmingsen (1513-1600) and the Development of Lutheran Natural-Law Teaching*, in *Journal of Markets and Morality*, vol. 17(2), 2014, 595-617 (603-605).

142 Egloffstein, von, *Selneccer, Nicolaus*, in *Allgemeine Deutsche Biographie* 33 (1891), 687-692 (accessed 17.12.2015), http://www.deutsche-biographie.de/pnd118613073.html?anchor=adb; T.R. Jungkuntz, *Formulators of the Formula of Concord. Four Architects of Lutheran Unity*, Eugene, Wipf and Stock Publishers, 1977, 89-109; E. Coch, *Selnecker, Nikolaus*, in *TRE*, Vol. XXXI, 2000, 105-8; W. Sommer, *Selnecker, Nikolaus*, in *RPP*, Vol. XI, 2012, 602.

143 T.R. Jungkuntz, *Formulators*, 108.

(1565), in the commentary on the seventh commandment. Contract doctrine is discussed among the genres of theft. After some general principles based on Christian charity and the Aristotelian virtue of commutative justice, Selnecker delves into the issue of the interest prohibition, loans at moratory interest and the purchase of annuities.

2.2.3.4 Gerhard: The First Lutheran Moralist

In the same traditional line of the *Loci* method can be placed Johann Gerhard.[144] Gerhard, 'the Most Erudite and Famous Theologian of the Lutheran Orthodoxy', was born in Quedlinburg in 1582. Johann Arndt[145] (1555-1621) was his parish priest, and it was on his advice that Gerhard decided to study medicine at the University of Wittenberg and later theology in Jena, then Marburg and again Jena, where he obtained his doctorate in 1606. In the same year, the Duke Johann Casimir of Coburg (1564-1633) appointed him as superintendent in Heldburg and general superintendent of Coburg in 1615. One year later, Gerhard received a chair at the University of Jena where he remained till his death, despite over 22 offers to teach in other places. With his illuminating judgment, Gerhard was a theological advisor of religious and secular authorities and battled against Calvinists and Roman Catholics.

Gerhard wrote a 'smorgasbord' of books concerning almost every field of theology. Still, his most influential work was the *Loci theologici*, a systematic treatment of Lutheran theology divided into 23 volumes. Together with Chemnitz, Gerhard provided an important contribution for the relation between political and ecclesiastical power.[146] His *Loci theologici* built the theological structure

---

144 F. Lau, *Gerhard, Johann*, in *Neue Deutsche Biographie* 6 (1964), 281 (accessed 05.01.2016), http://www.deutsche-biographie.de/pnd118538624.html; M. Honecker, *Gerhard, Johann (1582-1637)*, in *TRE*, Vol. XII, 1983, 448-53; J. Wallmann, *Gerhard, Johann*, in *RPP*, vol. V, 2009, 362-3. On Gerhard's theology see J.A. Steiger, *Johann Gerhard (1582-1637). Studien zu Theologie und Frömmigkeit des Kirchenvaters der lutherischen Orthodoxie*, Stuttgart-Bad Cannstatt, frommann-holzboog, 1997; J.A. Steiger, *Johann Gerhard. Ein Kirchenvater der lutherischen Orthodoxie*, in P. Walter, M.H. Jung (eds.), *Theologen des 17. und 18. Jahrhunderts. Konfessionelles Zeitalter – Pietismus-Aufklärung*, Darmstadt, Wissenschaftlische Buchgesellschaft, 2003, 54-69; M. Friedrich, S. Salatowsky, L. Schorn-Schütte (eds.), *Konfession, Politik und Gelehrsamkeit. Der Jenear Theologe Johann Gerhard (1582-1637) im Kontext seiner Zeit*, Stuttgart, Franz Steiner, 2017.

145 F.W. Bautz, *Arndt, Johann*, in *BBKL*, vol. I, 1990, 226-7.

146 B.C. Schneider, *Ius Reformandi. Die Entwicklung eines Staatkirchenrechts von seinen Anfängen bis zum Ende des Alten Reiches*, Tübingen, Mohr Siebeck, 2001, 174-177.

for the *Kirchenordnung* 'Casimiriana', drawn up by Gerhard after the visitation of the superintendency of Heldburg[147] and issued by the duke in 1626.[148]

Gerhard's *Loci* was considered among the first Lutheran books that dealt with moral theology.[149] It was quite influential in the formulation of the main topics of Lutheran ethics: the Decalogue and the three orders doctrine.[150] Gerhard's fundamental premises are in Luther and Melanchthon's doctrine of the law and the Gospel. Human nature is corrupted by sin, but innate knowledge of the image of God remains. However, this is only sufficient for the punishment of external crimes, and it does not recognise the sins. God wanted to place a witness of the natural laws in the Decalogue so that men could be reinforced in resisting their evil inclinations. In the state of integrity (before the Fall), natural law and moral law were intermixed and interdependent. But in the state of corruption, natural law is obscured, though God left the remaining knowledge (moral law) to direct men's external actions. This knowledge is a 'pedagogy' or schoolmaster used by God for the restoration of His image through Christ. After justification, the Gospel becomes *causa efficiens* of men's actions, and the law is the norm and rule for of the good works of those reborn.[151]

Gerhard treats extensively contract law in the 14th volume, the locus XXV (*de magistrato politico*).[152] Precisely, his analysis finds place in the *pars* II, cap. VII, sect. V, dedicated to the duties of the magistrate towards his subjects (*De officiis magistratus erga subditos*), membrum II, on the magistrate's concern for honourableness and justice (*de cura magistratus circa honestatem et iustitiam*), art. I on the civil laws (*de legibus politicis*). The paragraph 234 concerns the interest-taking prohibition and the lawfulness of the various credit instruments. Gerhard shows an eminently practical approach. As he had pre-

147 On the visitation see J.A. Steiger, *Kirchenordnung, Visitation und Alltag. Johann Gerhard (1582-1637) als Visitator und kirchenordnender Theologe*, in *Zeitschrift für Religions- und Geistesgeschichte*, Vol. 55/3, 2003, 227-52; S. Westphal, *Gerhards Tätigkeit als Superintendent und seine Visitationspraxis*, in M. Friedrich, S. Salatowsky, L. Schorn-Schütte (eds.), *Konfession*, 51-68.

148 See the classic study of M. Honecker, *Cura religionis magistratus christiani. Studien zum Kirchenrecht im Luthertum des 17. Jahrhunderts insbesondere bei Johann Gerhard*, München, Claudius, 1968, 51-136.

149 J.M. Lang, *De origine et progressu theologiae moralis systematicae*, n. XXIV, in J.K. Dürr, *Compendium theologiae moralis*, Altdorfi Noricorum, 1698.

150 M. Honecker, *Sozialethik des Luthertums*, in H.C. Rublack (ed.), *Die lutherische Konfessionalisierung*, 316-40 (321-7).

151 See E. Uhl, *Die Sozialethik Johann Gerhards*, München, Kaiser, 1932, 10-16.

152 Concerning the topic of the magistrate see M. Schmoeckel, *Ein Denker des Ausgleichs. Die Rechtslehre des Johann Gerhard*, in M. Friedrich, S. Salatowsky, L. Schorn-Schütte (eds.), *Konfession*, 20-35.

viously drawn up a counsel on this matter, here he provides a systematic revision. He is not interested in formulating general principles of contract law, but in giving a new formulation of the interest prohibition, which admits the lawfulness of the most common financial instruments. On this point he elaborates a consistent doctrine grounded on the interpretation of Scripture and scholastic arguments.[153]

2.2.4 *Biblical Commentaries and Sermons*

2.2.4.1 Georg Major: Between Paul's Letters and Melanchthon

The legacy of Luther and Melanchthon took also the form of biblical commentaries and sermons, which also addressed legal issues. We look at three examples: Georg Major (1502-1574), Jacob Andreae (1528-1590) and Aegidius Hunnius (1550-1603). Major[154] studied in Wittenberg (M.A. 1523), and among his professors were Luther and Melanchthon. In 1528 he became rector of the Latin School of Magdeburg. In 1537 he was ordained priest by Luther, was appointed assistant preacher at the Castle Church in Wittenberg and professor at the University. In 1540 and 1544 Major was elected rector, but in 1546, because the turmoil of the Schmalkald War, he was forced to flee to Magdeburg and Nordhausen. Then he found a position as court preacher in Merseburg. In this period he composed sermons on the Apostle's Creed, which will lead to a theological dispute, so called 'Majoristic'. In 1548 Major came back to Wittenberg, where he remained till his death.

Two threads identify Major's activity: he was a devoted interpreter of Paul's letters and a propagator of Melanchthon's ideas. Between 1540 and 1568, Major lectured on Paul's letters and published many homilies, *enarrationes* and *Auslegungen*. Major employed Melanchthon's method: the classification of Paul's letters following a rhetorical scheme and the analysis through dialectical categories. Major even used the same material produced by Melanchthon. He borrowed Melanchthon's crucial works on the *argumentum*, a description of the biblical author's method, and the topics (the *loci communes*).[155] In

153 In general, for the use of scholastics arguments see R.D. Preus, *The Theology of Post-Reformation*, 140-1.

154 On Major's biography, see H. Junghans, *Major, Georg*, in *Neue Deutsche Biographie* 15 (1987), 718 (accessed 18.12.2018) https://www.deutsche-biographie.de/gnd116689781.html#ndbcontent; K.F. Ulrichs, *Major, Georg (eig. Maier)*, in *BBKL*, vol. XIV, 1998, 1224-1227; T.J. Wenger, *Georg Major (1502-1574) Defender of Wittenberg's Faith and Melanchthonian exegete*, in H. Scheible (ed.), *Melanchthon in seinen Schüler*, 129-56. I. Dingel, G. Wartenberg (eds.), *Georg Major (1502-1574). Ein Theologe der Wittenberger Reformation*, Evangelische Verlagsanstalt, Leipzig, 2005.

155 T.J. Wenger, *Georg Major (1502-1574) Defender of Wittenberg's Faith*, 150-53.

the *Enarratio* to Paul's second letter to the Corinthians (*Enarratio secundae epistolae Pauli ad Corinthios*), published in 1558 and 1561, Major also wrestles with property law and contract law. Following Melanchthon, he investigates the lawfulness and right acquisition of goods and devises general principles for the lawful exchange of goods.

2.2.4.2 Andreae: Chancellor and Provost at the Tübingen University

Andreae[156] studied at the University of Tübingen (1541-1546). In 1546 he was appointed deacon in Stuttgart. During the imperial occupation of Württemberg, he fled to Tübingen, where he obtained a doctorate in 1553. In the same year, Duke Christoph of Württemberg appointed him superintendent of Göppingen. Andreae represented the Church of Württemberg in several occasions, was arbiter of theological disputes (both among Protestants and within Lutheranism), and was in correspondence with important reformed theologians. In 1561 Andreae became professor of theology, chancellor and provost at the University of Tübingen. Concerned for the unity of Lutheranism, in 1568 Duke Christoph tasked him to join a team of other theologians, among which Chemnitz and Selnecker, in order to find a harmonious settlement of the divisions. As seen before, this group ended their works with the *Formula of Concord.*

Andreae was also engaged with pastoral and administrative work. He sought to establish a model of a 'state church' in Saxony and worked actively for the enforcement of the provisions included in the *Formula of Concord.* He published a number of sermons and polemical writings about controversial topics, in the defense of Lutheran doctrine. In particular, in 1587 he was called to solve a dispute in Regensburg, where he preached four sermons: *Vier Christliche Predigten uber ettliche Evangelia im Advent* (1588), which include his opinions on matters of finance and the interest prohibition.

2.2.4.3 Hunnius: Between Tübingen and Wittenberg

A final example of contract law discussed in commentaries is Aegidius Hunnius[157] (German: Hunn). Hunnius studied theology at the University of

---

156 On Andreae's biography, see: M. Brecht, *Andreae Jakob (1528-1590)*, in *TRE*, Vol. II, 1978, 672-80; T.R. Jungkuntz, *Formulators*, 19-45; R. Kolb, *Andreae Jakob*, in H.J. Hillerbrand (ed.), *The Oxford Encyclopedia of the Reformation*, Vol. 1, 1996, 37-8; S. Hermle, *Andreae, Jakob*, in *RPP*, vol. I, 2007, 217-8.

157 On Hunnius' biography, see: F. Lau, *Hunnius, Ägidius*, in *Neue Deutsche Biographie* 10 (1974), 67 (accessed 26.04.2016), http://www.deutsche-biographie.de/pnd100295886.html; F.W. Bautz, *Hunnius, Aegidius*, in *BBKL*, Vol. II, 1182-3; W.R. Russell, *Hunnius, Aegidius*, in H.J. Hillerbrand (ed.), *The Oxford Encyclopedia of the Reformation*, vol. 2, 1996, 276;

Tübingen; his professors were excellent theologians such as Jakob Andreae, Jakob Heerbrand (1521-1600), Erhard Schnepff (1495-1558) and Johannes Brenz, with whose catechism he grew up. In 1574 he was deacon in Tübingen, and two years later became professor of theology in Marburg. He made decisive steps for the diffusion of Lutheranism in (Upper) Hesse and Kursachsen. In 1592 he was called to serve as professor of theology and provost at the University of Wittenberg, where he died in 1603. Hunnius published a large number of polemical treatises and commentaries on the Holy Scripture.[158] Among them, his commentary on the second letter of Paul to the Corinthians, published in 1605, contains a discussion on the lawfulness of the purchase of annuities and in a special way, the *widerkaufflicher Zins*. In addition, he was asked to write a counsel concerning the interest-taking prohibition and the financial instruments reported in the *Consilia theologica witebergensia* (1644). Reflections on contract law can be also found in his catechism (1592).

2.3 Penance, Casuistry and Moral Theology

2.3.1 *Introduction*

In the second half of the seventeenth century, the Lutheran casuist Johann Nikolaus Misler (1614-1683),[159] professor of theology and superintendent in Giessen, published his *Opus novum quaestionum practico-theologicarum, sive casuum conscientiae* (1676), a collection of cases of conscience. Among the cases dedicated to merchants, he wondered whether anyone could imperil the health of his soul through a particular form of bill of exchange, a chirograph. Misler answered that as the magistrate is not the lord of the souls and consciences, which belong to God, it is not licit to invade God's jurisdiction and lordship, and rule over the other's soul.[160] The 'court of conscience' is distinct from the court of the magistrate, he stressed.[161] This issue struck at the very roots of the delicate problem of pecuniary debts and the salvation of the soul.

M. Matthias, *Theologie und Konfession. Der Beitrag von Ägidius Hunnius (1550-1603) zur Entstehung einer lutherischen Religionskultur*, Leipzig, Evangelische Verlagsanstalt, 2004; M. Matthias, *Hunn (Hunnius), Aegidius*, in *RPP*, Vol. VI, 2009, 344.

158 J. Kunze, *Hunnius Aegidius*, in S.M. Jackson (ed.) *The new Schaff-Herzog encyclopedia of religious knowledge*, Vol. 5, 1909, 409-10.

159 J. Wallmann, *Misler, Johann Nikolaus*, in *RPP*, Vol. VIII, 2010, 396-7.

160 J.N. Misler, *Opus novum quaestionum practico-theologicarum, sive casuum conscientiae*, Francofurti, 1676, 244.

161 For practical reasons, we use the term 'court of conscience' as in the Roman Catholic tradition. However, in the Lutheran tradition this type of 'court' presents specific features, which will be examined in the following pages.

Indeed, in late Middle Ages unpaid debts could led to excommunication.[162] More generally, it is an example of the dynamics between the *forum internum* or court of conscience and the *forum externum*.

The relation between these two courts is certainly not a new phenomenon, as already in the Middle Ages theologians and canonists dictated norms for the conscience.[163] Yet the period from the end of the sixteenth century to the beginning of seventeenth century presents particular features and has been rightly labelled as 'the crisis of the European conscience'.[164] The fragmentation of Christendom was reflected in the regulation of the *forum internum* or court of conscience, with the emergence of plural forms of morality.[165] The different religious confessions translated their theological teachings into instruments and institutions to govern the Christian's behaviours and guarantee conformity to the doctrinal truth.[166] Not only did this movement respond to faith controversies and religious wars, but it also reacted against the advance of a rational and secular approach promoted by the modern natural lawyers.[167]

In a context of multiple normative orders, the Christian was both subject to the prince and his conscience. He was trapped between the legal rule and the moral rule.[168] State and church were concurrent and competing sources of

---

162 See T. Lange, *Excommunication for Debt in Late Medieval France*, Cambridge, Cambridge University Press, 2016.

163 See I/1.

164 P. Hazard, *La Crise de la Conscience europeenne 1680-1715*, three vols., first time published in Paris, 1934.

165 Roman Catholic, Lutheran and Calvinist theologians all nuanced their definitions of conscience. For the Roman Catholic theologians, see I/1; For the Calvinists, see for instance, T. Kirby, *Public Forum and Forum of the Conscience: John Calvin's Theological Groundwork of the Modern Public Sphere*, in T. Kirby (ed.), *Persuasion and Conversion: Essays on Religion, Politics, and the Public Sphere in Early Modern England*, Leiden, Boston, Brill, 2013, 36-51; H.J. Selderhuis, *Calvin's views on Conscience and Law*, in M. Germann, W. Decock (eds.), *Das Gewissen in den Rechtslehren der protestantischen und katolischen Reformationen. Conscience in the Legal Teachings of the Protestant and Catholic Reformations*, Leipzig, Evangelische Verlagsanstalt, 2017, 33-52; On Luther's idea of conscience, see M.G. Baylor, *Action and Person: Conscience in the Late Scholasticism and the Young Luther*, Leiden, Brill, 1977, 157-272; H. Maihold, *'Himmel und Erde'. Die Abrenzung von* forum internum *und* forum externum *in der frühen Neuzeit*, in M. Germann, W. Decock (eds.), *Das Gewissen*, 51-71 (53-5).

166 On the control of consciences, see J. Tully, *Governing Conduct*, in E. Leites (ed.), *Conscience and Casuistry*, 12-71.

167 See next paragraph.

168 T. Duve, *Katholisches Kirchenrecht und Moraltheologie im 16. Jahrhundert: Eine globale normative Ordnung im Schatten schwacher Staatlichtkeit*, in S. Kadelbach, K. Günther (eds.), *Recht ohne Staat?, Zur Normativität nichtstaatlicher Rechtsetzung*, Frankfurt, New York, Campus, 2011, 147-74 (158-9); T. Duve, *Global Legal History – A Methodological Approach*

jurisdiction.[169] They defended different interests, which sometimes conflicted, but sometimes gave birth to episodes of mutual cooperation.[170] Jurists and theologians were both involved in the analysis of the distinction and interaction between the *forum internum* and the *forum externum*.[171] Jurists aired their views on conscience not only in dogmatic treatises, but also in dissertations.[172] Even masters of Samuel Stryk's (1640-1710) and Justus Henning Boehmer's (1674-1749) calibre dealt with this topic.[173] For the preparation of the pastors and the education of the faithful, instead, the theologians sketched out casuistical books and moral theology manuals.[174]

---

in *Oxford Handbooks Online – Law*, Jan. 2017, DOI: 10.1093/oxfordhb/9780199935352.013.25 (accessed 7.12.17).

169 P. Prodi, *Una storia della giustizia*, 327-8; L. Waelkens, *The forum internum and its External Features in the legal history of Early Modern Times*, in M. Germann, W. Decock (eds.), *Das Gewissen*, 17-32 (27).

170 W. Decock, *Collaborative Legal Pluralism*, passim.

171 M. Scattola, *Gewissen und Gerechtigkeit in den Beichtbüchern der Frühen Neuzeit*, in *Journal of Early Modern Christianity*, 2015 (2), 117-58; W. Decock, C. Birr, *Recht und Moral*, 23-7.

172 We recall just some titles, but the list could be longer. J. Berghauer, (Supervisor: Heinrich Linck), *De exoneratione conscientiae*, Jenae, 1673; J. Goedde, (Supervisor: Johannes Tesmar), *Dissertatio iuris prima de conscientia*, Marburg, 1675; S.N. Orth, *Disputatio inauguralis iuridica de erronea conscientia in foro exteriori nos obligante vel excusante*, Giessae, 1678; H. Schütz, (Supervisor: Godofredo Suevo), *Disputatio inauguralis de probatione pro exoneranda conscientia*, Wittenbergae, 1695; J.H. Riensche, (Supervisor: Conrad, Lüdeking), *Disputatio inauguralis iuridica de casibus a quibusdam conscientiae in iure occurrentibus*, Wittenbergae, 1732.

173 C.E. Charisius, (Supervisor: Samuel, Stryk), *Disputationem de conscientiae foro* [...], Francofurti ad viadrum, 1683; S. Stryk, *Tractatus de iure sensuum* [...], Francofurti ad Oderam, 1671; On these and other works see M. Scattola, *Gewissen und Gerechtigkeit*, 153-6; J.H. Böhmer, *Dissertatio praeliminaris de iure circa libertatem conscientiae*, cited in M. Germann, *Justus Henning Böhmers Abhandlung über die Gewissensfreiheit. Eine Stichprobe zum Gewissensdiskurs aus der prostestantischen Kirchenrechtslehre zu beginn des 18. Jahrhunderts*, in M. Germann, W. Decock (eds.), *Das Gewissen*, 313-33.

174 On casuistry, secondary literature is abundant. See among the recent works: E. Leites (ed.), *Conscience and Casuistry*, passim; A.R Jonsen, S. Edelston Toulmin (eds.), *The Abuse of Casuistry*, passim; L. Gallagher, *Medusa's Gaze: Casuistry and Conscience in the Renaissance*, Stanford, Calif, Stanford University Press, 1991; H.D. Kittsteiner, *Die Entstehung des modernen Gewissen*, passim; M.W.F. Stone, *The Adoption and Rejection of Aristotelian Moral Philosophy in Reformed 'Casuistry'*, in J. Kraye, M.W.F. Stone (eds.), *Humanism and Early Modern Philosophy*, London, Routledge, 2000, 59-90; E Vallance, H. Braun (eds.), *Contexts of Conscience in Early Modern Europe, 1500-1700*, Basingstoke, Palgrave Macmillan, 2003; P. Hurtubise, *La casuistique*, passim; S. Knebel, *Casuistry and the Early Modern Paradigm Shift in the Notion of Charity*, in J. Kraye, R. Saarinen (eds.), *Moral Philosophy on the Threshold of Modernity*, Dordrecht, Springer, 2005, 115-39; S. Boarini (ed.), *La casuistique classique*, passim; D.R. Klinck, *Conscience, Equity and the Court of Chancery in Early Modern England*, Aldershot, Burlington USA, Singapore, Sydney, Ashgate, 2010;

A specific feature of Lutheran, and more generally, Protestant casuistry, is that it configured the court of conscience as a direct relationship between man and God.[175] While in the Roman Catholic tradition, the confessor was a judge and had to know sins and circumstances and inflict a punishment, the reformers adopted a new type of penance where the pastor had not such a role. He had to verify the knowledge of the Christian basic teachings, listen to the sins expressed in general, but not to impose acts of penance. This favoured a more direct contact between man and his conscience, without any external intermediation. Among the English casuists excellent examples in this sense are the works of puritans William Perkins (1558-1602), William Ames (1576-1633), Richard Baxter (1615-1691) and the Anglicans Robert Sanderson (1587-1663), Joseph Hall (1574-1656) and Jeremy Taylor (1613-1667).[176]

Lutheran casuists and moral theologians built their works on the basis of the theological principles already set out by Luther and Melanchthon and implemented by other theologians. Concerning contract doctrines, they did not bring profound innovations, but gave to these doctrines a more direct normative dimension and guarantee of enforcement in the court of conscience. They did not develop integrally new solutions but appealed to the authorities of the first or second generation of Lutheran theologians or also to Roman Catholic theologians to integrate or corroborate the answers to cases of conscience. After a brief examination of the new attitude towards private confession and

B.T.G. Mayes, *Counsel and Conscience*, passim; P.J. Holmes (ed.), *Caroline Casuistry: The Cases of Conscience of Fr Thomas Southwell, SJ*, London, Catholic Record Society, 2012; R. Palaia (ed.), *Coscienza, nella filosofia della prima modernità*, Firenze, Leo S. Olschki, 2013; A. Stoll, *Conscience in Early Modern Literature*, Cambridge, Cambridge University Press, 2017. On the Lutheran casuistry and moral theology also see also among the less recent works: L. Pelt, *Die christliche Ethik in der lutherischen Kirche*, passim; W. Gass, *Geschichte der christlichen Ethik*, passim; C.E. Luthardt, *Geschichte der christlichen Ethik*, passim; O. Dittrich, *Geschichte der Ethik*, passim.

175 See M. Scattola, *Gewissen und Gerechtigkeit*, 145-8; For the Reformed casuistry see among others J.F. Keenan, *William Perkins*, 112.

176 For a more detailed list see now W. Decock, C. Birr, *Recht und Moral*, 53-6. For the English casuistry see T. Wood, *English Casuistical Divinity During the Seventeenth Century, with Special Reference to Jeremy Taylor*, London, SPCK, 1952; P.J. Holmes (ed.), *Elizabethan Casuistry*, London, Catholic Record Society, 1981; A.W. Lindsley, *Conscience and Casuistry in the English Puritan Concept of Reformation*, Diss., University of Pittsburg, 1982; J.F. Keenan, *William Perkins (1558-1602) and the Birth of British Casuistry*, in J.F. Keenan, T.A. Shannon (eds.), *The Context of Casuistry*, 105-30; L. Witchel, *Casuistry in 17th Century England, English Protestant Casuistry, Conscience and Oath-Taking*, Saarbrücken, VDM Verlag Dr. Müller, 2009; C. Selzner, *Les forges des philistins, La problématique d'une casuistique réformée en Angleterre de William Perkins à Jeremy Taylor*, in S. Boarini (ed.), *La casuistique classique, genese, formes, devenir*, 73-86.

penance, our discourse revolves to the description of the different types of literature related to conscience. There is a long list of these works, and for this reason we will only focus on some examples.

2.3.2 *Towards a New Type of Penance*

Medieval theologians were concerned with the type of remorse a man was able to feel with his spiritual efforts.[177] For Luther the question was not about the sufficiency of penance and contrition. Man's nature is irreparably corrupted by sin, and the pain of repentance cannot bring any consequences to bear on salvation. The human person is not saved by his feelings, or spiritual emotions, but only by receiving the righteousness of Christ. The pain for sins is a requisite for faith, though. Then faith only justifies man.[178] Luther's doctrine of justification changes radically the attitude towards penance and the role of the priests.[179] Man is not saved by his personal spiritual effort, but only externally through the grace of Christ.

Following this vision, in the second editions of the *Loci*, Melanchthon explores the two parts of penance: confession and satisfaction. Private confession with the detailed enumeration of sins is not necessary, he writes, as there is no statement about that in the Scripture. Furthermore, the two powers (*potestates*) of the pastors are to be intended in very different way from the Roman Catholic Church. The first power, the ministry (*ministerium*), concerns

---

177 R.J. Bast (ed.), *The Reformation of Faith in the Context of Late Medieval Theology and Piety. Essays by Bernt Hamm*, Leiden, Boston, Brill, 2004, 140-1.

178 R.J. Bast (ed.), *The Reformation of Faith*, 147-52. On suffering and penance in Luther, see R.K. Rittgers, *Embracing the "True Relic" of Christ: Suffering, Penance, and Private Confession in the Thought of Martin Luther*, in A. Firey (ed.), *A New History of Penance*, Leiden, Boston, Brill, 2008, 377-95.

179 On this topic see E. Roth, *Die Privatbeichte und Schlüsselgewalt in der Theologie der Reformatoren*, Gütersloh, 1952; E. Kinder, *Beichte und Absolution nach den lutherischen Bekenntenisschriften*, in *Theologische Literaturzeitung*, 77,2 (1952), 543-50; L. Fendt, *Luthers Reformation der Beichte*, in *Luther: Mitteilungen der Luthersgesellschaft*, 24,3 (1953), 121-37; K. Aland, *Die Privatbeichte im Luthertum von ihren Anfängen bis zu ihrer Auflösung* in K. Aland, *Kirchengeschichte Entwürfe: Alte Kirche, Reformation und Luthertum, Pietismus und Erweckungsbewegung*, Gütersloh, Gerd Mohn, 1960, 452-519; B. Lohse, *Die Privatbeichte bei Luther*, in *Kerigma und Dogma*, 14 (1968), 207-28; J. Vercruysse, *Schlüsselgewalt und Beichte bei Luther*, in H. Junghans (ed.), *Leben und Werk Martin Luthers von 1526 bis 1546: Festgabe zu seinem 500. Geburtstag*, Göttingen, Vandenhoeck & Ruprecht, 1983, 153-69. On the role of the priests according to Luther see C. Voigt-Goy, *Potestates und ministerium publicum. Eine Studie zur Amtstheologie im Mittelalter und bei Martin Luther*, Tübingen, Mohr Siebeck, 2014, 85-181. For an excellent summary see R.K. Rittgers, *Confession (Private) and the Confessional* in T.J. Wengert, *Dictionary of Luther and the Lutheran Traditions*, Grand Rapids MI, Baker, 2017.

the preaching of the Gospel, the administration of the sacraments, and the announcement of the remission of sins. Melanchthon argues that this power is neither a mandate to know and deal with a lawsuit (*mandatum cognoscendi*), nor a judgment (*iudicium*), but only a mandate to communicate absolution. It also concerns hidden sins, which we do not remember or recount. Therefore, this task does not require the knowledge of sins, because it is not a judgment (*non est enim iudicium*). Concerning then the satisfaction, Melanchthon opines that the power of the pastor is to teach the gratuitous remission of sins and not to impose punishments. There is no need of a punishment inflicted by the confessor, because the remission of sins is gratuitous. The punishment inflicted by the magistrate does not mitigate any eternal punishments, because they are already remitted by Christ.[180]

These words are sufficiently clear to understand that penance is completely reshaped. No more a judgment with the detailed enumeration of sins, the evaluation of the circumstances and the imposition of a punishment. In this vision, the *forum internum* loses much of its juridical character. The minister is no more conceived as a judge, and punishments are no longer essential elements in the eschatological process. Instead, the *forum externum* follows the same road traced in the Roman Catholic Church. The other power of the pastors, the jurisdiction (*iurisdictio*), is for Melanchthon a judgment that only concerns the manifest crimes. It can be concluded with excommunication or absolution. Here, there is no sentence without cognition. This is not a judgment of conscience, Melanchthon stresses, but concerns external actions.[181]

Luther's and Melanchthon's teachings on penance did not remain void speculations but were adapted to different contexts by sermons preached by other theologians.[182] They were put into practice by official documents (Schmalkaldic Articles III, 8.1; *Confessio Augustana*, 25,1),[183] and Church Ordinances (*Kirchenordnungen*). Private confession was not abolished, but meant as preparation for the Lord's Supper.[184] For example, a provision

180 P. Melanchthon, *Loci communes* (*secunda eorum aetas*), in CR XXI, 497-8.

181 P. Melanchthon, *Loci communes* (*secunda eorum aetas*), in CR XXI, 494. On the development of the Lutheran ecclesiastical jurisdiction see M. Schmoeckel, *Der Pastor als Richter? Der Einfluss der lutherischen Reformation auf die untere kirchliche Gerichtsbarkeit*, in M. Engammare, A. Vauautgaerden (eds.), *L'intime du droit à la Reinassance. Actes du cinquantenaire de la FISIER*, Droz, Genève, 2014, 307-35.

182 See for instance M.J. Haemig, *Communication, Consolation and Discipline: Two Early Lutheran Preachers on Confession*, in K. Jackson Lualdi, A.T. Thayer (eds.), *Penitence in the Age of Reformations*, 30-48.

183 M. Ohst, *Confession II. Church History*, in *RPP*, vol. III, 2007, 371.

184 E. Bezzel, *Beichte III*, in *TRE*, vol. V, 1980, 421-5 (423-4). See also E. Bezzel, *Frei zum Eingeständnis: Geschichte und Praxis der evangelischen Einzelbeichte*, Stuttgart, Calwer, 1982.

included in the 1533 Church Ordinance of Brandenburg-Nürnberg required the Christians to be examined in their faith and conduct before taking part to the Lord's Supper. Pastors had to control the Christians' knowledge of the Ten Commandments, the Apostle's Creed, the Lord's Prayer and the doctrine of sacraments. Private confession was recommended, even though not always mandatory. Christians did not have to enumerate their sins; no interrogation of conscience was prescribed; and priests were forbidden to impose punishments.[185] The Church Ordinance of Hildesheim (1544) also recommended private confession, but if a Christian's conscience did not convict him of any sin, he could receive the Holy Eucharist without confession.[186] At length, in Lutheran lands, a new type of penance took place, even though, as we are going to see in the next paragraphs, with different shades.

2.3.3 *Catechetical Books, Manuals for Confessors and Collections of Theological Counsels*

The necessity of educating ministers and the new practice of confession brought along the creation of specific books for the preparation of the pastors. Comments on and the practical exposition of Luther's catechisms addressed this issue. We can recall the *Institutiones catecheticae* (1613) and the *Welt- und Geldsorge* (1621) of the Giessen professor of ethics, Conrad Dieterich[187] (1575-1639) and the work of the theology professor in Rostock, Lucas Bacmeister[188] (1605-1679), *Skiagrafia sive analysis et catena catechismi minoris doctoris Martini Lutheri* (1667), which displays the analysis of Luther's small catechism in schematic tables.

Other works realised a synthesis of the essential teachings of the Reformation, as for instance those included in Luther's catechism and Melanchthon's *Loci*. We can mention Erasmus Sarcerius'[189] (1501-1559) *Pastorale oder Hirtenbuch vom Ampt, Wesen vnd Disciplin der Pastorn vnd Kirchendiener* (1559) and Conrad

185 R.K. Rittgers, *The Reformation of the Keys. Confession, Conscience, and Authority in Sixteenth-Century Germany*, Cambridge Mass., Harvard University Press, 2004, 132-4. See also R.K. Rittgers, *Private confession and religious authority in Reformation Nürnberg*, in K. Jackson Lualdi and A.T. Thayer (eds.), *Penitence in the Age of Reformations*, 49-70.

186 R. Dürr, *Politische Kultur in der Frühen Neuzeit*, Göttingen, Gütersloher Verlagshaus, 2006, 304-5.

187 On Dieterich's biography see M. Huber, *Dieterich, Konrad*, in *Neue Deutsche Biographie* 3 (1957), 672 (accessed 18.12.2018); https://www.deutsche-biographie.de/gnd118891804.html#ndbcontent.

188 See http://thesaurus.cerl.org/record/cnp01012421 (accessed 17.11.2017).

189 H. Holstein, *Sarcerius, Erasmus*, in *Allgemeine Deutsche Biographie* 33 (1891), 727-9 (accessed 18.12.2018), https://www.deutsche-biographie.de/gnd122057635.html#adbcontent. For additional information see C.T. (Kees) de Groot, *Erasmus Sarcerius' Pastorale 1559. En de vorming van predikanten in de zestiende eeuw*, Apeldoorn, Labarum, 2016.

Porta's[190] (1541-1585) *Pastorale Lutheri* (1582). In some of these books, it must be noticed, private confession was intended again as a judgment. Yet, it kept the new specific features already seen: the priest could not impose punishments at the end of the confession; confession was meant as test for the knowledge of ecclesiastical teachings. Priests were asked to verify whether the Christians knew the catechism or also the summary of evangelical doctrine, as ignorance was understood as a symptom of sinfulness.[191]

Before the rise of the Lutheran casuistry, practical indications for pastors and parishioners were displaced in the collections of theological counsels,[192] such as Felix Bidenbach's[193] (1564-1612) *Consilia theologica* (1608-1612) in ten volumes, and the *Thesaurus consiliorum et decisionum* (1623)[194] by Georg Dedekenn[195] (1564-1628) written in four volumes in 1623.[196] These writings gathered responses given by faculties or authoritative theologians to practical cases, often involving conflicts between pastors and believers. We find different responses concerning contract law. For instance, Felix Bidenbach reports the opinion of Jakob Heerebrand and Theodor Schnepf on a case occurred in 1578 about a possible breach of the interest prohibition. Georg Dedekenn cites the opinions of Luther, Melanchthon, Brenz, Hunnius and Gerhard concerning loans and purchase of annuities.

Later, the *Consiliorum theologicorum centuria oder theologisch Fragbuch* published in Leipzig in 1626 by Joachim Pollio[197] (1577-1644), pastor in Breislau, includes the opinions of Melanchthon, Brenz, Hemmingsen and others on the lawfulness of various lending operations. The *Consilia theologica witebergensia*[198]

---

190 H. Holstein, *Porta, Konrad*, in *Allgemeine Deutsche Biographie* 26 (1888), 445 (accessed 18.12.2018), https://www.deutsche-biographie.de/gnd116269014.html#adbcontent.

191 R. Dürr, *Confession as an Instrument of Church Discipline: A Study of Catholic and Lutheran Confessional Manuals from the 16th and 17th Centuries*, in S. Müller, C. Schweiger, *Between Creativity and Norm-Making. Tensions in the Later Middle Ages and the Early Modern Era*, Leiden, Boston, Brill, 2013, 215-40 (234-7).

192 On the theological counsels see T. Kaufmann, *Konfession und Kultur*, 323-9.

193 F.B. Bautz, *Bidenbach (Bidembach), Felix*, in *BBKL*, vol. I, 1990, 582.

194 On this book see B.T.G. Mayes, *Counsel and Conscience*, 54-162.

195 A. Gössner, *Dedeken (Dedeckennus), Georg*, in *BBKL*, vol. XXXVIII, 2017, 295-300.

196 B.T.G. Mayes, *Counsel and Conscience*, 37. Porta's and Bidembach's books were recommended to the students of theology for the care of souls and the practice of confession. See C.E. Luthardt, *Geschichte der christlichen Ethik, Zweite Hälfte: Geschichte der christlichen Ethik*, 225-6; M. Nieden, *Die Erfindung des Theologen: Wittenberger Anweisungen zum Theologiestudium im Zeitalter von Reformation und Konfessionalisierung*, Mohr Tübingen, 2006, 170 fn. 36; B.T.G. Mayes, *Counsel and Conscience*, 30.

197 See http://thesaurus.cerl.org/record/cnp01878135 (accessed 17.11.2017).

198 A. Hunnius, *Ob und wie viel man* interesse *nehmen soll*, in *Consilia theologica witebergensia*, Franckfurt am Mäyn, 1664, 150-2.

(1644) comprises a counsel drafted by Aegidius Hunnius about the compatibility of financial instruments with the interest-taking prohibition. All these books document the topicality and concreteness of the legal and contractual issues and the persistent necessity of answers from theological authorities.

2.3.4 *Casuistry*

2.3.4.1 Balduin and Meisner: The School of Wittenberg

Collections of theological counsel were not specific enough and not disposed in a systematical and uniform order. Besides, the creation of specific confessional books of casuistry in the Roman Catholic context required the formation of similar instruments for the Lutherans.[199] The first Lutheran work of this genre was Friedrich Balduin's famous *Tractatus de casibus conscientiae* published posthumously in 1628. Balduin[200] (1575-1627) studied theology, philosophy and mathematics at the University of Wittenberg. In 1601 he was appointed adjunct faculty member of the philosophy department and in 1604 he became professor of theology. In the *epistola dedicatoria* of his work, Balduin explains that his theological discipline deals with the eternal man's health, offering to show man life and death, heaven and hell, so that he can know if he is disposed towards the first or the second.[201] The aim of casuistry is therefore to make man aware of his disposition: towards damnation or towards heaven.[202]

The content of Balduin's treatise is not completely new, as previously the same material was included in different genres of literature like dogmatic and pastoral treatises, biblical commentaries, catechisms, and sermons. Yet, the work of Balduin is characterized by the legal analysis of conscience and by the strict relation between the Christian and Scripture without any intermediations. Melanchthon conceived of conscience as a practical syllogism between

199 F. Balduin, *Tractatus loculentus, posthumus, toti reipublicae christianae utilissimus, de materia rarissime ante hac enucleate, casibus nimirum conscientiae*, Wittembergae, 1628, praefatio; B.T.G. Mayes, *Counsel and Conscience*, 34-5.

200 On Balduin's biography, see W. Gaß, *Balduin, Friedrich*, in *Allgemeine Deutsche Biographie* (), (accessed 1.11.2017), https://www.deutsche-biographie.de/gnd116883391.html#adbcontent; T. Mahlmann, *Balduin, Friedrich*, in *RPP*, vol. I, 2007, 559; R.H. Martin, *The Reformation of Conscience: Rhetoric in the Lutheran Casuistry of Friedrich Balduin (1575-1627)*, Diss., University of Virginia, 2008.

201 F. Balduin, *Tractatus*, epistola dedicatoria.

202 On the Protestant and Catholic conceptions about heaven and hell see D.P. Walker, *The Decline of Hell. Seventeenth-Century Discussions of Eternal Torment*, London, Routledge, 1964. For the Protestants see also the recent L. Throness, *A Protestant Purgatory: Theological Origins of the Penitentiary Act, 1779*, 2nd ed., Abigdon, Oxon, New York, Routledge, 2016.

the law of God and the real fact.[203] For Balduin conscience is a place for the cognition and examination of daily actions. Conscience is a tribunal (*forum*) where every man is actor, registrar and judge. Justice is always enforced, as nobody can escape and can avoid what conscience accepts and concludes.[204] Balduin knows the numerous works of Roman Catholic casuists, but he avows that his analysis of the cases of conscience will only be based on the Scripture.[205]

Balduin's treatise is comprised of four books: 1) on conscience and its cases in general; 2) on the human actions concerning God and religion; 3) on the human actions concerning the heavenly spirit; and 4) on the human actions concerning human affairs. The fourth book, chapter three deals with the cases of conscience about goods of fortune (*De casibus conscientiae circa bona fortunae*). Here, Balduin looks into the lawfulness and right mode to acquire and possess goods. He handles with the contract of sale, loan and different types of purchase of annuities.

Balduin authored the first book of Lutheran casuistry, but his solutions were often founded on other sources. The first reference is Scripture, but Balduin also cites Roman Catholic writers, for instance Thomas Aquinas, and Lutheran theologians like Brenz, Gerhard and others. Among Balduin's quoted authors, one needs to be mentioned in particular: Balthasar Meisner (1587-1626). Meisner[206] never published a casuistical handbook. But he authored a lecture on the Roman Catholic canon law and casuistry (*Oratio de Romani pontificis theologia casuidica vel de iure canonico*, 1617) and dealt with a number of cases of conscience in his philosophical writings.[207] Balthasar was the brother of Dorothea, first wife of Balduin and also one of his students. Not only did he study in Wittenberg but also in Gießen, Straßburg and Tübingen. In 1611 he came back to Wittenberg, where he served as professor of ethics and in 1613 as professor of theology. Meisner's approach to philosophy shows a refusal of the Stoic and Aristotelian doctrine of virtues and looks for a universal Christian

---

203 P. Melanchthon, *Definitiones*, in H. Engelland, R. Stupperich (eds.), *Loci praecipui theologici von 1559 (2 Teil) und Definitiones*, Gütersloh, Bertelsmann, 790, cited in B.T.G. Mayes, *Counsel and conscience*, 17.

204 F. Balduin, *Tractatus*, epistola dedicatoria: "*Hic ergo quilibet quotidiana cognitione vel exploratione sui opus habet, quae sit per conscientiae scrutinium, in quo homo habet forum suum, in quo ipse actor, scriba atque iudex est, forum in quo semper viget iustitia, quod nemo effugere, nemo declinare potest, semper enim conscientia assumit, simul ac concludit*".

205 F. Balduin, *Tractatus*, epistola dedicatoria: "*... secundum unicam Scripturae normam ...*".

206 On Meisner biography see P. Tschackert, *Meisner, Balthasar*, in *Allgemeine Deutsche Biographie* 21 (1885), 243 (accessed 20.10.2017), https://www.deutsche-biographie.de/gnd10434539X.html#adbcontent; W. Sparn, *Meisner, Balthasar*, in *BBKL*, vol. V (1993), 1172-4; K.G. Appold, *Meisner, Balthasar*, in *RPP*, vol. VIII, 2001, 215.

207 See B.T.G. Mayes, *Counsel and conscience*, 120-1.

natural law.[208] Meisner knows and employs the early modern scholastics' opinions: sometimes accepting them,[209] sometimes refusing them.[210]

In his 1616 *Dissertatio de legibus*, Meisner sustains the natural law foundation of the civil order, but does not address contract law. Instead in his *Dissertatio de summo bono* (1614) and in the third part of his masterpiece *Philosophia sobria*, published in 1623, he delves into issues concerning contract law. The *Dissertatio* deals with practical philosophy. In chapter three, article one, dedicated to human conscience, Meisner treats the binding effects of promises in conscience. In the *Philosophia*, discussing about the virtue of justice, he wrestles with the interest-taking prohibition and the most diffused credit instruments. In addition, he explores the complex debate on the contract of prostitution. As in other parts of his work, Meisner starts by looking at the opinions of the early modern scholastics and then formulates his own.

2.3.4.2 König and Dannhauer: Altdorf and Strasbourg

Following on the echoes of Balduin's treatise, in the seventeenth century a river of Lutheran casuistical books emerged. A student of Balduin and Meisner, Arnold Mengering (1596-1647) published three casuistical books: *Refectorium conscientiae evangelicum: Evangelischer Gewissens-Ruhe* (1638); *Scrutinium conscientiae cathecheticum: Das ist gewissensrüge und Sündenregister aus dem Catechismo*, (1642); and *Informatorium conscientiae evangelicum: Evangelisches Gewissens-Recht, Rath und Unterricht, wie man bey den ordentlichen Sontags-Evangelien sein Gewissen also in acht nehmen … lerne, daß man weder zur Rechten noch zur Lincken im Christentub verstossen* (1644). In Jena Andreas Kessler[211] (1595-1643) published his *Theologia casuum conscientiae* in 1658. Some of these works did not include cases about contract law. Among those who did examine contract law, we focus on some of works produced by Balduin's students in Wittenberg or those who were inspired by him. We begin with Georg König (1590-1654) and Johann Konrad Dannhauer (1603-1666).

---

208 W. Sparn, *Die Schulphilosophie in den lutherischen Territorien*, in H. Holzhey, W. Schmidt-Biggemann (eds.), *Die Philosophie des 17. Jahrhunderts*, vol. 4, *Das Heilige Römische Reich deutscher Nation Nord-und Ostmitteleuropa*, Basel, Schwabe & Co., 2001, 508-9.

209 Concerning the concept of 'religion', Meisner observes the contribution of Gregorio de Valencia (1549-1603). K.G. Appold, *Orthodoxie als Konsensbildung*, Tübingen, Mohr Siebeck, 2004, 257.

210 See for instance S.K. Knebel, *Casuistry and the Early Modern Paradigm Shift in the Notion of Charity*, in J. Kraye, R. Saarinen, *Moral Philosophy on the Thresold of Modernity*, Berlin, Springer, 2005, 115-40 (134).

211 P. Tschackert, *Kesler, Andreas*, in *Allgemeine Deutsche Biographie* 15 (1882), 655 (accessed 14.11.2017), https://www.deutsche-biographie.de/gnd124224644.html#adbcontent.

König[212], son of an official of the Electoral Palatinate, studied theology and philosophy in Altdorf, Wittenberg and Jena. He obtained a doctorate at the University of Marburg in 1626. Then he was pastor and professor of theology in Altdorf. König published his treatise on cases of conscience, *Casus conscientiae*, in 1654. He writes that God, who knows what he ordained and approved for men, built in men's heart a court, in order to make men able to know what they can or cannot do according to the divine prescriptions. This court is called conscience. Conscience is a spark of right reason, 'the most skillful judge and indicator of the goods and the evils'.[213]

Conscience is treated as a court regulated by the law. The law of conscience includes divine law, natural law and human law. As König illustrates, the Word of God is absolutely the principal norm (*norma principalissima*), which obliges conscience by reason of its author. Then, conscience is governed by natural law. Natural law does not derive from a certain institution but from natural instinct. It generates the distinction between honourable and shameful actions. As natural law is in agreement with the Word of God, it has the force and value of a norm. Although it does not oblige so strictly as the Word of God itself, because it was in some measure altered by Adam's Fall, it has more binding force than positive laws, because it derives from the light of the eternal law instilled in us.[214] Human laws, lastly, embrace ecclesiastical law and civil law and oblige the conscience to the extent that they are in agreement with the Word of God and help promote ecclesiastical discipline and public peace.[215] The law of conscience also concerns contracts. König proposes cases of conscience related to the interest prohibition and the effects of promises on the conscience.

König's pupil, Johann Konrad Dannhauer[216] (1603-1666), was the master of Philipp Jakob Spener (1635-1705) founder of Pietism, and studied theology in

---

212 On König see J.A. Wagenmann, *König, Georg* in *Allgemeine Deutsche Biographie* 16 (1882), 507-8 (accessed 19.05.2015), http://www.deutsche-biographie.de/ppn116292008.html?anchor=adb.

213 G. König, *Casus conscientiae, qui in sex capitibus doctrinae catechetizae, una cum tabula oeconomica subinde solent occurrere, erudite et fideliter decisae*, Altdorfii, 1654, proemium, 1: "*Nam Deus primum scit, quid in iudiciis suis, quoad nos, praescripserit et probaverit, nec ne: deinde huius rei tribunal etiam in nostris cordis erexit, ut et nos consciamus, quid iuxta praescriptum et approbationem divinam recte vel secus fieri possit, vel fiat, vel factum sit: aut non! Et hoc in nobis appellatur conscientia, nempe reliqua rectae rationis scintillula, bonorum malorumque judex et index dexterrimus ...*".

214 G. König, *Casus conscientiae*, proemium, 3.

215 G. König, *Casus conscientiae*, proemium, 3-4.

216 H. Schüssler, *Dannhauer, Johann Konrad*, in *Neue Deutsche Biographie* 3 (1957), 512 (accessed 08.01.2016), http://www.deutsche-biographie.de/pnd120227649.html; F.W. Bautz,

Marburg, Jena (with Johann Gerhard) and Altdorf. In 1629 he was appointed professor of rhetoric at Strasbourg University, and from 1658 till his death he was professor of theology there. Dannhauer assumed many roles in Strasbourg and was the most important theologian of Strasbourg University in the seventeenth century. He published two casuistry books: the two tomes of the *Liber conscientiae* (first tome published 1662, second tome in 1667) and the *Theologia casualis*, published posthumously in 1706. He also worked on a commentary on the Decalogue *Deuteronomium dannhawerianum* (1669), first edited under the name *Collegium decalogicum* (1638).

Dannhauer's *Liber conscientiae* describes conscience in medical terms, an approach also proposed by Meisner for the study of theology.[217] This book also shows Puritan influences.[218] The first tome is divided in two parts, each one including two sections. The first section is dedicated to 'physiology' and deals with conscience in general; the second section, 'pathology', is dedicated to the illnesses of conscience; section three includes semiotics and physiognomy. The second part includes two sections: general hygiene and symbology and cases.[219] To Dannhauer, conscience has its origin in God, who inscribed His law both on the tables of Moses and on man's heart, where He also built His divine tribunal.[220] In the *Liber conscientiae* Dannhauer does not deal with contract law. Instead, in the *Deuteronomium dannhawerianum* and in the *Theologia casualis*, Dannhauer shows interest for contract law and offers some reflections in the chapters dedicated to the seventh and eighth commandments of the Decalogue.

Dannhauer, Johann Konrad, in *BBKL*, vol. I, 1990, 1211-12; J. Wallmann, *Die Eigenart der Strassburger lutherischen Orthodoxie im 17. Jahrhundert*, in J. Wallmann (ed.), *Theologie und Frömmigkeit im Zeitalter des Barock*, Tübingen, Mohr Siebeck, 1995, 87-123; W. Sparn, *Die Schulphilosophie in den lutherischen Territorien*, in H. Holzhey, W. Schmidt-Biggemann (eds.), *Die Philosophie des 17. Jahrhunderts*, 544-46; J. Wallmann, *Dannhauer, Johann Konrad*, in *RPP*, vol. III, 2007, 664.

217 See W. Sparn, *Die Krise der Frömmigkeit und ihr theologischer Reflex im nachreformatorischen Luthertum*, in H.C. Rublack (ed.), *Die lutherische Konfessionalisierung*, 54-82 (72-3). For Meisner theology is designed as a spiritual medicine or therapeutics for reaching salvation. This new concept is the consequence of a professionalization based on the necessity to educate priests for preaching, pastoral care and church administration.

218 J. Wallmann, *Dannhauer, Johann Konrad*, passim.

219 J.K. Dannhauer, *Liber conscientiae sive theologia conscientiaria*, vol. 1, Argentorati 1662.

220 J.K. Dannhauer, *Liber conscientiae sive theologia conscientiaria*, 38: "*Originem suam et natales conscientia DEO debet, qui ut in tabulas Mosis, ita in tabulas cordis opus legis divino digito inscripsit, forumque divinum erexit* ... ".

2.3.4.3 Dunte, Prückner and the Pastoral Practice

Casuistry books were not only published by academics but also by pastors specialized in pastoral care. Already in 1636, eight years after the publication of Balduin's treatise, Ludwig Dunte[221] (1597-1639), pastor of Tallinn, printed his *Decisiones casuum conscientiae sexcentorum et ultra.* In this enormous collection of cases of conscience, the complete block of Lutheran theology is reviewed in the light of these cases, according to the *loci theologici*'s structure.[222] At the beginning of this book, Dunte avows that he intends to continue the line traced by Dedekenn, Bidenbach and Balduin, but also other excellent theologians like Gerhard and Hunnius, and Reformed theologians like Perkins and Rasmussen. Chapter 10, second section is dedicated to the second table of the Decalogue. Here, in the cases 42-5, Dunte addresses the issue of the interest prohibition and the purchase of annuities (*Zins*).

Andreas Prückner[223] (1610-d.?) was also primarily involved in the pastoral practice. He studied in Jena and then was pastor in Geldersheim (1634). He was appointed professor at the Gymnasium in Schweinfurt, deacon and archdeacon. In the following years he assumed different functions: in 1660, court chaplain in Castell; in 1661, pastor in Friesenhausen; and in 1663, pastor in Rüdenhausen. In his *Manuale mille quaestionum* (1662), which also spread in Norway, mostly among the clergy of Bergen and Trondheim,[224] Prückner follows Balduin's structure and division of topics. He also explores a good number of cases of conscience involving contract law. He focuses on the contracts of sale, loan, purchase of annuities and lease. For the solutions, Prückner even recalls scholastic authors like Francisco de Toledo Herrera (1532-1596) and Reformed thinkers like William Ames.

2.3.5 *Moral Theology*

2.3.5.1 Georg Calixt and the Theologians of Helmstedt

The casuistical books we examined were all composed by theologians who were educated in Wittenberg or other universities that adhered to the *Formula of Concord.* The University of Helmstedt, however, the first Protestant university

221 See Katalog der deutschen Nationalbibliothek, https://portal.dnb.de/opac.htm?method=simpleSearch&cqlMode=true&query=idn%3D124738265.

222 L. Dunte, *Decisiones casuum conscientiae sexcentorum et ultra, e diversis theologorum scriptis collectae, contractae,* [...], Lübeck, 1636.

223 See Katalog der deutschen Nationalbibliothek, https://portal.dnb.de/opac.htm?method=simpleSearch&cqlMode=true&query=idn%3D123188148 (accessed 31.10.2017).

224 See G. Dahl, *Book Collections of Clerics in Norway, 1650-1750*, Leiden, Boston, Brill, 2010, 89, 99, 186, 192, 210, 214, 293; G. Dahl, *Books in Early Modern Norway*, Leiden, Boston, Brill, 2011, 76.

in northern Germany, founded in 1576, represented a particular case.[225] Duke Julius of Brunswick-Wolfenbüttel (1528-1589) refused to sign the *Formula of Concord*,[226] leading to the emergence of a more liberal approach towards theology and philosophy. Jacopo Zabarella's (1533-1589) neo-Aristotelian theology inspired the humanist Johannes Caselius (1533-1613) and his pupil Cornelius Martini (1568-1621), which were appointed professors in Helmstedt. Caselius and Martini had as students Georg Calixt (1586-1656) and Conrad Horneius (1590-1649), to which the following pages are mainly dedicated.

2.3.5.1.1 *Calixt and the Rise of Lutheran Moral Theology*

Calixt[227] was selected for the chair of controversial theology in 1614, and in 1616 obtained his doctorate. Calixt's father had been a student of Melanchthon and privately taught him till his twelfth birthday. Then, Calixt was influenced by his master Martini. Calixt undertook an innovative theological approach and sought to reconcile the positions of the Lutherans, the Reformed and the Roman Catholics, by formulating a body of teachings that could be accepted by all.[228] In 1634, he published his incomplete treatise of moral theology *Epitome theologiae moralis*.[229] In the *epistola dedicatoria*, Calixt reveals the reasons for the creation of such a text. He declares the necessity to clarify the mistakes of the papal Church. The Church of the Pope, he writes, has been infected with many superstitions and deceits, in addition to absurd and dishonest pictures of the true doctrine. This Church recognises the superiority of the priests over every mortal and the claim for the universal authority of the Pope over the world. Such contaminations prevent man from understanding if conscience is

---

225 I. Mager, *Helmstedt, University of*, in *RPP*, vol. VI, 2009, 50.

226 L. Schorn-Schütte, *Lutherische Konfessionalisierung? Das Beispiel Brauchweig-Wolfenbüttel (1589-1613)*, in H.C. Rublack (ed.), *Die lutherische Konfessionalisierung in Deutschland (1589-1613)*, Gütersloh, Gerd Mohn, 1992, 163-94.

227 On Calixt's biography, see J. Wallmann, *Calixt, Georg*, in *TRE*, vol. VII, 1981, 552-9; I. Mager, *Calixtus, Georg*, in *RPP*, vol. II, 2007, 315-6.

228 I. Hunter, *The Secularisation of the Confessional State. The Political Thought of Christian Thomasius*, Cambridge, Cambridge University Press, 2007, 44. On Calixt's theology, see J. Wallmann, *Der Theologiebegriff bei Johann Gerhard und Georg Calixt*, Tübingen, Mohr Siebeck, 1961; J. Wallmann, *Zwischen Reformation und Humanismus. Eigenart und Wirkungen Helmstedter Theologie unter besonderer Berücksichtigung Georg Calixts*, in *Zeitschrift für Theologie und Kirche*, 1977, 348-70.

229 G. Calixt, *Epitomes theologiae moralis pars prima*, Helmestadii, 1662. Known editions are two: Helmaestadii 1634; Helmestadii, 1662. On Calixt's moral theology, see I. Mager, *Georg Calixts theologische Ethik und ihre Nachwirkungen*, Göttingen, Vandenhoeck & Ruprecht, 1969.

pure and in a state of grace before God.[230] The rise of moral theology is thus tangled with the need to correct the Roman Catholic Church's errors.

Calixt's method integrates morality in a theological perspective where faith is the primary requisite.[231] Indeed, the subject of moral theology is man regenerated by faith: the reborn man. The natural and supernatural actions of the born-again find their originating principle in the grace of the Holy Spirit: the Spirit dwells in them.[232] Then, the aim of moral theology is that the faithful may remain in state of grace and may not sin freely against conscience.[233] These words betray a conception of human freedom already seen in Melanchthon; a true freedom of will is only possible with faith.

Calixt's treatise is articulated in four parts: on the goal of moral theology; on the subject of moral theology; on the principles of human actions for the born-again; on the laws. Calixt follows the analytical method and employs as main sources the Holy Scriptures and the Church Fathers.[234] Roman Catholic authors, Calixt affirms, are mentioned when they are not in contrast with the fundamentals of Christendom and do not incline toward atheism.[235]

To Calixt, conscience determines what should be done in a specific case. Natural law and divine law are the norms of every human action, but for performing their function they need to be known and applied in works.[236] Natural law includes practical principles, which constitute the moral law or the Decalogue. The law of the public authority is (Calixt employs Aquinas's definition) a rational ordinance directed to the common good. Sometimes natural law presents special conditions or indeterminate solutions and positive

230 G. Calixt, *Epitomes theologiae moralis*, epistola dedicatoria: "*Dicimus, inquit, Ecclesiam in qua Romanus Pontifex sedet et dominatur* tot et tantis infectam esse superstitionibus et corruptelis et absurdis improbisque figmentis certae et verae doctrinae superadditis, ad enormem quaesitum et adferendam presbyteris super omnes mortales eminentiam et vindicandum Pontifici universale quoddam orbes imperium comparatis, ut qui intelligat, si sibi conscientiam suam illesam et gratiam Dei integram esse cupiat, probare et adstipulari nullo modo possit".

231 I. Mager, *Georg Calixts theologische Ethik*, 59.

232 G. Calixt, *Epitomes theologiae moralis*, 17: "*Actuum itaque supernaturalium in homine renato, tum etiam naturalium, quatenus ad finem supernaturalem referuntur, principium est habitans in renato Spiritus sanctus …*".

233 G. Calixt, *Epitomes theologiae moralis*, 3, IV: "*Finis igitur partis ejus, quam ex disciplina theologica modo tractamus et moralem vocamus, hic est, ut homo fidelis in fide et statu gratiae perseveret, nec eo per peccata liberé et contra conscientiam perpetrata excidat*".

234 I. Mager, *Georg Calixts theologische Ethik*, 66-7.

235 G. Calixt, *Epitomes theologiae moralis*, epistola dedicatoria.

236 G. Calixt, *Epitomes theologiae moralis*, 18.

law – either divine or human[237] – determines them.[238] Human law cannot forbid or admit what is not forbidden or admitted by natural law and the divine law.[239]

Calixt's textbook does not confront issues of contract law, on which he in 1667 published a separate treatise: *Dissertatio theologica moralis de usuris.* However, as a first work of moral theology, the *epitome* exercised a sensitive influence on the shaping of the discipline.

2.3.5.1.2 *Horneius, Uffelmann and Niemeier*

Conrad Horneius,[240] the other pupil of Caselius and Martini, studied philosophy, philology and theology in Helmstedt, before being appointed professor of logic and ethics in 1619. In 1622 he succeeded Martini in the chair of metaphysics and finally in 1628 he became professor of theology. Horneius shared the theological doctrine of his colleague Calixt and similarly adopted the analytical method.[241] In 1624 he published a treatise on moral philosophy (*Philosophia moralis*), while his *Compendium theologiae*, published posthumously in 1655, contains a treatment of contract law. The second part of the *compedium* is dedicated to moral theology and follows the scheme of the Decalogue. The comments on the seventh and eighth commandments also take into consideration the analysis of contract law. Like Calixt before him, Horneius does not only refer to Scripture and Church Fathers, but also to Roman Catholic authors.

In the same line of Calixt and Horneius, Heinrich Uffelmann (1641-1680) and Johann Bartold Niemeier (1644-1708) were also professors in Helmstedt. Uffelmann was professor of ethics (1665) and theology (1677). In his *Variorum eorumque illustrium conscientiae casuum fasciculus*, published posthumously in 1709, he addresses contract law cases of conscience in the comments on the seventh commandment. He looks at sale, just price theory, restitution, interest-taking prohibition and purchase of annuities. Among the sources used, we find both Calixt and Horneius, but again also Roman Catholic authors like Leonard Lessius. In his *De jure quo homo homini in sermone obligatur liber*

---

237 G. Calixt, *Epitomes theologiae moralis*, 64: "*Lex itaque positiva alia* divina est, *alia* humana".

238 G. Calixt, *Epitomes theologiae moralis*, 63.

239 G. Calixt, *Epitomes theologiae moralis*, 76-7: "*Manifestum profecto est, legem humanam non posse prohibere, quae lege divina sive naturali sive positiva fuerint mandata; neque mandare, quae fuerint prohibita*".

240 On Horneius biography see I. Mager, *Hornejus, Conrad*, in *Neue Deutsche Biographie* 9 (1972), 637 (accessed 30.10.2017), https://www.deutsche-biographie.de/gnd116993901.html#ndbcontent; F.W. Bautz, *Hornejus Konrad*, in *BBKL*, vol. II, 1990, 1062-3; W. Sparn, *Horneius, Konrad*, in *RPP*, vol. VI, 2009, 253.

241 I. Mager, *Georg Calixts theologische Ethik*, 66.

unus (*Helmaestedii*, 1676), instead, Uffelmann tackles the topics of truth in judgments, but also oaths, and contractual fidelity. In a special way Uffelmann condemns the Jesuit doctrine of mental reservations.

Johann Bartold Niemeier studied in Helmstedt were he became professor of metaphysics (1675), logic (1690) and theology (1698). Niemeier authored a manual of moral theology, *Theologia moralis*, published 1696 and 1704. The book gathers several theological disputations and follows the structure of the Decalogue. Contract doctrine is again addressed in the comments on the seventh and eighth commandments. Niemeier does not go in depth, but only articulates some principles about the protection against fraud and the binding nature of promises and contracts.

2.3.5.2 Dürr, Baier and the Theologians of Altdorf

Calixt's manual of moral theology was, by his own admission, incomplete. But the road he inaugurated found two excellent proselytes at the University of Altdorf: Johann Konrad Dürr (1625-1677) and Johann Wilhelm Baier (1647-1695). Dürr[242] studied theology and philosophy in Altdorf, Jena (where he was student of Gerhard), and Helmstedt. In 1654 he was appointed professor of moral philosophy at the University of Altdorf, in 1655 professor of poetry, and finally in 1657 professor of theology. Following the example of Calixt, Dürr committed himself to the development of the new discipline of moral theology. In 1662 he published the *Enchiridion theologiae moralis*, which later received a new refined version, in 1675. A third edition was published posthumously in 1698. The first and second editions differ notably, as the first one appears as a collection of dissertations, while the second one shows a more systematic elaboration. The *Compendium theologiae moralis* edited in 1698 also incorporates a treatise on the origins of moral theology, *De origine et progressu theologiae moralis systematicae*, written by Johann Michael Lang (1664-1731),[243] first a student of Baier then professor and pastor in Altdorf. The structure of Baier's book presents two parts. The first one is devoted to the characters of the discipline and the Christian duties in general. The second part treats the duties of the Christians according to their differing statuses (ecclesiastical, political and economic).

242 J.A. Wagenmann, *Dürr, Johann Konrad*, in *Allgemeine Deutsche Biographie* 5 (1877), 490-1 (accessed 17.12.2015), http://www.deutsche-biographie.de/pnd100112544.html?anchor=adb.

243 J.A. Wagenmann, *Lang, Johann Michael*, in *Allgemeine Deutsche Biographie* 17 (1883), 601-602 (accessed 9.11.2017), https://www.deutsche-biographie.de/gnd100299662.html#adbcontent.

Contract law critical questions are tackled in the common part, subpart III, dedicated to the forms of virtues for Christian men, which are primarily estimated in agreement with divine law, secondarily with the judgment of conscience, and where the different species of conscience act. Section IV, Chapter XVI regards the virtues of Christian men regarding the goods of fortune. This chapter deals with the acquisition and lawful possession of goods. Dürr investigates principally the lawfulness and right application of the contracts of sale, lease and various lending operations.[244]

The discipline of moral theology was also fostered by Dürr's student Johann Wilhelm Baier.[245] Baier studied in Altdorf, but also in Jena. In 1694 he became professor at the newly founded University of Halle and in 1695 was appointed senior court chaplain and general superintendent of Weimar. His *Compendium theologiae moralis* was published in 1697 and 1698. It presents a structure similar to Dürr's book and includes the analysis of contract law in chapter X, section VII, on Christian men's duties to the neighbour in contracts (*De officio hominis renati circa proximum in contractibus*). Baier's work was fairly influential. In 1703 Johann Michael Lang published annotations on Baier's compendium, *Ad B. D. Joh. Guil Baieri compendium theologiae moralis supplementa*. In addition, together with Buddeus' *Institutiones theologiae moralis*, Baier's work constituted the basis of the *Breviarium theologiae moralis* (1723) of Gustav Georg Zeltner (1672-1738),[246] also professor of theology in Altdorf. This manual includes synoptic tables of the Christian's duties.

2.3.5.3 Strauch and Schelwig: from Wittenberg to Danzig

The syncretistic trend inaugurated by Calixt met with a violent reaction from the famous orthodox theologian Abrahm Calov (1612-1686), whose students were Aegidius Strauch (1632-1682)[247] and Samuel Schelwig (1643-1715).[248] Strauch and Schelwig are examples of the more conservative side among the Lutheran theologians. Strauch, son of the professor of law and Electoral Councilor of Wittenberg Johann Strauch, studied history, mathematics and

244 J.K. Dürr, *Compendium theologiae moralis*, Altdorfi Noricorum, 1698.

245 A. Kreiner, *Baier, Johann Wilhelm der Ältere*, in *Neue Deutsche Biographie* 1 (1953), 543-4 (accessed 18.12.15), http://www.deutsche-biographie.de/pnd116040149.html.

246 P. Tschackert, *Zeltner, Gustav Georg*, in *Allgemeine Deutsche Biographie* 45 (1900), 52-3 (accessed 9.11.17), https://www.deutsche-biographie.de/gnd115540806.html#adbcontent.

247 A. Schimmelpfennig, *Strauch, Aegidius*, in *Allgemeine Deutsche Biographie* 36 (1893), 525-7 (accessed 15.01.18), https://www.deutsche-biographie.de/pnd117311421.html#adbcontent. J. Wallmann, *Strauch, Aegidius*, in *RPP*, vol. XII, 2012, 302.

248 D. Erdmann, *Schelwig, Samuel*, in *Allgemeine Deutsche Biographie* 31 (1890), 30-6 (accessed 15.01.18), https://www.deutsche-biographie.de/pnd104256621.html#adbcontent. J. Wallmann, *Schelwig, Samuel*, in *RPP*, vol. XI, 2012, 473.

Oriental languages at the Wittenberg University. In 1649 he moved to Leipzig, where he continued his training in Oriental languages and studied theology. In 1650 he returned to Wittenberg, obtained his doctorate in philosophy (1651) and was appointed professor of the same discipline (1653). An erudite scholar, in 1664 Strauch completed his doctorate in theology, and in 1666 he became assessor at the Wittenberg theological faculty. In 1669, Strauch served as rector of the Gymnasium in Danzig and pastor of the Trinity Church. Strauch fully polemized against the theologians of Helmstedt claiming for the purity of the Lutheran creed according to the Augsburg confession. In his *Theologia moralis*, which gathers a number of dissertations and was published posthumously in 1708, Strauch presents a number of cases concerning private property, interest and usury.

Samuel Schelwig was also educated in Wittenberg, where he attended lessons by some of the greatest Lutheran theologians like Calov, Meisner and Strauch. In 1673 he was appointed professor of philosophy and librarian at the Gymnasium of Danzig, and later professor of theology to replace Aegidius Strauch. In 1681 he was preacher at the *Katharinenkirche*, and in 1685 he became rector of the Gymnasium. Schelwig fully opposed the pietism initiated by Spener defending the integrity of the Lutheran faith. In his *Cynosura conscientiae* (1692), a collection of cases of conscience, he answered cases about lending, annuities (*Zins*), interest and usury. His main sources were, together with the Scriptures, Meisner's *Philosophia sobria* and Dedekenn's *Thesaurus*.

2.4 The Challenges of the Modern Natural Lawyers

2.4.1 *Introduction*

As seen previously, the ethical treatises, books of casuistry and moral theology, commonplaces and other dogmatic treatises of Lutheran theologians looked at natural law from the theological perspective devised by Luther and Melanchthon.[249] Yet, in the second half of the seventeenth century, other natural law theories put the notion of Christian revelation to the side, stirring

249 See the classic work of M. Scattola, *Das Naturrecht vor dem Naturrecht. Zur Geschichte des >ius naturae< im 16. Jahrhundert*, Tübingen, Max Niemeyer Verlag, 1999. Among the most recent surveys see W. Sparn, *Naturrecht und Verfassungsfrage im frühneuzeitlichen Luthertum – am Beispil religiöser Toleranz*, in R. von Friedeburg, M. Schmoeckel (eds.), *Recht, Konfession und Verfassung im 17. Jahrhundert. West-und mitteleuropäische Entwicklungen*, Berlin, Duncker & Humblot, 2015, 129-49 (130-1); M. Scattola, *Natural Law Part II: The Protestant and Philosophy Traditions*, in H. Lagerlund, H. Hill (eds.), *The Routledge Companion to Sixteenth Century Philosophy*, New York, Routledge, 2017, 580-613.

heated debates.[250] In particular, Samuel Pufendorf[251] (1632-1694) introduced a secular vision of natural law. He argued that this is founded on the state of corruption (the human nature after the Fall), and its content is to promote peaceful sociality.[252] Pufendorf's view triggered a bitter reaction among the most orthodox Lutheran theologians, who replied to the *pessimus calumniator et atheus*[253] that natural law could not be founded in the *socialitas*. The new theory led to a rationalistic drift, forgetting the indispensable correlation with divine revelation. These scholars resisted the rationalization of natural law and defended its divine characteristics.[254]

---

250 For a general overview see L. Daston, M. Stolleis (eds.), *Natural Law and Laws of Nature in Early Modern Europe. Jurisprudence, Theology, Moral and Natural Philosophy*, London and New York, Routledge, first ed. 2008, 2016; R. von Friedeburg, *The Rise of Natural Law in the Early Modern Period*, in U.L. Lehner, R.A. Muller, A.G. Roeber (eds.), *The Oxford Handbook of Early Modern Theology, 1600-1800*, 625-41; K. Haakonssen, *Early Modern Natural Law Theories*, in G. Duke, R.P. George (eds.), *The Cambridge Companion to Natural Law Jurisprudence*, Cambridge, Cambridge University Press, 2017, 76-102. A more detailed analysis in K. Haakonssen, *Natural Law and Moral Philosophy: From Grotius to the Scottish Enlightenment*, Cambridge, Cambridge University Press, 1996.

251 On Pufendorf there is a vast literature, see among the recent works: F. Palladini, G. Hartung (eds.), *Samuel Pufendorf und die europäische Frühaufklärung: Werk und Einfluss eines deutschen Bürgers der Gelehrtenrepublik nach 300 Jahren (1694-1994)*, Berlin, Akademie, 1996; H. Dreitzel, *Samuel Pufendorf*, in H. Holzhey, W. Schmidt-Biggemann (eds.), *Die Philosophie des 17. Jahrhunderts*, vol. 4, 757-812; T. Behme, *Pufendorf's Doctrine of Sovereignty and Its Natural Law Foundations*, in I. Hunter, D. Saunders (eds.), *Natural Law and Civil Sovereignty, Moral Right and State Authority in Early Modern Political Thought*, Basingstoke, Palgrave Macmillan, 2002, 43-58; Y. Ikadatsu, *Der Paradigmawechsel der Privatrechtstheorie und die Neukonstruktion der Vertragstheorie in seinem Rahmen, Pufendorf, Wolff, Kant und Savigny*, Ebelsbach, Aktiv Druck, 2002; D. Döring, *Wirkungen des konfessionellen Denkens auf das juristische Werk Samuel Pufendorfs*, in C. Strohm, H. De Wall (eds.), *Konfessionalität und Jurisprudenz in der frühen Neuzeit*, Berlin, Duncker & Humbolt, 2009, 415-30 D. Döring, *Samuel Pufendorf in der Welt des 17. Jahrhunderts, Untersuchungen zur Biographie Pufendorfs und zu seinem Wirken als Politiker und Theologe*, Frankfurt am Main, Klostermann, 2012; M. Schmoeckel, *Das Recht*, 63-5.

252 A. Raunio, *Natural Law in the Lutheran Tradition*, in N. Doe (ed.), *Christianity and Natural Law: An Introduction*, Cambridge, Cambridge University Press, 2017, 77-97 (88).

253 These terms are used by N. Beckmann, *Legitima defensio contra magistri Samuelis Puffendorffii ...*, 21 cit. in F. Palladini, *Discussioni seicentesche su Samuele Pufendorf. Scritti latini: 1663-1700*, Bologna, Il Mulino, 1978, 204.

254 For an account of the debate see M. Scattola, *Scientia iuris and ius naturae: The Jurisprudence of the Holy Roman Empire in the Seventeenth and Eighteenth Centuries*, in E. Pattaro, D. Canale, P. Grossi, H. Hofmann, P. Riley (eds.), *A Treatise of Legal Philosophy and General Jurisprudence, Vol. 9: A History of the Philosophy of Law in the Civil Law World, 1600-1900*, Berlin, Springer, 2009, 1-41. For a report of the critics of Pufendorf's natural law works and their opinions see F. Palladini, *Discussioni seicentesche*, 163-271.

As a strategy to fight the new approach, theologians like Johann Adam Osiander (1622-1697), Valentin Alberti (1635-1697), Johann Joachim Zentgrav (1643-1707), and Johann Wolfgang Jäger (1647-1720) turned back to Grotius' *De iure belli ac pacis* (1635).[255] They commented on his work either in the light of a strict orthodox theology, or combining the prescriptions of Scripture with the teachings of the early modern scholastics. Grotius was used as platform for opposing Pufendorf's theory. Another stream of theologians reacted in a different way, distinguishing between moral theology based on faith and revelation and moral philosophy based on reason and conservation of society. Moral theology is then fabricated by adjusting Grotius', Pufendorf's and Thomasius' (1655-1728) positions in the light of Scripture, or by looking back at orthodox theologians like Chemnitz or Dannhauer. We consider the examples of Johann Franz Buddeus (1667-1729), Johannes Olearius (1639-1713), and Johann Kaspar Haferung (1669-1744).

The dynamics of this discussion are reflected, indirectly, in the study of contract law. Methods, sources and solutions are different with respect to the various responses adopted. One element, however, is common to these works. The analysis of contract law does not only engage the principles of single contracts, but it is also concerned with the binding effects of promises and the general theory of contract law. The dialogue with the natural lawyers and early modern scholastics induced the Lutheran theologians to confront and examine more in-depth questions that before were, with a few exceptions, sporadically treated.

2.4.2 *The Defense of the Orthodox Doctrine*

2.4.2.1 Alberti and Zentgrav: Reactionary Theologians

Valentin Alberti,[256] son of a Lutheran minister killed in the Thirty Years' War, studied philosophy at the University of Leipzig, where he was appointed professor of logic and metaphysics. In 1672 he became professor of theology and in 1678 obtained a doctorate in theology. In his *Compendium iuris naturae, orthodoxae theologiae conformatum* (part I, 1676, part II, 1678), Alberti

---

255 For the use of Grotius see F. Grunert, *The Reception of Hugo Grotius's* De Jure Belli ac Pacis, *in the Early German Enlightenment*, in T.J. Hochstrasser, P. Schröder (eds.), *Early Modern Natural Law Theories. Contexts and Strategies in the Early Enlightenment*, Berlin, Springer, 2003, 89-106 (90-2); M. Scattola, *Scientia iuris*, 18-20.

256 R.C. Jenkins, *The Life of Valentin Alberti*, London, 1889; M. Petzoldt, *Konfessionalisierung als Identitätssuche*, in H. Baier (ed.), *Konfessionalisierung vom 16.-19. Jahrhundert: Kirche und Traditionspflege*, Neustadt an der Aisch, Degener, 1989, 67-86 (74-6). M. Petzoldt, *Alberti, Valentin*, in *RPP*, vol. I, 2007, 123.

is preoccupied with strengthening the natural law's roots in the Christian revelation.[257] He accepts Grotius' definition of natural law, but stresses that natural law translated from the state of integrity (human condition before the original sin) to the state of corruption (human condition after the original sin).[258] Furthermore, he claims *contra* Pufendorf that the state of creation (*status creationis*) is revealed only to Christians and not to pagans. When the grace of a universal and common God joins nature, it does not produce the knowledge of the state of integrity in the pagans, but the desire to look for the true religion of God.[259] Consequently, to Alberti natural law can only be conceived in the light of the revelation.

Alberti respects then the traditional division of the divine law: moral law, ceremonial law and forensic law, as already clarified by Melanchthon. The divine moral law corresponds to natural law. Natural law is innate in human beings, while the moral law is repeated by God in the Decalogue.[260] To Alberti, the source of natural law is in the orthodox doctrine of the state of integrity. Man is created as an image of God and maintains a remaining image of natural

---

257 On Alberti's natural law see J. Ihmels, *Das Naturrecht bei Valentin Alberti, Die Lehre des Compendium Iuris Naturae von 1678/96*, Diss., Leipzig, 1957; H.P. Schneider, *Justitia Universalis. Quellenstudien zur Geschichte des Christlichen Naturrechts bei Gottfried Wilhelm Leibniz*, Frankfurt am main, Klostermann, 1967, 247-53; E.D. Osterhorn, *Die Naturrechtslehre Valentin Albertis. Ein Beitrag zum Rechtsdenken der lutherischen Orthodoxie des 17. Jahrhunderts*, Diss., Freiburg im Breisgau, 1962; F. Palladini, *Discussioni seicentesche*, 212; F. Grunert, *Normbegründung und politische Legimität: zur Rechts- und Staatsphilosophie der deutschen Frühaufklärung*, Tübingen, Niemeyer, 2000, 36-62; H.P. Schneider, *Christliches Naturrecht*, in H. Holzhey, W. Schmidt-Biggemann (eds.), *Die Philosophie des 17. Jahrhunderts*, 813-35 (824-5). On Alberti's opinion on the right of just war, see H.H. Aure, *The Right to Wage War (jus ad bellum). The German Reception of Grotius 50 years after De iure belli ac pacis*, Berlin, BWV, 2015, 103-32.

258 V. Alberti, *Compendium iuris naturae*, pars secunda, Lipsiae, 1678, 22: "*Ius naturale est* dictatum rectae rationis (*e statu integritatis in corruptum, vel formaliter, vel normaliter tantum, translatum*) indicans, actui alicui ex eius convenientia aut disconvenientia cum ipsa natura rationali (*quatenus ex parte adhuc recta est*), inesse moralem turpitudine aut honestatem moralem, ac consequenter ab autore Naturae Deo talem actum aut vetari aut praecipi".

259 V. Alberti, *Compendium iuris naturae*, 8: "*Gratia enim, Dei communis ac universalis, quam cum natura jungitis non producit in Gentilibus notitiam de statu integritatis, sed desiderium, inquirendi verum cultum Dei*". On this point Alberti follows the Reformed professor of theology and rector of the University of Frankfurt (Oder), Samuel Strimesius (1648-1730), who claimed that Pufendorf had ignored the link between the two states, which is unavoidable. See S. Strimesius *Praxiologia apodictica seu philosophia moralis dimostrativa, pythanologiae hobbesianae opposita*, Francofurti ad Oderam, 1677, 43.

260 V. Alberti, *Compendium iuris naturae*, 30: "*Lex enim divina moralis maximam partem eadem est cum Jure N. Hoc enim diversis respectibus* utroque titulo *gaudet*: Juris N. *prout nobis innatum est*; Legis moralis, *in quantu a DEO in Decalogo repetitum extat*".

law.[261] Thus, Alberti attempts to derive norms from a survey of the state of integrity. In the second part of his work, and more in specific in 'the obligations concerning other men, which can be deduced from the appetite of freedom', Alberti studies the binding effects of promises and arguments about general theory of contract law.

Johann Joachim Zentgrav[262] studied philosophy at Strasbourg University (M.A. 1661) under the rectorate of Dannhauer and then theology and Oriental languages until 1665. After some travels in Germany, in 1676 he obtained a chair in moral philosophy at the University of Strasbourg, where from 1695 he was professor of theology. Zentgrav fully polemicized Pufendorf, arguing, among other things, that he had reduced natural law to the external actions, forgetting that these are signs of internal actions.[263] Zentgrav published a number of works dedicated to natural law: *De origine, veritate et immutabili rectitudine juris naturalis* (1678); *Origines juris naturalis secundum disciplinam Christianorum* (1681); *De origine, veritate et obligatione juris gentium instituta disquisitio* (1684). In his monumental work *Summa iuris divini sive isagogica institutio doctrinae de justitia et jure* (1699), he seeks to insert the Roman Catholic natural law tradition in a Lutheran perspective.[264] The fundamental assumption is the link with the Christian revelation. The divine law is divided in natural divine law, divine positive law and the new divine law or the evangelical law. As Alberti, Zentgrav utilizes Grotius' definitions, but corrects them. The structure of his work can give an impression of his ideas:

Section I
Art. 1 On the Divine Law
Subsection 1 On the Natural Divine Law
Subsection 2 On the Positive Divine Law, on the Decalogue, on the Ceremonial Law, on the Forensic Law
Subsection 3 On the New Divine Law or the Evangelical Law
Art. 2 On the Human Law
Subsection 1 On the Law of the People
Subsection 2 On the Civil Law
Subsection 3 On the Ecclesiastical law

261 V. Alberti, *Compendium iuris naturae*, 46.

262 See P. Tschackert, *Zentgraf, Johann Joachim*, in *Allgemeine Deutsche Biographie* 45 (1900), 66-67 (accessed 29.11.2017), https://www.deutsche-biographie.de/gnd10406742X.html#adbcontent; H.P. Schneider, *Justitia Universalis*, 274-86.

263 J.J. Zentgrav, *De origine, veritate et immutabili rectitudine juris naturalis*, Argentorati, 1678, Art. III, § 13, cit. in F. Palladini, *Discussioni seicentesche*, 218-9.

264 H.P. Schneider, *Christliches Naturrecht*, in H. Holzhey, W. Schmidt-Biggemann (eds.), *Die Philosophie des 17. Jahrhunderts*, 813-35 (826-7).

Section II
Art. 1 On the Power to Act and to Have a Morality Founded on Human Nature
Subsection 1 On the Law of the Intellect
Subsection 2 On the Law of Senses
Subsection 3 On the Law of Passions
Subsection 4 On the Law of Body
Art. 2 On the Law of the Christian and Human Society
Art. 3 On the Law of Sacred Affairs
Subsection 1 On the Law of Religion
Subsection 2 On the Law of the Emperor and the Priest on Sacred Affairs
Subsection 3 On the Law of Ecclesiastical Goods
Section III
Art. 1 On the Law of Necessity
Art. 2 On the Law of Charity
Art. 3 On the Law of Patience
Section IV
On the Law of War
Section V
Art. 1 On the Perfect and Imperfect Law and their Principles
Art. 2 On the Principles or the Origins of Just and Decorum and on the Law and Power Divinely Reserved

Zentgrav does not deal with contract law in a systematic way, but his observations are spread among different parts. For instance, reflections on the nature of duress are included in the chapter about the law of senses. The theme of law fascinated Zentgrav, as he was the promoter of several dissertations dedicated to Mosaic law – for example, the *Moses legislator ebraeorum charactere politico expressus* (1685) of Johann Balthasar Starck; *De legibus ebraeorum forensibus contra idololatriam* (1692) of Nicolaus Fridericus ab Avenheim; *Ex legibus ebraeorum forensibus contra magiam de maleficio magico* (1694) of Johann Daniel Wolff; and *Ex legibus ebraeorum forensibus de jure egenorum in specie* (1695) of Johann Daniel Gerberus.

2.4.2.2 Osiander, Jäger and the Early Modern Scholastics

Johann Adam Osiander[265] reacted in a different way to Pufendorf's hypothesis. Osiander studied theology at the University of Tübingen, where he became lecturer (1647), professor of Greek and associate professor of theology (1656). In 1657 he attained his doctorate and served as chief pastor. From 1680 till his

265 T. Schott, *Osiander, Johann Adam*, in *Allgemeine Deutsche Biographie* 24 (1887), 488-9 (accessed 31.10.2017), https://www.deutsche-biographie.de/gnd104279427.html#adbcontent, W. Bossert, *Osiander*, in *RE*^{3}, vol. 14, Leipzig, 1904, 513; H. Ehmer, *Osiander, Johann Adam*, in *RPP*, vol. IX, 2011, 420.

death, he was chancellor of the same university, and provost and preacher of the Collegiate Church. In his 1671 Osiander published his *Observationes maximam partem theologicae in libros tres de iure belli ac pacis Hugo Grotii*. Osiander is not the first German author to write a commentary on Grotius' *De iure belli ac pacis*, but his work also deals with contract law.[266] Osiander criticizes Grotius' definition of natural law as unclear, incomplete, and not legally binding.[267] Nonetheless, he utilizes Grotius as an instrument for restoring an orthodox natural law. He comments upon *De iure belli* not only in the light of Scripture, but also referring to the early modern scholastics. The scholastics are used either to support the necessity to correct Grotius' errors, or to show the points where they are mistaken and Grotius is right. In this way, Osiander's commentary is a fascinating melange of sources.

Osiander's contract doctrine provides solutions concerning general theory of contract law, but also about sale, loan and monopolies. These solutions are repeated and integrated with others in Osiander's *Theologia casualis* (1680-1682), a huge collection of cases of conscience divided in four tomes and six parts, comprising more than two thousand pages. The third part, which faces legal issues, is divided in five chapters: 1) on the law and justice; 2) on the judgment; 3) on the transfer of property by promises and donations; 4) on the transfer of property by usucapion and prescription; and 5) on the transfer of property by last will.

Osiander's method was replicated by his pupil, Johann Wolfgang Jäger.[268] Jäger (who married Osiander's daughter) attended courses in theology at the Tübingen University (PhD, 1693). He became professor of philosophy in 1678 and professor of theology in 1690. Jäger was not only an erudite academic, but also served as general superintendent of Württemberg from 1695. From 1699 on, he was consistorial councilor in Stuttgart. In 1704 he came back to the Tübingen University in the position of chancellor. In his *Observationes* to Grotius' *De jure belli ac pacis* (1710), Jäger describes natural law as fastened at the pole of Scripture and mostly to St. Paul's rule: the natural law is divinely inserted by God in the human mind to oblige Christians to love God, themselves and the neighbor.[269]

266 On the commentary genre see H.P. Schneider, *Justitia Universalis*, 122-58.

267 J.W. Jäger, *Hugonis Grotii libri tres observationibus theologicis, moralibus et politicis illustrati*, Tubingae, 1710, 43-4. He gives an account of Osiander's opinion.

268 M.H. Jung, Jäger, *Johann Wolfgang*, in *RPP*, vol. VI, 2009, 643.

269 J.W. Jäger, *Hugonis Grotii libri tres*, 46: "Nostra *itaque* sententia *est, jus naturae seu legem naturae stylo* Scripturae *et inprimis Paulino esse REGULAM* menti nostrae divinitus inscriptam, obligantem ad AMOREM DEI, SUI ET PROXIMI".

Jäger vehemently attacks the natural law proposed by modern natural law interpreters like Pufendorf, Philipp Reinhard Vitrarius (1647-1720) and Thomasius. He writes that they mainly focus on society as the source and decisive factor of natural law. The law of Sinai, instead, is the repetition of natural law and does not have society as its source, but only addresses society remotely, externally. It is absurd to say that the holy natural law grounds its precepts on the dishonourable and depraved actions of society.[270] Jäger repudiates the view that the source of natural law can be the conservation of society and insists on the idea that natural law is expressed in the Decalogue.[271]

The consequence of Jäger's stance is the firm research of a solid foundation in Scripture and the orthodox Lutheran tradition. However, like Osiander before him, Jäger also turns to Grotius and the early modern scholastics to support his construction. Concerning contract law, in the *Observationes* Jäger copes with the binding effects of pacts and promises. In his *Theologia moralis* (1704) he adresses issues about sales, purchase of annuities and the interest prohibition, in the paragraph dedicated to the virtue of justice and the seventh commandment.

2.4.3 *Buddeus: Separating Moral Theology from Natural Jurisprudence*

Alberti, Osiander and Jäger are examples of a reaction against Pufendorf that came back to Grotius as a valid alternative to repristinate a theologically orthodox natural law. Other theologians, however, focused on moral theology as a science, with a different source in respect to the modern natural law theories. Johann Franz Buddeus (Budde)[272] is the clearest example of this attitude. Buddeus graduated in Wittenberg (M.A. 1687) and was appointed professor of philosophy in Jena in 1689. In 1693 he became professor of moral philosophy

---

270 J.W. Jäger, *Hugonis Grotii libri tres*, 47-8: "*Plane itaque* absonum est, *quod hodierni juris naturae interpretes*, Pufendorf, Vitrarius, Thomasius *et alii volunt, quasi illud primario societatem respiciat; aut ex illa ceu fonte quodam pollulet; aut ab ea determinationem accipiat. Quemadmodum enim Lex Sinaitica, quae est repetitio legis naturae primitus datae, non respicit pro fonte societatem, sed illam remote demum tangit; uti porro absurdissimum est dicere, legem illam sanctissimam a societate humana in ratione honesti et turpis determinationem accipere: ita de lege naturae pariter est pronunciandum*".

271 J.W. Jäger, *Hugonis Grotii libri tres*, 48.

272 A.F. Stolzenburg, *Die Theologie des Joh. Franc. Buddeus und des Chr. Matth. Pfaff*, Berlin, 1926, 236-58; K. Aland, *Buddeus, Johann Franz*, in *Neue Deutsche Biographie* 2 (1955), 715 (accessed 11.12.2015), http://www.deutsche-biographie.de/pnd11851685X.html; E.H. Pältz, *Buddeus (Budde), Johann Franz*, in *TRE*, vol. VII, 1981, 316-7; W. Sparn, *Budde*, in *Lexikon für Theolgie und Kirche*, vol. 2, 1993, 755-6; E. Koch, *Buddeus, Johann Franz*, in *RPP*, vol. II, 2007, 248. For Buddeus' theology see F. Nüssel, *Bund und Versöhnung. Zur Begründnung der Dogmatik bei Johann Franz Buddeus*, Göttingen, Vandenhoeck & Ruprecht, 1996.

at the same university, after which he was appointed professor in Halle (1704) and again Jena (1705). Buddeus was in contact with moralists like Friedemann Becmann and Johann Wilhelm Baier, but also with contemporary philosophers like Descartes (1596-1650), Locke (1632-1704) and the natural lawyers, Grotius, Pufendorf and Thomasius. He refused Aristotelian philosophy, as well as the philosophy of Christian Wolff (1679-1754).

In his *Institutiones theologiae moralis* (1711), Buddeus treats natural law as part of the universal divine laws.[273] The universal divine laws, he writes, are natural laws and positive laws. Although the divine image has been damaged by original sin, the knowledge of practical principles about just and honourable actions is still present in man.[274] Because this knowledge has been weakened, however, God repeated the natural divine law in the Decalogue, so that first the Jews and then the Apostles could propagate it among all humanity.[275]

Although Buddeus admits that he will use Pufendorf's method for his manual, he takes a totally different position with regard to the principles. He stresses that Pufendorf dealt with the natural jurisprudence according to reason and in this way contemplated society and its conservation as sources of natural law. Instead, he will concentrate on the revelation of the divine laws and the union between God and the regenerated men. From this union all men's duties can be derived. Buddeus pinpoints that he will not only explain the single duties of the born-again men and confirm them in the light of the whole Scripture, but he will also derive every order from the divine law principle of men's union with God.[276] With respect to Alberti, Osiander and Jäger, Buddeus takes another road. He separates moral theology from the natural jurisprudence. He did

273 On Buddeus' natural law, see W. Sparn, *Naturrecht und Verfassungsfrage im frühneuzeitlichen Luthertum – am Beispil religiöser Toleranz*, in R. von Friedeburg, M. Schmoeckel, *Recht, Konfession und Verfassung*, 144-9. Buddeus' opinion was used by jurists such as Böhmer, see M. Germann, *Justus Henning Böhmers Abhandlung über die Gewissensfreiheit. Eine Stichprobe zum Gewissensdiskurs aus der prostestantischen Kirchenrechtslehre zu beginn des 18. Jahrhunderts*, in M. Germann, W. Decock (eds.), *Das Gewissen*, 315-6.

274 J.F. Buddeus, *Institutiones theologiae moralis, variis obseruationibus illustratae*, Lipsiae, 1727, 398.

275 J.F. Buddeus, *Institutiones theologiae moralis*, 401.

276 J.F. Buddeus, *Institutiones theologiae moralis*, praefatio: "*Quod autem ad principia attinet, cum nec nobis secundum rationis ductum iurisprudentiam naturalem tractantibus, PUFENDORFII institutum, ex societatis custodia cuncta derivantis se adprobaverit, nunc secundum revelatione leges divinas investigantibus, longe sublimius, idem tamen evidens et adaequatum succurrit principium, unio videlicet, hominum regenitorum cum Deo, ex quo omnia illorum officia, accurate et iusta serie, derivari possunt. Hoc ergo operam dedi, ut praemissa de legibus ipsis tractatione luculenta, non tantum singula regenitorum officia explicarem, et ex scriptura sacra cuncta confirmarem, sed ex nostro iuris divini principio, unione scilicet cum Deo, omnia ordine derivarem*".

not seek to reconcile the two disciplines but simply confesses the difference among them. This choice does not imply that he will not refer to the natural lawyers (he sometimes quotes Grotius, Thomasius and others), but that the primary source is not human reason but divine revelation, the union between man and God.

The second part of Buddeus' *Institutiones* concerns divine jurisprudence. Here Buddeus examines issues regarding various duties of men in general, and in specific according to the different orders.

> Second Part
> Prologue: On the Nature and Character of the Divine Jurisprudence
> I On the Human Actions, in Special Way on those concerning the Reborns, which Have to Be Directed by the Law
> II On the Universal Divine Laws in General
> III On the Divine Laws in Special
> Sect. I On the Human Duties before God, in a Special Way concerning the Internal Cult of God
> Sect. II On the External Cult of God, according to the Absolute and Hypothetical Laws
> Sect. III On the Human Duties in Front of Men Themselves
> Sect. IV On the Absolute Human Duties to the Others
> Sect. V On the Hypothetical Human Duties to the Others
> Sect. VI On the Duties of the Spouses, Parents and Sons, the Masters and the Slaves
> Sect. VII On the Duties of the Emperors and Citizens
> Sect. VIII On the Duties of the Ministers of God and Auditors
> IV On the Legal Means, which Compel Men to Observe the Divine Laws

Buddeus' contract doctrine is divided in two parts. In chapter III, section IV, dedicated to men's absolute duties to towards others, Buddeus looks at the binding nature of promises and pacts, while in the following section, concerning men's hypothetical duties towards others[277], he grapples with the lawfulness of the use of the single contracts and especially the issue of the interest-taking prohibition. The same issues are also discussed in Buddeus' *Elementa philosophiae practicae*, a treatise of moral philosophy, first published in 1697.

2.4.4 *Olearius and Haferung: Coming Back to the Tradition*

A line of differentiation and not integration of moral theology and natural jurisprudence can also be traced in the contributions of Johannes Olearius and

277 The *hypothetical duties* are established by the positive law, but they depend on the *absolute duties* based on the divine law. See P. Prodi, *Settimo non rubare*, 218.

Johann Kaspar Haferung.[278] Unlike Buddeus, these authors did not employ the contributions of the modern natural lawyers in their works, but only looked at the Scriptures in the gaze of the confessional theology. Olearius studied in Leipzig (M.A. 1660; Ph.D. 1679) where in 1664 was appointed professor of Greek and Latin and in 1677 professor of theology. Olearius was a colleague of Alberti but took a different path. His *Doctrina theologiae moralis* (1694) shows a singular aspect: the content of his doctrine is expounded in tables following a schematic order designed for teaching. In the fashion of the classical Lutheran creed, Olearius distinguishes the divine laws in natural law and positive law. God instilled the natural law in human heart and gave the universal positive law to humanity through the Jews. The natural law and positive universal law are contained in the Decalogue.[279] Contract doctrine is displayed in the tables dedicated to the virtues concerning the neighbour, in particular the virtues of fidelity and justice, and also in the part concerning the duties according to the specific vocations, which addresses the duties of the merchants.

Olearius' *Doctrina* received comments by Friedemann Bechmann (1628-1703), in the *Doctoris Johannii Olearii theologiam moralem annotationes*, published in 1704. Bechmann,[280] a theologian formed in Jena, also authored a treatise dedicated to the topic of conscience: *Theologia conscientiaria* (1692).[281] This work shows eighth chapters, which do not contemplates cases about business and contract law: 1) on the duties of Church ministers; 2) on the magistrate and its subjects; 3) on the marriage; 4) on the vows; 5) on the oaths; 6) on the prayers to God; 7) on the cult of God to do on Sunday or feasts; 8) on 'the obsessed'.

Johann Kaspar Haferung[282] also follows the traditional Lutheran natural law. Haferung studied theology in Wittenberg, where in 1702 became adjunct in the local superintendency, consistorial counselor and pastor of Greussen. In

278 G. Lechler, *Olearius, Johannes*, in *Allgemeine Deutsche Biographie* 24 (1887), 280-2 (accessed 05.01.2016), http://www.deutsche-biographie.de/pnd100618030.html?anchor=adb; U. Sträter, *Olearius, 4. Johannes*, in *RPP*, vol. IX, 2011, 305.

279 J. Olearius, *Doctrina theologiae moralis totius, in usum incipientium, certis paediae ac methodi limitibus circumscipta, et tabulis LXXII comprehensa*, Lipsiae 1681, Tab. IX.

280 J.A. Wagenmann, *Bechmann, Friedemann*, in *Allgemeine Deutsche Biographie* 2 (1875), 205 (accessed 13.11.2017), https://www.deutsche-biographie.de/gnd100030378.html#adb content.

281 F. Bechmann, *Theologia conscientiaria sive tractatus de casibus conscientiae*, Francofurti et Lipsiae, 1700. The book was edited several times: Lipsiae 1692; Francofurti et Lipsiae 1694; Francofurti et Lipsiae 1696; Ienae 1696; Lipsiae 1700; Francofurti et Lipsiae 1705; Francofurti et Lipsiae 1713.

282 Heppe, H. *Haferung, Johann Kaspar*, in *Allgemeine Deutsche Biographie* 10 (1879), 317 (accessed 18.12.2018). https://www.deutsche-biographie.de/gnd122687442.html#adbcontent.

1726 he was appointed professor of theology at the University of Wittenberg, where he remained until his death. In 1737 Haferung published his *Theologia moralis*. After the exposition of the aim and subject of moral theology, he goes through the Christian virtues. The rule of external human actions is the divine law, which is divided into natural law and moral law. The natural law is a command impressed by God at Creation. The moral law is added to the natural law and corresponds to Moses' law promulgated on Mount Sinai. Both the natural law and the moral law are included in the Decalogue and are prescribed for all men.[283] Haferung refers here to Chemnitz' *Loci theologici* and Dannhauer's *Collegium decalogicum*.[284] In the paragraph dedicated to the virtues of fidelity and gratitude, Haferung dedicates a few pages to the discussion on the binding effects of promises and pacts.

2.5 Conclusion

At the beginning of this chapter, we observed the creation of theological teachings that erected a body of principles and solutions to the different needs of contract law. The justification by faith, with the consequent analysis of the volitive process in born-again Christians and the perspective of charity towards God and the neighbour; the centrality of the Decalogue, instilled in human heart and repeated in the Mosaic law; and the two kingdoms doctrine remained fundamental pillars of the Lutheran theological and legal attitude. They founded a general regulation of contract law set in the seventh and eighth commandments of the Decalogue, but also the articulation of more detailed responses to specific problems, such as the lawfulness and right use of common financial instruments. In this way, the resulting contract doctrine mirrored the coordinates of the general assumptions of Reformation theology.

The theologians of the second generation gave more consistency to the teachings of their predecessors, integrating and expanding them in a variety of types of writings: ethical treatises, dogmatic treatises, catechisms, biblical commentaries and sermons. These are typical literary genres of the Reformation, which confronted many issues, including contract law. Thus, the contract law doctrines of the first reformers were interpreted and enriched through different methods and styles to meet the necessities of Christians. On top of that, they were updated and further developed through the resolution of disputes concerning the lawfulness and application of the primary credit instruments.

283 J.C. Haferung, *Theologia moralis per theses concinnatas*, Vitembergae, 1737, 51-53.
284 J.C. Haferung, *Theologia moralis per theses concinnatas*, 53 and 55.

The analysis of contract law acquired then a more pervasive normative dimension within the horizon of the casuistical and moral theological literature. Penance received a new configuration without the need of a detailed enumeration of sins and the imposition of acts of penance. The conscience was conceived of as a judge, also governed by rules concerning contract law. The shape of the conscience was determined by scriptural norms, without the obligatory intercession of priests. In contrast with the Roman Catholic casuistry, the Lutheran version emphasized the primacy of Scripture for the resolution of cases of conscience. In addition, the Lutheran moral theologians and casuists centred on faith as the starting point of Christian morality, and structured their works on the basis of the Decalogue and the doctrine of the three orders.

Finally, in the second half of the seventeenth century, tensions related to the emergence of new secular theories on the natural law brought about a withdrawal on orthodox positions that was combatted with different procedures. On the one hand, a direct challenge to the progressivist theories was effected by turning back to Grotius and early modern scholastics' works, which were corrected by the directives of Scripture. Others confronted the secularist tendency by advocating for a strategic separation between moral theology and philosophy, leaving the disciplines with completely different criteria of judgment. Moral theology considers the activity of the reborn as urged by faith, while philosophy elaborates on rational premises.

All of that allows studying, as we are going to see in the following chapters, the articulation of multiform approaches to contract law, in relation to different needs to which they were called to respond and to the analysis of the sources employed. The description of contract law was thus not homogeneous, but rather nuanced in different tones. It remained consistent with the theological background launched by Luther and Melanchthon and reinforced by the theologians of the first generation. This background accompanied the diverse solutions as the final cohering factor of the Lutheran works.

PART II

A Biblical Framework for Contract Law: Basic Elements

CHAPTER 1

The Conceptualization of Agreements

After having briefly explored the relation between law and theology according to both Roman Catholic and Lutheran theologians, we are now at the heart of our work: the illustration of the Lutheran system of contract law. The three chapters of this section concern the theologians' efforts to provide general rules for each type of agreement. The first relates to the preliminary issue of definitions and concepts; the second deals with rules derived from the seventh commandment of the Decalogue (you shall not steal); and the third chapter, with rules mostly associated with the eighth commandment (you shall not bear false witness). We present this distinction because it keeps faith with the Lutheran organization of arguments. As seen earlier, the Decalogue was a vital component of Lutheran moral theology.

1.0 Introduction

Our research on the contract doctrine forged by the Lutheran theologians commences with the analysis of the concepts and definitions used to identify the agreement of the parties. We need to grasp the conceptualizations of the theologians for what we now call 'contract', but that in the sixteenth century was related to a cluster of concepts. The word 'contract' is relative, because the theologians principally worked with 'promise' and 'pact' in addition to 'contract'.

The formation of these concepts and their meanings reflects the contribution of several traditions. Speaking metaphorically, while the skeleton derives from the medieval elaboration of Roman law and canon law, the organs originate from Aristotelian-Thomistic philosophy, and the skin from the early modern scholastics and natural lawyers. In this variegated body, the Lutherans implanted their genes. The centrality of the Decalogue, which fulfilment was granted by faith and the Holy Spirit, played an extensive role.

Contract doctrine was included in the comments to the seventh and eighth commandments. These two precepts acted as catalysts for a number of arguments, including the economic view of business, property and contracts, the normativity for social relationships, containing pacts and promises, and the reaction to certain theological debates. After a brief summary of the

 DOI:10.30965/9783657701506_005

conceptualizations of agreements before the Reformation, this chapter will explore the Lutheran approach.

1.1 Towards a Consensualist Theory of Contract Law

The Roman jurists did not develop a general theory of contract law, but were mostly concerned with particular legal problems.[1] Justinian's law required the parties' agreement to present objective elements to produce legal effects. These objective elements were the formal scheme of the nominate contracts (*emptio venditio, locatio conductio, mandatum, societas*) or of an exchange (*do ut des, do ut facias, facio ut des, facio ut facias*), when one of the parties executed the performance.[2] The agreement that did not possess these objective elements was not actionable. This agreement was called *pactum* (pact) and gave rise only to an *exceptio* (exception)[3].

The medieval glossators elaborated on the dialectics between *contractus* and *pactum* and formulated two theories: the theory of the 'garments of the pacts' (*vestimenta pactorum*) and the theory of the substantial, natural and accessory elements. The *vestimenta pactorum* theory is usually attributed to Piacentino (d. 1192) and centres around the concept of *pactum*. The pacts were categorized into accessory pacts and principal pacts.[4] The principal pacts were divided into 'naked pacts' and 'clothed pacts'. The naked pact (*nudum pactum*)

1 On the Roman law of contracts, resources are abundant. See for instance: E. Betti, *Der Typenzwang bei den römischen Rechtsgeschäften und die sogenannte Typenfreiheit des heutigen Rechts*, in *Festschrift für L. Wenger zu seinem 70. Geburtstag dargebracht von Freunden, Fachgenossen und Schulern*, I, München, Institut für Papyrusforschung, 1944, 249-83; E. Betti, *La tipicità dei negozi giuridici romani e la cosiddetta atipicità del diritto odierno*, in *Annali della Facoltà giuridica dell'Università di Macerata*, I (1966), 5-35. This was also collected in E. Betti, G. Grifò (eds.), *Diritto, metodo, ermeneutica. Scritti scelti*, Milano, Giuffrè, 1991, 325-59; M. Talamanca, *La tipicità dei contratti romani fra 'conventio' e 'stipulatio' fino a Labeone*, in F. Milazzo (ed.), *Contractus e Pactum. Tipicità e libertà negoziale nell'esperienza tardo-repubblicana. Atti del convegno di diritto romano e della presentazione della nuova riproduzione della* littera fiorentina, Napoli, ESI, 1990, 35-108; G. Melillo, *Contrahere, pacisci, transigere. Contributi allo studio del negozio bilaterale romano*, Napoli, Liguori, 1994, 3-40; For further references see: A. Massironi, *Nell'officina dell'interprete. La qualificazione del contratto nel diritto comune (secoli XIV-XVI)*, Milano, Giuffrè, 2012, 15. For an overview see L. Waelkens, *Amne Adverso*, 323-90.

2 I. Birocchi, *Causa e categoria generale del contratto. Un problema dogmatico nella cultura privatistica dell'età moderna 1. Il cinquecento*, Torino, Giappichelli, 1997, 46-7.

3 R. Zimmermann, *The Law of Obligations. Roman Foundations of the Civilian Tradition*, Oxford, Oxford University Press, 1990, 508.

4 I. Birocchi, *Causa e categoria*, 48.

did not give rise to an action: *ex nudo pacto non oritur actio*. The naked pact only gave rise to an *exceptio* (exception). In order to produce an action, the pact must be clothed, namely united with something that was able to confer binding effect: the garment (*vestimentum*). Garments were the *res, verba, litterae, consensus* and the delivery of the thing.[5]

In another attempt to generalize, the glossators shaped the theory of the substantial, natural and accessory elements. This theory seeks to understand the structure of contract law by using the concepts of *substantia* (essence), *natura* (nature) and *accidentalia* (accidental events).[6] These three elements can be individuated in each contractual type. The essence corresponds to the essential elements that define a specific type of contract. The natural elements are those included in the contract by custom, even though the parties can expressly change or delete them. The accidental elements are not tied to the structure of the agreement, but are added by the parties for circumstances.[7]

The solemnities of the civil law were not familiar to the canonists. As it is well known, starting from moral considerations, they recognized the efficacy of the *nudum pactum*. Three canonists played a primary, substantial role in providing the normative sources for this principle: Gratian (ca. 1075/1080-1145/1147), Huguccio (d. 1210) and Bernhard of Pavia (d. 1213). Gratian sowed the first seeds by inserting in his *Decretum* (1140) the canon *Quicumque suffragio* (C.66, c.12, q.2), the canon *Quia Johannes* (C.12, q.5, c.3) and the canon *Iuramenti* (C.22, q.5, c.12).[8] These canons set out the obligation to keep one's word on the given promise. Glossing on the canon *Quicumque suffragio*, Huguccio wrote that naked pacts should be enforced. He corroborated this statement by referring to the canon *Iuramenti* (C.22, q.5, c.12), which essential argument rested on the

5 I. Birocchi, *Causa e categoria*, 50-1. On the theory of *vestimenta pactorum* see also R. Volante, *Il sistema contrattuale del diritto comune classico*, Milano, Giuffrè, 2001.

6 According to the most qualified secondary literature this theory is a creation of the glossators. Yet, they found starting points in the Byzantine concept of *natura contractus* and in the Aristotelian philosophy. See I. Birocchi, *Causa e categoria generale*, 58-9. On the first one: G. Grosso, *Il sistema romano dei contratti*, Torino, Giappichelli, 1963, 186-7; H. Coing, *Zum Einfluss der Philosophie des Aristoteles auf die Entwicklung des römischen Rechts*, in *Zeitschrift der Savigny-Stiftung für Rechtsgeschichte*, Rom. Ab., vol. LXIX (1952), 24-59 (32); G. Otte, *Dialektik und Jurisprudenz: Untersuchungen zur Methode der Glossatoren*, Frankfurt am Main, Klostermann, 1971, 50-8. For theological influence see: P. Grossi, *Sulla 'natura' del contratto*, 607.

7 U. Santarelli, *La categoria dei contratti irregolari: lezioni di storia del diritto*, Torino, Giappichelli, 1984, 177-84; P. Grossi, *Sulla 'natura' del contratto*, 607-19; I. Birocchi, *Causa e categoria*, 56. For more references see: A. Massironi, *Nell'officina dell'interprete*, 185.

8 F. Calasso, *Il negozio giuridico. Lezioni di storia del diritto italiano*, 2nd ed., Milano, Giuffrè, 1959, 264-5.

equivalence between the breach of an oath and the breach of a promise: in both cases the Christian commits a sin.[9]

Other influential canons were provided by Bernhard of Pavia, who gathered in his *Breviarium extravagatium* (1187-1191) two important sources for the binding nature of the pacts: the canon *Antigonus* (X 1,35,1) and the canon *Qualiter* (X 1,35,3). These canons were then inserted in the title *De Pactis* of Gregory IX's *Liber Extra* and remained fundamental to the debate.[10] The enforceability of naked pacts was the consequence of the canonists' interpretation, but the principle in itself derived from conciliar decisions, like those made at the Council of Carthage (348 AD) and the Council of Toledo (633 AD). Furthermore, these decisions found correspondence in the writings of the Church Fathers and in the Scriptures.[11] The moral-theological background of these sources fixed the canonistic theory and justified its operativity.

The moral concern was certainly quite important for the medieval theologians as well. Inspired by Aristotle, Thomas Aquinas argued that a simple promise (*promissio simplex*) is binding, according to the virtue of fidelity and honesty. Moreover, he solidly grounded the binding effects of the promises on natural law.[12] Following Aquinas, the early modern scholastics founded their constructions on natural law, and in this way they freed the contract law from the formalities of Roman law. Clothed or not, the *pactum* is binding in conscience.[13] They also reflected on the concept of promise. The Roman law knew the concept of *pollicitatio*, as when a person chartered a public work or some improvement or entertainment for the city in gratitude for an honour he had received. The *pollicitatio* was based on the consent of one party, while the *pactum* required the consent of both the parties. Therefore, the early modern scholastics concluded that a promise offered was a *pollicitatio* and a promise accepted was a *pactum*.[14]

The solution of the early modern scholastics is destined to prevail, with the crisis of the *vestimenta pactorum* theory playing its part. Already commentators started to look for exceptions to the principle *ex nudo pacto actio*

---

9 P. Landau, *Pacta sunt servanda. Zu den kanonistischen Grundlagen der Privatautonomie*, in M. Ascheri, F. Ebel, M. Heckel, A. Padoa-Schioppa, F. Ranieri (eds.), *"Ins Wasser geworfen und Ozeane durchquert": Feschrift für K.W. Nörr*, Köln, Weimar-Wien, Böhlau Verlag, 2003, 457-74 (458, 464-7).

10 F. Calasso, *Il negozio giuridico*, 268-9; P. Landau, *Pacta sunt servanda*, 464-7.

11 K.P. Nanz, *Die Entstehung*, 46-9.

12 T. Aquinas, *Summa theologica*, IIaIIae, q. 88, a. 3; q. 88, a. 3, ad I; J. Gordley, *The Philosophical Origins*, 10-1.

13 W. Decock, *Theologians and Contract Law*, 146-7.

14 J. Gordley, *The Philosophical Origins*, 72-3.

non oritur,[15] and this paved the road for overturning this principle.[16] In the sixteenth century, the jurist Matthaeus Wesenbeck (1531-1586) declared that the *pactum nudum* is binding in civil courts. He writes that the canon law is applied in civil law through *communis opinio* and *usus*. The justification is that breaching a pact is an act against nature, conscience, and most of all, it is an act against the duty of the good man (*officium boni viri*) and a sin.[17] Beside the

---

15 I. Birocchi, *Causa e categoria*, 63-7.

16 W. Wiegand, *Die privatrechtlichen Rechtsquellen des usus modernus*, in D. Simon (ed.), *Akten des 26. Deutschen Rechtshistorikertages*, Frankfurt, 1987, 242; I. Birocchi, *Saggi sulla formazione storica della categoria generale del contratto*, Cagliari, Cuec, 1988, 51; R. Feenstra, *Pact and Contract in the Low Countries from the 16th to the 18th century*, in J. Barton (ed.), *Towards a general law of contract*, Berlin, Duncker & Humblot, 1990, 196-213 (198-9).

17 M. Wesenbeck, *Paratitla in pandectas iuris civilis*, Basileae, 1568, 110: "*Etsi autem hac de re, plura subtiliter disputari possunt, tamen modus aliquis adhibendus est, maxime cum hae iuris veteris subtilitates, hodie non sint in usu. Nam primum iure pontificio, ex quolibet pacto oritur actio* c. 1 et 3. ubi canonistae Extra eodem [X 1,35,1 et 3]. *Deinde hodie idem obtinet in omni foro, ubi ex aequo et bono, et ex suprema potestate iudicatur, ut sunt curiae summorum principum, arbitratorum, mercatorum, et similium*, Bartulus et doctores, in l. § Quinimo. [Quintus?; D. 17,1,29,4] Per illum textum hoc titulus et in 1 Si fideiussor. 29 § Quaedam, mandati [D. 17,1,29,4]. *Etsi autem longa disputatio est, an in reliquis curiis, in quibus secundum ius civile pronunciatur, ius pontificium obtinere debeat, tamen communis opinio est, et ita usus observat, ut indistincte ex pactis nudis, etiam in foro civili hodie detur actio.* Baldus et Salicetus in 1. Petens, 21 C. eodem [C. 2,3,27] et idem Baldus in l. Legitima, 6, in principio hoc titulo [D. 2,14,6 pr.] et Iason qui dicit esse communem, in dicta l. 7 §, Sed cum nulla, num. 4 [D. 2,14,7,4]. *Quod verum puto et sequendum. Nam pacta cum obligent naturaliter, et ex bono et equo*, l. 1. in principio hoc titulo, [D. 2,14,1pr] l. 1 de constituta pecunia [C. 4,18,1]. *Sequitur eum, qui pacta non servat, contra naturam, coscientiam, atque adeo contra ufficium boni viri facere, ac peccare, ut volunt canonistae, mortaliter*, glossa in c. 1 de pactis [D. 2,14,1?]. *Et certe divus Paulus ad Romanis 1, ἀσύνθετος, hoc est, eos qui pacta non servant, in illis numerat, qui capitaliter delinquunt. Est autem definitum inter doctores ut quotiescunque agitur de cavendo peccato, deque causa conscientia, toties etiam in foro civili ius pontificium debeat observari*, c. 1 et 2. ubi doctores, De operis novi nuntiatione [C. 8,11,1], Castrensis In authentica, At qui semel. num. 3 et 4 [C. 4,19,19, in authentica n. 3 et 4] C. De probatio cum simil". L. Seuffert, *Zur Geschichte der obligatorischen Verträge*, Verlag der C.H. Beck'schen Buchhandlung, Nördlingen, 1881, 107; K.P. Nanz, *Die Entstehung*, 91; I. Birocchi, *Saggi sulla formazione*, 42; R. Feenstra, *Pact and Contract*, 199. R. Feenstra, *Matthäus Wesenbeck (1531-1586) und das römisch-hollandische Recht (mit einer Bibliographie seiner juristischen Schriften)*, in H. Lück, H. de Wall (eds.), *Wittenberg. Ein Zentrum europäischer Rechsgeschichte und Rechtskultur*, Böhlau, Köln, 2006, 175-243 (204-5); W. Decock, *Theologians and contract law*, 156-7. As Feenstra rightly noted the word *serio et deliberate initis* are not in the edition of 1568 and were added later from the Basel 1575. However, there are also later linguistic changes. In the editions after 1568, the incipit is different, it starts with "*Quanquam autem hac de re*" and in the middle of the discourse is written "*Etsi vero est longa disputatio*". Furthermore, Wesenbeck points out *Rom. 1,31*.

Christian motivation, these statements triggered the reaction of the German jurists: they debated the reasons for justifying the enforceability of the *nudum pactum* in civil law. The majority ended up appealing to a nationalist perspective, referring to the simplicity of the old Germans.[18] The natural lawyers, however, provided another solution based on the conceptualization developed by the early modern scholastics. The foundation of contractual obligation lies not on a moralistic duty of truth but in the will of the parties.[19] The parties can freely dispose of their acts so that when a promise is accepted, the obligation is undertaken.[20]

1.2 The Seventh Commandment: Private Property and Contracts

1.2.1 *Introduction*

The Lutheran theologians did not attempt to shape new legal concepts; rather, they combined the already-formed ones with their theological vision. When the Reformation began, the civil law was governed by the theory of the *vestimenta pactorum* and its exceptions. The consensualist trend was still limited to canon law and moral theology. Thus, the Lutherans looked at contracts as legal instruments for the conveyance of property rights, governed by the seventh commandment of the Decalogue (you shall not steal). Instead, pacts and promises, as moral agreements, fell under the purview of the eighth commandment (you shall not bear false witness against thy neighbour), which forbids lies. Not only does this distinction show a specific feature of Lutheran morals, but also it reveals a persistence of the medieval theory of the *vestimenta pactorum*. A contract is a pact provided with legal effects and therefore is suitable for the transfer of property rights (seventh commandment). A pact is devoid of such effects, but still requires moral observance (eighth commandment).

The Lutheran theologians regarded contracts as instruments to transfer property rights. For this reason we will need to briefly deal with their attitudes towards property rights and only then can we address their contract theory.

18 I. Birocchi, *Saggi sulla formazione storica*, 61-75.

19 H. Grotius, *De iure belli ac pacis*, II, 11, § 4. (curavit B.J.A. De Kanter-Van Hettinga Tromp; annotationes novas addiderunt R. Feenstra et C.E. Persenaire), Aalen, Scientia, 1993; W. Decock, *Theologians and Contract law*, 212-3. For a brief survey see L. Moccia, *Promessa e contratto (Spunti storico-comparativi)*, in *Rivista di diritto civile*, 27 (1994), parte I, 818-52 (830).

20 A brilliant analysis is in K.P. Nanz, *Die Entstehung*, 135-69. See also the essays included in J. Barton (ed.) *Towards a general law of contract*, passim. For a more elaborated analysis of the problem see R. Feenstra, M. Ahsmann, *Contract. Aspecten van de begrippen contract en contractsvrijheid in historisch perspectief*, Deventer, Kluwer, 1980, 3-14; D. Deroussin, *Histoire du droit des obligations*, 2nd ed., Paris, Economica, 2012, 107-81.

After all, the scholastics also considered contracts as legal instruments to convey property rights.[21] They insisted on the freedom of the owner to use the thing for the accomplishment of his individuality. From this freedom derives the freedom of the parties to decide about their personal goods in contracts.[22] Instead, the Lutherans sustained that the essential content of property is determined by the relationship with God and the neighbour – a context of faith and charity animates their view. Private property derives from God and must be used according to God's will. God distributed properties unequally, so that the Christians can help each other by practicing charity in alms and contracts.

1.2.2 *The Defense of Private Property*

1.2.2.1 Not a Communion of Goods, but a Private Property for the Neighbour's Needs

"Fanatic and seditious" (*fanaticas et seditiosas*) – with these words Melanchthon labelled the opinions of the Anabaptists who claimed that Scripture reveals that everything should be held in common among Christians.[23] The Anabaptists' radical approach stirred an inflamed discussion on the nature of property and the lawfulness of contracts. Aside from the theological dispute with the Anabaptists, the Lutheran theologians defended private property against the practice of voluntary poverty developed by monasticism. In the Roman Catholic environment, the renunciation of goods was intended as work toward perfection, for obtaining salvation.[24] This is the opposite of the

21 W. Decock, *Theologians and Contract Law*, 164-5.

22 P. Grossi, *La proprietà nel sistema privatistico della seconda scolastica*, in *La seconda scolastica della formazione del diritto privato moderno. Incontro di studio. Firenze, 16-19 Ottobre 1972, Atti*, Milano, Giuffrè, 1973, 117-222, (148-72); I. Birocchi, *Notazioni sul contratto* (*a proposito di un recente lavoro di G. Alpa*), in *Quaderni fiorentini*, 19 (1990), 637-59 (647).

23 The bibliography on Anabaptism is abundant. I only selected some works: G.H. Williams, *The Radical Reformation*, Philadelphia, The Westminster Press, 1962; C.P. Clasen, *Anabaptism, a Social History, 1525-1618: Switzerland, Austria, Moravia, South and Central Germany*, Ithaca and London, Cornell University Press, 1972; R. Friedmann, *The Theology of Anabaptism. An Interpretation*, Scottdale, Pennsylvania, Herald Press, 1973; W. Klaasen, *Anabaptism in Outline: Selected Primary Sources*, Waterloo ont., Herald Press, 1981; W.O. Packull, G.L. Dipple, *Radical Reformation Studies, Essays presented to J.M. Stayer*, Aldershot, Brookfield USA, Singapore, Sydney, Ashgate, 1999; C.A. Snyder, *Anabaptist History and Theology: An Introduction*, 3ed., Kitchener, Pandora, 2002; J.D. Roth, J.M. Stayer (eds.), *A Companion to Anabaptism and Spiritualism, 1521-1700*, Leiden, Brill, 2007. For a contemporary view on Anabaptism and economics, see: J. Haltemann, *Anabaptists Approaches to Economics*, in P. Oslington (ed.), *The Oxford Handbook of Christianity and Economics*, Oxford, Oxford University Press, 2014, 246-61.

24 See previous I/1. For a brief survey see D. Flood, *Armut VI*, in *TRE* vol. IV, 1979, 88-98; C. Lindberg, *Beyond Charity. Reformation Initiatives for the Poor*, Minneapolis, Fortress Press, 1993, 17-67.

Reformation doctrine. The Lutheran theologians rejected the medieval ideal of ascesis and privation of goods, developing instead a vision of property oriented to the exercise of charity towards the neighbour. Private property is an ordinance of God, and it must be used for neighbour's advantage. By giving alms, the Christian helps the poor, while with contracts he meets the other Christians' needs. The exchange of goods becomes a way to benefit the other.

The debate on the lawfulness of private property was not unknown among the Roman Catholics. The Franciscan theories on the necessity of abandoning property rights had already led to numerous discussions.[25] Theologians like Ockham, Gerson, Summenhart (ca. 1455-1502) and others all faced this issue.[26] In the writings of the early modern scholastics, we also find several arguments in favour of private property, based on Scripture and Aristotelian-Thomistic philosophy.[27] In a move to the contrary, the approach adopted by the Lutherans centred on the interpretation of Scripture.

The Lutheran theologians used the seventh commandment of the Decalogue as a decisive argument in favour of private property. In the *Tischreden* (1540-44), Martin Luther[28] affirms that the seventh commandment set the lordship (*dominium*) of property as divine law, contrary to the superstitious vows of the ascetic monks and the ruinous communion of the Anabaptists.[29] In addition, in the small catechism (1529), on the seventh commandment, he writes:

25 M.D. Lambert, *Franciscan Poverty. The Doctrine of the Absolute Poverty of Christ and the Apostles in the Franciscan Order, 1210-1323*, London, SPCK, 1961; V. Mäkinen, *Property Rights in the Late Medieval Discussion on Franciscan Poverty*, Leuven, Peeters, 2001. For further references see N. Şenocak, *The Making of Franciscan Poverty*, in *Revue Mabillon*, 24 (2013), 5-26.

26 On Summenhart see, J. Varkemaa, *Conrad Summenhart's Theory of Individual Rights*, Leiden-Boston, Brill, 2012, 188-90.

27 A.A. Chafuen, *Faith and Liberty. The Economic Thought of the Late Scholastics*, Oxford, Lexington, 2003, 31-8.

28 On Martin Luther and property see: H. Barge, *Luther and der Frühkapitalismus*, 28-33; P. Althaus, *Die Ethik Martin Luthers*, Gütersloh, Gerd Mohn, 1965, 109-115; H.J. Goertz, *Eigentum VI*, in *TRE* vol. XXVIII, 1997, 423-28 (426-7); V. Mäkinen, A. Raunio, *Right and Dominion in Luther's Thought and Its Medieval Background*, in V. Mäkinen (ed.), *Lutheran Reformation and the Law*, 63-92; A. del Vigo Gutiérrez, *Economía y ética en el siglo XVI. Estudio comparativo entre los Padres de la Reforma y la Teología española*, Madrid, Biblioteca de autores cristianos, 2006, 312-8.

29 M. Luther, *Tischreden aus Anton Lauterbachs Sammlung B.*, in WA-TR 5, 6163: "*Ideo septimum praeceptum constituit iure divino proprietatis dominium contra monachorum superstitiosa vota et anabaptistarum perniciosam communionem* (...)".

> *we should fear and love God that we may not take our neighbor's money or property, nor get them by false ware or dealing, but help him to improve and protect his property and business.*[30]

Private property is not seen in an absolutistic view, for the enjoyment of the individual Christian, but it is socially determined in its proper use: helping the neighbour. Private property is therefore intrinsically connected to the Christian love for the neighbor.[31] The fundamental rule of charity is expressed in two dimensions: 'protecting' the neighbour's property and business and 'improving' his property and business.

In the first edition of the *Loci theologici* (1521), Melanchthon did not use the seventh commandment to justify the institution of private property, but followed a different line of argumentation. He states that the natural law can be summarized in three precepts: 1) worship God; 2) harm no one; and 3) possess all things in common.[32] However, because of human greed it is impossible to enjoy all things in common; thus the third law must be governed by the second and higher law: harm no one. The law that all things must be commonly held therefore needs to be replaced by the law stipulating that property must be divided for the sake of public peace. The human condition, though, requires a variety of goods, necessitating that things be exchanged. Since by nature things should be held in common, Melanchthon writes, it has been established that they can be exchanged in their use by contracts, purchases, sales, rent, lease, etc.[33] People can serve each other, relieving what the other lacks, through the establishment of contracts.[34]

In the *Prolegomena in officia Ciceronis* (1530), Melanchthon argues that the division of properties is established by the divine law because the seventh commandment of the Decalogue – *you shall not steal* – means that God

30 M. Luther, *Kleiner Katechismus*, in WA 30, 1, 245. I used the English translation from F. Bente (ed.), *Triglot Concordia: The Symbolical Books of the Evangelical Lutheran Church: German-Latin-English*, St. Louis, Concordia Publishing House, 1921. The book is available online: www.bookofconcord.org (accessed 03.08.2017). It is also available a more recent translation by F.S. Janzow, *Luther's Large Catechism: A Contemporary Translation with Study Questions*, St. Louis, Concordia Publishing House, 1978.

31 P. Althaus, *Die Ethik Martin Luthers*, 109; H.J. Goertz, *Eigentum VI*, in *TRE*, vol. XXVIII, 1997, 426; A. del Vigo Gutiérrez, *Economía y ética*, 313-4. For the implications of this concept see C. Lindberg, *Beyond charity*, 161-9.

32 P. Melanchthon, *Loci communes*, (prima eorum aetas), in CR XXI, 117.

33 P. Melanchthon, *Loci communes*, (prima eorum aetas), in CR XXI, 119. C. Bauer, *Melanchthons Wirtschaftsethik*, 128.

34 P. Melanchthon, *Loci communes*, (prima eorum aetas), in CR XXI, 120.

intends the division of properties.[35] The right to possess goods is not given by human authority, but by God himself. The magistrate is only the guardian and defender of the divine orders.[36] This statement is both against the communion of property advanced by the Anabaptists and contrary to the voluntary poverty practiced by the monks, which, Melanchthon says, are individual vocations and not the universal precept.[37] The seventh commandment also orders justice in selling, buying and evaluating goods and almsgiving.[38] Melanchthon explains that in Rom. 13,8, *owe no man any thing, but to love one another*, Paul is giving two precepts: the first one refers to the civil obligation, and the second one to the natural and divine obligation. The first precept is to observe contractual rights, pay what it is due to creditors, sellers, landlords etc. But the second asks Christians to practice love (*dilectio*) in the way established by Prov. 5,16, 2 Cor. 8,13 and 1 Tim. 5,8.[39] These passages describe how almsgiving should be performed.

In the third collection of the *Loci theologici* (1543-1559), Melanchthon posits again that the seventh commandment orders the division of properties (*dominiorum distinctio*).[40] The division of properties is not presupposed, but established in this precept. To Melanchthon the wording of this precept testifies that private property is an ordinance of God. Since God forbids the theft, he intends for individual men to retain possession of their things.[41] The argument of the divine institution of private property by the seventh commandment is repeated in the *Catechesis puerilis*, where Melanchthon also justifies the possession of goods by referring to 1 Tim. 6,17:

> *charge the rich of this world not to be highminded, nor to trust in the uncertainty of riches, but in the living God, (who giveth us abundantly all things to enjoy).*

35 P. Melanchthon, *Prolegomena in officia Ciceronis*, in CR XVI, 549.

36 P. Melanchthon, *Prolegomena in officia Ciceronis*, in CR XVI, 557-8.

37 P. Melanchthon, *Prolegomena in officia Ciceronis*, in CR XVI, 554 and 557; C. Bauer, *Melanchthons Wirtschaftsethik*, 130.

38 P. Melanchthon, *Prolegomena in officia Ciceronis*, in CR XVI, 551.

39 P. Melanchthon, *Prolegomena in officia Ciceronis*, in CR XVI, 553.

40 A more extended list of arguments against the communion of goods is offered in Melanchthon's *Prolegomena in officia Ciceronis*, but their detailed analysis would lead us away from our main topic. See P. Melanchthon, *Prolegomena in officia Ciceronis*, in CR XVI, 549-60. On Melanchthon's conception of property see C. Bauer, *Melanchthons Wirtschaftsethik*, in *ARG* 49 (1958) 1/2, 115-60; H.J. Goertz, *Eigentum VI*, 426-7; A. del Vigo Gutiérrez, *Economía y ética en el siglo XVI*, 318-25.

41 P. Melanchthon, *Loci communes*, (tertia eorum aetas), in CR XXI, 709: "*Sancitur enim dominiorum distinctio, quam haec ipsa vox praecepti testatur ordinationem Dei esse. Quia enim prohibet furta, vult singulos tenere res suas*".

As a further element of clarification, he mentions the rule of Solomon in Proverbs 5,16: "*let thy fountains be conveyed abroad, and in the streets divide thy waters*". This rule applies to property and alms: the fountains are compared to properties that shall be open to the poor, rivers.[42] Hence, to Melanchthon private property is a divine ordinance not destined to promote individual enjoyment but to help the poor and relieve the lack of others by contracts.

A few years later, Georg Major echoes these statements: the seventh commandment makes clear the ownership and the distinction of goods, because if everything had to be in common, there would be no room for theft, which is the illegal appropriation of a thing without the consent of the owner.[43] The seventh commandment ordains the exchange of goods through contracts approved by the laws and the consent of the people and alms, as introduced by natural law and divine law.[44] Major explains this point through the example of the rich man and the poor Lazarus in Luke 16. The rich man was debtor of the poor Lazarus: his duty was to raise Lazarus from poverty by his riches. Since he did not solve the debt, he committed a sin against the seventh commandment. Indeed, Major comments, Christians are obliged to act according to Prov. 5,16: "*let thy fountains be conveyed abroad, and in the streets divide thy waters*". We are the owners of our fountains. Yet, we are divinely obliged not to close the rivers, but to distribute them out and to give to the poor.[45]

The seventh commandment indicates that property is an ordinance of God. Property can be exchanged through alms and contracts, the modes for exchanging goods that God allowed. Property is not given for self-wellbeing, but to meet the neighbour's needs. This is a kind of refrain among the Lutherans. Another example is the catechism of Johannes Brenz:

> *but this law that forbids stealing clearly means that the division of properties and the property of riches among men is a divine ordinance.*[46]

---

42 P. Melanchthon, *Catechesis puerilis*, in CR XXIII, 164.

43 G. Major, *Enarratio secundae epistolae*, 137b: "*Quod autem liceat tenere proprium, patet ex septimo praecepto, non furtum facies, quo dominia et distinctiones rerum approbantur. Nam si omnia omnibus communia esse deberent, non esset locus furto, quod est contrectatio rei alienae invito domino*".

44 G. Major, *Enarratio secundae epistolae*, 138b.

45 G. Major, *Enarratio secundae epistolae*, 138b: "*Peccavit item dives Epulo contra septimum praeceptum, non furtum facies, quia quod ex sua copia Lazaro inopi debebat, non persolvit. Et si enim fontium nostrorum domini sumus, sicuti proverbiorum cap. 5 dicitur, tamen ad hoc divinitus sumus obligati, ne fontium rivos occludamus, sed eos foras derivemus et aliis egentibus communicemus*".

46 J. Brenz, *Catechismus, pia et utili explicatione illustratus*, Francofurti, 1556, 552: "*Sed haec lex de non furando, perspicue significat, quod distinctio dominiorum et proprietas facultatum inter homines sit divina ordinatio*". On the concept of *divina ordinatio* see also II/2.

Indeed, Brenz continues, the passage in Genesis where man is ordained in the property of the earth is not to be understood as condoning the exercise of tyranny on earth according to man's lust, but as showing that it is lawful for him to use the earth and earthly things according to the divine ordinance, the natural law and the positive or civil law.[47] Hence, if the Christians will acquire something through lawful contracts, inheritance, donation or other just and lawful reasons, they could lawfully use it, following their free will, but in the Lord and according to God's will.[48]

Here, the acknowledgement of property does not grant absolute freedom to the owner, but this freedom is limited by the divine ordinance, natural law and civil law. Property has a clear purpose: use in obeying God's will. This will is clarified in the seventh commandment, which forbids stealing and commands alms and justice in contracts. In this law, Brenz clarifies, it is ordered that with their riches, Christians come to the assistance of the destitute by giving bountiful alms, or by giving loans or donations for the sake of God.[49] Then, justice in contracts is commanded, particularly in sale. This justice is reverence of God and a duty pleasing to God.[50] Therefore, God's will expressed in the seventh commandment institutes private property and spurs Christians to assist the poor through almsgiving, donations and loans, and to practice justice in contracts.

1.2.2.2 Chemnitz' Refusal of the Arguments in Favour of a Communion of Goods

This conception of property is steadfastly linked to the dispute with the Anabaptists and to the refusal of an ascetic privation of goods. A relevant example is provided by Martin Chemnitz in his *Loci theologici*. He begins by reflecting that the issue of the lawfulness of private property is not new, but it had been previously discussed. Philosophers argued that the division of properties was against natural law. They were worried that the rich could wear out

---

47 J. Brenz, *Catechismus*, 552: "*Nam quod in Genesi homo ordinatur in dominum terrae, non est intelligendum, quod liceat homini exercere in terra tyrannidem secundum suam libidinem, sed quod liceat ei, iuxta divinam ordinationem, iuxta legem naturalem et positivam seu civilem, terra ac terrenis rebus uti*".

48 J. Brenz, *Catechismus*, 553: "*Itaque si quid acquirimus aut legitimis contractibus aut hereditate, aut donatione, aut aliis iustis et legitimis rationibus, eo licebit nobis, pro nostro arbitrio, sed in Domino, et secundum voluntatem Dei, uti*".

49 J. Brenz, *Catechismus*, 554: "*Et tamen praecipitur in hac lege, etiam sua quaedam rerum communitas, videlicet, ea, quam exigit caritas proximi, ut opibus tuis liberaliter subvenias egenti, et largiaris eleemosynam, vel mutuum dando, vel donando propter Deum*".

50 J. Brenz, *Catechismus*, 554: "*Tertio, mandatur iustitia in contractibus, in emptione et venditione. Haec iustitia est cultus Dei et officium Deo gratum*".

and oppress the poor with unequal contracts, and this would have been against nature, which decrees the sharing of goods and performances.[51] Gratian, for instance, writes that the division of properties was introduced by custom and regulation: before, everything was in common for natural law.[52] Chemnitz employs Gratian's *Decretum* not as a source of dogmatic content, but for testifying that the debate on private property was already discussed.[53] His discourse lacks a polemic vein, as he does not criticize Gratian; he only mentions him to attest that the debate was not new.[54]

Then, Chemnitz moves on the real aim of his work: the confutation of the positions against private property. He summarizes the reasons for holding the communion of properties and rebuts them one by one. The first argument in favour of common holdings was that, as God created the universe for the use of all humanity, He did not want to assign the things in the world to a specific human person, but to the universal human race. Similarly, the privilege to tend and fill the earth (Gen. 1,28) was given to the entire community. Thus, the division of ownership and properties is against the very point of Creation. By the very fact of the splendour of the sun and the use of the elements, God shows that everything must be shared.[55] At the creation of the world, God's command to rule over and fill the earth, given to the universal human species, is therefore an injection against the division of creation.

Chemnitz replies that after the creation, already Cain and Abel had their personal possessions, and after the universal flood, the land was distributed by God and not by human free will. In Acts 17,26 Paul affirms that when God created the world, He determined the times and bounds (*ὁροθεσίας*) of their habitation.[56] Thus, the privilege to fill the earth was given, in the sense that

51 M. Chemnitz, *Loci theologici*, pars secunda, Francofurti et Wittenbergae, 1653, 144-5.

52 M. Chemnitz, *Loci theologici*, pars secunda, 145: "Ita *Gratianus* distinct. 8 dicit: *distinctionem dominiorum, et consuetudine et constitutione introductam, iure autem naturae omnia esse communia*". The passage quoted does not correspond to Gratian's Distinctio VIII in such a form, but was probably paraphrased. Later he also mentions C 12, q.1, c.2.

53 This way of using the *Decretum* was also embraced by other Protestant theologians. See P. Astorri, *Il diritto canonico nella prima teologia pratica protestante*, passim.

54 Melanchthon used the same passage, but he argued that Gratian's opinion was false. See below paragraph 1.2.2.3.

55 M. Chemnitz, *Loci theologici*, pars secunda, 146: "*1. Ex articulo creationis: cum in principio Deus universa crearet ad usum generis humani, non fuit apud ipsum respectus personarum; sed universo generi humano, non quibusdam tantum, sed omnibus et singulis, similiter et eodem modo datum est privilegium illud Gen. 1 v. 28, subiicite terram et c. Ergo distinctio dominiorum et proprietas rerum pugnat cum articulo creationis. Nam et in splendore solis et in usu elementorum, Deus ipso facto adhuc ostendit, omnia debere esse communia*".

56 M. Chemnitz, *Loci theologici*, pars secunda, 146.

God by His power (hand) distributes to everyone, as He wants.[57] God gives poverty and riches. In Proverbs 22,2 and Sirach 11,14, the Scripture says that rich and poor both are from the Lord, namely that such inequal distribution derives from God, so that some have more and others less; some are abounding in wealth, and some are needy. God willed such an order, because in this way human individuals are reciprocally bound by the exchange of goods and performances.[58] Chemnitz is very clear: God gave this unequal distribution in order to practice charity. Indeed, every day the splendour of the sun and the use of the earth show that God's will was that the exchange of goods and services occurs according to His order: by alms, contracts, loans, etc.[59] The response to this claim fully reveals the character of property. God gives property in an unequal way, so that men can practice charity towards each other in the exchange of goods.

This argument is important because it illustrates again the aim of property. Yet, other arguments held by the partisans of the communal theory are criticised by Chemnitz. One such reasoning goes: in the redemptive activity of Jesus Christ there is no distinction; Christ saves all the Christians (Gal. 3,28; Col. 3,11). Thus, there should be no distinction between rich and poor. In the Christian community, all are equal. Chemnitz responds that Christ has indeed obtained the justification for all the believers, but this does not necessitate the communion of goods. There must be a distinction between the spiritual life and the social and political life. In the spiritual life, there is no distinction between men, and all are equal. But in the external life, there is a difference.[60]

Again, for the communitarians, the Holy Scripture orders several times *κοινωνία* – communion (Hebr. 13,16; 2 Cor. 8,4 and 9,13; Rom. 12,13; Gal. 6,6; Phil. 4,14) and equality (2 Cor. 8,14; Col. 4). Communion would conflict with private property, and equality would contravene the division of ownership.[61] Chemnitz replies that the Scripture clearly says that there is no conflict between

57 M. Chemnitz, *Loci theologici*, pars secunda, 146: "*Ita igitur datum est privilegium, subiicite, dominamini, etc., quod Deus ipse manum aperit, et distribuit cuique prout vult*".

58 M. Chemnitz, *Loci theologici*, pars secunda, 146: "*Scriptura enim dicit Prov. 22, v. 2 Syrach 11, v. 14 divites et pauperes esse a Domino, id est, talem inaequalem distributionem esse a DEO, quod alii plus alii minus possident, alii abundent, alii egeant. Voluit autem Deus, hoc modo consociatum et sibi invicem devinctum esse genus humanum communicatione rerum et officiorum*".

59 M. Chemnitz, *Loci theologici*, pars secunda, 146: "*Praebuit igitur inaequali distributione occasionem excercendae charitatis. Nam splendore solis et usu elementorum quotidie ostendit, voluntatem suam esse, ut fiat communicatio rerum et officiorum, iuxta ordinem a Deo praescriptum, eleemosynis, contractibus, mutuo etc.*".

60 M. Chemnitz, *Loci theologici*, pars secunda, 146.

61 M. Chemnitz, *Loci theologici*, pars secunda, 146.

private property and communion (Prov. 5,17 and 1 Tim. 6,17). The word *κοινωνία* is not employed to invite Christians to renounce to their goods and confer all to a common pot, but to encourage Christians to give spontaneously to the poor, as much as they freely want to give (1. Cor. 16,2; 2 Cor. 8,8 and 10): it is a suggestion and not a command. Paul, Chemnitz continues, describes equality not to remove the division between rich and poor, but so that the rich could relieve the poor with their abundance, that there could be equality.[62] Equality is a goal and does not imply renouncing private property and creating a communion; this equality can be reached through alms and other free donations to the poor.

Finally, one last argument against private property was that the primitive Church is an example of communion. The group of Christians, guided by the Apostles, shared everything. Those who had properties, lands or homes, sold them and gave the profits to the apostles (Acts 2,44 and 4,32).[63] Chemnitz counters this statement with a long discourse, where he also condemns the Catholic ideal of a spiritual merit in the renunciation of property (by disposing of his wealth, the Christian could gain spiritual merits), though we cannot examine this topic in depth here. In short, Chemnitz sustains that the Apostles created the primitive ecclesiastical community not because the doctrine of the Gospel postulates it, nor as a reverence for the more excellent life, as it is ordered in the Law; this community rather was an indifferent and temporal institution, not a perpetual one.[64] Indeed, Paul did not suggest such a communion to the nations (2 Cor. 8,13; and 9,7; 1 Cor. 16,1; 1 Tim. 6,17 and 1 John 3,17).[65]

It is time to formulate our concluding reflections on this point. The discussion with the Anabaptists and the refusal of an ascetic ideal of poverty gave the Lutherans the occasion to shed some light on the specific characteristics of property. God did not institute a communion of goods, but ordered private property. This is especially clear in the seventh commandment of the

62 M. Chemnitz, *Loci theologici*, pars secunda, 146: "*Respond. Scriptura manifeste dicit, non pugnare proprietatem et communionem. Prov. 5. v. 17 1 Tim. 6, vers. 17. Non enim vocat κοινωνία, ut abdicato dominio omnia conferantur in commune; sed ut de suo, quod proprium cuique est, aliquid communicet egentibus, quantum voluerit, 1 Cor. 16, v. 2. 2 Cor. 8, v. 8 et 10. non secundum imperium hoc dico; sed consilium do.* (…) *Ita Paulus aequalitatem describit, non ut tollatur distinctio divitis et pauperis, sed vestra copia illorum sublevet inopiam, ut ita fiat aequalitas*".

63 M. Chemnitz, *Loci theologici*, pars secunda, 146.

64 M. Chemnitz, *Loci theologici*, pars secunda, 147: "*Susceptam fuisse illam communionem ab apostolis, non quod doctrina Evangelii ita postularit, nec tanquam cultum praestantiorem, quam qui in lege mandati sunt; sed fuit institutum indifferens et temporale, non perpetuum*". This argument was also proposed by Melanchthon. See P. Melanchthon, *Prolegomena in officia Ciceronis*, in CR XVI, 551-2.

65 M. Chemnitz, *Loci theologici*, pars secunda, 147.

Decalogue. God assigned goods in different ways: some people are rich and some are poor. Nevertheless, the Christians are called to use their property according to God's will. They are bound to practice charity in order to meet the neighbour's needs. Goods are ordained to be exchanged with alms and lawful contracts.

1.2.2.3 A Divine Order: Luther and Melanchthon's Definition of Property

The aim of property is to practice charity towards the neighbour. Then, for the definition and extent of property, the theologians borrowed the concepts of *dominium* (lordship), *usus* (use), *ius* (right) and *facultas* (faculty) as elaborated in the medieval discussions. They used them in conjunction with their fundamental assumption that private property is ordered by the divine law. The result is that property derives from God, and it is the right of the single owner to use the thing according to God's will, as expressed in the seventh commandment.

Luther uses the term 'lordship' (*dominium*) and distinguishes between the extension of the right in state of integrity and the state of corruption. Before the Fall, he writes, lordship was based on Adam's power and wisdom. In the state of corruption, after the Flood, lordship has to be exercised according to God's will. Lordship thus corresponds to the permission granted to men to use the things created by God for their sustenance. Such oversight is therefore not a sin, but a gift of God.[66] It not only serves the one who has it, but helps those who are in poverty.[67] For Luther, lordship is necessarily linked to God: it is God's gift, to be used according to His will.

Melanchthon presents a more detailed and technical formulation. Property (*proprietas*) is the lordship (*dominium*) of a thing acquired according to just modes. The owner has the right to decide with his will about the thing, unless it is forbidden by law or an agreement.[68] Melanchthon stresses the power of the single owner over the thing. The right (*ius*) is attributed to the owner and not to another person, and it can be limited by the law or agreement. Then, Melanchthon defines lordship (*dominium*) as a right (*ius*), namely the faculty

---

66 M. Luther, *Vorlesungen über 1 Mose*, in WA 356 [6-17] cit. in V. Mäkinen-A. Raunio, *Right and Dominion in Luther's Thought and Its Medieval Background*, 82-5.

67 M. Luther, *Sommerpostille* (1520) – *Evangelium am 15 Sonntag nach Trinitatis Matth. 6, 24*, in WA 10, I, 376 [6-21] cit. in V. Mäkinen, A. Raunio, *Right and Dominion in Luther's Thought and Its Medieval Background*, 85.

68 P. Melanchthon, *Loci communes* (*tertia eorum aetas*), *Appendix II Definitiones multarum appellationum*, 1552-3, CR XXI, 1093: "*Proprietas est dominium rei iustis modis acquisitum, quo dominus et non alius, ius habet de ea re disponendi suo arbitrio, nisi quantum lege aut pacto prohibetur*".

(*facultas*) ordered by divine and human law, which the owner and no other person has to the thing, to decide according to his will about the thing, to the extent that it is permitted by law or an agreement.[69]

This definition adopts the terms *ius* (right), described as *facultas* (faculty) ordered by divine law and human law. These terms mirror the medieval debates among canonists and theologians,[70] and in particular seem to reveal the influence of Gerson.[71] Gerson had defined the term *ius* in a subjective sense as a *facultas* according to the right reason, or according to primary justice.[72] Melanchthon uses the term *facultas* in relation to the divine law and human law. The human law is the law of the magistrate as guardian and executor of the commandments.[73] The divine law corresponds to the seventh commandment of the Decalogue, which establishes private property.[74]

That private property is ordered by the divine law is the main argument used by Melanchthon to defend private property. This argument also rejects the traditional scholastic teachings on the origins of property. Gratian and many other scholastic authors had argued that natural law instituted a communion

69 P. Melanchthon, *Loci communes (tertia eorum aetas), Appendix II Definitiones multarum appellationum*, in CR XXI, 1093: "*Dominium est ius, id est, facultas ordinata lege divina vel humana, qua rem tenet dominus, et non alius, et de ea re disponit suo arbitrio, nisi quantum lege aut pacto prohibetur*".

70 For the development of these concepts see D. Willoweit, Dominium *und* Proprietas: *Zur Entwicklung des Eigentumsbegriffs in der mittelalterlichen und neuzeitlichen Rechtswissentschaft*, in *Historisches Jahrbuch* 94 (1974), 131-56.

71 On Gerson's conception of property see the classic works of M. Villey, *La formation de la pensee juridique moderne*, Paris, PUF, 2003 (first ed. 1968); R. Tuck, *Natural Rights Theories. Their Origin and Development*, Cambridge, Cambridge University Press, 1995 (first ed. 1979); B. Tierney, *The Idea of Natural Rights: Studies on Natural Rights, Natural Law, and Church Law, 1150-1625*, Grand Rapids, Eerdmans, 2001 (first ed. 1997); A.S. Brett, *Liberty, Right and Nature: Individual Rights in Later Scholastic Thought*, Cambridge, Cambridge University Press, 1997. On Summenhart, see J. Varkemaa, *Justification through Being: Conrad Summenhart on Natural Rights*, in J. Kraye, R. Saarinen (eds.), *Moral Philosophy on the Threshold of Modernity*, Dordrecht, Springer, 2005, 181-93; J. Varkemaa, *Conrad Summenhart's Theory of Individual Rights*, passim.

72 J. Gerson, *De vita spirituali animae* (1402), lectio 3, 26 in P. Glorieux, *Jean Gerson: Oeuvres complètes*, Paris, Desclée de Brouwer, v. 3 : "*Jus est facultas seu potestas propinqua conveniens alicui secundum dictamen rectae rationis*". See also *Oeuvres complètes*, v. 9, 242: "*Ius est facultas seu potestas propinqua conveniens alicui secundum dictamen primae justitiae*".

73 P. Melanchthon, *Prolegomena in officia Ciceronis*, CR XVI, 560. I. Deflers, Lex *und* Ordo, 257-8.

74 P. Melanchthon, *Loci communes (tertia eorum aetas), Appendix II Definitiones multarum appellationum*, CR XXI, 1093.

of goods: human laws introduced private property.[75] If private property derives from human law, men can renounce it and live in common. But Melanchthon wants to refuse this conclusion. He explains that 'the natural things', namely the natural knowledge of skills and precepts, are immutable, but not 'the useful things' (*utilitates*), as the perpetual health of body and other advantages, which were in the state of natural integrity. These useful things could be in common in the state of natural integrity, but this was not the precept.[76]

Melanchthon also affirms that Gratian's stance that according to the divine law, everything must be in common is false. The divine law, in the seventh commandment, orders the division of properties.[77] Gratian's opinion is false because the seventh commandment ordains private property. In fact, claiming that the divine law dictates private property brings Melanchthon to refuse the scholastic teaching of a communion of goods ordered by natural law. The divine law mandates private property.

1.2.2.4 The Nexus with the Revelation

In general terms, to Luther and Melanchthon property derives from God and must be used according to God's will. This vision was inherited by their disciples. David Chytraeus, in his *Regulae vitae: virtutum descriptiones methodicae* (1556) does not employ the term *dominium* in order to define property, but makes use of the two concepts of possession (*possessio*) and use (*usus*). He

75 See for instance B. Tierney, *The Idea of Natural Rights: Studies on Natural Rights, Natural Law, and Church Law*, 138-45.

76 P. Melanchthon, *Loci communes (tertia eorum aetas), Appendix II Definitiones multarum appellationum*, CR XXI, 1093-4: "*Naturalia sunt immutabilia, videlicet notitiae naturales artium et praeceptorum, sed non utilitates, quae fuissent in natura integra, ut perpetua sanitas corporis et aliae commoditates. Talis potuit esse in natura integra communio, nec tamen fuisset praecepti*". See also P. Melanchthon, *Prolegomena in officia Ciceronis*, CR XVI, 549: "*Naturalia sunt immutabilia, videlicet notitiae, quae sunt praecepta, ut notitia numerorum est immutabilis: sic immutabilia sunt praecepta moralia: agnosce et invoca verum Deum, honora parentes, non occides, non moechaberis, non furtum facies, non dices falsum testimonium etc. Sed bona utilia sunt mutabilia, ut quanquam sic condita est natura hominis, ut retineret vitam, sanitatem corporis et tamen haec bona propeter peccatum postea mutata sunt. Sic facultas communiter utendi rebus, fuisset bonum utile, quod mutatum est post peccatum propter multas causas*".

77 P. Melanchthon, *Disputationes de rebus politicis* (1541), in J. Haussleiter (ed.), *Melanchthon-Kompendium, eine unbekannte Sammlung ethischer, politischer, philosophischer Lehrsätze Melanchthons in Luthers Werken*, Greifswald 1902, 64: "13. *Falsa est haec sententia in decretis Gratiani, iure divino omnia esse communia (Gratianus D. 8). Nam ius divinum sancit proprietatem rerum in hoc praecepto: non furaberis (Exod. 20,15)*". The text is cited in P. Prodi, *Settimo non rubare*, 214, fn. 20. Melanchthon considers the Decalogue to reflect the divine law and reports Gratian's passage as *ius divinum*, while Gratian had written *ius naturae*.

writes that the just possession and good use of the things, riches or wealth, is a virtue. It is the virtue by which the possessor keeps his riches in fear of God, with faith and clear conscience. Furthermore, the possessor acknowledges that his wealth is given and guarded by God; he diligently strives after conserving and increasing it by honourable business; he collects it for the use ordained by God.[78]

Possessio and *usus* indicates two dimensions of the same right on the thing. *Possessio* seems to indicate the rights to properties or riches in general, while the *usus* seems to signify the finalization. The aim of property emerges again and is conjoined with the divine origins of wealth. As Chytraeus explicates, God desires that we keep our things and rightly use them for several reasons, among which are the acknowledgement of God's existence; the practice of faith and God's invocation for demanding the things we need; and the gratitude for the things received for realizing our vocation.[79] Possession and use of things are conceived in a relation with God: God gives the riches and commands that we use them according to His will. A dimension of faith drives the Christian in possessing and using his goods. Goods are given so that we recognise God, thank Him, and follow His will.

For Chytraeus, private property is ordered by the divine law, in the seventh commandment. Indeed, he explains, if all the goods were in common, there would be no need for the prohibition against theft.[80] Furthermore, natural law, that is the same law of God inserted in human nature, justifies private property. Natural reason, in this corruption of nature, understands that the reasons for seeking and for conserving the goods are not equal: since some people are lazy, others prodigal, others eager for power, etc., there is a need for the division of property.[81] Chytraeus considers men's evil attitude as justification for private property. There is a difference between men, due to sin, and this difference evidences the necessity of private property. In substance, Chytraeus' argument seems to say that a communion of goods is impossible, because the

78 D. Chytraeus, *Regulae vitae*, septimi praecepti virtutes: "*Iusta possessio et bonus usus propriarum rerum, seu facultatum, seu divitiarum est virtus, quae in timore Dei et fide, ac bona conscientia tenet proprias facultates et agnoscens eas a Deo dari et custodiri, sedulo studet eas conservare et honestis rationibus augere et ad usus a Deo ordinatos conferre*".

79 D. Chytraeus, *Regulae vitae*, septimi praecepti virtutes.

80 D. Chytraeus, *Regulae vitae*, septimi praecepti virtutes: "*1 A lege divina. Septimum praeceptum decalogi prohibet furta. Iam si omnia bona essent communia, nihil opus esse prohibitione furti*".

81 D. Chytraeus, *Regulae vitae*, septimi praecepti virtutes: "*II A lege naturae, quae est ipsa lex Dei insita naturae. Rom. 2. Intelligit autem naturalis ratio in hac corruptione naturae, cum non sint pares causae quaerendi et conservandi bona, cum alii sint ignavi, alii prodigi, alii cupidi potentiae etc. opus esse distinctione dominiorum*".

men who want to conserve the goods oppose those who are thirsty for them. He also indicates other reasons based on biblical passages and the examples of biblical characters, like Abraham, Isaac, etc., which cannot be examined in depth here.[82]

In the seventeenth century, the vision of private property as divinely ordered by divine law was challenged by the natural lawyers. For instance, Hugo Grotius (1583-1645) in *De jure belli ac pacis* (1625) advocated that at the creation of the world everything was in common, and the property of things only developed in a following moment.[83] Such a vision disappointed the chancellor and then-rector of the University of Tübingen, Johann Adam Osiander, who claimed that this conjecture was not in accordance with the holy history. Indeed Adam, and through him the whole humanity, received directly from God the property of things (the precept 'you shall not steal' would not make any sense otherwise).[84] To Osiander, the holy history does not record a period where everything was in common and Grotius' conception is founded not in the Holy Scripture but in the scholastics' assertion that for the law of nature, everything is in common (*de iure naturae omnia esse communia*).[85]

Osiander's firm rejection of a communion at the origins of the world was anything but unanimous among the Lutheran theologians. Johann Wolfgang Jäger refuted Osiander's opinion, pointing out that there are no reasons for holding that the Decalogue was inserted in Adam's heart, because it punishes sins (like adultery), and there were no sins in the state of integrity. Aegidius Strauch in his *Theologia moralis* distinguishes between implanted nature and deceived nature for the original sin. The divine command to replenish the earth (*replete terram*) was not directed to a single man, but to all men, and therefore it created a communion of goods (*communio bonorum*). The law of nature did not order immediately and directly the division of goods and property. The law of nature ordered it later, in occasion of the multiplication of human genre, when unfairness prevailed among men.[86]

This idea of the division of property originated by man's tendency to sin had been defended by Samuel Pufendorf in his *De jure naturae et gentium* (1672). Pufendorf held that from an original communitarian state, human beings

82 D. Chytraeus, *Regulae vitae*, septimi praecepti virtutes.

83 H. Grotius, *De iure belli ac pacis*, II, 2.

84 J.A. Osiander, *Observationes maximam partem theologicae in libros tres de iure belli ac pacis Hugo Grotii*, Tubingae, 1671, 650-1.

85 J.A. Osiander, *Observationes*, 652.

86 A. Strauch, *Theologia moralis*, 271: "*Non dicimus quod ius naturae* directe et immediate *rerum divisionem et proprietatem praeceperit, sed quod ius naturae fecerit* ex occasione humani generis multiplicati et iniquitatis inter homines invalescentis".

passed to property, due to a subsequent deformity of intellect (*ingenii pravitatem*), avarice and cupidity. Hence, all the things held in common were divided through an agreement and assigned to men as needed.[87] This vision was vehemently denied by the Lutheran jurist Johann Georg von Kulpis (1652-1698). He considered this communion an invention of the pagans adopted by the scholastics that could have never taken place either in the state of nature or in the state of corruption.[88]

Entering into the details of this debate would take us off topic. In this context, however, other theologians investigated the concept of property. Valentin Alberti in his *Compendium iuris naturae, orthodoxae theologiae conformatum* (1678) writes that not only the universal but also particular property derived directly from God.[89] The lordship (*dominium*) over things depends on the free will of the owner (*arbitrium*) in quantity and extension. Alberti notices that property should not only be considered in terms of extension but also of intensity, which is the degree it can be exercised. In the state of integrity, the extent of property was more ample and the intention was easier and happier than in the state of corruption.[90] Nevertheless, after the original sin, men have a different use of things, determined by necessity. God allowed this different use, but it is imperfect.[91] In the state of corruption, we must use and dominate the things for the glory of God.[92] This means that the owner can transform the things for his advantage, according to natural and Christian freedom, except for the limit imposed by a very just human positive law.[93] The adjective 'very fair' is inserted because human law must comply with the divine law.[94]

Alberti's definition is not far from Luther and Melanchthon's. He insists on the freedom of the owner within the limits imposed by God and human law. Alberti derives this definition from the comparison between the state of integrity and the state of corruption and stresses the different use of things. He

87 S. Pufendorf, *De jure naturae et gentium*, lib. 4, cap. 4, §. 3 and lib. 5 cap. 4 §. 4. See also A. Saether, *Natural Law and the Origin of Political Economy. Samuel Pufendorf and the History of Economics*, Abington, New York, Routledge, 2017, 76-86.

88 J.G. von Kulpis, *Collegium Grotianum*, Stutgardiae, 1697, exercitatio III, 34-5.

89 V. Alberti, *Compendium iuris naturae*, pars secunda, Lipsiae, 1678, 136-7.

90 V. Alberti, *Compendium iuris naturae*, 132.

91 V. Alberti, *Compendium iuris naturae*, 133-4.

92 V. Alberti, *Compendium iuris naturae*, 134: "*Quibuscunque rebus hodie utimur aut dominamur, iis simul in gloriam Dei uti ac dominari debemus*"; 135: "*Quicunque modus dominii potest in honorem Dei meumque commodum tendere, is est licitus*".

93 V. Alberti, *Compendium iuris naturae*, 134: "*Hunc finem si intendas, licet tibi res omnes dominio tuo subjectas in commodum tuum, ex naturali (et christiana) libertate vertere. Unde nec haec per legem positivam humanam, nisi aequissima sit, est circumscribenda*".

94 V. Alberti, *Compendium iuris naturae*, 134-5.

points out that the lordship (*dominium*) is imperfect in the state of corruption, but in any case derives from God, and for this reason it must be used for the glory of God.

The whole tension in setting the origins of private property is expressed in the definition of property formulated by Johannes Franz Buddeus in his *Institutiones theologiae moralis* (1711). Buddeus writes that according to the Holy Scripture, God granted the first man and woman the faculty (*facultas*) to use the things that He created for their self-preservation (Gen. 1,28-29). God repeated such a concession after the Flood to Noah and his descendants (Gen. 9,2). This power to use the things for personal support can be defined as lordship (*dominium*) in a general sense. If the *dominium* may be understood as the power to exclude other men from the thing, it is said to be less just, he writes. Yet, the origins of every property are to be sought in this divine concession.[95]

Buddeus notices that on this point there is a discussion among scholars.[96] Indeed, some authors refute the idea of a communion of goods at the origins of the world, while others argue that God created private property immediately. Buddeus distinguishes the power to use from the power to exclude in order to save the direct concession of God. The power to use is directly given by God, while the power to exclude others originated later. Some authors, writes Buddeus, refer to a division or a pact to explain the introduction of private property, while others speak about an occupation due to human nature. Others, instead, determine the formal content of the right of property in the power of exclusion. In both cases, the divine will is supposed to act.[97]

Buddeus is preoccupied with safeguarding the divine origins of property, but is also aware of the discussion among theologians, jurists and natural lawyers. Thus, he seeks to find a balance and separates the power to use from the power to exclude. The lordship of goods derives from divine concession or donation,

95 J.F. Buddeus, *Institutiones theologiae moralis*, 529: "*Alterum institutum universale est* dominium rerum, *de cuius origine, iuxta scripturae sacrae ductum, rectissime ita statuitur. Cum Deus primos humani generis parentes condidisset, facultatem quoque, rebus creatis ad sui conservationem utendi, illis concessit (Gen. I, 28.29). Quae concessio, in humani generis post diluvium restauratione, repetita fuit Noacho, eiusque posteris (Gen. IX, 2). Et haec ipsa facultas, utendi rebus creatis ad sui conservationem, potest* dominium, *si vox in latiori significatione accipiatur, vocari. Quod si vero quis vocem illam strictius accipiat, prout denotat possessionem rerum cum exclusione aliorum, coniunctam, minus recte ita dicetur. Interim origo omnis dominii ex ista concessione divina repetenda*".

96 J.F. Buddeus, *Institutiones theologiae moralis*, 529-30. He mentions Pufendorf, Kulpis, Gottlieb Gerhard Titius ? (1661-1714) and Jean Barbeyrac (1674-1744).

97 J.F. Buddeus, *Institutiones theologiae moralis*, 530.

then a division or occupation followed, but this was divinely approved.[98] The definition of property derives from the original command of God to fill the earth (faculty to use). Private property comes after, as the faculty to exclude.

In conclusion, the Lutheran theologians proposed a vision of property strongly anchored in their interpretation of Scripture. Property derives from God and must be exercised according to divine law, which has to be reflected in human law. The *dominium* indicates the *facultas* of the single owner on the thing, according to God's will. This will is manifested in the seventh commandment of the Decalogue, which ordains private property and dictates the conditions of its use. The divine origins of property, albeit expounded in different and not unanimous forms, represent a critical point. This argument excludes irrevocably the possibility to renounce the goods for instituting a communion. The structure of private property is determined by the divine law, which has to model human law.

1.2.3 *Contracts are a Creation of God*

1.2.3.1 Exploiting the Definitions already in Existence

The seventh commandment of the Decalogue ordains private property and determines its character and extension. Property is meant for the personal needs of the owner but also to serve the neighbour in lawful exchanges. The neighbour is supported by alms and by contracts. Hence, the Lutheran conception of property is reflected in contracts, conceived as instruments for exchanging property. Contracts are a divine institution founded on natural law. The Gospel does not abolish this ordinance but asks Christians to use it in faith and charity. Faith allows the recognition that contracts are a gift of God. Charity invites believers to support the neighbour by providing him with the goods he needs, but also to the practice of the virtue of justice, which regards the equality of performances and the lack of fraud. This fundamental perspective seems to be univocal and consistent among the theologians. Yet, on the specific point of the definitions of contract, the theologians undertook two attitudes. The first one is only based on the analysis of the concepts formulated by jurists, philosophers and those included in the Scriptures. The second one integrates the juridical and philosophical definitions in a theological context of the seventh commandment.

Melanchthon promoted both of these attitudes. In his *Prolegomena in officia Ciceronis*, written in 1530 and published in 1562, he adopts Labeo's definition

98 J.F. Buddeus, *Institutiones theologiae moralis*, 531: "*Constat namque ex dictis: quod ex concessione seu donatione divina, dominia rerum originem habeant, et licet deinde aut divisio, aut occupatio accesserit, hoc tamen itidem volente et adprobante Numine factum*".

of contract (*contractus est ultro citroque obligatio*), as it was frequent in the *ius commune*. A contract is a reciprocal obligation deriving from the expression of consent or a lawful agreement, or expressed consent by which it derives an obligation; in German, dealing (*Handlung*), expressed consent (*Bewilligung*) and obligation (*Verpflichtung*); in Greek reciprocal exchange (*συνάλλαγμα* – synallagma) of the things that are conveyed by the parties or are conferred for the conveyance.[99] This definition gathers the Roman law tradition as elaborated in the Middle Ages, the Aristotelian approach, and a German translation of the key words. The German words seem to describe the different stages of the agreement formation: the negotiation, expressed consent and obligation. The adjective 'lawful' (*legitima*) related to 'agreement' (*pactio*) stresses that only the agreements admitted by the law are capable of producing an obligation. And the adjective 'expressed' (*expressus*) related to 'consent' (*consensus*) excludes the non-expressed or internal consent, which also was questioned, especially among the Catholic theologians. As we will see with the concept of pact, it also designates the necessity of a free and non-vitiated consent.

For Melanchthon the aim of a theologian is not to establish what contracts are, but to show that the Gospel approves of their use.[100] What defines a contract is no longer in the realm of the theologian, as the indications of the medications for an illness;[101] on this topic Christians must follow the decisions of the magistrate.[102] This conclusion arises from the new configuration of the relationship between ecclesiastical and secular power that we have previously noted. The theologians preach the Gospel, while the magistrates enforce the law.

Paul Von Eitzen, one of Melanchthon's first followers, begins with an etymological interpretation. The name "contract" comes from contracting, and

99 P. Melanchthon, *Prolegomena in officia Ciceronis*, in CR XVI, 575: "*Contractus est ultro citroque obligatio, orta ab expresso consensu: seu est legitima pactio seu expressus consensus, ex quo oritur obligatio, germanice Handlung, vel Bewilligung vel Verpflichtung, graece συνάλλαγμα a rebus quae transferuntur utrinque, vel quae conferuntur ad translationem*". The word *Handlung* can also be translated as 'action', but the context suggests the use of 'dealing' or 'negotiation'. Similarly, the word *Bewilligung* can also be translated as 'approval' or 'permission' but the context suggests to opt for 'express consent'. See also I. Deflers, Lex *und* Ordo, 258-9.

100 P. Melanchthon, *Propositiones (III) De contractu redemptionis*, in CR XII, 686. The editor does not indicate the date of publication. However, a letter written in 1531 attaches this text. See W. Thüringer, C. Mundhenk, *Melanchthons Briefwechsel*, vol. 5, Stuttgart, Bad Cannstatt, frommann-holzboog, 2003, 123, n. 1158.

101 P. Melanchthon, *Propositiones (III) De contractu redemptionis*, in CR XII, 687: "*Quales debeant esse contractus, non magis ad theologum pertinet, quam qualia pharmaca debeant in singulis morbis dari*".

102 P. Melanchthon, *Propositiones (III) De contractu redemptionis*, in CR XII, 687.

it means the action of those who conclude a contract or an agreement about the exchange or barter of goods or services. Then, he resorts to Labeo's definition, like Melanchthon.[103] Martin Chemnitz takes into consideration several sources. Considering the names, he writes, the philosophers call *συνάλλαγμα* (synallagma – reciprocal exchange) an exchange with a certain compensation by which you can get what you need from another; the Gospel speaks about *πράγμα*, negotiation or business (Luke 19,13; 1 Thess. 4,6). Indeed, everyone has to live not alone, but in society, so that one has to deal and to support each other, in the exchange of goods and services. Therefore, the word 'contract' is relative. Matt. 22,5 and John 2,16 use '*ἐμπορία*', (commerce, business), and the Jews have three names that have their etymology from 'surrounding' (*circumeundo*) and 'bringing to the market' (*deferendo*): אוניתא (sale), זבון (purchase) and אשאלתא (transaction). Chemnitz analyses the words employed by philosophers (only cited in general) and in the Scripture for what we today would call a 'sale'. He observes that the term 'contract' is relative. The issue is that we do not live alone but we need to exchange goods with other people and this can be designed in different ways.[104]

No surprise, then, that Chemnitz does not articulate a new definition of contract. Since the definition of contract can be found in the works of philosophers and jurists, he refers to them without spending so much time in finding a better solution. The Romans defined contract as an act that produces a reciprocal obligation (Labeo's definition). Philosophers described the mutual exchange in terms of commutative justice as arithmetical proportion that has to be observed in the exchange of goods. The Roman Catholic theologian Jean Gerson depicted a contract as a lawful civil exchange.[105]

---

103 P. von Eitzen, *Ethicae doctrinae, pars altera, continens quinque libros posteriores*, Witebergae, 1573, 469: "*Nomen contractus a contrahendo venit et significat actionem eorum, qui de rerum aut laborum communicatione seu permutatione inter se contrahunt, seu conveniunt. Et sic definitur: contractus est ultro citroque obligatio orta ab expresso consensu, seu est legitima pactio, vel expressus consensus ex quo oritur obligatio*".

104 M. Chemnitz, *Loci theologici*, pars secunda, 155: "*Considerentur appellationes. Philosophi vocant συνάλλαγμα a commutatione, cum certa compensatione ab alio potes accipere, quo tu indiges. Luc. 19 v. 13. 1 Thess. 4, v. 6 vocatur πράγμα, id est negotiatio. Non enim quisque sibi tantum debet vivere; sed sit talis consociatio: das einer mit dem andern zuhandeln und zuthun habe/ in communicatione rerum et operarum. Ita etiam vocabulum contractus est relativum. Matth. 22. v. 5. Joh. 2, v. 16 vocatur ἐμπορία, vocabulo latino. Hebraei habent tres appellationes, quae a circumeundo et deferendo etymologiam habent, veluti* אוניתא, זבון *et* אשאלתא".

105 M. Chemnitz, *Loci theologici*, pars secunda, 155: "*Quae sint species seu formae legitimorum contractuum, ex scriptis philosophorum et jurisconsultorum petatur. Pauca igitur de iis annotabimus. Contractum ita definiunt jureconsulti, quod sit ultro citroque obligatio, ex pacto surgens partium. Philosophi iustitiam commutativam describunt, quae in commutatione*

Following Gerson (who in turn drew upon Roman law), Chemnitz divides contracts in nominate contracts and innominate contracts. Nominate contracts are purchase and sale (*emptio venditio*), lease-hire (*locatio condutio*), gratuitous agency (*mandatum*), deposit (*depositum*), partnership (*societas*), pledge (*pignus*), loan for use (*commodatum*), loan for consumption (*mutuum*), barter (*permutatio*), free giving and gratuitous reception (*datio liberalis et receptio gratuita*). Innominate contracts are *do ut des, do ut facias, facio ut facias, facio ut des*. The terms *datio liberalis* and *receptio gratuita* seem to have been taken from Thomas Aquinas, interpreted by Gerson. They represent two reciprocal and correlated acts, the act of giving spontaneously and the act of receiving gratuitously.[106]

Chemnitz keeps theology, philosophy and law separate. As a theologian, for him the point is not the legal or philosophical description of a contract, but the relation with God. Using the Aristotelian doctrine of causes, he writes that the matter and form of contracts is to be asked of philosophers and jurists. The theologian adds the efficient cause, which is the ordinance and approval of God.[107] This perspective reveals a definite border between law and theology. It is again a context of faith that guides the understanding of contracts: they are an ordinance of God. Because God approves them, they can be lawfully used.

1.2.3.2 Instruments of Faith and Charity

We come now to the other approach initiated by Melanchthon, which is founded on the integration of the legal concepts in the theological view of the seventh commandment. In the appendix to the last editions of his *Loci theologici* (1552-53), Melanchthon elaborated another definition of contract. He describes a contract as a mutual and honourable agreement between two or more parties, having as its object the lawful transfer of a certain thing, with respect to property rights, use or obligation divinely ordered by God. He points out that the agreement is *honourable*, the transfer is *lawful* and the obligation exchanged is *divinely* ordered.[108] In that way the pattern is on a profile of lawfulness related to divine law. Furthermore, since the parties need things they

---

rerum servat proportionem arithmeticam. Gerson dicit: contractus est communicatio civilis legitima".

106 M. Chemnitz, *Loci theologici*, pars secunda, 155. See J. Gerson, *Opuscolum de contractibus*, in *Opera omnia*, vol. 3, Antwerpiae 1706, 167; T. Aquinas, *Commentaria in in decem libros ethicorum aristotelis*, in *Opera omnia*, Pariis, 1660, 128.

107 M. Chemnitz, *Loci theologici*, pars secunda, 157: "*Materia igitur et forma contractuum a philosophis et iureconsultis petenda est. Theologus vero addit causam efficientem, esse Dei ordinationem et comprobationem ...*".

108 On the lawfulness of contracts and business see more specifically II/2.

do not have, God wanted men's lives to remain united by equality performed in lawful contracts and lawful exchanges. Entering into contracts, men understand that justice must promote equality to show that God is equality.[109] Thus, contracts are instruments to know God. They are a divine institution, an example that remembers God.[110] Contracts are also lawful; it is confirmed by the advice of a passage of Leviticus to avoid inequality in judgment and rules.[111]

Melanchthon insists on two aspects that derive from the seventh commandment of the Decalogue. First, contracts are divinely ordered means to acquire property rights. Second, by contracts men practice charity – they meet their neighbour's needs and exercise justice and equality. The seventh commandment orders the division of properties and the exchange by lawful contracts. Since the distribution of goods is unequal, contracts must be used to give the neighbour what he needs. In the execution of contracts, then, this commandment forbids fraud and injustice.

By practicing equality in contracts, the Christian can know that God is just and equal. Indeed, the virtue (not only the virtue of justice, but any virtue) shows a distinction between the 'honourable' and the 'shameful' acts. This distinction testifies that human nature is not generated by chance, but by a creating mind. The virtue is therefore a testimony of God's existence and allows a natural knowledge of God. The virtue also teaches God's corresponding attributes whether wisdom, freedom, truth, justice, truth, generosity, chastity, mercy etc. The virtue of justice teaches us that God is just.[112]

---

109 P. Melanchthon, *Loci communes* (*tertia eorum aetas*), Appendix II, *Definitiones multarum appellationum, quarum in ecclesia usum est*, 1552-1553, in CR XXI, 1094: "*Contractus est mutua et honesta consensio duorum vel plurium de re aliqua legitimo modo transferenda, vel quoad dominium vel quoad usum vel quoad obligationem divinitus ordinata, quia, cum singuli indigeant rebus, quas ipsi non habent, vult Deus servata aequalitate legitimis contractibus et communicatione legitima vitam hominum copulatam esse, ut intelligamus iustitiam esse aequalitatem et sciamus ipsum aequalem esse*".

110 P. Melanchthon, *Dissertatio de contractibus*, in CR XVI, 496: "*Amemus ergo hanc in contractibus divinam ordinationem, et sciamus in eis proposita esse exempla, commonefacentia nos de Deo*".

111 P. Melanchthon, *Loci communes* (*tertia eorum aetas*), Appendix II, *Definitiones multarum appellationum, quarum in ecclesia usum est*, 1552-1553, in CR XXI, 1094: "*Et sunt contractus confirmati Levitici 19* (*vs.35*). *Non facite inaequalitatem in iudicio, in regula etc.*".

112 P. Melanchthon, *Ethicae doctrinae elementorum libri duo*, in CR XVI, 166: "*Prima: Quia earum notitia testimonium est, quod sit Deus. Nam aeternum et immotum discrimen honestorum et turpium in mente, testatur, hanc naturam non esse casu ortam, sed ab aliqua aeterna mente architectatrice. Secunda: Quia docet, qualis sit Deus. Cum enim discernimus honesta et turpia, intelligimus, Deum esse sapientem, liberum, veracem, iustum, beneficum, castum, misericordem etc.*". See also before I/2.

This construction is based on the biblical and patristic idea of man as the image of God. The image refers to the Creator as maximum good.[113] Hence, by the virtue of equality in contracts, man can have a natural knowledge of God and His justice. However, because of original sin, man can only perform external actions. The image of God in man is deformed and must be renewed. The image is restored with the Word of God, through the Holy Spirit. In this way, it begins a new light and new obedience.[114]

Melanchthon's definition integrates the traditional definition of contract with his teachings on the virtues and the seventh commandment. It influenced other theologians like Victor Strigel, David Chytraeus and Johann Konrad Dürr. Strigel states that God instituted the contract in order to be a bond for society, in which He wants us to exercise justice, so that we can learn what justice and equality is and know that God is just and equal.[115] David Chytraeus in his *In Deuteronomium Mosis enarratio* (1575) writes that a contract in general is a mutual and honourable agreement between two or more parties, having as its object the lawful transfer of a certain thing, with respect to property rights, use or obligation divinely ordered, so that men's lives can be kept united and may be constructed by lawful exchange, that we may recognize that God is equal and just.[116] For Johann Konrad Dürr, a contract is a lawful means to acquire goods of fortune. Indeed God did not only introduce men in a state of reciprocal necessity and need, but He also willed contracts as instruments to keep connected human society, as perpetual matter for practicing Christian charity, friendship, integrity and knowing the wisdom of God.[117] This addition

113 P. Melanchthon, *Commentarius de anima*, Parisiis, 1540, 263. S. Kusukawa, *The Transformation of Natural Philosophy*, 96.

114 P. Melanchthon, *Commentarius de anima*, Parisiis, 1540, 263: "*Postquam vero contaminata est haec imago, restituitur verbo Dei per Spiritum Sanctum, qui novam lucem et novam obedientiam per verbum Dei inchoat*". The text is cited in S. Kusukawa, *The Transformation of Natural Philosophy*, 96.

115 V. Strigel, *In epitomen philosophiae moralis*, 765-766: "*Deus sanxit contractus, ut sint vincula societatis, in quibus vult exerceri iustitiam, ut discamus quid sit iustitia, videlicet aequalitas et agnoscamus ipsum esse iustum, id est, aequalem*".

116 D. Chytraeus, *In deuteronomium*, 453: "*Contractus in genere est mutua et honesta consensio duorum vel plurium de re aliqua legitimo modo transferenda, vel quo ad dominium, vel quo ad usum, divinitus ordinata, ut vita hominum legitima rerum communicatione copulata sit et construetur, ac ut Deum aequalem et iustum esse agnoscamus*".

117 J.K. Dürr, *Compendium theologiae moralis*, Altdorffi, 1675, 219. Under chapter XVI, *de virtutibus Hominis Christiani circa bona fortunae occupatis*, he describes contracts: "*Tertio comparantur bona fortunae per legitimos contractus. Non tantum autem invexit eos necessitas et mutua indigentia, verum etiam Deus extare eosdem et vigere vult, ut perpetuam materiam et exercitium Christianae charitatis, amicitiae, integritatis et ut agnoscamus sapientiam Dei, contractuum vinculis humanam societatem connexam retinentis*".

of charity and friendship might depend on the conception of property as destined for charity towards the neighbour.

Johann Wilhelm Baier again employs the term "contract", in his chapter on the contractual duties for the re-born regarding the neighbour (*De officio hominis renati circa proximum in contractibus*). Beside the free transfer of goods, he says that it pertains to the duty of Christians to conserve and to increase the riches of the neighbor with contracts. Contracts should be entered and served according to good faith. And love should be exercised in contracts to the advantage of both parties. Indeed the person we are contracting with should also benefit from the contract.[118] This definition emphasizes the aim of contracts as instruments for transferring property: practicing love (*dilectio*) towards the neighbour. The use of contracts is finalized to the enrichment of both the parties and not of only one.

In conclusion, Melanchthon gave rise to two slightly different ways of conceptualizing contracts. One is based on the distinction between theology and law. Contracts are legal concepts to be interpreted in a context of faith, which reveals that they are a divine institution. Another way combines the legal definitions with the teaching of the seventh commandment. The seventh commandment invites Christians to recognize that contracts are a creation of God. The law teaches that they must be used according to charity, to support and benefit the neighbour, to practice equality and justice and to avoid fraud.

1.3 The Eighth Commandment: Observance of Agreements

1.3.1 *Introduction*

The seventh commandment is the area of 'property', and a contract is conceived as an economic and legal instrument for the conveyance of the property rights. A contract is considered to be a platform for the exchange of goods, which must observe charity towards the neighbour. Instead, the eighth commandment treats the area of 'word'. It concerns the observance of the given word, the virtue of truth, which is violated by the *mendacium* (lie). Such a precept does not only involve contracts, but in general every type of agreement, down to the simple *pactum*.

118 J.W. Baier, *Compendium theologiae moralis*, Jenae, 1697, 489: "*Praeter gratuitam rerum communicationem ad officium hominis Christiani circa facultates proximi conservandas et amplificandas, hoc etiam pertinent, ut contractus bona fide ineantur et serventur, in iisque sic exerceatur dilectio, ut non solum nostri, verùm etiam illorum, cum quibus contrahimus, ratio habeatur illique adjuventur*".

Initially, the term *pactum* was used to identify the agreement devoid of the legal requirements and thus not legally actionable. During the late sixteenth and seventeenth centuries, however, this concept was destined to suffer a profound transformation, which led to a general theory of contract centred on the efficacy of the *nudum pactum*. This occurs, as seen before, for the analysis of the early modern scholastics and natural lawyers. They configured the pact as the result of a promise and an acceptance, and classified it as category including the contract. Some of the Lutheran theologians inserted notions gleaned from the scholastics and natural lawyers in their discourses. Others remained tied to the virtue of truth as a category to express contractual fidelity.

1.3.2 Pactum *and* promissio

At the beginning of the Reformation, the analysis of *pactum* and *promissio* is scarcely realized. These terms are employed to define binding statements in general, and forbid the *mendacium* (lie). In this sense, the first comments to the eighth commandment set out a general principle of agreement observance, but generally no definitions are proposed. In his *Loci theologici*, Melanchthon writes that the eighth commandment concerns the truth in judgments and pacts;[119] in his *Catechesis puerilis* he speaks about the truth in judgment, contracts and pacts and forbids the breach of pacts and promises in contracts.[120] This description gives a hint that the *contractus* should be considered as the legally binding category, while the *pactum* and *promissio* are more general concepts, devoid of the necessary garments for enforceability, and therefore are only morally binding.

Similarly, David Chytraeus speaks about pacts and promises all in treaties and contracts (*pacta seu promissiones omnes in foederibus et contractibus*).[121] In his *Catechismus*, Johannes Brenz distinguishes between the truth in contracts and the truth, faith and perseverance in pacts and covenants.[122] Martin Chemnitz writes that the eighth commandment prohibits breach of promises in pacts, covenants and contracts;[123] while Aegidius Hunnius reports that the truth (*Warheit*) governs all contracts (*Contracten*), sale (*keuffen und verkeuffen*), pacts (*Pacten*), alliances (*Bündnissen*), agreements (*Verträgen*), testaments

119 P. Melanchthon, *Loci communes* (*tertia eorum aetas*), in CR XXI, 709-710.

120 P. Melanchthon, *Catechesis puerilis*, in CR XXIII, 171-172.

121 D. Chytraeus, *Regulae vitae*, octavi praecepti virtutes.

122 J. Brenz, *Catechismus*, 567-568: "*Adhaec mandatur veritas in contractibus* (...) *praeterea mandatur veritas, fides et constantia in pactis et conventis*".

123 M. Chemnitz, *Loci theologici*, pars secunda, 85.

(*Testamenten*) and where one of the parties has promised (*versprochen*).[124] In these examples, *promissio* and *pactum* seem to be more general concepts destined to identify single statements and morally binding agreements, while the *contractus* represents legally binding agreements that are therefore suitable to transfer property. After all, in the comments on the seventh commandment, dedicated to the exchange of goods, the theologians only refer to contracts, while the eighth commandment includes contracts, pacts and other agreements in general. This distinction seems to betray a persistence of the medieval contractual theory among the Lutheran theologians.

Alongside this approach centred on the mere indication of obedience to the eighth commandment, some theologians also inquired into the requisites for the concrete insurgence of the binding effect. In his *Prolegomena in officia Ciceronis*, title *de pactis*, Melanchthon investigates the conditions for a pact (*pactum*) to be binding in conscience. He defines a pact as the agreement between two or more parties, by express words, to give or to take something honourable.[125] Setting aside the details of his argument, which we will examine later, it is worthwhile to notice not only the consensual structure of this definition but also the use of the adjective *honestus*. The consent concerns the capacity of the parties. To Melanchthon, here the traditional definition of pact needs to be corrected, because the consent is absent if the pact is formed with a madman. The consent is also absent in the promises extorted by fear, as when money is promised to a thief, to prevent him from taking one's life.[126] The *honestus* means that the pacts that have a shameful cause (*turpem causam*) and especially are against the divine law are not licit.[127] This approach inspired Von Eitzen who, though he studies the exceptions to the rule *pacta sunt servanda*, does not offer any definitions of pact.[128]

1.3.3 *Towards a New Conceptualization*

In the seventeenth century, in the wake of the early modern scholastics and natural lawyers, some Lutheran theologians explored in greater depth the

124 A. Hunnius, *Catechismus oder Kinderlehre von den Hauptpuncten Christlicher Religion*, Wittemberg, 1604, 103.

125 P. Melanchthon, *Prolegomena in officia Ciceronis*, in CR XVI, 560: "*Pactum est consensus duorum vel plurium, verbis expressis, ad aliquid honestum dandum aut capiendum*".

126 P. Melanchthon, *Prolegomena in officia Ciceronis*, in CR XVI, 561: "*Hic fit correctio ex definitione pacti, quia consensus deest, ut si furiosus pacisceretur. Sic et consensus deest in promissionibus terrore extortis, ut cum latroni promittitur pecunia, ne vitam eripiat*".

127 P. Melanchthon, *Prolegomena in officia Ciceronis*, in CR XVI, 561: "*Sed consideranda est particula honestum. Recte enim dicitur, pacta quae turpem causam habent, non sunt observanda. Ac praesertim hoc sic intelligatur, quae praecipiunt facere contra legem Dei*".

128 P. Von Eitzen, *Ethicae doctrinae pars altera*, 603-604.

concepts of promise and pact. Some of the first attempts are those of Balthasar Meisner, Georg König, and Conrad Horneius. In his *Dissertatio de summo bono* (1614), Meisner discusses the following question: *Is a simple promise binding in conscience?* He does not define promises, but only focuses on the possible effects in conscience.[129] Though there are no direct references, it is likely that he based his work on the early modern scholastics.[130] Similarly, in his *Casus conscientiae* (1654), Georg König mentions promises in order to analyse the requirements that make them binding, but he does not seek to define them.[131] Likewise, Horneius, in his *Compendium theologiae* (1655), deals with the requirements a promise must have in order to be binding, without attempting any definitions.[132] These authors do not enquire into the concepts themselves, but only into the conditions for the operativity of the bond.

The circulation of natural law theories caused the emergence of a new vision. Some theologians examined the interaction and effects of parties' free will. For instance, Osiander and Jäger comment upon Grotius' *De iure belli ac pacis* and conclude that an act of will is sufficient for the conveyance of property rights. The natural law does not require the delivery of the thing, but only the expression of will.[133] In his *Compendium iuris naturae* (1678), Valentin Alberti starts with the description of human freedom: freedom is the dominion over actions.[134] The freedom leans on principles of free actions, which originate from the intellect and will and from the knowledge of moral circumstances.[135] Since everyone has principles of free actions, he can act freely among equals.

---

129 B. Meisner, *Dissertatio de summo bono, cui praemissa sunt praecognita ethica et annexa coronis de virtute*, Wittenbergae, 1614, 241-2. Then, when he describes the vices of consent he also uses the word *"contractus"*.

130 His positions appear to be similar to the Jesuit Martinus Becanus (1563-1624). See in particular M. Becanus, *Disputatio theologica an haereticis servanda sit fides?*, in *Opuscola theologica*, vol. 2, Mainz, 1614, cap. 1, nr. 1, 7, and cap. 5, nr. 7, 22 both quoted in W. Decock, *Trust Beyond Faith Re-Thinking Contracts with Heretics and Excommunicates in Times of Religious War*, in *Rivista internazionale di diritto comune*, 27 (2016), 301-28 (317-8). Becanus offered a synopsis of early modern scholastics' contract law. See W. Decock, *Trust Beyond Faith Re-Thinking Contracts*, 2-3.

131 G. König, *Casus conscientiae*, 17.

132 C. Horneius, *Compendium theologiae quo universa fidei christianae tam credendorum quam agendorum doctrina tribus libris dilucide pertractatur*, Brunsvigae, 1655, 183-4.

133 J.A. Osiander, *Observationes*, 800-5; J.W. Jäger, *Hugonis Grotii libri tres*, 258-61.

134 V. Alberti, *Compendium iuris naturae*, 102: *"Dominium in actiones meas proprio nomine vocatur libertas"*. He quotes T. Maccius Plautus, *Miles gloriosus*, Act. 3, Sc. 1, 80. On the dominion over actions in scholastic setting see the good book of M.S. Testuzza, "Ius corporis, quasi ius de corpore disponendi". *Il* Tractatus de potestate in se ipsum *di Baltasar Gómez de Amescúa*, Milano, Giuffrè, 2016, 127-35.

135 V. Alberti, *Compendium iuris naturae*, 102-3.

Alberti bases his construction upon Aristotle's *Nicomachean Ethics* and the doctrines of Grotius. In turn, Grotius' doctrines reflect the classical scholastic agency theory.

Human freedom can be limited, Alberti continues. A general limit is imposed by honesty (*honestas*). Since we are the image of God, only the lawful exercise of freedom is admitted, therefore every action against honesty is unlawful. Then, there are two special limits. The first special limit regards the people subjected to a superior person, for instance to the magistrate.[136] This limit derives from the authority of the superior person, who can allow or forbid certain actions. The second special limit concerns the freedom of the promisor. He is limited by lawful pacts and promises. Promises and pacts are the way by which the human freedom is bound. They create an obligation between two men.[137] It is not a superior authority that produces the limit, but the promisor, with his will, can choose to be bound by a promise or a pact. Thus, promises and pacts are considered to be voluntary limits to human freedom.

Alberti is not the only Lutheran to adopt the Catholic teachings. Profoundly in debt to the early modern scholastics and to Grotius is the work of Johann Adam Osiander. Osiander dedicated one chapter of his *Theologia casualis* (1680) to the transfer of property due to promises. He suggests that the name *promissio* is general and can be extended to any contracts. Yet, in a special sense the term *promissio* designates the *gratuita promissio* (gratuitous promise), where something is promised gratuitously, while at other times it is customary to give a *promissio simplex* (simple promise), which concerns a deliberate and spontaneous obligation of faith, made to the other party about a certain thing.[138] Borrowing from the scholastics' categories, Osiander stresses that the promise needs free will (*spontanea*); it must be deliberate (*deliberata*); and the subject matter must be lawful and possible. Furthermore, this promise only produces an obligation of faith (*fidei obligatio*). Indeed, Osiander hastens to specify: according to the *doctores* (supposedly the medieval glossators and canonists), *promissio* does not have the power to transfer property rights according to the

136 V. Alberti, *Compendium iuris naturae*, 105.

137 V. Alberti, *Compendium iuris naturae*, 106: "*Limitatio secunda specialis, libertatis in promittente*: quicquid repugnat pacto aut promisso meo in se licito, id libere agere nequeo".

138 J.A. Osiander, *Theologiae casualis in qua quaestiones, dubia et casus conscientiae circa credenda et agenda enucleantur, pars tertia et quarta*, Tubingae, 1680, 97: "*Accipitur autem, cum agitur de promisssione specialiter, prout notat promissionem gratuitam, qua aliquid promittitur gratis, atque alias dici solet promissio simplex, quae deliberata et spontanea fidei obligatio, facta alteri de re quapiam bona possibili*".

positive law.[139] Indeed, for glossators and canonists the transfer of property required the delivery (*traditio*) of the thing, while following the scholastics, Grotius opted for a consensualist approach.[140]

A *promissio* is distinguished from *pollicitatio* (offer). A *pollicitatio* is the promise of the offerer, a naked promise still not followed by acceptance: every offer is a promise, but not every promise is an offer[141]. The *pollicitatio* is distinguished from a *pactum*. A *pactum* is the consent of two parties or *conventio* (agreement, covenant), so that for a *pactum* the consent of two parties is required, while the *pollicitatio* only requires the consent of one of the parties. The *pollicitatio* passes into a *pactum* when the party toward whom it is directed accepts it.[142] From the conceptual viewpoint, this analysis includes a dynamic of the agreement structurally centred in the consent of the parties. It is not the original contribution of Osiander, but rather the reception of a scholastic doctrine, as he frankly admits.[143] Osiander quotes the commentary of Antonio Gomez (ca. 1500-ca. 1572), a Spanish jurist and priest and the *Summa summarum* of Sylvester Mazzolini (1456/57-1523), who was a strenuous defender of the Roman Catholic Church's infallibility and opposer of Luther's *95 Theses*. A brief look at Gomez' texts reveals that our Lutheran theologian cut some parts of the text. For instance, Gomez describes the *pactum nudum* with the traditional Ulpian definition: as the consent of two or more parties *in idem placitum*. Osiander cuts the *nudum* (naked) and also part of the definition. Perhaps, he deleted the *nudum* because realized that this adjective was

---

139 J.A. Osiander, *Theologiae casualis*, 97: "Promissio *natura sua, supposito iure positivo, secundum doctores non habet vim transferendi dominii*".

140 Bibliography is abundant on this delicate topic. See W.M. Gordon, *Studies in the Transfer of Property by Traditio*, Aberdeen, University of Aberdeen, 1970; I. Birocchi, *Vendita e transferimento della proprietà nel diritto comune*, in L. Vacca (ed.), *Vendita e trasferimento della proprietà nella prospettiva storico-comparatistica*. Atti del Congresso Internazionale Pisa-Viareggio-Lucca, 17-21 aprile 1990, Milano, Giuffrè, 1991, 139-67; E.J.H. Schrage, *Traditionibus et usucapionibus, non nudis pactis dominia rerum transferuntur Die Wahl zwischen dem Konsens- und dem Traditionsprinzip in der Geschichte*, in M. Ascheri, F. Ebel, M. Heckel, A. Padoa-Schioppa, F. Ranieri (eds.), "*Ins Wasser geworfen und Ozeane durchquert*, 913-58.

141 J.A. Osiander, *Theologiae casualis*, 97: "Pollicitatio *est offerentis solius promissum, sive nuda promissio nondum secuta acceptatione; unde omnis pollicitatio est promissio, sed non contra*".

142 J.A. Osiander, *Theologiae casualis*, 97: "Pactum *est duorum consensus, atque conventio; unde ad rationem pacti requiritur consensus duorum; ad rationem pollicitationis solum unius. Transit autem pollicitatio in pactum, quando is, cui facta est, eam acceptat*".

143 Osiander quotes A. Gomez, *Commentariorum variarumque resolutionum iuris civilis* [...] *tomi tres*, Francofurti, 1616, t. 2, Cap. 9,§ 1, 2 and 3, 279-280; S. Mazzolini, *Summa summarum quae Sylvestrina dicitur*, Argentorati, 1518, under the heading 'Pollicitatio'.

no longer relevant. The natural law does not distinguish between the naked or clothed pact, and Osiander might have grasped this inutility and removed the *nudum*. But this is just a speculation.

1.3.4 *The Virtue of Truthfulness*

If some Lutheran theologians imported concepts from the early modern scholastics, others kept a slightly more conservative attitude. Johann Konrad Dannhauer, Johannes Olearius, and later Johann Caspar Haferung set the virtue of truthfulness and fidelity at the core of their system. In the dispute number eight entitled *On the truthfulness and lie in general and on the vow especially* (*De veracitate et mendacio in genere et de voto in specie*) of his original *Deuteronomium dannhawerianum* (1669), first edited under the name *Collegium decalogicum* (1638), Dannhauer analyses the virtue of truthfulness (*veracitas*). He writes that moral truthfulness (*veracitas moralis*) is different from the truth of physical reality and transcendental truthfulness (*veracitas rei ac transcendentali*) that relate to metaphysics.[144] Truthfulness in general is harmony. In the state of integrity, harmony was perfect, without dissimulations. After the original sin, however, in the state of corruption, harmony between internal disposition and external sign was reduced.[145]

Dannhauer distinguishes two types of truthfulness: verbal truthfulness and real truthfulness. Verbal truthfulness (*veracitas verbalis*) is in turn subdivided into two kinds of truthfulness: assertory truthfulness (*veracitas assertoria*) and promissory truthfulness (*veracitas promissoria*). The first one simply concerns the confirmation of things, which formally consists in the compliance of concept and word. The second one, promissory truthfulness, regards candour, faith, sincerity, and consists in the conformity of word and action.[146] Dannhauer does not take into consideration the promise in itself but the promise as an expression of truthfulness. The virtue of truthfulness exhorts the promisor to keep the words uttered. It implies the conformity between what pronounced and what offered.

In his *Doctrina theologiae moralis* (1703), Johannes Olearius seeks to combine the teachings on promises with the traditional system of virtues. Thus, the

144 J.K. Dannhauer, *Deuteronomium Dannhawerianum. id est: Collegium Decalogicum denuò typis*, Argentorati, 1669, 436. Dannhauer's Latin is somehow weird, as he uses the ablative *trascendentali*.

145 J.K. Dannhauer, *Deuteronomium Dannhawerianum*, 437.

146 J.K. Dannhauer, *Deuteronomium Dannhawerianum*, 437: "*Veracitas verbalis est vel* assertoria *quae nude rem confirmat, et consistit formaliter in conformitate conceptus et vocis,* vel promissoria *alias candor, fides, sinceritas, quae consistit in conformitate vocis et rei praestitae …*".

starting point is neither the doctrine of promises, nor the conceptualization of agreements. Olearius begins again from the virtues of fidelity and truthfulness, following a path that might even recall Aquinas. Unlike Dannhauer, the virtue that governs pacts and promises is fidelity. Truthfulness concerns every word expressed by the human mind; instead fidelity refers particularly to promises and oaths. Fidelity is the virtue by which a man keeps pacts and promises with another person firmly and without any fraud.[147] Again the pattern is not in pacts and promises but in the virtue that governs the bond. Similarly, in his *Theologia moralis per theses concinnatas* (1737), Haferung depicts fidelity as the Christian virtue that teaches keeping pacts and promises inviolable and without violence.[148] This virtue is not realised by the single Christian, but it follows from the grace of the Holy Spirit. The help of the Holy Spirit upholds the sanctity of the bond.[149]

1.3.5 *Attempting a Synthesis*

Despite this approach centred on virtue, the spread of early modern scholastics' and natural lawyers' contributions continued vigorously. Already Friedemann Becmann in his notes on Olearius' manual of moral theology uses the scholastic terms of 'gratuitous or naked promises'.[150] Then, in his *Elementa philosophiae practicae* (1697) and his *Institutiones theologiae moralis* (1711), Johann Franz Buddeus defines the *pactum* with the traditional Ulpian statement: "*consensus duorum pluriumve in idem placitum*". But he goes on with the analysis of the *promissio*. A pact is distinguished from a perfect promise (*promissio perfecta*), which is much stronger than a simple assertion and imperfect promise (*promissio imperfecta*). Indeed, in promises the faith is given by a solitary act, while in pacts, acceptance is also required. Against one's will no right is acquired: an offer has to precede and be responded to by an acceptance.[151]

147 J. Olearius, *Doctrina theologiae moralis*, Tab. XLVII: "[*Fidelitas*] *est virtus, per quam homo constanter et absque ulla fraude, cum altero pacta, eique promissa servat*".

148 J.C. Haferung, *Theologia moralis*, 248-249.

149 See I/2 and II/3.

150 F. Becmann, *Ad D. Joh. Olearii theologiam moralem annotationes*, Francofurti et Lipsiae, 1704, 348.

151 J.F. Buddeus, *Elementa philosophiae practicae*, Halae Magdeburgicae, 1720, 271: "*Est autem pactum consensus duorum pluriumve in idem placitum. Quo ipso* a promissione perfecta, *multo magis autem* a simplici assertione *et promissione* imperfecta, *discernitur. In promissionibus enim fides datur per actum solitarium: interim in iis etiam acceptatio requiritur, cum invito nullum ius acquiratur, nisi rogatio praecesserit, eique oblatio respondeat*". J.F. Buddeus, *Institutiones theologiae moralis*, 508-9. Promises are divided in three degrees: simple assertion, imperfect promise and perfect promise. However Buddeus does not clarify this distinction, only referring to Grotius and Pufendorf. He quotes H. Grotius,

Not only does Buddeus use Roman law concepts, but also he employs Grotius' concepts of perfect and imperfect promises and the early modern scholastics' reflections on offer and acceptance.

In his *Institutiones*, Buddeus also deals with contracts but fails to give a definition: he only observes that they are lawful and not forbidden to the Christians.[152] Yet, in the *Elementa* he uses Pufendorf's definition and calls a contract an act concerning things and actions to be sold in commerce, which only differs from pacts as genus and species.[153] Contract indeed is a species of pact. Then, Buddeus classifies contracts according to the Roman law categories: nominate contracts and innominate contracts. Nominate contracts are real contracts, consensual contracts and verbal contracts. Innominate contracts consist of four main species: *do ut des, do ut facias, facio ut facias, facio ut des*. Contracts are distinguished between bilateral or unilateral contracts; beneficent (*beneficus*) contracts, lucrative contracts, simple contracts or mixed contracts.[154]

Buddeus presents an effective synthesis between the Roman law and the theories proposed by the early modern scholastics and the natural lawyers. He uses the Ulpian definition and the classic classification between nominate and innominate contracts, but also the Grotian concepts of perfect promise (*promissio perfecta*) and imperfect promise (*promissio imperfecta*). The development of a more systematic contract law centred on the pact, the doctrines of promises and acceptance, and the centrality of consent have been received and assimilated.

This new conceptualization endured in the eighteenth century and seems to lead to a revision of the previous differentiation between the seventh and eighth commandment. Not only contracts, but also pacts, are considered valid to transfer property, and for this reason are included in the comments on the seventh commandment. An example is the *Theologia moralis* (1740) of Johann

---

De iure belli ac pacis, II, 2, § 2.3 and ff. and S. Pufendorf, *De iure naturae et gentium*, III, 5, § 6 et 7.

152 J.F. Buddeus, *Institutiones theologiae moralis*, 538: "*De contractibus etiam generatim id saltem observamus, quod christianis eos inire neutiquam sit prohibitum*".

153 J.F. Buddeus, *Elementa philosophiae practicae*, 305: "*Actus itaque circa res et actiones in commercium venientes, vocantur* contractus: *qui adeo a pactis non aliter a genere species, differunt*".

154 J.F. Buddeus, *Elementa philosophiae practicae*, 305: "*Sunt autem contractus vel* veri, *vel* quasi contractus: *illi vel* nominati *sunt, vel* innominati: *nominati sunt vel* reales, *vel* consensuales, *vel* verbales: *innominatorum plures sunt species, praecipue tamen quatuor solent constitui* do ut des, do ut facias, facio ut facias, facio ut des. *Sunt etiam contractus vel* bilaterales, *vel* unilaterales: *item vel* benefici, *vel* onerosi, *et denique vel* simplices, *vel* mixti".

Peter Reusch (1691-1758),[155] professor in Jena. He writes that property rights can be acquired only through the consent of the owner stated in a pact, of which there are various species.[156] The pact is regarded as a general category suitable for transferring property rights. The old distinction between contracts, as legal agreements, and pacts, as morally binding agreements, seems to be overcome.

To summarize what has been said up to now, at the beginning of the Reformation, pacts and promises were addressed in the context of the eighth commandment, which set out an obligation of truth and fidelity in pacts, promises and contracts. Some theologians attempted to define the requisites for the binding effect on the conscience. In particular, to Melanchthon, a binding agreement must be honorable and expressed through free consent.

A more detailed conceptualization came at a later time, through the reception of scholastics' and natural lawyers' solutions. A promise is a statement where one of the parties undertakes his obligation. By the other's acceptance, it becomes a pact. A pact is a general category that includes contracts, as instruments for business. Some theologians did not analyse these concepts, however, but only focused on the virtue of truth and fidelity. They did not spend words on the legal definition, but rather on the essential moral precept: keeping faith to the given word.

1.4 Conclusion

The question formulated at the entrance of this chapter was about the conceptualizations used by the Lutheran theologians for the binding agreement. We can now answer that the Lutheran theologians did not generate new legal concepts; rather they utilized those formulated by jurists, scholastic theologians and natural lawyers. In this sense, they suffered the lack of juridical formation and were indebted to external sources. Nonetheless, a reading that only focused on this point would be superficial; it would neglect to mention that the theologians deliberately did not grapple with new legal notions. The theologians aimed not to change legal definitions but to give them a theological horizon. They imbued the juridical structure with moral-theological meaning. They related contracts, pacts and promises to God's will for men. This relation with the divine is central, and as we are going to see better in the next chapter, finds its expression in a setting of faith and charity.

155 C. von Prantl, *Reusch, Johann Peter*, in *Allgemeine Deutsche Biographie* 28 (1889), 296 (accessed 16.01.2018); https://www.deutsche-biographie.de/pnd115536884.html#adbcontent.

156 J.P. Reusch, *Theologia moralis*, Jenae, 1740, 380, 380-1.

Contracts are regulated by the seventh commandment and are to be seen as means to exchange property rights. God allowed private property, but it is not confined to an egoistic enjoyment. Its aim is to meet one's neighbour's needs. God distributed properties unequally, so that Christians can help each other by contracts and alms. Contracts are lawful, but they must comply with the seventh commandment's regulation. They are modes to practice charity towards the neighbour: by supporting his needs and by following justice and equality.

Pacts and promises are governed by the eighth commandment, which sets out the virtue of truth in social relationships. The promisor is bound to keep faith to his word. Though this pattern generally remained stable, the theologians did not go much deeper into the definitions. They mostly relied on the illumination of the early modern scholastics and natural lawyers. This discourse ended up in the abandonment of the formalities of contracts; pacts were deemed also suitable for transferring property rights.

In short, the elements of Lutheran contract doctrine that we examined present two interrelated characters. First, they issue from a distinction between the juridical sphere and the theological sphere. The law is not intended as an instrument to direct Christians towards salvation. Rather, the law is a collection of concepts and definitions that do not need major modifications. Second, contracts, promises and pacts have to be intended and used in relation to God's will expressed in the Revelation. This profound revealing sense shapes the whole contract doctrine. In essence, it indicates both charity and truth.

CHAPTER 2

The Seventh Commandment: The Lawfulness and Right Use of Contracts

The initial analysis has permitted to show the interrelation between the conceptualizations of the theologians and the Decalogue. The Decalogue, and especially the seventh and eighth commandments, are also essential for the configuration of a series of contract law principles. Therefore, we now examine the principles related to the seventh commandment, while in the following chapter we will deal with those associated with the eighth commandment.

2.0 Introduction

This chapter investigates the way that Lutheran theologians regulated contracts. It does not examine every type of contract, which will be the goal of the following part, but explicates the basic principles that theologians employed. As has already been established in the previous chapter, the Lutheran theologians adopted the division between pacts and contracts. Contracts were considered to be fundamental instruments for operating in the market and were subject to the specific regulation of the seventh commandment. Following the Roman law classification, each contract, sale, loan and so on received a detailed treatment. The just price and usury were only two of the main issues that the theologians faced. To disentangle these issues, theologians used a complex of principles destined to guarantee the protection and the promotion of the contracting parties.

We now study the sources, the content and the interplay of these principles. Essentially, this chapter is composed of two parts: the lawfulness of business and contracts, and the right use of contracts. As these elements might suggest, the kind of evaluation made by the Lutheran theologians was founded on the Holy Scripture. The theologians applied to contracts the illuminating judgment of Scripture, which was for them the lighthouse that guided men towards salvation.

 | DOI:10.30965/9783657701506_006

2.1 The Lawfulness of Business and Contracts

2.1.1 *Anabaptists' Rejection of Business*

As seen earlier, a Protestant faction called Anabaptism claimed that property must be in common, and exchange of goods is not allowed in the Holy Scripture. The idea that business is forbidden to Christians is not new. Church Fathers such as Basil the Great (329/330-379) and Gregory Nazianzus (329-390) previously had reproached merchants, and in the Middle Ages a multitude of discussions had involved theologians and canonists on the lawfulness specifically of interest-taking and in general of business.[1] These discussions were directed to the Christian world as united body, while in the context of the Protestant Reformation, the disapproval of business practices was associated with the proposal of a sharing of goods that found a tangible possibility of application in the Anabaptist communities. The Anabaptists aimed to exercise the apostolic sharing of goods described in Acts 2,4 and 5.[2] They considered the concrete aspects of Christianity and did not accept that Christians could possess riches while at the same time poor people were starving in the streets. Being true Christians, they said, implies the rejection of riches and the care of the poor. Furthermore, trade and business are considered to be sinful means to acquire riches,[3] and interest on loaned money is condemned, as the surplus of money should be given to the poor.[4]

Anabaptism was a large and varied movement with different theological interpretations. But the arguments against business and contracts faced by

---

1 Many studies have been written on this topic. See: J.T. Noonan, Jr., *The Scholastic Analysis of Usury*, passim; J.W. Baldwin, *The Medieval Theories of the Just Price. Romanists, Canonists, and Theologians in the Twelfth and Thirteenth Centuries*, in *Transactions of the American Philosophical Society*, New Series, vol. 49, part. 4, 1959; J.A. Baldwin, *Masters*, passim; R. De Roover, *Le pensée économique des scholastiques, doctrines et méthodes*, Paris, Inst. d'Etudes médiévales, 1971; O. Langholm, *Economics in the Medieval Schools*, passsim; J. Kaye, *Economy and Nature in the Fourteenth Century: Money, Market Exchange, and the Emergence of Scientific Thought*, Cambridge, Cambridge University Press, 1998; O. Langholm, *The Legacy of Scholasticism in Economic Thought. Antecedent of Choice and Power*, Cambridge, Cambridge University Press, 1998; G. Todeschini, *I mercanti e il tempio, la società cristiana e il circolo virtuoso della ricchezza fra Medioevo ed età moderna*, Bologna, Il Mulino, 2002; O. Langholm, *The Merchant in the Confessional*, passim; P. Prodi, *Settimo non rubare*, passim.

2 C.A. Snyder, *Anabaptist History and Theology*, 237.

3 C.P. Clasen, *Anabaptism, A Social History*, 194-6; C.A. Snyder, *Anabaptist History and Theology*, 247.

4 C.P. Clasen, *Anabaptism, A Social History*, 196-200; C.A. Snyder, *Anabaptist History and Theology*, 248.

the Lutheran theologians were in general three.[5] First, business is discouraged in the Old Testament. The book of Sirach warns that it will be difficult that a merchant be exempt from sin (Sirach 26,20) because the sin is in the middle between the purchase and the sale (Sirach 27,2).[6] Apoc. 18,3 reports that in Babylon, merchants were fornicating with prostitutes; Zec 14,21 writes that there will be no more merchants in the house of God. In Tyre and Egypt, business is considered to be the cause of punishment by God (Is. 23,2; 45,14; Ez. 26,12; 28,5).[7] These are just some of the passages quoted; the actual list may be much longer.

Second, in the New Testament, business is also treated with contempt. In the parable of the wedding banquet, the king invited many people, but those who had to do their business paid no attention to the invitation (Matt. 22,5). In a similar way, the people of Sodom were selling and buying when they were destroyed (Luke 17,28).[8] In both passages trade and business seem to be a distraction from the spiritual life. However, the central point is that Christ expelled merchants from the temple, defining the place where they were selling as a 'hideout of thieves' (*spelunca latronum*) (John 2,16).[9] As the merchants were expelled from the temple, so trade and business are not licit. This passage had been used many times in medieval discussions.

The third and final argument is based upon the fact that many frauds are committed via business and contracts in the pursuit of profit. As this kind of behaviour is not suitable for Christians, they should not use contracts.[10] The basis for the three arguments – the Old and New Testament and the practical consideration that in commerce there are many frauds – led the Anabaptists to refuse business and trade. They do not mention the Church Fathers; nor do they refer to the *Decretum Gratiani* as many of the medieval theologians did.[11]

The Anabaptists' claim could be a seditious threat, as it drastically forbade any kind of business. It aimed at a communitarian form of Christianity, where everything is held in common and exchange is not allowed. It assumed a form of economy totally contrary to the development of capitalism. The merchants,

---

5 Anabaptists' arguments are extrapolated from the Lutheran texts. I did not have the possibility to analyze original Anabaptist treatises.

6 L. Osiander, *Enchiridion controversiarum, quae Augustanae confessionis theologis cum Anabaptistis intercedunt* [...], Witembergae, 1610, 234; F. Balduin, *Tractatus*, 953.

7 M. Chemnitz, *Loci theologici*, pars secunda, 156.

8 M. Chemnitz, *Loci theologici*, pars secunda, 156.

9 M. Chemnitz, *Loci theologici*, pars secunda, 156; L. Osiander, *Enchiridion controversiarum*, 234; F. Balduin, *Tractatus*, 953.

10 L. Osiander, *Enchiridion controversiarum*, 233; F. Balduin, *Tractatus*, 953.

11 J.W. Baldwin, *The Medieval Theories of the Just Price*, 64.

however, played a strategic role in the contemporary economic system. Foreign trade was especially crucial for the nation's general supply of money.[12] This explains why the Anabaptists' view on business captured the attention of the Lutheran theologians, as we are going to see in the following paragraph.

2.1.2 *Luther and Melanchthon's Reaction*

The Anabaptists raised the problem of the legitimacy or illegitimacy of business, which in turn involved contracts, as instruments of business, and their regulation. The question regarded the values behind the norms. For the Anabaptists, business is a valueless enterprise, and therefore it cannot have a legal platform. Sales, loans, deposits and so on are all instruments of business and so are totally prohibited. The Holy Scripture forbids any market activity and its legal means. The Lutheran theologians tackled the problem, but did not approve the Anabaptists' solution. In his treatise on trade and usury (*Von Kaufshandlung und Wucher*, 1524) Martin Luther declares that buying and selling are necessary. They cannot be dispensed with and can be practiced in a Christian manner.[13] Afterwards he adds that the patriarchs also used to buy cattle, wool, grain, butter and other goods.[14] The example of the patriarchs, which is taken from the Holy Scripture, justifies the lawfulness of trade and business. The need to use contracts is certified by patriarchs' adoption of contracts. It is not that contracts per se are forbidden, but only their wrong use.

The approach of Philip Melanchthon is different and more structured.[15] For instance, in his *Catechesis puerilis* (1541) he discusses the following question: 'Is it lawful for Christians to use contracts?'[16]. Melanchthon's answer is articulated in two levels. First, he writes that the Gospel does not abolish political or economic ordinances and therefore does not abolish the natural laws.[17] Contracts

12 We will discuss it more in detail in the following paragraphs. K. Glamann, *The Changing Patterns of Trade*, in E.E. Rich, C.H. Wilson, *The Cambridge Economic History of Europe Vol. V, The Economic Organization of Early Modern Europe*, Cambridge, London, New York, Melbourne, Cambridge University Press, 1983, 185-289 (192).

13 M. Luther, *Von Kaufshandlung und Wucher*, in WA 15, 293: "*Das kan man aber nicht leucken, das keuffen und verkeuffen ehn nottig ding ist, des man nicht emperen und wol Christlich brauchen kan sonderlich ihn den dingen, die zur nott und ehren dienen*".

14 M. Luther, *Von Kaufshandlung und Wucher*, in WA 15, 293.

15 J.S. Oyer, *Lutheran Reformers Against Anabaptists*, 140-78.

16 P. Melanchthon, *Catechesis puerilis*, in CR XXIII, 166: "*Licetne Christianis uti contractibus?*".

17 P. Melanchthon, *Catechesis puerilis*, in CR XXIII, 166: "*Licet, iuxta usitatam regulam: Evangelium non abolet ordinationes politicas aut oeconomicas, et quidem iura naturae non abolet*".

are of natural law because human life requires the mutual exchange made through contracts.[18] Second, Melanchthon argues:

> *Christians must know that a contract is an ordinance of God as other political ordinances; in a similar manner, Solomon said that the balance and the weight are the judgments of God, which means that they are justly ordained by God.*[19]

The passage contains two parts. In the first part Melanchthon states that contracts are *ordinances of God as other political ordinances* (*contractus esse ordinationem dei, sicut alias politicas ordinationes*). He adopts the term: 'political ordinance' (*ordinatio politica*). This term derives from an ensemble of sources, including Paul's letter to the Romans.[20] The original Greek word *διαταγή* was translated with the Latin *ordinatio*, which in modern English means 'ordinance' or 'command'. Indeed, in the passage of Rom. 13,1-2 Paul writes:

> *Let every soul be subject unto the higher powers. For there is no power but of God: the powers that be are ordained of God. Whosoever therefore resisteth the power, resisteth the ordinance of God: and they that resist shall receive to themselves damnation.*

God assigns the political ordinance, and the only power belongs to God; the political ordinance is therefore a creation of the power of God.

In the second part of the passage, Melanchthon harks back to the book of Proverbs (Prov. 11,1), where Solomon said: "*a false balance is abomination to the Lord: but a just weight is his delight*". Solomon recognises that the balance and weights are instruments of God, derived from the power of God. The balance is the judgment of God, and if it is used wrongly, God intervenes, preserving his creations.[21] The passage, clarifies Melanchthon, also contains a threat: God punishes atrocious crimes in this life too, as it is written: "*all they that take the sword shall perish with the sword*" or "*the plunderer who plundered will be in*

18 P. Melanchthon, *Catechesis puerilis*, in CR XXIII, 166: "*Sunt autem contractus iuris naturae, quia vita humana habet opus mutua communicatione, quae fit per contractus*".

19 P. Melanchthon, *Catechesis puerilis*, in CR XXIII, 166: "*Quare sciat Christianus, contractus esse ordinationem dei, sicut alias politicas ordinationes, quemadmodum et Salomon dixit: libra et pondus, iudicia Domini sunt, id est, res a Deo iuste ordinatae*".

20 R.B. Huschke, *Melanchthons Lehre vom Ordo politicus*, 151. For a more complete description see I/2.

21 P. Melanchthon, *Explicatio proverbiorum Salomonis*, in CR XIV, 27: "... *et efficaciter a Deo conservari, quantum ordinis relinquum manet, etiamsi a diaboli et ab organis diaboli interea magni tumultus moventur*".

turn plundered".[22] This aspect is an important feature of Melanchthon's thinking on contract regulation that we will examine later. The admonition, though, Melanchthon insists critically, is against the madness of the Anabaptists,[23] who should be warned that God will punish their errors.

Recapitulating, contracts are founded on natural law. The use of contracts is a necessity that even the patriarchs acknowledged. But even more, contracts are a divine ordinance, which God himself guarantees. Scripture further reveals that contracts are a creation of God, which makes them fully useable and which forms the foundations for the Lutheran regulation of contracts.

2.1.3 *The Response of the Lutheran Orthodoxy*

The *Palea Ejiciens* appended to Gratian's *Decretum* contained a passage erroneously attributed to John Chrysostom (349-407) forbidding Christians to be merchants because merchants will never follow God; and if any wish to be merchants, they have to leave the Church.[24] Martin Chemnitz observes that this is proof that the question of the lawfulness of business is not new, but was already discussed by medieval philosophers and jurists. The *Palea Ejiciens* was indeed the traditional location used by canon lawyers and scholastic theologians to discuss the question of the lawfulness of business and interest.[25] Now the question involves not only merchants but also the legal instruments of commercial enterprise. Contracts, inasmuch as they are instruments of business, lead to damnation.

Drawing upon Melanchthon, Chemnitz argues that:

> *the Gospel does not abolish the political and economic ordinances, which are built on the natural law (because it is the truth of God instilled in human hearts), but teaches how* (quomodo) *these ordinances must be piously used. The Holy Scripture includes several evidences that lawful contracts are not against faith, but they are*

---

22 P. Melanchthon, *Explicatio proverbiorum Salomonis*, in CR XIV, 27: "*Et comminatio saepe repetita: atrocia delicta puniuntur atrocibus poenis, etiam in hac vita*".

23 P. Melanchthon, *Explicatio proverbiorum Salomonis*, in CR XIV, 27.

24 M. Chemnitz, *Loci theologici*, pars secunda, 156: "Gratianus *distinctio 88 cap. eiiciens* (D. 88 C. 11), *citat sententiam Chrysostomi*: "quod nullum Christianus debet esse mercator, quia mercator nunquam potest Deo placere. Et si quis voluerit esse mercator, debet eiici de Ecclesia". The words do not exactly correspond to the *Decretum*. Perhaps he paraphased the text.

25 See bibliography quoted before. In particular, J.T. Noonan, Jr., *The Scholastic Analysis of Usury*, 38; J.A. Baldwin, *Masters*, 261-9. For a concrete example in the scholastic texts, see L. Lessius, book 2, chapter 20, dub. 1, nr. 4 L. Lessius *De iustitia et iure*, book 2, chapter 20, dub. 1, nr. 4 = L. Lessius, *On Sale, Securities, and Insurance*, translated by W. Decock, N. De Sutter, Grand Rapids MI, CLP Academic, Refo500, 2016, 11.

> *a divinely approved ordinance that pious men have used and can continue to use without harming their conscience.*[26]

The Gospel, therefore, does not abolish contracts but teaches the right way of using contracts. In other words, Scripture fixes the limits of contractual norms. It admits contracts, but requires that they be regulated. To Chemnitz Scripture does not only concede contracts but also requires and provides a regulation for them.

The medieval theologians and canonists argued for the lawfulness of commerce mainly on the basis of Aristotle and practical considerations, like the fact that merchants produce a good service for society.[27] Chemnitz' approach is different, because the Holy Scripture is the central authority. Chemnitz sounded out the whole Scripture to determine the exact nature of contracts. Eventually, he singled out three arguments that justify the lawfulness of business and contracts. The first argument is that the seventh commandment decrees the lawful exchange of goods. The exchange is allowed only towards people who have goods to exchange. It thus is not theft; and it is forbidden to ask a payment from the poor. God wants lawful and determinate forms of exchange, Chemnitz continues, because in the book of Proverbs, the wife who has the fear of God "*considereth a field and buyeth it; with the fruit of her hands she planteth a vineyard*", because "*she perceiveth that her merchandise is good*" and "*she maketh fine linen and selleth it, and delivereth girdles unto the merchant*" (Prov. 31,16, 18 and 24). Because in all these passages, buying, trading and merchants are described in positive terms, for Chemnitz this is a first proof of the permissibility of contracts.

The second argument is similar to Luther's and concerns the government of the Jews under Moses (*politia mosaica*). God ordained several forms of contracts: sale, rent, employment, deposit, pledge, loan, works, supply and services contracts, as some examples demonstrate. Abraham, Jacob and Joseph all employed contracts, and as examples of faith, their actions should be considered. Third, in the New Testament contracts were not abrogated. Contracts can be used if they do not harm charity. For example, the rule of 1 Cor. 7,30 and

---

26 M. Chemnitz, *Loci theologici*, pars secunda, 156: "*His opponantur firma et solida fundamenta ex Scriptura, ut regula illa, quae certa et immota est, quod Evangelium non abolet ordinationes politicas et oeconomicas, quae ex iure naturae extructae sunt* (*quia ius legis scriptum in cordibus, est veritas Dei patefacta ab ipso Deo*) *sed docet, quomodo illis ordinationibus pie utendum sit. Et extant testimonia in Scriptura, quae probant, usum legitimorum contractuum non adversari fidei; sed esse ordinationem, quae Deo probatur, qua pii et usi sunt et uti possunt, sine laesione conscientiae*".

27 J.W. Baldwin, *The Medieval Theories of the Just Price*, 63-7.

1 Thess. 4,6 indicate the way of using contracts. Another valid argument comes from Luke, 3,13. The tax collectors asked John the Baptist what they should do in their lives, and John answered: "*Exact no more than that which is appointed you*". Chemnitz observes that John does not forbid them from collecting taxes, but only asks them to do it lawfully. It applies to business too, because John uses the word *πράσσετε* (to transact public business, to exact revenue), which is appropriate for business.[28] It is not that contracts are forbidden, but it is the abuse of them that is not allowed.

Thus, Chemnitz concludes that without any doubt, contracts are divine ordinances and God ordained some types of contracts in the Mosaic government (*politia mosaica*). However, after the Mosaic law, the pagans constituted other forms of contracts by political legislation. The question is whether Christians can use such contracts in good conscience. The answer, Chemnitz says, is simple and plain. The solution he proposes comes again from the letters of Paul and the Gospel of Luke. In Corinth, Chemnitz explains, many shops existed and many contracts were used, some of them also constituted by pagan legislators. Paul wrote to them neither to return to the Mosaic forms, nor to become legislators and prescribe peculiar forms. Paul wrote to them to use the contracts that were in agreement with natural law. These contracts must be used according to faith (1 Cor. 7,30) without defrauding the neighbour (1 Thess. 4,6).[29] Although pagans instituted new contractual forms, they can be used when they are in agreement with natural law and faith. Natural law serves as a parameter to verify the lawfulness of these new forms of contract.

To sum up, Chemnitz does not only argue that contracts are lawful, but also that Scripture both requires that contracts are regulated and includes contractual norms for the right use of them. It is the wrong use of contracts that is forbidden by the Holy Scripture and not the contracts themselves.

Conrad Dieterich and Johann Franz Buddeus followed Martin Chemnitz' opinion. In his *Institutiones catecheticae* (1613), Dieterich wondered whether contracts and business are lawful. His answer is that contracts and business are lawful if they are executed in a just and lawful manner (*si iusto modo et legitime perficiantur*). He classifies five reasons for the lawfulness of contracts. Four of them are the same as Chemnitz. The fifth instead concerns the fact that society cannot be conserved without contracts and bargains.[30] This last argument is new and not developed by Chemnitz. It is based on the works

---

28 M. Chemnitz, *Loci theologici*, pars secunda, 156.

29 M. Chemnitz, *Loci theologici*, pars secunda, 156-7.

30 K. Dieterich, *Institutiones catecheticae e B. Lutheri catechesi depromptae*, (ed. A.W. Dieckhoff), Berolini, 1864, 125.

of Jean Bodin[31] (1529-1596) and the Roman Catholic jurist Petrus Gregorius Tholosanus[32] (1540-1597). Contracts, Dieterich argues, are useful and necessary. Indeed, in his *Les Six Livres de la République* (1576), Jean Bodin remembers that there are many cities and regions that are infertile and without trade cannot permit citizens to live comfortably. The merchants are as ministers, labourer and carriers, because they transfer the necessary goods to these places, writes Gregorius Tholosanus. Therefore, the Anabaptist opinion that condemns contracts, Dieterich concludes, is wrong.[33]

Johann Franz Buddeus reused some of the reasons proposed by Chemnitz and then Dieterich in his *Institutiones theologiae moralis* (1711). Buddeus observes that using contracts was never prohibited to Christians. Except in cases when contracts provide something against divine law, the Holy Scripture approves them (Prov. 11,1; 16,2; Lev. 19,35). Furthermore, God prescribed certain forms of contracts, as sale, rent etc. in the *politia mosaica* (Lev. 25,14; Deut. 15,2, 12). Finally, in the New Testament, contracts were not prohibited; only fraud and deceit were forbidden (Luke 3,13; 1 Thess. 4,6; James 4,13).[34]

Chemnitz and his followers countered wisely the most of Anabaptists' arguments against business and contracts. However, they did not tackle directly the last claim of the Anabaptists (frauds are committed in business and contracts because of the desire for profit). Other authors who examined the issue, such as Lucas Osiander[35] (1571-1638), noted that Anabaptists were focusing on an accident and not on the substance of contracts.[36] Similarly, Friedrich Balduin

31 M. Turchetti, *Jean Bodin*, in *The Stanford Encyclopedia of Philosophy* (Spring 2015 Edition, revision 2018), Edward N. Zalta (ed.), http://plato.stanford.edu/archives/spr2015/entries/bodin/ (accessed 13.12.2017).

32 K. Dieterich, *Institutiones catecheticae*, 126. The reference is to the fourth book of the *De republica*, c. 7, 121, n. 2. Tholosanus is not unknown among the Lutheran theologians. He was also quoted by Gerhard about the role of the magistrate. See J. Gerhard, *Loci theologici*, (ed. Preuss, 1878), tomus sextus, locus XXIV, p. I, c. 5, nr. 122, 319; M. Schmoeckel, *Ein Denker des Ausgleichs*, in M. Friedrich, S. Salatowsky, L. Schorn-Schütte (eds.), *Konfession, Politik und Gelehrsamkeit*, 31.

33 K. Dieterich, *Institutiones catecheticae*, 126.

34 J.F. Buddeus, *Institutiones theologiae moralis*, 538: "*De contractibus etiam generatim id saltem observamus, quod christianis eos inire neutiquam sit prohibitum. Praeterquam enim quod in se nihil contineant, quod iuri divino repugnet, scriptura sacra diserte eos adprobat Proverb. XI, 1, XVI, 11, Levit. XIX, 35. Ipse quoque Deus, certas contractuum formulas, ut emtionis, venditionis, locationis et c. in politia Mosaica praescripsit, Levit. XXV, 12. Deut. XV, 2, 12. Nec in novo testament interdicti leguntur. Admonemur saltem, ne fraudi et imposturae in illis locum concedamus, Luc. III, 13, 1 Thessal. IV, 6, Iacob IV, 13*".

35 T. Schott, *Osiander, Lucas II*, in *Allgemeine Deutsche Biographie* 24 (1887), 495-6 (accessed 13.12.2017); http://www.deutsche-biographie.de/pnd117154547.html?anchor=adb.

36 L. Osiander, *Enchiridion controversiarum*, 233-4.

maintained that Anabaptists are not refusing contracts themselves, but the abuse of contracts. When merchants are focusing on profit, forgetting the law of charity, or defrauding the neighbour, they commit sins, but the contract in itself is lawful. Christ does not expel contracts from the temple, but its exercise in a sacred place.[37] The Holy Scripture therefore allows contracts, but their use must be regulated.

In the end, the Anabaptists maintained a claim for the illegitimacy of business and contracts. The Holy Scripture, they said, decrees that they should be avoided because they are sinful. The Lutheran theologians responded to the Anabaptists' claim, proving that it is not that business and contracts are unlawful, but it is only their abuse that is forbidden. The Holy Scripture authorizes the use of contracts, but requires keeping them in line with norms that it dictates. The Lutheran theologians in some ways treated the Holy Bible as the modern jurists approach the constitution. They determined the lawfulness of contracts in the light of superior principles and fixed the limits within which contractual forms are valid and can be applied. The question of the lawfulness of contracts is therefore not a banal one. Rather, it represents a valid attempt to judge the validity of a system of norms in the light of a complex body of values. It shows the method of reasoning of Lutheran theologians, who found in the Holy Scripture the fundamental pillars of their normative system.

2.2 The 'Right Use' of Contracts

2.2.1 *Introduction*

The Lutheran theologians acknowledged the lawfulness of contracts and advocated that only their wrong use is forbidden. What is, though, the use of contracts that is admitted? The question concerns the foundations of contract law: the guideline principles of contract regulation. As discussed in the previous paragraph, it is also not a new question, because first the Church Fathers and then medieval theologians and canonists were concerned with something very similar: they looked for a solution against avarice and the fraudulent practices of merchants. The Roman law contained a system of protection against fraud that was adopted by canonists and medieval theologians.[38]

37 F. Baldwin, *Tractatus*, 954.

38 J.A. Baldwin, *The Medieval Theories of the Just Price*, 54-7; 67-8 and J.A. Baldwin, *Masters*, 264-5. For a more detailed analysis see W. Ernst, *Irrtum. Ein Streifzug durch die Dogmengeschichte*, in R. Zimmermann (ed.), *Störungen der Willensbildung bei Vertragschluss*, Tübingen, Mohr Siebeck, 2007, 1-34.

The scholastics elaborated a theory of fairness in exchange based on the natural law in relation to Aristotelian-Thomistic virtue of commutative justice, the Ulpian's do-no-harm principle and the seventh commandment of the Decalogue (*you shall not steal*).[39] According to Thomas Aquinas, equality must be maintained between what is given and what is received in an exchange. The early modern scholastics further explained that natural law commands that you should not do unto others what you would not have them do unto you; and equality must be observed between the objects of exchanges as is required by commutative justice.[40] The virtue of commutative justice, in turn, is comprised in the three basic rules of Ulpian: living honestly (*honeste vivere*), not harming the other (*alterum non laedere*) and giving everyone his due (*suum cuique tribuere*). Commutative justice and the rules of Ulpian were eventually attributed to the significance of the seventh precept of the Decalogue: you shall not steal.[41] Therefore, the scholastic theory of fairness in exchange was based upon a series of sources that in the end rested on the natural law as an expression of natural reason.

Behind this theory stood the idea that life is a road for the purification of sins. As some medieval theologians had established, the justice of God requires the payment of the debt into which our sins place us, and salvation is obtained only by reparation for committed sins. In the words of Aquinas, the satisfaction removes the offence through a reparatory punishment. It is an act of justice that restores the equality between God and the sinner.[42] In the end, as we will see also later, divine justice is reflected in a number of ramifications related to contractual justice.

In total antithesis to this view, Martin Luther contended that justice is the faith given by the word of God.[43] Man is justified by his faith without the need of any reparatory punishment.[44] On this basis, the Lutheran theologians

---

39 W. Decock, *Theologians and Contract Law*, 507-19.

40 W. Decock, *Theologians and Contract Law*, 511-2.

41 W. Decock, *Theologians and Contract Law*, 514.

42 T. Aquinas, *Summa theologiae*, III[a] q. 49 a. 3 ad 2: "*Unde oportet quod illi qui post Baptismum peccant, configurentur Christo patienti per aliquid poenalitatis vel passionis quam in seipsis sustineant*". T. Aquinas, *Summa theologiae*, IaIIae, q. 87, art. 6, ad. 3: "*Requiritur autem adhuc poena ad sanationem aliarum virium animae, quae per peccatum praecedens deordinatae fuerunt, ut scilicet per contraria curentur. Requiritur etiam ad restituendum aequalitatem iustitiae; et ad amovendum scandalum aliorum, ut aedificentur in poena qui sunt scandalizati in culpa; ut patet ex exemplo de David inducto*".

43 M. Luther, *Preface to the Letter of St. Paul to the Romans* (1552), in LW 6, 447-62.

44 On this problem see I/2. For a brief account see: O.H. Pesch, *Theologie der Rechtfertigung bei Martin Luther und Thomas von Aquin: Versuch eines systematisch-theologischen Dialogs*, Mainz, Grünewald-Verlag, 1985.

shaped three general principles: faith and charity, protection against fraud, and contractual equality. These principles recall partially the medieval solutions but positioned them most of all on the solid stronghold of the Holy Scripture, despite recourse to other sources like Aristotle, the scholastic theology and Roman law.

2.2.2 *Faith and Charity*

2.2.2.1 Introduction

The scholastic theory of fairness in exchange centred on justice in contractual relationships. Justice is giving to each one what is due so that if one of the parties does not do it he must pay for the offence. As already noted, behind this rigid theory remains the justification by law, where salvation is gained through the payment of the debts for the offences made. The Lutherans, however, followed the theory of justification by faith. According to this approach, faith in Christ's atoning work, granted by the Holy Spirit, justifies man. From faith follows charity or love[45] as thanksgiving for the salvation obtained.[46] This dynamic interaction between faith and charity affects contracts too. Faith allows the full recognition that contracts are a creation of God, while charity operates in two ways. On the one hand, charity pushes each party to take care of the needs of the other party. In this sense it stimulates right behaviours and aims to promote the other contracting party's interest. On the other hand, charity forbids fraudulent acts and tricks against the other party. In this sense it prohibits wrong behaviours and aims to protect both contracting parties.

2.2.2.2 Genesis: Melanchthon and Chemnitz

Luther was not concerned with contracts in general but only focused on determinate aspects. Melanchthon, instead, assumed that contracts are a divine ordinance, a creation of God founded on natural law. The Gospel does not abolish this ordinance.[47] The Christian must know that contracts are divine ordinances and that God ordained contracts to promote our practice of mutual charity.[48] The Christian must use contracts in faith, as a gift of God, and

45 The theologians adopted both the terms: *dilectio* (love) and *charitas* (charity). We have opted for charity.

46 See for instance M. Luther, *Commentary on Galatians* (1535), in LW 26, 133: "*Quia apprehendisti fide Christum per quem iustus es, nunc eas et diligas Deum et proximum*".

47 P. Melanchthon, *Catechesis puerilis*, in CR XXIII, 166.

48 P. Melanchthon, *Catechesis puerilis*, in CR XXIII, 166: "*Sed in primis consideret Christianus finem illarum ordinationum principalem. Deus enim haec dona ordinavit ad hunc finem, ut per ea mutuam charitatem exerceamus*".

know that charity towards the neighbour must be practiced in these duties.[49] Christians must not defraud the other party nor use the contract to trick the neighbour.[50]

The so-called 'second Martin', Martin Chemnitz, has the principal merit to have developed the thinking of Melanchthon. Chemnitz begins his section on contracts by writing that there are two universal rules: the first one is that God does not abolish political ordinances that are in agreement with natural law, as we already discussed it in the previous paragraph. The second rule derives from Paul, Col. 3,17: "*and whatsoever ye do in word or deed, do all in the name of the Lord Jesus, giving thanks to God and the Father by him*".[51] This passage does not only concern spiritual issues, but also everything of this world, as Paul says in 1 Cor. 10,31: "*whether therefore ye eat, or drink, or whatsoever ye do, do all to the glory of God*". Thus Chemnitz comments: "*the Word of God is needed so that by faith it is sure that contracts are an ordinance of God and that God likes them*".[52] In other words, faith allows the full recognition of contracts as divine creation.

Faith is, however, inevitably conjoined with charity, prompting Chemnitz to carry on with the following principle: "*civil contracts must be practiced so that in those civil duties faith is looked to attentively and charity is practiced*".[53] Faith is seen as the measure which prevents the Christian from doing something with a doubting and corrupted conscience, and which lets him know that the contract is not against the Word of God, but rather is approved by Him: "*He* (the Christian) *must commit his way of life to God, he must hope and ask for benediction, and if an evil event occurs, obey God*".[54] Chemnitz is very clear that using faith in contracts means acknowledging that they are a just ordinance of God and praying for God's guidance in forming contracts and for His blessing over contracts that are made. He encourages believers not to exclude contracts from the spiritual life, but rather use them as a divine instrument given by God.

At the same time, charity follows faith:

---

49 P. Melanchthon, *Catechesis puerilis*, in CR XXIII, 166: "*Quare Christianus in fide utetur contractibus, tanquam dono Dei et sciet his officiis exercendam esse charitatem erga proximum*".

50 P. Melanchthon, *Catechesis puerilis*, in CR XXIII, 166.

51 Col. 3,17.

52 M. Chemnitz, *Loci theologici*, pars secunda, 155: "*Requiritur itaque verbum Dei, ut fide certa sit, esse Dei ordinationem, Deo placere*".

53 M. Chemnitz, *Loci theologici*, pars secunda, 157: "*Regula enim est: ita esse exercendos contractus civiles, ut in illis civilibus officiis conspiciatur fides et exerceatur dilectio*".

54 M. Chemnitz, *Loci theologici*, pars secunda, 157: "*Fides hoc modo, ne quid geratur dubitante vel faucia conscientia; sed sciat non pugnare cum verbo Dei; sed probari, Deo commendet viam, speret, petat benedictionem et siquid sinistri acciderit, Deo obediat*".

> *God desired that humanity be linked by varied duties, for which reason he allocated goods and works, so that the members of the human race require exchange with others.*[55]

One who has money does not very often have goods and vice versa. So one who has money but not goods and one who has goods but not money can practice charity by the contract of sale. Or, if both of them have goods but not money, they can opt for barter. If the owner does not want to transfer completely the property right, and another one does not have enough money to buy it, they can agree to transfer the right to use the good for a certain time through a contract of rent. If one does not have goods or money, he can offer to work. If one has neither goods nor money nor work to offer, he can be raised up by loan or donation. If one fears that his counterpart in the bargain may not pay in full, they can make a pledge. In this way, Chemnitz annotates, God wanted that charity be practiced: not only towards the poor, but also towards every man in the whole political society.[56] Charity is therefore exercised in using the right form of exchange depending upon the neighbour's need. Correct appraisal of the need is the key concept for understanding Chemnitz' idea of charity. Every man needs something, not only the poor. Since my neighbour needs something, I can help him by establishing a contract. At the same time, he will help me, giving something else I need. The mutual exchange that is realized by contracts becomes an instrument to help each other.

Chemnitz' view on faith and charity arises from an economic view that is set forth in the thirty-first chapter of the book of Proverbs: Prov. 31,20: "*she stretcheth out her hand to the poor; yea, she reacheth forth her hands to the needy*"; Prov. 31,21: "*she is not afraid of the snow for her household, for all her household are clothed with scarlet*"; and Prov. 31,23: "*her husband is known at the gates, where he sitteth among the elders of the land*". Chemnitz interprets these passages by asserting that the aim of business is: 1) providing to yourself, family and home; 2) giving something to the poor; and 3) contributing to support the financial burdens of the state.[57] This interpretation makes clear that charity is also a way to harmonize the allocation of goods. Contracts are instruments

55 M. Chemnitz, *Loci theologici*, pars secunda, 157: "*Charitas ita exerceatur: voluit Deus genus humanum variis officiis consociatum esse, ideo et res et operas ita distribuit, ut alterius communicatione indigeat*".

56 M. Chemnitz, *Loci theologici*, pars secunda, 157: "*Ita voluit Deus exercere charitatem, non tantum erga pauperes; sed in tota politica societate erga omnes homines*".

57 M. Chemnitz, *Loci theologici*, pars secunda, 157: "*Sunt igitur fines: 1. Si sibi, domui, familiae prospicit, pro conditione status sui, non peccat; 2. Pauperibus inde aliquid largiatur 3. Conferatur aliquid ad sustinenda onera reipub.*".

of this allocation, because they allow the exchange of goods. Charity affects the exchange of goods as a positive impulse to give to the other party what he needs. Obviously charity does not only have this meaning, remarks Chemnitz. It also means the absence of deceit, fraud, etc. in both the forming and execution of the contract. Indeed, when the right form of contract has been selected, it cannot permit fraud or deceit in the formation – but it also must be fulfilled without sins.[58] In short, charity both invites Christians to take care of the neighbour's needs and forbids fraud.

2.2.2.3 Further Applications: Dieterich, Selnecker, Dürr, Baier and Buddeus

Other theologians followed the approach centred on faith and charity. For example, Nikolaus Selnecker, a disciple of Melanchthon and author of the *Formula of Concord* together with Martin Chemnitz, also makes use of the idea of charity in contracts. He writes that "*charity deriving from faith must shine in every contract, and in contracts nothing must be done that is in conflict with the charity of the law*".[59] He does not explain clearly what he wants to say; but it seems to be clear that he intends charity as a prohibition of wrongdoing against the other contracting party. Conrad Dieterich (1575-1639), in his *Institutiones catecheticae*, quotes Chemnitz: "*civil contracts must be practiced so that in those duties faith be looked to attentively and love* (dilectio) *be practiced*". Yet, he does not accurately report Chemnitz' entire idea. Faith is contemplated, Dieterich specifies, so that the conscience is not wounded, while love is exercised so that deceit, fraud and illusions do not harm the neighbour.[60] Dieterich quotes Chemnitz and refers to charity as the absence of frauds.

Some theologians used charity to define the aim of contracts. Referring to Aristotle's *Politics*, the scholastics assumed that contracts were introduced for the common good and for the benefit of both parties.[61] By contrast, Johann Konrad Dürr in his *Compendium theologiae moralis* (1675) argues that God introduced contracts not only on account of human contractors' mutual need, but also because through them we exercise Christian charity, friendship and

---

58 M. Chemnitz, *Loci theologici*, pars secunda, 157.

59 N. Selnecker, *Paedagogiae christianae pars prima continens decalogi explicationem*, Jenae, 1568, 212: "*In omni contractu caritas ex fide manans praelucere debet, et nihil in contractibus faciendum, quod cum legis caritate pugnat*".

60 K. Dieterich, *Institutiones catecheticae*, 126: "*Placebit nobis* Dominus Chemnitii *regula*: ita exercendos esse contractus civiles, ut conspiciatur in illis civilibus officiis fides, et exerceatur dilectio. *Fides, ne qua conscientia saucietur; dilectio, ne quoquo modo imposturis, fraudibus, praestigiis proximo noceatur*".

61 W. Decock, *Theologians and Contract Law*, 510-1.

integrity.[62] Similarly, Johann Wilhelm Baier in his *Compendium theologiae moralis* (1697) states that contracts are instituted so that Christians can exercise love (*dilectio*) and so that the people that are negotiating with us also receive benefits.[63] These authors set contracts in a context of faith and charity. They do not give further details, but it seems to be clear that they use charity, as the promotion of the other party's interest.

Johann Franz Buddeus merits a special consideration because he proposed a further meaning of charity in contracts. Charity is associated with justice and signifies the prohibition of wrongdoing in contracts.[64] But it also specifies duties for gratuitous contracts and onerous contracts. In gratuitous contracts, as for example a donation, the neighbour must always receive a benefit, and the benefit must not create damage.[65] Under onerous contracts, charity means keeping contractual norms but also not being too rigorous against the other party who could not fulfil the contractual norms without his fault.[66]

To Buddeus charity not only forbids offences but also guarantees that the other party gains effectively some benefit from the contract. Furthermore, and this point was not developed by his predecessors, charity is utilized as a general principle of equity in the relationship between the parties. It tempers the rigidity of law in favour of the other party. So, in case the terms of contracts are breached without fault, charity urges the wronged party not to blame the defaulting party and possibly not to ask for compensation. In this way, Buddeus carries even further the meaning of charity, as compassion for and restraint from (even legally justified) retaliation against the other party.

In conclusion, faith allows the recognition that contracts, as a creation of God, are therefore to be used in charity. Charity in contracts tended to remain somewhat open. On the one hand, charity worked as a general clause prohibiting all the possible offences against the other party, especially fraud and other deceit. On the other hand, charity pushed to use contracts in order to benefit and to fulfil the needs or assist the difficulties of the less powerful party. If these principles seem too theological, we do not have to forget that they were formulated for the *forum internum* and not for the *forum externum*. They aimed to be applied in confessions or for the education of the Christians. There

62 J.K. Dürr, *Compendium theologiae moralis*, Altdorffi, 1675, 219.

63 J.W. Baier, *Compendium theologiae moralis*, 489.

64 J.F. Buddeus, *Institutiones theologiae moralis*, 544: "*Charitatis scilicet pariter ac iustitiae ratio postulat, ne quid committamus, unde damnum aliquod in alterum redundare queat*".

65 J.F. Buddeus, *Institutiones theologiae moralis*, 544.

66 J.F. Buddeus, *Institutiones theologiae moralis*, 544: "*In* onerosis *idem demonstratur, si leges contractus accurate observemus: sed tamen charitatis quoque est, ne erga illos, qui praeter culpam suam leges istas tam accurate observare nequeunt, nimis rigorosi simus*".

were not designed for the secular courts, but for the spiritual courts and for the conscience.

2.2.3 *The Protection against Fraud*

2.2.3.1 Introduction

Faith and charity do not have to be understood as abstract, sentimental and in essence vague principles of contract law. Conversely, they were intended to have a very concrete meaning. On the one hand, as we have already seen, faith and charity formed a general framework of contract regulation, establishing an open catalogue of duties between the contractual parties. On the other hand, they found an appropriate objective form in relation to two other principles established by the seventh commandment of the Decalogue: the prohibition of fraud and equality in contracts. In relation to these principles, they were expanded upon, yielding more detailed accounts, which we are now going to examine.

2.2.3.2 Luther: *sola Scriptura*

According to Martin Luther, the seventh commandment forbids gaining any kind of advantage in trade that works to the disadvantage of the neighbour.[67] In particular, these abuses include:

> *where one openly defrauds another with bad merchandise, false measures, weights, coins, and by nimbleness and queer finances or dexterous tricks takes advantage of him; likewise, when one overcharges a person in a trade and wantonly drives a hard bargain, skins and distresses him.*[68]

Luther proposes a body of rules: exchanged goods must be without defects; measures and weight must be real and not false; money must be authentic; no frauds in contracts are admitted; and goods must be sold at a just price. These duties are a derivation of charity, lending to it greater substance.

In another passage Luther states:

> *let every one know that it is his duty, at the risk of God's displeasure, not only to do no injury to his neighbor, nor to deprive him of gain, nor to perpetrate any act*

---

67 M. Luther, *Der große Katechismus, nach der Fassung des deutschen Konkordienbuches*, Dresden, 1580, 224. See also 250-1.

68 M. Luther, *Der große Katechismus*, 227: "*Also auch fort auf dem Markt und Gemeinden Händeln geht es mit voller Macht und Gewalt, da einer den anderen öffentlich mit falscher Ware, Maß, Gewicht, Münze betrügt und mit Behendigkeit und seltsamen Finanzen oder geschwinden Fündlein übervorteilt, weiter mit dem Kauf übersetzt und nach seinem Mutwillen beschwert, schindet und plagt*".

of unfaithfulness or malice in any bargain or trade, but faithfully to preserve his property for him, to secure and promote his advantage, especially when one accepts money, wages, and one's livelihood for such service.[69]

Luther not only condemns the offences against the other contracting party, but also endorses preserving his property and promoting his interests. This last aspect fully reveals the significance of charity: promoting the other contracting party's interest. In addition, to Luther charity consists in a particular attention to the poor. The 'poor' are not only the people who do not have anything, but the poor are also those who are victims of the wrong use of the market, as it is revealed in another passage:

no more shall all the rest prosper who change the open free market into a carrion pit of extortion and a den of robbery, where the poor are daily overcharged, new burdens and high prices are imposed, and every one uses the market according to his caprice, and is even defiant and brags as though it were his fair privilege and right to sell his goods for as high a price as he please, and no one had a right to say a word against it.[70]

Luther attacks all the intentional alterations of the market, vicious distortions of prices and abuses of powers: any weakening of the other party's capital is banned. In summary, he indicates a body of duties that are related to charity. They concern the other contracting party but also alteration of market equilibrium. This description drafts the framework of a contract regulation that will be expanded by his successors. The fundamental elements are already laid down: transparency, absence of fraud and iniquities; diligent conservation and protection of goods; and enjoining against any alterations of the market.

2.2.3.3 A Detailed Categorization?

The legacy of Luther assumed several forms in the works of his followers. In general, commenting to the seventh commandment, they all condemned illicit acts in contracts, but using different terms: fraud (*fraus*), imposture

69 M. Luther, *Der große Katechismus*, 233: "*Darum wisse ein jeglicher, dass er schuldig ist bei Gottes Ungnaden, nicht allein seinem Nächsten keinen Schaden zu tun noch seinen Vorteil zu entwenden noch im Kaufe oder irgendeinem Handel irgendwelche Untreue oder Tücke zu beweisen, sondern auch sein Gut treulich zu verwahren, seinen Nutzen zu verschaffen und fordern, sonderlich so er Geld, Lohn und Nahrung dafür nimmt*".

70 M. Luther, *Der große Katechismus*, 240: "*Also soll es allen andern gelingen, so aus dem offenen freien Markt nichts denn ein Schindleich und Raubhaus machen, da man täglich die Armen übersetzt, neue Beschwerung und Teuerung macht und jeglicher des Marktes braucht nach seinem Mutwillen, trotzt und stolzt dazu, als habe er gut Fug und Recht, das Seine so teuer zu geben als ihn gelüstet, und soll ihm niemand dreinreden*".

(*impostura*), greediness (πλεονεξία), circumventing (*circumventio*), deceit (*dolus*). Only a few theologians were interested in giving these acts a definition, and an organic classification was lacking. One of the theologians who presented a more accurate description was the famous casuist Friederich Balduin. Contracts, he writes, are a lawful mean to acquire goods only if there are no deceits. Christians should not sell the goods of the other without his consent; they should not impede the buying of goods; they should not sell goods that have no value as valid goods; the buyers should not use false money, but follow the example of Abraham in Gen. 23,16 and weigh out the money according to the common current money.[71] The concept of deceit (*dolus*) includes here a wide range of wrongdoings that affects contracts and the market.

Likewise, the great theologian Johann Gerhard, in his *Loci theologici* describes frauds (*fraudes*) as a species of theft. Contractual frauds (*fraudes in contractibus*) are the following: taking advantage of the neighbour by selling vitiated goods or quoting an unfair price or using an unequal measure, false money, verbal frauds and other impostures.[72] The list is very similar to that of Balduin but not identical. Balduin mentions the prohibition to impede the purchase of goods but not the false measures that are instead reported by Gerhard. The distinction, however, does not permit the argument that they developed a different concept of fraud and deceit. Rather, it seems that the lists are only illustrative and that they wanted to prohibit every kind of trick against the other party. The *dolus* seems not to be distinguished sharply from the *fraus* as it was for the some of the medieval theologians.[73]

Johann Konrad Dannhauer, professor of theology in Strasburg, adopted a different approach. In his *Theologia casualis*, published posthumously in 1706, he also presents a description of the fraud (*fraus*), but focused on the limits. In particular, fraud occurs when you assess the good of the neighbour with shrewdness and not with sagacity.[74] Indeed, if I determine and work toward the good of the neighbour with sagacity, there is no fraud, and the conscience

71 F. Balduin, *Tractatus*, 935: "… *in his contractibus autem omnia fiant absque dolo, ne venalia faciamus alterius bona, praeter eius voluntatem, ne impediamus emptores alios, ne vendamus merces nullius pretii pro bonis, nec emptores pecuniam numerent adulterinam, sed ad exemplum Abrahmi, appendant pecuniam probatae monetae publicae* (Gen. 23,16)".

72 J. Gerhard, *Locorum theologicorum tomus quintus*, Tubingae, 1766, 339. This edition includes annotations that are useful for our topic. However, the most recent edition is the one by E. Preuss, *Ioannis Gerhardi loci theologici* […], 9 vols., Berolini, 1863-1885.

73 J.W. Baldwin, *The Medieval Theories of the Just Price*, 69.

74 J.K. Dannhauer, *Theologia casualis*, Gryphiswaldiae, 1706, 434: "… *fraus est, quando bona proximi mea facio non prudentia sed astutia*".

is safe.[75] Dannhauer resorts to the biblical example of Jacob and Laban (Gen. 30,37-42) to explain his statement; in this example, Laban had promised Jacob all the mottled animals. In order to obtain the best livestock, Jacob took fresh-cut branches from several trees and made white stripes on them. Then he placed the branches in all the watering troughs, so that they would be directly in front of the flocks when they came to drink. When the flocks were in heat and came to drink, they mated in front of the branches. And they bore young that were streaked or speckled or spotted.[76] Whenever the stronger females were in heat, Jacob would place the branches in the troughs in front of the animals so they would mate near the branches, but if the animals were weak, he would not place them there. So the weak animals went to Laban and the strong ones to Jacob.[77] This is not a fraud, Dannhauer comments, but sagacity. Dannhauer's definition is therefore deduced from the Holy Scripture, and it is based on the distinction between shrewdness (*astutia*) and sagacity (*prudentia*). Where there is shrewdness there is fraud; but where there is sagacity, the action is licit.

In many other cases, an accurate description of fraud was lacking. Dieterich uses the term 'deceit' for contracts, by forbidding fraudulent contracts. At the same time he forbids various impostures (*imposturis variis*)[78], the substitution of low-quality good for high-quality ones. Similarly, Johann Konrad Dürr in his *Compendium* classifies contracts with fraud and imposture as illicit ways of acquiring goods.[79] Other prohibitions are for example that of Christian Kortholt[80] (1633-1694), who in his *Theologia moralis* (1716) depicts various arts and frauds (*variae artes et fraudes*) as unlawful means to acquire goods, and he reproaches the people who act fraudulently (*fraudolenter*).[81] Henrich Uffelmann also includes imposture in contracts in the definition of theft.[82]

On the whole, the Lutheran theologians prohibited every contractual fraud, deceit, imposture and wrong action against the other contractual party in an extended meaning, even though they did not always make efforts to define the concepts used. Sometimes, as with Balduin and Gerhard, they gave a list of

75 J.K. Dannhauer, *Theologia casualis*, 434: *"Ubi enim cum prudentia bona conscientia bona proximi mea facere possum, ibi proprie fraus nulla est"*.

76 Gen. 30,37-39.

77 Gen. 30,41-42.

78 K. Dieterich, *Institutiones catecheticae*, 122-3.

79 J.K. Dürr, *Compendium theologiae moralis*, 226.

80 W. Göbell, *Kortholt, Christian*, in *Neue Deutsche Biographie* 12 (1979), 601 f. (accessed 19.01.2018); https://www.deutsche-biographie.de/pnd116341793.html#ndbcontent.

81 C. Kortholt, *Theologia moralis synoptice tractata*, Hafniae, 1716, 55.

82 H. Uffelmann, *Variorum eorumque illustrium conscientiae casuum fasciculus*, Lipsiae et Goslariae, 1709, 128.

examples. But in general they wanted to leave the list of the wrong behaviours open-ended, to be specified in the analysis of the single types of contracts. They therefore configured a principle of not wronging the other contracting party in any manner whatsoever. In this sense, this principle, as an expression of a duty to protect the other party, is an application of charity.

Among the biblical sources, three were frequently quoted.[83] First and foremost, 1 Thess. 4,6: "*That no man go beyond and defraud his brother in any matter: because that the Lord is the avenger of all such, as we also have forewarned you and testified*". This passage assumed capital importance and was the main basis for the prohibition of fraud and, as we will see in the following chapter, was also relevant for the principle of equality in contracts. Second, the passage of Luke 3,13 where John the Baptist said to the tax collector: "*Exact no more than that which is appointed you*". Third, James 4,13: "*To day or to morrow we will go into such a city, and continue there a year, and buy and sell, and get gain*". To understand it we need to quote also the verses 14 and 15:

> *Whereas ye know not what shall be on the morrow. For what is your life? It is even a vapour, that appeareth for a little time, and then vanisheth away. For that ye ought to say, If the Lord will, we shall live, and do this, or that.*

Scripture affirms not focusing on business alone but doing it according to the will of God. Alone or together, these passages were quoted when arguing for the necessity of fair behaviour, without duplicity or fraud, towards the other contractual party.

As already said, 1 Thess. 4,6 received great attention.[84] In particular, the words *ὑπερβαίνω* (go beyond) and *πλεονεκτέω* (taking advantage of, defraud) were interpreted by Melanchthon as a breach of lawful equality in contracts.[85] Indeed, etymologically the word *πλεονεκτέω* means "having more". In this way, as we will see in the following paragraphs, Melanchthon reintroduced the Aristotelian-scholastic virtue of commutative justice. Consequently, many theologians also added commutative justice to the prohibition of frauds. Others, instead, did not mention contractual equality or commutative justice. They did not associate

83 J. Gerhard, *Locorum theologicorum tomus quintus*, 339; J.B. Niemeier, *Theologia moralis*, Helmstadii, 1696, disp. XXV, n. XXIV; J.F. Buddeus, *Institutiones theologiae moralis*, 538.

84 The importance of this passage for contract law was also quite clear to the medieval and early modern theologians and jurists. See for instance H.G. Hermann, *Eigennutz und Übervorteilung: kanonistische Sichtweisen auf eine prekäre Optimierungsstrategie im Vertrag*, in M. Schmoeckel, D. Von Mayenburg, O. Condorelli, F. Roumy (eds.), *Der Einfluss der Kanonistik auf die europäische Rechtskultur 5: Das Recht der Wirtschaft*, Köln, Böhlau, 2016, 203-33.

85 See also the next paragraph.

any further meaning and kept to the literal biblical words. For example, in addition to the aforementioned theologians, we can add Nikolaus Selnecker who describes circumventing (*circumventiones*) and fraud (*fraudes*) in contracts as species of theft.[86] And Johann Bartold Niemeier, professor in Helmstedt, in his *Theologia moralis* (1696) writes that frauds, impostures and taking advantage of another are prohibited in every contract.[87]

Concluding this point, some of the Lutheran theologians condensed the observations of Martin Luther into a general principle of not wronging, not harming and protecting the other contractual party, with several addendums. These theologians remained strongly anchored in the literal meaning of the Holy Scripture, while others, who we are going to examine now, found in the Holy Scripture the inspiration to reintroduce the Aristotelian notion of commutative justice.

2.2.4 *Equality in Contracts*

2.2.4.1 Melanchthon: Equality as Obedience towards God

The duty to protect the other party from fraud was often associated or incorporated in the principle of 'equality in contracts'. The notion of equality in contracts is not explicitly stated in the Holy Scripture, but rather derives from the interpretation of Scripture in relation to Aristotle's *Nicomachean Ethics*. As already seen, Luther adhered more closely to Scripture by only forbidding fraud in contracts, while Melanchthon reintroduced Aristotle's virtue of commutative justice and argued for the necessity to maintain equality in contracts.[88] The use of Aristotle by Melanchthon must not be viewed in the same light as his use by the scholastics, but in the context of Melanchthon's philosophy. The virtue of commutative justice aims to recognise that God is just and teaches God's justice. A natural knowledge of God is possible, because the virtue is a testimony of God's existence. Equality in contracts is also a precept of the seventh commandment and requires perfect obedience. Man can perform external actions. However, because of his sin, he cannot perform the internal

86 N. Selnecker, *Paedagogiae christianae*, 211: "*Tertium genus furti sunt omnes πλεονεξίαι et fraudes in contractibus, in emptione, venditione, mensuris etc.*".

87 J.B. Niemeier, *Theologia moralis*, disp. XXV, n. XXIV: "*Prohibentur etiam fraudes, imposturae, Luc. III, 13, 1 Thess. IV, 6. Jac. IV, 13 et circumventiones per singula contractuum genera ...*".

88 On the use of Aristotle's philosophy see before I/2. See also: R. Schäfer, *Aristoteles/Aristotelismus V*, in *TRE*, v. III, Berlin-New York, 1978, 782-96; N. Kuropka, *Philip Melanchthon and Aristotle*, in I. Dingel, R.Kolb, N. Kuropka, T.J. Wengert (eds.), *Philip Melanchthon, Theologian in Classroom, Confession and Controversy*, Göttingen, Vandenhoeck & Ruprecht, 2012, 19-28. More in general see: P. Petersen, *Geschichte*, passim.

actions that are necessary to fulfil the precept of the law. Thus, the fulfilment of contractual equality depends upon faith and the work of the Holy Spirit.

The doctrine of equality is mainly set forth in Melanchthon's ethical commentaries and is subsequently described in the *Loci theologici*, the *Catechesis puerilis* and in the *Dissertatio de contractibus*. In his *Philosophiae moralis epitome* (1538) and *Ethicae doctrinae elementa* (1550)[89] Melanchthon comments upon Aristotle's doctrine of justice. He observes that because Plato proposed many definitions of justice, it can be difficult to distinguish between them. Aristotle wisely solved the problem by differentiating between universal justice and particular justice. Particular justice is the virtue that governs the duties towards other men in relationship: the order of people, equality in contracts, compensations of crimes and punishments. The definition of particular justice derives from Simonides of Ceos: *justice is the virtue of giving everyone his due* (*suum cuique tribuens*).[90] Melanchthon refers, although it is not cited, to Plato's *De republica*, where Simonides of Ceos is mentioned. Plato's definition of justice is quoted to suggest that Aristotle took his definition from Plato and assigned to it the name 'particular justice'. Subsequently Roman jurists adopted this form of justice and codified it in the Digest.

Particular justice has two species: distributive justice and commutative justice. Distributive justice promotes the civic order that is enforced by magistrates, empires, and families.[91] Commutative justice governs the exchange of goods that are necessary to live. For the conservation of society, the exchange of goods must be perpetual. This exchange occurs by contracts, and in order to perpetuate the exchange, it is necessary to maintain equality in contracts.[92] Indeed, without mutual reciprocity there will never be perpetual exchange, because eventually the supply of goods will end, and people will die from lack of anything to eat.

---

89 They were among his most influential writings and must be understood in the wider context of the reception of Aristotle. See I/2.1.3. In particular on this point: G. Frank, *The Reason of Acting*, 217-8.

90 P. Melanchthon, *Philosophiae moralis epitomes libri duo*, in CR XVI, 65; P. Melanchthon, *Ethicae doctrinae elementorum libri duo*, in CR XVI, 224: "*Est igitur definitio iustitiae particularis, quam recitant iurisconsulti, sumpta a Simonide: iustitia est virtus, suum cuique tribuens*".

91 P. Melanchthon, *Philosophiae moralis epitomes libri duo*, in CR XVI, 65; P. Melanchthon, *Ethicae doctrinae elementorum libri duo*, in CR XVI, 224.

92 P. Melanchthon, *Philosophiae moralis epitomes libri duo*, in CR XVI, 66; P. Melanchthon, *Ethicae doctrinae elementorum libri duo*, in CR XVI, 224: "*Res autem communicamus per contractus, et cum haec communicatio, quae fit victus causa, in infinitum vagetur, necesse est in ea summam aequalitatem effici, hoc est, aequalia pro aequalibus reddi*".

Commutative justice is the justice that preserves equality by arithmetic proportion. Arithmetic proportion consists in the equal distance between different numbers, as for example 3, 6, 9. As is the equality between the numbers, so must be the equality between seller and buyer, so that the human race can be preserved.[93] The exchange of goods can be perpetual only if there is equal compensation between the duties, insists Melanchthon in the *Catechesis puerilis*. If only one of the parties gives and the other one only receives, there will be no eternal exchange.[94] If one of the parties only gains and the other one only loses, after a while the second one will not have anything to exchange. Equality in contracts is therefore necessary for the conservation of society.

Equality in contracts is not only prescribed by Aristotle but also established in the Scriptures. In the *Loci theologici* (third editions) Melanchthon recalls justice in contracts in his comment to the seventh commandment.[95] In another passage he also states that equality has a twofold theological foundation. First, it is an example of the justice of God and of equality in placating God's wrath for human sins. Our sins are only remitted through the 'equal', the Son of God. The daily contracts, like sale, loans, lease and the compensation for damages, recall for us this equality.[96] Salvation came through Christ, who is the divine and human 'equal'. Contractual equality is an image of the equality manifested in Christ; it is a signpost in our daily lives of the divine sacrifice given for humanity.

Second, this equality that is required in contracts teaches us about the love for the neighbour. To Melanchthon, the precept to love the neighbour should be interpreted as requiring equality between you and the neighbour. You shall not increase your advantages with his disadvantages; you shall not oppress him to grow your social standing; you shall not seize his wealth in order to accumulate goods; and finally you shall not seek gain (*πλεονέκτημα*) in things, but love equality, giving to the neighbour what you judge should be given to

93 P. Melanchthon, *Philosophiae moralis epitomes libri duo*, in CR XVI, 66; P. Melanchthon, *Ethicae doctrinae elementorum libri duo*, in CR XVI, 224-5: "*Sicut enim hic omnes termini distant simpliciter aequalibus numeris, sic quaeritur summa aequalitas inter emptorem et venditorem, ut conservari genus humanum possit*".

94 P. Melanchthon, *Catechesis puerilis*, in CR XXIII, 166: "*Ut autem possit esse perpetua communicatio, necesse est effici aequalem compensationem. Si enim una pars tantum daret, altera tantum acciperet, non esset perpetua communicatio*".

95 P. Melanchthon, *Loci communes* (*tertia eorum aetas*), in CR XXI, 709.

96 P. Melanchthon, *Loci communes* (*tertia eorum aetas*), in CR XXI, 1014: "*Cernitur et exemplum iustitiae Dei et aequalitatis in placatione irae Dei. Non sunt remissa peccata nisi aequale λύτρον esset pro nobis, scilicet filius Dei. De hac equalitate quotidiani contractus, emptiones, venditiones, mutuationes, locationes, conductiones, deinde et delictorum compensationes nos admoneant*".

you.[97] Equality is therefore an expression of the fundamental precept to love the neighbour.

In the *Dissertatio de contractibus* Melanchthon writes that God ordered mankind to preserve equality, when he says: *you shall not steal* (Ex. 20,15) and *not go beyond* and *not gain more in business* (1 Thess. 4,6). These passages speak against breaching lawful equality.[98] Melanchthon solders the biblical text to Aristotle's equality, the regulation included in Scripture with Aristotle's ethics. In contractual arrangements, both parties have to strive for equality, which requires that each of the parties obtains the same amount that he gives, and that neither of them is impoverished or enriched by the contract.

Equality does not need to be practiced for our tranquillity, Melanchthon explains, but most of all for God. Because God desires that we love his justice, he admonishes us to keep his justice. God teaches that justice is equality so that we can know that he is impartial and does not have any preference of persons.[99] God invites us to love his divine ordinance in contracts and to know that contracts are examples that remind us of him.[100] To understand this point, we need to recall what was already said in the first part. The Church Fathers and the scholastics distinguished between the image of God in men that was destroyed by original sin and the similarity between men and God that was preserved. Martin Luther maintains that all similarity was lost because of original sin. Melanchthon, however, contends that while original sin destroyed the image, the similarity can be still recovered. God inserted in the human mind the theoretical and practical notions that allow the human mind to participate

---

97 P. Melanchthon, *Loci communes* (*tertia eorum aetas*), in CR XXI, 1014-5: "*Postremo haec ipsa aequalitas, quae in contractibus postulatur, docet nos de dilectione proximi et interpretatio est particulae, sicut, in hoc mandato: dilige proximum sicut te ipsum, id est, sit aequalitas inter te et proximum, non augeas tua commoda cum illius incommodo, non premas eum, ut tua existimatio crescat, non decerpas de eius facultatibus, ut tuas cumules, denique nulla in re quaeras πλεονέκτημα, sed ames aequalitatem, tribuas proximo ea, quae tibi tribuenda esse iudicas*".

98 P. Melanchthon, *Dissertatio de contractibus*, in CR XVI, 495: "*Ideo et de hac aequalitate praecipit Deus, cum inquit (Exod. 20, 15): non furtum facies. Item (1 Thessal. 4,6): non transgredi, nec plus auferre in negotio, id est, non recedere in contractibus a legitima aequalitate*".

99 P. Melanchthon, *Dissertatio de contractibus*, in CR XVI, 495: "*Primum igitur sciamus, non tantum propter nostram tranquillitatem servandam esse hanc aequalitatem, sed multo magis propter Deum. Ideo vult nos amare iustitiam, ut de sua iustitia nos admoneat. Docet iustitiam aequalitatem esse, ut se quoque sciamus aequalem esse, non tyrannum, non acceptatorem personarum*".

100 P. Melanchthon, *Dissertatio de contractibus*, in CR XVI, 496: "*Amemus ergo hanc in contractibus divinam ordinationem, et sciamus in eis proposita esse exempla, commonefacientia nos de Deo*".

in God's own mind.[101] Thus, the knowledge of the virtues is a testimony of God's existence and teaches men the attributes of God: God is just.[102]

Equality is lived as thanksgiving to God for the goods He gave to us. In another passage of the *Loci theologici* Melanchthon writes:

> *you must observe equality for the sake of God who commands you to abstain from other people's things, and thank God who gives you the goods and protects them.*[103]

The desire to establish equality finds its beating heart in the believer's gratitude towards God, who gave the goods and ordained that equilibrium is maintained in the exchange of goods. Contracts are divinely instituted so that through the mutual duties, men declare their obedience towards God. For this reason, Melanchthon insists, they must be observed piously and devoutly.[104]

Together with obedience to God, another essential element is that disobedience of God's law is punished. Breaching the law kindles the wrath of God. In Rom. 13,5, Paul writes that he who resists the ordinance of God shall provoke the wrath of God, and God punishes contractual injustice both by the punishments meted out by civic magistrates and by the disgraces of natural consequences,[105] as in the passages of Isaiah (33,1): "*when thou shalt cease to spoil, thou shalt be spoiled*" and Matthew (26,52): "*all they that take the sword shall perish with the sword*". Atrocious crimes are penalized with proportionate punishment, not only in the eschaton, but also in this life (*etiam in hac vita*), specifies Melanchthon.[106] In the German translation of the *Loci communes* (1559), he explicates that the sin is not only penalized by the magistrate, but also by God himself as the Just Judge (*gerechte Richter*) and Executioner (*Henker*) when the magistrate fails to meet his obligation.[107] God intervenes to punish the disobedience and so protects His law.

101 See I/2.1.3. G. Frank, *The Reason of Acting*, 221-2. See also G. Frank, *Die theologische Philosophie Philipp Melanchthons (1497-1560)*, Leipzig, Benno, 1995.

102 P. Melanchthon, *Ethicae doctrinae elementorum libri duo*, in CR XVI, 166.

103 P. Melanchthon, *Loci communes* (*tertia eorum aetas*), in CR XXI, 725: "*Et non conturbes eam aliis defraudandis, ut saepe divites crescunt iniquis contractibus; sed serves aequalitatem propter Deum, qui iussit te ab alieno abstinere: quare gratitudinem tuam in tuenda aequalitate declares, et agas Deo gratias, qui attribuit tibi et conservat facultates*".

104 P. Melanchthon, *Loci communes* (*tertia eorum aetas*), in CR XXI, 709: "*Et quia contractus divinitus instituti sunt, ut homines inter se mutuis officiis declarent obedientiam suam erga Deum, pie et sancte exercendi sunt*".

105 P. Melanchthon, *Loci communes* (*tertia eorum aetas*), in CR XXI, 709: "*Nam et iniustiam in contractibus punit Deus non solum poenis magistratum, sed etiam aliis cladibus ...*".

106 P. Melanchthon, *Explicatio proverbiorum Salomonis*, in CR XIV, 27: "*Atrocia delicta puniuntur atrocibus poenis, etiam in hac vita*".

107 P. Melanchthon, *Loci theologici germanice*, in CR XXII, 241.

In short, the principle of equality in contracts is based upon Aristotle's commutative justice but is inserted in a theological structure where obedience and disobedience to God appear to be the constitutive elements. God commanded equality in contracts. The virtue of commutative justice is a testimony of the fact that God exists and that He is just. Consequently, equality in contracts must be observed as obedience towards God. The fulfilment of this justice, though, is impossible to man but is entrusted to faith and the Holy Spirit. Faith permits not only the complete realization that contracts are ordinances of God and that God wants equality in contracts, but also allows a humanity disfigured by sin to fulfil this justice while loving God and the neighbour. Disobedience suffers the wrath of the Magistrate but also of God Himself.

Melanchthon nails Aristotle's virtue of commutative justice to the lively interplay between faith and charity. The engine of commutative justice is in this relationship and not in Aristotle's philosophy, which ignores the true ultimate end of human life and the corruption of the original sin.[108] Furthermore, the meaning of commutative justice is, in its entirety, different from the scholastics. Aquinas separated natural virtues (like justice) from supernatural virtues (like charity). Although the natural virtues are imperfect, they nevertheless permit happiness in this life. The supernatural virtues lead to the perfect happiness that is possible only in the afterlife. The critical distinction lies in the thinkers' differing conceptions of the Fall of man. To Aquinas, the virtue of charity is not considered to be the form of all virtues, because human nature is not totally corrupted by the original sin.[109] On the contrary, for Melanchthon commutative justice is a form of charity as obedience towards God. This obedience is only possible by faith.

A further element of distinction between Melanchthon and the scholastics is the role of the reason and will. To the scholastics, the reason is not totally corrupted by original sin; it is therefore capable of leading the will towards the good, of practicing justice as a natural virtue. By contrast, Melanchthon affirms that the will, which has been corrupted by sin, is not able to fully obey God under its own power.[110] The true freedom of the will thus is experienced only with the help of the Holy Spirit.[111] Therefore, to the scholastics the reason

108 See bibliography in part I/2.1.3. In particular, B. Kent, *Virtues of the Will. The Transformation of Ethics in the Late Thirteenth Century*, Washington D.C., The Catholic University of America Press, 1995, 24.

109 B. Kent, *Virtues of the Will*, 30.

110 P. Melanchthon, *Loci communes* (*secunda eorum aetas*), in CR XXI, 376.

111 See I/2.1.3. See also T.J. Wengert, *Human Freedom, Christian Righteousness: Philip Melanchthon's Exegetical Dispute with Erasmus of Rotterdam*, New York, Oxford University Press, 1998, 143-4.

for maintaining contractual equity is the personal interest of the believer to gain his salvation, for which the observance of equality in contracts is a mean. By contrast, the solution adopted by Melanchthon rests instead on charity as gratitude for the salvation received by faith. In this viewpoint the focus is spiritual, considering the fulfilment of equality in a context of faith. Contractual equality as obedience towards God is practiced as a form of charity towards the neighbour.

2.2.4.2 Chytraeus, Brenz and Gerhard: Specifying the Meaning of Equality

The doctrine of equality in contracts proposed by Melanchthon found a large following among Lutheran theologians and established itself as the most common principle of contract law. In its essential content, the doctrine was grounded on the Holy Scripture (the seventh commandment) and Aristotle. Equality formed the foundation of the doctrine of just price and usury but also endorsed further attributes. Some of the theologians saw equality as a form of protection of the other party's interest, while others placed equality in a context of promotion of the other party's interest.

We now give a brief look to some examples among the Lutheran theologians who worked on commutative justice in the sixteenth century: Chytraeus, Brenz and Gerhard. These theologians investigated the nature of commutative justice, trying to fluently articulate its fundamental meaning. Melanchthon's disciple David Chytraeus in his *Regulae vitae: virtutum descriptiones methodicae* (1556) produced an excellent summary of Melanchthon's doctrine of equality in contracts. Chytraeus depicts commutative justice as a virtue that preserves arithmetical equality in contracts and exchanges.[112] In the exposition, he follows Aristotle's doctrine of four causes (cause, form, matter and end). The efficient *cause* is God, who commanded justice and equality, so that nobody deceives and defrauds the neighbour in contracts (1 Thess. 4,6). *Matters* are the Roman law contracts divided for species: (*re, verbis, litteris, consensu*). *Form* is the will to serve equality in contracts. *Ends* are the following: obeying God, conserving society, practicing love toward the neighbor, and remembering the equality and justice of God, who is impartial towards everybody, demonstrating no preference of people.[113] In his later work, *In deuteronomium Mosis enarratio* (1575), Chytraeus repeats that equality obliges men to practice reciprocal love and reverence.[114]

---

112 D. Chytraeus, *Regulae vitae*, septimi praecepti virtutes, II, 3: "*Iusticia commutativa est virtus, quae in contractibus seu commutatio rerum servat aequalitatem arithmeticam*".

113 D. Chytraeus, *Regulae vitae*, septimi praecepti virtutes, II, 3.

114 D. Chytraeus, *In deuteronomium*, 452.

Aristotle's commutative justice is framed in a theological context, and Roman law contracts are considered to be subjects of commutative justice. It is not only the conservation of society but also a theological structure that supports Chytraeus's doctrine of equality, and this structure is based on the conviction that God ordained contracts. Then, commutative justice must be kept as an act of obedience towards God and for the love of the other contracting party.

The importance of the theological context might be seen also in the prohibition against discrimination due to social or physical condition. The only distinction admitted is between believers and non-believers. Chytraeus explicates that equality of prices and people in contracts must be observed independently from the people involved. Indeed, God is equal towards kings, princes, peasants, rich, poor, intellectual, ignorant, male and female. The ultimate basis of judgement is one's faith: everyone who believes in the Son of God will have eternal life. Everyone who does not believe in the Son of God will be condemned.[115]

In his *Catechismus*, commentary on the seventh commandment, Johannes Brenz states that justice in contracts (*iustitia in contractibus*) is reverence to God (*cultus Dei*) and a duty pleasing to God. This justice consists in giving everyone his due and lawfully negotiating, without deceit or substitutions.[116] It also involves the payment of debts on time and in the way established in the agreement. If you will not pay debts though you are able to, or you will not take care to pay with all your power, and thus defraud the creditor with your negligence and carelessness, you perpetrate theft.[117] With these words Brenz emphasizes that justice requires the fulfilment of the obligation and severely condemns the breach of contract, which is seen as theft. If the debtor can, he must pay the debt, otherwise he robs his creditor.

Brenz's view of contractual justice does not only detail a prohibition against fraud, but he also decries failure to comply with the obligations underwritten in the agreement. In this way, he further details the description of commutative justice. In addition, he points out that the fulfilment of the seventh

115 D. Chytraeus, *Regulae vitae*, septimi praecepti virtutes, II, 3: "… *Sic Deus iuxta unam normam aequalis est erga reges, principes, rusticos, divites, pauperes, doctos, indoctos, mares, foeminas etc. Omnis enim qui credit in Filium, habet vitam aeternam, qui autem non credit in Filium, condemnatur*".

116 J. Brenz, *Catechismus*, 554.

117 J. Brenz, *Catechismus*, 554-5: "*Complectitur debitorum solutionem definito suo tempore et promisso. Nam, cum non solveris, cum possis, debita, aut non curaveris pro tua virili, ut sis solvendo, ac defraudaveris tua negligentia et socordia creditorem, designas furtum*".

precept requires perfect love for God and the neighbour. Hence, obedience to the precept is only possible by and through faith.[118]

Johann Gerhard discussed commutative justice in the fifth volume of his *Loci communes theologici*. He writes that the virtue of commutative justice preserves equality in contracts.[119] It concerns restitution of the deposited thing, the payment of debt, and restitution of stolen things.[120] Consequently, sins against commutative justice are considered: the refusal to pay the salary, the refusal to return the thing deposited, the malicious deferment of payment, or the denial of payment.[121]

To Gerhard, commutative justice is meant as a command to fulfil contractual obligations, and in substance it prescribes restitution of what is due. In addition to commutative justice, the seventh commandment also forbids every fraud in contracts (*fraudes in contractibus*) that takes advantage of the neighbour; it likewise prohibits sales of vitiated wares or sales with an unequal price or unequal measure, false money, verbal frauds and other impostures.[122] In this way Gerhard gathers commutative justice and the prohibition against fraud under the seventh precept of the Decalogue. Within the range of the same precept, he distinguishes two different contents: commutative justice and the prohibition of fraud.

2.2.4.3 Olearius, Osiander and Jäger: Equality as Protection against Fraud

In the seventeenth century, other theologians continued to explore the meaning of commutative justice. Particularly, they aimed to describe commutative justice as a form of protection of the other party's interest. In his *Doctrina theologiae moralis* (1681) Johannes Olearius describes commutative justice as arithmetic proportion in exchanges.[123] He explicates, though, that commutative justice considers both people and goods exchanged in contracts and corrects every inequality due to fraud or deceit. Commutative justice excludes fraud as a whole, without the necessity of a specific provision. In addition, Olearius points out that commutative justice leads toward the maintenance of equality

---

118 J. Brenz, *Catechismus*, 556-8.

119 J. Gerhard, *Locorum theologicorum tomus quintus*, 338: "*altera igitur huius praecepti virtus est* justitia commutativa, *quae in contractibus servat aequalitatem rectae rationi et honestis legibus congruentem*".

120 J. Gerhard, *Locorum theologicorum tomus quintus*, 338: "*Ad hanc virtutem pertinet redditio depositi, solutio debiti, redditio eorum, quae furto vel rapina subtracta*".

121 J. Gerhard, *Locorum theologicorum tomus quintus*, 339.

122 J. Gerhard, *Locorum theologicorum tomus quintus*, 339.

123 J. Olearius, *Doctrina theologiae moralis*, Tab. XXXVII De Justitia: "*Haec observat proportionem* simplicem *seu* arithmeticam, *et exaequat rem rei*".

in contracts, but such equality does not require the same precision as an eye for an eye, because an eye for an eye may also be unjust or totally illicit.[124]

Slightly different from Olearius is the approach of Johann Adam Osiander. In his *Theologia casualis* (1680), Osiander presents commutative justice as a principle of fairness towards the other party: "*justice consists of acting in good faith towards the neighbour and not taking advantage of a man who is having an exchange of goods with us*". He first applies this idea of commutative justice to certain contracts: barter (*permutatio*), sale (*emptio et venditio*), and exchange (*cambium*).[125] He then also relates commutative justice to the transformation realized through the exchange of money or grain, wine or other things that are necessary for our life, for equivalent goods. It concerns loans for use, leases, pledges, deposits and other similar contracts. Commutative justice forbids coercion and fraud (*omnis vis et fraus*).[126] Similarly, Johann Wolfgang Jäger in his *Theologia moralis* (1704) considers commutative justice as the way to escape from the risks of fraud in business.[127] The practice of commutative justice becomes, in this way, the solution against fraud.

In conclusion, Olearius, Osiander and Jäger conceived commutative justice as a general principle of protection of the other contractual party, which is explicated as the duty of acting according to good faith and not defrauding the other party. Commutative justice is not only about price, but it aims to protect the neighbour against fraud.

2.2.4.4 Buddeus and Bertling: Equality as a Form of Promotion of the Other Party's Interest

Melanchthon considered equality in contracts as the obligation to avoid producing inequalities based on Christian charity. Following in these footsteps, some theologians tried to bring the content of the doctrine of equality to a wider precept of promoting the good of the other contractual party. The most brilliant example of this theological approach is Johann Franz Buddeus. Buddeus does not cite Aristotle's commutative justice but identifies equality in contracts as a species of charity:

---

124 J. Olearius, *Doctrina theologiae moralis*, Tab. XXXVII De Justitia.

125 J.A. Osiander, *Theologiae casualis*, 24-5: "*Iustitiae est, bona fide agere cum proximo, nec circumvenire illum, cum quo nobis res est, sive res pro rebus, aut pro pecunia res aut pecuniam pro pecunia commutemus; quorum* primum *dicitur permutatio*, secundum *emptio et venditio*, tertium *cambium*".

126 J.A. Osiander, *Theologiae casualis*, 25.

127 J.W. Jäger, *Theologia moralis, seu practica synoptice tractata*, Tubingae, 1714, 182: "*Periculum tamen a negotiantibus evitari potest, si utraque venditio atque ac emtio legitima sit ac iustitiae commutativae regulis conformis*".

> *he who loves the neighbour will make the effort to apply justice towards him, will strive to avoid the slightest harm to the neighbour, will not deny his duties towards him, and will make sure to avoid that his own benefices are damaging to other people.*[128]

Equality must be preserved in every contract (*servanda est in omnibus contractibus aequalitas*),[129] but Buddeus distinguishes the effects between gratuitous contracts and onerous contracts. In gratuitous, or more literally beneficent (*beneficis*) contracts, equality is fulfilled if the service that is performed does not cause damage. But in lucrative or onerous contracts, equality must carefully be observed: concerning the acts preliminary to the conclusion of the agreement, equality is fulfilled if the hidden vices are revealed or a warning is given. Equality is also fulfilled if the freedom of will is not annulled by duress (*metus*). Concerning the principal act, equality is fulfilled if it is not demanded more than what is equal; concerning the subject of the bargain, equality is fulfilled if what is more of the thing is not kept by us, except in the case that it is taken without our fault.[130]

As a species of charity, equality is a precept of promotion of the other contractual party. It includes both the correct fulfilment of contractual obligations, precaution against damages, and equality of performances. Buddeus distinguishes between preliminary acts, such as disclosing vices of the goods on sale, and principal acts, like an equal price and the correct measurement of the goods. With Buddeus we see the shift from a doctrine of equality in contracts based on commutative justice, intended as form of protection of the other party's interest, towards equality in contracts as a dynamic movement towards the interests of the other contractual party. If to the scholastics commutative justice was mainly observed for the personal interest of the believer who practiced it, for Buddeus the duty is all directed towards the other party.

---

128 J.F. Buddeus, *Institutiones theologiae moralis*, 544: "*Qui alterum amat, iustitiae quoque erga illum studebit, cavebitque sibi, ne illum ulla ratione laedat, nec sua illi unquam denegabit officia, operamque dabit, ne ex beneficiis quae in se conferuntur, damnum redundet in alios*".

129 J.F. Buddeus, *Institutiones theologiae moralis*, 544; J.F. Buddeus, *Elementa philosophiae practicae*, Halae Magdeburgicae, 1720, 307.

130 J.F. Buddeus, *Elementa philosophiae practicae*, 307: "*Officia contrahentium huc redeunt*: servanda est in omnibus contractibus aequalitas. *Et in beneficis quidem hactenus servatur aequalitas, si opera detur, ne quis ex iis sentiat damnum.* (…) *Sed in onerosis cumprimis accurate aequalitas observanda: idque respectu* actuum praecedaneorum, *si vitia rei, de qua agitur inducentur, sique caveatur, ne metu volendi libertas tollatur: respectu* actus principalis, *ne plus exigatur quam par est: respectu* eius de quo agitur, *ne retineatur, quod plus esse ex re apud nos, licet sine culpa nostra deprehenditur*". Buddeus might have been inspired by Grotius. See H. Grotius, *De iure belli ac pacis*, II, 12, § 8-13.

Another example might be considered to be the interpretation proposed by Ernest August Bertling (1721-1769),[131] who argues that commutative justice is a pursuit (*studium*) that the party must have in order to ensure that the party who contracts with him does not have less than before the contract was executed.[132] Commutative justice is exercised in both unilateral and bilateral contracts. In unilateral contracts, the party who receives the benefit practices commutative justice. For example, in a donation, the donee must not accept the donation if the donor is causing damage to his family with the donation, or if the donor is making the donation out of imprudence or for an illegal aim (as corruption). In bilateral contracts justice is practiced in the pursuit (*studium*) for perfect equality of the thing that must be produced or given by both of the parties.[133] The breach of commutative justice is considered from the theological point of view as a theft. Indeed, this is the sense of the seventh commandment of the Decalogue (Lev. 19,11,13,15), and every sin in contracts is a form of injustice (1 Thess. 4,6).[134] Also in this case, we see that this interpretation of the principle of equality stresses the promotion of the other contractual party, requiring an effort to guarantee the interest of the other party. Furthermore, the recipient must take care of the economic health of the other party, and refuse the benefits when they could damage the party or are illicit.

Bertling adds that some categories of people have a special consideration: widows, orphans and the needy. In Zech. 7,10 it is written: "*Do not oppress the widow or the fatherless, the foreigner or the poor. Do not plot evil against each other*"; therefore he who acts unjustly towards them commits a very grave sin. In this sense, commutative justice implies also a particular concern towards some particular subjects.[135]

In these examples, commutative justice is more than preserving equality between the actors, but also tends towards a more general principle of active promotion of the other contractual party. It implies a 'beneficial tension' towards the other contracting party that results in the complete safeguarding of his position. Although in his essential core the doctrine of equality remains

131 T. Hirsch, *Bertling, Ernst August*, in *Allgemeine Deutsche Biographie* 2 (1875), 514 (accessed 18.12.2018): http://www.deutsche-biographie.de/pnd116149566.html?anchor=adb.

132 E.A. Bertling, *De officiis et virtutibus christianorum libri tres sive theologiae moralis elementa*, Halae Magdeburgicae, 1753, 196: "*IUSTITIA COMMUTATIVA, est studium contrahentis, ne alter, cum quo contrahit, per hunc contractum minus, quam antea habuit, accipiat*".

133 E.A. Bertling, *De officiis et virtutibus*, 197: "*In contractibus bilateralibus exserit haec iustitia se per studium perfectae aequalitatis, vel dandorum vel faciendorum ex utraqua parte*".

134 E.A. Bertling, *De officiis et virtutibus*, 197.

135 See also III/2.

based on commutative justice, it is extended. The Spirit of the Bible, that is pure love given by God, permeates it and invites Christians to a kind of attention for the other contracting parties that goes further than mere equality.

2.3 Conclusion

The Anabaptists' claim pushed the Lutheran theologians to point out the lawfulness of business and contracts. Contracts are an ordinance of God and therefore can be lawfully used. The right use of contracts depends upon three basic principles: faith and charity, protection against fraud and contractual justice. Faith allows the full recognition that contracts are a creation of God and are to be used in charity. Charity forbids all the possible offences and exhorts to benefit and fulfil the needs of the other party.

Faith and charity can be seen as general context in which the other two principles take place. In a sense, these two principles are a derivation of faith and charity. Some theologians put forward a general principle of not wronging, not harming, and protecting the other party. Others added or anyhow reintroduced the Aristotelian commutative justice. To Melanchthon, equality needs to be practiced as obedience to God. It is a species of charity and its perfect fulfilment depends from faith. His followers followed various paths. Some theologians placed equality as a form of protection of the other party's interest, while others as a form of promotion. All these principles were generally stated in the comments on the seventh commandment.

The character of the principles we examined can be summarized in two interrelated points. First, we should note the theological, rather than juridical, approach adopted by the theologians. Many early modern scholastics were refined jurists, while the Lutherans tended to describe everything through the lens of the theological view, which in the last resort depends on the doctrine of justification by faith and on the core role of Scripture. Second, when they recur to Aristotelian-Thomistic philosophy, they do so in this theological context. Justice is inseparably related to faith and charity.

CHAPTER 3

The Eighth Commandment: Contractual Fidelity

Together with the seventh commandment of the Decalogue, the eighth commandment is a source of contract law principles. The theologians interpreted this last precept as requiring conformity between words and actions, between a promise or pact and its execution. Although this commandment sets out the general observance of promises and pacts, it does not say when the agreement is binding. This issue was faced by combining the spirit of the Scriptures with the opinions of the early modern scholastics and natural lawyers' writings. This chapter, then, tells a story of tension between the of reasoning of the scholastics and the faithfulness to the Scriptures.

3.0 Introduction

The early modern scholastics elaborated a contract theory centred on the free consent of the parties. This theory comprised a set of concepts and norms, including offer and acceptance, vices of the will and lawfulness of the subject matter, that were virtually applicable to every contract. The Lutheran theologians also worked on the foundation and requirements for a valid agreement. They relied on Scripture as their principal source: biblical rules and examples were constant in their discourses. Yet this approach was problematic, for the Bible does not contain detailed solutions for some issues of contract law. The theologians therefore embraced different strategies. A more conservative stream refused compromises and only formulated rules soundly confirmed by Scripture. This minimalistic approach opted for the creation of fundamental principles that the Christians should apply in concrete circumstances with their own conscience.

A more progressive stream of thinkers entered into details and imported concepts and solutions from the early modern scholastics and the natural lawyers, shoring them up with scriptural references. If it was necessary, these theologians reacted against positions irreconcilable with their moral vision. Indeed the primacy of Scripture remained irreplaceable, and the final judgment on every issue was left to it. Instead, when Scripture was silent or not clear, they simply conformed to the opinions of the scholastics and the natural lawyers. The outcome is a sort of mixture between old scholastic conceptions and the

 | DOI:10.30965/9783657701506_007

new contribution of the Reformation, which in the end seems destined to prevail. Indeed, in the eighteenth century, the theologians went towards a purer separation between reason and faith, creation and revelation. The moral theology of the day thus only focuses on the people justified by faith and eschews references to sources other than the Scriptures.

3.1 *Pacta sunt servanda*: Towards a New Foundation

3.1.1 *Introduction*

Canonists and scholastic moral theologians built a contract law theory around the principle *pacta sunt servanda*, which became the core and the ground for general rules applicable to every contract. The fundament of this principle was the moral prohibition against lies. This prohibition secured the spiritual interest of the promisor to gain his salvation. Freedom of decision and intention were therefore essential, as they led towards salvation or damnation. The early modern scholastics, then, placed the ground of the rule on natural law and argued that a non-vitiated consent generates the obligation to fulfil the pact, independently from the civil law formalities.

The Lutheran theologians received the principle *pacta sunt servanda*, but overturned its moral foundations. The fulfilment of the pact is a precept of the divine law and natural law. The eighth commandment includes the virtues of truthfulness and fidelity, and forbids falsehoods. It requires obedience with love towards God and the neighbour. This obedience, however, is impossible for man. Due to sin, man can only provide an external, performative obedience. Internal obedience, with heart, derives from the Holy Spirit. For the justified people, then, the solidity of the pact is determined by the love of God. This love inspires charity towards the neighbour and faith in agreements.

In the seventeenth century, the emergence of moral theology and the claims of a secular natural law prompted new formulations of this doctrine. Alberti, for instance, derived the precept to keep agreements from the state of integrity, as painted in the Scriptures. Dannhauer, Olearius and Haferung anchored it on the virtues of truthfulness and fidelity. Buddeus looked at the Christian love inspired by God. With the exception of Alberti, who focused on natural law, these theologians only considered the actions of the people justified by faith (the reborn). The peculiarity of this approach is that the solidity of the bond depends upon the work of faith and the Holy Spirit in guiding the Christians' behaviour. It is not the result of the Christian's own efforts. For the Lutheran theologians, it is not the Christian that strives to keep pacts to procure his salvation; it is a work of the Holy Spirit, after salvation has been bestowed. Thus, the attention of the Christian is fully directed to God and the neighbour as recipients of love.

3.1.2 *The Legacy of Canon Law*

As seen earlier, the medieval glossators analysed the Roman law system of contracts starting from the concept of pact (*pactum*).[1] The naked pact (*nudum pactum*) did not have binding effects and gave only rise to an exception: *ex nudo pacto non oritur actio*. In order to give rise to an action the pact must be clothed, namely united with something that was able to confer binding effect: the garment (*vestimentum*). Garments were the *res, verba, litterae, consensus* and the delivery of the thing.[2]

The canonists of the late eleventh and twelfth centuries developed a contract theory centred on the opposite principle, *ex nudo pacto oritur actio*.[3] This construction originated from the moral rule 'you shall not lie'. This rule did not distinguish between a sworn promise, a simple promise and a promise with the legal requisites.[4] In the eyes of God, the breach of an oath and the breach of a promise are both sins.[5] This moral rule aimed to safeguard the spiritual interest of the Christian to reach his salvation.[6] And the intention played a significant role, because it determined the good or evil nature of the moral action. The good action led to gaining moral merits, while the evil action brought the Christian closer to damnation.[7]

The canonists shared the opinion that the naked pacts are enforceable, but were divided on the type of remedy to use. Huguccio (d. 1210) opted for the *officium iudicis*; Johnannes Teutonicus (1180-1252) proposed the *conditio ex canone*;

1 R. Volante, *Il sistema contrattuale*, 24.

2 A. Söllner, *Die causa im Kondiktionen- und Vertragsrecht des Mittelalters bei den Glossatoren, Kommentatoren und Kanonisten*, in *Zeitschrift der Savigny Stiftung, rom. Abt.*, 77 (1960), 182-269 (216-7); I. Birocchi, *Causa e categoria*, 50-1.

3 F. Spies, *De l'observation des simples conventions en droit canonique*, Paris, 1928; J. Roussier, *Le fondement de l'obligation contractuelle dans le droit classique de l'Eglise*, Paris, 1933; M. Roberti, *L'influenza cristiana nello svolgimento storico dei patti nudi*, in *Cristianesimo e diritto romano*, Milano, 1935, 87-169; P. Fedele, *Considerazioni sull'efficacia dei patti nudi nel diritto canonico*, in *Annali dell'Università di Macerata*, Vol. XI, Tolentino, 1937, 5-90; G. Astuti, *I contratti obbligatori nella storia del diritto italiano*, vol. I, Milano, Giuffrè, 1952; P. Bellini, *L'obbligazione da promessa con oggetto temporale nel sistema canonistico classico, con particolare riferimento ai secoli XII e XIII*, Milano, Giuffrè, 1964; T. Mayer-Maly, *Der Konsens als Grundlage des Vertrages*, in H. Hübner, E. Klingmüller, A. Wacke (eds.), *Festschrift für Erwin Seidl zum 70. Geburstag*, Köln, P. Hanstein, 1975, 118-29; P. Landau, *Pacta sunt servanda*, 457-74.

4 P. Bellini, *L'obbligazione da promessa*, 43-7.

5 C.22, q.5, c.12.

6 P. Bellini, *L'obbligazione da promessa*, 21, 25-6.

7 P. Bellini, *L'obbligazione da promessa*, 30-4.

and Innocent IV (1195-1254) was in favour to the *denunciatio evangelica*.[8] In addition, the enforcement was later conditioned to the presence of a *causa*, which derived from the medieval elaboration of Roman law. This further requisite developed in two stages. First, Jacques de Révigny (1230-1296) reduced the garments of the pacts (*vestimenta pactorum*) we saw before only to one: the delivery of the thing (*traditio rei*). This was the only *causa* of the pact. Then, Baldus de Ubaldis (1327-1400) added the Roman law idea of this single garment (*vestimentum*) to the canonistic principle.[9] The naked pact was actionable if it was provided with a *causa*. The canonist Niccolò Tedeschi (*Panormitanus*, 1386-1445) and others followed this approach and required the presence of a *causa* for enforcing the naked pact.[10]

The early modern scholastics looked especially at the natural law foundation of the rule. The court of conscience does not request the same formalities as Roman law: the pact is enforceable because it is based on natural law. Before God, the crucial point is the keeping of contractual faith. Hence, the *causa* was more intended as true cause of the promise, which does not need to be expressed. This idea led the discourse towards the consent. And the notion of *causa* ended up in the requisite of a pure (non-vitiated) consent. The natural law required a non-vicious consent to produce a valid agreement.[11] The natural law overcomes the distinction between a naked pact and a non-naked pact. As Decock has pointed out, the primary interest of the early modern scholastics was the will of the parties and the impediments to the will (the vices of consent).[12]

3.1.3 *The Eighth Commandment*

The Lutheran theologians elaborated on a new moral configuration of the principle *pacta sunt servanda*. Faith in promises, pacts and contracts is a natural law rule repeated in the eighth commandment of the Decalogue. This commandment includes the virtues of truth and fidelity. Every man is bound to

8 E. Bussi, *La formazione dei dogmi di diritto privato nel diritto comune*, Padova, Cedam, 1937, 221-9; F. Calasso, *Il Negozio giuridico*, 279; P. Landau, *Pacta sunt servanda*, 467-9; W. Decock, *Theologians and Contract Law*, 123-5.

9 A. Guzmán Brito, *Causa del contrato y causa de la obligación en la dogmática de los juristas romanos, medievales y modernos y en la codificación europea y americana*, in *Rev. estud. hist.-juríd.* [online]. 2001, n.23, 209-367, see XVIII, IV, 2. http://dx.doi.org/10.4067/S0716-54552001002300006 (accessed 7.4.2017).

10 A. Söllner, *Die causa*, 257-9.

11 W. Decock, *Theologians and Contract Law*, 150-1. For Luis de Molina see also A. Guzmán Brito, *Acto, negocio, contrato y causa en la tradición del derecho europeo e iberoamericano*, Cizur Menor (Navarra), Aranzadi, 2005, 407-39.

12 W. Decock, *Theologians and Contract Law*, 152.

keep faith in agreements. By keeping faith in agreements, men obey God. This obedience, though, can only be perfect if motivated by love for God and the neighbour. This love is instilled in man by faith and the Holy Spirit. Without faith, man cannot fulfil the law, for man's nature is corrupted such that he can only perform external actions. Therefore, the dynamic of contractual fidelity rests substantially on the activity of faith and charity.

In his large catechism, Luther did not mention pacts and promises, but mostly focused on bearing false witness.[13] It is Melanchthon then who gave impulse for the blossoming of the new view. He wrote a few, still important, sentences about content and the foundation of this rule. The rule by which honourable pacts are binding (*honesta pacta sunt servanda*) is governed by natural law.[14] The addition *honesta* concerns the quality of the agreement, which must not offend the divine law, as we will see later.[15] Natural law is defined as the knowledge of divine law divinely instilled in man.[16] The precepts of the natural law are included in the Decalogue and thus, the rule that all honourable agreements are binding is repeated in the eighth commandment (*you shall not bear false witness against thy neighbour*). This law defends judgements and pacts and includes the virtue of truth, 'the most beautiful of all virtues'. The truth must be loved and defended while lies (*mendacia*) must be avoided.[17] The truth forbids the breach of pacts and every deceit and fraud.[18]

The rule to keep honourable pacts concerns every man, but the perfect adherence (with love) to this precept is impossible because of the taint of sin. As seen before, for Melanchthon, man can only perform external actions. Internal actions, actions with love, need the intercession of the Holy Spirit. Melanchthon stresses that the internal obedience cannot begin without the knowledge of the Gospel and without the Holy Spirit.[19] For love to grow, it is necessary to hear the voice of the Gospel and the remission of sins.[20] In other

13 M. Luther, *Der große Katechismus, nach der Fassung des deutschen Konkordienbuches*, Dresden, 1580, 625-33.

14 P. Melanchthon, *Loci communes* (*tertia eorum aetas*), in CR XXI, 712 and 715.

15 See II/3.3.2.1.

16 P. Melanchthon, *Loci communes* (*tertia eorum aetas*), in CR XXI, 712.

17 P. Melanchthon, *Philosophiae moralis epitomes libri duo*, 1538 in CR XVI, 151-2, P. Melanchthon, *Loci communes* (*tertia eorum aetas*) in CR XXI, 709: "*Haec lex munit iudicia et pacta, et continet virtutem omnium pulcherrimam, veritatem ...*"; P. Melanchthon, *Loci communes* (*tertia eorum aetas*), in CR XXI, 715.

18 P. Melanchthon, *Loci communes* (*tertia eorum aetas*), in CR XXI, 709-10.

19 P. Melanchthon, *Loci communes* (*tertia eorum aetas*), in CR XXI, 765: "*Sed interior obedientia non potest inchoari sine agnitione Evangelii et sine Spiritum sanctum*".

20 P. Melanchthon, *Loci communes* (*tertia eorum aetas*), in CR XXI, 765.

words, faith must go before.[21] Without faith, man is only capable of an external obedience.[22] Hence, unlike the scholastics, the fulfilment of the *honesta pacta sunt servanda* is not grounded on the strength of the Christian but on the grace of the Holy Spirit. It is not only a rational process, but a spiritual consequence.[23]

Melanchthon founded the *honesta pacta sunt servanda* on natural law and the divine law, but the fulfilment of this rule requires faith. Only faith gives man the necessary love for God and the neighbour. Without the grace of the Gospel, man is only capable of external actions. Melanchthon's followers implemented and improved this path. In his catechism, Brenz distinguishes contracts and pacts, but remembers all of them in his comment to the eighth commandment. Truth is requested in contracts, as it is written in Jeremiah 9,4-5:

> *take ye heed every one of his neighbour, and trust ye not in any brother: for every brother will utterly supplant, and every neighbour will walk with slanders. And they will deceive every one his neighbour, and will not speak the truth: they have taught their tongue to speak lies, and weary themselves to commit iniquity.*

Then, truth, fidelity and steadfastness are requested in pacts and covenants. Again the source quoted is Jer. 5,1:

> *run ye to and fro through the streets of Jerusalem, and see now, and know, and seek in the broad places thereof, if ye can find a man, if there be any that executeth judgment, that seeketh the truth.*

The fulfilment of this commandment and thus truth, fidelity and perseverance depend on faith and Holy Spirit. Brenz alludes to Gal. 5,22: "*but the fruit of the Spirit is love, joy, peace, longsuffering, gentleness, goodness, faith*".[24] Indeed, as he repeats, the implementation of the commandment is only possible by faith or by the power of the Holy Spirit.[25] Finally, he points out that in Rom. 1,31[26] the 'covenantbreakers' are mentioned among those whom 'God gave to a reprobate mind'.[27]

---

21 P. Melanchthon, *Loci communes* (*tertia eorum aetas*), in CR XXI, 765: "*Ut igitur dilectio oriatur, necesse est pracecedere fidem ...*".

22 P. Melanchthon, *Loci communes* (*tertia eorum aetas*), in CR XXI, 716-7.

23 See I/2.

24 J. Brenz, *Catechismus*, 567-8.

25 J. Brenz, *Catechismus*, 569-70.

26 Rom.1,31 will also be used by the great Protestant jurist Matthaeus Wesenbeck to justify his opinion that the *nudum pactum* is actionable in a civil court. See II/1.1. On Wesenbeck see also IV/2.3.2.

27 J. Brenz, *Catechismus*, 568.

Sharing the same orientation as Melanchthon, Chemnitz declares that the eighth commandment forbids deceiving the neighbour in pacts and other business. The Decalogue adds the words *against thy neighbour*, because the aim of the precept is not the truth towards God, but the truth in political society and in the actions towards the neighbour.[28] The breach of promises in pacts, treatises and contracts is a form of lie (*mendacium*) and therefore a sin against the eighth commandment. To lend weight to the argument, Chemnitz quotes the first letter of Paul to the Romans (Rom. 1,31), where Paul declares that God condemns men who breach promises: they are called covenant-breakers (*ἀσυνθέτους*) and 'implacable' (*ἀσπονδεί*), ignorant of the covenants. Then, he mentions several examples of people who broke covenants: Zedekiah (Jer. 37) and Moab (2 Kings 3,5); and the famous example of steadfastness in keeping pacts and promises: the covenant between Joshua and the Gibeonites (Joshua 9,18). Finally, he refers to 1 Tim. 1,10, where liars and perjured persons are joined together.[29] As for Melanchthon, to Chemnitz the content of natural law is the Decalogue.[30] Thus, every man is bound to keep faith in agreements. Yet, he remarks that the good works that the law teaches can only be performed by the renovation of the Holy Spirit: when the Holy Spirit writes the law in the heart of the Christians, only then do their activities become good works.[31]

Finally, Johann Gerhard also attributes the foundation of the rule *pacta sunt servanda* to the eighth commandment of the Decalogue. He points out that the virtue of truthfulness is the main virtue of this precept, which must 'shine' in works as the keeping of promises and pacts.[32] The use of fraudulent or ambiguous words, then, is a sin against the eighth commandment.[33] Natural law corresponds to the moral laws, which are summarized in the Decalogue.[34] Thus, knowledge of the eighth commandment is also divinely imbued in the human mind.[35] Because of sin, however, the light of natural law is obscured, and for this reason God repeated the law in the Decalogue.[36] Until men are

28 M. Chemnitz, *Loci theologici*, pars secunda, 84.

29 M. Chemnitz, *Loci theologici*, pars secunda, 85: "*Tertia mendacia et violatio promissionum in pactis, foederibus et contractibus. Rom. 1,31 ἀσυνθέτους, ἀσπονδεί, nescii foederis. Jer. 37 Sedechias, 4 Reg. 3,5 Moab. Insigne exemplum constantiae in pactis et promissis servandis, extat in Josua cum Gibeonitis Jos 9.v.18, 1 Tim.1.v.10 coniunguntur mendaces et periuri*".

30 M. Chemnitz, *Loci theologici*, pars secunda, 96-7.

31 M. Chemnitz, *Loci theologici*, pars tertia, 28-32.

32 J. Gerhard, *Locorum theologicorum tomus quintus*, Tubingae, 1766, 341: "*Ex his fundamentis facile intelligitur, quod veritas seu veracitas sit* primaria *ac principalis virtus huius praecepti, quae lucere debet: (...) in opere, ut pacta et promissa inviolata servemus*".

33 J. Gerhard, *Locorum theologicorum tomus quintus*, 342.

34 J. Gerhard, *Locorum theologicorum tomus quintus*, 223.

35 J. Gerhard, *Locorum theologicorum tomus quintus*, 229-30.

36 J. Gerhard, *Locorum theologicorum tomus quintus*, 230-1.

reborn they can only obtain an external obedience to the law. An inner obedience, with the heart, needs faith and the Holy Spirit.[37]

In conclusion, the Lutheran theologians individuated in natural law, the eighth commandment and the virtues of truth and fidelity the solid foundation of contractual fidelity. Man should obey God by keeping faith in agreements, but because of sin, perfect obedience is impossible to achieve. The love of God received by faith stimulates the Christian to love the neighbour and therefore to keep faith in promises and pacts. The vibrant content of contractual fidelity is in faith and charity. The sterility of man is converted to a good seed. Because God loves man, he can love the neighbour and commit himself to keep the word given.

3.1.4 *Natural Law*

The route inaugurated by Melanchthon and imitated by the Lutheran theologians was cast in doubt in the second half of the seventeenth century. As an example of this movement, Pufendorf put forward a different perspective on natural law. As seen in the first part, he argued that natural law was founded on the state of corruption, and its purpose was to promote peaceful sociality.[38] The Lutheran theologians reacted to these claims in different ways. For instance, Valentin Alberti attempted to derive natural law from the divine revelation and particularly from the state of integrity before the original sin.[39] This natural law was divinely inspired in man.[40] This method is also reflected in the foundation of the contractual bond. Alberti posits that in the state of integrity, marriage was indissoluble, as is proved by Gen. 2,24: "*and they shall be one flesh*", and Matt. 19,9:

> *and I say unto you, Whosoever shall put away his wife, except it be for fornication, and shall marry another, committeth adultery: and whoso marrieth her which is put away doth commit adultery.*

Since marriage was based on a promise and marriage was inviolable, Alberti concludes that in the state of integrity promises were always faithfully observed.[41]

---

37 J. Gerhard, *Locorum theologicorum tomus quintus*, 349: "*Nos contra statuimus, homines nondum renatos*, externam *quidem disciplinam praestare posse* (…) *sed* interiorem *obedientiam cordis sine fide et Spiritu Sancto ab eis non posse inchoari* …".

38 See I/2.4.

39 V. Alberti, *Compendium iuris naturae*, pars prima, editio secunda, Lipsiae, 1696, 46.

40 V. Alberti, *Compendium iuris naturae*, pars prima, 39.

41 V. Alberti, *Compendium iuris naturae*, pars secunda, 106: "*Promissio cecidisset omnino in statum integritatis, hominique praestita fuisset ab homine, quamdiu integer, fidelissime*".

In the state of corruption, man must strive to restore the integrity he lost after the original sin. Hence, man draws near the original integrity by keeping promises pronounced towards other men.[42] The natural law orders that everything that is promised from a man to another man must be performed.[43] Alberti draws the general effect of promises from the comparison between the original state of integrity and the current state of corruption. Man must strive to recover his lost integrity, and for this reason he must keep promises and pacts, which were always kept in the state of integrity.

Alberti claims that in his *De iure belli ac pacis*, Grotius unconsciously considered the obligation deriving from promises in the same way. Grotius' argument is that the eternal law obliges both God and men. The promises must be kept because the eternal law (or the nature of immutable justice) is in a way common to God and those who have the use of reason. According to Alberti, this implies that the aim of keeping promises is to make us similar to God, because the eternal law is instilled in us through natural law, once in the divine image, now in its remains.[44] To Alberti, the eternal law is transmitted to us through the natural law inscribed in the image of God that we had in the state of integrity. Now, in the state of corruption, there is a remainder of it.

Alberti was a strenuous defender of the orthodox doctrine of natural law. He sought to maintain the connection between natural law and the divine revelation that Pufendorf had cast in doubt. He looked at Scripture, where the book of Genesis reveals that in the state of integrity, pacts and promises were always faithfully observed. Therefore, he concluded that the natural law orders the observance of promises and pacts. Keeping promises is a precept of natural law. By observing such a precept in the state of corruption, man recovers part (at least) of the integrity he lost for the original sin.

42 V. Alberti, *Compendium iuris naturae*, 106-7: "*Unde sequitur, in statu corruptionis fidem servandam esse tum ab omni homine, quia omnis homo integritati reducendae studere debet, tum omni homini, quia servanda est homini ut homini*".

43 V. Alberti, *Compendium iuris naturae*, 107: "*quicquid homini promittitur ab homine, illud eidem ab hoc praestandum est*".

44 V. Alberti, *Compendium iuris naturae*, 117-8: "*Ubi non possum non notare modum, quo H. Grotius obligationem promissionum, nostrae de iuris naturae hypothesi conformiter, nescius deducit. Argumentum enim eius hoc est*: ad quoad deus lege aeterna obligatur, ad id obligantur etiam homines. Atqui ad promissa praestanda etc. E. ratio maior est: quia lex aeterna aut natura, immutabilis iustitiae, Deo et omnibus his, qui ratione utuntur, suo modo communis est. *In quam vero finem communis est, nisi ut Deo assimilemur? Quomodo communis est, nisi quatenus lex aeterna per ius naturae olim in imagine divina, hodie in reliquiis eius, in nos derivata est?*".

3.1.5 *The Virtue of Truthfulness and Fidelity*

Another solution against the attack of the secular natural law was the separation between reason and revelation. The Lutheran moral theologians focused only on the born again and the work of the Holy Spirit for the maintenance of agreements. One strain of thought individuated the reason, founding the duty of keeping pacts and promises in the virtues of truthfulness and fidelity. Olearius for instance clarified that truthfulness is a general concept that includes every word pronounced, while fidelity relates specifically to pacts and oaths.[45] Fidelity is the virtue by which a man firmly and without fraud keeps promises and pacts with another man.[46] The principal efficient cause of the virtues is the Holy Spirit, while the secondary principal cause is the will of the reborn men acting freely according to the Holy Spirit.[47]

In a very similar way, in his *Theologia moralis* (1737) Johann Caspar Haferung founds the rule on the virtue of fidelity. Fidelity is the Christian virtue that promotes adherence to pacts and promises. It is derived from faith and means keeping faith. It differs from truthfulness, which is concerned with every word. Fidelity is more comprehensive, taking into account property, pacts and promises. It is also different from candour, which includes every sign and action as expressing a sign of the will, while fidelity only regards the performance and the fulfilment of promises.[48] The virtue of fidelity is included in the Christian virtues towards other men. The efficacy of these virtues stems from the Holy Spirit and is the supernatural fruit of the faith.[49]

Olearius and Haferung might have found encouragement for their construction by reading some of the erudite words of Dannhauer. In his *Deuteronomium dannhawerianum* (1669) Dannhauer grapples with the virtue of truthfulness, and particularly he writes that the promissory truthfulness (*veracitas promissoria*) regards candour, faith, sincerity, and consists in the conformity between the word and the thing offered.[50] Christ established such conformity in Matt. 5,37: "*but let your communication be, Yea, yea; Nay, nay: for whatsoever is more than these cometh of evil*". Dannhauer uses biblical hermeneutics for the

45 J. Olearius, *Doctrina theologiae moralis*, Tab. XLVII: "Fidelitas *praecipue ad promissa et iuramenta refertur.* Veracitas *vero latius se extendit ad omnia verba* (…)".

46 J. Olearius, *Doctrina theologiae moralis*, Tab. XLVII: "[*Fidelitas*] *est virtus per quam homo constanter et absque ulla fraude, cum altero pacta, eique promissa servat*".

47 J. Olearius, *Doctrina theologiae moralis*, Tab. IV.

48 J.C. Haferung, *Theologia moralis*, 249: "… *cum fidelitas tantum praestationem et impletionem promissorum involvat*".

49 J.C. Haferung, *Theologia moralis*, 27: "*Sed eas quae efficacia, seu* operatione Spiritus Sancti *fiunt, adeoque sunt supernaturales fidei fructus*".

50 J.K. Dannhauer, *Deuteronomium Dannhawerianum*, 437: "… *vel* promissoria *alias candor, fides, sinceritas, quae consistit in conformitate vocis et rei praestitae* …".

interpretation of this passage and acutely notices that the first *yes* denotes the promise, while the second one the completion: if one does not speak clearly it makes a complication (πλοκή). Indeed, the *yes* (ναὶ) belongs to the promisor and therefore through the *so be it* (ἀμήν) is explained Revelation 1,7.[51] In substance, a promise implies the conformity between what is pronounced and what is offered. Dannhauer adds that the same principle is prescribed in the popular German maxim:

> *a man, a man, a word, a word, as one deals with the ox through its horns, so a man deals with another man through the words* (*Ein Mann, ein Mann, ein Wort, ein Wort, den Ochsen halt man bei den Hörnern, den Mann bei den Worten*).[52]

This maxim was also used by many jurists to justify the duty to keep simple agreements.

The approach adopted by Dannhauer, Olearius and Haferung remained tied to the Scriptures without recourse to other sources. Indeed, they are only focusing on the justified people, the reborn. As we are going to see in the following paragraphs, they considered the virtue and its offences as the central elements, and the efficacy of the virtue issues from the Holy Spirit.

3.1.6 *Christian Love*

Buddeus offered another type of solution for the foundation of the *pacta sunt servanda*. He laid the architecture of his discourse on the principle that the agreements are binding as an act of love towards the neighbour. He writes that love towards the neighbour (Matt. 22,39) is the summary of the teachings of how to treat other people. Love of the neighbour (*amor proximi*) derives from the love and will of God, and it is to be sincerely directed also towards one's enemies. This love aims to avert the potential for harm, to believe that others are equals and to behave towards them justly, even to strive to promote the advantage of their soul, body and temporal goods.[53] Love is not the fruit of man's endeavour; as Buddeus points out, the reason for such love is the will and love

---

51 J.K. Dannhauer, *Deuteronomium Dannhawerianum*, 537: "*... de hac proprie agit Servator Matth. 5. 37.* Sermo vester sit, EST, est, non, non, *prius* est, *notat promissum; posterius, complementum rhetorica quadam πλοκή. Est enim ναὶ promittentis atque ideo per ἀμήν explicantur Apoc. 1. 7*".

52 J.K. Dannhauer, *Deuteronomium Dannhawerianum*, 437.

53 J.F. Buddeus, *Institutiones theologiae moralis*, 502-3: "*Summa officiorum erga alios continetur in* amore proximi Matth. XXII, 39. *Est autem amor proximi, etiam inimicos, propter voluntatem et amorem Dei, sincero prosequitur, ut non tantum eos nullo modo laedat, sed eos sibi aequales credat, iuste se adversus eos gerat, immo commoda illorum qua animam, qua corpus, et fortunae bona, promovere omni studio annitatur*".

of God.[54] Indeed, as he said at the beginning of his manual of moral theology, he directs his attention towards born-again Christians.[55]

The love for the neighbour has several degrees: abstaining from damaging the neighbour; practicing equality with the neighbour; keeping pacts and promises; and promoting the neighbour's interest.[56] The third degree of love is that which we demonstrate to others when it cannot be denied to them without injustice, among which mostly is the upholding of pacts and promises.[57] If we do not keep pacts and promises, Buddeus continues, the sociableness of a community cannot be saved. Indeed, if not the only means, pacts are certainly the primary means of acquiring goods we need, when other people do not decide to give them spontaneously. Therefore, if it is not certain that the word given will be respected, people will no longer enter into pacts or be induced to promise something.[58] It follows that reneging on a pact harms the promisee in a very serious way, which is surely an act against love.[59] This idea of the breach of pacts as an act against sociableness harks back to the scholastics, as we will see later.

Buddeus' approach does not look immediately at the Decalogue, but at the core of Christian ethics, the love for the neighbour. This love descends from God and does not result from the Christian personal endeavour. Buddeus also grounds the *pacta sunt servanda* on the virtues of integrity, truthfulness, fidelity and justice. He writes that for the Christians, keeping promises and pacts is also an inviolable duty dictated by these four virtues. The addition of the virtue of justice is important, because, as we are going to see in the next paragraph, it also alludes to the legal effects of the agreement.

The observance of the agreements is certainly a duty established in the Scriptures. To Buddeus the sincerity of love cannot coexist with perfidy (*perfidia*). Rightly, Paul in the first letter to the Corinthians (13,6) affirms that love

54 J.F. Buddeus, *Institutiones theologiae moralis*, 504: "*Fundamentum amoris huius, sed id, quod praecipue, ut proximum nostrum amemus, nos impellere debet, est voluntas, et amor Dei*".

55 See I/2.4.3.

56 J.F. Buddeus, *Institutiones theologiae moralis*, 504.

57 J.F. Buddeus, *Institutiones theologiae moralis*, 508: "*Tertius amoris gradus est, ut ea praestemus aliis, quae illis sine iniuria denegari nequeunt, quorsum cumprimis illud pertinet, ut pacta atque promissa servemus*".

58 J.F. Buddeus, *Institutiones theologiae moralis*, 508: "*Hoc ratio ipsa docet, cum si pacta et promissa non serventur, socialitas salva esse nequeat, pacta quoque, si non unicum, certe praecipuum sint medium, ea acquirendi, quibus indigemus, si alii sua sponte ea nobis praestare nolint. Si quis autem certus non sit, fidem sibi datam servandam, non temere ut pacta ineat, aut promissis fidat se induci patietur*".

59 J.F. Buddeus, *Institutiones theologiae moralis*, 508: "*Accedit, quod gravissime laedatur, cui fidem datam non servamus, quod adeo vel maxime cum amore pugnat*".

does not delight in injustice but rejoices with the truth. The virtue of integrity, justice, truthfulness and fidelity are Christian virtues recommended in various passages of the Scriptures. In particular, the virtue of fidelity is mentioned in Matthew 5,37: "*But let your communication be, Yea, yea; Nay, nay: for whatsoever is more than these cometh of evil*" and James 5,12: "*but let your yea be yea; and your nay, nay; lest ye fall into condemnation*".[60]

In conclusion, to Buddeus the rule *pact sunt servanda* is founded on the Christian love for the neighbour. The pact is kept through the love given by God. Moreover, the pact has to be kept because a breach would mean damage to the other and consequently the whole society. The duty to keep pacts is also established by the virtues of integrity, truthfulness, fidelity and justice; and it is also set in Scripture. This variety of arguments is an expression of Buddeus' attempt to synthesize and harmonize different traditions. As we will see also later, he conglomerates scholastics' and natural lawyers' ideas with the Lutheran supremacy of faith and Scripture.

3.2 Moral or Legal Effects

3.2.1 *Introduction*

The Lutheran theologians firmly affirmed the natural law principle that agreements are binding. This precept is also repeated in the Decalogue. Man must keep faith in promises, pacts and contracts. Yet, the perfect obedience to this precept requires love for God and the neighbour. This love is only given by faith and the Holy Spirit. The benefic fruit of faith pushes the Christian to obey the dictates of Scripture.

The Lutheran theologians were mostly concerned with the moral obligations, leaving the legal obligations to jurists and natural lawyers. Like their Roman Catholic colleagues, though, some Lutheran theologians also questioned the relationship between law and morality, and in particular the elements necessary to distinguish a morally binding agreement from a legally binding agreement. As we are going to see, the majority recognized in the will of the promisor the most important element to determine the moral or legal effects.

3.2.2 *The Early Modern Scholastics*

The early modern scholastics had differentiated moral duties and legal duties through the virtue of justice and the virtue of honesty. Indeed, Thomas

60 J.F. Buddeus, *Institutiones theologiae moralis*, 509.

Aquinas had distinguished between a moral debt (*debitum morale*), governed by the virtue of honesty, and a legal debt (*debitum legale*), founded on the virtue of justice. Drawing upon Aristotle, Thomas asserted that certain human relationships must be based on equality, which means giving to the other what it is due. Other relationships, instead, do not require such rigidity, as for example, the duty of truthfulness in speaking with the others, gratefulness in compensating another person for a benefit, and vindication in compensating another person for an evil act.[61]

The scholastics used the virtue of truth and the virtue of justice to distinguish moral and legal obligations. The debate, then, was largely dominated by the provocative claim of the Cardinal Cajetan, who advocated that simple promises are only morally binding and as a matter of venial sin. The French humanist François Connan (1508-1551) held the same opinion and considered the simple promises as not legally binding.[62] On the contrary, the great part of the scholastics and the natural lawyers refused this view. According to Lessius, objective factors (such as the matter and the nature of the promise) and subjective factors are equally important to determine the moral or legal effects of the promises. Other theologians, spearheaded by Molina, relied on the intention of the promisor.[63]

3.2.3 *Onerous Promises and Gratuitous Promises*

The effects of the debate triggered by Cajetan and Connan were also felt among the Lutherans. The strong majority of the theologians refused their opinions, but there also were supporters. Rarely the theologians arranged new solutions, but principally relied on the opinions of the scholastics and the natural lawyers. This topic is therefore a clear example of the influence these scholars exercised on the Lutherans. In his *Dissertatio de summo bono* (1614), Balthasar Meisner seems to be inclined towards Cajetan and Connan's opinion, though he does not make any clear reference to them. Meisner distinguishes between the obligation deriving from a gratuitous promise, an onerous promise and a sworn promise. The gratuitous promise is binding for the virtue of truth and fidelity, but it is not binding for the virtue of justice. He who breaches a gratuitous promise commits a sin two times, because he lies against the virtue of

61 T. Aquinas, *Summa theologiae*, IIaIIae, q. 80 art. 1; W. Decock, *Theologians and Contract Law*, 197-9.

62 J. Gordley, *The Philosophical Origins*, 73; I. Birocchi, *Causa e categoria*, 120.

63 W. Decock, *Theologians and Contract Law*, 201-2.

truth and breaks faith with the virtue of fidelity.[64] This promise is therefore only binding in conscience, and it does not produce legal effects.

The onerous promise, instead, creates an obligation based on the virtue of truth, fidelity and justice. So he who does not keep the promise can be defined as mendacious, perfidious and unjust.[65] The promise is not only morally binding but also gives rise to an action in the civil court.

The sworn promise adds to the other virtues the virtue of religion. The gratuitous sworn promise is binding for the virtue of truth, fidelity and religion. The onerous sworn promise makes an obligation for the virtue of truth, fidelity, justice and religion. The man who breaches such a promise therefore is mendacious, perfidious, unjust and perjurer. Each one of these acts constitutes a grave sin,[66] and the promise is binding in the civil courts.

In conclusion, the onerous promise, with an oath added or not, produces effects in the *forum externum*. Instead, the gratuitous promise, with an oath or not, is only valid in the *forum internum*. This construction relies on the gratuitous or onerous nature of the agreement. It presumes that a gratuitous promise is only binding in conscience, while an onerous promise is also legally binding.

3.2.4 *The Promisor's Intention*

Meisner's view did not gain many admirers among the Lutherans. Other theologians, as Osiander and Jäger, held the opposite view and strongly rejected Cajetan and Connan's thesis. In his *Theologia casualis*, Johann Adam Osiander argues that every accepted promise in a serious matter obliges one on pain of mortal sin. Three motivations support this statement. First, Psalm 15 affirms that he who spoke the truth in his heart, he who has not used deceit in his tongue, shall dwell in God's tabernacle. Second, Osiander mentions a passage of Gregory of Nyssa, where God is described as faithful.[67] The third reason is rational. Osiander condemns the opinion of Cajetan and his followers de Soto,

---

64 B. Meisner, *Dissertatio de summo bono*, 244: "*Obligatio* gratuitae *promissionis oritur ex duplici virtute*, veritatis *et* fidei. *Unde si quis non praestat dupliciter peccat*; 1 quia *mendax est, contra virtutem veritatis*, 2. quia *perfidus est, contra virtutem fidei*".

65 B. Meisner, *Dissertatio de summo bono*, 244: "*Obligatio promissionis* onerosae *oritur ex triplici virtute*, veritatis, fidelitatis, iustitiae. *Unde qui non praestat, tripliciter peccat sit enim* 1. mendax, 2. perfidus, 3. iniustus".

66 B. Meisner, *Dissertatio de summo bono*, 245.

67 J.A. Osiander, *Theologiae casualis*, 107. Unfortunately, he only alludes to Gregory of Nyssa without quoting any specific works.

Ledesma, Henriquez and others.[68] He opts for Molina's view, which he says Lessius considers as being likely, and which mainly rests on the intention.

According to Molina, an accepted promise on a serious matter is binding for the virtue of justice, and as a matter of mortal sin, if the promisor wanted to produce such a bond. If the promisor only wanted to be obliged according to the virtue of fidelity, he is not obliged by mortal sin.[69] Osiander observes that the subject matter of a promise can be gratuitous or onerous, but this does not change the nature of the bond. Even a gratuitous promise can imply an obligation based on the virtue of justice, if the promisor wants. The will of the promisor is the decisive element.[70] Despite the recourse to the Scriptures and the Church Fathers, which can be certainly used to establish the binding nature of the agreements, Osiander also turns to the scholastics. The problem had been raised in the scholastics' context, and the solution had already been found. Therefore, our theologian follows the easy way and repeats Molina's solutions. The promisor's will is the only useful element to distinguish the nature of the obligation.

In his observation on Grotius' *De iure belli ac pacis*, Osiander comes to similar conclusions when he discusses the opinion of Connan. Connan set forth the idea that the production of legal effects depends from objective elements. The naked pacts do not produce legal effects; they are only binding if the performance is executed or if a legal stipulation is added.[71] Osiander does not agree and responds that adding the stipulation does not make the promise more stable in the court of conscience (*forum conscientiae*), but only in the external court (*forum exterior*), because it can be presumed that the promise was made with a superior deliberation.[72] Then, he claims that if the accepted

---

68 J.A. Osiander, *Theologiae casualis*, 108: "*Male itaque* Cajetanus, Sotus, Ledesma, Henriquez et alii *statuunt, promissionem simplicem, acceptatam in re gravi, non obligare sub mortali*".

69 J.A. Osiander, *Theologiae casualis*, 108: "*Ergo existimo, promissionem in re gravi acceptatam obligare sub mortali, si promittens se velit ex iustitia obligare; si autem solum ex fidelitate se obligare velit, sub lethali minime obligare. Mecum* Molina tomo secundo d. 262 *et probabile* Lessius *fatetur*".

70 J.A. Osiander, *Theologiae casualis*, 108.

71 On Connan's opinion see: M. Diesselhorst, *Die Lehre des Hugo Grotius vom Versprechen*, 31-4; U. Petronio, *Sinallagma e analisi strutturale dei contratti all'origine del sistema contrattuale moderno*, in J. Barton (ed.), *Towards a General Law of Contract*, Berlin, Duncker & Humblot, 1990, 215-47; Birocchi, *Causa e categoria*, 95-136. As it has been suggested by Schmoeckel, Connan was close to Calvin's ideas, See M. Schmoeckel, *Das Recht der Reformation*, 264-70.

72 J.A. Osiander, *Observationes*, 898: "*Verum respondentur* (1) *formulam stipulationis non reddere promissionem firmiorem in foro conscientiae, sed solum in foro exteriori, quia praesumitur majori cum deliberatione facta*".

onerous promise is binding because of the virtue of justice, the gratuitous promise is binding in the same way. The consequence is sharp: even though with the onerous promise, there is a more perfect obligation, namely that in addition to the original obligation of the promisor there is an equal obligation of the promisee, this does not make the promisor's obligation of another genre, or it does not belong to the virtue of justice, but it only indicates a difference in the degree of promise.[73] In other words, the fact that one kind of promise is onerous and another is gratuitous does not change the nature of the obligation, but it is only a difference in the extent of the promise.

The virtue of fidelity is the virtue that binds the promisor to fulfil the promise, because he promised and bound himself to his words. Hence, the extent of the binding effect is not to be judged from the virtue of fidelity, but it is to be judged from the nature of the promise. The promise is binding from its nature, writes Osiander, even if it is only a simple assertion.[74] This type of reasoning begins from the etymology of the word 'promise' and not from the consensual nature of the agreement.[75] It remembers somehow Dannhauer's approach on the virtue of truthfulness, which associates the definition with the content of the precept. Yet, Osiander wants to take distance from the virtue of truthfulness and fidelity. A promise is binding for its own nature and not because of the virtue of fidelity. In the court of conscience every promise – even if it is only a statement devoid of the legal requirements, for the same fact that it is a promise – must be observed.

Osiander continues: the basis of the obligation can only be differentiated if the promise creates a personal right, viz. a right to claim the thing from the promisee (*ius ad rem*). The subtle distinction is revealed by the will. The testator promises to give a personal right to the heir. The heir receives the right to claim the thing from the promisee, which means an actionable right, as an

73 J.A. Osiander, *Observationes*, 898-899: "(2) *si promissio onerosa acceptata obligat ex lege iustitiae, etiam gratuita ita obligabit, consequentia est evidens, quia etsi in onerosa sit perfectior obligatio, eo quod pro obligatione rependatur aequalis obligatio, non tamen hoc facit, obligationem promittentis esse alterius generis, aut non pertinere etiam ad virtutem iustitiae, sed tantum gradualem quandam differentiam indicat*".

74 J.A. Osiander, *Observationes*, 899: "(3) *virtus fidei est qua quis servat promissum, quia promisit et se verbis obstrinxit. Hinc quomodo obliget promissio non est diiudicandum ex virtute fidei, sed potius quomodo fides obliget, diiudicandum ex natura promissionis; promissio autem ex natura sua obligat, etiam quantum ad simplicem assertionem*".

75 This attempt to prove the binding effect from the nature of the promise seems very similar to the approach that Christian Wolff will later use. See *Ius naturae methodo scientifica pertractatum*, Frankfurt am Main, 1764, III, § 363. Wolff left the discussion on the virtues as basis for the binding effect of promises by focusing on the nature of promises. See J. Gordley, *The Philosophical Origins*, 75-6.

obligation of the promisor. Consequently, there is an obligation of justice even if it is a gratuitous promise. The fact that the promisee can demand or remit the debt is for Osiander a univocal sign of an obligation of justice.[76]

In conclusion, in his *Theologia casualis* Osiander battled against Cajetan's opinions, opting for a solution very close to Molina's. It is not the nature of the promise, gratuitous or onerous, that makes the difference. The intention of the promisor is fundamentally the criterion to determine the moral or legal effect of the promise. Next to this solution, Osiander makes use of the Scriptures and the Church Fathers, which he says should be considered at the first and second place, respectively. Scripture is very useful to prove the necessity to keep pacts, but less for determining the nature of the bond. The solution is therefore rational and constructed on the early modern scholastics.

In the *Observationes*, Osiander repudiates Connan's opinion. He insists on the fact that a promise is binding for its own nature. It is not an issue of virtues, but in the court of conscience a promise is binding for its nature: both naked and clothed, a promise is binding. Of course this reasoning can only be valid in the court of conscience. And this precisely is the context of Osiander's reasoning. Here no criterion is proposed to distinguish between moral or legal effects.

3.2.5 *Every Just and Honourable Promise is Binding in Conscience*

Johann Wolfgang Jäger also discards Cajetan's opinion. In his commentary on Grotius' *De iure belli ac pacis*, Jäger contends that every just and honourable promise, even if it is simple (not accepted by the promisee), is binding in conscience: because of the promise, the promisor is obliged in his conscience to make true his word, namely to keep the promise. Otherwise the promisor commits a lie, which is not a venial sin, but as the moralists (supposedly the Roman Catholics) say, a mortal sin in its nature. Jäger refers to the Gospel of Matthew 5,37 and comments that since Christ says that we will be accountable for our superfluous words, we should also be responsible for our lies.[77] Scripture does not make any difference between legal or simple promises. Every just and honourable promise is binding.

---

76 J.A. Osiander, *Observationes*, 899.

77 J.W. Jäger, *Hugonis Grotii libri tres*, 322: "*Nos extimamus* primo, *omnem promissionem* iustam et honestam, *etiam simplicem, ad sui observationem* obligare in conscientia. *Ratio est, quia ex promissione tenetur quis in conscientia verum facere dictum suum, hoc est, adimplere promissum; alias mendacium committit, quod nobis non tantum est peccatum, ut moralistae volunt, veniale, sed ex natura sua mortale. Quod evidenter constare potest ex illo dicto Salvatoris apud Matthaeum, ubi ait, nos obligatos esse ad reddendam rationem coram tribunali divino de verbo otioso. Si ergo de quovis otioso verbo reddenda est ratio, cur non de mendacio*".

To bolster the argument, Jäger observes that a breach of promise harms the quietness and common good of human society. On this point he mentions Augustine and Thomas Aquinas. According to the former, man is naturally obliged to keep whatsoever promise he makes; similarly, Thomas holds that the promisor who does not keep the promise acts unfaithfully towards the promisee. Indeed, he who promises has bound himself to keep faith to what said and an infringement of the faith is against natural law. Hence, he who breaches natural law, breaches at the same time the law that is the guardian of society.[78]

Having proved that the breach of a promise implies a sin, Jäger discusses the requirements by which a promise can have effect. He holds that every promise – simple, true, deliberate, voluntary, with a licit and possible subject matter, if the circumstances and the condition of the parties remain unchanged – is binding in conscience, and he who breaches it commits a mortal sin.[79] In support of this statement he quotes the 'best moralists': Miguel Bartolomè Salon (1539-1621), Gregorio di Valencia (1550-1603), Emmanuel Rodriguez (1545-1619) and Gregory Sayer (1560-1602).[80]

These authors, Jäger continues, assume that observance of promises is not only governed by the virtue of truth, but also by the virtue of commutative justice. Therefore, what has been promised is already due, not only for the

78 J.W. Jäger, *Hugonis Grotii libri tres*, 321. Unfortunately, Jäger does not mention any detailed reference to the works of Augustin and Thomas. It is possible, however, that he found this formulation in G. Sayer, *Clavis regia sacerdotum, casuum concientiae sive theologiae moralis*, Venetiis, 1615, Libr. 6, cap. VI, n. 15, 329. Jäger's and Sayer's texts are very similar and Jäger cites Sayer later. Sayer quotes Thomas who seems the true author of this consideration. T. Aquinas, *Summa theologiae*, IIaIIae, q. 88, a. 5 arg. 1; IIa IIae, q. 110, a. 3, arg. 5. The first quote might come from T. Aquinas, *Summa theologiae*, IIaIIae, q. 88, a. 3.

79 J.W. Jäger, *Hugonis Grotii libri tres*, 322: "*Unde* secundo *a fortiori dicimus, omnem promissionem simplicem, veram, deliberatam, voluntariam, rei licitae, possibilis, immutato manente rerum et personarum statu, ita in conscientia obligare*, ut peccet mortaliter qui non servet *promissum*".

80 J.W. Jäger, *Hugonis Grotii libri tres*, 322: "*In hac assertione meliores moralistae conveniunt, eamque defendunt* Michael Salon in 2.2 de dominio, Gregorius de Valentia Tom. 3, disp. 6. Emmanuel Rodriquez part. 2 Summ. 27. Sayrus in clav. reg. libr. 6. cap. 6". M. Salon, *Commentariorum in disputationem de iustitia* [...] *tomus primus*, Venetiis, 1592, 134 ff.; G. de Valentia, *Commentariorum theologicorum tomus tertius*, Lugduni, 1603, 1344 ff.; E. Rodriguez, *Summa casuum concientiae*, Duaci, 1614, Pars secunda, c. 29, 668. Jäger's quotation is wrong because chapter 27 treats the pledge, while chapter 29 deals with promises. G. Sayer, *Clavis regia sacerdotum, casuum concientiae sive theologiae moralis*, Libr. 6, cap. 6, n. 16, 355. It is possible that Jäger took the reference to Salon, de Valentia and Rodriguez from Sayer's work. Indeed, Sayer quotes all these works and commits the same mistake of Jäger in the quotation of Rodriguez. Furthermore, Jäger's statements closely resemble Sayer's.

virtue of truth, but also for the virtue of justice.[81] The reason is that the obligation is not only based on the moral virtue of truthfulness, which commands us to speak the truth, but also on commutative justice, according to which we are obliged to pay the debt we promised. Cajetan's opinion is wrong, because what has been promised is already due and not only on account of the virtue of truthfulness, but also in view of the virtue of justice.[82] The interpretation of Scripture is useful for proving a morally binding effect, but for the legally binding effect, Jäger is constrained to refer to the scholastics. Jäger hangs on their opinion, which finds in the virtues of truth and commutative justice the motivation for the creation of a moral and legal bond.

Unlike Osiander, Jäger adheres to the scholastics' distinction between obligations based on the virtue of truthfulness and fidelity, and obligations also based on the virtue of justice. Promises are not only binding for the virtue of truth but also from the virtue of commutative justice. For this reason they produce a moral and juridical bond. Scripture is only quoted for attesting the obligation in conscience. Indeed, it cannot offer solutions for distinguishing moral and legal promises, and for this reason Jäger needs the assistance of the scholastics.

Although it is not said explicitly, the final criterion for establishing the effects of the promise seems to be promisor's intention. If the promisor intended to be civilly bound, he formed an obligation based on the virtue of justice that therefore is legally actionable. In the opposite case, he will be only morally bound.

3.2.6 Pollicitatio *and* perfecta promissio

Osiander and Jäger remained close to the early modern scholastics and insisted on the promisor's intention. Alberti's conclusions are not too far, but he proposes a slightly more original approach. He distinguishes between a justiciary (*iustitiaria*) promise and a beneficial (*benefica*) promise. The first one, he writes, occurs when I promise to give you something that is already yours. In this case I create only an accessory obligation with my promise, because the thing I promise to give back is already yours. The second one occurs when I promise to give you something mine. In this case a principal obligation is produced, because the thing is not yours, but mine, and there is no obligation

81 J.W. Jäger, *Hugonis Grotii libri tres*, 322. On Soto's and Lessius's criticism of Cajetan see W. Decock, *Theologians and Contract Law*, 200-1.

82 J.W. Jäger, *Hugonis Grotii libri tres*, 322: "Ratio *est, quia observantia promissi non solum* pertinet *ad virtutem moralem veritatis, qua praecipitur nobis, ut verum dicamus, ut male putat Cajetanus; sed* etiam ad iustitiam commutativam, *qua tenemur reddere debitum ei, cui fuit promissum*".

to give you the thing. Thus, the promise can produce an accessory obligation or a principal obligation. This does not change the moral or legal nature of the promise. Unfortunately, Alberti does not adduce any examples, which might help to clarify the meaning of these statements.

For identifying the nature of the promise, Alberti undertakes another strategy: he distinguishes between a simple promise or offer (*pollicitatio*) and a perfect promise (*perfecta promissio*).[83] From both of them originates an obligation to perform what has been promised, but from the first one, it only derives a moral obligation, while the perfect promise produces both a moral and a civil obligation.[84] A moral obligation binds only conscience. When it is broken, it does not offend the right of the other person. Instead when a civil obligation is breached, the right of the other is damaged.[85] In other words, the moral obligation affects conscience, while the civil obligation pertains to the judicial courts. Alberti does not clearly explain why there is a difference between the promise and the perfect promise, but one might argue that the perfect promise implies the will to confer a right and a legal obligation, which is not stated in the *pollicitatio*, that only remains a moral enunciation.

The civil and moral obligation of keeping perfect promises concerns also pacts and contracts. Indeed, Alberti writes, if there is an obligation deriving from a perfect promise, much more can an obligation be discerned in case of agreements, pacts and contracts, where the binding effect is intended not only by words, but it is also expressed in reciprocal bond. The mutual bond is stronger than the perfect promise.[86]

In conclusion, despite the opinion of Meisner, who seemed to follow Cajetan and Connan (although he does not cite them), the majority of the Lutheran theologians refused this view. Osiander and Jäger sustained that every promise gives birth to a moral obligation. They justified this point by referring to Scripture and the scholastics. Every promise can also produce a civil obligation, if the promisor wants. On this aspect they generally turned to the early modern scholastics. It should be remembered, though, that the majority of the early modern scholastics also requested the acceptance of the promisee. Alberti made a further step and separated promises (*pollicitatio*) from perfect

83 Alberti does not define them, but we can suppose he was inspired by Grotius. See H. Grotius, *De iure belli ac pacis*, II, 11, § 3-4.

84 V. Alberti, *Compendium iuris naturae*, 117: "*Ex utraque nascitur obligatio ad praestandum id, quod promissum est; sed illa in pollicitatione est moralis tantum; in perfecta promissione moralis et civilis simul*".

85 V. Alberti, *Compendium iuris naturae*, 18-9.

86 V. Alberti, *Compendium iuris naturae*, 118.

promises (*perfecta promissio*). The first one only produces a moral bond, while the second a moral and legal obligation.

3.3 Formation of the Agreement

3.3.1 *Introduction*

The theologians were unanimous on the principle that agreements are binding. The strength of the agreement is sustained by a moral obligation founded in the Holy Scripture, especially in the eighth commandment of the Decalogue, natural law, the virtue of truthfulness and fidelity and Christian love. The Christian is called to obey the Word of God and keep the faith given in promises, pacts and contracts. The fulfilment of this obligation derives from faith and Holy Spirit.

But when does the binding effect arise? What are the requirements for a binding agreement? Looking at the Scriptures, some theologians required the consent of the parties, the absence of mistakes and deceit, the lawfulness of the subject matter. Some other theologians performed a more detailed analysis, but they mostly drew upon the early modern scholastics' and natural lawyers' works. These theologians also sought to appeal to the Holy Scripture, but this offers scarce support for some issues, and for this reason they needed other sources. In addition to the abovementioned elements, they investigated the necessity of a declaration, acceptance, and the effects of duress.

We first examine in general the different sets of requisites proposed by the theologians, and then we get into the details. Starting from the formation of the agreement, we will then deal with the vices of consent and the licitness of the performance.

3.3.2 *Requirements for the Obligation*

3.3.2.1 Commenting on Cicero: Melanchthon and Von Eitzen

In his *Prolegomena in officia Ciceronis*, Philip Melanchthon addressed the issue of the requirements for a pact to be observed. He essentially designates two requirements for a valid obligation: the free consent and the honourable promise (*ut promissa sint honesta*). As seen before in the paragraph on definitions, the first requisite relates to the capacity of the parties and to the lack of fraud. The second one regards the conformity of the promise to the divine law.[87] This approach is minimalistic but is sufficient to emphasize the basic requirements for a pact to be binding: the subjective requirement of a free will and the

87 P. Melanchthon, *Prolegomena in officia Ciceronis*, in CR XVI, 561. See II/1.3.2.

objective requirement of a licit performance. Melanchthon does not analyse separately the different stages of formation of the agreement and does not talk about the acceptance of the promisee. The starting point of his work is indeed the pact as a result of the consent of two or more parties. Manifest sources of inspiration are the Scriptures and Cicero's *De officiis*, which is indeed studied by Melanchthon.

Melanchthon's approach stimulated the reflections of Paul von Eitzen. In his *Ethica doctrina, pars altera* (1573), in the title dedicated to the eighth commandment, Von Eitzen writes that there are few exceptions where the faith of promises can be broken without sin (*fides promissorum sine scelere violari possit*).[88] He indicates five exceptions, which we briefly summarize here and then see in details in the following chapters: 1) The promise harms the church, the native land (*patria*), the community where the promisor lives or innocent men, or the promise is against the good morals (*contra bonos mores*), namely it is shameful and dishonorable (*turpe et inhonestum*)[89]. 2) The promise is useless or harms the promisee.[90] 3) The condition of the promise subject is changed that the promise cannot be kept without evident danger.[91] 4) The promise must not be observed if it harms more the promisor's position than benefits the promisee.[92] 5) The promise must not be observed if it has been extorted by duress or deceit.[93] The last two points have been drawn from Cicero, as Von Eitzen puts bluntly. For the rest, Von Eitzen looked at the potential damages or perils that the promise can cause to the parties, to the offences against the morality and the necessity of a free will. He justifies the promisor who does not keep the promise because it can damage him, more than profiting the promisee. Same in the event of changed circumstances, if the fulfilment of the promise is dangerous. Also, like Melanchthon, he does not deal with the necessity of the acceptance for the production of the binding effects. No references

88 P. von Eitzen, *Ethicae doctrinae pars altera*, 603b.

89 P. von Eitzen, *Ethicae doctrinae pars altera*, 603b: "*Prima exceptio, si promissum est noxium Ecclesiae, patriae, civitati, in qua vivis, aut aliis innocentibus hominibus, vel si est contra bonos mores, hoc est turpe et inhonestum*".

90 P. von Eitzen, *Ethicae doctrinae pars altera*, 604a: "*Secunda, si promissum est inutile, aut noxium ei cui facta est promissio*".

91 P. von Eitzen, *Ethicae doctrinae pars altera*, 604a: "*Tertia, si eius, cui facta est promissio, conditio ita mutata fuerit, ut sine evidenti periculo servari promissio haud possit*".

92 P. von Eitzen, *Ethicae doctrinae pars altera*, 604a–604b: "*Quarta exceptione ita tradit Cicero lib. 1 Officiorum (...) promissa servanda non esse, si tibi plus noceant, quam illi prosint, cui promiseris*". Cicero, *De officiis*, 1, 32.

93 P. von Eitzen, *Ethicae doctrinae pars altera*, 604b: "*Quinta exceptio etiam traditur a Cicerone: illis, inquit, promissis standum non esse, quis non videt? quae coactus quis metu, aut deceptus dolo, promiserit*". Cicero, *De officiis*, 1, 32.

to Scripture are adduced, and it seems that the basic criterion adopted for formulating this exception is the 'do no harm' principle, united with the principle that the common good must be served, as in Cicero's *De officiis*.[94]

3.3.2.2 Drawing upon the Scholastics: Meisner, Horneius and Jäger

Balthasar Meisner tackled in a systematic way the issue of the requirements necessary for a promise to be binding in conscience, but he undertook an approach different from Melanchthon and Von Eitzen. In his *Dissertatio de summo bono* (1614), he imitates the scholastic model. A simple promise: 1) must be free, namely not unjustly extorted with duress or deceit; 2) deliberate, there is no room for a change of mind; 3) with the intention to bind oneself; 4) the thing promised must be pleasing for the promisee, because the promise of something that is displeasing to the promisee is not a promise but a threat; and 5) the promisor must have the power to bind himself.[95] If he does not have the power to bind himself, or the subject matter of the promise is impossible, the promise is invalid. If these conditions are respected, a promise is binding in conscience.

This kind of solution is anything but new: it echoes the discourses of the early modern scholastics on the validity of promises. They, in turn, took inspiration from the Thomistic doctrine on the requisites for the lawfulness of the oath:[96] judgment (*iudicium*), truth (*veritas*) and justice (*iustitia*). The judgment establishes that the oath be deliberate and motivated; the truth requires the correspondence between will and oath; and justice addresses the lawfulness of the subject matter.[97] Then, this is not only a transposition of a theory developed by the early modern scholastics, but also of a construction that in the final analysis was shaped by Thomas Aquinas.

At a first glance, it might seem that Meisner does not require the acceptance of the promisee for the binding effects of the promise. Yet, a few pages later, he distinguishes three types of promises: gratuitous promises, onerous promises and sworn promises. The gratuitous promise is not binding until it becomes a pact through the acceptance by the promisee. As a consequence, the naked promise is not binding and not enforceable until it becomes a pact through

94 Cicero, *De officiis*, 1, 10, 31.

95 B. Meisner, *Dissertatio de summo bono*, 239: "Promissio simplex dicitur, quae sit *homini*, cujus conditiones quinque commemorant: 1) *Ut sit libera, non metu vel dolo injuste extorta*; 2) *Ut sit deliberata, ne postmodum promissi nos poeniteat*; 3) *Ut fiat cum intentione se obligandi*; 4) *Ut res promissa sit grata promissario. Promittere enim cuipiam, quod ei displicet, non est promittere, sed minari*; 5) *Ut promissor possit se obligare*".

96 I. Birocchi, *Causa e categoria*, 237.

97 T. Aquinas, *Summa theologiae*, IIa-IIae, q. 89, a. 3.

the acceptance.[98] Same for the onerous promise that produces a reciprocal bond.[99] For Meisner, acceptance is therefore an essential requirement for the binding effects.

The contrary opinion, that a promise is binding without acceptance, seems however to have existed within the Lutheran orthodoxy. Conrad Horneius and then Johann Wolfgang Jäger followed the famous casuist Martín de Azpilcueta, also named Dr. Navarrus.[100] Conrad Horneius affirms that the Christian who does not keep a promise – true, voluntary, on a morally licit subject matter, possible and with unchanged conditions – commits a grave sin.[101] Similarly, Jäger holds that every promise simple, true, deliberate, voluntary, with a licit and possible subject matter, if the condition of the people and of the subject matter remains unchanged, is binding in conscience and he who breaches it commits a mortal sin. Horneius and Jäger consider the effects of a promise in conscience and do not recall the acceptance of the promisee.

3.3.2.3 Looking at the Virtues: Olearius and Haferung

On this last route, other theologians, such as Olearius and Haferung, did not require the promisee's acceptance. Their approach is characterized by a better adherence to the Scriptures, a link with the doctrine of virtues and a lack of references to early modern scholastics and natural lawyers. As requirements for a valid obligation, they individuated: the expressed consent of the parties, the absence of mistakes and deceits, the lawfulness of the subject matter.[102] As we are going to see, these authors will mostly focus on principles rather than on norms, but they will attempt to use just the Aristotelian doctrine of virtues in combination with the Scripture.

To summarize, following Cicero's *De officiis* and the Scripture's guidelines, Melanchthon and Von Eitzen drafted a body of requirements for the application of the rule *pacta sunt servanda*. To Melanchthon, they include the honesty of the promise and a free consent. To Von Eitzen they are the honesty of the promise, absence of damages for the parties, utility for the promisee and free

98 B. Meisner, *Dissertatio de summo bono*, 241: "*Gratuita promissio ut sit valida et obliget, requirit* (…) *ex* parte promissarii, *ut acceptet promissionem. Unde nuda promissio, antequam in pactum transeat, quod sit per acceptationem, ordinarie non obligat, nec actionem parit in foro civili*".

99 B. Meisner, *Dissertatio de summo bono*, 240-1.

100 M. de Azpilcueta, *Enchiridion sive manuale confessariorum et poenitentium*, Antverpiae, 1608, 430-1.

101 C. Horneius, *Compendium theologiae*, 783.

102 J. Olearius, *Doctrina theologiae moralis*, Tab. XLVII; J.C. Haferung, *Theologia moralis*, 248-50.

consent. Later, some theologians imported from the early modern scholastics the requirements for the binding effects of a promise. Essentially, they relied on the intellect and will of the promisor and on the subject matter. The promise must be free, deliberate and intentional. The subject matter must be pleasing for the promisee, and the promisor must have the power to bind himself. Meisner also specifies that the promisee's acceptance is necessarily required for gratuitous and onerous promises, while others, like Horneius and Jäger, did not include the acceptance. More orthodox theologians also did not request acceptance, but demanded expressed and free consent, and lawful subject matter. We now focus on the subjective requirements and then on the objective requirements. For the sake of clarity we will keep one compact treatment, distinguishing each time the different approaches used.

3.3.3 *The Intention*

As said earlier, for the scholastics the intention played an essential role, because an evil intention led to damnation, while a good intention drove towards Paradise. Intention was therefore essential for an agreement. But what happens if a declaration is placed without intention? This question had been addressed by the scholastics mostly with regard to marriage. Indeed it occurred that parties declared to marry, but they internally did not want to bind themselves (fictious promise, *promissio ficta*). The majority of the scholastics concluded that the lack of intention renders impossible the production of a bond. A minority opinion, however, held that the declaration is sufficient to cause the binding effect.[103]

Some Lutheran theologians also required the intention to be bound. They focused on the moral requirement of the correspondence between intention and declaration. The promisor who promises something but internally does not have the intention to bind himself is a liar, but there is no binding effect. For instance, Horneius requires that the promise be true, which excludes a fictious promise, because he who promise something by words, but does not have the intention to bind himself, notably harms the neighbour and commits a mortal sin.[104]

Jäger seems to be close to the early modern scholastics when he writes that the binding effect derives from the intention to bind oneself: only a true intention creates the bond. A true promise is a promise made with the intention to

103 W. Decock, *Theologians and Contract Law*, 192-7.

104 C. Horneius, *Compendium theologiae*, 183-4: "*Dixi vera, ad excludendam fictam promissionem, cum quis verbis quidem promisit, sed animum se obligandi non habuit, quamvis etiam hic si notabiliter proximum laedat, vel laedere in animo habeat, mortaliter peccet*".

bind oneself (*cum animo se obligandi*). Nobody can be bound except for his intention, because it is precisely in the intention that is located the power of binding oneself. Therefore, if someone promises something only by external signs, but internally he does not want to be bound, he is a false and a liar, and the other does not acquire the right to reclaim what has been promised.[105] This solution plainly reflects the scholastic centrality on the intention.

Other theologians did not examine in depth this problem but limited their observations to the necessity of a free and spontaneous consent. Alberti points out that in order to create an obligation, the consent of both parties is necessary.[106] Consent is an act of both the intellect and the will and must be spontaneous: the act must be produced through a deliberate will. A deliberate will is surely directed to that pact, without any doubt, and it is sufficiently informed by intellect.[107] Buddeus only stresses the spontaneity of consent. In every case, he writes, a spontaneous and un-impeded consent is required for the validity of pact.[108]

3.3.4 *The Expression of Consent*

3.3.4.1 Introduction

In order to create a valid agreement, the consent must be expressed with a declaration. Certainly, the necessity of a declaration was a topic largely discussed by the early modern scholastics. They investigated the efficacy of the so-called internal promises (not externally declared). The majority concluded for the necessity of a declaration, while a minority faction maintained that the internal promise was binding, without the declaration. The Lutherans again imitated the early modern scholastics. Already Gerhard, concerning marriage, investigated whether deaf or mute individuals could pronounce a valid consent, and similarly whether a tacit consent is sufficient or if an expressed consent should be requested.[109] Concerning promises, two opinions circulated: Osiander concluded for the necessity of the declaration, while Jäger, looking at the special nature of the *forum conscientiae*, answered the opposite. However,

105 Jäger, *Hugonis Grotii libri tres*, 323: "*Diximus autem* primo *de promissione* vera, *hoc est ut sit facta* cum animo se obligandi; *nemo enim potest obligari, nisi animum habeat se obligandi; potissima enim vis obligativa, stat in intentionem. Interim si quis per verba exteriora aliquid promisit, et interius non habuit intentionem se obligandi: ille fallax est et turpiter mendax, quanquam alteri ius proximum ita non nascatur petendi promissum*".

106 V. Alberti, *Compendium iuris naturae*, 108-9.

107 V. Alberti, *Compendium iuris naturae*, 109-10.

108 J. F. Buddeus, *Institutiones theologiae moralis*, 509.

109 J. Gerhard, *Locorum theologicorum tomus quintus*, 127-8.

others did not grapple with this issue: they demanded the declaration and only concentrated on the types of declarations.

3.3.4.2 Osiander: The Necessity of a Declaration

Osiander faces this problem differently in his *Observationes* and in his *Theologia casualis.* In the *Observationes*, he first summarizes the argument proposed by the minority voices among the early modern scholastics and then rebuts it. He mentions the Dominicans Domingo de Soto (1494-1560) and Pedro de Ledesma (1550-1616) and the Jesuit Luis de Molina (1535-1600), who claimed that the intention is sufficient to cause the bond according to natural law and there is no need of a declaration.[110] They listed three reasons: 1) the internal promise adds something to a simple purpose, a so-called naked purpose (*nudum propositum*), and therefore the internal promise is binding more than a naked purpose. 2) A man who does not want a certain good can release it through an internal act. 3) A man can also cause an obligation by an internal act. If he promised with an internal act yesterday, and today he declares externally his intention, the promise can be accepted. If the other party accepts the promise, the promisor is bound without a new internal act. He is bound by virtue of his previous internal act, because he did not make another internal act, but merely declared externally the previous one.[111] The assertions of these scholars pivoted on the intention as essential element to make the obligation and excluded the necessary nature of the external sign. If the power of binding is rooted in the intention, the sign is not a necessary element but only an accessory element.

Osiander does not share this view, maintaining rather that the internal promise is not binding, but requires an external declaration. He endorses Grotius, who opted for the necessity of an external declaration. If promises and donations are practical signs, they are included in the same act of promising or donating. There is no distinction between donation or promise and the act of donating or promising. There is no promise and no donation without an external declaration.[112] This perspective considered as fictitious the separation between an internal and an external promise: the promise only exists with a declaration; without a declaration, there is no promise.

Osiander is convinced by this solution and carefully rejects the claim of the majority of the scholastics expounded previously. To the first argument, he

110 J.A. Osiander, *Observationes*, 901. Unfortunately, Osiander does not quote any works of these authors but only proposes a short summary.
111 J.A. Osiander, *Observationes*, 901.
112 J.A. Osiander, *Observationes*, 901.

responds that an internal promise adds something to the purpose, but it is not the completion of a promise: it is just the beginning of a promise, which is not enough to produce any obligation.[113] To the second argument, he replies that the ownership and property of goods can be dismissed through an internal act, surely if they are abandoned, but they cannot be transferred, because more acts are required to transfer goods.[114]

To the third argument, Osiander responds that such a construction supposes that the obligation is derived from a real internal act, but the obligation is derived from both an internal act and an external act. Although the power of binding is in the will, this is not able to generate any obligation without an external act, which works like an interposing instrument. As the jurisdiction is not conferred without an external act, so external signs are not only required to express the will to donate, but also to make the same donation and promise, as through organs of transferring and applying.[115] Osiander concludes by refusing the opinion of these theologians and by following Grotius, who contended the necessity of the declaration. He first analysed the early modern theologians' positions and then engaged in the discussion.

Osiander's solution might seem disappointing because he mainly relies on sources other than the Scriptures and does not attempt to find an original idea. In his *Theologia casualis*, however, he tries to face the same problem (the necessity of an external declaration) in a different way. He distinguishes between promises before God and promises towards men.[116] Promises to God are binding also without an external declaration. First of all, Scripture guarantees this statement in Ecclesiastes 5,4: "*When thou vowest a vow unto God, defer not to pay it; for he hath no pleasure in fools: pay that which thou hast vowed*". The

113 J. A. Osiander, *Observationes*, 901: "*Quapropter respondemus ad objecta, et quidem ad (1) internam promissionem addere utique aliquid supra propositum, sed non promissionis complementum, sed inchoationem solum promissionis, quae nondum sufficit ad causandam aliquam obligationem*".

114 J.A. Osiander, *Observationes*, 901-2: "*Ad (2) respondetur quamvis possessio et dominium possint amitti actu interno, scilicet si res habeatur pro derelicta, non tamen possint transferri in alium actu solo interno, quia ad translationem plura requiruntur ...*".

115 J.A. Osiander, *Observationes*, 902: "*Ad (3) respondetur quamvis tota vis obligandi sit a voluntate, non tamen causatur immediate obligatio absque actu externo, tamquam instrumento interveniente; sicut nec jurisdictio confertur sine externo actu, et consequenter signa externa non solum requiruntur ut voluntas donandi per illa significetur, sed etiam ut per illa ipsa donatio et promissio fiat, tamquam per organa transferendi et applicandi*".

116 This distinction was also quite familiar to the scholastics. See for instance W. Decock, *Theologians and Contract Law*, 179-80.

Church Fathers Augustine and Bernhard support this conclusion.[117] Finally, Osiander adds a theological reason: God is not like men who need exterior signs; God is the knower of hearts (*καρδιογνώστης*). To Him is also accessible the inner realm of men, the profundity of his thoughts.[118] Save the third reason, these arguments are not totally clear. Indeed the Scriptures and the Church Fathers affirm that the vow must be kept, but they do not say anything about the way it must be pronounced.

Concerning promises towards men, the solution is different. If the promise is merely an internal one, not declared through an external sign, it is not binding.[119] According to Osiander, when the Scripture refers to promises towards human society and the neighbour, it always uses the word 'discourse' (*sermo*) because it wants to mean that promises have this name and strength through an external sign.[120] For instance, in Esther 5,3: "*Then said the king unto her, What wilt thou, queen Esther? and what is thy request? it shall be even given thee to the half of the kingdom*"; Matt. 14,7: "*Whereupon he promised with an oath to give her whatsoever she would ask*"; Mark 14,11: "*And when they heard it, they were glad, and promised to give him money*". According to Osiander, these passages testify that between men a promise must be expressed through an external sign in order to be valid.

The second reason is that Church Fathers, when they deal with promises, always describe them as uttered through an external sign. For instance, regarding the promise made by Jephthah to God, Ambrose says: "*the promise was harsh, but more bitter was the payment, because even he who made it necessarily deplored*".[121] Indeed this passage seems to allude to a spoken promise.

The third reason is that the promise is manifested to the other party through a sign, because God granted man the use of the word in order to bind himself to the neighbour[122] Osiander bolsters this statement by making reference to Jesuit scholastics. For example, he quotes the Spanish theologian Juan de

---

117 Augustinus Hipponensis, *Enarrationes in psalmos*, 115, 8, 28, in *PL* 36; Sermone de tempore 117, n. 5, in *PL* 38, p. 1979; Bernardus, *Liber de modo bene vivendi*, in *PL* 184, LXII, 147, p. 1292.

118 J.A. Osiander, *Theologiae casualis*, 99: "Tertio *ratio theologica. Est Deus καρδιογνώστης qui non, ut homines, opus habet figuris externis, sed cui etiam interiora, profundum nostrarum cogitationum, patet*".

119 J.A. Osiander, *Theologiae casualis*, 99: "*Si verò* posteriori modo *spectetur, promissio non videtur illa obligare, si sit merè interna, nullo signo manifestata*".

120 J.A. Osiander, *Theologiae casualis*, 99.

121 J.A. Osiander, *Theologiae casualis*, 99: "*Dura promissio, acerbior solutio, quam necesse habuit lugere etiam ipse, qui fecit*". Ambrosius, *De officiis ministrorum*, Lib. III, c. 12, § 78.

122 J.A. Osiander, *Theologiae casualis*, 99: "... *nec alio fine Deus sermonem homini concessit, quam ut inter alia etiam per illum sese proximo obliget et obstringat*".

Dicastillo (1584-1653), who makes a comparison with the promulgation of law. As a law is not binding until it has been promulgated, so a human act cannot be binding before the acceptance. Internal promises cannot be accepted because they cannot be known.[123]

Then, Osiander quotes a large passage of the work of the great moralist Antonio Escobar y Mendoza (1589-1669). Mendoza asserts that an internal promise is not enough to cause an obligation, because an obligation based on the virtue of fidelity cannot arise from a mere internal promise: truthfulness and fidelity require external signs between men. The virtue of truthfulness requires that intentions correspond to facts, and the virtue of fidelity expects facts to be in agreement with what has been said. It follows that an obligation based on the virtue of justice cannot arise: if there is no obligation of fidelity, there cannot be an obligation of justice. Indeed the obligation of justice presupposes the existence of an obligation of fidelity.[124]

To sum up, in his *Observationes* Osiander admires Grotius' solution: the promise only exists with a declaration, for without a declaration, there is no promise. Yet, he is not only satisfied with a mere reference. He goes in depth by reporting the opposing opinion and by criticizing it. In his *Theologia casualis*, Osiander follows a different method: Scripture takes the first place, then the Church Fathers and finally the reasoning of the scholastics. The scholastics mainly used rational arguments and employed a speculative analysis of the problem. Osiander instead begins from the Holy Scripture and the Church Fathers and only at a third level inserts rational arguments.

Despite the praiseworthy attempt to derive a solution from the Scriptures and the Church Fathers, Osiander draws upon the early modern scholastics. Scripture helps, because it seems to associate promises with a declaration. But it appears that our theologian wanted to engage in the discussion and found persuasive some scholastic reasonings that substantially corroborate his argument.

3.3.4.3 Jäger: Everything is binding in the Court of Conscience

The necessity of a declaration is similarly questioned by Johann Wolfgang Jäger. Jäger is also imbued with the scholastic arguments: he reports the discussion between the early modern theologians and then formulates his own

123 J.A. Osiander, *Theologiae casualis*, 99-100.

124 J.A. Osiander, *Observationes*, 902-3. A. Escobar, *Universae theologiae moralis receptiores absque lite sententiae nec non problematicae disquisitiones* [...], Lugduni, 1663, vol. 5, pars prima, p. 112, § 128-9. Such an opinion is also maintained by the majority of the early modern theologians. For instance, Escobar refers to Gabriel Vásquez (1549-1604), Leonard Lessius (1554-1623), Tomás Sánchez (1550-1610), Ludovico López (d. 1595) and others.

opinion, although he does not add any original motivation. The starting points are Molina's and Ledesma's positions and particularly other two arguments against the necessity of a declaration. The first one regards an oath added to a promise. If a mental promise is strengthened by an oath, this promise will not only be binding for the oath, but also for the mental promise. The oath indeed does not create a new obligation, but it merely confirms the previous one. The second argument concerns a promise made by a deaf person or made to an absent person, although in the presence of another person. This promise is binding in conscience, even though an external sign does not express it.[125]

To these reasons, Jäger counterposes the opinions of the French Catholic theologian Jacques Almain[126] (1480-1515) and the German Jesuit Christoph Haunold (1610-1689).[127] They maintain that the expression of concepts through words is absolutely natural. Consequently, without an expressed promise, it is impossible to have an obligation. The internal promise confirmed by an oath is binding due to the power of the oath, and not for the promise in itself: it is the reverence to God that makes the promise effective. The promise pronounced to an absent person is not binding until the person who was absent accepts it or another person accepts it in the absentee's name.[128]

After the careful examination of the scholastics' stances, Jäger makes his conclusion that is, though, rather surprising. He writes that because in the *forum conscientiae* everything is binding, what has been mentally promised is also binding.[129] Unfortunately, he does not substantiate this position, but rather makes a kind of practical consideration. He seems to conclude that in the *forum conscientiae* there is no need of an external declaration in order to produce a binding agreement.

To summarize, Osiander and Jäger grappled with the problem of the efficacy of internal promises following the traces of the early modern scholastics. They studied the scholastics but reached opposite conclusions from each other. Osiander espouses the view that internal promises are not binding. Jäger holds the contrary. Osiander mainly justifies his opinion by mentioning the scholastics, but also through the Scriptures and the Church Fathers, which he declares

125 J.W. Jäger, *Hugonis Grotii libri tres*, 327.

126 T.M. Izbicki, *Jacques Almain*, in H. Lagerlund (ed.), *Encyclopedia of Medieval Philosophy: Philosophy Between 500 and 1500*, vol. 1, London, Dordrecht, Heidelberg, London, New York, Springer, 2011, 579-81.

127 B. Schneider SJ, *Haunold, Christoph*, in *Neue Deutsche Biographie* 8 (1969), 98 (accessed 01.09.2015); http://www.deutsche-biographie.de/ppn124773664.html.

128 J.W. Jäger, *Hugonis Grotii libri tres*, 329.

129 J.W. Jäger, *Hugonis Grotii libri tres*, 329: "*Nos interim id notamus*, totius esse in foro conscientiae, etiam *ea, quae* mentaliter promissae *sunt*, servare".

to have the first and second place respectively. On the other hand, Jäger states that everything is binding in *forum conscientiae*, but he does not add any validation. He fails to develop a complete argument, as he simply chooses between the two solutions presented by the scholastics.

3.3.4.4 The Types of Declarations

As noted earlier, several Lutherans did not enter into the discussion on the consent formulated in mind and the necessity of an exterior sign but took it for granted and pragmatically examined the way this exterior sign can be formulated. They analysed the means used to communicate the consent to the other party. For instance, Johannes Olearius speaks about pacts and promises formulated expressly or tacitly, with a nod or a sign or testified with any other indication.[130] Haferung differentiates between an explicit pact and an implicit pact, and then between a pact expressed by signs or a consent expressed by words. He depicts these forms of pacts through examples taken from Scripture. The 'explicit pact' is a pact established by words, as for instance the statement of Laban pronounced to Jacob in the book of Genesis 31,50-51:

> *if thou shalt afflict my daughters, or if thou shalt take other wives beside my daughters, no man is with us; see, God is witness betwixt me and thee. And Laban said to Jacob, Behold this heap, and behold this pillar, which I have cast betwixt me and thee.*

In this passage consent is verbally pronounced from Laban to Jacob. Instead, the 'implicit pact' is clear from the nature of pact or from the relationship with the other party. For example, as a truce is not only valid during the day but also by night, so a son is supposed to obey his parents.[131]

To Haferung, consent can be expressed through signs, as nod, gesture or a similar expression as in Luke 1,62 and Judith 9,4. In the discussion between Elizabeth, the mother of St. John the Baptist, and her neighbour and relatives about the name to give to the baby (St. John), the neighbour and relatives "*made signs to his father, asking how he would have him called*". This is a clear fact that proves consent can also be expressed by sign. Less clear is the second

---

130 J. Olearius, *Doctrina theologiae moralis*, Tab. XLVII. Furthermore, he warns the party to indicate clearly his intentions, because every ambiguity should be avoided.

131 J.C. Haferung, *Theologia moralis*, 249: "Pactum [1] *circa quod obligat fidelitas est* (a) *vel* explicitum, *quod expressis utrinque verbis initur et stabilitur. Gen. XXXI, 50. 51. Vel* implicitum, *quod in natura pacti explicite, vel ex* relatione *nostri in alium intelligi existimatur. Ut, qui dierum inducias* pactus est, *servet et noctium; qui* filius *est, etiam obsequatur parenti*".

passage, the apocryphal book of Judith, because there seem be no references to gestures or signs. The passage just tells that Judith prays God asking for help.

The necessary consent for the pact can also be expressed by words: the promisor should keep his word if the other party proves to have understood the words. Haferung refers to the case of an oath made by Shimei and ordered by Solomon in 1 Kings 2,42:

> *and the king sent and called for Shimei, and said unto him, Did I not make thee to swear by the Lord, and protested unto thee, saying, Know for a certain, on the day thou goest out, and walkest abroad any whither, that thou shalt surely die? and thou saidst unto me, The word that I have heard is good.*

The fact that Shimei understood the words makes the promise valid. The consent is declared and understood.[132] As seen, even if this discourse can seem to be not entirely original, Haferung uses Holy Scripture as a source of inspiration for his analysis. He takes words and episodes to draw conclusions on the means to communicate the consent.

If Haferung seems to be tied to the Scriptures, Johannes Franz Buddeus more openly refers to external sources such as the natural lawyers. He distinguishes between expressed consent, tacit consent and presumed consent. Consent can be declared by words, facts, gestures, etc. Silence can be considered as consent under determined circumstances. Presumed consent is not a valid form of consent because it is against equity. Buddeus does not explain this issue clearly; instead he just refers to Christian Thomasius, who should provide the reader with a further explanation.[133]

In conclusion, there is no doubt that the theologians gave the parties the possibility to express their consent in different ways and not only through words. The interesting aspect is again the method employed. Haferung seeks solutions in the Scriptures, while Buddeus trusts external sources, like the natural lawyers.

3.3.5 *The Necessity of Acceptance*

The creation of a binding agreement depends on the expressed will of the parties. A necessarily linked issue is about the acceptance of the promise: if the promise could take effect before the acceptance by the promisee. As seen earlier,

---

132 J.C. Haferung, *Theologia moralis*, 249: "(b) *Est vel* signo *tantum, e.g. nutu, gestu aut simili expressum. Luc. 1, 62. 63. Iud. IX, 4. vel* verbo *declaratum; Quod ita intelligendum et servandum est, ut alter, cui promissio fit, innuit, se intelligere. 1 Reg. II, 42*".

133 J.F. Buddeus, *Institutiones theologiae moralis*, 509. He cites C. Thomasius, *Institutiones iurisprudentiae divinae*, lib. 2, cap. 7 § 19.

certain Lutheran theologians do not request the acceptance, but the promise is binding in conscience due to the sole consent of the promisor. Horneius and Jäger followed Martín de Azpilcueta: a promise true, voluntary, on a morally licit subject matter, possible and if the conditions remain unchanged is binding in conscience. They do not specify the necessity of acceptance.

Other theologians answered the opposite and demanded the acceptance. For instance, Friedemann Becmann plainly writes that acceptance is requested, because a naked promise is not binding without acceptance and does not give rise to any actions in the civil courts. The reason is that the obligation arises from the mutual consent of two parties. Therefore, if the promisee does not consent, the promisor is not obliged.[134] Despite the lack of references, this solution seems to have been inspired by the early modern scholastics and the natural lawyers, as they centred their contractual doctrine on the parties' consent.

Osiander is an example of a more structured analysis. In his *Theologia casualis*, he sustains that in order to transfer a right, the promisee's acceptance is required and lists three reasons: Scripture, the Church Fathers and rational arguments.[135] The first reason is based upon the authority of Scripture. Osiander cites Joshua 6,17:

> *and the city shall be accursed, even it, and all that are therein, to the Lord: only Rahab the harlot shall live, she and all that are with her in the house, because she hid the messengers that we sent*"; v. 22-23: "*but Joshua had said unto the two men that had spied out the country, Go into the harlot's house, and bring out thence the woman, and all that she hath, as ye swore unto her. And the young men that were spies went in, and brought out Rahab, and her father, and her mother, and her brethren, and all that she had; and they brought out all her kindred, and left them without the camp of Israel.*

As it is evident, Scripture is not very clear on this point, and Osiander does not add any explanation. In the quoted passage, there are no direct references to promises, and no plain solution to the problem. The only relevant aspect is Joshua's order that is executed. Maybe it is for this reason that Osiander needs to add other justifications.

134 F. Becmann, *Ad D. Joh. Olearii theologiam moralem*, 348: "*Ex parte* eius, cui promissio facta est, *requiritur ut promissionem acceptet. Nam nuda promissio sine acceptatione alterius non obligat, nec in foro civili actionem parit. Ratio est, quod obligatio nascatur ex mutuo duorum consensu. Si ergo promissarius non consentit in promissum, promissor non obigatur*".

135 J.A. Osiander, *Theologiae casualis*, 103-4: "*An promissio obliget ante acceptationem? Requiri acceptationem regulariter, constat primo ex Josuae 6, v. 17, 22,23. Secundo ex Gregorio M. Homilia 32 in Evangelia* (...) *Tertio ex ratione*".

The second motivation Osiander indicates is a statement of Gregory the Great. To Gregory, something was promised to the new disciples in the present life, so that they could be stronger in the future life. People are made of flesh, and if they do not see, they do not believe. God indicates the celestial things by bestowing lands, so that by perceiving what it is possible to see, people can hope in what they cannot see.[136] This discourse is about promises, but again there seems not to be any reference to the necessity of acceptance.

The third and last motivation is rational: the obligation arises from the reciprocal consent of the parties because the promisor can change his mind and revoke his promise before the other contracting party's consent is expressed.[137] Osiander justifies this statement through the opinions of the early modern scholastics. The method is the same we saw a few moments ago regarding the internal promises: a summary of the scholastics' opinions, often without specific bibliographical references. Covarrubias and Molina, he writes, affirm that likely the necessity of acceptance derives from the fact that the positive law ordains it, but if we remain in the area of natural law, the promisor's consent might only be necessary in order to cause a valid obligation. These authors observe that: 1) in the public offer (D. 50,12) an obligation arises without acceptance, and therefore the promise is binding *per se*; 2) in the gratuitous promises, the obligation does not arise by the acceptance, but by the promise in itself, because there is no reciprocal obligation. Diego de Covarrubias (1512-1577) and Molina quote the opinion of the canonist Felinus Sandaeus (1444-1503), who in turn quotes Bartolus, Baldus and Panormitanus. Sandaeus holds that such promises are valid in canon law, without acceptance.[138]

Osiander continues in the scholastics' line of reasoning, writing that it is more probable that the promise and the donation do not have binding effects before the acceptance, and this does not only come from civil law, but also from natural law and the *ius gentium*. This is the common opinion. Although he is not expressly cited, Lessius was a prominent advocate of this solution.[139] To the first objection, Osiander continues, it is possible to answer that the civil

136 J.A. Osiander, *Theologiae casualis*, 103-4; Gregorius, *Homiliae in Evangelia*, Homilia XXXII, in *PL* 76, 6, 1237.

137 J.A. Osiander, *Theologiae casualis*, 104: "Tertio *ex ratione. Obligatio non nascitur, nisi ex mutuo duorum consensu. Quapropter priusquam alterius consensus accedat, prior potest poenitere, et suam promissionem revocare*".

138 J.A. Osiander, *Theologiae casualis*, 104; F. Sandaeus, *In quinque libros decretalium commentaria*, Lugduni, 1535, ad X. 1.35, num. 7; D. de Covarruvias, *Relectio in cap. Quamvis pactum de pactis*, Lugduni, 1558, secunda partis, § 2 num. 8; L. Molina, *Disputationes de contractibus*, (De iustitia et iure, vol. 2), Venetiis, 1601, Disputatio 263, p. 23ff.

139 L. Lessius, *De iustitia et de iure ceterisque virtutibus cardinalis libri quatuor*, Lovanii, 1605, lib. 2, cap. 18, dub. 6, 199-201. On Lessius's opinion see: W. Decock, *Theologians and Contract Law*, 187-92.

law does not establish that the public offers have binding effects before the acceptance, but that the offers cannot be revoked freely. The obligation does not arise from the acceptance as a direct cause, Osiander points out, but as a condition necessarily requested.[140]

Roman law, canon law and natural law require the acceptance. The decretal *Si tibi absenti* (VI 3,4,17) states that in case of the absence of the recipient, the benefit (*beneficium*) will be assigned to the bishop. The assignment is possible, but the recipient will not acquire any right on the benefit until he has ratified it. The canon law, therefore, requires an acceptance, and the text could not be clearer.[141] Osiander trusts the interpretation of the great Jesuit moralist Antonio Escobar y Mendoza, who affirms that in the cited passage, the obligation only arises after the acceptance and not before. Furthermore, nowhere is it said that the canon law corrects the civil law for the necessity of acceptance. The acceptance is necessary for natural law, and therefore it is also requested by the positive canon law.[142]

To recapitulate, some Lutheran theologians did not believe that the acceptance of the promisor was necessary for the binding effects of a promise. Other theologians, however, held the opposite. In a few sentences, Becmann answers that the obligation arises from the mutual consent of two parties, and therefore acceptance is necessary. Osiander attempts to find solutions to this problem in the Scriptures and in the Church Fathers. Yet it is plain that he wishes to import solutions from the early modern scholastics, as neither the Scriptures nor the Church Fathers are clear on this issue. Because the solution could not come from these preferred sources, it was necessary to look elsewhere. Granted, Scripture retains its place of primacy, but de facto Osiander's work relies on the early modern scholastics. On top of that, the summary he presented includes an important reference to the canon law that, in this way, indirectly becomes part of Osiander's argument.

3.3.6 *The Subjects of the Agreement*

There is one last point that needs to be explored: the rule *pacta sunt servanda* applies to pacts between men and its efficacy regards every man. Johann Franz

140 J.A. Osiander, *Theologiae casualis*, 104.

141 J.A. Osiander, *Theologiae casualis*, 103-4: "*Imo satis clare habetur in illo ipso capitulo, quod adversarii objiciunt, nempe* cap. 7 de praebend. in 6 (VI 3,4,17) *ubi dicitur.* [*Si tibi absenti per tuum Episcopum conferatur beneficium: licet NB. Per collationem hujusmodi* (*NB.* Donec eam ratam habueris) *ius in ipso beneficio, ut tuum dici valeat, non acquiras*]. *Quid clarius?*".

142 J.A. Osiander, *Theologiae casualis*, 106-7. A. Escobar, *Universae theologiae moralis*, vol. 5, dubium 14, n. 131-2, p. 112.

Buddeus designates the extent of the binding effect of pacts with these words: "*the word given in pacts and promises has to be respected towards every single person*".[143] Within this general principle, the theologians took into consideration special categories of subjects, who were analysed because of their peculiar characteristics in terms of morality and confession of faith.

Alberti suggests an exception to the *pacta sunt servanda* in the case of criminals. Since the contractual obligation has to be licit, agreements with criminals are not binding, except in the case that the crime is of small extent, so that the punishment can be remitted without breaching natural law.[144] Indeed, the natural law requires always punishment for its violation, and a promise that is against a punishment cannot be considered valid.[145] Alberti seems to apply to the person a requisite that was commonly applied to the subject matter of the agreement. Mostly the theologians looked at the case of the criminals as a case of immoral subject matter. Yet, to Alberti it concerns the person, who as a criminal, cannot produce a valid agreement with his consent.

Another category of person that was the subject of particular consideration was the heretic. The sixteenth to seventeenth centuries were periods of religious wars. Europe was sharply divided between various confessions. Merchants traveled and needed to negotiate agreements with people of different confessions. Among the Catholics, erudite scholars as Lessius, Suarez and Becanus explored the issue.[146] In the Lutherans' circles, Olearius and Haferung assume that the people who must keep fidelity in pacts are men who have made a promise: believers or unbelievers, orthodox men or heretics.[147] Similarly, Alberti considers as valid the effect of promises both in the state of integrity and in the state of corruption. In the state of corruption, it regards enemies, dishonest people, heretics and unbelievers.[148]

For Buddeus agreements with heretics are licit and must be observed. He claims that there is a common bond produced by natural law, and the Holy Scripture indicates that certain agreements were stipulated with the heretics. For example, Abraham entered into a contract with Abimelech, and David and

---

143 J.F. Buddeus, *Institutiones theologiae moralis*, 510: "*Fides in pactis et promissis data, erga omnes ac singulos servanda est*".

144 V. Alberti, *Compendium iuris naturae*, 108: "*Quia vero promissio alias debet esse licita, obligatio eius iure naturae non est extendenda ad maleficos, nisi crimen eorum sit tantillum, ut poena non invito iure naturae ipsis possit remitti*".

145 V. Alberti, *Compendium iuris naturae*, 108.

146 W. Decock, *Trust Beyond Faith Re-Thinking Contracts*, passim.

147 J. Olearius, *Doctrina theologiae moralis*, Tab. XLVII; J.C. Haferung, *Theologia moralis*, 249-50.

148 V. Alberti, *Compendium iuris naturae*, 108.

Salomon with Hiram, king of Tyre.[149] Agreements with heretics are approved, but Buddeus deems that agreements with atheists are not binding. He affirms that it is a foolish man who concludes a pact with an atheist; since the atheist does not have any religion, he also does not have any natural law. Agreements with atheists are excluded from the application of the rule *pacta sunt servanda*, because the atheists do not profess any religion and do not acknowledge any natural law or divine law. The rule *pacta sunt servanda* is founded on the divine law and on the existence of God as the legislator. Without God there is no divine law, which renders the agreements with the atheists void.[150]

In conclusion, for the Lutherans the efficacy of agreements is to be related to every man, though some categories of people were the subject of a more detailed consideration. Alberti considered the agreements to be invalid for criminals, while Buddeus maintained that agreements with atheists are void. Agreements with heretics are instead valid, as they remain nonetheless bound to a natural law. In this analysis the moral concern stands out, and for this reason the theologians exclude certain people from the range of application of the *pacta sunt servanda*.

3.4 Vices of Consent

3.4.1 *Introduction*

The mutual consent of the parties creates a binding agreement. As a further requisite for the validity of the contractual obligation, the theologians asked that the consent be free and spontaneous. The early modern scholastics already arrived at this conclusion, in line with Grotius and other natural lawyers. Inspired by the Roman law, canon law and Aristotelian-Thomistic philosophy, they individuated various obstacles to the freedom of consent: duress (*metus*), mistake (*error vel dolus*) and incapacity.[151]

Generally speaking, the Lutherans gathered the fruits of the discussion ripened in the Roman Catholic context, though some theologians used the virtue of fidelity and the interpretation of Scripture as dominant elements of their

149 J.F. Buddeus, *Institutiones theologiae moralis*, 511.

150 J.F. Buddeus, *Institutiones theologiae moralis*, 511: "*Cum atheis, si modo constet, eos tales esse, pacta inire stultum foret, cum nulla religione teneantur, adeoque nec leges naturales admittant*". Then he continues the discourse in the footnotes: "*Non tantum stultum est, cum atheis pacta aut foedera inire, sed ipsa illa foedera nulla plane sunt, cum omne pactum aut foedus supponat legem divinam, pacta esse servanda. Lex autem divina sine Deo, seu legislatore, concipi nequit*".

151 W. Decock, *Theologians and Contract Law*, 215-327.

analysis. They do not speak about impediments to will, but they examine the breach of the bond, which in turn is based on the virtue of fidelity. According to Dannhauer, for example, the virtue of truthfulness is opposed to the fallacy or fraud (*fallacia*), and the fallacy encompasses deceit (*dolus*) and mistake (*error*).[152] In a similar way, Olearius considers the opposites of the virtue of fidelity: perfidy (*perfidia*), deceit, betrayal (*proditio*) and, as its species, treason (*traditio*).[153] He concludes that they are all nullifying conditions for the fidelity to promises.

Haferung holds that the promisor must have full mental capacity (*mentis compos*) and lists the same points of Olearius, adding 'desertion' (*desertio*), probably meant as denial of the obligation.[154] This group of theologians does not focus on the lack of consent, but looks more at its consequences: the bond is breached. The subject of the analysis is not the will of the parties, but the virtue of fidelity and when it is dishonored. As a consequence, these theologians do not include duress in their treatments of general contract law, but they analyse the execution of the agreement. In other words, in these authors we see a shift from the centrality of consent to the centrality of the bond.

A second stream of theologians imitated the early modern scholastics and natural lawyers, and connected the setting-aside directly to the lack of consent. Balthasar Meisner, for example, indicates as vices of consent: duress, mistake and deceit.[155] Georg König mentions duress and deceit.[156] According to Buddeus, the consent is the most important requisite; if it is lacking or was impeded, the obligation to fulfil promises or pacts is consequently nullified.[157] Impediments to consent are divided in two types: those concerning the intellect and those regarding the will. Impediments that affect the intellect are the following: age (*aetas*), insanity (*furor*), mistake and drunkenness (*ebrietas*). The impediment regarding the will is duress and coercion (*metus et coactio*).[158] Similarly, Alberti holds that a promise is only valid when it is produced by an act of intellect and will. The party should not promise without a detailed knowledge of the pact, because in this case, he cannot fully utilize or express

152 J.K. Dannhauer, *Deuteronomium Dannhawerianum*, 438, 443, 444.

153 J. Olearius, *Doctrina theologiae moralis*, Tab. XLVII.

154 J.C. Haferung, *Theologia moralis*, 250-1.

155 B. Meisner, *Dissertatio de summo bono*, 242.

156 G. König, *Casus conscientiae*, 17.

157 J.F. Buddeus, *Institutiones theologiae moralis*, 509: "*Cumque ante omnia consensus ad ea requiratur, si hic non adfuerit, aut impeditus fuerit, obligationem quoque pactorum aut promissorum nullam esse, sua sponte sequitur*".

158 J.F. Buddeus, *Institutiones theologiae moralis*, 509. In the *Elementa philosophiae practicae*, 272, Buddeus explicates that he refers to a single impendiment.

his will. Alberti distinguishes two impediments: mistake, which affects the intellect, and duress, which concerns the will.[159]

Next to the early modern scholastics and natural lawyers, this second stream may have found inspiration in the moral regulations on marriage.[160] Marriage has in common with promises and pacts the necessity of a free consent. For instance, one of the first Lutheran authors to deal with this topic, Hemmingsen, observes that the consent must be free, namely with judgment and will. Indeed, he who consents does so with a sane judgment, without mistake. He who commits a mistake is erroneous in judgment and thus does not consent purely. He who does not consent purely does not truly promise: what prevents the cause also prevents the effect.[161] This is just an example of the theologians' analysis of free consent in marriage law, an example that demonstrates how the Church's marriage laws might have influenced the general treatment of vices of consent.

In conclusion, the theologians used different methods. One is based on rational arguments, while the other tends to derive solutions from the interpretation of Scripture. The reason is submitted to Scripture. For the sake of clarity, we will examine the vices according to a modern division: incapacity, mistake and duress. We will describe the methodological similarities and dissimilarities within the subsequent paragraphs.

3.4.2 *Incapacity*

As often seen in the early modern treatises on contract law, the first requirement the theologians placed for a valid binding effect is mental capacity. They did not have a deep insight into the problems of the will and for this reason relied on external sources. Taking inspiration from Cicero, Melanchthon stated that a pact with a minor or an insane person is to be considered void, because of the lack of consent.[162] In the case of minors, almost two centuries later, Buddeus suggests a similar solution. Yet, he adds that the law should determine

---

159 V. Alberti, *Compendium iuris naturae*, 110: "*Vis enim et metus mutilant actum volendi; error, sciendi*".

160 This approach is quite similar to the scholastics'. See W. Decock, *Theologians and Contract Law*, 234-47.

161 N. Hemmingsen, *Libellus de coniugio, repudio et divortio*, Lipsiae, 1572, 103-4: "*Debet praeterea legitimus consensus esse liber, idque et iudicio et voluntate. Iudicio quidem, ut qui consentit, sano iudicio, sine errore hoc faciat. Nam qui errat, iudicio fallitur: qui fallitur iudicio, non pure consentit: qui non pure consentit, non vere promittit. Quicquid enim impedit causam, impedit etiam effectum*".

162 P. Melanchthon, *Prolegomena in officia Ciceronis*, in CR XVI, 561.

the required age to perform valid acts. No universal rule can be fixed, because there are differences of personality, education and other causes.[163]

Consent is also impeded when people are affected by insanity. Olearius and Haferung write that the promisor must be sane.[164] Haferung does not add anything, but Osiander takes up the issue of the lucid intervals, which was examined by the Roman Catholic theologians. Following the Jesuit Thomas Sanchez' (1550-1610) treatise on marriage (1602), Osiander stresses that mental illness has to reflect an integral damage to the brain, while a partial damage can permit a valid consent. During the so-called lucid intervals, periods when the ill person is conscious, the person can effectively promise or enter into a pact. Likewise a person can enter into a pact when he is not capable of dealing with certain matters, but he is able to deal with other matters.[165] Buddeus also admits the validity of a pact in the case of a party with lucid intervals, if the consent was expressed when the party was conscious.[166] Although framed in different terms, the issue of the lucid intervals still finds a place in the contemporary canon law of marriage.[167]

Drunkenness is the last obstacle to a legitimate consent. Osiander explains that in this case, as for insanity, it is possible to promise by an attorney that received the mandate when the party was sober or before getting ill.[168] Again, this is a case still discussed in the canon law concerning marriage.

3.4.3 *Mistake* (error vel dolus)

3.4.3.1 Introduction

The pact is also invalid if one of the parties commits a mistake (*error*) or the mistake results from a deceit (*dolus*). As seen in the previous chapter, the deceit (*dolus*) and the fraud (*fraus*) were already abundantly discussed with regards to contracts and in the comments to the seventh commandment, but some authors proposed a specific treatment applicable in general to every agreement.

---

163 J.F. Buddeus, *Institutiones theologiae moralis*, 509-10.

164 J. Olearius, *Doctrina theologiae moralis*, Tab. XLVII: "*Qui promisit*, mentis suae compos, *non* amens *sit*"; J.C. Haferung, *Theologia moralis*, 250: "... *promittens sit mentis compos* ...".

165 J.A. Osiander, *Observationes*, 906: "... *sed hoc intelligendum de illis furiosis, qui simpliciter sunt tales, et dilucida non habent intervalla, alioquin tempore sane mentis possint valide promittere et alios contractus celebrare. 2 non est intelligendum hoc de eo furioso, qui in una vel altera materia insanus est, in reliquis autem sanam mentem habet, quem casum contingere posse probat Sanchez*".

166 J.F. Buddeus, *Institutiones theologiae moralis*, 510.

167 See for instance P.J. Viladrich, *El consentimiento matrimonial*, Pamplona, Eunsa, 1998, 72 and 108-10.

168 J.A. Osiander, *Observationes*, 906: "*quamvis tempore insaniae, furoris aut ebrietatis talis promittere nequeat, potest tamen per procuratorem, cui cum sobrius esset mandatum dedit*".

We see two examples: a more conventional one proposed by Meisner has its sources of inspiration in the Roman law of sale, the moral regulation of marriage and the writings of the early modern scholastics; while a more orthodox Lutheran view designed by Dannhauer pivots on the central role of Scripture. They reveal two different methods. The first is based on rational speculations; the second extracts solutions from the Scriptures. Of course, we must bear in mind that these authors write that in two different genres of books. Meisner is producing a philosophical treatise, while Dannhauer is explaining the Decalogue. Still, they represent two ways chosen by our Lutheran theologians to tackle the same issue.

3.4.3.2 Meisner: A Rational Approach

The Roman law of sale already distinguished between a mistake related to the substance of the agreement and a mistake related to a quality. If the mistake pertains to the substance, the agreement is invalid, while if it concerns only an accident, the agreement is valid, but the damaged party has the right to receive compensation.[169] Drawing upon this division, Balthasar Meisner opines that if a mistake regards the substance, the promise or contract is void. It is the case of a seller who believes that the object of the agreement is a gem, but instead it is just a glass.[170] If the mistake is about a quality, instead, the agreement is valid, unless the decision to enter in the contract was determined by the quality of the subject matter. If the contract remains valid, it is possible to get the thing for a different, appropriately adjusted price.[171]

Having determined the consequences of the two different types of mistake, Meisner looks at the possibility of declaring the agreement void when the party discovers the mistake. He indicates two solutions depending upon the gratuitous or onerous nature of the agreement. If the contract or promise is gratuitous, the party can revoke its intention. Indeed, Meisner writes that in a donation, the donor is only bound by his intention. When the donor knows the mistake, he can revoke his donation, because he no longer has the intention

169 R. Zimmermann, *The Law of Obligations*, 592-4.

170 B. Meisner, *Dissertatio de summo bono*, 242: "*An error vel dolus promissum, contractum faciat irritum? Resp. Si error circa substantiam rei contingat, est irritus, ut si venditor gemmam putet esse vitrum*".

171 B. Meisner, *Dissertatio de summo bono*, 242: "*Si error tantum sit circa qualitatem rei, nec dederit causam contractui, validus est contractus. Etsi enim scivisses rei qualitatem, voluisses tamen contrahere, licet non eo pretio*".

to donate.[172] This solution rests on the scholastic centrality of intention, even though no source is quoted.

If the promise or contract is onerous, Meisner suggests looking at the subject matter. If the subject matter is still intact (*res integra*) or the obligation has not yet been fulfilled, the party can be free from the contract, but only in its conscience, because it could be forced to perform the contract by a judicial decision. Meisner takes this solution from the regulation of the betrothal (*sponsalia*): a betrothal with a prostitute is not binding.[173] The moral aspect is certainly relevant in the court of conscience, but Meisner hastens to point out that in a civil court, the case is different, and the party might be asked to perform the obligation.

If the execution of the contract has already started (*res non integra*), there are two options. If the other party did not know the defect, no voiding is possible according to the law, but the party can use the *actio quanti minoris* and in this way recover the unjust cost. The *actio quanti minoris* is a Roman law remedy conceded to recover part of the price of the defective good. In particular, the damaged party could recover the difference between what the good was actually worth and what it would have been worth without the defect.[174] If the other party knew the flaw, however, the defrauded party can choose to confirm or to annul the agreement. The reason is that the other party must have contributed to the deceit, because by positive law he must declare every hidden defect.[175] Meisner takes again inspiration from the regulation of the sale of goods and in particular from the duty to reveal the defects of goods.

The mistake might also be caused by a deception by the other contracting party or by a third party. If Meisner earlier drew upon the medieval elaboration of Roman law and the doctrine of marriage, on this point he seems to have been inspired by the early modern scholastics. Indeed, the Roman law distinguished between contracts *stricti iuris* and contracts *bonae fidei*. Contracts *stricti iuris* were not automatically void in case of deceit, but the offended party could use the *exceptio doli* and the *actio de dolo*. Instead, contracts *bonae fidei* were

---

172 B. Meisner, *Dissertatio de summo bono*, 243: "*Quaeritur autem* Num rescindi possit, errore cognito? *Resp. si sit contractus vel promissio gratuita, potest. Donator enim ultra intentionem suam non obligatur. Cognito igitur errore potest revocare, quia non fuit intentio, hoc aut tali modo donandi*".

173 B. Meisner, *Dissertatio de summo bono*, 243: "*Si* adhuc integra est, *non teneris in conscientia implere contractum, nisi fortè per sententia judicis cogaris, ut patet in sponsalibus cum meretrice contractis*". It might be noted that although the discussion is about promise, Meisner uses the word contract in these cases.

174 R. Zimmermann, *The Law of Obligations*, 318.

175 B. Meisner, *Dissertatio de summo bono*, 244: "*Ratio est quia in tali casu alter censetur particeps doli. Tenebantur enim saltem iure positivo aperire tibi omnia occulta rei vitia*".

immediately void. This classification was combined with the distinction between a deceit that had been essential for the conclusion of the agreement (*dolus causam dans contractui*) and a deceit that had not been essential (*dolus incidens contractui*).[176]

These categories were familiar to the canonists and the glossators, but a significant change occurred with the early modern scholastics. In particular, Diego de Covarruvias stated that in the court of conscience, the distinction between contracts *stricti iuris* and contracts *bonae fidei* does not make sense, because this court pays attention to natural law. Molina, then, stated that if the deceived party still desires the contract, notwithstanding the fact he suffered a deception, this is possible. The party who has been the victim of deceit can choose to invalidate the contract, though if he opts to affirm the validity, the other party must perform the obligation.[177]

The erudite reflections of the early modern scholastics might have inspired Meisner, who argues that if the deceit had been incurred by the other contracting party and determined the contract, then the deceived party can choose whether to invalidate the pact.[178] Similar to Molina, Meisner grants the offended party the possibility to keep the agreement. Molina might also have suggested to him the solution of a linked problem: the effects of a deceit made by a third person and not by the other contracting party. Molina argued that the deceit was not sufficient in this case to invalidate the agreement, but the party could file suit against the deceiver.[179] Likewise, Meisner writes that if the mistake or deceit determined the contract, but a third person made it, or it derived from an opinion of the offended party, the contract is valid. The reason is that there is no damage occasioned by the other party, and there is no right that makes this contract void.[180] Meisner does not focus on the lack of will

176 W. Decock, *Theologians and Contract Law*, 274-6.

177 D. de Covarruvias, *Relectio in regulam possessor malae fidei, de regulis iuris, lib. 6*, in *Opera omnia*, Augustae Taurinorum, part. 2, par. 6, num. 6, 394; L. Molina, *De iustitia et iure*, Moguntiae, 1659, vol. 2, tract. 2, disp. 352, col. 412, n. 2 both cited in W. Decock, *Theologians and Contract Law*, 297 and 299, who also notices that these authors elaborated on the works of the jurist Pierre de Belleperche and the theologian and canonist Conrad Summenhart.

178 B. Meisner, *Dissertatio de summo bono*, 242: "*Si vero dolus interveniat et causam det contractui et proveniat ab eo qui tecum paciscitur, potest contractus arbitrio tuo, qui deceptus es, irritari*".

179 W. Decock, *Theologians and Contract Law*, 300-1.

180 B. Meisner, *Dissertatio de summo bono*, 243: "*Si vero error vel dolus det causam contractui et non proveniat ab eo, qui tecum, contrahit, sed ab aliquo tertio, vel a propria opinione, tunc contractus est validus. Nulla injuria partis intervenit, nec nullum est ius, quod talem contractum reddat irritum*".

of the deceived party, but looks at the subjects who caused the mistake. The deceit that damaged the party was made by a third party and not by the other contracting party.

In conclusion, Meisner delved into the complex problems of the contractual mistake and developed a regulation that goes beyond the specific contracts, but can be virtually applied to every agreement. To deal with this issue, he focuses on rational categories and sets aside appeals to the Scriptures. However, he proposes detailed solutions on the effects of the mistake on the agreement. He goes beyond the dictates of Scripture, but the price is a specific and technical answer to the possible doubt of conscience. Likely, Meisner benefited from the accurate analysis of the early modern scholastics and natural lawyers, although he does not cite one in particular. He also seems clearly to depend upon the Roman law regulation of sale contracts and the moral treatment of marriage. Drawing upon these sources, he produces a precious blending of traditions and a brilliant example of the general treatment of mistakes.

3.4.3.3 Dannhauer: Obedience to the Scriptures

Unlike Meisner, Dannhauer sticks to the Holy Scripture and derives his arguments from its interpretation. Scripture is for him the essential source, and on this topic, he does not refer to the early modern scholastics or the natural lawyers. However, as we are going to see, his conclusions are far less detailed than Meisner's. Dannhauer assumes that the virtue of truthfulness produces the fulfilment of promises and analyses the fallacy (*fallacia*), which is the opposite of truthfulness. A fallacy can be made by words (*fallacia verbalis*) or by actions (*fallacia realis*). The first one is a lie (*mendacium*) while the second one is a deceit (*dolus*).[181] Olearius and Haferung probably drew upon this statement and distinguished the deceit perpetrated by words from the deceit executed through actions. Olearius specified that deceit realized by actions regards fraudulent suggestions.[182] Haferung added the biblical example of the deception of the people of Gibeon, in the book of Joshua 9,4.[183]

Coming back to Dannhauer, he says that the fallacy can be studied in a general sense or in a strict sense. In general the fallacy can be seen as every event that produces a deception (*frustratio*). He refers to Matthias Flacius' *Clavis Scripturae Sacrae*, a formidable dictionary based on biblical hermeneutics. There, the word fallacy is said to derive from 'I am absent' (*desum*),

181 J.K. Dannhauer, *Deuteronomium Dannhawerianum*, 438: "Veracitati *opponitur* fallacia, *quae vel* verbalis *est, vel* realis: *illa proprie est mendacium, haec dolus*".

182 J. Olearius, *Doctrina theologiae moralis*, Tab. XLVII.

183 J.C. Haferung, *Theologia moralis*, 251.

'I am missing' (*deficio*), and 'I am standing apart' (*disparo*)[184]. In a strict sense, Dannhauer describes the fallacy as vicious (*vitiosa*) because it damages the right of the neighbour.[185]

In a general sense, the fallacy does not necessarily produce damages. Dannhauer proposes three types of this fallacy: the fallacy made for exploratory reasons and to rouse up a major desire (*exploratoria et maioris desiderii excitatoria*); the fallacy made as a strategy of war (*stratagematica in bellis*); the fallacy to prevent or to correct an error (*erroris vel praeservativa vel correctoria*). These three types of fallacy in the broad sense are entirely derived from biblical episodes. Here, the biblical dependence of Dannhauer's reasoning clearly emerges.

The first type is the fallacy that God used to instill faith in men. For instance, in Genesis 32, Wisdom feigned an enemy in the conflict against Jacob; in Luke 24, Christ hid His presence from the disciples of Emmaus to test their faith; finally, in Matthew 15, Christ said that He did not want to help the woman of Canaan in order to elicit a faithful reaction of the disciples.[186] Christ used the fallacy in order to confirm the disciples in the truth, and not as a result of a mistake.[187] The second type of fallacy that Dannhauer considers to be lawful is the fallacy made for reasons of war. He refers to 2 Sam. 5,23, where David asked the Lord how to defeat the Philistines, and God told him to come upon them from a way they could not expect.

The final type of fallacy is the fallacy to prevent or to correct an error. Man towards whom the simulation takes place is not presumed to have undergone this experience grievously, especially because it is not an injury towards him, as he is grateful for it afterwards. In this case the pact is valid, because it does not provoke any injury.[188] It is like a doctor that gives to the patient a bitter medicine disguised in a sweet drink.[189] Dannhauer cites the biblical example of Rebecca, which he says it is often used to explain this type of fallacy. Rebecca perpetrated a deceit in order to correct an error of her husband Isaac. Jacob, son of Rebecca, had acquired the right to be blessed by his father Isaac in virtue of a sale contract. However, his father Isaac wanted to bless the other son,

---

184 J.K. Dannhauer, *Deuteronomium Dannhawerianum*, 438. M. Flacius, *Clavis Scripturae Sacrae*, pars prima, Basileae, 1567, 396.

185 J.K. Dannhauer, *Deuteronomium Dannhawerianum*, 444.

186 J.K. Dannhauer, *Deuteronomium Dannhawerianum*, 441.

187 J.K. Dannhauer, *Deuteronomium Dannhawerianum*, 442.

188 J.K. Dannhauer, *Deuteronomium Dannhawerianum*, 443: "Erroris vel praeservativa vel correctoria, *cum scilicet is, erga quem simulatio sit, non aegre eam laturus praesumitur, adeoque cum volenti post factum, non sit injuria*".

189 J.K. Dannhauer, *Deuteronomium Dannhawerianum*, 443.

Esau. Rebecca, knowing the situation, gave to Jacob the clothes of his brother Esau. Isaac confused one son with the other and blessed Jacob instead of Esau.

Dannhauer explains the passage through the words of Aegidius Hunnius.[190] To Hunnius, it is not permissible to deceive one's parent by a trick, but Rebecca and Jacob followed the Word of God. Moreover, Jacob had acquired this right by a sale contract, as Genesis 26 states. Thus, for a double reason, based on divine law and human law, this right of primogeniture with all annexed benefits, prerogatives and privileges belonged to Jacob. Rebecca prudently and piously deemed it was necessary to prevent Isaac from bestowing the blessing in error, and aided Jacob in deceiving his father in order to receive the benefice of primogeniture. Thus, also this fact cannot be reproached, as it was based on the clear Word of God.[191]

All these instances regard the fallacy in general. They might be scarcely important for contract law, but we report them to indicate the method adopted by Dannhauer. Indeed, he takes from biblical examples solutions that then are generalized. The analysis of this biblical passage is an example of the way Dannhauer looked at the Scripture as endless resource for moral knowledge.

More linked to contract law is the fallacy in a strict sense. To Dannhauer, this fallacy can be defined as a simulation or dissimulation of an opinion that is false, easy to be accepted (*ingestiva*) and harmful (*iniuriosa*) per *se*. The fallacy constitutes a simulation or dissimulation per *se*. Indeed, Dannhauer notices, it can also happen that the other party is impressed by a false concept deriving from a thing perceived by senses and intellect, such that the vice lays not in the thing but in the senses and in his judgment.[192] The fallacy is properly harmful of the rights. For example, it influences the freedom of judgements about friendship, contracts, sales, obligations, promises and treatises.[193] Dannhauer presents many biblical examples. He quotes Gen. 29, where Laban deceived Jacob by giving his daughter Leah, instead of Rachel; or Gen. 37, the deceit of the sons of Jacob who sent Joseph's coat with blood marks, so that he would believe Joseph had been eaten by a ferocious beast; Gen. 38, the deceit of Tamar

190 A. Hunnius, *Articulus de providentia Dei et aeterna praedestinatione seu electione filiorum Dei ad salutem*, Witebergae, 1605, 86-7.

191 J.K. Dannhauer, *Deuteronomium Dannhawerianum*, 444.

192 J.K. Dannhauer, *Deuteronomium Dannhawerianum*, 444: "*Definiri potest hujusmodi fallacia, quod sit* simulatio vel dissimulatio per se falsae opinionis ingestiva et injuriosa, per se, dico, *quia fieri potest, ut alter falso conceptu imbuatur, è re aliqua sensu ac intellectu percepta, ut sensus potius ac judicii vitium sit, quam rei iudicatae*".

193 J.K. Dannhauer, *Deuteronomium Dannhawerianum*, 445: "*Fallacia enim proprie est iurium laesiva, e.g. iudicandi libertatis, amicitiae, contractuum, emtionis, venditionis, obligativum* (?), *promissionum, foederum etc.*".

towards Judah; Jer. 41, the deceit of Ishmael; and similar cases.[194] Again the notion and negative impact of fallacy on pacts and contracts is derived from biblical analysis. Scripture is for Dannhauer a 'tank' of examples from which he draws his conclusions.

Since the fallacy has a negative impact, it must be stopped. Indeed, the fallacy is a sin that is forbidden by the law of God (*fallacia demum peccatum est lege divina prohibitum*).[195] Dannhauer's analysis is completely immersed in the Scriptures. He asserts that someone might argue the opposite, and so that fallacy would be allowed, on the basis of Jer. 4,10: "*then said I, Ah, Lord God! surely thou hast greatly deceived this people and Jerusalem, saying, Ye shall have peace; whereas the sword reacheth unto the soul*"; and Paul 2 Cor. 12,16: "*but be it so, I did not burden you: nevertheless, being crafty, I caught you with guile*". Dannhauer responds that in the first case the word is used in Hiphil Stem,[196] which does not necessarily denote a direct causative type of action. The meaning of the deceit is not positive but negative, because it is associated with the sin. In the second case, Dannhauer claims that Paul was referring to the opinion of those who made a simulation against him.[197] Again, Dannhauer performs with great care the interpretation of Scripture. Particularly, he founds his conclusions in the analysis of the Hebrew text.

To conclude, Dannhauer offers an example of a treatment of mistake and deceit almost entirely grounded on the Scriptures. He finds in the biblical words the key for his analysis. He accurately investigates the meaning and the use of the words. In this sense it appears to be significant, not only the large number of biblical quotations and examples that support his arguments but also the reference to Flacius' dictionary of biblical hermeneutics. Dannhauer seems not interested in the rational dynamics of the mistake. Rather, he infers the consequences of mistakes and deceit from the interpretation of the Bible. The solution, then, does not come from reasoning but from the mere obedience to the dictates of Scripture.

The problem with such a method is the total lack of detailed solutions, which instead Meisner provides. Dannhauer remains general and does not touch significantly upon contract law. In substance, he only writes that mistakes and deceits are harmful. He suggests some exceptions, like the fallacy to prevent or correct an error, but they are hardly applicable to contract law.

194 Dannhauer also mentions 1 Maccabees 12,42; 16,15; 2 Maccabees 12,3.

195 J.K. Dannhauer, *Deuteronomium Dannhawerianum*, 446.

196 For the Hyphil Stem see R.J. Williams, *Williams' Hebrew Syntax*, 3rd ed., Toronto, Buffalo, London, University of Toronto Press, 2007, 61; J.A. Hackett, *A Basic Introduction to Biblical Hebrew*, Peabody, Hendrickson, 2010, 127.

197 J.K. Dannhauer, *Deuteronomium Dannhawerianum*, 446.

The effects of mistakes on the agreement need to be analysed according to a rational and juridical approach, which goes beyond the mere interpretation of Scripture. Dannhauer leaves these problems to the jurists, whereas Meisner faces them.

3.4.4 *Duress*

3.4.4.1 The Law of Marriage

Canonists, early modern scholastics and natural lawyers examined in depth the impact of duress (*metus*) not only on contractual consent, but also on matrimonial consent.[198] The law of marriage was indeed an excellent battlefield for exploring the effects of duress. The Lutherans mainly discussed the innovations to marriage regulation, as the marriage of priests and the parental consent, but some authors also tackled the issue of duress. It is beyond of the scope of this book to study the Lutheran theologians' contribution to marriage law. We propose instead to examine the similarity between marriage law and the general theory of contract law and to see the inspirational role that the treatment of duress on marriage could have had.

Tapping into Roman law, canon law and the early modern scholastics, Johan Gerhard sketches out a description of duress. Duress is defined as a force and constraint, a pressure that is not possible to reject (*maioris rei impetum qui repelli non queat*), so that the party acts reluctantly and unwillingly.[199] Duress has to be current,[200] and can be classified as just duress or empty duress. The former describes the threatening of those who justly and rightly tremble, as for instance death, prison, damages, or torment. The latter, empty duress (*vanum*), is insignificant, and it is caused by the fault of those who fear, and not by those who generate the fear.[201]

For marriage as for other contracts, the crucial problem is the qualities that the duress must present in order to invalidate the agreement. Gerhard distinguishes two main causes: duress by divine providence, as for instance in a fortuitous case, and duress by human action, like when the duress is caused by the magistrate or parents. If duress is provoked by a fortuitous case, by divine providence, such that one party promises in danger of war, shipwreck, plague, death or plundering of goods, then the betrothal is not invalid, because this duress is not caused by God, but rather results from the fear experienced by

198 W. Decock, *Theologians and Contract Law*, 215-74.

199 D. 4,2,2.

200 X 4,1,14; X 4,1,28.

201 J. Gerhard, *Locorum theologicorum tomvs decimvs qvintus*, Tubingae, 1776, 124.

the person.[202] Instead, if the magistrate causes the duress, it is necessary to look whether the person who suffered duress was a minor. If the parents exercised duress or coercion, Gerhard suggests looking at the intensity: whether the threat is atrocious or soft. On top of that, he considers not only the people who caused the duress and the means by which the duress was caused, but also the personal quality of the people who suffered duress.[203]

On the whole, Gerhard affirms that the excessive strength of the magistrate or the parents contrasts with the will of God, and the marriage is void. Whereas if the duress is caused because of fortuitous case, God does not prohibit the marriage and therefore it is valid. This is an interesting aspect on Gerhard's view of duress and marriage. Apart from that, these statements could serve for a broader treatment applicable in general to every contract.

3.4.4.2 Does Duress Invalidate an Agreement?

As for marriage, the crucial issue for duress in contract law is whether it is strong enough to eliminate consent. Already Melanchthon viewed as void any agreement extorted by great fear, unless it was established with an oath.[204] In this case, Melanchthon opined, the Christian must fulfil the oath, because in the oath there must not be any dissimulation, and the promises cannot be frustrated with a breach of an oath. It is not licit to do something evil to obtain something good. Therefore, as the canon law (X 2,24,8) sets out, the oath is binding and the agreements extorted by fear must be performed, when the Christian did not swear to do something against the law of God.[205] Melanchthon endorsed the canonical doctrine according to which a promise ratified with an oath must be fulfilled, even if the promise had been extorted by duress. This solution does not apply when the oath is against the law of God. However, for the canon law the person who promised under duress could

202 J. Gerhard, *Locorum theologicorum tomvs decimvs qvintus*, 125: "*Si casu fortuito divinitus incutiatur metus, videlicet si quis matrimonium promittat in discrimine belli, naufragii, pestis, mortis; direptionis bonorum, etc. tunc sponsalia non redduntur irrita, quia is metus ad illum actum sponsionis efficiendum non est a Deo illatus*".

203 J. Gerhard, *Locorum theologicorum tomvs decimvs qvintus*, 125: "*Notandum etiam illud, quod semper habendus sit respectus non solum ad eos, qui vim inferunt, et ad obiecta sive media, per quae vis infertur, et quarum rerum comminatio proponitur; sed etiam et quidem cumprimis ad eos, qui vim sustinent ...*".

204 P. Melanchthon, *Prolegomena in officia Ciceronis*, in CR XVI, 561: "*Haec pactio irrita est, nisi sit sancita iuramento*".

205 P. Melanchthon, *Prolegomena in officia Ciceronis*, in CR XVI, 561: "*Nam in iuramento prorsus debet abesse simulatio, et non sunt eludenda promissa violatione iuramenti, quia non sunt facenda mala, ut eveniant bona. Ideo recte docent canones* (X 2,24,8), *talia pacta iuramento sancita servanda esse, cum non iurasti te ipsum facturum aliquid contra legem Dei*".

be absolved and his conscience was not guilty if he did not perform his oath. Melanchthon firmly disapproves this conclusion because, he says, no man can invalidate the bond between man and God.[206]

Other Lutheran theologians faced the issue of duress differently. They adopted various solutions, which have in common a rational method, typically accompanied by a plethora of references to the early modern scholastics or the natural lawyers. To start with, Meisner settles the matter once and for all in a few words. He suggests distinguishing between a contract concluded under just grave duress versus unjust grave duress. In case of *just* grave duress the contract is valid.[207] Instead, if the duress is *unjust* and grave, the contract can be rescinded by the party who suffered the duress.[208] Unfortunately, Meisner does not define just and unjust duress; neither does he add further explanations.

Osiander's analysis is integrally dominated by references to the early modern scholastics. Martín de Azpilcueta or Doctor Navarrus, Fortunius Garcia (1494-1534), Fernando Rebello (d. 1608), Gabriel Vasquez (1549-1604), Diego de Covarruvias and others argued that the promise extorted by duress, even if it was a light duress or mere reverential fear, harms the promisor and consequently the promisee does not acquire the right that the promisor must keep the promise. Thus, the party who suffered duress has the right to receive back its things. The reason is that the promise damaged the innocent party, and it is not just that the other party acquires a right through an unjust and harmful action.[209] No appeal to Scripture is made, and a totally rational solution is offered.

Osiander continues, citing the Italian Jesuit Emanuele Tesauro (1592-1675), who observed duress effects in the *forum internum* and in the *forum externum*. In the court of conscience, the promise extorted by duress or deceit is void, and the guilty party has to return the received things. But in the civil courts,

---

206 P. Melanchthon, *Prolegomena in official Ciceronis*, in CR XVI, 460-1. X 2,24,8. For the canon law theory see R. H. Helmholz, *The Spirit of Classical Canon Law*, Athens & London, The University of Georgia Press, 2010, 167-8, 231.

207 B. Meisner, *Dissertatio de summo bono*, 242: "*Si gravi metu, sed tamen iuste coactus es contrahere vel pacisci, validus est contractus*".

208 B. Meisner, *Dissertatio de summo bono*, 242: "*Quod si vero gravi metu et quidem injuste coactus es contrahere, dicunt ejusmodi contractum rescindi potest pro arbitrio ejus, qui metum injuste passus est, eo quod ipsi facta sit injuria*".

209 J.A. Osiander, *Observationes*, 907: "*Rationem allegant, quia extorquens promissionem per dolum vel metum etiam levem facit injuriam promittenti, et consequenter non acquirit jus, ut promittens stet promissioni: non enim justum est, ut per actionem injustam et injuriosam acquiramus jus. Hinc etiam Navarrus, Garzias, Rebellus, Vasquez et Covarruvias existimant promittentem talem non teneri promissionem adimplere et promissarium adimpleta promissione teneri restituere*".

in order to avoid a multiplication of litigations, the light duress or deceit is not recognized and the promise is valid. On this point, Tesauro refers to Martín de Azpilcueta (Dr. Navarrus), Sylvester Mazzolini (1456/7-1527) and Gabriel Vasquez.[210] A duress-extorted promise is invalid even if an oath was added. Indeed, the oath follows the same rules of the promise: if the promise is invalid, the oath is also invalid. The case is different, and the oath must be kept, if the oath does not concern the promise but the things that were the subject matter of the promise. In this case, the oath must be observed for the reverence of the name of God.[211] Osiander does not add anything to these conclusions, but simply seems to follow them. In the court of conscience a promise uttered under duress is void, even if an oath is added.

Zentgrav does not look at the scholastics, but at the natural lawyers: he reports both the opinion of Grotius and Pufendorf. Grotius followed in turn the opinion of the Dominican priest Sylvester Mazzolini, stating that a pact concluded by the party under duress is valid, because the consent was already fully and not conditionally expressed. On the contrary, Pufendorf maintained that a pact or promise concluded by a party under unjust duress is not valid. The natural law requires that the party who extorted a profit through an unjust duress returns it and pays what the other party lost because of the pact. As compensation the natural law removes the obligation for the offended party, if the other does not immediately pay the damage.[212]

Zentgrav agrees with Grotius because (he says) his justifications appear to be stronger. Although promisor's consent was extorted by duress with the consequent damage, the right was effectively transferred to the other party,

---

210 J.A. Osiander, *Observationes*, 907: "*Audiamus Taurinensem Patritium Tom. 2 pag. 427.* Sciendum, quod licet in foro conscientiae promissio metu, aut dolo extorta sit invalida et accepta sint restituenda, tamen in foro externo accepta per promissionem metu levi, aut dolo factam non sunt restituenda, cum pro metu levi non detur actio, ne multiplicentur lites Navar. Silvester, Vasquez, locis citatis et alii".

211 J.A. Osiander, *Observationes*, 908.

212 J.J. Zentgrav, *Summa juris divini*, 355: "Ego, *inquit*, Hugo Grotius, d) omnino accedo illorum sententiae qui existimant, seposita lege civili quae obligationem potest tollere aut minuere, eum qui metu promisit aliquid, obligari: quia consensus hic adfuit, nec conditionalis, sed absolutus. *Cui* Pufendorfius *e*) *contradicens*, enimvero, *inquit*, invalida judicamus illa pacta et promissa, ad quae ab illo ipso cui promittit, aut qui cum paciscitur, injusta eiusdem vi quis compellitur. Cum enim jure naturali, qui per injustum metum alteri quid extorsit, id restituere teneatur, adeoque tanto debeat pensare, quantum isti per tale pactum decedit, per compensationem velut tolli obligatur intelligitur, si non solvitur id, quod statim restituti debebat". He cites: H. Grotius, *De iure belli ac pacis*, II, 11, § 7; S. Pufendorf, *De iure naturae et gentium*, lib. 3, cap. VI § 11.

and it also seems that he wanted it in good faith.[213] To lend weight to this position, Zentgrav cites the Lutheran professor Samuel Rachel (1628-1691): notwithstanding the damage, for which an adequate compensation is needed, the promise cannot be nullified. Rachel explains that the promise is binding in its nature and not as a result of the way it was extorted. The act of duress, however, generates a right of restitution by natural law.[214]

In addition, Zentgrav observes that an oath extorted by duress is binding. The Roman tribune Marco Pomponio kept his oath pronounced under duress, as Cicero and Livio reported.[215] And the English reformer Robert Sanderson (1587-1663) sustains that the incautious party who tied the bond at its soul, pronouncing a sworn promise, must keep the promise.[216] This position is different from the one held by Osiander. Following the early modern scholastics, Osiander affirmed that an oath under duress is not valid, while for Zentgraf it is binding regardless.

Buddeus' solution rests on the intensity of duress. Duress causes the voiding of a pact only when it completely removes or overwhelms the use of reason. If the duress did not have such strength, the pact is valid.[217] Then, referring to Pufendorf, Grotius and Thomasius, Buddeus examines the effects on a pact when the duress is exercised by a third person or by the other party. If duress was induced by a third person, the pact is valid. The third person must however pay damages. If the other party provoked duress, it is necessary to distinguish again, whether the party had legally the power to constrain the innocent party or not. If the party had the power to force the innocent party to do something, the pact is valid. Otherwise, if he did not have that power, the pact is invalid. The reason is not a vice of consent. Rather, it is the fact that the coercing party

213 J.J. Zentgrav, *Summa juris divini*, 355: "*Sed firmior Grotius videtur ratio. Et iste promittentis paciscentisque metu elicitus consensus, cum non obstante ejus cui sit promissio injuria, damnoque ab eodem dato, in eundem jus adversus consentientem transtulerit, atque etiam id bona fide is transtulisse videri voluerit*".

214 J.J. Zentgrav, *Summa juris divini*, 355-6. He cites S. Rachel, *De principio actionum moralium liber*, Helmestadii, 1664, disp. 1, 27.

215 J.J. Zentgrav, *Summa juris divini*, 356: "*Juramentum etiam per vim metumque extortum obligare, alibi docuimus, laudato M. Pomponio, tribuno plebis Romae, qui juramentum, quod terrore coactus juraverat, sancte servavit, quod prolixius* Ciceroni, *atque* Livio *explicatur*".

216 J.J. Zentgrav, *Summa juris divini*, 354. He quotes R. Sanderson, *De iuramenti promissorii obligatione libellus*, Cothena Anhaltinorum, 1674, prael. IV, Sect. 14, 121-2.

217 J.F. Buddeus, *Institutiones theologiae moralis*, 510: "*Si metus tam vehemens non fuerit, ut omnem rationis usum excusserit, pactum per se non reddit irritum*". Similarly see in the *Elementa philosophiae practicae*, 272: "*Metus, hoc est terror animi, nisi ita vehemens fuerit, ut omnem rationis excusserit usum, pactum per se non reddit irritum*".

did not have the right to accept what was promised.[218] If the pact is invalid, the guilty party must return the things he received from the pact.[219] Buddeus takes the first solution from Pufendorf and the second from Grotius.

To recapitulate, basing their discourses mostly on the early modern scholastics and the natural lawyers, the Lutheran theologians gave different answers to the problem of duress. Scripture is completely silent in this discourse. Meisner posits that the pact can be invalidated in case of unjust grave duress. Osiander follows the early modern scholastics and distinguish the *forum internum*, where even the light duress is relevant, and the *forum externum*, where light duress is not considered. Zentgrav compares the opinion of Grotius and Pufendorf, siding with the former. Grotius grants a compensation for duress, but the agreement is valid. In fact, the promise is binding in its nature. To the contrary, Buddeus follows Pufendorf and concludes that when the duress is strong enough to counter the use of reason, the pact is not valid. Then, if duress was caused by a third person, the pact is valid; if it was unjustly generated by the other contracting party, the pact is invalid and the guilty party must return the goods.

With respect to duress effects of a sworn pact or promise, we also find contrasting opinions. Following the medieval canon law, Melanchthon holds that a promise extorted by duress but ratified with an oath must be fulfilled. Instead, drawing upon the early modern scholastics, Osiander maintains that the sworn promise exacted by duress is void. On the contrary, Zentgrav argues that it is valid, even if duress was exercised. He appeals to the Reformed theologian Sanderson. In the end, the Lutheran theologians were unable to develop a proper theory of duress. Since this point lacks a solid biblical reference, they had no other choice than grasp at the solutions prepared by others. The result clearly shows this weakness.

3.5 The Performance

3.5.1 *Introduction*

In order to be binding, a promise needs to be expressed and accepted. Furthermore, the promisor must be free, not deceived or mistaken. The Lutheran theologians reached this conclusion, although using different

218 J.F. Buddeus, *Institutiones theologiae moralis*, 510. He quotes S. Pufendorf, *De iure naturae et gentium*, lib. 3, cap. 6 § 10 and lib. 4 cap. 2 § 8.

219 J.F. Buddeus, *Institutiones theologiae moralis*, 510. He quotes H. Grotius, *De iure belli ac pacis*, II, 17, § 17.

methods. A more rational approach delved into the technicalities, while a more orthodox one focused on the content of biblical revelation. Of course the distinction is anything but sharp, because sometimes the theologians tried to combine the Scriptures with the rational approach.

Other limitations concern the performance, as the moral or physical impossibility. Both the more progressive and the conservative theologians agreed on these points. Yet, only some of them dealt with other aspects as the execution. Again the general thread is constituted by an approach based on the rational argument and another on the submission of reason to Scripture.

3.5.2 *Moral Impossibility*

3.5.2.1 General Clauses

The immorality of subject matter was commonly recognized by the early modern scholastics as an obstacle for the validity of the agreements. They in turn referred to Roman law and canon law sources.[220] Following in the scholastics' footsteps, the Lutherans formulated general clauses by which they required pacts and promises to be morally lawful. In the comment to the eighth commandment in the *Loci theologici*, Melanchthon stated that only honourable promises must be observed (*honesta pacta sunt servanda*).[221] The addition, honourable pacts, is explained in the *Prolegomena in officia Ciceronis* and concerns the pacts that have a shameful cause (*turpem causam*) and especially go against the divine law.[222] Melanchthon specifies that it is not licit to wish, to seek, to promise and to keep a promise against the divine law. The superior rule (you shall not wish anything against the precepts of God) restricts the inferior rule (you shall keep the pacts). This last rule is therefore confined to those precepts that are admitted by the law of God.[223]

Melanchthon's concept of honesty relates unavoidably to the divine law. Instead, Paul von Eitzen utilized a different notion of morality, which is apparently unmoored from the divine law. As an oath, he writes, the faith of covenants must not be a bond of injustice (*vincolum iniquitatis*). Agreements

220 W. Decock, *Theologians and Contract Law*, 422-5; 478-81. The Roman law contains indeed numerous passages that nullify immoral contracts. See for instance Inst. 3,19,24; D. 45,1,26.

221 P. Melanchthon, *Loci communes* (*tertia eorum aetas*), in CR XXI, 712 and 715.

222 P. Melanchthon, *Prolegomena in officia Ciceronis*, in CR XVI, 561: "*Sed consideranda est particula honestum. Recte enim dicitur, pacta quae turpem causam habent, non sunt observanda. Ac praesertim hoc sic intelligatur, quae praecipiunt facere contra legem Dei*".

223 P. Melanchthon, *Prolegomena in officia Ciceronis*, in CR XVI, 561: "*Contra legem divinam nihil velle, nihil petere, nihil promittere, nec promissa facere licet. Ac superior regula hic restringit inferiorem: Nihil velis contra praecepta Dei. Inferior regula est: serves pacta. Haec regula restringitur tantum ad ea, quae praecepta ac concessa sunt lege Dei*".

against good morals must not be ratified. A breach of morality is a valid cause of discharge (*excusatio*) from the *pacta sunt servanda*.[224] The party who wants to enter into an agreement that could harm the Church, his native land or his community, could do injustice to innocent men, or could perpetrate something shameful, all of which provide grounds for the annulment of the *pacta sunt servanda*. Von Eitzen alludes to a general concept of morality that includes the protection of the common good and especially the Church as institution, the native land (*patria*), the community (*civitas*), innocent men and the reproach of shamefulness (*turpitudo*). He does not make any reference to the divine law or Scripture; rather he seems to have been inspired by Cicero's *De officiis*, which is also cited in other parts of his work.[225]

Several theologians, Meisner, König and Olearius among them, stipulated that for a promise to be binding, it must have a 'licit' and 'honourable' subject matter.[226] For instance, Olearius holds that the promise must concern a licit and honorable subject matter (*fiat de re licita ac honesta*);[227] if the promise concerns an illicit and dishonorable subject matter, it is not binding (*si facta sint promissa de re illicita aut inhonesta, non obligant*).[228] These authors do not explain in detail the notion of *honestas*, but put these assertions as general clauses forbidding immoral agreements.

Haferung likewise points out that the subject matter must be licit and honorable. Yet, in order to explain this statement clearer, he adds biblical references. Concerning the honorable subject matter, he mentions Matt. 26,15, when Judas sold Christ for thirty pieces of silver; about the licit subject matter, Haferung quotes Mark 4,24: Jesus Christ warns to measure justly, because the measure you use will be used to measure you.[229] Here, Scripture helps to enlighten the precept.

Alberti opted for a different road and admitted an exception (partial) to the rule on the illicit and dishonorable promise or pact. Following a moral line of reasoning, he reflects that if the subject matter is illicit but necessary for a

224 For a detailed analysis on the debt relief among the Catholics see W. Decock, *Law, Religion and Debt Relief: Balancing above the 'Abyss of Despair' in Early Modern Canon Law and Theology*, in *American Journal of Legal History*, 2017, vol. 57 (2), 125-41.

225 Cicero, *De officiis*, 1, 10, 31. See before II/3.3.2.1.

226 B. Meisner, *Dissertatio de summo bono*, 241: "*PROMISSIO ONEROSA, ut obliget, eadem ferme requirit:...5) in re licita et honesta*"; G. König, *Casus conscientiae*, 17: "*de rebus licitis et honestis*".

227 J. Olearius, *Doctrina theologiae moralis*, Tab. XLVII.

228 J. Olearius, *Doctrina theologiae moralis*, Tab. XLVII.

229 J.C. Haferung, *Theologia moralis*, 250: "*Videndum enim, ut,* quod promittitur, *sit* (α) honestum, *non inhonestum, Matth. XXVI, 15.* (β) licitum, *non illicitum aut prohibitum I. Marc. IV, 24 seqq.*".

good aim, the promise can be performed. The promisor, however, must carefully evaluate the moral circumstances before making the choice.[230]

A particular form of illicit and dishonest promise or pact occurs if the party does not have the power over the subject matter, viz. the party has not the right of property on what he wants to sell. As seen before, the theologians understood contract law as a form for transferring property rights, and for this reason this aspect is not less important. Alberti argues that it is not licit to deal with something that is not yours or belongs to another person.[231] I can promise everything that is subject to my power, and it is honorable or indifferent, neither good nor evil, but I cannot promise what is dishonorable.[232] Similarly, Buddeus deems that if the party lacks the power to transfer the subject matter, he cannot be bound. Depraved and illicit goods cannot be the subject matter of a contract, because the party has no power over them. The pact is illicit whether the performance is fulfilled or the performance is not fulfilled.[233]

3.5.2.2 Natural Law vs. Moral Theology

The Lutheran theologians were not only passive imitators but also careful readers. They did not always accept the solutions developed by external sources, for instance by the natural lawyers. A provoking case concerns Grotius' opinion on the promise performed on a shameful subject matter. Grotius famously maintained that the immoral promises are illicit, but after performance, a vicious promise can still provoke juridical effects. This conclusion triggered blistering criticism among the Lutherans, especially by Osiander. The interesting point is that Osiander uses the opinions of some early modern scholastics (and not only the Scriptures) to criticize Grotius.

Grotius justified his conclusion by referring to the prodigal donation (*prodiga donatio*) and to the biblical example of Tamar, also frequently cited among the early modern scholastics.[234] He insinuated that once the prodigal donation had been made, there was no more corruption (*vitiositas*), because the things remained with the donee without any vice.[235] Osiander replies that the prodigal

---

230 V. Alberti, *Compendium iuris naturae*, 116-7: "quaecunque, res in se quidem est illicita, sed ad bonum finem simpliciter necessaria, eam potes, instar permittentis morali aestimatione Te habendo, promittere".

231 V. Alberti, *Compendium iuris naturae*, 111-2.

232 V. Alberti, *Compendium iuris naturae*, 112: "Quicquid ex iis, quae potestati mea subjecta sunt, est indifferens vel honestum, illud promitti potest ... Quicquid est inhonestum, illud promittere non debes".

233 J.F. Buddeus, *Institutiones theologiae moralis*, 510.

234 W. Decock, *Theologians and contract law*, 494-6.

235 H. Grotius, *De iure belli ac pacis*, II, 11, § 9.

donation can be considered in two different ways. It can show an excess of generosity, if the subject matter and the aim are honorable. On the other hand, this donation can denote enormous excess where other vicious circumstances also concur. In the first case, the donation is perfectly licit and cannot be compared with a promise on a shameful subject matter. The second type of donation cannot be seen in the same way, because it has no legal effect, and in conscience, the recipient is obliged to return to the donor the excess received.[236]

To lend weight to his argument, Osiander quotes the scholastic theologians Domingo de Soto and Domingo Bañez (1527-1604), who aim to say that the prodigal promise does not bind, except in case of an added oath. First, if it is prodigal, its execution is absolutely illicit. Second, if something has been promised as a price and the promisor does not want to give more, then he is not obliged to pay the excess, save the case of an added oath. Third, the promise can be prodigal because the promisor was deceived or the promise was not pronounced freely.[237] Using these three rational motivations, the theologians reached a conclusion contrary to Grotius, and Osiander uses them to confute Grotius.

Concerning the other argument proposed by Grotius, the example of Tamar, we need to briefly recall the biblical episode in Gen. 38. Tamar was the widow of Er, son of Judah. Because Judah had unjustly refused to give her as wife to his other son Shelah, she perpetrated a deceit. She covered herself with a veil to be disguised, and then sat down at the entrance of a city, like a prostitute. Judah thought that she was a prostitute and invited her to have sex with him. The price was fixed at a goat, but she demanded Judah's seal, its cord, and its staff as pledge. Then they slept together. Subsequently Judah sent the goat to her by his friend, who did not find her, and Judah kept the goat. Grotius noticed that Judah paid the price, even though he spent the night with a prostitute, and concluded that after the execution of the wrong action the pact is binding.[238]

Responding to this biblical argument, Osiander does not need to cite the scholastics. He replies that because promises and pacts that include an evil action are ineffective, none of the parties are bound, for nobody can be bound

236 J.A. Osiander, *Observationes*, 910: "*Quod concernit prodigam donationem, potest illa dupliciter considerari, aut in quantum dicit excessum liberalitatis qualemcunque, posita alias honestate objecti et finis; aut in quantum notat excessum enormem, in quo concurrunt etiam aliae vitiosae circumstantiae: priori modo non potest prodiga donatio accusari tanti vitii, multo minus comparari cum promissione ob rem turpem; posteriori autem modo si consideretur, utisque effectu iuris caret, et in conscientiae tenetur restituere donatarius illud ipsum, quod enormiter fuit superfluum*".

237 J.A. Osiander, *Observationes*, 910.

238 H. Grotius, *De iure belli ac pacis*, II, 11, § IX.

to commit a sin. This applies not only before the execution, but also after the execution of the shameful action. The parties are not obliged to fulfil the obligations, as the fulfilment is a continuation and confirmation of the sin.[239] The example of Tamar, Osiander continues, is quoted without any reason, because everything is illicit: the fornication is illicit, the promise is illicit, the transmission of the seal and the goat is illicit. Therefore, he concludes that this example cannot be invoked to support Grotius' thesis.[240] Grotius grounded his statements on two arguments. The first one (prodigal donation) is rational, and Osiander destroys it by making use of scholastic reasonings. The second one (Tamar's example) is based on the Scriptures, and here our Lutheran theologian performs his task without references to other sources.

This polemic raised by Grotius did not only involve Osiander, but also other theologians. Horneius, Jäger and Buddeus also spent some words on this. Horneius writes that the subject matter must be licit. If it becomes illicit, the promise must be remitted or not fulfilled.[241] Jäger also maintains that the promise has to be licit in order to have binding effects. If the promise was illicit, it was also sinful, and thus it cannot be performed.[242] On the same line, Buddeus disagrees with Grotius.[243] Yet disappointingly, he does not explain its reasoning but refers to Philipp Reinhard Vitrarius and John Selden, who, he claims, refute Grotius adequately.[244]

In conclusion, the Lutheran theologians criticized Grotius' position on the immoral promise. Yet, they did not formally build any solid counterargument. Their answers are likely suggested by external sources. Osiander deliberately uses the opinion of the early modern scholastics to discredit Grotius. Horneius and Jäger were also probably inspired by the scholastics. Buddeus refers to Protestant authors.

---

239 J.A. Osiander, *Observationes*, 909: "*Nam (1) promissio et pactio quae sit propter opus malum, invalida est non tantum ante opus praestitum et neutram partem obligat; quia nemo potest se obligare ad peccatum, sed etiam post patratum flagitium, adeoque non tenetur ad promissum implendum, etiam opere secuto et patrato, promissos quia haec impletio nihil aliud est quam peccati semel coepti continuatio et confirmatio*".

240 J.A. Osiander, *Observationes*, 910-1.

241 C. Horneius, *Compendium theologiae*, 784.

242 J.W. Jäger, *Hugonis Grotii libri tres*, 323.

243 J.F. Buddeus, *Institutiones theologiae moralis*, 510. He quotes H. Grotius, *De iure belli ac pacis*, II, 11, § 9.

244 J.F. Buddeus, *Institutiones theologiae moralis*, 510. See P.H. Vitriarius, *Institutiones juris naturae et gentium*, Francofurti ad Moenum, 1752, lib. 2, cap.11, q. 21 (22), 149; J. Selden, *De jure naturali et gentium juxta disciplinam Ebraeorum libri septem*, Lipsiae et Francofurti, 1695, lib. 5, cap. 4, 572-6 (576).

3.5.2.3 Noxious or Useless Subject Matter and Changed Circumstances

The impact of changed circumstances on the contractual bond has been the subject of analysis since the Romans.[245] In his *De officiis*, Cicero justified the breach of faith in promises in the case of changed circumstances. The reason he adduced was the contrariety of two fundamental principles of justice: do not harm anyone and conserve the common interest. He wrote that if, under changed circumstances, these principles are modified, the moral duty that obliges keeping the pacts also undergoes a change.[246] In particular, Cicero explored the case of a promise that became noxious or useless and formulated some examples: the lawyer who cannot assist his client because his son got ill;[247] the depositary of a sword should not return it to the proprietor who became insane.[248] Cicero's example of the sword was used by Augustine in his exposition on the Psalms.[249] Then, it was inserted in Gratian's *Decretum*,[250] from which the canonists began their discussions.[251] Canonists and then civilians sought to limit the validity of a contract by stating that every contract would be valid on the tacit condition that the circumstances are not changed.[252]

---

245 Bibliography on this topic is abundant, see for instance G. Osti, *La clausola "rebus sic stantibus" nel suo sviluppo storico*, in *Rivista di diritto civile*, 1-58; G. Osti, *Clausola "rebus sic stantibus"*, in *Novissimo digesto italiano*, vol. III, Torino, UTET, 1974, 353-60; R. Feenstra, Impossibilitas *and* Clausola rebus sic stantibus. *Some aspects of frustration of contract in continental legal history up to Grotius*, in A. Watson (ed.), *Daube Noster: Essays in Legal History for David Daube*, Edinburgh, Scottish academic press, 1974, 77-104; M. Rummel, *Die 'clausola rebus sic stantibus'. Eine dogmengeschichtliche Untersuchung unter Berücksichtigung der Zeit von der Rezeption im 14. Jahrhundert bis zum jüngeren Usus Modernus in der ersten Hälfte des 18. Jahrhunderts*, Baden Baden, Nomos, 1991; M. Beck-Mannagetta, *Die Clausola Rebus sic Stantibus und die Geschäftsgrundlage in der Dogmengeschichte*, in *La formazione storica del diritto moderno*, vol. III, Firenze, Olschki, 1997, 1263-76; A. Thier, *Legal History*, in E. Hondius, H.C. Grigoleit, *Unexpected Circumstances in European Contract Law*, Cambridge, Cambridge University Press, 2011, 15-32; W. Decock, *Theologians and Contract Law*, 202-8.

246 Cicero, *De officiis*, 1, 31: "*Sed incidunt saepe tempora, cum ea, quae maxime videntur digna esse iusto homine, eoque quem virum bonum dicimus, commutantur fiuntque contraria, ut reddere depositum,* [*etiamne furioso?*] *facere promissum quaeque pertinent ad veritatem et ad fidem; ea migrare interdum et non servare fit iustum. Referri enim decet ad ea, quae posui principio fundamenta iustitiae, primum ut ne cui noceatur, deinde ut communi utilitati serviatur*".

247 Cicero, *De officiis*, 1, 32.

248 Cicero, *De officiis*, 3, 95.

249 Augustinus Hipponensis, *Enarrationes in psalmos*, 5, 7.

250 C. 22, q. 2, c. 14.

251 See R. Feenstra, Impossibilitas, 81; A. Thier, *Legal history*, 17-8.

252 A. Thier, *Legal History*, 17-8.

Seneca continued Cicero's discourse. He declared that the moral duty to keep promises only concerns promises where circumstances remain unchanged. A wise man does not change his will, if the conditions remain the same as when the promise had been undertaken.[253] Drawing upon Seneca, Thomas Aquinas argued that the promisor who does not keep his promise can be excused if the conditions of the persons and of the business are changed (*mutatae conditiones personarum et negotiorum*).[254] This principle was inherited and updated by the early modern scholastics.[255]

The Lutheran theologians seem to have been inspired by Cicero's and Seneca's writings, although they might have read them through the medieval filter. Melanchthon analyses Cicero's example of a sword that should not be returned to a promisee who became insane. He claims that returning the sword to the promisee who became insane is not honorable (*honestum*).[256] In a similar way, following Cicero, Von Eitzen concludes that the promise is not binding if it is useless or harms the promisee.[257] The frustration of the promise is admitted if the condition of the promise's subject is changed, so that the promise cannot be kept without evident danger.[258] On this point, he reports the example of the sword.[259] The example of the lawyer is instead quoted concerning the promise that harms more the promisor than benefits the promisee.[260] In this case, the promise should not be performed.

To Alberti a promise must benefit the promisor, the promisee or both of them and must not damage anyone. The promise must not have as subject matter something that harms the other party or a third party.[261] Furthermore, the natural law rule is *pacta sunt servanda* and only an 'apparent change in

253 Seneca, *De beneficiis*, 4, 34-5.

254 T. Aquinas, *Summa theologiae*, IIaIIae, q. 110, a. 3, ad. 5.

255 W. Decock, *Theologians and Contract Law*, 206.

256 P. Melanchthon, *Prolegomena in officia Ciceronis*, in CR XVI, 561-2: "*Ad honesta et hic casus pertinet: deposuit gladium sanus: si repetat furens, non est dandus, quia desinit honestum esse reddere furenti*".

257 P. von Eitzen, *Ethicae doctrinae pars altera*, 604a.

258 P. von Eitzen, *Ethicae doctrinae pars altera*, 604a: "*Tertia, si eius, cui facta est promissio, conditio ita mutata fuerit, ut sine evidenti periculo servari promissio haud possit*".

259 P. von Eitzen, *Ethicae doctrinae pars altera*, 604a.

260 P. von Eitzen, *Ethicae doctrinae pars altera*, 604a–604b: "*Quarta exceptione ita tradit Cicero lib. 1 Officiorum (…) promissa servanda non esse, si tibi plus noceant, quam illi prosint, cui promiseris*". See Cicero, *De officiis*, 1, 32.

261 V. Alberti, *Compendium iuris naturae*, 113: "quicquid in commodum alterius, vel tuum, vel utriusque, sine ullius praejudicio, dirigitur, id promittere potes … quicquid alteri vel tertio nocet, id promittere non debes".

circumstances' can be approved.[262] This unusual term is explained in the following sentences. For Alberti, the *pacta sunt servanda* never suffers a true modification, and the agreement should always be kept. Nonetheless, there are 'apparent changes' that occur because the subject matter changes or because a superior precept commands another behaviour.[263] The subject matter changes when its essence is modified per *se* or by the other party.[264] The first case – the subject matter changes – concerns changed circumstances. Here, Alberti quotes expressly Seneca's *De beneficiis*.[265] Instead, the second change in circumstances concerns reciprocal promises as in covenants, pacts and contracts, when the other party does not keep the promise.[266]

Finally, Jäger holds that the promise that is noxious and useless for the promisee must not be kept. He again proposes the example of a man who promised a sword and in the meantime the promisee became insane. Similarly, the promise must not be kept if it is more noxious for the promisor than useful for the recipient. Jäger mentions the example of the lawyer formulated by Cicero. A lawyer has to take part to a trial in the tribunal, but the day before his child got sick and requires the care and presence of the father. In this case, Jäger affirms, the love for the child must be preferred.[267]

These authors were evidently moved by the contributions of Cicero and Seneca as handed down by the medieval discussion. Slightly different, although in the same track, seem to be the reflections of Olearius and Haferung. Olearius subordinates the efficacy of the promise to the condition that there are no damages predicted for the future. If the fulfilment of the obligation

---

262 V. Alberti, *Compendium iuris naturae*, 128: "*Hujus nimirum praeceptum est*: promissa sunt servanda; *ejusque mutationem, nisi apparentem, non admittit*". Alberti describes this concept in V. Alberti, *Compendium iuris naturae*, 24: "*Est tamen, ubi aliquando mutationi apparenti, cum veram nunquam subeat, tam in axiomatibus, quam in rebus ipsis, obnoxia est*".

263 V. Alberti, *Compendium iuris naturae*, 128.

264 V. Alberti, *Compendium iuris naturae*, 129: "*Materia pervertitur, tum, quando in se, quoad essentialia, mutatur, tum, quando ab altero promittentium, mutilatur*".

265 Seneca, *De beneficiis*, 4, 35.

266 V. Alberti, *Compendium iuris naturae*, 129-30: "*Altera mutatio propria est promissionibus reciprocis, quales in conventionibus, pactis et contractibus fiunt. Sufficit hic, si alter partem promissionis suae non servet*".

267 J.W. Jäger, *Hugonis Grotii libri tres*, 325: "*Ex dictis* infertur, non esse servandam promissionem, quando *id, quod promittitur, vel* sit inutile, aut nocivum, *ei, qui promissio facta. Ut si quis promisisset alicui ensem, et interim efficitur furiosus; vel quando promissionis observatio facta sit magis nociva promittenti, quam esset utilis ei, cui sit promissio; ut si quis promisisset, se fore advocatum in causa eius in crastinum, et accidat proprii filii infirmitas, exigens paternam curam et praesentiam. In talibus casibus amor sui praerogativam tenet*".

harms the promisee, the promise must not be fulfilled.[268] Instead, if the fulfilment of the promise causes damages to the promisor in the future, the obligation must be fulfilled, because by promising, we renounce the right on our thing and transfer it to the other party.[269] This solution is based on the stability of the bond. Once the agreement is concluded, the promisor is obliged to fulfil the obligation, even in case of future damages. Olearius also states that the promise must not be fulfilled in case of an unexpected and unpredicted event, that the promisor, had he predicted it, would have expressly withdrawn from negotiations on the promise.[270] Olearius does not explicitly refer to Cicero or other sources.

For Haferung useless and noxious promises must not be performed. He recalls the same example of the sword and the insane party and adds that the promise with an undefined or unknown subject matter is invalid. He explains that such a requirement is necessary because the open-ended promise could result in destruction of the goods. The idea is taken from Matt. 14,7: on Herod's birthday, the daughter of Herodias danced so well that Herod promised to give her whatever she asked. Then she asked the head of Saint John the Baptist.[271]

In short, following a tradition that harks back to Cicero and Seneca, the Lutheran theologians concluded that a promise is no longer binding if the circumstances are changed, and the alteration creates damage for the promisee or the promisor. A useless and noxious promise should not be fulfilled. If the conditions changed, making a promise useless or noxious, the promise should not be fulfilled. Among the theologians examined is lacking an extensive analysis of the problem, as they mostly relied on the Romans. Melanchthon, Von Eitzen and Jäger followed Cicero. Alberti quoted Seneca and separated the two cases of the damage and the unchanged circumstances, which were united in Cicero. Similarly, but without any references, are the positions of Olearius and Haferung. For these authors, as for the scholastics, the mere changed circumstances, if not willed by the promisor, are sufficient for a lawful dissolution of the promise.

268 J. Olearius, *Doctrina theologiae moralis*, Tab. XLVII: "*Ipsi, cui promissum factum est, illius impletio* noxia *non sit futura: tum enim res ipsa docet, non esse implendum*".

269 J. Olearius, *Doctrina theologiae moralis*, Tab. XLVII: "*Si promissi impletio noxia sit futura* promittenti, *praestari tamen debet, quia per promissum ius in rem nostram abdicavimus, et in alterum transtulimus*".

270 J. Olearius, *Doctrina theologiae moralis*, Tab. XLVII: "*Interim eiusmodi casus incidere posse credimus, qui promissi praestationem impediant, nempe inopinati ac non praevisi, quos ipse promittens, si praevidisset, expresse excepisset*".

271 J.C. Haferung, *Theologia moralis*, 250.

3.5.3 *Physical Impossibility*

Like the Roman Catholics, the Lutheran theologians separated moral impossibility from physical impossibility. The former concerns the licitness of the agreement and the absence of damages, while the latter regards the material possibility of fulfilling the obligation. For example, Jäger and Buddeus cite the well-known principle: *nobody can be obliged to do the impossible* (*ad impossibilia nemo obligatur*).[272] As a consequence, the obligation that became impossible after the conclusion of the agreement should not be fulfilled. Jäger proposes the case of a party that cannot return the received money because of misfortune.[273] Buddeus refers to Pufendorf, insisting that if the performance was possible at the time of the conclusion of the pact, but became impossible afterwards, and the party knew it when entered in the agreement, the party must pay something.[274] In this case the party is penalized, because he should have declared that the obligation would become impossible in the future.

Alberti sustains that a promise with an impossible subject matter is invalid because of the natural law.[275] Yet, the impossible subject matter can be classified. Drawing upon Aristotle's *Nicomachean Ethics*, Alberti distinguishes a subject matter impossible for everybody, from the subject matter only impossible for some. This type of reasoning was also applied to marriage law, from which he might have drawn inspiration. The impossibility for everybody concerns death or hazardous circumstances that can lead to death. The second regards what is a disadvantage for someone, but could be different for others.[276] Both types of performance cannot be the subject matter of a promise.[277] Alberti warns not to confuse the two genres: what is impossible for one is not what is impossible for everyone.[278]

---

272 J.W. Jäger, *Hugonis Grotii libri tres*, 324; J.F. Buddeus, *Institutiones theologiae moralis*, 510.

273 J.W. Jäger, *Hugonis Grotii libri tres*, 324: "... *ut si promittat pecuniam, quam postea ob infortunium reddere non potest, non tenetur servare promissum, cum ad impossibile nemo teneatur*".

274 J.F. Buddeus, *Institutiones theologiae moralis*, 510. S. Pufendorf, *De jure naturae et gentium*, lib. 3, cap. 7 § 2.

275 V. Alberti, *Compendium iuris naturae*, 110: "*Hinc promissiones etiam rerum impossibilium natura sunt invalidae*".

276 V. Alberti, *Compendium iuris naturae*, 111; Aristotle, *Nicomachean Ethics*, III. 7 and VI. 5.

277 V. Alberti, *Compendium iuris naturae*, 111: "*Neutra possunt fieri materia promissionis*".

278 V. Alberti, *Compendium iuris naturae*, 111: "*Cave itaque, diversa impossibilitatis genera confundas et quod alicui tantum impossibile est, a nemine promitti posse statuas*". On this point, Alberti criticizes Thomas Hobbes, who held that one could not be bound not to resist injuries or death, and responds citing Samuel Pufendorf, who remembers that there are categories of people that are bound to risk their life, as for example soldiers. The impossibility may be artificial – although apparent, but it does not remove the obligation. T. Hobbes, *De cive*, cap. 2 § 18; S. Pufendorf, *De jure naturae et gentium*, lib. 3, cap. 7 § 5.

3.5.4 *Rules for the Execution*

A number of Lutheran theologians only focused on the theory that we described so far. They expounded rules for the formation of pact, but did not investigate other issues concerning the execution. Meisner and König, for instance, listed the conditions that a promise needs to be legally binding. Similarly, Osiander and Jäger discussed the legal requisites for the binding effects of pacts and promises. The reasons for this restricted treatment may be many. Likely, these theologians deemed not essential dealing with other aspects, as the execution of the agreement.

Another possibility is that they avoided delving into these issues because other authors had already done it fully. Buddeus, for example, avows that much could be said on questions like the interpretation, the conditions, the messengers (*internunciis*), the acceptance of pacts and promises, and that these are only slightly extraneous from the teachings of moral theology, because from time to time there are also theological questions where these doctrines can be useful. However, Grotius, Vitrarius, Pufendorf, Barbeyrac and Thomasius, who consider natural law according to reason (*secundum rationem*), examined them in depth, and thus he will not add anything.[279] In substance, Buddeus focused on the requirements for the efficacy of the pact, but left other issues open. The reader is invited to look for solutions in the works of the natural lawyers.

Other theologians drafted a set of general rules for performing the obligations created for the main transactions. The centrality of the bond, more than the intention and the fidelity to Scripture, is possibly one of the reasons that motivated these authors. For example, Olearius writes that if the performance

---

Certain authors admit that in the state of corruption, perpetual virginity is impossible. Alberti refers to Francisco Suarez, who holds that God does not command to everybody to remain virgin, because it is not possible according to nature. But, Alberti critically remarks, the Roman Catholic Church should have admitted this impossibility for everybody and not just for some. F. Suarez, *De legibus*, L. I c. 9 n. 19.

279 J.F. Buddeus, *Institutiones theologiae moralis*, 511-2: "*Non tantum de interpretatione, sed et de conditionibus, internunciis, acceptatione pactorum, atque promissorum, multa dici possent, ab instituto nostro eo minus aliena, quod in theologicis etiam subinde quaestiones occurrant, ubi harum doctrinarum aliquis usus esse queat. Verum, cum ab illis, qui ius naturae secundum rationem considerant, haec omnia exquisito studio pertractata sint, nihil addimus. Conferendi itaque Hugo Grotius,* de iure bellis ac pacis, lib. 2 cap. 11 et 16 *et commentatores, ad haec loca*; Philippus Reinhardus Vitrarius, *Institutiones juris naturae et gentium ad Methodum Hug. Grotii, itidem lib. 2 cap. 11 et 16*; Samuel Pufendorfius, *De iure naturae et gentium*, lib. 3, cap. 8 et 9, lib. 5 cap. 12; Johannes Barbeyracius, *ad* haec loca; Christianus Thomasius, *Institutiones iurisprudentiae divinae*, lib. 2, cap. 12 et quae in compendium dicimus, *Elementa philosophiae practicae*, part. 2, cap. 4 sect. 4 § 14 seqq."

concerns goods, they have to be conserved with the same care as the zealous family father (*sedulus Paterfamilias*) and returned only to the creditor; if the goods must be administered, it must be done judiciously; if a duty is requested to us, we have to obey faithfully, as St. Paul in 1 Cor. 4,2 states: "*it is required in stewards, that a man be found faithful*"; if a consultation is demanded of us, we have to make it without disappointing the other party.[280]

Along the same line, Haferung writes that if the promise guarantees help or benefit, this must be performed according to the mode, time and place set out in the agreement, as God does in Psalm 33,4: "*For the word of the Lord is right; and all his works are done in truth*".[281] If the agreement is a deposit, we must diligently observe it and return the thing at the time established (Exodus 22).[282] If it is a loan for use (*commodatum*), the goods have only to be diligently used for the granted use and returned in time. If the goods must be administered, we have to take care that there will be a profit for the other party.[283] Indeed, the proper manner of administering is illustrated in Matt. 25,14, the parable of the talents.

In a sense, the formulation of these general rules based on the Scriptures is indicative of two aspects. First, it shows again the clear dependence of the Scriptures. Second, it might be a clue of an attention to the obligation more than to the consent. Both the centrality of the Scriptures and the importance of the obligation will be explored by other theologians in the late eighteenth century.

3.6 From the Will to the Bond: A Brief Gaze towards the Future

It is not the aim of this dissertation to deal with authors throughout the whole eighteenth century. Yet, it might be interesting to have a brief look at some of them in order to see what is the outcome of the discussion we studied and the path the theologians followed. As we are going to see, two aspects need to be mentioned. First, the tension between a rational approach and a moral approach only based on Scripture seems to end. The more orthodox perspective, which only drew upon the Holy Scripture without any external references, gets the upper hand. External sources such as early modern scholastics and natural

280 J. Olearius, *Doctrina theologiae moralis*, Tab. XLVII.

281 J.C. Haferung, *Theologia moralis*, 250.

282 J.C. Haferung, *Theologia moralis*, 250-1: "*Si est* depositum, *nostrae fidei commissum, id diligenter asservetur, et convento tempore restituatur ...*".

283 J.C. Haferung, *Theologia moralis*, 251.

lawyers are no longer quoted, even though some aspects of their contributions are received. The consequence appears to be a stricter distinction between law and morality, between reason and faith.

Second, the approach of the Lutheran theologians tends more to focus on the compliance with the rule *pacta sunt servanda* rather than on the consent as the essential element for the constitution of the agreement. Consent remains an important aspect, but some theologians stress the firmness of the bond, because of the rule *pacta sunt servanda* and the necessity of the fulfilment. This view might be derived from the essential principle of the Reformation: the obedience to the Scriptures. The gaze is then not on the parties, but on the obligation that must be obeyed.

To start with, the professor of theology in Tübingen, Israel Gottlieb Canz, dedicates a brief chapter to contract law in his *Unterricht von den Pflichten der Christen oder theologische Moral* (1749). The essential content is that the Christians keep good faith (*Treu und Glauben*) in the foundation of the various contracts. Canz indicates several biblical passages for justifying this duty, but mainly he refers to Rom. 13,7: "*Render therefore to all their dues: tribute to whom tribute is due; custom to whom custom; fear to whom fear; honour to whom honour*". To Canz this precept requires the Christian to give to everyone what he owes him. Yet, the contract is also an action that depends on the consent of the parties. Here, Canz integrates the contribution of the early modern scholastics imported by other Lutheran theologians before him. He writes that the consent must be spontaneous, without fear, according to one's convenience and allowed. The subject matter must be morally possible.[284] Remarkably, Canz does not require acceptance of the promisee. Promise only depends upon the will of the promisor.

A second author we review is Ernst August Bertling. In his *De officiis et virtutibus christianorum libri tres, sive theologiae moralis elementa* (1753), Bertling associates the breach of pact and promises to the seventh commandment of the Decalogue and not to the eighth commandment. This change might be due to the development of a contract doctrine, more and more removed from the Roman law formalities, as seen earlier. Bertling maintains that pacts and promises are binding because Matt. 5,37 and 2 Cor. 1,17 establish it. He also adds other references, for example Matt. 23,23, where Christ warns the scribes and Pharisees that they have neglected the precepts of the law, such as justice, mercy and faithfulness; and Lev. 19,2, where God tells Israel to be saint. Bertling requires that the subject matter be known, because the subject matter that the

284 I.G. Canz, *Unterricht von den Pflichten der Christen oder theologische Moral*, Berlin, 1749, 426-7.

party receives must have the same characteristics of the subject matter known and promised. If the received goods do not have the same qualities, it is not the same subject matter, and therefore the pact is vitiated by a deceit that is a kind of theft.[285]

The conservative trend supported by Dannhauer, Olearius and Haferung was still in force in the second half of the eighteenth century. Ernest Schubert in his *Institutiones theologiae moralis* (1759) maintains that the binding effect of the pact is because of the virtue of truth. He declares that the breach of pacts and promises is an act against truth. The truth is offended in two ways: firstly when we decide to promise something that we do not want to perform. Secondly, when we promised something, which we wanted to perform, but later we do not satisfy. Therefore, it is necessary that the parties sincerely promise and observe their pacts.[286] Likewise against the truth are ambiguous words and mental reservations, immoral subject matters and breaches of contract.[287] Notably, Schubert insists that neither the fear of damage nor an imminent danger can free one from an obligation. The agreement is even maintained if the party promised something that is shameful, or without having the power to be bound, and then he does not want to fulfil the obligation due to his will or a fortuitous case.[288] In this author, we see the exasperation of the doctrine of the solidity of the bond based on the obedience to the Scriptures. When the bond is created, the party must fulfil it, no matter the state of his will or the possibility of the subject matter.

The gigantic work of Johann Lorenz von Mosheim, *Sitten Lehre der Heiligen Schrift*, deals with contract law in his seventh part, first published in 1778. The brief discourse begins with the request of reciprocal fidelity (*Treue*) and integrity (*Redlichkeit*) in contracts, which is justified with several biblical passages (Rom. 13,7; Psalm 15,2; 1 Thess. 4,6) and derives from the general human love (*allgemeinen Meschenliebe*).[289] Then, Mosheim lists three requisites for the observance of the contracts: the subject matter of the agreement must be morally and physically possible; the Christian must understand that God is witness to

285 E.A. Bertling, *De officiis et virtutibus*, 195-6.

286 J.E. Schubert, *Institutiones theologiae moralis*, Lipsiae, 1759, 338: "*In hoc negotio veritas duplici modo laedi potest: primo, cum quid nos praestituros esse pollicemur, quod tamen praestare nolumus; secundo, cum, quod promissimus, et tunc praestare volebamus, postea non adimplemus. Quare necessum est, ut paciscentes et sincere promittant, et pacta sua servent*".

287 E. Schubert, *Institutiones theologiae moralis*, 342-3.

288 E. Schubert, *Institutiones theologiae moralis*, 343-4.

289 J.L. von Mosheim, *Sitten Lehre der Heiligen Schrift*, Siebenter Theil, Leipzig, 1778, 395-6.

the agreement and every violation (such a deceits or intrigues) is also an insult to God; and the Christian must punctually fulfil the agreement.[290]

In conclusion, a brief look at some of the Lutheran moral theologians in the eighteenth century allows observation of a closer relation with the Scriptures and the abandonment of reference to external sources, such as the natural lawyers or Catholic authors. Even though these sources are not formally cited, however, the scholastic requirements for the validity of the agreement are now assimilated into the discourse. The analysis of the Lutheran theologians of the sixteenth and seventeenth century paved the way for the subsequent treatment of contract law. To this more orthodox approach corresponds the intensifying of attention to the bond, rather than to the consent of the parties. This is a symptom of a shift from the freedom of the parties to create a bond, to the obedience to a biblical commandment, upheld by the Holy Spirit. Once the agreement has been drawn up, the parties must fully keep faith to their words. For some theologians the fulfilment must occur even if the subject matter became legally or morally impossible.

3.7 Conclusion

The Lutheran theologians inherited from the Catholic canonists and moral theologians the principle according to which agreements are binding (*pacta sunt servanda*) and transformed its moral constitution. This principle was founded on natural law and directed to safeguard the Christian's spiritual interest to gain salvation. For the Lutherans, *pacta sunt servanda* is a precept of the natural law repeated in the eighth commandment of the Decalogue and expressed by the virtue of truthfulness or fidelity. Every man must obey, but because of sin he can only obey with external actions. The obedience with heart rests on the grace of God obtained by faith. Encouraged by the Holy Spirit, the Christian is pushed to keep faith in agreements. During the seventeenth century, because of attacks by the natural lawyers, the theologians had to defend this view in various ways. Alberti grounded it on a natural law derived from the state of integrity. Other theologians paid attention only to the born-again believers and founded the rule on the virtues of truthfulness and fidelity or on Christian love given by God. They separated the order of creation and reason from the order of revelation and faith.

Starting from the natural law rule *pacta sunt servanda*, canonists and early modern theologians propped up a general theory of contract centred on the free

290 J.L. von Mosheim, *Sitten Lehre der Heiligen Schrift*, 398-400.

consent of the parties. They advocated that an agreement is binding when certain requirements are present: free, deliberate and expressed will, acceptance, licit subject matter, and the promisor's ability to be bound. The Lutherans faced the same issue, but were limited by the scarce support of Scripture. Scripture does not include clear solutions for determining when the agreement is binding. Therefore, the theologians followed various strategies. Melanchthon and Von Eitzen drew inspiration from Cicero's *De officiis*. Meisner undertook a rational approach inspired by the early modern scholastics; Horneius, Osiander, Jäger and Alberti commented upon the early modern scholastics and the natural lawyers on the basis of Scripture; while Buddeus sought to find a synthesis between these attitudes: he proposed a brief treatment of the crucial issues, referring then to the natural lawyers for a more pointed analysis. A stream of thought spearheaded by Dannhauer, Olearius and Haferung remained strictly tied to Scripture and the doctrine of virtues. Yet, these theologians only formulated some general rules, without delving into details and controversial issues.

The outcome is a blending of these different approaches, which leaves no room for a systematic and coherent contract theory. Granted, it must be kept in mind the different genre of the works: some of them were manuals of moral theology, some philosophical treatises, still others commentaries on natural law. However, the theologians only erected the 'scaffold' of a general theory: some elements solidly cemented in the Scriptures. The expressed consent of the parties, the absence of mistakes and deceit, and the lawfulness of the subject matter are certainly well stated and grounded in the Scriptures. Other issues, though, such as the necessity of the declaration and acceptance, the consequences of mistakes or the quality that duress must have in order to invalidate the agreement, are solved by reference to early modern scholastics and natural lawyers. These are also crucial moral issues. But the Lutherans failed to invent new solutions.

Another aspect that merits highlighting is that some theologians centred their discourse around the virtue of truthfulness or the virtue of fidelity. They did not begin their analysis from the consent, but from the virtue. They gave attention to the bond more than to the will of the parties. They looked at the possible breaches of the agreement and not at the lack of consent. As a consequence, they stressed the obligatory structure of the relationship, the fulfilment of the obligation and the performance. This might be the effect of the Lutheran hegemony of Scripture. The centre is not the will of the parties, but the obedience to the obligation, as imposed by the Word of God. A brief look at some authors in the late eighteenth century reveals that this approach continued to be followed.

In conclusion, the general theory proposed by the Lutheran theologians of the sixteenth and seventeenth centuries is a hybrid of the Lutheran and the Catholic way of thinking. Scripture remains at the fore, as well as the arguments that can be drawn from it. The theologians based their conclusions on biblical hermeneutics and on episodes narrated in Scripture. At a second level, rational arguments, original or more often imported by other sources, found their space. They were utilized to disentangle technical issues that Scripture does not explicate clearly. In this framework, two different spirits coexisted: the scholastic trust in reason, and the Lutheran obedience to the Scriptures – the Catholic idea of human freedom and the Lutheran view of the supernatural effects given by the Holy Spirit. This might seem a paradox, but it actually demonstrates an effective combination of the new and the old. It is a transitional stage, towards a sharper separation between morality and law that will take place in the eighteenth century.

PART III

Selected Issues from Particular Types of Contract

CHAPTER 1

Sale, Lease and Restitution

The second part of this work illustrated concepts and general principles of contract law. Now we proceed to more concrete aspects involving the regulation of the specific contracts. We will study the sale, lease and the various forms of loans. Because the theologians of the day viewed these contracts as instruments for the lawful or unlawful acquisition of property, the formulation of rules to guarantee the righteousness of profit was therefore an essential element. Together with this, the analysis of the relations between different categories of people, such as rich and poor, played an important role. The theologians considered both these aspects in the light of the illuminating judgment of Scripture, which constituted the fundamental criterion for their solutions. Yet, for some issues, they also adopted many of the medieval and early modern scholastic contributions.

1.0 Introduction

In the dedicatory letter of his *Annotationes* to Olearius' manual of moral theology, Friedemann Bechmann denounced the commixture between scholastic theology and Aristotelian philosophy. In his view, Aristotelian philosophy was polluted by a multitude of errors needing correction by the light of the divine Revelation. Bechmann argued that the Lutheran theology, on the other hand, was founded on the divine Revelation as expressed in the Scripture.[1] Despite such definitive statements, the Lutheran theologians nonetheless utilized the opinions of the scholastic theologians. As this chapter will reveal, they wisely recognised the primacy of Scripture, but they did not neglect appeals to different sources, mostly the scholastics' contributions. These completed the points not detailed by Scripture, making possible a more specific treatment.

Based on Aristotle, Roman law and Cicero, the scholastics' theory of just price encompassed rules about pricing, protection against malicious alterations of prices and other commercial fraud. Violations of these teachings were sanctioned with restitution. In brief, this required the unjust possessor

1 F. Bechmann, *Annotationes in celeberrimi Dn. D. Joh. Olearii Theologiam Moralem* [...], Francofurti et Lipsiae, 1704, epistola dedicatoria.

 | DOI:10.30965/9783657701506_008

to return the things he had stolen. Restitution was effective through the sacrament of penance. After confession the priest ordained the specific amount of restitution and identified acts of penance for the Christian to do. Penance was a vital element of the road towards salvation. Restitution of the stolen goods was just the end of the offence; the Christian needed to do the acts of penance to extinguish the temporal punishment ordained by God for his sin.

The Lutheran theologians subordinated the scholastic teachings to the fundamental gaze of Scripture. This was a necessity, as Scripture provided a solid foundation for general rules, but not for more detailed regulations. Thus, Luther recycled the scholastic ethics of pricing, but founded them on Scripture versus Aristotelian philosophy. Melanchthon spoke about the just price and used Roman law concepts, but he inserted them in a theological horizon. On these premises, the theologians who supported Luther and Melanchthon undertook a twofold path. A stream of moralists spearheaded by the theologians of Helmestedt and Altdorf ratified the scholastic answers to a number of cases of conscience. Yet, other theologians, such as Dannhauer, Osiander and Meisner, even if they did not ignore the scholastics' solutions, refused or restricted them, looking rather at Scripture as the core or sole criterion of judgment. The outcome shows this oscillating tendency: positions open to accepting the scholastic solutions stand together with others more conservative. The Lutheran moral theology appears in this way somewhat polychromatic.

Regarding restitution, the Lutheran theologians diverged from the scholastics on the basic assumptions, but they shared some conclusions. Like the scholastics, they stressed the necessity of restitution as an element of contrition, necessary for the remission of sin. However, they did not request Christians to perform acts of penance after restitution. Salvation already derives from the sacrifice of Christ, and another sacrifice is not required from His followers. The act of restitution flows from the grace of faith, which stimulates the Christian to return the stolen goods. No following acts of penance are requested. Then, the operativity of restitution is left to a rather small body of rules that do not gain the same technical precision reached by the scholastics. The impression is that the Christian is firmly asked to perform restitution, but not driven through the obstacles its application might present. He is called to follow his conscience and the bright light of Scripture.

1.1 Sale: Roman Law, Aristotle and Orthodox Theology

1.1.1 *Introduction*

In the medieval analysis of sale, under the umbrella of the just price theory, the scholastic theologians included not only the ethics of pricing, but also frauds of goods, compulsions, monopolies and other alterations of prices.[2] The Lutheran theologians looked at the use of the sale of goods in a context of faith, which avers that a contract is divinely ordered and must comply with God's rules. These rules are dictated by the divine law, especially the seventh commandment of the Decalogue. On the interpretation of the divine law, however, the theologians followed two different roads. On the one hand, Luther based his considerations on the seventh commandment to forbid fraud on goods and any kind of counterfeiting or deceit, although the rules on the ethics of pricing are not explicated in this commandment. Luther appealed to the summary of the divine law: the natural law (*all things whatsoever ye would that men should do to you, do ye even so to them*) and Christian charity (*thou shalt love thy neighbour as thyself*). He did not mention fairness in exchange but grounded his ethics of pricing on the natural law and Christian charity. On the other hand, Melanchthon likewise used the seventh commandment of the Decalogue, but he also called upon commutative justice, although this must be seen from a perspective of faith, as in the case of the contractual equality we have seen earlier.

Luther and Melanchthon's followers adopted both of these models, resulting in fragmentary doctrine. We find general statements carved in Scripture. The seventh commandment, natural law and Christian law are accompanied by numerous quotations of other scriptural passages. But we also find several allusions to the just price or commutative justice, skirted by references to scholastic theologians' works. The scholastic solutions are particularly important for the analysis of detailed circumstances and practical problems, even though the Lutheran theologians did not always accept their opinions pleading for a different interpretation of Scripture.

2 On the scholastic doctrine of just price there is a vast literature. J.T. Noonan, Jr., *The Scholastic Analysis of Usury*, 82-99; R. De Roover, *The Concept of the Just Price Theory and Economic Policy*, in *Journal of Economic History*, 18 (1958), 418-34; J.W. Baldwin, *The Medieval Theories of the Just Price*, passim; O. Langholm, *Price and Value in the Aristotelian Tradition*, Bergen, Universitetsforlaget, 1979; J. Gordley, *Equality in Exchange*, in *California Law Review*, vol. 69, n. 6 (1981), 1587-1656; O.F. Hamouda, B.B. Price, *The Justice of the Just Price*, in *The European Journal of the History of Economic Thought*, 4:2, 1997, 191-216; O. Langholm, *The Legacy of Scholasticism*, 77-89. For more references see A. Del Vigo Gutiérrez, *Economia y ética*, 511-719.

We will first have a look at the definitions of sale. Then, we go through two different sets of obligations. The first one centres on the determination and qualities of the goods sold. It includes the seller's property rights, the just measure of the goods, and the declaration of defects. A second body of duties concerns the ethics of pricing, price alterations, and monopolies.

1.1.2 *Lawfulness and Structure*

In Roman law texts, the sale of goods was conceived as a consensual contract, where no particular requirement was necessary except the agreement between the parties.[3] The conclusion of the agreement set the obligations of the parties. Then, for the acquisition of ownership, a separate act of conveyance was required.[4] Originally, the price of goods derived from the free determination of the parties.[5] Yet, a constitution issued by Diocletian (C. 4,44,2) said that 'it was humane' that he who sold a piece of land for less than half its true value (the so-called *laesio enormis*) could rescind the contract, unless the purchaser paid the true, full value. This text encompassed a legal principle that could be extended to a large number of cases. When a disproportion in the value is too high, it is the role of the public authority to protect the disadvantaged party.[6]

In addition, other texts from the Digest established that the price of goods derives from the common estimation.[7] These passages stimulated the interest of scholastic theologians and canonists of the Middle Ages and early Modern Era.[8] They used them together with Aristotelian philosophy to state that every sale must be concluded at a just price. Indeed, for the doctrine of equality in exchange, the parties must agree on the price, which has to correspond to a determinate value: the market price or the price fixed by the public authority.

---

3 R. Zimmermann, *The Law of Obligations*, 230. More in general on the contract of sale in Roman law see: D. Daube (ed.), *Studies in the Roman Law of Sale: Dedicated to the Memory of Francis de Zulueta*, Oxford, Clarendon University Press, 1959; L. Waelkens, *Amne Adverso*, 374-83.

4 R. Zimmermann, *The Law of Obligations*, 271. See also W. Ernst, *vor § 433. Der Kauf als Vertragstyp*, in M. Schmoeckel, J. Rückert, R. Zimmermann (eds.), *Historisch-kritischer Kommentar zum BGB*, 3, Tübingen, Mohr Siebeck, 2013, 36-58 (38-46).

5 R. Zimmermann, *The Law of Obligations*, 255-6.

6 R. Zimmermann, *The Law of Obligations*, 259-62. The authenticity of the passage was already cast in doubt by the humanist jurists. See W. Decock, *Elegant Scholastic Humanism? Arias Piñel's (1515-1563) Critical Revision of Laesio Enormis*, in P.J. du Plessis, J.W. Cairns (eds.), *Reassessing Legal Humanism and its Claims. Petere fontes?*, Edinburgh, Edinburgh University Press, 2016, 137-53.

7 D. 35,2,63; D. 36,1,16; D. 14,2,4.

8 J.W. Baldwin, *The Medieval Theories of the Just Price*, 42-6. For the early modern theologians see W. Decock, *Theologians and Contract Law*, 519-28.

If a good is sold for a price higher than the just price, the equality of justice is broken and must be restored.[9]

The Lutheran theologians did not formulate new legal concepts, but elaborated on those already in existence. What has been said for the contracts in general is also true for the sale of goods. Based upon the medieval elaboration of Roman law and the doctrine of just price, Melanchthon defines sale as that contract by which the lordship (*dominium*) of a thing is transferred for a just price and where the buyer does not have the right to withdraw the price.[10] He also emphasizes that the substantial elements of the sale are the following: merchandise, price and the consent of the seller and the buyer. Three elements stand out in this definition. First, the concept used to identify property rights is *dominium*. Second, the price must be *just*, which clearly alludes to the theory of just price. Third, Melanchthon identifies the substantial elements of sale. This last point seems clearly to refer to the medieval theory of the substantial, natural and accidental elements of the contract we saw earlier.[11]

In his *Prolegomena in officia Ciceronis*, Melanchthon sets forth a slightly different treatment of sale. He believes that the delivery of the corporeal thing (*traditio*) can be added to the substantial elements of the contract.[12] The classification of the *traditio* among the substantial or natural elements of the contract is an intricate issue, and several opinions had been proposed among medieval and early modern jurists.[13] Baldus, for instance, maintained that the *traditio* was part of the natural elements. Alciato did not consider the *traditio* to be an essential element, while Zasius with a subtle argument answered that the *traditio* was an inseparable natural element.[14] Unfortunately, Melanchthon does not substantiate his statement, which makes it more difficult to understand his argument. The practical effect of his conclusion would essentially be that a pact excluding the transfer of the thing would be void.

---

9 J. Noonan Jr., *The Scholastic Analysis*, 83 and 89; J.W. Baldwin, *The Medieval Theories of the Just Price*, 72-3.

10 P. Melanchthon, *Loci communes* (*tertia eorum aetas*), in CR XXI, *Appendix II Definitiones multarum appellationum*, 1552-1553, 1094: "*Emtio est contractus, quo res transfertur quoad dominium pro iusto pretio, nec retinet emtor ius retrahendi pretii. Et nominatur substantialia emtionis merx, pretium et consensus emtoris et venditoris*".

11 See II/1.1.

12 P. Melanchthon, *Prolegomena in officia Ciceronis*, in CR XVI, 581: "*... credo recte addi posse traditionem de re corporali*".

13 I. Birocchi, *Vendita e transferimento della proprietà nel diritto comune*, in L. Vacca (ed.), *Vendita e trasferimento della proprietà nella prospettiva storico-comparatistica*. Atti del Congresso Internazionale Pisa-Viareggio-Lucca, 17-21 aprile 1990, Milano Giuffrè, 1991, 139-67.

14 I. Birocchi, *Vendita e transferimento della proprietà nel diritto comune*, 160-3.

Melanchthon then discusses the lawfulness of this contract, providing three reasons why it is lawful. First, the examples of Abraham, Jacob, David and Jeremiah, who used the sale and other lawful contracts, show that sale is granted to Christians, for the Gospel does not abolish political and economic ordinances. God wants His people to know that politics and economics are His ordinances and work, and He wants them to be used with reverence.[15] As seen before, regarding the contracts in general, to Melanchthon the sale is a creation of God and must be used according to His will.

Second, God wanted men united by mutual love – as in the words of Matt. 22,39: *thou shalt love thy neighbour as thyself* – for we consider the neighbour in this way: it is good to conserve him, to exchange with him and to be united with him. In that manner humanity coheres: everyone needs assistance and goods, and such deficiency or dependency is a kind of 'reminder' (*commonefactio*) of God's will. In order to keep this exchange perpetual, Melanchthon explains, God wanted us to observe mutual equality,[16] which He names 'justice'. He wanted humankind to understand it, so that we might learn that God is just and equal.[17] The sale is a creation of God and must be used to meet the neighbour's needs; the law teaches us God's pleasing works.

Third, sale is expressly approved by two scriptural passages.[18] 1 Cor. 7,30-1 says:

> *and they that weep, as though they wept not; and they that rejoice, as though they rejoiced not; and they that buy, as though they possessed not; And they that use this world, as not abusing it: for the fashion of this world passeth away;*

---

15 P. Melanchthon, *Prolegomena in officia Ciceronis*, in CR XVI, 581: "*Extant exempla emptionum et venditionum, Abrahae, Iacob, Davidis, Hieremiae, quae et hunc contractum et alios legitimos contractus ostendunt concessos esse Christianis, iuxta regulam: Evangelium non abolet politicas et oeconomicas ordinationes: imo Deus vult nos agnoscere politiam et oeconomiam esse suas ordinationes et opera, et vult nos illis reverenter uti*".

16 P. Melanchthon, *Prolegomena in officia Ciceronis*, in CR XVI, 581-2: "*Cum enim Deus velit homines copulatos esse mutua dilectione, iuxta dictum (Matth. 22, 39): dilige proximum tuum sicut te ipsum, ut cogitemus nos ab ipso quoque diligi, iuxta dictum: bonum est conservativum sui, communicativum et congregativum, sic condidit genus humanum, ut singuli multorum laboribus et rebus indigeamus, et haec ipsa indigentia commonefactio esset de voluntate Dei. Ut autem possit esse perpetua communicatio, vult servari mutuam aequalitatem*".

17 P. Melanchthon, *Prolegomena in officia Ciceronis*, in CR XVI, 582: "*Et hanc aequalitatis conservationem nominat Deus iustitiam, eamque vult intelligi, ut discamus et ipsum iustum et aequalem esse*".

18 P. Melanchthon, *Prolegomena in officia Ciceronis*, in CR XVI, 582.

and Prov. 16,11: "*A just weight and balance are the Lord's: all the weights of the bag are his work*".

The lawfulness of sale and more in general, the lawfulness of business and contracts, was a point specifically questioned by the Anabaptists.[19] In responding to these pleas, Melanchthon designs a perspective of faith for the sale of goods. The sale is lawful and must be used according to God's will: reflecting that we love our neighbour and exchange with him in order to provide him with what he needs. This exchange is regulated by contractual justice. By keeping this justice, we learn God's justice. The law teaches the Christian the justice of God. This scheme mirrors what we have seen for the contract in general.

Melanchthon's analysis of sale influenced Paul Von Eitzen. In his *Ethica doctrina*, Von Eitzen defines the *venditio* and *emptio* as:

> *those contracts where the seller obligates himself to deliver the merchandise to the buyer, and to transfer the lordship* (dominium) *and possession* (possessio) *over it for a certain price. As the merchandise belongs to the buyer, so the price belongs to the seller.*[20]

Von Eitzen seems to identify in one single act the passing of lordship (*dominium*) and possession (*possessio*). Indeed, repeating Melanchthon, he adds that the substantial elements of the sale are price, consent and the delivery (*traditio*) of the corporeal thing.[21]

Even though Von Eitzen recalls justice in exchange at the beginning of his contract law treatment, he does not say anything about the just price in the definition of sale. He warns Christians that the use of the contract of sale is licit, as the examples of the patriarchs in Scripture teach. God has ordained the sale, as one needs the things of others; the same need is a reminder of God's will and approval. The theft of the goods we need is forbidden; therefore sale is allowed.[22] As seen before, the seventh commandment justifies the

19 See before II/2.1.1.

20 P. von Eitzen, *Ethicae doctrinae pars altera*, 474: "*Sunt autem venditio et emptio contractus, in quo obligat se vendens ad tradendam mercem ementi, atque ita ad transferendum dominium et possessionem mercis, pro certo pretio, et vicissim emptor obligat se ad dandum precium et sicut merx sit ementis, sic precium sit vendentis*".

21 P. von Eitzen, *Ethicae doctrinae pars altera*, 474: "*Suntque substantialia venditionis et emptionis merx precium, et consensus quibus addi potest traditio de re corporali*".

22 P. von Eitzen, *Ethicae doctrinae pars altera*, 474: "*Contractum venditionis et emptionis inter Christianos licitum esse, docent exempla Sanctorum in scriptura sacra, et quidem cum sic a Deo ordinatum sit ut alii aliorum rebus indigeant, ipsa indigentia est commonefactio de Dei voluntate et approbatione. Prohibitum est furtum earum rerum, quibus indigemus, ergo concessa est emptio*".

lawfulness of the sale. The sale is useful because God ordained it to provide people with the goods they need. This attention to the lawfulness of the contract is a consequence of the dispute with the Anabaptists. The Anabaptists refused business and contracts, and in this way constrained the Lutheran theologians to defend the lawfulness of this agreement.

Another author that can be associated with Melanchthon, David Chytraeus, also deals with the contract of sale. His definition seems however not to add substantial changes to the definition formulated in the *ius commune*. In his *In Deuteronomium Mosis enarratio*, Chytraeus defines the contract of sale as the contract where thing and price are exchanged; for that reason the seller is obliged to deliver the thing and to transfer its lordship or to perform the eviction. Inversely, the buyer is obliged to pay the price to the seller and does not have the right to receive back that price.[23] This definition neither mentions the just price, nor any justification of the contract. Yet, as with Von Eitzen, Chytraeus described commutative justice at the beginning of his chapter dedicated to contract doctrine, as a principle applicable to every contract.[24]

Later authors like Johann Konrad Dürr continued on the road traced by Melanchthon. For his definition of sale, Dürr drew from a passage included in the Digest. This text observed that the sale of goods originated from the barter, which did not require money, while money is a constitutive element of a sale.[25] To Dürr, the sale is that contract used in place of barter, by which useful goods are acquired for a necessary price. The price is established through public estimation and corresponds to the worth, the quantity and value of the good.[26] Dürr does not recall the Roman law concept of property and possession, electing instead to use the less juridical concept of *res utiles*. In other terms, he does not identify the relationship between a person and a good, but only speaks about a category of goods. He also does not say anything regarding the just price, though he points out that the price must be accurately determined. With Melanchthon and Von Eitzen, he adds some statements on the justification of

23 D. Chytraeus, *In deuteronomium Mosis enarratio*, 456-7: "*Emptio venditio est contractus, quo res precio commutantur, ea ratione, ut venditor obligetur ad rem tradendam, eiusque aut transferendum dominium, aut praestandam euictionem. Emptor contra ad dandum pretium venditori, nec habet ius aut tempus ullum repetendi pretium*".

24 D. Chytraeus, *In deuteronomium Mosis enarratio*, 451.

25 D. 18,1,1pr.

26 J.K. Dürr, *Compendium theologiae moralis*, 219: "*Emtio est contractus in locum permutationis succedens, quo acquiruntur res utiles necessario pretio, publica aestimatione definito et rerum ipsarum dignitatem, quantitatem et valore exaequante*". As we see further, Horneius's, Dürr's, and Baier's works were studied and updated by Johann Michael Lange in his *Ad B. D. Joh. Guil. Bajeri theologi etiam post fata celeberrimi, compendium theologiae moralis supplementa*, Jenae, 1700.

the contract, reasoning that God approved the contract of sale in order to raise up the human race from its need, as it is proved in the Holy Scripture. Because not everything can be obtained from agriculture, through inheritance or by our work, the sale is necessary.[27] Sale is a useful contract to acquire the goods we need and therefore can lawfully be used.

On the whole, the Lutheran theologians grasped the meaning of sale through the spectrum of the medieval elaboration of Roman law, the doctrine of just price and the debate on the lawfulness of business and contracts. Melanchthon employs the medieval theory of the substantial elements, describes the delivery as an essential element of the sale, and insists on the just price and on the lawfulness of the contract. Von Eitzen uses the two concepts of lordship and possession, considers the delivery as an essential element of the sale, and justifies the lawfulness of this agreement. Chytraeus speaks about the delivery and the transfer of property in return of a price. Von Eitzen and Chytraeus do not emphasize that the price must be just. But both of them recognize commutative justice as valid for the contracts in general. Dürr does not refer to the just price, but adds some statements to justify the contract. He does not say explicitly that the price must be just, but explains the ways it must be determined: common estimation and public authority.

1.1.3 *Rules Concerning the Goods*

1.1.3.1 The Right of Property

Selling implies the existence of the seller's valid right of property. As seen before, the seventh commandment of the Decalogue sets out the right to private property by forbidding stealing. For this reason, the theologians insisted that only the real proprietor can sell the goods. For example, Jäger points out that a lawful and just sale needs the seller be the lawful owner (*dominus*) and possessor, who therefore has the right to sell the good.[28] Baier specifies that the buyer is obliged not to buy goods that he knows are not on sale.[29] The seller must not sell what he does not own; the buyer must not buy or attempt for what is not saleable. These duties aim to safeguard the right of property.

A particular exception regards the relationship between husband and wife. Can the husband sell his wife's goods without her consent? Johann Dannhauer answers not only by referring to the Holy Scripture but also to the Roman

27 J.K. Dürr, *Compendium theologiae moralis*, 219.

28 J.W. Jäger, *Theologia moralis*, 183: "*Legitima et iustitiae congruens venditio est, cum et is qui vendit, rei venditae legitimus dominus ac possessor sit, adeoque ius vendendi habeat* ...".

29 J.W. Baier, *Compendium theologiae moralis*, 490: "*Ut res venales fiant, cum bona possidentis seu venditoris voluntate, non contra eius voluntatem ab emtore venales reddantur*".

Catholic theologian Martín de Azpilcueta (Dr. Navarrus).[30] Azpilcueta writes that save the goods that are in the dowry, husband and wife can transfer the other's goods, if his/her consent can be virtually predicted according to right reason and conscience.[31] This solution is confirmed by the biblical example of Abigail, the wife of Nabal (1 Sam. 25). Nabal was rich and possessed many herds. King David was having troubles in the desert and asked for help from Nabal, who refused. David, because of the offence received, decided to attack Nabal and massacre all the males in his household. Abigail was informed of the imminent attack and, without Nabal knowing, sent to David a large quantity of supplies belonging to her husband, which assuaged David's vengeful spirit.[32] Dannhauer comments that Abigail sought the good of her husband, even though she 'sold' his goods.[33] She did not steal anything, but protected her family by making use of the goods which had been given by God.[34] Thus, Dannhauer allows a spouse to sell the other's goods, if the other would likely have agreed according to right reason and conscience.

Another case, Dannhauer says, is more complex: can a man steal food, if he is going to starve, having no other mean of nourishment? Dannhauer reports that Leonard Lessius, Gregory of Valencia and Roberto Bellarmino[35] maintain that in the case of extreme necessity, every good is held in common, and for this reason the seizure of bread is to be considered licit. Dannhauer refuses this opinion. Drawing upon classical Lutheran teachings on private property, he affirms that a communion of goods is against natural law and the *ius gentium*. A division of goods was probably even in Paradise, if Adam would have not committed his sin. What is established by natural law cannot be changed, he holds. A communion of goods could only be founded on the *ius gentium*. However, this would require the consent of people. Even if everyone agreed to a communion of goods, this still excludes an order. As homicide is forbidden, theft is condemned. Therefore, Dannhauer concludes, it is not licit to steal in

30 Dannhauer only cites their names. No references to any writings are proposed.

31 J.K. Dannhauer, *Theologia casualis*, 425: "*... licet ei aliquid abalienare, si videatur maritus consensurus, si recta ratio et conscientia id suadet*".

32 1 Sam. 25.

33 J.K. Dannhauer, *Theologia casualis*, 425.

34 J.K. Dannhauer, *Theologia casualis*, 426: "*Ibi igitur nullum furtum commissum, quoties Deus rem quasi destinavit*".

35 Unfortunately he does not include any references to their works. For a gaze on the scholastic analysis see V. Mäkinen, *Rights and Duties in Late Scholastic Discussion on Extreme Necessity*, in V. Mäkinen and P. Korkman (eds.), *Transformations in Medieval and Early-Modern Rights Discourse*, Dordrecht, Springer, 2006, 37-62; W. Decock, *Law, Religion and Debt Relief*, passim. Lessius and Azpilcueta pointed out that only the use of the goods became common and not the property.

case of necessity (*ergo non licet in casu necessitatis furari*). He invites the magistrate to follow this opinion, adding the following consideration. Men who are starving are of two types. Either they can walk and work, and therefore can avoid stealing, or they are sick and cannot steal. Means to conserve life that contravene the divine order can never be justified.[36]

To sum up, the right of property is not only ordered by civil law but also by the seventh commandment of the Decalogue. This prompts the theologians to underscore the necessity that the seller be the real proprietor of the goods. This rule admits an exception concerning marriage; the husband can market his wife's goods, with the reasonably presumed consent of his wife. The solution is both provided by the early modern scholastics and Scripture. Exceptions are instead not admitted concerning the case of extreme necessity. We saw the rigid approach by Dannahuer, who refuses the opinions of some scholastic authors and does not justify stealing. Here, we really encounter the practical consequences of the scholastic and the Lutheran views on property law.

1.1.3.2 A Just Measure

After having the right of property, the theologians require the sellers to evaluate correctly the quantity of goods that are for sale. Olearius for instance writes that the sellers should be cautious and not measure inaccurately,[37] a rule that is formulated in the Holy Scripture. Lev. 19,35-36 is explicit:

> *Ye shall do no unrighteousness in judgment, in measuring length, weight, or number. Just balances, just weights, a just ephah, and a just hin shall ye have: I am the Lord your God, who brought you out of the land of Egypt.*

Also frequently quoted is Deut. 25,13-26:

> *Thou shalt not have in thy bag divers weights, a great and a small. Thou shalt not have in thine house divers measures, a great and a small. But thou shalt have a perfect and just weight, a perfect and just measure shalt thou have, that thy days may be lengthened in the land which the Lord thy God giveth thee.*

Scripture clearly outlaws false evaluations or calculations in order to protect the buyer from acquiring an incorrect amount of goods and suffering fraud. Indeed, if the seller transfers less than the amount established, he defrauds the other party.

---

36 J.K. Dannhauer, *Theologia casualis*, 426-8.

37 J. Olearius, *Doctrina theologiae moralis*, Tab LXXI.

The amount to sell might have been established by the public authority. Can exemptions be admitted? This question was already debated by the early modern scholastics.[38] According to Osiander, the possibility for a fixed amount is instituted by God in Lev. 19,35, and the Church Fathers many times reproached avarice and hoarding. However, drawing upon some scholastic authors, Osiander tackles particular cases concerning the possibility to diminish the measure of the goods sold. He first approves the opinion of Alonso Rodriguez (1526-1616), Pedro de Aragón (1545/1546-1592), Francisco de Toledo Herrera and Luis López (1520-1596). These authors stated that in the event that the buyer does not want to buy the merchandise for its actual worth, because a monopoly was made, or because the prince did not want to value the merchandise for the just price, the seller can diminish the measure, so that the quantity that he trades is justly commensurate with the price that is received.[39] The seller does not make a false measurement, but rather decreases it for a just reason. He is therefore allowed to do so. Furthermore, the prince did not adapt the price to the circumstances of the market and had been negligent. This is the solution of the early modern scholastics, which Osiander merely accepts, without adding any caveats.

Osiander also takes the opinion of those, like the Roman Catholic moralist Carlo Mallet (d. 1658), who said that the bakers who prepare smaller loaves of bread or sell more for less can be excused, considering the work and the price of grain and so on; there are times that they do not have the just and moderate salary by selling the bread according the fixed rate.[40] Here an emergency situation justifies the baker to sell for more or less than what it is legally established. He is permitted to do this, because he otherwise would not have a just salary to sustain his household and business. The issue was resisted, however controversially, among the early modern scholastics, and the majority refused Mallet's position.

---

38 See W. Decock, *Collaborative Legal Pluralism*, passim.

39 J.A. Osiander, *Theologiae casualis*, 30: "*Quomodo itaque probari potest* primo *assertio Rodriquezii, Arragonii, Toleti, Lopezii, statuentium, in casu, quo emptores nolent emere merces, quanti revera valent, aut quia factum est monopolium, aut quia princeps noluit iusto pretio merces taxare, licitum esse venditori minuere mensuram, ita ut quantitas, quam tradit, iustissime valeat illud pretium, quod recipitur*".

40 J.A. Osiander, *Theologiae casualis*, 31: "*Secundo, qui cum* Malleto *dicunt, aliquando excusari pistores, qui panes minores taxa conficiunt, aut vendunt supra taxam, si omnibus consideratis, videlicet pretio tritici, labore, etc. non remaneat illis iustum et moderatum stipendium sui laboris etc. vendendo panem ad taxam*". Osiander refers to the Catholic moralist Carlo Mallet (d. 1658), who wrote several books about moral theology. Anyway, the same passage reported by Osiander is in M. Bonacina, *Tractatus de restitutione et de contractibus*, in *Operum de morali theologia* […] *compendium*, t. 2, Venetiis, 1683, 500.

In conclusion, the duty to make a just measuring has a clear biblical foundation. Yet, for special exceptions the theologians did not develop a novel framework; rather they relied on the early modern scholastics, revealing again the limit of an approach purely based on Scripture. Scripture does not provide detailed solutions for some issues, and for that reason the Lutherans needed the support of external sources.

1.1.3.3 Defects of Goods I: Following the Scholastics

Roman law already provided several solutions to the problem of non-declared defects of goods. For instance, the buyer could use the *actio empti* against the seller who fraudulently did not disclose a flaw he knew; or against the seller who had assured the buyer that the good was free from certain or all imperfections. Alternatively, the buyer could ask a stipulation where the seller guaranteed the lack of certain defects[41] or could make use of the Aedilitian remedies, among others the *redhibendi iudicium*, the *actio redhibitoria* and the *actio quanti minoris*.[42]

Theologians and canonists of the Middle Ages and the early Modern Era linked the presence of undeclared deficiencies to the just price theory. In the *quaestio* 77 of his *Summa theologiae*, Thomas Aquinas stated that defects of substance, quantity and quality are fraud and cause restitution.[43] Following the Roman law of sale, but also the Aristotelian theory of commutative justice,[44] Aquinas affirmed that the seller is obliged to reveal two kinds of limitations of his goods. Firstly, he must declare the imperfection that can damage the neighbour, because the thing is sold for a price that is superior to its actual value. Secondly, he must reveal the defect that can be risky because it can make the use of the thing difficult, hazardous or impossible. Moreover, Aquinas foresaw instances when the defect must have to be revealed: the seller then has to clearly specify the hidden flaw to the buyer. If the flaw is self-evident and the price is consequently reduced, then the seller is not bound to explicitly reveal it.[45] The failure to declare a defect influences the price and therefore generates the right of the innocent party to receive back the price paid in excess.[46]

---

41 R. Zimmermann, *The Law of Obligations*, 308-10.

42 R. Zimmermann, *The Law of Obligations*, 316-8; L. Waelkens, *Amne Adverso*, 378-80.

43 T. Aquinas, *Summa theologiae*, IIaIIae, q. 77.

44 See W. Decock, J. Hallebeek, *Pre-contractual duties to inform in Early Modern Scholasticism*, in *Tijdschrift voor Rechtsgeschiedenis*, 78 (2008), 89-133, (97).

45 T. Aquinas, *Summa theologiae*, IIaIIae, q. 77, a. 3.

46 W. Endemann, *Studien in der romanisch-kanonistischen Wirtschafts-und Rechtslehre bis gegen Ende des Siebenzehnten Jahrhunderts*, vol. II, 1883, 88. An extended analysis is in O. Langholm, *Economics in the Medieval Schools*, 221-48.

A number of Lutheran theologians remained in the same vein of Aquinas. For example, Johann Konrad Dürr maintains that the imperfection that must be revealed should be hidden, possibly harmful, dangerous or useless. It is *possibly harmful*, if for example a dog or a horse that is the subject of the sale might become crazy; the defect is *dangerous* when a house is not well built; and it is *useless* when for example the sale concerns a horse that is unable to be ridden.[47] He honestly avows that these are not his personal reflections, but rather the contributions of Aquinas and Juan Azor.[48]

Andreas Prückner does not show such accurate description but insists that only the hidden flaws must be revealed. If the defect is instead evident, it needs not be indicated – and if the purchasing party does not see it, it is his own fault.[49] Prückner refers to the *Summa casuum sive de instructione sacerdotum* (1599) of the Jesuit Cardinal Francisco de Toledo Herrera.[50] On the same line, quoting Aquinas, Horneius states that only the hidden flaw must be declared; if it is undisguised, the seller is not obliged to declare it.[51] Likewise, Baier asserts that the imperfection that can cause damage or peril must sincerely be indicated.[52]

The incorporation of the scholastic theology might be associated with the doctrine of contractual justice that Melanchthon proposed. Being inspired by the scholastic doctrine of just price, Melanchthon's theory gave free reign to the application of scholastic solutions. These solutions can be well-integrated in this doctrine by delimiting the particular framework.

1.1.3.4 Defects of Goods II: The Rigorist Version

In contrast to Melanchthon, Luther introduced a view based upon natural law, Christian charity and the Decalogue, without mentioning commutative justice or equality. As seen before, Luther condemned every fraud in contracts. For instance, in his *Skiagrafia sive analysis et catena catechismi minoris d. Martini*

---

47 J.K. Dürr, *Compendium theologiae moralis*, 220.

48 J.K. Dürr, *Compendium theologiae moralis*, 220. T. Aquinas, *Summa theologiae*, IIaIIae, q. 77, a. 3; J. Azor, *Institutionum moralium, tomus tertius*, Coloniae agrippinae, 1618, l. 7, c. 23, 694-9.

49 A. Prückner, *Manuale mille questionum*, Norimbergae, 1662, 143: "*An venditor tenetur mercis vitium emptori manifestare? Resp. Tenetur, vitium mercis sit* occultum, *cum id vergat in emptoris damnum: non tenetur, si vitium mercis sit* manifestum, *quia emptor culpa sua id non advertit, cum advertere potuisset ac debuisset*".

50 A. Prückner, *Manuale mille questionum*, 143. F. Toledo, *Summa casuum conscientiae sive de instructione sacerdotum*, l. 8, cap. 49, conclus. 2, 742.

51 C. Horneius, *Compendium theologiae*, 768.

52 J.W. Baier, *Compendium theologiae moralis*, 490: "*Ut vitium rei vendendae, per quod emptori damnum aut periculum obtingit, sincere indicetur*".

Lutheri (1667), Lucas Bacmaister indicates that Luther prohibited the fraud of selling defective goods.[53] The foundation of this rule was in Scripture, particularly the seventh precept, and no reference was made to the just price.

Luther's fidelity to Scripture might have inspired the more rigorous approach followed by other theologians. They requested the parties to indicate every defect of the goods, whether evident or not and whether possibly damaging or not. Dannhauer observes that in the *forum conscientiae*, merchants must reveal every flaw of the goods in order to avoid cheating the imprudent man.[54] Similarly, Osiander speaks in general about every single excess or defect of goods according to conscience.[55] He quotes Lev. 19,18, where readers are exhorted to love the neighbour as themselves, and Syr. 21,1-3, which invites them to pay attention to their daily practices, because due to avarice many sins are committed in exchanges.[56] Scripture keeps a very general tone and protects the neighbour against every offence, especially from the sins of greed. Hence, for Osiander any limitations of the general duty of disclosure cannot be tolerated. To bolster the argument, he cites John Chrysostom's homily on the first letter of Paul to the Corinthians, where he asserts that God gave goods to men so that they can be used for the neighbour's utility: men should not only look at the value goods pose to themselves, but first at their utility for the neighbour. For instance, Chrysostom writes that:

> *the husbandman sows not only so much corn as is sufficient for himself, but seeks the profit of the many; he takes to the field against dangers, not that he may save himself, but that he may also place his cities in security; the merchant brings home not so much as may be sufficient for himself alone, but for many others also.*[57]

---

53 L. Bacmeister, *Skiagrafia sive analysis et catena catechismi minoris d. Martini Lutheri* [...], Rostochi, 1667, Tab. III: "*Committitur autem furtum dolosa defraudatione qua fit merce vitiosa*".

54 J.K. Dannhauer, *Theologia casualis*, 435: "*Sed in conscientiae foro omnino tenetur mercator vitia mercium significare et hominem imprudentem non fallere*".

55 J.A. Osiander, *Theologiae casualis in qua quaestiones, dubia et casus conscientiae circa credenda et agenda enucleantur, pars prima et secunda*, Tubingae, 1680, 1405: "*An in emptione et venditione cavendus sit omnis excessus vel defectus per conscientiam?*".

56 J.A. Osiander, *Theologiae casualis*, 1405: "*Ita dictat Scriptura, quae iubet* proximum diligere ut seipsum Levit. 19 *et propterea respiciendo ad praxin cottidianam illud ingeminat* Syr 27, v. 1.2.3".

57 J.A. Osiander, *Theologiae casualis*, 1405. I used the translation by Rev. T.W. Chambers in P. Schaff (ed.) *Saint Chrysostom: Homilies on the Epistles of Paul to the Corinthians, Nicene and Post-Nicene Fathers*, vol. 12, 1889, 148. http://www.ccel.org/ccel/schaff/npnf112.html (accessed 5.12.2017).

Finally, Osiander recalls 'right reason', which for him corresponds to classical principles: *neminem laedere* and *suum cuique tribuere*.[58]

Osiander advocates a general duty to reveal any defects in goods. He stresses that the seller must always disclose a problem, even though the seller thought it was not relevant and was not interrogated on the point by the buyer. To justify this point, the necessity of a declaration even in lack of a specific question, Osiander follows the same method. He first quotes the Scripture, then the Church Fathers and finally puts forth an argument based on 'right reason' (*recta ratio*). The Scripture (Matt. 7,12), he writes, advises a general duty of protecting the neighbour and particularly exhorts Christians to tell the truth, Eph. 4,15: "… *but speaking the truth in love, may grow up into Him in all things, who is the Head, even Christ*". Ambrose similarly commands truthfulness in exchanges: "*but the law of justice is plain, namely, that a good man ought not to go aside from the truth, nor to inflict an unjust loss on anyone, nor to act at all deceitfully or to take part in any fraud*".[59] He points out that:

> *in everything, therefore, good faith is seemly, is pleasing; justice, due measure in equity, is delightful. But what shall I say about contracts, and especially about the sale of land, or agreements, or covenants? Are there not rules just for the purpose of shutting out all false deceit, and to make him whose deceit is found out liable to double punishment? Everywhere, then, does regard for what is virtuous take the lead; it shuts out deceit, it expels fraud. Wherefore the prophet David has rightly stated his judgment in general, saying: He has done no evil to his neighbour. Fraud, then, ought to be wanting not only in contracts, in which the defects of those things which are for sale are ordered to be recorded (which contracts, unless the vendor has mentioned the defects, are rendered void by an action for fraud, although he has conveyed them fully to the purchaser), but it ought also to be absent in all else. Candour must be shown, the truth must be made known.*[60]

Finally, Osiander alludes to right reason: he who enters into a contract must be sure not to commit deceit (*dolus*).[61]

The consequence of this inflexible position is that Osiander discredits the opinions of a number of early modern scholastic theologians. First, he writes

---

58 J.A. Osiander, *Theologiae casualis*, 1405-6.

59 J.A. Osiander, *Theologiae casualis*, 1406. Ambrosius, *De officiis ministrorum libri tres*, in PL 16, lib. III, cap. 11, n. 73. I used the translation by H. de Romestin, E. de Romestin and H.T.F. Duckworth, in P. Schaff, H. Wace (eds.), *Nicene and Post-Nicene Fathers*, Second Series, vol. 10, 1896. Revised and edited for New Advent by K. Knight http://www.newadvent.org/fathers/34013.htm (accessed 5.12.2017).

60 J.A. Osiander, *Theologiae casualis*, 1406. Ambrosius, *De officiis ministrorum libri tres*, in PL 16, lib. III, cap. 10, n. 66, 164; I used the translation as before.

61 J.A. Osiander, *Theologiae casualis*, 1406-7. See also *Theologia casualis*, vol. 3 and 4, 28-9.

that the opinions of Juan Azor, Martín de Azpilcueta and Manuel de Sá[62] (1530-1596) cannot be ratified. These authors maintained that if the defect is not noteworthy (*notabilis*), the seller is neither obliged to disclose it, nor to offer restitution. To Osiander this opinion is erroneous, because the buyer rationally contravenes his will, both when the seller transfers to him a harmful defect and when the imperfection impinges upon the use for which the good was bought.[63]

Second, Osiander rebukes Fernando Rebello and Molina's solutions, which denied that the seller must indicate the obvious defect that the buyer did not notice.[64] Third, Osiander condemns Azor, Lessius and Rebello's viewpoint that the seller (even if interrogated by the buyer) is obliged to reveal the hidden defects only if they are noteworthy, because in this case he would only commit a 'white lie' (*mendacium officiosum*) and not a harmful lie (*mendacium nocivum*).[65] To Osiander it does not matter whether the defect is hidden, evident or noteworthy. Scripture and the Church Fathers make no distinction and therefore any flaw must always be declared. He does not trust rational classification, but opts for a radical duty to reveal every imperfection the conscience suggests. As seen before, the characters of the defects derived from a complex of sources such as Aristotle, Cicero and the medieval elaboration of Roman law, which are refused by Osiander because they are not included in the Scriptures. The Scriptures and the Church Fathers are the first criterions to determine the moral duties regarding the defects of goods. Here, we can clearly grasp the difference between the scholastic way of thinking and the Lutheran.

Osiander's fight against the scholastics does not conclude here. He is again very critical towards the scholastics in the following cases: is it possible to sell a

62 A. Leite, *Sà, Manuel de*, in C. O' Neill, J. Domcnguez (eds.), *Diccionario histórico de la Compañia de Jesús biográfico-temático*, Roma, Madrid, Institutum Historicum, 2001, vol. 4, 34-54.

63 J.A. Osiander, *Theologiae casualis*, 1407: "*Non possumus itaque probare sententiam* Azorii, Emanuel Sa et Navarri *statuentium: si defectus non sit notabilis, non obligari venditorem illum aperire, neque obligari ad aliquam restitutionem, quia emptor esset rationabiliter invitus, cum non tribuamus vitium ei nocivum, et quod sit notabile ad usum, ad quem emitur*".

64 J.A. Osiander, *Theologiae casualis*, 1407: "Secundo *neque sententiam* Rebelli, Mollina *et aliorum, qui negant teneri venditorem emptori manifestare defectum patentem, quem emptor non advertit*".

65 J.A. Osiander, *Theologiae casualis*, 1407: "Tertio *sententiam* Azorii, Lessii *atque* Rebelli *scriptitantium: venditorem etiam interrogatum de occultis defectibus obligari eos manifestare, tantum si sint notabiles, non autem si sint non notabiles, quia committat in tali casu occultando vel negando defectum illum non mendacium nocivum, sed officiosum tantum*". On the use of the term 'mendacium officiosum' among the early modern scholastics see W. Decock, J. Hallebeek, *Pre-contractual duties*, 122.

debt when I secretly know that the debtor will not pay it at the ordinary price? Is it possible to sell at the ordinary price grain or wine when I know that it will soon spoil? Is it possible to sell grain that is not cleaned? These questions regard the Christian who knows that what he is selling could damage the neighbour, but the damage concerns an uncertain future.

Osiander answers firmly that this is against the Holy Scripture, the Church Fathers and right reason. He only trusts the Scriptures, as he refuses compromises based on rational circumstances. Lev. 25,14 establishes that nobody must harm the neighbour: "*and if thou sell aught unto thy neighbor or buyest aught of thy neighbor's hand, ye shall not oppress one another*"; Ecclus. 27,2-3 proclaims that in the contract of sale, many sins are committed, and the culprit will be punished; also Ecclus. 42,3-5 enjoins readers to avoid shame and not sin in negotiations.[66] In addition, Ambrose affirms that nothing is more against nature than not helping the neighbour.[67]

These issues were already debated by the early modern scholastics.[68] Influenced by a scrupulous respect for the neighbour, Osiander refuses the following opinions: 1) the opinion of Lessius (concerning the sale of toxic debts), who proposed that it is not against justice, if the seller does not entice the buyer with lies or fraud; 2) the opinions of Pedro de Aragón[69] and Alonso Rodriguez, according to whom, he who sells something that he knows will be or will likely be soon damaged, is not immediately damaging the buyer by not declaring such a defect, and can thus sell the good at its ordinary price. Having the good available for present use, the human estimation is valid such that the good can be sold at the ordinary price, and keeping silent on the defect does not produce any damage, even though the seller probably knows that the good will not maintain its usefulness; 3) the opinions of Miguel Bartolomé Salòn (1539-1621) and Luis López (1520-1596), who said that the merchant does not breach justice by mixing dust in perfectly clean wheat, so long as he does not

66 J.A. Osiander, *Theologiae casualis*, vol. 3 and 4, 29. It is interesting to note that Osiander also inserts a quotation from the *Ecclesiasticus*, a book that was included in the *Vulgata* but not in Luther's Bible translation.

67 J.A. Osiander, *Theologiae casualis*, vol. 3 and 4, 29. Osiander only cites Ambrosius' *De officiis* in general.

68 See W. Decock, *Lessius and the Breakdown of the Scholastic Paradigm*, in *Journal of the History of Economic Thought*, vol. 31, N. 1, March 2009, 57-78; W. Decock, J. Hallebeek, *Pre-contractual duties*, 89-133; W. Decock, *Spanish Scholastics on Money and Credit*, in D. Fox, W. Ernst (eds.), *Money in the Western Legal Tradition: Middle Ages to Bretton Woods*, Oxford, Oxford University Press, 2016, 267-83.

69 For the role of Aragón in this debate see W. Decock, *Lessius and the Breakdown*, 65; W. Decock, J. Hallebeek, *Pre-contractual duties*, 110-1; 121-2.

mix in more than it is possible to gather from the ground, for thus it is commonly sold. Medina already contested this opinion.[70]

These opinions that Osiander counters defended the seller on the basis of justice. To Lessius, selling a debt that I know the debtor will not repay at the ordinary price is not against justice, as long as the market price of the debt reflects the inferior quality of the letter of debt.[71] To Aragón and Rodriguez, the estimation is valid as long as the good can be sold at the ordinary price and keeping silence on the defect does not produce any damage. To Bartolomé Salón and Luis López the merchant does not breach justice by mixing dust in clean wheat, so long as he does not mix it more abundantly than it would have gathered from the ground. All these three solutions are refuted by Osiander, because Scripture heightens one's general duty to reveal all the defects because of its call to charity and not merely to justice. Osiander's main criterion of judgment is Scripture, and for this reason he cannot accept these compromises. Scripture requires an absolute protection of the neighbour, without excuses. He seeks to eliminate references to criteria other than Scripture. In this way the moral discourse tends to become more moral and less juridical.

To this rigorous duty of the seller corresponds a similar strict obligation for the buyer. For Osiander, the buyer must indicate the if the seller underestimates the quality of the good and then must let him change the price or decide not to sell the thing. Indeed, this is a precept of justice and even more of charity. Here, Osiander agrees with Aquinas, Azpilcueta and Rebello.[72]

In conclusion, on this point the Lutheran theologians embraced different paths. They all agree that flaws of defective goods must be disclosed, but then they are divided on the type of defect. A more open faction followed closely

70 J.A. Osiander, *Theologiae casualis*, vol. 3 and 4, 29-30: "*Non igitur possumus probare illa* Lessii, *quae proponit, dicendo, non esse contra iustitiam, modo mendaciis vel fraudibus non alliciam emptorem; de quo vide* illum *pag. 235. dub. 10* [see L. Lessius, *De iustitia et iure*, dub. 10, 261]. *Nec secundo illa* Arragonii et Rodriquezii, *statuendum, quod qui aliquid vendat, quod novit cito corrumpendum, et probabiliter putet, emptorem statim illud esse consumpturum, tacendo talem defectum, posse pretio currenti id vendere; quia cum habeat valorem in ordine ad usus humanos, et ad usum praesentem, hominum aestimatione tanti valeat, pretio currenti posse id vendi, et taciturnitatem defectus, nullum afferre damnum; cum probabiliter scio, emptorem id non esse conservaturum.* Tertio *nec illa* Salonii et Lopezii, *dicentium, non violare iustitiam mercatorem, immiscendo pulverem tritico optime purgato; dummodo non amplius immisceat, quam ex area colligi possit, et communiter vendatur; quibus se opponit* Medina *in* Instructione Confessariorum". For the opinion of Medina see W. Decock, *Lessius and the Breakdown*, 61; W. Decock, J. Hallebeek, *Pre-contractual duties*, 109-10.

71 W. Decock, *Spanish Scholastics on Money and Credit*, in D. Fox, W. Ernst (eds.), *Money in the Western Legal Tradition: Middle Ages to Bretton Woods*, 277-83.

72 J.A. Osiander, *Theologiae casualis*, vol. 1 and 2, 1407.

the scholastics and indicated that the flaw must be noticeable or harmful in order to cause an obligation of restitution. This solution comes from a rational approach. Others instead remarked the primacy of strict interpretation of the Scriptures and condemned every lack of admission for the buyer. In particular, Osiander drew upon Scripture, but also upon the Church Fathers. He believed in a general duty to protect the neighbour, based on charity. He closed the door to more flexible opinions proposed by some scholastic authors with regard to the case of the seller who knows that what he is selling could damage the neighbour. The Holy Scripture fully expresses this intention; therefore no compromises based on rational justifications can be accepted. After this flaming attack, however, Osiander slowed down and presented more mitigated positions on the issue of the positive quality of the goods that the seller does not know. In this case he agreed with the scholastics: the buyer must indicate the quality to the seller, who can change the price or decide not to sell the thing.

1.1.4 *Rules Concerning the Price*

1.1.4.1 The Ethics of Pricing: Common Estimation, Public Authority and Conscience

The medieval and early modern scholastics' doctrine of equality in exchange did not look at the parties' personal benefits or advantages, but affirmed that transactions must be performed according to the just price of goods.[73] The parties must agree on the price, which has to correspond to a determinate value: the market price, the price obtained by a common estimation under normal conditions, or the price fixed by the public authority.[74] For their teachings, the scholastics took inspiration from Aristotle and the Roman law. In his *Nicomachean Ethics*, Aristotle wrote that the 'need' is the key factor to measure the value of things,[75] while Roman law granted a remedy for the 'unjust price'.[76] An old maxim dictated that a thing is worth as much it can be sold for (*Res tantum valet quantum vendi potest*).[77] The scholastics limited its efficacy by stating that is only valid within the framework of the just price.[78] They interpreted the Roman law by saying that the price is determined by the common estimation,

73 J. Gordley, *The Philosophical Origins*, 94-5.
74 O. Langholm, *The Legacy of Scholasticism*, 82-8; J. Gordley, *The Philosophical Origins*, 98.
75 Aristotle, *Nicomachean Ethics*, V, 5.
76 D. 35,2,63. See also before about the *laesio enormis*.
77 D. 13,1,14,pr; D. 36,1,1,16; D. 47,2,52,29. Cfr. O. Langholm, *The Legacy of Scholasticism*, 78.
78 W. Decock, *Theologians and Contract Law*, 538.

and not from the affection or utility of single persons, temporary circumstances or rare necessities.[79]

In his treatise dedicated to commerce and usury (*Von Kaufshandlung und Wucher*), Luther substantially followed the scholastics. He writes that first, the public authority should make the estimation, appointing wise and honest men to appraise the cost of goods and to fix the price at which the merchant would get his due and have an honest living. Second, he suggests selling goods at the market price or the customary price of a certain place.[80] The price of goods should be determined by the public authority according to the costs incurred by the merchants. As a second option, the price should be fixed following the market price.

Luther's view of the ethics of pricing did not abandon the perspective outlined by the scholastics.[81] One point, however, needs to be emphasized. Luther never uses the concept of just price,[82] but grounds his considerations on natural law (Matt. 7,12) and Christian love (Lev. 19,18).[83] The merchants, writes Luther, want to sell the goods as dear as they can.[84] This is, though, a price fixed on the basis of the merchants' interests without considering the need of the neighbour. At the roots of this vision lies the evil desire to satisfy self-interest, which is totally against the love of the neighbour and the natural law.[85] The selling must therefore be governed by law and conscience, so that the neighbour is not harmed.[86] The practical criteria are the same as the scholastics, but the foundation is different. Luther puts the ethics of pricing in relation to Scripture: it is obedience to Scripture, notably to natural law and Christian charity, to avoid damaging the neighbour.

Luther's immediate followers did not examine *in extenso* the issue of goods' pricing. They were apparently more interested in forbidding frauds in general

79 J. Noonan Jr., *The Scholastic Analysis*, 82-3. For a more extended analysis see A. Del Vigo Gutiérrez, *Economia y ética*, 568-650.

80 M. Luther, *Von Kaufshandlung und Wucher*, WA 15, 296.

81 J. Höffner, *Wirtschaftsethik und Monopole im fünfzehnten und sechzehnten Jahrhundert*, Jena, Fischer, 1941, 148-9; O. Langholm, *Martin Luther's Doctrine on Trade and Price in Its Literary Context*, 89-107.

82 H. Barge, *Luther und der Frühkapitalismus*, 26; H.J. Prien, *Luthers Wirtschaftethik*, 112, fn. 221; O. Langholm, *Martin Luther's Doctrine on Trade and Price*, 94.

83 The biblical references are explained in M. Luther, *Ein (grosser) Sermon von dem Wucher*, in WA 6, 48-9.

84 This description calls to mind the medieval view of commerce as buying cheap and selling dear, which can be found in Augustine, *De trinitate*, Lib. XIII, cap. III. It was popular among scholastic theologians and canonists. See D. Wood, *Medieval Economic Thought*, 113.

85 M. Luther, *Von Kaufshandlung und Wucher*, in WA 15, 294.

86 M. Luther, *Von Kaufshandlung und Wucher*, in WA 15, 295.

than in discussing rules on pricing. At a later moment, however, the Lutheran theologians set forth the same guidelines for determination of price that Luther proposed or ones even more closely related to the scholastics. Dürr writes that the price should be determined by the magistrate or by common estimation.[87] Similarly, Baier maintains that an equitable price for the things for sale (*res vendendis atque emendis aequum pretium*) is established by the magistrate (*vel iuxta definitionem Magistratus*) or according to the common estimation.[88] This common estimation must be founded on several factors: the value of things, common utility and necessity, abundance or rarity, and the facility or difficulty in acquiring and conserving them.[89] Similarly, to Jäger, the equal price is calculated on the basis of an estimation of the usefulness of goods, labour and peril that the seller suffered.[90]

For the scholastics, the ethics of pricing strongly depended on the community,[91] but they also granted the parties the possibility of an individual negotiation when there is no fixed price (*pretium conventionale*).[92] In a similar way, Luther did not only propose the price fixed by law or the market, but also appealed to the seller's individual conscience. The seller can also set the price, Luther writes, if neither the law nor the market fixed it. The seller must follow his conscience in order to avoid overcharging the neighbour and not to harm or injure him.[93] The seller should pay attention to honest living, costs, trouble, labour and risks.[94] Here, the criterion for establishing the price includes not only the costs, but also trouble, labour, and risks the merchants supported for selling their goods. Furthermore, Luther is conscious of the impossibility of determining the exact amount and suggests that Christians who unintentionally get too much profit 'let that go into' the Lord's Prayer, where we pray 'forgive us our debts', because no man's life is without sin.[95]

87 J.K. Dürr, *Compendium theologiae moralis*, 220: "*1. ut res eo pretio vendantur, quod a magistratu est determinatum aut morali hominum intelligentium aestimatione statutum*".

88 J.W. Baier, *Compendium theologiae moralis*, 490.

89 J.W. Baier, *Compendium theologiae moralis*, 490: "*... vel iuxta aestimationem communem hominum peritorum ac bonorum, in ipsarum rerum dignitate, utilitate et communi necessitate, item abundantia aut raritate, facilitate aut difficultate acquirendi aut conservandi, fundatam*".

90 J.W. Jäger, *Theologia moralis*, 183.

91 A.A. Chafuen, *Faith and Liberty*, 86.

92 A. Del Vigo Gutiérrez, *Economia y ética*, 644-47.

93 M. Luther, *Von Kaufshandlung und Wucher*, in WA 15, 295: "*Sondern weyl solch deyn verkeuffen eyn werk ist, das du gegen deynem nehisten ubest, soll es mit solchem gesetz und gewissen verfasset seyn, das du es ubest on schaden und nachsteyl deynes nehisten*".

94 M. Luther, *Von Kaufshandlung und Wucher*, in WA 15, 296.

95 M. Luther, *Von Kaufshandlung und Wucher*, in WA 15, 297.

Luther's approach tends towards an individual estimation of price. Conscience should be led by the intention to avoid damage to the neighbour, but also to get an honest reward. A similar indication is included in *De conscientia et eius iure* (1632) of the famous Reformed casuist William Ames. Ames appeals to Prov. 20,14 and the merchant's conscience in order to forbid malicious price hikes that harm the neighbour.[96]

To summarize, not too far from the scholastics' teachings, Luther's ethics of pricing did not only include the market price and the price fixed by the public authority, but also called upon the seller's conscience. If the market and the law do not establish the price, the seller is allowed to follow his conscience. For the various aspects not determined by the law or the customary price, the seller should use his conscience. Certainly, conscience should factor in some parameters, like the costs, trouble, labour, and risks the merchants supported for selling their goods. But in general this seems to be an invitation to the single Christian to consider the necessity of the neighbour.

1.1.4.2 Market Abuse I: Conscience, the Holy Scripture and the Magistrate

Luther's appeal to the merchant's conscience was particularly welcomed by Johann Nicolaus Misler. In his *Opus novum quaestionum practico-theologicarum, sive casuum conscientiae*, Misler articulates a general regulation of market which not only includes the ethics of pricing but also price distortions. He claims that to operate in the market, merchants should follow three guides: conscience, the Holy Scripture and the precepts set by the magistrate. The first is the conscience that God naturally carved in the human heart, as St. Paul reminds us in Rom. 1,14.[97] It illuminates what is fair or unfair, and forbids lacerating the name of God with insults, inflicting damage on the neighbour, and robbing his goods and defaming him with lies and calumnies. Conscience commands us to love the neighbour as ourself, do not to another what we would not have him do to us, do not reject what we would not reject.[98] In short: in this natural light it is clearly seen what is licit and illicit in the contract of sale.[99]

---

96 W. Ames, *De conscientia et eius iure libri quinque*, Franekerae, 1635, Book 5, Cap. 43, 369: "*Regula illa est primaria, quae traditus a Spiritu sancto*, Prov. 20, 14, *ne emptor, ut pretium possit minuere, dolose detrahat quidquam mercibus emendis; aut venditor, ad pretium augendum, contra conscientiam suam amplificet mercium suarum dignitatem*".

97 J.N. Misler, *Opus novum*, 246: "*Primum est conscientia, quae naturalis et cordibus a Deo insculpta lex est, cuius S. Paulus meminit Rom. 1, 14*".

98 J.N. Misler, *Opus novum*, 246: "*Omnis verò lex ostendit, quid aequum vel iniquum sit, vetatque Dei nomen convitiis lacerare, proximum damno afficere, eiusque bona rapere et famam mendaciis vel calumniis proscindere; contra praecipit, ut quis proximum amet ac seipsum, neque alteri faciat quod sibi nolit fieri, vel deneget id, quod sibi denegari inique ferat*".

99 J.N. Misler, *Opus novum*, 246: "*Ex hoc naturae lumine apparet, quid in emptione liceat vel non*".

The second criterion Misler proposes is the Holy Scripture. The merchants, writes Misler, should observe what the Holy Scripture indicates or what it forbids. Psalm 119,9 declares, indeed: "*how shall a young man cleanse his way? By taking heed thereto according to Thy word*". Misler comments that this can be applied to every work, to merchants and to other vocations, so that anyone preserves his way keeping the Word of God.[100] The third rule the merchants should follow is the judgment of the magistrate, which is founded on the political ordinances. Misler contends that everything the magistrate deems to be inexcusable for the merchant, or that he maintains as shameful to be done, will be unjust and illicit.[101]

In an authentic Lutheran spirit, Misler devised a moral regulation centred on these three pillars: conscience, Scripture and the magistrate. The merchants have no need for rational rules or commutative justice, but are regulated by these principles. Concerning the ethics of pricing, then, Misler allows merchants to ask the price due for the purchase of goods; expenses for travel, transport and taxes; a small gain for labour, care and perils they suffered; the compensation (*interesse*) for money expended when, because of business, in which his vocation consists, he does not have other means to acquire in the quest for the nourishment of his family.[102] Nobody shall deny such a kind of profit, Misler points out, except when it is against natural equity and the love for the neighbour.[103] The price can be raised for rarities, but Misler warns the merchants that if the increase is not due to scarcity but to a necessity of the seller, this is against equity and charity.[104] Natural equity and Christian love for the neighbour seems to be the criteria for regulating the price, as for Luther.

Christians should follow conscience to avoid inexcusable price raisings, Misler continues. The laws cannot consider all the particular circumstances for variation of prices. Price of merchandise varies from region to region, and the amount of expenses and the difficulty of the travel and other innumerable circumstances certainly cannot be excluded from consideration. Thus, the

100 J.N. Misler, *Opus novum*, 247: "*Itaque quid Sacra Scriptura permittat vel vetet, mercator attendat. Nam quod de tota hominis vita David pronunciat*: quomodo mundam servabit adolescens viam suam? Custodiendo sermones tuos, *Psal. 119, v. 9 id ad cuiuslibet opificium, mercaturam vel vocationem aliam applicari potest, ut quisque viam servet custodiendo verba DEI*".

101 J.N. Misler, *Opus novum*, 247: "*Accedit tertium iudicium magistratus, quod in ordinationibus politicis fundatum est: quicquid hoc in iudicio mercator putat inexcusabile, vel ipsum fateri pudet, illud iniustum erit et illicitum*".

102 J.N. Misler, *Opus novum*, 245.

103 J.N. Misler, *Opus novum*, 245: "*Tale lucrum mercatori nemo invidebit, nisi qui aequitatem naturalem et dilectionem proximi tollere velit*".

104 J.N. Misler, *Opus novum*, 249.

merchant should weigh them carefully according to conscience and natural equity and not go against them.[105]

Furthermore, the merchants should take into account the distinction between rich and poor and decrease the sale price for the poor.[106] It is not just that the merchants profit from the poor buyers; Christian charity forbids gaining profit from the other's calamity.[107] They should consider a particular situation in formulating the prices and reduce them when appropriate, in order to participate in alleviating the suffering of these people[108]. This attention to the poor and particular natural events that harm the position of the other is an aspect that we will also see later, when discussing the lending and interest prohibition. The rule of love does not imply a strict observance of price rules, but to consider the negative circumstances that afflict the neighbour.

In conclusion, Misler suggested merchants to follow their conscience, Scripture and the magistrate in their business. The merchants should diminish the sale price for the poor, not adding an extra profit against them and diminishing the price, in order to help people in case of calamity. This way of determining the price reveals some specific features of Lutheran theology. Conscience must look at the neighbour according to natural law and charity and avoid any kind of offence. Especially in the case of calamity, the seller should help the poor buyer. The law can be mitigated according to charity in order to help the neighbour.

1.1.4.3 Market Abuse II: Scholastic Argumentation Applied

The scholastic doctrine of just price forbade any kind of fraud, economic compulsions, market distortions and alteration of prices.[109] It aimed to preserve equality in exchanges, so that none of the parties received more than what has given.[110] Melanchthon followed this approach in formulating his doctrine

---

105 J.N. Misler, *Opus novum*, 247: "*Sed mercatori certa praescribi lex nequit, ob circumstantiarum, quae in mercatura occurrunt, variationes: cum in singulis regionibus pretia mercium varient, et sumptuum magnitudo atque itinerum difficultas aliaeque innumerabiles circumstantiae non patiantur certis eam includere cancellis. Itaque perpendenda est mercatori conscientiae aequitatisque naturalis, ne quid contra illam delinquat*".

106 J.N. Misler, *Opus novum*, 248: "*… deinde distingui quoque debet inter pauperes et divites, ut illis pretio minori res vendatur*".

107 J.N. Misler, *Opus novum*, 249: "*Itaque fas non erit mercatorem augere pretia, eaque ab emtore egeno exigere: charitas namque christiana prohibet, ne aliorum calamitas in mercatoris emolumentum cedat*".

108 J.N. Misler, *Opus novum*, 248.

109 O. Langholm, *The Legacy of Scholasticism*, 82-8.

110 J.T. Noonan, Jr., *The Scholastic Analysis of Usury*, 87; R. De Roover, *The Concept of the Just Price Theory*, 418-34; J.W. Baldwin, *The Medieval Theories of the Just Price*, 71-4; O. Langholm, *The Legacy of Scholasticism*, 83.

of contractual justice and also recalled the just price in his definition of sale. Luther, however, did not refer to contractual equality but only appealed to the seventh commandment of the Decalogue, natural law and Christian charity. He reproached Christians who sell the goods at a higher price than the common market value or than is customary. In particular, he condemned people who raise the price because they know that the supply will shortly cease, and people who sell their goods on credit for a higher price than if they were sold for cash.[111]

Apart from the foundation used, whether equality in contracts or the seventh commandment, natural law and Christian charity, the Lutheran theologians forbade market abuse in general and faced singular cases. Some theologians stuck to the Scriptures, but others referred to the scholastics and to Reformed authors. Indeed, price manipulations were common, and already the medieval manuals for confessors and penitents included a long list of cases.[112] The theologians utilized the scholastic elaborations of these cases, even though they did not always reach the same conclusions.

The first consequence of the ethics of pricing is that the buyer cannot fraudulently decrease the price and the seller cannot increase it. For example, Dürr forbids deceitfully lowering the price and value of merchandise as, he says, the buyers often do. The justification is Prov. 20,14: *"'it is nought, it is worthless!' saith the buyer; but when he has gone his way, then he boasteth"*.[113] To Baier the seller can never increase the price for a singular necessity (*pro singulari necessitate*) of the buyer. Likewise, the buyer cannot fraudulently decrease the price beneath its just worth.[114] Prückner also insists that it is not licit to sell a thing of great price for a price that is less than its value, if the seller is ignorant of the higher value, while the buyer knows it. Although he is unaware of it, the seller is harmed.[115] Finally, referring to 1 Thess. 4,6, Olearius prohibits selling goods that have false or small value as precious and useful ones.[116]

---

111 M. Luther, *Von Kaufshandlung und Wucher*, in WA 15, 305.

112 See for instance O. Langholm, *The Merchant in the Confessional*, passim.

113 J.K. Dürr, *Compendium theologiae moralis*, 219-20: "*Mercium precium ac dignitas dolose non elevetur, ut saepe fieri solet ab emtoribus Prov. XX, 14*".

114 J.W. Baier, *Compendium theologiae moralis*, 490: "*Non autem pro singulari necessitate emtoris a venditore nimis augeatur pretium, vel ab emtore fraudolenter elevetur infra iustam dignitatem*".

115 A. Prückner, *Manuale mille quaestionum*, 141: "*Siccine magni precii rem licet ab aliquot minoris emere, quam valet? Resp. Non licet, si venditor rei precium non intelligat, emptor vero intelligat: quia venditor, quantumvis inscius, laeditur*".

116 J. Olearius, *Doctrina theologiae moralis*, Tab. LXXI: "[Ne scilicet:] *Adulterinas aut viles* merces *pro pretiosis et utilibus supponant*, 1 Thess. 4, 6".

The seller and the buyer are forbidden to illicitly raise or lower the price of goods. The case is different if the seller knows the price of the goods he sells and decides spontaneously to decrease it for the buyer. This is a sale mixed with a donation, and it was considered to be perfectly lawful.[117] To Prückner, the seller can donate and reduce the price without any injustice. In support of this stance, he refers to the Reformed philosopher Marcus Friedrich Wendelin (1584-1652) and the great casuist William Ames.[118] In a similar way, Conrad Horneius distinguishes between the pure contract of sale where the rigidity of equality of thing and price must be observed.[119] And the exchange in a sale, just as united with a donation, where the seller consciously and voluntarily decreases the price and the rigidity of equality (*rigor aequalitatis*) is not observed. Indeed, the seller can reduce the price in consideration of the buyer. The buyer can be a friend of the seller, consanguineous, poor and miserable, or even powerful. In this last case, the seller might decide to reduce the price in order to be able to receive something for himself in turn.[120] In short, the seller can meet the buyer's needs by diminishing the price, in consideration of a special quality or the necessity of the buyer.

Other cases analysed include, for example, the price for the goods sold on credit and the price for the goods paid in advance. These two cases were faced by Prückner. Basing his considerations on the Roman Catholic Francisco de Toledo Herrera and the Reformed Marcus Friedrich Wendelin, Prückner ends up affirming that a good can be sold for a higher price than its value, if the good is sold for a credit. In this way, the greater profit is licit, because it compensates for the lack of immediate payment.[121] This is the opposite of what Luther

117 See L. Lessius *De iustitia et iure*, book 2, chapter 21, question 4 n. 37 = L. Lessius, *On Sale, Securities, and Insurance*, translated by W. Decock, N. De Sutter, 35.

118 A. Prückner, *Manuale mille quaestionum*, 141: "*Licet vero, si* rei precium venditor non ignoret, *et ex libera voluntate de eo aliquid emptori remittat: nam sine ulla injustitiae labe emptori potest donare, nedum aliquid de precio remittere* Wendelin. *part. 2. Philosos. moral. lib. 1. cap. 30. quaest. 21. p. 52 Confer. Ames lib. 5. de Conscient. cap. 43. quaest. 1. p. 379 seq*". M.F. Wendelin, *Philosophia moralis*, Francofurti, 1666, lib. 1, cap. 30, quaest. 21?. This reference seems not corresponding. W. Ames, *De conscientia et eius iure*, 369-72.

119 C. Horneius, *Compendium theologiae*, 767.

120 C. Horneius, *Compendium theologiae*, 767: "*... vel est commutatio ex venditione quasi et donatione mixta, ut vendens sciens et volens intuitu personae ementis, quia singularem cum ea amicitiam habet, vel quia consanguineus est, vel pauper et miser, vel potens etiam, ut commodare sibi vicissim queat, de pretio aliquid remittit et ibi rigor aequalitatis non spectatur: sicut enim totum si velit, donare potest, ita etiam partem pretii quantam voluerit*".

121 A. Prückner, *Manuale mille quaestionum*, 141: "*Licetne rem suam pluris vendere, quam in se valet? Resp. Licet, si* precium mercis iustum sit, et merx credito vendatur: *quia lucrum illud iustum venditori loco pensionis est*".

stated. Indeed, Luther reproached people who sell their goods on credit for a higher price than if they were sold for cash.

According to Prückner, it is also illicit to obtain an inferior price, if the payment is made in advance, because the good must be sold for its value.[122] The seller may sell the goods over the just price, if in return he gets a credit on the sale. Yet, Prückner finds a reason for this, like for instance the expenses that the seller will suffer in case of not fulfilling the obligation.[123]

Conrad Horneius took from the scholastics two different cases.[124] The first one concerns the owner of a good who asks a seller to sell it for 10 gulden, but it instead sells for 12 gulden. Can the seller keep the two extra gulden gained? Horneius answers that if the rule of just price was broken, the seller has to return to the buyer the two extra gulden. If instead the rule was not broken and he used the required diligence, the money belongs to the owner. If the seller used more than the required diligence, however, and improved the thing, he can keep the money. But if the market price increased, the money belongs to the owner.[125]

A second case regards the merchant who knows that the price of his goods will decrease because other merchants will begin selling the same goods. Is he obliged to sell his goods at a lower price than the market price, or must he indicate that in the future will be other merchants? This is the famous case of the Merchant of Rhodes included in Cicero's *De officiis* and copiously treated among the scholastics.[126] Horneius follows Thomas Aquinas, who answered that the merchant is obliged neither to reveal the presence of other merchants nor to lower the price. For justice this is not requested, it is just for virtue. Horneius also refers to Gabriel Biel, who adds that future events are uncertain, and the merchant cannot be sure that the price will change. The merchant must therefore use the current market price.[127]

---

122 A. Prückner, *Manuale mille quaestionum*, 142: "*Utrum licet anticipata pecunia rem, v.g. vinum, frumentum etc. emere infra infimum pretium? Resp. Quod non: quia sic emptor venditorem identidem defraudat. Res enim tanti debet emi, quanti valet, aut valitura probabiliter creditur eo tempore, quo res ipsa traditur*".

123 A. Prückner, *Manuale mille quaestionum*, 142.

124 See L. Lessius *De iustitia et iure*, book 2, chapter 21, question 5 and 19 = L. Lessius, *On Sale, Securities, and Insurance*, translated by W. Decock, N. De Sutter, 37-44; 121-122.

125 C. Horneius, *Compendium theologiae*, 770.

126 See Cicero, *De officiis*, 3, 12, 50; W. Decock, *Lessius and the Breakdown*, 57-8; W. Decock, J. Hallebeek, *Pre-contractual duties*, 94-5.

127 C. Horneius, *Compendium theologiae*, 769-70: "*Quaeritur, an mercator in locum aliquem appellens et plures mercatores se subsequi sciens, unde precium mercium suarum paulo post imminuendum sit, aut minoris sua vendere teneatur, quam communis aestimatio fori est, aut praesentiam futuram plurium mercatorum indicare? R. Thomas loc. cit. a. 3 ad. ult.*

This case is very similar to another one discussed by Osiander and concerning the defects of the goods. As seen before, Osiander opted for a rigoristic position based on the primacy of Scripture. The merchant must always indicate what he knows. Conversely, here Horneius follows Aquinas and allows the merchant to sell his goods, even though he suspects the price will go down. This solution is grounded on justice, while Osiander adopts a strict interpretation of Scripture united with charity. In this way, he tightens the area of the neighbour's safeguard. The merchant must use the knowledge he has to protect the neighbour, no matter if this knowledge is uncertain. The neighbour comes first and must be protected.

In conclusion, market abuse includes a vast range of illicit activities. Luther forbade the generality of wrong behaviours by using the seventh commandment, natural law and Christian charity and faced some particular cases. Melanchthon prohibited unjust profit in general as breach of contractual justice. The Lutheran theologians followed these approaches but also relied on scholastic and Reformed theologians. For analysing the innumerable cases, the Lutherans could not avoid the abundant experience of the Roman Catholics, who for centuries had developed solutions for these issues.

1.1.4.4 Private Monopolies Are Against Charity

Monopoly is a complex theme that would require detailed treatment, which is not possible in the scope of this work. Our observations are therefore limited to a brief sketch.[128] On the whole, the Roman Catholic theologians and canonists saw unfavourably the purchase in stock and the sale of a particular type of good by a single merchant or association of merchants. The code of Justinian

---

Mercatorem qui vendit mercem suam secundum precium, quod invenit, non videri contra iustitiam facere, si, quod futurum est, non indicet, si tamen indicarit, aut eo respectu de precio aliquid detraxerit, esse id abundantioris virtutis, quamvis ad illud ex iustitiae debito teneri non videatur. Addit Gabriel, futura contingentia incerta esse, et multa intervenire posse, ut certus mercator non sit, adventuros, quos putarat, et proinde posse eum precio usitato mercem suam vendere". See T. Aquinas, *Summa theologiae*, IIaIIae, q. 77, art. 3, r. 4.

128 For a more detailed account on the issue of monopolies in the period of the Reformation see: C. Bauer, *Conrad Peutingers Gutachten zur Monopolfrage: Eine Untersuchung zur Wandlung der Wirtschaftsanschauungen im Zeitalter der Reformation*, in *ARG*, 45 (1954), 1-44, 145-96, 147-73; C. Bauer, *Conrad Peutinger und der Durchbruch des neuen ökonomischen Denkens in der Wende zur Neuzeit*, Freiburg, Herder, 1965; K.N. von Stryk, *Die Monopolgutachten des rechtsgelehrten Humanisten Conrad Peutinger aus dem frühen 16. Jahrhundert. Ein Beitrag zum frühneuzeitlichen Wirtschaftrecht*, in *Zeitschrift für neuere Rechtsgeschichte*, 10 (1988), 1-18; B. Mertens, *Im Kampf gegen die Monopole*, Tübingen, Mohr Siebeck, 1996; For a general overview see J. Höffner, *Wirtschaftsethik und Monopole im fünfzehnten und sechzehnten Jahrhundert*, Jena, Fischer, 1941.

already contained a norm that banned the use of monopolies.[129] The canonists commented on it, exalting and condemning the aspects of conspiracy that the monopolies involved. Late medieval theologians like Antonino of Florence (1389-1459) followed this line but also considered the coercion to buy goods as a motivation to prohibit monopolies. Monopolies entail conspiracy and compulsion to buy goods and for that reason are sinful.[130]

The early modern scholastics carried on this tradition, but presented two different attitudes towards the monopolies. A more conservative one maintained that even if authorized by a public authority, monopolies harm the freedom of purchasers and must be forbidden. The coercion to buy goods at a price determined by the seller is again the central reason to reproach monopolies.[131] Another interpretation observed that the monopolists do not act against justice in buying, because they do so at the current price. Nor do they act against justice, if they refrain from selling the goods, because they have no duty to sell the goods.[132] Considering the lack of a breach of justice, this interpretation saw monopolies in a different way.

In his treatise on trade and usury, Martin Luther criticized monopolies.[133] Starting from the idea that price should be set according to natural law and Christian charity, he writes that monopolies are prohibited because the sellers set the price as dear as they wish. Instead, the political authority and common market must determine the price. The monopolists act for self-interest and are also condemned by the public authority.[134] Luther adds that the biblical example of Joseph in Gen. 41,48 should not be used to argue for the lawfulness of monopolies. Luther notices that: "*accumulation of this kind is not self-interest, or monopoly, but a really good Christian providence for the community and for the good of others*".[135] Joseph accumulated the goods to follow God's

129 C. 4, 59.

130 O. Langholm, *The Legacy of Scholasticism*, 95-6.

131 O. Langholm, *The Legacy of Scholasticism*, 96-7.

132 O. Langholm, *The Legacy of Scholasticism*, 98-9. See L. Lessius *De iustitia et iure*, book 2, chapter 21, question 21 n. 150-153 = L. Lessius, *On Sale, Securities, and Insurance*, translated by W. Decock, N. De Sutter, 130-3.

133 On this topic see the bibliography indicated about Luther and the interest prohibition. In particular, see also A. Pawlas, *Zur Kalkulation einer 'gerechten' Preis bei Luther*, in *Luther* 60 (1989), 97-9; C. Lindberg, *Beyond Charity*, 110-8; A. Del Vigo Gutiérrez, *Economia y ética*, 651-8.

134 M. Luther, *Von Kaufshandlung und Wucher*, in WA 15, 305.

135 M. Luther, *Von Kaufshandlung und Wucher*, in WA 15, 306: "*Und ist doch solch Einsammlen kein Eigennütz oder Monopolion, sondern ein recht gut christliche Fursichtikeit, fur die Gemeine und Andern zu gut*".

instructions and not because of avarice. Therefore, the story of Joseph is not an argument in favour of monopolies.[136]

Luther's followers defended this thesis. For example, Dannhauer affirms that nobody is obliged to sell his goods. If the grain market is saturated such that everybody can have grain, the seller is not obliged to sell his goods. Nonetheless, in the case of imminent famine, because of charity he is bound to sell his grain. Regarding the price, he can profit, but always must remain subject to the law of charity.[137] The example of Joseph cannot be invoked to assert the opposite, because he acted with public authority and in accordance with justice.[138]

Osiander replied to Grotius' opinion, which was in favour of monopolies. Returning to the teachings of the early modern scholastics, Grotius advocated that not all forms of monopolies are against natural law, as political authorities can allow them for a just cause and with a fixed price. The use of monopolies is approved by the biblical example of Joseph, he wrote. Monopolies instituted by private people can also be allowed if the price is fair. Then, if these people hinder the importation of goods, or buy them up, so that they can sell them at a higher price, but not at an unjust price, they breach the rule of charity, but they do not breach the rights of their fellow man.[139]

Grotius considered four types of monopolies: 1) when the sellers agree on the price, preventing others from selling goods for a lower price; 2) when the sellers only sell certain products, both on their own authority or by a privilege granted by the prince; 3) when the sellers acquire large quantities of goods and destroy or hoard them until the price rises and they can sell their goods for an higher price; 4) similarly when the sellers forbid or impede the sale of a certain type of good so that they can sell their competing goods for a higher price.[140]

Osiander responds that the sellers deciding on the price do not defraud natural law, but charity.[141] The case is different for the monopolies authorized by the political authority, because princes have the authority to allow monopolies,

---

136 M. Luther, *Von Kaufshandlung und Wucher*, in WA 15, 305-6.

137 J.K. Dannhauer, *Theologia casualis*, 424: "*Si forum frumentarium frumenti plenum est, et quilibet habere potest, unde emat, nec ullus defectus ad venditionem cogat, non teneris vendere frumenta, sed potius ad parsimoniam teneris; imminente vero annonae caritate vendere debes, et praecavere ne nimium lucri capias; quamvis liceat aliquid lucrari, interim tamen, ne trascendas legem charitatis, videndum*".

138 J.K. Dannhauer, *Theologia casualis*, 424.

139 H. Grotius, *De iure belli ac pacis*, II, 12, § 16.

140 H. Grotius, *De iure belli ac pacis*, II, 12, § 16. The approach is very similar to L. Lessius *De iustitia et iure*, book 2, chapter 21, question 21 = L. Lessius, *On Sale, Securities, and Insurance*, translated by W. Decock, N. De Sutter, 2016, 127ff.

141 J.A. Osiander, *Observationes*, 932.

avoiding any offence.[142] The third and fourth types of monopolies indicated by Grotius, then, absolutely cannot be admitted. The example of Joseph cannot be used to establish the lawfulness of monopolies. First, Joseph purchased the goods after having predicted the famine. Second, Joseph gathered and paid for wheat without extortion, because every citizen could conserve as much wheat as he wanted. Then, during the period of famine, he sold the wheat at a just price and with the consent of the population. Third, even if the work of Joseph might be called a monopoly, he did for the sake of the health of the state and the population.[143]

Grotius distinguished between what is against justice and what is against charity. Osiander doubts that this distinction is sufficiently solid because, he writes, he who sins against charity also sins against the second table of the Decalogue, but all the juridical norms are derived from the second table. Therefore, he who commits a sin against charity also commits a sin against justice.[144] And, he continues, the issue is made much clearer if we consider what is proper of justice: giving each one his due (*suum cuique tribuere*). But giving each one his due is very much contained in charity. Therefore, it proceeds from the inverse that he who does not love the neighbour is also unjust, because without loving he does not give to him his due.[145] In substance, Osiander wants to avoid a schism between justice and charity and draws a wide definition of charity that includes justice. Charity is necessary for justice, and he who commits a sin against charity also commits a sin against justice. As seen previously, for him Scripture brings forth a single concept of charity that does not admit compromises.

---

142 J.A. Osiander, *Observationes*, 932-3.

143 J.A. Osiander, *Observationes*, 933-4.

144 J.A. Osiander, *Observationes*, 934: "*Nam qui contra charitatis normam peccat, ille peccat contra secundam tabulam Decalogi, atqui per secundam tabulam eiusque praecepta omnia diffunditur quoque iustitia, eo ipso quo peccat contra charitatem aliquis, peccat quoque contra iustitiam*".

145 J.A. Osiander, *Observationes*, 934: "*Et res magis luculenter patet si consideremus quid sit iustitiae proprium, nempe suum cuique tribuere. At quid maximè charitati inest, quam ut proximo etiam suum tribuat. Denique ex opposito hoc ipsum dispalescit, qui enim non amat proximum, non amando enim non tribuit quod tribuendum*".

1.2 Lease: Between the Scholastics and the Scriptures

1.2.1 *Introduction*

The theologians structured the lease around four essential points. First, they stressed the lawfulness of this agreement, allowing Christians to use it in accordance with God's will. Second, as a consequence of the doctrine of equality, they insisted on the just price of rent and the ban of fraud. Third, they extended the responsibility of the lessee for damages caused to the item leased, even without an express provision in the contract. Fourth, they stated that the use of the thing and the performance must not be shameful. On this last point, the theologians tackled the issue of prostitution contracts.

The greater part of the regulation on leases derives from the medieval elaboration of Roman law and Melanchthon's interpretation of justice in equality. Sporadic references to the early modern scholastics are also useful to complete the discourse. On the prostitution contracts, the link with the scholastics is evident, as much as their criticism or clear approval. We begin with an analysis of the definitions and main obligations. Then, we conclude with the special case of prostitution.

1.2.2 Locatio rei *and* locatio personae

1.2.2.1 Equality in Lease: Melanchthon and His Immediate Followers

In Roman law, the consensual type of agreement called *locatio conductio* included rent, contracts of service and contracts for work.[146] The medieval glossators considered two legal relationships, the *locatio conductio rei* (letting and hiring of things) and the *locatio conductio operarum* (letting and hiring of services). The third one, the *locatio conductio operis* (letting and hiring of work) was viewed as a species of the *locatio conductio operarum*.[147] The *locatio conductio rei* corresponds to the lease. The *locatio conductio operarum* involves the employment of one person for performing a service. In the *locatio conductio operis*, one person promises to execute a particular task, achieving a specific objective.[148] In the early modern era, a different classification took place and these relationships were intended as three agreements.[149]

---

146 L. Waelkens, *Amne Adverso*, 383.

147 R. Fiori, *La definizione della 'locatio conductio'. Giurisprudenza romana e tradizione romanistica*, Napoli, Jovene Editore, 1999, 306-7.

148 R. Zimmermann, *The Law of Obligations*, 351, 384, and 393.

149 See M. Kaser, *Das römische Privatrecht*, vol. I., 2nd ed., Münchern, Beck, 1971, 565; R. Fiori, *La definizione della 'locatio conductio'*, 308-13; P. Oestmann, *§§ 535-580a. Mietvertrag*, in M. Schmoeckel, J. Rückert, R. Zimmermann (eds.) *Historisch-kritischer Kommentar zum BGB*, 464-594 (474-5); W. Decock, *De strijd om de juridische kwalificatie*

The Lutheran theologians followed the medieval framework and analysed two agreements: *locatio rei* and *locatio personae seu operarum*. In his *Prolegomena in officia Ciceronis*, Melanchthon defines *locatio* as the granting of the use of a thing or a performance of a person, in return for a certain agreed-upon amount of money. When it is said 'use', he emphasizes, the abuse and corruption of the rented thing is excluded.[150] In this definition, Melanchthon focuses immediately on the responsibility of the lessee, who pays to use the thing and not to abuse it. Then, to explain this point better, he draws upon the Roman law distinction between contracts of good faith (*contractus bonae fidei*) and contracts of strict law (*contractus stricti iuris*). The *locatio* is a contract of good faith (*contractus bonae fidei*) and therefore the lessee is obliged to compensate the lessor if he damaged the thing with fault, even in absence of an expressed provision in the contract.[151]

To Melanchthon, the contracts of good faith are those where something is due for the sake of equality, even though it is not expressly named in the provisions.[152] These contracts are sale, lease, *locatio conductio*, deposit, society and loan for use, and, he continues, there is inequality if the seller consciously deceives the buyer, as if he sells for a price a useless thing. There is also inequality if the lessee damages the thing he rents and does not pay the damages owed.[153] By contrast, in the contracts of strict law, the parties are only requested to keep the expressed contractual provisions. In the loan for consumption, for instance, the debtor is only requested to return the sum he received. Because the lease is a contract of good faith, Melanchthon concludes that the lessee should not damage the thing, make a shameful use of it or defraud the lessor.[154]

The Roman law distinction between contracts of good faith and contracts of strict law is used by Melanchthon in order to point out the parties' obligations and principally to insist on the responsibility of the lessee, even if it is not specified in the contract. Furthermore, it indicates again Melanchthon's vision

van de advocaat-cliëntverhouding. Rechtshistorische kanttekeningen, in *Tijdschrift voor Privaatrecht*, 2014, 1209-53 (1243).

150 P. Melanchthon, *Prolegomena in officia Ciceronis*, in CR XVI, 589: "*Locatio est personae vel rei ad usum facta concessio pro pecunia numeranda, de qua convenit: cum dicitur ad usum, excluditur abusus et corruptio rei locatae*".

151 P. Melanchthon, *Prolegomena in officia Ciceronis*, in CR XVI, 589-90: "*Quare conductor si quid sua culpa corrumpit, compensare debet, etiamsi non est expresse mentio facta illius compensationis. Numeratur ergo locatio inter contractus bonae fidei*".

152 P. Melanchthon, *Prolegomena in officia Ciceronis*, in CR XVI, 590: "*Contractus bonae fidei sunt, in quibus aliqua non nuncupata lingua, tamen propter aequalitatem debentur*".

153 P. Melanchthon, *Prolegomena in officia Ciceronis*, in CR XVI, 590.

154 P. Melanchthon, *Prolegomena in officia Ciceronis*, in CR XVI, 590.

of equality.[155] Equality permeates the definitions of contracts of good faith and substantiates the obligations of the parties. Parties must comply with equality, which shapes the obligations not explicitly stated in the contract. If the lessee damages, abuses or abases the thing leased, he shall pay compensation to the lessor.

Contractual equality is a precept of God and corresponds to His will. Melanchthon explains that the rules for these cases (leases) are not only known because of public disputes, but much more because of the customs, and the very nature of the exchange, which prompts us to think of God's will. God established contracts as a bond for human society, that we can learn what is justice, what is equality, and thus recognize that He is just and equal. For this reason it is written in Lev. 19: "*Ye shall do no unrighteousness in judgment, in measuring length, weight, or number*".[156] Melanchthon's conception of contracts emerges again. They are a divine ordinance where God teaches man His justice.

Melanchthon's approach was persuasive for his followers. For instance, Paul Von Eitzen defines the *locatio* as the concession to use the performance of one person or one thing in return for an established price. Repeating Melanchthon, he points out that the term 'use' excludes every 'abuse' or 'spoiling' of the rented thing. He also immediately focuses on the responsibility of the lessee. When the lessee damages the thing, because of his fault, he must pay a compensation for the damages to the landlord or owner, even though this was not mentioned in the contract.[157] With Melanchthon, Von Eitzen draws on the Roman distinction between contracts of good faith and contracts of strict law.[158] Since the *locatio* is a contract of good faith, Von Eitzen concludes that the lessee shall not damage the thing he rents, nor make a shameful use of it, nor defraud the lessor.[159] As it is plain, these statements closely resemble Melanchthon's.

155 See II/2.2.4.1.

156 P. Melanchthon, *Prolegomena in officia Ciceronis*, in CR XVI, 591: "*Horum casuum regulae non tantum propter forenses disputationes notae sint, sed multo magis propter mores, ut cogitemus de voluntate Dei, qui sanxit contractus, ut sint vincula societatis humanae, et vult in eis exerceri iustitiam, ut discamus quid sit iustitia, videlicet aequalitas, et agnoscamus ipsum esse iustum, aequalem etc. Ideo praeceptum est Levit. 19 (35): "non facias corruptelam in libra, pondere*".

157 P. Von Eitzen, *Ethicae doctrinae pars altera*, 482-83: "*Locatio est persona vel rei ad usum facta concessio, pro pecunia numeranda, de qua convenit. Cum dicitur ad usum, excluditur abusus et corruptio rei locatae, quare conductor si quid sua culpa corrumpit, compensare debet, etiamsi non est expresse facta mentio istius compensationis*".

158 P. Von Eitzen, *Ethicae doctrinae pars altera*, 483.

159 P. Von Eitzen, *Ethicae doctrinae pars altera*, 483: "*Cum igitur locatio sit contractus bonae fidei, conducens non corrumpat res locatas, nec conferat ad turpem usum, nec defraudet*

Another of Melanchthon's followers, David Chytraeus, focused on the lawfulness of the agreement. After having noticed that it is a very common and honourable contract, Chytraeus states that the *locatio conductio* is the contact by which the service or work of a person, the use of an estate, home or other thing is conceded in return for a certain price.[160] The Word of God verifies that the *locatio conductio* is a lawful contract. In order to prove this point, Chytraeus quotes several biblical passages. However, they refer mostly to the *locatio conductio operarum* rather than to the *locatio rei*. He mentions Matt. 7,10: "*for the workman is worthy of his meat*" and Gen. 3,19: "*In the sweat of thy face shalt thou eat bread till thou return unto the ground*"; 1 Cor. 9 refers to the biblical law: "*Thou shalt not muzzle the mouth of the ox that treadeth out the corn*". This last passage applies to men that need their salary when they have done their job. Chytraeus explains that it pertains not only to people who do manual work as handworkers or mercenaries, but also to people who do intellectual work, like teachers, governors and counselors, both for the Church and state. God ordered that he who teaches the Gospel should be paid for what he has taught, as in Gal. 6,6: "*Let him that is taught in the Word share with him that teacheth, in all good things*".[161] In these passages the *locatio conductio* is meant more as an employment contract or contract for work than as a lease.

The lessor can use the thing, but he must agree with the lessee on a fair price. Chytraeus writes that payment or wage can be asked and required for the lease or usufruct of fields, houses, and other things, although they are added to the principal. Indeed, the risk and ruin of the rented thing belongs not to the lessee but to the lessor. The lessor departs from the use of the rented thing, while allowing another to profit from it, and for this an equal compensation is justly asked.[162] Chytraeus cares to stress the lawfulness of profit and warns that this is not usury. The lessor can lawfully demand a payment and gain an equal

---

locatores. Ideo res conducentis invecta in domum locatam obligatae sunt locatori, tanquam pignus, non solum propter locationis mercedem sed etiam ad compensationem rerum corruptarum".

160 D. Chytraeus, *In deuteronomium*, 454-5: "*Maxime autem usitatus in communi vita contractus et honesissimus rei familiaris agendae et locupletandae modus est locatio conductio, qua personae seu operarum, laborum alicuius vel fundi, domus, alteriusque rei, usus, pro certa mercede alteri conceditur*".

161 D. Chytraeus, *In deuteronomium*, 455.

162 D. Chytraeus, *In deuteronomium*, 455-6: "*Iuste etiam ex agrorum, vel domuum, aliarumve rerum ad usum vel usumfructum concessarum locationibus, pensiones seu mercedes, tametsi sorti accedant, peti et exigi possunt. Nam rei elocatae periculum et interitus, non ad utentem, sed ad locatorem spectat, et usu nonnihil rei locatae decedit, cuius compensatio aequalis iustissime petitur*".

profit for the rent of the thing. Indeed, he renounces the thing for a certain period, and for this sacrifice an equal profit is lawful.

Concluding on this point, Melanchthon, Von Eitzen and Chytraeus started from the general view that God established contracts as a bond for human society and wanted the practice of His justice. Contractual justice means the just price, but also that the lessee has to pay for any damage, even if this is not set out in the contract. Particularly, he has to avoid shameful use or abuse of the thing, as this runs counter to equality. Chytraeus adds some words on the lawfulness of the contract and especially of profit, which is justified by his renunciation of his use of the thing or property.

1.2.2.2 Horneius, Dürr, Baier and Prückner: Gaining Precision

As seen, Melanchthon and his immediate followers depicted the lawfulness and equality necessary in a lease, without delving into particular duties of the parties. They underscored the necessity of a just price and of the proper use (and not abuse) of the leased item. They did not list the obligations of the parties, however, as some later authors did. Examining the association between the sale and lease, Horneius, Dürr and Baier made a more specific description.[163] For instance, Horneius begins by comparing a lease with a sale. In a sale, property is conveyed; in a lease, the use is conceded, while the property remains the owner's. Consequently, the subjects of the *locatio rei* can only be things for which use and property can be separated. Food or other consumable things cannot be the subjects of lease. In this way, Horneius proposes to adapt the same rules designed for a sale to a lease, as they are applicable.[164]

Horneius notes that the goods that can be sold can also normally be rented. For this reason, the same conditions on the use of the thing that are requested for the sale of goods have to be observed for the goods leased. For instance, if the lessor rents the item for a price higher than its worth, and in this way defrauds the lessee, the lessee must receive restitution or be compensated.[165] After having compared the contract of sale and lease, Horneius concludes that, indeed, the same goods that can be sold, can also be rented. The same rules pertaining to a sale can also be applied to the lease, for the good of both lessor and lessee. Horneius does not enter into details, then, but only issues a reminder of the just price rule, which, he says, also informs the lease.

---

163 The similarity between the rules for sale and lease is already noticed in D. 19,2,2.

164 C. Horneius, *Compendium theologiae*, 770-1.

165 C. Horneius, *Compendium theologiae*, 771: "*Cetera autem quae vendi queunt, regulariter etiam locari possunt. Quapropter in illis quoque omnes eae conditiones observandae sunt, quod ad usum rei pertinet, quae in emtione venditione requiruntur, ex gr. si iusto carius quis rem locarit aut conduxerit, ut id, in quo alter defraudatus est, ei restituatur seu compensetur*".

Dürr observes that as in the sale of goods, the lordship over the thing (*dominium rei*) is transferred, while in the *locatio* the faculty to use and enjoy the thing (*facultas utendi vel fruendi*) are transferred to another person in exchange for a certain price. When the owner of a thing does not want to sell it, but he can be deprived of the use of the thing for a certain time, and the other does not have sufficient wealth to buy the necessary thing, he can obtain the use of the thing for a certain time, the first one becomes the lessor and the second one, the lessee.[166] Dürr stresses the distinction between sale and lease and the different opportunities to use the former or the latter. In this way he justifies the contract, and especially the profit derived from it.

In contrast to the theologians we examined in the last paragraph, Dürr and then his disciple Baier present a more specific evaluation of the parties' obligations. For the lawfulness of the contract, it is required from the lessor: 1) that he gives that thing for a fixed time; 2) that he reveals the hidden defects to the lessee; 3) that he pays the necessary expenses to assure the utilization of the good to the lessee; 4) that he pays damages that the lessee suffered for deceit (*dolus*) or fault of the lessor, either light or heavy; and 5) that he does not rescind the contract before the time determined.[167] Reciprocally, the lessee shall devote himself to the following duties: 1) he shall pay in the prescribed time; 2) he shall not transform the use of the thing that was originally assigned by the lessor; 3) after the use of the thing, he shall return the thing intact and without damages; 4) he shall not leave the contract before the time established without a just and probable cause.[168] These rules define accurately the obligations of the parties. This accuracy is probably the consequence of the necessity to help the Christians to follow their conscience in practical circumstances. Dürr is

---

166 J.K. Dürr, *Compendium*, 222: "*Porro sicut venditione dominium rei, ita locatione facultas utendi vel fruendi transfertur in alterum, sub conditione certae pensionis aut mercedis. Quando enim dominus rei non vult prorsus a se abalienare dominium rei, cuius usu ipse potest aliquantisper carere, vel alteri non suppetunt tantae facultates, ut rem necessariam emere possit, potest usum eius rei ad tempus obtinere, ille quidem locatione, hic vero condutione*".

167 J.K. Dürr, *Compendium*, 220: "*Qui contractus legitime se habeant, requiritur 1. ex parte locatoris, ut rem locatione usui conducibilem ad tempus praefinitum praestet. 2. Ut occultum vitium conductori indicet. 3. Ut solvat impensas factas in res necessarias, sine quibus conductor re locata uti non potest. 4. Ut resarciat damna, quae passus est conductor dolo aut culpa lata, vel levi ipsius locatoris. 5. Ne contractum locationis ante tempus praefinitum rescindat*". See also in a very similar way J.W. Baier, *Compendium theologiae moralis*, 491.

168 J.K. Dürr, *Compendium*, 221: "*Conductori vicissim incumbit, 1. Ut statuto tempore debitam pensionem solvat. 2. Ne rem conductam in alium usum convertat, quam inter ipsum et locatorem primo conventum est. 3 Ut rem locatam post destinatum locationis tempus integram et indemnem restituat. 4. Ne eandem ante illud tempus sine iusta et probabili causa deserat*".

writing in a manual for moral theology, with a clear pastoral aim. In contrast, the preceding discussions initiated by Melanchthon had a more theoretical approach, and consequently they were less detailed.

For Baier the tenant should use the thing with the diligence of a good father; he shall pay the rent in due time; he should not leave the rented item before the fixed time or neglect to pay the agreed rent; he shall compensate the lessor for the damages that were produced by his fault.[169] Horneius and Dürr only considered the *locatio rei*. Baier, however, also takes into consideration the position of the worker or employee and the employer in the *locatio operarum*. He maintains that the worker (who leases out his own work) must perform the job faithfully and with the maximum diligence. Furthermore, if he causes damages, he must pay a compensation for them. The employer must pay the wages in due time.[170]

These duties are enumerated without reference to Scripture or other authors. Nonetheless, the derivation from the law of sale seems clear. References to the scholastic theologians can be found in the work of Prückner. He stresses that the payment of damages due to the loss of the good is only necessary in the case of fault. He draws upon the early modern scholastic Francisco de Toledo Herrera and states that the lessee who used the good as a true owner but lost the good is not obliged to make restitution. Indeed, if he performed his duties with diligence and the good was secretly stolen, this occurred without his fault. If instead he did not heed to the good or turned it to another use that was not established in the contract, he is obliged to pay compensation. The loss of the good shall be attributed to his negligence or fraud.[171]

In conclusion, Melanchthon, Von Eitzen and Chytraeus gave a first brilliant sketch of the law of lease. Later theologians, such as Horneius, Dürr, Baier and Prückner, improved it by giving a more precise description of the parties'

---

169 J.W. Baier, *Compendium theologiae moralis*, 491: "*Ut conductor re conducta ad eum, de quo convenit, usum atque instar boni patrisfamilias utatur; ut statuto tempore mercedem solvat; ne rem conductam ante tempus praefinitum sine iusta causa deserat, ac pensionem de qua convenit, solvere recuset; immo etiam, ut damna, quae sua culpa evenerunt, resarciat*".

170 J.W. Baier, *Compendium theologiae moralis*, 491: "III *Ut, qui operas suas locat, fideliter eas, et in artificiis quidem, exactissima diligentia praestet, aut si quid damni a se illatum est, id non aegre compenset. IV Ut, qui operas alterius conduxit, mercedem pro illis promissam, ac tempore quidem iusto solvat*".

171 A. Prückner, *Manuale mille quaestionum*, 107-8: "Utrum locatarius locatum, in usu suo, quem verus dominus intendit, relicto, deperditum tamen, iure tenetur ad restitutionem? *Resp. Non tenetur, cum locatum, debita licet adhibita diligentia*, clam fuit surreptum, *quia idipsum praeter culpam suam periit: tenetur vero, si locatum vel* supine neglexit, *vel* in alios usus, *ad quos ipsum non accepit*, convertit, *quoniam hoc suae incuriae aut fraudi imputabit*. Tolet. lib. 5. Instruct. Sacerd. cap. 18, n. 1, p. 793".

obligations. While the first observations have a more refined theorical analysis and are included in theological treatises or philosophical comments, the posterior indications are geared to a reader who needs practical solutions and are devised for manuals for moral theology and collection of cases of conscience. The discourse can be seen on these two different levels and give evidence of the different necessities of the Christians.

1.2.3 *The Lease of Body* (locatio corporis)

1.2.3.1 The Debate among the Early Modern Scholastics

Prostitution was generally classified as lease of the right to use the body (*locatio corporis*) and was fully discussed by the scholastic theologians. Already Thomas Aquinas and Peter John Olivi addressed the question whether the prostitute should make restitution for the profit she gained. Both of them concluded that the contract is valid. Aquinas distinguished between shameful gain and illicit profit and affirmed that the prostitute does not act against the law, even though her performance is immoral. More precisely, Olivi argued that although the subject matter is iniquitous, the contractual form is juridically licit.[172]

The debate remained vivid among the sixteenth-century scholastics. In particular, drawing from Augustine, Medina held that the prostitute should return her profits. He substantiated this conclusion by stating that a sinful act could not be sold, because it has no market price, and consequently equality could not be guaranteed.[173] In addition, he pointed out that prostituting is an intrinsically evil act and can only be rewarded by a sum that is viewed as extrinsic to the transaction, like a donation.[174] Other theologians, like Soto and Covarruvias y Leyva, reaffirmed the classical teachings: the prostitute can keep her wage.[175] Due to the complexity of the debate, we cannot examine it in detail. Regardless, it constituted the background for the analysis of the Lutheran theologians.

1.2.3.2 Meisner: Four Reasons Against the Prostitute's Right to Keep Her Salary

Luther stated briefly that prostitutes should not return their wages because they gained them through a sin against God and the law. Restitution would

172 T. Aquinas, *Summa theologiae*, IIaIIae, q. 32, a. 7; P.J. Olivi, *De contractibus*, part. 3, art. 3, reg. 4, 310-1 (ed. Piron 1999). They are quoted by W. Decock, *Theologians and Contract Law*, 426-30.

173 W. Decock, *Theologians and Contract Law*, 440-1.

174 W. Decock, *Theologians and Contract Law*, 444-5.

175 W. Decock, *Theologians and Contract Law*, 447-52; 455-70.

therefore be absurd because the neighbour is not offended but is involved in the sin.[176] Among the Lutherans, Meisner and Osiander tackled the issue of whether the prostitute can keep the price of her shameful act, but they undertook opposite roads. Meisner was radically against the possibility of keeping the payment for prostitution and rejected many of the scholastic opinions. Conversely, Osiander appeared to accept them. For Meisner, the starting point is the debate within the early modern scholastics. He first summarizes Gregory of Valencia's view that the prostitute can keep the price of the agreement. Gregory of Valencia (1550-1603) observed that some Roman law texts allowed prostitutes to retain their profit. For this reason they can also keep it in conscience. Then, Meisner alludes to the contrary opinion held by Medina: a sin does not have an estimable value and cannot be sold.[177]

Meisner firmly opposes the prostitute keeping his wage and enumerates four reasons for this position, which we are now going to examine in depth. First, he argues that this papal opinion that permits the prostitute retaining his wage is scandalous (*scandalosam*), because prostitutes are confirmed in their evil acts. If prostitutes hear that they can keep their profit, they continue in their business (*pergunt in illo suo mercimonio*) and rarely think of amending their life choices.[178] This argument lies in the pastoral nature of the Church. The Church should call penitents to repent. But by allowing prostitutes to keep their salary, the Church would encourage them.

Second, for Meisner the scholastic opinion contradicts right reason. A price derives from an estimation of a licit thing; but if the thing is evil per se, although licit due to some reasons, the price nonetheless cannot be estimated, because sins cannot be sold, nor can a wage be justly demanded for them. In no way can fornication be licit, Meisner continues; it is a thing evil in itself, and forbidden by divine and natural law.[179] Meisner reflects that as sex outside the wedlock, prostitution is illicit, and an illicit act cannot be valued and sold.[180]

---

176 M. Luther, *Decem praecepta Wittenbergensi praedicata populo* (1518), WA 1, 394-521 (504-5).

177 B. Meisner, *Philosophia sobria*, pars tertia, Wittebergae, 1623, 432-3.

178 B. Meisner, *Philosophia sobria*, 435: "*Dicimus ergo, Papisticam opinationem esse 1. Scandalosam. Meretrices enim per eam confirmantur in sua malitia, siquidem quando audiunt, sibi juste mercedem dari, pergunt in illo suo mercimonio, et de vita emendanda raro cogitant*".

179 B. Meisner, *Philosophia sobria*, 435-6: "*II Rectae rationi contrariam. Quicquid enim pretio aestimatur, illud eo respectu, quo estimatur, oportet esse rem licita, ad minimum indifferentem: Si vero mala sit per se, nulloque respectu licita, tum precio aestimari nequit, quia peccata nequeunt vendi, nec iuste pro iis ulla merces exigitur. At vero fornicari nullo modo est licitum, est res per se mala, iure divino et naturali prohibita*".

180 This solution seems to be inspired by Medina.

Still, the scholastics replied that the sum transferred is not the price of the sin but the price of the lease, because the prostitute rents her body for the utility of another. Meisner rebuts: this lease is the same sin of fornication. There can be no distinction between the sin as an illicit thing and the lease of body, as a licit thing. Indeed, the same act of prostituting the body is a sin, and a sin cannot have a saleable price, nor can the *locatio corporis* for this act have a valid price.[181] For Meisner, the legal act and the moral act cannot be separated. Because prostitution is an evil act, the contract with such an object is void, and the prostitute cannot keep the salary.

Third, the opinion that allows prostitutes to retain their payment is against honourable laws. This argument is plainly the same used by other early modern scholastic theologians, as it is reported by Gregory of Valencia and attributed to the rigorist faction.[182] Meisner quotes the same passages quoted by the scholastics: D. 45,1,26 (*Generaliter*); D. 45,1,123 (*Si plagii*); C. 4,7,5 (*Mercalem*); and D. 2,14,7,3 (paragraph *Si ob maleficium*). These laws generally stated that no shameful action can gain a payment, nor is the pact or an illicit condition valid.[183] Gregory, who held the opposite, objected that these laws should be understood as concerning shameful actions and offences that are against justice. Meisner answers that these laws judge that nothing can be given for 'offences' (*maleficiis*). The *special* cause of this statement is that the offences are against justice but much more, the *general* cause is that they are sins and illicit acts *per se*. Therefore, nothing can be given or accepted for them. If for an act against justice, no payment can be given, then more certainly nothing is to be given for the act of prostitution, which is not only against *general* justice, but also against *particular* justice.[184]

Meisner here employs a double concept of justice: a general one and a particular one. He adduces two reasons to justify this concept. The nature of justice, he explains, is the steady disposition to give to every man his due. Whatever act does not give to everyone his due, but deprives him of it, is unjust. But in the act of prostitution, the prostitute's body is not given its due; rather its honour is taken away as a result of the shameful act. Therefore, the act of prostitution is unjust and nothing can be justly given or demanded as a consequence of that act.[185] Meisner casts an eye on the body and honor of the

181 B. Meisner, *Philosophia sobria*, 436.

182 See W. Decock, *Theologians and Contract Law*, 457.

183 B. Meisner, *Philosophia sobria*, 437.

184 B. Meisner, *Philosophia sobria*, 438: "*Si pro illo actu, qui contra iustitiam est, nulla merces solvenda; tum neque aliquid dandum erit pro actu meretricio, quia hic etiam contra iustitiam est, non tantum generalem; sed etiam contra particularem, quod gemina ratione probo*".

185 B. Meisner, *Philosophia sobria*, 438.

prostitute, which is also worthy of receiving justice. The act of prostitution is an act against justice, because it does not respect the honour of the prostitute. Due to this breach of justice, no payment can be given or demanded.

This double and extended concept of justice can also be derived from the additional shamefulness. Meisner takes expressly this argument from the Jesuit Juan Azor. Whatever is given and taken in a shameful way (*turpiter*) is not given and taken according to justice, and in the same manner remain a wage for a performance. But what is given to the prostitute and taken from her for the shameful act is given and taken in a shameful way. Therefore, it is not given and taken according to justice and has to be returned.[186] The virtue of justice is opposed to shamefulness (*torpitudo*). Thus, remunerating the shameful act with a wage is in a certain manner to approve it, which is absolutely shameful.[187] This argument is based on a syllogism, which in the last instance rests on the equivalence between the moral and the legal lawfulness. Given the fact that what is given or accepted shamefully is against justice, and that the work of the prostitute is shameful, nothing can be given or accepted for the act of prostitution.

In his fourth point, Meisner engages in a bitter discussion with Gregory of Valencia: he reports Gregory's motivations for allowing the prostitute to keep her wage and rejects them. According to Gregory, in Gen. 38, Judah promised a young goat to Tamar as a price for prostitution. In the Scripture this act is neither reproached, nor does Judah himself indicate that this was reprehensible.[188] Meisner shrewdly responds that the consequence of this argument is void, because prostitution should not be judged by facts, but by laws. The Scripture only tells about what Judah did, but the same fact is not approved.[189] Meisner spells out: an approval cannot be deduced from the silence. The Scripture in this passage does not give clear elements to deduce an approval, but only narrates facts.

Then, Gregory refers to *Sed quod meretrici* (D. 12,5,4,3), where Ulpian states that what has been given to the prostitute cannot be asked back. To Gregory, these words are a clear approval of the payment of prostitute. He also mentions

186 B. Meisner, *Philosophia sobria*, 438-9: "*Quodcunque datur et accipitur turpiter, non utique datur et accipitur secundum iustitiam, ac proinde neque ut merces operis. Sed quod datur meretrici, et ab ea accipitur pro actu turpi; datur et accipitur turpiter. Ergo non datur et accipitur secundum iustitiam, et consequenter debet restitui*".

187 B. Meisner, *Philosophia sobria*, 439.

188 The example of Tamar was also used by other Roman Catholic authors, as for instance Pope Adrian VI, Covarrubias and even Grotius. See W. Decock, *Theologians and Contract Law*, 438-9, 457, 495.

189 B. Meisner, *Philosophia sobria*, 440: "*Nulla inest huic argumento consequentia, quoniam non factis sed legibus iudicandum. Narratur tantum, quid Judas egerit, non vero ipsius factum probatur, licet ipse pro licito habuerit*".

Thomas Aquinas (q. 32 a. 7) and Dr. Navarrus, who shared this interpretation. Meisner replies that the text speaks about a *datus* (giving) in general. Yet, it can be given to the prostitute in two senses: as a salary due or as an undue gift. The jurist does not affirm that it is licit to give something to the prostitute as a salary nor for her to accept it. But it seems more to talk about gifts given to the prostitute. Such gifts cannot be asked back.[190] In this view, the prostitute would not be paid, but would receive a donation.

Finally, Gregory repeats an opinion of Cajetan, according to whom the act of prostitution has an estimable price. Prostitution is indeed the giving of pleasure, and it has a price, as the giving of drink or food. Meisner strongly denies that the act of prostituting can have an estimable price, because it is illicit and degenerate. No sin can have an estimable price, he avers. By the act of prostituting, something is indeed given for the use of a man and for his pleasure. However, this giving and using of the body of the prostitute, is *per se* wicked and against the divine law.[191]

In conclusion, these four reasons clearly show that Meisner was involved in the discussion on prostitution contracts and wanted to maintain a steady position. Generally speaking, he repudiates the division between law and morality: the moral illicit can never give rise to something legal. The act of the prostitute is illicit and her salary is consequently illicit. This moral rigorism does not look at the concrete situation of prostitute, who needed money to survive, but focuses instead on the purity of conscience as the supreme good to be preserved.

1.2.3.3 Osiander: Resuming the Scholastic Approval

Meisner expressed a fervid criticism of the scholastic opinion that the prostitute can keep her wage. Countering him, his Lutheran colleague Osiander seems to approve the opinion promoted by Gregory of Valencia, Soto, Molina and Aragón. Osiander neither agrees with them explicitly, nor confutes their opinion. The rent of body (*locatio corporis*) has an estimable value. The donation made by the prostitute has a price and therefore is valid according to natural law, even though it is illicit from an extrinsic view.[192] The prostitutes can demand what has been given before and after the act.

---

190 B. Meisner, *Philosophia sobria*, 441: "*Loquitur lex de dato in genere: potest autem meretrici aliquid dari dupliciter: vel ut merces debita; vel ut donum indebitum.* Priori *modo aliquid meretrici licite dari, vel ab ea accipi posse, jurisconsultus non affirmat; sed videtur potius loqui de* donis, datisque indebitis; *quando meretrici aliquid donatur: talia dona non repeti posse, ibi asseritur*".

191 B. Meisner, *Philosophia sobria*, 443-4.

192 J.A. Osiander, *Theologiae casualis*, vol. 1 and 2, 1453.

The client is obliged to pay the prostitute, because she did not give her services for free, but for a fixed price. The prostitute can take the promised price, demand it (*exigere*), and keep it in conscience. The reason is that even though such a body rent is illicit, it nonetheless has an estimable value. The rent of body by public prostitutes is has an easily discerned market price. Because the price is not given for the sin, but for the body rent for the pleasure of the other, the lessee does not pay for the sin, but for the act of the woman who serves to pleasure.[193]

On other topics Osiander showed moral rigidity, but in this case he seems to entertain the more pragmatic solution. The prostitute can keep her salary because the price is not given for the sin but for the body rent for pleasure. The distinction between the moral and the legal act is admissible for Osiander as he merely follows the more traditional scholastic opinion that allowed the prostitutes to retain their wages.

1.3 Guidelines for Restitution

1.3.1 *Introduction*

The overreaching principle of the scholastic doctrine of justice in exchange was restitution. To the scholastics every breach of the equality triggered an obligation of restitution of the unjust profit. Restitution was an indispensable requisite for salvation, because it determined the end of the offence. It was the first step on the road of salvation, as a penance for the offence committed. For this reason, in a rain of words, the scholastics made clear all the specifics of restitution, with such attention that it became one of the main subjects of their treatises. The Lutherans also proposed the doctrine of restitution. The thing unjustly taken must be returned to the lawful owner. Yet, for them restitution had no direct causality in salvation. Restitution is a benefic consequence of

193 J.A. Osiander, *Theologiae casualis*, vol. 1 and 2, 1454: "Secundo *posse pretium promissum accipere, et exigere, et acceptum in conscientia retinere. Et ita Sotus*, lib. 4. quaest. 7. art. 1. Bannez. 2.2 quaest. 62. art. 5. Arragonius ibidem, Molina tom 1 disput. 94. Lopez 1 par. cap. 105. Petrus Navarrus lib. 4 cap. 2 n. 11 et alii. *Ratio, quia talis locatio corporis licet illicita sit, sentamen pretio aestimabilis, imo pluris aestimatur, quam locatio corporis publicae meretricis. Tum quia pretium non datur pro peccato, sed pro locatione corporis in delectationem alterius, nec is, qui dat, dat propter peccatum, sed propter actum, quo mulier ei servit ad voluptatem*". D. de Soto, *De iustitia et iure libri decem*, Lugdunum, 1559, 264-5; D. Báñez, *Scholastica commentaria in* [...] *partem Angelici Doctoris S. Thomae*, Duaci, 1615, 120-32; P. de Aragonia, *In secundam secundae Divi Thomae Doctoris Angelici commentaria*, Lugduni, 1597, 174-88; L. de Molina, *De iustitia et iure*, t. 1, Moguntiae, 1659, 380-7; P. de Navarra, *De restitutione in foro conscientiae, tomus secundus*, Lugduni, 1595, 409-10.

the salvation already granted by Christ. It still determines the end of sin, but is not seen as a necessary act of penance – rather it is a grateful response to the forgiveness of God.

The eschatological difference is also reflected in the approach to more practical issues. The scholastics dictated numerous norms for the execution of restitution. The Lutherans only formulated general principles. However, this does not mean that they underestimated the importance of making restitution. They denied the possibility to practice almsgiving in place of restitution and considered restitution replaceable or renounceable only in a limited number of hypotheses. The Lutherans were instead in sync with the scholastics about the refusal to apply the Roman law remedy of the *laesio enormis* in the court of conscience. Here they were of the same opinion. We first examine the theoretical features related to the foundation and consequences on salvation. Then, we move on the more practical aspects, such as the execution and the inapplicability of the *laesio enormis*.

1.3.2 *Theoretical Features*

1.3.2.1 Foundation: Augustine, the Scriptures and Rational Arguments

The doctrine of restitution harks back to Augustine.[194] In a famous passage of a letter to Macedonius, a vicar of Africa, the bishop of Hippo argued that the sin is not remitted if what has been taken off is not returned (*non remittitur peccatum, nisi restituatur ablatum*).[195] The passage received enormous attention. It was first inserted in Yves of Chartres' *Decretum*, then Gratian's *Decretum*, partially in Peter Lombard's *Sentences* and finally in the *Liber Sextus* as one of the general principles of law.[196] Restitution was applicable to a large number of cases, not only related to tangible things but also intangible goods, such as honour and marriage.[197] Particularly, it counteracted the offences related to the market and to the seventh commandment.[198] The Roman law had a similar

194 J. Hallebeek, *The Concept of Unjust Enrichment in Late Scholasticism*, Nijmegen, GNI, 1996, 7-18; N. Jansen, *Theologie, Philosophie und Jurisprudenz in der spätscholastischen Lehre von der Restitution*, Tübingen, Mohr Siebeck, 2013, 25-8.

195 Augustinus Hipponensis, *Epistola ad Macedonium*, in *PL* 33, ep. 153, 6, 20, c. 662.

196 K. Weinzierl, *Die Restitutionslehre der Frühscholastik*, München, Heuber, 1936, 54-174; K. Weinzierl, *Die Restitutionslehre Der Hochscholastik Bis Zum Hl. Thomas Von Aquin*, München, Heuber, 1939, 89ff.; C. Bergfeld, *Katholische Moraltheologie und Naturrechtslehre*, in H. Coing (ed.), *Handbuch der Quellen und Literatur*, 1000-1; J. Hallebeek, *The Concept of Unjust Enrichment in Late Scholasticism*, 22; N. Jansen, *Theologie, Philosophie*, 25; W. Decock, *Theologians and Contract Law*, 516-7.

197 G. Dolezalek, *The Moral Theologians' Doctrine of Restitution and its Juridification in the Sixteenth and Seventeenth Centuries*, in *Acta Juridica*, 104, 1992, 104-14 (107-8).

198 P. Prodi, *Settimo non rubare*, 114-5.

remedy, the 'unjust enrichment'.[199] But it regarded a more restricted area of illicit acts,[200] and confronted with restitution, it became almost superfluous.[201]

Like the scholastics, the Lutherans followed Augustine. Melanchthon writes that the Augustinian rule is true and concerns all Christians who consciously and voluntarily hold what belongs to another person and can return it, as Paul says in Eph. 4,28: "*Let him that stole steal no more*". Now, he who steals is a thief until he consciously and voluntarily relinquishes the other's possession.[202] Melanchthon explains this passage with an example: if a man kidnaps another man's wife, he will remain a kidnapper and an adulterer while he keeps the woman. Therefore, when Paul forbids stealing, he wants the return of the stolen things, because in this way he who has been stealing ceases to be a thief.[203] Paul's letter confirms the opinion of Augustine. Restitution is ultimately necessary for the remission of the sin. If the thief does not return the unjust gain or the thing belonging to the other party, he is still a sinner. The fact that he does not return the goods or the unjust gain is a clear sign that he still wants to be a sinner. The lack of restitution is evidence of a sinful will, and while this persists, the sin cannot be remitted.

Together with Augustine and with Paul's letter to the Ephesians, some biblical passages played a strategic role in the Lutheran arguments in favour of restitution.[204] Luke 19,8 concerns the conversion of the wealthy tax collector Zacchaeus. Accused of being a sinner, Zacchaeus answered: "*Behold, Lord, the half of my goods I give to the poor; and if I have taken any thing from any man by false accusation, I restore him fourfold*". Commenting this passage, Luther states that he who has stolen must become like Zacchaeus and give back what he has robbed to those he has 'fleeced'; otherwise he does not atone for his sin rightly. According to the positive law, he cannot keep the goods with right or good conscience and much less according to divine law. The divine law urges the return of the stolen things. If things are not returned, the thief does not make a right repentance and is still a sinner. And, Luther adds, he who is eating and

199 On the analysis of the Glossators see K. Weinzierl, *Die Restitutionslehre*, 31-53.

200 J. Hallebeek, *The Concept of Unjust Enrichment in Late Scholasticism*, 19.

201 W. Decock, *Theologians and Contract Law*, 514.

202 P. Melanchthon, *Catechesis puerilis*, in CR XXIII, 169: "*Haec regula vera est in genere de omnibus, qui scientes et volentes alienum detinent, et habent unde reddant, seu possunt reddere, sicut Paulus inquit: qui furatus est, deinceps non furetur. Atqui ille qui furatus est, tantisper est fur, dum alienum sciens ac volens detinet*".

203 P. Melanchthon, *Catechesis puerilis*, in CR XXIII, 169.

204 For an overview of the biblical passages used by the medieval scholastics see K. Weinzierl, *Die Restitutionslehre*, 11-30.

drinking with him shares his sins.[205] Luther does not explicitly mention restitution, but states that the thief must return his goods in order to make a right repentance. This fragment was utilized to argue that he approved restitution.[206]

Another oft-quoted passage is Ezekiel 33,13-15, which regards the necessary conversion of the Jews proclaimed by the prophet Ezekiel:

> *When I shall say to the righteous, that he shall surely live; if he trusts to his own righteousness, and commits iniquity, all his righteousnesses shall not be remembered; but for his iniquity that he hath committed, he shall die for it. Again, when I say unto the wicked, Thou shalt surely die; if he turn from his sin, and do that which is lawful and right; If the wicked restore the pledge, give again that he had robbed, walk in the statutes of life, without committing iniquity; he shall surely live, he shall not die.*

Paul von Eitzen, Friedrich Balduin, Johann Adam Osiander considered this passage as a confirmation of the necessity of restitution.[207]

Eph. 4,28, Luke 19,8 and Ez. 33,13-15 do not only show the positive value of restitution, but also that the restitutive act follows the conversion of the sinner as a concrete act of repentance. What is indeed requested by the Lutherans is a true sign of repentance that ends the sinful behaviour. As we will see, this act does not merit salvation, which has been already granted by Christ. The act of restitution stems properly from faith, as an act of thanksgiving for the salvation obtained.

In addition to the Scriptures, the theologians added other reasons for supporting restitution. Osiander, for instance, argued that the duty of restitution is supported by right reason (*recta ratio*). He took the argument from Cicero's *De officiis*.[208] For Cicero, justice requires giving to everyone his due, therefore to preserve justice, it is necessary to return the stolen thing.[209] Olearius instead took a position closer to the scholastics and held that restitution is properly an

---

205 Martin Luther, *Colloquia oder Tischreden Doctor Martini Lutheri*, Frankfurt 1567, 80: "*Das hat seine Masse / er muss aber ein Zacheus werden / und was er zu viel geraubet hat / wieder geben / denen ers abgeschunden hat / oder er buesset nicht recht. Nach beschriebenen Rechten kan ers auch nicht mit Recht und guten Gewissen behalten / geschweige denn nach Goettlichen Rechten. Und wer mit ihm isset und trincket / der machet sich theilhafftig an seinen Sunden*".

206 C. Meyer, *Disputatio theologica de restitutione ablati*, Regiomonti, 1707, 22.

207 P. von Eitzen, *Ethicae doctrinae pars altera*, 488; F. Balduin, *Tractatus*, 957; J.A. Osiander, *Theologiae casualis*, vol. 3 and 4, 31.

208 Cicero, *De officiis*, III, 23.

209 J.A. Osiander, *Theologiae casualis*, vol. 3 and 4, 31: "Tertio *recta ratio. Si enim iustitia exigit, ut unicuique suum tribuatur, tum si res aliena detinetur, necessario erit restituenda, ut iustitiae suus maneat locus*".

act of commutative justice.[210] These sources were, however, generally put in a secondary level, while the Holy Scripture maintained a position of primacy.

1.3.2.2 An Issue of Salvation?

The doctrine of restitution took on great importance for the scholastics because they considered it to be an essential prerequisite for salvation.[211] Thomas Aquinas interpreted the above-mentioned passage of Augustine in the light of his view of justice as equality: restitution of the unjustly stolen thing is an act of commutative justice that restores equality. The preservation of equality is necessary for salvation of the soul, and is attained by restitution.[212] Restitution, however, is not sufficient for salvation. Indeed, restitution is not part of the satisfaction, but only the preamble of it, he writes. Restitution corresponds to the end of the offence.[213] When the sinful act terminates, the debt of punishment (*debitum poenae*) still remains for the sin committed.[214] Restitution does not remove the guilt of the sin. When a man took someone's thing unjustly, Aquinas explains, two different aspects must be considered. One is the inequality of the 'thing', the other is the sin of injustice. The guilt of injustice is different from the injustice of the 'thing'. Restitution is the remedy for the injustice of the thing and restores equality by returning what has been taken unjustly. But the guilt is remitted by the punishment (*poena*), which has to be inflicted by the judge.[215]

To Aquinas, the 'stain' of sin cannot be removed unless man accepts the order of Divine justice, and either takes upon himself the punishment of his

---

210 J. Olearius, *Doctrina theologiae moralis*, Tab. XXXVII De Justitia.

211 The Roman Catechism of 1566, issued after the Council of Trent also emphasized that restitution was a condition necessary for absolution. Catechismus ex decreto Concilii Tridentini ad parochos Pii V pont. max. iussu editus, Romae, 1566, cap. 5, num 78.

212 T. Aquinas, *Summa theologiae*, IIaIIae, q. 62, a. 2, concl.: "*Respondeo dicendum quod restitutio, sicut dictum est, est actus iustitiae commutativae, quae in quadam aequalitate consistit. Et ideo restituere importat redditionem illius rei quae iniuste ablata est, sic enim per iteratam eius exhibitionem aequalitas reparatur. Si vero iuste ablatum sit, inaequalitas erit ut ei restituatur, quia iustitia in aequalitate consistit. Cum igitur servare iustitiam sit de necessitate salutis, consequens est quod restituere id quod iniuste ablatum est alicui, sit de necessitate salutis*". See also N. Jansen, *Theologie, Philosophie*, 28-33. On the impact of Aquinas's statements see J. Gordley, *Foundations of Private Law. Property, Tort, Contract, Unjust Enrichment*, Oxford, Oxford University Press, 2006, 424-5.

213 T. Aquinas, *Commentum in quatuor libros sententiarum*, Liber IV, Dist. 15, q. 1, art. 5: "*... constat quod non est pars satisfactionis proprie acceptae, sed est praeambulum ad satisfactionem ...*".

214 T. Aquinas, *Summa theologiae*, IaIae, q. 87, a. 6: "*Unde patet quod, cessante actu peccati vel iniuriae illatae, adhuc remanet debitum poenae*".

215 T. Aquinas, *Summa theologiae*, IIaIIae, q. 62, a. 3.

past sins or bears patiently the punishment that God inflicts on him. In both ways, punishment avails for satisfaction.[216] Thus, satisfaction for sin comes from penitential acts (good works: fasting, prayers, etc.) according to the judgment of the priests.[217] In Aquinas's view, restitution and satisfaction are two different but essential stages for the salvation of the soul. Restitution determines the end of the offence, but the offence in itself must be restored through a reparatory punishment.[218]

For the Lutherans, restitution is necessary, but it does not concern salvation, which is already granted by Christ. To Melanchthon, restitution is not part of the satisfaction but concerns the contrition. Contrition is a trembling and pain for the sin, with the intention not to commit actions against the conscience and God's will. In the example of the kidnapped woman we saw earlier, the remission of sin cannot occur until the woman is returned.[219] Indeed, he who does not return the woman does not have any trembling and pain because of his sin. He is still sinning and to remit the sin is indispensable for restitution.

Hitherto, the solution is similar to the scholastics'. The point of the departure comes further. For Melanchthon, the scholastics' idea of satisfaction is completely wrong. He polemically writes that the Roman Catholics teach that God is merciful and remits the sin, but because he is also just and vengeful, he commutes the eternal punishment into a temporal punishment in Purgatory.[220] Part of the sin is remitted through the power of the keys and another part through acts of penance. The compensation of the punishment, Melanchthon remarks, is absurd. The remission of the fault and eternal death are united. The sacrifice of Christ eliminates both the sin and the eternal death without any human action.[221] To Melanchthon, another sacrifice is not requested. Restitution is the only condition requested for the remission of sins. And it

---

216 T. Aquinas, *Summa theologiae*, IIaIIae, q. 62, a. 3: "*Unde macula peccati ab homine tolli non potest nisi voluntas hominis ordinem divinae iustitiae acceptet, ut scilicet vel ipse poenam sibi spontaneus assumat in recompensationem culpae praeteritae, vel etiam a Deo illatam patienter sustineat, utroque enim modo poena rationem satisfactionis habet*".

217 T. Aquinas, *Summa theologiae*, III, q. 84, a. 8.

218 For a more detailed account see R. Cessario, O.P., *The Godly Image. Christ and Salvation in Catholic Thought from Anselm to Aquinas*, Petersham, MA, St. Bede's Publications, 1990, 116-21.

219 P. Melanchthon, *Catechesis puerilis*, in CR XXIII, 169.

220 P. Melanchthon, *Loci communes* (*tertia eorum aetas*), in CR XXI, 903: "*Sic enim docent, Deum, cum sit misericors, remittere culpam, sed cum sit etiam iustus et vindex, mutare poenam aeternam in temporalem purgatorii*".

221 P. Melanchthon, *Loci communes* (*tertia eorum aetas*), in CR XXI, 903: "*Sciamus igitur culpam et mortem aeternam simul tolli propter Christum, non propter ullam nostram compensationem*".

is requested because otherwise the believer would still be sinning. No punishment remains and no acts of penance are necessary. Instead, for Aquinas restitution is only the preamble of satisfaction, the punishment for the sins remains and is only removed by penance.

The particular character of the Lutheran restitution is also brought to light by other authors. Commenting the passage of Luke 19,8, Johannes Brenz explains that the remission of sins is gained by the sacrifice of Christ. Zacchaeus' restitution of stolen things is not a work that produces the remission of sins in front of God. His sins were already forgiven by Christ in whom he believed, and who aroused in him great joy, before restitution of the stolen things.[222] Restitution is the peak of a process that God creates in the heart of Zacchaeus. Hence, it is not a work that Zacchaeus makes in order to gain salvation, but it is an effect of his conversion prompted by God. This point is absolutely central in whole Lutheran moral scheme. The good works are not done to gain salvation, but are performed because of the salvation already granted. Pushed by the grace of the Holy Spirit, the Christian makes restitution. This is exactly the opposite of the Roman Catholic view.

Johann Adam Osiander says the same with a different terminology. He explains that restitution is necessary for the *salus aeterna* only negatively, in the sense that it removes an impediment (the sin) to salvation. By contrast, the 'pontifical doctors' are wrong when they consider restitution as positively essential for salvation, as a condition, or that it has a certain causality for salvation, in the sense that it is a mean, a work that gains the salvation.[223] Although Osiander uses other terms (positive or negative effects for salvation), he makes clear the distance between the Lutheran and the scholastic view. The Lutherans only meant restitution as a condition for the remission of sins. Instead, the scholastic considered it as the first step toward salvation, which derives from walking a laborious road of making satisfaction through acts of penance.

---

222 J. Brenz, *In evangelii quod inscribitur secundum Lucam, duodecim posteriora capita, homiliae octoginta*, 548: "*Solus enim Christus est peccatorum expiator. Et Zacheus non restituit aliena ut merito huius operis consequeretur peccatorum suorum remissionem coram Deo. Peccata enim eius erant iam per Christum in quem credidit, et quem magno gaudio suscepit, remissa, priusquam aliena bona restitueret*".

223 J.A. Osiander, *Theologiae casualis*, vol. 3 and 4, 32: "Secundo *illud nimium est, quod quidam* Pontificii Doctores, *et alii etiam disputant, restitutionem alieni esse ita necessariam, ut ab illa pendeat salus aeterna; adeoque esse necessariam necessitate tum praecepti, tum medii ad salutem, cum multa sint necessaria homini Christiano, quae tamen non necessaria ad salutem et quaedam necessaria possint dici* positive, *per modum conditionis, aut sub ratione cuiusdam causalitatis ad salutem; quaedam autem* negative vel privative tantum *se habeat, in quantum removent prohibens sive impediens salutem. Quemadmodum remotio purulentae materiae necessaria est sanitatem sub ratione impedientis removens*".

1.3.3 *Practical Features*

1.3.3.1 Instructions for Executing Restitution

Despite the concern for the theological issues of the foundation and necessity for salvation, the Lutheran theologians dedicated far fewer words than their Roman Catholic colleagues to the more practical aspects. They determined rules for the execution of restitution, but without the precision afforded by the sophisticated framing of the scholastic theology. Aquinas planned a distinction that turned out to be seminal among the early modern scholastics.[224] He distinguished two essential reasons for restitution: restitution by reason of having someone else's thing (*ratione rei*) or restitution by reason of having taken someone else's thing in a previous act (*ratione acceptionis*). In the first case, the possessor of someone else's thing is bound to return the thing to the lawful owner, according to commutative justice.[225] This hypothesis concerns the recovery of possession or property by real actions.

The second reason for restitution, however, encompasses both delictal actions and contractual actions.[226] Aquinas describes three cases. First, the thing is taken against the will of the owner by robbery or theft. The thief is bound to restitution because of the thing (*ratione rei*), but also because of the injurious action (*ratione iniuriosae actionis*). He is bound to make compensation for the loss incurred, but he also merits punishment for the injustice committed. Secondly, a man takes another's property with the consent of the owner and for his own profit, as in a loan. To Aquinas, the borrower is bound to restitution, not only by reason of the thing (*ratione rei*), but also by reason of the taking (*ratione acceptionis*), even if he has lost the thing. Third, a man takes another's property without profit, as in the case of a deposit. He is bound to restitution on account of the thing taken (*ratione rei*). If this thing is taken from him without his fault, he is not bound to restitution.[227]

Such an elegant classification guided the more specific solutions of the early modern scholastics. Yet, it cannot be found among the Lutheran theologians. In a general way, Melanchthon and Brenz only affirm the necessity of restitution. Balduin states that the main point of the divine law and human law is restitution of the taken thing, if it still exists. Following an opinion of Juan Azor (1535-1603), he specifies that only the stolen thing must be returned and not the profit gained by the use of the thing.[228] Balduin limits his statements to

224 J. Hallebeek, *The Concept of Unjust Enrichment in Late Scholasticism*, 47-53; N. Jansen, *Theologie, Philosophie*, 49-60.

225 T. Aquinas, *Summa theologiae*, IIaIIae, q. 62, a. 6.

226 J. Hallebeek, *The Concept of Unjust Enrichment in Late Scholasticism*, 50.

227 T. Aquinas, *Summa theologiae*, IIaIIae, q. 62, a. 6.

228 F. Balduin, *Tractatus*, 958.

this declaration without delving into the motivations that might have justified Azor's solution.

Apparently following Aquinas, Olearius argues that restitution is an act of commutative justice. To be bound to restitution is either the man who produced an unjust damage to the other, with compulsion, deceit, fraud or other inexcusable fault, or the man who participated in the injustice by his counsel, cooperation or material support, ordered it or approved actions made in his name.[229] The second range of cases was also discussed by Aquinas, who stated that the person who collaborated to damage is also bound to restitution.[230] Yet, for the first one, Olearius formulates a more general solution. Restitution is subordinated to an act of injustice caused by inexcusable fault, and no distinction between restitution *ratione rei* and *ratione acceptionis* is offered. The standard criterion to determine restitution is given by the unjust damage, caused by fault. Further distinctions do not matter.

Olearius' doctrine of restitution seems to be expressed in general terms and is applicable to a vast array of situations. This interpretation is reinforced by looking at the description of the subject of restitution. To him the subject of restitution is: a) in general (*in genere*) everything in which someone has a right; b) properly (*proprie*), external and corporeal things, mostly possessions; c) analogically (*analogice*), internal and incorporeal goods, like those that consist in honor and reputation.[231] For Olearius, restitution then is suitable for the recovery of property or possession, but also honour and reputation.

A linked problem the scholastics had discussed was the unavailability of the thing due to it being lost or sold to a third person. Among the various solutions, the majority of the scholastics affirmed that in the case of restitution *ratione rei* the selling price cannot replace the thing, but the position of the possessor of good faith must be more accurately evaluated. He has to pay the price only if he is enriched by the transaction.[232] Olearius' approach is again very general. He writes that the possessor of someone else's thing has to return the same thing if it still exists and is in his power. If the same thing is

229 J. Olearius, *Doctrina theologiae moralis*, Tab. XXXVII De Justitia: "*Is qui ad restitutionem teneatur. Omnis scilicet, qui a) alteri injuste damnum intulit, sive per* vim, *sive* dolum, fraudem, *aliamve* culpam, *non* excusabilem *b) injustitiae illius particeps fuit, sive* consilio *ac* jusso suo, *sive* ratihabitione *actionis suo nomine patratae, sive etiam* cooperatione et auxilio".

230 T. Aquinas, *Summa theologiae*, IIaIIae, q. 62, a. 7.

231 J. Olearius, *Doctrina theologiae moralis*, Tab. XXXVII De Justitia: "*Subjectum, in quo restitutio locum habeat. Sunt sempe a*) In genere *omnia, in quae aliquis ius habet. b*) Proprie *res externae ac corporeae, praecipue possessiones.* c) Analogice *Bona interna et incorporea, item ea, que in honore ac fama consistunt*".

232 J. Hallebeek, *The Concept of Unjust Enrichment in Late Scholasticism*, 60.

ruined or is no longer in the possession of the thief, or by his fault it was damaged or depreciated in value, the price of the thing must be paid. Finally, the possessor has to pay the damage or lack of profit caused to the owner by the lack of availability of the thing.[233] The issue of the damages or dearth of profit was also discussed by the early modern scholastics, but with more precision.[234] Olearius sketches the edges of a doctrine of restitution, but does not enter in the subtle and elaborated distinctions formulated by the scholastics. He simply concludes that the stolen thing is to be returned if it still exists; otherwise its monetary value is to be paid. Moreover, the damage or *lucrum cessans* must be relinquished.

To sum up, the early modern scholastics founded their elaborated conclusions on Aquinas's scheme of restitution *ratione rei* and restitution *ratione acceptionis*. On the opposite side, the Lutherans only formulated principles, without delving into detailed norms. It could be added that the Lutheran vision of private confession, without the enumeration of sins, did not help the practice of restitution. Maybe this is the reason why the theologians did not need to explore more in depth the practical aspects of restitution.

1.3.3.2 General Exceptions

The Lutheran theologians did not write the same rivers of pages as their Roman Catholic colleagues, but they nonetheless cared about restitution. The duty of restitution terminates the sin and is therefore essential. The scholastics already proposed some exceptions, as in case of damages for the debtor's soul or family. The Lutherans also admitted exceptions in particular difficult situations, showing even more inflexible positions. Balduin and Olearius describe three general cases. First, no one must make restitution if it is impossible, as the old adage says: *ad impossibilia nemo tenetur*. The theologians warn that at least there must be the intention to make restitution, because otherwise there is no contrition and no remission of sin.[235] It must be an objective impossibility and not a subjective impossibility.

Second, restitution is not necessary if the creditor decides for the remission of debt spontaneously, that is, without compulsion, fraud or duress.[236] The act

233 J. Olearius, *Doctrina theologiae moralis*, Tab. XXXVII De Justitia: "Objectum, quod sit restituendum. *Est nimirum vel a) ipsa* res, *si adhuc existat, ac in potestate illius sit, qui alterum ea fraudavit. b) Rei* precium, *si res ipsa vel periit, vel in istius non sit potestate, aut eius culpa deterior facta sit. c)* Damnum *aut* lucrum cessans *Domino per rei suae ablationem illatum*".

234 N. Jansen, *Theologie, Philosophie*, 97-100.

235 F. Balduin, *Tractatus*, 958; J. Olearius, *Doctrina theologiae moralis*, Tab. XXXVII De Justitia.

236 F. Balduin, *Tractatus*, 958; See also J. Olearius, *Doctrina theologiae moralis*, Tab. XXXVII De Justitia; J.A. Osiander, *Theologiae casualis*, vol. 3 and 4, 32.

of grace made by the creditor nullifies the obligation of restitution. Finally, the third case concerns the debtor in extreme necessity, if the creditor is not poor. As we are going to see better in the next chapter, in case of loans or annuities, the debtor fallen in extreme poverty is not obliged to restitution.[237] Apart from these main exceptions, the theologians followed a rigid path. We see this in the analysis of two particular issues: the possibility to convert the duty of restitution in almsgiving and the possibility to escape restitution in case of damages for the debtor.

1.3.3.3 Almsgiving in Place of Restitution

Restitution of the stolen things cannot be substituted with other practices, such as almsgiving. The practice of giving alms in place of restitution belonged to a group of Greek schismatics and had been described by the Roman Catholic canon lawyer and philosopher Guido Terrena (1270-1342). The early modern scholastics cited this author to discuss and criticize this opinion. Indeed, Friedrich Balduin takes it from Leonard Lessius.[238] To support their view, the Greeks used the passage of Luke 11,39-41:

> *and the Lord said unto him, Now do ye Pharisees make clean the outside of the cup and the platter; but your inward part is full of ravening and wickedness. Ye fools, did not he that made that which is without make that which is within also? But rather give alms of such things as ye have; and, behold, all things are clean unto you.*

The words '*But rather give alms of such things as ye have*' were intended as an invitation to the use of alms for repairing sins.

Balduin replies that it is not Christ's intention that alms seek to compensate robberies and unjust fraud. Christ only commands almsgiving in place of the robberies because, as a sign of true repentance, it will purify what is impure. It is better to give than to receive. But he who believes that satisfaction for his robberies can only come through alms is very much mistaken and is entangled in his sins much more.[239] He who still keeps the goods, even if he gives alms,

237 F. Balduin, *Tractatus*, 944-5.

238 L. Lessius, *De iustitia et iure*, lib. 2, cap. 7, dub. 10, 73-4.

239 F. Balduin, *Tractatus*, 956: "*Sed haec non est mens Christi, quod duntaxat eleemosyna rapine et fraudes hominum iniquorum compensari queant; sed tantum dare iubet eleemosynam, loco rapinarum, quod quia signum est verae poenitentiae, facile mundabit id, quod in patinis et calicibus vestris immundum videbatur: melius enim est dare quam accipere. Qui autem putant, se pro rapinis suis satisfacere posse eleemosynis, vehementer falluntur, et peccatis magis magisque implicantur*".

does not want to repent. It is not a true repentance but hypocrisy, Balduin concludes.[240]

Almsgiving is admitted, though, if the beneficiary of restitution is no longer alive and has no heirs. God indeed is considered to be the beneficiary of restitution through almsgiving. But the amount of money must be the same value as the stolen things. In other words, it is not requested a symbolic donation to the poor, but a real restitution.[241]

The discussion over the role of almsgiving is an example that shows the stability of the doctrine of restitution among the Lutheran theologians. Behind the polemics with the Greeks, indeed, there is a strong intention to reaffirm the centrality of restitution for the remission of sins. Alms alone are not sufficient; remission of sin can only occur with restitution.

1.3.3.4 Restitution in the Event of Damages to the Debtor and His Family

One of the most intricate cases recorded on this topic regarded whether it was necessary to perform restitution, when the act of restitution might create powerful damages or losses for the debtor and his family. This question looks the dramatic effects of restitution. Restitution moves wealth: it can impoverish one family and enrich another one. These dramatic effects had led some of the Roman Catholic theologians to claim that the debtor is not obliged to restitution when this caused remarkable damages to him or his family or to his reputation and honor. As Osiander reports, John Duns Scotus (1266-1308), Giovanni Cagnazzo (d. 1521), Battista Trovamala (-), Sylvester Mazzolini (1456/57-1527) and other Roman Catholic authors followed this opinion.[242]

Osiander deems that conscience is the most important aspect to safeguard and contends that notwithstanding the damages, the family should proceed with restitution regardless.[243] He justifies this opinion by referring to the Holy Scripture and the Church Fathers. In Matt. 19,8, Zacchaeus decided to donate to the poor half of his goods and return four times the amount to the people he defrauded, even though he suffered remarkable losses and damage to his

240 F. Balduin, *Tractatus*, 956.

241 F. Balduin, *Tractatus*, 959-960.

242 The account is given by Osiander. J.A. Osiander, *Theologiae casualis*, vol. 3 and 4, 35. For an analysis of the debate see W. Decock, *Law, Religion and Debt Relief*, passim.

243 J.A. Osiander, *Theologiae casualis*, vol. 3 and 4, 34: "*Nos existimamus, utut iactura familiae videatur obstare, utut discrimen aliquod famae et existimationis, teneri tamen, qui laesit, ad restitutionem, nec conscientiam tutam et serenam esse, nisi fiat compensatio, exoneretur id, quod iniuste receptum*".

honour and reputation, Osiander comments.[244] John Chrysostom observed that Zacchaeus' riches were not only unjustly gained, but also accumulated in a patrimony, because he could not return four times the amount of the fraud without adding something from his personal patrimony. Furthermore, Theodoret of Cyrus (393-457) noticed that Zacchaeus would probably have lost all of his riches in this operation, because he gave one half to the poor and four times to the people defrauded. Zacchaeus actually did so, Theodoret stressed, because in the Gospel it is not written that *he will do it*, but *he does*. The text of the Scripture and the comment of the Fathers seem therefore to be univocal. Osiander concludes that if Zacchaeus destroyed his riches to follow Christ, the Christian should do the same.[245]

To bolster the argument, Osiander adds a subtle evaluation. If we put on one side of a scale the damage for the family and the risk for the reputation, and on the other side, the quietness of conscience, certainly the purity of conscience must be more than everything, more than all riches, more than the vanishing splendour of any honour.[246] Osiander considers the weight of the riches and the weight of a pure conscience, the weight of temporal goods versus the weight of spiritual goods. It is patently clear that it is more important to have a pure conscience than to be rich.

Osiander also discusses a different solution that circulated among the early modern scholastics.[247] This solution rested on the distinction between superior goods like honour and reputation, and inferior, temporal goods. The temporal goods could not be returned if this produced an offence to the superior goods (*res superioris ordinis*). Thomas de Vio (*Cajetan*) was strongly in favour of this option,[248] while other theologians held that the debtor is obliged to return the inferior goods, even though this can produce damage to the superior

---

244 J.A. Osiander, *Theologiae casualis*, vol. 3 and 4, 34: "*Nam* primo *cum notabili etiam damno rerum suarum et citra attentionem ad famae et honoris periculum, Zachaeus id praestit, de quo Lucae 19, v. 8*".

245 J.A. Osiander, *Theologiae casualis*, vol. 3 and 4, 35.

246 J.A. Osiander, *Theologiae casualis*, vol. 3 and 4, 35: "Tertio *ponamus in libram damnum familiae, discrimen famae et conscientiae tranquillitatem; conferamus haec duo inter se: sane pluris unicuique esse debet conscientiae puritas, quam omne pondus opum, omnis honoris evanidi splendor*".

247 For this solution see W. Decock, *Law, Religion and Debt Relief*, passim.

248 J.A. Osiander, *Theologiae casualis*, vol. 3 and 4, 36: "Tertio *observamus disputari inter pontificios de restitutione rerum inferioris ordinis, cum detrimento proprio in rebus superioris, diffidentibus inter se circa hoc punctum* Cajetano, *qui absolute hoc negat*". Cajetanus, *In secundam secundae sanctissimi, ac preclarissimi doctoris Thome Aquinatis (...) commentaria*, 1519, quaest. 63, art. 2.

goods.[249] Some theologians said that it is never licit to postpone restitution, save the case of extreme necessity. Others argued that, except in the case of the creditor suffering great damage because of denied restitution, the debtor is not obliged to make restitution immediately, but he can wait until a favourable moment. Osiander doubts that this solution would be valid in the court of conscience, but does not formulate a complete counter-argument. Rather, he refers to the Reformed theologian Gisbert Voetius.[250]

Friedrich Balduin also looked at the scholastic opinion that the *res inferioris ordinis* should not be returned with damage to the *res superioris ordinis*.[251] Nevertheless, he only admitted the possibility of not returning the goods in exceptional cases. First, restitution can be avoided in case of spontaneous (not obtained by fraud or duress) remission of debt, because in this way the goods are donated to the debtor.[252] Second, restitution is not needed in case of ignorance of fact (*ignorantia facti*) or ignorance of the law (*ignorantia iuris*). The ignorance of fact occurs when the debtor does not know that the goods belongs to others because he received them in good faith, as for example in a donation, inheritance or sale.[253] The ignorance of the law concerns, instead, the cases when the debtor is ignorant that the contract that allows him to possess the goods is unlawful, as for example when the contract is affected by usury.[254] Third, if restitution inflicts harm on the body or soul of the creditor, debtor, or others.[255] Following a principle that harks back to Cicero,[256] Balduin explains that this can happen for weapons, which must not be returned to insane men or to possible thieves. Christians are not obliged to return money, if they know for sure that it will be used for evil purposes, such as corruption.

---

249 J.A. Osiander, *Theologiae casualis*, vol. 3 and 4, 36: "… *aliis vero affirmantibus, quod scilicet teneatur quis restituere res inferioris ordinis, cum detrimento in rebus superioribus, sive superioris ordinis*".

250 J.A. Osiander, *Theologiae casualis*, vol. 3 and 4, 36. See G. Voetius, *Selectarum disputationum theologicarum pars quarta*, Amstelodami, 1667, 608-31.

251 F. Balduin, *Tractatus*, 958.

252 F. Balduin, *Tractatus*, 958: "*Verum haec locum habere possunt in certis tantum casibus, ut* (*1*) *cum creditor debitori sciens ac volens, non vi aut metu coactus, non dolo aut fraude circumventus, sed sponte debitum remittit, tunc enim amittit ratione debiti et sit donatio*".

253 F. Balduin, *Tractatus*, 958: "Ignorantia facti *ut cum ignorat debitor, rem esse alienam, quia bona fide eam accepit inter bona haereditaria a patre, vel bonae fide emit, vel accepit donatam ab alio*".

254 F. Balduin, *Tractatus*, 958.

255 F. Balduin, *Tractatus*, 958-9: "(*3*) *cum restitutio vergit in damnum animae aut corporis creditoris, vel debitoris, aut alterius tertii*".

256 See before II/3.5.2.3.

They can, however, postpone restitution or lend to a friend of the creditor or the heir.[257]

In short, restitution is grounded on a precept of Scripture. And Scripture requires obedience. Conscience is of primary importance, and it can only be clean following restitution. Regardless of whether this damages the debtor, both Osiander and Balduin conclude that restitution must be performed. Osiander shows an intransigent attitude and firmly rejects granting the debtor the possibility of not making restitution. Balduin consents that the debtor can be free from the obligation of restitution, referring to more general arguments, such as remission of debt, ignorance, and damage to the creditor or third parties.

1.3.3.5 The *laesio enormis*

As said before, a passage of Justinian's code forbade the seller to recover the just price if the violation was less than a half of the just price.[258] The so-called *laesio enormis*, the transgression surpassing half of the value, became very popular with the canonists and the civilians during the Middle Ages, but it did not find acceptance among the theologians. In the court of conscience every single violation could obtain satisfaction and not only that which was beyond the moiety (*laesio ultra dimidium*). Equality must be preserved in the *forum internum*, and every breach of equality is a sin that entails restitution.[259]

The Lutheran theologians followed closely the scholastic model. Chemnitz differentiates the Roman law from the court of conscience: the civil laws only rescind the deceiving that are beyond the half of the just price, but in the *foro conscientiae* the rule of 1 Thess. 4,6 and Matt. 7,12 must be observed. Diocletian, the author of the Roman law constitution on the *laesio enormis*, must not govern consciences.[260] Chemnitz puts the stress on the different legal orders: the Scripture regulates conscience, while the Roman emperors provided laws for the external courts. For this reason, the *laesio enormis* cannot be applied in the court of conscience.

The assumption of two different regulations and the necessity of restitution even in case of a small violation is also frequent in other theologians. For instance, Uffelmann states with very clear words:

---

257 F. Balduin, *Tractatus*, 959.

258 C. 4,44,2.

259 W. Decock, *Theologians and Contract Law*, 532-4.

260 M. Chemnitz, *Loci theologici*, pars secunda, 158: "*Leges civiles tantum illas circumscriptiones rescindunt, quae dimidietatem justi pretii excedunt: sed in foro conscientiae servanda est regula Pauli, 1 Thess. 4, 6. Item quicquid volueritis, ut faciant vobis homines, Matth. 7, 12. Diocletianus enim, qui constitutionis illius auctor fuit, conscientias non debet gubernare*".

> *although the civil law permits deceits within the boundaries of the half of the just price, in the* foro conscientiae *every deceit is forbidden, and so even he who slightly defrauds the neighbour commits a sin and must compensate the damage.*[261]

Similarly, Horneius writes that everyone who defrauds the neighbour for less than a half of the just price (*intra dimidium iustii pretii*) is not obliged to compensate in *foro exteriori*. Yet, he commits a sin in *foro conscientiae* and must compensate the damage.[262] To justify this statement, he harks back to Thomas Aquinas's *Summa theologiae*: the civil law is given to all people, among whom there are many lacking virtue, and it is not given to the virtuous alone. Hence, human law was unable to forbid all that is contrary to virtue, and it suffices for it to prohibit whatever is destructive of the human intercourse, while treating other matters as though they were lawful, not by approving of them, but by not punishing them. The divine law and natural law forbid what is against virtue and nothing is left unpunished. Therefore, every breach of the just price is opposed to divine law and natural law but not to civil law.[263] The violation, Horneius points out, must be made consciously and intentionally, because if the seller was not aware of it he is excused and must not return the amount gained.[264]

Osiander first proves the necessity of restitution and then looks at the different rationales of the civil law and the court of conscience. 1 Thess. 4,6 forbids defrauding the neighbour, because in a sale equality must be observed. Yet, equality is not observed if the price is not equal to the sold thing and either exceeds it or is inadequate.[265] Augustine, in his *De Trinitate*, writes that malicious men believe that acquiring at a good price and selling at a dear price is a common practice. Since it is a vice, however, everyone can resist this inclination by acquiring the sense of justice.[266] Equality is therefore required in sale,

261 H. Uffelmann, *Variorium*, 130: "*Quamvis verò ius civile permittat deceptionem infra dimidium iusti precii, in foro tamen conscientiae omnis omnino deceptio penitus est prohibita, adeò ut et qui leviter defraudat proximum peccet, atque ad restituendum damnum teneatur*".

262 C. Horneius, *Compendium theologiae*, 768: "*Licet qui defraudat proximum intra dimidium iusti pretii in foro exteriori ad restituendum damnum non teneatur; in foro tamen conscientiae peccat et compensare damnum debet*".

263 T. Aquinas, *Summa theologiae*, IIaIIae, q. 77, a. 1, concl. 1.

264 C. Horneius, *Compendium theologiae*, 768.

265 J.A. Osiander, *Observationes*, 929-30: "*Probamus autem illam restitutionem tum ex aperto textu I. ad Thessalon. IV. v.6, ubi Paulus diserte*: Ne quis supergrediatur, neque circumveniat in negotio fratrem suum, quoniam vindex est Dominus de his omnibus; *tum ex ratione, quia in emtione et venditione debet servari aequalitas: non autem illa servatur, si pretium non sit aequale rei venditae, sed excedat vel deficiat*".

266 Augustinus Hipponensis, *De trinitate*, Lib. XIII, cap. III.

but in the civil law restitution is not always due in order to avoid innumerable controversies; but this is not a valid excuse to avoid restitution in conscience.[267]

On the same pattern of the scholastic theologians, the Lutherans remarked the difference between the *forum internum* and the *forum externum*. Conscience is governed by the precepts of Scripture and demands restitution even of small quantities. On the other hand, the *laesio enormis*, the remedy granted in the tribunals, only applies to infractions surpassing half of the just price. Conscience and earthly tribunals remain two different jurisdictions, governed by different norms. Conscience is sensible to even tiny offences and requires meticulous attention, while the civil law has to take into account other factors, like the necessity to avoid an excessive number of disputes.

1.4 Conclusion

In this chapter we examined sale, lease and restitution. The Lutheran theologians relied on the medieval elaboration of Roman law for the basic notions on sale and lease. Then they formulated general rules founded on Scripture. Concerning sale, the theologians required the seller to be the lawful proprietor the goods. Indeed, the seventh commandment of the Decalogue institutes private property and forbids theft. Another rule the theologians drew from Scripture is that goods must be diligently measured: Scripture outlaws false evaluations or calculations. Scripture also contains a general duty to inform about defects of goods, as an expression of the love for the neighbour. Some theologians admitted exceptions based on the scholastics' rational considerations and in particular on the virtue of justice. Others opted for a more rigid attitude to reveal every vice that conscience suggests, as Scripture does not enumerate exceptions. For example, Osiander corroborated the dictates of the Scripture with the contribution of the Church Fathers. Thus, he gained more precision on the Christians' duties and refused many of the scholastics' conjectures. He believed in a general duty to protect the neighbour, based on charity.

With regard to the ethics of price, the theologians followed the framework traced by the scholastics, and affirmed that the price of goods must be fixed by the market or the public authority. In case there is no price fixed, the merchants can negotiate the price, but conscience must drive them. Scripture manifestly condemns every fraudulent alteration of prices, but it does not offer solutions for practical cases. Misler adopted a pure Lutheran spirit and identified in conscience, the Holy Scripture and the magistrate the pillars for the

267 J.A. Osiander, *Observationes*, 930.

merchant's business activity. However, other theologians borrowed the results of the scholastic casuistry. Regarding monopolies, Luther condemned them, but the Lutheran theologians almost never addressed this issue. One author who did was Osiander, who refuted Grotius' position. Grotius first used the biblical example of Joseph to justify monopolies; then he asserted that private monopolies are only against charity and not against justice. For Osiander, as for Luther, this example cannot be invoked to permit monopolies. Moreover, every breach of justice is also a breach of charity, which cannot be condoned. Charity cannot be compromised.

The Lutheran regulation of leases substantially followed the scheme used for sales. Rules impede fraud on price; the defects of the thing must be declared, damages must be paid for the shameful use of it, and it must be returned at the end of the contract. Some theologians also considered a particular form of lease, the lease of the body or contract of prostitution. Meisner and Osiander both studied the opinions of the scholastic theologians. Meisner showed disappointment for that scholastic faction who allowed the prostitute to keep her wage. He firmly concluded that a sin has no price. On the other hand, Osiander limited his statements to an account of the scholastic opinion in favor of it.

Like the scholastics, the Lutheran theologians considered restitution to be necessary, as it represented the end of the offence. However, they did not ask the performance of acts of penance afterwards, as the scholastics did. For the Lutherans, God forgives the sins by the grace of the Holy Spirit and faith. It is by this faith that the Christian returns the stolen goods. Restitution is then the natural consequence of the conversion and does not require any following act of penance. The Lutheran theologians did not devote much time to a number of aspects that the scholastics examined in depth, like the reasons for restitution or the exact amount, fruit, damages, etc. They stated that restitution concerns an unjust acquisition of property, and it is applicable to a vast range of situations. It must be always performed, save a limited number of exceptions. In contrast to the opinion of some scholastic theologians, the reformers held that damages for the debtor or his family are not comprised among these exceptions. Restitution is an essential duty and cannot be easily avoided. It can be perfectly understood, then, that the Lutheran theologians did not admit the *laesio aenormis*. As for the scholastics, this is a Roman law remedy confined to the *foro externo*.

In conclusion, the Lutheran theologians mapped out a set of basic principles for the regulation of sales, leases and restitution in the light of Scripture. But they did not write more than a few words on the more concrete cases of conscience. The scholastics were much more productive in this respect. Some Lutherans simply built their logic of contract law following the scholastics. Others, instead, did criticize the scholastics, reaffirming the primacy of Scripture over rational justifications. In particular, they refused to separate the virtue of justice from the virtue of charity, as some scholastics and natural lawyers did. Every offence against charity cannot be tolerated, even if it does not breach justice. Thus, the different attitude towards the scholastics makes the Lutheran contract doctrine heterogeneous and open to multiple interpretations.

On one point, however, the Lutherans seemed to be consistent. They sought to free the scholastic teachings from the chains of the medieval vision of justice. They grounded their statements on the fundamental idea that man is justified by faith, without the efficacy of good works. They intended private confession as a general indication of sins without their enumeration. In this way the work of the priest was more focused on the principles than on the concrete circumstances. Hence, the Lutheran doctrines of sale, lease and restitution remain a complex of principles rooted in the words of Scripture, which are summarized in the love for the neighbour. These principles have their strength in the call to Christians' consciences. It is the conscience that, illuminated by the spirit of Scripture, has to look for more specific rules. The theologians set sales, leases and restitution on a path of faith where the revealing gaze of charity dominates and conscience is called to obedience.

CHAPTER 2

Lending and the Interest Prohibition

Today usury consists in lending money at excessive rate of interest. At the threshold of the sixteenth century, usury was the practice of lending at interest. Whatsoever interest in a loan, not only a high rate of interest, was prohibited. The interest prohibition originated in the tradition of the Roman Catholic Church but continued to be effective among the reformers. A number of financial contracts, which produced effects similar to loans at interest, satisfied the economic needs of society. Theologians and jurists were equally involved in the discussion on the compliance of these contracts with the interest prohibition. In this chapter we see the theoretical approach of the theologians and the formulation of a Lutheran theory of interest. The contribution of the jurists, the construction of a legal framework and the relation with the theologians are instead discussed in part IV.

2.0 Introduction

Nikolaus Selnecker, a student of Melanchthon and later a professor of theology in Leipzig, concluded the chapter on usury in his moral treatise *Paedagogia christiana* (1565) with a worried tone:

> *today, Germany is suffocated by this crime* [*usury*] *and other nations as well. It is to fear that this evil will eventually destroy Germany, although the whole world is laughing now when this is said.*

He compared his struggle with merchants to the conflict that allegedly rose between Luther and a rich merchant when Luther was condemning usury. The merchant mocked himself of Luther: "*what is this good man and theologian doing? He should rather have commanded me, a usurer, to pursue this business, since I know what usury is and what it effectuates*".[1] Selnecker was anxious about the consequences of the accepted and widespread practice of usury (charging

1 N. Selnecker, *Paedagogiae christianae*, 214: "*Hodie etiam Germania suffocata est hoc scelere, et aliae nationes. Et verendum est, ne hoc malum destruat tandem Germaniam, quamvis nunc omnis mundus rideat, quando talia dicuntur, sicut opulentus iste mercator dixerat, cum Lutherus de usuris scripsisset, quid facit bonus ille vir, et theologus, commendare debebat mihi hoc negocium, qui usuras exerceo, et scio quid sint, et quid efficiant*".

 | DOI:10.30965/9783657701506_009

interest) and noticed the arrogant reaction of merchants when this was reproached. The tension with the merchants was especially due to the diffusion of a new financial instrument, very similar to a loan at interest, and called 'the German contract' or 'the five per cent contract'. The German contract infringed upon the interest prohibition and Luther condemned this contract as usurious, triggering the gruelling protests of merchants and bankers.

The battle with merchants became more difficult when, in 1530, Holy Roman Emperor Charles V legalized the essential elements of this contract. The interest prohibition was the purview of theologians, but the emperor's ordinance – ruling that an instrument that practically produced the same effects of a loan at interest could be lawfully practiced- countered the religious authorities. Luther's disciples struggled with the decision to be idle or to take a stand: to condemn the German contract or to approve it; to refuse the secular law or to accept it. How was one to reconcile the interest prohibition with the new law of finance? The answer was radical: the theologians replaced the old medieval theory of interest with a new theory of interest. They argued that not every loan at interest is forbidden. Only if charity towards the neighbour is offended, does a loan at interest go against the interest prohibition. They did not prohibit every loan at interest in general, as did their Catholic colleagues, but left to the individual Christian to choose whether a contract is against charity and thus a violation of the interest prohibition.

The Roman Catholic Church, as a legal and political body, imposed the prohibition against interest by means of a number of canon law norms. These legal norms pertained to the Christian society and punished sins against the virtue of justice. Justice teaches that nobody can take the property of another against his will. The usurer forces the borrower to pay interest and in this way he robs his goods. Usury was considered a form of robbery, because the borrower is forced to pay something to the lender because of the former's need for money. Justice does not distinguish between poor and rich; robbery is an evil act regardless of the people involved. The Christian who breaches the law must pay the price of his sin and return the stolen goods and the damage. The prohibition was justified by references to Scripture: especially Psalm 15,5 and Luke 6,35: the injunction to lend hoping for nothing in return (*mutuum date nihil inde sperantes*). Nevertheless, rational arguments were more often used, for example that the usurer sells the time that belongs to God or the Aristotelian conception of the sterility of money.

The Lutheran theologians claimed that the interest prohibition is only formulated in the Scriptures, next to which canon law norms and rational arguments, if mentioned, assume a subsidiary position. The prohibition concerned the Christian community and was embedded in a set of biblical rules, most of all Luke 6,35. This passage received a new interpretation, however: it does not forbid every loan at interest, but only those loans that harm the neighbour. The interest prohibition thus merely concerns loans against charity towards the neighbour and not every loan at interest. Usury therefore is a sin against charity. The prohibition is a precept of the Gospel and not a legal norm. The legal norm for the Christian society becomes then a precept of charity for the community of believers. The magistrate can issue laws about usury, interest and financial contracts but they must comply with the rule of charity and must be applied through the rule of charity.

Christians are responsible with their own conscience to make sure that charity is observed. They have to protect the other contracting party from damages, meet his needs and assist in case of necessity. This is a personal judgment that concerns the detailed circumstances of every agreement. Charity is not incorporated in any legal norm, but it implies the mitigation of law under particular circumstances. Aware of the need to act in accordance with charity, Christians must decide for themselves whether to apply the law, whether to execute a certain financial operation or whether to enact a specific contractual term on the basis of charity. It is not a matter of asking dispensation from the priests. When there is an apparent conflict between the law and charity, Christians must look inward and rely on their own conscience to make a decision. In this way charity acts as a form of equity, mitigating the strict law.

2.1 Requisites for a Revolution

2.1.1 *Introduction*

The development of a Lutheran theory of interest arises from two linked issues: the rigidity of medieval prohibition against interest and the vast diffusion of the German contract. Canonists and scholastic theologians forged a severe doctrine according to which every loan at interest is forbidden. The German contract, however, was a financial operation quite similar to a loan. The contrast between the prohibition and the new agreement produced the sparks for the renewal of the theory of interest. The Lutheran theologians will be summoned to examine the problem and give an answer. Before dealing with their writings, however, we need to summarize the essential characteristics of the medieval interest prohibition and the German contract.

2.1.2 *Scholastic Theologians and Canonists on the Prohibition Against Interest*

2.1.2.1 Roman Law and Canon Law

In Roman law, the loan for consumption (*mutuum*) was defined as a real contract by which the ownership of things that can be measured, numbered, and weighed is transferred to a borrower. The borrower must return the things to the lender after a certain time, not the very things, but things of the same kind, quantity, and quality.[2] The loan was not gratuitous, but a payment beyond the principal, what we today call 'interest', was admitted. The term '*usura*' or '*foenus*' designated this interest. The term '*interesse*' did not have the same meaning as today, but it was the compensation the creditor should receive because of the damage he suffered in a loan.[3]

In the Roman republic, the interest rate was established in 1% monthly and 12% yearly on the principal (*centesima usura* or also *foenus unciarum*), and for the sea loan (*foenus nauticum*) an even higher interest was admitted.[4] The emperor Justinian (482-565), with the legislation *Eos qui* (C. 4,32,26) reduced the regular interest rate (*usura*) to 6%; it was set at 8% for merchants and bankers and 12% for sea loans (C. 4,32,26,2). Justinian's reform, (as we will see in IV), was very important for the Lutheran theologians: they looked to this law as an example of good legislation. Justinian was a Christian emperor and observed the provisions of the Council of Nicaea (325) that, referring to Psalm 15 (14), condemned the Roman law *usura centesima*.[5]

---

2 Gaius, Gai. III, 90; R. Zimmermann, *The Law of Obligations*, 153. On the loan for consumption in Roman law see: D. Daube, *Money and Justificiability*, in *Zeitschrift der Savigny Stiftung, rom. Abt.*, 96 (1979), 1-16; G. Diósdi, *Contract in Roman Law: From the Twelve Tables to the Glossators*, Trans. J. Szabó, Budapest, Akadémiai Kiado, 1981; E.A. Meyer, *Legitimacy and law in the Roman world: tabulae in Roman belief and practice*, Cambridge, Cambridge University press, 2004. For further references see R. Fiori, *Contracts, Commerce and Roman Society*, in P.J. Du Plessis, C. Ando and K. Tuori (eds.), *The Oxford Handbook of Roman Law and Society*, Oxford, Oxford University Press, 2016, 581-95.

3 J.T. Noonan, Jr., *The Scholastic Analysis of Usury*, 105.

4 O. Bazzichi, *Dall'usura al giusto profitto. L'etica economica della scuola francescana*, Cantalupa (Torino), Effatà editore, 2008, 19; H.J. Becker, *Das Zinsverbot im lateinischen Mittelalter*, in M. Casper, N. Oberhauer, F. Wittreck (eds.), *Was vom Wucher übrigbleibt. Zinsverbote im historischen und interkulturellen Vergleich*, Tübingen, Mohr Siebeck, 2014, 15-45 (18).

5 C.H. Turner, *Ecclesiae occidentalis monumenta iuris antiquissima*, 1, Oxford, 1899, 270: "*XVII De clericis usuras accipientibus. Quoniam multi sub regula constituti avaritiam et turpia lucra sectantur, oblitique divinae scripturae dicentis QUI PECUNIAM SUAM NON DEDIT AD VSVRAM mutuum dantes centesimas exigunt; iuste censuit sancta et magna synodus, ut si quis inventus fuerit post hanc definitionem usuras accipiens aut ex adinventio ne aliqua vel quolibet modo negotium transigens aut hemiola (id est sescupla) exigens vel aliquid tale prorsus excogitans turpis lucri gratia, deiciatur a clero et alienus exsistat a regula*". H. Siems, *Handel und*

The Council of Nicaea condemned clerics who profited from a loan, but a letter from Pope Leo I in the fifth century extended the prohibition against interest to lay people.[6] Both these decisions were reported in the *Decretum Gratiani*,[7] together with a provision of the Nynweger capitulary (806)[8] that gives the first definition of interest-taking (usury): "*when more is asked than is given*", then specified by Gratian: "*whatever is demanded beyond the principal*". In addition, the *Palea eiciens* (appended to the *Decretum*) formulated a strong attack against usurers.[9] The reason is that the usurer sells time, a good that

---

Wucher im Spiegel frühmittelalterlicher Rechtsquellen, Hahn, Hannover, 1992, 508; H.J. Becker, *Das Zinsverbot*, 18.

6 Bibliography on usury is boundless. We report here a short selection. B.N. Nelson, *The Idea of Usury*, passim; G. Le Bras, *Usure* in *Dictionnaire de théologie catholique*, XV, 2, Paris 1950, 2336-72; J.T. Noonan, Jr., *The Scholastic Analysis of Usury*, passim; R. de Roover, *Scholastic Economics: Survival and Lasting Influence from the Sixteenth Century to Adam Smith*, in *The Quarterly Journal of Economics*, vol. 69, n. 2 (May, 1955), 161-90, also in J. Kirschner (ed.), *Business, Banking, and Economic Thought in Late Medieval and Early Modern Europe*, Chicago-London, Chicago University Press, 1974, 306-35; T.F. Divine, *Interest: an historical & analytical study in economics & modern ethics*, Milwaukee, The Marquette University Press, 1959; E. Bianchi, *In tema d'usura. Canoni conciliari e legislazione imperiale del IV secolo*, in *Athenaeum*, Jan 1, 61, 1983, 321-42; O. Langholm, *The Aristotelian Analysis of Usury*, Bergen, Oslo, Stavanger, Tromsø, Universitetsforlaget, 1984; A. Spicciani, *Capitale e interesse tra mercatura e povertà nei teologi e canonisti dei secoli XIII-XV*, Jouvence, Roma, 1990; O. Langholm, *Economics in the Medieval Schools*, passim; H. Siems, *Handel und Wucher*, passim; O. Langholm, *The Legacy of Scholasticism*, passim; G. Andenna, *Riflessioni canonistiche in materia economica dal XII al XV secolo*, in Università Cattolica del Sacro Cuore, *Chiesa, usura e debito estero. Giornata di studio in occasione del Cinquantennio della Facoltà di Economia (Milano 19 dicembre 1997)*, Milano, Vita e Pensiero, 1998, 21-42; J. Lockwood O' Donovan, *The Theological Economics of Medieval Usury Theory*, in *Studies in Christian Ethics*, vol.14 (1), 2001, 48-64; G. Todeschini, *I mercanti ed il tempio. La società cristiana e il circolo virtuoso della ricchezza fra Medioevo ed Età Moderna*, Il Mulino, Bologna, 2002; D. Wood, *Medieval Economic Thought*, Cambridge, Cambridge University Press, 2002; F. Wittreck, *Geld als Instrument der Gerechtigkeit. Die Geldrechtslehre des Hl. Thomas von Aquin in ihrem interkulturellen Kontext*, Paderborn, München, Wien, Zürich, Ferdinand Schöningh, 2002; C. Gamba, *Licita usura. Giuristi e moralisti tra medioevo ed età moderna*, Viella, 2004; P. Vismara, *Oltre l'usura: la Chiesa moderna e il prestito a interesse*, Soveria Mannelli, Rubbettino, 2004; G. Todeschini, *La riflessione etica sulle attività economiche*, in E. Greci (ed.), *Economie urbane ed etica economica nell'Italia medievale*, Roma-Bari, Laterza, 2005, 151-228; D. Quaglioni, G. Todeschini, G. M. Varanini (eds.), *Credito e usura fra teologia, diritto e amministrazione. Linguaggi a confronto (sec. XII-XVI)*. Convegno internazionale a Trento, 3-5 settembre 2001, Roma, Ecole Française de Rome, 2005; C.R. Geisst, *Beggar Thy Neighbor, A History of Usury and Debt*, Philadelphia, University of Pennsylvania Press, 2013; H.J. Becker, *Das Zinsverbot*, 15-45.

7 C. 14, q. 4, c. 7 and C. 14, q. 4, c. 8.

8 H. Siems, *Handel und Wucher*, 738-46.

9 The attack was erroneously attributed to John Chrysostom. See also II/2.1.3.

belongs only to God. This argument was based on the Stoic-Platonic tradition and assumed a damage produced by the usurer in the stealing of a good that belongs to God and is shared by all creatures.[10]

The canon law ordered that nothing can be demanded over the principal and loans must be gratuitous. During the years of the papal monarchy, many other canons were issued, and some of them were gathered in the *Liber extra*. Canon 13 of *Porro detestabilem* from the 1139 Second Lateran Council declares that usury is forbidden both by the Old Testament and the New Testament, although it does not quote any particular passage. Similarly, in a passage from the Synod of Tours (1163), Pope Alexander III condemns as usurious the credit sale at a price higher than the cash price (X 5,19,6). Then, the canon 25 of the Third Lateran Council (1179) declares that the manifest usurers (*usuraii manifesti*) are forbidden to receive the sacraments, even Christian burial (X 5,19,3). Finally, the decretal *Consuluit* of Pope Urban III (1185-1187) interpreted the passage of Luke 6,35 as interest prohibition (X 5,19,10).[11] With the canon law norms, the popes assured that in the whole Christian society usury (lending at interest) was forbidden.

The canon law prohibited receiving any profit from a loan, while the Roman law admitted it. Nevertheless, the interpretation of the canonists and legists considered the prohibition against interest to be valid also for the Roman law. An opinion circulated among canonists, such as Huguccio, that the Novella of Justinian contained a provision that the laws do not disdain to imitate the canons. The law in favor of interest-taking would be therefore abrogated by this provision, giving preference to the canons.[12] Other canonists, Hostiensis among them, recognised that the Roman law admitted the charging of interest, but observed that the acceptance of the Council of Nicaea implied the change of any laws contrary to these canons. Furthermore, the canon law must prevail over the Roman law in a question of sins.[13] On this line, legists like Azzo, Cinus and Bartolus maintained that the Roman law could not admit what the divine law forbade.[14] The Roman law's permission of interest could have no force, because it was against divine law. The canon law prohibition of interest became therefore universal: loans must be gratuitous both for Roman law and canon

10 J.T. Noonan, Jr., *The Scholastic Analysis of Usury*, 38-44; J. Lockwood O' Donovan, *The Theological Economics of Medieval Usury Theory*, 52-3; H.J. Becker, *Das Zinsverbot*, 21-2.

11 J.T. Noonan, Jr., *The Scholastic Analysis of Usury*, 18-20; H.J. Becker, *Das Zinsverbot*, 22-5.

12 T.P. McLaughlin, *The Teaching of the Canonists on Usury*, in *Medieval Studies* 1 (1939), 81-147 (84).

13 T.P. McLaughlin, *The Teaching of the Canonists*, 86.

14 T.P. McLaughlin, *The Teaching of the Canonists*, 88-90.

law. Canonists and legists interpreted the interest prohibition as a matter of divine law that cannot be violated by any subordinate law.

2.1.2.2 A Sin Against Justice and a Breach of Natural Law

The canon law prohibition against interest sought to prevent a sin against the virtue of justice. The scholastic theologians conceived of interest-taking (usury) as an invasion of the right to private property and a sin against the virtue of justice, treated under the seventh commandment of the Decalogue and based only on the intention to gain profit from a loan.[15] In the Carolingian period, usury was a form of avarice or uncharitableness, but Anselm of Canterbury, Hugh of St. Victor (1096-1141), Peter Comestor (d. 1178), and Peter Lombard defined usury on a par with robbery and a sin against justice.[16] Usury was considered to be an invasion of the right of property, because the borrower does not pay interest freely but is forced.[17] Thomas Aquinas maintained that the borrower pays interest because he is forced by a certain necessity. The need pushes the borrower to accept a loan under the condition that he returns more than what he received.[18] Such a constriction expropriated the borrower's property unjustly. As a consequence, the usurer was excommunicated and must return the damage or the loss.[19] Only in this way, could he pay the price of his sin and obtain absolution. Usury put the soul at great danger:[20] the medieval theory of atonement required the punishment for the sins in order to obtain salvation. The usurer was a robber and must return the robbed goods to be forgiven.

The prohibition against interest was based upon a number of sources: the Bible, councils, and Church fathers. As Noonan writes, the Holy Scripture was not the most important source, which rather was the tradition of the Church: the councils and Church fathers.[21] Two of the preferred scriptural passages quoted were Psalm 15,5 and Luke 6,35.[22] Psalm 15,5 affirms "*he that putteth not out his money to usury, nor taketh a bribe against the innocent*". It was used by the Church fathers when they dealt with the problem of usury and then by the Council of Nicaea.[23] Luke 6,35: "*lend, hoping for nothing in return*", was

15 J.T. Noonan, Jr., *The Scholastic Analysis of Usury*, 32-3.
16 J.T. Noonan, Jr., *The Scholastic Analysis of Usury*, 17.
17 O. Langholm, *The legacy of scholasticism*, 59-62. The similarity between usury and robbery has biblical roots (Ez. 18, 5-13) but the argument developed through appeal to natural reason.
18 O. Langholm, *The legacy of scholasticism*, 63-4.
19 J.T. Noonan, Jr., *The Scholastic Analysis of Usury*, 30.
20 See J. Le Goff, *La bourse et la vie. Économie et religion au Moyen Age*, Paris, Hachette, 1986.
21 J.T. Noonan, Jr., *The Scholastic Analysis of Usury*, 11.
22 F. Wittreck, *Geld als Instrument der Gerechtigkeit*, 120.
23 E. Bianchi, *In tema d'usura*, 323.

authoritatively interpreted by Pope Urbanus III (1120-1187) in the decretal *Consuluit* as a general interest prohibition. This passage assumed a relevant place in the debate on interest-taking, even though other interpretations were proposed.[24] To these sources we can add Exodus 22,25; Leviticus 25,35-37; Deuteronomy 15,7-10; Amos 8,5-6; and Ezekiel 18,8, which were quoted by the Synod of Paris in 829.[25]

Beyond the Scriptures, the foundation of the prohibition against interest laid out a number of natural law arguments. Together with the idea of the sale of time, the scholastics elaborated other arguments based on Roman law and Aristotelian philosophy. In a loan for consumption (*mutuum*), what is mine becomes yours, and you cannot pay for what it is yours.[26] Interest is an unnatural use of money, because money cannot breed. According to its nature, money is sterile.[27] The substance of money is to be consumed in use. It has no use separate from its substance. The usurer sells the use of money and its substance separately; therefore, either he sells two times the same thing, or he sells something that does not exist.[28]

The scholastics considered usury (lending at interest) as a sin against justice and breach of natural law, which was considered to be, in Thomistic terms, the law of reason. This construction perdured in the Middle Ages and in the early Modern era, because the Spanish scholastics did not change the main arguments, even though they brought some modifications.[29] Scripture was not at the first place, because the scholastics began their reasoning from different sources, both philosophical reflections and Scripture.[30]

---

24 For example, Pier Giovanni Olivi (1248-1298) maintained that Christ in this passage is not making a general prohibition against profit in loans, but he only indicates the road of absolute perfection: giving without the hope to receive something back. See G. Andenna, *Riflessioni canonistiche in materia economica dal XII al XV secolo*, 35.

25 J.T. Noonan, Jr., *The Scholastic Analysis of Usury*, 16.

26 J.T. Noonan, Jr., *The Scholastic Analysis of Usury*, 39-44.

27 O. Langholm, *The Aristotelian Analysis of Usury*, 54-69.

28 J.T. Noonan, Jr., *The Scholastic Analysis of Usury*, 51-7; O. Langholm, *The Aristotelian Analysis of Usury*, 70-90.

29 C. Gamba, *Licita usura*, 250-5, 266-9; F. Monsalve, *Late Spanish Doctors on Usury, and the Evolving Scholastic Tradition*, in *Journal of the History of Economic Thought*, vol. 36, n. 2, 2014, 215-35. On the early modern scholastic thought, see F. Gómez Camacho, *Economia y filosofia moral*, passim; A. Del Vigo Gutiérrez, *Economia y ética*, passim; A. Azevedo Alves, J. M. Moreira, *The Salamanca School*, New York, Continuum, 2010.

30 J. Porter, *Natural and Divine Law. Reclaiming the Tradition for Christian Ethics*, Grand Rapids, MI., Cambridge, U.K., W.B. Eerdmans, 1999, 140.

2.1.3 *The German Contract: A Formidable Weapon for Bankers and Merchants*

2.1.3.1 Introduction

In the first decades of the sixteenth century, Germany experienced an increase of profits from commerce and finance and a decrease or stability of profit or wages from agriculture and farming. The declining per capita resources and consistent inequality led to the Peasants' War of 1524-25.[31] In this context, a sophisticated financial instrument that guaranteed returns of 5% of the invested sum was disseminated, especially among bankers and merchants. The investor lent capital to the entrepreneur to use for business, with a clause that guaranteed the return after a certain time of the principal and a fixed percentage of the profits the entrepreneur gained.[32] This agreement was denominated 'the five percent contract' or 'the German contract' (*contractus germanicus*).

The nature of this contract was widely discussed among canonists, theologians and jurists. They tried to classify it through the structure of two medieval financial contracts: partnership and *census*. In addition to the issue of classification, the German contract was incredibly similar to a loan, triggering fierce disputes on its lawfulness. We first examine the medieval constructions, the two legal qualifications of the German contract, and finally the moral problems.

2.1.3.2 Antecedents: Partnership and *census*

By way of exceptions to the interest prohibition, and in order to allow circulating capital, a number of financial contracts flourished from the twelfth century on.[33] These contracts produced similar effects to a loan, but were constructed in alternative way, so that the interest prohibition was circumvented. Included among these were the partnership and the *census* contract. The partnership (*societas*) followed the Roman law model and indicated an agreement between people for making profit. The scholastics pointed out that merchants practiced the contract and that the investor and the entrepreneur must share the risk. The risk sharing (*ius fraternitatis*) between the parties constituted an essential element of this contract and distinguished it from a loan. Under this condition, the partnership was accepted without stifling discussions.[34]

---

31 M. Luther, *On Commerce and Usury*, ed. with introduction and notes by Philipp Robinson Rössner, 49.

32 I. Birocchi, *Tra elaborazioni nuove e dottrine tradizionali, Il contratto trino e la natura contractus*, in *Quaderni fiorentini*, 19, 243-322 (243-4).

33 M. Koyama, *Evading the 'Taint of Usury': The usury prohibition as a barrier to entry*, in *Explorations in Economic History*, 47 (2010), 420-42 (423-6).

34 J.T. Noonan, Jr., *The Scholastic Analysis of Usury*, 135-6. For a detailed analysis of this contract among the scholastic theologians see: L. Brunori, *Societas quid sit. La societé commerciale dans l'élaboration de la Seconde Scolastique*, Paris, Mare & Martin, 2015.

The practice of the *census* contract dates back to medieval feudal Europe.[35] The word *census* or phrase *redditus seu pensio*[36] was originally used to mean a performance based on the land (real fruits) that the land user must pay to the landlord. The economic expansion of the thirteenth century made it possible to create another type of *census*. The land user sold part of his income to someone else other than the landlord, in return for an amount of another income (*supercensus*).[37] This new *census* began to be considered as an independent wealth, which could be sold or donated. In this way, by selling the income of his land, the small land user like a farmer could obtain the capital he needed.[38]

The *census* contract was classified as a sale, where the buyer was the lender/investor and the seller was the borrower/entrepreneur. The buyer purchased the *census* (annuity from fruitful property) and in return he provided the seller with the necessary capital. As Noonan has classified, many types of *census* existed. The real *census* was based on real estate; the personal *census* was founded on the returns of the work of a slave or the debtor; or the census could be based on all the goods of the seller or similarly on tax revenues. The *census* could be associated with an annual fixed income, or the income could vary time to time. It could be for the life of the creditor or the debtor, perpetual or temporary.

35 F. Veraja, *Le origini della controversia teologica sul contratto di censo nel XIII secolo*, Roma, Edizioni di Storia e Letteratura, 1960, 6-7. On the *census* contract in general, see: B. Schnapper, *Les rentes au XVIe siècle. Histoire d'un instrument de crédit*, École pratique des hautes études – VIe section. Centre de recherches historiques. Affaires et gens d'affaires XII, Paris, S.E.V.P.E.N., 1957; R. Trifone, *Censi*, in *NssDI*, III, Torino, 1959, 91-98; B. Schnapper, *Les rentes chez les théologiens et les canonistes du XIIIe au XVIe siècle*, in E'tudes d'historie du droit canonique dédiées à Gabriel Le Bras, Paris, Sirey, 1965, 965-995; G.K. Schmelzeisen, *Zinsvertrag und Rentenkauf, Zeitschrift der Savigny-Stiftung für Rechtsgeschichte*, Germ. Abt. 95 (1978), 229-36; H.J. Gilomen, *Der Rentenkauf im Mittelalter* Habilitationsschrift, Universität Basel 1984; http://www.hist.uzh.ch/fachbereiche/mittelalter/emeriti/gilomen/publikationen/Rentenk.auf.pdf (accessed 05.01.2017); C. Montanari, *Rendita perpetua (diritto intermedio)*, in *Enc. Dir.*, XXXIX, Milano, 1988, 820-47; J.H. Munro, *The Medieval Origins of the Financial Revolution: Usury, Rentes, and Negotiability*, in *The International History Review*, 25, 3, 2003, 505-562; A. Landi, *Ad evitandas usuras. Ricerche sul contratto di censo nell'*Usus Modernus Pandectarum, Roma, Fondazione Sergio Mochi Onory, 2004; M. Leone, *The Theologian and the Contracts: Henry of Ghent and the emptio-venditio reddituum*, in *Recherches de Théologie et Philosophie Médiévales*, 75/1 (2008), 137-60; J.H. Munro, *Rentes and the European 'Financial Revolution'*, in G. Caprio (ed.), *Handbook of Key Global Financial Markets, Institutions and Infrastructure*, London, Waltham, San Diego, Elsevier, 2013, 235-49.

36 On the different denominations see F. Veraja, *Le origini*, 10. See also E. Cortese, *Intorno alla* causa impositionis *e a taluni aspetti privatistici delle finanze medievali*, in *Annali di storia del diritto*, Anno II (1958), 111-186 (155) reprint in I. Birocchi, U. Petronio, *Ennio Cortese, Scritti*, Spoleto, Centro italiano di studi sull'Alto Medioevo, I, 1999.

37 F. Veraja, *Le origini*, 7-8.

38 F. Veraja, *Le origini*, 8-9.

The *census* could be non-redeemable, or redeemable only at the option of the buyer or at the option of the seller, or it might be redeemable by either.[39]

The nature of the *census* contract was fiercely disputed among medieval canonists and theologians. If this contract had been classified as a loan, it would have been condemned as a usurious contract. Therefore, most of the theologians and canonists, among these also Pope Innocent IV, recognized that it was not a loan but a sale, a sale of the right to have an income from real properties.[40] Furthermore, in the fifteenth century, two papal bulls (Martin V – 1423 and Callixtus III – 1455) approved the real *census*.[41] In this way, the doors were opened wide for *census* contract to become one of the essential pillars of the German financial economy.[42]

2.1.3.3 Two Legal Qualifications

The German contract identifies a peculiar financial operation, but the legal qualification is twofold.[43] Jurists, canonists and theologians tried classifying the German contract through two of the already known financial contracts: partnership and *census*. Hence, the German contract received a double legal qualification: triple contract (*contractus trinus*) and mutually redeemable *census* (*census utrinque redimibilis*). The triple contract arose from the combination of a partnership (*societas*), an insurance (*assecuratio*), and a sale, while the other one exploited the *census* structure.

2.1.3.3.1 *The Triple Contract* (contractus trinus)

The scholastic theologian Conrad Summenhart discussed the German contract in his *Tractatus de contractibus* (1500). Summenhart was not the first, because a few years previously (1486), Angelo Carletti di Chivasso (1411-1495) classified

39 J.T. Noonan, Jr., *The Scholastic Analysis*, 159.

40 J.T. Noonan, Jr., *The Scholastic Analysis*, 160-9. See also B. Schnapper, *Les rentes chez les théologiens et les canonistes du XIIIe au XVIe siècle*, 965-95.

41 Extrav. Comm. 3.5.1; 3.5.2.

42 G. Schmoller, *Zur Geschichte der national-ökonomischen Ansichten in Deutschland während der Reformations-Periode*, in *Zeitschrift für die gesamte Staatswissenschaft / Journal of Institutional and Theoretical Economics*, 1 January 1860, vol.16 (3/4), 461-716 (557); M. Luther, *On Commerce and Usury*, ed. with introduction and notes by Philipp Robinson Rössner, 98-9.

43 E. Van Roey, *Le contractus germanicus ou les controverses sur le 5% au XVIe siecle en Allemagne*, in *Revue d'Histoire Ecclesiastique*, Jan. 1902 (39), 901-46 (945); J.T. Noonan Jr, *The Scholastic Analysis of Usury*, 240. A.J. Wilson, G. Kim, *Put-call parity, the triple contract and approaches to usury in medieval contracting*, in *Financial History Review*, 22 (2), 2015, 205-33. Wilson and Kim notice that the interest rate in the triple contract might not be 5 percent. For this reason they hold that the German contract is a special case of the triple contract.

the operation as the sum of two legal contracts: partnership and insurance. Summenhart classified the German contract as a partnership, because the parties agreed to make a profit. He investigated whether the clause stipulating that only one of the parties receives profits was admissible in a partnership. In this new agreement, the investor gets a fixed return, and the risk is supported only by the entrepreneur, but an essential element of partnership is that both of the parties have the same position and share profits and losses (*ius fraternitatis*). Being against the nature of partnership, this contract would constitute a loan and thus a usurious contract.[44] Summenhart solved the problem by observing that the *ius fraternitatis* is not broken if the risk is transferred to one of the parties, because they both have a share in the profits. The fact that the investor does not support the risk is not an essential element of a partnership, but it is an essential element of a loan. The parties can transfer natural elements of a contract to another contract.[45]

A few years later, Johannes Eck[46] classified the five per cent contract as the combination of three different contracts: a partnership (*societas*), an insurance (*assecuratio*), and a sale (*emptio-venditio*).[47] The partnership was the principal, but there was a sale, because the investor acquired a fixed part (5%) of the entrepreneur's profits, and there was a form of insurance because the repayment was guaranteed.[48] In this way, Eck avoided the contract being categorized as a loan, and consequently in fraud of the interest prohibition. The triple contract (*contractus trinus*), as this construction was called, was lawful, because the consent of the parties permitted changes to the natural elements of the contract that are not essential; thus the element of the sharing of profit and losses could be changed by the will of the parties.[49]

44 I. Birocchi, *Tra elaborazioni nuove e dottrine tradizionali*, 263.

45 I. Birocchi, *Tra elaborazioni nuove e dottrine tradizionali*, 266.

46 H.A. Oberman, *Werden und Wertung der Reformation. Vom Wegestreit zum Glaubenskampf*, Tübingen, Mohr, 1977, 161-200; J.P. Wurm, *Johannes Eck und der oberdeutsche Zinsstreit 1513-1515*, München, Aschendorff, 1997.

47 On the triple contract see: E. Van Roey, *Le contractus germanicus*, 901-46; J.P. Lévy, *Un palliatif à la prohibition de l'usure: le contractus trinus ou triplex*, in *Reue historique du droit* 63 (1939), 423-33; J.T. Noonan Jr, *The Scholastic Analysis of usury*, 202-29; I. Birocchi, *Tra elaborazioni nuove e dottrine tradizionali*, 243-322; W. Decock, *The Catholic Spirit of Capitalism? Contrasting Views on Profit-Making through Capital Investment in the Age of Reformations*, in W. Decock, J.J. Ballor, M. Germann and L. Waelkens (ed.), *Law and Religion*, 22-43; H.J. Becker, *Das Zinsverbot*, 38-9; A.J. Wilson, G. Kim, *Put-call parity, the triple contract*, 205-33; W. Decock, *In Defense of Commercial Capitalism: Lessius, Partnerships and the Contractus Trinus*, in B. Van Hofstraeten and W. Decock, *Companies and Company Law in Late Medieval and Early Modern Europe*, Leuven-Paris-Bristol, CT, Peeters, 2016, 55-90.

48 I. Birocchi, *Tra elaborazioni nuove e dottrine tradizionali*, 288.

49 W. Decock, *The Catholic Spirit of Capitalism?*, 23.

2.1.3.3.2 *The Mutually Redeemable Census* (*census utrinque redimibilis*)

Parallel to the triple contract, the German contract was analyzed as mutually redeemable personal *census*. This agreement presents some modifications of the original *census* contract. The buyer (lender/investor) bought the right to receive the 5% of the invested sum on annual basis. The seller (borrower/entrepreneur) could use the money for whatever business, because the contract was detached from a specific real estate. The buyer did not take part in the business of the seller and did not share profits and losses with him. The obligation of the seller was to pay a 5% annuity (*census*). The annuity could be redeemed either by the seller or the buyer. These two elements, the personal obligation and the mutual redeemability, represented an extension of the medieval theory of *census*.[50]

The triple contract and the mutually redeemable personal *census* were two substantially different classifications of the same financial operation. The qualification as a *census* contract probably was used to explain the agreement to people who were not merchants,[51] but also erased the criticism on the alteration of the partnership contract. Furthermore, the *census* scheme had the advantage of papal endorsement: the two papal bulls which officially accepted the real *census*. Perhaps it is for this reason, then, that based on these bulls[52] and despite the criticisms, the emperor Charles V at the Diet of Augsburg in 1530 issued an imperial police ordinance (*Reichspolizeiordnung*) where he permitted the substantial elements of the German contract. The emperor established that in the *widerkauffs gülten* – the redeemable *census* – the amount of the annuities must not exceed 5%. Moreover, he determined that the seller/borrower must always have the power to redeem the annuity.[53] The emperor did not formally recognize the German contract but set out two essential elements: the highest amount of annuity permitted is 5% of the invested sum, and the power to redeem the contract is in the hands of the borrower.

On the Catholic side, Pope Gregory XIII (1502-1585) condemned the mutually redeemable *census*; Pope Pius V (1504-1572), in the bull *Cum onus* in 1569, established that every census should have been constituted toward "*a fruitful, immobile good, specifically designated to pay the census returns*;" otherwise it would have been condemned as a usurious contract. No country received the bull, and only a few theologians defended it.[54] But it struck at the root of

50 J.T. Noonan Jr, *The Scholastic Analysis of Usury*, 230-1.
51 J.T. Noonan, Jr., *The Scholastic Analysis of Usury*, 238-9.
52 On the relation between the two papal bulls and the imperial ordinance see IV/1.3.3.
53 M. Weber, *Die Reichspolizeiordnungen von 1530, 1548 und 1577*, 156.
54 J.T. Noonan Jr., *The Scholastic Analysis of Usury*, 237.

the new financial operation, which was based on the non-specification of real estate. Sixtus V (1521-1590) with the bull *Detestabilis avaritia* (1586) judged the triple contract in violation of the interest prohibition. Yet, the Catholic theologians continued to debate the lawfulness of this agreement during the seventeenth century.[55]

2.1.3.4 The Approach of the Lutheran Theologians

Due to its extensive popularity and the problems connected to the breach of the interest prohibition, the German contract attracted the attention of the Lutheran theologians. Unfortunately, they often did not formulate detailed definitions, which makes it very difficult to understand precisely to which contract they refer in their writings. The theologians used varying language: buying of annuity (*Zinskauf*), buying of annuities (*emtio redituum*), redeemable annuity (*widerkaufflicher, widerkäufflicher or widerkeufflicher Zins*), contract with a clause of annual income (*contractus cum pactione pensionis annuae*), and the five per cent partnership (*Contract der geselschafft fünffe vom hundert*).[56] All these terms seem to refer to the German contract, but the theologians almost never gave clear definitions. For practical reasons we adopt one single appellation: redeemable annuity (*widerkauﬄicher Zins*), also used by the jurists.[57] Nonetheless, we see from time to time the strategies and denominations adopted by the theologians.

Very often the theologians were interested only in certain aspects of the agreement, which are reflected in the terms employed. For instance, Johann Gerhard adopted the term '*census*', and the agreement is simply described as the contract where for the use of 100 gulden, 5 gulden are yearly paid.[58] The focus is on the annuity (*census*) that the debtor/seller has to pay to the creditor/buyer: 5% of the lent sum, because this was the problem Gerhard wanted to tackle. Melanchthon used the term 'contract with the clause to resell' (*contractus cum pacto de revendendo*), including both the sale of an estate with the clause to resell, the sale of the right to receive an income from a single estate (real *census*) or from different estates (the German contract). He probably used this classification because he wanted to point out that this agreement is a sale and not a loan.

55 R. de Roover, *Scholastic Economics*, 173. For additional bibliography see H.J. Becker, *Das Zinsverbot*, 41.

56 The German word *Zins* that now means 'interest', derives from the Latin term *census*. See J. Grimm, W. Grimm, *Deutsches Wörterbuch*, Leipzig, 1956 http://woerterbuchnetz.de/cgi-bin/WBNetz/wbgui_py?sigle=DWB (accessed 22.12.2017).

57 See IV.

58 J. Gerhard, *Locorum theologicorum tomus decimus quartus*, Tubingae, 1776, 101.

Concerning the power to redeem the annuity, the theologians usually distinguished between three possible agreements: 1) the contract is perpetual, but the seller/borrower can redeem the annuity when he wants; 2) the contract has a fixed time when the seller/borrower must redeem the annuity[59]; 3) the contract is perpetual, but the buyer/lender the possibility to ask back the sum, under certain circumstances.[60] A good example of a definition that includes this distinction is given by a professor of theology in Tübingen, Theodor Thumm (1586-1630),[61] in his *Tractatus de usura licita et illicita* (1622). Thumm's definition seems to consider the real *census* contract (fruitful land specifically determined) and the German contract (no land is specified – personal obligation to pay a 5% annuity – mutual redeemability). The contract with the clause to resell (*Zinskauf – widerkaufflicher Zins*), as he designates this agreement, occurs when a man pays a certain amount of money to secure an annual income, the produce from one or more real estates. The seller is allowed to cultivate the lands and maintain the ownership until he can return the sum to the buyer and in this way terminate the annual payment. The payment can be in fruits or money. The contract is not perpetual, but the seller/borrower has always the power to redeem the annuity (*quovis tempore*).[62]

Thumm then examines another form of this contract where a buyer/creditor rents a certain amount of money in return for a certain annual payment, the amount of which the law establishes. The parties can agree that the contract ends after a certain period of time. When the agreed-upon time elapses, the buyer/lender has the power to ask back the sum. The parties can also agree that the contract is perpetual, but the buyer/creditor has the possibility to ask back the sum; in the case of this necessity, he must give six months' notice to the seller/debtor.[63] Thumm's definition highlights the flexibility of the *census* structure, which can be adapted to several uses, according to the needs of the parties.

The *widerkaufflicher Zins* was incredibly similar to a loan, raising the probing question of the possible breach of the interest prohibition. The theologians almost never discussed the whole contract, but limited their observations only to some aspects. They analyzed the problem of the risk of loss that belongs to

---

59 See for example A. Hunnius, *Commentarius in posteriorem epistolam D. Pavli Apostoli ad Corinthios*, Witebergae, 1605, 249-50.

60 T. Thumm, *Tractatus de usura licita et illicita*, Tubingae, 1622, 41.

61 P. Tschackert, *Thumm, Theodor*, in *Allgemeine Deutsche Biographie* 38 (1894), 169-71 (accessed 22.01.2018) https://www.deutsche-biographie.de/pnd123140528.html#adbcontent; H. Ehmer, *Thumm, Theodor*, in *BBKL*, vol. XI (1996), 1527-30; M.H. Jung, *Thumm, Theodor*, in *RPP*, vol. XII, 2012, 704.

62 T. Thumm, *Tractatus de usura licita et illicita*, 31.

63 T. Thumm, *Tractatus de usura licita et illicita*, 41.

the borrower/seller; the legal nature of the agreement; and the lawfulness of the annuity. These issues played a different role depending on the strategy adopted. Some theologians tried to demonstrate that, notwithstanding the clause to redeem, the *widerkaufflicher Zins* was a sale, not a loan. If this contract is not a loan, the interest prohibition does not apply. This approach, also used by the scholastics, functioned well to prove the lawfulness of the real *census*, but the German contract was more similar to a loan. It constituted a personal obligation to pay the 5% annuity, at times for a fixed period of time. In this way, this agreement was substantially identical to a loan at interest. Probably for this reason, distinguishing between a sale and a loan was no more satisfying.

The theologians elaborated on the framework of the interest prohibition and focused directly on the lawfulness of the annuity. Most of the time the question was formulated in these terms: "*can a lender take the annuity* (*census*) *from the borrower with clear conscience?*" as we find, for instance, in the collection of cases of conscience of Andreas Prückner in 1660.[64] The answer was often positive. The obligation to pay the 5% annuity is lawful because according to the new theory, the loans at interest are not forbidden if the neighbour is not harmed. Even though the contract was still classified as a sale and not a loan, this qualification was less important. Loans at interest were admitted, if none of the parties were damaged.

The problem of risk of loss also received different consideration. Luther strongly denied that the seller/borrower should support the risk alone and condemned the contract. He claimed that the only way to consider the *Zinskauf* licit would be that the seller and the buyer share the risk. Melanchthon and the other Lutheran theologians argued that even if a contractual term sets out that only one of the parties has to support the risk, nonetheless, both of them must support it, in case of unexpected circumstances (for instance, fire or flood). The risk sharing impedes the perception the contract as usurious.

These three issues – the risk, the nature of the agreement, and the lawfulness of profit – constitute in general the crux of the discourse. First, we will clarify some aspects of Luther and Melanchthon's theories of interest. Then we go through the Lutheran orthodoxy, observing the selected contribution of some authors and their different theories of interest. As we will see, the Lutheran theory of interest is created in a progressive development that proceeds through the integration of different doctrines.

---

64 A. Pruckner, *Manuale*, 110: "*Potestne* mutuans censum annuum, v.g. florenos 5. vel 6. a mutuatario illaesa conscientia sumere?"

2.2 Pillars for a New Theory of Interest: Luther's and Melanchthon's Formulations

2.2.1 *Introduction*

The diffusion of the German contract triggered the fierce reaction of Martin Luther, which first condemned this agreement and later allowed it only for special categories of people. Generally speaking, Luther followed the scholastic vision of the interest prohibition. Yet, he mapped out some principles, which were necessary for the development of the new theory of interest. Melanchthon reintroduced Aristotelian scholastic philosophy and canonists' theories, but more openly than Luther, allowed the German contract, which is not a loan but a sale, and also the *interesse* as lawful compensation for the damages incurred in a loan.

Abundant publications have already examined in depth Luther[65] and Melanchthon's[66] statements on interest-taking and usury, and for this reason

65 See bibliography in introduction, fn. 6. In addition see R.W. Elert, *Morphologie des Luthertums*, vol. II, 466-92; H. Wiesenmüller, *Die Wirtschaftsethik Thomas von Aquins, Luthers und Calvins und das deutsche Unternehmertum des Vor- und Frühkapitalismus*, diss, Erlagen, 1968; M. Honecker, *Art. Geld II.2.1.7 Reformation*, in *TRE*, vol. XII, 1984, 286-8; J. Wieland, *»Wucher muß sein, aber wehe den Wucherern«. Einige Überlegungen zu Martin Luthers Konzeption des Ökonomischen*, in *Zeitschrift für Evangelische Ethik*, 35 (1991), 268-84; C. Braun, *Vom Wucherverbot zur Zinsanalyse, 1150-1700*, diss., Zürich, 1994; A. Pawlas, *Die lutherische Beruf- und Wirtschaftsethik*; C. Hecker, *Lohn- und Preisgerechtigkeit. Historische Rückblicke und aktuelle Perspektiven unter besonderer Berücksichtigung der christlichen Soziallehren*, Marburg, Metropolis-Verlag, 2008, 59-62; H. Peukert, *Martin Luther. A First Modern Economist*, in J. Backhaus (ed.), *The Reformation as a Precondition for Modern Capitalism*, Münster, Lit, 2010, 13-64; J.D. Singleton, *"Money Is a Sterile Thing": Martin Luther on the Immorality of Usury Reconsidered*, in *History of Political Economy*, Winter 2011, vol. 43, 4, 683-98; M. Lapp, *»Denn es ist geld ein ungewis, wanckelbar ding«. Die Wirtschaftsethik Martin Luthers anhand seiner Schriften gegen den Wucher*, in *Luther: Zeitschrift der Luther-Gesellschaft*, 2012, vol. 83(2), 91-107; H.J. Becker, *Das Zinsverbot*, 39-40; M. Schmoeckel, *Das kanonische Zinsverbot und die Konfessionalisierung*, in W. Decock, J.J. Ballor, M. Germann, L. Waelkens, *Law and Religion*, 186-212; R. Rieth, *Luther's Treatment of Economic Life*, in R. Kolb, I. Dingel, L. Batka, *The Oxford Handbook of Martin Luther's Theology*, Oxford, Oxford University Press, 2014, 383-96. On Luther's importance for today's economy: A. Pawlas, *Die Wirtschaft des Menschen zwischen Fluch und Segen. Ökonomische Kritik bei Luther und Calvin* in *Paradoxie der Freiheit. Zur Relevanz von Luthers ökonomischer Kritik und Calvins Wirtschaftsmoral für das Verhältnis von Kirche, Staat und Wirtschaft*, epd-Dokumentation 21/2014, 12-33; J. Wieland, *Luthers Ökonomiekritik und ihre Ausläufer in der Wirtschaftsethik der Gegenwart*, in *Paradoxie der Freiheit. Zur Relevanz von Luthers ökonomischer Kritik und Calvins Wirtschaftsmoral für das Verhältnis von Kirche, Staat und Wirtschaft*, epd-Dokumentation 21/2014, 4-11; C. Hecker, *Wenn aus Kontingenz Notwendigkeit wird. Die neue Welt der Finanzmärkte und die alten Warnungen Martin Luthers*, in *Zeitschrift für Evangelische Ethik*, 59, 3 (2015), 191-204.

66 In addition to the mentioned works of Nelson, Honecker, Braun, Kerridge and Jones, see C. Bauer, *Melanchthons Wirtschaftsethik*, 115-60; I. Deflers, *Lex und Ordo*, 258-60;

our attention will only be devoted to some aspects that were influential among their followers. Together, Luther and Melanchthon established the pillars for the construction of a new theory of interest.

2.2.2 *Luther and the Spirit of the Scriptures*

2.2.2.1 Three Essential Innovations

Similarly to the scholastic theologians, Martin Luther looked at interest-taking as a problem of unlawful acquisition of property and reaffirmed the canon law prohibition of lending at interest.[67] Nevertheless, he proposed three essential innovations that paved the way for the new theory of interest. First, Luther tried to deal with the problem of interest and usury only on the basis of Scripture. In his *Sermon on Usury* (*Ein* (*grosser*) *Sermon von dem Wucher*, 1520) and in *On Trade and Usury* (*Von Kaufshandlung und Wucher*, 1524)[68] he presents an exegesis of the Sermon on the Mount (Matthew 5, 38-42). Although there are clear connections with the medieval conception, Luther's reasoning has an immediate and primary reference to Scripture. Luther's theology is essentially exegesis,[69] an exposition of Scripture. The authority of Scripture comes before and acts as an instrument of critical judgement over and against the tradition as councils and Church fathers.[70] This approach granted Scripture a leading role and reversed the traditional discourse on the interest-taking prohibition. According to Luther's logic, the interest prohibition is not incorporated in a canon law norm, but it is only established in Scripture. The Church is not a society governed by legal norms, but is a community of Christians that stands in front of God and follows Scripture. The interest prohibition is expressed by the precept of Luke 6,35: to lend hoping for nothing means that to profit from a loan is forbidden.[71] The interpretation of Scripture determines the framework of the interest prohibition.

Second, Luther grounds the interest prohibition on natural law and the Christian love for the neighbour.[72] Natural law is not the scholastic law of

---

N. Kuropka, *Philipp Melanchthon: Wissenschaft und Gesellschaft*, Tübingen, Mohr Siebeck, 2002, 192-8.

67 About the canon law prohibition see M. Schmoeckel, *Das Recht*, 249-50; M. Schmoeckel, *Das kanonische Zinsverbot*, 191-6, 205.

68 For the context of these works see: H.J. Prien, *Luthers Wirtschaftsethik*, 69-83.

69 P. Althaus, *The Theology of Martin Luther*, trans. R. C. Schultz, Philadelphia, Fortress, 1966, 3.

70 B. Lohse, *Martin Luther's Theology*, 187.

71 M. Luther, *Ein (grosser) Sermon von dem Wucher*, in WA 6, 47; M. Luther, *Von Kaufshandlung und Wucher*, in WA15, 301.

72 M. Luther, *Ein (grosser) Sermon von dem Wucher*, in WA 6, 49: "*Drumb were nicht richtigers noch kurzer unterweyssung ynn diessem und allen hendelln zeytlichs guts, das eyn iglich mensch, zo er mit seynem nehisten soll handelnn, ym fursezt dise gebott 'was du willt, das dyr eyn ander thet, das thu du nym auch,' und 'lieb deynen nehsten als dich selb'*".

reason but consists in the rule of reciprocal respect included in Luke 6,31 and Matthew 7,12: "*And as ye would that men should do to you, do ye also to them likewise*". Luther opines that charging of interest is against natural law, because Christians shall lend good wares and return good wares, so that the other party is not injured or offended. The usurer seeks to damage the neighbour with his advantage and for this reason he breaches natural law. Luther also affirms that the borrower pays interest because he is forced by necessity, but this argument only works as a confirmation of the scriptural dictates.[73] The scholastic Aristotelian arguments are relevant only in support of the Scriptures.

The practice of interest-taking is also against the Old and the New Law, which commands believers to love the neighbour.[74] Luther refers here to Lev. 19,18 and Mark 12,31: "*love your neighbour as yourself*". Usury is an act against the neighbour because the usurer seeks his own profit, with no regard for the neighbour, the borrower. The usurer seeks his own profit and therefore violates the rule of love. The interest prohibition is based on the precept of Luke 6,35, which commands to lend hoping for nothing in return, which is breached along with the rule of love for the neighbour, because the usurer seeks his own profit and does not care about any damage to the neighbour. Luther does not classify usury as a sin against justice, but as a sin against love. The scholastics reasoned in terms of justice, while Luther judges in terms of charity. The rule of Luke 6,35 is not about justice, because it is a precept of the Gospel, which in its essence is a statement of charity.

Third, Luther put forward a set of distinctions between lawful and unlawful acquisition of property. Following the Scriptures, he demarcates the different features of alms, loans and sale. He categorized the lawful and unlawful acquisition of goods in four different degrees and orders.[75] The first degree, he writes, is that if anyone takes some of our temporal goods by force, we shall not only permit it, and let the goods go, but even be ready to let him take more, if he will.[76] Luther comments on the passage of Matthew 5,40: "*And if any man will sue thee at the law and take away thy coat, let him have thy cloak also*". The second degree of dealing with temporal goods is to give goods freely to people

73 See for instance the motivations against the *Zinskauf* that we discuss in the following paragraph. M. Luther, *Ein (grosser) Sermon von dem Wucher*, in WA 6, 53-5.

74 M. Luther, *Ein (grosser) Sermon von dem Wucher*, in WA 6, 48-9. Concerning the love for one's neighbour see also H. Barge, *Luther und der Frühkapitalismus*, 14-5.

75 M. Luther, *Ein (grosser) Sermon von dem Wucher*, in WA 6, 36. For the analysis of the *Sermon von dem Wucher* see S. Doherty, *Theology and Economic Ethics. Martin Luther and Arthur Rich in Dialogue*, Oxford, Oxford University Press, 2014, 7-70.

76 M. Luther, *Ein (grosser) Sermon von dem Wucher*, in WA 6, 36; M. Luther, *Von Kaufshandlung und Wucher*, in WA 15, 300-1.

who need them.[77] The biblical foundation is in the passage of Matthew 5,42: "*Give to him that asketh thee*". To Luther, the aim of this precept is to gain faith in God. Trusting God in the matter of temporal goods helps the believers to trust in greater and eternal things.

The third degree is lending without charges or interest.[78] In lending, the believer takes the risk that the goods may not be returned: "*I give away my property and take it back if it is returned to me; if not, then I must do without it*".[79] According to Luther, if the good returns you can take it back; otherwise, you made a gift. The believer should not expect anything from the loan.[80] The Gospel indicates only one distinction between giving and lending: a gift is not taken back, while a loan is received back if it is returned. If the believers ask for money, they are not assuming the risk, but rather are looking for profit – thus, they are usurers,[81] because they deny the risk that the capital will not be remunerated.

The fourth degree (only expounded in Luther's *Von Kaufshandlung und Wucher*) is buying and selling.[82] In distinguishing these four categories, especially the last three, viz. alms, loans, and sales, Luther designed a method that inspired his followers. The alms concern the needy, and the loan must be free, but in a sale it is possible to earn a profit. Gratuitousness and profitability therefore remain two distinct spheres of activity, the first one related to alms and loans, and the second, to the sale.

In conclusion, Luther remained anchored in some of the scholastic conceptions. He viewed the interest-taking as a forced payment due to the necessity facing the borrower, and thus as an unlawful acquisition of property; he interpreted the passage of Luke 6,35 as a prohibition against interest. Nonetheless, the interest prohibition is not expressed in a canon law norm, but only in the Scriptures. The interest prohibition is founded on natural law and charity towards the neighbour. The sin of usury is not against the virtue of justice, as it

77 M. Luther, *Ein (grosser) Sermon von dem Wucher*, in WA 6, 41; M. Luther, *Von Kaufshandlung und Wucher*, in WA 15, 301.

78 M. Luther, *Ein (grosser) Sermon von dem Wucher*, in WA 6, 47; M. Luther, *Von Kaufshandlung und Wucher*, in WA 15, 301.

79 M. Luther, *Von Kaufshandlung und Wucher*, in WA 15, 301: "*Die dritte ist, leyhen odder borgen, dass ich mein gutt hyn gebe, und widder neme, so myrs widder bracht wird, und emperen mus, wo mans nicht widder bringt*".

80 M. Luther, *Von Kaufshandlung und Wucher*, in WA 15, 301.

81 M. Luther, *Von Kaufshandlung und Wucher*, in WA 15, 301: "*Denn wer also leyhet, das ers besser odder mehr widder nemen will, das ist ein offentlicher und verdampter wucher; Syntemal auch die noch nicht Christlich handeln, die also borgen, das sie widderumb eben dasselb foddern odder hoffen, und nicht frey dahyn wagen, obs widder kompt odder nicht*".

82 M. Luther, *Von Kaufshandlung und Wucher*, in WA 15, 303.

trespasses no laws, but rather is a slight against charity. The usurer possesses an egoist attitude that makes him look toward his profit without regard for the damage inflicted upon the neighbour. Finally, Luther distinguished the sphere of business from the sphere of alms and loans. These three elements can be seen as essential innovations, in the sense that they laid the foundations of the theory of interest developed by the Lutheran theologians.

2.2.2.2 The *Zinskauf*: From Criticism to Moderate Approval

In his first writings on usury, Luther condemned the *Zinskauf* (buying of annuity).[83] The text is not particularly clear, but concerning this nomenclature, he seems to refer to the German contract in the form of a redeemable annuity.[84] Luther looks at two distinct problems: the admission of the contract in itself and the element of profit. The *Zinskauf* goes against natural law and love for one's neighbour, he writes, because the business is not conducted for the sake of the seller, but only for the sake of the buyer. The buyer, Luther continues, does not aim to promote the neighbour but looks only at his profit.[85] The buyer receives the annuity (*Zins*), but does not take part in the risks. The annuity is due because the buyer might have earned other profits with the money given to the seller. Luther objects that the buyer could also possibly gain more or lose his capital altogether with a different enterprise. When

---

83 M. Luther, *Ein (grosser) Sermon von dem Wucher*, WA 6, 51; T. Strohm, *Luthers Wirtschafts- und Sozialethik*, in *Leben und Werk Martin Luthers von 1526 bis 1546. Festgabe zu seinem Geburstag*, vol. 1, Göttingen, Vandenhoeck und Ruprecht, 1983, 205-23; H.J. Prien, *Luthers Wirtshaftsethik*, 97-105; D.W. Jones, *Reforming the Morality of Usury*, 53-4; S. Doherty, *Theology and Economic Ethics*, 55-9; M. Schmoeckel, *Das kanonische Zinsverbot*, 192-3.

84 The definition is not detailed, but Luther refers to a *census* contract with a five per cent annuity, which is gained from a non-specified land. He describes this agreement referring to the *interesse*, used as justification for the payment of the annuity. M. Luther, *Ein (grosser) Sermon von dem Wucher*, in WA 6, 53: "*wen ich hundert gulden hab, damit ich mocht ym handelt durch meyn mühe und ʃorg eyn jar lang funff, sechß odder mehr gulden erwerben, die thu ich von myr zu einem andernn auff eyn fruchtpar gutt, das nit ich, ßondern er mag alßo damit handelln auff dem selben. Drumb nym ich von yhm funff gulden, die ich hett mocht erwerben, und alßo vorkaufft er mir die zinß, funff gulden vor hundert, und bin ich kauffer und er vorkauffer*". See also WA 6, 55: "*Darumb soll nit gestattet werden, das man zinß kaufft mit blossem gelt, unangezeygt, und unbestympt den grund der zinß in ʃunderheyt, wie itzt der prauch ist* (...)". On the definition of the *Zinskauf*, see M. Luther, *On Commerce and Usury*, ed. with introduction and notes by Philipp Robinson Rössner, n. 80, fn. 61. Robinson Rössner argues that the word *Zinskauf* would mean the purchase of all sorts of interest-bearing assets, mostly referred to the annuities. Yet, the agreement Luther discusses concerns a five per cent annuity, which is not linked to a specific land. This seems to reveal that he does not deal with the purchase of annuities in general, but with the five percent contract.

85 M. Luther, *Ein (grosser) Sermon von dem Wucher*, WA 6, 52-3.

the buyer takes the annuity, he does not have anymore the risk of losing his capital.[86] In this way, he is safe, and the seller/borrower only supports the risk. As an additional argument to refuse the contract, Luther alludes to the sterility of money.[87]

After this initial attack, Luther softened his opinion,[88] and then in the admonition *An die Pfarrherrn, wider den Wucher zu predigen* (1540),[89] he granted exceptions for special categories of people, as the elderly, the poor widows, and the orphans who do not have other support except the *Zinskauf.* Luther explains that this would not be interest (*Wucher*) – as the common adage says, the world cannot exist without interest – but should be considered as "*an interest out of need*" (ein Notwucherlin), a small form of interest in circumstances of necessity: "*a mere half work of mercy for the needy, who otherwise would have nothing and a form of interest that does not particularly harm the others*".[90] The elderly, widows, and orphans had already been considered in special way in canon law. The *miserabiles personae*, as they were named, deserved special protection, which resulted in the privilege of ecclesiastical jurisdiction.[91] Furthermore, the thesis that the special nature of these people justified a different treatment with regards to the *census* contract had already been maintained by some scholastics.[92] Luther recognises that for the elderly, widows, and orphans, it is necessary to admit an *interest out of need* (ein Notwucherlin)[93] as a form of mercy towards them, because without this permission, they would

---

86 M. Luther, *Ein (grosser) Sermon von dem Wucher*, WA 6, 53-5.

87 S. Doherty, *Theology and Economic Ethics*, 59-61 maintains that Luther derives the sterility of money from his understanding of the divine creation.

88 B. J. Nelson, *The Idea of Usury*, 30-31; E. Kerridge, *Usury*, 42.

89 M. Luther, *An die Pfarrherrn, wider den Wucher zu predigen*, in WA 51, 331-424.

90 M. Luther, *An die Pfarrherrn*, in WA 51, 372: "*Und hieher möcht der spruch gehören, der droben gesagt ist: Die welt könne nicht on Wucher sein, doch das es nicht stracks ein wucher, auch nicht ein recht, sondern ein not Wücherlin were, schier ein halb werk der barmherzigkeit, fur die dürfftigen, die sonst nichts hetten, und den andern auch nicht sonderlich schadet*".

91 R. Helmholz, *The Spirit of Classical Canon Law*, Athens, Georgia, University of Georgia Press, 1996, 116-45; T. Duve, *Sonderrecht in der Frühen Neuzeit. Studien zum ius singulare und den privilegia miserabilium personarum, senum und indorum in Alter und Neuer Welt*, Frankfurt am Main, Klostermann, 2008.

92 I. Birocchi, *Tra elaborazioni nuove e dottrine tradizionali*, 276-7.

93 A. Pawlas, *Luther zu Geld und Zins. Mit einem Vorwort über Lutherische Erwägungen zu Geld und Zins*, in Uppsala University Coin Cabinet Working Papers, Uppsala, Uppsala Universitet, 2013, 4-36 (28-9) (online: http://uu.diva-portal.org/smash/get/diva2:676716/FULLTEXT01.pdf – accessed on 27.06.2016). See also A. Pawlas, *Did Calvin Have a Better Understanding of Modern Economics as Luther? Max Weber's Ideas to the Test*, in *Research in World Economy*, vol. 6, n. 1, 2015, 36-57 (42).

have even fewer means of support. The magistrate, the preachers, and the jurists have to intervene with equity (*epieikeia*). The equity arises from mercy toward the condition of some people. This mercy liberates from sin, so that in this way it is possible to use the *Zinskauf* with clear conscience.

Luther's stand on the *Zinskauf* fluctuated from strong criticism to moderate approval. In the end, he finds a compromise between the interest prohibition and the necessity of the real economy. The solution is equity, as a form of mercy for special categories of people. The *Zinskauf* is forbidden by the interest prohibition, but in special cases, for old people, widows and orphans, an exception can be made, because they have relatively few other means to live.[94]

2.2.3 *Melanchthon: Turning Back to the Past?*

2.2.3.1 The Prohibition Against Interest

Melanchthon united the innovative spirit of Luther with Aristotelian philosophy. He writes that receiving and asking for interest is unjust because of the divine law, the breach of equality, and other arguments that he derives from Aristotle. First, the Holy Scripture (Lev. 25,36; Psalm 15,5; Luke 6,35) attests that interest-taking is forbidden.[95] Second, society cannot last if equality is not observed. And equality is not observed when interest is pretended, because he who borrowed not only receives back his goods but also something more.[96] Third, as Aristotle rightly asserted, money does not bear fruits, and the usurers deal with money as merchandise; but money is a price, not merchandise.[97] This is the argument of the sterility of money. Although he holds Scripture at the forefront, Melanchthon again considers rational arguments in support of the prohibition of interest.

Melanchthon's theory of interest entailed the analysis of the gratuitous loans, the contract with the clause to resell, and the lawful compensation in case of damages in a loan (the *interesse*). The borrowing (*mutuatio*) is defined as:

---

94 This approach persisted in the Protestant tradition, as for example in the work of M. Bucer and W. Musculus. For the first one see B.J. Nelson, *The Idea of Usury*, 70-1; For the latter see W. Decock, *The Catholic Spirit of Capitalism?*, 40-1. It was also discussed among the Catholics. See E. Van Roey, *Le contractus germanicus*, 928.

95 P. Melanchthon, *Dissertatio de contractibus*, in CR XVI, 497.

96 P. Melanchthon, *Dissertatio de contractibus*, in CR XVI, 497; *Philosophiae moralis epitomes libri duo*, in CR XVI, 128; P. Melanchthon, *Ethicae doctrinae elementorum libri duo*, in CR XVI, 249.

97 P. Melanchthon, *Dissertatio de contractibus*, in CR XVI, 498; *Philosophiae moralis epitomes libri duo*, in CR XVI, 128.

> *the contract by which money or another consumable thing is transferred for free, not only with regards to its use, but also its ownership; if the borrower accepts the transfer, he is obliged to return a thing of the same genus, or in equivalent.*[98]

This definition points out the gratuitous nature of the loan, which is justified by referring to the nature of the thing: it is a consumable thing that does not bear fruits. If the lender charges interest, he recuperates more than what he gave to the borrower. He thus takes advantage of an unfruitful thing, and arithmetical equality is not preserved.[99] Melanchthon's interpretation reflects the medieval approach, as he clearly refers to the Aristotelian arguments of the sterility of money and commutative justice.

2.2.3.2 The Contract with the Clause to Resell

As an alternative to the gratuitous loans, Melanchthon permits the 'contract with the clause to resell' (*contractus cum pacto de revendendo*),[100] or the 'contract with a clause of redemption' (*contractus redemptionis*),[101] which seems to include the real *census* contract and the redeemable annuity (*widerkaufflicher Zins*). In his *Philosophiae moralis epitome* (1538), he faces the objection formulated by Jacob Strauss[102] one of the agitators of the Peasants' war.[103]

---

98 P. Melanchthon, *Dissertatio de contractibus*, in CR XVI, 496: "*Mutuatio est contractus, in quo pecunia, vel alia res, quae usu consumitur, gratis transfertur, non modo quoad usum, sed etiam quoad dominium, illo tamen accipiente, obligato ad reddendum idem in genere, seu aequivalens*". Similarly in his *Loci theologici* (tertia eorum aetas), in CR XXI, 1094: "*Mutuatio est contractus, quo transfertur pecunia seu frumentum seu alia res utilis, cuius usus est consumtio, cum hac obligatione, ut tantundem post certum tempus reddatur, et dans mutuo retinet ius tantundem petendi, quantum mutuo dedit*".

99 P. Melanchthon, *Dissertatio de contractibus*, in CR XVI, 496-7.

100 This type of clause was also discussed by the scholastic theologians. See for example, L. Lessius *De iustitia et iure*, book 2, chapter 21, question 14 = L. Lessius, *On Sale, Securities, and Insurance*, translated by W. Decock – N. De Sutter, 93-100.

101 P. Melanchthon, *Propositiones (III) De contractu redemptionis*, in CR XII, 686-9.

102 P. Melanchthon, *Philosophiae moralis epitome*, in CR XVI, 131; See J. Strauss, *Haubstuck unnd Artickel Christlicher leer wider den unchristlichen wucher*, Erfurt, 1523, in J. Rogge, *Der Beiträge des Predigers Jakob Strauss zur frühen Reformationsgeschichte*, Berlin, Evangelische Verlagsanstalt, 1957. Strauss' positions on usury are summarized in B.N. Nelson, *The Idea of Usury*, 36-45; 60. See also J. McDurmon, *Reassessing Jacob Strauss and the Mosaic Code*, in *HTS Teologiese Studies/Theological Studies* 68(1), 2012, Art. #1253, 4 pages. http://dx.doi.org/10.4102/ hts.v68i1.1253. On his biography, see G. Kaller, *Strauß, Jacob*, in *BBKL* 11, 1996, 34-7.

103 On this topic in general, see K. Hill, *Baptism, Brotherhood, and Belief in Reformation Germany: Anabaptism and Lutheranism, 1525-1585*, Oxford, Oxford University Press, 2015; T. Scott, *The Early Reformation in Germany. Between Secular Impact and Radical Vision*, Abingdon, Routledge, 2016. On Melanchthon's view, see M. Schmoeckel, *Der Bauernkrieg und Melanchthons Kehre*, in G. Hasselhoff, D. von Mayenburg (eds.), *Die Zwölf Artikel*

Melanchthon observes that Strauss damned every contract and suggests that the Christians follow the authority of the magistrate:

> *the following useful rule must be kept: Christians can use the contracts that are approved by the laws and the authority of the magistrate, that is by a good, wise judge or jurist. The Christians can indeed use the political ordinances. Such ordinances are not only valid because of reason, but also because of the authority of the magistrate, which God approves.*[104]

A similar position was also included in a *Propositio* dedicated to the *contractus redemptionis*[105] and reaffirmed in a counsel about interest-taking and usury written in 1553, with regard to an imperial provision issued for the city of Regensburg in 1541.[106] The stress on the role of the magistrate represents a direct consequence of the Lutheran political theory: the magistrate, in this case the emperor Charles V, regulated the *widerkaufflicher Zins*, and the Christians can use this regulation in good conscience, because God empowers the magistrate.

In the *Dissertatio de contractibus* (1545) and the *Ethicae doctrinae elementa* (1550), Melanchthon does not mention Strauss, but probably he refers to the Anabaptists in general. He observes that these men damned every income and notices the necessity to warn people against these 'seditious opinions'.[107] Melanchthon argues that the contract with the clause to resell is not a loan but a true sale. The method he follows was previously employed by the scholastics and consists in proving that the contract is not a loan, but a sale, because in this way the prohibition against interest does not apply.[108] Melanchthon distinguishes three forms of the contract with the clause to resell: 1) when an estate

---

von 1525, 179-202. On the relationship between Strauss and the Anabaptists see J. Oyer, *The influence of Jacob Strauss on the Anabaptists. A problem in historical methodology*, in M. Lienhard (ed.), *The Origins and Characteristics of Anabaptism*, The Hague, Springer, 1977, 62-82.

104 P. Melanchthon, *Philosophiae moralis epitomes libri duo*, in CR XVI, 131: "*Tenenda est igitur utilis regula: contractus legibus, et autoritate magistratus, hoc est, boni et sapientis iudicis seu iurisconsulti approbatos, concessos esse christiano homini. Licet enim christiano uti politicis ordinationibus. Et hae ordinationes valent non solum propter rationem, sed etiam propter autoritatem magistratus, quam Deus approbat*".

105 P. Melanchthon, *Propositiones (III) De contractu redemptionis*, in CR XII, 687.

106 P. Melanchthon, *Bedenken: vom Verbot und Straff des Wuchers*, in CR VIII, 84-8.

107 P. Melanchthon, *Dissertatio de contractibus*, in CR XVI, 499: "*Constat enim quosdam turbolentos homines sine omni discrimine, omnes reditus damnasse. Adversus tales seditiosas opiniones praemuniendi sunt animi*". See also CR XVI, 441.

108 On the discussion about the substantial elements of the contract, see P. Grossi, *Sulla natura del contratto*, passim; Birocchi, *Tra elaborazioni nuove*, 243-73 and 287-304.

is purchased; 2) when the incomes produced by a certain estate are bought; 3) when the incomes produced by several estates are purchased. The first one is the regular sale; the second form is the real *census*; and the third one seems to be the German contract. Indeed, an essential character of this agreement was that the estate is not specified, because the buyer/lender has only the right to 5% of the lent sum, independently from the land.

In Melanchthon's view, the first two forms are a true sale, because the clause to resell does not eliminate the nature of sale.[109] He does not investigate whether the power to redeem should belong to the seller or to the buyer, but only focuses on the fact that the sellback clause does not change the nature of the contract.[110] The agreement contains the substantial elements of a sale: price, merchandise, and consent. The merchandise is the estate or a certain income produced by the estate. And the Roman law, Melanchthon observes, admits a similar agreement for restitution of an estate with the payment of a price.[111]

An objection that might be formulated is that the buyer is not a real owner, because he cannot sell the good to another person, only to the original seller. Melanchthon replies that the obligation to resell only to the original seller does not prohibit the buyer from being a true owner. The buyer is a real owner, albeit with the limitation of reselling. The good cannot be sold to another person, but only to the original seller. To bear this statement, Melanchthon refers to the Roman law again. In *Si ita quis* (D. 45,1,63) is said that a slave that is donated with the condition of not being transferred to another person is in fact a true slave of the new master.[112] The clause of reselling does not negate the nature of the contract. Since there is a real conveyance of property, the contract is a sale.

The third form of the contract with the clause to resell – where an income produced by several estates is sold – is more debated.[113] However, Melanchthon observes that the merchandise is the right to receive the income. This idea derives from Pope Innocent IV (1195-1254) who argued that in this contract is constituted an income on the goods and not an income on the people and the

109 P. Melanchthon, *Dissertatio de contractibus*, in CR XVI, 499: "*Porro hae duae formae sunt verae emptiones, nam pactum de revendendo non tollit naturam emptionis*".

110 The attribution of the right to resell to the investor had been discussed by the scholastics, and the imperial ordinance only admitted it in favour of the entrepreneur.

111 C. 4,54,2.

112 P. Melanchthon, *Dissertatio de contractibus*, in CR XVI, 500.

113 Melanchthon reports that Jean Gerson affirmed that in this contract equality is average respected and therefore it must be declared usurious.

income can be considered merchandise to sell.[114] Since the merchandise is the right to receive the income, the contract is not usurious: there is a price and merchandise, and it is licit to sell such a good.[115] Melanchthon concludes that the contract with the clause to resell is a real sale and not a loan, and therefore the interest prohibition does not apply.

Unlike Luther, Melanchthon advocated the lawfulness of the *widerkauffli-cher Zins*, without distinguishing between the categories of people who can employ it. He also admits the real *census* contract. He seems to be following the scholastics when insisting that these contracts are sales and not loans. Since these contracts are not loans, they are not against the interest prohibition. Melanchthon's approach looks at the nature of the contract and applies the distinction between sale and loan. This was a strategy employed by the scholastics to justify the *census* contract.[116] Instead, in the *Philosophiae moralis epitome*, Melanchthon extols the role of the magistrate and points out the fact that he regulates these contracts. This approach clearly reflects the two kingdoms doctrine. As political ordinances, the Christians can use these contracts without offending the conscience.

2.2.3.3 A Dialogue with the Canonists: The *interesse*

Scholastic theologians and canonists distinguished between the term '*usura*' that designated interest in a loan, and the term '*interesse*' which was the compensation the creditor should receive if he suffered damage in a loan. The *interesse* was admitted as title of compensation in particular cases: when the guarantor of a loan had been forced to borrow money at interest because the principal debtor failed to pay the debt; as a penalty in case the debtor did not pay in the time agreed; or in case of delay in making restitution of the sum.[117] These titles derived from the fault of the debtor who failed to return the sum in the time agreed. Instead, other titles were allowed at the beginning of a loan. Theologians and canonists examined the losses of the lender because of the lack of money and singled out two main titles of *interesse*: loss occurring (*damnum emergens*) and profit ceasing (*lucrum cessans*). The profit ceasing (*lucrum*

---

114 Innocentii IV, *In quinque libros decretalium commentaria absolutissima*, 2nd Ed., Francofurti ad Moenum, 1579, 517. X 5,19,5.

115 P. Melanchthon, *Dissertatio de contractibus*, in CR XVI, 501: "*Sed dictum Innocentii memorabile in hac quaestione tenendum est, qui inquit: videndum esse in hoc contractu, ut reditus constituatur in re, seu ad rem referatur, non ad personam vendentis, et addit Innocentius, talem contractum non esse usurarium, cum in eo sit merx et pretium, et talia iura realia licitum sit vendere*".

116 See before III/2.1.2.

117 J.T. Noonan, Jr., *The Scholastic Analysis of Usury*, 105-12.

cessans) remained particularly debated, but Hostiensis and other important theologians approved it.[118] At the end of the sixteenth century, both the loss occurring and the profit ceasing were generally accepted. Yet, other titles, like the capital risk (*periculum sortis*) and the loss of liquidity (*carentia pecuniae*) continued to be discussed.[119]

In *An die Pfarrherrn, wider den Wucher zu predigen*, Luther admits the *lucrum cessans* and *damnum emergens*, in case the creditor suffered damages due to the delay of the debtor.[120] Following in the scholastics' footsteps, in the *Philosophiae moralis epitome* (1538), Melanchthon distinguishes the concept of *usura* from *interesse* and concedes the *damnum emergens* and *lucrum cessans*, even if it was not established in the agreement. He draws upon Roman law, canon law, and the canonists. Because nobody must harm the neighbour, he writes, it should be attentively considered that the *Digestum* and Justinian's code distinguish between interest (*usura*) and compensation for damages (*interesse*).[121] And for this reason, the agreement for that compensation, if it is not fraudulent, is admitted. Pope Lucius III (1181-1183), in a decision included in the *Liber extra* concerning a similar case, judged that the guarantor of a surety must pay not only the credit but also the compensation for some kind of loss the creditor suffered (*interesse*).[122]

Furthermore, Hostiensis, glossing on X 5,9,16, admits the *lucrum cessans* also before the notice of default, but only if it is not a pretext for charging interest (*modo ne sit praetextus usurarum*). Although he grants an equitable compensation, Hostiensis limits it to the people who have their riches mainly in money and business.[123] In fact, the people that cannot be deprived of a large amount of money without damage should justly receive compensation. Melanchthon concludes that the payment of the *interesse* established in a commercial

118 J.T. Noonan, Jr., *The Scholastic Analysis of Usury*, 115-32.

119 T. Van Houdt, *Money, Time and Labour. Leonard Lessius and the Ethics of Lending and Interest Taking*, in *Ethical Perspectives* 2 (1995), 1, 11-27 (18-26); P. Vismara, *Oltre l'usura*, 87-112. See also T. Van Houdt, *Implicit intention and the conceptual shift from* interesse *to* interest. *An underestimated chapter from the history of scholastic economic thought*, in *Lias* 33 (2006) 1, 37-58.

120 M. Luther, *An die Pfarrherrn, wider den Wucher zu predigen*, in WA 51, 346. See also M. Schmoeckel, *Das kanonische*, 194.

121 D. 17,2,60; C. 4,32,15.

122 P. Melanchthon, *Philosophiae moralis epitomes libri duo*, in CR XVI, 139.

123 P. Melanchthon, *Philosophiae moralis epitomes libri duo*, in CR XVI, 139: "*Sic iudicat Hostiensis in cap. Salubriter, de usuris, deberi etiam id, quod interest lucri cessantis ante moram, sed addit: modo ne sit praetextus usurarum. Etsi enim aliquam aequam compensationem concedit, tamen metas certas constituit, ut in personis, quibus facultates suae praecipuae sunt in pecunia et negotiatione*".

contract of loan is lawful. The parties can agree that in the case of a real and not feigned *damnum emergens* and *lucrum cessans* the borrower has to pay the *interesse*. Besides, since the reason for this *interesse* is the compensation for damage, and nobody must cause damage to the other, the *interesse* can be requested even without a formal inclusion in the agreement.[124]

In his *Dissertatio de contractibus*, Melanchthon classifies the two damages the lender suffers in a slightly different way: they regard the period after the notice of default. The damage occurring (*damnum emergens*) is the damage caused by the non-fulfilment of the obligation to return the goods, and the profit ceasing (*lucrum cessans*) is the impediment to the lender's profit.[125] To Melanchthon, the *damnum emergens* attributes the right to receive a payment, if the sum is returned after the time agreed. Such a payment, which we today would call moratory interest, is a just compensation for the damage caused by the delay. It can be claimed even if it was not provided in the agreement, because the right to receive the *interesse* does not derive from the agreement, but from the damage.[126] Melanchthon justifies this statement by referring to natural law, which commands not to earn at the expense of the other. This rule corresponds to the equality established by the injunction to love one's neighbour as oneself and to the equality of book five of the *Nicomachean Ethics*.[127]

The topic of the *lucrum cessans* is more complex. Melanchthon draws on the medieval canonist Niccolò Tedeschi, Panormitanus (1386-1445) in his gloss on X 5,19,8,[128] but also adds some considerations based on the type of loan. Like Panormitanus, Melanchthon holds that the compensation for *lucrum cessans* is due only to merchants or people involved in business, because their riches are not in estates but in business – the flow of money – so if the borrower fails to pay in time, the lender suffers damage similar to the *damnum emergens*.[129] The particular quality of the businessman makes it possible for him to ask the *lucrum cessans*, because he needs the money for other financial operations.

Then, in order to further specify the range of application of this compensation, Melanchthon distinguishes between the loan in accordance with duty

124 P. Melanchthon, *Philosophiae moralis epitomes libri duo*, in CR XVI, 140.

125 P. Melanchthon, *Dissertatio de contractibus*, in CR XVI, 504: "*Interesse vocatur, quod debetur alicui, vel, quia damno affectus, vel quia lucrum aliquod impeditum est*".

126 P. Melanchthon, *Dissertatio de contractibus*, in CR XVI, 504-5.

127 P. Melanchthon, *Dissertatio de contractibus*, in CR XVI, 505: "*Iure naturae aequum est, neminem cum alterius detrimento et iniuria locupletari. Congruit enim haec regula ad aequalitatem, de qua dicit praeceptum: diligas proximum sicut te ipsum, et ad ea quae dicuntur quinto Ethicorum*".

128 Nicolai Siculi, Abbatis Panormitani, *Lectura super quinto Decretalium, cum glosis* (*sic*) *Bernardini de Landriano*, Venetiis, 1495, fol. 59.

129 P. Melanchthon, *Dissertatio de contractibus*, CR XVI, 505.

(*mutuatio officiosa*) and the loan that is not in accordance with duty (*mutuatio non officiosa*).[130] This classification, which is explained in the *Prolegomena in officia Ciceronis*, seems to emphasize the moral duty to lend (Luke 6,35).[131] On the opposite, the scholastics used the word '*officium*' to indicate any professional activity. The first type of loan is made to help the neighbour, if the lender can lend without impoverishing his resources. In this loan it is unjust to give or to expect something beyond the principal, except in case of a serious *damnum emergens* or *lucrum cessans*, and if the borrower caused the damage.[132] The loans that are not in accordance with duty are the loans for economic use (*usus oeconomicus*), as for instance when the kings ask a loan of their citizens and do not return the sum if they are not pressed by the payment of the damages. In this case, Melanchthon grants that a moderate compensation complies with equality and can be lawfully mandated.[133]

Melanchthon's distinction between dutiful and non-dutiful loans elucidates the profit or non-profit aims of loans. The compensation for *damnum emergens* and *lucrum cessans* should not be asked in the dutiful loans, because the lender did not break into his savings, but destined part of his assets to help the neighbour. Exceptionally, the *interesse* can be requested if the debtor caused the damage. In the other loans, the lender borrows over his capacities to assist the neighbour in a financial operation. In this case the *interesse* pushes the debtor to a prompt return and should be asked.

In his *Dissertatio de contractibus* the *interesse* before the delay is simply not discussed, but in the *Ethicae doctrinae elementa*, Melanchthon rehearses it, but without the references to the canonists and the Roman law. He insists that no one must damage the other, before or after the notice of default, and for this reason he concludes that the *interesse* for *damnum emergens* and *lucrum cessans* must be allowed.[134]

In conclusion, Melanchthon incorporates in his theology the most advanced solutions proposed by the medieval canonists. He applies them through the

130 A very similar distinction is described in a letter written to the political authority of Regensburg in 1554. Here, Melanchthon distinguishes between a *mutuatio officiosa* and a *mutuatio damnosa*. See CR VIII, 369-72; B.N. Nelson, *The Idea of Usury*, 63-4 holds that Melanchthon drafted the distinction even before in 1525. On this topic see also C. Bauer, *Melanchthons Wirtschaftsethik*, 142-5.

131 P. Melanchthon, *Prolegomena in officia Ciceronis*, in CR XVI, 579: "*Mutuatio, quae proprie officium est, est cum honestus homo honesto homini indigenti ad honestas causas dat mutuo talem summam, qua sine notabili detrimento suo carere potest* (...) *De hac officiosa mutuatione simpliciter servandum est dictum* (*Luc. 6, 35*)".

132 P. Melanchthon, *Dissertatio de contractibus*, in CR XVI, 505-6.

133 P. Melanchthon, *Dissertatio de contractibus*, in CR XVI, 506.

134 P. Melanchthon, *Ethicae doctrinae elementorum libri duo*, in CR XVI, 255-7.

spectrum of the natural law as protection against injuries and for this reason grants that the parties can ask for damages before the notice of default, even if this was not established in the agreement. Furthermore, he admits the compensation for the damage caused by the failure of the debtor to return the sum in time, but also the damage resulted by the lack of capital and the ceasing profit (*lucrum cessans*). On this point he distinguishes between loans for commercial purposes from the loans to help people in need. The *interesse* should be regularly permitted only in the first case. The element of profit plays a substantial role in the admission of the *interesse*: where the loan is for helping people in need, no compensation can be allowed.

2.3 Loans Towards the Poor and Business Contracts: A First Reformulation of the Interest Prohibition

2.3.1 *Introduction*

Martin Luther left his disciples with a tricky issue. He first refused the *Zinskauf* and then approved it, but only for certain people. Emperor Charles V, though, in 1530 and then in 1548, officially legalized an annuity (*Zins*) of 5%, opening wide the doors to the German contract. A literal interpretation of Luther's words would have led to disobedience of the imperial ordinance and also to notable insolvencies. Several disputes on the right interpretation of Luther's words led to an extensive interpretation, which also considered other categories of people, and not only the elderly, widows, and orphans.

We leave this problem for the moment (it will be the subject of another chapter) and now focus on the theoretical approach that some Lutheran theologians adopted. Already Melanchthon advanced a strategy to deal with the German contract. He classified this agreement as a sale, and in this way excluded the application of the interest prohibition. This solution could work well with the real *census*, which was based on the fruits of an estate, but had difficulty in applying to the *widerkauufflicher Zins*, where the personal obligation to pay a 5% annuity was almost identical to an interest. The Lutheran theologians addressed this problem, and the solution they found implied the reformation of the interest prohibition. Johannes Brenz and Johannes Aepinus were among the first who proceeded in this vein. They followed some of the essential aspects that Luther and Melanchthon had already drawn and designed a first reformulation, which would later be carried on by others.

The new theory of interest is founded on a fresh analysis of Luke 6,35: *mutuum date nihil inde sperantes*. The scholastics considered usury (interest-taking) as robbery, a sin against justice. Justice does not distinguish between subjects, because robbery is a wrong action both against rich and poor. Arguing to the contrary, Luther identified the sin of usury as a sin against charity. He did not develop this point, but sowed the seeds for his followers. It is by exploiting this perspective that the Brenz and Aepinus arrived at a new understanding of the passage of Luke 6,35, which separates loans towards the poor from the loans towards the rich. The precept of Luke only concerns the poor, while the rich can enter into business contracts.

The new theory of interest arises from the reinterpretation of the rule of Luke 6,35 and is rooted in Luther's two kingdoms doctrine, as follows. The rule of Luke 6,35 is based on charity and not on justice. It urges lending even without the possibility to receive back the goods. It does not concern the realm of business, but only the poor who can work and return the goods received. Loans must be gratuitous towards them. The rich must abide by the rule of 1 Thess. 4,6, protection against fraud. They can use the *widerkaufflicher Zins* and other contracts, which are regulated by the political ordinance. These contracts are not described by the Gospel, but are determined by the law of the magistrate, which must comply with the natural law, expressed in Matthew 7,12. It is no more the Church that governs the morality of contracts, but the civil magistrate in compliance with Scripture. Furthermore, the Christian is called to apply the ordinance with his own conscience. He must distinguish between a rich borrower and a poor borrower. In the first case he can practice the *widerkaufflicher Zins*, but in the latter he must assist the party with a gratuitous loan.

The new theory rests essentially on two points. First, the theologians reinterpreted the rule of Luke 6,35 as a precept centred on charity, and they distinguished the subjects of the loans from the subjects of business contracts. Second, they separated the regulation of loans from the other business contracts. The loans are regulated by Luke 6,35, in conjunction with 2 Cor. 8,13, which proposes that the lender shall lend according to his capacity and the borrower must strive to return the sum. The business contracts are regulated by the magistrate's ordinance, which must comply with natural law and equity (Matthew 7,12-1 Thess. 4,6).

2.3.2 Mutuum date nihil inde sperantes: *From a Rule of Justice to a Rule of Charity*

2.3.2.1 The Rich and the Poor

The distinction between the subjects of the loan and the subjects of the business contracts, particularly the *widerkaufflicher Zins*, came through scriptural interpretation. Johannes Brenz, in one of his homilies on the gospel of Luke (1541), gave a fundamental impulse for the new interpretation. Talking about the compensation of loss (*interesse*), Melanchthon interpreted the precept of

Luke 6,35 restrictively as only concerning the lending to indigents. In this way, he eliminated business transactions from the range of application of the prohibition on lending at interest. Brenz was probably inspired by this intuition. He considered the rule of Luke 6,35 as expression of the rule of love for one's neighbour (*dilectio proximi*):

> *if the love for the neighbour is really true, it does not only bring with it that civil form of justice, making you lend to somebody from whom you hope something in return; it also makes you lend to the needy and poor, from whom you hope nothing in return. Everyone in fact loves himself so much that he desires to receive a loan when he is oppressed by necessity or poverty, even if he cannot repay it.*[135]

The rule of Luke 6,35 teaches believers to lend even if the borrower cannot return the sum because of poverty or failure.[136] Brenz assumes that this rule derives from the more general love for the neighbour and stresses the distinction between civil justice and charity. The precept of Luke 6,35 goes beyond justice, because it commands to lend even without the possibility of receiving the goods back. Justice requires reciprocity, but the passage of Luke denies the importance of reciprocity. Lending expecting nothing in return is an action that gushes from charity towards the neighbour and is not a rule of justice. The Christian does not seek something in return, but lends because of love.

In Brenz's view, the precept to love the neighbour, as the precept to lend hoping for nothing in return, is directed towards two orders of people.[137] The first precept concerns enemies and friends: "*if indeed I turn towards the enemies it is commanded that I love enemies. Consequently, if I must love my enemies, will it not be licit for me to love friends, too?*".[138] Certainly, Brenz answers, but underlines that love, both for friends and for enemies, requires candour, passion, and that purity that we must have towards friends. Furthermore, the love for

---

135 J. Brenz, *In evangelii quod inscribitur secundum Lucam, duodecim priora capita homiliae centum et decem* Luke 6, Homilia 61, 183b: "*Dilectio enim proximi, si vera est, non hanc civilem tantum iusticiam secum affert, ut mutuum des ei, a quo speres vicissitudinem, sed etiam ut mutuum des ei, nimirum, egeno et pauperi, a quo nullam speres vicissitudine. Nam unusquisque seipsum in tantum diligit, ut necessitate et egestate oppressus cupiat sibi subveniri largitione mutui, etiamsi non sit vicissim solvendo*".

136 J. Brenz, *In evangelii*, Luke 6, Homilia 61, 183b.

137 J. Brenz, *In evangelii*, Luke 6, Homilia 61, 183b: "*Principio igitur, quod attinet ad sentenciam horum verborum: mutuum date, nihil inde sperantes, observandum est, quod sicut in diligendo, ita et in mutuo dando, duo nobis hominum ordines proponuntur*".

138 J. Brenz, *In evangelii*, Luke 6, Homilia 61, 183b: "*Et siquidem vertero me ad partem inimicorum, tunc praecipitur mihi, ut diligam inimicos. Ergo ne, quia praecipitur ut diligam inimicos, non licebit mihi diligere etiam amicum?*".

God must be set at the first place, as Christ said, "*he that loveth father or mother more than Me, is not worthy of Me*".[139]

As for the rule of love, the injunction to lend, hoping for nothing in return, is directed towards two categories of people: the rich, who possess estates, and the poor, who have nothing.[140] Brenz transfers the distinction of the two categories of people that are the subject to the precept of love, to the precept of loan. He writes that while love is a very general precept, for the loan there are two more specific categories: rich and poor. The rule of Christ in Luke 6,35 relates only to the poor and indigents that cannot return the borrowed goods: "*if indeed I turn towards the poor and those who do not have anything and see their necessity, the precept to lend to them hoping for nothing in return applies*".[141]

If the rule of Luke 6,35 only concerns the poor, it remains to be seen which law will apply to the rich parties. Brenz reflects on the nature of the biblical text:

> *if the precept of Luke is to relieve the poor and lend to them gratuitously, will it be illicit to use civil contracts, in which returns are equal, with the rich people and those who possess lands? Shall I lend hoping for nothing in return even to the rich and those possessing lands? Not at all. The rule of love asks me to love the enemies when I am turned towards the enemies, as we said earlier, while at the same time I must love the friends when I am turned towards them. The same is true in a loan: when I am turned towards the poor, I have to take care of them as much as I can, but, by the same token, when I am turned towards the rich, land-owners and those possessing other things, I will be allowed to use civil contracts with them.*[142]

Brenz interprets Luke 6,35 through the lens of the precept to love one's neighbour. As seen before, the rule of love does not request reciprocity, and consequently also the rule of lending hoping for nothing in return does not. But

---

139 J. Brenz, *In evangelii*, Luke 6, Homilia 61, 183b. The reference is to Matthew 10,37.

140 J. Brenz, *In evangelii*, Luke 6, Homilia 61, 183b: "*Sic et in mutuo dando, duo ordines hominum proponuntur nobis: alter ordo est pauperum, nihil possidentium, alter est divitium, aut eorum qui possident agros et alia bona terrena*".

141 J. Brenz, *In evangelii*, Luke 6, Homilia 61, 183b: "*Et siquidem vertero me ad ordinem pauperum et nihil possidentium, ac videro illic necessitatem, ibi tum praeceptum est, ut dem mutuo, nihil inde sperans*".

142 J. Brenz, *In evangelii*, Luke 6, Homilia 61, 184: "*Num ergo, quia praeceptum est ut pauperi subveniam, et gratis mutuo dem, non licebit erga divitem et possidentem agros civilibus contractibus, in quibus paria dantur paribus uti et necesse habeo etiam divitibus et possidentibus agros sine spe recipiendi mutuo dare? Minime omnium, sicut enim in diligendo, ut paulo ante diximus, necesse quidem habeo inimicos diligere, si me vertero ad ordinem inimicorum, interim tamen debeo et amicos, quos ab altera parte habeo, diligere, ita et in mutuo dando, necesse quidem habeo pauperibus pro virili mea succurrere, interim tamen licebit mihi cum divitibus et possidentibus agros et alia bona, civilibus contractibus uti*".

when it is possible to receive something back, the precept of free lending does not apply anymore. The love towards the enemies is indeed different from the love towards the friends. In the same way, the lending to the poor is different from lending to the rich.

Brenz explains that with the rich, the Christians do not have to observe the rule to lend hoping nothing in return, but rather should follow the rule not to defraud the neighbour in business (1 Thess. 4,6).[143] Paul designated this rule for the right use of contracts and did not condemn them. Therefore, the rule *mutuum date nihil inde sperantes* does not forbid using the civil contracts, but only obliges the parties to take care of the necessities of the neighbour.[144] The rule of Luke 6,35 is set in another perspective and only concerns the impoverished; the rich are in the sphere of application of 1 Thess. 4,6, which concerns business. In this way, Brenz separates the regulation of the loans towards the poor from the business contracts for the rich people. The conjunction between the love for the neighbour and the rule of Luke 6,35 casts new light on the prohibition against lending at interest and clarifies that it only applies towards to the poor.

2.3.2.2 *Almosen, leihen und contracten*

Brenz paved the way for Johannes Aepinus, who expanded the difference between rich and poor by introducing a third category: the people who are not completely poor but can work. The opinion of Aepinus, and most of all his distinction of three orders of Christians, became very influential among theologians and jurists. Charles Du Moulin also used it in his *Tractatus commerciorum et usurarum redituumque pecuniae et monetarum* (1546).[145]

In his exegesis on Psalm 15 (1543), Aepinus distinguishes three main activities that constitute society: alms, loans, and other contracts. Because men live

143 See II/2.2.3.

144 J. Brenz, *In evangelii*, Luke 6, Homilia 61, 184.

145 C. Du Moulin, *Tractatus commerciorum et usurarum, redituumque pecunia constitutorum, et monetarum*, Coloniae Agripine, 1584, n. 86, 101: "*Dum haec ad excudendum recognoscerem, commodo venit in manus meas libellus elegantissimus eruditissimi viri Io. Aepini in Psal 15, ubi tres facit hominum ordines, quos iuvare decet dissimili ratione et modo. Quidam (inquit) pauperes, qui ad mendicitatem inevitabili necessitate rediguntur, nec reddere queunt. Quidam indigentes, his ad tempus opus est, sed aliquando reddere poterunt. Quidam possessiones tenent quibus de suo satis est, qui ad tuenda vitae necessaria commoda alienis rebus ac bonis non indigent. Primis gratuita beneficentia seu eleemosyna; secundis mutuum debetur; tertiis permittitur inter se de lucro pacisci*". See also B. Nelson, *The Idea of Usury*, 73. Nelson notices that Aepinus's approach was also used one century before in the work of Annius of Viterbo, *Pro monte pietatis: Consilia*, 8v. R. Savelli, *Diritto romano e teologia riformata*, passim. For the popularity among the jurists, see IV/2.

together in the earth, he writes, these three interactions cannot be eliminated. Society on earth is likened to a body with nerves or veins, which cannot survive with one element missing.[146] The comparison with the human body helps to clarify the concept. As Aepinus explains, if these parts were abolished or not exercised, all the societies, all the business and the states of life would be stopped, and dissolved, as a body is drawn by lot and falls if the nerves or veins were cut.[147] Societal cohesion is guaranteed by three activities: giving alms, lending, and practising contracts. These three parts must remain united. They represent the fundamental bond of society, so that if one of these activities is lacking, society ends.

Although he does not quote any biblical passage, Aepinus adds that God ordered these three activities. He claims that there is an ordinance of God that is necessary for the conservation of the life and states on earth:

> *the law of God has not only commanded that one gives alms and lends to his neighbour; for the sake of the common good He has also ordained the use of contracts and business, viz. that people shall buy, sell, and negotiate amongst each other.*[148]

Alms, loans, and contracts are a creation of God. To Aepinus, God has ordained this so that we can be certain that we use the contracts with clear conscience, as we use the other ordinances of God. Furthermore, following God's ordinance, the secular law (*weltliche Recht*) has forged rules, form, matters, and mode, so that men can negotiate and do business with each other.[149]

Aepinus looks at the structure of society as an ensemble of these three God-approved activities – giving alms (*Almosen*), lending (*leihen*), and using contracts (*contracten*) – which correspond to three different classes of people, not only two, as with Brenz. This is the crucial point. Aepinus suggests that some people are absolutely poor and destitute (*ganz arm und notturfftig*); because of inescapable poverty, they beg or pray for God's will. They must live with alms and cannot give back what they received.[150] Then, some other people are also destitute but still strong, healthy and fresh (*wol notturfftig aber doch starck, gesund und frisch*); members of this group can work. They need help, but not

146 J. Aepinus, *Auszlegung D. Johannis Epini vber den XV. Psalm Davids*, Franckfurt am Meyn, 1543, 54.

147 J. Aepinus, *Auszlegung*, 54a.

148 J. Aepinus, *Auszlegung*, 54b: "*Gottes gesetz hat nicht allein gebotten das man Almusen geben, und seinem nechsten leihen soll, sondern hat auch, dem gemeinen besten zu gute, contract hantierung und hendele verordnet, dz ist, das sie undter einander sollen kauffen und verkauffen und vergleichen*".

149 J. Aepinus, *Auszlegung*, 55b.

150 J. Aepinus, *Auszlegung*, 68a.

forever, only until they can walk by themselves and return the sum received. Finally, a third category concerns the people who possess goods. They have enough for their preservation and need in this life. They do not require help.[151]

The division of people into these three categories is related to the activities: alms (*Almosen*) are given to the poor; funds are lent (*leihen*) to the able-bodied poor; and civil contracts (*contracten*) are formed between the wealthy. The prohibition of interest only concerns the poor who can work (*wol notturfftig aber doch starck, gesund und frisch*). Loans given to them cannot charge interest. Widows, elders, orphans, sick, unemployed or underemployed people, and people who suffered calamities or unfavorable events may not be completely lacking financial means, but regardless need particular assistance and are classified as poor.[152] Instead the rich people have the possibility to use business contracts, as the German contract, where a charge of an interest is included. Loans are not to be given to the poor and destitute (*ganz arm und notturfftig*), either with or without interest; monies given to them are to be regarded as gifts. In this way the range of application of the prohibition against interest is additionally circumscribed. The rule of Luke 6,35 is not a rule of justice for every Christian, but a precept of charity to help the poor who can work.

2.3.3 *Loans to the Poor*

2.3.3.1 *Relaxatio* and *adflictio*

The reinterpretation of Luke 6,35 and the consequent differentiation between orders of people separated sharply the loans for the poor who can work and the other contracts, especially the *widerkaufflicher Zins* that are for the rich. Luke 6,35 regulates the loans towards the poor, while the magistrate regulates the other contracts. This separation produces three effects: a new regulation for the loans, the reformulation of the interest prohibition, and a new regulation for business contracts. We take now the issue of the loans and the prohibition

---

151 J. Aepinus, *Auszlegung*, 68a.

152 W.J. Wright, *Capitalism the State, and the Lutheran Reformation: Sixteenth-Century Hesse*, Athens, Ohio University Press, 1988, 118. Wright stresses that theologians and lawmakers focused on these people because Luther forbade begging. On the relationship between the Lutheran Reformation and poor relief see H.J. Grimm, *Luther's Contribution to Sixteenth-Century Organization of Poor Relief*, in *Archif für Reformationsgeschichte*, 61 (1970), 222-34; A.P. Knobler, *Luther and the Legal Concept of the Poor in Sixteenth-Century German Church Ordinances*, Ann Arbor, MI, UMI Press, 1992; T.G. Fehler, *Poor Relief and Protestantism: The Evolution of Social Welfare in Sixteenth-century Emden*, Farnham, Ashgate, 1999; C. Lindberg, *Beyond Charity*, passim; R. Jütte, *Poverty and Deviance in Early Modern Europe*, Cambridge, Cambridge Univerisity Press, 2006; J. Witte Jr., *Martin Luther's Influence on Legal Reforms and Civil Law*, in *Oxford Research Encyclopedia of Religion* (March 2017) DOI: 10.1093/acrefore/9780199340378.013.503 (accessed 8.2.2018).

of interest that concerns the poor and then we discuss the other contracts destined to the rich.

Martin Luther stressed the gratuitous nature of the loan:

> *but if we look the word of Christ squarely in the eye, than he does not teach that we are to lend without charge, for there is no need for such teaching, since there is no other lending than without charge, since if a charge is made it is not a loan.*[153]

Nonetheless, in his admonition of 1540, he also individuated a rule for performing the loans. For Luther, the rule of Luke 6,35 must be interpreted in accordance with the rule of Paul in 2 Cor. 8,13: "*For I do not mean that other men should be eased and ye afflicted, but that there be an equality*". Paul, writes Luther, does not want believers to give to the other so that he receives a life of ease, and we receive a life of affliction.[154] If this were the sense of Christ's words, by lending we would damage ourselves. Christ does not want us to become mendicants, Luther continues, but he intends that we help the mendicant as well as we are able.[155] The rule of lending means for Luther that the Christians have to lend, but the time and quantity depend on their capability and should not harm their position. To Luther, the rule of Paul is the practical criterion for performing the loans.

Melanchthon distinguished between the loans in accordance with duty (*mutuatio officiosa*) and the loans that are not in accordance with duty (*mutuatio non officiosa*). The first type of loan is made to help the other, if the lender can lend without loss of his resources. This loan is regulated by Luke 6,35, but also by Prov. 5,16 and 2 Cor. 8,13. God wishes that the Christians lend to assist their neighbour, but without squandering their substances. The loan must not cause damage to the lender. The loans that are not in accordance with duty are the loans for economic use (*usus oeconomicus*), which normally admit the practice of the *interesse*.[156]

Aepinus endorsed Luther and Melanchthon's interpretation, but inserted it in his discourse on the three categories of people: poor, poor who can work, and rich. In the description of the second category, namely the people who can

---

153 M. Luther, *Ein (grosser) Sermon von dem Wucher*, in WA 6, 47-8: "*Aber ßo wir dem wort Christi recht unter augen sehen, ßo leret er nit leyhen on auff facz, dann das ist nit not zu leren, seyntemall keyn ander leyhen ist dan on auff faß, oder ists mit auff facz, so ists nit leyhen*".

154 As we will see also later, the two terms 'ease' (*relaxatio – Ruhe*) and 'affliction' (*adflictio – Trübsal*) assume a central role and are translated from the Greek New Testament: *ἄνεσις* and *ϑλῖψις*.

155 M. Luther, *An die Pfarrherrn, wider den Wucher zu predigen*, WA 51, 384-5.

156 P. Melanchthon, *Dissertatio de contractibus*, in CR XVI, 505-6.

work, he maintains that the Christians should lend to them, because they are not so poor and sick to beg and can give back the money lent after a certain time. The lender shall lend according to his capacity, so that he is not harmed by the loan. The borrower must strive to return the sum and not live in laziness. Aepinus bears this statement by referring to the rule of Paul in 2 Cor. 8,13:

> *and this teaches us also the Scripture clearly, in 2 Cor. 8 the Apostle Paul says that one should exercise the work of love with good assessment and wariness, so that equality is kept and one does not have a life of ease (Ruhe) because of the other one's affliction (Trübfal). It means that one should not live lazy, unworried and idle thanks to the sorrow and effort of another one.*[157]

The loan is not devoid of regulation, but it also must comply with equality, so that none of the parties is damaged. Aepinus explains that if one gave money to derelicts and bad people, there would not be equality. There would be only affliction and damage for one of the parties, and laziness and idleness for the other.[158] Thus, the Christians should lend carefully and to people who can work and will strive to return the goods.

The first effect of the separation between loans to the poor and business contracts for the rich is that the rule of Luke 6,35 in conjunction with Paul 2 Cor. 8,13, should regulate the loans. The rule of Paul sets out the way the loans should be performed and applies to the second category of people. These people are poor but can work and must return the sum, because if they do not do it, they damage the creditor. The lender shall lend according to his capacity and the borrower shall strive to return the sum, without harming the lender. Beneath this rule lies again charity, as fundamental principle of the Gospel. Charity pushes the lender to lend, and the borrower, to return the sum.

2.3.3.2 The Interest Prohibition Reformulated

The second effect of the separation between loans to the poor and business contracts to the rich is the reformulation of the interest prohibition, which only concerns lending to the poor and not to the rich. In his exegesis of Psalm 15, Aepinus concluded that all the biblical laws about loans and interest (*usura*) do not refer to people indistinctly but only to the second order:

---

157 J. Aepinus, *Auszlegung*, 69a: "*Und solches leret uns auch die Schrifft klerlich, zu den Corinthern in der andern im viii. cap. sagt der Apostel Paulus, das man die werk der liebe mit guten bescheide und fursichtigkeyt uben sol, das es gleich sei und gleich zughe, dass der eine nitt ruhe hab mit des andern trübsal, das ist, das der eine nit ein faul, mussig, unbesorget leben habe, mit eins andern sorg und mühe*".

158 J. Aepinus, *Auszlegung*, 69a.

to this second order of men pertain all the divine laws about loans and interest that we have talked about before and which these clearly speak about the poor and not about all men without distinction.[159]

In this way Aepinus fulfils his theory and reinterprets the interest prohibition as only referring to the poor. The *Zinskauf* is not a usurious contract, but it is approved by God. The interest prohibition only concerns loans towards the poor, and not the other contracts that are lawfully approved.[160]

Aepinus's interpretation probably inspired David Chytraeus, who in his commentary on the Deuteronomy defines usury as almost only related to the poor and interprets the passage of Scripture that regards the interest prohibition as only referring to the poor.[161] He states that usury only concerns the loan where something beyond the principal is demanded, most of all to the poor and the weak. Hence, only the immoderate interest and the charging of interest to the poor are forbidden. Exodus 22,25; Leviticus 25,35-37; and Deuteronomy 15,7-10 all refer to the poor.[162] The passage of Luke 6,35 is not an injunction to donate only the interest from a loan, but also the principal to the poor who are insolvent.[163] According to Chytraeus, the sinners lend to each other hoping to receive the equal in return, but the precept of Christ affirms lending hoping for nothing in return (not even the lent sum); the person pities the poor, and lending to them is actually lending to Christ and thus earning his credit.[164] Christ is not teaching to seek profit, but to help the poor. The passage of Luke 6,35 does not forbid business, but invites the Christian to assist the poor by lending, and since they are poor the Christian shall not expect something in return. It is a

159 J. Aepinus, *Auszlegung*, 69a: "*Auff diese andere ordnung der menschen gehören alle götliche gesetze vom leyhen und wom wucher, die wir vor hin erzelet haben, welche klerlich und deutlich von den nottürfftigen reden, und nit von allen menschen ins gemeine on unterschiedt*".

160 J. Aepinus, *Auszlegung*, 67b: "*Es ist aber der zinss kauff kein wucherischer contract, derhalben wirt solcher zinss kauff auch von Got nit verdampt, Denn wucher gehörtt und ist allein bei dem leihen und borgen, und nit in andern contracten, die die recht approbirn*".

161 D. Chytraeus, *In deuteronomium*, 431: "*Nos autem ex verbo Dei et Sacris literis iudicium formantes certo statuamus, usuras omnes, in quibus propter solum officium mutuationis, aliquid supra sortem a pauperibus praesertim et attenuatis ut scripturae verbo utar petitur aut accipitur, a Deo prohibitas et illicitas esse, eosque magis vituperandis et detestandas esse, si immoderatae sint et insuper ut dixi a pauperibus exigantur*".

162 D. Chytraeus, *In deuteronomium*, 432.

163 D. Chytraeus, *In deuteronomium*, 432: "*Et Christus non modo usuras, verum etiam sortem pauperibus, qui non sunt solvendo, donari iubet*".

164 D. Chytraeus, *In deuteronomium*, 432: "*Nam et peccatores peccatoribus dant mutua, ut recipiant aequalia (id est, sortem vel sortis valorem) sed mutuo date nihil inde sperantes (ne quidem de sorte) et erit merces vestra multa et foeneratur enim Domino, qui miseretur pauperis*".

precept of the Gospel that moves from charity towards the neighbour and not a precept of justice that concerns business.

Chytraeus reinterprets Scripture as saying that the interest prohibition only regards the poor. He does not consider all the passages (for instance, he does not reference Psalm 15,5), but beginning from the New Testament (Luke 6,35), he re-evaluates the Old Testament (Exodus 22,25; Leviticus 25,35-37; Deuteronomy 15,7-10). The Gospel illuminates the rest of the Scriptures and works as lighthouse for its reading. In this way, the essential content of the prohibition is reformulated: from a social rule for the whole business, to a precept for the poor; from a legal norm for the society to a rule for the community of Christians; from a rule of justice to a rule of charity. The scholastics had interpreted the passage as a rule that prohibited the whole society from profiting from a loan. Loan at interest (usury) is a form of robbery, forbidden by the virtue of justice. The rule had a universal character, and its violation led to excommunication. Justice does not distinguish between poor or rich, because robbery is wrong *per se*. Chytraeus' reinterpretation of the Gospel fills the rule with a new sense. Because of the call to exercise charity towards the neighbour, the lending to the poor is forbidden. The Gospel is not interpreted as a legal rule, but as a rule of charity towards the poor. The juridical element is removed in favour of charity. The result is that the rule to lend hoping for nothing in return is a precept of charity that only concerns the poor.

The new formulation of the interest prohibition was translated into practice by the resolution of the numerous disputes about the interest-taking prohibition and the acceptance of a five per cent annuity. For example, in his collection of theological counsels (*Consiliorum theologicorum decas VI*, 1609), Felix Bidenbach reported a dispute that occurred in 1578. The theologians Jakob Heerbrand and Theodor Schnepf wrote an opinion on the possibility to take a 5% annuity (*census* or *Zins*). The passage of Luke 6,35 had been invoked to designate such kind of contract as usurious. The theologians remarked that Christ considers here only the loan towards poor and indigent.[165] In this passage, Christ does not refer to the loan for business, which is allowed:

> *But here Christ is not discussing in general of each and every loan or lending, but only of the loan made for alms* (Mutuo Eleemosynario), *since everyone has the duty to help and to lend to the poor according to his capacity, especially when they (= the poor) are in need, but not in such a way that the other ones (= those who do not lend) are without sorrow (literally: have rest) and those who lend are afflicted.*[166]

165 F. Bidenbach, *Consiliorum theologicorum decas VI*, Franckfurt am Meyn, 1609, 66.

166 F. Bidenbach, *Consiliorum theologicorum decas VI*, 66: "*Aber es redet hie Christus nicht in gemein von jedem unnd allem Mutuo oder Leihen: Sondern allein von dem Eleemosynario,*

For the two theologians, Christ did not come to this world to give laws and ordinances and to restrain the secular business of sales; rather he left this task to the secular magistrate.[167] The resolution of this dispute synthetizes the discussion made before: the rule of Luke 6,35 only concerns the poor; and Christians must lend according to their capability and without harming their position.

In conclusion, the separation between orders of people brings out two fundamental consequences for the loans. The first one is that loans to the poor are regulated by Scripture, which protects the parties against harm. The lender must lend to the poor according to his capacity; the borrower must work hard to return the sum. The loan to the rich presents no equality, because the rich borrower would receive a benefit and the lender would suffer damages. The second consequence is the reformulation of the interest prohibition. Scripture does not forbid profit in financial loans, but only the profit from loans to the poor. The precept of Luke 6,35 is the cornerstone of the new interpretation. Christ does not instruct his followers to avoid business, but to help the poor as a work of charity. The precept is not founded on justice, but it is governed by charity. The legal norm the scholastics formulated is abolished. What remains is a rule of charity, to assist the poor.

2.3.4 *The* widerkaufflicher Zins

2.3.4.1 The Authority of the Magistrate

The distinction between the three orders of people made it possible to divide loans to the poor from the other contracts, especially the *widerkaufflicher Zins*, which was earmarked for the rich parties. In his homily on the Gospel of Luke that we examined before, and in a counsel entitled *Von wucherlichen Contracten und Zinsgelt* published by Felix Bidenbach in 1608,[168] Johannes Brenz wondered whether the German contract, the contract by which an annual incomes (*emptio annuorum redditiuum*) is purchased, was usurious.[169] He answers frankly that is not the Holy Scripture that determines it, but the magistrate:

---

da den Armen sonderlich in dem Nothfall, ein jeglicher nach seinem Vermügen, als einem armen Menschen zu helffen und zu leyhen schuldig, doch nicht der gestalt, dass die andern sollen ruhe haben, und die Leyhende trübsall".

167 F. Bidenbach, *Consiliorum theologicorum decas VI*, 66-7.

168 F. Bidenbach, *Consiliorum theologicorum decas I*, 20-2.

169 J. Brenz, *In evangelii*, Luke 6, Homilia 61, 184.

> *the Holy Scriptures teach clearly that unlawful contracts and unlawful interest must be avoided, but by no means they teach which contracts are unlawful and usurious. The Scriptures leave this task to the human laws, and to the ordinances and constitutions of the civil magistrate.*[170]

In the book of Genesis, God says to man:

> *be fruitful and multiply, and replenish the earth, and subdue it; and have dominion over the fish of the sea, and over the fowl of the air, and over every living thing that moveth upon the earth.*[171]

To Brenz, by giving humanity dominion over the earth, God is commanding man to order and administer the earth and what pertains to the civil life. The conservation of civil life and human society thus pertains to the civil magistrate and civil contracts. God gave to man, and especially to the magistrate, the power to conserve civil life and rule on the lawfulness of civil contracts.

Brenz accompanies this interpretation with the analysis of two other texts: Psalm 115,16 and Rom. 13,1. The Psalm proclaims: "*the heaven, even the heavens, are the Lord's; but the earth hath He given to the children of men*". Brenz interprets the text as saying that God dominates the earth and heaven and satiates it, but leaves to men the external administration of the earth, so that with their reason men judge the lawfulness of the civil contracts, and much more this task pertains to the magistrate. Paul says in Rom. 13,1: "*let every soul be subject unto the higher powers. For there is no power but from God; the powers that be are ordained by God*". To Brenz, Paul would not ask the Christians to submit to the magistrate if the magistrate did not have the power to judge in these matters. Thus, establishing which contracts are lawful and not lawful is a duty of the magistrate, and Christians do not have to look to the Holy Scriptures but to the laws, ordinances, and regulations of their ruler. The magistrate, Brenz points out, should not, however, be insane, but should judge according to right reason.[172]

Brenz is applying the Lutheran political theory, which sees in the magistrate a divine minister. The magistrate receives from God the authority to govern the world, and Christians must obey him. The evaluation of the magistrate is the key point to determine if the *widerkaufflicher Zins* is usurious. The civil

---

170 J. Brenz, *In evangelii*, Luke 6, Homilia 61, 184: "*Sacrae literae docent quidem illegitimos contractus, et illicitam usuram fugienda et vitanda esse, nequaquam autem docent, qui contractus sint illegitimi et usurarii, sed reiiciunt hoc iudicium ad leges humanas, et ad ordinationes atque constitutiones magistratus civilis*".

171 Gen. 1,28.

172 J. Brenz, *In evangelii*, Luke 6, Homilia 61, 184b.

ordinances of the magistrate are to be considered as a 'divine ordinance', writes Brenz in another homily.[173] In this ordinance the German contract is ordered with authority and majesty.[174] The ordinance was made with the counsellor of the electoral princes and the senate of the Holy Roman Empire. It is clear that the contract by which an annual income in a certain estate or goods is purchased is considered to be a just and lawful contract with a maximum annuity of 5% of the capital.[175]

Brenz's approach might be labelled as positivist. He insists dramatically on the authority and wisdom of the magistrate and the clearness of the text of his ordinance. However, even though he does not refer to natural law, Brenz adds some other considerations to justify the imperial ordinance. In the law, he writes, the *widerkaufflicher Zins* is classified as a sale. The classification is important to separate this contract from a loan.[176] In fact, it is a species of the contract of sale and has all the elements: merchandise, price and consent. Taking evidently inspiration from Melanchthon and the scholastics, Brenz asserts that the clause of re-selling is compatible with the nature of the sale. Furthermore, he maintains that the contract is not against equity. One of the parties possesses the estates and does not want to alienate them but can relinquish the fruits of the estates, while the other one has money. If this contract were not allowed, the party who needs money because of necessity would pay a large interest rather than sell his goods.[177] In this way, the sale of annuity appears equal.

On the whole, Brenz concludes that even if this contract might not appear to be useful and just, the magistrate authorized it. This is the central point. And the Holy Spirit commands that we obey the judgment of the magistrate. As Paul says, this is a divine ordinance, so that he who resists it resists God.[178] This conclusion might reveal some aspects of resignation. The magistrate judged in this way so there is no other solution than obeying. The subjects must obey the magistrate even when his decision might not seem correct.

173 J. Brenz, *In evangelii*, Luke 19, Homilia 29, 553: "*Tametsi dici posset, quod haec parabole tantum gratia recitentur, nec agatur hic, num usurae illae civiles sint licitae at illicitae, attamen quia hic fit earum mentio, paucissimis observandum est, quod usus eorum contractuum, qui publicis et civilibus legibus approbantur, sit licitus et honestus, propterea quod civiles ordinationes, sint ordinationes divinae*".

174 J. Brenz, *In evangelii*, Luke 6, Homilia 61, 185: "*In qua ordinatione videtis primum, quanta autoritate et maiestate de hoc contractu constituatur*".

175 J. Brenz, *In evangelii*, Luke 6, Homilia 61, 185.

176 F. Bidenbach, *Consiliorum theologicorum decas I*, 20-2.

177 J. Brenz, *In evangelii*, Luke 6, Homilia 61, 185.

178 J. Brenz, *In evangelii*, Luke 6, Homilia 61, 185.

2.3.4.2 Divine Ordinance

Aepinus also distinguished loans, which are governed by the evangelical rule of Luke 6,35, from the other contracts, especially from the *Zinskauf*, which are regulated by the ordinance of the magistrate. The Gospel regulates the free loans, but the law regulates the *Zinskauf* and other contracts. Aepinus writes that Christ did not set out ordinances or laws for the secular world, but left this task to the magistrate (*Obrigkeit*). The Christians must obey the ordinances of the magistrate and consider them as divine ordinances that can be used with good conscience.[179] The kingdom of Christ is not of this world and therefore Christ does not formulate rules of good policy for the secular business, but designates and entrusts the public authorities with this task.[180] This is a clear application of the two kingdoms doctrine. The magistrate receives a divine power, and for this reason, his ordinances are like divine ordinances.

Brenz claimed that it is not a task of the Scripture but of the magistrate to determine the regulation of contracts. Aepinus also insists on the necessity of the magistrate law because the Holy Scripture does not include the complete regulation of contracts:

> *the Gospel of our Lord Christ postulates justice, equity and equality in the secular business, but it does not set the form, manner and rules of these business. Furthermore, it does not show in particular what is just or unjust, equal or unequal, in a particular contract or affair. Therefore, in such secular business we have to follow the ordinances and statutes of the political authority that do not transform the contract into a loan, which would be a violation of the forum conscientiae, viz. God's court.*[181]

The Gospel does not provide the secular kingdom with a law of contracts, and for this reason, the Christians have to keep the magistrate's ordinances.

Unlike Brenz, Aepinus points out that the natural law must approve the positive law of the Magistrate. For this reason, he writes that the imperial ordinance

---

179 J. Aepinus, *Auszlegung*, 69-70.

180 J. Aepinus, *Auszlegung*, 70a: "*Das reich Christi ist nit von dieser welt, derhalben ordnet der Herr Christus auch nit policeien, machet kein gesetz von weltlichen hendeln, sonder weiset und wirffet solcher hendel erkentnuss auff die obrikeit*".

181 J. Aepinus, *Auszlegung*, 78a-b: "*Das Evangelium unsers Herrn Christi furdert in weltlichen hendeln gerechtigkeyt, billigkeyt, und gleichmessigkeyt. Aber die form weyse unnd regele solcher hendele, stellet er nicht, zeyget auch nicht an, was in eynem ietlichen contract unnd handele inn sonderheyt recht oder unrecht, billich oder unbillich sei. Derhalben ist von nöten dz wir in solchen weltlichen hendeln, folgen der Obrigkeyt ordnungen und Statuten, die nit wider die foro conscientie, wie mans heyst, das ist inn Gottes gericht, in den contract des leihens verwandelt*".

> *is not against the natural law, because it does not damage the common good. It does not destroy and spoil the (different) classes and the essence of this necessary human life, but rather preserves it much more. There is also justice and equality in it, neither is it against the love for the neighbour.*[182]

Natural law represents the criterion to judge the ordinance of the magistrate. Natural law is not the law of reason, but as for Luther, it corresponds to the rule of Matthew 7,12: "*all things whatsoever ye would that men should do to you, do ye even so to them*". Since the natural law is not against the magistrate's provisions, Aepinus concludes that the Christians can practice these contracts with a clear conscience.[183] The ordinance is a divinely inspired injunction that the Christians can apply with clear conscience.

God confers on the magistrate the power to rule the earthly world and to determine which contracts are lawful and which are unlawful. The magistrate, in this case the Holy Roman Emperor, decided that a 5% annuity is lawful. The Christians must keep the ordinances of the magistrate and consider them as divine directives that can be used with clear conscience. This approach is tremendously positivistic. However, Aepinus adds that the ordinance must not transform the contract into a loan, which would make it a violation against the *forum conscientiae*, and that it must abide by the natural law, which is the criterium to judge and apply the dictates of the ruler. He argues that this ordinance, however, is not against natural law and does not damage the neighbour.

2.4 Charity and Finance I: Early Guidelines

2.4.1 *Introduction*

After the divide between loans towards the poor and other contracts, especially the *widerkauflicher Zins* for the rich, other theologians made a further step towards a Lutheran theory of interest. For Brenz and Aepinus, the gratuitous loans and *widerkauflicher Zins* have different regulations. Luke 6,35 and 2 Cor. 8,13 govern the loans, while the *widerkauflicher Zins* is regulated by the magistrate's ordinance. The magistrate receives from God the authority to rule the world and the Christians must obey his ordinance as a divine precept. The

182 J. Aepinus, *Auszlegung*, 77b: "*Dieser abscheid des Reyches ist nicht wider das Naturliche Recht. Denn er schadet nicht dem gemeynen besten, er zerstöret unnd verderbt auch nicht die stende und das wesen dieses notwendigen menschlichenn lebens, sondern erhelts viel mehr, es ist auch darinn billigkeyt unnd equalitet, auch ists nicht wider die liebe des Nehesten*".

183 J. Aepinus, *Auszlegung*, 78b.

ordinance must comply with natural law, however, as expressed in the principle of Matthew 7,12.

Urbanus Rhegius formulated a new interpretation of Luke 6,35 in conjunction with the rule of love and natural law. If charity and natural law towards the neighbour are kept, the German contract is not usurious. A contract breaches the interest prohibition only if there is damage to the neighbour. Rhegius does not distinguish between rich and poor, but charity and natural law become the essential instruments for evaluating and applying the imperial ordinance. The ordinance does not condemn every contract, but leaves room for the Christians to judge in the concrete circumstances if the neighbour is offended. If the party is damaged, they cannot apply the ordinance, because Luke 6,35 exhorts the Christians to lend hoping for nothing in return. But if the neighbour is not offended, charging interest is allowed.

Niels Hemmingsen refused Rhegius' approach, because it does not correspond with the Scripture. Yet, he acknowledged that the magistrate might allow interest-bearing loans. Interest-taking (usury) is not a sin in itself but it is a sin because of the behaviour of the usurer who is greedy and idolatrous. The magistrate could therefore allow loans at interest. A stronger opponent of the new trend was Martin Chemnitz. He rejected not only Rhegius' interpretation, but also Aepinus and Hemmingsen's theories, and turned back to the scholastic conception of the interest-taking prohibition: any profit in a loan is forbidden. However, Chemnitz's approach conjugated the scholastic investigations on the nature of contract with Christian charity, which he converts to an essential principle of contract law.[184]

For Chemnitz, Christian charity rules the gratuitous loans, but also the contract with the clause of redemption (*contractus redemptionis*), the partnership and the *interesse*. In a loan, if the borrower cannot return the goods, the lender must not urge restitution. The lender must pay attention to the necessity of the borrower; he cannot take in pledge something that the borrower needs for his support. Among the rich, loans must not be used to cause damages. The contract with the clause of redemption must meet the needs of the parties. If the debtor is unable to pay the debt, charity pushes the creditor to remit the debt. In the partnership, the parties must share profits and losses. In the practice of the *interesse*, some precautional rules prevent offending charity.

Although charity emerges as the fundamental principle of contract law, both for loans and other business contracts, differences in the interpretation of Scripture and connections with the scholastic methods make it still difficult to

184 See II/2.2.2.

speak of a systematic Lutheran theory of interest. Rather a draft or a guideline for lending contracts rooted on charity is sketched out, which other theologians will bring to a conclusion.

2.4.2 *Rhegius: A Change of Perspective*

2.4.2.1 *So hab erstlich fur augen das natürliche gesetzt und des nehesten liebe*

A pioneer of the new approach was Urbanus Rhegius, yet he might have drawn on the work of Martin Bucer (1491-1551).[185] Rhegius has been almost ignored by all the historians who examined the problem of usury. Although not very famous, his writings were nonetheless cited by popular theologians as Chemnitz (who explicitly quotes him) and might have inspired John Calvin and Charles Du Moulin.[186] In 1536 Rhegius wrote a sermon on Psalm XV, in which he addressed some issues on interest (*Wucher*).[187] Although Rhegius does not define the contract, it is clear from the name that he discusses the five per cent contract, classified as a partnership (*Contract der geselschafft fünffe vom hundert*).[188] Rhegius' theory is divided in two parts. First, he elaborates a new definition on usury, combining the precept of Luke 6,35, natural law (Matthew 7,12), and Christian charity. He then applies this construction to the legal ordinance that allowed a 5% annuity.

Rhegius starts by analysing the usual definition of usury (interest-taking). Usury occurs when something is taken beyond the principal in a loan.[189] Such behaviour, he notices, is directly against the love for the neighbour, because the usurers seek only their profit and not the love.[190] The usurers, writes Rhegius, act in this way:

---

185 On Bucer's theory see: C. Hopf, *Martin Bucer and the English Reformation*, Oxford, Blackwell, 1946; B.N. Nelson, *The Idea of Usury*, 68-72; N. Jones, *God and the Moneylenders. Usury and Law in Early Modern England*, Oxford, Blackwell, 1989, 20-3. On Bucer and the law, see C. Strohm (ed.), *Martin Bucer und das Recht*, passim.

186 Rhegius writes before Calvin and Du Moulin. Neither cite him, but their statements are incredibly similar to his.

187 Short reflections can also be found in U. Rhegius, *Loci theologici e patribus et scholasticis neotericisque collecti*, Francofurti, 1550, 129-30. Rhegius repeats the same four degrees of dealing with temporal goods discussed by Luther. The purchase of annuity (*census*) is considered a form of business (fourth degree: buyng and selling).

188 U. Rhegius, *Derr XV psalm Davids*, [35].

189 For the description of usury see before III 2.1.2.

190 U. Rhegius, *Derr XV psalm Davids*, Magdeburg, 1538, [29]. Because the booklet has no page numbers, I numbered them. Index of the psalm (*Inhalt dieses psalmen*) = page 1. The part about usury begins at page 27: "*Wer sein geld nicht auff wucher gibt*".

> *if you are poor and need their money, they like to see that and would not want that you were to become richer, because they plan to lend you money and other things, making very sure to take back the principal and the interest they impose in surplus to the principal. The usurers do not want to bring themselves in danger with the debtor, in case that he dies or ruins, but they want to be sure of their money through an honest surety and pledge. So, they come to your house and sit behind the stove, without worry and risk, and leave their money for handling, then you must pay 5%, 6%, but also 9%, 10% or 20% annually.*[191]

In this way, Rhegius observes critically, the creditor earns a consistent profit, and the debtor is oppressed.[192] Rhegius views the behaviour of the usurer as an act of aggression towards the neighbour. The usurer lends the money, and by charging interest, he exploits the borrower. Such an aggression corresponds to the nature of interest-taking as is described in the Scripture. In the Scripture, the word 'interest' (*usura*) has two names: *Neschech* and *Tharbith*. *Neschech* means a bite, because the usurer damages the neighbour, while *Tharbith* connotes an increase – the usurer uses the portion gained to enrich himself.[193] The words used to designate interest in the Scripture thus confirm that interest-taking (usury) is a transgression against the love of the neighbour, as the increment is conjoined with the damage: "*therefore it is clear and without doubt for all Christians that usury is a big sin (and) in flagrant contradiction to the love for the neighbour*".[194]

Medieval theologians considered usury a sin against both justice and the seventh commandment of the Decalogue, classifying it as a form of robbery. To Rhegius, usury is a sin against the love for the neighbour. This new classification changes the perspective of the interest prohibition, opening new borders. Rhegius claims that the passage of Luke 6,35 should be read in relation with the rule of love for the neighbour:

191 U. Rhegius, *Derr XV psalm Davids*, [30]: "*Bistu arm an geld, und bedarffst ires gelds, das sehen sie gern, sie wolten nicht das du reicher werest, denn sie gedencken dir geld und andert zu thun, mit guter vergewissung der heubtsumma, und des wuchers, den sie vber die heubtsumma nemen, und wollen mit iren schuldenern inn keiner fahr stehen, die schuldener sterben oder verderben, so wollen sie ires gelds gewiss sein, durch redliche bürgschafft und underpfand. Da komen sie zu haus hinderm ofen sitzen, on alle sorge und fahr, und lassen ire gülden hantieren, da mus hundert gülden ein iar nicht allein fünff oder sechs, sondern neun, zehen, ia etwa funffzehen oder zwentig gülden ewuchern*".

192 U. Rhegius, *Derr XV psalm Davids*, [30].

193 U. Rhegius, *Derr XV psalm Davids*, [31].

194 U. Rhegius, *Derr XV psalm Davids*, [32]: "*So ist nu gewiss und ungezweivelt bey allen Christen, das der wucher ein grosse sunde ist, der liebe des nehesten gantz entgegen*".

> *Yes, our true master Christ speaks that one should lend and hope nothing in return, and from that it is clear that when one lends and takes something in addition to the sum, this is abhorrent from the teachings of Christ. But one must also look around in other places in the Bible what is important to know in this business. Christ and the apostles teach us everywhere that the love for the neighbour is the fulfilment of the second table of the Decalogue.*[195]

The love for the neighbour should be put at the fore, and the other precepts must be interpreted through it. The passage of Luke 6,35 should be read in conjunction with the rule of love, because every action or omission concerns the neighbour:

> *since this charity is truly the right rule, to which all our doings with regard to our neighbour should be directed. And what is based upon and done according to this rule, that is well done. And in this case one should very diligently see to the natural law, as Christ teaches in Matthew 7.*[196]

The natural law Rhegius means is expressed in Matthew 7,12: "*all things whatsoever ye would that men should do to you, do ye even so to them; for this is the Law and the Prophets*". The connection between the tenets of Luke 6,35, Matthew 7,12, and the love for the neighbour allows Rhegius to argue that usury is a sin against love.

Up to now Rhegius mostly followed Luther, but then he goes further. He does not consider that every loan is against the interest-taking prohibition because of the breach of the rule of Luke 6,35. To be considered as usurious, a loan must not only violate this rule, but must also offend the rule of love. The breach of Luke 6,35 is not against the interest prohibition if there is no offence against the neighbour:

195 U. Rhegius, *Derr XV psalm Davids*, [33]: "*Unser rechter Meister Christus spricht ia man sol leihen, und nichts davon hoffen, daraus denn erscheinet, wenn man leihet und uber die heubtsumma etwas nimpt, das ist der lere Christi zu wider. Aber man mus auch an andern orten weiter inn der schrifft umbsehen, was zu diesem handel zu wissen nötig ist. Christus und die Apostel leren uns allenthalben das die liebe des nehesten sey eine erfüllung der andern tafel Mosi* (...)".

196 U. Rhegius, *Derr XV psalm Davids*, [33]: "(...) *Denn diese liebe ist warlich die rechte Regel, darnach sich all unser thun und lassen, gegen unserm nehesten richten sol. Und was nach dieser Regel gericht und gehandelt wird, das ist wol gehandelt, und ist hie inn diesem handel gar vleissig auff das natürliche gesetz zu sehen, wie Christus uns leret Matth. vii*".

> *when a Christian keeps this rule (the rule of love) towards the neighbour in a contract or loan, we should not readily consider that contract as usurious.*[197]

The prohibition of interest changes its form because of the rule of love: a contract is not usurious if it does not damage the borrower.

Rhegius contends that Christians must judge with their conscience if the contract damages the neighbour. With an emphatic expression, he affirms that in each business transaction, a Christian must firstly have before his eyes the natural law and the love for the neighbour: "*So hab erstlich fur augen das natürliche gesetzt und des nehesten liebe*".[198] With regard to the payment of the annuities, Rhegius suggests that there is no offence when the gratitude (*danckbarkeit*) for the money received pushes the debtor to pay something beyond the principal. If the debtor wants to give to the creditor part of his profit, and this does not damage him, Rhegius writes, he can do so, and the contract should not be reproached as usurious.[199] Rhegius uses the gratitude to justify the attribution of a sum of money in addition to the principal.[200]

At the same time, charity invites the parties to share profits and losses. Rhegius holds that the investor shall not damage or lead the entrepreneur to ruin but should help him and share damages and benefits faithfully and safely.[201] In the German contract, the seller/entrepreneur must support the risk of losing the capital that he received from the buyer/investor. Rhegius alters the structure of the contractual obligation by inferring that the parties should share both damages and benefits. The risk should not belong only to one party, but should be shared.

When charity for the neighbour is used as the basis for determining the legality of potentially usurious contracts, Rhegius argues, the Christian must judge if there is a breach of charity, or damage to the borrower. The gratitude for the money received can lawfully motivate the concession of part of the

197 U. Rhegius, *Derr XV psalm Davids*, [33]: "*Wenn nu ein Christ diese Regel helt gegen seinen nehesten, inn einem Contract, oder lehen, so sollen wir den selben Contract nicht bald wucherlich urteilen*".

198 U. Rhegius, *Derr XV psalm Davids*, [34]. He could have found inspiration in M. Luther, *Decem praecepta Wittenbergensi praedicata populo*, 502-3.

199 U. Rhegius, *Derr XV psalm Davids*, [34].

200 The scholastic theologians also admitted this solution, see S. Piron, *Le devoir de gratitude. Émergence et vogue de la notion d'antidora au XIIIe siècle*, in D. Quaglioni, G. Todeschini, G. M. Varanini (eds.), *Credito e usura fra teologia, diritto e amministrazione*, 73-101.

201 U. Rhegius, *Derr XV psalm Davids*, [35]: "*Der Lehenherr dringet den kaufmann nicht inn schaden, und gedenckt in nicht zu verderben, sondern im auff zu helffen, hat schaden unde nutz gemein mit dem kauffmann trewlich und ungeferlich*".

profit to the entrepreneur and the receipt of something beyond the principal. For Rhegius, the creditor and debtor must share profits, but also losses.

2.4.2.2 Applying the Political Ordinance

The second part of Rhegius' theory entails the application of his interpretation of Scripture to the Lutheran political theory. Rhegius examines the ordinance of Charles V that admitted a 5% annuity, and as Melanchthon, Brenz and Aepinus before him, claims that it is a divine ordinance:

> *since the political authority (Obrigkeit) is an ordinance of God (Rom. 13), and all the ordinances that such an authority issues and approves, on the basis of the natural law and written law are also approved through the Word of God and recognized as legitimate. They should be observed.*[202]

Because the magistrate exercises a divine role, the magistrate's ordinances are as God's ordinances and must be obeyed.

Then, Rhegius adds the new interpretation he previously articulated. The natural law and Christian love imply that it is usury only that really offends the neighbour. The magistrate did not deem interest-taking as universally forbidden, but only when it is against natural law and Christian love. The magistrate did not condemn every loan at interest, because not every loan is forbidden. The Christians should operate in the same way and distinguish when charging interest is against the neighbour and when it is not:

> *so we should not quickly judge before we learn that the lender with his loan forgets the fraternal love (der brüderlichen liebe) and only considers his own benefit, regardless of how the debtor will be able to cope. We must work in this case with the mouth of God that designates interest with two names Neschech and Tharbith, that is suppress/suppressing and increase/increasing. When the money is lent and claimed back in this sense, only with the aim or the consequence that the usurer derives increase and splendour from it and the needy suppression and ruin, then this truly goes against the love for the neighbour and constitutes a dreadful sin.*[203]

---

202 U. Rhegius, *Derr XV psalm Davids*, [35]: "(…) *Denn Oberkeit ist ein ordung Gottes Rom. 13, und alle ordnung so ein Oberkeit aus dem natürlichen und geschriebenem gesetz macht und billicht, werden durch Gottes wort approbiert, und fur recht erkant, die man halten sol*".

203 U. Rhegius, *Derr XV psalm Davids*, [35-36]: "*Derhalben wir nicht geschwind urteilen müssen, bis wir erfaren, das der Lehenherr mit seinem ausleihen der brüderlichen liebe vergisst, und allein auff sein eigen nutz trachtet, unangesehen wie der schuldner bestehen möge. Denn wir müssen inn diesem handel auff Gottes mund werken, der den wucher nennet Neschech unde Tharbith, das ist, ausbeissung und mehrung, wenn gelt dieser meinung wird aus gelihen, und wider geheischet, das dadurch allein des wucherers zunemen und herrligkeit, und des dürfftigen ausbeissung und verderben gesucht wird, oder folget. Furwar das ist wider die liebe des nehesten, und grewliche sunde*".

Rhegius invites Christians to a practical judgment in the application of the political ordinance. The magistrate leaves Christians the freedom to apply the ordinance, making sure that nobody is offended. Interest-taking is not forbidden if there is no damage for the neighbour. The two Hebrew words for interest (Neschech and Tharbith) show that usury is when the lender seeks to increase his resources without regard for the impoverishment or bankruptcy of the borrower. The connection between these two words reveals that usury is against the love for the neighbour. When love is not offended, however, we can deduce that the lending at interest is lawful.

The burden therefore is on the Christians to distinguish if the neighbour is damaged or not in the concrete circumstances. Emperor Charles V, Rhegius writes, and a long time before him, the Christian emperor Justinian did not consider every sum beyond the principal to be usurious, and for this reason the Christians should also hold this judgment.[204] Rhegius uses the example of Justinian to claim that the magistrate's ordinance is a lawful legislation. The magistrate followed natural law and charity and approved the German contract, because interest-taking is not universally forbidden but only when the neighbour is damaged.

Christians must follow the same criteria and apply the ordinance in accordance with natural law and Christian love. Charity works here as a criterion to justify and apply the ordinance of the magistrate. The ordinance of the magistrate is lawful because it does not forbid every loan at interest but only when there is damage to the neighbour. This is a judgment that the single Christian must perform. However, Rhegius warns that the people who will follow the natural law and Christian love are only the kind-hearted Christians (*gutherzigen Christen*).[205] They do not put faith in temporal goods and will apply the imperial ordinance, avoiding injury to the neighbour. There are also 'worldlings' (*Weltkindern*) that place priority on temporal goods and do not respect the Gospel; they have impure hearts, are without faith, and consider the neighbour only for his goods. They want to to bite, rip, scratch and scrape the debtor.[206] For them, Rhegius continues, it is useless to cite the precept of Exodus 22,25. God says, *"thou shalt not lay upon the poor Neschech, that is interest"* (*Du solt kein Neschech, das ist, wucher auff den armen treiben*), using such language that we understand that he speaks about the damaging interest

204 U. Rhegius, *Derr XV psalm Davids*, [36].

205 The nature of the true Church and the distinction between Christians and non-Christians was an important topic for Rhegius. See S. Hendrix, *Urbanus Rhegius*, in C. Lindberg (ed.), *The Reformation Theologians*, 119.

206 U. Rhegius, *Derr XV psalm Davids*, [36].

(*schedlichen wucher*) that oppresses, damages, and bites the poor.[207] The difference between these two categories of people, kindhearted Christians and worldlings, reflects the new vision of the Church: no more a society governed by legal norms, but a community of Christians inspired by the Gospel. The rule of love cannot be imposed by a legal norm, as only the true Christians can put it into practice. Charity issues essentially from faith.[208] Rhegius speaks in terms of counsels that the Christians will apply, and which the worldlings, who are not concerned with the Gospel, will refuse.

In a nutshell, Rhegius analyses the interest prohibition in relation to natural law and Christian love. In this way he comes to the conclusion that interest-taking is not always damned, but only when the neighbour is offended. When the neighbour is not damaged, as for instance if the debtor gives something to the creditor out of gratitude, there is no usury. Natural law and Christian love are unified in one precept: not harming the neighbour. They are also the criteria to judge the ordinance of the magistrate. The magistrate admitted the German contract, because he did not consider charging interest as generally forbidden, but only when there is damage to the neighbour. Christians are therefore called to the same acute evaluation and use this contract only when it will not result in injury for the borrower. The real Christians, Rhegius points out, will have before their eyes the natural law and the love for the neighbour and will apply the magistrate ordinance in a way that ensures the neighbour is not harmed.

2.4.3 *Hemmingsen at the Crossroad of Interest Theories*

Rhegius' interpretation may have been an inspiration for John Calvin and Charles Du Moulin. They also contended that a loan at interest is not forbidden, if there is no damage for the neighbour. They observed that the term *usura* (interest) in the Holy Scripture is described with two names: *Neschech* (bite) and *Tharbith* (increase) because God wants to teach us that interest-taking harms the neighbour.[209] In the Lutheran orthodoxy, though, some theologians

207 U. Rhegius, *Derr XV psalm Davids*, [37].

208 See II/2.2.2.

209 For Calvin's theory see E. Ramp, *Das Zinsproblem*, 81-97; B.N. Nelson, *The Idea of Usury*, 73-82; M. Wykes, *Devaluing the Scholastics: Calvin's Ethics of Usury*, in *Calvin Theological Journal, 38* (2003), 27-51; M. Schmoeckel, *Das Recht*, 250-2. On Du Moulin: M. Le Goff, *Du Moulin et le prêt à intérêt: le légiste, son influence*, Genève, Mégariotis, 1905; R. Filhol, *Dumoulin Charles*, in R. Naz (ed.), *Dictionnarie de droit canonique*, vol. VI, Paris, 1950, 42-67; J. L. Thireau, *Charles du Moulin, 1500-1566: étude sur les sources, la méthode, les idées politiques et économiques d'un juriste de la Renaissance*, Genève, Librairie Droz, 1980, 372-79; R. Savelli, *Da Venezia a Napoli: diffusione e censura delle opere di Du Moulin nel cinquecento italiano*, in C. Stango (ed.), *Censura ecclesiastica e cultura politica in Italia tra*

reacted against this theory. The etymology of the words *Neschech* and *Tharbith* is not entirely clear, and Niels Hemmingsen, in his *Enchiridion theologicum* (1557) rejects Rhegius' view.[210] He argues that interest (*usura*) is not only designated with the word *Neschech* (bite) but also with the word *Tharbith* (increase). Lev. 25,36: *Take thou no interest* (*Neschech*) *from him or increase* (*Tharbith*), should therefore be interpreted as forbidding anything that exceeds the principal. Any increment beyond the principal is forbidden.[211] Hence, the prohibition against interest is generalized, and this distinction does not justify the usurers.[212] In Hemmingsen's view, the interpretation of Scripture must take into account the two meanings of interest. Interest is not only damage, but also increase. For this reason, every increase in a loan is prohibited.

Despite his refusal of the new thesis, Hemmingsen formulates an argument in favour of the admission of lending at interest. He distinguishes between sins by nature (*peccata sua natura*) and sins by an additional circumstance (*peccata quae peccati rationem ex adiuncto sumunt*). Sins by their nature are idolatry, blasphemy, murder, theft, adultery, and false witness. They can never be admitted and must be punished by the magistrate. Sin by an additional behaviour is usury. The magistrate, with prudence, could admit interest-bearing loans. Lending at interest is not a sin, but the sin is in the additional behaviour of the usurers who are greedy and idolatrous and burden the debtor with the payment of interest against the precept of love.[213]

Hemmingsen justifies this position by referring to the passage of Deut. 23,20: "*Unto a stranger thou mayest lend upon interest, but unto thy brother thou shalt not lend upon interest*". He comments that if interest-taking/usury were a sin by nature, God would have not admitted it to be charged to the foreigners;[214] but because God did not prohibit it, interest-taking is not a sin by nature. Hemmingsen leans on the admission of interest for the Jews towards the foreigners to claim that charging interest is not universally forbidden. He

---

Cinquecento e Seicento: VI Giornata Luigi Firpo; atti del convegno, 5 marzo 1999, Firenze, Olschki, 2001, 101-54; On both of them: J.T. Noonan, Jr., *The Scholastic Analysis of Usury*, 365-70; C. Gamba, *Licita usura*, 227-34.

210 N. Hemmingsen, *Enchiridion theologicum*, Viteberga, 1564, 417: "*Nec de usura ulla distinctio contra legem naturae et verbum Dei recipienda est*".

211 N. Hemmingsen, *Enchiridion theologicum*, 417.

212 N. Hemmingsen, *Enchiridion theologicum*, 417-8.

213 N. Hemmingsen, *Enchiridion theologicum*, 407: "*Non enim per se peccatum est dare mutuo pecuniam, iuxta pactionem interpositam, sed ex adiuncto peccati rationem sortitur, nimirum ex eo, quod et animus usurarii avarus sit et idolatra et proximus gravetur contra dilectionis praceptum*".

214 N. Hemmingsen, *Enchiridion theologicum*, 407: "*Nam si sua natura peccatum esset huiusmodi contractus, nequaquam suo populo permisisset Dominus usuras capere ab alienis*".

adds that this interest cannot be deemed admissible as a form of the so-called spoils of the Egyptians (*Spolia Aegiptiorum*), namely the authorized theft of the Egyptians' goods before the Exodus, because the stolen goods were the salary for the hard work they had been subjected during the slavery in Egypt.[215]

On the one hand, Hemmingsen closed the doors to the new theory that admitted loans at interest when there is no damage for the neighbour. On the other hand, he acknowledged that the magistrate can allow loans at interest. Interest-taking is not a sin in itself, but it is a sin (usury) because of the greed and idolatry of the usurer that spurs him to issue usurious loans. If it were universally forbidden, God would also have forbidden the Jews from charging interest on loans to foreigners. This passage of Scripture is for Hemmingsen a confirmation that interest-taking is not always damned, and the magistrate might allow it. Interest-taking is different from usury.

2.4.4 *Chemnitz: Trusting only the Scriptures*

2.4.4.1 The Real Meaning of *usura*

The progress towards the formation of a Lutheran theory of interest broke suddenly at the end of the sixteenth century. Martin Chemnitz rejected most of the new theories and turned back to a classic interpretation of the interest prohibition. Despite this criticism, however, he pursued the road traced by Luther and Rhegius on Christian charity as a fundamental criterion of proper behaviour in matters of finance. Chemnitz begins with a refined etymological interpretation of the word 'interest' (*usura*). Together with the Latin word *usura*, he takes into consideration the Greek term *τόκος*, which Aristotle used in his *Politics* to argue that money is not utilized as mean of exchange in usurious contracts, but rather breeds money, which is against its nature. Then he also examines the three Hebraic words. The word 'נֶשֶׁךְ' (*Neshech*) means corrosion and bite, which is similar to avarice, as is described in Micah 3,5. The term 'נָשָׁה' (*Nashah*) means trouble or burden, which is used in Deut. 24,10-11. Finally, the terms מַרְבִּית (*Marbith*) and תַּרְבִּית (*Tharbith*) which mean multiplication of quantity, as when repayment of the loan demands more than what is given, and when the lender does not aim to help the neighbour but only seeks to multiply his profit.[216]

After the examination of the different words used to mean interest in the Scriptures, Chemnitz concludes that in the Scriptures, interest-taking is not a good thing *per se* and in its kind. It is not a question of use or abuse, moderation or approval, so that only the excess is to be condemned. Interest-taking is

215 N. Hemmingsen, *Enchiridion theologicum*, 407.

216 M. Chemnitz, *Loci theologici*, pars secunda, 158.

per se an evil, vicious, and damned action.[217] Interest-taking is not only disapproved of but also prohibited by God, writes Chemnitz. In Deut. 23,19-20, God will bless the believer who does not engage in loans at interest with works and lands, but he will curse with works and expel from the homeland the believer who charges interest.[218] Moreover, the passage of Proverbs 28,8: "*he that by interest and unjust gain increaseth his substance, shall gather it for him that will pity the poor*", suggests that the usurers will suffer the malediction of God.[219]

Chemnitz's strong and steady conclusion already sounds like a refusal of the new theories of interest. The detailed examination of interest is only the basis for his subsequent work. In the light of his vision that interest-taking is generally and universally forbidden by the Scriptures, Chemnitz criticizes the new approaches towards a reformulation of the interest prohibition. Urbanus Rhegius, but also reformed theologians and jurists like John Calvin and Charles Du Moulin, assumed that God designated interest by two names: *Neschech* (bite) and *Tharbith* (increase), because he wanted to teach that charging interest damages the neighbour. Interest-taking is not *per se* harmful, but only when it is associated with damage against the neighbour. When it does not 'bite', as for example between two rich parties, the Scripture would not condemn the charging of interest.[220] Chemnitz refuses this view, because it is not clearly stated in the Scripture. First he observes that in the holy language, *usura* 'interest' can also be intended as multiplication of quantity, and not only as 'bite' or corrosion. Second, he reflects that if the Scripture really had wanted to create this difference, it would have made it clear. For instance, Christ made explicit the prohibition of divorce except in cases of fornication. But the Scripture simply speaks about interest (*usura*) without any distinction between rich and poor. For these reasons, Chemnitz concludes that the interpretation that interest-taking is not harmful *per se*, but only when effectively it damages the neighbour, is wrong. This interpretation is not true and complete, and it cannot give certainty to conscience.[221]

---

217 M. Chemnitz, *Loci theologici*, pars secunda, 158-9: "*Constituendum est ex certis et perspicuis Scripturae testimoniis, usuram non esse rem per se et suo genere bonam, nec ita mediam, ut ex usu, vel abusu iudicetur, et moderatio quidem probetur, excessus vero tantum damnetur: sed esse actionem per se et suo genere malam, vitiosam et damnatam*".

218 M. Chemnitz, *Loci theologici*, pars secunda, 160: "*... sed consideretur in singulis testimoniis atrocitas verborum, quibus damnatur usura: Deut. 23, v. 19. Non foeneraberis fratri tuo ad usuram, etc. sed absque usura, quo indiget, commodabis, ut benedicat tibi Deus in opere tuo in terra etc.. Ergo usurae puniuntur maledictione Dei, in operibus et ejectione ex patria*".

219 M. Chemnitz, *Loci theologici*, pars secunda, 160-1.

220 M. Chemnitz, *Loci theologici*, pars secunda, 162.

221 M. Chemnitz, *Loci theologici*, pars secunda, 162: "*Sed quia ex verbo Dei de hac quaestione iudicandum est, etymologicae illae notationes non possunt conscientiae eam, quae hac in re*

Having rejected Rhegius and Du Moulin's interpretation, Chemnitz goes on to deal with Aepinus and Chytraeus' view that the interest prohibition only concerns lending to the poor. Chemnitz replies to them that the Scripture (Psalm 15,5, Ez. 18,8, and Luke 6,35) forbids charging interest without any distinction of people. From the clear content of the Scripture, the conscience cannot be sure of this difference between poor and rich, Chemnitz holds that the definition of the interest prohibition must remain the traditional one, which concerns everybody.[222] He only trusts well-defined statements of Scripture that can assure conscience, and since Scripture is not univocal about the reference to the poor, it is not possible to reduce the interest prohibition only to them.

Chemnitz also rebuts Hemmingsen's view, which interpreted the passage of Deut. 23,20 as an admission of charging interest. In the eyes of Hemmingsen, interest-taking would not be a sin by nature, because God permitted it in loans to foreigners. Taking inspiration from Jean Gerson, Martin Chemnitz responds that in the Old Testament, God acted both as a theologian and legislator, dictating rules both for the sanctity of the soul and for the conservation of civil society. He regulated not only the *forum conscientiae* but also the *forum politicum*.[223] Therefore, in the care for society, some rules were adapted to the external preservation of society. Such rules should only be considered in front of the magistrate and not in the *forum conscientiae*.[224] One of these was about interest,

---

necessaria est, certitudinem praebere, idque propter duas potissimum causas: 1. quia usura in lingua sancta non tantum a mordendo nomen habet, verum etiam a superabundantia et amplius accipiendo, sicut supra dictum est. 2. Si ipsa Scriptura hanc differentiam manifeste ostenderet, quod scilicet cum divite usuram exercere non sit peccatum, tunc res plana esset, sicut de repudio Christus dicit, excepta causa fornicationis etc. (…) *Iam vero de usura simpliciter et in genere Scriptura loquitur, sine tali exceptione et differentia. Non igitur vera, plena et perfecta est etymologica illa definitio*".

222 M. Chemnitz, *Loci theologici*, pars secunda, 165: "*Sed illis et aliis omnibus similibus ratiunculis opponitur hoc simplex, firmum et solidum fundamentum. Si Scriptura in descriptione usurae talem constitueret differentiam, quando in mutuo a paupere aliquid ultra sortem exigitur, esse peccatum, quando vero a divite, esse legitimam et piam negotiationem, tunc plana esset responsio. Jam vero in genere et simpliciter damnat usuram et omnem superabundantiam, quae in mutuo ultra sortem exigitur, sine discrimine a quocunque accipiatur Psal. 15 v. ult. Ezech. 18 v. 8, Luc. 6 v. 35*".

223 M. Chemnitz, *Loci theologici*, pars secunda, 159: "*Deus in Veteri Testamento fuit et theologus et legislator. Alibi enim tradit, quomodo servendum sit Deo, in iustitia et sanctitate coram ipso. Alibi vero pro externa societate vitae civilis in republica israelitica, certas quasdam politicas constitutiones praescribit isti populo. Hoc est, sicut vulgo loquimur, tractat de iure fori et de iure poli, ordinat forum politicum et forum conscientiae*".

224 M. Chemnitz, *Loci theologici*, pars secunda, 159.

which was civilly admitted, but theologically condemned.[225] Charging interest was admitted, but only in the *forum politicum* and not in the *forum conscientiae*. For this reason, Chemnitz comes to the conclusion that God did not mean to permit sin in the law of heaven (*ius poli*), but for the preservation of society, tolerated lending at interest against the foreigners, according to the law of the land (*ius fori*).[226]

The new theories for the reformulation of the interest prohibition are all refused. Acutely Chemnitz explored the details of each theory and brought out their deficiencies. In conclusion, in order to shine light on the labyrinth of the possible false interpretations, Chemnitz singles out what he believes are the essential elements of interest (*usura*):

1) Interest pertains to the contract of a loan for consumption;
2) Interest includes what is beyond the money lent, established both by a pact or the intention of the parties;
3) Interest is when something is charged beyond the principal, because of the use of money or because of the duty to lend. A lawful compensation for the damage that the debtor caused to the creditor (the *interesse*) is not interest. Same if the debtor reckons that he is obliged by gratitude to give something to the creditor as recompense;
4) Interest is not only money, but also everything received in addition to the sum, in the same kind or another kind.[227]

225 M. Chemnitz, *Loci theologici*, pars secunda, 160: "*Ita civiliter permisit usuram erga extraneos, ne erga domesticos fidei exercertur. Ne vero illa permissio traheretur in forum conscientiae coram Deo, saepe repetita inculcatione, Deus generaliter et expresse atrocibus verbis usuram damnavit*".

226 On the origins of these two terms, see P. Prodi, *Una storia della giustizia*, passim; A. Fossier, *Le « for de la conscience ». l'invention d'une nouvelle frontiere juridictionnelle (xiiie siecle)*, in B. Garnot, B. Lemesle (ed.), *La justice entre droit et conscience du Moyen Âge à nos jours*, Éditions universitaires de Dijon, 2014, 115-23.

227 M. Chemnitz, *Loci theologici*, pars secunda, 162-3: "*Ad definitionem igitur usurae pertinet: 1. Quod sit in contractu mutui, Exod. 22. v. 25. Deut. 23. v. 20.* (…) 2. (…) *quod ultra restitutionem sortis aliquid, vel pacto, vel intentione interveniente, exigitur. Inde enim vocatur* מַרְבִּית *seu* תַּרְבִּית *sicut supra dictum est. 3. Quando ultra sortem aliquid exigitur, propter mutuo datae pecuniae usum, vel propter officium mutuationis. Nam legitima compensatio eius quod interest, quando debitor efficacem causam damni dedit, non est usura. Item, quando debitor usu mutuae pecuniae vel damnum aliquod evasit, vel lucratus est aliquid, et intelligens, se gratitudinis ergo obligatum esse ad antidora, aliquid creditori ultra sortem donaverit, si is absque pacto, exactione et intentione usuraria accipiat, non est usura. Honesta enim est sententia iurisconsultorum*: In officiis charitatis primo loco illis tenemur obnoxii, a quibus beneficium agnoscimus accepisse. 4. *Quicquid illud sit, quod ultra sortem exigitur, sive eiusdem, sive alterius generis, est usura*".

Chemnitz explains this last point by referring to St. Jerome and Thomas Aquinas. They both stress that interest is not only money, but also every benefit that the lender obtains in addition to the amount of money that he lent.[228]

With stunning precision, Chemnitz delimited the borders of the interest prohibition. In particular, he concedes the legality of the *interesse*, as a form of lawful compensation for damages suffered by the lender and caused by the borrower. He also permits the debtor to give something in addition to the borrowed sum to the creditor out of gratitude, when the capital saved the debtor from certain damage or earned a profit. As for Rhegius before, to Chemnitz, gratitude does not constitute only a spiritual obligation, but can also undergird an obligation to pay something to the creditor. He emphasizes that this obligation is justified by charity: if the debtor gained a large profit with the money from the creditor, charity commands him to transfer something to the creditor.[229]

On the whole, Chemnitz proposed a rigid and conservative interpretation, in contrast with those authors that maintained that usury is extant only when there is damage for the neighbour, or that it only concerns the poor, or that it is not a sin in its nature. To Chemnitz, interest-taking is always and generally forbidden. The prohibition does not change due to moderation, damage, or the subjects involved. Interest/usury is when something is expected in addition to the sum of money in a loan. Whatsoever thing received beyond the principal is usury. The only exceptions he admits are the *interesse* (compensation for loss) and the payment of a sum from gratitude.

2.4.4.2 *Tria genera christianorum*

Chemnitz outlawed brave and incorrect interpretations of Scripture, but also proposed a regulation on loans and business contracts. This regulation relies on Aepinus' distinction of three orders of people: poor, poor who can work, and rich. The first order concerns the beggars, as for instance Lazarus (Luke 16,20).[230] The beggars (*mendici*), Chemnitz explains, have neither goods, nor money, nor can work to purchase something. They cannot use the contract of sale, because they do not have anything to exchange. Furthermore, the contract of sale was not approved by God to be exercised with beggars. God wants their suffering to be relieved by the giving of alms.[231]

---

228 M. Chemnitz, *Loci theologici*, pars secunda, 163. Unfortunately, he does not mention the works.

229 M. Chemnitz, *Loci theologici*, pars secunda, 168.

230 M. Chemnitz, *Loci theologici*, pars secunda, 163.

231 M. Chemnitz, *Loci theologici*, pars secunda, 163: "*Et contractus illi Deo non probantur, sed est discrimen personarum. Non enim instituit Deus emptionem, ut cum mendicis exerceatur; sed talium inopiam vult sublevari largitione eleemosynarum*".

The second order includes the needy, those people who do not have money or goods, but can work (*sunt quidam, qui nec res, nec pecuniam habent, sed possunt operas praestare*), as in Lev. 25,35: "*and if thy brother be waxen poor, and fallen in decay with thee; then thou shalt relieve him: yea, though he be a stranger, or a sojourner; that he may live with thee*". The biblical text, Chemnitz writes, shows that the Christians have to seize and sustain the brother who is depressed and shaky but can still work, before he falls into poverty. The Christians cannot help him with the contract of sale, nor with alms, because Paul in 2 Thess. 3,12 and in 1 Thess. 4,12 encourages the Christians to work in order to have a respectable life and to need nothing.[232] Chemnitz individuates then two forms of helping these people: the hiring of labour and services and the contract of loan for consumption. The reason is that Lev. 25,39 clearly states: "*And if thy brother that dwelleth by thee be waxen poor, and be sold unto thee; thou shalt not compel him to serve as a bondservant*". If the hiring is not admitted or accepted, the Christian can raise your neighbour with the loan, but God wanted the loan to be gratuitous, so that the neighbour is not oppressed and worn out in the attempt to repay.[233]

To the third order belong the rich, those who God blessed with goods and riches. They can purchase what they need and care for their life,[234] but God did not provide them with all the necessary goods. Thus, they need to use contracts to procure what they need.[235] To Chemnitz, this order does not require alms, and when the Scripture mentions the duty to make free loan towards the poor, it does not refer to them. This order of people shall use the contracts of sale, lease, barter, etc.[236] The contract of loan should instead be used for helping the people of the first and second order.

To this classification, Chemnitz adds two general rules. First, he invites Christians to remember that the promises of alms and free loans are much

---

232 M. Chemnitz, *Loci theologici*, pars secunda, 164.

233 M. Chemnitz, *Loci theologici*, pars secunda, 164: "*Huic igitur hominum ordini Deus praescribit duas formas et modos, ut vel opera ipsorum conducatur. Nam in eodem, Levit. 25.v.39. preaecipit de mercеariis, et de servis, qui propter egestatem se vendunt aliis: vel si vocatio ipsorum elocationem operarum non commode patitur, ut officio mutuationis subleventur. Et illud officium Deus vult esse gratuitum, ne is, qui sublevari debet, opprimatur et exhauriatur*".

234 M. Chemnitz, *Loci theologici*, pars secunda, 164: "*Sunt qui Dei benedictionem habent, et res et facultates, quibus acquirere et tueri possunt vitae necessaria*".

235 M. Chemnitz, *Loci theologici*, pars secunda, 164. See also II/2.2.2.2.

236 M. Chemnitz, *Loci theologici*, pars secunda, 164: "*Manifestum autem est, cum hoc ordine, si qua nostra vel re vel opera indigent, non faciendam esse communicationem per eleemosynas. Et quando Scriptura praecipit, ut egentes et attenuatos gratuita mutuatione sublevemus, ostendit non praescriptum esse hoc officium propter illos, qui per se abundant. Huic igitur ordini propositi sunt reliqui legitimi contractus, ut emptio, locatio, permutatio, etc.*".

greater than other contracts, which have the promises of the seventh precept of the Decalogue. God will bless much more the Christian who give alms and free loans than the Christian who uses sale, *census*, partnership, and other contracts. Second, charity as master and moderator (*magistra et moderatrix*) must always come first.[237] As Chemnitz suggests: "*in the single orders, even the legitimate forms of exchange become unjust and illicit if they are not practiced according to charity or go against it*".[238] He insists on the crucial importance of charity in all the forms of exchange, both gratuitous and onerous. He holds that God wanted charity to be practiced not only towards the poor, but also towards every man in the whole political society.[239] Charity towards the neighbour applies to loans, the contract with the clause of redemption, the partnership, and the *interesse*, as we will see in the next few pages.

2.4.4.3 Lending According to Charity

Chemnitz's treatment of the loan for consumption is divided in two parts. First, he individuates the essential elements of this agreement. Second, he indicates how lending should be performed according to charity. A loan consists of four elements: 1) a thing is transferred to the borrower.[240] 2) The transfer occurs for free, because it is not a sale or a lease. 3) The power to use the thing is not perpetual but for a certain time: it is not a donation. 4) The recipient must return the thing in the same genre, quantity, and estimation. If the recipient does not return the thing, he is a sinner, as Psalm 35,21 testifies. The risk of capital (*periculum sortis*), as for instance in the case of fire or theft, pertains to the recipient.[241]

---

237 M. Chemnitz, *Loci theologici*, pars secunda, 164.

238 M. Chemnitz, *Loci theologici*, pars secunda, 164: "*Fiunt enim in singulis ordinibus, etiam legitimae formae communicationum iniquae et illicitae, si exerceantur sine charitate proximi, vel contra eam pugnant*".

239 M. Chemnitz, *Loci theologici*, pars secunda, 157.

240 Chemnitz suggests that the loan for consumption (*mutuum*) is so named because something that is mine becomes yours (*de meo fiat tuum*). The speculation over the etymology of the contract was already made by Gaius in his *Institutiones* and resulted to be false. The term '*mutuum*' is probably derived from '*mutare*', which means 'to exchange', 'to swap'. See R. Zimmermann, *The Law of Obligations*, 153.

241 M. Chemnitz, *Loci theologici*, pars secunda, 162: "*Et de substantia mutui sunt haec quatuor: 1. quando res ita transfertur, ut fiat accipientis. Mutuum enim inde dictum volunt, quia de meo fiat tuum 2. Debet esse officium gratuitum: alias enim esset vel venditio, vel locatio. 3. Datur potestas utendi mutuo, non in perpetuum; sed ad certum tempus: alias enim esset donatio. 4. Additur obligatio, ut restituatur, non quidem eadem res numero, sed alia eiusdem vel generis, vel quantitatis et aestimationis. Psal. 35. v. 21. Peccator mutuo accipit et non solvit et c. Et quidem de iure periculum sortis pertinet ad accipientem: ut si vel casu vel furto, vel incendio amittatur*".

Chemnitz's analysis breaks apart and illustrates separately the elements of the contract of loan already determined by the Roman law and the medieval discussion. In this way he elucidates the differences with other contracts, especially the donation, sale, and lease, and the main characteristics of the contract of loan for consumption: the gratuitous nature; the borrower must not return the very thing but a thing of the same genre after a certain time; the omission of returning is a sin; the risk pertains to the borrower; the loans must be used towards the people of the second order. He is not a fine jurist, as some formulations suggest. For instance, he seems to say that both loans and donation transfer the use of the thing; instead they produce a conveyance of property rights, which the use is only one aspect.

The loan for consumption is regulated by a number of rules that Chemnitz takes from Scripture and interprets in the light of charity. Morality demands that the lent sum is returned (Psalm 37,21: *the wicked borroweth and payeth not back*), but when the debtor is reduced to poverty, "*thou shalt not be to him as a usurer*" (Ex. 22,25).[242] Indeed, if meanwhile the debtor is reduced to poverty, by virtue of the law of charity, the loan is transformed to alms (*lege charitatis mutuum transit in eleemosynam*).[243] According to Luke 6,35, the Christians should not only borrow when they hope to receive back the things, but also when it is difficult to receive the goods back, as when the poor asks for them. If the debtor can pay, the lender has the right to keep the payment, because the contract of loan includes the obligation to return the goods.[244]

If the lender takes a pledge on a good that the borrower needs as a means of support, or he uses to dress or to sleep, the lender shall return it at the end of the day:

> *If thou at all take thy neighbour's raiment to pledge, thou shalt deliver it unto him by that the sun goeth down: For that is his covering only, it is his raiment for his skin: wherein shall he sleep? and it shall come to pass, when he crieth unto me, that I will hear; for I am gracious* (Ex. 22,26-27) and similarly, *when thou dost lend thy brother any thing, thou shalt not go into his house to fetch his pledge* (…) *and if the man be poor, thou shalt not sleep with his pledge* (Deut. 24,10 and 12).

On this point, Chemnitz seems to follow a literal interpretation, but this might be clarified by the interpretation of the next passage quoted. Deut. 24,6 proclaims that "*no man shall take the nether or the upper millstone to pledge, for he taketh a man's life in pledge*", which Chemnitz interprets as the lender shall not

242 M. Chemnitz, *Loci theologici*, pars secunda, 164.
243 M. Chemnitz, *Loci theologici*, pars secunda, 165.
244 M. Chemnitz, *Loci theologici*, pars secunda, 164.

take in pledge such a thing that the borrower cannot be deprived for the necessary life sustenance.[245] The political laws do not punish this taking pledge, but charity proclaims that this is unjust.[246] The summary of this teaching might be that lender must pay attention to the necessity of the borrower; he cannot deprive him of something needed for his support and in case he does take something like this, he shall return it 'at the end of the day'.

Chemnitz points out that nobody must be damaged by the loan. The precept of 2 Cor. 8,13 sets out that among the rich people, the gratuitous loan must not cause damages and that it is not admitted to anyone, whether rich or poor, to gain profit from a loan. Interest-taking is generally damned and can never be practiced with good conscience.[247] Both Luther and Aepinus employed this passage to maintain that the debtor must not live in laziness and must strive to return the sum. Chemnitz seems to follow this interpretation, by requiring that nobody be damaged because of the contract. Yet, he specifies that the precept protects the people of the third order (the rich people). Furthermore, he insists on the prohibition of interest, barring the way to more liberal interpretations. As we will see later, the passage of 2 Cor. 8,13 was also used to justify profit in a loan.

Lending according to charity means for Chemnitz to abide by a set of rules dictated by Scripture. The borrower must return the goods, but if he is reduced to poverty and cannot return the goods, the loan is transformed to alms. The gratuitous loans do not only concern the poor, but Christians are especially invited to lend to them. Among the wealthy, loans must not be used to cause damages. In any case, the lender should not take in pledge something that is necessary for the borrower's livelihood; if he needs it, the lender has to return it at the end of the day, according to the dictates of charity.

245 M. Chemnitz, *Loci theologici*, pars secunda, 164: "*Ibidem vers. 6. Non accipies loco pignoris inferiorem et superiorem molam, quoniam animam oppignoraverit tibi, id est, rem talem, qua debitor non potest carere ad necessariam vitae sustentationem*".

246 M. Chemnitz, *Loci theologici*, pars secunda, 164.

247 M. Chemnitz, *Loci theologici*, pars secunda, 166: "*Nam igitur Evangelium iubet, ut in tali casu, de quo nunc quaerimus, alter, qui non est attenuatus, mea pecunia ita utatur, ut cum meo damno locupletetur: hoc certe non iubet sicut manifesta est sententia 2 Cor. 8 v. 13. Duo igitur iam constituta sunt. 1 Quod in hoc casu hominibus tertii ordinis, non debetur gratuita communicatio, cum damno alterius. 2 Quod propter officium mutuationis, supra sortem lucrum exigere, nec a pauperibus, nec a divitibus licet. Usura enim generaliter damnata est, ut in nullo casu bona conscientia exerceri possit*".

2.4.4.4 The Contract with a Clause of Redemption (*contractus redemptionis*)

The people of the third order, the rich people, can also use the contract with a clause of redemption (*contractus redemptionis*) in order to gain profits. The essential elements of this contract are the following: 1) the subject of the agreement must be an estate or an income deriving from certain estates; 2) to the contract of sale is added the clause or obligation to resell when the creditor has the power to redeem: when the price is offered the buyer is forced to return the estates or the right to receive the income; 3) until the seller restitutes the price, the buyer has the ownership and usufruct of the estates he bought or obtains the right to receive a certain income from the estates, which income he can use until the seller redeems; 4) the price must be fair and should be estimated by a wise man; and 5) the contract must not lead to the circumvention of the interest prohibition.[248]

This contract, which mirrors closely the contract that Melanchthon analysed,[249] is qualified as a sale of an estate or of the income from several estates with a clause of reselling.[250] It includes the sale with the clause to resell and the real *census*. It also seems to include the German contract, because an income from different lands is allowed, which is one of the essential elements of this agreement. As Melanchthon did, Chemnitz insists on the qualification as a sale, and not a loan, so that this contract does not constitute a breach of the interest prohibition. Furthermore, Chemnitz proves that this contract does not lead to a circumvention of the interest prohibition and does not breach Christian charity.

248 M. Chemnitz, *Loci theologici*, pars secunda, 166: "*Sed cum tertio ordine hominum, qui gratuito mutuo non indigent, et volunt alieno aere uti ad sua lucra et commoda, conceditur contractus redemptionis, illis praecipue, de quibus in hoc casu disputamus. Multa autem in hoc contractu requiruntur, ut legitime fiat. 1 Emuntur vel possessiones, vel reditus certi constituti in possessionibus. 2. Emptioni additur pactum seu obligatio, de retrovendendo, quod creditor habet potestatem redimendi, ut quando obtulerit pretium cogatur emptor restituere, vel possessiones, vel ius percipiendi reditus. 3. Donec venditor restituerit pretium, emptor in possessionibus ita emptis habet dominium et usufructum, vel acquirit ius percipiendi certos reditus ex possessionibus, quo utitur donec venditor redemerit. 4. Debet esse aequalitas pretii, et quia manifestum est, esse differentiam, quando absolute aliquid venditur et quando additur obligatio, unus seu servitus de retrovendendo. Arbitrio igitur bonorum virorum aestimabitur pretium. 5. Non fiat in fraudem usurariam, scilicet quando illis denegatur gratuitum mutuum, qui propter egestatem indiget hoc officio, et offertur illis contractus redemptionis, quo exhauriantur, cum mutuatione gratuita essent sublevandi*".

249 See before 2.2.3.

250 A similar approach was also adopted by Salomon Gessner. See *Commentationes in psalmos Davidis*, 147.

2.4.4.4.1 *The Clause to Resell* (pactum de revendendo)

A crucial element of the contract with a clause of redemption (*contractus redemptionis*) is the clause to resell (*pactum de revendendo*). Chemnitz is not a jurist and he lacks precision when he discusses the clause to resell. Many refined jurists distinguished clearly between the redemption, which belongs to the entrepreneur/seller, and the resale, which belongs to the buyer/investor.[251] For Chemnitz, they seem to be the same thing, because he calls this a contract with a clause of redemption (*contractus redemptionis*), but then he considers the clause to resell (*pactum de revendendo*).

Chemnitz describes the clause to resell (*pactum de revendendo*): it can be perpetual or for a limited period of time until the seller or his heirs can pay the price. If the seller triggers the clause, the buyer is obliged to return the goods. The clause to resell might also include a particular provision according to the seller or his heirs must pay the price by a certain date, after which they lose the right of redeem.[252] The clause to resell that he admits only pertains to the entrepreneur/borrower. The investor/lender is not entitled to redeem the contract.

The lawfulness of this clause flows from Scripture. In Chemnitz's view, God allowed the clause to resell expressly in Lev. 25,23-30, of which we report only the first lines:

> *The land shall not be sold for ever: for the land is mine, for ye are strangers and sojourners with me. And in all the land of your possession ye shall grant a redemption for the land.*

The passage of Lev. 25,23-30, also employed by Jean Gerson for the same aim,[253] concedes effectively the possibility that an estate can be sold with a clause to resell. Since Scripture approves the redemption, the magistrate can also admit a sale with a clause of redemption, and the Christians can use it.

The clause to resell can also be triggered only after a certain period of time. Such a clause to redeem after a certain period of time, writes Chemnitz, can

---

251 See for instance W. Druwé, *Transregional Normativity in Learned Legal Practice. Loans and Credit in* Consilia *and* Decisiones *in the Northern and Southern Low Countries* (*c. 1500-1680*), Diss., Leuven, 2018.

252 M. Chemnitz, *Loci theologici*, pars secunda, 166-7.

253 Chemnitz explicitly refers to Gerson in another part of his work. M. Chemnitz, *Loci theologici*, pars secunda, 157. See also J. Gerson, *De contractibus*, in P. Glorieux (ed.), *Oeuvres complètes*, vol. IX, Paris, Desclée de Brouwer, 1973, 389-90. Leonard Lessius also used this biblical passage. See L. Lessius, *On Sale, Securities, and Insurance*, translated by W. Decock, N. De Sutter, 93.

be a pretext of usury, if an honest and lawful cause is lacking.[254] He warns to proceed with caution, so that conscience is not offended.[255] The honest and lawful cause represents a criterion to evaluate the possible usurious nature of the contract. As today in the modern civil law systems, the cause works as an essential instrument to establish the contract that can lawfully be enforced, so for Chemnitz it determines the lawfulness of the contract.

2.4.4.4.2 *The Contract Should not be Used to Escape the Interest Prohibition*

In the contract definition, Chemnitz specifies that the price must be just and the contract must not be in fraud of the interest-taking prohibition. The element of a just price corresponds to the nature of the sale, and the parties should consider the difference between a regular sale and a sale with a clause to resell. The transgression of the interest prohibition, Chemnitz points out, occurs if at the moment of the redemption, the buyer obtains something more of what he originally purchased.[256] The contract is also usurious if the risk of the sold thing remains on the seller and is not transferred to the buyer.[257] It is against the law, Chemnitz explains, because according to the law, the good that has been sold belongs to the buyer, and he must support the risk. Since this agreement is a sale, when the good is sold, the risk belongs to the buyer and not to the seller. If the contract contains a term that passes the risk to the seller, the contract is usurious. Chemnitz does not mention a single provision, but it seems clear that he refers to the medieval elaboration of Roman law. Finally, the contract with a clause of redemption is in violation of the interest prohibition if it is proposed to people who would need a gratuitous loan; while the contract is more convenient for the investor, if it oppresses the entrepreneur, it should not stand.[258]

Chemnitz's analysis is built on the nature of the contract of sale. First he points out that the clause to resell does not change the nature of the contract. God indeed admitted the sale with clause to resell. Then, he states that the price must be just; and if the risk of the sold thing remains to the seller, it is

---

254 M. Chemnitz, *Loci theologici*, pars secunda, 167: "*Sed hae conditiones de certo tempore ut plurimum sunt pratextus usurarii, nisi subsit honesta et legitima causa*".

255 M. Chemnitz, *Loci theologici*, pars secunda, 167: "*Caute igitur hic agendum est, ne conscientia faucietur*".

256 M. Chemnitz, *Loci theologici*, pars secunda, 166: "*Fiat enim hic contractus usurarius, quando adjicitur tale pactum, ut in redemptione aliquid plus solvatur qua emptor dederit*".

257 M. Chemnitz, *Loci theologici*, pars secunda, 166: "*Item, ut periculum rei venditae pertineat ad ipsum venditorem, usque ad tempus sibi concessum ad redimendum. Hoc enim est contra naturam emptionis, sicut leges dicunt*: res empta debet pertinere ad periculum emptoris".

258 M. Chemnitz, *Loci theologici*, pars secunda, 166.

not a sale but a loan. In a sale the risk is sold with the thing and only the buyer supports it. Finally, he remarks that only rich people can practice the contract.

2.4.4.4.3 *The Contract is not against Charity*

The *contractus redemptionis* is not against charity, if lawfully used.[259] So far Chemnitz has been bound to issues related to the nature of the contract: he worked with the differences between the sale and the loan. Now, he explores the observance of Christian charity. A specific character of the nascent Lutheran theory of interest is the compliance with Christian charity. It is not enough that a contract is not a loan and does not breach the interest prohibition. It must also maintain Christian charity towards the neighbour. To Chemnitz, charity entails first that both the parties receive benefits from the contract, and then that they help each other in case of need, by repaying or remitting the debt.

The *contractus redemptionis* presents several advantages for the parties: the buyer can rent his money and receive a profit; the seller can redeem the goods, if he does not want to sell them definitively. The seller of an annuity conserves the property and usufruct of the good, so step by step, he can scrape together something and eventually pay the price to redeem the annuity. When, instead, the estate is sold, the party has no more the right of property and the usufruct, so he can find the price to redeem in other ways.[260] The contract is therefore useful for both the parties and does not produce any damage. Chemnitz seems to look at the *contractus redemptionis* as an instrument to help the neighbour, more than a financial operation aimed only at profit. He requests the parties to use this contract to benefit each other and not for self-centred accumulation of wealth. Before entering into the contract, the parties are called to evaluate their needs, and to ensure that the contract meets them. In this way the contract does not stymie charity.

Chemnitz stresses that the parties also have to consider the requirements of charity while performing the contract. The precept of charity shows that among the people of the third order, if an obligation overtaxes and oppresses the neighbour, the debt must be remitted. Chemnitz justifies this statement by referring to Isaiah 58, 6: "*is not this the fast that I have chosen? to loose the bands of wickedness, to undo the heavy burdens, and to let the oppressed go free, and that ye break every yoke?*" He interprets this passage as concerning promissory notes, setting aside *bounds of impiety*, paying oppressing assets. He explains

259 M. Chemnitz, *Loci theologici*, pars secunda, 167: "*Nec pugnat contra charitatem, si legitime usurpetur*".

260 M. Chemnitz, *Loci theologici*, pars secunda, 167.

that asking the payment of a debt, as a promissory note, is not a sin, but if it is against charity, even a just promissory note becomes unjust.[261] In general, charity implies that the creditor remits the debt, if the debtor is unable to repay. As for the gratuitous loans, the investor must not oppress the entrepreneur. The detailed framework of this rule, and especially the cases when it applies, are not indicated. Other theologians will solve this lack later.

The *contractus redemptionis* therefore is not against charity, if the parties abide by some rules. The contract can help the neighbour, if both the parties receive benefits. The buyer receives a profit, while the seller obtains the capital, with the power to terminate the contract. It is clear, however, that before entering into the contract, the parties must estimate their respective needs that the contract should meet. While performing the obligations, if the contract burdens the debtor, the creditor should remit the debt.

2.4.4.5 Partnership

Chemnitz offers another solution to the people who cannot or do not want to use the *contractus redemptionis*. They can sell a promissory note on a *census*, or they can use the partnership. Chemnitz does not write much on the promissory note, except as we have seen, that the creditor must remit the debt in the case of the debtor's need. He focuses instead on the partnership. The scholastic theologians already considered lending constructions based on partnership contracts lawful. Melanchthon also admitted the partnership, but emphasized that the parties must share losses and profits: the contract is a vicious if one of the parties gains more.[262] Similarly, he condemned the clause where only one of the parties is guaranteed against every risk and the other suffers damages (*pactum de salvo capitali*). This contract is not a partnership, he observed, but a loan.[263]

Chemnitz leans on Melanchthon and maintains that when one of the parties has the capital and the other can work, they can make a partnership. Chemnitz points out that a partnership is different from a loan, because in the partnership, the property of the money is not transferred to the entrepreneur, but the risk, profit, and damages are shared between the parties. If there is a clause of insurance for the investor (*pactum de salvo capitali*), and it

261 M. Chemnitz, *Loci theologici*, pars secunda, 164: "*Ita in tertio ordine, quando contractus proximum exhauriunt et opprimunt, praecipit Scriptura de remissione debiti, sicut Esa. 58, v. 6. loquitur de syngraphis, dissolvere colligationes impietatis, solvere fasciculos deprimentes, et c. Et per se quidem, repetere debitum juxta syngraphas, non est peccatum, sed si pugnet contra charitatem, etiam legitimae et justae syngraphae fiunt iniquae*".

262 P. Melanchthon, *Philosophiae moralis epitomes libri duo*, in CR XVI, 142.

263 P. Melanchthon, *Philosophiae moralis epitomes libri duo*, in CR XVI, 142.

includes the case when the other incurred in damage without its negligence, the contract becomes a loan, and the money paid to the investor contravenes the interest prohibition.[264] Again, as before with the *contractus redemptionis*, Chemnitz plays with the distinction between loan and partnership. The partnership is based on the sharing of profit and losses between the parties. If one of the parties, by a clause of insurance, gets only profit, the contract should be requalified as a usurious loan. This clause transforms the contract into a loan at interest, because the investor gives the capital to the entrepreneur and receives a certain guaranteed profit.

2.4.4.6 The *interesse*

The scholastics already allowed the *interesse* as a lawful compensation for damage incurred in a loan and distinguished it from *usura*. They individuated several titles of *interesse*.[265] Melanchthon allowed two titles: loss occurring (*damnum emergens*) and profit ceasing (*lucrum cessans*). Melanchthon's immediate followers, e.g. Von Eitzen and Chytraeus, repeated his positions.[266] Rhegius stressed that in a purchase of annuities the *interesse* (compensation) for *lucrum cessans* and *damnum emergens* is usurious when it is requested of the debtors who were less prosperous than the creditors.[267] Martin Chemnitz followed Melanchthon, but added four rules based on commutative justice and charity towards the neighbour.[268] First, the amount of the compensation should be determined by referring to the creditor and not to the debtor. Second, the creditor must receive the compensation only to repay the damage, so that he can be unscathed. Third, the compensation must be founded on an effective and near cause. In fact, Chemnitz points out that a remote and accidental cause can be a pretext for charging interest. Fourth, the debtor is obliged not to seek to gain profit from damaging the lender.[269]

---

264 M. Chemnitz, *Loci theologici*, pars secunda, 167: "*Est autem haec differentia inter mutuationem et contractum societatis, quod hic dominium pecuniae non transfertur in accipientem; sed pericula, lucra et damna communia sunt. Si enim fiat pactum de salvo capitali, etiamsi alter sine sua negligentia damno affectus sit, incidit in mutuationem, et est usura, quicquid ultra sortem exigitur*".

265 See before 2.2.3.3.

266 P. Von Eitzen, *Ethicae doctrinae: pars altera*, Lib. VI, Cap. XII, 478; D. Chytraeus, *In deuteronomium*, 427.

267 U. Rhegius, *Loci theologici e patribus et scholasticis neotericisque collecti*, 129b.

268 Particular rules were also formulated by the scholastics. See C. Zendri, *L'usura nella dottrina dei giuristi umanisti: Martin de Azpilcueta (1492-1586)*, in D. Quaglioni, G. Todeschini, G.M. Varanini (eds.), *Credito e usura fra teologia, diritto e amministrazione*, 265-90 (288-90).

269 M. Chemnitz, *Loci theologici*, pars secunda, 168.

Chemnitz relies on Melanchthon, but does not make any explicit reference to the canonists. As he did before with other contracts, Chemnitz applies charity as essential principle of contract law to the *interesse*. Charity includes specific duties for the lender and the borrower. He who creates the damage must pay, because it would be unjust if the lender suffers damage from the borrowers without a just recompense. The amount of the compensation must be determined on the basis of the damage suffered, but only the damages caused directly by the borrower should be paid. Furthermore, the lender shall not ask more than the payment of the damage, and the borrower shall not gain profit from the injury of the lender.

Chemnitz is sceptical with regard to the *interesse* agreed at the beginning of a loan, and most of all about the ceasing profit (*lucrum cessans*), because he deems that this remedy can be an easy way out for usurers.[270] In the end, Chemnitz allows the *lucrum cesssans*, but with some conditions. First, the profit concerns only the people involved in business, because there is certainly damage when a negotiation is interrupted. Second, the *lucrum cessans* must be current or 'quasi-current' (*in actu vel quasi in actu*). The creditor can be impeded in a possible profit, but not from a profit that he would have never obtained. It is called *lucrum cessans* because a current damage takes place, not a possible damage. Third, if the lender advances funds to people who are not indigent, it is possible to assume that he is looking to accrue real interest, but to gain profit without labour and the risk of lending. Fourth, the amount of the compensation must not be established by the creditor but by the magistrate.[271]

Since the *lucrum cessans* might be a pretext for breaching the interest prohibition, Chemnitz formulates a series of precautionary rules. The *lucrum cessans* can only be applied to business contracts; the loss must be concrete; the cause of the compensation must be clearly determined; and the magistrate must define the amount. In short, Chemnitz substantially follows Melanchthon's attitude towards the *interesse*, which in turn draws upon the canonists. However, he tends to be more careful and rigorous to the possible breaches of the interest prohibition. Charity exhorts the parties not to abuse of the *interesse* and ask for it only when necessary.

---

270 M. Chemnitz, *Loci theologici*, pars secunda, 168: "*Et de interesse damni emergentis, certa et manifesta est ratio. Sed interesse lucri cessantis obscuriores habet latebras, quibus usurarii se tegunt*".

271 M. Chemnitz, *Loci theologici*, pars secunda, 168.

2.5 Charity and Finance II: Systematic Treatment

2.5.1 *Reforming the Interest Prohibition*

2.5.1.1 Introduction

Chemnitz' restrictive interpretation of the interest prohibition added fuel to the debate on the lawfulness of the German contract. The problem is made clear in a counsel of Jean Gerhard published in Dedekenn's *Thesaurus consiliorum et decisionum* (1623). Since Chemnitz damned interest-taking in general, the question was whether the taking of five per cent annuities (*Zins*) has to be considered usury.[272] Gerhard responds that it is not usury and adds a series of considerations centred on the idea that interest-taking is only forbidden when it is against charity towards the neighbour. Before Gerhard, Aegidius Hunnius restored the new approach towards usury and interest-taking, ensuing the result of the dispute of Regensburg, which had admitted the German contract. Hunnius and Gerhard were the undisputed protagonists of a liberal trend in the Lutheran orthodoxy, also followed by the jurists, which led to definitive refounding of the interest prohibition.[273]

The problem Hunnius and Gerhard tackled was about the lawfulness of the German contract in the form of a redeemable annuity (*widerkaufflicher Zins*). The question raised was whether the investor was authorized to take not only the principal but also part of the profits that emerged from the entrepreneur's business. Both Gerhard and Hunnius answered that the contract was lawful, but in order to support this conclusion they could not accept Chemnitz' conservative position, and opted instead for a more progressive view. Through a delicate interpretation, they came to the conclusion that in the Scriptures, lending at interest is only forbidden when the neighbour is harmed. The passage of Luke 6,35 only concerns the poor, and not business contracts. The *widerkaufflicher Zins* can be used under the condition that none of the parties breach the rule of charity.

2.5.1.2 Hunnius and the Rule of Paul – 2 Cor. 8,13

In 1594, in Wittenberg, Aegidius Hunnius drew up a counsel dedicated to the annuity taken in the *widerkaufflicher Zins* and the *interesse* in a loan. This counsel was published in German in the *Consilia theologica witebergensia*

272 G. Dedekenn, *Thesauri consiliorum et decisionum volumen secundum, politica continens* [...], Jenae, 1671, 155. The conflict of interpretations is also noticed by Paul Tarnov (1562-1633) in his *De sacrosancto ministerio libri tres*, Rostochi, 1624, 282-3.

273 B.N. Nelson, *The Idea of Usury*, 92. Nelson also includes Jacob Andreae among the progressive theologians. We examine Andreae's analysis of usury in IV/1.

(1644).[274] A similar analysis was included in his commentary on the Second Letter of Paul to the Corinthians (1605). The main thesis Hunnius defends is that charging interest is not forbidden in general, but only when the debtor is damaged. An identical position had also been put forward by other theologians and jurists, primarily the Reformed jurist Charles Du Moulin, who Hunnius mentions. The argument Hunnius proposes, however, differs slightly from Du Moulin's. Hunnius interprets the Old Testament passages against charging interest – Exodus 23, Lev. 25, Deut. 23, Psalm 15,5 and Ez. 18 – as founded on Paul 2 Cor. 8,13: "*for I do not mean that other men should be eased and ye burdened, but that there be an equality*". This rule sets out that Christians do not have to enhance the neighbour's position, to their own detriment. The two Latin words *relaxatio* (ease) and *adflictio* (affliction) play a particular role. Interest-taking, Hunnius carries on, is against the rule of Paul 2 Cor. 8,13:

> *the reason of the prohibition is clear, since in this kind of interest, the loan is given to the neighbour so that the lender gets surely a life of ease (relaxatio), but for the borrower there is affliction (adflictio), because his resources are reduced little by little and eventually exhausted.*[275]

The cause, he explains, is that 'interest' (*usura*) derives from the Hebrew word 'to bite', because it gnaws at the neighbour's substances and reduces him to poverty.[276] The rule of Paul exhorts Christians to help the neighbour without damaging him, but the lender acts to the contrary, taking advantage of the borrower with the payment of interest. Lending at interest impoverishes the borrower and enriches the lender. Since the borrower is damaged, charging interest is forbidden.

This interpretation is also confirmed by the passage of Deut. 23,20 that admits an exception for the foreigners: "*unto a stranger thou mayest lend upon interest; but unto thy brother thou shalt not lend upon interest*". Hunnius contends that the passage is not meant to apply to every stranger, but only to the people who were living close to the Jews, the people of Canaan whom God wanted to be ruined, because of the abominable acts they made. The people of Canaan were unjust possessors of the land, and for this reason God allowed the Jews to squeeze them with lending at interest. Because the people of Canaan could not be expelled or exterminated, the Jews were allowed to deprive them of

274 A. Hunnius, *Ob und wie viel man* interesse *nehmen soll*, 150-2.

275 A. Hunnius, *Commentarius*, 245: "*Prohibitionis ratio manifesta est, quandoquidem in hoc usurae genere, sic datur mutuum proximo, ut danti quidem sit relaxatio, accipienti vero mutuum sit adflictio, siquidem ipsius substantia paulatim imminuitur et exhauritur denique*".

276 A. Hunnius, *Commentarius*, 245.

their goods by charging interest.[277] Such a case, concludes Hunnius, confirms that the charging of interest is an action that harms the neighbour, and for this reason, it is forbidden.

The final and crucial point of the new interpretation is the passage of Luke 6,35. Hunnius claims that the words of Christ in Luke 6,35 must not be interpreted as a simple refusal to loans at profit, but for comparison.[278] He suggests considering the context, namely Luke 6,33-35:

> *And if ye do good to them which do good to you, what thank have ye? for sinners also do even the same. And if ye lend to them of whom ye hope to receive, what thank have ye? for sinners also lend to sinners, to receive as much again. But love ye your enemies, and do good, and lend, hoping for nothing again; and your reward shall be great, and ye shall be the children of the Highest: for he is kind unto the unthankful and to the evil* and Matthew 5,39-42: *But I say unto you, That ye resist not evil: but whosoever shall smite thee on thy right cheek, turn to him the other also. And if any man will sue thee at the law, and take away thy coat, let him have thy cloak also. And whosoever shall compel thee to go a mile, go with him twain. Give to him that asketh thee, and from him that would borrow of thee turn not thou away.*

The context reveals that Christ is teaching the love for the enemies. Christ is not talking about loans where a return is demanded, as the Evangelist says: 'the same amount' (*τὰ ἴσα*), but about loans to the poor, from which the Christians cannot hope to receive the capital back.[279] In Luke 6,33 the term *τὰ ἴσα* (the same amount) concerns the loans made by the sinners. Instead, the Christians must lend to the neighbour even if he is poor and cannot return the capital.[280] The passage of Luke 6,35 therefore only refers to the poor.

Hunnius puts in the cornerstone of his reasoning the rule of Paul in 2 Cor. 8,13, which states that Christians must not ease the neighbour's situation with their own suffering. The interest prohibition is based on this principle, because in the lending at interest is embedded an aggressive stance towards the neighbour. Charging interest is then forbidden because of this aggression. The logical consequence is that if there is no aggression, there is no usury. In Hunnius' view, Deut. 23,20 expresses the harming nature of usury; and in Luke 6,35, Christ was not referring to business contracts, but only to the treatment of the

277 A. Hunnius, *Commentarius*, 245: "*Ideo Dominus inter reliqua media hoc etiam concessit Israelitis, ut possessiones eas, quae alioquin ipsis decretae fuerant, hoc interveniente medio, a Cananaeis tanquam injustis possessoribus ad se traducerent*".

278 A. Hunnius, *Commentarius*, 246.

279 A. Hunnius, *Commentarius*, 247: "*Christus enim non hic egit de mutuo, in quo redduntur vel etiam exiguntur, eadem, seu ut Evangelista loquitur, τὰ ἴσα, sed in in quo propter indigentiam proximi ne quidem restitutio sortis certa sperari potest*".

280 A. Hunnius, *Commentarius*, 247-8.

poor. The conclusion of this complex reinterpretation is that interest-taking is only forbidden when the neighbour is harmed.

2.5.1.3 Gerhard: Etymology and Context

Gerhard dealt with the problem of the interest prohibition and the lawfulness of the German contract in the collection of political cases published under his supervision, *Centuria quaestionum politicarum* (1608), and then in his *Loci theologici*. Following the path already traced by Hunnius, Gerhard identifies the meaning of interest with an aggression towards the neighbour. He motivates this statement by an etymological interpretation of the words used in the Scriptures to mean interest/usury (*usura*).[281] Usury is condemned, writes Gerhard, but it must be clear when effectively the charging of interest occurs. Several passages of the Old Testament forbid charging interest, but the prohibition regards certain cases only. Deut. 23,20 and Psalm 15,5 employs the word נֶשֶׁךְ (*Neschech*), that means 'corrosion' and 'bite'. For this reason, Gerhard holds that in these passages the prohibited interest is only the interest that harms the neighbour. Then, the terms מַרְבִּית (*Marbith*) and תַּרְבִּית (*Tharbith*) that are used in Deut. 23,21, Prov. 27, Ez. 18,8 mean 'multiplication of quantity', and are also to be interpreted as an accumulation of resources at the expense of the neighbour.[282] Exodus 22,25 and Leviticus 25,35-37 forbid charging interest, but against the poor only, because the text refers only to them.[283] The result of this interpretation is again that interest-taking is only forbidden when the debtor is harmed:

> *in these and similar passages interest is described by oppression, burden and diminution of the neighbour's resources. Such a description does not concern the annuities we are discussing here.*[284]

The charging of interest implies an injury to the neighbour by reducing his resources. To Gerhard, the annuity does not deprive the debtor of his goods, and therefore it is not against the interest prohibition.

The new interpretation of Scripture stresses that lending at interest is only forbidden when the borrower is harmed, as when he is an impoverished man.

281 Gerhard's analysis is very long. We only propose some aspects. A complete examination would lead us away from the main topic.

282 J. Gerhard, *Locorum theologicorum tomus decimus quartus*, 109.

283 J. Gerhard, *Locorum theologicorum tomus decimus quartus*, 109.

284 J. Gerhard, *Locorum theologicorum tomus decimus quartus*, 110: "*In his et similibus dictis usura describitur per oppressionem, onerationem, facultatum proximi diminutionem, quae descriptio non competit censibus illis annuis, de quibus hoc loco agimus*".

The closing step is the analysis of Luke 6,35. Gerhard claims that in this passage, Christ does not speak about the interest prohibition, but only about the poor. Similarly to Hunnius, Gerhard explains that the context shows the righteousness of this interpretation: Luke 6,33, 6,34 and 6,35 make it clear that Christ does not refer here to the loan according to duty (*mutuum officiosum*), where a certain amount of money is given to the neighbour under the condition that the same amount (*τὰ ἴσα*) is given back, but he refers only to the 'alms loan' (*mutuum eleemosynarium*), where the capital is donated to the poor neighbour.[285]

Christ is inviting the believers to love their enemies, because even the sinners can love their friends. The correct interpretation of Luke 6,35 is that the sinners give money for business only to the people who can give back the money and repay the loan, but the Christians are enjoined to a greater work, lending to the poor who cannot repay. The sinners lend to the people to whom they hope to receive something in return (*a quibus sperant se recepturos*). They practice the loan according to duty (*mutuum officiosum*). Instead, the honest men and the Christians lend to people from whom nothing can be expected in return (*a quibus nihil sperare possunt*). They are required to practice a higher degree of beneficence and charity.[286] The antithesis between these two categories of people shows that in Luke 6,35 Christ is referring to the 'alms loan' (*mutuo eleemonsynario*).

Gerhard distinguishes four types of loans. The first is the 'alms loan' (*mutuum eleemosynarium*), in which the *census* and the capital are remitted. The second type is the 'gratuitous loan' (*mutuum gratuitum*) or 'loan according to duty' (*mutuum officiosum*), when the capital is given without the *census*. The third is the 'compensatory loan' (*mutuum compensatorium*), which the lawyers call 'loan with stipulation' (*mutuum cum stipulatione*), when the *census* is demanded with the money given. The fourth is the 'usurious loan' (*mutuum usurarium*), when the illicit and immoderate interest, prohibited by human and divine laws, is demanded, and the neighbour is burdened, and his income

285 J. Gerhard, *Locorum theologicorum tomus decimus quartus*, 116: "*Ex antithesi sole clarius elucescit, Christum nequaquam loqui de* mutuo officioso, *in quo certa pecuniae summa proximo datur ea lege et conditione, ut constituto tempore eamdem et sic τὰ ἴσα reddat; sed de* mutuo eleemosynario, *in in quo ipsa sors egenti proximo donatur, ut nihil plane redeat ad creditorem, qui pecuniam proximo erogaviti*".

286 J. Gerhard, *Locorum theologicorum tomus decimus quartus*, 116: "*Nam de peccatoribus dicit, quod mutuum officiosum exerceant, hoc est, quod dent illis mutuum, a quibus sperant se recepturus; sed a piis et christianis altiorem aliquem beneficentiae et caritatis gradum exigit, iubet ipsos mutuum dare etiam illis, a quibus nihil sperare possunt* …".

is garnished.[287] The first two types are works of charity and mercy towards the neighbour. The third type is a licit contract, only if some conditions (which will be examined later) are observed. The fourth type identifies the interest which is prohibited by the laws.[288]

While Melanchthon used the term '*mutuum officiosum*' but did not speak about '*mutuum eleemosynarium*',[289] Gerhard makes a further distinction. The gratuitous loan or loan according to duty (*officiosum*) requires the borrower only to return the capital. In an 'alms-loan' (*mutuum eleemosynarium*), the creditor remits the capital and the annuity (*census*). The compensatory loan (*mutuum compensatorium*) refers to the *widerkaufflicher Zins*, which is not classified as a sale, but as a loan. This classification is possible, Gerard avers, because Christ does not refer to loans given to the rich, but about loans taken out by the poor. Thus, whether the *widerkaufflicher Zins* is a sale or a loan does not matter;[290] what matters here is that this contract can only be practiced between the wealthy.

The passage of Luke 6,35 only concerns loans/alms towards the poor and not the business loans that can be practiced by rich people. The corollary of this reasoning is Aepinus's distinction of three orders of people, which Gerhard puts forward again. He considers the German contract to be lawful, but only for the people of the third order, the rich (*opulenti*). The extreme poor (*extreme pauperes*) need indubitably the benefit of alms (*eleemosyna*), according to Luke 6,35. The duty to give gratuitous loans (*gratuitum mutui officium*) is towards the working poor (*indigentes*).[291] Hence, the German contract practiced between rich people is an entirely licit form of business.

Concluding this point, Gerhard argues that the etymology of the words used to designate interest in the Old Testament reveals that interest-taking (usury)

287 J. Gerhard, *Locorum theologicorum tomus decimus quartus*, 117: "*Primum est* mutuum eleemosynarium, *quando census et ipsa sors condonantur. Alterum est* mutuum gratuitum, *quod etiam vocari potest* officiosum, *quando quis absque censu sortem recipit. Tertium est* mutuum compensatorium, *quod iurisconsulti vocant* mutuum cum stipulatione, *quando ob erogatam pecuniam praeter sortem etiam census aliquis a proximo exigitur. Quartum est* mutuum usurarium, *quando scilicet usurae illicitae et immoderatae legibus divinis et humanis prohibitae exiguntur, quibus proximus gravatur, oneratur et ipsius facultates exhauriuntur*".

288 J. Gerhard, *Locorum theologicorum tomus decimus quartus*, 117: "*Priores duae species sunt peculiaria opera caritatis et misericordiae proximo debitae. Tertia species est contractus licitus, modo observetur conditiones superius propositae. Quarta species est usura legibus damnata*".

289 See III/2.2.3.

290 The jurists' opinion is different. See IV/2.3.4.2.

291 J. Gerhard, *Locorum theologicorum tomus decimus quartus*, 101.

is connected with an offence against the neighbour. The passage of Luke 6,35 should be read according to the context, which shows that Christ is not talking about financial operations, but about lending to the poor, which means almsgiving. Thus, the *widerkaufflicher Zins* can lawfully be practiced. The essential condition for its admission is that the parties do not breach the rule of charity.

2.5.2 Widerkaufflicher Zins: *Justification*

2.5.2.1 Introduction

According to the new theory, lending at interest is forbidden when one of the contracting parties acts against charity. The rule of charity regulates not only loans given to the poor, but also loans to the rich, for which charging interest is permitted. The *widerkaufflicher Zins* is now substantially viewed as a loan at interest, and the rules dictated for the gratuitous loans apply to it. These rules are used to justify the obligation to pay the annuity. The seller/entrepreneur is obliged by gratitude to return the lent sum and part of the profits he gained with the buyer/investor's money. Gratitude is founded on the natural law expressed in Matthew 7,12, which exhorts the parties to reciprocal respect.

Furthermore, the investor should receive the annuity because he must provide for his family, according to the rule of 2 Cor. 8,13 connected with 1 Tim. 5 and 2 Cor. 8,14, which requires the investor to take care of his family before other people. These rules request the parties to protect each other against injuries. The annuity should be paid, because without compensation for the money given, the investor suffers damage. The ordinance of the magistrate on the *widerkaufflicher Zins* therefore is licit, because it impedes a breach of charity and an offence to the neighbour.

2.5.2.2 The Political Ordinance as Specification of the Scriptures

A specific feature of Lutheran political theory is obedience to the political authority. Brenz and Aepinus already celebrated the divine power of the magistrate's ordinances. Johann Gerhard continues in this vein, stating that the Gospel does not abolish the political ordinances and the lawful contracts that are in agreement with natural law (Rom. 13,1 and 1 Peter 2,13).[292] In support, he quotes David Lobeck (1560-1603),[293] professor of theology in Rostock, who published a commentary on the Augsburg Confession. Lobeck writes that the way the negotiations must be conducted, and the determination of the

292 J. Gerhard, *Locorum theologicorum tomus decimus quartus*, 103.

293 Indexeintrag *Lobeck, David*, in *Deutsche Biographie*, https://www.deutsche-biographie.de/gnd124752039.html (accessed 12.01.2018).

contracts that have to be considered lawful, is not the duty of a theologian, but it is a task for the magistrate and the jurists.[294] These assertions, Gerhard comments, should be interpreted in the sense that the word of God forbids every fraud, injustice and breach of charity in general, while the magistrate applies these prohibitions in special regulations.[295] The law of *widerkaufflicher Zins* is a special regulation of the general biblical prohibition of frauds; thus with his law the magistrate specifies the Scriptures.

The ruler's ordinances are not an intrusion into the sphere of the theologians, Gerhard continues, but are the exercise of his task. The ordinance does not intend to placate consciences but to assure a better good for the believers. The magistrate is a minister of God and must guarantee that his subjects observe both tables of the Decalogue. He is a guardian of the Decalogue and avenger of the transgressions of the divine law.[296] The law of the magistrate does not contradict Scripture, but converts biblical precepts into legal norms.

The ordinance on the *widerkaufflicher Zins* has to be in agreement with the divine law. To Gerhard, the ordinance remains close to the divine law, because the annuity is nothing but the possibility to pay in installments the *lucrum cessans* and *damnum emergens* that the creditor suffers by lending his money.[297] Gerhard is using an argument typical for the *interesse* (compensation for loss), as distinguished from the *usura* (interest). The *interesse* was a compensation in case of damages in a gratuitous loan, while the *usura* was the profit from gratuitous loans. Gerhard goes beyond this distinction and relates this argument to the annuity. As we will see in the following pages, the investor/buyer is damaged by the entrepreneur/seller if he does not receive the annuity. The annuity compensates the investor for the damage deriving from the lack of his money. In the new theory of interest, the traditional barriers between sale and loan tend to soften. In this way, arguments that were before a prerogative of the loans are translated to the *widerkaufflicher Zins*.

2.5.2.3 An Obligation Founded on Gratitude and Natural Law

Chemnitz utilized the argument of the borrower's gratitude for the money received to justify the attribution of a certain amount of money to the lender in

294 D. Lobeck, *Disputationes theologicae XX articulorum Augustanae confessionis*, Rostochii, 1599, disp. XVIII, th. 93.

295 J. Gerhard, *Locorum theologicorum tomus decimus quartus*, 103: "*id quod de contractuum equitate* in specie *accipiendum, nam* in genere *verbum Dei praecipit, cavendam esse iniustitiam, fraudes, violationem caritatis etc.*".

296 J. Gerhard, *Locorum theologicorum tomus decimus quartus*, 104.

297 J. Gerhard, *Locorum theologicorum tomus decimus quartus*, 104.

a loan. He founded this duty on charity. Hunnius and Gerhard relate the argument of gratitude to the annuity in the *widerkaufflicher Zins*. The *widerkaufflicher Zins* is substantially considered on par with a loan at interest. In the new theory, loans at interest are admitted, which implies that the arguments that previously justified the gratuitous loans then pass to the loans at interest.

Hunnius contends that natural law, equity, Christian charity, and the rule of Matthew 7,12 admonish and exhort to pay the annuities. If someone asks you for money, he writes, and then uses it for his business, he makes a profit with your money. He uses your money for his profit, but you could also have used your money for business purposes. Hence, it is licit for you to ask a payment for the use of your money.[298] According to Hunnius, the duty of gratitude postulates that the debtor keeps the creditor unscathed and pays him for his disadvantage. It pertains to the law then, to determine the right quantity of this compensation.[299] Christian charity, natural law, and equity together generate a duty of gratitude towards the investor. This duty is utterly lawful and justifies the attribution to the investor of a sum of money in addition to the lent sum.

Hunnius does not stress the distinction between charity, natural law, and gratitude. Gerhard, instead, differentiates natural equity from gratitude. For Gerhard, the *widerkaufflicher Zins* is a financial instrument that was admitted only for the members of the third order, rich people. The extremely poor and the needy cannot use this contract. The reason for this prohibition is not only related to the patrimonial assets of the rich people, but also to the destination of the money in the latter case: to business and profit. Money could be used for business both by the investor and the entrepreneur. Since the investor is in essence lending his right to engage in business, he should be equally compensated. In fact, Christ established the natural equity when he said in Luke 6,31: "*And as ye would that men should do to you, do ye also to them likewise*". The rule of Christ means that none of the parties must be damaged by the contract.[300] Since the entrepreneur is using the capital for business purposes, the investor should be equally compensated.

The compensation is also a matter of gratitude. Gerhard explains that what is requested from gratitude belongs to natural law and consequently the obligation that results from gratitude is an obligation of natural law. Gratitude requires that the debtor who used other people's money to establish a profitable

298 A. Hunnius, *Commentarius*, 251.

299 A. Hunnius, *Commentarius*, 251: "*Sed et gratitudinis referendae officium postulat, ut debitor te suum creditorem, imo benefactorem indemne praestet, nec cum tuo damno et incommodo suum commodum parare satagat, sed in compensationem officii aliquid tibi pendat, quod quantum esse debeat, constituunt et moderantur leges*".

300 J. Gerhard, *Locorum theologicorum tomus decimus quartus*, 101-2.

business be obliged to give to the creditor something more than the received sum. He must pay a compensation for the benefits he gained.[301] The natural law requires this remittance. And because the debtor is bound by natural law, he can also be constrained by the civil law. The magistrate can promulgate laws that allow the debtor to compensate the creditor for the benefits he received.[302]

Hunnius held that because of Christian love and natural law, the debtor's payment of the annuity to the creditor for the use of the money is legitimate. This payment is a form of gratitude and therefore is lawful. Gerhard formalized the argument distinguishing between natural law and gratitude, claiming that both of them require that the debtor pay the annuity on the sum that he received. Natural law lays the foundation for a civil obligation that the magistrate, as he did, can lawfully admit. Natural law commands the parties to look at their reciprocal benefit; in this way it represents a form of charity. Charity urges the parties to respect each other and avoid unjust behaviours.

2.5.2.4 *Relaxatio* and *adflictio*

Luther and Aepinus interpreted the rule of Paul 2 Cor. 8,13, as a rule for the loans: the lender shall lend according to his capacity, and the borrower shall strive to return the sum. As before with the argument of gratitude, in the new theory of interest, this rule is applied also to the business contracts. The rule of Paul is not invoked for the gratuitous loan, but to justify the payment of the annuity in the *widerkaufflicher Zins*. Charity insists that none of the parties be damaged by the contract. If the entrepreneur gains profit from the money of the investor and does not pay the annuity, he obtains a life of ease, while the investor is afflicted. This is against charity. Principally, the investor's family is damaged, because the investor cannot use the lent funds to support it.

The rule of Paul in 2 Cor. 8,13 founds the duty to return the sum in a loan. According to Hunnius, Paul admonishes that charity has to be practiced to the extent that we do not suffer afflictions or scarcity.[303] For example, if a rich man

---

301 J. Gerhard, *Locorum theologicorum tomus decimus quartus*, 102: "*Praeterea, quod debita gratitudo postulat, illud iure naturali etiam exigi certum est; gratitudo enim est iuris naturalis, ac proinde obligatio, quae ex gratitudine nascitur, est iuris naturalis. Iam vero in praedictu casu debita gratitudo exigit, ut is, qui pecunia alterius negotiatur et lucratur, vel etiam magno onere bonis ipsius immobilibus inhaerente levatur ac liberator, gratum sese praestet erga eum, a quo hoc beneficio adfectus est, id quod sit non sola sortis restitutione, sed etiam liberali aliqua compensatione*".

302 J. Gerhard, *Locorum theologicorum tomus decimus quartus*, 102.

303 A. Hunnius, *Commentarius*, 248-9.

demands a loan of 100, 200 or 1000 florins it is licit (because of equity) to ask for restitution of the sum.[304] The apostle, in fact, claimed:

> *it is not in order to make a life of ease (*relaxatio*) to the other that you should suffer (*adflictio*), but even the charity that begins with oneself urges that you have superior regard for the people that God and nature connected closer to you.*[305]

The rule of Paul in 2 Cor. 8,13 justifies restitution of the sum, because the investor would otherwise suffer damages.

The restitution of the sum occurs in a gratuitous loan, but in the *widerkaufflicher Zins*, the debtor returns not only the principal but also something more: the 5% annuity. To motivate this further payment, Hunnius insists on the necessity that the investor looks after his family. He writes that if the investor is lacking such a large sum of money for such a long time, and the entrepreneur promotes his affairs and enriches his fortune with the investor's money:[306]

> *who would be of such poor judgement as not to complain with a loud voice that you* [the investor] *have been treated unjustly and against the rule of the Apostle who does not want that the neighbour be benefited in such a way, that he receives a benefit at your expense. Indeed, in this way your relatives would also be defrauded, while you should take care of them before the others, as the Apostle testifies in 1 Tim. 5.*[307]

The rule of Paul in 2 Cor. 8,13 sets out that the investor does not have to benefit the entrepreneur with his disadvantage, because in this case he would defraud his relatives.[308] They have to be preferentially considered, as Paul says in 1 Tim. 5,8: "*but if any provide not for his own, and specially for those of his own house, he hath denied the faith, and is worse than an infidel*". The connection between 2 Cor. 8,13 and 1 Tim. 5,8 entails that the investor can request the annuity,

304 A. Hunnius, *Commentarius*, 249.

305 A. Hunnius, *Commentarius*, 249: "*Non ut alteri sit relaxatio, vobis autem angustia: sed et charitas quae a semetipsa incipit, suadebit ut potiorem habeas rationem eorum, quos et Deus et natura tibi arctius coniunxit*".

306 A. Hunnius, *Commentarius*, 251.

307 A. Hunnius, *Commentarius*, 251: "*Quis tam sit nullius iudicii, qui non clamet, inique tecum agi, et contra regulam Apostoli, qui non vult sic benefieri proximo, ut illi quidem sit relaxatio, tibi vero angustia. Quin defraudarentur hac ratione tui domestici, quorum potiorem tibi habendam esse rationem Apostolus ipse testatur, inquiens, 1 Tim. 5*".

308 A very similar approach is proposed by John Mair about the case of the 'Merchant of Rhodes', see W. Decock, J. Hallebeek, *Pre-contractual duties*, 117-8. On the 'Merchant of Rhodes' see also W. Decock, *Lessius and the Breakdown*, 57-78. This problem is also faced in III/1.1.4.3.

because he has to take care of his family. If he cannot look after his family, he suffers damage, and the rule of Paul is broken.

Hunnius remarks that nothing is committed against Christian charity if in this case the debtor pays the annuity.[309] The annuity is given not only for compensation for the received sum but also for the damages that the creditor might have if the loan were gratuitous. In actuality, the rule of Paul would be broken if the entrepreneur does not pay the annuity to the investor.

Gerhard relied upon Hunnius and presented the argument in a more systematic version. He writes that although the rule of Paul concerns especially alms, in general it teaches Christians to benefit others so far as the Christians do not suffer losses.[310] The proverb of Solomon (Prov. 5,16-17) refers to this situation properly: "*let thy fountains be dispersed abroad, and rivers of waters in the streets. Let them be only thine own, and not strangers' with thee*". Gerhard explains that if others use our money for profit in business, commerce, or buying real estate, without any compensation, they earn money. Hence, the benefits or life of ease (*relaxatio*) that we permitted our neighbour by giving the money has been caused by our affliction (*adflictio*), since we could also have used our money for business. In order to have equality between the parties, equity and Christian charity require that the rich people that used our money pay compensation to us, for the losses we received for the unavailability of the money, as Paul says in 2 Cor. 8,14.[311]

Then Gerhard links 2 Cor. 8,13 not only with 1 Tim. 5,8 as Hunnius did, but also with 2 Cor. 12,14: "*for the children ought not to lay up for the parents, but the parents for the children*". He wants to draw the attention to the investors' children:

> *Furthermore, no care of ours would be mobilized and even less would treasures of wealth be collected by them, if our neighbour got his advantage but did not allow us to take part in his profits and to be in partnership with him. This is against the duty*

309 A. Hunnius, *Commentarius*, 252.

310 J. Gerhard, *Locorum theologicorum tomus decimus quartus*, 102.

311 J. Gerhard, *Locorum theologicorum tomus decimus quartus*, 102: "*Iam vero si alii nostra pecunia pro lubitu uterentur ad negotiationes, mercimonia, praediorum emtiones etc. eaque absque ulla compensatione nobis facta plurimum lucrarentur, tunc ipsis quidem esset* relaxatio, *nobis vero ac nostris* adflictio, *siquidem nos non minus, ac illi ipsimet nostra hac pecunia potuissemus contractus emtionis, vel alios ad rem faciendam idoneos exercere, ac commoda nostra parare; equitas igitur et illi respondens christiana charitas requirit,* ut fiat equalitas, *hoc est, ut divitis illius negotiatoris, qui pecunia nostra lucratus est, abundantia nostram ac nostrorum inopiam suppleat* (…) *ut in simili apostolus loquitur 2 Cor. VIII, 14*".

> *of Christian charity. An ordered charity starts from oneself and urges us to take better care of the people who God and nature created as our closer relatives.*[312]

If the investor provides an advantage to the entrepreneur without receiving part of his profits, first the investor cannot take care of his own children, and second he cannot save up anything for them. This is against charity, because charity requires Christians to care for their relatives before other people.[313] Charity urges that none of the parties is damaged in legal relations. A gratuitous loan towards a businessman harms the investor and breaches the rule of charity; the entrepreneur therefore should compensate the investor for his disadvantage with the payment of the annuity.

Gerhard bolsters the argument by reflecting on the use of money among the three orders of people: the extreme poor, the needy, and the rich. He observes that it is unequal and against Christian charity, that the people of the second class (the needy) receive money by alms and earn profit without returning the sum to the investor. It is also unequal and against charity if the rich people of the third order (the rich) obtain money by which they promote their business and earn profit, without any compensation. The investor should take part of the entrepreneur's profit. As it is against charity if the people of the second class ask some money through the alms and with them they earn profit, so it is also against charity if the people of the third order ask for money from people of the same order, and profit from receipt of a gratuitous loan.[314] Gerhard points out that the entrepreneur is enriched and the investor is impoverished, against Paul's teaching in 2 Cor. 8, 13. Because rich people can pay for the use of money, the rule of Paul implies that they should pay.

In this new theory, the rule of Paul concerns not only to the gratuitous loans, but also justifies the payment of the annuity in the *widerkauﬄicher Zins*. The creditor must help the debtor but without suffering losses, and for this reason he can demand the annuity in addition to the borrowed sum. If it were not

312 J. Gerhard, *Locorum theologicorum tomus decimus quartus*, 102-3: "*Iam vero nulla nostrorum ageretur cura, multo minus thesauri ipsis colligerentur, si proximus nostra pecunia suum duntaxat pararet commodum, nec in ejusdem participationem ac κοινωνία ullam nos admitteret. Ergo id pugnat cum christianae caritatis officio. Ordinata charitas incipit a se ipsa, ac suadet, ut potiorem rationem habeamus eorum, quos Deus et natura arctius nobis conjunxit*".

313 Gerhard writes that *an ordered charity starts from oneself* (*ordinata charitas incipit a se ipsa*). This construction was also used by the scholastics to indicate that before loving the other, the Christian must take care of himself. See W. Decock, J. Hallebeek, *Pre-contractual duties*, 103; W. Decock, *Theologians and Contract Law*, 596.

314 J. Gerhard, *Locorum theologicorum tomus decimus quartus*, 103.

paid, the creditor and his family would suffer losses. Behind the rule of Paul lies charity, as an essential guarantee of respect between the parties.

2.5.2.5 Social Utility and Equality with Lawful Contracts

The lawfulness of the *widerkaufflicher Zins* was a controversial topic, and in order to provide a further defence of this financial operation, Gerhard formulated two additional arguments. The first one regards the practical consideration that the *widerkaufflicher Zins* is useful for society. In 1 Cor. 14,33 Paul declares that: "*God is not the author of confusion, but of peace, as it is in all churches of the saints*". From this, Gerhard perceives that God is not an unstable God (*ἀκαταστατέω*); but if the annuity, which is asked for funds to be used in business, were absolutely and simply forbidden, an enormous disorder (*ἀταξία*) would result, not only in the political order, but also in the church. The people who have money would refuse to give their money to others, because they would not receive an adequate compensation. In this way, commerce and business, which are not only useful but also necessary for the human genre, would be impeded.[315] The argument rests on the general utility of the circulation of capital for society and the negative effects that the prohibition of annuity would cause.[316] God desires peace on earth, but the ban of annuities would produce chaos.

Many authors have noticed the social damage in absence of lending at interest. Gerhard quotes the jurists Johannes Petrus de Ferrariis (1389-1416), Baldus, and the Byzantine emperor Leo VI (866-912). De Ferrariis asserts that without interest-taking, the world could not be sustained or governed.[317] Baldus writes that without usurers, many people could not eat. Finally, the constitution of Emperor Leo VI (866-912) in the *novella* 83 re-introduced loans at interest after his father, Emperor Basilius I the Macedonian (811-886), had forbidden them. The regulation imposed by the previous emperor, writes Leo, caused damage to the empire, because the situation did not improve but devolved. The people who lent money at interest were no longer allowed to do this by law and consequently forced the borrower to swear oaths to pay interest that then were breached.[318] The emperor, therefore, decided to grant loans at interest because

315 J. Gerhard, *Locorum theologicorum tomus decimus quartus*, 106.

316 Lessius adopts a similar approach. See W. Decock, *The Catholic Spirit of Capitalism?*, 34-5.

317 J.P. De Ferrarijs, *Practica*, Francoforti ad Moenum, 1581, 398: "*Hic ergo diligenter advertas: quia mundus hodie non sustinetur, nec regitur, nisi de usuris*". J. Gerhard, *Locorum theologicorum tomus decimus quartus*, 106: "*mundum vix sustineri, aut regi posse sine usuris*". The quotation is reported also by C. Besold, *Operis politici editio nova*. Argentorati, 1626, 6: "*Mundum vix sustineri, aut regi, ait, nisi de usuris*".

318 J. Gerhard, *Locorum theologicorum tomus decimus quartus*, 106.

of the positive effects on society. Using these examples, Gerhard tries to demonstrate the positive effects on society of the charging of interest. If interest, which is basically the annuity paid in the *widerkaufflicher Zins*, would be forbidden, society would experience several negative effects.

The second argument is completely different and is based on Chemnitz' analysis of contracts. Chemnitz had proved the lawfulness of several contracts, even though he did not admit explicitly the *widerkaufflicher Zins*. Gerhard contends that the *widerkaufflicher* is lawful because of its equality with other lawful contracts like *emphyteusis, antichresis*, partnership, and promissory note. These contracts are similar to the *widerkaufflicher Zins* from the viewpoint of natural equity. As they are lawful, so the *widerkaufflicher Zins* is also lawful.[319] The argument is evidently an attempt to force Chemnitz' position. Chemnitz had been conservative. Although he granted the use of the contract with a clause to redeem, he never mentioned explicitly the *widerkaufflicher Zins*. Gerhard tries to solve the problem by equating the *widerkaufflicher* to other lawful contracts.

2.5.3 **Widerkaufflicher Zins:** ***Application***

2.5.3.1 Introduction

The reinterpretation of Luke 6,35 – understanding the charging of interest as only forbidden when it damages the neighbour – is rooted in the central role of Christian charity. A loan can be lawful only if it complies with charity. The rule of charity applies both to loans towards the poor, which must be gratuitous, and to the loans between rich, where the charging of interest is permitted. The *widerkaufflicher Zins* is lawful, but the parties must observe charity.

In the *widerkaufflicher Zins* this precept is translated to three particular rules: only certain orders of people can use the contract; the amount of money and the time for restitution must meet the demands of the parties; and in case of calamities or events due to random chance, the creditor shall remit the debt. These rules demand that Christians exercise practical judgement on the circumstances of the contract, both at the stage of negotiations and during the execution of its terms. In a situation where charity is contravened, the Christian is called to follow his conscience and disobey, or neglect to invoke the law. Charity operates as a form of equity and intervenes to mitigate the severity of the law.

319 J. Gerhard, *Locorum theologicorum tomus decimus quartus*, 104-5.

2.5.3.2 Condition of the Parties

The first judgment that charity asks the Christian to perform concerns the quality of the people involved in the bargain. The medieval scholastic prohibition against interest repressed a sin against the virtue of justice. The sin of usury was conceived as a form of robbery: the usurer robs the goods of the entrepreneur. Justice does not distinguish between rich and poor, because theft damages the poor man and the rich man alike. In the new theory, the interest prohibition punishes a sin against charity, so that if charity is not offended, no sin is committed. The interest prohibition becomes a rule of charity that adapts to different circumstances. The Christian is called to judge whether the individual contract breaks the rule of charity. Particularly, he is called to pay attention to the quality of the parties. The *widerkaufflicher Zins* is a form of business and may only be practiced between rich people, and should not be entered into with the gravely poor or the working poor. Even if the legal norms admit the contract, the Christian shall refrain from signing a contract with a person who cannot pay the annuity and return the principal or he shall not charge the annuity. Gerhard stresses that there must be a financial goal: the annuity cannot be requested from people who do not use the money for business and to gain profit, but desire it for their personal support and that of their family, and who can hardly return even the principal of the loan.[320] The *widerkaufflicher Zins* is a complex financial operation that has to be used only for profit and not for ordinary family sustenance. If the people who are looking for the capital do not specifically need the money to fund an economic operation, the annuity must not be charged.

The *widerkaufflicher Zins* has different spiritual effects from loans and alms. Drawing upon Chemnitz, Gerhard holds that alms and loans have wider divine promises. The other contracts are included in the promises of the seventh precept of the Decalogue. Thus, the Christians have to employ first and foremost loans and alms, and only secondarily the *widerkaufflicher Zins*. They should not focus only on that contract, as if it was the only or the primary option.[321] Gerhard adds that the rich merchants who want to preserve their riches ought not use the contract to secure their capital and live idly without work. God commanded men to work for living, as cited in Psalm 128,2: "*for thou shalt eat the labor of thine hands; happy shalt thou be, and it shall be well with thee*"; and

320 J. Gerhard, *Locorum theologicorum tomus decimus quartus*, 106: "*Ne ab illis census annuus exigaur, qui pecunia mutuo accepta non utuntur ad negotiationes exercendas et lucra comparanda, sed ad necessariam sui ac suorum sustentationem pecuniam a nobis expetunt, atque ipsa sortem vix ac ne vix quidem reddere possunt*".

321 J. Gerhard, *Locorum theologicorum tomus decimus quartus*, 107.

he similarly references 1 Thess. 3,2 and 2 Thess. 3,10. Orphans, widows, and the elderly, who cannot use their substances without diminishing them and are less suitable to business, deserve to be treated leniently, because they want to sell their money for their sustenance and not for business purposes.[322] It is evident that Gerhard follows Luther: orphans, widows, and the elderly may use the German contract for their sustenance, while merchants should also work to secure their means of support.

In the new theory, the interest prohibition becomes a rule of charity. The Christian is called to assess whether the rule of charity is broken. He must be sure that both contracting parties are rich, because the *widerkaufflicher Zins* can only be used for commercial ventures. With the poor he cannot use the contract, even though the legal norms might admit it. In this case, the Christian should not invoke the laws and should refuse the contract or not charge the annuity. Furthermore, the other contracts with the poor, loans and alms, have greater divine promises, and Christians should privilege their use.

2.5.3.3 Reciprocal Benefit

The second judgement regards the proportion between the annuity and the lent sum. The annuity must be calculated on the basis of the time and amount of the lent sum and must be a multiple of the sum, according to geometrical proportion. This rule was originally dictated for the alms on the basis of 2 Cor. 8,13. Georg Major, a Melanchthon's immediate follower, in his comment on the second letter of Paul to the Corinthians (2 Cor. 8,13), observed that Paul gave this rule for alms:

> *I do not want that alms be given so that they, who receive that benefit, will have ease and will live in splendour and idleness and gourmandize your goods, and you are drained and in scarcity because of these alms. But I want you to give according to equality.*[323]

Major advocates an approach very similar to the scholastics and holds that equality consists in the reciprocity between people who have material riches, but are spiritually poor, and people who are materially poor, but spiritually rich. The Gospel promises the poor benefits in the spiritual life, albeit their

---

322 J. Gerhard, *Locorum theologicorum tomus decimus quartus*, 107.

323 G. Major, *Enarratio secundae epistolae*, 144: "Non enim scilicet ita conferri eleemosynas volo, *ut alijs, in quos haec beneficia conferuntur, sit relaxatio, ut illi in delicijs et ocio vivant et de bonis vestris, vestro sudore et labore partis, helluentur* (…) *et* ut vobis per has elemosynas exhaustis sit angustia (…) *sed volo conferri* (*inquit Paulus*) ex aequabilitate". Melanchthon advanced a similar opinion. See P. Melanchthon, *Dissertatio de contractibus*, in CR XVI, 505-6.

temporal lives lack resources. The rich instead have many goods, but do not receive the same spiritual promises. Hence, Major suggests the rich to give to the poor part of their goods and receive from the poor prayers and part of the spiritual goods of the poor. It is thus an exchange between spiritual goods and material goods. There is no equality if only one party receives and only one gives, but the teaching of Christ should be observed: "*give, and it shall be given unto you*".[324] In this way, there is an equal exchange between spiritual and temporal goods. Equality, Major highlights, should not be assessed according to arithmetical proportion, but geometrical proportion. In this way the poor can be clothed and can eat, but not live and dress as a prosperous man. The affluent are obliged by both natural and divine law to observe this equality.[325]

To Major equality according to geometrical proportion regulated alms. Hunnius transferred this equality from alms to the redeemable annuity (*widerkaufflicher Zins*). He admonishes the parties that in the *widerkaufflicher Zins* they shall estimate the amount of the given sum according to the geometrical and not arithmetical proportion. The creditor might lend a small sum, but the annuity will be consequently reduced. Or he might lend for one year, so the annuity should be regulated.[326] Geometrical proportion must govern the *widerkaufflicher Zins*, so that the import of the annuity is based on time and amount of money lent.

Gerhard defined more specifically how the profit must be adjusted according to the time and the sum. It is necessary, he writes, to distinguish between the major or minor amount of money that is requested and the short or long time for restitution of the sum. If the amount is small, and the time is short (as for instance one or two months), the annuity should not be requested.[327] The amount of the sum must be judged not absolutely (*ἁπλῶς*) but in a comparable way (*σύγκριτικῶς*) to the wealth of the investor, not according to arithmetical proportion but to the geometrical proportion.[328] In this way the precept of Paul in 2 Cor. 8,13 balances the terms of the contract so that both the parties have advantages. Arithmetical proportion implies an equal difference between the goods, while geometrical proportion suggests that one of the goods is a multiple of the other. The parties should follow this proportion in calculating the amount lent money and the annuity.

324 Luke 6,38.

325 G. Major, *Enarratio secundae epistolae*, 146.

326 A. Hunnius, *Commentarius*, 252-3.

327 J. Gerhard, *Locorum theologicorum tomus decimus quartus*, 106-7.

328 J. Gerhard, *Locorum theologicorum tomus decimus quartus*, 107: "*Monendum interim, de pecunia summa maiore vel minore iudicandum non ἁπλῶς, sed σύγκριτικῶς, respectu ad erogantem habito, nec* secundum arithmeticam, *sed* geometricam proportionem".

The magistrate must determine the amount of the annuity, but Hunnius and Gerhard also advocate that in the negotiations between merchants, the official number established by the laws might be adjusted. It is important that the profit is reciprocal, so that the amount of annuity corresponds to the time and amount given. For instance, if the entrepreneur can use 100 florins only for 1 year, the profit for the investor shall be less. In this calculation, however, the merchants must observe the rule of charity as the supreme moderator.[329]

In short, charity implies a direct control over the amount of the lent money and the annuity. Charity urges adaptation of the laws when their strict observance damages the neighbour. Conditions of the agreement and in particular the amount of money, interest, and duration must be proportioned so that both the parties are satisfied.

2.5.3.4 Remission of Debt

Probably the strongest precept of charity concerns the remission of debt when the debtor experiences some adversity. When the burden is too heavy for the debtor, because he suffers damages for unforeseen and unexpected circumstances, charity pushes the creditor to remit the sum and also the annuity. The remission of debt because of charity represents the solution the Lutheran theologians found to the problem of the risk of loss. The *widerkaufflicher Zins* implies the assignation of a certain capital to the entrepreneur to make profit. But the entrepreneur might experience unexpected circumstances that make him unable to meet his obligations. Luther already raised this problem and noticed that although the investor receives the annuity, he does not take part in the risks of the entrepreneur. This is especially true when the annuity is not related to a specific estate, but comes from all the properties in general. In this way, the risk vanishes even more, because it is not connected with a property (that may perish or be destroyed by flood, fire etc.) but only to the people, which must pay interest anyway.[330] He insisted that every bargain requires a risk: *"for if this risk is not taken, the purchase of annuity (Zinskauf) is simply usury"*.[331]

To the contrary, as seen before, Melanchthon maintained that the *widerkaufflicher Zins* is lawful. The investor/buyer must support the risk, and if the estate is destroyed by flood, the right to demand the payment is terminated. Similarly, when serious damage affects the estate, the investor should return part of the

---

329 A. Hunnius, *Commentarius*, 253.

330 M. Luther, *Ein (grosser) Sermon von dem Wucher*, in WA 6, 53-5.

331 M. Luther, *Ein (grosser) Sermon von dem Wucher*, in WA 6, 57: "*Dan wo dise fahr nit ist im zinskauff, da ist kurzt und entel wucher*".

income to the entrepreneur. The problems, Melanchthon observes, arise because very often this rule of equality is not practiced.[332] The equality is for Melanchthon the response to the problem of risk, and the lack of equality in the common usage does not suffice to consider the contract to be illicit.

Melanchthon's rule of equality was translated in terms of charity by Urbanus Rhegius and then by other theologians, e.g., Chemnitz, Hunnius, and Gerhard. Rhegius only drafted the argument; Chemnitz followed this position; and Hunnius continued further on this road. Hunnius observes that if, after the stipulation of the contract, the debtor incurs some adversity, like a fire or plundering of the goods, he is reduced to poverty, and he could return the borrowed sum and also the annuity only with difficulties. The creditor must preserve his clear conscience in front of God, not imposing the strict observance of law, but remembering the precept of Leviticus 25 and fraternal charity. Thus, in consideration of the circumstances, the creditor must partially or totally remit the debt.[333] The passage of Leviticus he references is probably Lev. 25,35: "*and if thy brother be waxen poor, and fallen in decay with thee; then thou shalt relieve him: yea, though he be a stranger, or a sojourner; that he may live with thee*". The gaze, points out Hunnius, must absolutely be turned on the fact that none of the parties breach Christian charity, which is the moderator of the parties, so that none of them are encumbered or oppressed.[334]

Following Hunnius, Gerhard writes that charity must be reciprocal, which means that both the parties must seek to benefit each other also in this contract.[335] Reciprocal charity is not observed when the risk of losing the capital is charged only to the debtor who is exercising business with the money of the creditor:

332 P. Melanchthon, *Dissertatio de contractibus*, in CR XVI, 503.

333 A. Hunnius, *Commentarius*, 252: "*Adiicimus autem, si post initum contractum debitor adverso aliquo infortunio, puta incendio, direptione bonorum et consimilibus ad eiusmodi paupertatem redigatur, ut vix habeat, unde sortem reponat, nedum ut ultra sortem aliquid praestet amplius: debere creditorem, ut suae conscientiae coram Deo recte consulat, non strictum urgere ius, sed meminisse divini praecepti Levit. 25 et fraternae charitatis, ideoque circumstantiarum ratione habita, pensionem vel totam vel ex parte ei remittere*".

334 A. Hunnius, *Commentarius*, 252: "*Omnino enim eo collimandum est, ne ulla ex parte violetur Christiana dilectio, quae moderatrix sit utrinque, ne alterutra pars praegravetur aut opprimatur*".

335 J. Gerhard, *Locorum theologicorum tomus decimus quartus*, 103: "*Denique in omnibus legitimis contractibus* caritatem oportet esse reciprocam, *hoc est, utriusque partis contrahentium commoda sunt promovenda, ergo etiam in hoc speciali contractu, et creditoris et debitoris habenda est ratio*".

> *if by fortuitous case, unexpected and unavoidable, [the debtor] is reduced to indigence, charity as a moderator and director* (moderatrix ac directrix) *of every contract shall mediate between the parties, and after consideration of the circumstances shall order to remit the annuity or also the principal. When men of the third class are reduced to the second class, then loans towards them must be gratuitous, and when they are reduced to the first class, they are to be helped with alms. Annuities should certainly not be expected from them.*[336]

The annuity must not be asked of people who received money for business and subsequently were reduced to indigence, not because of their fault but because of a fortuitous event, like fire, shipwreck, etc. If in fact, they became part of the second class, the loan must be gratuitous for them. The same is true if they were reduced to the first class (dire poverty). Because of the changed situation, the investor should not ask even the return of the loaned sum. In these cases, Christian charity, as magister and moderator, must drive the actions of the investor.[337]

In a more systematic way, Gerhard recurs to the three categories of people (poor, poor who can work, and rich) to explain the necessity of the remission of debt. The *widerkaufflicher Zins* is directed to the rich, but if one of the parties is not rich anymore, the sale of income cannot be practiced. Indeed, only a free loan can be given to a poor man who can work, and alms to the poor. The remission of debt guarantees against the risk and protects the weaker party. The debtor and the creditor must share disadvantages from unexpected circumstances. Charity pushes the investor to help the entrepreneur by accepting a partial payment of the principal or not demanding it at all. This behaviour implies rejecting a strict application of the law, but corrects the law, where a strict application would damage the neighbour. Christian charity seeks to safeguard the position of the debtor and assure that he can receive benefits from the contract.

336 J. Gerhard, *Locorum theologicorum tomus decimus quartus*, 103: "*Sin vero casu aliquo fortuito, insperato atque inevitabili ad inopiam redigatur, tunc caritas christiana tanquam moderatrix ac directrix omnium in christiana republica contractuum, sese mediam interponat, ac ratione circumstantiarum habita annuum illum censum, vel ipsam etiam sortem debitori remittendam esse iubeat, quando enim homines tertii ordinis rediguntur ad secundam classem, tunc mutuum erga ipsos debet esse gratuitum, quando ad primam, eleemosyna sunt iuvandi, tantum abest, ut census annui ab illis exigendi*".

337 J. Gerhard, *Locorum theologicorum tomus decimus quartus*, 106: "*Si enim ex divite quis fit pauper, tum debeo etiam modum cum ipso agendi mutare. Breviter dicendo, christiana charitas ut omnium reliquorum, ita etiam hujus contractus directrix ac moderatrix statui debet*".

2.6 Corollaries and Reception

2.6.1 *Introduction*

The reformulation of the interest prohibition in the sense that lending at interest is only forbidden when it is against Christian charity presents two corollaries. First, the interest prohibition is expressed in and founded on Scripture, while the Aristotelian scholastic arguments based on natural law have a secondary place, if still mentioned at all. Second, because lending at interest to the poor is categorically forbidden, a particular financial operation called *mons pietatis*, when directed towards the poor, is also forbidden.

These two issues are structurally different, but they represent effects of the new theory of interest and for this reason are treated together. A few words should be spent also for illustrating the general acceptance of the new theory among the Lutheran theologians throughout the seventeenth century. The building block of the new theory was constructed approximately between the 1530s and the first two decades of the seventeenth century. Afterwards, the theologians relied on the previous positions, occasionally making small improvements.

2.6.2 *Natural Law: Two Opposite Opinions*

The largest part of the discussions about the *widerkaufflicher Zins* and its compatibility with the interest prohibition concerned the interpretation of Scripture. The Lutheran theologians mainly worked with the divine law to reformulate the interest prohibition. The scholastic arguments based on natural law were somehow put aside. Gerhard, for instance, affirmed that interest-taking has been condemned by many sources, which he classified in five categories: 1) divine law; 2) canon law; 3) consent of people; 4) authority of the fathers and councils; and 5) numerous inconveniences that derive from charging interest.[338] The natural law is not mentioned, and when he refers to it, always means the rule of Matthew 7, 12 or Luke 6, 31. Thus, Aristotelian arguments in support of the interest prohibition were often abandoned.

The natural law was invoked by Melanchthon to justify the interest prohibition. As seen before, he alluded to the Aristotelian scholastic arguments against interest. Along the same line, Conrad Horneius in his *Compendium theologiae* (1655) borrowed from the Roman Catholic theologians arguments of the consumptibility of money, conveyancing of property, and sterility of money. In the first place, Horneius founds the prohibition of interest on divine law. But ancillarily he employs the scholastic argument based on natural law,

338 J. Gerhard, *Locorum theologicorum tomus decimus quartus*, 98-100.

referring to Thomas Aquinas, John Duns Scotus, and Aristotle. Horneius draws upon Thomas Aquinas's statements on the consumptibility of things: he who takes interest on the lent money sells something that does not exist, or he sells one thing two times. The reason is that the use of certain things consists in the consumption. For such things the use cannot be distinguished from the ownership of the thing, because when the use is sold, the ownership is sold as well. For instance, if someone wants to sell some wine and its use separately, he sells the same thing two times, or he sells something that does not exist. As the use of the wine is the consumption, so the use of money is to be spent in the exchange.[339]

Horneius reproduces faithfully the Thomistic argument, but also refers to the argument of Scotus: if the property of the lent thing is transferred, the lender is no more the owner and cannot take something more from the money he gave. The fruits of the money belong to the borrower and not to the lender. Otherwise the lender acquires a thing that he does not possess.[340] Finally, Horneius adopts the Aristotelian argument of sterility of money. The money does not breed money, but only exists to be exchanged. The usurer earns money on the money, which is against nature.[341]

All these scholastic arguments are still considered to be valid to justify the prohibition against interest. If Horneius is an example of a conservative trend, Heinrich Uffelmann held an opposing position. In his *Variorum eorumque illustrium conscientiae casuum fasciculus* (1709), Huffelmann drives back the Aristotelian-scholastic arguments. He seems following Summenhart and other scholastic theologians who criticized these arguments.[342] Concerning the natural sterility of money, Uffelmann asserts that money is naturally sterile, but not according to civil law. Money does not produce fruits because of its nature, but because of other causes, such as the damage for the creditor and the compensation for the danger of losing the capital.[343]

Aristotle's second reason was that the money must be used to exchange and not to produce profit. Interest-taking is therefore a perversion of the use of money. Uffelmann replies that there is no reason that money must be used only for what it has been created. The primary goal of money is exchange, but

339 C. Horneius, *Compendium theologiae*, 775.

340 C. Horneius, *Compendium theologiae*, 775.

341 C. Horneius, *Compendium theologiae*, 775-6.

342 See J.T. Noonan Jr., *The Scholastic Analysis of Usury*, 340-62.

343 H. Uffelmann, *Variorum*, 131: "*ad Minorem aliquam sterilem esse dupliciter, vel naturaliter, vel civiliter, nummum priori modo sterilem esse concedo, posteriori modo nego. Quid? quod fructus non ex ipso nummo sed ex alia plane causa proveniat, nempe ex detrimenti, sive damni emergentis lucri cessantis et periculi compensatione*".

it can also be used for a profitable bargain. For these reasons, Uffelmann concludes that lending at interest is not against natural law.[344]

In short, after the precepts of Scripture, Aristotelian-scholastic arguments based on natural law resurfaced. These arguments had a secondary place but were still considered to be valid evidence of the wrong nature of interest-taking. At a later point only, they were criticized. For the Lutherans, the Scriptures played the central role in their logic, while the rational arguments remained in the background.

2.6.3 Mons pietatis

The topic of the so-called *montes pietatis* is abundantly discussed in the literature,[345] but we need to examine some of the positions that the Lutheran theologians held. The *montes* were public pawnshops with the aim to help the poor. A small fee was requested for the care of the goods pawned and the administration, while donations provided the *montes* with the necessary amounts of money.[346] The *montes* created enormous disputes between Catholic theologians, especially between the Franciscans and the Dominicans. We cannot delve deeply, but substantially the Franciscans were in favour of them and maintained that they were a remedy against usury, and that the charging of a small fee for the expenses was the only possible way to keep them working. On the contrary, the Dominicans asserted that they were against the precept of Luke 6,35. Pope Leo X's bull *Inter multiplices* (1515), accepted by the Fifth Lateran Council (1512-1517), approved the *mons pietatis*. The bull attempted to

344 H. Uffelmann, *Variorum*, 131-2.

345 Recent literature in this field includes: M.G. Muzzarelli, *Il denaro e la salvezza: l'invenzione del Monte di Pietà*, Bologna, Il Mulino, 2001; L. Armstrong, *Usury and Public Debt in Early Renaissance Florence. Lorenzo Ridolfi on the 'Monte Comune'*, Toronto, Pontifical Institute of Mediaeval Studies, 2003; G. Todeschini, *Ricchezza francescana. Dalla povertà volontaria alla società di mercato*, Bologna, Il Mulino, 2004; P. Vismara, *Oltre l'usura*, 117-27; A. Toaff, *Jews, Franciscans, and the First monti di Pieta in Italy (1462-1500)*, in S.J. McMichael, S. E. Myers (eds.), *Friars and Jews in the Middle Ages and Renaissance*, Leiden, Brill, 2004, 239-54; N.L. Barile, *Contratti di censo e monti di pietà. Problemi e prospettive di ricerca*, in P. Maffei, G.M. Varanini (eds.), *Honos alit artes. Studi per il settantesimo compleanno di Mario Ascheri. Il cammino delle idee dal medioevo all'antico regime. Diritto e cultura nell'esperienza europea*, Firenze, Firenze University Press, 2014, 139-46; M. Carboni, M.G. Muzzarelli (eds.), *I conti dei Monti: teoria e pratica amministrativa nei Monti di Pietà fra Medioevo ed Età Moderna*, Venezia, Marsilio, 2008. For a more detailed bibliography, see N.L. Barile, *Credito, usura, prestito a interesse*, in *Reti medievali*, Vol. 11 n. 1 (2010), http://www.rmojs.unina.it/index.php/rm/article/view/4757/5347?acceptCookies=1 (accessed 1.3.2017).

346 J.T. Noonan, Jr., *The Scholastic Analysis of Usury*, 295.

settle the matter by arguing that a moderate fee was charged only because of the expenses and not for the profit of the *mons*.[347]

Luther and Melanchthon did not deal with the lawfulness of the *montes*, but among the Lutheran theologians, Balthasar Meisner and Friedrich Balduin tackled the issue. Meisner discusses the *montes* in the third part of his *Philosophia sobria* (1623). He follows Gerhard's theory on the interest prohibition and applies it to the *mons*: the *mons* is usurious because is directed towards the poor.[348] The new theory of interest is certainly less rigid than the old one, but it cannot tolerate that loans towards the poor are not gratuitous. In the *montes pietatis* the poor do not borrow money for free, but some fees are gathered, and a pledge is given. When a loan harms the properties of the poor it is usurious, and Meisner concludes that the *montes* are usurious loans.[349] He also alludes to the Scripture (Exod. 22,46; Ez. 18,7-8) that forbids asking in pledge goods that the person needs.[350] If this happened the poor would be pressed and thrown into greater difficulties.

To bear this argument, namely that *montes pietatis* are illicit because they harm the poor, Meisner adds a long quotation of Domingo de Soto's *De iustitia et iure*.[351] Before Soto, Cardinal Cajetan had totally rejected the *montes pietatis* with a brilliant argument founded on commutative justice. Following Cajetan,

347 J.T. Noonan, Jr., *The Scholastic Analysis of Usury*, 299-300.

348 B. Meisner, *Philosophia sobria*, 409: "*Censemus igitur, quod Mons ille, licet aliquam videatur pietatis speciem habere, et in usus pauperum vergere; adprobari tamen et commendari minime possit*".

349 B. Meisner, *Philosophia sobria*, 410: "*Omne mutuum, quod indigentem proximum mordet, suaque substantia paulatim privat est usurarium: sed mutuum montis pietatis, indigentem proximum mordet, suaque substantia paulatim privat, per exactionem pretii ultra sortem dandi. Ergo mutuum montis pietatis est usurarium*".

350 B. Meisner, *Philosophia sobria*, 410.

351 B. Meisner, *Philosophia sobria*, 413; D. de Soto, *Libri decem de iustitia et iure*, Lugduni, 1582, Libr. 6 quaest. I, art. 6, fol. 192b. Concerning Soto's economic thought, see J. Barrientos García, *Un siglo de moral económica (1526-1629), Tom. 1: Francisco de Vitoria y Domingo de Soto*, Salamanca, Ediciones Universidad de Salamanca, 1985; J.M. Garrán Martínez, *La prohibición de la mendicidad. La controversia entre Domingo de Soto y Juan de Robles en Salamanca (1545)*, Salamanca, Ediciones Universidad de Salamanca, 2004; S. Orrego-Sanchez, *La actualidad del ser en la Primera Escuela de Salamanca. Con lecciones inéditas de Vitoria, Soto y Cano*, Ediciones Universidad de Navarra, Pamplona, 2004; H. Rodriquez Penelos, *Contribución de Domingo de Soto a la gestación del pensiamiento económico hispanoamericano*, in J. Cruz Cruz (ed.), *La ley natural como fundamento moral y jurídico ed Domingo de Soto*, Pamplona, Eunsa, 2007, 223-40; Th. Duve, *La teoría de la restitución en Domingo de Soto: Su significación para la historia del derecho privado moderno*, in J. Cruz Cruz (ed.), *La ley natural*, 181-98; S. Contreras, *La determinación del Derecho en Domingo de Soto y Francisco Suárez*, in *Revista de Estudios Histórico-Jurídicos*, XXXV, (2013), 655-80.

and holding a conservative view, Soto condemns the *montes pietatis*.[352] He argues that the lender should lend for free to the poor, but in the *montes* obtains the pledge for his benefit. Furthermore, the borrower must pay the expenses for the conservation of the pledge; but how can he pay them if he has already given in pledge what he possessed? The only solution is to deduct some money from the money he borrows. The loan must be gratuitous, but if the poor has to pay the expenses, it is not gratuitous.[353] Hence, perceiving it as an onerous loan, Soto concludes the *montes* are usurious.

Meisner's judgment is firmly against the *montes pietatis*, because in this financial operation, the poor are forced to pay something beyond the principal. The poor are requested to pay a small fee for the expenses of the pledge, and it betrays a breach of the interest prohibition. A few years after Meisner, the great casuist Friedrich Balduin also condemns the *mons pietatis* because, he writes, it is an unjust method to obtain riches. By 'unjust' Balduin means that it is against the Scripture's provisions. Scripture allows Christians to take a pledge when they lend money, but it requires two conditions.[354] First, the deadline for the payment must not be too narrow: many people make it in order to easily get the property of the pledge. God forbids this practice in Ex. 22,25: "*if thou lend money to any of My people who are poor among thee, thou shalt not be to him as a usurer*"; and Sirach (Ecclesiasticus) 29,11 commands the Christian to be patient with the neighbour and leave him the necessary time to pay the debt.[355] Second, Scripture forbids Christians to extort the neighbour's pledge, especially if the item in question belongs to the poor.[356] Ex 22,26-27 establishes:

> *if thou at all take thy neighbor's raiment in pledge, thou shalt deliver it unto him by the time the sun goeth down, for that is his only covering. It is his raiment for his skin. Wherein shall he sleep? And it shall come to pass, when he crieth unto Me, that I will hear, for I am gracious.*

And Ez. 18,7 puts as a requisite for the just man the restitution of the pledge: "*but hath restored to the debtor his pledge*". Thus, Balduin comes to the conclusion that the contract that states that the pledge can become property of the

352 J.T. Noonan, Jr., *The Scholastic Analysis of Usury*, 296-300.

353 B. Meisner, *Philosophia sobria*, 414-5.

354 F. Balduin, *Tractatus*, 948-9.

355 F. Balduin, *Tractatus*, 949.

356 F. Balduin, *Tractatus*, 949: "*Vult Scriptura, ne proximi pignus ad nos rapiamus, praesertim si sint pignora pauperum* …".

lender after a certain time and without the payment of the debtor is usurious, evil, and illicit. The creditor must incur the same punishment as the usurers.[357]

Meisner and Balduin hold the same opinion: the *montes pietatis* are usurious. Meisner clearly states that the *montes* hide onerous loans towards the poor, which is against the interest prohibition. Quoting the scholastic theologian Soto, he points out that the pledge is a burden for the poor, because he must pay the expenses for its conservation. The fee the poor has to pay is similar to an interest and thus goes against the interest prohibition. Balduin trusts only the Scripture. The *montes* are usurious because the pledge can become the property of the lender after a certain time without a payment by the debtor. Scripture allows using pledges, but establishes detailed requisites that the *montes* do not keep. Such a strong refusal of the *montes* is not complemented by any original solution for helping the poor. The only possibility seems to be gratuitous loans.

2.6.4 *Spreading the Good Word*

The Lutheran theory of interest illuminated the theological science throughout the seventeenth century, during which it was generally integrated in moral treatises and collections of cases of conscience. An in-depth analysis of the reception of this theory would require a separate study. Here we only look at some examples. Friedrich Balduin cites Brenz, Hunnius, Gessner, Gerhard, Meisner, and Dedekenn.[358] Similarly, in his *Compendium theologiae moralis*, Johann Conrad Dürr refers to Chemnitz, Gerhard, Balduin, and Gessner.[359] Samuel Schelwig, in the *Cynosura conscientiae*, alludes to Meisner and Dedekenn.[360] Joann Franz Buddeus draws on Gerhard, Chemnitz, and Dannhauer.[361] These references testify to the progressive assimilation and consolidation of the Lutheran theory of interest.

Johann Konrad Dannhauer backs the Lutheran theory in his *Deuteronomium*, but uses an innovative style. He distinguishes between usurious avarice (*avaritia usuraria*), interest according to duty (*usura officialis*), natural interest (*usura naturalis*), and the alms-interest (*usura eleemosynaria*). Usurious avarice is forbidden, while the others are allowed. The interest according to duty

357 F. Balduin, *Tractatus*, 949: "*Contractus ergo illum, quo pignora post statutum tempus et deficiente solutione veniunt in possessionem mutuantis habemus pro usurario, impio et illicito, quo opes iniuste augentur, imo creditor hanc unicam ob causam in poenas usurariorum merito incurrit*".

358 F. Balduin, *Tractatus*, 946.

359 J.K. Dürr, *Compendium theologiae moralis*, 224.

360 S. Schelwig, *Cynosura conscientiae*, Lipsiae, 1692, 272-9.

361 J.F. Buddeus, *Institutiones theologiae moralis*, 542.

is described by the English famous casuist William Ames in his *De conscientia et eius iure vel casibus*, to whom Dannhauer refers.[362] In Matthew 25,27 Christ sets forth the parable of the talents, concluding: "*thou ought therefore to have placed my money with the exchangers, and then at my coming I should have received mine own with interest*". Ames comments that interest-charging bankers constituted an accepted profession among the Jews, and Christ did not condemn it; rather, under such a similitude he alludes to a spiritual duty, without any insinuation about the condemnation of usury.[363] Lending at interest as practiced by bankers for financial gain is therefore permitted.

Then, natural interest (*usura naturalis*) corresponds to the breeding of sheep or the planting of crops. It is mentioned in Gen. 26,17, but most of all in Matt. 16,23: "*but he that received seed into the good ground is he that heareth the Word and understandeth it; who also beareth fruit and bringeth forth, some a hundredfold, some sixty, some thirty*". Natural interest is a multiplication of fruits grown from seeds or of domesticated animals like sheep. Finally, the alms-interest (*usura eleemosynaria*) derives from alms to the poor, which multiply the benefits of God.[364] Dannhauer looks at the different types of interest that exist in reality and describes them: his horizon is wider than Gerhard and others, because he looks not only at the lawfulness and unlawfulness of loans at interest but also to their effective use. With regard to other interpretations, as for instance Chemnitz's, Dannhauer does not intend usury (lending at interest) as a negative behaviour only, but considers it as a means of increasing money that can have different applications.

The Lutheran theory of interest was also adopted in specific treatises concerning interest-taking and in theological treatises. Theodor Thumm's treatise on interest (1622) is a practical explication of the new theory.[365] The father of Lutheran moral theology, Georg Calixt, also worked on a treatise dedicated to interest in 1667: *Dissertatio theologica moralis de usuris*. While he does not quote any theologian, the arguments expounded substantially reflect the Lutheran theory of interest.[366]

In theological treatises, then, theologians explored the interpretation of certain scriptural passages on interest. The passage of Deut. 23,20 was particularly questioned. For instance, Wolfgang Franz maintained that this passage

362 W. Ames, *De conscientia et eius iure vel casibus*, editio nova, Franekerae, 1635, 375.

363 J.K. Dannhauer, *Deuteronomium Dannhawerianum*, 866.

364 J.K. Dannhauer, *Deuteronomium Dannhawerianum*, 866-7.

365 T. Thumm, *Tractatus de usura licita et illicita*, Tubingae, 1622.

366 G. Calixt, *Dissertatio theologica moralis de usuris*, Helmestadi, 1667, in I. Mager (ed.), *G. Calixt. Ethische Schriften*, Göttingen, Vandenhoeck & Ruprecht, 1970, 220-45. See also I. Mager, *Georg Calixts theologische Ethik und ihre Nachwirkungen*, 138-41.

forbade the Jews to lend at interest among themselves, but they were allowed to charge interest to foreigners (not the poor foreigners, but only the rich), so that they could faithfully adhere to the true religion.[367] Pfeiffer instead observed that this is not a precept but a naked permission. God wanted the Jews to forego the charging of interest against other Jews. Interest is against natural equity, and exacting interest from the strangers was also against natural equity, except in the case of the people of Canaan, who were particular enemies of Jews.[368] In contrast, some other Lutheran theologians, such as König, argued that the Jews were allowed to charge interest against the stranger because of natural equity. He drew upon the Reformed jurist Francois Hotman, who, in his treatise on interest, suggested that the foreigners did not observe the Decalogue and extorted interest from the Jews. For that reason, as a natural reciprocity, the Jews were allowed to require interest from loans to them.[369]

As we will see better with the jurists, the theory of interest was an argument quite debated also among the Reformed theologians. Overlaps and cultural exchanges among Reformed thinkers and Lutherans surely occurred, although among the theologians is rare to find the explicit admissions. In his manual of moral theology (1714), Johann Wolfgang Jäger again describes the old theory of interest, which he writes is followed by several Reformed theologians – William Ames, Wolfgang Musculus, and Benedict Aretius – and the new one, which he attributes to Samuel Pufendorf. Jäger endorses the new theory and warns Christians to remember the precepts of charity.[370]

Finally, the Lutheran theory of interest was considerably employed to solve the numerous disputes on usury that spread across Germany – not only the dispute of Regensburg, which we treat in IV/1, but also the dispute of 1578 reported by Felix Bidenbach, which we have seen before. Heerbrand and Schnepf pointed out that the civil magistrate approved the 5% *census*, and

367 W. Franz, *Tractatus theologicus novus et perspicuuis, de interpretatione sacrarum scripturarum maxime legitima*, VVittebergae, 1708, 950: "*His ita standibus, dicendum est, quod noluerit usuras accipi ab Israelitis, et ab illis qui fide Israelitis erant pares, indulserit vero illis accipere ab Ethnicis non conversis, sive intra sive extra Judaeam habitantibus, longe vel prope, in primis vero propius habitantibus, et ut quilibet facile videbit, tantum hanc ob causam, ut religioni verae citius favere et adhaerere ipsi quod discerent*".

368 A. Pfeiffer, *Dubia vexata Scripturae Sacrae*, editio quartae, Lipsiae, 1699, 275.

369 G. König, *Casus conscientiae*, 67; F. Hotman, *De usuris libri duo*, Lugduni, 1558, 140. Hotman also writes that this opinion derives from the theologian Cephas Tervius. The pseudonimous should correspond to the Calvinist theologian Pierre Viret (1511-1571). G. Berthoud, *Antoine Marcourt, Réformateur et Pamphlétaire du "Livre des Marchans" aus Placards de 1534*, Geneve, 1973, 248.

370 J.W. Jäger, *Theologia moralis*, 184-6. On Pufendorf see C. Gamba, *Licita usura*, 342-53.

such approval is not against Christian charity (*Christliche lieb*). Christian charity must rule every contract, including the contract where an amount of money is sold for an annuity. It would be against Christian charity, write the theologians, if someone pursued avenues to become rich with another's money and to their detriment.[371] In a similar way, Conrad Schlüsselburg (1543-1619), in his collection of cases of conscience (*Vier und zwantzig hochwichtige Fragen und Bedencken, mit ihren klaren deutlichen und gründlichen Antwortungen*, 1625), presents a case which occurred in Mecklenburg.[372] The issue was whether accepting a 5% or 6% *census* was to be considered usury. The decision was pronounced by theologians like David Chytraeus, Simon Pauli (1534-1591), Lucas Backmeister senior (1530-1608), and Konrad Becker (1561-1604).

On the whole, the Lutheran theory of interest gained energic vitality in the seventeenth century. It circulated abundantly in collections of cases of conscience and manuals of moral theology; dedicated treatises on interest were composed and the theologians faced the topic of the interest prohibition also in their theological treatises. Reformed theologians were also sometimes cited and their theory examined, and lastly the Lutheran teachings on interest were employed to solve disputes on interest and usury. The new path grew and became entrenched; the good news, charity towards the neighbour, spread through Germany.

2.7 Conclusion

The Lutheran theologians resolved the tensions between finance and law by freeing the law of interest from the teachings of scholastics and canonists. The Roman Catholic Church incorporated the interest prohibition in a legal norm, which was supported by a mixture of scriptural and philosophical arguments. The Lutheran theologians demolished this construction. The magistrate regulates the business contracts, but his legislation must comply with natural law and charity, and the Christians should apply it according to charity. The Lutheran theologians insisted on the responsibility of the Christians to apply the law with charity. It is not the Church as a legal and political body that dictates norms, but it is the Church as a community of Christians who put the

371 F. Bidenbach, *Consiliorum theologicorum decas VI*, 69: "*Das were wider das Gesetz der Liebe, dass einer mit dess andern Schaden und Geld ohne widerlegung sollte unnd wolte reich werden*".

372 C. Schlüsselburg, *Vier und zwantzig Hochwichtige Fragen und Bedencken, mit ihren klaren deutlichen und gründlichen Antwortungen*, Rostock, 1625, 144-62.

Gospel into practice. The creation of law is a prerogative of political power, but its application depends on Christians' individual conscience. The conscience must follow the Gospel, the essential principle of which is charity. Charity exhorts the parties to look at the reciprocal benefit and to assist each other in case of need. It operates as a form of equity: it mitigates the law and restrains believers from avid thirst for profit.

The formation of a Lutheran theory of interest was associated with the analysis of a series of financial contracts, the most discussed of which was the German contract or five per cent contract. In this operation, the investor lent to the entrepreneur the capital, to use for a business, with a clause that guaranteed that the investor would recoup not only the capital but also a fixed part of the profits of the entrepreneur (5% of the invested sum). This operation received a double legal classification. Scholastic theologians defined it as a combination of a partnership, insurance and a sale, the so-called triple contract (*contractus trinus*). The Lutheran theologians principally utilized another legal qualification, very common in the practice, which built the contract on the *census* structure. The *census* was a medieval contract that permitted the purchase of a right to receive an annual income from fruitful property. The German contract was classified as redeemable *census* (*widerkaufflicher Zins*). The investor/buyer purchased the right to receive a certain annuity (5% of the invested sum). The contract could be for a fixed period of time or perpetual, redeemable at the option of the seller or at the option of the buyer. This *census* was detached from a specific productive acreage, but constituted a personal obligation to pay the 5% annuity.

The German contract was extremely similar to a loan at interest and attracted the attention of the Lutheran theologians, who suspected it was an infraction of the interest prohibition. The theologians were not expert jurists. They almost never discussed the whole contract and limited their observations only to some aspects: the problem of the risk of loss that belongs to the entrepreneur/seller; the nature of the contract; the profit that does not derive from a specific fruitful property; and the redemption after a certain period of time. These issues played a different role for each interpreter. For instance, Luther rejected the German contract because only the borrower bears the risk. Conversely, Melanchthon and other theologians insisted on addressing the nature of the agreement, claiming that because it is not a loan but a sale, the interest prohibition does not apply. This approach imitated the scholastics, which considered the real *census* as a sale of a right to receive an annual income from fruitful property. The argument functioned well with a *census* based on a single tract of land, but the German contract established a personal obligation of the seller/entrepreneur to pay the 5% annuity. Without any reference to a specific acreage this obligation was identical to the payment of an interest. The Lutheran orthodoxy solved the problem by reformulating the interest prohibition. The obligation to pay the 5% annuity is lawful, they decided, because loans at interest are not forbidden if the neighbour is not harmed. Even though the contract was often still classified as a sale and not a loan, this qualification was less important. Loans at profit were deemed admissible, if none of the parties are damaged.

The debate on the lawfulness of the German contract dominated the attention of the Lutheran theologians. Nonetheless, the theologians also examined other financial operations as for instance the real *census*, the partnership, the *interesse* (compensation for loss), and the *montes pietatis*. These contracts had all been discussed at length among the scholastic theologians and canonists. With the *census* contract, the buyer/investor bought the right to receive an annuity from a real estate. This contract could be formulated in various ways, but generally the seller/borrower could use the capital received and when he returned the capital, the contract ended. The partnership was constituted as a joint venture where the parties must share profits and losses. The '*interesse*' was the compensation the creditor should receive, should he suffer damage in a loan. The damage was considered according to a double classification: occurring damage (*damnum emergens*) and profit ceasing (*lucrum* cessans). The *montes pietatis* were public pawnshops with the aim to help the poor. A small fee was requested, however, for the care of the goods pawned, which made the *montes* similar to a loan at interest. The Lutheran theologians accounted for all these operations with a new regulation.

The Lutheran theory of interest was forged progressively by the integration of different doctrines. The theologians did not fabricate a single consistent theory; rather they elaborated a number of different doctrines that gradually came together. This process began around at the end of the 1530s and stabilized approximately by the first decades of the seventeenth century. Later theologians did not bring substantial changes and constructed their works on the basis of the precedent analysis. With the only aim to depict a clearer image, we might distinguish four virtual stages of formation: a first stage where Luther and Melanchthon laid down the foundations (2.2); a second stage when the first reformulation of the interest prohibition, founded on the distinction between business contracts and loans to the poor, took place (2.3); a third stage where the essential ethical element of charity towards the neighbour was established as general principle of contract law (2.4); a fourth stage when the elements of these theories were collected and systematized (2.5). This classification should not mislead; the words have a vivid character that tends to escape from conceptualizations. The writings examined conserved their dynamism beyond the scheme we use today. They had a value in the building of a Lutheran theory of interest, but also independently from the connections we draw.

The fresh start began, obviously, with Martin Luther. He endorsed the traditional interpretation of Luke 6,35 - lending at interest is forbidden- but also stated that the interest prohibition is not established by a canon law norm, but only by Scripture. The interest prohibition punishes a sin against natural law and Christian charity. His approach towards the German contract was oscillating: initially, Luther refused this agreement, but later admitted it only for old people, orphans and widows. Melanchthon resurrected the Aristotelian scholastic arguments against interest-taking, but they have a secondary role; for him as well the prohibition is mainly justified in the Scriptures. More openly than Luther, however, he accepted the German contract, distinguishing it from a loan by classifying it a sale.

The followers of Luther inherited the problematic issue of the lawfulness of the German contract. Based on Luther's writings on usury and interest, and on the doctrine of the two kingdoms, a number of theologians designed theoretical solutions. The centre of the debate was the right interpretation of Scripture. The Aristotelian scholastic natural law arguments in favour of the interest prohibition were in large part not touched. Some theologians used these arguments merely as a secondary source, while others criticized them. An essential role was played by the 1530 imperial ordinance of the Emperor Charles V, which fixed the maximum amount of annuities at 5% of the invested sum and set out that the power to redeem only pertains to the seller/entrepreneur. As a matter of fact, the ordinance legalized the crucial elements of the German contract: especially the admission of the 5% annuity troubled the theologians, because the obligation to pay the annuity was practically identical to an interest. Johannes Brenz and Johannes Aepinus did not protest the ordinance, but appealed to the divine authority of the magistrate to justify it. Meanwhile, they reflected on the interpretation of the precept of Luke 6,35: it does not concern every Christian but only the poor. It is not a rule of justice that concerns every man and every loan, but a rule of charity for the Christians regarding the poor. The outcome was that Luke 6,35 governs the loans given to the working poor. The German contract can be only used for transactions between prosperous individuals and is regulated by the magistrate, whose ordinance follows natural law and can be used in good conscience.

Urbanus Rhegius put forward another theory. The passage of Luke 6,35 is a specification of the rule of charity, which governs the whole Gospel. In order to be usurious, a loan must not only require interest, but also harm the neighbour.

The imperial ordinance that permits a 5% annuity is not wrong, because it does not condemn every loan at interest, but leaves to the Christians to decide if there is damage in the concrete circumstances. The Christians are called to apply the ordinance and practice the German contract according to natural law and Christian charity. They must judge if the other party is damaged or not. If the party is damaged, they cannot apply the ordinance and charge interest, because Luke 6,35 exhorts the Christians to lend hoping for nothing in return. But if the payment of interest does not harm the neighbour, it can be charged. Rhegius specifies that the payment of the annuity out of gratitude is not against charity, and that the parties must not only share profits but also losses.

The wave of change was not univocal. Theologians as Niels Hemmingsen and most of all Martin Chemnitz struck down the new approaches and turned back to the traditional concept of interest, which relates to everybody and independently of the question of damages. Chemnitz only accepted two points of the previous theories. First, only rich people can practice the business contracts. Second, all the contracts must have as a master and moderator (*magistra et moderatrix*) the rule of charity. God wanted charity to be practiced not only towards the poor, but also towards every man. Chemnitz accepted the contract with the clause to resell, the *interesse*, and the partnership. In the contract with the clause to resell, which includes a sale with the clause to resell, the real *census* and the German contract, the parties are called to evaluate their needs and ensure that the contract meets them. If the debtor is unable to pay the debt, charity pushes the creditor to remit the debt. In the partnership, Chemnitz exhorts the parties to share profits and losses. For the *interesse*, he dictates a set of rules taken from Scripture.

A decisive impulse towards the reformulation of the interest prohibition came from Aegidius Hunnius and Johann Gerhard, halfway between the sixteenth and the seventeenth centuries. They adopted a liberal and modern attitude and restored the theories Chemnitz had criticized. They held that the passage of Luke 6,35 should be interpreted as forbidding only the loans that harm the neighbour. It occurs especially with the loans at interest towards the poor. The German contract, albeit still formally classified as a sale, is considered on a par with a loan at interest. Some of the rules that previously concerned the gratuitous loans passed to the German contract. The Christian is called to apply this agreement and magistrate ordinance in compliance with his own conscience and according to charity. Charity consists in protection against damages, but also as assistance for the less powerful party. Charity justifies the obligation to pay the annuity, because without the payment the investor is damaged, and the borrower is advantaged. Charity invites the parties to a concrete judgement of obedience and disobedience of the law. The Christian should pay attention to the capacities of the other party: the German contract can only be practiced among rich people; the amount of the annuity must be proportionate to the lent sum and the parties' needs; and in case of unforeseen and unexpected circumstances, the creditor must remit the debt.

At the end of the road, we see that the interest prohibition as it was conceived in the Middle Ages is completely overturned by the Lutheran theologians. The old theory of interest is replaced with a new one. The crucial point is the reinterpretation of Luke 6,35 as a precept founded on charity and not on justice. In the light of the Gospel, then, the theologians reconsidered the interpretation of the other passages of Scripture which expressed the interest prohibition. In the scholastic world, lending at interest was simply forbidden. The prohibition was embedded in a legal norm. In the new theory, the precept of Luke 6,35 does not forbid every loan, but only the loan that harms the neighbour. The legal norm becomes a precept of equity rooted in charity; the law, therefore, does not belong to the Gospel but to the magistrate. The magistrate can regulate business contracts, but Christians have to apply them according to charity, which acts as an equalizer and mitigates the strict law. The German contract can be practiced under the condition that charity is kept. Charity implies a set of rules that protects the neighbour against damages and guarantees that he benefits from the contract. The Christian is called to apply the law and the contractual terms according to charity and to judge with his own conscience the observance of charity while performing the contractual obligations.

PART IV

From Lutheran Theology to Legal Practice

CHAPTER 1

The Dispute of Regensburg (1587)

In the first part of this work we described the Lutheran theologians and their attitude towards contract law in general. In the second and third parts we focused on their theoretical reflections on basic elements and particular types of contract. Now, we turn to the impact of these reflections on the works of the jurists. In the sixteenth-seventeenth centuries, contract law in Lutheran Germany was shaped by theologians and jurists in synergy. The contribution of the theologians did not remain confined in the *foro interno*, but was used by the jurists for the *foro externo*.

As Harold J. Berman has maintained, theologians and jurists explore two interrelated dimensions of social relations, for a Christian society needs both spiritual direction and normative order. Theologians, concerned with the ultimate end of salvation, interpret biblical teachings. Jurists convert these teachings for application to the social order – they give to faith and hope a normative structure.[1] The work of the theologians is therefore not isolated but opened towards the jurists.

The fourth part of this work examines the relationship between Lutheran theologians and jurists over the course of two chapters. The former is dedicated to a dispute on the violation of the interest prohibition where both theologians and jurists were involved. The latter regards the doctrinal writings of the Lutheran jurists and their correspondence with the Lutheran orthodoxy.

The 'German contract' was very much in vogue in sixteenth-century Germany. Five ecclesiastical ministers of Regensburg accused this contract of being in violation of interest law. The local political authority reproved the ministers and contended that the contract was lawful, but the ministers stood on their positions. As a consequence, a controversy arose between the two parties. The resolution was first entrusted to the theologian Jacob Andreae and then to the jurists of the law faculty of Tübingen.

As this chapter will show, the arguments and reasoning of Andreae and the jurists of Tübingen are deeply interrelated and often draw on the theoretical elaboration of the Lutheran theologians. Andreae's refined biblical interpretation lacks legal precision, which the jurists provide. On the other hand, the jurists need the spiritual legitimation to ground their conclusions. Both Andreae and the Tübingen jurists relied on the earlier debates of other theologians that

1 H.J. Berman, *The Interaction between Law and Religion*, London, Scm Press Ltd, 1974.

 | DOI:10.30965/9783657701506_010

we have previously studied. The Regensburg dispute is therefore an example of the fruitful cooperation between theologians and jurists.

1.1 The Origins of the Dispute

1.1.1 *Prior Events*

1.1.1.1 Luther and the German Contract

As seen before, the German contract received a double qualification: triple contract and mutually redeemable annuity (*census-Zins*). In the latter, the theologians used various denominations and allowed different options for the redemption of the contract. In the case we discuss now, the investor (lender/buyer) buys the right to receive 5% of the invested sum on an annual basis (*Zins-census*). The entrepreneur (borrower/seller) can use the money for any business he chooses, because the contract is detached from a specific real estate. The obligation of the entrepreneur is to pay 5% annuity and to return the capital at the time established: the parties agree that the contract ends after a certain period of time.[2]

In his first writings on the interest prohibition, Luther rehearsed the Roman Catholic interpretation of Luke 6,35: lending at interest is forbidden. He also condemned the German contract, which he calls *Zinskauf*, because it is against natural law and Christian charity. The business is not conducted for the sake of the seller, but always for the sake of the buyer. The buyer receives the annuity (*Zins*) but does not take part in the risks. To those who argued that the annuity is due because the buyer might have earned other profits with the money given to the seller, Luther objects that the buyer could also gain more or lose his capital. When the buyer elects to pursue the annuity, he no longer risks the loss of his capital.[3]

In the admonition *An die Pfarrherrn, wider den Wucher zu predigen* (1540), Luther changed his mind and admitted the possibility of using the *Zinskauf* to aid special categories of people, such as the elderly, the poor widows and the orphans who do not have other support except that gained by using this contract. He writes:

> *If it should happen that e.g. elderly people, poor widows or orphans or otherwise needy persons who until then had learnt no other means of sustaining life, would make business with 1000 or 2000 florins and* [*if it were the case*] *that they would have nothing else if they had to give that up and would have to warm their hands*

2 See III/2.1.3.

3 M. Luther, *Ein (grosser) Sermon von dem Wucher*, in WA 6, 53-5.

> *at their beggar's staff or would have to starve, in that case I would like that that the jurists make an alleviation to the strict law.*[4]

Luther spells out that this would not be usury, but "an interest out of need", (*ein Notwucherlin*):

> *and here the above mentioned saying could be applicable: the world cannot be without interest, but [in my view] it would not exactly be usury, nor a law, but a little/insignificant interest out of need, almost half a work of mercy for the poor who would otherwise have nothing, and [it] would not particularly harm the others.*[5]

Luther thus permits the *Zinskauf* but only for these special categories of people: the elderly, widows, orphans and other indigents. He distinguishes between the needy and the not-needy.[6] For the people in need it is necessary to admit *interest out of need*, because without this permission they would not have any means of support. They cannot work, but they can use this contract to get the earnings that are necessary to live. Luther does not want anyone to despair and so he recognises that:

> *if the sovereign were called upon and together with wise jurists, preachers and counselors he would find a tolerable mean (of) epieikeia or amnesty, the conscience could be eased/at peace.*[7]

In this way, as an exception for the needy, the *Zinskauf* could be lawfully used. The magistrate should fix the amount of *Zins*, and the ecclesial ministers and the jurists should address the controversies on this contract.[8]

These new teachings represent a breakthrough in respect to the previous position, which was stridently against the *Zinskauf*. One of the reasons that might have conducted to this change of mind is the fact that at the Diet of

4 M. Luther, *An die Pfarrherrn*, in WA 51, 371: "… *Wenn der fal furkeme, das etwa alte leute, arme Witwen odder waisen, odder sonst durfftige personen, die bis daher kein andere narung gelernt, hetten im handel ein Tausent floren odder zwey, Und solten sie davon lassen, so hetten sie sonst nichts, und musten die hand am bettelstab wermen, oder hungers sterben. Hie wolt ich wol gern, das die Jüristen ein linderung des scharffen rechten setzen* (…)".

5 M. Luther, *An die Pfarrherrn*, in WA 51, 372: "*Und hieher möcht der spruch gehören, der droben gesagt ist: Die welt könne nicht on Wucher sein, doch das es nicht stracks ein wucher, auch nicht ein recht, sonder ein not Wücherlin were, schier ein halb werk der barmherzigkeit, fur die dürfftigen, die sonst nichts hetten, und den andern auch nicht sonderlich schadet*".

6 M. Luther, *An die Pfarrherrn*, in WA 51, 372-3.

7 M. Luther, *An die Pfarrherrn*, in WA 51, 372: "*Darumb acht ich, wo hierin der landsfurst wurde angeruffen und der selb mit vernunfftigen Juristen, predigern und Reten ein leidlich mittel Epiikia oder Amnistiam finden wurde, mochte als denn das gewissen zu frieden gestellet werden*".

8 M. Luther, *An die Pfarrherrn*, in WA 51, 373-4.

Augsburg in 1530, Charles V, the emperor of the Holy Roman Empire, had permitted this contract. The imperial provision facilitated the circulation of this agreement that become more popular. Another hypothesis is that Luther was induced to moderate his position by the counsel of his followers. For instance, Brenz openly favoured the *Zinskauf* and defended the imperial ordinance. Pushed by these factors, Luther might have decided to reconsider his opinion and concede the *Zinskauf* for specific categories of people.

One little note needs to be made about the instrument selected by Luther for granting this exception. The magistrate, the preachers and the jurists have to intervene with equity (*epieikeia*). Equity arises from mercy toward the condition of some people. Mercy liberates from sin, so that in this way it is possible to use the *Zinskauf* with a good conscience. To Luther, equity embodies mercy, and this mercy forgives from sins. In this way equity can be seen as a reflection of the divine mercy of God.[9] The magistrate, the preachers and the jurists have to apply this divine mercy to the faithful and mitigate the law. The correction of law derives from the grace of God and becomes in this way an instrument of mercy.

Luther's opinion was widely discussed in the ambit of the Lutheran orthodoxy. Luther relied on the scholastic assertion that Luke 6,35 forbids loans at interest. On the other hand, he granted an exception for special categories of people. The imperial ordinance of 1530 (replied in 1548), though, allowed a 5% annuity (*Zins*) in the *widerkaufflicher Zins*. The ordinance did not make a distinction between people, but was applicable to everyone. The contrast between Luther's statement and the imperial ordinance constituted a serious problem, especially considering the general popular acceptance of the German contract. As seen before, a number of Lutheran theologians tried to solve the problem by articulating a new theory of interest. At the same time, several disputes were raised on the right interpretation of both the interest prohibition and Luther's words.

1.1.1.2 The Dispute of Rudolstadt

One of the disputes about the lawfulness of taking 5% annuities occurred in 1564 Rudolstadt. Following Luther's *An die Pfarrherrn, wider den Wucher zu predigen*, Bartholomaeus Gernhard (1525-1600),[10] pastor of the church of

9 J. Gehrke, *The Virtue of Epieikeia: A Study in Luther and his Sources*, in *Seminar Ridge Review*, Autumn 2014, v. 17 (1), 68-101 (91).

10 E. Anemüller, *Gernhard, Bartholomäus* in *Allgemeine Deutsche Biographie* 9 (1879), 35-37 (accessed 4.10.2017); URL: https://www.deutsche-biographie.de/gnd100143687.html#adbcontent.

St. Andrew, refused to absolve and to admit to the Lord's Supper the nobles Georg von Schonberg and Georg von Schonfeld. According to Gernhard and his followers, they had taken 4-6% annuities (*Zins*) in loans and therefore they were usurers.[11] The nobles replied that they were had no other possibility than invest money with annuities (*Zins*) and that these had been allowed by the imperial legislation.

The following dispute ended with the defeat of Gernhard but triggered a debate that inflamed the whole Germany. The issue was intricate: not less than ten counsels were pronounced by theologians and jurists, many of whom fought against the five percent *Zins*. Universities such as Leipzig, Wittenberg, Jena, Tübingen, Erfurt and Marburg sent their counsels. And theologians as Maximilian Mörlin (1516-1584) of Coburg, Nikolaus von Amsdorff (1483-1565) of Eisenach, and Simon Musaeus (1521-1576) of Gera were also consulted.

The theologians of Wittenberg (via the pen of Paul Eber) wrote that it is impossible to formulate a universal rule, but each superintendent with the help of the *Obrigkeit* must decide case by case. It is necessary to distinguish between the loans in accordance with duty (*mutuationibus officiosis*), which must be gratuitous, and those intended for profit. The parish priest cannot solely dictate excommunication, but the *Konsistorium* must be consulted.[12] Similarly, the jurists of Leipzig and Johannes Stoeffel from Jena's university recommended the intervention of the *Konsistorium*.[13]

Maximilian Mörlin and Nikolaus von Amsdorff condemned the 5% annuities as usurious. The jurists of the theology faculty of Erfurt decided the same and referred to Luther's first writings against usury.[14] The theologians of Tübingen, Jacob Andreae, Dietrich Schnepf, Lucas Osiander the elder (1534-1604), Johannes Brenz, and Felix Bidenbach condemned a 5% annuity in a loan as usurious, sinful and damned. However, the arguments used (the imperial ordinance is an ordinance of God; if there is no breach of Matthew 7,12, there is no usury) give a hint that they might have approved the 5% annuity in the

11 B. Anemüller, *M. Bartholomäus Gernhard und der Rudolstädter Wucherstreit im 16. Jahrhundert*, Rudolstadt, 1861, 8-9. See also M. Neumann, *Geschichte des Wuchers in Deutschland bis zur Begründung der heutigen Zinsengesetze (1654)*, Halle, 1865, 483 n. 2, 484-5; G. Arndt, *"Christoph Fischer und seine Tätigkeit als Generalsuperintendent im Thüringer Lande"*, in *Beiträge zur thüringischen und sächsischen Kirchengeschichte: Festschrift für Otto Dobenecker zum siebzigsten Geburstage am 2. April 1929*. Jena, 1929, 294-326 (315-321); H. Barge, *Luther und der Frühkapitalismus*, 43-4; B.N. Nelson, *The Idea of Usury*, 93.

12 B. Anemüller, *M. Bartholomäus Gernhard*, 13.

13 B. Anemüller, *M. Bartholomäus Gernhard*, 14.

14 B. Anemüller, *M. Bartholomäus Gernhard*, 14-7.

Zinskauf but not in a loan.[15] The first contract is indeed a sale, and a lawful form of business, while a loan should only be used for helping the poor, gratuitously. Later the jurists of Marburg (the text is signed by the dean Anton Heistermann [1538-1568]), the theologian Simon Musaeus, superintendent in Gera, and others supported the pastor Gernhard. In the end, however, the progressivists won and the opinion of Gernhard was rejected.

1.1.1.3 *Nicht als ein Recht, sondern als ein Dispensation*: Gallus' Teachings on the Interest Prohibition and the Imperial Ordinance

A conservative interpretation of Luther's statements was again proposed by Nikolaus Gallus (1516-1570), the superintendent of Regensburg. Gallus was promoted as *magister* by Melanchthon and studied theology in the ascendant of Luther. He followed the orthodox Lutheran Matthias Flacius in the Adiaphoristic Controversy. In 1543, Gallus was deacon in Regensburg, but then traveled in other towns, and finally returned in Regensburg, where he influenced the expansion of Lutheranism.[16] In a series of sermons and in his catechism,[17] Gallus countered Brenz's opinion on the authority of the imperial ordinance[18] and argued that the ordinance only concerns the worldlings (*weltkindern*), while the Christians in contrast should keep in mind the precept of Luke 6,35 and lend hoping for nothing in return.[19] According to Gallus, the imperial law admitted a 5% annuity in virtue of the great infidelity of the world,

15 B. Anemüller, *M. Bartholomäus Gernhard*, 18. The counsel is included in a manuscript, which is not easy to read. Anemüller reports that these theologians concluded that the 5% is usurious, sinful and damned. Yet, these accusations are for the 5% in a loan (*mutuo*), while in sale of an income *Zins* seems to be allowed, as it is reported in the manuscript: "*… venditio et emptio annui redditus ex utraque parte, sit licita et minime usuraria*". See *Gutachten über den Wucherstreit in Rudolstadt* (*Forschungbibliothek Gotha*), Chart. A 103, Bl. 113r-116v, (113v). This might explain why these liberal theologians opted for a declaration of usury in this case. However, a deeper examination of the manuscript would be necessary to draw definitive conclusions.

16 G. Moldaenke, *Gallus, Nicolaus* in *Neue Deutsche Biographie* 6 (1964), 55 f. (accessed 4.10.2017); https://www.deutsche-biographie.de/gnd118537369.html#ndbcontent; H. Voit, *Nikolaus Gallus. Ein Beitrag zur Reformationsgeschichte der nachlutherischen Zeit*, Neustadt a. d. Aisch, 1977; F.W. Bautz, *Gallus (eigentlich: Hahn), Nikolaus*, in *BBKL*, v. II (1990), 174; R. Kolb, *Nikolaus Gallus critique of Philip Melanchthon's teaching on the freedom of the will*, in *ARG* 91(2000), 87-110. On the Reformation in Regensburg see H. Schwarz (ed.), *Reformation und Reichsstadt. Protestantisches Leben in Regensburg*, Regensburg, Universitätsverlag, 1994.

17 N. Gallus, *Catechismus, predigweise gestelt für die Kirche zu Regenspurg zum Methodo: das ist ordentlicher Summa christlicher Lere wider allerlei Newerung und Verfelschung*, Regensburg, 1554, die zehend Predig, von dem siebenden gebot.

18 See before III/2.3.4.1.

19 N. Gallus, *Zwo Predigten Wider den Wucher*, Jhena, 1572, [6].

which does not serve the neighbour unless a profit is made.[20] The Gospel requires service of the neighbour, but Charles V's imperial ordinance justifies a selfish quest for advantage. Therefore, the Christians should not treat this ordinance as law (*Recht*), but as a dispensation (*Dispensation*) due to the infidelity of the world. They have to consider it in a Christian way, according to God's order.[21] Gallus compares this situation with the biblical policy started after the fall of Adam because of human malice and advises Christians to consider the ordinance in light of the divine law.[22] He cites Psalm 15,5 and Luke 6,35. About the latter, drawing on the Spanish canonist Diego de Covarrubias,[23] he comments that no power on the earth and no angel in the heaven can change the divine law. Hence, all the laws that allow charging interest against the divine law are wrong.[24]

Gallus looks at life from to a spiritual perspective, which refuses to build certainty on the material goods but emphasizes faith in God and man's personal work. He lends weight to his argument with the following Scriptural passages: Matthew 6,31-34:

> *Therefore take no thought, saying, What shall we eat? or, What shall we drink? or, Wherewithal shall we be clothed? (For after all these things do the Gentiles seek), for your heavenly Father knoweth that ye have need of all these things. But seek ye first the kingdom of God, and his righteousness; and all these things shall be added unto you. Take therefore no thought for the morrow: for the morrow shall take thought for the things of itself. Sufficient unto the day is the evil thereof*; Genesis 3,19: *In the sweat of thy face shalt thou eat bread*; Psalm 37,3: *Dwell in the land and you shall be fed*; Psalm 128,1-2: *Blessed is every one that feareth the Lord; that walketh in his ways. For thou shalt eat the labour of thine hands: happy shalt thou be, and it shall be well with thee*; 2 Thess. 3,10: *if any would not work, neither should he eat*; Luke 16,3: *Then the steward said within himself, What shall I do? for my lord taketh away from me the stewardship: I cannot dig; to beg I am ashamed*; and 1 Thess. 4,11: *to work with your own hands, as we commanded you.*

These passages plainly command the Christians to work and trust the Lord. Interest-taking is indirectly considered to be wrong, because the lender relies on the profits he receives from the work of the borrower and not from his own work.

---

20 N. Gallus, *Zwo Predigten Wider den Wucher*, [7].

21 N. Gallus, *Zwo Predigten Wider den Wucher*, [7].

22 N. Gallus, *Zwo Predigten Wider den Wucher*, [7].

23 D. De Covarrubias, *Variarum ex iure pontificio regio et caesareo resolutionum*, Venetiis, 1566, *Libro III*. Gallus quotes the book n. 1, but the discussion on usury is included in book n. 3 and for this reason we suppose that his quotation was referred to book n. 3.

24 N. Gallus, *Zwo Predigten Wider den Wucher*, [8].

The situation is different with the people who are incapable (*untüchtig*) of work. The teachings of the New Testament spur the Christians to take care of the sick, the poor citizens, widows, orphans and others in need. Gallus quotes 1 Tim. 5: "*But if any widow has children or nephews, let them learn first to shew piety at home, and to requite their parents: for that is good and acceptable before God*"; and also 1 Tim. 6,18: "*that they do good, that they be rich in good works, ready to distribute, willing to communicate*". Thus, Gallus concludes that normally nobody is allowed to request interest, and a true Christian would not allow anyone to charge interest. But since those in need cannot always receive aid or have a trade, these categories of people can charge interest in order to have an income.[25] This represents an interest out of need, to assist the downtrodden, as Luther admonished.[26]

In conclusion, Gallus castigates the new approach designed by Brenz and followed by other theologians and opts for a strict application of Luther's teachings on the interest prohibition. The imperial ordinance is against the divine law, and the Christians must obey Luke 6,35. An exception is possible for the people in particular need, as Christian charity commands the Christians to take care of them and one way to care for the lower-income people is for them to receive something in addition to the capital when they loan to others. Gallus' attitude towards the German contract paved the way for the dispute of Regensburg that we are going to examine in the next pages.

1.1.2 *The Discussion in Regensburg*

1.1.2.1 The Five Zealous Ministers

In his *Epitome historiae ecclesiasticae* (1603), Lucas Osiander recounts:

> *in Regensburg there were five among the ministers of the evangelical church who were gifted with a sharp mind but only moderately learned. They were so zealous that they did not govern with the appropriate knowledge.*[27]

These ministers not only inveighed against what actually is usury, continues Osiander, but also condemned the contracts that are not against Christian charity and had been approved by the political magistrate, as when an annuity (*Zins*) has been received in addition to the invested sum. Consequently, in

25 N. Gallus, *Zwo Predigten Wider den Wucher*, [10].

26 N. Gallus, *Zwo Predigten Wider den Wucher*, [11].

27 L. Osiander, *Epitomes historiae ecclesiasticae centuriae XVI*, pars altera, Tubingae, 1603, 1047: "*Erant autem Ratisbonae inter Evangelicos Ecclesiae Ministros quinque, viri acri quidem ingenio, et mediocriter docti, sed tali zelo praediti, qui non secundum scientiam ab ipsis gubernabatur*".

their sermons, the ministers designed the people who used these contracts with the epithet of "*four times thieves, robbers and plunderers*" and "*refused to absolve and to admit them at the Lord's Supper, and called to remove them, even when they were about to die, so that they should die without any consolation, like dogs.*"[28]

The judgment of Osiander is visibly against these five ministers, because they followed their opinions and did not govern with good wisdom. Furthermore, it is implicit that the ministers meant to enforce the canon law. Indeed, the designation as robbers and the consequences of the sin of usury reflect the canon law theory of usury and interest. Usury was conceived as a form of robbery, the usurer was excommunicated, and Christian burial denied.[29]

Osiander's account also reveals that a dispute originated from the refusal of the *widerkaufflicher Zins*. In June 1587 these ministers – Dietrich Rosinus, Michael Linsenbarth, Paulus Schnetter, Abraham Rorer and Johannes Roet[30] – accused the people who used this contract of being thieves, robbers and plunderers. In a series of sermons, they argued that the *widerkaufflicher Zins* is unlawful, invoking Luther's statements and the teachings of the reformer of Regensburg, the superintendent Nikolaus Gallus.[31]

The reasons of the protest were substantially based on the Roman Catholic theory of interest and can be resumed in four points:

1) In the passage of Luke 6,35 Christ meant to teach that nobody could receive more than what he lent. The loan must therefore be gratuitous, and profit is forbidden. The *widerkaufflicher Zins* is illicit, because the entrepreneur returns to the investor not only the capital but also the 5% annuity.

---

28 L. Osiander, *Epitomes historiae ecclesiasticae*, 1047: "*Et eos, qui eiusmodi contractibus utebantur, pro concionibus appellabant, quatruplices fures, latrones, praedones, et tales neque absolvendos, neque Coenam Domini illis exhibendam: sed prorsus, etiam morituros, deferendos esse, ut absque omni consolatione, tanquam canes, morerentur*".

29 See III/2.1.2.1.

30 I could not find any biographical information.

31 F. Loy, *Der Regensburger Wucherstreit: ein Beitrag zum Kampf des Luthertums gegen den Kapitalismus*, Erlangen, 1925, 12, 14-6. A summary of the dispute is also in B. Duhr S.J., *Der 5% Streit im protestantische Regensburg: Ausweisung vom 5 Predigern*, in *Zeitschrift für katholische Theologie*, XXXII (1908), 608-10; B.N. Nelson, *The Idea of Usury*, 93-4. See also J.G. Walch, *Historische und theologische Einleitung in die Religions-Streitigkeiten der evangelisch-lutherisch Kirchen*, IV, Jena 1739, 426-33; G. Arnold, *Unpartheyische Kirchen- und Ketzerhistorien, vom Anfang des Neuen Testaments biss auf das Jahr Christi 1688*, v. I, Schaffhausen, 1740, 1148-50. A further account is in A.D. Carolus, *Wirtenbergische Unschuld*, Ulm, 1708, 293-6. However, both Walch and Arnold raise doubts about its accuracy.

2) The five ministers applied strictly Luther's teachings on usury and interest. Luther declared that special categories of people: old people, poor, indigent, widows and orphans should be allowed to use the *widerkaufflicher Zins*. Thus, the five ministers allowed old people, poor, indigents, widows and orphans to take the annuity, but condemned other categories of people who did it.
3) The two imperial ordinances of Charles V (1500-1558) that allowed a 5% annuity are against the divine law. In the opinion of the ministers, the emperor may not intervene in the divine law. He is the sovereign of the earthly kingdom but not of the heavenly kingdom. In the court of conscience the precept of Luke 6,35 forbids acceptance of the 5% annuity, and the emperor cannot change it. Consequently, the ministers considered the Christians who followed the ordinance and took the annuity to be usurers.
4) In the second stage of the controversy, in front of the jurist of Tübingen, the ministers (or most likely their lawyers) claimed that other two contractual terms, the redeemability after a certain period of time and the personal obligation, were in violation of interest law. Two papal bulls of Martin V (1369-1431) and Callixtus III (1378-1458) in the fifteenth century had approved the real *census* redeemable by the seller, but not by the buyer, as the contract practiced in Regensburg allowed. Another papal bull of Pius V (1504-1572) in the sixteenth century had condemned the *census* on multiple productive properties, which was an essential aspect of the *widerkauﬄicher Zins*. The ministers advocated the binding force of these bulls and the consequent usurious nature of the agreement.

The accusations of the five ecclesiastical ministers raised a political, economic and primarily theological issue, as they hung on the canonist theory of interest and refused the imperial law and the nascent Lutheran theory that supported it. The five ministers' stand presented notable repercussions on the spiritual life of Christians. Not only did the ministers preach sermons, but also they absolved and condemned the penitents in the confessional. The five ministers absolved the elderly, the orphans and the widows who used the *widerkaufflicher Zins* but refused or reserved the absolution of the rich.[32] To be absolved the rich were required to return the annuities they had received.

1.1.2.2 The Theological and Political Response

In July 1587, Christoph Binder (1519-1596) responded to the five minister's claims. Binder graduated in Tübingen, follower of Jacob Andreae's theology

32 J. Andreae, *Vier Christliche Predigten*, 287.

was for more than thirty years abbot of the monastery of Adelberg but was often sent to other destinations in order to offer advice on religious affairs.[33] After hearing the case of the ministers of Regensburg, he argued that in the passage of Luke 6,35, Christ only refers to loans; the *widerkaufflicher Zins* is not a loan but a business contract, and therefore Christians can accept a 5% annuity with clear conscience. One of the five ministers, Dietrich Rosinus, accused Binder of propagating a new and false doctrine on interest.[34] Indeed, the ministers put forward again the canonist theory of interest, while Binder tended to back the new formulation we discussed in the previous chapter.

The chamberlain (*Kammerer*) and the councilman (*Rath*) of the city of Regensburg (who supported Binder) tried mediation, but the five ministers maintained their positions. Thus, these authorities asked Duke Ludwig von Württemberg (1554-1593) to invite to Regensburg the provost and chancellor of the University of Tübingen, Dr. Jacob Andreae (1528-1590), together with the theologian Jakob Heilbrunner (1548-1618), to settle the dispute. In October 1587, Andreae and Heilbrunner came to Regensburg.[35] Andreae remained there until January 1588 and preached four sermons on interest and usury during the Advent period:[36] *Vier Christliche Predigten uber ettliche Evangelia im Advent* (1588).[37] With this text, Andreae powerfully condemned the arguments of the five ministers.

In December 1587 the councilman of Regensburg pronounced a decree by which the five ecclesiastical ministers were outlawed.[38] However, the ministers rejected the decision and published a heated reply to the councilman and chamberlain: *Gegenbericht und notwendige Verantwortung auff den Bericht und Vermahnung eines Erbarn Cameren und Raths der Stadt Regensburg an ihre liebe Burgerschafft und Gemein, deren im December der vergangenen 87 jars geurlaubten fünff Kirchendienern* (1588). In this writing, they accused Andreae of twisting the sense of Luther's words and appealed to the authority of two

33 C. Palmer, *Binder, Christoph* in *Allgemeine Deutsche Biographie* 2 (1875), 643-4 (accessed 25.10.2016); https://www.deutsche-biographie.de/gnd123508029.html#adbcontent.

34 F. Loy, *Der Regensburger Wucherstreit*, 6-7. The author also presents a detailed account of the first stage of the dispute, before the arrival of Andreae and Heilbrunner.

35 A. Westermayer, *Die Reformation überhaupt und ihre Einführung in Regensburg insbesondere*, Regensburg, 1843, 184.

36 J. V. Andreae, *Fama andreana reflorescens ...*, Argentorati, 1630, 285.

37 The sermons were also published in Tübingen in 1589 under the name: *Vier Christliche Predigten vom Wucher*. On Andreae's sermons Sabine Holtz has already proposed a brief investigation from the theological viewpoint: S. Holtz, *Theologie und Alltag. Lehre und Leben in den Predigten der Tübinger Theologen 1550-1750*, Tübingen, Mohr Siebeck, 1993, 228-36.

38 F. Loy, *Der Regensburger Wucherstreit*, 20.

famous Lutheran jurists – Hieronymus Schurpf and Johann Oldendorp. These jurists endorsed Luther's first treatises on usury and interest, where he refused the *Zinskauf* and supported the canonical view of the interest prohibition.[39]

The reaction of the councilman was firm and immediate. He sent the acts to the assessment of the local ecclesiastical tribunal: the consistorial court (*Konsistorium*).[40] The issue was subsequently submitted to the jurists of the faculty of Tübingen, who presented their counsels. The practice of the *Aktenversendung*, the submission of a case to a council (*Collegium*) of jurists with adjudicatory power, was common in the sixteenth century. In certain cases, a court did not decide the controversy by itself but sent the acts to an assembly of jurists asking for a decision.[41] The text of the so-called 'Christian Counsels' (*Christlich Bedenken*) of the Tübingen jurists was published together with the four sermons of Andreae, the considerations of the Regensburg Chancellor and the opinion of Marquard von Hattstein[42] (1560-1581), bishop of Speyer and judge in the imperial cameral tribunal (*Reichskammergericht*), in the dispatch of the case.[43] In the following pages we look at Andreae's sermons and then, in the second part of this chapter, at the counsels of the jurists.

39 *Gegenbericht und notwendige Verantwortung auff den Bericht und Vermahnung eines Erbarn Cameren und Raths der Stadt Regensburg an ihre liebe Burgerschafft und Gemein, deren im December der vergangenen 87 jars geurlaubten fünff Kirchendienern*, 1588, [24-25].

40 F. Loy, *Der Regensburger Wucherstreit*, 25.

41 P. Oestmann, *Aktenversendung* in *Handwörterbuch zur deutschen Rechtsgeschichte* (HRG), vol. I, 128-32. For a general overview: E. Klugkist, *Die Aktenversendung an Juristenfakultäten*, in *Juristenzeitung* 22 (1967), 155-8. For a more detailed bibliography: J. Schröder, *Wissenschaftstheorie und Lehre der "praktischen Jurisprudenz"*, Frankfurt am Main, Klostermann, 1979; K.A. Hake, *Juristenfakultäten, Aktenversendung und Reichskammergericht*, Aachen, Shaker Verlag, 2013. For the literature of *consilia*, especially in Tübingen, see J. Geipel, *Die Konsiliarpraxis der Eberhard-Karls-Universität und die Behandlung der Eherverletzung in den Tübinger Konsilien*, Müller & Gräff, Stuttgart, 1965; E. Isenmann, *Reichsrecht und Reichsverfassung in Konsilien reichsstädtischer Juristen (15.-17. Jahrhundert)*, in R. Schnur (ed.), *Die Rolle der Juristen bei der Entstehung des modernen Staates*, Berlin, Duncker und Humblot, 1986; E. Isenmann, *Wirtschaftsrecht und Wirtschaftsethik um 1500. Theologische und juristische Konsilien zum Barchenthandel in der Reichsstadt Ulm*, in R. Lieberwirth, H. Lück (ed.), *Akten des 36. Deutschen Rechtshistorikertages Halle an der Saale*, 10.-14. September 2006, Baden-Baden 2008, 195-259.

42 G. Christ, *Marquard von Hattstein* in *Neue Deutsche Biographie* 16 (1990), 242-244 (accessed 16.11.2016); URL: https://www.deutsche-biographie.de/gnd102322694.html#ndbcontent.

43 *Abfertigung de Ungegründten Gegenberichts der zu Regensburg Anno 1587 geurlaubten Prediger.*

1.2 Four Sermons for Christians' Education

1.2.1 *A Worried Conscience*

Andreae's four sermons present the same structure: they begin with the explanation of the Sunday Gospel and then continue with the analysis of the interest prohibition and the refusal of the five ministers' theological claims. The question Andreae addresses is the following: "*whether on the basis of the imperial law and of the ordinances of the Holy Roman Empire it is a reprehensible interest* (Wucher) *to take a 5% annuity* (Zins)".[44] This question does not look at the nature and other technical aspects of the contract, but only focuses on the given annuity (5% on the invested sum). Andreae must determine if the taking of an annuity (*Zins*) is against the interest prohibition. Furthermore, this question aims to clarify whether the provisions included in the imperial ordinance, which admitted the 5% annuity, are lawful according to the divine law. The provisions of the emperor's ordinance – ruling that an instrument that practically produced the same effects of a loan at interest could be lawfully practiced – might be against the divine law.

Andreae stresses that the issue of the lawfulness of the annuity involves Christians' consciences and the delicate relation with the sacramental life:

> *those who have taken a 5% annuity are alienated from baptism, are refused absolution in the confessional and are not admitted to the Lord's Supper, or at least their conscience is so burdened that they do not dare to access the Lord's Supper by themselves until they have repaid such annuities.*[45]

The five ministers considered taking a 5% annuity to be a sin with consequences on the soul: without restitution, there is no absolution. Andreae must verify this point to establish the right practice of Christian life.

The conscience of the Christians felt the effect of the unclear situation. Andreae even says that the lack of an answer on the spiritual implications of accepting the 5% annuity creates a doubt in conscience, which turns into despair. When such consciences are not redeemed from doubts, the devil can bring them into fear and temptations, inducing them to cry: "*Oh I am lost and*

---

44 J. Andreae, *Vier Christliche Predigten uber ettliche Evangelia im Advent*, Regensburg, 1588, 282: "*Ob vermoeg der Keyserlichen Rechten, und des Hey: Roe: Reichs verordnungen, fünff gulden Zins von Hundert zunemen, ein verdampter Wucher sey, oder nicht*".

45 J. Andreae, *Vier Christliche Predigten*, 283: "*Dann wölche vom Hundert fünff gulden Järlich Zins genommen, die sind entweder von der Tauff abgestossen, im Beichtstuel ihnen die Absolution vorgehalten, und nicht zum Sacrament zugelassen, oder auffs wenigst ihre Gewissen dermassen beschweret worden, das sie zum H. Sacrament für sich selbst nicht gehn dörffen biss sie solche Zins abgelöset haben*".

condemned forever, I am a usurer, a four times thief, I have murdered and robbed, I must be doomed forever". And if one consoles them and tells them: "*No, you are not a usurer, because the emperor has allowed it*", then the devil whispers (evil) thoughts and says: "*the emperor has allowed it that way in his empire, but in the kingdom of God it is not valid; the emperor tolerates it, but he does not say it is just*".[46] The conscience of the Christian is confused and tormented. And an answer is necessary.

1.2.2 *Propelling the Lutheran Theory of Interest*

1.2.2.1 Introduction

The five ministers' central argument is that the interest prohibition outlaws every profit in a loan. Consequently, in the imperial ordinances the *widerkauf-flicher Zins* is discussed in a paragraph entitled "On usurious contracts" (*Von wücherlichen Contracten*), because it is forbidden. Following the scholastic theory, the ministers deem that the *widerkaufflicher Zins* is a loan at interest and for this reason it must be declared usurious.

Andreae's response focuses on three points. First, he analyzes the interest prohibition in line with the new teachings that circulated among the Lutheran theologians. The interest prohibition only concerns the poor; loans towards the poor must be performed through charity; the business contracts are regulated by equality. Then Andreae interprets Luther's statements on the interest prohibition in the light of the new theory. Finally, he looks at the real root of the issue, the scholastic theory of interest, and demolishes it.

1.2.2.2 The Prohibition Against Interest, Gratuitous Loans and Business Contracts

Andreae is a formidable progressivist theologian and sustains the new developments in the interest theory that were already being promoted not only by Lutheran but also by other Protestant theologians. The starting point of his discourse is the meaning of the word 'interest' (*usura*) in the Holy Scripture. Andreae interprets meticulously the biblical passages concerning the interest prohibition and conclude that they only relate to the poor (Deut. 23,20 and

46 J. Andreae, *Vier Christliche Predigten*, 284: "*Dann aus dem zweifel kompt endlich verzweiflung. Darumb, wann solche Gewissen aus diesem zweifel nicht erlöset, kann der Teufel sie in solche Anfechtung und angst bringen, das sie ruffen und schreyen, O ich bin ewig verloren und verdampt, Ich bin ein Wucher oder Wucherin, bin ein vierfaltiger Dieb, ich hab gemord und geraubt, Ich muss ewig verloren sein. Und da man sie schon tröstet, und sagt, Nein, sie seyen kein Wucher, dann der Keyser hab es erlaubet, da bläset der Teufel gedancken ein, und sagt, der Keyser hab es in seinem Reich also geordnet, aber in Gottes Reich gellt es nicht, der Keyser und leide es, aber er heisse es nicht recht*".

Psalm 15,5; Ez. 18,8).[47] Andreae explicates that, if a Christian were poor, he would like to receive a loan without interest. For this reason, the Christians are obliged to lend to the poor gratuitously. The natural law included in Matthew 7,12 commands to do the other what you would expect he do to you.[48]

The rule of Luke 6,35 (*to lend hoping for nothing in return*) asks the Christians not to seek reciprocity from the poor: "*but He wants that we should lend to the poor in such a way that we do not hope to receive more in return than what we have lent to them*".[49] The sinners lend to each other hoping for something in return. However, the Christians are called to love even their enemies and not to seek reciprocity. Whether the poor are friends or foe, the Christians should lend to them hoping for nothing in return.[50] The interest prohibition, then, only concerns the poor and not the rich. The loans towards the poor must be performed according to charity and the business contracts must comply with equality within the relationship.

1.2.2.2.1 *Lending According to Charity*

To Andreae, charity is meant as rule not only for the borrower and one single lender, but it also involves the whole community of Christians:

> (However), *this humility and Christian love should no less be practiced in borrowing than in lending, to the effect that no sole person be encumbered or be put into danger of being ruined or of coming to harm by lending, due to the fact that in a city or a community one would put this burden on this person alone, and all the others would run no risk.*[51]

Charity invites the Christians to share the difficulties. So, when one needs money, he can ask the other Christians: not only a single person. Every Christian should lend part of the requested sum. Andreae explains this argument with a brilliant example. God could permit that the shack of an honest craftsman is burned to the ground. The craftsman has no job, but wants to re-build the

47 J. Andreae, *Vier Christliche Predigten*, 34-6.

48 J. Andreae, *Vier Christliche Predigten*, 37-8.

49 J. Andreae, *Vier Christliche Predigten*, 39: "*Sondern er will, das man den Dürfftigen also leyhen soll, das wir auch gleiches, das ist, was wir ihme gelihen haben, nicht mehr hoffen zu empfangen*".

50 J. Andreae, *Vier Christliche Predigten*, 39-40.

51 J. Andreae, *Vier Christliche Predigten*, 45: "*Es soll aber im borgen oder entlehnen auch diese bescheidenheit und Christliche liebe nicht weniger, als im leyhen gebraucht werden, das nicht einer allein beschweret, und in gfahr seines verderbens, oder grossen schaden durch Leihen gesetzt werde, also, das man einem allein in einer Stad oder Gemein diesen Last auff legen, und die andern alle läer aussgehen solten*".

shack, to have a shelter for his wife and his children. He has no money and needs to borrow from another person. The neighbour should help him, for it would be against the Christian love to allow him to fall into despair, as when one leaves the poor in the cold. Yet, since there are many other Christian brothers in the city, one is not obliged to donate out of mercy or to give the entire sum. A brother lends to the craftsman according to his capital and risks his money, because it might not come back. Then he tells the borrower: "there are other Christian brothers in the city and they are also responsible to lend money to you". Thus, this poor man can re-build his shack and with the blessing of God, little by little, can pay the debts.[52]

Lending according to charity implies that the lender shall lend an amount of money, but not necessarily the complete amount requested. Christian love is a rule for the community and every member has to do his own to help the neighbour. The rule of Luke 6,35 applies to loans and finds its concrete way of application through charity. Charity inspires, justifies and finally moderates it. The Christian is not obliged to lend the entire amount of money requested, but just one part. In this way the rule acquires a human dimension and does not place too great a burden on the lender.

1.2.2.2.2 *Doing Business According to Equality*

Lending (*leihen*) is separated from doing business (*handeln*). The former must be free, while for the latter a charge may be asked. Lending can be practiced towards the poor and indigent. Business is afforded to people who need money but are not poor or indigent.[53] This distinction is the fruit of the reflections ripened in the circle of the Lutheran theologians.[54] In business, both the parties can benefit, and neither of them has to suffer damages.[55] The parties should keep the rules dictated by Christ and St. Paul in the Holy Scripture: Matthew 7,12; 1 Thess. 4,6; and 2 Cor. 8,13-14.[56] These rules impose equality in business. In the *widerkaufflicher Zins*, one of the parties sells to the other the right to receive a certain annual income (*Zins*) in return for a sum. To Andreae, the annuity (*Zins*) is justified because this is an agreement made for business and not a loan for helping the poor. In business, the parties must observe equality. If one of the parties' profits while the other gains nothing, there is no equality. The annuity is therefore the just price paid for the use of the money. In this way the

52 J. Andreae, *Vier Christliche Predigten*, 46-7.
53 J. Andreae, *Vier Christliche Predigten*, 71-6.
54 See before III/2.
55 J. Andreae, *Vier Christliche Predigten*, 70-1.
56 J. Andreae, *Vier Christliche Predigten*, 78-9.

buyer of the *Zins* shares part of the profits with the seller. If there were no *Zins* there would be no equality, but one of the parties would get profits with the money of the other one. According to Andreae, Luther also shares this view:

> *therefore* (*writes Luther again well and true*) *no better or briefer instruction can be given about this, and about all dealing with temporal goods, than that everyone who is to have dealings with his neighbour set before himself these commandments*: "all things whatsoever ye would that men should do to you, do ye even so to them" *and* "thou shalt love thy neighbor as thyself".[57]

Andreae emphasizes the necessity to keep equality in business to advocate the lawfulness of the *widerkaufflicher Zins*. In order to convince the listeners, he uses a subtle strategy: he presents the argument with a suggestive example. A farmer had a farm on which he not only provided for himself, but also for his wife, for six, seven, eight or more children and also for food and wages for labourers and maids, and he was able to put something aside for himself as well. Then he was obliged to sell it, to prevent being bereft of the pure preaching of God's word and the correct use of the Holy Sacraments, and he obtained 1.000 florins, which he cannot reinvest in a profitable immovable property; but he has to spend it for a usual annuity to the effect that he gets 50 florins in return from someone who deals with his 1000 florins and gets a profit that is three to four times higher (than 50 florins). One should ask oneself whether in this case the rule of Christ and Saint Paul is abided by, that no party should be favoured before another.[58] Andreae emphasizes the difficulties of the farmer and draws the attention to the prejudice he suffers. If the seller gains a profit with the money he received from the buyer, according to the mentioned equality, he

---

57 J. Andreae, *Vier Christliche Predigten*, 80: "*Darumb (schreibt D. Luther abermal wol und recht) were nichts richtigers, noch kurtzere unterweisung, in diesen unnd allen Händeln, zeitlichs guts, denn das ein jeglich Mensch, so er mit seinem Nächsten soll handlen, ihme fürsetzte diese Gebot: Was du wilt, das dir ein anderer thet, das thue ime auch. Und: Liebe deinen Nächsten, als dich selbst*". M. Luther, *Ein (grosser) Sermon von dem Wucher*, in WA 6, 49.

58 J. Andreae, *Vier Christliche Predigten*, 83-4: "*Wil desselben ein deutlich wol bekant Exempel geben, das Jederman wol verstehn kan. Es hat ein Bawrsman ein Hofe gehabt, darauff er nicht allein sich selbst, sondern auch sein Weib, sechs, sieben, acht, oder mehr Kinder, sampt Knecht und Mägten mit Speiss und lohn erhalten und wol auch etwas für sich bringen können. Den hat er müssen verkauffen. Er wolte denn der reinen Predigt Gottes worts, und des rechten unverfelschten gebrauchs der H. Sacramenten beraubt sein, und hat daraus gelöset Tausent barer Gülden, die kan er aber nicht widerumb an ein ligend einträglich Gut anlegen, sonder muss es aussthon, umb ein Landleuffigen Zins, das er Järlich darvon nimpt funffzig Gülden, von einem, der mit solchen Tausent gülden handelt, und wol drey oder viermal so viel darmit gewinnet. Hie ist die frage, Ob hie auch die Regel Christi und S. Pauli gehalten werde, das kein theil von dem andern verfortheilt werde*".

should share part of the profit with the buyer. In this way the *Zins* contract would be entirely lawful.

In conclusion, the interest prohibition concerns only loans and not business contracts. Business agreements are subjected to another regulation that imposes equality between the parties. Because the *Zins* contract is also a business contract, it needs to comply with the rules of equality. The payment of the *Zins* is lawful: if the *Zins* were not paid, there would be a benefit for one of the parties and a loss for the other. This argument conjures up a similar idea of the canonists and scholastic theologians. They also tried to shift the agreement out of the sphere of the interest prohibition by arguing that it is a sale and not a loan.

1.2.2.3 Luther's Teachings on the Interest Prohibition and the German Contract

Having staked out the specific boundaries of the interest prohibition, Andreae goes on and applies them to Luther's statement on the interest prohibition. In his early formulations, Luther raged against the sin of usury and denounced usurers as thieves, robbers and murderers. Yet, in the admonition *An die Pfarrherrn, wider den Wucher zu predigen* (1540), he considered the widows, orphans and indigent people in a special way, because they can have no other profit than by investing their money.[59] Luther approved the *widerkaufflicher Zins* for these people and left the task to allow this agreement to the (unidentified) jurists. They shall mitigate the strict law (*scharff Recht*). The term 'strict law' is not precise, and Andreae wonders: what did Luther mean by the 'strict law'? Did he intend to say the human law or the divine law? The human law, he tries answering, can be mitigated, but what is a sin and what is not a sin cannot be changed. Neither the pope nor the emperor may change that. Hence, Luther could only refer to the human law in advising the jurists' emendation.[60]

The human law then, Andreae continues, is divided into two types: the law of the pope and the law of the emperor. The law of the emperor is the Roman law, which about the interest prohibition is subjected to the papal law.[61] The Roman (imperial) law surrenders to the papal law because this is a matter of divine law, in which it cannot intervene.[62] The law that the jurists shall mitigate is therefore the Roman (imperial) law. It is so strict because has been usurped

59 J. Andreae, *Vier Christliche Predigten*, 85.
60 J. Andreae, *Vier Christliche Predigten*, 86-7.
61 See III/2.1.2.1.
62 J. Andreae, *Vier Christliche Predigten*, 87.

by the papal law. The papal law, Andreae attacks fiercely, depraved the imperial law and made it too strict, to the extent that consciences become confused.[63]

The papal prohibition against interest was considered to be valid in the Roman law, which became strict because subjected to the papal law. The papal law, in turn, is strict because rests on a misunderstanding of Scripture. To Andreae, this is dramatically the root of the problem. The papal law teaches that everything in addition to the borrowed sum is usury and individuates the foundation of the prohibition in the passage of Luke 6,35. As seen before, indeed, the Second Lateran Council in 1139 and the decretal *Consuluit* (1187) of Pope Urban III (1185-1187) founded the prohibition of interest on Luke 6,35. Andreae argues that the prohibition is based on a false understanding of the passage. In this verse, he writes, Christ does not speak a word about interest-taking, nor about profit. Christ wants the Christians to risk the total amount of the money they lend, and to not anticipate its return.[64]

Because of the false interpretation of the Gospel, Andreae posits, the papal law condemns the Christian who receives a profit in addition to the borrowed sum. Such a condemnation entered into the Roman law, making it 'strict'. To Andreae, the rigorousness is visible in the fact that the papal law condemns widows, orphans and old indigent people that do not work and cannot trade when they ask a 5% annuity on the borrowed sum.[65] This is not usury as the Scripture describes usury, he points out, because it does not bite, nor corrupts the people. It does not damage. This is, as Luther wrote, a mere "interest out of need" (*Notwücherlin*), a work of mercy (*ein werk der Barmhergihkeit*) for the indigent that do not have almost anything and that not harm particularly the others.[66]

Andreae reads Luther through the lens of the new theory of interest. The canonists' interpretation of the Gospel is wrong, because Luke 6,35 only regards the poor. Luther admits the *widerkaufflicher Zins* for special categories of people. Luther uses the concept of 'interest out of need' (*Notwücherlin*), as it grants people in need the possibility to gain interest. Andreae hastens to add that usury is, according with the Scripture, only when there is a bite or damage

63 J. Andreae, *Vier Christliche Predigten*, 87-8: "*Das ist aber des Papst Recht, so man das geistlich Recht nennet, woelchs in diesem Handel das Keiserlich Recht verderbt, und zu scharff gemacht, unnd dardurch die Gewissen verwirret hat*".

64 J. Andreae, *Vier Christliche Predigten*, 89: "*So doch Christus an diesem Ort nicht ein wort vom Wucher, noch von gewinst redet. Sondern will, das die Christen die Hauptsumma des gelihnen Gelts wagen, und nicht wider hoffen sollen*".

65 J. Andreae, *Vier Christliche Predigten*, 89.

66 J. Andreae, *Vier Christliche Predigten*, 89-90.

for the neighbour. Since there is no damage for the parties, the contract is not usurious.

1.2.2.4 Crushing the Scholastic Theory of Interest

Having proved that the Scripture and Luther are against the five ministers, Andreae now moves to the final step of his argument and faces the core issue: the canonists' theory of interest and usury.

1.2.2.4.1 *The False Meaning of* Usura/Wucher

In the two imperial ordinances (1530-1548), the *widerkaufflicher Zins* is regulated in a paragraph entitled: *"on usurious contracts"* (*Von wücherlichen Contracten*).[67] The five ministers argued therefore that this was evidence that the contract is forbidden. The annuity is indeed contrary to the passage of Luke 6,35. The ministers referred time and again to the Word of Christ in Luke 6,35 in order to prove that Christ taught that whenever one gives money, whatever name it may have, and does not have both gain and loss in balance, it is condemnable interest (*Wucher*).[68] The loan must be gratuitous and cannot include something in return: the borrower must return only the sum he received; the lender is not allowed to ask the borrower to share part of his profits. Since in the *widerkaufflicher Zins* the investor gets more than what he lent, the ministers concluded that this is a usurious agreement.

Andreae responds promptly that the ministers ran into a confusion generated by the canonists (the word 'canonists' is used in general, without any specific reference). The canonists confused the meaning of the word 'interest' (*usura* – *Wucher*) in the Holy Scripture and the meaning in the imperial law:

> [so] *there is not an unambiguous meaning or explanation. Indeed, the jurists explain with it the meaning of the Latin word* (usura), *which corresponds to 'Wucher' in German, namely everything that one has and takes above what one has given, as a compensation for the use of the money. But they also use the word in another and broader sense than the canonists and the 'doctores' of canon law, as was shown above. Since for the canonists 'Wucher' is indeed to be condemned and a terrible sin against nature, God and law. And in such words the Holy Scripture speaks about 'Wucher' as well. However, in such a meaning the 'doctores' of imperial law do not*

67 On these provisions see before III/2 and later IV/2.

68 *Abfertigung de Ungegründten Gegenberichts der zu Regensburg Anno 1587 geurlaubten Prediger*, Tübingen, 1589, 11-2: "*Nach eingenommen solchem Bericht, haben sie fort und fort auff die Wort Christi, Luc. 6 getrungen, da geschrieben stehet: Leihet dass ir nichts darfür hoffet. Darmit zubeweisen, dass Christus gelehret haben soll, wann man Gelt aussthue, es habe Namen wie es wöllet, da man nicht Gewinn unnd Verlust mit einander gemein habe, unnd neme mehr, denn man gelihen habe, so seie es ein verdampter Wucher*".

> *use and interpret it (= the word Wucher/usura) at all, unless they add 'verbottner unzimmlicher' (= forbidden improper) 'Wucher'.*[69]

The jurists did not mean to condemn as usury everything that one person obtains because of the use of the money he received. Although they use the same word (*Wucher*) of the canonists, the jurists do not mean the same thing:

> *(Therefore), albeit the jurists in their description of the word (Wucher) use precisely the same words with which the canonists and the papist doctors described the blamable interest, they have by no means used that word (Wucher) in the sense of the Papist law (which misuses the description of the word (Wucher). But they have explicitly taught that not everything is blamable interest which exceeds the main sum in trading, either in giving or in taking.*[70]

The jurists distinguish between loans and doing business, between a lawful *Wucher* – interest (in business) and unlawful *Wucher* – interest (in loans). Even though in the imperial ordinance the *widerkauflicher Zins* is discussed under the title "On usurious contract", it is lawful because it is a business agreement and not a loan for helping the poor. The sin of usury is the practice of lending at unlawful interest (in loans). In business contracts the charging of interest is lawful. Here we can really see the problems related to the two different meanings of the word *usura* – *Wucher*.

The canonists did not make this distinction and assumed that *Wucher* is everything that has been received in addition to the borrowed sum (both in loans

69 J. Andreae, *Vier Christliche Predigten*, 199: "*So ist es doch nicht einerley verstand oder auslegung. Dann die Rechtsgelerten erkleren hiermit das Lateinisch wort (usura) so man verdeutscht Wucher, was es heisse, nämlich alles das, so man weitter hat und nimpt, wegen des brauchs des Gelts, denn man ausgethon hat. Demnach gebrauchen sie das wort (Wucher) viel in einem andern und weitleufftigern verstand, denn die Canonisten und* Doctores *des geistlichen Rechtens, wie droben angezeigt worden ist. Dann bey den Canonisten ist und heisset Wucher durchaus ein verdampt ding und ein grewliche Sünde, die wider die Natur, Gott und Recht ist. Unnd also redet die Heilige Schrifft auch vom Wucher. In solchem verstandt aber, brauchen und verstehn es die* Doctores *der Keyserlichen Rechten, gar nicht, Sie setzen denn darzu verbottner unzimmlicher Wucher*".

70 J. Andreae, *Vier Christliche Predigten*, 199-200: "*Darumb, ob wol die Juristen in beschreibung des worts (Wuchers) eben die wort gebraucht, mit wölchen die Canonisten und Bäptistische* Doctores, *den verdampten Wucher beschrieben haben. So haben sie doch solchs wort (Wucher) keines wegs in dem verstand gebraucht, wie das Bäptistisch Recht thut (wölchs die Beschreibung des worts (Wucher) wie es die Rechtsgelerten beschriben misbraucht). Sondern ausdruckenlich gelert, das nicht alles verdampter Wucher seye, was uber die Hauptsumma im Handel gegeben und genommen werde*".

and in business). They justified their statements with the Word of Christ in Luke 6,35.[71] But to Andreae the right meaning of the passage is totally different:

> *Christ wants to teach us that when we see a man in need, both a friend or an enemy, then we must lend money to him even with the peril to lose all the money, and* [*he wants to teach us*] *that we should not hope to get back one penny more than the main sum.*[72]

In this passage Christ does not talk about *Wucher* and for this reason the canonists' teachings are wrong:

> *since then Christ in this passage does not speak of interest* [*Wucher*]*, and even more so he does not describe in it what interest is, it must follow that the teachings of the canonists are false and wrong.*[73]

Andreae points out that the canonists make a twofold mistake. On the one hand, they do not distinguish the different understanding of the word *Wucher* in the Holy Scripture (that only condemns interest in loans) and the use of the word *Wucher* by the jurists in the imperial law (that distinguishes between loans and trades). On the other hand, they associate all borrowed sums with the word loan (*leihen*), without distinguishing between money given in the *widerkaufflicher Zins* and the money given in a loan. They call everything *Wucher*.[74] In that way, the canonists mixed divine and secular law and made a 'mush of shreds' (*lumpmus*), with the effect that they can hardly be distinguished.[75]

Andreae blames the canonists and hurls the fault of the misunderstanding at them. Their reasoning is based on a false interpretation of Scripture that produced an erroneous concept of interest (*Wucher*). This concept of interest

---

71 J. Andreae, *Vier Christliche Predigten*, 193.

72 J. Andreae, *Vier Christliche Predigten*, 195: "*Es will Christus lehren, wann wir ein Menschen in der noth sehen stecken, er sey freund oder feinde, so sollen wir ihm leyhen, und solten wir gleich in der gefahr stehn, das wir die ganze Summa verlieren solten, und nichts mehr von der Hauptsumma selbst hoffen, das uns ein häller mehr darvon werde zukommen*".

73 J. Andreae, *Vier Christliche Predigten*, 195: "*Weil dann Christus an diesem ort ganz und gar nichts vom Wucher redet, noch viel weniger hiemit den Wucher beschreibt, was er seye, So muss auch folgen, das der Canonisten lehr falsch und unrecht seye*".

74 J. Andreae, *Vier Christliche Predigten*, 195-6.

75 J. Andreae, *Vier Christliche Predigten*, 196: "*Dergestallt dann hernach die Canonisten das Göttlich und Weltlich Recht, unter einander gemischet, und ein Lumpmuss daraus gemacht, das man sie schwerlich mehr underscheiden mögen*". Andreae makes use of the singular expression *lumpmus*, which seems to be a neologism, and might be translated as 'mush of shreds'.

infested the language, so that there are now two different notions of interest – one is wrong, and one is good. The canonists do not distinguish between loans and business and condemn everything. But the jurists who made the imperial law use the same term with a different sense. They condemn interest as it is referred to loans. But they did not mean to condemn the *widerkaufflicher Zins*, because it is not a loan. The canonists are considered in general. Andreae does not mention the name of a single canonist, nor a decretal, nor a normative act. His criticism remains therefore vague and full of polemic. After all, it is a sermon and not a treatise. And there was nothing more attractive than a ferocious condemnation of canon law for a crowd that was hungry for a culprit.

1.2.2.4.2 *The Effects of the Wrong Interpretation*

In Andreae's view, the canonists' wrong interpretation of Scripture spread confusion among Christians. Because of the false teachings, the Christians find two distinct notions of interest: one that is included in the Holy Scripture and one that is included in the imperial law. The imperial law distinguishes two types of interest, one that is admitted by the divine law and another one that is instead forbidden.[76] The result, Andreae writes, is that the 'pious hearts' of the Christians are in doubt.[77]

The wrong interpretation of Scripture generated by the canonists gives birth to two practical consequences. First, Christians think that they should always lend hoping for nothing in return when they are asked. But this is, Andreae highlights, against natural law and the divine law. The Christians have to take care of their family and children first and only secondly the indigents. So, if a craftsman or an honest burgher with four or five children asks for money, the Christian should answer that he also has children that require attention until they will be well educated. It might happen that one of the members of the Christian's family gets ill and must go to the hospital, or another one die, what shall we have then? Shall they beg?[78] The Christians are not always obliged to loan hoping for nothing in return, but their primary responsibility is to look after their family, and only then can they lend to the downtrodden.

The second practical consequence Andreae suggests is that people believe that accepting a 5% annuity for business as established by the imperial ordinance is usury. But that is also wrong. Andreae responds passionately:

76 J. Andreae, *Vier Christliche Predigten*, 196.
77 J. Andreae, *Vier Christliche Predigten*, 201.
78 J. Andreae, *Vier Christliche Predigten*, 203.

> *where is written that one gives a certain sum without receiving anything and the other one can use it? In the Gospel or in the Letters? In the Prophets or in the Evangelists? In the Old or the New Testament? No, No.*[79]

The Christian can give something to the poor and indigents and then use other funds in business. The business transaction cannot require an annuity of 10%, 12% or 18%, but only 5% as the ordinance of the emperor prescribed in accordance with natural law and divine law.[80] The *widerkaufflicher Zins* is a lawful form of business. The canonists considered it to be unlawful because of the false interpretation of the Scripture.

Andreae's animated criticism aims to dash to pieces the canonists' conception of the interest prohibition. However, it is worthwhile to remember that the canonists had already attempted to classify the *census* contract as a sale. A sale was not subjected to the interest prohibition. Although in different forms, the *census* was contested, but was practiced in Roman Catholicism for centuries. The specific character of Andrea's analysis lies in the interpretation of the Gospel that, as a Lutheran theologian, he performs with great care. The interpretation of Scripture he offers shatters the old idea of interest and usury. In that sense this is a gust of fresh wind from the Reformation on the old medieval canon law.

1.2.3 *Only for the Elderly, Orphans, Widows and Other Indigents?*

1.2.3.1 Introduction

The second argument the five ministers defended was based on Luther's statements. As seen before, Luther admitted that special categories of people, as the elderly, orphans, widows and other indigents could practice the *widerkaufflicher Zins*, because they are in need. They cannot work or have other income. The five ministers fought for a strict interpretation of this permission. They claimed that only these people were allowed to receive the annuity and excommunicated all the others who expected the fee.[81]

With a reckless interpretation, Andreae replies that Luther's statements are meant to allow the *widerkaufflicher Zins* not only to the elderly, orphans and widows, but also to other categories of people. Luther meant to say that *particularly* old people, orphans, widows and other indigents are allowed to use the German contract. But he did not want to forbid this agreement for all the

79 J. Andreae, *Vier Christliche Predigten*, 205: "*Wo stehet das geschriben: im Evangelio, oder in der Epistel: in Propheten oder Evangelisten: im Alten oder Newen Testament: das er ein solche Summa aussgeben, und nichts darvon hoffen, und ein anderer sein eigen Nutzen darmit schaffen soll: Nein, nein*".

80 J. Andreae, *Vier Christliche Predigten*, 205-6.

81 J. Andreae, *Vier Christliche Predigten*, 238.

others. Luther approves the Justinian legislation on interest, which also regards it as available to other classes like the aristocracy, traders, burghers and peasants. Luther defines this concession as *interest out of need.* The need, Andreae holds, is the need to get the essential means to live. It concerns every person and not only a particular category. Every person, then, can use the *widerkaufflicher Zins.*

1.2.3.2 The Example of Justinian I

One might expect that in front of Luther's words a true Lutheran would kneel down or agree at least. But it is totally the opposite. Andreae advocates the lawfulness of the usage in Regensburg, where the *widerkaufflicher Zins* was used by all kind of people. Astonishingly, he claims that Luther did not mean to limit the annuity only to the elderly, orphans, widows and other indigents, but also made its use available to other people. To demonstrate this aspect, Andreae puts forward a Machiavellian reasoning. He begins by observing that Luther left the task of mitigating the *scharff Recht* to the jurists, the ecclesiastical ministers and the territorial princes. Luther advised that they should operate with equity (*epieikeia*), but the way equity should be put into practice is not explained in detail.

Andreae makes the most of this point to bear his argument and looks at the way the jurists, the ecclesiastical ministers and the territorial princes would propose their vision of equity if they were asked. When the magistrate asks the ecclesiastical minister what is 'just', he will certainly answer that the summary of the teachings contained in the New Testaments is in the rule of Matthew 7,12. Then, there are also the rules of Paul in 1 Thess. 4,6, and 2 Cor. 8,13-14, which as seen before, establish equality in business[82]. To Andreae, the ecclesiastical ministers will therefore give recommendations aimed toward a single end: maintaining equality.

After this request, Andreae continues, the magistrate will ask to the jurists what is a just ordinance according to them. Andreae notices cunningly that Luther himself gives the answer. Luther writes that the emperor Justinian also moderated interest and allowed the aristocracy to ask 4 florins, the traders to request 8 florins and the others 6 florins:

> *he (Justinian) wants to moderate the old difficult burden: if this (I say) can be useful to that end, I am gladly willing to agree with it and to help carry the burden for the sake of God.*[83]

82 J. Andreae, *Vier Christliche Predigten*, 95.

83 J. Andreae, *Vier Christliche Predigten*, 96: "*Er wölle damit die alte schwere Last messigen, Kan es (sage ich) hieher dienen, so will ich gern mit stimmen und helffen tragen für Gott*". See M. Luther, *An die Pfarrherrn*, in WA 51, 373.

The fact that Luther approved Justinian's law represents an essential point for the argument of Andreae:

> *here you have, dear Christian, a clear teaching of Luther not only for old people, poor widows and orphans or other indigent people, but also for other classes as more precisely the aristocracy, traders, burghers and peasants, namely that, if the regulation of the emperor Justinian were to be maintained, and if it pleased to the sovereigns (Landsfürsten) with their learned jurists and wise counselors, he (Luther) would also agree with it.*[84]

Andreae extends the permission of charging interest through the reference to Justinian. Luther, he declares, meant the ordinance of Justinian to be endorsed. Since Justinian's law concerned the aristocracy, traders, burghers and peasants, the permission to charge interest shall also take into account these categories. The subjects of the mitigation are not only old people, widows and orphans, but also the aristocracy, traders, burghers and peasants.

Luther's argument thus is completely overturned. Luther meant to affirm that only special categories of people as the old people, widows and orphans were allowed taking interest. He wrote that the rigid prohibition of interest should have been mitigated, through equity (*epieikeia*), as a work of mercy, for a meritorious case. Justinian was quoted as an example of that moderation. To Andreae, instead, the reference to Justinian means that the permission or 'work of mercy' also regards the aristocracy, traders, burghers and peasants. Luther meant through compassion to carve out an exception for a special case, an act of equity. Andreae's interpretation transforms the special case into a general rule.

1.2.3.3 The Example of Justinian II

The example of Justinian takes on great importance for Andreae. Not only does he use it to extend Luther's permission to use the German contract, but he also holds that Emperor Charles V followed Justinian's legislation, which complies with natural law and divine law. Indeed, Justinian is a Christian emperor who did not ordain anything that was against natural law or the precept of

84 J. Andreae, *Vier Christliche Predigten*, 96: "*Hie hastu, lieber Christ, ein lautern bescheid D. Luthers, nicht allein für alte Leut, arme Wittwen und Waisen, oder sonst dürfftige Leut, sondern auch für andere Stände, als nemlich die vom Adel, Kauffleut, Bürger und Bawren, Nemlich, wann es noch bey des Kaysers Iustiniani verordnung bleiben sollte, und es dem Landsfürsten mit sein gelerten Juristen und vernünfftigen Räthen also gefiel, so wöll er auch mit stimmen*".

Matthew 7,12.[85] Hence, in agreement with Luther's statements, Charles V adopted Justinian's model and admitted only a 5% annuity.

The imperial ordinances are portrayed as a continuation of Justinian's legislation. Justinian is a Christian emperor whose law would have never countermanded natural law. The argument, however, is lacking – it only relies on the presumption that Christian membership would have impeded Justinian from issuing a law in violation of natural law. But one might object that Justinian could also have committed a sin in issuing that law. Thus, to bolster the argument, Andreae hastens to add that Emperor Charles V promulgated the ordinances after having consulted his counselors, the electoral princes and the estates of the Holy Roman Empire. It is binding in the whole territory of the Holy Roman Empire and will be recognized by the Imperial Chamber Court (*Cammergericht*) as a divine, just, merciful and right ordinance, according to the law of nature and the precept of God.[86]

Because they perpetuate Justinian's model, Charles V ordinances are totally lawful and in compliance with Luther's statement. Luther agrees with Justinian's legislation and so, with a syllogism, Andreae maintains that Luther also approves that the subjects of the permission are not only the *miserabiles personae* but also the aristocracy, traders, burghers and peasants. Because Charles V continued Justinian's legislation, his ordinances are not founded on the papal law but on Justinian; the law of Justinian is not contaminated by the canon law and is therefore a just law. The remainder of Andreae's argument is an apologetic defense of the imperial ordinances, based on the fact that they have been made with the counsel of qualified people and are effective in the whole of Germany.

1.2.3.4 The Difference Between *sonderlich* and *allein*

Andreae's argument left him open to two attacks that he systematically counters. The extension of Luther's word is evident, and someone might protest that Luther meant to help only the indigents; he wanted to allow interest out of need or as a work of mercy. Andreae replies pungently that this person would have a misguided and flawed understanding of Luther's words. Here, Luther wrote anything but that he wanted to help alone (*allein*) indigent people, but he also meant to help also the aristocracy, traders, burghers and peasants. The key point is the second part of Luther's aforementioned statements:

85 J. Andreae, *Vier Christliche Predigten*, 96.
86 J. Andreae, *Vier Christliche Predigten*, 97.

> *that way, he wants to moderate the old difficult burden: If this (I say) can be useful to that end, I am gladly willing to agree with it and to help carry the burden for the sake of God especially, where there are indigent people and an interest out of need or an interest out of mercy (sonderlich, wo es durfftige personen und ein not wucher oder Barmhertziger wucher).*[87]

Andreae clings to this passage to defend his interpretation: Luther meant to help especially (*sonderlich*) the indigent people with the charging of an interest out of need (*Notwucher*):

> *Here once again Luther's words are cited in an unjust and wrong way. As a matter of fact, Luther did by no means write that he would only agree and carry (the burden) for the sake of God when indigent people are concerned, but that he would do this for the aristocracy, traders, burghers and peasants (as well), and he adds: 'in particular when indigent people and an interest out of need or an interest out of mercy are at stake'.*[88]

Now, Andreae writes, there is a great difference between the two words: 'especially/in particular' (*sonderlich*) and 'alone' (*allein*). Paul in Gal. 6,10, writes: "*as we therefore have opportunity, let us do good unto all men, especially* (sonderlich) *unto those who are of the household of faith*". As Paul did not want that we do good to those who are of the household of faith only, so then Luther meant to help not only to the orphans and the other indigents only but also the aristocrats, traders, burghers and peasants.[89] The reasoning sounds compelling. The good deeds are especially for certain people, but it does not exclude the others. The permission to use the *widerkaufflicher Zins* is especially directed towards the *miserabiles personae*, but it does not imply that others are excluded.

Andreae adds that the emperor did not create a special legislation for the widows, orphans and other indigent people, as they do not have a special heaven. But the law that he made for the aristocracy, merchants and other burghers and peasants also includes the widows, orphans, other indigents and their guardians.[90] In substance, the emperor did not have any reason to make

87 M. Luther, *An die Pfarrherrn*, in WA 51, 373: "*Er wölle damit die alte schwere Last messigen, Kan es (sage ich) hieher dienen, so will ich gern mit stimmen und helffen tragen für Gott, sonderlich, wo es durfftige personen und ein not wucher oder Barmhertziger wucher*".

88 J. Andreae, *Vier Christliche Predigten*, 101: "*Hie werden abermals D. Luthers wort unrecht und verkehrt angezogen. Dann D. Luther keines wegs geschrieben hat, das er allein mit stimmen, und vor Gott tragen helfen wölle, wenn es allein. Allein, allein Dürfftige Personen sind, sondern er wölle es thon für die vom Adel, Kauffleut, Bürger unnd Bawren und setzt darauff. Sonderlich wo es dürfftige Personen und ein Notwucher seye*".

89 J. Andreae, *Vier Christliche Predigten*, 101-2.

90 J. Andreae, *Vier Christliche Predigten*, 102.

a special legislation for certain categories of people. He had not to distinguish people, because their souls are all on the same level.

With a subtle distinction between the two words, especially (*sonderlich*) and alone (*allein*), Andreae defends the extension of Luther's statements. Luther was not only referring to the indigents but especially to them. Other categories of people are therefore also subject to the permission of interest (the interest out of need). The difference between the two is in the end so thin that the emperor does not make it. The emperor allows asking 5% annuity to everybody, widows, orphans, old people and other indigents included, but not limited only to them. The imperial ordinance is therefore lawful, as the practice in Regensburg.

1.2.3.5 The Concept of Need

The second point of Andreae's argument that might be contested is that the concept of need justified a different treatment for certain categories of people. Luther speaks about people in need. How then does Andreae admit the extension to other categories of people? Widows, orphans and elderly are certainly indigents and in need, but are the aristocrats at the same level? The needy and not-needy represented a valid criterion to select the people who could benefit from the permission. So, Luther would have meant to allow only the indigents, widows and orphans, and not everyone, to charge 50 florins for 1.000 florins or 100 florins for 2.000 florins.[91]

Astutely, Andreae looks at problem from another perspective: one could answer that if these people have 1.000 or 2.000 florins for making business, they are probably not indigent but rich. Luther calls them indigents who cannot work, albeit they have 1.000 or 2.000 florins. Thus, Andreae concludes that there is no distinction between the orphans and the rich, because both have 1.000 or 2.000 florins to invest.[92] Luther's criterion would not be so sharp, because rich, widows and orphans, all have money to invest.

The question however remains: what was Luther's intent with the 'interest out of need' (*Notwucher*)? The need, Andreae notices, cannot change what is right and what is not right. Adultery committed because the wife was ill for a long time, is adultery because of need, but it remains adultery. The jurists, the priests and the territorial princes cannot change what God condemned. They cannot admit interest if God condemned it. So, when Luther alluded to the interest out of need, he did not mean to say that the need justifies an evil

91 J. Andreae, *Vier Christliche Predigten*, 105.
92 J. Andreae, *Vier Christliche Predigten*, 106.

action. A murder is wrong and remains wrong into eternity.[93] Usury is a sin and remains a sin. The need cannot justify usury.[94]

The solution comes from a different interpretation of the concept of 'need'. There is another need, Andreae suggests brazenly, without which nobody can live on earth. This is when one should trade with another. But not everyone has the opportunity to buy goods, so one could make a fruitful use of his money to satisfy his need and not to lose the primary good. Otherwise he would become a mendicant.[95] This is the interest out of need (*Notwucher*). The need Luther refers is the need of the essential goods to live. These goods can be obtained through commerce or, for the people who cannot commerce, by the *widerkaufflicher Zins*. Therefore, Andreae concludes that 50 florins charged as annuity on a sum of 1.000 florins or 100 florins charged as annuity on 2.000 florins can be taken.[96]

The need that Luther considers is not the need of hunger that excuses a wrong action. The need regards the necessity to get the essential support for life. This need can be satisfied through commerce or for the people who cannot do it, by the *widerkaufflicher Zins*. Again, with an extended interpretation, Andreae defends his thesis on the lawfulness of the *widerkaufflicher Zins* and the conformity with Luther' words. The interest out of need is not the interest-taking for people in need, but concerns everybody, because everybody needs to have the essential goods to live.

1.2.4 *An Ordinance for Conscience*

The third and last issue raised by the five ecclesiastical ministers of Regensburg concerned the power of the emperor to quiet (*stillen*) the conscience. The emperor allowed a 5% annuity, but the ministers claimed that this was against the interest prohibition. The emperor is not God and cannot ordain what God has not approved. The emperor rules over his kingdom, which is terrestrial, mortal and changeable. The reign of Christ, however, is divine, eternal and immutable. Given these two different kingdoms, an ordinance of the terrestrial emperor could not placate the conscience of the Christians, which is subject to God alone.[97] The argument sounds genuinely a Lutheran one and relies on the two kingdoms doctrine. The magistrate cannot intervene in the heavenly kingdom, because the Word of God only governs it.

---

93 J. Andreae, *Vier Christliche Predigten*, 107.
94 J. Andreae, *Vier Christliche Predigten*, 108.
95 J. Andreae, *Vier Christliche Predigten*, 108-9.
96 J. Andreae, *Vier Christliche Predigten*, 109.
97 J. Andreae, *Vier Christliche Predigten*, 97-8.

Andreae responds shrewdly that Luther did not want that the imperial ordinance to be one that is deemed just before the emperor, but not before God. Luther meant that it should be an ordinance by which the conscience is put at peace.[98] The imperial ordinance neither changes what is a sin, nor reassure the sinners, because it is not in the power of the emperor to make sin what is not sin, but a sin remains a sin, even if the emperor admitted it.[99] The imperial ordinance, Andreae declares, is in agreement with the Holy Scripture. It is founded on the correct interpretation of Luke 6,35, which does not consider everything given in addition to the lent sum as usury, but distinguishes what is a loan from what is business.[100] Moreover, the ordinance keeps the divine precepts of Christ expressed in Matthew 7,12, 2 Cor. 8 and 1 Thess. 4,6.[101] These rules set out protection against damages and equality among the parties.

Since the imperial ordinance complies with these rules, Andreae deems that it is a divine law that pertains to the kingdom of God and to the imperial kingdom:

> *Thus, it is not only a human ordinance that the emperor ordained following Matthew 7, but a divine ordinance of which a Christian can make use with a calm and unharmed conscience.*

The consequence is therefore:

> *he who opposes such an ordinance and does not consider it as an ordinance of God does not have a calm and good conscience and will not remain unpunished.*[102]

Andreae quotes a groundbreaking passage of the Reformation, Paul's Rom. 13,5: "*therefore ye must be subject not only for wrath, but also for conscience's sake*"[103] and concludes that the imperial law is a Christian, divine and indeed a God-pleasing law (*Christlich, Goettlich, und Gott wol gefellig Recht*). It does not

---

98 J. Andreae, *Vier Christliche Predigten*, 99: "*Das es nicht ein solche Ordnung sey, die allein vor dem Keyser aber nicht vor Gott für gerecht gehalten werde. Sondern es sey ein solche ordnung, dardurch die Gewissen zu friden gestellt werden*".

99 J. Andreae, *Vier Christliche Predigten*, 99.

100 J. Andreae, *Vier Christliche Predigten*, 113.

101 J. Andreae, *Vier Christliche Predigten*, 232, 284-5.

102 J. Andreae, *Vier Christliche Predigten*, 207-8: "*So ist es nicht allein ein Menschliche ordnung, was der Keyser nach dem Gebott Christi, Matth. am 7. ordnet, Sondern ein Göttliche ordnung, deren ein Christ nicht allein mit ruhigen unverletzten Gewissen, sich gebrauchen kan, sonder wer sich solcher Ordnung widersetzt, und nicht für Gottes ordnung erkent, der werde kein ruhig gut Gewissen haben, auch nicht ungestrafft bleiben*".

103 J. Andreae, *Vier Christliche Predigten*, 208.

come from a profane but from an illuminated Christian emperor, and every Christian can use it with good faith.[104]

The imperial ordinance calms the conscience and eliminates the affliction. It abides by the new formulation of the interest prohibition and does not offend charity. The ordinance is not only a political instrument, but also has a theological character; it is not only a secular law but also a divine law. Andreae's words reflect the Lutheran teachings on the role of the magistrate as a divine institution. He roots his statements in Rom. 13,5, an essential text for theorizing on the relationship between church and state.[105]

Two considerations can be put forward. First, it is evident that Andreae wants to support the imperial authority – he defends and justifies the political order and attempts to avoid dissent or rebellion. Luther himself had adopted a similar solution for the peasants' war. There, he supported the office of the magistrate as a divine institution and condemned the rebels. Second, Andreae's statements push towards a transmission of power. The canon law was for centuries the instrument used by the Church to put its teachings into practice. It codified the results of the theological debates and the moral decisions. The canon law regulated the conscience of the Christians. In matter of sins, for instance, the canon law prevailed over the civil law. Now, this construction is dismantled – the magistrate is the ruler of Christian society.

1.2.5 *Conclusion*

The question placed at the beginning regarded the usurious nature of the *widerkaufflicher Zins*. Andreae responded that the interest prohibition only concerns loans towards the poor. The *widerkaufflicher Zins* is a business contract and as such must ensure equality among the parties, but is not subject to the interest prohibition. Equality means that the parties must have equal advantages and disadvantages – one should not be damaged while the other profits. The *widerkaufflicher Zins* complies with equality, because the annuity (*Zins*) is the price for the use of capital. After all, the investor could have made another profit with the capital he gives to the entrepreneur. Without the annuity the entrepreneur would have benefits and the investor would have losses. The annuity is therefore the just price paid in order to avoid the inequality of the contract.

---

104 J. Andreae, *Vier Christliche Predigten*, 285.

105 On the important role of this reference see: R.J. Ross, *Binding in Conscience: Early Modern English Protestants and Spanish Tomists on Law and the Fate of the Soul*, in *Law and History Review*, 33 (2015), 803-37.

Then, with an extensive interpretation Andreae affirms that Luther's statements are meant to allow the taking of annuity not only to widows, orphans and the elderly but also to other categories of people. Luther intended that particularly the elderly, orphans, widows and other indigents are allowed to use the five per cent contract – but he did not envision forbidding it for all the others. Indeed, Luther approves the Justinian legislation on the charging of interest, which also concerns other classes like the aristocracy, traders, burghers and peasants. Luther defines this concession as *interest out of need*, and the need, Andreae explains, is the requirement for the essential means to live. Because this concerns every person and not only a particular category, every person can use the *widerkaufflicher Zins*.

The imperial ordinance that permitted the 5% annuity complies with the Scripture and Luther's statements. It distinguishes between interest that is forbidden (in the case of loans) and interest (*Zins*-annuities) in business, which is allowed. The imperial ordinance is based on Justinian's legislation that does not violate the divine law.

The five ecclesiastical ministers, because of the papal law and the canonists, misunderstood the biblical teachings on interest-taking and mistakenly applied the passage of Luke 6,35 to the *widerkaufflicher Zins* too. They interpreted strictly Luther's statements and considered the imperial ordinance as referring only to elderly, poor, indigent, widows and orphans and refused to absolve the rich.[106] Andreae terminates with an apologetic tune, pointing out that the Scripture does not distinguish between different forms of rich people, nor between orphans and widows:

> *I am asking you where is it written in the Holy Scripture, in the Old and New Testaments, in the Prophets and the apostles, in the Gospel or in the letters that it is permitted to the widows and the orphans to receive interest and not the other people? And that for one rich (man) it is forbidden and to the other one it is allowed, where is it written?*[107]

The opinion defended by the five ecclesiastical ministers of Regensburg is therefore wrong and must not be followed.

Andreae proved the lawfulness of the payment of the annuity (*Zins*) as a central aspect of the *widerkaufflicher Zins* and guaranteed the spiritual

106 J. Andreae, *Vier Christliche Predigten*, 287.

107 J. Andreae, *Vier Christliche Predigten*, 287: "*Ich frage dich aber, wo stehet es in H. Schrifft alts und newes Testaments, in der Propheten oder Apostel Schrifften, im Evangelio oder in Episteln geschrieben, das den Wittwen und Waisen erlaubt sey zu Wuchern, und andern Leutten nicht: Item, das einem Reichen erlaubt sey zu Wuchern, und dem andern Reichen nicht, wo stehets geschrieben* ...".

legitimation of the two imperial ordinances. He granted to the emperor the power to intervene in the matter of interest and to heal Christians' consciences. The emperor holds a peculiar religious function: if his provisions comply with the Scripture, they obligate consciences. With Berman's words we might say that the emperor gives to the religious doctrine an appropriate normative form. He converts the biblical teachings into cohesive norms. He consolidates faith in the social order.[108]

Andreae put forward a detailed interpretation of Scripture and Luther's statements, but he also received much from the discussions that originated in the milieu of the Lutheran orthodoxy. Melanchthon, Brenz, Aepinus and Rhegius are some of the authors that might have inspired him. The Calvinist Du Moulin, which as we will see later is very important for the jurists, is never quoted. The judgment of Luther, instead, is abused and sacrificed at the altar of power and stability. Luther's restrictive opinion on interest and usury is substituted with new teachings that legalize the *widerkaufflicher Zins* for everybody. This represents an evident concession to the emergence of capitalism. We might certainly guess that Andreae defended the *widerkaufflicher Zins* for reasons of political stability and economic convenience for society. First, the application of Luther's writings would have caused the partial non-compliance with the imperial ordinance. Second, distinguishing between categories of people, as Luther had proposed, would have probably created negative effects on the economy. Considering the general propagation of the German contract, it would have produced numerous insolvencies. Nonetheless, these are mere speculations, because Andreae obviously does not document his reasons.

The four sermons of Andreae must be considered according to their nature. They are sermons directed to the citizens of Regensburg. They are neither a dogmatic treatise, nor a manual for confessors. The style is therefore vivid and captivating. Andreae recourses often to passionate and apologetic statements to express his opinion. And he is very polemic against the contrary opinion. Some concepts are rattled off in general without a detailed exposition. For instance, the attacks against the canonists and the canon law lack references. They paint a monolithic vision of the canonist science, as though all the canonists were sticking to the old concept of usury, while in reality, the subject of usury was very much debated between the canonists and scholastic theologians. And a number of them were in favour of the new type of *census* contract.[109]

108 H.J. Berman, *The Interaction between Law and Religion*, passim.

109 J.T. Noonan Jr., *The Scholastic Analysis of Usury*, 155-64, 230-48.

We conclude with Andreae's emphatic words on the importance of the dispute for the Christian faith. The dispute of usury at Regensburg was an essential one, he states, because it concerned the proper interpretation of the Word of God. Without this dispute the Christians would have remained with a false and impure teaching on the highest article of the Lutheran Christian faith.[110] For a Christian, he specifies, every single Word of God is an article of faith,[111] and this dispute involved the Word of God. Thus, if the issue had passed unnoticed, with time, not only the truth of the body and blood of Jesus Christ in the Holy Supper but also Christ himself would have been completely lost.[112]

1.3 Legal Counsels

1.3.1 *Introduction*

Beside the spiritual issue, the use of the *widerkaufflicher Zins* required a legal analysis. Thus, the proceedings of the controversy between the five ecclesiastical ministers and the magistrate of Regensburg were submitted to the jurists of the law faculty of Tübingen. The main question the jurists were asked to solve was formulated in these terms:

> *since up to then there was a custom in Regensburg, which was also deemed just and was allowed by the chamberlains and by the council, that it is not only permitted to the widows and orphans, but also to burghers and residents, to use in their business the normal annuity (Zins) rate – as it is deemed just, in the case of redeemable Zins, by the different classes in the empire to lend one hundred guilders for 5 guilders, not perpetually, but for a fixed number of years to someone, who can either buy goods or trade with that money or benefit from it in another way; that person does not share gains nor losses with the one who lent him the money, but is the sole loser or beneficiary. Would such a contract be in conflict with God's word, with the law, with nature, with the written imperial laws, with Christian love, with honour and equity? And would it be impossible for a Christian to either give or accept such a contract with clear conscience?*[113]

---

110 J. Andreae, *Vier Christliche Predigten*, 289.

111 J. Andreae, *Vier Christliche Predigten*, 222.

112 J. Andreae, *Vier Christliche Predigten*, 289.

113 *Abfertigung*, 8 (see also 127-8): "*Sonder das ist die Frage, dieweil bis daher in der Statt Regenspurg üblich unnd gebreuchlich gewesen, auch von Cammerer unnd Raht für recht gehalten unnd geduldet worden, dass nicht allein im Vormundampt, wegen der Witwen unnd Waisen, sonder auch undern Burgern und Einwohnern, in ihren Händlen, umb den landläuffigen Zins, wie derselbig von den Ständen des Reichs in widerkäufflichen Zinsen für billich und recht erkennet, hundert gulden umb fünff gulden, nicht eines ewigen Kauffs, sonder nur auff ettlich gewisse Jar einem aussgelihen, darumb Gütter zukauffen, zuhandthieren, oder in ander weg sein Nutzen darmit zuschaffen, welcher auch weder gewinn*

The jurists shall assess the lawfulness of the *widerkaufflicher Zins* concerning the divine law, natural law, Christian love, honour, equity and the civil law. The *widerkaufflicher Zins* contemplates three contractual terms: the payment of the annuity, the redeemability after a certain period of time and the absence of risk sharing. Andreae only investigated the lawfulness of the charging of an annuity while the jurists are also asked to analyse the other contractual terms. Therefore, the questions of Andreae and the jurists are overlapping on the lawfulness of the annuity, but not on the other two terms, where the work of the jurists completes in a way the work of Andreae.

Andreae explored the edges of the interest prohibition and the space for business. He attested that the *widerkaufflicher Zins* is not usurious and the imperial ordinances abide by the divine law. He provided the emperor with the necessary spiritual legitimation to operate in matters of divine law. The jurists used Andreae's writings as a basis for the definition of the interest prohibition and the legitimation of the political power in matter of interest. They reinforced and completed these statements, adding the interpretation of the imperial ordinance and the analysis of the lawfulness of the contractual terms. Theologians and jurists cooperated in the establishing of the law of the *widerkaufflicher Zins*. This law therefore is deemed irreproachable in the eyes of God and in compliance with the emperor.

Another point that needs to be spotlighted is that although it is classified as one main question (*Hauptfrag*), there are two questions instead. The jurists shall not only investigate the lawfulness of the *widerkaufflicher Zins* but also the lawfulness of a custom of using that contract in Regensburg. After having illustrated the main question, the Tübingen jurists notice that in the city of Regensburg there is maybe no recorded statute, law or ordinance that admitted the *widerkaufflicher Zins*.[114] However, the chamberlain and the council of the city of Regensburg, with a clear knowledge and will, and without being hindered, objected to the position of the ministers and allowed, maintained and acknowledged as proper, legitimate, even divine and Christian the common usage of lending with annuity (*Lehenzins*), as it was mentioned in the above main question. So, the jurists hold the view that Regensburg's burghers can benefit with clear conscience from their authority's accommodation, from its

---

noch verlust mit dem, so ihm das Gelt gelihen, gemein, sonder allein haben wolt: Ob solcher Contract dem Wort Gottes, dem Gesätzt der Natur, dem Keiserlichen geschribnen Rechten, der Christlichen Liebe, aller Erbar unnd Billicheit zuwider sey? Und demnach von einem Christen mit unverletztem Gewissen weder gegeben noch genommen werden könne?".

114 *Abfertigung*, 133.

consent and from this somewhat unclear but common practice.[115] The jurists do not say it explicitly, but with a subtle observation point out the lack of a formal legislation for the *widerkaufflicher Zins* in Regensburg. The practice of that contract is therefore justified by the existence of a custom. The jurists shall verify if the custom is reasonable. A binding custom requires two elements: a certain practice is observed with the consent of the authority; and this practice is reasonable and not against natural equity.

1.3.2 *A Reasonable and Just Custom in Regensburg*

1.3.2.1 Introduction

The imperial ordinances of 1530 and 1548 allowed a 5% annuity and established that the power to redeem must always be given to the seller/entrepreneur. Martin Luther in his 1540 sermon assumed that only old people, orphans and widows could practice the *widerkaufflicher Zins*. Following Luther, the five ministers of Regensburg contested the authority of the emperor to allow a 5% annuity for everybody. Furthermore, they claimed that no local legislation in Regensburg could authorize the practice of the *widerkaufflicher Zins*, neither it did so, because the interest prohibition cannot be changed by a provision of the political authority. The five ministers only allowed elderly, orphans and widows to enter into a *widerkaufflicher Zins* and refused to absolve any others.

The jurists of the law faculty of the University of Tübingen grappled with this problem. They decided that even though there is no statute, ordinance or legislation for the *widerkaufflicher Zins* in Regensburg, the use of this contract is authorized by customary law, as it meets both requirements of a binding custom: the practice is undertaken with the consent of the authority, and it is deemed reasonable and not in violation of natural equity.

1.3.2.2 The Approval of the Public Authority

A custom is legally binding when a public authority has recognized and assented to it. To ascertain that not only the elderly, orphans and widows but also other categories of people practiced the *widerkaufflicher Zins*, the jurists make use of a presumption: if the reproached five ecclesiastical ministers were right, and so the *widerkaufflicher Zins* was usurious, such a custom would have

---

115 *Abfertigung*, 132-3: "*Weil dann wir berichtet werden, dass die Oberkeit, als Kammerer und Rath der Statt Regensburg, mit gutem wissen und willen, ja auch unverhindert, diser und anderer ihrer Prediger widerfechtens und einredens, für zimlich, billich, ja Göttlich, und Christlich und ihrer Policen zuträglich geduldet, gehalten und erkennt, die jenige Lehenzins (darvon in oberzelter Hauptfrag meldung beschehen) bedunckt uns, es können ihre Burger, diser ihrer Obrigkeit vergünstigung, erlaubens, ja neblichen und gemeinen Brauchs, wol mit gutem Gewissen sich behelffen*".

been practiced in contradiction of the civil authority of Regensburg for many years. But this conclusion would be irrational. It seems instead that the whole population of Regensburg observed this practice with the consent of a civil authority that decided not to condemn it:

> *from what then de facto would be presumed, that the community of Regensburg not only under themselves, without knowledge and approval, but much less against the will, order and command of the public authority, deliberately and well considered, approved and endorsed such an annuity from loan, also for many years brought here, the public authority held therefore as a charitable work. But the community brought such use and practice, with the knowledge and will of the same public authority that did not condemn it.*[116]

Cleverly, the jurists reverse the burden of proof: if the practice of the *widerkaufflicher Zins* is usurious, why did the public authority never condemn it?

The five ministers argued that the charging of interest is generally forbidden in the Holy Scripture, as theologians and canonists proclaim, and therefore the magistrate cannot allow loans at interest.[117] The jurists respond, however, that this is in fact a task of the political magistrate, who holds the power to judge in matters such as the interest prohibition and to reassure the consciences of his people. The jurists sustain this statement by recalling Johann Brenz's homily n. 61 on the sixth chapter of the gospel of Luke, and homilies n. 19 and 29 on Luke 19, which we have already examined before.[118] Additionally, they draw on the opinions of two Protestant jurists: the Calvinist Charles du Moulin and the Lutheran Justin Göbler (1503/1504-1567).[119]

Charles du Moulin, often quoted in the text, refers to Conrad Summenhart's treatise on contract law:[120] "*the civil law must establish whether a contract is usurious*".[121] He adds:

116 *Abfertigung*, 133-4: "*Nach dem dann in facto presupponiert würdet, dass solche Lehenzins (...) die gemeine Burgerschafft zu Regenspurg nicht nur under ihen selbs, ohne wissen und bewilligung, vil weniger aber wider willen, geheiss unnd verbott der Obrigkeit, sonder auss derselben wissentlichen und wolbedachtem zulassen und gut heissen, also vil jar hergebracht, die Obrigkeit darob, als eim gemeinnutzigen Werk gehalten (...) sonder die Burgerschafft, bey deren, mit wissen unnd willen der Oberkeit daselbst, herbrachten gebrauch und übung, unverdampt lassen*".

117 *Abfertigung*, 129.

118 *Abfertigung*, 131-2.

119 von Eltester, *Göbler, Justinus* in *Allgemeine Deutsche Biographie* 9 (1879), 301 (accessed 17.05.2016); http://www.deutsche-biographie.de/pnd122200489.html?anchor=adb.

120 C. Du Moulin, *Tractatus*, passim.

121 *Abfertigung*, 135: "*... ius civile spectet definire, an contractus sit usurarius vel non*". C. du Moulin, *Tractatus*, n. 70, 83. Du Moulin quotes C. Summenhart, *De contractibus licitis atque illicitis*, Venetiis, 1580, q. 34.

> *in particular the judgment over the forms, equity or justice of contracts must not be sought on the basis of Scripture, but of the civil laws. The Gospel requires justice and equality in civil business, but it does not describe their forms and rules, neither indicates in particular what is just or unjust, equal or unequal in the single contracts.*[122]

Hence, he concludes: "(*therefore*) *it is necessary in these to follow the public ordinances agreeing with right reason*".[123] Du Moulin grounds his statements in Rom. 13,5 and explains that the political ordinances of a legitimate magistrate must be obeyed not only because of the sanctions, but also because of conscience.[124]

The jurist of Sankt Goar, Justin Göbler, agrees with this opinion and in his annotations on the Imperial Constitution of 1648[125] claims that the judgment whether contracts are honest and useful for the state is attributed to the magistrate. The theologians should only educate Christians that it is licit to follow political ordinances. Since contracts are political ordinances, they are under the judgment of the magistrate and not of the ecclesiastical ministers.[126] The magistrate (and not the theologians) holds the power to rule in matter of contracts, even when it regards the interest prohibition: what is actually interest (*usura*) and what is forbidden interest should not be learnt from any private opinion but from the civil authority (*Obrigkeit*).[127]

Both Du Moulin and Göbler follow the doctrine of two kingdoms, which is based on the distinction between the Gospel and the law. Preaching the Gospel is a task of the ecclesiastical ministers. Governing the world is a duty of the magistrate. Melanchthon and other theologians elaborated the concept of political ordinance. Here, Göbler uses it to reaffirm the sovereignty of the magistrate over the determination of usurious contracts. As Andreae and other theologians had strongly contended, the magistrate may intervene to regulate loans at interest, and these secular regulations should assuage the conscience.

---

122 *Abfertigung*, 135: "*et particulare iudicium de contractuum formis, aequitate et iustitia, non ex sacra Scriptura peti debeat: sed ex civilibus legibus* (…). *Itaque Evangelium iustitiam quidem et aequalitatem in civilibus negocijs exigit, sed formas et regulas earum non describit, nec indicat speciatim, quid in singulis contractibus iustum et iniustum, equum aut iniquum sit*". C. Du Moulin, *Tractatus*, n. 87, 102.

123 *Abfertigung*, 135: "*Ideo necesse est, in his sequi ordinationes publicas consentientes rectae rationi*". C. Du Moulin, *Tractatus*, n. 87, 102.

124 C. du Moulin, *Tractatus*, n. 87, 103: "*Non enim propter poenas tantum, sed etiam propter conscientiam obedientia debetur legitimo magistratui in politicis ordinationibus Roma. 13*".

125 J. Göbler, *Divi Caroli qvinti politiae ac reipvblicae imperialis constitutio*, Francofurti, 1566.

126 *Abfertigung*, 135-6. J. Göbler, *Divi Caroli qvinti politiae ac reipvblicae*, 80.

127 *Abfertigung*, 131: "*Was aber eigendtlich* usura *unnd eben* prohibita usura *seie, das möge und solle nit auss eines jeglichen privati* opinion, *sonder von der weltlichen Obrigkeit erlernet werden*".

1.3.2.3 Reasonableness and Natural Equity

The regulation of financial contracts is up to the civil magistrate and not to the ecclesiastical ministers. Then, the jurists advocate that the magistrate of Regensburg had the legitimate power to allow the practice of the *widerkaufflicher Zins* and rightly defended it against the five ecclesiastical ministers, because the custom is reasonable and not against equity.[128] The custom is just and rational because the magistrate followed the inspiration of Justinian's moderation of interest in *Eos, qui* (C. 4,32,26):

> *then something moved the honourable emperor Justinian, that he also approved interest in loans, in a proper sense, and yet moderated it in dimension, as in the law* Eos qui *is found. Without doubt this pushed the civil authority in Regensburg to allow and to approve the same for its burghers, for the opportunity of its city and the burghers' business.*[129]

The jurists endorse the account of Justinian's law put forward by Luther and extended by Andreae. In order to prove that *Eos qui* is not against natural equity they refer to 'the most qualified jurists': Matthaeus Wesenbeck[130] and Charles Du Moulin.

In his *Paratitla*[131] (first published in 1563) Wesenbeck distinguished between interest for punishment (*usura punitoria*), interest for profit (*usura lucratoria*), and interest for compensation (*usura compensatoria*). Yet, the jurists hold, in Regensburg only 'interest for compensation' is practiced. Wesenbeck refers to the *interesse*, as a lawful compensation the creditor should receive if he suffered damage in a loan:

> *it cannot be said that the interest for compensation is in general forbidden or shameful, since it is not the profit gained in addition to the capital on the grounds of the loan. Rather it is the price or the estimation for using the capital at the expense of the creditor.*[132]

---

128 *Abfertigung*, 136.

129 *Abfertigung*, 136-7: "*Dann was den Hochlöblichen Keiser Iustinianum bewegt, dass er auch usuras, proprie sic dictas, in mutuo* (…) *gebillichet, unnd doch vermassen moderiert, wie in l. eos qui, C. de usuris* (C. 4,32,26), *zufinden: Das hat zweifels ohne, die Oberkeit in Regenspurg verursacht, dergleichen ihren Burgern, nach gelegenheit ihrer Statt unnd burgerlichen Wesens, zuverstatten und zubillichen*".

130 See also IV/2.

131 M. Wesenbeck, *Commentaria quae olim paratitla in pandectas iuris civilis et codici iustiniani libros*, Antwerpiae, 1621, Dig. 22, n. 7, 234.

132 *Abfertigung*, 137: "*usuram compensatoriam interdictam in universum aut turpem esse, dici non potest: quia non est lucrum supra sortem exactum, propter officium mutuationis, sed precium vel aestimatio usus sortis consumptae, cum damno creditoris*".

As a Christian jurist, Wesenbeck believes that the evangelical duty to help the other does not imply that you preserve him unscathed: "*nobody is compelled to benefit the other with his loss. Neither does the apostle Paul* (2. Cor. 8,13) *wish that we promote the neighbour with our affliction*".[133] For this reason, an investor could use the money for profit, but could also lend the money he does not use and receive an interest for the damage he suffered. The emperor Justinian, in order to avoid the risk of avarice, admitted a certain tolerable interest with *Eos, qui*.[134] Wesenbeck affirms implicitly that *Eos, qui* is lawful. The Tübingen jurists likewise hold fast to this point in arguing the lawfulness of Justinian's legislation.

Charles Du Moulin, the other authority quoted, also permits Christians to follow Justinian's provision on loans at interest: "*I conclude that Christians cannot observe the imperial constitution* Eos, qui (C. 4,32,26) *in case of alms, but that they can observe it in case of civil commerce*".[135] Thus, the Tübingen jurists conclude that Justinian's regulation of loans at interest complies with natural equity, as Wesenbeck and Du Moulin attest.[136] The political authority of Regensburg appropriately accepted Justinian's inspiration and recognized a custom that is reasonable and does not go against the natural equity. *Eos qui* is the handhold to justify the usage of the *widerkaufflicher Zins*.

1.3.3 *The Lawfulness of the* widerkaufflicher Zins

1.3.3.1 Introduction

The political authority of Regensburg implicitly authorized the usage of the German contract. This usage was based on Justinian's legislation on interest. Hence, the Tübingen jurists ruled that in Regensburg a custom legitimized the *widerkaufflicher Zins* not only for the elderly, orphans and widows but also for other categories of people. Now, they address the question over the lawfulness of this contract, which is far more complex. The *widerkaufflicher Zins* provides essentially three contractual terms. First, the investor lends the capital to the entrepreneur, who in return has to pay 5% on the capital at annual intervals. The entrepreneur is free to use the money for any purpose but is obliged to pay back the 5% annuity: he does not share profits or losses with the investor.

---

133 *Abfertigung*, 137: "*... cum nemo alteri suo cum detrimento benigne facere cogatur, ne ipse quidem Apostolus vult, sic nos alijs commodare, ut nobis sit afflictio ...*". M. Wesenbeck, *Commentaria*, 234: "*Ne quidem Apostolus 2. Cor. 8.13...*".

134 *Abfertigung*, 137-8.

135 *Abfertigung*, 138: "*Concludo ergo quod non quidem in casibus eleemosynae ... sed in usu civilium commerciorum etiam a Christianis servari posset d. l. eos etc.* [C. 4,32,26]". C. Du Moulin, *Tractatus*, n. 80, 96.

136 *Abfertigung*, 138.

Second, the annuity is not perpetual but redeemable after a certain time. It is unclear whether the buyer or the seller specifies the length of contract, but somehow a time for the redemption is fixed by the parties. Third, the annuity does not derive from a specified real estate but is detached from the land and it only represents a personal obligation to pay the annuity.

Concerning the first term, the payment of a 5% annuity is allowed by the imperial ordinances, but this provision is expressed under the paragraph dedicated to usurious contracts. For this reason, the five ministers assumed that this payment was 'usurious', in violation of the interest prohibition. The Tübingen jurists respond following Andreae: the five ecclesiastical ministers' assumption flows from an incorrect interpretation of the Gospel made by the canonists. The canonists' improper interpretation contaminated first canon law and then the Roman law, establishing that every loan at interest is forbidden. In the imperial ordinances, the payment of the 5% annuity is stated in the paragraph entitled: "On usurious contracts" (*Von wücherlichen Contracten*), because of the inaccurate definition of usury advanced by the canonists.

The second main term of the *widerkaufflicher Zins* sets out the redeemability of the contract after a certain period of time. In the *widerkaufflicher Zins* is not stated explicitly which of the parties retains the power to ordain the date of redemption, but the ministers hold that the establishing of a certain time for the return of the sum would show that the buyer decides the end of the contract. The jurists reply that if the parties agree to the repayment after a certain time, the agreement is lawful and does not favour the buyer/investor.

The third main term indicates that the obligation to pay the annuity is not linked to a specific real estate, but to the income derived from many estates. The five ministers maintain that in this way the risk is only supported by the entrepreneur and not by the investor. The jurists reply that this term does not damage the entrepreneur if all the lands perish, and that such a clause is considered to be legal by the imperial cameral tribunal (*Reichskammergericht*).

As a matter of fact, the five ministers advocated the enforcement of the canon law provisions in the two papal bulls of Martin V and Callixtus III, the bull *Cum onus* issued in 1569 and a restrictive interpretation of the imperial ordinances of Charles V at the Diet of Augsburg in 1530 and 1548. They supported the old theory of interest and fought for its conservation. On the contrary, the jurists backed the new theory and struggled for its definitive affirmation. They pleaded for overcoming the canon law and for the correct interpretation of the new civil law provisions. In the following pages, we are going to examine in detail the arguments proposed by the two parties.

1.3.3.2 The Purchase of Annual Income

1.3.3.2.1 *The Canonists' False Understanding of the Holy Scripture*

For the Tübingen jurists, the essence of the quarrel lies in the inaccurate teachings on the interest prohibition put forward by the medieval canonists. In other words, the five ecclesiastical ministers defended the old theory of interest, according to which every loan at interest is forbidden, while the jurists endorsed a new approach, which considers usury to be only a loan against Christian charity. The jurists founded their conclusions on Du Moulin's celebrated treatise on interest and on the writing of the Lutheran jurist Peter a Vuell.[137] Du Moulin declares that canonists, legists and scholastic theologians interpreted the divine law more according to its literal sense (*ad literam*) than to its spirit (*ad spiritum*). In this way, they understood the prohibition against interest in a strict and rigorous way, so that no human law can change it, even in special cases.[138] They "*did not direct attention to the aim of the divine law that is charity, of which Christ is the witness (Matth. 7)*",[139] because if the divine law is interpreted in the light of charity, the true meaning is clear: the charging of interest is not forbidden by the divine law, except when it is against charity.[140] Thus, Du Moulin concludes that it is misguided what those (the canonists) wrote and taught – namely, that the divine law condemns any interest or whatever advantage that is taken by the creditor – because in truth lending at interest is not condemned if the neighbour is not defrauded.[141]

The canonists' improper teaching stems from a false interpretation of the passage of Luke 6,35. For Du Moulin, the Words of Christ do not concern the interest prohibition, but rather restitution of the borrowed sum, without asking for an equal benefit. Christ is talking about the indigents and the poor and does not forbid the annuity, if it is paid by someone who is not indigent. Christ does not anticipate lending without asking in return the lent sum, but desires that those with means assist the indigents. Certainly, he does not prohibit the borrower from returning the sum with a certain interest to the benefactor,

---

137 Vuell, Peter in J.H. Zedler, *Grosses vollständiges Universal-Lexicon aller Wissenschafften und Künste*, v. 51, Leipzig und Halle, 1747, 1233. I could not find further information.

138 *Abfertigung*, 139.

139 *Abfertigung*, 139: "*... quod non respexerunt ad scopum divinae legis quae est charitas, teste Christo, Matth. 7*". C. Du Moulin, *Tractatus*, n. 10, 10.

140 *Abfertigung*, 139: "*Non est igitur, (inquit ibi Molineaus) usura lege divina prohibita et illicita, nisi in quantum est contra charitatem*". C. Du Moulin, *Tractatus*, n. 10, 10.

141 *Abfertigung*, 140: "*Non esse igitur verum, sed erroneum, quod illi hactenus scripserunt et docuerunt, quamlibet usuram aut foenus, aut quicquid omnino commodi, ob mutuam pecunia recipiat creditor a lege divina damnari: quin imo non damnatur usura, nisi quae fraudi proximo est, eumque praegravat*". C. Du Moulin, *Tractatus*, n. 10, 11.

to the benefactor's advantage. He does not forbid restitution of the loan but wants the Christians to put charity towards the poor first. Therefore, charging an interest is not forbidden in itself, but it is only forbidden when damages the brother, because in this way it is against love.[142] If your brother earned profit with your money, and he decides spontaneously to give you part of the profit, this is not against the interest prohibition.[143] Du Moulin stresses the necessity of interpreting the passage of Luke 6,35 in the light of charity: Christ is not talking here about business but only about loans for indigents. The compensation given for the profit gained complies with charity, and it is thus totally licit.

Peter a Vuell expounds a similar reasoning in his treatise on interest (1564).[144] He deems that in Luke 6,35 Christ was not talking about loans in the juridical sense, as indicated in the civil law. Christ was referring to the indigents and to the poor, but not to the rich.[145] Furthermore, the contract of loan, like the other contracts, produces positive effects for the poor and also helps the other citizens to guard against the scarcity of money. In truth, a Vuell remarks, interest can be charged in the contract of loan to compensate the creditor for the damage he suffers in lending the sum.[146] This possibility, however, is only granted to certain people. To determine the people that are allowed to ask for interest, a Vuell recourses to the division of people in three classes formulated by Aepinus: extreme poor, poor who can work and rich.[147] Only the rich can charge interest.

1.3.3.2.2 *The 'Contamination' of Canon Law*

Through the canonists, the misinterpretation of Scripture was implanted into the canon law. The Tübingen jurists are more specific than Andreae and give appropriate references. They hold that the contamination of the canon law can be clearly seen in Pope Urban III's decretal *Consuluit* (X 5,19,10), where it is written to observe what in the Gospel of Luke is manifestly known: "*lend*

---

142 *Abfertigung*, 140: "*Ut ergo non vult Christus, non nisi certa spe restitutionis mutuari, sed magis spectari, quo indigenti subveniamus, quam quo pecunia sit in tuto, ita si frater, ita non egeat, quin possit cum suo commodo sortem cum aliquo foenore benefactori reddere, non prohibet: sicut non prohibet repetitionem mutui, etiam in publico iudicio, sed vult semper et ubique rationem haberi charitatis proximi pauperis etc. non ergo accipere usuram quamlibet, sed cum damno fratris accipere, dilectioni repugnat*". C. Du Moulin, *Tractatus*, n. 10, 11.

143 *Abfertigung*, 140-141. C. Du Moulin, *Tractatus*, n. 10, 11.

144 P. a Vuell, *Tractatus de usuris*, Coloniae, 1564.

145 *Abfertigung*, 141. P. a Vuell, *Tractatus de usuris*, arg. 2 and 13.

146 *Abfertigung*, 142. P. a Vuell, *Tractatus de usuris*, arg. 2 and 13.

147 *Abfertigung*, 142-4. P. a Vuell, *Tractatus de usuris*, arg. 2 and 13. On Aepinus see before III/2.3.2.2.

hoping for nothing in return".[148] The jurists claim that this statement is against the intention of Christ (*contra mentem Christi*), because in this way it makes sinful all the people who accept something in addition to the invested sum, without any distinction.[149] This false interpretation passed from the canonists to the canon law:

> *so, it is clear, without any doubt, that it is mainly on the incorrect interpretation of the Word of God (Luke 6), that the papal law and the whole canonical tradition is founded. On the basis of which, it has been concluded that the manifest usurers (as they interpret), those who accept every amount, even the slightest, on top of the borrowed sum, are not to be admitted to the Holy Eucharist and excluded from Christian burial if they died with this sin unconfessed.*[150]

The decretal *Consuluit* is evidence of the transmission of the Gospel's false interpretation into the canon law.

In addition to the decretal *Consuluit*, the jurists analyse another canon that has been victim of an inaccurate interpretation of Scripture: the palea *Ejiciens*. As mentioned in another chapter,[151] a passage falsely attributed to John Chrysostom asserted that since Christ had expelled the merchants from the temple, the merchants could not be pleasing to God, and the Christian must therefore abandon the Church if he wanted to practice business. The jurists object that the palea *Ejiciens* is based on an illogical misunderstanding of the Word of God. The palea condemns the charging of interest per se, without any distinction.

Furthermore, the palea says:

> *he who buys a good and sells it intact and unchanged is a merchant that is expelled from the temple of God. And above all the merchants, the most damned is the usurer. He sells a good received from God* [the time] *and not bought as the merchants do.*[152]

---

148 *Abfertigung*, 146 (D. 5,19,10): "*Verum quia quid in his casibus tenendum sit, ex evangelio Lucae manifeste cognoscitur, in quo dicitur: Date mutuum etc.*".

149 *Abfertigung*, 146.

150 *Abfertigung*, 146: "*Ist derwegen kein zweiffel, dass fürnämlich auff den unrechten Verstand der Wort Christi, Lucae 6. das ganze Paplistich Recht et tota canonistarum factio et traditio, diesorts gegründet seie unnd dass dannenher geschlossen worden, quod usurarij manifesti (hoc est, ut ipsi interpretantur) quicunque aliquid ad minimum ultra sortem ex mutuo qualicunque accipiunt, nec ad communione admittantur altaris, nec Christiana (si in hoc peccato decesserunt) accipiant sepultura etc.*".

151 See before II/2.1.3.

152 *Abfertigung*, 147: "*Qui vero rem comparat, ut integram et immutatam vendendo lucretur, ille est mercator, qui de templo Dei eijcitur. Unde super omnes mercatores, maledictus plus est usurarius. Ipse namque rem datam a Deo vendit, non comparatam, ut Mercator, etc.*".

The jurists conclude on this point that he who follows the canon law should be advised that it is not based on the right interpretation of the Scripture.[153] They do not polemically attack the canonists, as Andreae did. They only ascertain that there were mistakes in the old canon law. In this sense, they demonstrate that they are both humanists and reformers. They look at the old tradition with historical and critical minds but at the same time are solidly based on Scripture. In this way they pinpoint, analyze and remove the mistakes of the old canon law.

1.3.3.2.3 *The Abolition of Justinian's Law Relating to Interest*

In the opinion of the Tübingen jurists, the canonists misunderstood the Gospel and infected the canon law with their wrong interpretation. Then, the canon law transmitted the misinterpretation to Roman law and imperial law. The jurists refer to the medieval opinions in which the canon law's interest prohibition prevails over civil law.[154] Justinian's law allowed loans at interest, but after the conversion of the Roman emperors, the Roman law was made to comply with the papal law. The papal law forbade interest, and for this reason Justinian's legislation could not be applied anymore.

The jurists draw on the gloss to *Quid dicam* (C. 14, q.4, c.11), which reports that no interest may be required according to the civil laws, both because "*the laws do not disdain to imitate the sacred canons*", and because the emperor (Justinian) commanded observation of what was established at the Council of Nicaea (where receiving interest was condemned). Since the emperor Justinian confirmed the statutes of the Council of Nicaea, canonists and legists espoused the view that he meant to waive all the laws regarding interest.[155] Justinian's legislation on interest was therefore abrogated, because the Roman law must comply with the papal law.

On top of that, the jurists refer to the Italian jurist Johannes Petrus de Ferrariis. In his *Practica* (1501), he writes that Justinian meant to agree with the pope and to forbid and admit the same interest the pope forbade and admitted.[156] In the same line, Du Moulin also judges that in matter of interest the Roman law does not contrast with the Gospel and the canon law.[157] Hence, to the jurists it is evident that the canon law influenced the Roman law. The

153 *Abfertigung*, 147.
154 See before III/2.
155 *Abfertigung*, 147-8.
156 *Abfertigung*, 148. J.P. De Ferrarijs, *Practica*, Francoforti ad Moenum, 1570, in forma libelli in actione hypothecaria, n. 4, 379-80.
157 *Abfertigung*, 148-9. C. Du Moulin, *Tractatus*, n. 84, 99.

absolute prohibition of accruing interest entered in the civil law by the abolition of Justinian's regulation of loans at interest.

1.3.3.2.4 *The German Imperial Law*

The civil law legislation on loans at interest was abrogated in virtue of the canon law prohibition against interest. But the condemnation of interest-taking also affected the German imperial law. The jurists notice that the imperial recess (*Reichsabschied*) of 1500 and the imperial policing ordinances (*Reichspolizeiordnungen*) of 1530 and 1548[158] admitted an annuity of 5% and assigned the power to redeem to the seller/debtor and not to the buyer/creditor.[159] Yet in the imperial ordinances these provisions are made in the paragraph entitled: "On usurious contracts" (*Von wücherlichen Contracten*).[160] The purchase of annuities is however not usurious, the jurists claim. Even though it is described under the paragraph on usurious contracts, they assume that is a lawful contract, and that it is considered to be indecorous is due to the authority of the canonists.[161]

---

158 The jurists refer to three different imperial diets and related ordinances. Yet, as it is specified at the end of the text (*Abfertigung*, 167-169), the provisions on the usurious contracts that were discussed are included in the ordinance of 1530 and then repeated in the ordinance of 1548. Both the ordinances refer to the ordinance of 1500, which it does not establish the allowance of 5% annuity. The ordinance of 1500 condemns the usurious contracts and attests that the purchase of income is commonly used. It observes that is dangerous and indicates the necessity of a regulation. See *Augsburger Reichsabscheid* 1500, tit. 32 in Johann Jacob Schmauß, *Neue und vollständigere Sammlung der Reichs-Abschiede, Welche von den Zeiten Kayser Conrads des II. bis jetzo, auf den Teutschen Reichs-Tägen abgefasset worden*, Vol. 2. – Franckfurt am Mayn 1747, 81: "... *Dieweil aber die Widerkäuff allenthalben in den Landen gemein sind und unter dem Schein derselben mancherley Gefäharlichkeit und Unziemlichkeit geübt wird, befehlen wir hiemit unserm verordneten Reichs-Regiment, geben ihnen auch desz hiemit Unser vollkommen Gewalt und Macht, der Widerkäuff halben ziemliche Form, Maasz und Ordnung fürzunehmen und zu machen ...*".

159 *Abfertigung*, 149. M. Weber, *Die Reichspolizeiordnungen von 1530, 1548 und 1577*, 156, RPO 1530, tit. 26, par. 8: "*Und nachdem die widerkauffs gülten allenthalben inn landen gemeyn seind/ so soll hinfürther von dem hundert nit mer dann fünff/ wie gebreuchlich/ gegeben unnd genommen werden. Und hinfürther die verschreibung auff widerkauff/ wie widerkauffs recht beschehen/ was dar über gegeben/ genommen oder gehandelt/ wöllen wir das selbig für wucherlich geacht und gehalten/ und wie obgemelt/ gestrafft werd*". The ordinance of 1548 is more specific on the power to redeem. See M. Weber, *Die Reichspolizeiordnungen von 1530*, 190, RPO 1548, tit. 17, par. 8: "... *und die loßkündigung der gült verschreibung/ auff wider kauff/ wie widerkauffs/ wie widerkauffs recht, bey dem verkauffer/ und nit bey dem kauffer stehn/ unangesehn/ wie dieselbig gült verschreibung gestellt ist ...*".

160 *Romischer Kenserlicher Maiestat*, tit. 26 par. 1, Von wücherlichen Contracten.

161 *Abfertigung*, 150-1.

The reason because this agreement is lawful is that it is commonly practiced: a custom guarantees its lawfulness. The jurists of Tübingen draw on Matthaeus Wesenbeck and the Roman Catholic jurist Tiberio Deciani (1509-1582).[162] Wesenbeck states that: "*nothing forbids the purchase or sale of such an income also with the clause of redemption*".[163] He also reports that other jurists consider the contract to be usual and conventional. Jakob Henrichmann (1482-1561),[164] for instance, in the resolution of a case published in his *Consilia*,[165] writes that the purchase of annuity is practiced throughout Germany.[166] He also points out that if someone might say that an evil custom does not excuse one from committing a sin, as in the gloss in *Denique* (D.4, c.6), one could answer that this case occurs when the custom is illicit – but this is not the case. The argument is expounded in a similar case by Olradus de Ponte (d. ca. 1337), which Henrichmann quotes:

> *the regional custom according to which such contracts are practiced continuously makes this contract stronger and far from suspicion of being illicit.*[167]

And again, quoting Baldus, Henrichman writes:

> *this conclusion affirms that such contract is licit when in the city and in the region, it is frequently used by good and serious men and lawful merchants.*[168]

The purchase of annuity is therefore not a usurious contract, because it is commonly practiced.

---

162 M. Cavina (ed.), *Tiberio Deciani (1509-1582). Alle origini del pensiero giuridico moderno*. Atti del convegno internazionale di studi storici e giuridici, Udine 12-13 aprile 2002, Udine, Forum, 2004; M. Pifferri, *Generalia delictorum. Il Tractatus criminalis di Tiberio Deciani e la "parte generale" di diritto penale*, Milano, Giuffrè, 2006.

163 *Abfertigung*, 151: "*Quod hos reditus emere aut vendere nihil prohibeat, etiam cum pacto de revendendo ...*".

164 J. Franck, *Henrichmann, Jakob* in *Allgemeine Deutsche Biographie* 11 (1880), 782-783 (accessed 19.05.2016); http://www.deutsche-biographie.de/pnd116393378.html?anchor=adb.

165 J. Henrichmann, *Consiliorum sive responsorum iuris* [...] *tomus primus*, Dilingae, 1566, Consilium VI, 130.

166 *Abfertigung*, 152.

167 *Abfertigung*, 152-3: "*Corroborat etiam contractum ipsum et ab omni suspicione illiciti reddit alienum, ipsius regionis consuetudo, secundum quam tales contractus continuo celebrantur ...*". J. Henrichmann, *Consiliorum*, 131.

168 *Abfertigung*, 153: "*... hanc conclusionem assert, quod contractus sit licitus, quando in civitate et regione frequenter exerceatur per bonos et graves viros et legales mercatores*". J. Henrichmann, *Consiliorum*, 131.

Tiberio Deciani also advocates the lawfulness of the purchase of annuity. In his *Responsa* he writes: "*if someone makes a contract that is commonly considered to be licit by all, but it is not, he is not said for this reason to be committing usury*".[169] In addition, Deciani writes that in some regions the custom of using this contract is considered to be licit by the canon lawyers. The canon law he refers to is substantially two bulls of Martin V (1369-1431) and Callixtus III (1373-1458) that approve this contract (*Extrav. Com.* 3,5,1 and 3,5,2).[170] Indeed, Martin V in 1425 and Callixtus III in 1455 had admitted the lawfulness of the annuity on real estates and recognized that it was a widespread contract.[171] The canon law recognized the custom of using that contract.

In short, a false interpretation of Scripture was inserted in the canon law. The canon law, in turn, contaminated the civil law and the imperial law. In the imperial law the word '*usura/Wucher*' is used, but not to condemn the sale of annuity. The purchase of annuity is perfectly legal, because it is commonly practiced with the consent of the most qualified jurists and approved by two papal bulls. The reconstruction of the Tübingen jurists reinforces what Andreae said in his sermons.

1.3.3.3 The Redeemability After a Certain Period of Time

The contract practiced in Regensburg was also characterized by a clause of redemption with a fixed time limit. In the agreement it is not explicitly stated whether the power to redeem is assigned to the seller or to the buyer, but the parties agreed that the contract is not perpetual but ends after a certain period of time (*nicht eines ewigen Kauffs, sonder nur auff ettlich gewisse Jar*). The defense of the five ministers asserted that this term was usurious, insinuating that the two aforementioned papal bulls of Martin V and Callixtus III inspired Charles V's ordinances, especially with regard to the power to redeem. To safeguard the position of the seller/entrepreneur, the pope attributed to him an exclusive and undetermined power to redeem. In the imperial ordinance as well, the power to redeem is assigned only to the will or action of the seller, so that if the buyer/investor wants the redemption, he must nonetheless absolutely gain accord with the seller, otherwise the agreement is 'dishonourable, wrong and

169 *Abfertigung*, 153: "*... si quis faciat aliquem contractum, qui communiter ab omnibus habeatur pro licito, licet in veritate esset illicitus, ex hoc non propterea dicitur usuram committere ...*". T. Deciani, *Responsorvm D. Tiberii Deciani* [...] *volumen primum*, Venetiis, 1602, Responsum 2, n. 80, 27.

170 *Abfertigung*, 154.

171 J.T. Noonan Jr., *The Scholastic Analysis of Usury*, 160; P. Vismara, *Oltre l'usura*, 53.

criminal' (*ein unzimlich pactum und demnach unrecht unnd sträfflich*).[172] Such an addition, in the opinion of the ministers, was derived from the papal bulls.[173]

To reinforce this claim, the ministers, or most likely their lawyers, remember that the jurist Andreas von Gail (1526-1587),[174] who quotes the Spanish canon lawyer Diego de Covarrubias,[175] sustains this idea. Both Gail and Covarrubias condemn the purchase of annuity when a clause of redemption is placed in favour of the buyer. Gail points out that the contract is usurious when the capital has not been sold for an uncertain time, but by the decision of the buyer/investor it was established that the capital must be returned, and the annuity redeemed at certain time: this agreement would not be a sale but a loan.[176]

The Tübingen jurists defend the redeemability after a certain period of time. They believe that if the parties have fixed a date for the end of the loan, this does not make the contract usurious, because there is no explicit provision in favour of the buyer. Three motivations bear this statement. First, as the aforementioned jurist Jakob Henrichmann reports, this form of agreement is commonly practiced in the whole of Germany. Second, the redeemability after a certain period of time does not provoke the unlawfulness of the contract *per se*. Tiberio Deciani (who is talking about the power to redeem in favour of the seller after a certain period of time) writes that it is not against the law that such a clause does not consider the free and absolute will of the seller/entrepreneur, but can be exercised only after a certain period of time.[177] He explains that if I can buy an annuity lawfully, much more I can rebuy an annuity after a certain time if there is a just price. The power to redeem is described as the power to re-buy the annuity. The contract is a sale, and the essential point is thus the just price.[178]

Furthermore, Deciani refers to jurists, canonists and theologians. The jurist Andrea Alciato (1492-1550) and the canonist Niccolò Tedeschi, Panormitanus, advocate that the clause alone is not sufficient to declare that the contract

172 *Abfertigung*, 155.

173 *Abfertigung*, 155.

174 K. von Kempis, *Andreas Gail (1526-1587). Zum Leben und Werk eines Juristen der frühen Neuzeit*, Frankfurt a. M., Lang, 1988; C. v. Bar, H.P. Dopffel, *Deutsches Internationales Privatrecht im 16. und 17. Jahrhundert*, vol. 1, Tübingen, Mohr Siebeck, 1995, 85-7.

175 *Abfertigung*, 156.

176 *Abfertigung*, 156. Andreas Gail, *Practicarum observationum* [...] *libri duo*, Coloniae, 1583, lib. 2, obs. 7. n. 14. 270. Although it is not mentioned in the report of the Tübingen jurists, Gail also refers to D. de Soto, *Libri decem de iustitia et iure*, libr. 6, quaest. 5 art. 3, fol. 204b.

177 *Abfertigung*, 157: "*Non obstat (inquiens) quod tale pactum non est collatum in libera et absolutam voluntatem vendentis, sed est limitatum, ut possit redimere, tantum post 12 annos*". T. Deciani, *Responsorvm*, Responsum 2, n. 130-1, 29.

178 *Abfertigung*, 159.

is usurious, but it is necessary that there is a very low price. Theologians as Conrad Summenhart and Juan de Medina also maintain that such a clause is not illicit, but there must be a just price. Deciani concludes then that there is a common opinion of the jurists, canonists and theologians: all agree that the clause per se is not illicit, if there is a just price.[179] The common opinion guarantees the lawfulness of the power to redeem after a certain time. It must be noticed, however, that Deciani discusses the power to redeem in favour of the seller/entrepreneur, which can trigger the clause after a certain time. The Regensburg contract ends after the time elapsed, both if the seller/entrepreneur wishes or not. Hence, Deciani was discussing a very similar case, but not exactly the same.

Third, the aforementioned bull of Martin V does not outlaw the power to redeem the annuity after a certain period of time and consequently neither does the imperial ordinance, by which it was inspired. The Tübingen jurists offer a refined interpretation: at a first glance (*prima facie*), it seems that the bull condemns and deems to be usurious the clause of redemption after a certain time period. But, they observe sharply, this cannot be deducted from the tone used. The pope writes: "*here and always creditors were granted the power and grace to redeem the annuity whenever they wanted*".[180] These words are written in a narrative way and not in a regulatory way (*non dispositive, sed tantum narrative*). This is the crucial point: the words of the pope are included in the report made for the clergy, aristocracy and inhabitants of the places where the contracts are used. They therefore do not have a universal normative content.[181]

On top of that, the jurists maintain that the issue the pope was called to decide had not involved the power to redeem, but only the validity of the real *census* contract. In fact, it had occurred that many people did not want to redeem the annuity and accused the contract of being usurious. The pope responded that the contract in itself is licit; but he did not discuss the temporal limit of the redemption.[182] The jurists conclude then that if the sellers consciously and willingly accept that the redemption can only occur after a certain period of time, nobody can say that this is a usurious contract, as the pope does not say it.[183] The bulls of the popes did not condemn the clause of

179 *Abfertigung*, 159: "*Satis est ergo, quod communis opinio est tam canonistarum, quam iurisconsultorum ac etiam theologorum, tale pactum per se non esse illicitum, dum tamen concurrat iustum precium*". T. Deciani, *Responsorvm*, Responsum 2, n. 135, 29.

180 *Abfertigung*, 159: "*Ibi et semper in contractibus ipsis creditoribus data fuit facultas atque gratia quod ipsum annuum censum, quandocunque vellent, redimere possent*".

181 *Abfertigung*, 159-60.

182 *Abfertigung*, 160.

183 *Abfertigung*, 160-1.

redemption in a certain time (*pactum de redimendo intra certum tempus*). If both the parties agree, the contract can include a clause of redemption actionable only after a certain period of time. The will of the parties is sufficient to modify the agreement. To confirm this interpretation the jurists cite again Deciani:

> *I say that because of the two bulls of Martin V and Callixtus III, it is approved very clearly that the clause of redemption in favour of the seller, even if it is limited to a certain time (12 years), it is however valid.*[184]

Moreover, the clause is licit because there is a custom. Deciani writes that such a clause is practiced in several regions, as the two papal bulls also prove it.[185]

In conclusion, the purchase of an annual income with the power to redeem after a certain period of time is practiced in Germany; a common opinion of jurists, canonists and theologians does not consider this agreement unlawful if there is a just price; the bull of Martin V does not forbid the agreement. The Tübingen jurists hold therefore that the contractual term is lawful. It is worthwhile to observe that the jurists do not clearly respond to the objection raised on redeemability by the buyer. While they prove that redeemability after a certain time is lawful, none of the sources quoted ascertain the lawfulness of the redeemability of the buyer/investor. The contract provides the redeemability after a certain period of time (both for the seller and the buyer), but the sources quoted refer to the redeemability of the seller/entrepreneur limited to a certain time.

1.3.3.4 The Personal Obligation

Another contractual term that the five ecclesiastical ministers criticized was the seller's personal obligation of paying the 5% annuity. The borrower's responsibility in the contract is to return the capital and pay 5% annuity for the duration of the contract. The annuity is not linked up to a specific real estate, but the seller is free to invest the money as he wishes. In the real *census* contract, conversely, the obligation was connected to a specific real estate. This new form of *census* contract had been already discussed among the Catholic moral theologians and approved by most of them.[186] Nonetheless, Pope Pius V

184 *Abfertigung*, 163: "*Dico per extravag. Martini et Calixti clarissime probari, quod pactum de retrovendendo adiectum venditioni annui reditus validum est et admissum et licet sit limitatum ad certum tempus, id est 12 annorum, tamen id quoque valere*". T. Deciani, *Responsorvm*, Responsum 2, n. 146.

185 *Abfertigung*, 163. T. Deciani, *Responsorvm*, Responsum 2, n. 81.

186 J.T. Noonan Jr., *The Scholastic Analysis of Usury*, 231-7.

with the bull *Cum onus* in 1569 established that every *census* should have been constituted on *a fruitful, immobile good, specifically designated to pay the census returns*, otherwise it would have been condemned as a usurious contract. Among the scholastics, the only reason used to condemn this provision was that it was a way of hiding usury.[187]

The Tübingen jurists reply that in the *widerkaufflicher Zins*, the investor never damages the entrepreneur, even if the estates and goods obliged are completely destroyed. On top of that, the generally recognized custom is that the *census* contract is valid also when the subject is not a defined good but a combination of goods, so that it is constituted a personal obligation. The jurists draw on Andreas von Gail, who writes:

> *in every census contract the person is obliged to giving* (*dare*) *and performing* (*facere*) *annually. For that reason, if the real estate, which is accessorily attached to the obligation and to the contract for the best security of the buyer, perishes, the person remains nevertheless obliged to pay the income.*

Gail, the jurists emphasize, states that this opinion is followed by the highest German court, the imperial cameral court (*Reichscammergericht*).[188] Because the imperial cameral court endorses this opinion, the jurists conclude that the *widerkaufflicher Zins* is admissible, even if it creates only a personal obligation to pay a certain amount of money.[189]

The personal obligation to return to the buyer the 5% annuity is then lawful. Notwithstanding the lack of connection between the annuity and a determined productive property, this term does not damage the entrepreneur. This conclusion is the same of the imperial cameral court, the highest judiciary court in Germany. The jurists simply conform to the authoritative opinion of this court.

---

187 I used the translation in J.T. Noonan Jr., *The Scholastic Analysis of Usury*, 237-8.

188 *Abfertigung*, 166: "*Sed generali consuetudine passim, aliter receptum esse, valere scilicet emptionem annui census tam super incertis, quam certis fundis et rebus contractae, adeoque sola obligatione personali constitui posse, testis est Gail d. obs. 7. n. 13. Ubi docet, in huiusmodi emptionibus reddituum personam quotannis dare, facere, teneri. Ideoque perempto fundo, qui ad maiorem emptoris securitatem accessorie in obligationem et contractum venit, personam adhuc ad solutionem reditus obligari* (...). *Et hanc opinionem* (*inquid Gail ibid.*) *Camera sequitur*". A. Gail, *Practicarum observationum* [...] *libri duo*, Antverpiae, 1653, Lib. 2, *Observatio* 7, 290. On the opinion of the imperial cameral court see M. Neumann, *Geschichte des Wuchers*, 551-5. For the importance of this court in matter of business law see A. Amend Traut, *Die Akten und Beilagen von Reichskammergericht und Reichshofrat als Quellen des Handelsrechts*, in *Zeitschrift für neuere Rechtsgeschichte*, 37 (2015), 177-205.

189 *Abfertigung*, 167.

1.3.4 *Conclusion*

The jurists had been requested to address two questions: the existence of a general custom of using the *widerkaufflicher Zins* by every kind of people, and the lawfulness of the *widerkaufflicher Zins*. To answer the question of the custom, the Tübingen jurists focused on two points. First, they demonstrated that the magistrate has the power to intervene and regulate the charging of interest. Second, the magistrate followed the inspiration of Justinian legislation on interest, which is reasonable and not in contradiction of natural equity.

Then, the jurists analysed the three main terms of the contract: the purchase of the annuity, the power to redeem the annuity after a certain period of time, and the personal obligation. The purchase of annuity had been admitted by the two imperial ordinances of 1530 and 1548. Although the ordinances describe this agreement under the title 'On the usurious contracts', many jurists nonetheless attest that it was a lawful custom to use this contract. The error stems from a false interpretation of the Gospel made by the canonists. It entered into the canon law and then Roman law and imperial law. The redeemability after a certain period of time is practiced in Germany; a common opinion of jurists, canonists and theologians does not consider this agreement unlawful if there is a just price; and the bull of Martin V does not forbid the agreement. The personal obligation is also commonly practiced and admitted by the imperial cameral court.

In the part on the custom and the lawfulness of the annuity, the Tübingen jurists drew largely upon theological sources. They demonstrate an understanding of the theological discussion behind the *widerkaufflicher Zins*. The doctrine of interest elaborated in the circle of the Lutheran orthodoxy was received and applied. In addition, the jurists refer to the Calvinist jurist Charles Du Moulin. The Lutheran theologians most likely also read Du Moulin, but they almost never quote him. The jurists cite Du Moulin insistently, together with Lutheran jurists as Wesenbeck and Vuell.

On the other hand, concerning the two additional contractual terms, the work of the jurists was essentially a technical one. They established the lawfulness of the clause of redemption and the personal guaranteed obligation through the reference to customary law, supported by the opinion of qualified jurists and the legal practice in the courts. They cite Gail, Deciani, again Wesenbeck and Du Moulin. In turn, they conjure up humanists and medieval authorities as Alciato, Panormitanus and Olrandus de Ponte. The Tübingen jurists reveal in this way an erudite knowledge of the European legal science. This knowledge goes beyond the confessional membership, because sometimes we see quoted also Catholic theologians and canon lawyers as Summenhart and Covarrubias.

The jurists conclude their counsels by reaffirming the existence of a custom that was rightly in force in Regensburg and of which they determined the legal framework. As Tiberio Deciani writes, a custom operated in many regions on the basis of the aforementioned bulls of Martin V and Callixtus III. And again, Andreas von Gail maintains that the custom about the purchase of annuities was observed regularly. In the city of Regensburg, such a use was not started a few years before but about forty years prior, and therefore it can be said that is a custom, observed as law by the major and more aristocratic part of the population. The civil authority of Regensburg did not impede such behaviour but promoted it. Furthermore, the civil authority did not act against the law and the opinion of the jurists, canonists and theologians, as has been demonstrated.[190]

The Tübingen jurists therefore endorse the civil authority of Regensburg and reject the opinion of the five ecclesiastical ministers. In their words:

> *and it can be concluded with certainty that in Regensburg, the contested interest from loan (which is not only used here but also in many other places of the Empire of the German nation, and no more than 5% is given or taken), which has been contested for many years, is not against the Word of God, the law of nature, the positive law and above all the imperial ordinances and directions, nor against the Christian love, and even less against mercy and equity and therefore such interest can be very well given and taken by Christians with clear conscience.*[191]

The German contract can be lawfully practiced, and the profit granted is not usury. Again, as it was before with Andreae, this is the victory of the practical reasons of economy and politics over Luther's approach towards the prohibition against interest.

190 *Abfertigung*, 163-4.

191 *Abfertigung*, 171: "*... unnd lasst sich beständiglich schliessen, dass die zu Regenspurg nun lange zeit und vil jar gestrittene* usurae ex mutuo (*wie die nicht allein daselbsten, sonder an andern vilen orten im Reich Teutscher Nation gebräuchlich, als da mehr nicht dann fünff vom hundert gegeben und empfangen werden*) *dem Wort Gottes, dem Gesatz der Natur, den Key geschribnen Rechten, und sonderlichen den Reichsabschieden unnd Ordnungen* (...) *noch auch der Christlichen liebe, vil weniger aber aller Erbar und billichheit mit nichten zu wider, und demnach ein solcher Zins von eim Christen mit unverletzem Gewissen, wol möge gegeben und genommen werden*".

1.4 Conclusion

As we have also seen in another chapter,[192] the lawfulness of the *widerkauflicher Zins* was particularly questioned in sixteenth-century Germany. The dispute of Regensburg in 1587 was not isolated, because other similar disputes rose in the same period (as we have seen in Rudolstadt). The result of this dispute was however very influential. Contemporary historians as Lucas Osiander reported it; theologians such as Dedekenn, Hunnius and Gerhard and jurists as Peter Heige and Ernst Cothmann[193] mentioned the dispute or employed the proceedings in their writings.[194] This suggests that the dispute left an important mark in the history of lending at interest.

Besides the impact on the regulation of the German contract, the dispute of Regensburg can be seen as an example of the intense relationship between theologians and jurists. Jacob Andreae and the Tübingen jurists cooperated in settling the dispute. Andreae laid down the basis for the jurists' counsels and the jurists integrated Andreae's sermons. For instance, Andreae explores the biblical roots of the interest prohibition and clarifies the correct interpretation of Scripture. But his work lacks evidence and precision when he deals with the historical account of the alleged canonists' errors and the contamination of Roman law and imperial law. The jurists fill this gap. They provide the necessary references on the transmission of errors from the canon law to the Roman law and the imperial law. Furthermore, Andreae supports his view with a terrific interpretation of Luther's statements about interest. Yet, when he writes about the Justinian legislation on interest, he makes no references. The jurists complete his work and prove the lawfulness of the Roman legislation.

In a way Andreae completes the jurists' work. The excellent portfolio of legal quotations the jurists adduce to show the canon law errors is empty without his interpretation of the Gospel. He demonstrated that the canonists misunderstood the Gospel. Andreae also assured the spiritual legitimation of the emperor to judge in the matter of interest and to placate the consciences. These two aspects are based on a solid interpretation of Scripture, which only an

192 III/2.

193 On Heige and Cothmann see IV/2.

194 For example, the dispute was reported in L. Osiander, *Epitomes historiae ecclesiasticae centuriae XVI, pars altera*, Tubingae, 1603, 1047; G. Dedekenn, *Thesauri consiliorum et decisionum volumen secundum*, 150-1. It is quoted by A. Hunnius, *Commentarius in posteriorem epistolam*, 248; J. Gerhard, *Locorum theologicorum tomus decimus quartus*, 116; P. Heige, *Quaestionum*, 8; E. Cothmann, *Consultationum et responsorum iuris volumen II*, Francofurti, 1662, responsum 52, 19-20.

erudite theologian could make. The jurists completely miss the knowledge and legitimation to interpret the Holy Scripture. Andreae formulated the right teachings on the charging of interest; the jurists provided the legal framework.

Another aspect is important to realise: Andreae and the Tübingen jurists relied on the contribution of other Lutheran theologians. Their arguments are interwoven with the theory of interest put forward by the Lutheran orthodoxy. Andreae's distinction between loans and business lays its foundation in the work of Melanchthon, but also Brenz, Aepinus, Heerbrand, and Schnepf. Concerning the different subjects of lending and making business, Andreae most likely drew on Brenz and Aepinus. His view that there is usury only when one of the parties is damaged shows some similarities with Rhegius' interpretation of usury according to charity. The power of the magistrate to bind consciences in the matter of interest stems not only from Luther's two kingdoms doctrine, but undoubtedly Andreae was also inspired by the writings of Melanchthon and Brenz. Andreae was perfectly aware of the teachings promoted in the milieu of Lutheran orthodoxy, which constitute the background of his analysis.

The ideas ripened in the ambient of the Lutheran orthodoxy also circulated and bloomed among the jurists. Nonetheless, the jurists, more released from dogmatic bounds, also refer to the Calvinist jurist Du Moulin. This attitude is typical of the Lutheran jurists, as we will see again in the next chapter. The jurists quote Brenz to support the power of the Regensburg magistrate to accept as a custom the matter of interest. Peter a Vuell criticizes the canon lawyers' teachings on usury and interest with arguments likely suggested from Rhegius and Aepinus. Rhegius had previously advocated the necessity of interpreting the passage of Luke 6,35 in the light of charity. Aepinus designed the three categories of people that are the subject of donations, loans and business. Hence, Andreae and the Tübingen jurists' writings are impregnated with the Lutheran theory of interest. It lies behind the sentences, backs the arguments and provides the skeleton of the discourse.

In the end, the dispute of Regensburg reveals a profound relation between theologians and jurists. In the Christian society, the theologians need the jurists, and the jurists need the theologians. Theologians describe the spiritual end of actions. Jurists display the social effects. Theologians look at human salvation. Jurists look at social order. Theologians guarantee moral lawfulness; jurists establish juridical lawfulness. Together they mould norms for the religious growth and the human cohesion. Paraphrasing Berman, we might say that without the spiritual significance, people are overcome by despair. Without legal order, people are at the mercy of anarchy.

CHAPTER 2

The Contribution of the Jurists

The admission of the five per cent annuity by the imperial legislation and the new theory of interest developed by the Lutheran theologians were supported in parallel by the work of the jurists. We already glimpsed the jurists' approach in the previous chapter. Now, we concentrate directly on them in order to study their contribution to the elaboration of the new theory of interest. The Lutheran jurists relied on the theologians and implemented their teachings, but they also offered an innovative analysis on the interaction between two different normative orders: the moral and spiritual order governed by the divine law, and the juridical and social order ruled by the civil law. The purpose of this chapter, then, is to understand how the jurists reconciled these two orders.

2.0 Introduction

Benedict Carpzov the Younger (1595-1666),[1] whose enormous influence led the great German historian Stintzing to associate his name with the Italian

1 T. Muther, *Carpzov, Benedict* in *Allgemeine Deutsche Biographie* 4 (1876), 11-20 (accessed 15.09.2017); https://www.deutsche-biographie.de/gnd118667246.html#adbcontent; R. von Stintzing, E. Landsberg, *Geschischte der deutschen Rechtswissenschaft*, II, München, 1884, 55-100; Otto, J., *Carpzov, Benedikt*, in M. Stolleis (ed.), *Juristen. Ein Biographisches Lexikon*, München, C.H. Beck, 1995, 115-6; G. Kleinheyer, *Benedikt Carpzov*, in G. Kleinheyer, J. Schröder (eds.), *Deutsche und Europäische Juristen aus neun Jahrunderten*, 6 ed., Tübingen, Mohr Siebeck, 2017, 92-7; For further references see W. Schild (ed.), *Benedikt Carpzov 1595-1666, Werk und Wirken; Gesammelte Aufsätze, Vorträge und Dissertationen zu Carpzov aus drei Jahrhunderten*, Goldbach, Keip, 1997; G. Jerouschek, W. Schild and W. Gropp (eds.), *Benedict Carpzov: Neue Perspektiven zu einem umstrittenen sächsischen Juristen*, Tübingen, Diskord, 2000; C. von Bar, P. Dopffel (eds.), *Deutsches internationales Privatrecht im 16. und 17. Jahrhundert*, vol. 1, Tübingen, Mohr Siebeck, 1995, 300-3; C. von Bar, P. Dopffel (eds.), *Deutsches internationales Privatrecht im 16. und 17. Jahrhundert*, vol. 2, Mohr Siebeck, Tübingen, 2001, 192-5; M. Lipp, *Das privatrechtliche Wirken Benedikt (II) Carpzovs im Kontext der europäischen Zivilrechtswissenschaft*, in H. Lück, H. de Wall (eds.), *Wittenberg. Ein Zentrum europäischer Rechsgeschichte und Rechtskultur*, Böhlau, Köln, 2006, 245-73; J. Günter, *Carpzov, Benedikt (1595-1666)* in *Handwörterbuch zur deutschen Rechtsgeschichte* (HRG), I, 819-21, www.HRGdigital.de/HRG.carpzov_benedikt_1595_1666 (accessed 21.02.2018).

 | DOI:10.30965/9783657701506_011

Bartolus,[2] was one of the central members of the *Usus Modernus Pandectarum*.[3] In his *Jurisprudentia forensis romano-saxonica* (1638), he began the first definition of the constitution n. XXX, dedicated to loans with moratory interest, with these words:

> *Neither do I want to discuss here whether interest* (usurae) *is licit for the law, nor do I want to repeat what has been written on this topic by Peter Heige and Matthias Coler. It is sufficient to say that moderate interest is today tolerated not only by general custom but also by the imperial law and by the provincial law in the Electorate of Saxony.*[4]

Carpzov avowed that the question about the interest prohibition had now exhausted its dynamism and did not merit further discussion. First, the customary law, the imperial law and the provincial law now tolerated a moderate interest rate. With several provisions issued in the years 1500, 1530, 1548, 1577 and 1586, the imperial law authorized the charging of 5% annuity (*Zins*). Moreover, in Saxony the electoral princes amended the provincial law in 1550,

2 R. von Stintzing, E. Landsberg, *Geschischte*, 61.

3 In general on this movement see the classic studies: F. Wieacker, *Privatrechtsgeschichte der Neuzeit*, 2nd. ed., Göttingen, Vandenhoeck & Ruprecht, 1967, 204-24; G. Wesenberg, G. Wesener, *Neuere deutsche Privatrechtsgeschichte im Rahmen der europäischen Rechtsentwicklung*, Schauenburg, Lahr, 1969, 100-6; A. Söllner, *Die Literatur zum Gemein und partikularen Recht in Deutschland, Österreich, den Niederlanden und der Schweiz*, in H. Coing (ed.), *Handbuch der Quellen und Literatur der nueren europäischen Privatrechtsgeschichte*, II/1, C.H. Beck, München, 1973-77, 501-16; K. Luig, *Einleitung zur Sektion 2: Usus modernus und Dogmengeschichte des Privatrechts*, in D. Simon (ed.), *Akten des 26. Deutschen Rechtshistorikertages, Frankfurt am Main 22. bis 26 September 1986*, Frankfurt am Main, Klostermann, 1987, 233-5; K. Luig, *Usus Modernus*, in *Handwörterbuch zur deutschen Rechtsgeschichte* (*HRG*), vol. V, 1998, 628-36; K. Luig, *Samuel Stryk (1640-1710) und der "Usus modernus pandectarum"*, in M. Stolleis (ed.), *Die Bedeutung der Wörter. Studien zur europäischen Rechtsgeschichte; Festschrift für Sten Gagnér zum 70. Geburtstag*, München, Beck, 1991, 219-35; H.P. Haferkamp, T. Repgen, *Usus modernus pandectarum Römisches Recht, Deutsches Recht und Naturrecht in der Frühen Neuzeit*, Köln, Böhlau, 2007; More bibliography in M. Heger, *Recht im „Alten Reich" – Der Usus modernus*, in *Zeitschrift für das Juristische Studium*, 1/2010, 29-39.

4 B. Carpzov, *Jurisprudentia forensis romano-saxonica*, Lipsiae, 1668, part 2, constit. 30, 677: "*Nolo hic disputare, an jure licitae sint usurae, vel non? Nec repetere lubet ea, quae a Doctores praesertim a* Petr. Heig. part. 2 quaest. 1 et Matth. Coler. de process. execut. part. 1 cap. 10 num. 35 et mult. seqq. *in hanc rem scripta fuere. Sufficiat nosse usuras moderatas hodie non tam consuetudine generali, quam lege imperiali* Recess. Imp. 1500, 1539, 1548, 1577 sub. tit. Von wucherlichen Conträcten etc. in Recess. Wormatiens. de anno 1586. *et in Electoratu Saxoniae iure provinciali in* Const. Mauritii Electoris de anno 1550 tit. Von den Wuchern Costit. Augusti electoris de anno 1555, h. Costit. 30 in fin. de anno 1572 et Ordinat. Torgensi de anno 1583 tit. von Wucher / wucherlichen Conträcten etc. *tolerari*". See also B. Carpzov, cap. 1 n. 28-31. For a survey of the new imperial and provincial law see M. Neuman, *Geschichte des Wuchers in Deutschland bis zur Begründung der heutigen Zinsengesetze (1654)*, Halle, 1865, 539-51.

1555, 1572 and 1583 to authorize the same amount.[5] Second, Carpzov suggested that two jurists, Heige and Coler, had fully examined the problem of the lawfulness of interest-bearing loans so thoroughly that there was nothing he could add. For this reason, then, these two jurists are going to be the main subjects of this chapter. We focus on their works as case studies for the jurists' treatment of the interest prohibition.

Carpzov's statements on the interest prohibition did not conclude here. He also emphasized that the interest (*usurae*) that does not contravene equity is allowed by the divine law (Ex. 22,15; Lev. 25,37; Deut. 23,19; Luke 6,34). Indeed, jurists and theologians together (*pariter*) proved solidly, with reasons from the civil law and the divine law, that the magistrate may delimit the amount of legally charged interest, as much as the lowest interest can be legal, and the most outrageous ones are forbidden. Finally, he recommended that charity towards the neighbour must always be kept in view, and loans at interest cannot be given to the poor and indigent. He conjured up the authority of theologians and jurists as Martin Chemnitz, Aegidius Hunnius, Johannes Gerhard, Charles Du Moulin, Matthias Coler, Peter Heige, Ernst Cothmann and others.[6]

In substance, Carpzov not only referred to the customary law, the civil law and the works of two influential jurists, but also quoted the theologians and sharply adhered to the new theory of interest we have examined before. The charging of interest is not universally forbidden by divine law; the magistrate

5 See *Ordungen Hertzog Ernsten* (...), Dressden, 1597, 40b and 64a.

6 B. Carpzov, *Jurisprudentia forensis*, 677: "*Nec simpliciter iure divino usurae censentur prohibitae; Non certe hae, quae aequitate nituntur, Exod. 22. vers. 15. Levit. 25 vers. 37. Deut. 23 vers. 19. Luc. 6 vers. 34. Ac iamdudum a jurisconsultis pariter atque theologis praestantissimis decisum, atque rationibus ex iure divino et civili firmissimis probatum fuit, posse principem usurarum quantitatem in hac temporum necessitate definire, quam et moderatiores tenere iure possint et improbiores excedere prohibeatur; Ita tamen, ut semper charitatis proximo debitae ratio habenda ac pauperibus et indigentibus pecunia absque ulla usura mutuo danda sit,* Martin Chemnit. in loc. Philip. comm. Aegd. Hunn. in Consil. Theolog. An liceat ultra sortem erogata pecunia accipere pensionem. D.J. Gerh. decad. 8 quaest. polit. 1. Molin. in tract. de usur. n. 86. Heig. et Coler. dict. loc. Ernest Cothm. vol. a. resp. 52 n. 34 et seqq. Ant. Tesaur. decis. 57. Ventur. de Valent. in part. litig. lib. 2 cap. 11 n. 27". M. Chemnitz, *Loci theologici*, pars secunda, de paupertate, caput V, 155-170; A. Hunnius, *Ob und wie viel man* interesse *nehmen soll*, passim; J. Gerhard, *Centuria quaestionum politicarum*, Jenae, 1608, decas octava, quaestio 1; C. Du Moulin, *Tractatus*, n. 86, 102; P. Heige, *Quaestionum iuris tam civilis quam saxonici pars posterior*, Wittebergae, 1630, q. 1, 1ff.; M. Coler, *Tractatus de processibus executivis in causis civilibus et pecuniariis ad practicam fori saxonici passim accommodatus*, editio quarta, Jenae, 1615, cap. X, n. 35 ff, 223ff.; E. Cothmann, *Consultationum*, responsum 52, 15ff.; A. Tesauro (1521-1586), *Novae decisiones sacri senatus Pedemontani*, Augustae Taurinorum, 1609, Decisio LVII, 61b-64a; I.V. Winther (*Ventura de Valentia*), *Parthenius litigiosus sive discorsus politico-iuridicus*, Argentorati, 1628, lib. 2, cap. 11, n. 23?, 565-6.

can set the interest rate; charity towards the neighbour must always be upheld; and loans at interest towards the poor are forbidden. These points are the result of a discussion informed not only by the jurists but also by the theologians. The jurists' analysis alone is not enough to shape the new theory of interest. The interpretation of the divine law is a task for the theologians, on which the jurists necessarily relied. In this chapter, then, we need to understand the contribution of the jurists, but also their relationship with the theologians. We will investigate how the jurists integrated theological solutions in their works.

In the first part we will observe the melding of theological and legal arguments in the works of Coler and Heige. The remaining pages will be devoted to examining the impact of the new theory. We look more in general at the reception of the new theory among other jurists and at some of the consequences. Three main problems will be addressed: the relation between the conservative and progressive streams of thought; the reception of the main features of the new theory; and the effects on the canon law.

2.1 Matthias Coler: A Bold Claim

2.1.1 *Introduction*

Born in Altenburg, Matthias Coler (1530-1587) was initially a student of medicine in Wittenberg. On Melanchthon's advice, he studied canon law and civil law (*utroque iure*) in Leipzig. Following the example of his teachers Modestinus Pistoris (1516-65) and Christoph Zobel (1499-1560), he became a real reformer. After his graduation in 1558, Coler obtained a professorship in Jena and then was member of the court of appeal in Leipzig and Chancellor in Anhalt.[7] In his later work *Tractatus de processibus executivis* (1586), which had several editions before 1657, he treated cases concerning different types of enforcement proceedings. Coler deals with the interest prohibition in chapter 10, which is dedicated to enforcements in pecuniary lawsuits. The reason he touches on this topic is that the contract, the subject matter of a case, was a loan, and the creditor had demanded from the debtor something more than the principal.[8]

---

7 H. Zedler, *Grosses vollständiges Universal-Lexicon aller Wissenschafften und Künste*, vol. 6, Leipzig, 1733, 663; R. von Stintzing, E. Landsberg, *Geschischte*, 571-2; E. Wolf, *Colerus, Matthias* in *Neue Deutsche Biographie* 3 (1957), 320 (accessed 11.12.2016); https://www.deutsche-biographie.de/gnd124644988.html#ndbcontent; W. Wiegand, *Plus petitio*, Berlin, Schweitzer, 1974, 81-4., 85-8, 115-20; C. von Bar, P. Dopffel (eds.), *Deutsches internationales*, vol. 2, 11-3.

8 M. Coler, *Tractatus de processibus*, Jenae, 1615, pars I, cap. X, n. 36, 223. The first edition published in 1586 presents a different numeration, but the content seems to be the same. See

The debtor signed a chirograph,[9] where he committed himself to return the sum of 1000 florins of Saxony, received in loan, *cum omnibus usuris et interesse*.[10] Thus, Colerus wonders whether interest (*usurae*) can be asked in a loan and in which amount (*An usurae peti possint? et in qua quantitate?*).[11]

The answer is articulated in two parts. The first part looks at the defence of the charging of interest in light of the divine law. The charging of interest is a fruit of equality, and this equality is not against the divine law. Indeed, the natural law and Christian charity included in Matth. 7,12 are the essential principles of Christian life and require doing to others what you would have them do to you. The debtor should act as he were in place of the creditor. If he were the creditor, he would expect something in return as gratitude for the money received.[12] Gratitude, then, justifies the payment of interest. Furthermore, the risk of loss is not supported by the debtor alone, because charity spurs the creditor to remit the debt when, in case of unforeseen circumstances, the debtor is not able to pay it off.

The second part considers the civil law. For Coler the civil law never fully condemned the charging of interest. Justinian introduced a limitation of the interest rate, *Eos, qui* (C. 4,32,26) and *Quamvis* (C. 4,32,3), which had never been abrogated. Neither the subsequent emperors, nor the more recent imperial law, the imperial recess (*Reichs Abschied*) of 1500 nor the imperial policing ordinance (*Ordnung von Reformation guter Policey*) of 1548 expressly abrogated it.[13] Justinian's law was also in agreement with the divine law and the opinions of the theologians. These laws constitute then the legal platform for the creditor's claim for the payment of interest, which is an entirely lawful demand.

2.1.2 *Defending Interest-Taking as a Matter of Divine Law*

2.1.2.1 The Reason of Equality

2.1.2.1.1 *Barter and Loan*

In order to show that the divine law does not conflict the civil law that allows a moderate charge of interest on a loan, Coler proposes two arguments. The first

M. Coler, *Tractatus de processibus executivis in causis civilibus et pecuniariis ad practicam fori saxonici passim accommodatus*, Ienae, 1586, 257-370.

9 On this type of credit instrument see R. De Roover, *L'évolution de la lettre de change, XIV*^e^*-XVIII*^e^ *siècles*, Paris, Armand Colin, 1953. On the analysis of the early modern scholastics see W. Decock, *Spanish Scholastics on Money and Credit*, 277-83.

10 M. Coler, *Tractatus de processibus*, 216.

11 M. Coler, *Tractatus de processibus*, n. 36, 223.

12 As seen before, this is a scholastic idea, see S. Piron. *Le devoir de gratitude. Émergence et vogue de la notion d'antidora au XIII*^e^ *siècle*, in D. Quaglioni, G. Todeschini, G.M. Varanini (eds.), *Credito e usura fra teologia, diritto e amministrazione*, 73-101.

13 On these laws see the discussion in III/2 and IV/1.

is quite complex and might be divided into three steps. The first step is not a spiritual one, but a juridical one. As an erudite jurist, Coler starts looking at the common nature of the barter and the loan. Once, he writes, negotiations and contracts were based on the barter, and it was licit for diligent men to increase their patrimony day-by-day, by the further exchange of goods with someone who estimated them for a different value. Later, money replaced the barter, and now the merchant or another can borrow my money and use it for his profit and utility. Yet, the reason of equality (*aequalitatis ratio*) recommends that I be paid for my service with the benefit of a modest part of the profit. This should occur because the substitute (loan) follows the same nature of the thing it substitutes (barter).[14]

Coler's reasoning is founded on the assumption that barter and loan have an identical nature. In the barter, men could exchange unuseful goods for useful goods for a certain time. Then, if today someone lends his unused money, he should receive back something useful in return, because the barter and the loan have the same nature.[15] In other words, Coler argues that the successor of the barter is not the sale, as we might expect, but the loan. In both contracts something unuseful is exchanged for something useful. If in the barter something useful is received in exchange for what is unnecessary, in a loan it should occur the same. The lender gives the money, which is unuseful for him, and in return should receive part of the borrower's profits. The effort to maintain equality between the parties indicates the legitimacy of accruing interest in the form of sharing in the profits.

2.1.2.1.2 *Equality and Gratitude*

This equality that supports profit sharing complies with the divine law and natural law. This is the second step of Coler's reasoning. For example, an industrious merchant receives 100 florins from a loan, and with that he buys goods that he can subsequently sell to get another 100 or 50 florins. If the creditor received 5% on the sum the merchant makes beyond his recovery of the capital,

14 M. Coler, *Tractatus de processibus*, n. 48, 224-5: "*Sicut enim olim negociationes et contractus constituebantur ex permutatione mercium, adeo, quia ex ulteriore deinceps commutatione earum, quas quis sibi comparabat, licebat homini industrio augere de die in diem suum patrimonium, (...), ita postquam in locum permutationis successit nummus, hodie in forma publica cudi consuetus* l. 1 de contrah. empt. [D. 18,1,1] et l. 1. de rer. permut. [D. 19,4,1] *quem videlicet a me mutuo accipit mercator, aut alius, aucupando suum quaestum et utilitatem cum mea pecunia, aequalitatis ratio suadet, beneficium modici alicui lucri mihi pro officio meo retribui, ad hoc ut substitutum sequatur naturam eius, in cuius locum surrogatur*".

15 M. Coler, *Tractatus de processibus*, n. 70, 229.

this complies with the justice of equality, Coler comments.[16] There is no damage, nothing against the divine law and natural law, nothing against charity for the neighbour; rather this is the result of mutual charity. The lender gives a benefit to the borrower freely, and the borrower, without his damage, gives part of his profit to the lender.[17] Coler adopts here the opinion of the French jurist Du Moulin. The payment of part of the profits does not harm the debtor; therefore it is not against the divine law.

This payment, which does not harm the debtor, is suggested by gratitude. To Coler it is not only just, but absolutely in agreement with natural law, that in this case the debtor recognises the good faith of the creditor and is obliged to pay a modest recompense out of gratitude for the amount of profit he obtained as a result of the loan. This recompense would be given as for a certain genre of barter.[18] The debtor should give part of his profits to the creditor because of gratitude for the money received. Indeed, Matthew 7,12 commands that we do to the others what we wish the others do to us. If the debtor were in place of the creditor, he would expect something in return, because his money was used to gain profits. Therefore, he should do for the creditor what he would wish done if their roles were reversed: give part of the profits as a sign of gratitude. Similar to a barter, the creditor receives something in exchange for the use of his money. The debtor, Coler recommends, must not be 'an ingrate cuckoo' and deny what it would be like to be on the opposite side, to be the creditor, because Christ affirms we do to the others what we wish the others would do to us, as this is the fullness of the law and the prophets.[19]

Citing Du Moulin, Coler insists that the creditor should not brook that more is demanded from him than what he would have demanded from the debtor, if he were in the same necessity and the same amount of money had been

16 M. Coler, *Tractatus de processibus*, n. 55, 226.

17 M. Coler, *Tractatus de processibus*, n. 55, 226: "*Hic nihil noxiae, nihil contra ius divinum vel naturae, nihil contra charitatem proximi, sed potius ex mutua charitate geritur: alter beneficium mutui praestat debitori de suo, mutuatarius econtra benefactorem suum, absque omni suo damno, cum exigua parte lucri percepti ex pecunia creditoris, remunerat* Haec Molin. de commerc. post principium n. 10". C. Du Moulin, *Tractatus*, n. 10, 10-2.

18 M. Coler, *Tractatus de processibus*, n. 66-7, 228: "*Ideo non solum non iniquum est, sed iuri naturae maxime conveniens, debitorem isto casu agnoscere bonam fidem et gratitudinis ergo obligari, saltem pro eo, in quo locupletior est factus, ad mediocria ἀντιδωρεά (?) tanquam ad quoddam genus permutationis, suo creditori* (...)".

19 M. Coler, *Tractatus de processibus*, n. 66-7, 228: "(...) *adeo, quia isto casu non debet obligatus esse ingratus cuculus, et denegare id, cuius contrarium ipse postolaturus erat, si creditoris personam repraesentasset* (...) *per illud Christi: Matth. cap. 7 Omnia quaecunque vultis, ut faciant vobis homines, idem et vos illis facite in hoc pendent lex et prophetae*".

helpful.[20] This concession rises from the rule of Christian charity. A couple of elegant quotations help to corroborate this argument. Charity is considered by the famous canonist Hostiensis in his *Summa aurea* as expression of the law of heaven (*ius poli*).[21] And the Italian jurist Johannes Petrus de Ferrariis stresses that the vice of ingratitude 'burns the font of piety'.[22] Actually this is a passage from Bernard of Clairvaux's sermons on the Song of Solomon, where he writes that ingratitude dries up the divine mercy.[23] Ingratitude has moral implication: it is a mortal sin that harms the soul.

To sum up, the sharing of profits between the debtor and the creditor maintains equality and follows the precept of Matt. 7,12. Not only there is no damage for the debtor, but he is obliged to share his profits by gratitude. Indeed, if the debtor were in place of the creditor he would expect something in return, as a sign of gratitude, because his money was used to gain profit. Gratitude then should push the debtor to pay something to the creditor for the use of the money. If he would not do this, he would commit the sin of ingratitude. Thus, gratitude towards the neighbour is the moral foundation of sharing the profits. To the juridical reason (the shared nature of barter and loan), Coler thus adds a spiritual reason: the refusal to share the profits is both a breach of Matthew 7,12 and the sin of ingratitude.

2.1.2.1.3 *The Interest Prohibition and the Aristotelian Argument*

Coler's reasoning might seem convincing, except for the fact that it appears to plainly clash against the interest prohibition. Thus, and this is the third and last step, he strives to prove that the sharing of profits does not contravene the divine law and the Aristotelian argument against lending at interest. Concerning

---

20 M. Coler, *Tractatus de processibus*, n. 67, 228: "*Ac in summa, non debet aegre ferre reus, si ab illo non plus accipiatur, et exigatur, quam ipse a debitore voluisset accipere vel exigere, si is in tali necessitate et peristati constitutus et ipsius beneficio vel pecuniis adiutus fuisset*, prout erudite scriptum relinquit Molineaus in tract. commerc. in praef. num. 10 et idem Molinaeus de commerciu. quaest. 2 n. 71". C. Du Moulin, *Tractatus*, n. 10, 10-2; n. 71, 84.

21 Hostiensis, *Summa aurea*, Venetiis, 1574, Proemium, sub § unde habuit, n. 5, 6: "*Quod tibi vis fieri, mihi fac, quod non tibi, noli / Sic potes in terris vivere iure poli*". The term *ius poli* derives from a letter of Augustine included in the *Decretum*. See: B. Tierney, *The Idea of Natural Rights. Studies on Natural Rights, Natural Law, and Church Law 1150-1625*, Grand Rapids MI, Eerdmans, 2001, 118-30.

22 M. Coler, *Tractatus de processibus*, n. 67, 228: "et tradit Ferrar. in for. lib. pro act. hypothecar. verb. si ne aliqua usurarum. num. 2 *quod vitium ingratitudinis exurit fontem pietatis*". J.P. De Ferrarijs, *Practica*, Genevae 1594, 737.

23 Bernardus, *Sermones super Cantica Canticorum*, Sermon 51, ed. J. LeClercq, 8 vols., Roma, Editiones Cistercienses, 1957, 2, 87: "*Ingratitudo ventus urens, siccans sibi fontem pietatis, rorem misericordiae, fluentae gratiae*".

the divine law, Coler quotes again Du Moulin, who claims that the divine laws do not deny this solution, because they only condemn the payment of interest that oppresses and demeans the neighbour, as in the case of fraud. The divine laws do not condemn the interest on a loan that does not damage or diminish patrimony or disadvantage – the interest that can be given as a result of the acquisition of profit and can be paid.[24] The divine laws concerning the interest prohibition should be read through the precept of Matt. 7,12 and only forbid the interest that harms the neighbour. Coler does not examine this point in detail, but only follows the path traced by Du Moulin. As we are going to see later, Peter Heige instead gives more attention to this issue.

The Aristotelian argument of the sterility of money is similarly contrasted. To Aristotle, it was against the nature of money to bear fruits. Drawing upon Conrad Summenhart, Coler replies this can be said of many things that are not going to bear fruits unless the activity of men supplements them, such as cultivating fields, planting vineyards and tending gardens. Thus, Conrad Summenhart wrote that however great the thing given in a loan is, as for instance money, it is not suitable to bear fruits by itself, but it bears fruits through the additional activity of men.[25]

In conclusion, Coler's first argument to prove that the divine law is not against the civil law allowing a moderate charge of interest is based on three points. First, he observes that the barter and the loan have the same nature, the nature of equality: if I give you something unuseful for me, I need to receive from you something useful. If I give you my money, which now I do not need, I should receive back something I need. The parallel between barter and loan allows Coler to argue that there is an equality that justifies the payment of an interest to the lender.

---

24 M. Coler, *Tractatus de processibus*, n. 68, 229: "*Nec obstant, secundum eum, leges divinae superius allegatae, cum hae eam demum usuram damnent, quae proximum praegravat et exhaurit, ita, ut ipsi fraudi sit, non autem eam, quam mutuum rogans, sine aliquo damno, vel diminutione sui patrimonii, aut facultatum suarum incommodo, sed etiam cum magno earum lucro, et accessione solvere potest*".

25 M. Coler, *Tractatus de processibus*, n. 69, 229: "*Minus adversatur illud Aristotelis, quod contra naturam nummi est, fructificare et nummos parere, cum istud idem de plaerisque rebus nascentibus dici possit, quod videlicet per se et de sui natura non fructificent, nisi accedat industria hominis, colentis agrum, plantantis vineas, hortos et similia. Unde Conradus Sumanhardus in tract. de contractibus scriptum relinquit; quantumvis res mutuo data, puta nummus, per se non sit apta fructificare: tamen, accedente industria hominis, ad fructificandum nata est* Cunrad ubi supra tract. 2 q. 30 in 3 conclus. vers. contra hanc evasionem arguitur tripliciter". C. Summenhart, *De contractibus licitis atque illicitis*, 2, q. 30, concl. 4, 132.

Second, this equality is not against the divine law, but it fully complies with the rule of Matthew 7,12, which is the summary of the divine law. Indeed, the deep reason that pushes the debtor to give to the creditor part of his profits is gratitude. This duty of gratitude is based on Matt. 7,12. Third, a certain behaviour that complies with Matt. 7,12 cannot be defined as a sin. It is by this essential precept that all the laws about interest have to be interpreted. Charging interest is not forbidden, if none of the parties is harmed. Furthermore, the payment of a moderate interest is not against the nature of money, because money can bear fruits with the work of men, as is the case with many other sources of nourishment and comfort.

Though Coler is a jurist, he nonetheless attempts the interpretation of Scripture (with the help of Du Moulin), in combination with the analysis of the civil law. In this way, he provides the luminous evidence that the payment of interest does not contrast with the spirit of the divine law: the love of the neighbour. Although it is called charity, here the meaning attributed to the precept of Matt. 7,12 is equality. Equality among the parties justifies the payment of interest.

2.1.2.2 The Risk of Loss

2.1.2.2.1 *The Remission of Debt*

Coler's second argument to demonstrate that the divine law is not against the civil law's admission of interest regards the issue of risk. An objection often raised against the charging of interest was that creditor's profit would be certain, while for the debtor it remained uncertain. An unforeseen circumstance might occur and limit or destroy debtor's business. Even Luther had made this observation in his first writings on usury and concluded that the payment of *Zins* was unlawful. Coler does not ignore this problem:

> *what is going to happen if for several years unfruitfulness comes upon unexpectedly? What if lightning ruins every fruit, just as we frequently see occur? What if the merchandise is immersed in the surface of the sea, driven about by the waves? What if the businessman is robbed, stripped of his belongings and left alone like a dog?*[26]

26 M. Coler, *Tractatus de processibus*, n. 58, 226: "*Neque vero ignoro, quid proxime dictis objiciatur, lucrum videlicet usurarium, quantulumcumque illud sit, in persona creditoris esse certum, econtra vero lucrum debitoris versari sub incerto, quid enim si magna anni sterilitas incidat? quid, si fulgure prosternantur omnes fruges, prout crebro fieri videmus? quid, si fluctivago mergantur in aequore merces? quid, si negociator in latrones incidat, qui ipsum exutum et spoliatum omnibus rebus, semice [a]nem relinquunt?*".

He answers that some events occur only rarely. Then, the damage or sterility of one year are compensated with fertility and increased fruits in the subsequent years, and the same happens for trade on the sea.[27] Finally, if both the debtor's capital and profit perish, the creditor must recourse to the rule of Christian charity, and the debtor is not only deserving of commiseration, as Proverbs 14 and 19 write, but also the interest must be completely remitted. Indeed Ex. 22,25 affirms: "*if thou lend money to any of my people that is poor by thee, thou shalt not be to him as a usurer, neither shalt thou lay upon him usury*". The remission of interest is also associated with the remission of the principal. Because this event is supported by the family of the creditor, and can result in the indigence of the debtor and his family, Coler says, we also must remit the principal, or the part we can remit, and thus help to raise the debtor from his indigence, as Christ said: lend, hoping for nothing in return (Luke 6,35).[28]

In other words, if the debtor cannot repay the principal and interest, then the creditor must remit both. The creditor must support the same burden as the debtor. This assumption arises from Ex. 22,25 and Luke 6,35, both of which exhort Christians to relieve the neighbour's poverty, requiring the creditor to remit the debt of the poor debtor. It seems evident here that the theologians' interpretation of these passages played a role, even though Coler does not quote any theologian. He adds the decretal *Propter sterilitatem* (X 3,18,3) that commands in lease contracts the remission of the rent in case of sterility of the land. The meaning of this text is extended and applied to the charging of interest in a loan. The creditor shares the risk with the debtor; in case of failure to gain the expected profit, the former should remit the debt in part or in full. In this way, the imbalance of risk is overcome.

Coler states further that the reason underlying this conclusion is that Christian piety and natural law insist that we do to others what we wish them do to us; in this way, "*he that giveth unto the poor shall not lack*" (Prov. 28,27), as

---

27 M. Coler, *Tractatus de processibus*, nn. 58-9, 226.

28 M. Coler, *Tractatus de processibus*, n. 60, 226: "*Denique si contingat sortem perire una cum lucro, quod expectabatur ex parte debitoris, hic iterum ad regulam charitatis Christianae recurrendum est, ut talem debitorem non solum commiseratione dignum esse judicemus* secundum illud proverb. cap. 14 *Honorat Deum, qui miseretur pauperis*, item 19. *Foeneratur domino, qui misericordiam pauperi exhibet, sed eidem etiam in totum remittam usuras, juxta supra dicta: non urgebis pauperem debitorem, quasi exactor, nec usuris opprimes* Exod. 22 cum aliis allegatus et d. c. propter sterilitatem ibi remissio pro rata pensionis facienda [X 3,18,3], *imo, in quantum res familiaris creditoris patitur, et expetit inopia debitoris, eiusque familiae, debemus etiam sortem, aut saltem quantum possumus de sorte remittere, ut eius inopiam sublevemus, iuxta illud Christi: mutuum dantes nihil inde sperantes*".

he can trust that he will likewise be greeted with mercy in times of need.[29] Yet, the poverty that needs to be assisted is the fatal poverty (*de paupertate fatali*), into which the debtor fell without any fault.[30] The Roman rule in *Cunctis* (C. 11,26,1) institutes an examination to verify the people with uncertain beggary (*mendicitas*). Indeed, Coler concludes, the voluntary poverty which derives from prodigality or laziness does not require assistance, and the debtor must be treated as: "*a slothful man* [*who*] *hideth his hand in his bosom, and will not so much as bring it to his mouth again*" (Prov. 19,24); because of his sloth, "*so shall poverty come as a marauder, and want as an armed man*" (Prov. 6,11).

2.1.2.2.2 *Advantages and Losses*

The risk the debtor supports is compensated by the remission of debt in the case of subsequent poverty. This argument does not only work to disentangle the issue of risk, but it also helps to defend the charging of interest. Coler contends that the opposite conclusion – a gratuitous loan, where the debtor benefits while the creditor suffers loss – would be against justice.[31] For instance, he wonders, if someone manages to scrape together a certain amount of money by inheritance, fortune or honourable works during his youth, and due to misfortune, or because of his senility, he cannot seek a more abundant sustenance – or if he were an orphan – would he commit a sin against natural law by lending his money without interest?[32]

Lending at interest would then be necessary to avoid a sin, because advantaging the neighbour with proper loss is against natural law. Coler does not ignore the injunction that property must be used to assist the poor, but, he says, the charging of interest does not conflict with what has been said by Solomon in Prov. 5,16-17: "*let thy fountains be dispersed abroad and let them be only thine*

---

29 M. Coler, *Tractatus de processibus*, n. 60, 226: "*Quod et pietas Christiana ac ius naturae superius allegatum flagitat, ut videlicet quaecunque nobis fieri volumus, eadem faciamus et aliis. Qui enim dat pauperi, non indigebit* Solom. cap. 28".

30 M. Coler, *Tractatus de processibus*, n. 60, 226: "*Quod ipsum tamen de paupertate fatali, in quam absque culpa sua praecipitatur reus, non autem de voluntaria, quae ex prodigalitate vel desidia veint, accipiatur de qua legitur* Proverb. cap. 19 *abscondit piger manus in sinum, nec ad os quidem admovet* et in l. 1 C. de validis mendit. [C. 11,26,1] *Illis enim* (ut idem Salomon cap. 5 inquit) *ceu viator veniet inopia, et obruet eos paupertas ut latro*".

31 M. Coler, *Tractatus de processibus*, n. 60, 227: "*Deinde ex adverso cogitemus, quanta sit injuria, benefacere proximo, cum detrimento ipsius creditoris*".

32 M. Coler, *Tractatus de processibus*, n. 60, 227: "*Pone enim, quod quis ex haereditate paterna, vel beneficio fortunae, et honestis laboribus iuventutis, aliquantulum corrasit pecuniae, et ob adversam valetudinem, vel etiam ratione senectutis, ex operibus manuum suarum victum amplius quaerere impeditur: aut finge, pupillum esse: nonne is peccaret in legem naturae, si mutuo det proximo sine usuris?*".

own". This formulation had been used before by Melanchthon and other theologians to mean that property must be oriented to assist the poor.[33] To Coler, the payment of interest is not against this view of property, because in Prov. 5,10 it is commanded, "*lest strangers be filled with thy wealth; and thy labours be in the house of a stranger*"; and for this reason, Paul in 2 Cor. 8,13 wrote that you would not pursue a life of ease at the others' affliction, but that with your wealth you should assist his indigence.[34] In brief, property must be used to help the neighbour, but without impoverishing oneself.

As seen before in the theologians' works, these passages concern the relation between property and alms. They set out the duty of the Christians to consider first their own necessities and only secondarily the neighbour's needs. Coler explains it with an example. If a person owns the capital but cannot work, he does not commit a sin if he lends his money at interest. If this payment were unjust, the elderly who cannot work anymore and similar categories of people would not lend their money, but they would just keep it safe at home. But they also need to eat and so, day-by-day, the money would diminish until the whole amount is gone, and they will be forced to beg, as in Luke 16: "*what shall I do? For my lord taketh away from me the stewardship. I cannot dig; to beg I am ashamed*".[35]

In conclusion, in order to solve the problem of risk of loss due to unexpected events (not resulting from the laziness of or excessive prodigality of the debtor), Coler advocates for the remission of debt. The risk should be shared between the creditor and the debtor. It does not belong only to the debtor, because the creditor should remit the debt – the sum he gave plus the interest – if the debtor suffers unforeseen negative circumstances. Charity, as an effective promotion of the debtor inspired by Luke 6,35 and other biblical passages, determines this solution.

At the same time, this solution also guarantees the payment of part of the debtor's profits to the creditor. Indeed, without this payment, the creditor would give an advantage to the debtor, with his loss. Scripture commands that the Christian helps the neighbour without losses for him (Prov. 5,10, 16-17; 2 Cor. 8,13). It is a precept of justice that imposes that in parallel to the share of

---

33 P. Melanchthon, *Philosophiae moralis epitomes libri duo*, in CR XVI, 155.

34 M. Coler, *Tractatus de processibus*, n. 60, 227: "(…) *nonne impingeret adversus illud Salomonis* cap. 5. *Fontes tui deriventur foras et tu dominus ipsorum maneto. Item ibidem iubet ita misericordiam exhiberi proximo, ne nobis desit, et forsan extranei proventibus nostris et labores nostri pristini sint in domo aliena* d. cap. 5 *Ideo divus Paulus scriptum relinquit* in 2. epist. ad Corinth. cap. 8. *Non ut aliis sit relaxatio vobis autem angustia, sed ut vestra copia illorum succurrat inopiae*".

35 M. Coler, *Tractatus de processibus*, n. 60, 227.

risk, there must also be the share of profits. Otherwise, the creditor would be impoverished and the debtor enriched. Behind the lines, we can notice that Coler's reasoning lays on a theological structure given by the interpretation of certain scriptural passages. Even though the Lutheran theologians are never directly quoted here, it seems difficult to deny their contribution in providing at least the skeleton of the discourse.

2.1.3 *The Law of Justinian*

2.1.3.1 A Repudiated Law

Having established that the charging of a moderate interest in a loan is not against the divine law, Coler shifts to the civil law. His thesis is that Justinian's law admitting the payment of interest kept the divine law and has never been abrogated. This law constitutes the legal platform for the right to claim interest, which was Coler's goal. As seen before, the case he was dealing with regarded a chirograph concerning a loan at interest, and he argued on behalf of the creditor's entitlement to the interest.

Coler begins his reasoning with a brief summary of the traditional opinion: by virtue of the divine law and canon law, theologians, legists and canonists all agree that the creditor cannot have an action for the interest, except in case of delay (moratory interest).[36] Indeed, the common opinion followed by the contemporary jurists is that the imperial laws also forbid every kind of interest (*usurae*), save the annuities in the purchase of annuities with power to redeem, admitted by the recent imperial law (*Reichs Abschieden zu Augsburg*, 1548). The old laws admitting the payment of interest in a loan, *Quamvis* (C. 4,32,3) and *Eos, qui* (C. 4,32,26), had been abrogated by the law *Cunctos*[37] (C. 1,1,1) and the norms in *De ecclesiasticis titulis* (Nov. 131,1; Auth. 9,6), where the subjects of the empire were commanded to live 'the religion of the Gospel', one of the precepts of which is to lend, hoping for nothing in return.[38] In addition, *Novissime* (C. 5,37 ante leg. 1; Nov. 72,6-8) stipulated that the guardians of the orphans were no longer allowed to loan the money of the orphans at interest.[39] Thus, for the traditional opinion, as we also saw before, the civil law does not admit charging interest, because it submits to the canon law.

In particular, this opinion was also held by a great Lutheran jurist, Hieronymus Schurpf[40] (1481-1554), to whom Coler refers. We need to spend a

36 M. Coler, *Tractatus de processibus*, n. 43, 224.
37 About this passage see L. Waelkens, *Amne Adverso*, 68-9.
38 M. Coler, *Tractatus de processibus*, n. 44-5, 224.
39 M. Coler, *Tractatus de processibus*, n. 46, 224.
40 On Schurpf's biography see C. von Bar, P. Dopffel (eds.), *Deutsches internationales*, vol. 1, 14-5.

few words on this author, because his opinion represented a potential obstacle to the emergence of the new theory. Schurpf was not only a gifted jurist, but also a close friend of Luther and Melanchthon, and an active reformer.[41] In his collection of juridical counsels,[42] *Consilia seu responsa iuris* (1564), counsel n. 3, he deals with the interest prohibition. He contends that interest-bearing loans are generally forbidden by the divine law, natural law, canon law and civil law. Even though the charging of interest was admitted by certain Roman laws, he writes, 'the very Christian Justinian' (*Christianissimus Iustinianus*) abrogated them. By the norms included in *De ecclesiasticis titulis* (Nov. 131,1; Auth. 9,6), Justinian ordered his subjects to observe the provisions of the four main councils: Nicaea (325), Constantinople (381), Ephesus (431) and Chalcedon (451).[43] At the first council, the charging of interest was forbidden (D. 47, c. 2) and so the following civil law derogated from previous laws admitting the payment of interest.[44]

Schurpf also points out that the civil law did not have the power to permit loans at interest, because the interest prohibition was founded on the divine law, and the civil law is inferior to the divine law.[45] Schurpf's conservative view was quoted by the five ministers of Regensburg to support their claims. In short, Schurpf believed that Justinian's laws admitting the payment of interest had been abrogated by the subsequent Christian emperors, who obeyed the dictates of the Christian councils. Besides, they would not have the power to allow charging of interest, because human law is inferior to divine law. Therefore, no law admitting the payment of interest was in force.

---

41 On Schurpf's involvement with the Reformation and on his friendship with Luther see J. Witte Jr., *Law and Protestantism*, 67-68; H. Berman, *Law and Revolution II*, 422, nt. 32. On the relationship with Melanchthon, see for instance C. Strohm, *Ethik im frühen Calvinismus*, 220.

42 On this type of literature see U. Falk, *Consilia. Studien zur Praxis der Rechtsgutachten in der frühen Neuzeit*, Frankfurt am Main, Klostermann, 2006; For further references see H. Gehrke, *Konsilien, Konsiliensammlungen*, in *Handwörterbuch zur deutschen Rechtsgeschichte* (HRG) www.HRGdigital.de/HRG.konsilien_konsiliensammlungen (accessed 25.09.2017), vol. III, 117-21.

43 H. Schurpf, *Consiliorum seu responsorum iuris centuria secunda*, Francofordiae ad Moenum, 1564, cons. III, 23: "*Hodie tamen per d. titul 1 de ecclesia civil. colla. 9* [N. 131,1; A. 96] *sunt etiam de iure civili prohibitae, ubi Christianissimus Iustinianus mandat quatuor concilia principalia, Nicaenum, scilicet Constantinopolitanum, Ephesinum, et Calcedonense servari*".

44 H. Schurpf, *Consiliorum*, 23: "*Sed in concilio primo, Niceno scilicet usurae fuerunt prohibite d. c. quoniam 46 distinct* [D. 47, c. 2] *Et sic posterius ius civile derogat omnibus prioribus legibus usuras permittentibus*".

45 H. Schurpf, *Consiliorum*, 23.

2.1.3.2 Reversing Schurpf's Opinion

Coler does not agree at all with his Lutheran colleague. He rebuts bluntly that the law allowing interest did not contrast with the divine law and has never been abrogated. To prove this statement, he looks at the origins of Justinian's law and at the reasons that led to the false idea of an abrogation. The Roman emperors, he writes, considered that it was impossible to avert commerce between men, and that without money commerce could not be practiced. At the same time, they saw that loans were like taxes that reduced the party who had to pay them to extreme poverty. Among these two evils, they judged to choose the lesser and thus the more tolerable. By *Quamvis* (C. 4,32,3) they permitted not only charging interest on a loan, but also demanding payment of interest in court. Furthermore, in order to prevent the neighbour from being ruined by the payment of interest, they established a certain mode and amount of interest that was licit with *Eos, qui* (C. 4,32,26). Over that amount, the stipulation or claim for interest was unlawful. In this way, Coler continues, the emperors subjected the authoritative statements of the Old and the New Testament setting the interest-taking prohibition to the rule of charity and natural law, which dictates: whatever you would like another do to you, do so to another.[46] The Roman emperors did not issue a law against the divine law, but they subordinated the precepts of the Old Testament and New Testament banning loans at interest to the rule of Christian charity and natural law, Matt. 7,12. The emperors limited the interest rate to prevent the neighbour from being harmed by the payment of interest. Here Coler follows again the French Calvinist Du Moulin, who also held that Justinian's law observes the precept of Matt. 7,12.

Since the civil law of interest is not against the divine law, Coler goes a step further and claims that *Eos, qui* and *Quamvis* have never been abrogated. The usual thesis, he says, is that these provisions had been abrogated by the newest law of the *Authenticum* (*per ius novissimum authenticorum*), especially by the norms included in *De ecclesiasticis titulis* (N. 131,1; A. 9,6). However, this thesis is

46 M. Coler, *Tractatus de processibus*, n. 47, 224: "*Caeterum, quicquid huius sit, divi imperatores, habito respectu ad commercia hominum, quibus in hac societate humana carere non possumus, et, quae absque pecuniis paratis exerceri nequeunt, quia videbant mutuationes eius temporis esse tales exactiones, per quas pars mutuo accipiens plane redigebatur ad extremam paupertatem, et ex duobus malis minus et tolerabilius eligendum iudicabant, usuras pro mutuo non tam in stipulatum deduci, quam etiam exigi recte posse permiserunt* l. quamvis 3. C. de usur. [C. 4,32,3] *Et ne proximus exhauriretur per istud lucrum, quod exigitur ultra sortem, certum modum et quantitatem praefiniverunt, ultra quam usuras vel stipulari vel exigere non liceret* l. eo 26 C. de usur. [C. 4,32,26] *restringendo videlicet dicta veteris et novi Testamenti, prohibentia usuras, ad regulam charitatis et iuris naturae, dictantis: quicquid vultis, ut faciant vobis homines, idem et illis praestate*, Matth. 7, prout testatur Molin. in tract. commerc. quaest. 2 num. 71". C. Du Moulin, *Tractatus*, n. 71, 84.

not proved. In this last law it is decreed that the ecclesiastical rules of the four councils of Nicaea (325), Constantinople (381), Ephesus (431) and Chalcedon (451) should be observed. But this law was promulgated principally to conserve and defend the articles of faith and Christian doctrine against the errors of Nestorius, Eutyches and similar heretics, which were condemned in the mentioned councils. Coler avers that the emperor did not intend to overturn or overthrow the laws of contract, 'devised with so much attention for the conservation of the political state'.[47] Even the provisions of *Novissime* (C. 5,37 ante leg. 1; Nov. 72,6-8) were not touched. The emperors did not intend to abolish integrally the interest that helps to support orphans, but only to take care to secure their guardians from loss. Indeed, the guardians who admitted to lending the orphans' money at interest had to refund to the children the interest with their money, as it is established in *Si pecuniam* (C. 5,56,3).[48] Coler rejects the traditional position neatly here. The norms in *De ecclesiasticis titulis* were not issued to derogate from all the provisions on usury and interest, but to defend the Church against the opinions of some heretics. Hence, the content of these norms has nothing to do with loans at interest. The emperors did not want to intervene on these pecuniary laws, which have therefore not been abrogated.

The other objection expressed by Schurpf was that the emperors could not authorize the charging of interest, because they did not have the power to modify the divine law. It is undoubted, Coler replies, that an imperial law cannot negate a divine law, because human law is inferior to the divine law.[49] Nonetheless, the prince can limit the divine law for a cause of public utility or other cause, as the canonist Felinus Sandaeus affirms;[50] Rochus Curtius

47 M. Coler, *Tractatus de processibus*, n. 71, 229: "*Quod autem de sublatis usuris per ius novissimum authenticorum, maxime per rub. de ecclesiast. titul.* § 1 coll. 9 [N. 131,1; A. 9,6] *obiicitur, id ibidem non probatur. Etsi namque eo in loco praecipitur, servari regulas ecclesiasticas quatuor synodorum, Nicenae, Constantinopolitanae, Ephesinae et Calcedonensis: tamen illa constitutio promulgabatur principaliter ad conservandum et propugnandum articulos fidei et doctrinae Christianae, contra errorem Nestorii, Eutychis, et similium haereticorum, in dictis conciliis damnatorum, non autem intelligitur, leges contractuum, pro conservando statu politico multis vigiliis excogitatas, per hoc evertere, vel labefactare voluisse, prout in simili loquitur Imperator* in l. si quando 35. C. de inoff. testam. [C. 3,28,35] et ita solvit Bald. in l. cunctos populos. 1 num. 3 C. de summ. trin.". Baldus de Ubaldis, *In primum, secundum et tertium codicis librum*, Venetiis, 1599, in l. *Cunctos*, C. 1,1,1, num. 3, in *Commentaria omnia von Baldus de Ubaldis*, ed. Keip Verlag, vol. 5, 2004, 5b.

48 M. Coler, *Tractatus de processibus*, n. 72, 230.

49 M. Coler, *Tractatus de processibus*, n. 74, 230.

50 M. Coler, *Tractatus de processibus*, n. 75, 230: "... *tamen potest princeps leges divinas, ex causa utilitatis publicae, vel aliter, restringere ac limitare*, prout late Felin. in d c. quae in ecclesiarum". F. Sandaeus, *In quinquem libros decretalium commentaria*, Lugduni, 1535, in X. 1,2,7, n. 2, 23.

(d. 1495) likewise extends the permission to a statute or custom.[51] Therefore, he who objects to the ordinance of the magistrate shows disobedience to God and is said to be a rebel, according to Paul in Rom. 13.[52] Coler exploits the opinions of Sandaeus and Curtius to argue that the laws of interest, *Quamvis* (C. 4,32,3) and *Eos, qui* (C. 4,32,26), only restricted the divine law, but did not go against it. For this reason, the emperors held the power: they did not change the divine law, but only renegotiated its limits, fixing a certain amount of interest that is licit.

2.1.3.3 The New Imperial Law and the Theologians' Approval

The civil laws permitting the payment of interest in a loan, *Quamvis* (C. 4,32,8) and *Eos, qui* (C. 4,32,26), have never been abrogated. Yet, the imperial recess (*Reichs Abschied*) of 1500 and the imperial policing ordinance (*Ordnung von Reformation guter Policey*) of 1548 in the section about usurious contracts (*Von Wucherlichen Contracten*), which we saw before, introduced new provisions and allowed a five per cent annuity in the *widerkaufflicher Zins*. To Coler these laws did not abrogate the previous legislation. If the new imperial laws are inspected and examined more acutely, he argues, it is possible to see that they never clearly state that the 5% interest is forbidden or that *Eos, qui* and *Quamvis* are expressly abrogated.[53] In other words, the new law does not interfere with the previous law.

An objection that might be raised is that the new imperial provisions only grant the charging of annuities in the purchase of annuities with clause of redemption (*widerkaufflicher Zins*), and consequently all other forms of interest must be considered forbidden. Coler replies that a correction of the law cannot be determined from an argument *a contrario*, but certainly in case of doubt,

---

51 M. Coler, *Tractatus de processibus*, n. 76, 230: "*Imo, quod etiam statutum vel consuetudo, restringes ius divinum ex legitima causa, publicae videlicet utilitatis, valeat, testatur Rochus Curt.* in c. cum tanto sect. 1. n. 19 et sect. 2 n. 6 et 8 extra de consuet. ". R. Curtius, *Enarrationes in celeberrimum iuris cap. cum tanto*, Lugduni, 1550, sectio I, n. 19, 25; sectio II, n. 6 et 8, 29b–30.

52 M. Coler, *Tractatus de processibus*, n. 76, 230: "*… adeo, ut, qui deinceps tali ordinationi magistratus resistit, Deo ipsi inobedientiam exhibere, et rebellis esse dicatur, secundum Paulum Rom. 13*".

53 M. Coler, *Tractatus de processibus*, n. 77, 230: "*Ac, si quis dicat: per istas solutiones, nondum esse dissolutum saltem eum nodum, quo constringuntur ex ordinationibus imperii* in den gemeinen Reichs Abschieden/ *tales usurarii, quae cum novissimum ius sint, merito derogant omnibus prioribus (…) replicatur: si penitius constitutiones imperii introspiciamus et examinemus, nusquam clare et in terminis exprimi, quod usurae quincunces prohibeantur, aut quod nominatim fuerint abrogatae* l. eos 26. [C. 4,32,26] l. quamvis 8 C. de usur. [C. 4,32,8]".

when the previous law does not clearly seem to be abrogated, the amendment of law is not to be presumed.[54] The amendment of law must be explicitly stated both in canon law and civil law, Coler continues, as *Expediat* (VI 1,6,29) and *Si quando* (C. 3,28,35) confirm. Thus, in the absence of an explicit statement, the Roman law granting permission to charge interest cannot be said to have been abrogated or amended.

The Roman laws *Quamvis* (C. 4,32,8) and *Eos, qui* (C. 4,32,26) have never been abrogated, even by the most recent law. One last point, though, needs to be examined. The interpretation of the divine law is a task of the theologians and not the jurists. Coler does not ignore this problem,[55] and recurs directly to the highest authority in the theological field: Martin Luther. This conclusion is validated, he stresses, by 'the purer restorer of the doctrine in this Church', Martin Luther, who in the admonition *An die Pfarrherrn, wider den Wucher zu predigen* (1540), does not only approve the regulation of interest made by the emperor Justinian in *Eos, qui*, but also adds that the emperor's amendments can help avoid the old, severe, and difficult usurary burden: "*so I am gladly willing to agree with it and to help carry the burden for the sake of God especially where there are indigent people and an interest out of need or an interest out of mercy*".

This passage is exactly the same that will be examined at the dispute of Regensburg in 1587 (Coler publishes his book one year before in 1586). For Coler, Luther does not stop condemning usury, but reached this new view by abandoning the canonists' opinions with which he was initially imbued, and observing that in this life, mostly in this case, not everything can exactly be demanded according to the divine rules, because of the necessities of men.[56]

---

54 M. Coler, *Tractatus de processibus*, n. 78-79, 231: "*Ac si dicatur, non fieri ibi mentionem, nisi unius usurae permissae, puta quincuncis, in uno videlicet casu tantum, reemptionis nempe perpetuae, (…), adeoque per consequens omnes alias usuras intelligi prohibitas respondetur: correctionem iuris non induci per argumentum a contrario sensu (…) Ac certe, quod in dubio, quando videlicet non expresse apparet derogatum esse praecedentibus legibus, correctio iurium non praesumatur, habetur ad hoc apertus tex.* in c. cum expediat. de elect. in 6. [VI 1,6,29] et l. si quando 35 C. de inoff. testam [C. 3,28,35]".

55 M. Coler, *Tractatus de processibus*, n. 91, 235.

56 M. Coler, *Tractatus de processibus*, n. 98, 236: "*Pro qua conclusione non parum facit, quod purioris doctrinae in his ecclesiis restaurator D. Lutherus, bonae memoriae, in 7. Tomo Jenensis literae, recedens in hic a canonistis, quorum opinionibus ab initio fuerat imbutus, quamvis usura damnare non cessat, tamen, quia animadvertit, in hac vita, isto praesertim casu, non praecise omnia ad amussim regulae divinae, propter necessitates hominum, exigi posse (…) moderationem illam usurarum, factam per imperatore Justinianum in* l. eos 26. C. de usuris [C. 4,32,26] *non modo non improbat, sed addit*: Kan diese Messigung des Keysers/ zu Abwendung des alten/harten/schweren/wucherlichen Lastes dienen/ so wil ich gerne mitstimmen/ und helffen tragen vor Gott/ sonderlich/ wo es dürfftige personen/

Coler also carefully specifies that Luther's opinion is followed by 'the healthier judgments' of the theologians with great authority.[57] In demonstrating that the opinion of the theologians is taken into consideration, Coler does not go into details but appeals to the supreme authority, Martin Luther, who praises Justinian's legislation. Luther's blessing is the final confirmation that the civil law can be applied.

In conclusion, the laws admitting the payment of moderate interest for a loan, Justinian's *Eos, qui* and *Quamvis*, have never been abrogated. To Coler the emperor did not change the divine law, but only restricted it to its essential rule: Matthew 7,12. The new imperial provisions of 1500 and 1548 set the amount at 5% of the lent sum, but do not explicitly overturn the previous legislation. For this reason, the concession of a moderate interest in a loan can be lawfully claimed. Furthermore, this old law is approved by Luther, which guarantees that this law is not against the interest prohibition and can be lawfully applied.

In this way, Coler reached his aim. He proved that the civil law allowing the payment of a moderate interest is not against the divine law and had never been abrogated. This is a more extended result than many of the theologians'; indeed, they mostly focused on the purchase of annuities. Coler defended the bold claim that interest (*usurae*) on a loan can be lawfully required from the beginning of the contract. This is the complete reversal of the interest prohibition as canonists and Roman Catholic theologians conceived it.

2.2 Peter Heige: Reading the Law with the Eyes of Charity

2.2.1 *Introduction*

The second protagonist of the new theory of interest indicated by Carpzov is Peter Heige. Peter Heige (1559-1599) was born in Stralsund, studied at the universities of Helmstedt and Basel, and received a doctorate in civil law and canon law (*in utroque iure*). From 1584 on, he was a professor of law and assessor at the *Hofgericht* in Wittenberg. One of his major works, the *Quaestiones iuris tam civilis quam saxonici* was published posthumously in 1601 and was included in the index of condemned books.[58] In the first question of the

---

und ein Nothwucher oder barmhertziger Wucher were". M. Luther, *An die Pfarrherrn*, in WA 51, 373.

57 M. Coler, *Tractatus de processibus*, n. 98, 236.

58 M. Adami, *Vitae Germanorum iureconsultorum et politicorum*, Heidelberg, 1620, 339-40; J.H. Zedler, *Grosses vollständiges Universal-Lexicon aller Wissenschafften und Künste*, v. 12, Leipzig, 1735, 1144ff.; A.R. von Eisenhart, *Heige, Peter* in *Allgemeine Deutsche Biographie*,

Quaestiones, Heige investigates whether charging interest is lawful by divine and human law and whether the new provincial law admitting five per cent interest (*usurae*) without the necessity of proving the loss (*quod interest*) is just.[59] He writes that not only it is custom in these lands (Saxony) to ask and receive a five per cent interest, but also that after Justinian's law this is approved by the provincial laws.

The provincial laws Heige deals with are very probably the same quoted earlier by Carpzov, but he does not present an accurate list. Rather, in his work he refers to the *Ausschreiben* of the *Kurfürst* August of Saxony (1526-1586), issued on 8 May 1583.[60] With this law, the electoral prince of Saxony authorized *Zins* in the amount of 5%, but recommended the use of Christian charity (*Christliche Liebe*). The neighbour shall not be harmed, and in case of need, no advantage must be taken, and the neighbour must be assisted[61]. In particular, when the debtor has not enough goods to satisfy the creditor, he must only return the principal and not the *Zins*. Furthermore, the law remembers that Christian charity must be applied towards the poor and the indigent. He who demands the *Zins* from them shall answer for his action in front of God.[62] This law essentially put into practice the new theory of interest and is a vivid example of its influence. Heige's analysis is intended to defend this law and others permitting the charging of interest. Indeed he explains that there are some who still doubt the justice of these laws, and therefore it is worth seeing if there are reasons that support this conclusion.[63]

Heige follows a general path and does not investigate any specific contracts. Rather he focuses on the lawfulness of interest (*usurae*). Heige starts with a brief survey of the opinion that loans at interest are fundamentally condemned. He adduces scriptural passages as they were interpreted by Church Fathers, Councils, scholastic theologians and canonists, but also by Lutheran

11 (1880), 307 f. (accessed 14.09.2017): https://www.deutsche-biographie.de/gnd100290469.html#adbcontent.

59 P. Heige, *Quaestionum iuris tam civilis quam saxonici pars posterior*, q. 1, 1: "*Usurae an iure divino vel humano licitae et proinde iustane sit constitutio provincialis, quae absque probatione eius, quod interest, quincunciales usuras exigi permittit*". Disappointingly, here Heige only refers to the provincial law in a very general way and does not mention any specific law.

60 *Chur-Fürst Augusti Ausschreiben*, Torgau, 8 Maj. Anno 1583, in J.C. Lünig, *Codex Augusteus*, Leipzig, 1724, 137ff. See for instance P. Heige, *Quaestionum*, 28.

61 *Chur-Fürst Augusti Ausschreiben*, 142.

62 *Chur-Fürst Augusti Ausschreiben*, 144.

63 P. Heige, *Quaestionum*, 6.

theologians such as Martin Luther, Philip Melanchthon, Leonhard Culman[64] (1497-1562) and Niels Hemmingsen, and Reformed authors like Benedict Aretius (1522-1574) and Wolfgang Musculus (1497-1563). Then, he mentions the five ministers at the dispute of Regensburg. Finally, Heige alludes to the Roman emperors and the Greek philosophers who condemned taking interest.[65] For all these authorities the charging of interest is forbidden *per se*, absolutely. Yet, Heige rejects this view and holds that charging interest is not forbidden in general; what is forbidden is excess in the profit demanded, an evil behaviour that harms the neighbour.[66] Usury then corresponds not to a general prohibition of lending at interest, but to the abuse in the charging of interest. The concept of 'usury' tends to assume a meaning similar to the current one: not a prohibition of lending for profit, but a prohibition of the abuse of lending.

Heige's discourse might be divided into three virtual parts. First, he offers an interpretation of the divine law in line with his thesis. Then, he looks at the provincial law to give evidence that this fulfils the divine law. Finally, he explains how the provincial law must be enforced. The enforcement of human law requires particular diligence in order to avoid breaching the divine law. In doing this, we will see that the contribution of the theologians is incorporated in Heige's teachings. He employs not only the writings of the Lutheran theologians but also those of the Reformed theologians.

2.2.2 *Reinterpreting the Divine Law*

2.2.2.1 The Permission to Charge Interest on Loans to Foreigners

As previously noted, Heige's essential thesis is that the charging of interest is not forbidden *per se* and absolutely, but it is only the damage to the neighbour that is forbidden. The sin is not in charging interest, but in offending the neighbour. The demonstration of this thesis is entrusted to three arguments. The first one, which we see in this paragraph, is based on the reading of Deut. 23,20, where God allowed the Jews to charge interest from the pagans.[67] Heige is a jurist, but tries to interpret Scripture, with the help of the theologians. He

---

64 J. Hartmann, *Culmann, Leonhard*, in *Allgemeine Deutsche Biographie*, 4 (1876), 639 (accessed 25.01.2018) https://www.deutsche-biographie.de/pnd118638572.html#adbcontent.

65 P. Heige, *Quaestionum*, 1-10.

66 P. Heige, *Quaestionum*, 11-2.

67 On the prohibition among the Jews and its Christian reception see E. Klingenberg, *Das israelitische Zinsverbot in Torah, Mišnah und Talmud*, Mainz, Akademie der Wissenschaften und der Literatur, 1977; E. Otto, *Gerechtigkeit und Erbamen im Recht des Alten Testaments und seiner christlichen Rezeption*, in E. Otto, *Kontinuum und Proprium: Studien zur Sozial- und Rechtsgeschichte des Alten Orients und des Alten Testaments*, Wiesbaden, Harrassowitz, 1996, 342-57.

holds that interest is of that genre of things that are not *per se* and plainly sins.[68] In Deut. 23,20 God permitted the Jews to charge interest when loaning to foreigners, but forbade that interest be charged to a Jew, because they were brethren. To Heige, God would have never allowed the Jews to require interest if that were a sin. What constitutes a sin is never permitted, even for a good end. God is indeed the Lord of both Jews and pagans (Rom. 3) and commanded His people to abstain from all evil (1 Thess. 5,22).[69] What is forbidden is always forbidden in every time and place. An evil action can never become good because of favourable circumstances.[70]

In Heige's view, the prohibition from loaning at interest to other Jews is not enacted because this was a sin; indeed, God allowed charging interest towards the outsiders, and He would have never permitted a sin, even towards the pagans. When an action is evil in itself, it remains evil even if there is a good reason or condition. Therefore, if God really meant to forbid the charging of interest He would have forbidden it in the case of both Jews and pagans. Heige borrows this solution from the *Ethices christianae libri tres* (1579) of the French moral theologian Lambert Daneau (1530-1595).

The motivations for the permission of Deut. 23,20 remain however difficult to explain, and several hypotheses were advanced. Heige remembers that among the scholastics the passage of Deut. 23,20 was interpreted in the sense that the permission was justified because of the war against the foreigners.[71] He refers to the canonist Diego de Covarrubias, but the theologians Summenhart, De Medina and others also used this interpretation. They assumed that lending at interest was admitted against war enemies, so that it could not be called a 'proper interest' (*usurae propriae*) but rather 'just taxes' (*iustae exactiones*)[72]. Heige rejects this interpretation and adopts the interpretation of François Hotman (1524-1590).[73] To Hotman, God would have never

---

68 P. Heige, *Quaestionum*, 12: "*Esse autem usuram, per se consideratam, ex eo genere rerum, quae per se et ἁπλῶς peccata non sunt, ex sequentibus constare potest*".

69 P. Heige, *Quaestionum*, 12: "*Principio enim ex Deut. c. 23 v. 20 liquet Dominum permisisse ab extraneo usuram capere, utcunque a fratre Judaeo vetitum esset: quod ille certe non fecisset, si usura per se peccatum esset. Nam quae per se peccata sunt, non permittit Dominus, etiam ad finem bonum. Rom. 3. 1 Thess. 5,22, Danae. Ethic. lib. 1 c. 9. fol. 39. lib. 2 c.16 fol. 282b. sed omnino, omnique loco, tempore et omnibus vetat et fieri prohibet, Danae Ethic. Christia. lib. 2 c. 15*". L. Daneau, *Ethices christianae libri tres*, Genevae, 1579, lib. 1, cap. 9, 38-39; lib. 2, cap. 16, 282; lib. 2 c. 15.

70 P. Heige, *Quaestionum*, 12.

71 D. Covarruvias, *Variarum ex iure pontificio, regio et caesareo resolutionum*, Venetiis, 1566, lib. 3, c. 1, n. 7, 703-4.

72 D. Covarruvias, *Variarum*, lib. 3, c. 1, n. 7, 704.

73 P. Heige, *Quaestionum*, 12.

permitted something against natural law. The Jews can charge the foreigners interest because the Jews could not receive money by gratuitous loans from them, as the foreigners asked the Jews to pay interest. The other populations did not have the Mosaic law that forbade charging interest among citizens and so imposed harsh fees on the Jews. As a consequence, the Jews were permitted to loan to them at interest.[74]

Regardless, the real motivation for the permission is not decisive for Heige. He concludes that, whatsoever cause justified the permission, it appears clear that in the Jewish community, charging interest on loans to foreigners was tolerated. This is evidence, therefore, that lending at interest is just and lawful according to the divine law.[75] This thesis was also sustained by the Lutheran theologian Niels Hemmingsen, to whom Heige refers. Lending at interest does not constitute the sin of usury. The sin of usury is in the additional behaviour of the usurers who are greedy and idolatrous and burden the debtor with the payment of interest against the precept of love. Hemmingsen added that it is in accordance with the Jews' permission to lend at interest to outsiders that the so-called spoil of the Egyptians (*Spolia Aegiptiorum*) – namely the authorized theft of the Egyptians' goods before the Exodus – occurred, because the stolen goods were the salary for the manual labour to which they had been subjected during the slavery in Egypt.[76]

In conclusion, looking at the Scripture and drawing on the works of the Reformed theologian Daneau, the Reformed jurist Hotman and the Lutheran Hemmingsen, Heige maintains that charging interest is not a sin *per se*. Indeed, in Deut. 23,20 God allowed the Jews to charge the pagans interest, and He would have never condoned a sin. Lending at interest is therefore not a sin, universally forbidden, but it is forbidden only in particular circumstances, such as when the Jews lent to other Jews.

2.2.2.2 *Tarbith* and *Neshek*

The charging of interest is not universally forbidden; when, then, is it forbidden? Heige's answer is that the charging of interest is forbidden when the

74 F. Hotman, *De usuris*, 140.

75 P. Heige, *Quaestionum*, 13: "*Atque utut se res habeat, et quaecunque tandem causa hujus permissionis fuerit, satis apparet, ex eo colligi potest: usuram in extraneis et alienis a Republica Israelitarum (…) tolerari atque ita casum dari, in quo usura iusta et legitima sit, etiam secundum divinam legem*".

76 P. Heige, *Quaestionum*, 13: "*Neque contra haec objici possunt spolia Aegiptiorum, cum ea fuerint stipendia pro durissimis laboribus, quae cum negarent Aegyptii, Dominus, ut supremus judex, ea mutuo accepta ab Aegyptijs auferri pracipit*". N. Hemmingsen, *Enchiridion theologicum*, 407.

neighbour is harmed. To come to this conclusion, Heige delves into the etymological analysis of the word 'interest' (*usura*) in Scripture. Again, Heige is not a theologian, but nonetheless ventures into the exegesis of the biblical text. In the Scripture, he notes, different terms designate 'interest'. Interest is called *Tarbith* (תַּרְבִּית), which means an 'increment' as in Lev. 25,36; interest is also called *Neshek* (נֶשֶׁךְ), which derives from the root נשך that means 'to bite', as is used in Deut. 23,19 (20), Ex. 22,25 and Psalm 15,5. Finally, the word 'interest' is found in Psalm 72,14: *mit·tō·wḵ* (מִתּוֹךְ), which means 'oppression'.

Heige observes that in several biblical passages – Lev. 25,36; Prov. 28,8; Ez. 18,8, 13 and 22,2 – the terms *Neshek* (bite) and *Tarbith* (increment) are used jointly.[77] These passages forbid the 'increment' that is connected with the 'bite' (*morsus*) against the neighbour.[78] Thus, he concludes that the conjunction of these two words shows that it is not the charging of interest in itself that the Scripture means to forbid, but only the damage to the neighbour. To confirm this interpretation, he specifies that in addition to the word *Neshek* (נֶשֶׁךְ) is sometimes mentioned the word נֹשֶׁא, which derives from the root נשא that means to lend on interest and to be a creditor, a tax collector and a usurer, as in Isaiah 24,2, Jer. 15,10 and 1 Sam. 22,2. All these terms unify the meaning of creditor and usurer. The usurer is a creditor, notes Heige, because typically the charging of interest is not damned, and the epithet of usurer is not negative.[79]

This interpretation of the Scripture can only be satisfying if the passages are interpreted jointly. It is difficult to remove every doubt, Heige explains, except when one passage is explained with the other. Hence, the 'increment that bites' is condemned and not an increment or interest *per se*. The pressure or bite that is added (*adiunctam pressuram et morsum*) is reproached, Heige avers, because the Scripture is one cohesive unit.[80] The whole Scripture is linked together in a coordinated (copulative) way, and the disparate passages are meant to be understood by mutual interpretation. This interpretation reveals that the increment or the payment of interest that 'bites' is forbidden, but not the increment in itself. This is the crucial point: it is only the added oppression and bite that are condemned. To Heige, in Scripture the use of the word 'interest' is associated with oppression or damage for the neighbour. This word is always used

---

77 Please note that this etymology is now debated. Currently, the word נשך correspond to two different etymologies: 'interest' and 'to bite'.

78 P. Heige, *Quaestionum*, 24-5.

79 P. Heige, *Quaestionum*, 24.

80 P. Heige, *Quaestionum*, 25: "*Vix est, ut per huiusmodi interpretationem dubitatio omnis tollatur, nisi dixeris, unum locum per alterum explicari, et illam tantum abundantiam, quae mordet, improbari, et ita non per se abundatiam aut usuram, sed illi adiunctam pressuram et morsum, reprehendi, quod Scriptura tota sit una copulativa*".

to mean an increment conjoined with damage. Usury is therefore forbidden for the damage suffered by the neighbour, but charging interest in itself is not forbidden.

The Scripture does not condemn the increment, but only condemns the increment that harms the neighbour, repeats Heige:

> *certainly nobody ignores that the following are the two main precepts of the divine law: that before everything we love God and the neighbour as ourself, and this law about interest is similarly suitable to pertain to the appendix of this last precept. Wherefore when it is forbidden to give money at interest, this means that we must not do anything in that business against the charity and the love that we owe our neighbour or, put differently, that we do not harm him for the sake of our profit.*[81]

Heige assumes that the law of interest is a sort of appendix to the precept to love the neighbour. In this way, the prohibition against lending at interest means that we should not breach the law of charity towards the neighbour and harm him because of our profit. The use of the terms in the Scripture is not casual but corresponds to a logic that is completed in the precept of charity. Such an interpretation is not integrally new, but can be found in other works, as for instance in Rhegius and Du Moulin, who wrote before Heige. Furthermore, Gerhard writes after Heige and follows this interpretation in his *Loci*, while in the *Centuria quaestionum politicarum*, he explicitly quotes Heige.[82]

Heige's interpretation is also reinforced by two references: the French jurist Hugues Doneau[83] (1527-1591) and the Danish Lutheran theologian Niels Hemmingsen. In his treatise on interest, Doneau holds the opinion that the charging of interest that does not damage the neighbour is licit. Similarly, Hemmingsen holds that lending money at interest is not *per se* a sin, but it

81 P. Heige, *Quaestionum*, 25: "*Certe duo esse legis divinae summa capita, nemo ignorat: videlicet, ut supra omnes res DEUM amemus et proximum, tanquam nos ipsos: et ad hujus posterioris praecepti appendicem, hanc de usuris legem pertinere similiter convenit. Quapropter cum pecunia proximo ad usuram dari prohibetur, hoc significari intelligitur, ne quid in ea re adversus charitatem et dilectionem, proximo debitam, faciamus: sive ne illi, lucri nostri causa, noceamus*".

82 J. Gerhard, *Locorum theologicorum tomus decimus quartus*, 108-10; J. Gerhard, *Centuria*, decas octava, q. 1.

83 K. Stapelfeldt, J. Schröder, *Hugo Donellus*, in G. Kleinheyer, J. Schröder (eds.), *Deutsche und Europäische Juristen aus neun Jahrhunderten*. 6 ed., Tübingen, Mohr Siebeck, 2017, 118-21; E. Holthöfer, *Doneau, Hugues*, in M. Stolleis (ed.), *Juristen, Ein biographisches Lexicon, Von der Antike bis zum 20. Jahrundert*, München, C.H. Beck, 1995, 182. About his theory of interest see C. Gamba, *Licita usura*, 235-48.

becomes a sin if the creditor acts with usurious intentions, is mean and idolatrous, and the neighbour is oppressed in violation of charity.[84]

On the whole, Heige maintains that Scripture is fulfilled by Christ's commandment of charity. Consequently, the charging of interest is only forbidden when the neighbour is harmed. Damaging the neighbour is prohibited, and for this reason Scripture uses the term 'to bite', together with the term 'interest'. Scripture is conceived as a coherent system, where all corresponds to the law of charity, and the adoption of the two words jointly confirms this argument.

2.2.2.3 Using and Abusing

To bear out the thesis that the charging of interest is not banned in general, but it is only the harmful behaviour which is prohibited, Heige sketches out a final argument founded on biblical exegesis. The divine law does not forbid contracts and negotiations between men. The divine law clearly makes them firm, and it is only because of the added frauds and deceptions that men are condemned. Heige suggests that in 1 Thess. 4,6 Paul openly admonishes that in business no one shall oppress or take advantage of his brother, because neither thieves, nor covetous, nor rapacious people shall possess the kingdom of God (1 Cor. 6,10).[85] Contracts and transactions are not forbidden in the Scripture; swindling and other evil behaviours are forbidden. The use of contracts is not forbidden, but only the abuse of contracts.

Contracts are not forbidden in general, but only the abuse of contracts in particular cases. In a pledge, says Heige, there is a difference between a rich man and a poor man: what is just for the rich is not just for the poor, as in Deut. 24,12 it is stated: "*and if the man be poor, thou shalt not sleep with his pledge*". The creditor is allowed to keep the pledge of the rich, but he has to return the pledge of the poor. Besides, the sale of real estates is permitted but parties have to comply with justice. Following the works of the Roman historian Flavius Josephus *Antiquitates iudaicae* (Antiquities of the Jews) and Joachim

---

84 P. Heige, *Quaestionum*, 25; H. Doneau, *In titulum de usuris in pandectis et sequentem commentarius*, Lugduni, 1558, c. 2, 47-52; N. Hemmingsen, *Enchiridion theologicum*, 407.

85 P. Heige, *Quaestionum*, 25: "*Argumento sit, quod contractus et negotiationes inter homines lex divina nullibi prohibeat sed manifeste stabiliat, et tantum propter adiunctas fraudes et imposturas homines damnet et aperte quidem* Paulus 1 Thessalon. 4, v. 6 *monet, ne quis opprimat, aut circumveniat in negocio fratrem suum: quia neque fures, neque avari, neque rapaces, regnum Dei possidebunt 1 Corinth 6, v. 10.*".

Stephani's *De iurisdictione judaeorum, graecorum, romanorum et ecclesiasticorum* (1599),[86] Heige quotes Lev. 25,15:

> *according to the number of years after the Jubilee thou shalt buy from thy neighbor, and according unto the number of years of the fruits he shall sell unto thee*; and Lev. 25,50: *and he shall reckon with him that bought him from the year that he was sold to him unto the Year of Jubilee; and the price of his sale shall be according unto the number of years, according to the time of a hired servant shall it be with him.*

Again, 1 Kings 9,11 and 1 Kings, 10,28-29 are examples of transactions carried out by the King Solomon;[87] and a profitable transaction, without offence for the neighbour, is also recommended in the Gospel, in the parable of the talents, reported in Matt. 25,20, 22 and 27 (and similarly Luke 19,13, 16 and 23 and Rom. 13,7-8).

These passages impose conditions on the validity of contracts, but do not forbid them. It is the abuse of contracts that is forbidden, but not the use. The same is true for the charging of interest, sustains Heige: the charging of interest is not forbidden, but only its abuse. To Heige, the 'added qualities' (*ad qualitates adiunctas respiciendum*) must be taken into account. The argument is that the Scripture simply forbids some other 'added qualities': we can rightly charge interest except when the conscience is offended.[88] The charging of interest is not forbidden *per se*, but only in conjunction with the 'added quality' of an evil behaviour, such as fraud.

Heige finds again examples in Scripture. Christ forbids judging and swearing (Matt. 7,1), and none of his disciples can be called 'master' (Matt. 23,8). However, he comments, by doing this, imposed judgments, oaths and degrees of disciplines and doctrines are never forbidden, but the abuse of things that are lawful *per se* is reproached, as Paul condemns the custom to dispute before judgements (Matt. 5,24, 1 Cor. 6,1ff.).[89] To Heige, the Scripture always sus-

86 J. Stephani, *Libri quatuor de iurisdictione judaeorum, graecorum, romanorum et ecclesiasticorum*, Francofurti, 1661, l. 3, cap. 10, 177.

87 He uses a particular way to quote the Scripture diffused in Eastern Christian Church. For instance, he writes 3 Kings 9,11 and Paralipomen 2,8,1. The Holy Fathers called the third and fourth books of Kings but for the Hebrews they correspond to the first and second book, as we now find them. Paralipomen is the Greek name for the book of Chronicles. It is possible that Heige found these quotations in an Eastern Church Father's book.

88 P. Heige, *Quaestionum*, 26: "*Esse praeterea in proposito exemplo usurarum ad qualitates adiunctas respiciendum, illud argumento sit, quod nonnulla alia simpliciter scriptura prohibet, quibus tamen, salva conscientia, recte utimur*".

89 P. Heige, *Quaestionum*, 26: "*Ita enim prohibet Salvator iudicare, et iurare: item, ne se quisquam ex suis Patrem aut Doctorem, vocari permittat: in quo tamen nequaquam iudicia*

tains the gravity of interest-taking, and in this it can especially be noticed 'the oblivion of charity' that is due to the neighbour as a work of mercy and eagerness for the benevolence towards the oppressed (*studia benignitatis erga oppressos*).[90] The prohibition against lending at interest has as its inherent concern the lack of charity towards the neighbour, as if Scripture wanted to forbid the offences against charity.

Then, Heige carries on, Christ added to those all passages 'a very beautiful rule' (*pulcherrimam regulam*): do to others what you would have them do to you – by which all the passages of the Scripture where interest is damned became clearer:[91] Ex. 22,21ff.; Ex. 22,52; Lev. 25,35ff.; Deut. 23,19-20; Deut. 28,11 and 43; Ezra 5,3ff.; Psalm 15,2-5; Prov. 13,22; 18,8, 20, 27; Prov. 29,13; Isaiah 58,3, 6-7, 9-10; Jeremiah 17,1, 9, 11; Ezek. 18,5, 7, 12-13, 16-17 and Ezek. 22,7, 12; Matthew 7,12; Luke 6,30, 34-36. In Heige's view, Scripture must be read in the light of charity. In this way it is clear that the all the biblical passages concerning interest never forbids its *use*, but always its *abuse*, because this violates the injunction of charity toward the neighbour. With this interpretation Heige proves again his knowledge of Scripture. He is a jurist, but before engaging with the civil law, he seeks to explore the profound meaning of Scripture.

The passages of Luke 6,30 and Luke 6,34-36 (where it is stated *lending hoping for nothing in return*), require a more detailed elucidation. Heige explicates that others remarked that in the passage of Luke, Christ does not discuss charging interest, but in these passages, He admonished that if charity towards the neighbour requires it, we fully remit the debt of the neighbour. Here, Heige asks the assistance of the Bruges jurist Jacques de Corte,[92] *Curtius*, (1505-1567) who writes that Christ in this passage invites us not to avert our eyes from our brother but to give freely, even if we do not receive anything back, as it is also indicated in Matthew 5,24 and Deut. 15,2-3,7.[93] These passages illustrate

---

aut iuramenta ἔπακτα, gradus item disciplinarum et doctrinae prohibentur, sed abusus rerum, per se licitarum taxatur, quomodo et Paulus Apostolus *litigandi in iudiciis consuetudinem in suis damnat* Matthaei 5 v. 24. c. 7 v. 1. c. 23 v. 8 et seq. Paul 1 Corinth 6. v. 1 et seqq.".

90 P. Heige, *Quaestionum*, 27: "(…) *de foenoris gravitate semper Scripturam conqueri videmus, atque in eo praecipue notari oblivionem charitatis, proximo debitae, ad opera misericordiae, studia benignitatis erga oppressos*".

91 P. Heige, *Quaestionum*, 27: "*Denique a Salvatore nostro et Interprete optimo λόγῳ istis omnibus pulcherrimam regulam adjici: ut quaecunque volumus, ut faciant nobis homines, eadem et nos illis faciamus: quae omnia, collatis scripturae locis, ubi usura damnatur, fient illustriora* …".

92 On this jurist see E.I. Strubbe, *Jacobus Curtius Brugensis, hellenist en jurist uit de zestiende eeuw*, in *Anamnheie. Gedenkboek E.A. Leemans*, Brugge, 1970. See also *The History of Leuven's Faculty of Law*, Brugge, Die Keure professional publishing, 2014, 58.

93 P. Heige, *Quaestionum*, 27: "*Et de hoc postremo*, apud Lucam *loco, alii annotarunt, in eo de usura nihil tradi: imo praecipiunt mutuam pecuniam, si charitas seu dilectio proximi exigat,*

a vision also shared by some theologians: in Luke 6,34-36 Christ is not talking about the charging of interest for profit, but he is talking about the poor. Yet, Heige does not quote any theologians, opting instead for the jurist of Bruges, *Curtius, vir exquisitae doctrinae*.[94]

From all these passages, Heige comes to the conclusion that it is clear enough that this denial of interest is not a moral law but a political law, and requiring the payment of interest is not forbidden absolutely (ἁπλῶς), but only when charity towards the neighbour is violated.[95] It was not a moral law, always valid, but a political law, applicable only for certain periods and circumstances, as it was for the Jews. These examples confirm that Scripture does not universally forbid transactions and contracts, but requires the parties to keep certain rules that protect the neighbour from offences. The same is true for the charging of interest. It is not forbidden *per se* but in view of an additional quality, the potential damage. The abuse of interest is forbidden and not the use of interest. This interpretation pivots on the coherency of Scripture, which prohibits the abuse of several activities that normally would be licit. Again Heige plays the part of a theologian and dives into biblical interpretation.

2.2.3 *Defending the Civil Law*

2.2.3.1 Compliance with the Divine Law

For Heige, the interest prohibition must be read through the eyes of charity. The following stage is then to give evidence that the civil law does not provide anything against charity. He avers that the purpose of the divine law is charity, and all our actions are to be recalled to charity. Thus, if it is not set at an unjust rate (but at a reasonable 5%), neither charging nor paying interest is contrary to the divine law.[96] Charity is the best moderator of all actions (*optima est actionum omnium moderatrix*), and this also applies to the charging of interest.[97]

---

debitori omnino ut condonemus, quod et Curt. d. lib. 3. q. 29. *innuere voluit: invitat autem ibi praecipue Dominus suos ad beneficentiam, ne a fratre oculos avertamus, libenter demus, etiamsi nihil simus recepturi, quod et traditur* Matthaei 5. v. 24 Deuteron. 15, v. 2.3.7. et seq.". See J. de Corte, *Coniecturarum, sive variarum iuris civilis quaestionum explicatarum* [...] *libri tres*, Hanoviae, 1605, book 3, chapter 29, 296-7.

94 Rivier, *Curtius, Jakob*, in *Allgemeine Deutsche Biographie* 4 (1876), 649-50 (accessed 22.09.2017); https://www.deutsche-biographie.de/gnd119646277.html#adbcontent.

95 P. Heige, *Quaestionum*, 27: "*Ex quibus omnibus satis constat, legem istam de usuris, non plane moralem, sed politicam fuisse, (...) et usuram ipsam ἁπλῶς non prohiberi, nisi quatenus per eam charitas proximi violatur*".

96 P. Heige, *Quaestionum*, 19: "*Quinto: Ne quis iniquitatem usurarum deinceps praetendat, dicimus, aequissimum esse, ut usurae quincunces pendantur, neque ideo contra legem divinam committi. Etenim finis Legis Divinae est charitas, ad eamque omnia nostra sunt revocanda*".

97 P. Heige, *Quaestionum*, 19: "*Haec eadem optima est actionum omnium moderatrix: et ut plane de usura, quid statuendum sit, liqueat, ex planissime definiri potest*".

The Heige's argument is divided into two parts. First, he illustrates the reason behind the payment of interest in civil law; then, he shows that this reason is not against charity. The starting point is the examination of the different types of interest recognized by civil law. The compensatory interest or punitive interest (*usura compensatoria aut punitoria*), Heige says, is commonly considered to be just, because it compensates for damage due to the failed return of the capital on time – even the most ardent critics of the charging of interest do not deny its legitimacy.[98] Instead, when one looks at interest for profit (*usura lucratoria*), it seems unjust to gain a certain guaranteed profit only because of the act of lending, when there is no concern for the possibility of damage.[99] However, Heige comments, it appears that the civil law also closed its eyes and considered the demand of interest as just and tolerable, not only for the delay in the payment but also before it.[100]

The reason for this permission is that the laws assume that not only the debtor but also the creditor can make profit with the money given on loan. For any profit the debtor had with the creditor's money, and the creditor was devoid of due to his lack of it, the laws consider it to be just that some part of the profit is given to the creditor. A certain amount can be taken from an uncertain future profit deriving from the debtor's business, and assumed as the damage of the creditor from his unpursued business. This amount can be taken without evidence of damage, Heige points out, because it is difficult to prove the loss, which sometimes can even exceed the established amount of interest.[101] Thus, the reason that the civil laws admit the *usura lucratoria* is the same as the argument for the moratory interest: the creditor's damage from the lack of his

98 P. Heige, *Quaestionum*, 19: "*Namque si de usura compensatoria, aut punitoria, ut vocant, quaeratur, nemo inficiari potest, aequam esse eius petitionem, qui damnum, ob non solutam sua die pecuniam sibi sarciri postulat, quod etiam hi, qui iniquiores sunt usurarum aestimatores, non negant*".

99 P. Heige, *Quaestionum*, 19.

100 P. Heige, *Quaestionum*, 19-20: "*Tamen apparet, leges civiles ad hoc quoque connivisse, exemplo medicorum: et proinde usurarum petitionem iustam et tolerabilem censuisse, non tantum, quae commissa mora, verum etiam quae ante ullam moram exiguntur, quasque adeo ab ipso numerationis die stipulati sumus*".

101 P. Heige, *Quaestionum*, 20: "*Ratio autem huius permissiones ex eo est, quod praesumunt iura, non tantum debitorem, sed et creditorem cum pecunia mutuo data lucrari posse: ideoque non iniquum putant, pro eo lucro, quo creditor interea caruit, ab eo, quod debitor ex pecunia creditoris habuit, partem aliquam decidi (…), et ita quasi super incerto eventu futuri emolumenti, ex negociatione debitoris, et praesumto damno creditoris, ob huius omissam negociationem, modico in praesens accepto, transigi magis quam postea singularem probationem, nomine eius, quod interest, suscipere, cuius upote probatio difficilis est, et definitam usurarum quantitatem aliquando potest excedere*".

money. The creditor could have gained profits that are instead gained by the debtor. For this reason the civil laws authorize the loans at interest.

Heige shifts then to the second part of his reasoning: the admission of interest to recoup damages is due to a principle of equality between the parties, to prevent one from being damaged while the other benefits. This equality corresponds to the equilibrium in the relation between private property and the needs of the neighbour. Heige explains that it is not against duty to help the other in a way that that will keep the helper unscathed, as the laws *Sed si quis* (D. 29,3,7) and *Sancimus* (C. 5,37,25) confirm. The first law concerns the sealers of wills, who need not suffer damage in their services. The second passage regards the creation of guardians or administrators for orphans, again, as the text specifies, 'without damages'.

Besides, Paul in 2 Cor. 8,13 exhorts that we give advantage to the other in such a way that there is neither affliction because of one's duties, nor utter reprieve from them.[102] As seen before with Coler, and also with the theologians, this passage plays a role of capital importance in justifying the equality of charging interest. Yet, the interpretation given by Heige slightly differs from the others. He writes that we ought to benefit the other without diminishing our resources or having an 'ease' (*ne nobis ipsis sit afflictio, vel remissio*). He applies the two key words of the passage, 'affliction' (*afflictio*) and 'ease' (*remissio*), to the creditor. The creditor is not to receive either an affliction or a benefit in lending his money. On the contrary, the large part of the interpreters we saw apply the first word 'affliction' to the creditor who gives the money without interest, and the second one for the debtor who receives a 'relaxation': use of the capital without payment of interest.

To Heige the creditor is neither to be harmed by lending his money, nor to be benefited. 2 Cor. 8,13 is meant as a criterion for the just amount of interest the debtor should pay. In addition, he points out that requiring interest is not an unlawful mode of acquiring property. As seen before, property has a precise aim: helping the neighbour. This conception was incorporated in Prov. 5,16-17, a passage often quoted by theologians: "*let thy fountains be dispersed abroad, and rivers of waters in the streets? Let them be only thine own, and not for strangers with thee*". Heige opines that Solomon did not want the fountains to *be dispersed abroad*, such that in keeping possession of them and showing mercy towards the neighbour, so that the close community lacks for nothing,

102 P. Heige, *Quaestionum*, 20: "*Non est officio contrarium, sic alium iuvare, ut te serves indemnem* l. sed si quis ex lignatoribus 7. [D. 29,3,7] quemad. testa. aper. l. sancimus 25 C. de admin. tuto. [C. 5,37,25] Paulus Apost. 2 Corinth. 8 v. 12 (13?) *sic nos aliis commodare iubet, ne nobis ipsis sit afflictio, vel remissio*".

it may be that the stranger remains unenriched by the profits.[103] Indeed, he who does not take care of his own family is judged worse than an unbeliever (1 Tim. 5,8 and Gal. 6,10).[104] This argument resembles that of Hunnius and Gerhard. Before assisting the neighbour, the Christian has to take care of his family. As the Scripture asks the Christians to first consider their own necessities and only then to help the neighbour, so the creditor has the right to use his money to purchase real estate or an annuity or whatever transaction earns him profits.[105] The creditor has the right to receive interest because it is presumed that his money profits both by buying real estate or an annuity. If he lends his money, he loses the possibility of making another more useful transaction. He suffers damage, and for this damage he has the right to receive interest from his loan.

Finally, the compliance with equity (*aequitas*) is also manifest from the fact that a relatively low rate of interest is asked, while the debtor stands to make the greatest degree of profit with the borrowed capital. The donation of part of the profit, which he can give to the creditor without his damage, is an indication of gratitude. As with Coler before, Heige comes to the conclusion that the moral foundation of the payment of interest is gratitude. The creditor and others are stimulated to act in a similar way because they are frightened by the sin of ingratitude.[106] The obligation at recompense or 'return-gift' (*ἀντιδωρεά*) has in it natural equality for sure, Heige insists. If receiving a wage is against the duty to give a free recompense, it is however a benefit, even if it is not gratuitous. Even the people who have a gratuitous duty are allowed to ask for a salary for the work they did, as an honorarium.[107] Heige quotes *Salarium* (C. 4,35,17), *A tutoribus* (D. 26,7,33), *Qui negotiationem* (D. 26,7,58), *Titium* (D. 26,7,47,6). These passages concern all performances that are not normally

---

103 P. Heige, *Quaestionum*, 20: "*Salomon Proverb. 5, 16.17 fontes nostros ita foras derivari vult, ut nos tamen dominium eorundem retineamus et ita misericordiam proximo exhiberi, ne nobis desit, et forte extranei impleantur proventibus nostris*".

104 P. Heige, *Quaestionum*, 20.

105 P. Heige, *Quaestionum*, 20.

106 P. Heige, *Quaestionum*, 21.

107 P. Heige, *Quaestionum*, 21: "*Obligationem ad ἀντιδωρεά naturalem aequitatem in se habere certum est.* l. sed si lege 25 § consuluit. de petit. haered. [D. 5,3,25] *et ut maxime officio contraria sit merces l. 1 manda* [C. 4,35,1?]: *tamen non desinit esse beneficium, etsi non sit gratuitum,* l Titius 4 de obseq. paren. et patro. praestan. [D. 37,15,3] *et nihilominus etiam his, qui gratuitum officium praestare debent, conceditur, aliquod auctoramentum operae honorarium exigere.* l. salarium. C. manda. l. 1 § in honoratis. de extraord. cognition [C. 4,35,17]: a tutoribus 33 § fin. de admini. et peric. tut. [D. 26,7,33] l. qui negotiationem 58. in fin. princ. [D. 26,7,58] l. Titium. 47. § altero 6 eod. tit. [D. 26,7,47]".

paid (uncertain promises; guardianships, etc.), but that should justly receive remuneration.

In conclusion, Heige claims that charging interest complies with equality, because without such payment, the creditor would receive damage. The creditor is not obliged to benefit the debtor with his losses. He must first consider the welfare of his family. Furthermore, gratitude in virtue of the profits the debtor makes with the creditor's money is the justification for the payment of interest. This gratitude urges the debtor to reward the creditor for the money he received. As a matter of fact, Heige identifies the very meaning of charity with equality. The breach of equality due to the damage for the creditor justifies the payment of interest, as otherwise equality – and therefore charity – would be offended.

2.2.3.2 The Power of the Magistrate

The second argument to defend the legitimacy of the civil law is that the magistrate holds the power to rule on the charging of interest, and his law is not against charity. Heige calls upon 'famous theologians and excellent lawyers', who openly wrote that the prince can set the amount of interest.[108] Concerning the theologians, Heige first cites Martin Luther's passage in *An die Pfarrer wider den Wucher* (1540), also quoted by Coler and discussed at the dispute of Regensburg. Luther, Heige comments, said that Justinian's legislation can be sufficiently excused, because the magistrate has the power to execute the distribution of temporal things, and therefore a five per cent interest cannot be grievous to the debtor, especially when paid to orphans, widows and miserable people who lend their principal because they lack other means of support or income. Then he cites other theologians who also permitted the same: Wolfgang Musculus, Martin Chemnitz, David Chytraeus, Philip Melanchthon, Niels Hemmingsen and Johannes Aepinus. They approve the mitigation of interest set by emperors and princes, which set a limit to 'the increasing frauds of usurers', granted a certain profit, and invited 'the most honourable people' to give loans more easily.[109]

108 P. Heige, *Quaestionum*, 22: "*Septimo et ultimo rationes superiores adeo et theologos magni nominis et iurisconsultos egregios, permoverunt, ut aperte scriberent: posse principem usurarum quantitatem in hac temporum necessitate definire ...*".

109 P. Heige, *Quaestionum*, 22-3: "*Nam inter theologos supra nominatus* Martinus Lutherus lib. sing. de usura ad parochos Tom. 7 Jenens. fol. 405 in § Aber wie wann der fall keme/ rc. *Iustiniani sanctionem ad temperanda antiqua onera graviorum usurarum inductam, satis excusari posse ait: cum magistratus potestatem habeat, de rebus temporalibus disponendi, et usura quincunx non possit adeo molesta esse debitori: maxime, si pupilli, viduae et miserabiles sint personae, quae aliunde victum nullum habeant, quibus et* Musculus d. lo. *easdem*

A number of authorities in the field of theology, mostly Lutheran, defended the power of the rulers to issue laws on the matter of interest-taking. In addition to them, Heige appeals to French theologians and jurists. First, he cites the Calvinist Daneau, according to whom if a loan is given to the brother looking for profit, or willing to increase his good, the amount of interest defined by the law can be taken justly. The underlying reason is that it is lawful to buy from the same party an income or real estate, on the condition that the conscience is clear and in this transaction, Christian charity is not intended to be trespassed.[110] Daneau confirmed the validity of the civil law by referring to the legitimacy of the purchase of annuities or the sale of real estate, if charity is observed. Then, Heige refers to Hotman, Du Moulin and Doneau.

Lastly, the Roman Catholic jurists Antonino Tesauro[111] (1521-1586) and Alfonso Villagut[112] (1566-1623) also accept this conclusion, albeit only in reference to the rule of the magistrate over the Jews who lent money in their domain. To Heige the reference to the Jews does not diminish the strength of the argument: the charging of interest should also be admitted among the Christians. There is no reason, he explains, that Christians should not also charge interest. Indeed, Christians should not cause a scandal among non-Christians or invite them to commit a sin; but a sin does not change its nature depending upon what people group commits the offense. If charging interest were against the divine law, it would have been forbidden universally, for both

permisit et David Chytraeus Deuteron. 23 post Phil. Melanchth. in epit. Moral. philos. *cumque his* Martinus Chemnitius in locis Philip. communib. Nicol. Hemmin. d. class. 4 c. 2 de legibus Joan. Aepin. in Psalm 15 *moderationem imperatorum et principum probant, quod grassantibus foeneratorum fraudibus modum ponere, et concesso aliquo augmento, honestiores ad facilius mutuandum, invitare simul voluerint*". M. Luther, *An die Pfarrherrn*, in WA 51, 373; W. Musculus, *De usuris ex verbo Dei appendix* [...], Tubingae, 1558; D. Chytraeus, *In deuteronomium*, 431ff.; P. Melanchthon, *Philosophiae moralis epitomes libri duo*, in CR XVI, 128-42; M. Chemnitz, *Loci theologici*, pars secunda, de paupertate, caput V, 155-70; N. Hemmingsen, *Enchiridion theologicum*, 407; J. Aepinus, *Auszlegung*, 54ff.

110 P. Heige, *Quaestionum*, 23: "*Eodem modo et Danae. Ethices Christian. c. 15. si quidem fratri de lucro certanti, vel suam rem augere volenti, mutuum detur, definitam a lege usurarum quantitatem, tam aequo iure accipi posse, ait, quam ab eodem licet partem reditus vel fundi emere, salva bonaque conscientia, nec in eo Christianam charitatem violari contendit*". L. Daneau, *Ethices christianae libri tres*, lib. 2 c. 15.

111 P. Casana, *Note biografiche su un giurista del XVI secolo: Antonino Tesauro*, in *Bollettino storico bibliografico subalpino*, XC (1992), fasc. I, 281-309; P. M. T. Guerra Medici, *Principi e giuristi nella prima età moderna. Antonino e Gaspare Antonio Tesauro magistrati del duca di Savoia*, Napoli, ESI, 1993.

112 J.F. von Schulte, *Die Geschichte der Quellen und Literatur des Canonischen Rechts von der Mitte des 16. Jahrhunderts bis zum Gegenwart*, Stuttgart, 1880, 475. See also C. Gamba, *Licita usura*, 263-6.

Christians and Jews.[113] Heige follows the interpretation of Deut. 23,20 we have seen before: a sin is always clearly and universally forbidden. On top of that, to corroborate this argument, he refers to Rom. 1,18-20:

> *for the wrath of God is revealed from Heaven against all ungodliness and unrighteousness of men, who hold the truth in unrighteousness, because that which may be known of God is manifest in them, for God hath shown it unto them. For from the creation of the world the invisible things of Him are clearly seen, being understood through the things that are made, even His eternal power and Godhead, so that they are without excuse.*

and Acts 21,20ff., where Paul explains that the Jews' customs can be abandoned, but not the law. Finally, Heige refers to Jacques de Corte and Matthias Coler for a more detailed analysis on this point.[114]

In short, Heige does not defend the power of the magistrate to regulate the amount of interest with a proper argument. Rather, he invokes the authority of theologians and jurists, not only Lutheran, but also Reformed and even Roman Catholic. In this way he reveals not only a skill in interpreting Scripture, but also a significant knowledge of the most influential theological and juridical minds of his day. Heige corrects the opinion of the Roman Catholics by a biblical interpretation, which reflects his vision on the prohibition against interest among the Jews. As seen before, the charging of interest was not forbidden universally, but for particular reasons. If loaning at interest were a sin, it would have been forbidden always and everywhere. Thus, being that the charging of interest was not universally forbidden, the political authorities hold the power to regulate the interest rate.

---

113 P. Heige, *Quaestionum*, 23: "*Eandem sententiam inter iurisconsultos late defenderunt* Molinae et Hotoman., dictis locis Hugo donell. de usuris c. 2 et novissime Anton. Tessa., decis. 57 *post* Alphon. Villag. Neap. de usu., q. 13, conclu. 4 nu. 11, *qui duo, licet de Judaeis tantum loquantur, quod nempe his usura permitti possit: tamen nulla ratio prohibet, quo minus idem Christianis licere debeat: cum neque inimicis fidei scandalum aut offendiculum ponere, aut ad peccandum eosdem invitare debeamus, peccata enim sunt uniusmodi, neque personis distinguuntur, et si lege divina usurae prohibentur, eadem tam Judaeos, quam Christianos et omnes in universum gentes teneat*: secundum Paul. Rom. 1, v. 28.19.20. Actor. 21 v. 20 et seq.". C. Du Moulin, *Tractatus*, n. 44ff. (?); F. Hotman, *De usuris*, Lugduni, 1551, L. 2, c. 1, 113ff. (?); H. Doneau, *In titulum de usuris in pandectis et sequentem commentarius*, Lugduni, 1558, c. 2, 47ff; A. Villagut, *Tractatus de usuris*, Venetiis, 1589, quaestio 13, conclusio 4, 107-8; The opinion is included in the work of Antonino Tesauro (1521-1586), but it has been written (as the text says), by Gaspare Antonio Tesauro (1563-1628), son of Antonino. See A. Tesauro (1521-1586), *Novae decisiones sacri senatus Pedemontani*, Augustae Taurinorum, 1609, Decisio LVII, 61b-64a.

114 P. Heige, *Quaestionum*, 23.

2.2.3.3 The Sterility of Money

The third and final argument in defence of the charging of interest implies the refusal of the scholastic argument of the sterility of money. The sterility of money had been for centuries one of the standard arguments employed to uphold the interest prohibition, and even Luther endorsed it.[115] This argument comes from Aristotle's *Politics*, where Aristotle assumed that money, as an artificial good, cannot breed.[116] In a loan at interest, money breeds money, which is against nature. Heige replies that money cannot only be considered as a number, but it can also be considered as use, fruits, which are devoted to the necessity of human trade. In fact, the Roman jurists defined interest (*usura*) as fruit and income from the money in several provisions: *Qui quadrigenta* (D. 35,2,88), *Generaliter* (D. 40,5,24), *Titius* (D. 22,1,38), and *Defuncta* (D. 7,1,58). This conclusion is also confirmed by Jacques Cujas and Charles Du Moulin, to whom Heige refers.[117]

Heige offers a solution that already circulated among the scholastic theologians:[118] artificial goods can bear fruits. Houses, horses and ships are sterile and not fungible goods, but they can be rented, and the owner gets the rent payment as a civil fruit. Similarly, the land can bear fruits from the work of peasants.[119] Hence, he concludes that not only the civil law but also experience and common sense show that the use of money has its utility in accordance with the use of men. This utility is measurable because of the consumption or restitution of money, and the payment of interest is demanded because of the creditor's lack of money during the term of the loan.[120] In substance, by repeating solutions already formulated, Heige criticizes the scholastic argument of

115 See before III/2.2.2.

116 Aristotle, *Politics*, 1, X, 4, 1258b.

117 P. Heige, *Quaestionum*, 16-17: "*Hoc enim modo iurisconsulti usuram, fructum et reditum ex pecunia redactum appellant l. qui quadrigenta 88. § fin. ad l. Falcid.* [D. 35,2,88] *l. generaliter 24 § si cui legatum de fidei com. libert.* [D. 40,5,24] *l. usura 24.* [D. 22,1,34] *l. videamus 38. de usur.d. l. Titius de praescript. verb.* [D. 22,1,38] *l. defuncta 58 § pen. de usufruct.* [D. 7,1,58] *Molinae d. lib. num. 511 Cujac. lib. 9 obs. 15*". C. Du Moulin, *Tractatus*, n. 512, 652-4; J. Cujas, *Observationum et emendationum Libri XXVIII*, Coloniae Agrippinae, 1598, lib. 9, cap. 15, 166-7.

118 O. Langholm, *The Aristotelian Analysis of Usury*, 61, 75-6. Already Gerard of Siena (d. before 1336) proposed this solution. On Gerard see the recent contribution: L. Armstrong, *The Idea of a Moral Economy: Gerard of Siena on Usury, Restitution, and Prescription*, Toronto, University Press, 2016.

119 P. Heige, *Quaestionum*, 17.

120 P. Heige, *Quaestionum*, 17: "*Et denique non ius tantum civile, sed ipsa rerum experientia et communis sensus ostendit, usum, seu fruitionem pecuniae, habere suam utilitatem, usibus hominum commodam, et aestimabilem, praeter ipsius sortis consumptionem, vel restitutionem Molinae. d. lo. n. 530. Ex quo etiam, propter ipsum illum usum usura exigitur, eoque cessante, deberi definit l. deducta 58 § cum autem 6. ad SC. Trebell.* [D. 36,1,58] *l. socium 60*

the sterility of money. Money can bear fruit with the work of men. This argument, therefore, does not constitute an obstacle to the validity of charging a moderate interest.

2.2.4 *The Judgment of Conscience*

2.2.4.1 Charity as a General Criterion

The divine law and the civil law permit a moderate interest rate if the neighbour is not harmed. Yet Heige advises that just because interest is allowed does not mean that it can be always and indiscriminately charged. Indeed, it is necessary for the Christian to follow 'the judgment of his mind and healthy conscience' (*mentis suae et conscientiae sanae iudicium*).[121] This judgment concerns not only the magistrate, who must not approve what God forbids, but also the parties who charge interest.[122] Here we are facing one of the greatest examples of the interaction between law and morality, between the *forum internum* and the *forum externum*. Heige expounds that the law on the charging of interest must not be enforced strictly, but it requires an analysis of the concrete circumstances. In particular, he alludes to circumstances concerning the parties, their qualities, times and places, all of which have to be considered according to equity, utility, and honesty and together assessed in compliance with 'degrees of Christian charity' (*dilectionis Christianae gradibus*).[123]

An analysis of the concrete circumstances thus determines the terms of the loan. This analysis is concretely a judgement operated by conscience. Following the Scripture, Heige describes this assessment in greater detail. It concerns first of all the absence of damages:

> *if someone protects himself through a stipulation of interest for a presumed profit or damage, the judge of the conscience of this man shall permit him to evaluate whether he harms the neighbour, or not, and shall not inquire any further.*[124]

---

in princ. pro socio [D. 17,2,60] *l. 7 § 4. de admi et peric. tuto* [D. 26,7,4] *l. si navis 62 in pr. de rei vind.* [D. 6,1,62]". C. Du Moulin, *Tractatus*, n. 530, 674-76.

121 P. Heige, *Quaestionum*, 27: "*Hoc vero cum dicimus, meminisse omnes, qui usuras accipiunt, volumus: non ideo, quod lege aliqua usurae concessae sunt, semper et indistincte eas exigi posse: Nam hic quoque unusquisque mentis suae et conscientiae sanae iudicium adhibeat oportet*".

122 P. Heige, *Quaestionum*, 27.

123 P. Heige, *Quaestionum*, 28: "... *ita et de hoc toto usurarum genere, non ex sese, sed ex circumstantiis pro personarum contrahentium, temporum locorumque qualitate, adhibitis aequitatis, utilitatis, honestatis formulis, et collatis dilectionis Christianae gradibus, statuendum*".

124 P. Heige, *Quaestionum*, 28: "*Si quis igitur stipulatione usurarum, ob praesumtum lucrum vel damnum, sibi caverit, iudex conscientiae illius permittet, ut aestimet, an proximum laedat, vel non, ultra non inquiret*".

The conscience of the single Christian must determine whether the contract harms the other party, as 1 Cor. 11,28 affirms: "*but let a man examine himself, and then let him eat of that bread and drink of that cup*", and similarly 1 Cor. 11,31: "*for if we would judge ourselves, we should not be judged*", which Heige quotes later.

Then, the judgement of conscience is not only about compliance with the law, but the Christian must seek what is truly beneficial: "*everyone is the best judge and witness of his actions, and must examine every action and consider not only what is lawful, but also what is expedient*".[125] Indeed, Gal. 6,4 affirms: "*but let every man put to the proof his own work, and then shall he have rejoicing in himself alone, and not in another*"; and similarly 1 Cor. 6,23 (and equally 1 Cor. 6,12): "*all things are lawful for me, but all things are not expedient. All things are lawful for me, but all things do not edify*". Heige follows closely Scripture and encourages the parties to attain an acute evaluation of the agreement and the circumstances, so that concretely no one is offended, but all are 'edified'.

The judgment of conscience is founded on charity. To Heige, everyone shall bear in mind the precepts of charity and thus use the things of the world, and not abuse of them.[126] Again, Heige draws on Scripture, especially 1 Cor. 7,31: "*those who use this world, as not abusing it. For the fashion of this world passeth away*". Charity invites the party not to seek his own good but the goods of others, as in 1 Cor. 10,24: "*let no man seek his own, but every man another's wellbeing*"; and in Phil. 2,4: "*look not every man to his own things, but every man also to the things of others*". Charity commands the parties to beware avarice, which is the root of all evil, as 1 Tim. 6,10 avers: "*for the love of money is the root of all evil; and while some have coveted after it, they have erred from the faith and pierced themselves through with many sorrows*". Furthermore, the observance of charity can imply that the party remains in the situation he was when God called him – 1 Cor. 7,20: "*let every man abide in the same calling as when he was called*".

Finally, Heige concludes:

> *the Christian must know that there is a large profit in a pious soul, satisfied with its condition, and that the end of the whole law is charity out of a pure heart, a good conscience and an unfeigned faith.*[127]

125 P. Heige, *Quaestionum*, 28: "*Unusquisque enim suarum actionum optimus est arbiter et testis. Probet unusqusque opus suum et non tantum quid liceat, sed et quid expediat, cogitet*".

126 P. Heige, *Quaestionum*, 28: "*Meminerit charitatis ubique mandata et sic mundo utatur, ut non abutatur*".

127 P. Heige, *Quaestionum*, 29: "*Denique sciat quaestum esse magnum pietatem cum animo, sua sorte contento, finemque legis totius esse charitatem ex puro corde, et conscientia bona et fide non simulata*. Galat. 6, v. 4. 1 Corinth 6. v 12. Roman. 12, v. 9 et seq. 1 Corinth. 13 et c. 7 v. 31.20 et c. 10, v. 23.24 et c. 11 v. 28.31 Philippen 2 v. 4. 1 Timoth. 6 , v. 10 et c. 1 v. 5. 19. Tit. 3, v 8.".

This results brilliantly from the words of Scripture. Heige lists a set of key passages including 1 Tim. 1,5: "*now the aim of the commandment is charity out of a pure heart, with a good conscience and with faith unfeigned,*"; 1 Tim. 1,19: "*holding faith and a good conscience which some, having put aside, have suffered shipwreck concerning faith*"; Titus 3,8: St. Paul's hymn of charity in Rom. 12,9 ff. and 1 Cor. 13. All these passages limpidly reveal how the core of Christian ethics, the love for the neighbour, affects one of the crucial aspects of finance. The charging of interest must be applied with the eyes of charity.

The civil law does not require a strict enforcement, but the analysis of the circumstances by a judgement of conscience performed not by the person of the judge in court, but by the Christian's individual conscience. The conscience is therefore the judge and witness of the Christian's actions, deciding not what is lawful, but what is advantageous. The conscience must be guided by charity towards the neighbour. Charity is not a vague concept because, referring to a number of biblical passages, Heige offers a full, detailed description of charity's meaning. Charity means not harming the neighbour; not abusing the things of this world; seeking the other's profit; being aware of avarice; and renouncing one's profit, if necessary. In short, charity acts as a form of equity for the mitigation of the law. Heige is a jurist, but the number of scriptural passages gives a hint to presume that he cared about this point. The application of the law passes through the judgement of a charity-formed conscience. Even St. Paul's hymn of charity is quoted to support this conclusion.

2.2.4.2 The Qualities of the Parties

In general the judgment of conscience is grounded on charity. In particular, it focuses on the personal qualities of the parties. Following the Lutheran theologian Aepinus as cited by Du Moulin, Heige distinguishes three classes of people: the poor who cannot return the goods received; the indigent who can work and return the goods received; the people who possess enough goods and do not need the other's goods for maintaining the necessary advantages of life. The first category is associated with alms (Luke 6,35); the second category with the gratuitous loan (Lev. 25,35-36; Ps. 112 (111),5; Prov. 19,17; Eccl. 12,1; Sir. 29,1ff.);[128] the third category can gain a moderate profit. Only this last

128 P. Heige, *Quaestionum*, 29: "*Huc igitur spectant et collimant, quae de distinctis in proposito hominum ordinibus ex* Ioh. Aepino in Psal. 15, *retulit* Molinae d. tr. nu. 86 *et ad duos gradus redigit* Danae d. c. 15. *Quosdam videlicet esse pauperes, qui ad mendicitatem inevitabili necessitate rediguntur, nec reddere queunt: Quosdam indigentes, quibus ad tempus opus sit, sed qui aliquando reddere possunt: Quosdam denique possessiones tenere, quibus de suo satis sit, nec opus habeant ad tuenda vitae necessaria commoda alienis rebus et bonis. Primis gratuitam beneficentiam, seu eleemosynam, dandam* Luc. 6, 35. *Secundis mutuum*

category of people is allowed to give and receive loans at interest. But Heige insists that in the contracts within the third category, charity towards the neighbour must still be observed, as it is clear in 1 Thess. 4,6 and Matt. 7,12.[129] Heige inserts the biblical passages that are not quoted explicitly by Aepinus. They cast a clear image on the regulation of these three classes. Charity works in particular as attention to the personal quality of the parties. If one of the parties is extremely poor, the other one shall give him alms. If one of the parties is poor but can still work, the other one cannot charge interest. The loan at interest can only be contracted between rich parties, who still must fulfil the contract without fraud and in accordance with equality.

In conclusion, Heige recognizes the lawfulness of the new law relating to interest, but invites the Christian not to enforce it strictly. A judgment of conscience, performed according to charity, is necessary. In particular, the Christian must consider the quality of the people involved in the bargain. Heige resorts Aepinus' distinction in three categories of people: the extreme poor, the poor who can work, and the rich. A moderate profit is only allowed to the rich, whereas for the other two categories the charging of interest is forbidden. Heige draws his conclusions on Scripture and Aepinus' work. However, it is possible that he found inspiration in other works of the Lutheran theologians, which already pointed out the centrality of charity in contract law.

2.3 The Impact of the New Theory

2.3.1 *Introduction*

As it is well known, the *Usus Modernus Pandectarum* movement takes this name from the *Specimen usus moderni pandectarum* (1690-1712), a work created on the model of Carpzov's,[130] by the great German jurist Samuel Stryk.[131] Stryk was not only a formidable jurist, but also a fervent Lutheran. It is not without meaning, then, that he also accepted the new theory of interest:

---

officiosum et gratuitum exhibendum Levit. 25, 35-36. Psal. 112 v. 5. Proverb. 19, v. 17. Eccl. c. 12, v. 1; Ecclesiast. 29, v. 1 e seq. cum similibus, supra ex vetere foedere allegatis". C. Du Moulin, *Tractatus*, n. 86, 101. L. Daneau, *Ethices christianae*, lib. 2 c. 15.

129 P. Heige, *Quaestionum*, 29: "*Tertii permitti inter se de lucro moderato pacisci: ubi tamen, ut in caeteris contractibus, charitatis, proximo debitae, ratio habenda est* 1 Thess. 4, 6. Matthae 7, 12".

130 K. Luig, *Samuel Stryk (1640-1710)*, 222.

131 On his biography see K. Luig, *Stryk, Samuel (1640-1710)*, in M. Stolleis (ed.), *Juristen, Ein biographisches Lexicon*, 607-8; H. Hof, *Samuel Stryk* in G. Kleinheyer, J. Schröder (eds.), *Deutsche und Europäische Juristen aus neun Jahrunderten*, 6 ed., 432-6.

> *actually this excessive rigidity on the charging of interest damaged societies more than benefited them. I admit that excessive interest rates have been practiced, but why had all kinds of interest to be forbidden, indiscriminately, on that account?.*

In the Old Testament, Stryk continues, the charging of interest was not absolutely forbidden, but the charging of interest among the Jews was forbidden, so that they would have an incentive to practice the duties of humanity even more strenuously among themselves. In the New Testament (Luke 6,35), Christ does not even speak about interest-taking, but he talks about the capital: "*he says that because of the laws of love we need to support the people from which we cannot get back the capital in case of indigence*".[132]

Stryk adhered manifestly to the new orientation in matter of interest prohibition. It was not the charging of interest in itself that had to be forbidden, but only its abuse. Scripture does not condemn the charging of interest in general, but was subjected to incorrect interpretation, because even Christ did not forbid interest. Christ was saying that because of the *laws of love* (*ex legibus amoris*) we should not ask that impoverished people return the money loaned to them.

Samuel Stryk's blessing of the new theory is a clear example of the overwhelming diffusion of this theory. The purpose of the following paragraphs is then to grasp some of the changes the new understanding determined. The spreading acceptance of the new theory brought along a series of effects. First of all, the theory's diffusion led to fierce criticism of the old interest-taking prohibition. The case of the Lutheran Matthaeus Wesenbeck is a brilliant example in this sense. Wesenbeck held a conservative position – charging interest is always forbidden – which was overturned by his commentators Bachov von Echt and Hahn.

The new theory also turned significant attention to the implementation of the civil law. The qualities of the parties have to be carefully examined. As we are going to see, several jurists wrote that financial agreements can only be stipulated among rich parties and not with the poor, because only in this way Christian charity is not offended. In addition, in case of calamity, charity

---

132 S. Stryk, *Continuatio altera usus moderni pandectarum a libro XIII usque ad XXII*, Halae Magdeburgicae, 1728, 783-4: "*Verum hic nimius rigor et censura circa usuras plus obfuit rebuspubl. quam profuit. Concedo, semper magnos circa usuras excessus fuisse, sed an propterea in totum et indisticte damnari debuerunt? Nec enim in veteri testamento absolute prohibitae fuerunt, sed tantum eatenus, ne judaei inter se foenus exercerent, ut divinum Numen eos eo magis ad mutua officia humanitatis inter se exercenda alliceret. Christus in N. T. nequidem in adducto effato de usuris loquitur, sed de ipsa sorte, quod scilicet etiam illis subveniendum sit ex legibus amoris in casu inopiae, a quibus restitutionem sortis impetrare non possumus*".

towards the neighbour recommends the creditor to remit the debt. Certain authors even argued that the creditor should abstain from the enforcement proceedings.

Lastly, the canon law was also affected by the new theory. Canon law norms regarding the interest taking prohibition began to be interpreted in the sense that they do not forbid the charging of interest in general, but only when the neighbour is harmed. Furthermore, a collateral effect of the new theory was a dispute on the nature of the purchase of annuities (*emptio reddituum*), a contract we discussed earlier. Some jurists insinuated that this contract is not a sale but a loan, as in the new theory loans at interest are lawful. However, this opinion was severely criticized and refused. The purchase of annuities had gained peculiar characteristics that differentiated it from the loan.

2.3.2 *Wesenbeck's* Paratitla *Reconsidered by Bachof von Echt and Hahn*

Matthäus Wesenbeck (Mattheus van Wesembeke),[133] the most Christian of all jurists and the most learned jurist among the Christians (*Jusperitorum christianissimus et Christianorum jurisperitissimus*), was born in Antwerp on 25 October 1531, and was the twelfth of thirteen brothers, all named after the Apostles. He studied at the University of Leuven, and was a pupil of Gabriel Mudaeus (Brecht 1500-Leuven 1560).[134] His parents (Petrus Wesenbeck, alderman in Antwerp, and Barbara Cylia, descendant of a rich and prosperous family) were Roman Catholics, but apparently he converted to Lutheranism during his stay in Leuven.[135] On 18 June 1550 he became *licentiatus iuris* and visited

133 On Wesenbeck's biography see: M. Adam, *Vitae germanorum iureconsultorum et politicorum*, Heidelbergae, 1620, 270-6; N.H. Gundling, *Otia*, v. III, Frankfurt und Leipzig, 1707, 213-74; A.R. von Eisenhart, *Wesenbeck, Matthäus*, in *Allgemeine Deutsche Biographie* 42 (1897), 134-8 (accessed 8.2.2018); https://www.deutsche-biographie.de/pnd11757287X.html#adbcontent; R. von Stintzing E. Landsberg, *Geschichte der deutschen Rechtswissenschaft*, I, München-Leipzig 1880, 351-5; R. Dekkers, *Mattheus van Wesenbeke*, in R. Dekkers *Het humanisme en de rechteswetenschap in de Nederlanden*, Antwerp, 1938; H. Lück, *Ein Niederländer in Wittenberg. Der Jurist Matthäus Wesenbeck (1531-1586)* in *Zentrum für Niederlande Studien. Jahrbuch 2 (1991)*, 199-209; M. Ahsmann *Wesenbeck, Matthaeus*, in M. Stolleis (ed.), *Juristen, Ein biographisches Lexicon*, 651; R. Feenstra, *Matthäus Wesenbeck (1531-1586) und das römisch-hollandische Recht (mit einer Bibliographie seiner juristischen Schriften)*, in H. Lück, H. de Wall, *Wittenberg*, 175-243.

134 On Mudaeus see: M. Wesenbeck, *Oratio de Gabriele Mudaeo* ..., Wittenbergae, 1572; Schulz, *Mudäus, Gabriel*, in *Allgemeine Deutsche Biographie* 22 (1885), 439-440 (accessed 8.2.2018) https://www.deutsche-biographie.de/pnd100215785.html#adbcontent.

135 The legend, reported by more than one bibliographer, says that during Wesenbeck's stay in Leuven, a farmer was captured and imprisoned because he was Lutheran. Hearing this farmer singing Luther's Psalms with obstinacy, Wesenbeck decided to embrace Luther's Bible and confession. Other bibliographers, however, affirm that Wesenbeck converted to Lutheranism slowly.

Paris and other parts of France for his education. In 1552, after his return to the Netherlands, he decided to move to Germany to avoid the attentions of the Spanish Inquisition. In 1557 he obtained a lectureship in Jena, and in 1558 became *doctor juris* and started to teach as a professor. In 1569 the old Johann Schneidewin died, and Wesenbeck obtained a professorship in Wittenberg, where he remained until his death. Wesenbeck was a man of faith but was not member of the Lutheran orthodoxy. He was considered instead to be a *crypto-Calvinist*.[136]

In 1563 Wesenbeck published the first edition of his *Paratitla in Pandectarum iuris civilis libros quinquaginta*. Following Charles Du Moulin, Wesenbeck distinguishes between three types of interest: interest for profit (*usura lucratoria*), interest for compensation (*usura compensatoria*), and interest for punishment (*usura punitoria*). Interest for punishment derives from a delay in a payment; interest for compensation is to compensate the creditor for the lack of his money; interest for profit, Wesenbeck judged, is by its nature dishonest and unlawful.[137]

The verdict against this last type of interest is reinforced by six motivations. First, the divine law (Lev. 25; Psalm 15; Ez. 18; Luke 6) outlaws loans at interest. Second, the creditor demands a wage for a service that should be gratuitous. Third, the payment of interest is not a lawful mode of acquiring property according to the *ius gentium* and civil law, but it is plainly condemned. Fourth, the payment of interest contradicts the nature of loan, because the loan must be gratuitous. Fifth, the payment of interest is against nature itself, because money does not breed. Sixth, the creditor cannot demand the payment of interest because the risk does not pertain to him but to the debtor.[138] All in all, these reasons reflected the traditional theory of interest. Wesenbeck endorsed a rather traditional orientation and considered the charging of interest to be generally forbidden. He was an esteemed jurist, and his authoritative opinion certainly weighted on the debate, but did not find acceptance among his Lutheran colleagues. At the dispute of Regensburg, the jurists of Tübingen already sought to force his conservative vision.[139] Furthermore, as we are going to see, Wesenbeck's commentators made a profound revision of his view, according to the directives of the new theory.

---

136 C. Strohm, *Calvinismus und Recht*, 16. On Cryptocalvinism see I. Crusius, *"Nicht calvinisch, nicht lutherisch": Zu Humanismus, Philippismus un Kryptocalvinismus in Sachsen am Ende des 16. Jahrunderts*, in *Archiv für Reformationgeschichte. Archive for Reformation History.* Jahrgang 99 (2008), 139-73.

137 M. Wesenbeck, *In pandectas iuris civilis et codicis iustinianei libros commentarii*, Basileae, 1629, 490.

138 M. Wesenbeck, *In pandectas iuris civilis*, 490-1.

139 See IV/1.

The *Paratitla* received a remarkable acclaim, and many editions were published, some of them also with observations, comments or annotations.[140] The *Notae et animadversiones in Matthaei Wesenbecii Pandectas Iuris Civilis* of the Reformed jurist and Heidelberg professor Reiner Bachof von Echt[141] (1575-1640) appeared in 1640. A few years later Heinrich Hahn[142] (1605-1668) printed his *Observata theoretico practica, ad Matthaei Wesenbecii in L libros digestorum commentarios* (1659). Both Bachof von Echt and Hahn overturned Wesenbeck's stance: loans at interest, even for profit, are lawful. Bachof notices the dissonance of Wesenbeck's opinion with the new imperial legislation: the loan is gratuitous in virtue of a simple civil law provision, and therefore the lawmaker can change it and allow the charging of interest.[143] At the same time, Bachof maintains that the debtor supports the risk, but he also uses the capital of the creditor, and for this reason the creditor can justly insist upon the payment of interest.[144]

In addition to Bachov van Echt's remarks, Hahn also refuted the arguments founded on the divine law and natural law. Hahn replies to Wesenbeck that the divine law does not prohibit interest in general, but distinguishes between interest going against charity or justice and interest that does not.[145] Prov. 28,8 permits the charging of interest, Hahn says, but the text recommends that the profit be given to the poor. In the parable of talents (Matt. 25,30 and Luke 19,23) Christ considers the lending at interest as an example of a good action for the good servant.[146] Lev. 25,35-37 and Ex. 22,25 clearly concern the prohibition against interest on loans to the poor and those which faculties are on

140 R. Feenstra, *Matthäus Wesenbeck*, 186-7.

141 R. von Stintzing, E. Landsberg, *Geschichte*, I, 683-7. See also R. von Stintzing, *Bachof von Echt, Reiner*, in *Allgemeine Deutsche Biographie* 1 (1875), 756 unter Bachoff (accessed 25.09.2017): https://www.deutsche-biographie.de/gnd100021174.html#adbcontent.

142 R. von Stintzing, E. Landsberg, *Geschichte*, II, 230-2; W. Hinz, *Die Entwicklung des gutgläubigen Fahrniserwerbs in der Epoche des usus modernus und des Naturrechts*, Berlin, Duncker und Humblot, 1991, 77-8; Further references in M.J. Schermaier, *Die Bestimmung des wesentlichen Irrtums von den Glossatoren bis zum BGB*, Böhlau, Wien, Köln, Weimar, 2000, 153-4.

143 M. Wesenbeck, *Commentarii in pandectas iuris civilis et codicem justinianeum olim dicti paratitla, aucta subinde ab Arnoldo Vinnio, cum notis et observationibus Rehinardi Bachovii Echtii*, Amstelodami, 1665, 327-8. I am quoting Bachov von Echt's observation.

144 M. Wesenbeck,, *Commentarii in pandectas*, 328.

145 H. Hahn, *Observata theoretico practica ad Matthaei Wesenbecii in L. libros digestorum commentarios*, Pars posterior, Coloniae Agrippinae, 1675, 30: "*Ad primum reponitur, iure divino distingui inter usuras quae* contra charitatem proximi, vel iustitiam et qua non tales".

146 H. Hahn, *Observata*, 30.

the verge of ruin, because this is against charity.[147] Psalm 15,20 and Ez. 18,8 forbid the charging of interest, Hahn comments. Yet they should not be interpreted simply as a general prohibition. The Jews did not deny that there was a type of interest that was licit. In Ez. 8 interest is associated with oppression of the poor. And in this light, closes Hahn, Luke 6,35 should also be understood.[148] The divine law thus associates the prohibition against interest with the damage to the neighbour and does not forbid the payment of interest in general. This interpretation is very similar to Heige's and Coler's, seen before.

Together with this first group of passages, Hahn also analyses the dictate of Deut. 23,20. He holds that the Jews were allowed to charge interest on loans to foreigners, because it was easier to practice equality, charity and mercy between brethren. Brethren can give more than the others, so that the souls are reinforced and bound fast through reciprocal services.[149] Thus, loaning at interest among kin might result in unjustice, to the detriment of the entire community. Another answer he frames is that the approbation of interest against the foreigners was a ceremonial legislation: a law given only for the Jews for a limited period of time. Citing Aristotle's *Nicomachean Ethics*, Hahn writes that what is equal is better than what is legal. This is true not only about the human 'legal', but also about the divine 'legal', as the law to sanctify the Sabbath is limited in the case of works intended for the health of the neighbour.[150] Hahn seems to say that the charging of interest was fully limited against brethern for a certain period of time, because this was the 'equal', but the 'legal' gives permission to charge interest. Hence, Deut. 23,20 does not constitute an obstacle for the new interpretation, but rather supports it.

Finally, Hahn also counters another two of Wesenbeck's arguments. He opposes Wesenbeck's thesis of the unlawfulness of the acquisition of property through interest by referring to Aristotle's *Nicomachean Ethics*. Aristotle affirms that if a contract, also a loan, keeps commutative justice, a lawful exchange takes place.[151] Therefore, the charging of interest is a lawful means for the acquisition of property. Then, Hahn refuses the idea that interest goes against the nature of money. Although money is a thing that is sterile in its

147 H. Hahn, *Observata*, 30: "*Nam* Lev. 25.35.36.37 et Exod. (not 23) 22.25 *manifeste agitur de usura quae a paupere exigitur et ab eo cuius facultates attritae manusque nutaverit, quae contra caritatem*".

148 H. Hahn, *Observata*, 30.

149 H. Hahn, *Observata*, 30: "*Nam dici potest, hoc verum esse ex aequitate, charitate et misericordia facilius exercenda erga fratres, quibus plus aliquantum tribuendum quam reliquis, ut animi inter se coalescerent et mutuis officiis devincirentur*".

150 H. Hahn, *Observata*, 30.

151 H. Hahn, *Observata*, 30.

nature, it can bear fruits with the work of men, civil fruits, which are gained not naturally but civilly.[152] This is the argument articulated by Summenhart, which we have seen before repeated by Coler.

In conclusion, Wesenbeck's opinion on the prohibition against interest is torn to pieces and substituted with the new theory in its essential elements. The interest taking prohibition is not a general interdiction, but the charging of interest is forbidden only when the neighbour is harmed. Hahn dictates some conditions that we have already seen: loans towards poor must be gratuitous; the magistrate fixes the interest rate; the creditor cannot abuse the neighbour in pursuit of the payment of interest.[153] As the criticisms of Wesenbeck indicate, the new current seems to take the upper hand. Bachof van Echt and Hahn are expressions of the dominant trend among the jurists of the *Usus Modernus Pandectarum*, which determines the end of the previous conceptions and assumes a position of supremacy. It is especially a change in the image of the divine law, which was triggered not only by the jurists' elaboration, but also by the theologians', as we will see in the next paragraph.

2.3.3 *The Influence of the Theologians on the Jurists*

2.3.3.1 Denying the Payment of Interest Goes Against Charity

The adoption of the new theory is a consequence of the fact that the jurists studied and employed the opinions of the theologians. This concerns especially two features of the new theory: the evaluation of the parties' qualities before the stipulation of the agreement and the remission of debt in case of calamity, as can perhaps be best illustrated by some examples. In his juridical dissertation *De mohatra contractu* (1663) published under the supervision of a genuine Lutheran jurist, Kaspar Ziegler[154] (1621-1690), Heinrich Gregorii clearly states that the interpretation of the Holy Scripture is beyond the tasks of a jurist, and he does not want to invade the field of the theologians.[155] Hence, he declares:

152 H. Hahn, *Observata*, 31: "*In quinto negatur, usuram naturae nummi simpliciter contrariari; quia, ut res natura steriles et infoecundae, ita et nummus potest fructus ferre industria hominis, civiles, qui ideoque non natura sed iure percipiuntur* (…)".

153 H. Hahn, *Observata*, 32.

154 C. von Bar, P. Dopffel (eds.), *Deutsches internationales*, vol. 1, 561-3; H.P. Schneider, *Die Lehre vom christlichen Naturrecht bei Caspar Ziegler*, in H. Lück, H. de Wall (eds.), *Wittenberg. Ein Zentrum europäischer Rechsgeschichte und Rechtskultur*, Böhlau, Köln, 2006, 273-91.

155 H. Gregorii, (Supervisor: K. Ziegler), *Dissertatio iuridica de mohatra contractu*, Ienae, 1747, 19: "*Caeterum cum ad theologos pertineat, et cathedram nostram transcendat, Scripturae Sacrae expositio, nolumus nos ea, quae nostra non sunt, invadere*".

> *we learn from the theologians* (he mentions Johann Gerhard) *that the authoritative statements against interest included in the Old Testament concern the duty to give a free loan to the poor. Thus, beyond the given sum nothing must be demanded to them with their detriment and oppression*[156].

The charging of interest is forbidden against the poor, because they may be harmed. This is the new meaning of the interest prohibition: not a general prohibition of lending at interest, but a prohibition to harm the neighbour with an abuse of the charging of interest. Indeed, Heinrich Gregorii explains that the charging of interest that is forbidden is that which, against Christian charity, bites and gnaws the neighbour (*contra Christianam charitatem proximum mordent et arrodunt*). If we charge interest on loans to the poor, who already have nothing, we are afflicting them, he says. Similarly, loaning at interest is forbidden for the rich if it exceeds the rate established by the magistrate,[157] but may be charged on loan contracts between the rich, provided it is at or under the rate set by the magistrate. In this way, the meaning of the term 'usury', as an excessive rate of interest or the requirement that the poor pay interest on a loan is moving closer to the contemporary meaning.

An analogous opinion is included in the dissertation *Asylum generale debitorum* by the jurist Hans Jakob von Ryssel (1627-1669) published for the first time in 1651 under the supervision of Benedikt Carpzov. Von Ryssel writes that according to the desire of the theologians and honourable jurists:

> *it is allowed to take the lawful interest, and a moderate profit can be negotiated with the debtors that are not reduced at beggary, not the poor or temporarily indigent, but with those who have properties and sufficient riches, who do not need of the others' goods for getting the necessary advantages to live. This permission, however, only applies if charity towards the neighbour is not neglected.*[158]

---

156 H. Gregorii, K. Ziegler, *Dissertatio iuridica*, 19: "*Ita tamen ab illis edocemur, dicta V. T. usuras prohibentia agere de officio mutui indigentibus gratis praestando, ita ut praeter sortem cum ipsorum detrimento et oppressione nihil ab illis exigi debeat. Gerhard.* Loc. de magistrat. n. 249 seq.". J. Gerhard, *Loci theologici*, Vol. 13-14, n. 249, 112ff.

157 H. Gregorii, K. Ziegler, *Dissertatio iuridica*, 29: "*Prohibitae enim omni iure sunt illae usurae, quae contra Christianam charitatem proximum mordent et arrodunt, quaeque a debitoribus illis, qui vel prorsus sunt pauperes aut indigentes cum eorum afflictione, aut etiam a divitibus ultra modum legitimum exiguntur*".

158 H.J. von Ryssel, (Supervisor: B. Carpzov), *Asylum generale debitorum*, Lipsiae, 1651, caput I, 10, nn. 28-30: "*Sed in medio tuti subsistimus, voto nostratium theologorum piorumque iurisconsultorum subscribentes, ut cum debitoribus non ad mendicitatem, usque pauperibus, vel ad tempus indigentibus, sed possessiones ac facultates tenentibus, quibus de suo satis est, nec ad vitae necessaria commoda tuenda alienis bonis ac rebus opus habent, de lucro moderato pacisci, licitasque usuras accipere permissum sit, ita tamen, ne charitatis proximo*

The reference is to the well-celebrated 1 Thess. 4,6, but also to works of Lutheran theologians and jurists: Martin Chemnitz's *Loci communes*, Martin Luther's *An die Pfarrherrn, wider den Wucher zu predigen*, Johann Gerhard's *Centuria quaestionum politicarum* (decade 8, quaestio 1), Peter Heige's *Quaestionum* and Matthias Coler's *Tractatus*. Together with the references to the Lutheran theologians and jurists, this passage reveals von Ryssel's determination to identify carefully the categories of people who can charge and be charged interest. Von Ryssel is quick to point out that the debtor must possess goods for the advantages or privileges of life. The debtor has to be able to return the principal and interest.

Finally, Johannes Aepinus' distinction in three categories was also common among the jurists. As seen before, in his sermon on Psalm 15, the Lutheran theologian distinguished between three categories of people: the poor, the poor who can work and the rich. This distinction is expressly recalled by many jurists, as for instance, Heinrich Hahn,[159] Ernst Cothmann[160] and Benedict Carpzov[161]. The charging of interest is only admitted for the rich, while for the poor no interest can be suffered.

As these examples show, the jurists incorporated the theologians' teachings into their works. In particular, they followed the theologians' interpretation that the interest taking prohibition only concerns the poor. Charity as an essential principle of contract law imposes first of all the prohibition to grant loans at interest to the poor. They can however be negotiated with the rich and those who possess enough goods to repay the loan with interest.

2.3.3.2 The Remission of Debt

The new theory of interest does not only include the prohibition to charge interest on loans to the poor, but also stipulates that if the debtor is on the verge of poverty, the creditor must remit the debt. In this sense, the dissertation *Asylum generale debitorum* by Hans Jakob von Ryssel, written under the supervision of Benedikt Carpzov, is again an extraordinary example of the

debitae ratio negligatur, 1 Thess. 4, vers. 6 *Chemnit.* in loc. Philipp. commun. *B. Luther* in lib. singul. de usur. ad paroch. tom. 7 Jenens. fol. 405, *Gerhard* decad. 8. quaest. polit. 1, *Heig.* p. 2 q. 1 *Coler* de process. execut. p. 1 cap. 10 n. 35 et multis seqq.". M. Chemnitz, *Loci theologici*, pars secunda, de paupertate, caput V, 155-70; M. Luther, *An die Pfarrherrn, wider den Wucher zu predigen*, in WA 51, 331 ff.; J. Gerhard, *Centuria quaestionum politicarum*, decas octava, quaestio 1; P. Heige, *Quaestionum iuris tam civilis quam saxonici pars posterior*, q. 1, 1ff.; M. Coler, *Tractatus de processibus executivis*, cap. X, n. 35 ff, 223ff.

159 H. Hahn, *Observata*, 32.

160 E. Cothmann, *Consultationum*, responsum 52, 17.

161 B. Carpzov, *Jurisprudentia forensis*, pars 2, constit. 30, 677.

theologians' influence.[162] Von Ryssel strongly believes that a rigid execution of the law which allows creditors to recoup their losses from the debtors would be against charity towards the neighbour. Perhaps, he writes, if the Roman legislators had stated something on this point and had been indulgent with the debtors suffering calamity, we would not have so many indigents; and we would not have to recourse to the universal rule and make examples of those who had thought to be licit in challenging the divine law (Deut. 15,7. Lev. 25,35-36, Luke 6,35), which detests the rigidity against the debtors who were impoverished.[163]

The interpretation of Scripture is a task of the theologians, and von Ryssel does not want to interfere. Yet the theologians, he continues, opine that the not-indigent creditor is obliged, under pain of mortal sin, not to demand from the debtor the thing the debtor needs for his nourishment or for averting serious damage. Furthermore, the theologians generally require that the creditors likewise be affected in the move to equilibrium, and in case of damage suffered by the debtor in a critical case, not only they do not get the profit, but they also abandon the quest to recover the unpropitious capital from the debtors.[164] The creditor thus is obligated to leave the debtor what he needs for his nourishment or to live without ruinous damage.

The theologians exhort the creditors not to sue both for the expected profit and the capital. Von Ryssel not only repeats their opinion, but also quotes *in extenso* a number of excerpts from theologians' works. He begins with Luther's *Von Kaufhandlung und Wucher*, where Luther admonishes that in the third degree of dealing with temporal goods, the creditor must give the sum without asking back, as the precept of Luke 6,35 commands: lend hoping for nothing in return.[165] Others, continues von Ryssel, restrain this principle to the case of poverty due to an accident. For instance, Friedrich Balduin in his *Tractatus de casibus conscientiae* suggests that the creditors remit the debt when the debtor is reduced to poverty because of an accident.[166] For Lucas Osiander,

162 H.J. von Ryssel, B. Carpzov, *Asylum generale*, caput III, nn. 55-6.

163 H.J. von Ryssel, B. Carpzov, *Asylum generale*, caput III, 55, n. 52: "*Ac si forsan, quid legislatores romani statuerint, et debitoribus calamitosis indulserint, non magni habendum, nec ad exemplum et regulam universalem trahendum quis putaverit,* (2) *ad ius divinum provocare licebit, quod rigorem adversus debitores depauperatos valde detestatur,* Deut. 15 vers. 7. Lev. 25, 35 et 36 Luc. 6 vers. 45…".

164 H.J. von Ryssel, B. Carpzov, *Asylum generale*, caput III, 55, n. 53: "… *unde theologi inferunt creditorem non indigentem teneri sub peccato mortali non exigere a debitore rem, qua ille indiget vel ad sustentandam naturam, vel ad notabile damnum vitandum: idque nostrates communiter operam dant, ut creditoribus aequilibrium pervadeant, damno casu fatali debitoribus dato, ne solum illi percipiant lucrum, damnum vero cedat debitoribus*".

165 H.J. von Ryssel, B. Carpzov, *Asylum generale*, caput III, 55, n. 54-5.

166 H.J. von Ryssel, B. Carpzov, *Asylum generale*, caput III, 55, n. 56; F. Balduin, *Tractatus*, 944.

the remission of debt derives from equity, as moderator of the laws.[167] Martin Chemnitz in his *Loci theologici* reproaches people who do not want to use the contract with the clause of redemption or the partnership, to respect 1 Thess. 4,6.[168] Aegidius Hunnius, in a passage we saw before, writes that the creditor must remit the debt when the debtor is reduced to poverty because of a fire, shipwreck, or other accident.[169] Finally, Johann Gerhard recommends that the creditor remit the principal and interest, if the debtor is reduced to indigence by fortuitous event, unexpected and unavoidable. When men of the third class are reduced to the second class, loans towards them must be gratuitous, and when they are reduced to the first class, they are to be helped with alms.[170]

It is plain that von Ryssel knows the theologians' opinions, as he uses them to bear out the thesis that the creditor must remit the debt if the debtor is suffering negative circumstances. Thus, after this brief survey, von Ryssel closes:

> *to what end these admonitions of the theologians? They certainly instruct the creditors that if the debtors suffer damages or their resources are fallen, without their fault, they are bound to remit the interest or part of the credit. Rigorous debt execution can certainly not be demanded against them with a clear conscience. When the creditors insist in their rigidity and remit nothing, why could not the magistrates and princes restrain the creditors by public law and make them observe the duty of charity?*[171]

Von Ryssel argues that the magistrate should intervene to punish the creditors who do not remit the debts of the poor debtors. The rigidity of the law ought to be mitigated by charity. The Lutheran theologians' influence is clearly manifest here. The theologians ask the creditors to act with charity towards the debtors.

---

167 H.J. von Ryssel, B. Carpzov, *Asylum generale*, caput III, 55, n. 57; L. Osiander, *Vom Wucher in dem Regespurgischen Streit*, in G. Dedekenn, *Thesauri consiliorum et decisionum volumen secundum*, 150.

168 H.J. von Ryssel, B. Carpzov, *Asylum generale*, caput III, 55, n. 58; M. Chemnitz, *Loci theologici*, pars secunda, 167-8.

169 H.J. von Ryssel, B. Carpzov, *Asylum generale*, caput III, 55, n. 59; A. Hunnius, *Commentarius in posteriorem epistolam*, 252.

170 H.J. von Ryssel, B. Carpzov, *Asylum generale*, caput III, 55, n. 60; J. Gerhard, *Auff 12 nachfolgende Fragen*, in G. Dedekenn, *Thesauri consiliorum et decisionum volumen secundum*, 168.

171 H.J. von Ryssel, B. Carpzov, *Asylum generale*, caput III, 55, nn. 61-2: "*Sed quorsum haec theologorum monita? Informant nempe creditores, quod si debitores praeter culpam suam damnum passi et facultatibus lapsi fuerint, iis usuras, vel partem etiam ipsius crediti remittere sint obstricti, tantum abest, ut bona conscientia executio rigorosa ab iis intentari queat. Quidni ergo magistratus ac principes, creditores refractarios de rigore, nihil remittentes per legem publicam compescere et in charitatis officio continere possint?*".

Charity is the tenet that justifies the remission of debt and impedes inequality among the parties. Von Ryssel observes that it is unequal if one of the parties has already lost his goods because of a war, and he is subsequently deprived of the rest due to rigid enforcement procedures. Similarly it is unequal if misfortune kept his goods from selling, and then the rest of his assets are seized.[172] Thus, Von Ryssel underlines:

> *Equity and Christian charity do allow neither; charity alone will instantly remove any doubt of conscience, should one trouble our mind because of a legal provision or enforcement procedure. One should always keep in mind that all sanctions imposed by the legislators and all imperial prescripts and edicts must give way to Christian charity.*[173]

Von Ryssel conjures up the authority of Luther, who wrote that all the laws, divine laws and human laws, are not binding against love (*Liebe*). Love should guide the interpretation of all laws, as when this does not happen, the law harms. A law against love must immediately be repealed, because the laws are directed to upholding love, as St. Paul said: love is the fulfilment of the law (Rom. 13,10).[174]

Christian charity is therefore the solution to avoiding injustice produced by the strict enforcement of the law. Von Ryssel illuminates the application of the law with the bright light of charity. Charity denies any rigorous enforcement that would damage the neighbour. When the creditor is called to choose whether to apply the law and proceed with a harsh punishment or remit the debt, charity enlightens his decision. All the laws and all the authorities must surrender in front of charity, as indeed, charity is the fulfilment of the law. If Christian charity will be in the heart of creditors, von Ryssel concludes, they

---

172 H.J. von Ryssel, B. Carpzov, *Asylum generale*, caput III, 56, n. 63.

173 H.J. von Ryssel, B. Carpzov, *Asylum generale*, caput III, 56, nn. 64-5: "*Neutrum sane aequitas et charitas christiana admittit, quae vel sola omnem scrupulum, si quis ex praescripto legum et processu executionis animum nostrum turbaret, uno ictu removebit; semper enim cordi infigendum, omnes legumlatorum sanctiones, omnia principum rescripta et edicta cedere charitati christianae* ...".

174 H.J. von Ryssel, B. Carpzov, *Asylum generale*, caput III, 56, nn. 64-5: "... *quo de notabiliter scripsit B. Lutherus: Dass alle Gesetze, göttliche und menschliche, so von eusserlichen Thun gebiethen, nicht weiter binden, dann die Liebe gehet: die Liebe soll seyn eine Ausslegung aller Gesetze, wo die nicht ist, so ist es schon aus, so schadet das Gesetze balde, es sey, wie es wolle. Wann ein Gesetze wieder die Liebe lauffen will, so soll es bald auffhören, Ursach: Dann alle Gesetze sind gegeben allein, dass sie Liebe auffrichten sollen, wie S. Paulus saget, die Liebe ist des Gesetzes erfüllung*, in Postill. ecclesiast. super epist. dominic. 17 post festum Trinitat." G. Plochmann, *Dr. Martin Luther's Kirchenpostille*, II Predigten über Evangelien, Fünfter Band, Erlangen, 1828, 128-9.

will not so pursue the enforcement proceedings but will spontaneously repudiate their rights, preferring love towards the neighbour to stringency (*sed sua sponte iuri suo repudium dabunt, dilectionem proximi rigori praeferentes*).[175] Here we have one of the clearest examples of the juridical implications of the new theory. Inspired by Christian charity (*charitas*) or Christian love (*dilectio-Liebe*), the creditor should waive the enforcement procedures and remit the debt. This conclusion comes out after the diligent examination of the theologians' statements, which represent the moral background.

In conclusion, to von Ryssel, charity towards the neighbour should always guide the creditors. If the debtor suffered from calamity, as for instance flood or war, the creditor should listen to charity and refrain from legal proceedings. This is a vibrant example of the practical impact of the new theory, and it also reveals the importance of the contribution of the theologians. Charity, as the illuminating principle of Christian life, should inspire creditors to have mercy on the poor debtor, although the law would rule in the creditor's favour.

2.3.4 *Rethinking the Canon Law*

2.3.4.1 A New Gaze on the Interest Prohibition

This new theory of interest had also an impact on the interpretation of the canon law. As a matter of fact, the canon law stipulating the interest prohibition was gradually considered to be abrogated by general custom.[176] The canon law and the contribution of the canonists were, however, reviewed by the Lutheran jurists in the light of the new theory. We look at two examples. On the one hand, some jurists reinterpreted the canons to only forbid the charging of interest when the neighbour is harmed. On the other hand, others concluded that the purchase of annuities (*emptio reddituum*) – the canonists' creation to work around the interest-taking prohibition – is in actuality a loan disguised as a sale. This contract is nothing more than a creation of canonists and scholastic theologians to avoid the interest-taking prohibition. This opinion was discarded and the purchased of annuities was still considered to be a sale. We look now at the former issue and in the following paragraph at the latter.

Some jurists sought to read the canon law through the spectrum of the new theory. Peter Heige, for example, maintains that the decretal *Quoniam* (D. 47, c. 2), which reports the canon 17 of the Council of Nicaea, forbade usury to clerics and lay people for two reasons. The first reason is that it was believed

---

175 H.J. von Ryssel, B. Carpzov, *Asylum generale*, caput III, 56, n. 66: "*Charitas ergo christiana si creditoribus cordi erit, non multum fiduciae in regulis processus executivi collocabunt sed sua sponte iuri suo repudium dabunt, dilectionem proximi rigori praeferentes*".

176 R. Zimmermann, *The Law of Obligations*, 175.

that the profit provided by the payment of interest was shameful and dishonourable. The second is that it wanted to limit the high interest rate placed by the Roman law with the *centesima et sesquicentesima usura*.[177] Thus, he deems that this decretal does not condemn the 'use' of interest in itself, but its 'abuse'.[178] This interpretation is confirmed by the fact that canon law permitted the creditor to take something in addition to the principal in several cases (*Salubriter* X 5,19,16 and *Conquestus* X 5,19,8), as it was not deleterious for the neighbour.[179] These passages concern the possibility of keeping the fruits of a pledge in special cases. As seen before, Heige's thesis is that the charging of interest in itself is not prohibited: it is the abuse that is forbidden. Thus, the canon law only denies the charging of interest insofar as it harms the neighbour.

A similar opinion is included in the *Tractatus de usu usurarum* (1631), of Christoph vom Hagen (1596-1664), jurist in Mecklenburg and assessor at the local provincial court.[180] This work is primarily a collection of the best opinions on the interest-taking prohibition among jurists and theologians. On the cover of his book, vom Hagen engraves the dictates of Matthew 7,12, '*do to others what you would have them do to you, for this is the law and the prophets*', which clearly reveals his progressive position. He contends that canonists, legists and their followers 'boldly' affirmed that the canon law forbids all forms of interest. However, no text can be reported where the charging of non-'biting interest' (*de usuris mordacibus*), and interest that do not offend the love for the neighbour and Christian charity are prohibited.[181] Vom Hagen holds that the civil laws governing the charging of a 'moderate and just' interest are never corrected or condemned by the canons, and therefore they should be considered as approved. Everything they say concerns the 'biting' interest and the like, which violates Christian charity. It appears from new and old canons, and from the canonists' opinions, that only 'immoderate, unlawful, condemned,

---

177 The interest rate was established in 1% monthly or 3/2 % monthly. See before III/2.1.2.1.

178 P. Heige, *Quaestionum*, 29-30: "*Ad canones et concilia deinde quod attinet, fateri necesse est, ut plurimum clericis, interdum et laicis, usurarum exercitia interdici: sic tamen, ut propter turpem et inhonestum quaestum, quem inde parari existimabant, id constituatur, partim propter graviores usuras, centesimas scilicet et sesquicentesimas, ex concilii niceni sententia* c. quoniam multi 47 distinct. [D. 47, c. 2] *Existimo autem et hic magis abusum rei, per se non malae quam ipsum usum damnatum*".

179 P. Heige, *Quaestionum*, 30.

180 Information on him is limited. See CERL Thesaurus (accessed 26.09.2017): http://thesaurus.cerl.org/record/cnp00996256 .

181 C. vom Hagen, *Tractatus*, 68: "*Ad ius canonicum quod attinet, etsi canonistae et legistae, ac horum sequaces, omnes omnino usuras hoc iure prohibitas esse audacter affirmant: tamen nullus textus afferri potest, in quo huiusmodi usurae non mordaces, neque dilectionem proximi et charitatem christianam offendentes, sunt prohibitae* (…)".

shameful and harmful interest' is condemned.[182] Vom Hagen alludes to several canons: *Quoniam* (D. 47, c. 2), *Sedicionarios* (D. 46, c. 8), *Non licet* (D. 46, c. 9), *Si feneravis hominem* and the following (C. 14, q. 3., c. 1,2,3 and ff.), the title *De usuris* in the Liber Extra (X 5,19,1 and 2) and *Usurarum voraginem* (VI 5,5,1).[183] These canons represent in great part the discussion on usury and interest as elaborated by the canonists.

A particular example of this interpretation concerns the decretal *Naviganti* (X 5,19,19), issued by Pope Gregory IX in 1236 to outlaw the charging of interest on maritime loans, when the 'sailors' or traders who borrowed the money assumed the risk of loss. This decretal had an extreme importance for the discussion of the interest-taking prohibition.[184] Vom Hagen states that the civil law on maritime loans included in Justinian's code (C. 44,33) is not corrected by the decretal *Naviganti*, because the prohibition does not concern the activity of lending, but the immoderate interest that is taken because of the creditor's unjust fear of losing his money. Vom Hagen lists three reasons. First, the decretal is founded on the false premise that the charging of any interest – both the interest that harms the neighbour and goes against charity, and the interest that does not abuse the neighbour and does not offend charity – harms the neighbour, and therefore the charging of interest is considered a thing evil and forbidden in itself.[185] This premise is wrong, because for vom Hagen only the interest that harms the neighbour is forbidden.

Second, the decretal does not address the actual and probable danger of sea travel, but about the void danger (*de periculo vano*) that is less probable and imaginary. It is because of this danger that the creditor, without having any just fear, is sure to receive a certain immoderate profit beyond the principal.

182 C. vom Hagen, *Tractatus*, 68-9: "*Nusquam quoque in eodem iure legitur, vel in genere, vel in specie, ius civile, quo ad dictas usuras iustas ac moderatas esse correctum vel reprobatum, ideoque approbatur censetur, iuxta c. 1 et 2 de novi oper . nunciat.* (C. 8,11,1-2) *c. cum expediat. de Elect. in 6* (VI 1,6,29), *sed omne id, quod affertur, loquitur de usuris mordacibus, et dilectionem proximi offendentibus, immoderatis, illegitimis et improbis, turpibus et nocivis, uti apparet tam ex veteribus, quam novis canonibus et canonistis*".

183 C. vom Hagen, *Tractatus*, 69.

184 J.T. Noonan Jr., *The Scholastic Analysis of Usury*, 137ff. On the historical context of the decretal *Naviganti* see R. De Roover, *The cambium maritimum contract according to the Genoese Notarial Records of the Twelfth and Thirteenth Centuries*, in D. Herlihy, R. Lopez, V. Slessarev (eds.), *Economy, Society and Government in Medieval Italy. Essays in Memory of Robert L. Reynolds*, Kent, Kent State University Press, 1969, 15-33.

185 C. vom Hagen, *Tractatus*, 76: "*Primo, quia falso nititur praesupposito, quasi omnis omnino usura, sive mordeat proximum, et offendat dilectionem proximi, damnum inferat debitori, vel non, per se et sui natura sit mala ac prohibita, cuius tamen contrarium supra late probavi*".

This immoderate profit is condemned. This interpretation is confirmed by the analysis of the words 'or he who is going to a fair' (*vel eunti ad nundinas*), and 'sailor' (*naviganti*) that for vom Hagen might relate to cases different from the actual maritime danger.[186]

Third, the decretal does not refer to the moderate, just and legal interest but to the unjust and immoderate fee that results from the assumption of danger or risk.[187] To vom Hagen *Naviganti* does not prohibit lending money at interest, but only forbids creditors from taking an immoderate interest because of an unjust fear of losing their money. This fear is unjust because it is not related to the real danger of the sea, but rather it is related to an imaginary and void danger, which is for vom Hagen a fantasy that results in clear damage to the neighbour, and it is for this reason that the charging of interest is forbidden. The charging of interest is forbidden by the decretal because it is absolutely harmful, a claim which vom Hagen has already addressed.

In short, the new theory brings about a reinterpretation of the canon law. According to the Lutheran theologians and jurists, the canons only forbid the charging of interest that is detrimental to the neighbour. The jurists sought this new interpretation of the law to defend the new theory and make it firmer, which resulted in a new standard of evaluation of the canon law of usury, namely through the lens of charity. This analysis implies a new gaze on the canon law. The canons are not completely abandoned, but interpreted differently. Here we can really see the impact of the Lutheran theory of interest on the canon law. The theological context determined a new vision of the canon law.

2.3.4.2 The Nature of the *emptio reddituum*

The reformulation of the interest prohibition gave also rise to a collateral debate on the nature of the purchase of annuities (*emptio reddituum*). As seen before, Coler argued explicitly that loans, including provisions on interest from the beginning of the loan (lucrative, not moratory interest), can be stipulated. Then, other jurists observed the equivalence between annuity and interest (*usurae*).[188] Following this reasoning, two estimated jurists, Ernst Cothmann (1557-1624) and Christoph vom Hagen, insinuated that the purchase of annuities is not a sale but a loan. The same opinion was also held by the French Reformed theologian Claude Saumaise (1588-1653). Then the Lutheran Heinrich Hahn refused Cothmann's and vom Hagen's claims, while Johann Otto Tabor (1604-1674) pointedly replied to Saumaise that this contract is a true sale and not a

186 C. vom Hagen, *Tractatus*, 76-7.

187 C. vom Hagen, *Tractatus*, 78.

188 See A. Landi, *Ad evitandas usuras*, 97-119.

loan. Eventually, the majority of the Lutheran jurists shared Tabor's and Hahn's conclusions. It is worthwhile to have a brief look at this discussion, as an example of the new vision on loans and purchase of annuities and of the conservation of a canonists' construction.

Ernst Cothmann was a Lutheran jurist, assessor of the *Hofgericht*, later of the *consistorium* in Rostock, and finally chancellor of the dukes of Mecklenburg-Güstrow. Cothmann was also a professor at the university of Rostock, where he became dean of the law faculty and rector of the university.[189] In his *responsum* n. 52 of the *Consultationes et responsa iuris* (1597), he deals with a loan at interest, and the possibility of obtaining the payment of interest (*usurae*). Cothmann agrees with the new theory of interest and cites in support a number of authorities. First, he remembers the theologians: Melanchthon, Brenz, Hemmingsen and Chytraeus, and he adopts the three classes of people devised by Aepinus.[190] Then, he recalls the opinions of Du Moulin, the counsel made by the jurists of the faculty of Tübingen at the dispute of Regensburg, Peter a Vuell and Justin Göbler, which we have already seen before. Finally, Cothmann mentions the work of Coler and two other jurists that support the theory: Peter Friderus,[191] *Mindanus* (d. 1616), who refers to Luther and Brenz,[192] and the Reformed Italian Giulio Pace (1550-1635),[193] who does not quote any authors, but substantially adopts the new theory.[194] These works cast an image of the vast diffusion of the new theory.

Supported by the large number of authors quoted, Cothmann insists that he does not want to defend anything other than the lawful interest, as it is condoned by the magistrate and is just and proportionate. This lawful interest is not against the divine law, because the Scripture only concerns the poor. Neither it is against natural law, because money can bear fruits with men's work. Finally, a moderate interest is not against the new regulations and ordinances of the Holy Roman Empire. On this point, Cothmann develops his theory that the purchase of annuities is not an actual sale, but a loan. The key argument is that annuity and interest are equivalent, and therefore the new

189 C. von Bar, P. Dopffel (eds.), *Deutsches internationales*, vol. 2, 54-7.

190 E. Cothmann, *Consultationum*, responsum 52, 18.

191 T. Muther, *Friderus, Peter*, in *Allgemeine Deutsche Biographie* 7 (1878), 385 (accessed 29.10.2017): https://www.deutsche-biographie.de/gnd100126944.html#adbcontent.

192 P. Friderus, *De processibus, mandatis et monitoriis* [...] *tractatus*, editio novissima, Wetzlariae, 1737, liber II, caput 72, 633-44. Brenz and Luther are mentioned at p. 644.

193 On his biography see L. Bianchin, *Pace, Giulio*, in *Dizionario Biografico degli Italiani*, Vol. 80, 2014 (accessed 29.10.2017): http://www.treccani.it/enciclopedia/giulio-pace_%28Dizionario-Biografico%29/.

194 G. Pace, *De rebus creditis, seu de obligationibus quae re contrahuntur, et earum accessionibus* [...] *commentarius*, Spirae Nemetvm, 1696, tit. 32, n. 125ff., 117.

imperial legislation, which refers to annuities, also approves a moderate interest on a loan.

Cothmann writes that given the authority of these imperial laws, 'the disciples of the pontifical religion' condemn loans at interest and in their place receive and approve the annual incomes; thus their theoretical views have the same practical effect.[195] The creation of the purchase of annuities issued from Roman Catholic theologians and canonists. 'The followers of the pontifical religion', Cothmann judges, interpreted the passage of Luke 6,35 as referring to every loan. They substituted the sale for the loan and gave their money to the neighbour not in a loan but as the price for a certain annual income.[196] Hence, the purchase of an annual income is nothing other than a loan. While Roman Catholic authors contrived a strategy to bypass the interest-taking prohibition, the contract they engineered is actually not a sale but a loan.

For Cothmann, this statement is proved by the fact that the civil regulation applied to the sale concerns instead the loan. All the laws that belong to 'the false and artful sale' do not suit the true and lawful contract of sale, but the loan. They do not contain what departs from the loan's nature. For instance, both in the purchase of annuities and in the loan, the creditors are inhibited in their power to receive back the amount given: a certain amount of money is given, and its property is transferred to the recipient.[197] Then, as with a loan, in the purchase of annuities, the seller/borrower can use the goods. If he wishes to be free from the obligation to pay the annuity, he must return the same amount and genre of money to the buyer/lender. Finally, as in a loan, the buyer's gain is always certain while the seller's gain is uncertain.[198]

Thus, Cothmann concludes that the laws that are applied to the purchase of annuities exceed the terms of sale. A provision, according to the buyer only

---

195 E. Cothmann, *Consultationum*, responsum 52, 18: "*Non etiam obstant constitutiones et ordinationes novissimae sacri Imperii Romani. Quamvis enim auctoritate earum imperialium constitutionum pontificiae religionis sectatores usuras damnent, et earum loco annuos reditus recipiant et probent, tamen in effectu res eodem redit*".

196 E. Cothmann, *Consultationum*, responsum 52, 18: "*Contractui enim mutui substituerunt contractum emptionis, et pecunias suas proximo non ex mutuo subministrarunt, sed velut precium pro certis annuis reditibus tradiderunt et numerarunt*".

197 E. Cothmann, *Consultationum*, responsum 52, 19: "*Omnes tamen et singulae leges, quae huic commentitiae et fucatae emptioni insunt, non tam vero et legitimo emtionis contractui, quam mutuo conveniunt, neque quicquam continent, quod a mutui natura discedat, praeter id, quod emptori quantitatem datam repetendi potestatem inhibeant, nam in redituum emptione aeque atque in mutuo quantitas pecuniae certa datur, eiusque dominium in accipientem transfertur*".

198 E. Cothmann, *Consultationum*, responsum 52, 19.

cannot get back the amount of money[199] does not change the substance of the agreement, but adds to the loan a harsher condition.[200] Indeed, while in the loan the interest rate cannot exceed a certain limit (*Si non sortem*, D. 12,6,26), in the temporary redeemable annuity, the amount of the annuity can grow endlessly.[201] In other words, the limit for the buyer/lender is a reason to charge a higher annuity.

For Cothmann, the provisions applied to the purchase of annuities are the same used for the loans: the conveyance of property, the possibility to dispense with the obligation to pay the annuity by returning the goods and the uncertain profit for the debtor. The recent imperial provision that the buyer cannot get back the capital, but only the seller can terminate the contract by redeeming the annuity, only makes the loan harsher, because the buyer can charge a greater amount of annuity, while the civil laws fixed a limit on the interest on a loan. Therefore, both the contracts receive the same regulation. It follows that that they are the same contract, a loan and not a sale.

With these intrepid statements, Cothmann aimed to argue that the recent imperial law on the purchase of annuities did not put any obstacles to the practice of loans at interest. Annuities are like interest payments, and the purchase of an annuity is a loan. Therefore, the emperor intended to approve loans at interest and in the case Cothmann was dealing with, a loan at interest, the creditor could have the right to receive interest.

The same thesis was defended by Christoph vom Hagen, but with a different goal. Vom Hagen faced no practical case, but dealt with the theme of the interest-taking prohibition in a theoretical way, according to the new formulation. He meant to condemn an operation started by the papists that allowed for the possibility of an immoderate interest and that benefited churches and monasteries. Vom Hagen repeats Cothmann's observations and also formulates other arguments we cannot examine in detail.[202] Then, he polemically attacks the purchase of annuities. For him nothing in this contract is a true and lawful sale, but it was created to conceal immoderate and damaging interest, also to the advantage of ecclesiastical and canonical churches.[203]

---

199 On this provision see before the new imperial law. III/2.1.3.3.

200 E. Cothmann, *Consultationum*, responsum 52, 19: "*Leges igitur, quae emptioni redituum apponuntur, emptionis notissimos terminos excedunt. Neque una illa lex, quod scilicet soli emptori repetere pecuniae quantitatem non liceat, mutui substantiam mutat, sed mutuo duriorem tantum conditionem iniicit*".

201 E. Cothmann, *Consultationum*, responsum 52, 19.

202 C. vom Hagen, *Tractatus*, 91-100.

203 C. vom Hagen, *Tractatus*, 97.

Cothmann and Vom Hagen's thesis was met with bitter criticism. In particular, Heinrich Hahn, in his observations on Wesenbeck's *Paratitla*, replied to their arguments, stating that the purchase of annuities is a true sale and different from a loan. First, he writes, according to the principles of human actions, the parties wanted to stipulate a true sale and not a loan.[204] Second, this contract is concluded by the consent of the parties on price and goods, which are the proper elements of the consensual contract of sale, and there is no loan without the intervention of a thing.[205] Third, the nature of the act that is concluded proves that it is a sale. Indeed the parties sell the right to receive an income, which has an estimable price.[206] Fourth, the loan and the purchase of annuities represent two different possibilities for the parties who need money. In particular, the annuity redeemable by the seller is not a loan, because a sale can provide the clause of re-selling. This clause does not transform the sale into a loan, and it is not against the nature of a sale. The seller sells the good to the buyer for a price. Finally, the purchase of annuities is considered to be a sale, as approved in the recent imperial recess of 1530.[207]

In essence, Hahn gave priority to the will of the parties and the will of the emperor. The former wanted to negotiate a sale. The latter explicitly characterised the annuity contract as a sale. Then, Hahn looked at the different nature of the sale, a consensual contract, and the loan, which is a real contract. In the purchase of annuities, the parties agree on the price and goods, while the loan instead requires the delivery of the thing. Finally, the right to receive a certain annual income has an estimable price and can be sold; the clause to resell is not against the nature of sale and can be lawfully included in this agreement. This last point had already been discussed many times by theologians, canonists and jurists, as seen before.[208]

Hahn's refusal of the thesis that the purchase of annuities is a loan and not a sale reflected the majority opinion among the Lutheran jurists and theologians. Cothmann was aware of that and already mentioned Johann Aepinus, Johann Oldendorp, Charles Du Moulin, Andreas Gail and Matthaeus Wesenbeck.[209] In

---

204 H. Hahn, *Observata*, 35: "*Nam 1 iuxta principia humanarum actionum, contrahentes hic non mutuum, sed veram emptionem venditionem celebratam voluerunt*".

205 H. Hahn, *Observata*, 36: "*Hic contractus consensu de pretio et merce perficitur, quod proprium contractus consensualis qui emptio venditio vocatur, cum mutuum nullum fiat nisi rei interventu*".

206 H. Hahn, *Observata*, 36.

207 H. Hahn, *Observata*, 36.

208 See III/2.

209 The list is in E. Cothmann, *Consultationum*, responsum 52, 18. J. Aepinus, *Auszlegung*, 54ff. (Cothman refers to Aepinus, 32 but it seems that the discussion on the annuities is explained later); J. Oldendorp, *De emptione et venditione reddituum*, Frakfurt, Oder, 1525;

addition, Benedikt Carpzov[210] and Samuel Stryk[211] also followed this trend. Carpzov and Stryk insisted on the will of the parties and claimed that the provisions of the imperial law of 1548 attributed the power to redeem only to the seller/borrower. This provision clearly makes the purchase of annuities different from a loan.[212] This is the crucial point: the power to redeem being only granted to the seller/borrower is a specific feature of *emptio reddituum*. The regulation of the loan does not contemplate such a provision, with the consequence that there are two different agreements: the purchase of annuities and the loan.

The thesis that the purchase of annuities is not a sale but a loan was also held by the French humanist Claude Saumaise, in his *Dissertatio de foenore trapezitico* (1640). As a matter of fact, he asserted, the purchase of annuities is a papist creation and equivalent to a loan at interest.[213] The Lutheran Johann Otto Tabor countered these accusations in his *Consultatio academica de praesidiis debitorum infelicium et inprimis de exceptione alterius tanti usurarii* (1652). He even recurred to the authority of Catholic and Lutheran theologians to prove the nature of the sale of the purchase of annuities. Becanus, Navarrus, Soto, Molina, Luther, Hunnius and Balduin were all quoted together in support of this view.[214]

In conclusion, the adoption of the new theory of interest brought along with it a ferocious attack on the nature of the purchase of annuities (*emptio reddituum*). The theory of the identical nature of the purchase of annuities and the loan at interest went however straight to the point. The purchase of annuities had been invented by canonists and scholastic theologians to avoid the interest prohibition and provide the parties with a financial instrument that produced effects similar to a loan. For centuries they sought to classify this contract as a sale and not a loan, in order to avoid the application of the interest prohibition. Cothmann, vom Hagen, and later Saumaise strove to affirm exactly the opposite. The purchase of annuity is not a sale but a loan, an

---

C. Du Moulin, *Tractatus*, n. 20-21, 21-2; M. Wesenbeck, *In paratitla*, D. 22, n. 14, 26; A. Gail, *Practicarum observationum* Antverpiae, 1653, Lib. 2, *Observatio* 7, 288ff.

210 B. Carpzov, *Jurisprudentia forensis romano-saxonica*, Lipsiae, 1674, part. 3, cost. 24, def. 12, 1164-5.

211 S. Stryk, *Continuatio altera*, 808ff.

212 B. Carpzov, *Jurisprudentia forensis*, part. 3, cost. 24, def. 16, 1166; S. Stryk, *Continuatio altera*, § XL, 813.

213 C. Saumaise, *Dissertatio de foenore trapezitico*, Lugduni, 1640, 80-2. A summary is also included in G.A. Struve, *Syntagma iuris civilis, pars altera, cum additionibus Petri Mülleri*, editio tertia, Francofurti et Lipsiae, 1738, excerc. 27, lib. 22, tit 1, n. 58, 142ff.

214 J.O. Tabor, *Consultatio academica de praesidiis debitorum infelicium et inprimis de exceptione alterius tanti usuraii*, Giessae Hassorum, 1686, pars 3, articulus 5, 169ff.

instrument created by the Roman Catholic theologians and canonists to circumvent the canon law's interest-taking prohibition. Hahn and Tabor refused this view and reaffirmed the nature of sale of this agreement. This was also the majority opinion. The new imperial law explicitly dictated provisions that distinctly characterized this agreement as a sale. In the end nothing changed. Still, this discussion on the nature of the most diffused financial instrument is a genuine fruit of the new theory of interest. If the interest prohibition is not general, and loans at a moderate interest can be admitted, there is no need to conceal loans as sales.

2.4 Conclusion

This chapter opened with the words of Benedict Carpzov who acknowledged Matthias Coler and Peter Heige as the promoters of a new theory of interest and usury. In 1586 Coler defended the audacious claim that interest on a loan, even if it is not moratory interest, can be charged. Loans at a moderate interest rate can be allowed if the neighbour is not harmed. Before him, two formidable Lutheran jurists, Wesenbeck (1563) and Schurpf (1564) had kept the old conception that the charging of interest is always forbidden. In contrast, Coler picked up the thread of a discourse already started among the Lutheran theologians, even though he mostly referred to the French Du Moulin. He put forward arguments based on the divine law and the civil law. Concerning the divine law, Coler claimed that the reason of equality warrants the payment of interest, in accordance with Matthew 7,12, which requires the debtor to act as if he was a creditor. The creditor would expect something in return for the use of his money, because the debtor gained a profit with it. Thus, the debtor should pay interest to the creditor as gratitude for the money received. Ingratitude is a mortal sin, and the debtor commits a sin if he does not pay interest. Furthermore, the payment of interest does not burden the debtor for the sake of an uncertain profit, because in case of calamity the creditor is called to remit the interest and also the principal, if necessary. On the contrary, if the debtor did not pay interest, the creditor would suffer damage. According to Prov. 5,10, and 16-17, and 2 Cor. 8,13, nobody is called to benefit the neighbour with his losses. Hence, the divine law is not against the expectation of interest payments.

Regarding the civil law, Coler's view is that the old laws *Quamvis* (C. 4,32,3) and *Eos, qui* (C. 4,32,26) respect the divine law and have never been abrogated. As evidenced by the law *Cunctos* (C. 1,1,1) and the norms in *De ecclesiasticis titulis* (Nov. 131,1; Auth. 9,6), the Roman emperors did not want to abolish them, and even the new provisions of Charles V did not intend their overturning. The cherry on the top is the reference to Luther's approval of Justinian's law, which allows Coler to demand the necessary theological blessing. Coler does not ignore the fact that the interest-taking prohibition belongs to the theologians' sphere, but Luther's statements back his solution. Despite the fact that Luther is the only theologian quoted, Coler might have found inspiration in the works of other Lutheran theologians, as some of the arguments he proposed might suggest. The inverse is also possible: Coler influenced some Lutheran theologians, like Hunnius and Gerhard, which wrote after Coler, who also present arguments founded on equality and gratitude. Coler is never quoted, but Gerhard cites Heige, who reported Coler's conclusions.

A few years later, Peter Heige mounted a trenchant defence of the new theory of interest. He begins with a rich interpretation of Scripture supplied with elegant references to the Reformed theologians Daneau, the jurist Hotman and the Lutheran theologian Hemmingsen. His idea is that requiring interest is not forbidden in itself, but for the additional evil behaviour – it is the damage to the neighbour that the Scripture wants to reproach, but not the charging of interest. Thus, the Jews were not forbidden to charge foreigners interest, because the charging of interest is not a sin. God otherwise would have never permitted it, even in the case of the foreigners. Moreover, the etymology of the word 'interest' in Scripture is always associated with damage, as opposed to reasonable sums that do not detrimentally affect the borrower. Finally, Scripture always forbids the abuse of contracts, not their use. The charging of interest is not forbidden *per se*, but rather any abuse that harms the neighbour.

Heige endorses the new 1583 provincial law of the *Kurfürst* August of Saxony, which included provisions that reflected the new theory. He follows the path laid by Coler, using divine law to justify the validity of loaning at interest. Concerning the power of the magistrate to authorize the charging of interest, he relies upon the authority of the Lutheran theologians, Melanchthon, Aepinus, Chemnitz, Chytraeus, beyond referring to Luther himself. Yet, he also refers to Reformed Du Moulin, Hotman, Doneau and Daneau, and the Roman Catholic Tesauro and Villagut. This reveals that his horizons are far wider than the orthodox Lutheran theology. Finally, Heige counters the scholastic argument of the sterility of money.

One interesting feature of Heige's theory is his approach to the way the civil law must be enforced. The law allowing a charge of interest must not be enforced strictly, but through the judgement of conscience. This assessment must look not only at the lawfulness of the agreement but at what is truly profitable for both parties. It is founded on charity and enjoins the parties to avoid mutual damages and seek the benefit of the neighbour. In particular, this judgment implies the appropriate collaboration of the parties. No charge of interest is admitted towards the poor, but can only be required of the rich. On this point Heige adopts Aepinus' distinction of three classes of people.

The new theory of interest supported by Coler and Heige was broadly accepted by other jurists. The acclaim of the new theory is so ubiquitous that Wesenbeck's conservative opinion was integrally corrected by his commentators Bachov von Echt and Hahn. They affirmed neatly that the charging of interest is not forbidden in general but only when the neighbour is harmed. Besides, the new theory implies two central aspects, which were essentially constructed by the theologians. First, no charge of interest is admitted towards the poor. Ziegler, Carpzov, Cothmann and others do not venture in the interpretation of Scripture, but rely on the contributions of the theologians, especially on Aepinus' distinction of three classes of people. Second, the debt should be remitted if the debtor suffered adverse circumstances. In this case, Von Ryssel under the supervision of Carpzov provides one of the greatest examples of the theologians' influence. Inspired by charity, the creditor should exercise mercy, foregoing the intransigent though legally justified litigation and remitting interest and even the principal, if necessary.

Lastly, the new theory brings about a reinterpretation of the canon law. The prohibition against lending at interest is only dictated by Scripture, and the canon law loses its power. However, it is anything but abandoned. Unlike certain theologians, Heige and vom Hagen do not repudiate the canon law, but maintain that the canons intended to forbid only evil behaviour against the neighbour and not the charging of interest *per se.* This reinterpretation shows a peculiar feature of the new theology. The canon law is read through the lens of Christian charity, which is not only a criterion for the enforcement of the law but also an interpretative principle. It drives the understanding of the canon law.

The purchase of annuities (*emptio reddituum*) is re-evaluated by Cothmann, vom Hagen and later Saumaise, who held that is not a sale but a loan. This opinion is not accepted by the larger part of the Lutheran jurists. The purchase of annuities, though a creation of the canonists and scholastic theologians, is still estimated a sale. The consolidated use of this agreement produced a specific regulation that identifies this agreement and differentiates it from the loan. Again the work of the canonists is not abandoned but revalued.

In substance, the contribution of the jurists focused on establishing the legal framework for loaning at interest. They argued that not only the purchase of annuities but also the charging of interest on a loan can be allowed. In this way they went further than some of the theologians, who only directly considered interest-bearing loans, while other theologians only discussed the purchase of annuities. The jurists interpreted and defended Justinian's law, the imperial law and the provincial law. They provided these laws with robust roots and opened the doors to the new theory of interest, particularly altering the concept of usury. Usury thus came to be understood not as receiving profit in addition to the capital, but as the charging of an excessive interest rate, or the harmful behaviour that defrauds and impoverishes the neighbour.[215] In this sense, it becomes closer to the current meaning of the term.

The jurists endeavoured to clarify not only the interpretation of the civil law, but they also looked at the divine law. The law of interest could not be valid without a moral justification. The divine law represented an unavoidable point of contention that needed to be overcome. The contribution of the theologians, then, remained fundamental. The theologians guaranteed the necessary moral support and spiritual legitimation for the civil law.[216] But they also devised the criteria for the application of the provisions on the charging of interest. Charity was again the keystone of the discussion, as it casts a glance towards the poor and promotes the remission of debt. In this way it acts as equity for the mitigation of the rigid law.

In a more liberal way, some jurists referred to theologians and jurists belonging to other confessions, mostly Calvinism. The French Du Moulin, Daneau, Doneau and Hotman played certainly a role. Especially Du Moulin has been widely quoted. Is it then possible to say that the jurists simply received Du Moulin's theory? Behind the scenes, Du Moulin is a role model for many Lutheran jurists. Yet, two aspects are equally important. First, many of Du Moulin's conclusions are in a way stimulated by the Lutheran elaboration we saw previously. Du Moulin based his thoughts on Luther's, Melanchthon's, Aepinus', Rhegius' and others. Second, the adherence to the orthodox Lutheran faith required necessarily the approval of the Lutheran theologians. The quotation of Du Moulin was not enough to prove a statement in matter of divine law, without the endorsement of the theologians belonging to the Lutheran confession. Even Coler, who often refers to Du Moulin, in the end calls upon the authority of Martin Luther.

In conclusion, the progressive elaboration of the new theory of interest is the fruit of the cooperation between theologians and jurists. The theologians are the guardians of the spiritual and moral order established in the divine law.

---

215 This trend in the German doctrine is also noted by W. Endemann, *Studien in der romanisch-kanonistischen Wirtschafts- und Rechtslehre*, 1, Berlin, 1874, 69.

216 On this point and mostly concerning Roman Catholic authors, see W. Decock, *Collaborative Legal Pluralism*, passim.

They placed the foundations, the structure of the new theory, by engraving in a block of stone the interpretation of some biblical passages. The conception of property and alms is set by Prov. 5, 16-17 and 2 Cor. 8,13; the interest prohibition must be read in the light of Matt. 7,12; Lev. 25,35-37, Ex. 22,25; Luke 6,35 and other passages concerning the poor; Deut. 23,20 does not imply an absolute prohibition; and Christians are called to obey the political authority, according to Romans 13. The fundament of the new construction lies in the understanding the theologians gave of these passages.

The jurists set out the social and legal order governed by the civil law. They integrated the theological underpinnings into their arguments and implemented them. They used the theologians' contributions to shore up the licitness of charging interest and to determine its application criteria. At the same time, the jurists renewed the vision on the old Roman law and recovered it. The Roman law permitting the charging of interest has never been abrogated, but rather constitutes the antecedent of the new imperial law. The jurists adopted a clear position: the civil law supplants the canon law. The latter loses its power, but it is not totally dismissed. It remains alive in the discussions of the jurists, reinterpreted to corroborate the new theory. There is thus a change in the social and moral order, which is no longer guaranteed by the Church of the canonists and the canon law, but by the theologians and the jurists. A new standard for evaluating the legitimacy of lending is accepted.

General Summary

1 Christian Spirituality and Law: Developments and Sources

1.1 *Care for the Souls before the Reformation and in the Early Roman Catholic World*

Before addressing the contribution of the Lutheran theologians to contract law, we needed to illustrate the salient features of the Roman Catholic theology in the Middle Ages and the Early Modern Era. Indeed, canon lawyers and scholastic theologians of this time devised sophisticated contract doctrines that were later utilized by the Lutherans. The Catholics viewed the morality of contract law in the framework of the sacrament of penance. Penitential theology was shaped by the combination of different influences like monasticism, penitential books, Aristotelian philosophy, Roman law and canon law. Christian spiritual life was oriented towards the last judgment, when God will judge man for his sins. Sins are offences against God and the neighbour and entail a punishment. Man is free to perform good or evil actions; he can reject or accept natural law or the human laws that comply with it. In this way, he either ascends towards God or descends towards Hell. As compliance with rules was linked to salvation, man was encouraged to look to the neighbour's good as an instrument for gaining his own salvation.

Priests were viewed as representatives of God in this world. In the court of conscience, they examined attentively men's sins and imposed acts of penance. The assessment of the penitent's guilt was a crucial moment, as penance removed the temporal punishment imposed by God for one's sins. The Christian moral life also concerned decisions about legal obligations. Priests had to be trained as jurists, and moral literature (manuals for confessors and penitents, collections of cases of conscience, manuals of moral theology, systematic treatises) revolved on a detailed description of all human relationships in legal terms. Doctrines about just price, restitution and the prohibition of interest were mapped out, together with the construction of a general theory based on the canon law principle of the binding effect of simple agreements. In substance, contract law consisted of a jungle of norms to limit the Christian's sins and to drive him towards salvation. The last horizon of the scholastic theology was to restore justice wounded by sin.

1.2 *The Engagement of the Lutheran Theologians with Contract Law: Principles and Literature*

Luther, Melanchthon and their followers turned against the Roman Catholic vision of spiritual life, instead advocating the primacy of Scripture. In their

DOI:10.30965/9783657701506_012

view, the Word of God is Gospel and law, as two distinct but inseparable elements. Salvation is revealed in the Gospel and accepted by faith, without the need of good works. The law serves the Gospel. It governs the world through the hands of the magistrate, reveals to man his sins and teaches the justified people the good works. Compliance with the law is therefore detached from salvation, which only comes from the Gospel and faith.

The distinction between the law and the Gospel founded the two kingdoms doctrine. To Luther, every Christian is simultaneously citizen of a physical and temporal kingdom, the 'earthly kingdom', and of the spiritual kingdom, the 'heavenly kingdom', illuminated by the Word of God. The Christian is born into sin and is called to obey the secular authority and to follow its justice. God is present in this temporal kingdom especially through three orders: family, state and Church. However, through faith, the Christian is also a citizen of the heavenly kingdom. Here he is renovated by grace, justified and bound by the Gospel.

Justified by faith, the Christian looks at the law with a spirit of love and charity towards God and the neighbour. Moved by this love, he seeks to perform the good works that the law teaches. Penance was not abolished but received a new configuration. Confession did not include the enumeration of sins, but only their general indication. The imposition of acts of penances was often forbidden. Christians' moral education was promoted in various genres of works. At the beginning, sermons, catechisms, treatises and collections of theological counsels contained moral guidance, also concerning issues of contract law. Later, casuistical and moral theological handbooks were developed. The conscience was conceived of as a judge operating according to the norms of Scripture and especially the natural law.

The Lutheran theologians believed that natural law was divinely instilled in the human mind, but because of sin, it was obscured. For this reason, God repeated the content of the natural law in the Decalogue, summarized in the Golden Rule: *love your neighbour as yourself*. The theologians also insisted that the magistrate was called to issue his law in accordance with natural law. In the second half of the seventeenth century, this vision was challenged by the secular theories on natural law, theories which erased the connection with the divine revelation, holding that natural law merely aims to guarantee peaceful sociality. The theologians sought to restore the orthodoxy in various ways. One stream of thought concentrated only on the actions of the people justified by faith, distinguishing the sphere of creation from that of Revelation. Another line of thinking drew upon Grotius and early modern scholastics, correcting their stances in the light of Scripture and the fundamental principles of the Lutheran confession.

2 A Biblical Framework for Contract Law: Basic Elements

2.1 *The Seventh Commandment: Private Property and Contracts*

The seventh and eighth commandments of the Decalogue were the starting point for the analysis of contract law in the Lutheran tradition. The seventh commandment (*you shall not steal*) included the analysis of property and contracts, while the eighth commandment (*you shall not bear false judgment*) concerned the observance of agreements. Generally speaking, the treatment of the commandments comprised definitions and principles. In chapter 1 we discussed the definitions related to the seventh and eighth commandments. In chapter 2 we focused on the principles related to the seventh commandment, while in chapter 3 we examined those associated to the eighth commandment. In this paragraph we deal with definitions and principles related to the seventh commandment, while in the following one we examine those associated to the eighth commandment.

The Lutheran theologians espoused the view that private property is a divine institution ordained by the seventh commandment. This conception went deliberately against a communion of goods propelled by the Anabaptists, but also against the voluntary abandoning of property professed by the monks. The defence of private property did not mean the promotion of an egoistic tendency, however; private property was intrinsically connected to the Christian love for the neighbour. It should be understood as a gift of God, to be used for supporting the neighbour through alms (Prov. 5,16) or contracts.

Property was defined as lordship (*dominium*) over the things acquired according to just means. The lordship is a right (*ius*), namely the faculty (*facultas*) ordered by divine law and human law. In the seventeenth century, Pufendorf held that from an original communal state, human beings transitioned to private property, due to the influence of avarice and cupidity. The Lutheran theologians reacted with different strategies: Osiander and Alberti restated the divine origins of private property, lambasting those who contended the existence of a primaeval communal state. Buddeus formed a compromise position, distinguishing the power to use the thing as directly given by God, from the power to exclude others from the thing that originated later.

Contracts were generally defined by adopting Roman law or philosophical definitions. Melanchthon repeated Labeo's definition. Chemnitz relied on definitions posited by other authors and the Scriptures, pointing out that the theologians do not have to shape new legal definitions but must only add the efficient cause that is God's ordination and approval. In addition to this approach, however, Melanchthon also argued that contracts are divinely ordered means to acquire property rights, to meet the neighbour's needs and to practice the virtue of justice and equality. In this way, he integrated the contract definition with the theological perspective fixed by the interpretation of the seventh commandment.

Melanchthon's definition emphasized the aim of contracts: to fulfil the neighbour's needs and to exercise the virtue of justice and equality. In general, the virtue (not only the virtue of justice, but any virtue) shows a distinction between shameful and honourable acts. This distinction proves that human nature cannot be generated by chance, but that a God must exist. Furthermore, the virtue reveals God's corresponding attribute, whether justice, truth, etc. Thus, for Melanchthon, by practicing the virtue of justice, man can recognise the existence of God and that He is just. Melanchthon's definition also underscored the divine institution of contracts: contracts are divinely ordered means to acquire property rights. Other theologians – Strigel, Chytraeus, Dürr and Baier – followed, more or less exactly, this definition. For instance, Strigel stated that God instituted the contract in order to provide a bond for society, in which He wants us to exercise justice, so that we can learn what justice and equality is and know that God is just and equal. For Baier, contracts should be established and fulfilled according to good faith, and love should be exercised in contracts to ensure the advantage of both parties.

In addition to definitions, the seventh commandment was the ideal kernel for the formulation of a body of principles to oversee the main economic transactions. First of all, the theologians reaffirmed the lawfulness of business and contracts against the claims of the Anabaptists. The Anabaptists advocated that business and contracts were forbidden by the Scriptures. Luther answered back that the example of the patriarchs justifies the lawfulness of trade and business. Melanchthon, Chemnitz and other theologians argued that contracts are a creation of the power of God founded on natural law, a divine ordinance. God does not abolish his ordinance but only teaches how it must be used. It is not that contracts are forbidden, but only their abuse is forbidden. The theologians substantiated this vision with abundant biblical arguments and examples.

As the wrong use of contracts is forbidden, the theologians determined what is the 'right' use of contracts. Essentially, contracts have to be used in in accordance with the principle of faith and charity. To Melanchthon, the Christian must use contracts in faith, as a gift of God, and know that charity towards the neighbour must be practiced in these duties. Chemnitz developed Melanchthon's idea, stating that faith prevents the Christian from doing something with a doubting and corrupted conscience, and lets him know that the contracts are not against the Word of God, but rather are approved by Him. Charity forms a general framework for contract regulation, to determine the right form of exchange through accurate assessment of the neighbour's need. In addition, charity was interpreted as a general principle of equity. The Christian must not be legally rigorous against the neighbour who could not fulfil the contractual provisions through no fault of his own.

Faith and charity formed a general framework of contract regulation, establishing an open catalogue of duties between the contractual parties. On the other hand, they found an appropriate objective form in relation to two other principles established by the seventh commandment of the Decalogue: the prohibition against fraud and the injunction for contractual equality. Mostly referring to 1 Thess. 4,6, Luke 3,13 and James 4,13-15, the theologians forbade every genre of fraud, deceit, imposture and wrong action against the other contractual party. Yet only a few of them were interested in giving these acts a definition, and an organic classification was lacking. Luther, and similarly Balduin and Gerhard, alluded to commercial fraud as selling spoiled or defective merchandise, or using false measures, weights, coins or other tricks aimed at overcharging a person in trade or to impose a high price and take advantage of weaker or impoverished parties. Dannhauer attempted a definition of fraud based on the biblical example of Jacob and Laban (Gen. 30,37-42), determining that fraud occurs when there is shrewdness, but not when there is sagacity. On the whole, the majority of the theologians did not propose a definition of deceit or fraud.

The duty to protect the other party from fraud was often associated or incorporated in the principle of 'equality in contracts'. Luther and a few other theologians did not speak about contractual justice; it was rather an approach initiated by Melanchthon. To Melanchthon, the precept of 1 Thess. 4,6 and the seventh commandment reveal that God orders humanity to preserve equality in contracts. Contractual equality remembers the justice of God, who sent his own Son to save us from our sins. At the same time, this equality is a form of charity towards the neighbour. The practice of equality is an act of love towards God and the neighbour, moved by the Holy Spirit. The principle of equality in contracts is based upon Aristotle's commutative justice but is inserted in a theological structure where obedience and disobedience to God appear to be the constitutive elements. Equality in contracts must be observed as obedience towards God. This obedience, though, is impossible to man but is entrusted to faith and the Holy Spirit.

The doctrine of equality proposed by Melanchthon found a large following among the Lutheran theologians, who further developed it and nuanced its characteristics. For example, to Brenz justice in contracts involves the payment of debts and the prohibition of deceit. To Gerhard, contractual inequality means the refusal to pay the salary, the refusal to return the thing deposited, or the malicious deferment or denial of payment. To Osiander, justice consists of acting in good faith towards the neighbour and not profiting from his disadvantage. Finally, for Buddeus, contractual equality is an act of love for the neighbour that also implies precontractual duties of disclosure of defects and absence of duress. These viewpoints reveal a rather dynamic doctrine with numerous coloured pixels, which might be seen as a symbol of the variety of approaches within the Reformation.

2.2 *The Eighth Commandment: Observance of Agreements*

The seventh commandment regulated contracts as platforms for the exchange of property rights. In addition, the eighth commandment imposed the observance of the given word in whatever type of agreement, even without the legal formalities. Again, the theologians did not create new legal definitions but relied on those formulated by other authors. Thus, starting from Cicero, Melanchthon stressed that a pact must be honourable and requires that the consent of the parties is not coerced. In the seventeenth century, following the traces of the early modern scholastics and the natural lawyers, theologians like Osiander and Buddeus differentiated simple promises from offers and pacts. An offer is a naked promise still not followed by acceptance, while a pact is the consent of two parties. Some theologians argued that an act of will is sufficient for the transfer of property, without the delivery of the thing requested by Roman law. Other theologians, however, did not employ these concepts but only adopted the virtue of truthfulness and fidelity as categories to express contractual faith.

The eighth commandment was read in the sense that every agreement is binding. The canon law rule *pacta sunt servanda* was welcomed by the Lutheran theologians and inserted in the new theological perspective. Agreements are binding because of the natural law as repeated in the eighth commandment of the Decalogue. This commandment is expressed by the virtue of truthfulness and fidelity. The implementation of this precept is an act of love towards God and the neighbour deriving from faith. In the seventeenth century, the natural lawyers held that natural law is founded on the state of corruption (the human nature after the Fall), and its content is to promote peaceful sociality. Alberti reacted by grounding the *pacta sunt servanda* on the natural law derived from the state of integrity. Other theologians only revolved the attention towards the justified people and founded the rule on the virtues of truthfulness and fidelity or on Christian love given by God. They distinguished the order of creation and reason from the order of revelation and faith.

The principle *pacta sunt servanda* was further specified by the analysis of the requirements for the binding effect. As Scripture only provides general indications, the theologians drew upon Cicero and other classical authors, the early modern scholastics and the natural lawyers. A basic solution inspired by Cicero only requires the free consent of the parties and the lawfulness of the performance. A more detailed one, suggested by the scholastics, demands for the validity of the agreement a free, deliberate, intentional consent, where the thing must be pleasing to the promisee, and the promisor must have the power to bind himself. Finally, some theologians only concentrated on the virtue of fidelity and requested the expressed consent of the parties, the absence of mistakes and deceits, and the lawfulness of the subject matter.

In discussing these requirements, the theologians floated in a sea of different opinions, which derived from the more or less close adherence to the fundamental theological underpinnings and from the embracing of different strategies. For example, drawing upon arguments in the Church Fathers and the Scriptures, Osiander held that an external declaration is necessary for the validity of the agreement. When Scripture refers to promises towards human society and the neighbour, it always uses the word 'discourse' (*sermo*), suggesting that promises are external signs of internal belief. When the Church Fathers deal with promises, they always describe them as uttered through an external sign. Finally, Osiander backed this view by references to scholastic authors. On the opposite side, Jäger explored the debates among the early modern scholastics and concluded that because everything (even simple promises) is binding in the *forum conscientiae*, what has been only mentally promised is also binding. This was not the thesis supported by the majority of the scholastics.

Acceptance of the promisee was anything but a foregone conclusion. Indeed, based on the Scriptures, the Church Fathers and mostly the early modern scholastics, Osiander required this acceptance. The obligation arises from the reciprocal consent of the parties, because the promisor can change his mind and revoke his promise before the other contracting party's consent is expressed. The same position was espoused by Meisner and Bechmann. However, Horneius and Jäger followed Martín de Azpilcueta and did not explicitly recall the acceptance. Such a solution (without quoting the scholastic author) was also employed by Canz in the middle of the eighteenth century. The majority of the scholastics, however, rejected Azpilcueta's position.

Debate arose about the effects of mistake and duress on the agreement. Meisner contended that an unjust grave duress makes the pact invalid. Similarly, Buddeus argued that the pact is not binding if it is sufficiently strong to remove the use of reason. Following the early modern scholastics, Osiander admitted that in the *forum internum* even a light duress is relevant. Zentgrav stated that the agreement remains binding, but the party who suffered duress can claim for damages. On the promise accompanied by an oath, we also find different conclusions. Melanchthon and Zentgrav deemed that a sworn promise extorted by duress is binding, while Osiander maintained the opposite. On mistakes, Meisner designed a complex rational solution, which contemplated several sample cases. On the contrary, referring to the interpretation of Scripture, Dannhauer only affirmed that mistakes and deceits are harmful. These different results show the absence of a single consolidated viewpoint and the coexistence of different methods.

Finally, the theologians unanimously required the moral and physical lawfulness of the agreement, citing a morality centred on the Decalogue. As a consequence, they utterly rejected the opinion held by Grotius that the immoral promises performed can still cause valid juridical effects. These promises are ineffective, as nobody could be bound to commit a sin. Furthermore, following a tradition that harks back to Cicero and Seneca, the theologians maintained that agreements can be frustrated on account of noxious or useless subject matter and changed circumstances. Parties could not enter into a contract with criminals and atheists, while they were allowed to do so with heretics. To Alberti the obligation must be licit and therefore agreements with criminals are not valid. To Buddeus agreements with heretics are conceded in the Scripture, but as the atheists have no natural law, pacts with them are not valid.

Together with the requirements for the binding effect, the Lutheran theologians entered into the debate on the elements necessary to distinguish a morally binding agreement from a legal agreement. Despite the opinion of Meisner, who seemed to follow Cajetan and Connan in separating gratuitous from onerous promises, the majority of the theologians drove back this view. Osiander and Jäger sustained that every promise (for Osiander it must be accepted, but not for Jäger) gives birth to a moral obligation. They justified this point by referring to the Scriptures. Every promise can also produce a civil obligation, if the promisor wants. On this aspect they generally turned to some of the early modern scholastics.

In the end, the Lutheran theologians were unable to articulate an innovative general theory of contract law. Despite a few references, Scripture did not provide elaborate solutions but only sketches out general principles. Thus, the theologians undertook various paths: they only relied on Scripture, the virtue of truthfulness and fidelity; they followed Cicero, as previously the Roman Catholics did; they imitated or were inspired by the early modern scholastics and the natural lawyers. This lack of homogeneity and coordination impedes discussion of a systematic theory; rather the theologians committed individual explorations, attempting to resolve the problems of a consensualistic theory of contract law and to reconcile different sources with the essential theological statements of the Reformation.

3 Selected Issues on Particular Types of Contract

3.1 *Sale and Lease*

Together with general principles, the theologians also analysed specific types of contract. For the regulation of the sale of goods, the theologians both drew rules from the interpretation of the Bible and from the scholastics' works. For example, Lev. 19,35-36 and Deut. 25,13-26 were generally read as establishing the duty of the seller to evaluate correctly the quantity of goods that are for sale (fraud on calculations was forbidden). Osiander interpreted the passages of Lev. 19,18 and Syr. 21,1-3 as a general duty to inform the buyer about whatever defect of goods. Dürr forbade deceitfully lowering the price and value of merchandise, based on Prov. 20,14. Referring to 1 Thess. 4,6, Olearius prohibited selling goods that have false or small value as precious and useful ones.

Because Scripture was not sufficiently detailed, the theologians employed solutions devised by the scholastics. The scholastics' opinions were either accepted and inserted in the new moral context, or refuted in the name of an intransigent duty of charity towards the other contracting party. Indeed, the scholastics considered as valid in the court of conscience not only solutions grounded in the virtue of charity, but also in the virtue of justice, which was repudiated by some Lutherans. For example, in the matter of duties to inform the buyer about the defects of goods, Dürr and Prückner restated Aquinas's solution in the *quaestio* 77 of his *Summa theologiae*: the defect that must be revealed is one that is hidden, possibly harmful, dangerous or useless. Instead, looking at the Scriptures (Matt. 7,12; Eph. 4,15) and the homilies of Ambrose and John Chrysostom, Osiander insisted that the buyer must be informed about every vice, hidden or clear, noteworthy or not, with a possible damage or not, with a diminution of price in the future or not.

Osiander's rigid position also countered the solution to some cases discussed by the early modern scholastics. Under certain conditions, the scholastics allowed the Christian to sell what he knows could damage the neighbour, on the basis of justice, as long as the seller lowered the price accordingly. For instance, Lessius authorized the seller to sell a debt when he secretly knows that the debtor will not pay it at the ordinary price, as long as the market price of the debt reflects the inferior quality of the letter of debt, because it is not against justice, if the buyer is not intentionally misled. Drawing upon the indications of Lev. 25,14, Ecclus. 27,2-3, Ecclus. 42,3-5 and Ambrose, Osiander replied that

Scripture heightens one's general duty to reveal all the defects because of its call to charity and not merely to justice. The scholastic opinion grounded on justice was therefore generally dismissed. However, discussing the very similar case of the merchant who knows that the price of his goods will decrease because other merchants will begin selling the same goods, Horneius followed Thomas Aquinas, who answered that the merchant is obliged neither to reveal the presence of other merchants nor to lower the price. As a matter of justice, this is not requested.

The same double attitude towards the scholastics, accepting or refusing their solutions, can be seen with regard to the analysis of the ethics of pricing and market abuse. For example, Luther and later Dürr and Baier set forth the same criteria for setting the price as were dictated by the scholastics. Horneius and Prückner solved a number of cases concerning variation of prices by borrowing solutions from the scholastics. To Horneius, a diminution of price because of a donation could be tolerated. Indeed, the seller can reduce the price in consideration of the buyer. Prückner assumed that a good could be sold for a higher price than its value, if the good is sold on credit. However, other authors did not refer to the scholastics or opposed their opinions. Misler advocated for a market regulation grounded on conscience, Scripture and the magistrate. He did not offer more than general indications: the price can be raised for rarities but not for a necessity of the seller, and it should be reduced for the poor. Osiander refused to justify acts of private people who hinder the importation of goods, or buy them up, so that they can sell them at a higher price. If the price is just, Lessius and Grotius asserted that these people were acting not against justice, but only against charity. Osiander rebutted that he who commits a sin against charity also commits a sin against justice. He who does not love the neighbour is also unjust, because without loving he does not give to him his due. Therefore, these types of monopolies could not be accepted.

On the whole, the theologians designed a body of rules for the sale of goods, despite the lack of uniformity. Different angles reflected the more or less close observance to the standard teachings of the Reformation and the opening or closure towards sources coming from a different confession.

For the regulation of lease, the theologians followed the structure of sale, borrowing solutions from the medieval elaboration of Roman law and placing them in the new theological context. For instance, Melanchthon drew upon the Roman law distinction between contracts of good faith (*contractus bonae fidei*) and contracts of strict law (*contractus stricti iuris*). The *locatio* is a contract of good faith (*contractus bonae fidei*), and therefore the lessee is obliged to compensate the lessor if he damaged the thing through his fault, even in absence of an expressed provision in the contract. To Melanchthon the contracts of good faith are those where something is due for the sake of equality. Contractual equality means the just price, but also that the lessee has to pay for any damage, even if this is not set out in the contract. In addition, the thing must not have a shameful use.

Starting from these general indications, Horneius, Dürr, Baier and Prückner proposed a more systematic body of rules for the lessor and the lessee. This also includes the duty to reveal defects and the impossibility for the lessor to rescind the contract before the time determined. The lessee cannot transform the use of the thing that was originally assigned by the lessor and cannot leave the contract before the time established without a just and probable cause. About lease of body, or contract for prostitution, the theologians studied the debate among the early modern scholastics. Meisner rigidly refused to allow the prostitute keeping her wage: a sin cannot be sold. Osiander did not examine the issue in depth but simply applied the opposite solution without stating any motivation.

3.2 *Financial Operations*

One of the most remarkable contributions of the Lutheran theologians was the discussion about a widespread, supposedly usurious, financial instrument. This agreement was a particular type of purchase of annuity having various denominations, *Zinskauf, widerkaufflicher Zins*, or five per cent contract. It was characterized by annual returns of 5% of the invested sum. In 1530 the Emperor Charles V fixed the maximum amount of annuities at 5% of the invested sum, practically opening wide the doors to this agreement. In his first writings against usury, Luther condemned the new financial instrument as usurious and remained faithful to many of the scholastics' and canon lawyers' essential arguments, e.g. lending at interest is forbidden, interest-taking is an unjust acquisition of property, and money cannot bear fruits. Later, in 1540, Luther allowed the *Zinskauf* for the elderly, orphans and widows (a classification already existing in the Roman Catholic world), as an 'interest out of need', a *Notwucherlin*.

Despite his rather conservative view, Luther also proposed three innovations that will be developed by his disciples. First, while the scholastics incorporated the interest prohibition in a canon law norm supported by a mixture of scriptural and philosophical arguments, Luther lifted Scripture to prominence. To Luther the Church is not a society governed by legal norms, but is a community of Christians that stands before God and follows the Scriptures. The interest prohibition is not expressed in the canon law, but in the Scriptures. Second, Luther founded the interest prohibition on natural law and the Christian love for the neighbour (Matt. 7,12; Lev. 19,18). The scholastics distinguished between sins of charity and sins of justice. Usury was a sin against justice: it concerned both rich and poor and implied the duty of restitution. Luther did not restate the scholastic distinction between sins of charity and sins of justice. For him, usury is a breach of the rule of charity, an offence towards the neighbour. Third, referencing Matthew 5, Luther distinguished between three different degrees of dealing with temporal goods: alms, loans and sales.

Melanchthon discussed the contract with the clause to resell, which includes both the sale of a good with a clause of reselling, the purchase of an annuity deriving from a single land, and the purchase of an annuity deriving from different lands (the five per cent contract). Following a line of thought that harks back to medieval canonists and scholastic theologians, Melanchthon wrote that this contract is a sale and not a loan, and for this reason it does not breach the interest prohibition. He also appealed to the divine authority of the magistrate to justify the imperial ordinance on the five per cent contract. Because God approves the political power, the Christians can lawfully use financial tools endorsed by the political ordinances. Furthermore, talking about the compensation of loss (*interesse*), Melanchthon interpreted the precept of Luke 6,35 restrictively as only concerning the lending to indigents. In this way, he eliminated business transactions from the range of application of the prohibition on lending at interest.

Brenz was probably inspired by this intuition and interpreted the precept of Luke 6,35 as not pertaining to every Christian but only the poor. It is not a rule of justice for every man and every loan, but a rule of charity regarding the poor. Thus, he distinguished two categories of people, the rich who can practice the *widerkaufflicher Zins* and the poor to whom it is forbidden. Aepinus went further and proposed a threefold classification: the beggars, the working poor and the rich. Alms regard the first class, loans are for the second class, and business contracts can be stipulated among people of the third class. The effect of the new interpretation is that Luke 6,35 only concerns gratuitous loans to the poor. The poor are not the beggars, but the people who can work: unemployed or underemployed people, people who suffered calamities or unfavorable events, sick, elderly and similar. They should receive loans according to the rule of Paul in 2 Cor. 8,13, which means that the lender shall lend according to his capacity, while the borrower must strive to return the sum.

Rhegius put forward another theory on the foundations of the interest prohibition. To him in the Scriptures the use of the word *usura* does not reveal any absolute prohibition of lending at interest. In Hebrew this word has two names, *Neschech* (bite) and *Tharbith* (increase), which mean that the usurer increases his profit with damage to the neighbour. Usury is thus an infraction of the rule of love, and the passage of Luke 6,35 is a specification of the rule of charity. In order to be usurious, a loan must not only provide a charge of interest, but also harm the neighbour. Therefore, the Christians are called to apply the ordinance and practice the five per cent contract according to natural law and Christian charity. The charging of interest is only forbidden when it harms the other contracting party. With an emphatic expression, Rhegius wrote that the Christian must firstly have before his eyes the natural law and the love for the neighbour.

These innovative perspectives did not find unanimous consensus among the Lutheran theologians. Hemmingsen drove back Rhegius' stance, arguing that in the Scriptures interest (*usura*) is not only designated with the word *Neschech* (bite), but also with *Tharbith* (increase), which means that anything that exceeds the principal in a loan is forbidden. However, he distinguished between sins by nature and sins by an additional circumstance. Sins by their nature can never be admitted. Sin by an additional behaviour is usury. Lending at interest is not a sin, but the sin is in the additional behaviour of the greedy and idolatrous usurers who burden the debtor with the charging of interest, contravening the precept of love. The magistrate could therefore allow the payment of interest.

More incisively, Chemnitz criticized all the new theories (even Hemmingsen's one). For him, Scripture shows that interest-taking is always and in every instance forbidden. He only accepted two points of the previous theories. First, only rich people can practice the business contracts. Second, all the contracts must have as a master and moderator (*magistra et moderatrix*) the rule of charity. If the debtor is unable to pay the debt, charity pushes the creditor to remit it. In addition, Chemnitz allowed the contract with clause of redemption, also discussed by Melanchthon. He claimed that this contract is a sale and not a loan, and the clause of reselling is explicitly permitted in Lev. 25,23-30. Regardless, this contract must not breach the interest prohibition and must comply with the rule of charity. Concerning the first requirement, Chemnitz stressed that the contract should have a just price, the risk of loss should pass to the buyer, and the agreement should not be stipulated with poor people. The second requirement meant that both the parties must receive benefits from the contract, and if the debtor cannot repay the debt, the creditor must remit it. Lastly, to Chemnitz gratuitous loans were governed by the precept of 2 Cor. 8,13, Luke 6,35 and a body of rules from the Old Testament (Ex. 22,26-27; Deut. 24,10-12; Deut. 24,6), which established that the lender cannot take as pledge goods that are necessary for the borrower's life sustenance.

The tension between the progressive and the conservative theologians reached the apex at the dispute of Regensburg, where five ministers interpreted Luther's words restrictively. They argued that Luther only allowed the elderly, widows and orphans to use the *widerkaufflicher Zins* and excommunicated all the others who practiced this operation. Jakob Andreae replied to them in three steps. First of all, he proved that the interest prohibition only concerns loans directed to the poor. The old canonistic theory of interest was based upon a false interpretation of Scripture. Business contracts are not in the range of the interest prohibition and have to comply with contractual equality. The *widerkaufflicher Zins* complies with equality because the annuity is the price for the use of money. The creditor could have used it for other financial operations.

Second, with a formidable interpretation, Andreae extended the meaning of Luther's words. Luther did not aim to allow the German contract to old people, widows and orphans only, but also to other categories of people. Indeed, he approved Justinian's regulation of interest rate in *Eos, qui* (C. 4,32,26), which regards also citizens, aristocrats, merchants, etc. Furthermore, the need he was referring to was the need of everyone to earn the means to live. Luther granted no special permission for a few people, but a general permission for everyone. The third and last argument of Andreae was grounded on the reading of the political ordinance of Charles V according to Rom. 13,5. As this ordinance complies with natural law, it is like a divine ordinance that the Christian must obey in his conscience.

The dispute of Regensburg marked the victory of the new theory of interest and usury, which was subsequently systematized in the works of Aegidius Hunnius and Johann Gerhard. To Hunnius usury is forbidden by the Scripture because it is an act against charity. Usury breaches Paul's rule in 2 Cor. 8,13, for it impoverishes the borrower and enriches the lender. In Deut. 23,20 the charging of interest was authorized to the Jews against the people of Canaan because God wanted the Canaanites to be ruined. Luke 6,35 only concerns loans at interest towards the poor, because in this way they are oppressed. Thus, if there is no aggression, there is no usury. With similar arguments, Gerhard also held that usury is an act against the neighbour and oppresses the poor. He specified that in Luke 6,35 Christ talks about the almsgiving loan (*mutuum eleemosynarium*) and not about the compensatory loan (*mutuum compensatorium*), where for the money given, an annuity is also demanded. This compensatory loan also seems to include the *widerkaufflicher Zins*, which is therefore considered on a par with loan in which the charging of interest is lawful. Indeed, according to the new theory, it is no longer the legal classification of the contract (sale or loan) that determines whether the charging of interest is allowed, but the personal quality of the contracting party and in particular the necessity not to damage him.

Natural law, equity and charity justify the obligation to pay the annuity, for without the payment the investor is damaged, and the borrower is benefited. On top of that, gratitude implies that the debtor pays the creditor for the disadvantage deriving from the lack of the money that was lent to him. Yet, the Christian is called to apply the *widerkaufflicher Zins* and the magistrate's ordinance in compliance with his own conscience and according to charity. Charity invites the parties to a concrete judgement of obedience and disobedience of the law. The Christian should pay attention to the capacities of the other party: the *widerkaufflicher Zins* can only be practiced among rich people; the amount of the annuity must be proportionate to the lent sum and the parties' needs; and in case of unforeseen and unexpected circumstances, the creditor must partially or totally remit the debt.

In short, the prohibition against lending at interest is not founded on Aristotelian scholastic arguments and the canon law but on the Scriptures. The precept of Luke 6,35 does not forbid every loan at interest, but only the loan at interest towards the poor. What medieval canonists and scholastic theologians interpreted as a legal norm became a precept of equity rooted in charity; the law, therefore, does not belong to the theologians but to the magistrate. The magistrate can regulate business contracts; but Christians, justified by faith, have to apply them according to charity. Charity implies a set of rules that protects the neighbour against damages and guarantees that both parties benefit from the contract. These fundamental assumptions were cultivated by Lutheran theologians and jurists throughout the seventeenth century. Yet, they also stimulated the works of important Reformed theologians and jurists, especially Calvin and Du Moulin, who started from the fundamental intuitions of the Lutherans.

Despite the vast concern for the *widerkaufflicher Zins* and gratuitous loans, the theologians also examined other financial operations: purchase of real annuity (*census*), the *interesse* (compensation for loss), the partnership (*societas*), and the *montes pietatis*. Real annuities were generally admitted following arguments devised by canonists and scholastics theologians, viz. this contract is a sale and not a loan. Titles of compensation for loss (*interesse*) were only conceded after the notice of default. Luther admitted the *damnum emergens* and *lucrum cessans*. Melanchthon held the same opinion, but pointed out that *lucrum cessans* is due only to merchants or people involved in business, because their riches are not in estates but in business. They need money for other financial operations. Besides, if the loan was made to the poor, no *interesse* could be tolerated, save the borrower caused a serious damage.

Von Eitzen and Chytraeus repeated Melanchthon's positions. Rhegius stressed that in a purchase of annuities the *interesse* (compensation) for *lucrum cessans* and *damnum emergens* is usurious when it is requested of the debtors who were less prosperous than the creditors. Chemnitz followed Melanchthon, but specified four rules: the amount of the compensation should be calculated by referring to the creditor and not to the debtor; the creditor must receive the compensation only to repay the damage; the compensation must be founded on an effective and near cause of the damage; and the debtor is obliged not to seek to profit from damaging the lender. Chemnitz also permitted the charging of the *lucrum cessans*, but with some conditions. First, the profit concerns only the people involved in business. Second, the *lucrum cessans* must be current or 'quasi-current'. Third, if the lender advances funds to people who are not indigent, it is possible to assume that he is looking to accrue real interest. Fourth, the amount of the compensation must not be established by the creditor but by the magistrate.

Both Melanchthon and Chemnitz allowed participation in partnerships but, like the scholastics before them, they emphasized that the parties must share losses and profits: the contract is vicious if one of the parties gains more. They also condemned the clause where only one of the parties is guaranteed against every risk and the other suffers damages (*pactum de salvo capitali*). Drawing upon the new theory of interest, Meisner concluded that the *montes pietatis* are usurious because they are directed towards the poor. In order to lend weight to the argument, he referred to the scholastic Domingo de Soto, famous for his conservative views. In a similar way, Balduin condemned the *montes*, but he only appealed to the authority of Scripture. In conclusion, the discussion of these additional issues again reveals certain features of the Lutheran theology: the attribution of important tasks to the magistrate, the role of charity as guideline of contract law, and the protection of the poor.

3.3 *Restitution*

The closing chapter of the contract law doctrine developed by the theologians was restitution. The infraction of contract law rules produced an unjust profit from one of the parties at the cost of the other. It therefore entailed an obligation to make restitution. Like the scholastics, the Lutherans claimed the inevitability of restitution, yet they proposed a substantially different arrangement. First of all, the Lutherans did not estimate restitution as a prerequisite for salvation. Acts of penance are not required, because salvation only comes from faith. It is because of faith that the Christian makes restitution, as an act of love towards God and the neighbour. Secondly, the Lutherans only dictated general principles for executing restitution without delving into detailed norms, while the scholastics issued a flood of prescriptions.

The Lutherans insisted that restitution must occur even if it implies that the debtor and his family suffer damage. Only a limited number of exceptions were permitted, as for instance when the debtor is poor, or the creditor spontaneously remits the debt. In actuality, restitution was obligatory, but the modality of its execution was left for a good part to the Christian's individual conscience. Here again we see the novelty of the Reformation theology at work. There is no need of detailed regulation for restitution, because the Christian does not do it by the force of legal norms, nor moved by the desire to earn his own salvation. He provides restitution as urged by the grace of faith and as an act of love towards God and the neighbour.

4 From Lutheran Theology to Legal Practice

The analysis of contract law realized by the theologians did not remain in the sphere of moral theology, but was enhanced by the jurists. In the limited space of this dissertation we only focused on the relation between theologians and jurists concerning the theory of interest and usury. This relation can be summarized in three points: the jurists adopted the fundamental conclusions reached by the theologians, added further arguments, and built the necessary legal structure. First, the jurists adopted the fundamental conclusions reached by the theologians. They derived from the theologians the new asset of political and ecclesiastical powers. For instance, the jurists of Tübingen, called to settle the dispute of Regensburg, drew upon Brenz' teachings to establish that the magistrate has the power to intervene and regulate interest. Likewise, Coler and Heige referred to Luther's blessing of Justinian's regulation of interest *Eos, qui* (C. 4,32,26) to legitimize the power of the political authority to determine the interest rate. Furthermore, the jurists adhered to the new theological interpretation of the interest-taking prohibition. The jurists of the law faculty of Tübingen endorsed Andreae's orientation. Coler, Heige, Cothmann, Ziegler, Carpzov, Stryk, Hahn and others followed the theologians in assuming that the interest prohibition only concerns loans towards the poor. Charity should oblige creditors to remit debts when debtors are in need; similarly, to protect the neighbour, the interest rate must be based on a certain proportionality. Finally, the jurists relied on the theologians' utilization of a number of biblical passages concerning the conception of property and alms (Prov. 5,16-17; 2 Cor. 8,13) and the protection against fraud (1 Thess. 4,6).

Second, in addition to the reception of the theologians' contribution, the jurists strove for the construction of the new theory. For instance, Heige interpreted Scripture to reinforce the positions of the theologians, arguing that it is not the use of interest that is forbidden but the abuse of interest, the damage towards the neighbour. In addition, he claimed that the law allowing a charge of interest must not be enforced strictly, but through the judgement of conscience. This assessment is founded on charity and enjoins the parties to avoid mutual damages and seek the benefit of the neighbour. The contribution of the jurists also influenced the theologians. Indeed, Gerhard probably adopted Coler's and Heige's arguments to defend the charging of interest by invoking equality and gratitude.

Third, the jurists provided the new theory with the necessary legal framework. The Tübingen jurists proved the lawfulness of the three main terms of the *widerkaufflicher Zins*. The purchase of annuity was admitted by the two imperial ordinances of 1530 and 1548. The redeemability after a certain period of time was commonly practiced in Germany. The personal (and not real) obligation was not only commonly practiced, but also admitted by the imperial cameral court (*Reichskammergericht*). Besides, Coler reevaluated and legitimated the Roman law of interest. Heige defended the *Ausschreiben* of the *Kurfürst* August of Saxony, issued in 1583. Incidentally, we saw how this legislation reflected the new theory, showing that legislators implemented the theologians' statements. Further research is necessary, however, with regard to this profile.

Even more liberally than the theologians, the jurists quoted different sources, among which appeared Reformed authors and the Roman Catholic canon law. Nevertheless, these were often used in combination with references to Lutheran authors in order to guarantee the adherence to a complex of doctrinal principles that determined the Lutheran confession. For example, the Tübingen jurists connected Du Moulin's opinion with references to Brenz, Wesenbeck and Vuell. Coler cited Du Moulin, but also referred to Luther. The discourse is similar with regard to the canon law, which was reinterpreted in the light of the new theory. Heige and vom Hagen reasoned that the canon law wanted to prohibit evil behaviour against the neighbour that derived from an abuse of interest and not the charging of interest in itself. Thus, external sources were assimilated and integrated in the new perspective.

The majority of the jurists welcomed the new theory, but important scholars, such as Schurpf and Wesenbeck, held a conservative view. They recapitulated the old arguments, according to which charging interest is always forbidden. Coler countered Schurpf's thesis, arguing that the Roman law of interest is not against the divine law, and that the political authority has the power to regulate interest. Hahn and Bachov of Echt definitively overcame the old vision of the interest prohibition supported by Wesenbeck. Therefore, usury came to be understood not as receiving profit in addition to the capital, but as the charging of an excessive interest rate, or the harmful behaviour that defrauds and impoverishes the other contracting party.

Concluding Remarks

After this brief summary of the main points treated in this book, we propose now an overall interpretation of the theologians' contribution to contract law. We will discuss the hypothesis formulated in the introduction and related to the supposed existence of a Lutheran doctrine of contracts. Then, we will seek to highlight some of the insights this research has produced relating to the history of contract law and the history of economic thought and ethics. Lastly, we will articulate some hypotheses for the possible future analyses of Lutheran teachings of contract law.

1 A Lutheran Theory of Contract Law?

Luther and Melanchthon gave birth to a new vision of Christian spiritual life centred on the primacy of Scripture. Scripture must be interpreted according to the distinction between law and the Gospel. Salvation does not come from compliance to legal norms, but only by faith in the Gospel. The law governs the world, reveals man's sins and guides the justified people. This distinction does not mean that law and the Gospel are completely separated. Justified by faith man obeys the law as moved by the Holy Spirit and looks at God and the neighbour with a spirit of love. He performs the good works that the law teaches out of gratitude for the salvation already obtained.

Luther and Melanchthon applied these and other fundamental teachings in their treatments of contract law. The theologians who followed them, Rhegius, Brenz, Aepinus, Chytraeus, Chemnitz, Balduin, Gerhard, Meisner, Buddeus and many others interpreted Luther's and Melanchthon's principles and norms, elaborating detailed responses to most crucial issues of contract law. Generally speaking, they remained faithful to their masters, but at times they moved away from them. Especially in the matters of usury and interest, the Lutheran theologians undertook paths that contradicted or deliberately altered Luther's statements. Besides, occasionally authors remained more faithful to Luther than to Melanchthon and vice versa. This aspect might be seen with regard to the virtue of commutative justice, for example.

The Decalogue, summarized in the rule of charity, constituted the basis for the Lutheran normativity. Rules stemming from Scripture were placed at the core of the system. Yet this new perspective did not lead to an immediate purification of Scripture from external sources. This radical approach only seems more to be followed in the second half of the eighteenth century. Before

 | DOI:10.30965/9783657701506_013

that time, Aristotelian philosophy, scholastic or Reformed theology and the natural lawyers' works were utilized, following a dual approach. Theologians either borrowed concepts and solutions, setting them in the context determined by the new interpretation of Scripture, or substituted them.

The virtue of commutative justice and the virtue of truthfulness and fidelity were implanted in a framework of faith and charity. Concepts and resolutions in the matters of the ethics of pricing, duties to inform, market abuse, general theory, and contracts of prostitution were also imported and placed within the new context. On the same issues, however, other theologians scorned the scholastic conclusions rooted in the virtue of justice and replaced them with other solutions which were only based on the virtue of charity. A typical example is the duty to inform the other party about the defects of the goods to sell. Among the scholastics, this duty tolerated conclusions based on justice, which were not always accepted in a model illuminated by charity. Every defect of the ware, present or future, possible or expected, must be declared.

The Lutheran theologians also reversed certain interpretations of Scripture given by scholastic theologians and canon lawyers. This is plain from looking at the theory of interest and the requirement for restitution. Here, the theologians dismantled the scholastic interest prohibition and loosened restitution from the knots of the scholastic regulation. The interest prohibition had been constructed on a legalistic interpretation of Luke 6,35 that was rejected by the Lutherans who pleaded for the interpretation of the Gospel in the light of charity. They recognized in this way that the subjects of that rule are not all the Christians, but only the poor. By the same token, Eph. 4,28, Luke 19,8 and Ez. 33,13-15 showed the necessity of making restitution, but also that the restitutive act follows the conversion of the sinner as a concrete act of repentance. The act of restitution stems properly from faith, as an act of thanksgiving for the salvation obtained, and not as a good work to merit salvation.

Whether the outcome reveals a Lutheran theory of contract law might be debatable. If one looks for a contract theory with the same systematic integrity and legal strength of the Roman Catholic one, the answer would probably be negative. Certainly, the Lutheran theologians were constant in setting a number of theological principles. With regard to specific problems, however, they seem not to have developed a completely organic and coherent treatment. We have seen single immersions in the intricacy of contract law, rather than uniform and systematic approaches. Besides, the theologians were not educated in law, and this is reflected in their reasoning, which often lacked legal subtlety. Lastly, the amount of works realized is scarcely comparable with the gigantic contribution left by the Catholic scholastics. The scholastics compiled an impressive body of volumes, while the Lutherans' production was far less copious.

Nonetheless, if one treasures the specific features of Reformation theology, then elements of a Lutheran contract doctrine surface. The Lutherans distinguished the law, which belongs to the magistrate and the jurists, from the Gospel, which pertains to the theologians. Contract law was therefore promulgated by the political authority and mapped out by the jurists, but it was accompained by a parallel structure determined by the moral theologians and based on the elucidation of Scripture. This regulation concerned both the guidance of the legislators for the drafting of the law and the concrete implications for the Christians regarding the application of the law. Hence, 'legal' norms issued by the political authority were complemented by 'moral' norms formulated by the theologians, which dictated the 'right' use of contracts.

The content of these norms was principally rooted in Scripture and natural law, despite the recourse to other extra-confessional sources. The theologians identified in the Scriptures a set of general principles, such as charity, equality, prohibition against fraud, and observance of the agreements. In addition, they devised more specific regulations for the standard economic transactions: sale, loan and all the principal financial operations. The theologians mandated rules on prices, interest, diligence in performance, precontractual duties to inform, monopolies and other topics. This body of principles and norms was consistent and formally expressed, so that it could be designated as a theory.

Granted, the Lutheran teachings of contract law did not boast the same homogeneity and compactness as the scholastic ones. Some theologians swore an oath of fidelity to the theological underpinnings of the Reformation, while others also accepted solutions devised by the Roman Catholic theologians and the natural lawyers. Still, this does not negate the fact that the theologians faced all the most current problems of contract law. In their answers they progressively articulated a complex of ideas that in substance complied with the basic assumptions of the Reformation. Although the theologians showed different shades of orthodoxy and originality, they regardless realized an effective 'Lutheran' treatment of contract law.

2 The Collaboration between Theologians and Jurists in Regulating Contracts

The contract law teachings developed by the Lutheran theologians should not be read in an isolated way but in relation with the jurists, who also made their contribution. Theologians and jurists cooperated in resolving contract law problems, especially those concerning interest and usury. The jurists considered the Scriptures and the divine law as the supreme cornerstones of the legal system. They also hazarded at biblical interpretation, but essentially relied on the theologians. The theologians were the authentic guardians of interpretation of the Scriptures. They established the balance of powers between the ecclesiastical and the political authority, and delimited the dogmatic boundaries for the formulation and enforcement of political ordinances. In return, they also needed the support of the jurists for giving legal depth to their teachings.

The new vision on the Scriptures did not imply the obliteration of the *forum internum*, but rather its new relationship to the *forum externum*. The *forum internum* became governed by theology and not by law. Principles and norms were no longer fabricated by legal experts, but only by the doctors of the Scriptures, the theologians. These principles and norms were therefore often formulated through Scriptural (versus legal) references and in general terms, to be applied by the individual conscience. The court of conscience remained in force, but lost much of its legalistic attitude. It was not the struggle to reach salvation that guaranteed the enforcement of norms in the court of conscience, but the generous potential of faith and charity. Morality and law appeared in this way to be distinct but intertwined spheres. The regulation of contract law in the *forum internum* lost its precision and became an ensemble of rules to be specified by the magistrate with the counsel of his jurists, and applied by the Christians. The magistrate, the jurists and the contractual parties were called to implement the divine law: the magistrate, through the legislation; the jurists, through the formulation of norms, the arguments expounded in their treatises and counsels; the parties, by tempering the rigidity of law according to the needs of the other party. The Christian's individual conscience became the hero of this process.[1]

Looking back at Gordley's study on the Aristotelian-Thomistic tradition,[2] we might observe that the Lutheran theologians and jurists did not disrupt it, but the way of looking at Aristotle changed. Aristotelian philosophy was studied in a theological horizon, according to which every virtue recalled God's attributes and required the grace of God for its ultimate fulfilment. The Lutheran gaze started not from human freedom, but from the grace of God. The virtue testifies that God exists and reveals His attributes. By practicing the virtue, man can know God. But through his own effort, man could never completely obey God and fulfil the virtue. Because of sin, the grace of faith only is capable

1 The increasing importance of the merchant's conscience in this period is an aspect that has been already noticed by P. Prodi, *Settimo non rubare*, 204-5.
2 J. Gordley, *The Philosophical Origins*, passim; J. Gordley, *Foundations of Private Law*, passim.

of pushing man to obey God and accomplish the virtue. The Lutherans insisted on faith as the true engine of morality, but they did not break with Aristotelian philosophy.[3]

At length, the panorama of contract law in the early modern era was more complex than what has been described up to now. The study of contract law was not only the monopoly of the natural lawyers, jurists and scholastic theologians, but the Protestant theologians also played their role. Certain legal historiography has disregarded the connections between law and moral theology in the early modern era, and thus removed the theologians from legal history.[4] As Berman claimed, scholars have ignored the impact of values on law.[5] However, social order derives from the cooperation between law and morality. In the words of Malinovski, the sacredness of words and especially promises and contracts is a crucial factor for keeping social order. The meaning that society entrusts to them is not only the fruit of legal but also moral institutions.[6] Legal history cannot avoid looking at the interplay between legal and moral agents in society. In the early modern era, contract law was not only statal rules engraved by jurists, but it was the blending of values and norms, faith and reason together.

3 The Lutheran Theory of Interest and the Morality of the Marketplace

From an economic viewpoint, the Lutheran theory of interest merits special consideration. Even though in practice the Lutheran and the scholastic theory of interest might have wrought similar effects, it seems that the Lutheran theory was more restrictive than the Roman Catholic one. Scholastics and canon lawyers built an absolute prohibition against lending at interest, established in the canon law. But then by way of exceptions, they allowed a myriad of

3 In general terms, the thesis of an abandoning of Aristotelian morality has been recently defended by B.S. Gregory, *The Unintended Reformation. How a Religious Revolution Secularized Society*, Cambridge, Mass., London, Harvard University Press, 2012, 206-7. However, see the criticism by J.J. Ballor, *A Society of Mutual Aid. Natural Law and Subsidiarity in Early Modern Reformed Perspective*, in W. Decock, J.J. Ballor, M. Germann, L. Waelkens (eds.), *Law and Religion*, 9-21.

4 This has been observed by I. Birocchi, *Causa e categoria*, 204 and W. Decock, *Theologians and Contract Law*, 25.

5 H.J. Berman, *Law and Revolution II*, 449.

6 B. Malinowski, *Coral Gardens and Their Magic: A Study of the Methods of Tilling the Soil and of Agricultural Rites in the Trobriand Islands*, vol. 2: *The Language of Magic and Gardening*, George Allen & Unwin, London, 1935, 234-5, cited in H.J. Berman, J. Witte Jr. (ed.), *Law and Language. Effective Symbols of Community*, Cambridge, Cambridge University Press, 2013, 91.

financial transactions, far more than the Lutherans did. The Lutherans placed the Scriptures, and not the canon law, at the centre of the system. From an absolute prohibition of interest, the theologians devised a prohibition to harm the neighbour by charging an excessive interest rate. This prohibition was especially geared in favor of the weaker party, the poor. The Lutherans stressed the responsibility of the single Christian to avoid damaging the other contracting parties in the concrete situation, while the Roman Catholics permitted a larger number of financial techniques by the authorization of priests, canon lawyers and theologians, who circumvented *de facto* the strict prohibition. Once these authorities gave green light, however, the conscience could be free to pursue one's personal interest, unconcerned for the real situation of the other party.

The Lutheran theory of interest should also not only be read in an insulated way, but in the vaster and more influential perspective of the Protestant theory of interest, to which the Lutherans gave a formidable stimulus. Without underestimating the importance of Calvin, Du Moulin and others, the contribution of the Lutherans laid down the foundation of the new Protestant theory of interest and usury. Many of the essential aspects of the new theory, such as the crucial role of natural law and charity, the new interpretation of key biblical passages about *usura* and the division in three classes of people, were already sketched out by the Lutherans before the writings of the French authors. Hence, the inception of the new theory in the Lutheran thought is an aspect to take into consideration in order avoiding a partial or incomplete depiction.

Echoing Max Weber's thesis, Erich Fromm has argued that Lutheranism was at the origin of the 'industrial religion', which proclaimed, among other things, the supremacy of personal interest and reciprocal antagonism.[7] As said in the introduction, Weber's thesis was refuted by historians of economics. However, this research has once more proved that the idea that Lutheranism promoted competition and individualism seems to be manifestly wrong. The emergence of the economic power separated from the political and the sacred power is a long process that started in the late Middle Ages.[8] Indeed, the dialectical tension between the material and spiritual has been a constant factor in the development of the Western legal tradition.[9] The solution proffered by the Lutheran theologians and jurists was to avoid emphasizing competition and profit. The reformers legitimated private property, contracts, business and interest; meanwhile, though, they insisted on their 'right' use according to faith and charity.

7 E. Fromm, *To Have or To Be*, (transl. F. Saba Sardi) *Avere o essere*, Milano, Mondadori, 1977, 160-1.

8 P. Prodi, *Cristianesimo e potere*, Bologna, Il Mulino, 2012, 8-9.

9 H.J. Berman, *Law and Revolution II*, 197.

The Lutherans spurred the Christian to undertake the protection and promotion of the neighbour's goods, for the sake of his own good and the glory of God. Contractual rules were decreed to protect the neighbour against any fraud. Charity encouraged the care for the economically weaker party and the abstention to legal claims in case the debtor could not fulfil the contractual provisions. In particular, the Lutherans introduced a judgment of conscience in the application of the law. The interpretation of the rules was to be fitted to the needs of the other contracting party and especially the personal quality played a role. Certain contractual rules were only valid when both promisor and promisee were rich. When one of them was poor or became poor, the other party must assist him. Widows, elders, orphans, sick, unemployed or underemployed people, and people who suffered calamities or unfavorable events may not be completely lacking financial means, but regardless needed particular assistance and were classified as poor. Thus, the charging of interest was not allowed towards them, and their debt should be remitted. They were also excluded from the duty of restitution.

These obligations towards the poor stipulated by theologians and jurists were both directed to the contracting parties and the magistrate to be followed in their conscience. The magistrate as a divine institution was called to regulate prices and interest and to issue laws against fraud and for the safeguard of the poor. On the other hand, the individual Christian must enforce them according to charity towards the neighbour. Charity acted as a form of equity and mitigated the rigidity of law. Therefore, the Lutheran model seems to be clearly tilted towards solidarity, rather than the individualism and competition that fostered the emergence of the 'industrial religion', as Fromm has contended.

4 The Fate of the Lutheran Contract Law: Some Hypotheses

An in-depth analysis of the impact of the Lutheran theologians' teachings of contract law on German or more in general on European legal thought would require a separate study. Here we only put forward some hypotheses, some ideas for further investigations into the possible developments of the Lutheran contribution to contract law. The strain of the Lutheran theologians for the regulation of contract law could be read in the vaster horizon of providing the legitimation, guide and supplement for the public governance and state legislation.[10] The results of the Lutheran analysis of contract law might have

10 See the illuminating reflections of H.J. Berman, *Law and Revolution II*, 194-5. See also A. Wijffels, *Law and Religion in Early-Modern Europe: Some Tentative Conclusions*, in W. Decock, J.J. Ballor, M. Germann, L. Waelkens (eds.), *Law and Religion*, 266-75.

flowed into the *Polizeiordnungen*.[11] These regulations were instruments to establish a Christian discipline (*christliche Zucht*),[12] and in sixteenth-seventeenth century Germany, many of them included provisions about price setting, *Zins*, length of the lending operation and monopolies.[13] The common man was forbidden to receive credit when the contract could harm him, and especially mortgages were not allowed towards the poor. In some cases, the magistrate appointed an officer to verify the conditions of the people who wanted to borrow money and the reasons for such claims. Without authorization the concession of credit was forbidden.[14] Particular rules granted to the poor more favourable economic conditions for loans and other financial instruments.[15]

Certainly, the theologians did not propel an unconditional subjection to the directives of the magistrate, but guided the legislators in the light of Scripture and invited Christians to follow their consciences when these were in conflict with the law. Brad S. Gregory has recently stated that 'the most important social virtue among early modern Lutherans and Reformed Protestants' was not *caritas* but obedience.[16] Concerning contract law, this conclusion does not seem to be proved. It is true that the theologians praised the divine authority of the magistrate and gave his decrees the weight of divine ordinances. It is however also worthwhile that they often determined the legislative interventions and dictated the operative conditions for their enforcement. A law against natural law could virtually have never been observed. The theologians insisted on the role of the legislator to temper the economic differences and

11 On the *Polizeyordnungen* see K. Härter, *Disciplinamento sociale e ordinanze di polizia nella prima età moderna*, in P. Prodi (ed.), *Disciplina dell'anima, disciplina del corpo e disciplina della società tra medioevo ed età moderna*, Bologna, Il Mulino, 1994, 635-58; M. Stolleis, K. Härter, L. Schilling (eds.), *Policey im Europa der Frühen Neuzeit*, Frankfurt am Main, Klostermann, 1996; K. Härter, *Policey und frühneuzeitliche Gesellschaft*, Klostermann 2000. Further references in K. Härter, *Security and "Gute Policey" in Early Modern Europe: Concepts, Laws, and Instruments*, in *Historical Social Research*, vol. 35, 4 (2010), 41-65. An edition of the ordinances is W. Kunkel, G.K. Schmelzeisen (eds.), *Polizei- und Landesordnungen*, Köln, Böhlau, 1968.

12 Fürstlich-Hessische Landesordnung in der obern Grafschaft Katzenelnbogen (ca. 1587), cit. in K. Härter, *Disciplinamento sociale*, 643.

13 G.K. Schmelzeisen, *Polizeiordnungen und Privatrecht*, Münster, Köln, Böhlau Verlag, 1955, 475-500. For a more general perspective see P. Prodi, *Settimo non rubare*, 332-9.

14 G.K. Schmelzeisen, *Polizeiordnungen*, 462-75.

15 W.J. Wright, *Capitalism*, 187-216; K. Härter, *Disciplinamento sociale*, 648-54. S. Kreiker, *Armut, Schule, Obrigkeit. Armenversorgung und Schulwesen in der evangelischen Kirchenordnungen des 16. Jahrhunderts*, Bielefeld, Verlag für Regionalgeschichte, 1997; H.J. Berman, *Law and Revolution II*, 190ff. M. Stolleis, *History of Social Law in Germany*, Berlin, Springer, 2013, 11-28.

16 B.S. Gregory, *The Unintended Reformation*, 209.

at the same time stimulate the parties' conscience to apply financial devices without harming the neighbour.

The contribution of the theologians might have found also another channel to be effective. At the end of the seventeenth century, the secular vision of natural law got the upper hand. Thomasius proclaimed that only the positive law can be defined as law in a strict sense, while natural law had the role of a counsel.[17] The legal science was subordinated to the authority of the state, and moral theology was marginalized. At the very least moral theology was no longer expected to provide legal rules for the regulation of civil society.[18] Nevertheless, gleams of the theologians' ideas might have leaked out in the reflections of the natural lawyers and then filtered through the codifications.[19] For instance, charity as a theme is present in the works of Domat (1625-1696),[20] Leibniz (1646-1716)[21] and Wolff (1679-1754)[22]. Even though it is very difficult to trace their teachings back to the Lutherans, it is definitely a fact that all of these scholars were Protestants.

The contours of the Lutheran contract law teachings, then, like the early modern scholastic ones, were lost out of sight in the mist of secularization. Throughout the eighteenth century, moral theological works were still produced, but they progressively declined to confront legal problems and focused only on a biblical morality. This was one of the consequences of an increasing individualization of conscience. Because Christians became accustomed to finding by themselves the solutions to moral problems in the Scriptures, the

17 C. Thomasius, *Fundamenta iuris naturae et gentium*, Halae et Lipsiae, 1718 (4nd. ed. Aalem 1963), 139 cit. in P. Prodi, *Una storia della giustizia*, 407.

18 See S. Pufendorf, *De officio, Ad lectorem*, in G. Hartung (eds.), *Samuel Pufendorf, De Officio*, in W. Schmidt-Buggeman (ed.), *Samuel Pufendorf, Gesammelte Werke*, vol. 2, Berlin, 1997, 5, cit. in W. Decock, *Theologians and Contract Law*, 49.

19 P. Prodi, *Settimo non rubare*, 343. See also the works of F. Todescan, *Le radici teologiche del giusnaturalismo laico*, 3 vols., Milano, Giuffrè, 1983-2001; For a survey on the codifications see A. Padoa Schioppa, *Storia del diritto in Europa. Dal medioevo all'età contemporanea*, Bologna, Il Mulino, 2007, 456-72.

20 On Domat in general see J.L. Halpérin, *French Legal Science in the 17th and 18th Centuries: To the Limits of the Theory of Law*, in E. Pattaro, D. Canale, P. Grossi, H. Hofmann, P. Riley (eds.), *A History of the Philosophy of Law in the Civil Law World, 1600-1900*, 43-68.

21 G.W. Leibniz, *De justitia*, ed. Mollat, 35. cit. in H.P. Schneider, *Justitia Universalis*, 386. Leibniz speaks about justice as *charitas sapientis*. See also P. Riley, *Leibniz on Justice as "The Charity of Wise"* in P. Riley (ed.), *A Treatise of Legal Philosophy and General Jurisprudence, Vol. 10: The Philosophers' Philosophy of Law from the Seventeenth Century to Our Days*, Berlin, Springer, 77-106.

22 D. de Levie, *Christian Wolff und der Begriff der Menschenliebe. Festvortrag aus Anlass der Verleihung der Ehrensenatorwürde der Universität zu Köln*, Krefeld, Scherpe, 1972.

assistance of the theologians was less demanded.[23] The religious wars led to the turning to the state authority to determine the true faith and to indoctrinate moral behaviours.[24] In addition, promoters of Christian enlightenment accused private confession of being a papal instrument and obtained its abolition in many Lutheran lands.[25] Thus, the theological roots of the contract law doctrines were sterilized in a secular faith for an individual freedom, only limited by considerations of social utility.[26]

Secularized will theories pivoted on the freedom of the parties in order to promote individual interests.[27] Yet, in the second half of the nineteenth century, the transformation towards an industrial society brought out the gaps in this conception. Abuses of contractual freedom damaged the economically weaker parties. Hence, contract law became to be considered as an instrument having a social function. The legislator should intervene for the regulation of social and economic disparity and the protection of the weaker party.[28]

Many years before, in a different context, the Lutheran theologians and jurists reconciled the tensions between private interest and economic disparity by stating the duty to use contracts within the bounds of faith and charity. They stressed the appraisal of the different qualities of the contracting parties and fought for the protection and promotion of the weaker party. They advocated the intervention of the state, but also the judgment of the personal conscience of the Christians driven by Scripture. In a secularized world, this vision could never persist, as it relied on the central role of religion. When religion was marginalized in the public debate, the teachings of the Lutheran theologians and jurists became obsolete.

---

23 D.R. Klinck, *Conscience, Equity and the Court of Chancery*, 264-5.

24 J. Tully *Governing conduct*, in E. Leites (ed.), *Conscience and Casuistry*, 12-71 (15).

25 R.K Rittgers, *Confession (Private) and the Confessional* in T.J. Wengert, (ed.) *Dictionary of Luther and the Lutheran Traditions*, Grand Rapids MI, Baker, 2017.

26 H.J. Berman, *The Christian Sources of General Contract Law*, in J. Witte Jr., F.S. Alexander (eds.), *Christianity and Law: An Introduction*, Cambridge, Cambridge University Press, 125-41 (140).

27 J. Gordley, *The Philosophical Origins*, 161-213.

28 G. Chiodi, *La funzione sociale del contratto: riflessioni di uno storico del diritto*, in F. Macario, M.N. Miletti (eds.), *La funzione sociale nel diritto privato tra XX e XXI secolo. Atti dell'incontro di studio, Roma, 9 ottobre 2015*, Roma, Roma Tre Press, 2017, 151-68 (156 and 158). See also T. Repgen, *Die soziale Aufgabe des Privatrechts*, Tübingen, Mohr Siebeck, 2001. In Germany, the abuse of the economic condition was forbidden by the § 226 BGB and by the § 138 BGB, which set out that contracts including usurious interest are invalid, because they are antithetical to good customs. See G. Cazzetta, *Abuso del diritto e forma di unità del giuridico*, in *Rivista di diritto civile*, 3 (2017), 559-81 (570-2).

Bibliography

1 Primary Sources

1.1 *Roman Law, Canon Law, Provincial Law and Imperial Law*

Corpus iuris civilis. P. Krüger, Th. Mommsen, R. Schöll, G. Kroll, eds., Berolini, 3 vols., 1872-1895.

Corpus iuris canonici. E. Friedberg, ed. Lipsiae, 1879-1881.

Corpus juris canonici emendatum et notis illustratum. Gregorii XIII. pont. max. iussu editum. Romae, in aedibus Populi Romani, 1582.

Lünig, J.C., *Codex Augusteus*, Leipzig, 1724.

Ordungen Hertzog Ernsten (...), Dressden, 1597.

Reichspolizeiordnungen 1530 and 1548. M. Weber ed., *Die Reichspolizeiordnungen von 1530, 1548 und 1577. Historische Einführung und Edition*. Frankfurt am Main: Klostermann, 2002.

1.2 *Holy Bible*

The Holy Bible, King James Version, 1611 (King James Easy Reading Version, 1987).

Luther Bibel: Biblia Das ist Die gantze Heilige Schrifft Deudsch Auffs new zugerich, Wittemberg, 1545.

Biblia Sacra iuxta vulgatam versionem. R. Weber, ed. Wurttembergische Bibelanstalt: Stuttgart, 1994.

1.3 *Classical Authors*

Ambrosius Mediolanensis, *De officiis ministrorum libri tres*. J.P. Migne, ed. *Patrologiae cursus completus, series latina* vol. 16, Parisiis, 1845.

Aristoteles, *Nicomachean Ethics*. C. Rowe, ed. and transl. Oxford: Oxford University Press, 2002.

Aristoteles, *Politica*. L. Canfora, ed. Milano: Mondadori, 2014-2015.

Augustinus Hipponensis, *De trinitate*. J.P. Migne, ed. *Patrologiae cursus completus, series latina* vol. 42, Parisiis, 1865.

Augustinus Hipponensis, *Enarrationes in psalmos*. J.P. Migne, ed. *Patrologiae cursus completus, series latina* vol. 36, Parisiis, 1865.

Augustinus Hipponensis, *Epistola ad Macedonium*. J.P. Migne, ed. *Patrologiae cursus completus, series latina* vol. 36, Parisiis, 1865.

Augustinus Hipponensis, *Sermone de tempore* 117. J.P. Migne, ed. *Patrologiae cursus completus, series latina* vol. 38, Parisiis, 1865.

Augustinus Hipponensis, *De civitate Dei contra paganos*. J.P. Migne, ed. *Patrologiae cursus completus, series latina* vol. 41, Parisiis, 1864.

Cicero, Marcus Tullius, *De officiis*. W. Miller, ed. and trans. Cambridge: Harvard University Press, 1975.

Gregorius, *Homiliae in Evangelia*. J.P. Migne, ed. *Patrologiae cursus completus, series latina*, vol. 76, Parisiis, 1857.

Plautus, Titus Maccius, *Miles gloriosus. Ed. with introd. and notes by Mason Hammond e.a.; rev. by Mason Hammond*, Cambridge Mass.: Harvard University Press, 1970.

Seneca, Lucius Annaeus, *De beneficiis*. J.W. Basore, ed. *Moral Essays*, v. 3, London and New York: Heinemann, 1935.

1.4 *Late Medieval Authors*

Abelardus, Petrus, *Commentaria in epistolam Pauli ad Romanos*. E.M. Buytaert, ed. *Petri Abaelardi opera theologica*, v. 1, Turnhout: Brepols, 1969.

Anselmus Cantauriensis, *Cur Deus homo*. J.P. Migne, ed. *Patrologiae cursus completus, series latina*, vol. 158, I, Parisiis, 1864.

Aquinas, Thomas, *Commentaria in in decem libros ethicorum aristotelis*. J. Nicolai, ed. *Opera omnia*, Pariis, 1660.

Aquinas, Thomas, *Summa theologiae. Opera omnia iussu impensaque Leonis XIII edita*, tom. 4-12, Romae, 1888-1906.

Astesanus, *Summa Astensis*, Romae, 1728.

Bernardus Clarae-vallensis, *Liber de modo bene vivendi*. J.P. Migne, ed. *Patrologiae cursus completus, series latina*, vol. 184, Parisiis, 1862.

Bernardus Clarae-vallensis, *Sermones super Cantica Canticorum*. J. LeClercq ed., 8 vols., Roma: Editiones Cistercienses, 1957.

Franciscus Assisiensis, *Regula non bullata*. K. Esser, ed. *Opuscola sancti patris Francisci Assisiensis*, Grottaferrata: Collegio S. Bonaventura, 1978.

Gerson, Jean, *De contractibus*. P. Glorieux, ed. *Oeuvres complètes*, vol. IX, Paris: Desclée de Brouwer, 1973.

Gerson, Jean, *De vita spirituali animae* (1402). P. Glorieux, *Oeuvres complètes*, vol. III, Paris: Desclée de Brouwer, 1962.

Hostiensis, Henricus, Cardinalis, *Summa aurea*, Venetiis, 1574.

Innocentius IV (Sinibaldo de' Fieschi), *In quinque libros decretalium commentaria absolutissima*, 2nd. ed., Francofurti ad Moenum, 1579.

Lombardus, Petrus, *Liber sententiarum*. J.P. Migne, ed. *Patrologiae cursus completus, series latina*, vol. 192, Parisiis, 1855.

Panormitanus, Abbas (Nicolaus de Tudeschis), *Lectura super quinto Decretalium, cum glosis* (*sic*) *Bernardini de Landriano*, Venetiis, 1495.

Pennaforte, Raimundus de, *Summa de paenitentia*. S.J. Ochoa-A. Diez ed., Roma: Commentarius pro religiosis, 1976.

Sandaeus, Felinus, *In quinque libros decretalium commentaria*, Lugduni, 1535.

Ubaldis, Baldus de, *In primum, secundum et tertium codicis librum*, Venetiis, 1599, ed. Keip Verlag, *Commentaria omnia von Baldus de Ubaldis*, vol. 5, 2004.

1.5 *Early Modern Authors*

Abfertigung de Ungegründten Gegenberichts der zu Regensburg Anno 1587 geurlaubten Prediger, Tübingen, 1589.

Adam, Melchior, *Vitae germanorum iureconsultorum et politicorum*, Heidelbergae, 1620.

Aepinus, Johannes, *Auszlegung D. Johannis Epini vber den XV. Psalm Davids*, Franckfurt am Meyn, 1543.

Aepinus, Johannes, *In psalmum XV. Davidis D. Iohannis Aepini commentarius*, Argentorati, 1543.

Alberti, Valentin, *Compendium iuris naturae*, pars prima, editio secunda, Lipsiae, 1696.

Alberti, Valentin, *Compendium iuris naturae*, pars secunda, Lipsiae, 1678.

Ames, William, *De conscientia et eius iure vel casibus libri quinque*, editio nova, Franekerae, 1635.

Andreae, Johannes Valentin, *Fama andreana reflorescens* [...], Argentorati, 1630.

Andreae, Johannes, *Vier Christliche Predigten uber ettliche Evangelia im Advent*, Regensburg, 1588.

Arnold, Gottfried, *Unpartheyische Kirchen-und Ketzerhistorien, vom Anfang des Neuen Testaments biss auf das Jahr Christi 1688*, v. I, Schaffhausen, 1740.

Azor, Juan, *Institutiones morales*, Coloniae Agrippinae, 1612.

Azor, Juan, *Institutionum moralium tomus tertius*, Coloniae agrippinae, 1618.

Azpilcueta, Martin de, *Enchiridion sive manuale confessariorum et poenitentium*, Antverpiae, 1608.

Bacmeister, Lucas, *Skiagrafia sive analysis et catena catechismi minoris d. Martini Lutheri* [...], Rostochi, 1667.

Baeza, Diego de, *Commentaria moralia in evangelicam historiam*, vol. 4, Lugduni, 1631.

Baier, Johan Wilhelm, *Compendium theologiae moralis*, Jenae, 1697.

Balduin, Friedrich, *Tractatus loculentus, posthumus, toti reipublicae christianae utilissimus, de materia rarissime ante hac enucleate, casibus nimirorum conscientiae*, Wittembergae, 1628.

Bechmann, Friedemann, *Annotationes in celeberrimi Dn. D. Joh. Olearii Theologiam Moralem* [...], Francofurti et Lipsiae, 1704.

Bechmann, Friedemann, *Theologia conscientiaria sive tractatus de casibus conscientiae*, Francofurti et Lipsiae, 1700.

Berghauer, Johannes (Supervisor: Heinrich Linck), *De exoneratione conscientiae*, Jenae, 1673.

Bertling, Ernst August, *De officiis et virtutibus christianorum libri tres sive theologiae moralis elementa*, Halae Magdeburgicae, 1753.

Besold, Christoph, *Operis politici editio nova*, Argentorati, 1626.

Bidenbach, Felix, *Consiliorum theologicorum decas I*, Franckfurt am Meyn, 1608.

Bidenbach, Felix, *Consiliorum theologicorum decas VI*, Franckfurt am Meyn, 1609.

Bonacina, Martino, *Tractatus de restitutione et de contractibus. Operum de morali theologia*[...] *compendium*, t. 2, Venetiis, 1683.

Brenz, Johannes, *In evangelii quod inscribitur secundum Lucam, duodecim posteriora capita, homiliae octoginta*, Halae Svevorum, 1540.

Brenz, Johannes, *In evangelii quod inscribitur secundum Lucam, duodecim priora capita homiliae centum et decem*, Francofurti, 1541.

Brenz, Johannes, *Catechismus, pia et utili explicatione illustratus*, Francofurti, 1556.

Buddeus, Johann Franz, *Elementa philosophiae practicae*, Halae Magdeburgicae, 1720.

Buddeus, Johann Franz, *Historia critica theologiae dogmaticae et moralis*, Francofurti ad Moenum, 1724.

Buddeus, Johann Franz, *Institutiones theologiae moralis, variis obseruationibus illustratae*, Lipsiae, 1727.

Buddeus, Johann Franz, *Isagoge historico-theologica ad theologiam universam*, vol. 1, Lipsiae, 1730.

Calixt, Georg, *Epitomes theologiae moralis pars prima*, Helmestadii, 1662.

Calixt, Georg, *Dissertatio theologica moralis de usuris*, Helmestadi, 1667. I. Mager, ed. *G. Calixt. Ethische Schriften*. Göttingen: Vandenhoeck & Ruprecht, 1970.

Canz, Israel Gottlieb, *Unterricht von den Pflichten der Christen oder theologische Moral*, Berlin, 1749.

Carolus, Andreas David, *Wirtenbergische Unschuld*, Ulm, 1708.

Carpzov, Benedict, *Jurisprudentia forensis romano-saxonica*, Lipsiae, 1668.

Carpzov, Benedict, *Jurisprudentia forensis romano-saxonica*, Lipsiae, 1674.

Catechismus ex decreto Concilii Tridentini ad parochos Pii V pont. max. iussu editus, Romae, 1566.

Charisius, Christian E., (Supervisor: Samuel Stryk), *Disputationem de conscientiae foro* [...], Francofurti ad viadrum, 1683.

Chemnitz, Martin, *Loci theologici*, Francofurti et Wittembergae, 1653.

Chytraeus, David, *Regulae vitae: virtutum descriptiones methodicae*, Wittenbergae, 1556.

Chytraeus, David, *In deuteronomium Mosis enarratio*, Witebergae, 1575.

Coler, Matthias, *Tractatus de processibus executivis in causis civilibus et pecuniariis ad practicam fori saxonici passim accommodatus*, Ienae, 1586.

Coler, Matthias, *Tractatus de processibus executivis in causis civilibus et pecuniariis ad practicam fori saxonici passim accommodatus*, editio quarta, Jenae, 1615.

Corte, Jacob de, *Coniecturarum, sive variarum iuris civilis quaestionum explicatarum* [...] *libri tres*, Hanoviae, 1605.

Cothmann, Ernst, *Consultationum et responsorum juris* [...] *volumen II*, Francofurti, 1662.

Covarrubias, Diego de, *Variarum ex iure pontificio, regio et caesareo resolutionum libri III*, Venetiis, 1566.

Covarruvias, Diego de, *Relectio in cap. Quamvis pactum de pactis*, Lugduni, 1558.

Cujas, Jacob, *Observationum et emendationum Libri XXVIII*, Coloniae Agrippinae, 1598.

Curtius, Rochus, *Enarrationes in celeberrimum iuris cap. cum tanto*, Lugduni, 1550.

Daneau, Lambert, *Ethices christianae libri tres*, Genevae, 1579.

Dannhauer, Johann Konrad, *Liber conscientiae sive theologia conscientiaria*, t. 1, Argentorati, 1662.

Dannhauer, Johann Konrad, *Deuteronomium Dannhawerianum, id est: collegium decalogicum denuò typis*, Argentorati, 1669.

Dannhauer, Johann Konrad, *Theologia casualis*, Gryphiswaldiae, 1706.

Deciani, Tiberio, *Responsorvm D. Tiberii Deciani* [...] *volumen primum*, Venetiis, 1602.

Dedekenn, Georg, *Thesauri consiliorum et decisionum volumen secundum, politica continens* [...], Jena, 1671.

Dieterich, Conrad *Institutiones catecheticae e B. Lutheri catechesi depromptae*. A.W. Dieckhoff, ed. Berolini, 1864.

Doneau, Hugues, *In titulum de usuris in pandectis et sequentem commentarius*, Lugduni, 1558.

Du Moulin, Charles, *Tractatus commerciorum et usurarum, redituumque pecunia constitutorum et monetarum*, Coloniae Agripine, 1584.

Dunte, Ludwig, *Decisiones casuum conscientiae sexcentorum et ultra, e diversis theologorum scriptis collectae, contractae* [...], Lübeck, 1636.

Dürr, Johann Konrad, *Compendium theologiae moralis*, Altdorffi, 1675.

Dürr, Johann Konrad, *Compendium theologiae moralis*, Altdorfi Noricorum, 1698.

Eitzen, Paul von, *Ethicae doctrinae: pars altera continens 5 libros posteriores*, Witebergae, 1573.

Eitzen, Paul von, *Ethicae doctrinae libri novem, pars prima*, Slesvigae in isthmo cimbrico, 1585.

Escobar, Antonio de, *Universae theologiae moralis receptiores absque lite sententiae nec non problematicae disquisitiones* [...], vol. 5, Lugduni, 1663.

Ferrarijs, Johannes Petrus de, *Practica*, Francoforti ad Moenum, 1581.

Ferrarijs, Johannes Petrus de, *Practica*, Genevae 1594.

Flacius, Matthias, *Clavis Scripturae Sacrae*, pars prima, Basileae, 1567.

Flamborough, Robert of., *Liber Poenitentialis*. J.J.F. Firth, ed. Toronto: Pontifical Institute of Mediaeval Studies, 1971.

Franz, Wolfgang, *Tractatus theologicus novus et perspicuuis, de interpretatione sacrarum scripturarum maxime legitima*, VVittebergae, 1708.

Friderus, Peter, *De processibus, mandatis et monitoriis* [...] *tractatus*, editio novissima, Wetzlariae, 1737.

Gail, Andreas von, *Practicarum observationum* [...] *libri duo*, Antverpiae, 1653.

Gail, Andreas von, *Practicarum observationum* [...] *libri duo*, Coloniae, 1583.

Gallus, Nikolaus, *Catechismus, predigweise gestelt für die Kirche zu Regenspurg zum Methodo: das ist ordentlicher Summa christlicher Lere wider allerlei Newerung und Verfelschung*, Regensburg, 1554.

Gallus, Nikolaus, *Zwo Predigten Wider den Wucher*, Jhena, 1572.

Gegenbericht und notwendige Verantwortung auff den Bericht und Vermahnung eines Erbarn Cameren und Raths der Stadt Regensburg an ihre liebe Burgerschafft und Gemein, deren im December der vergangenen 87 jars geurlaubten fünff Kirchendienern, 1588.

Gerhard, Johann, *Auff 12 nachfolgende Fragen*. G. Dedekenn, *Thesauri consiliorum et decisionum volumen secundum*, Jena 1671, 168.

Gerhard, Johann, *Centuria quaestionum politicarum*, Jenae, 1608.

Gerhard, Johann, *Locorum theologicorum tomus decimus quartus*, Tubingae, 1776.

Gerhard, Johann, *Locorum theologicorum tomus decimus quintus*, Tubingae, 1776.

Gerhard, Johann, *Locorum theologicorum tomus quintus*, Tubingae, 1766.

Gessner, Salomon, *Commentationes in psalmos Davidis*, Witebergae, 1609.

Göbler, Justinus, *Divi Caroli qvinti politiae ac reipvblicae imperialis constitutio*, Francofurti, 1566.

Goedde, Johann (Supervisor: Johannes Tesmar), *Dissertatio iuris prima de conscientia*, Marburg, 1675.

Gomez, Antonio, *Commentariorum variarumque resolutionum iuris civilis* [...] *tomi tres*, Francofurti, 1616.

Gregorius Petrus Tholosanus, *De republica libri sex et viginti*, Pont-à-Mousson, 1596.

Gregorii, Henricus (Supervisor: Caspar Ziegler), *Dissertatio iuridica de mohatra contractu*, Ienae, 1747.

Grotius, Hugo, *De iure belli ac pacis*, (curavit B.J.A. De Kanter-Van Hettinga Tromp; annotationes novas addiderunt R. Feenstra et C.E. Persenaire), Aalen, Scientia, 1993.

Gundling, Nicolaus Hieronymus, *Otia*, vol. III, Frankfurt und Leipzig, 1707.

Gutachten über den Wucherstreit in Rudolstadt (*Forschungbibliothek Gotha*), Chart. A 103, Bl. 113r-116v.

Haferung, Johann Caspar, *Theologia moralis per theses concinnatas*, Vitembergae, 1737.

Hahn, Heinrich, *Observata theoretico practica ad Matthaei Wesenbecii in L. libros digestorum commentarios*, pars posterior, Coloniae Agrippinae, 1675.

Heige, Peter, *Quaestionum iuris tam civilis quam saxonici pars posterior*, Wittebergae, 1630.

Hemmingsen, Niels, *Enchiridion theologicum*, Witebergae, 1564.

Hemmingsen, Niels, *Libellus de coniugio, repudio et divortio*, Lipsiae, 1572.

Henrichmann, Jakob, *Consiliorum sive responsorum iuris* [...] *tomus primus*, Dilingae, 1566.

Horneius, Conrad, *Compendium theologiae quo universa fidei christianae tam credendorum quam agendorum doctrina tribus libris dilucide pertractatur*, Brunsvigae, 1655.

Hotman, Franciscus, *De usuris libri duo*, Lugduni, 1558.

Hotman, Franciscus, *De usuris*, Lugduni, 1551.

Hunnius, Aegidius, *Catechismus oder Kinderlehre von den Hauptpuncten Christlicher Religion*, Wittemberg, 1604.

Hunnius, Aegidius, *Articulus de providentia Dei et aeterna praedestinatione seu electione filiorum Dei ad salutem*, Witebergae, 1605.

Hunnius, Aegidius, *Commentarius in posteriorem epistolam D. Pavli Apostoli ad Corinthios*, Witebergae, 1605.

Hunnius, Aegidius, *Ob und wie viel man* interesse *nehmen soll.* Consilia theologica witebergensia, Franckfurt am Mäyn, 1664, 150-2.

Ignatius of Loyola, *Racconto di un pellegrino*. G. de Gennaro, ed. and trans. Roma: Città Nuova, 1988.

Jäger, Johann Wolfgang, *Hugonis Grotii libri tres observationibus theologicis, moralibus et politicis illustrati*, Tubingae, 1710.

Jäger, Johann Wolfgang, *Theologia moralis, seu practica synoptice tractata*, Tubingae, 1714.

König, Georg, *Casus conscientiae, qui in sex capitibus doctrinae catechetizae, una cum tabula oeconomica subinde solent occurrere, erudite et fideliter decisae*, Altdorfii, 1654.

Kortholt, Christian, *Theologia moralis synoptice tractata*, Hafniae, 1716.

Kulpis, Johann Georg von, *Collegium Grotianum*, Stutgardiae, 1697.

Lang, Johann Michael, *Dissertatio prooemialis de origine et progressv theologiae moralis systematicae*. J.K. Dürr, *Compendium theologiae moralis*, Altdorfi Noricorum, 1698.

Lang, Johann Michael, *Ad B.D. Joh. Guil. Bajeri theologi etiam post fata celeberrimi, compendium theologiae moralis supplementa*, Jenae, 1700.

Lessius, Leonardus, *De iustitia et de iure ceterisque virtutibus cardinalibus libri quatuor*, Lovanii, 1605.

Lessius, Leonardus, *De iustitia et iure ceterisque virtutibus cardinalibus libri quatuor. On Sale, Securities, and Insurance*. W. Decock and N. De Sutter, trans. Grand Rapids MI: CLP Academic, Refo500, 2016.

Lilienthal, Theodor Christoph, *Bibliotheca lilienthaliana sive apparatvs librorvm*, Regiomonti, 1782.

Lipenius, Martin, *Bibliotheca realis theologica omnivm materivm, rerum et titulorum*, t. 2, Francofurti ad Moenum, 1685.

Lobeck, David, *Disputationes theologicae XX articulorum Augustanae confessionis*, Rostochii, 1599.

Luther, Martin, *(Kleiner) Sermon von dem Wucher* (1519). *D. Martin Luthers Werke*, vol. 6, Weimar, 1888.

Luther, Martin, *Sommerpostille* (1520) – *Evangelium am 15 Sonntag nach Trinitatis Matth. 6, 24*. D. *Martin Luthers Werke*, vol. 10, I, Weimar, 1910.

Luther, Martin, *An den christlichen Adel deutscher Nation* (1520). *D. Martin Luthers Werke*, vol. 6, Weimar, 1888.

Luther, Martin, *Ein (Grosser) Sermon von dem Wucher* (1520). *D. Martin Luthers Werke*, vol. 6, Weimar, 1888.

Luther, Martin, *Von weltlicher Oberkeit* (1523). *D. Martin Luthers Werke*, vol. 11, Weimar, 1900.

Luther, Martin, *Von Kaufshandlung und Wucher* (1524). *D. Martin Luthers Werke*, vol. 15, Weimar, 1899.

Luther, Martin, *Von Kaufshandlung und Wucher* (1524). ed. with introduction and notes by Philipp Robinson Rössner, London and New York: Anthem, 2015.

Luther, Martin, *Fastenpostille 1525, Epistel auf den 4 Sonntag nach Epiphanias Rom. 13, 8ff. D. Martin Luthers Werke*, vol. 17, Weimar, 1907.

Luther, Martin, *In epistolam S. Pauli ad Galatas commentarius* [1531] 1535. *D. Martin Luthers Werke*, vol. 40, Weimar, 1911.

Luther, Martin, *Commentary on Galatians* (1535). *Luther's Works*, vol. 26, Philadelphia, 1963.

Luther, Martin, *Vorlesungen über 1 Mose* (1535-1545). *D. Martin Luthers Werke*, vol. 43, Weimar, 1912.

Luther, Martin, *Die erste Disputation gegen die Antinomer* (1537). *D. Martin Luthers Werke*, vol. 39, I, Weimar, 1926.

Luther, Martin, *Die Thesen zu den Disputationen gegen die Antinomer* (1537). *D. Martin Luthers Werke*, vol. 39, I, Weimar, 1926.

Luther, Martin, *Die dritte Disputation gegen die Antinomer* (1538). *D. Martin Luthers Werke*, vol. 39, I, Weimar, 1926.

Luther, Martin, *Die Zirkulardisputation über das Recht des Widerstands gegen den Kaiser* (1539). *D. Martin Luthers Werke*, vol. 39, II, Weimar, 1932.

Luther, Martin, *An die Pfarrherrn, wider den Wucher zu predigen* (1540). *D. Martin Luthers Werke*, vol. 51, Weimar, 1914.

Luther, Martin, *Tischreden aus Anton Lauterbachs Sammlung B.* (1540-44). *D. Martin Luthers Werke, Tischreden*, vol. 5, Weimar, 1919.

Luther, Martin, *Preface to the Letter of St. Paul to the Romans* (1552). *Luther's Works*, vol. 6, Philadelphia, 1970.

Luther, Martin, *Colloquia Oder Tischreden Doctor Martini Lutheri*, Frankfurt, 1567.

Luther, Martin, *Der große Katechismus, nach der Fassung des deutschen Konkordienbuches*, Dresden, 1580. Friedrich Bente, ed. *Triglot Concordia: The Symbolical Books of the Evangelical Lutheran Church: German-Latin-English*. St. Louis: Concordia Publishing House, 1921.

Luther, Martin, *Predigt am sechzehenten Sonntage nach Trinitatis*. G. Plochmann, ed. *Dr. Martin Luther's Kirchenpostille*, II Predigten über Evangelien, vol. 5, Erlangen, 1828.

Major, Georg, *Enarratio secundae epistolae Pauli ad Corinthios*, VVitebergae, 1561.

Mayer, Johann Friedrich, *Bibliotheca scriptorum theologiae moralis et conscientiariae*. A. Strauch, *Theologia moralis*, Gryphiswaldiae, 1708.

Mazzolini, Sylvester, *Summa summarum quae Sylvestrina dicitur*, Argentorati, 1518.

Meier, Gebhard Theodor, *Introductio in universum theologiae moralis, cum dogmaticae, tum pragmaticae, studium, aua, quae propria, quae aliena sunt theologiae morali, unde illa & in quantum possint debeantque accipi,* [...] *exhibetur*, Francofurti, Lipsiae, Helmstadii, 1671.

Meisner, Balthasar, *Dissertatio de summo bono, cui praemissa sunt praecognita ethica et annexa coronis de virtute*, Wittebergae, 1614.

Meisner, Balthasar, *Philosophia sobria*, pars tertia, Wittebergae, 1623.

Melanchthon, Philip, *Loci communes theologici prima eorum aetas* (1521). K.G. Brentschneider and H.E. Bindseil, eds. *Opera quae supersunt omnia*, vol. XXI, Halis Saxonum: Schwetschke, 1854.

Melanchthon, Philip, *Loci communes* (1521). C. Preus trans. *Commonplaces, Loci communes 1521*. Saint Louis: Concordia Publishing House, 2014.

Melanchthon, Philip, *De locis communibus ratio* (1521). K.G. Brentschneider and H.E. Bindseil, eds. *Opera quae supersunt omnia*, vol. XX, Halis Saxonum: Schwetschke, 1854.

Melanchthon, Philip, *Compendiaria dialectices ratio* (1523). K.G. Brentschneider and H.E. Bindseil, eds. *Opera quae supersunt omnia*, vol. XX, Halis Saxonum: Schwetschke, 1854.

Melanchthon, Philip, *Prolegomena in officia Ciceronis* (1530). K.G. Brentschneider and H.E. Bindseil, eds. *Opera quae supersunt omnia*, vol. XVI, Halis Saxonum: Schwetschke, 1850.

Melanchthon, Philip, *Loci communes theologici secunda eorum aetas* (1535-1541). K.G. Brentschneider and H.E. Bindseil, eds. *Opera quae supersunt omnia*, vol. XXI, Halis Saxonum: Schwetschke, 1854.

Melanchthon, Philip, *Philosophiae moralis epitome libri duo* (1538). K.G. Brentschneider and H.E. Bindseil, eds. *Opera quae supersunt omnia*, vol. XVI, Halis Saxonum: Schwetschke, 1850.

Melanchthon, Philip, *Catechesis puerilis* (1541). K.G. Brentschneider and H.E. Bindseil, eds. *Opera quae supersunt omnia*, vol. XXIII, Halis Saxonum: Schwetschke, 1855.

Melanchthon, Philip, *Loci communes theologici tertia eorum aetas* (1543-1559), Appendix II, *Definitiones multarum appellationum, quarum in ecclesia usum est*, 1552-1553. K.G. Brentschneider and H.E. Bindseil, eds. *Opera quae supersunt omnia*, vol. XXI, Halis Saxonum: Schwetschke, 1854.

Melanchthon, Philip, *Dissertatio de contractibus* (1545). K.G. Brentschneider and H.E. Bindseil, eds. *Opera quae supersunt omnia*, vol. XVI, Halis Saxonum: Schwetschke, 1850.
Melanchthon, Philip, *Ethicae doctrinae elementorum libri duo* (1550). K.G. Brentschneider and H.E. Bindseil, eds. *Opera quae supersunt omnia*, vol. XVI, Halis Saxonum: Schwetschke, 1850.
Melanchthon, Philip, *Explicatio proverbiorum Salomonis* (1550). K.G. Brentschneider and H.E. Bindseil, eds. *Opera quae supersunt omnia*, vol. XIV, Halis Saxonum: Schwetschke, 1847.
Melanchthon, Philip, *Liber de anima* (1552). K.G. Brentschneider and H.E. Bindseil, eds. *Opera quae supersunt omnia*, vol. XIII, Halis Saxonum: Schwetschke, 1846.
Melanchthon, Philip, *Bedenken: vom Verbot und Straff des Wuchers* (1553). K.G. Brentschneider and H.E. Bindseil, eds. *Opera quae supersunt omnia*, vol. VIII, Halis Saxonum: Schwetschke, 1841.
Melanchthon, Philip, *Loci communes* (1559). J.A.O. Preus, trans. *The Chief Theological Topics. Loci Praecipui Theologici 1559*. 2nd English ed. Saint Louis: Concordia Publishing House, 2011.
Melanchthon, Philip, *Propositiones (III) De contractu redemptionis*. K.G. Brentschneider and H.E. Bindseil, eds. *Opera quae supersunt omnia*, vol. XII, Halis Saxonum: Schwetschke, 1844.
Meyer, Christoph (Supervisor: Gottfried Wegner), *Disputatio theologica de restitutione ablati*, Regiomonti, 1707.
Misler, Johann Nikolaus, *Opus novum quaestionum practico-theologicarum, sive casuum conscientiae, quorum decisiones juxta seriem ac ordinem locorum communium vulgo receptum, digestae*, Francofurti, 1676.
Molina, Luis de, *Disputationes de contractibus*, (De iustitia et iure, vol. 2), Venetiis, 1601.
Mosheim, Johann Lorenz von, *Sitten Lehre der Heiligen Schrift*, Siebenter Theil, Leipzig, 1778.
Musculus, Wolfgang, *De usuris ex verbo Dei appendix* [...], Tubingae, 1558.
Niemeier, Johann Bartold, *Theologia moralis*, Helmstadii, 1696.
Oldendorp, Johann, *De emptione et venditione reddituum*. S. Pettke and H.P. Gloeckner, eds. Rostock: Universitätsbibliothek, 1995.
Olearius, Johannes, *Doctrina theologiae moralis totius, in usum incipientium, certis paediae ac methodi limitibus circumscipta, et tabulis LXXII comprehensa*, Lipsiae, 1681.
Orth, Simon Nikolaus, *Disputatio inauguralis iuridica de erronea conscientia in foro exteriori nos obligante vel excusante*, Giessae, 1678.
Osiander, Johann Adam, *Observationes maximam partem theologicae in libros tres de iure belli ac pacis Hugo Grotii*, Tubingae, 1671.
Osiander, Johann Adam, *Theologiae casualis in qua quaestiones, dubia et casus conscientiae circa credenda et agenda enucleantur, pars tertia et quarta*, Tubingae, 1680.

Osiander, Johann Adam, *Theologiae casualis in qua quaestiones, dubia et casus conscientiae circa credenda et agenda enucleantur, pars prima et secunda*, Tubingae, 1680.

Osiander, Lucas, *Epitomes historiae ecclesiasticae centuriae XVI, pars altera*, Tubingae, 1603.

Osiander, Lucas, *Enchiridion controversiarum, quae Augustanae confessionis theologis cum Anabaptistis intercedunt* [...], Witembergae, 1610.

Osiander, Lucas, *Vom Wucher in dem Regespurgischen Streit*. G. Dedekenn, *Thesauri consiliorum et decisionum volumen secundum*, Jena 1671, 150.

Pace, Giulio, *De rebus creditis, seu de obligationibus quae re contrahuntur, et earum accessionibus* [...] *commentarius*, Spirae Nemetvm, 1696.

Pfaff, Christoph Matthäus, *Introductio in historiam theologiae literariam notis amplissimis: quae novum opus conficiunt, illustrata*, vol. I, Tubingae, 1724.

Pfeiffer, August, *Dubia vexata Scripturae Sacrae*, editio quartae, Lipsiae, 1699.

Prückner, Andreas, *Manuale mille quaestionum*, Norimbergae, 1662.

Pufendorf, Samuel, *De iure naturae et gentium libri octo*, Londini Scanorum, 1672.

Rachel, Samuel, *De principio actionum moralium liber*, Helmestadii, 1664.

Reimmann, Jacob Friederich, *Catalogus bibliothecae theologicae, systematico-criticus, in quo libri theologici in bibliotheca Reimanniana extantes* [...] *enumerantur: et quid in unoquoque sit peculiare vel vulgare, quae laudes et labes* [...] *at non intemperanter tamen* [...] *indicatur*, Hildesiae, 1731.

Reusch, Johann Peter, *Theologia moralis*, Jenae, 1740.

Rhegius, Urbanus, *Derr XV psalm Davids*, Magdeburg, 1538.

Rhegius, Urbanus, *Loci theologici e patribus et scholasticis neotericisque collecti*, Francofurti, 1550.

Riensche, Joahnn Heinrich (Supervisor: Conrad Lüdeking), *Disputatio inauguralis iuridica de casibus a quibusdam conscientiae in iure occurrentibus*, Wittenbergae, 1732.

Ryssel Hans Jacob von, (Supervisor: Benedict Carpzov), *Asylum generale debitorum*, Lipsiae, 1651.

Rodriguez, Emmanuel, *Summa casuum concientiae*, Duaci, 1614.

Salmasius, Claudius, *Dissertatio de foenore trapezitico*, Lugduni, 1640.

Salon, Miguel Bartolomè, *Commentariorum in disputationem de iustitia* [...] *tomus primus*, Venetiis, 1592.

Sanderson, Robert, *De iuramenti promissorii obligatione libellus*, Cothena Anhaltinorum, 1674.

Sayer, Gregory, *Clavis regia sacerdotum, casuum concientiae sive theologiae moralis*, Venetiis, 1615.

Schelwig, Samuel, *Cynosura conscientiae*, Lipsiae, 1692.

Schlüsselburg, Conrad, *Vier und zwantzig hochwichtige Fragen und Bedencken, mit ihren klaren deutlichen und gründlichen Antwortungen*, Rostock, 1625.

Schubert, Ernst, *Institutiones theologiae moralis*, Lipsiae, 1759.

Schurpf, Hieronymus, *Consiliorum seu responsorum iuris centuria secunda*, Francofordiae ad Moenum, 1564.

Schütz, Heinrich (Supervisor: Godofredo Suevo), *Disputatio inauguralis de probatione pro exoneranda conscientia*, Wittenbergae, 1695.

Selden, John, *De jure naturali et gentium juxta disciplinam Ebraeorum libri septem*, Lipsiae et Francofurti, 1695.

Selnecker, Nicolaus, *Paedagogiae christianae pars prima continens decalogi explicationem*, Jenae, 1568.

Senckenberg Heinrich Christian von and Schmauß, Johann Jacob, *Neue und vollständigere Sammlung der Reichs-Abschiede, Welche von den Zeiten Kayser Conrads des II. bis jetzo, auf den Teutschen Reichs-Tägen abgefasset worden*, vol. 2, Franckfurt am Mayn, 1747.

Soto, Domingo de, *Libri decem de iustitia et iure*, Lugduni, 1582.

Stephani, Joachim, *Libri quatuor de iurisdictione judaeorum, graecorum, romanorum et ecclesiasticorum*, Francofurti, 1661.

Stolle, Gottlieb, *Anleitung zur Historie der theologischen Gelahrheit*, Jena, 1739.

Strauch, Aegidius, *Theologia moralis*, Gryphiswaldiae, 1708.

Strauss, Jacob, *Haubstuck unnd Artickel Christlicher leer wider den unchristlichen wucher*, Erfurt, 1523. J. Rogge, ed. *Der Beiträge des Predigers Jakob Strauss zur frühen Reformationsgeschichte*. Berlin: Evangelische Verlagsanstalt, 1957.

Strigel, Victorin, *In epitomen philosophiae moralis Philippi Melanchthonis, Hypomnēmata*, Neapoli Nemetum, 1582.

Strimesius, Samuel, *Praxiologia apodictica seu philosophia moralis dimostrativa, pythanologiae hobbesianae opposita*, Francofurti ad Oderam, 1677.

Struve, Georg Adam, *Syntagma iuris civilis, pars altera, cum additionibus Petri Mülleri*, editio tertia, Francofurti et Lipsiae, 1738.

Stryk, Samuel, *Tractatus de iure sensuum* [...], Francofurti ad Oderam, 1671.

Stryk, Samuel, *Continuatio altera usus moderni pandectarum a libro XIII usque ad XXII*, Halae Magdeburgicae, 1728.

Summenhart, Conrad, *De contractibus licitis atque illicitis*, Venetiis, 1580.

Tabor, Johann Otto, *Consultatio academica de praesidiis debitorum infelicium et inprimis de exceptione alterius tanti usuraii*, Giessae Hassorum, 1686.

Tarnov, Paul, *De sacrosancto ministerio libri tres*, Rostochi, 1624.

Tesauro, Antonio, *Novae decisiones sacri senatus Pedemontani*, Augustae Taurinorum, 1609.

Thomasius, Christian, *Institutiones iurisprudentiae divinae libri tres*, Halae, 1710.

Thomasius, Christian, *Fundamenta iuris naturae et gentium*, Halae et Lipsiae, 1718, 4th. ed. Aalem: Scientia, 1963.

Thumm, Theodor, *Tractatus de usura licita et illicita*, Tubingae, 1622.

Uffelmann, Heinrich, *De jure quo homo homini in sermone obligatur liber unus*, Helmaestedii, 1676.
Uffelmann, Heinrich, *Variorum eorumque illustrium conscientiae casuum fasciculus*, Lipsiae et Goslariae, 1709.
Valentia, Gregorio de, *Commentariorum theologicorum tomus tertius*, Lugduni, 1603.
Villagut, Alfonso, *Tractatus de usuris*, Venetiis, 1589.
Vio, Tommaso de, (Cajetan), *In secundam secundae sanctissimi, ac preclarissimi doctoris Thome Aquinatis* [...] *commentaria*, 1519.
Vitriarius, Philipp Reinhard, *Institutiones juris naturae et gentium*, Francofurti ad Moenum, 1752.
Voetius, Gisbert, *Selectae disputationes theologicae*, pars quarta, Amsteloadami, 1667.
Vuell, Peter a, *Tractatus de usuris*, Coloniae, 1564.
Walch, Johann Georg, *Historische und theologische Einleitung in die Religions-Streitigkeiten der evangelisch-lutherisch Kirchen*, IV, Jena 1739.
Walch, Johann Georg, *Bibliotheca theologica selecta litterariis adnotationibus instructa*, vol. 2, Jenae, 1758.
Wendelin, Marcus Friedrich, *Philosophia moralis*, Francofurti, 1666.
Wesenbeck, Matthaeus, *Paratitla in pandectas iuris civilis*, Basileae, 1568.
Wesenbeck, Matthaeus, *Oratio de Gabriele Mudaeo* [...], Wittenbergae, 1572.
Wesenbeck, Matthaeus, *Commentaria quae olim paratitla in pandectas iuris civilis et codici iustiniani libros*, Antwerpiae, 1621.
Wesenbeck, Matthaeus, *In pandectas iuris civilis et codicis iustinianei libros commentarii*, Basileae, 1629.
Wesenbeck, Matthaeus, Bachovius Echtius, Reinhardus, Vinnius, Arnoldus, *Commentarii in pandectas iuris civilis et codicem justinianeum olim dicti paratitla, aucta subinde ab Arnoldo Vinnio, cum notis et observationibus Rehinardi Bachovii Echtii*, Amstelodami, 1665.
Winther, Georg Valentin von (Ventura de Valentia), *Parthenius litigiosus sive discorsus politico-iuridicus*, Argentorati, 1628.
Wolff, Christian, *Ius naturae methodo scientifica pertractatum*, Frankfurt am Main, 1764.
Zedler, Johann Heinrich, *Grosses vollständiges Universal-Lexicon aller Wissenschafften und Künste*, v. 6, Leipzig, 1733.
Zedler, Johann Heinrich, *Grosses vollständiges Universal-Lexicon aller Wissenschafften und Künste*, v. 12, Leipzig, 1735.
Zedler, Johann Heinrich, *Grosses vollständiges Universal-Lexicon aller Wissenschafften und Künste*, v. 51, Leipzig und Halle, 1747.
Zentgrav, Johann Joachim, *Summa juris divini, sive isagogica institutio doctrinae de iustitia et iure* [...], Argentorati, 1699.

2 Secondary Sources

2.1 *Dictionaries and Encyclopedias*

Ahsmann, Margreet (1995). "Wesenbeck, Matthaeus." Michael Stolleis, ed. *Juristen, Ein biographisches Lexicon, Von der Antike bis zum 20. Jahrundert*. München: C.H. Beck, 651.

Aland, Kurt (1955). "Buddeus, Johann Franz." *Neue Deutsche Biographie* 2, 715 http://www.deutsche-biographie.de/pnd11851685X.html. (December 11, 2018).

Anemüller, Ernst (1879). "Gernhard, Bartholomäus." *Allgemeine Deutsche Biographie* 9, 35-7 https://www.deutsche-biographie.de/gnd100143687.html#adbcontent. (December 18, 2018).

Appold, Kenneth G. (2001). "Meisner, Balthasar." *Religion Past and Present*, VIII, 215.

Barton, Peter F. (1981). "Chyträus, David (1531-1600)." *Theologische Realenzyklopädie* VIII, 88-90.

Bautz, Friedrich W. (1990). "Arndt, Johann." *Biographisch-Bibliographisches Kirchenlexikon* I, 226-7.

Bautz, Friedrich W. (1990). "Bidenbach (Bidembach), Felix." *Biographisch-Bibliographisches Kirchenlexikon* I, 582.

Bautz, Friedrich W. (1990). "Brenz, Johannes." *Biographisch-Bibliographisches Kirchenlexikon* I, 743-4.

Bautz, Friedrich W. (1990). "Chemnitz, Martin." *Biographisch-Bibliographisches Kirchenlexikon* I, 991-2.

Bautz, Friedrich W. (1990). "Dannhauer, Johann Konrad." *Biographisch-Bibliographisches Kirchenlexikon* I, 1211-2.

Bautz, Friedrich W. (1990). "Eitzen, Paul von." *Biographisch-Bibliographisches Kirchenlexikon* I, 1483-4.

Bautz, Friedrich W. (1990). "Gallus (eigentlich: Hahn), Nikolaus." *Biographisch-Bibliographisches Kirchenlexikon* II, 174.

Bautz, Friedrich W. (1990). "Hornejus Konrad." *Biographisch-Bibliographisches Kirchenlexikon* II, 1062-3.

Bautz, Friedrich W. (1990). "Hunnius, Aegidius." *Biographisch-Bibliographisches Kirchenlexikon* II, 1182-3.

Bezzel, Ernst (1980). "Beichte III." *Theologische Realenzyklopädie* V, 421-5.

Bianchin, Lucia (2014). "Pace, Giulio." *Dizionario Biografico degli Italiani* 80. http://www.treccani.it/enciclopedia/giulio-pace_%28Dizionario-Biografico%29/ (October 10, 2017).

Bossert, Wegenmann (1904). "Osiander." *Realenzyklopädie für protestantische Theologie und Kirche*. 3nd. Ed., 14, 513.

Brecht, Martin (1978). "Andreae Jakob (1528-1590)." *Theologische Realenzyklopädie* II, 672-80.

Christ, Günter (1990). "Marquard von Hattstein." *Neue Deutsche Biographie* 16, 242-4 https://www.deutsche-biographie.de/gnd102322694.html#ndbcontent (November 16, 2016).

Coch, Ernst (2000). "Selnecker, Nikolaus." *Theologische Realenzyklopädie* XXXI, 105-8.

Collet, Giancarlo (2012). "Strigel, Victorinus." *Religion Past and Present* XII, 304.

De Blic, Jacques (1924). *Jésuites. Théologie morale*, in *Dictionnaire de théologie catholique* VIII, Paris: Letouzei et Ané, 1069-70.

Düfel, Hans (1977). "Aepinus, Johannes." *Theologische Realenzyklopädie*, vol. I, 1977, 535-44.

Egloffstein von (1891). "Selneccer, Nicolaus." *Allgemeine Deutsche Biographie* 33, 687-92 http://www.deutsche-biographie.de/pnd118613073.html?anchor=adb (December 21, 2018).

Ehmer, Hermann (1996). "Thumm, Theodor." *Biographisch-Bibliographisches Kirchenlexikon* XI, 1527-30.

Ehmer, Hermann (2011). "Osiander, Johann Adam." *Religion Past and Present* IX, 420.

Eisenhart, August R. von (1880). "Heige, Peter." *Allgemeine Deutsche Biographie* 11, 307 f. https://www.deutsche-biographie.de/gnd100290469.html#adbcontent (December 21, 2018).

Eisenhart, August R. von (1897). "Wesenbeck, Matthäus." *Allgemeine Deutsche Biographie* 42, 134-8 https://www.deutsche-biographie.de/pnd11757287X.html #adbcontent (December 21, 2018).

Eltester von (1879). "Göbler, Justinus." *Allgemeine Deutsche Biographie* 9, 301 http://www.deutsche-biographie.de/pnd122200489.html?anchor=adb (December 21, 2018).

Erdmann, D. (1890). "Schelwig, Samuel." *Allgemeine Deutsche Biographie* 31, 30-6 https://www.deutsche-biographie.de/pnd104256621.html#adbcontent (January 15, 2018).

Filhol, René (1950). "Dumoulin Charles." Raoul Naz, ed. *Dictionnarie de droit canonique*. VI, Paris, 42-67.

Fitzgerald, Allan et al., eds. (1990). *Augustine Through the Ages: An Encyclopedia*. Grand Rapids, MI: Eerdmans.

Flood, David (1979). "Armut VI". *Theologische Realenzyklopädie* IV, 88-98.

Gaß, Wilhelm (1875). "Balduin, Friedrich." *Allgemeine Deutsche Biographie*, https://www.deutsche-biographie.de/gnd116883391.html#adbcontent (November 1, 2017).

Gehrke, Heinrich (2016). "Konsilien, Konsiliensammlungen." *Handwörterbuch zur deutschen Rechtsgeschichte* (HRG), vol. III. 117-121. www.HRGdigital.de/HRG.konsilien_konsiliensammlungen (December 18, 2018).

Göbell, Walter (1979). "Kortholt, Christian." *Neue Deutsche Biographie* 12, 601 f. https://www.deutsche-biographie.de/pnd116341793.html#ndbcontent (January 12, 2018).

Goertz, Hans Jürgen (1997). "Eigentum VI." *Theologische Realenzyklopädie* XXVIII, 423-8.

Gössner, A. (2017). "Dedeken (Dedeckennus), Georg." *Biographisch-Bibliographisches Kirchenlexikon* vol. XXXVIII, 295-300.

Grimm, Jacob and Grimm, Wilhelm (1956 [1854]). "Deutsches Wörterbuch." Leipzig http://woerterbuchnetz.de/cgi-bin/WBNetz/wbgui_py?sigle=DWB (December 12, 2017).

Günter, Jerouschek (2008). "Carpzov, Benedikt (1595-1666)." *Handwörterbuch zur deutschen Rechtsgeschichte* (HRG), I, 819-21. https://www.hrgdigital.de/id/carpzov_benedikt_1595_1666/_sid/HDVA-632785-PF9d/stichwort.html (December 18, 2018).

Hartmann, Julius (1876). "Culmann, Leonhard." *Allgemeine Deutsche Biographie* 4, 639 https://www.deutsche-biographie.de/pnd118638572.html#adbcontent (December 18, 2018).

Hendrix, Scott (1998). "Rhegius, Urbanus." *Theologische Realenzyklopädie* XXIX, 155-7.

Heppe, Heinrich (1879). "Haferung, Johann Kaspar." *Allgemeine Deutsche Biographie* 10, 317 https://www.deutsche-biographie.de/gnd122687442.html#adbcontent (December 18, 2018).

Hermelink, Heinrich (1955). "Brenz, Johannes." *Neue Deutsche Biographie* 2, 598 f. http://www.deutsche-biographie.de/pnd118515128.html (December 18, 2018).

Hermle, Siegfried (2007). "Andreae, Jakob." *Religion Past and Present* I, 217-8.

Hirsch, Theodor (1875). "Bertling, Ernst August." *Allgemeine Deutsche Biographie* 2, 514 http://www.deutsche-biographie.de/pnd116149566.html?anchor=adb (December 18, 2018).

Hof, Hagen (2017) "Samuel Stryk." Gerd Kleinheyer and Jan Schröder eds. *Deutsche und Europäische Juristen aus neun Jahrunderten.* 6 ed., 432-6.

Holstein, H. (1888). "Porta, Konrad." *Allgemeine Deutsche Biographie* 26, 445 https://www.deutsche-biographie.de/gnd116269014.html#adbcontent (December 18, 2018).

Holstein, H., *Sarcerius, Erasmus,* in *Allgemeine Deutsche Biographie* 33 (1891), 727-29 https://www.deutsche-biographie.de/gnd122057635.html#adbcontent (December 18, 2018).

Holthöfer, Ernst (1995). "Doneau, Hugues." Michael Stolleis, ed. *Juristen, Ein biographisches Lexicon, Von der Antike bis zum 20. Jahrundert.* München: C.H. Beck, 182.

Honecker, Martin (1983). "Gerhard, Johann (1582-1637)." *Theologische Realenzyklopädie* XII, 448-53.

Honecker, Martin (1984). "Geld II.2.1.7 Reformation." *Theologische Realenzyklopädie* XII, 286-8.

Honnefelder, Ludger, Möhle, Hannes and Söder, Joachim (2000). "Scholastik." *Lexikon für Theologie und Kirche,* 3. ed., 9, 199-202.

Huber, Max (1957). "Dieterich, Konrad." *Neue Deutsche Biographie* 3, 672 https://www.deutsche-biographie.de/gnd118891804.html#ndbcontent (December 18, 2018).

Izbicki, Thomas M. (2011). "Jacques Almain." Henrik Lagerlund, ed. *Encyclopedia of Medieval Philosophy: Philosophy Between 500 and 1500* 1, Dordrecht: Springer, 579-81.

Jakubowski-Tiessen, Manfred (2009). “Hemmingsen, Niels.” *Religion Past and Present* VI, 52-3.
Jung, Martin H. (2009). “Jäger, Johann Wolfgang.” *Religion Past and Present* VI, 643.
Junghans, Helmar (1987). “Major, Georg.” *Neue Deutsche Biographie* 15, 718 f. https://www.deutsche-biographie.de/gnd116689781.html#ndbcontent (December 18, 2018).
Kaller, Gerhard (1996). “Strauß, Jacob.” *Biographisch-Bibliographisches Kirchenlexikon* XI, 34-7.
Kaufmann, Thomas (1997). “Martin Chemnitz (1522-1586) Zur Wirkungsgeschichte der theologischen Loci.” Heinz Scheible, ed. *Melanchthon in seinen Schülern*. Wiesbaden: Harrassowitz. 183-254.
Keller, Rudolf (1994). “Orthodoxie, altprotestantische.” *Evangelisches Lexikon für Theologie und Gemeinde* 3, 1492-4.
Keller, Rudolf (1997). “David Chytraeus (1530-1600). Melanchthons Geist im Luthertum.” Heinz Scheible, ed. *Melanchthon in seinen Schülern*. Wiesbaden: Harrassowitz, 361-71.
Kleinheyer, Gerd (2017). “Benedikt Carpzov.” Gerd Kleinheyer and Jan Schröder, eds. *Deutsche und Europäische Juristen aus neun Jahrunderten*. 6 ed., Tübingen: Mohr Siebeck, 92-7.
Knolle, Theodor (1953). “Aepinus, Johannes.” *Neue Deutsche Biographie* 1, 91 http://www.deutsche-biographie.de/pnd116296283.html. (December 20, 2018).
Koch, Ernst (1997). “Victorin Strigel (1524-1569). Von Jena nach Heidelberg.” Heinz Scheible, ed. *Melanchthon in seinen Schülern*. Wiesbaden: Harrassowitz, 391-404.
Koch, Ernst (2001). “Strigel, Victorin[us].” *Theologische Realenzyklopädie* XXXII, 252-5.
Koch, Ernst (2007). “Buddeus, Johann Franz.” *Religion Past and Present* II, 248.
Kolb, Robert (1996). “Andreae Jakob.” Hans J. Hillerbrand, ed. *The Oxford Encyclopedia of the Reformation* 1, 37-8.
Kreiner, Arthur (1953). “Baier, Johann Wilhelm der Ältere.” *Neue Deutsche Biographie* 1, 543 f. http://www.deutsche-biographie.de/pnd116040149.html (December 20, 2018).
Kunze, Johannes (1909). “Hunnius Aegidius.” Samuel M. Jackson, ed. *The new Schaff-Herzog encyclopedia of religious knowledge* V, Grand Rapids, MI: Baker, 409-10.
Lau, Franz (1964). “Gerhard, Johann.” *Neue Deutsche Biographie* 6, 281, http://www.deutsche-biographie.de/pnd118538624.html (December 21, 2018).
Lau, Franz (1974). “Hunnius, Ägidius.” *Neue Deutsche Biographie* 10, 67 f. http://www.deutsche-biographie.de/pnd100295886.html (December 21, 2018).
Le Bras, Gabriel (1950). “Usure.” *Dictionnaire de théologie catholique* XV, 2, Paris, 2336-72.
Lechler, Gotthard (1887). “Olearius, Johannes.” *Allgemeine Deutsche Biographie* 24, 280-2 c URL: https://www.deutsche-biographie.de/pnd100618030.html#adbcontent (December 21, 2018).

Leite, A. (2001). "Sà, Manuel de." Charles E. O' Neill and Joaquin M. Domínguez, eds. *Diccionario histórico de la Compañia de Jesús biográfico-temático*, Roma, Madrid, Institutum Historicum, 2001, vol. 4, 34-54.

Loesche, Georg (1952). "Chytraeus, David." Samuel Macauley Jackson, ed. *The New Scharzog Encyclopedia of Religious Knowledge* III, Grand Rapids MI: Baker, 116-7.

Luig, Klaus (1995). "Stryk, Samuel (1640-1710)." Michael Stolleis, ed. *Juristen, Ein biographisches Lexicon, Von der Antike bis zum 20. Jahrundert*. München: C.H. Beck, 607-8.

Luig, Klaus (1998). "Usus Modernus." *Handwörterbuch zur deutschen Rechtsgeschichte* (*HRG*) V, 1998, 628-36.

Mager, Inge (1972). "Hornejus, Conrad." *Neue Deutsche Biographie* 9, 637 f. https://www.deutsche-biographie.de/gnd116993901.html#ndbcontent; (December 21, 2018).

Mager, Inge (1993). "Mörlin, Joachim." *Biographisch-Bibliographisches Kirchenlexikon* VI, 8-11.

Mager, Inge (2007). "Calixtus, Georg." *Religion Past and Present* II, 315-6.

Mager, Inge (2009). "Helmstedt, University of." *Religion Past and Present* VI, 50.

Mahlmann, Theodor (1981). "Chemnitz, Martin." *Theologische Realenzyklopädie* VII, 714-21.

Mahlmann, Theodor (2007). "Balduin, Friedrich." *Religion Past and Present* I, 559.

Mahlmann, Theodor (2007). "Chemnitz, Martin." *Religion Past and Present* II, 509-10.

Mahoney, John (1997). "Probabilismus." *Theologische Realenzyklopädie* XXVII, 465-8.

Matthias, Markus (2009). "Hunn (Hunnius), Aegidius." *Religion Past and Present* VI, 344.

Freedman David N., ed. (1987). *The Eerdmans Bible Dictionary*. Grand Rapids: Eerdmans.

Moldaenke, Günther (1964). "Gallus, Nicolaus." *Neue Deutsche Biographie* 6, 55 f. https://www.deutsche-biographie.de/gnd118537369.html#ndbcontent. (December 21, 2018).

Montanari, Carlo (1988). "Rendita perpetua (diritto intermedio)." *Enciclopedia del diritto* XXXIX, Milano: Giuffrè, 820-47.

Munro, John (2008). "Price Revolution." *The New Palgrave Dictionary of Economics*, 2nd. ed., vol. 6, Basingstoke, Palgrave Macmillan, 2008, 631-4.

Muther, Theodor (1876). "Carpzov, Benedict." *Allgemeine Deutsche Biographie* 4, 11-20 https://www.deutsche-biographie.de/gnd118667246.html#adbcontent (December 21, 2018).

Muther, Theodor (1878). "Friderus, Peter." *Allgemeine Deutsche Biographie* 7, 38: https://www.deutsche-biographie.de/gnd100126944.html#adbcontent (December 21, 2018).

Oestmann, Peter (2008). "Aktenversendung." *Handwörterbuch zur deutschen Rechtsgeschichte* (*HRG*) I, 128-32. https://www.hrgdigital.de/HRG.aktenversendung.

Ohst, Martin (2007). "Confession II. Church History." *Religion Past and Present* III, 371.

Osti, Giuseppe (1974). "Clausola "rebus sic stantibus"." *Novissimo digesto italiano* III, Torino: UTET, 353-60.

Palmer, Christian (1875). "Binder, Christoph." *Allgemeine Deutsche Biographie* 2, 643-4 https://www.deutsche-biographie.de/gnd123508029.html#adbcontent (December 21, 2018).

Pältz, Eberhard H. (1981). "Buddeus (Budde), Johann Franz." *Theologische Realenzyklopädie* VII, 316-7.

Petzoldt, Martin (2007). "Alberti, Valentin." *Religion Past and Present* I, 123.

Pfundner, Thomas (2013). "Strigel, Victorin." *Neue Deutsche Biographie* 25, 555-6 https://www.deutsche-biographie.de/gnd124408494.html#ndbcontent (December 21, 2018).

Prantl, Carl von (1889). "Reusch, Johann Peter." *Allgemeine Deutsche Biographie* 28, 296 https://www.deutsche-biographie.de/pnd115536884.html#adbcontent (December 21, 2018).

Rivier (1876). "Curtius, Jakob." *Allgemeine Deutsche Biographie* 4, 649-50 https://www.deutsche-biographie.de/gnd119646277.html#adbcontent (December 21, 2018).

Russell, William R. (1996). "Hunnius, Aegidius." Hans J. Hillerbrand, ed. *The Oxford Encyclopedia of the Reformation* 2. Oxford: Oxford University Press, 276.

Sauter, Gerhard (1997). "Rechtfertigung IV." *Theologische Realenzyklopädie* XXVIII, 315-28.

Schäfer, Rolf (1978). "Aristoteles/Aristotelismus V." *Theologische Realenzyklopädie* III, 782-96.

Scheible, Heinz (2007). "Aepinus, Johannes." *Religion Past and Present* I, 73.

Scheible, Heinz (2008). "Eitzen, Paul v." *Religion Past and Present* IV, 387.

Schilling, Johannes (2003). "Paul von Eitzen – ein Kirchenvater Schleswig-Holsteins." Marion Bejschowetz-Iserholt and Reimer Witt, eds. *Kirchliches Leben in Schleswig-Holstein im 17. Jahrhundert. Vorträge zu einer Ausstellung im Landesarchiv Schleswig-Holstein.* Schleswig: Schleswig-Holsteinischen Landesarchivs, 41-58.

Schimmelpfennig, Adolf (1879). "Geßner, Salomon." *Allgemeine Deutsche Biographie* 9, 121-2 https://www.deutsche-biographie.de/gnd117543640.html#adbcontent (December 21, 2018).

Schimmelpfennig, Adolf (1893). "Strauch, Aegidius." *Allgemeine Deutsche Biographie* 36, 525-7, https://www.deutsche-biographie.de/pnd117311421.html#adbcontent (December 21, 2018).

Schmoeckel, Mathias (2008). "Beichtstuhljurisprudenz." *Handwörterbuch zur deutschen Rechtsgeschichte* (*HRG*) I, 505-8. https://www.hrgdigital.de/HRG.beichtstuhljurisprudenz (December 21, 2018).

Schneider, Burkhart SJ (1969). "Haunold, Christoph." *Neue Deutsche Biographie* 8, 98 http://www.deutsche-biographie.de/ppn124773664.html (December 21, 2018).

Schott, Theodor (1887). "Osiander, Johann Adam." *Allgemeine Deutsche Biographie* 24, 488-9 https://www.deutsche-biographie.de/gnd104279427.html#adbcontent (December 21, 2018).

Schott, Theodor (1887). "Osiander, Lucas II." *Allgemeine Deutsche Biographie* 24 (1887), 495-6 http://www.deutsche-biographie.de/pnd117154547.html?anchor=adb (December 21, 2018).

Schulz (1885). "Mudäus, Gabriel." *Allgemeine Deutsche Biographie* 22, 439-40 https://www.deutschebiographie.de/pnd100215785.html#adbcontent (December 21, 2018).

Schüssler, Hermann (1957) "Dannhauer, Johann Konrad." *Neue Deutsche Biographie* 3, 512 http://www.deutsche-biographie.de/pnd120227649.html (December 21, 2018).

Schüssler, Hermann (1959). "von Eitzen, Paul." *Neue Deutsche Biographie* 4, 426 f. http://www.deutsche-biographie.de/ppn129922706.html (December 21, 2018).

Sommer, Wolfgang (2012). "Selnecker, Nikolaus." *Religion Past and Present* XI, 602.

Sparn, Walter (1993). "Budde." *Lexikon für Theolgie und Kirche* 2, 755-6.

Sparn, Walter (1993). "Meisner, Balthasar." *Biographisch-Bibliographisches Kirchenlexikon* V, 1172-4.

Sparn, Walter (2009). "Horneius, Konrad." *Religion Past and Present* VI, 253.

Speer, Heino and Deutsch, Andreas, eds. *Deutsches Rechtswörterbuch*. http://drw-www.adw.uni-heidelberg.de/drw-cgi/zeige (December 21, 2018).

Stapelfeldt, K. and Schröder, Jan (2017). "Hugo Donellus." Gerd Kleinheyer and Jan Schröder, eds. *Deutsche und Europäische Juristen aus neun Jahrhunderten*. 6 ed., Tübingen: Mohr Siebeck, 118-21.

Stark, Werner (1973-4). "Casuistry." Philip P. Wiener, ed. *Dictionary of the History of the Ideas*. New York: Scribner. http://web.archive.org/web/20060618095059/http://etext.lib.virginia.edu/cgi-local/DHI/dhi.cgi?id=dv1-35 (December 21, 2018).

Stintzing, Roderich von (1875). "Bachof von Echt, Reiner." *Allgemeine Deutsche Biographie* 1, 756 unter Bachoff https://www.deutsche-biographie.de/gnd100021174.html#adbcontent (December 21, 2018).

Sträter, Udo (2011). "Olearius, 4. Johannes." *Religion Past and Present* IX, 305.

Teetaert, Amédée (1937). "La <<Summa de poenitentia>> de saint Raymond de Penyafort." *Dictionaire de théologie catholique* XIII, Paris : Letouzey et Ané, 1806-23.

Trifone, Romualdo (1959). "Censi." in *Novissimo digesto italiano* III, Torino: UTET, 91-8.

Tschackert, Paul (1885). "Meisner, Balthasar." *Allgemeine Deutsche Biographie* 21, 243 https://www.deutsche-biographie.de/gnd10434539X.html#adbcontent (December 21, 2018).

Tschackert, Paul (1882). "Kesler, Andreas." *Allgemeine Deutsche Biographie* 15, 655 https://www.deutsche-biographie.de/gnd124224644.html#adbcontent (December 21, 2018).

Tschackert, Paul (1894). "Thumm, Theodor." *Allgemeine Deutsche Biographie* 38, 169-71 https://www.deutsche-biographie.de/pnd123140528.html#adbcontent (December 21, 2018).

Tschackert, Paul (1900). "Zeltner, Gustav Georg." *Allgemeine Deutsche Biographie* 45, 52-3 https://www.deutsche-biographie.de/gnd115540806.html#adbcontent (December 21, 2018).

Tschackert, Paul (1900). "Zentgraf, Johann Joachim." *Allgemeine Deutsche Biographie* 45, 66-7 https://www.deutsche-biographie.de/gnd10406742X.html#adbcontent (December 21, 2018).

Turchetti, Mario (2018 [2015]). "Jean Bodin." Edward N. Zalta, ed. *The Stanford Encyclopedia of Philosophy* http://plato.stanford.edu/archives/spr2015/entries/bodin/ (December 21, 2018).

Ulrichs, Karl F. (1998). "Major, Georg (eig. Maier)." *Biographisch-Bibliographisches Kirchenlexikon* XIV, 1224-7.

Wagenmann, Julius A. (1875). "Bechmann, Friedemann." *Allgemeine Deutsche Biographie* 2, 205 https://www.deutsche-biographie.de/gnd100030378.html#adbcontent (December 21, 2018).

Wagenmann, Julius A. (1877). "Dürr, Johann Konrad." *Allgemeine Deutsche Biographie* 5, 490-1 http://www.deutsche-biographie.de/pnd100112544.html?anchor=adb (December 21, 2018).

Wagenmann, Julius A. (1882). "König, Georg." *Allgemeine Deutsche Biographie* 16, 507-8 http://www.deutsche-biographie.de/ppn116292008.html?anchor=adb (December 21, 2018).

Wagenmann, Julius A. (1883). "Lang, Johann Michael." *Allgemeine Deutsche Biographie* 17, 601-2 https://www.deutsche-biographie.de/gnd100299962.html#adbcontent (December 21, 2018).

Wallmann, Johannes (1981). "Calixt, Georg." *Theologische Realenzyklopädie* VII, 552-9.

Wallmann, Johannes (2007). "Dannhauer, Johann Konrad." *Religion Past and Present* III, 664.

Wallmann, Johannes (2009). "Gerhard, Johann." *Religion Past and Present* V, 362-3.

Wallmann, Johannes (2010). "Misler, Johann Nikolaus." *Religion Past and Present* VIII, 396-7.

Wallmann, Johannes (2012). "Schelwig, Samuel." *Religion Past and Present* XI, 473.

Wallmann, Johannes (2012). "Strauch, Aegidius." *Religion Past and Present* XII, 302.

Wenger, Timothy J. (1997). "Georg Major (1502-1574) Defender of Wittenberg's Faith and Melanchthonian exegete." Heinz Scheible, ed. *Melanchthon in seinen Schülern*. Wiesbaden: Harrassowitz, 129-56.

Wenley, R.M. (1910). "Casuistry." James Hastings, ed. *Encyclopedia of Religion and Ethics* 3 Edinburgh, 239.

Witte, John Jr. (2017). "Martin Luther's Influence on Legal Reforms and Civil Law." *Oxford Research Encyclopedia of Religion* DOI: 10.1093/acrefore/9780199340378.013.503 (February 12, 2018).

Wolf, Erik (1957). "Chemnitz, Martin, evangelischer." *Neue Deutsche Biographie* 3, 201 f. http://www.deutsche-biographie.de/pnd118829157.html (December 21, 2018).

Wolf, Erik (1957). "Colerus, Matthias." *Neue Deutsche Biographie* 3, 320 https://www.deutsche-biographie.de/gnd124644988.html#ndbcontent (December 21, 2018).

Zschoch, Hellmut (1994). "Rhegius Urbanus." *Biographisch-Bibliographisches Kirchenlexikon* VIII, 122-34.

Zschoch, Hellmut (2012). "Rhegius, Urbanus." *Religion Past and Present* XI, 191.

2.2 *Monographies and Articles*

Adam, Karl (1921). *Die geheime Kirchenbusse nach dem heiligen Augustin. Ein Auseinandersetzung mit B. Poschmann*. Kempten: Kösel & Pustet.

Agamben, Giorgio (2013). *The Highest Poverty. Monastic Rules and Form-of-Life*. Stanford: Stanford University Press.

Aland, Kurt (1960). "Die Privatbeichte im Luthertum von ihren Anfängen bis zu ihrer Auflösung." Kurt Aland, *Kirchengeschichte Entwürfe: Alte Kirche, Reformation und Luthertum, Pietismus und Erweckungsbewegung*. Gütersloh: Gerd Mohn, 452-519.

Albanesi, Nicola (2002). *Cur deus homo: la logica della redenzione. Studio sulla teoria della soddisfazione di S. Anselmo arcivescovo di Canterbury*. Roma: Pontificia Università Gregoriana.

Alberigo, Giuseppe et al., eds. (1973). *Conciliorum oecumenicorum decreta*. Bologna: Istituto per le scienze religiose.

Allegro, Giuseppe (2010). *Teologia e metodo in Pietro Abelardo*. Palermo: Officina di studi medievali.

Allman, Dwight D. (2007). "Sin and the Construction of Carolingian Kingship." Richard Newhauser, ed. *The Seven Deadly Sins. From Communities to Individuals*. Leiden, Boston: Brill.

Althaus, Paul (1965). *Die Ethik Martin Luthers*. Gütersloh: Gerd Mohn.

Althaus, Paul (1966). *The Theology of Martin Luther*. Trans. Robert C. Schultz, Philadelphia: Fortress.

Amend Traut, Anja (2015). "Die Akten und Beilagen von Reichskammergericht und Reichshofrat als Quellen des Handelsrechts." *Zeitschrift für neuere Rechtsgeschichte* 37, 177-205.

Andenna, Giancarlo (1998). "Riflessioni canonistiche in materia economica dal XII al XV secolo." Università Cattolica del Sacro Cuore, ed. *Chiesa, usura e debito estero. Giornata di studio in occasione del Cinquantennio della Facoltà di Economia (Milano 19 dicembre 1997)*. Milano: Vita e Pensiero, 21-42.

Anemüller, Bernhard (1861). *M. Bartholomäus Gernhard und der Rudolstädter Wucherstreit im 16. Jahrhundert*. Rudolstadt: F. priv. Hofbuchdruckerei.

Angelozzi, Giancarlo (1981). "L'insegnamento dei casi di coscienza nella pratica educativa della Compagnia di Gesù." Gian Paolo Brizzi, ed. *La 'Ratio studiorum'. Modelli culturali e pratiche educative dei gesuiti in Italia tra Cinque e Seicento*. Roma: Bulzoni, 121-62.

Angelozzi, Giancarlo (1986), "Interpretazioni della penitenza sacramentale in età moderna." *Religioni e società* I.2, 73-87.

Angelozzi, Giancarlo (2012). "I gesuiti e la confessione." *Lo Sguardo. Rivista di filosofia* 10.3, 39-53.

Appold, Kenneth G. (1998). *Abraham Calov's Doctrine of Vocatio in its Systematic Context*. Tübingen: Mohr Siebeck.

Appold, Kenneth G. (2004). *Orthodoxie als Konsensbildung*. Tübingen: Mohr Siebeck.

Appold, Kenneth G. (2008). "Academic Life and Teaching in Post-Reformation Lutheranism." Robert Kolb, ed. *Lutheran Ecclesiastical Culture, 1550-1675*. Leiden, Boston: Brill, 65-115.

Arbesmann, Rudolph (1954). "The concept of "Christus medicus" in St. Augustine." *Traditio* 10, 1-28.

Armstrong, Lawrin (2003). *Usury and Public Debt in Early Renaissance Florence. Lorenzo Ridolfi on the 'Monte Comune'*. Toronto: Pontifical Institute of Mediaeval Studies.

Armstrong, Lawrin (2016). *The Idea of a Moral Economy: Gerard of Siena on Usury, Restitution, and Prescription*. Toronto: University Press.

Arndt, Georg (1929). "Christoph Fischer und seine Tätigkeit als Generalsuperintendent im Thüringer Lande." *Beiträge zur thüringischen und sächsischen Kirchengeschichte: Festschrift für Otto Dobenecker zum siebzigsten Geburstage am 2. April 1929*. Jena, 294-326.

Arnould, Emile J. (1940). *Le Manuel des Pèchès, ètude de littèrature religieuse anglo-normande (XIIIme siècle)*. Librarie e. Droz: Paris.

Assel, Hans Günther (1948). *Das kanonische Zinsverbot und der "Geist" des Frühkapitalismus in der Wirtschaftsethik bei Eck und Luther*. diss., Erlagen.

Astorri, Paolo (2016). "Il diritto canonico nella prima teologia pratica protestante: la formazione dei ministri ecclesiastici secondo Hyperius, Zepper e Voetius." *Glossae* 13, 5-29.

Astuti, Guido (1952). *I contratti obbligatori nella storia del diritto italiano*. vol. I, Milano: Giuffrè.

Aure, Harald H. (2015). *The Right to Wage War (jus ad bellum). The German Reception of Grotius 50 years after De iure belli ac pacis*. Berlin: BWV.

Azevedo Alves, Andre A. and Moreira, Jose M. (2010). *The Salamanca School*. New York: Continuum.

Baldwin, John W. (1959). "The Medieval Theories of the Just Price: Romanists, Canonists, and Theologians in the Twelfth and Thirteenth Centuries." *Transactions of the American Philosophical Society, New Series* 49.4, 1-92.

Baldwin, John W. (1970). *Masters, Princes and Merchants. The social views of Peter the Chanter and his Circle*, vol. I, Princeton, Princeton University Press, 1970.

Ballor, Jordan J. (2014). "A Society of Mutual Aid. Natural Law and Subsidiarity in Early Modern Reformed Perspective." Wim Decock, Jordan J. Ballor, Michael Germann and Laurent Waelkens, eds. *Law and Religion. The Legal Teachings of the Protestant and Catholic Reformations*. Göttingen: Vandenhoeck & Ruprecht, 9-21.

Bar, Christian von, and Dopffel, Peter, eds. (1995). *Deutsches internationales Privatrecht im 16. und 17. Jahrhundert*. vol. 1. Tübingen: Mohr Siebeck.

Bar, Christian von and Dopffel, Peter, eds. (2001). *Deutsches internationales Privatrecht im 16. und 17. Jahrhundert*. vol. 2. Tübingen: Mohr Siebeck.

Barge, Hermann (1951). *Luther und der Frühkapitalismus*. Gütersloh: C. Bertelsmann Verlag.

Barile, Nicola Lorenzo (2010). "Credito, usura, prestito a interesse." *Reti medievali*, vol. 11 n. 1 http://www.rmojs.unina.it/index.php/rm/article/view/4757/5347?acceptCookies=1 (December 5, 2018).

Barile, Nicola Lorenzo (2014). "Contratti di censo e monti di pietà. Problemi e prospettive di ricerca." Paola Maffei and Gian Maria Varanini, eds. Honos alit artes. *Studi per il settantesimo compleanno di Mario Ascheri. Il cammino delle idee dal medioevo all'antico regime. Diritto e cultura nell'esperienza europea*. Firenze: Firenze University Press, 139-46.

Barrientos García, José (1985). *Un siglo de moral económica (1526-1629), tom. 1: Francisco de Vitoria y Domingo de Soto*. Salamanca: Ediciones Universidad de Salamanca.

Bast, Robert J., ed. (2004). *The Reformation of Faith in the Context of Late Medieval Theology and Piety. Essays by Bernt Hamm*. Leiden-Boston: Brill.

Bauer, Clemens (1950). "Die Naturrechtsvorstellungen des jüngeren Melanchthon." Richard Nürnberger, ed. *Festschrift für Gerhard Ritter zum 60. Geburstag*. Tübingen: Mohr, 244-55.

Bauer, Clemens (1951). "Melanchthons Naturrechtslehre." *Archiv für Reformationsgeschichte* 42, 64-100.

Bauer, Clemens (1954). "Conrad Peutingers Gutachten zur Monopolfrage: Eine Untersuchung zur Wandlung der Wirtschaftsanschauungen im Zeitalter der Reformation." *Archiv für Reformationsgeschichte* 45, 1-44, 145-96, 147-73.

Bauer, Clemens (1958). "Melanchthons Wirtschaftsethik." *Archiv für Reformationsgeschichte*, 49 1/2, 115-60.

Bauer, Clemens (1965). *Conrad Peutinger und der Durchbruch des neuen ökonomischen Denkens in der Wende zur Neuzeit*. Freiburg: Herder.

Bayer, Oswald (2007). *Martin Luthers Theologie*. 3rd ed. Tübingen: Mohr Siebeck.

Baylor, Michael G. (1977). *Action and Person: Conscience in the Late Scholasticism and the Young Luther*. Leiden: Brill.

Bazzichi, Oreste (2008). *Dall'usura al giusto profitto. L'etica economica della scuola francescana*. Cantalupa (Torino): Effatà editore.

Beck-Mannagetta, M., *Die Clausola Rebus sic Stantibus und die Geschäftsgrundlage in der Dogmengeschichte*, in *La formazione storica del diritto moderno*, vol. III, Firenze, Olschki, 1997, 1263-76.

Becker, Hans-Jürgen (2014). "Das Zinsverbot im lateinischen Mittelalter." Matthias Casper, Norber Oberhauer and Fabian Wittreck, eds. *Was vom Wucher übrigbleibt. Zinsverbote im historischen und interkulturellen Vergleich*. Tübingen: Mohr Siebeck, 15-45.

Behme, Thomas (2002). "Pufendorf's Doctrine of Sovereignty and Its Natural Law Foundations". Ian Hunter and David Saunders, eds. *Natural Law and Civil Sovereignty, Moral Right and State Authority in Early Modern Political Thought*. Basingstoke: Palgrave Macmillan, 43-58.

Belda Plans, Juan (2000). *La escuela de Salamanca y la renovación de la teología en el siglo XVI*. Madrid: Biblioteca de autores cristianos.

Bellini, Piero (1964). *L'obbligazione da promessa con oggetto temporale nel sistema canonistico classico, con particolare riferimento ai secoli XII e XIII*. Milano: Giuffrè.

Benton, Lauren and Ross, Richard J., eds. (2013). *Legal Pluralism and Empires, 1500-1850*. New York-London: New York University Press.

Benton, Lauren and Ross, Richard J. (2013). "Empires and Legal Pluralism: Jurisdiction, Sovereignty, and Political Imagination in the Early Modern World." Lauren Benton and Richard J. Ross, eds. *Legal Pluralism and Empires, 1500-1850*. New York-London: New York University Press, 1-20.

Bergfeld, Christoph (1973). "Katholische Moraltheologie und Naturrechtslehre." Helmut Coing, ed. *Handbuch der Quellen und Literatur der neueren europäischen Privatrechtsgeschichte*. vol. II, first part, München: C.H. Beck, 999-1033.

Berman, Harold J. (1974). *The Interaction between Law and Religion*. London: Scm Press Ltd.

Berman, Harold J. (1983). *Law and Revolution. The Formation of the Western Legal Tradition*. Cambridge Mass.- London: Harvard University Press.

Berman, Harold J. (1988). "Toward an Integrative Jurisprudence: Politics, Morality, History." *California Law Review* 76 n. 4, 779-801.

Berman, Harold J. and Witte John Jr. (1989). "The Transformation of Western Legal Philosophy in Lutheran Germany." *Southern California Law Review* 62 n. 6, 1575-1611.

Berman, Harold J. (2003). *Law and Revolution II. The Impact of the Protestant Reformations on the Western Legal Tradition*. Cambridge Mass.-London: Harvard University Press.

Berman, Harold J. (2008). "The Christian Sources of General Contract Law." John Witte Jr. and Frank S. Alexander, eds. *Christianity and Law: An Introduction*. Cambridge: Cambridge University Press, 125-41.

Berman, Harold J. and Witte John Jr., ed. (2013). *Law and Language. Effective Symbols of Community*. Cambridge: Cambridge University Press.

Berthoud, Gabrielle (1973). *Antoine Marcourt, Réformateur et Pamphlétaire du "Livre des Marchans" aus Placards de 1534*. Geneve: Droz.

Betti, Emilio (1944). "Der Typenzwang bei den römischen Rechtsgeschäften und die sogenannte Typenfreiheit des heutigen Rechts." *Festschrift für L. Wenger zu seinem 70. Geburtstag dargebracht von Freunden, Fachgenossen und Schulern.* Vol. I, München: Institut für Papyrusforschung.

Betti, Emilio (1966). "La tipicità dei negozi giuridici romani e la cosiddetta atipicità del diritto odierno." *Annali della Facoltà giuridica dell'Università di Macerata* I, 5-35. This is also in Betti, Emilio and Grifò, Giuliano, eds. (1991). *Diritto, metodo, ermeneutica. Scritti scelti*. Milano: Giuffrè, 325-59.

Beutel, Albrecht, ed. (2005). *Luther Handbuch*. Tübingen: Mohr Siebeck.

Beutel, Albrecht (2005). "Theologie als Unterscheidungslehre." Albrecht Beutel, ed. *Luther Handbuch*. Tübingen: Mohr Siebeck, 450-4.

Beyer, Hermann Wolfgang (2017 [1935]). *Luther und das Recht*. Nikosia: Verone.

Bezzel, Ernst (1982). *Frei zum Eingeständnis: Geschichte und Praxis der evangelischen Einzelbeichte*. Stuttgart: Calwer.

Bianchi, Ernesto (1983). In tema d'usura. Canoni conciliari e legislazione imperiale del IV secolo. *Athenaeum* 61, 321-42.

Biller, Peter (1998). "Confession in the Middle Ages: Introduction." Peter Biller and Alastair J. Minnis, eds. *Handling Sin: Confession in the Middle Ages*. York: York Medieval Press, 1-34.

Billeskov Janson, F.J. (1993). "From the Reformation to the Baroque." Sven Hakon Rossel, ed. *A History of Danish Literature*. Lincoln: University of Nebraska Press, 71-120.

Birocchi, Italo (1988). *Saggi sulla formazione storica della categoria generale del contratto*. Cagliari:Cuec.

Birocchi, Italo (1990). "Tra elaborazioni nuove e dottrine tradizionali, Il contratto trino e la natura contractus." *Quaderni fiorentini* 19, 243-322.

Birocchi, Italo (1990). "Notazioni sul contratto (a proposito di un recente lavoro di G. Alpa)." *Quaderni fiorentini* 19, 637-59.

Birocchi, Italo (1991). "Vendita e transferimento della proprietà nel diritto comune." Letizia Vacca, ed. *Vendita e trasferimento della proprietà nella prospettiva storico-comparatistica*. Atti del Congresso Internazionale Pisa-Viareggio-Lucca, 17-21 aprile 1990. Milano: Giuffrè, 139-67.

Birocchi, Italo (1997). *Causa e categoria generale del contratto. Un problema dogmatico nella cultura privatistica dell'età moderna 1. Il cinquecento*. Torino: Giappichelli.

Black, Antony (1992). *Political Thought in Europe 1250-1450*. Cambridge: Cambridge University Press.

Blicke, Peter (1975). *Die Revolution von 1525*. Münich-Wien: Oldenbourg.

Blomme, Robert (1958). *La doctrine du péché dans les écoles théologiques de la première moitié du XIIe siècle*. Louvain: Publications universitaires de Louvain.

Bloomfield, Morton W. (1952). *The Seven Deadly Sins: An Introduction to the History of a Religious Concept, with Special Reference to Medieval English Literature*. East Lansing: Michigan State College Press.

Boarini, Serge, ed. (2009). *La casuistique classique: genèse, formes, devenir*. Saint-Étienne: Publications de l'Université de Saint-Étienne.

Böckenförde, Ernst-Wolfgang (2007). *Der Staat als sittlicher Staat, Der säkularisierte Staat: sein Charakter, seine Rechtfertigung und seine Probleme im 21. Jahrhundert*. München: Von Siemens Stiftung.

Bode, Gerhard (2008). "Instruction of the Christian Faith by Lutherans after Luther." Robert Kolb, ed. *Lutheran Ecclesiastical Culture, 1550-1675*. Leiden-Boston: Brill, 159-204.

Bossy, John (1975). "The Social History of Confession in the Age of the Reformation." *Transaction of the Royal Historical Society* 25, 21-38.

Bossy, John (1988). "Moral Arithmetic: Seven Sins into Ten Commandments." Edmund Leites, ed. *Conscience and Casuistry in Early Modern Europe*. Cambridge: Cambridge University Press, 214-43.

Boyle, Leonard E. (1962). "The Constitution Cum ex eo' of Boniface VIII: Education of Parochial Clergy." *Mediaeval Studies* 24, 263-302.

Boyle, Leonard E. (1977). "Aspects of Clerical Education in Fourteenth-Century England." Paul E. Szarmach and Bernard S. Levy, eds. *The Fourteenth Century*. Proceedings of the State University of New York Conferences in Medieval Studies. Binghamton, N.Y.: Center for Medieval and Early Renaissance Studies, 19-32.

Boyle, Leonard E. (1981). *Pastoral Care, Clerical Education and Canon Law, 1200-1400*. London: Aldershot.

Boyle, Leonard E. (1982). "Summae confessorum." *Les genres Littéraires dans les sources théologiques et philosophiques médiévales. Définition, critique et exploitation, Actes du Colloque international de Louvain-la-Neuve 25-27 Mai 1981*. Publications de l'institut d'études médiévales, 2e série: Textes, études, congrès, vol. 5, Lovain-La-Neuve: Université catholique de Louvain, 227-37.

Brady, Thomas A. (2007). "Emergence and Consolidation of Protestantism in the Holy Roman Empire to 1600." R. Po-chia Hsia, ed. *The Cambridge History of Christianity, Reform and Expansion 1550-1660*. Vol. 6. Cambridge: Cambridge University Press, 20-36.

Brambilla, Elena (2000). *Alle origini del Sant'Uffizio. Penitenza, confessione e giustizia dal medioevo al XVI secolo*. Bologna: Il Mulino.

Brambilla, Elena (2006). *La giustizia intollerante: inquisizione e tribunali confessionali in Europa (secoli IV-XVIII)*. Roma: Carocci.

Braun, Christian (1994). *Vom Wucherverbot zur Zinsanalyse, 1150-1700*. diss., Zürich.

Braun, Harald and Vallance, Edward, eds. (2003). *Contexts of Conscience in Early Modern Europe, 1500-1700*. Basingstoke: Palgrave Macmillan.

Brett, Annabel S. (1997). *Liberty, Right and Nature: Individual Rights in Later Scholastic Thought*. Cambridge: Cambridge University Press.

Brock, Stephen L. (2015). *The Philosophy of Saint Thomas Aquinas: A Sketch*. Eugene, Oregon: Cascade Books.

Brockmann, Thomas and Weiss, Dieter J. (2013). *Das Konfessionalisierungsparadigma. Leistungen, Probleme, Grenzen*. Münster: Aschendorff.

Bruchhold, Ullrich (2010). *Deutschsprachige Beichten im 13. und 14. Jahrhundert: Editionen und Typologien zur Überlieferungs-, Text- und Gebrauchsgeschichte vor dem Hintergrund der älteren Tradition*. Berlin: De Gruyter.

Brunori, Luisa (2015). *Societas quid sit. La societé commerciale dans l'élaboration de la Seconde Scolastique*. Paris: Mare & Martin.

Burr, David (1985). "The Correctorium Controversy and the Origins of the *Usus Pauper* Controversy." *Speculum* 60, 331-42.

Bussi, Emilio (1937). *La formazione dei dogmi di diritto privato nel diritto comune*. Padova: Cedam.

Calasso, Francesco (1959). *Il negozio giuridico. Lezioni di storia del diritto italiano*. 2nd ed., Milano: Giuffrè.

Callewier, Hendrik (2007). Anti-jezuïtisme in de Zuidelijke Nederlanden (1542-1773). *Trajecta* 16, 30-50.

Capitani, Ovidio (1984). *L'Italia medievale nei secoli di trapasso: La riforma della Chiesa (1012-1122)*. Bologna: Pàtron.

Capobianco, Pacifico Pasquale (1935-6). "De ambitu fori interni in iure ante codicem." *Apollinaris* 8, 591-605 and *Apollinaris* 9, 364-374.

Cappellini, Paolo (1981). "Sulla formazione del moderno concetto di 'dottrina generale del diritto', (*a proposito di M. Lipp, Die Bedeutung des Naturrechts für die Ausbildung der allgemeinen Lehren des Deutschen Privatrechts, Schriften zur Rechtstheorie, Heft. 88, Berlin, 1980*)." *Quaderni fiorentini* 10 323-54.

Carboni, Mauro and Muzzarelli, Maria Giuseppina, eds. (2008). *I conti dei Monti: teoria e pratica amministrativa nei Monti di Pietà fra Medioevo ed Età Moderna*. Venezia: Marsilio.

Carpin, Attilio (2006). *La confessione tra il XII e il XIII secolo: teologia e prassi nella legislazione canonica medievale*. Bologna: Edizioni Studio Domenicano.

Carty, Jarret A. (2017). *God and Government: Martin Luther's Political Thought*. Montreal: McGill-Queen's University Press.

Casagrande, Carla and Vecchio, Silvana (1994). "La classificazione dei peccati tra settenario e decalogo (XIII-XV)." *Documenti e studi sulla tradizione filosofica medievale, Rivista della Società Internazionale per lo Studio del Medioevo Latino* V, 331-95.

Casagrande, Carla and Vecchio, Silvana (2000). *I sette vizi capitali: storia dei peccati nel Medioevo*. Torino: Einaudi.

Casana, Paola (1992). "Note biografiche su un giurista del XVI secolo: Antonino Tesauro." *Bollettino storico bibliografico subalpino* XC, fasc. I, 281-309.

Cavina, Marco, ed. (2004). *Tiberio Deciani (1509-1582). Alle origini del pensiero giuridico moderno*. Atti del convegno internazionale di studi storici e giuridici, Udine 12-13 aprile 2002. Udine: Forum.

Cazzetta, Giovanni (2017). "Abuso del diritto e forma di unità del giuridico." *Rivista di diritto civile* 3, 559-81.

Cessario, Romanus O.P. (1990). *The Godly Image. Christ and Salvation in Catholic Thought from Anselm to Aquinas*. Petersham, MA: St. Bede's Publications.

Cessario, Romanus O.P. (2001). *Introduction to Moral Theology*. Washington D.C.: The Catholic University of America Press.

Chafuen, Alejandro Antonio (2003). *Faith and Liberty. The Economic Thought of the Late Scholastics*. Lanham-Boulder-New York-Oxford: Lexington.

Chiodi, Giovanni (2017). "La funzione sociale del contratto: riflessioni di uno storico del diritto." Francesco Macario and Marco Nicola Miletti, eds. *La funzione sociale nel diritto privato tra XX e XXI secolo. Atti dell'incontro di studio, Roma, 9 ottobre 2015*. Roma: Roma Tre Press, 151-68.

Cipolla, Carlo Maria (2002 [1974]). *Storia economica dell'Europa pre-industriale*. Bologna: Il Mulino.

Clasen, Claus Peter (1972). *Anabaptism, a Social History, 1525-1618: Switzerland, Austria, Moravia, South and Central Germany*. Ithaca and London: Cornell University Press.

Coing, Helmut (1952). "Zum Einfluss der Philosophie des Aristoteles auf die Entwicklung des römischen Rechts." *Zeitschrift der Savigny-Stiftung für Rechtsgeschichte*, Rom. Ab., vol. LXIX, 24-59.

Collin, Peter, ed. (2016). *Justice without the State. Judicial Self-Regulation in the Past and Present*. Frankfurt am Main: Klostermann.

Collin, Peter (2016). "State and Perspectives of the History of Social Law in Germany." *Rechtsgeschichte, Legal History* 24, 393-401.

Conte, Emanuele (2008). "Per una storia del diritto medievale nel XXI secolo." *Eadem Utraque Europa* Año 4, n. 7, 57-87.

Conte, Emanuele (2009). *Diritto comune. Storia e storiografia di un sistema dinamico*. Bologna: Il Mulino.

Contreras, Sebastián "La determinación del Derecho en Domingo de Soto y Francisco Suárez." *Revista de Estudios Histórico-Jurídicos* XXXV, 655-80.

Cortese, Ennio (1999 [1958]). "Intorno alla causa impositionis e a taluni aspetti privatistici delle finanze medievali." *Annali di storia del diritto*, Anno II, 111-86 reprint in Italo Birocchi and Ugo Petronio, ed. *Ennio Cortese, Scritti*. Spoleto: Centro italiano di studi sull'Alto Medioevo, I.

Crislip, Andrew T. (2005). *From Monastery to Hospital. Christian Monasticism & the Transformation of Health Care in Late Antiquity*. Ann Arbor: The University of Michigan Press.

Crusius, Irene (2008). "Nicht calvinisch, nicht lutherisch": Zu Humanismus, Philippismus un Kryptocalvinismus in Sachsen am Ende des 16. Jahrunderts." *Archiv für Reformationgeschichte. Archive for Reformation History* 99, 139-73.

Cummins, Stephen and Kounine, Laura, eds. (2016). *Cultures of Conflict Resolution in Early Modern Europe*. London: Routledge.

Cusack, Carole M. (1998). *Conversion Among the Germanic People*. Midsomer Norton: Bookcraft.

D'Avray, D.L. (1985). *The Preaching of the Friars. Sermons diffused from Paris before 1300*. Oxford: Clarendon Press.

Dahl, Gina (2010). *Book Collections of Clerics in Norway, 1650-1750*. Leiden- Boston: Brill.

Dahl, Gina (2011). *Books in Early Modern Norway*. Leiden-Boston: Brill.

Daston, Lorraine, Stolleis, Michael, eds. (2016 [2008]) *Natural Law and Laws of Nature in Early Modern Europe. Jurisprudence, Theology, Moral and Natural Philosophy*. London-New York: Routledge.

Daube, David, ed. (1959). *Studies in the Roman Law of Sale: Dedicated to the Memory of Francis de Zulueta*. Oxford, Clarendon University Press, 1959.

Daube, David (1979). "Money and Justificiability." *Zeitschrift der Savigny-Stiftung für Rechtsgeschichte*, Rom. Ab., vol. 96, 1-16.

David, Joseph E. (2017). *Gesetzreligion und Rechtspluralismus*. Stefan Grundmann and Jan Thiessen, eds. *Religiöse Werte im Recht*. Tübingen: Mohr Siebeck. 19-42.

Deckers, Daniel (1991). *Gerechtigkeit und Recht. Eine historisch-kritische Untersuchung der Gerechtigkeitslehre des Francisco de Vitoria (1483-1546)*. Freiburg-Wien: Universitätsverlag.

Decock, Wim (2009). "Lessius and the Breakdown of the Scholastic Paradigm." *Journal of the History of Economic Thought* 31, n. 1, 57-78.

Decock, Wim (2011). "From Law to Paradise: Confessional Catholicism and Legal Scholarship." *Rechtsgeschichte, Legal History* 18, 12-34.

Decock, Wim (2013). *Theologians and Contract Law: The Moral Transformation of the Ius Commune*. Leiden-Boston: M. Nijhoff.

Decock, Wim (2014). "The Catholic Spirit of Capitalism? Contrasting Views on Profit-Making through Capital Investment in the Age of Reformations". Wim Decock, Jordan J. Ballor, Michael Germann, and Laurent Waelkens, eds.), *Law and Religion. The Legal Teachings of the Protestant and Catholic Reformations*, Göttingen, Vandenhoeck & Ruprecht, 2014, 22-43.

Decock, Wim (2014). "De strijd om de juridische kwalificatie van de advocaat-cliëntverhouding. Rechtshistorische kanttekeninge." *Tijdschrift voor Privaatrecht* 2, 1207-57.

Decock, Wim (2016), "Spanish Scholastics on Money and Credit." David Fox and Wolfgang Ernst, eds. *Money in the Western Legal Tradition: Middle Ages to Bretton Woods*. Oxford: Oxford University Press, 267-83.

Decock, Wim (2016). "Trust Beyond Faith Re-Thinking Contracts with Heretics and Excommunicates in Times of Religious War." *Rivista internazionale di diritto comune* 27, 301-28.

Decock, Wim (2016). "Elegant Scholastic Humanism? Arias Piñel's (1515-1563) Critical Revision of Laesio Enormis." Paul J. du Plessis and John W. Cairns, eds. *Reassessing Legal Humanism and its Claims. Petere fontes?* Edinburgh: Edinburgh University Press, 137-53.

Decock, Wim (2016). "In Defense of Commercial Capitalism: Lessius, Partnerships and the Contractus Trinus." Bram Van Hofstraeten and Wim Decock, eds. *Companies and Company Law in Late Medieval and Early Modern Europe*. Leuven: Peeters, 55-90.

Decock, W. (2017). "Collaborative Legal Pluralism. Confessors as Law Enforcers in Mercado's Advice on Economic Governance (1571)." *Rechtsgeschichte, Legal History* 25, 103-14.

Decock, Wim (2017). "Law, Religion and Debt Relief: Balancing above the 'Abyss of Despair' in Early Modern Canon Law and Theology." *American Journal of Legal History* 57 (2), 125-41.

Decock, Wim and Hallebeek, Jan (2010). "Pre-contractual duties to inform in Early Modern Scholasticism." *Tijdschrift voor Rechtsgeschiedenis* 78, 89-133.

Decock, Wim and Birr, Christiane (2016). *Recht und Moral in der Scholastik der Frühen Neuzeit 1500-1750*. Berlin-Boston: De Gruyter.

Deflers, Isabelle (2005). *Lex und Ordo. Eine rechtshistorische Untersuchung der Rechtsauffassung Melanchthons*. Berlin: Duncker & Humbolt.

Deflers, Isabelle (2009). "Konfession und Jurisprudenz bei Melanchthon." Christoph Strohm and Heinrich de Wall, eds. *Konfessionalität und Jurisprudenz in der frühen Neuzeit*. Berlin: Duncker & Humbolt, 33-46.

De Jong, Mayke (2005). "Charlemagne's Church." Joanna Story, ed. *Charlemagne: Empire and Society*. Manchester-New York: Manchester University Press, 103-35.

Dekkers, René (1938). "Mattheus van Wesenbeke". René Dekkers, *Het humanisme en de rechteswetenschap in de Nederlanden Nicolas Everaerts, 1462-1532, Wigle Van Aytta, 1507-1577, Gabriel Vander Muyden, 1500-1560, Jacob Reyvaert, 1535-1568, Mattheus Van Wesembeke, 1531-1586*. Antwerp: De Sikkel.

De Levie, Dagobert (1972). *Christian Wolff und der Begriff der Menschenliebe. Festvortrag aus Anlass der Verleihung der Ehrensenatorwürde der Universität zu Köln*. Krefeld: Scherpe.

Delumeau, Jean (1983). *La péché e la peur. La culpabilisation en Occident (XIIIe-XVIIIe siècles)*. Fayard: Paris.

Delumeau, Jean (1990). *L'aveu et le perdon. Les difficultés de la confession XIIIe-XVIIIe siècle*. Paris: Fayard.

Del Vigo Gutiérrez, Abelardo (2006). *Economia y ética en el siglo XVI, Estudio comparativo entre los Padres de la Reforma y la teología española*. Biblioteca de Autores Cristianos: Madrid.

De Roover, Raymond (1953). *L'évolution de la lettre de change, XIV*e*-XVIII*e *siècles*. Paris: Armand Colin.

De Roover, Raymond (1958). "The Concept of the Just Price Theory and Economic Policy." *Journal of Economic History* 18, 418-34.

De Roover, Raymond (1969). "The cambium maritimum contract according to the Genoese Notarial Records of the Twelfth and Thirteenth Centuries." David Herlihy, Robert S. Lopez and Vsevold Slessarev, eds. *Economy, Society and Government in Medieval Italy. Essays in Memory of Robert L. Reynolds*. Kent: Kent State University Press, 15-33.

De Roover, Raymond (1971). *Le pensée économique des scholastiques, doctrines et méthodes*. Paris: Inst. d'Etudes médiévales.

De Roover, Raymond (1974 [1955]) "Scholastic Economics: Survival and Lasting Influence from the Sixteenth Century to Adam Smith." *The Quarterly Journal of Economics* 69, n. 2, 161-90. Reprint in Julius Kirschner, ed. *Business, Banking, and Economic Thought in Late Medieval and Early Modern Europe*. Chicago-London: Chicago University Press, 306-35.

Deroussin, David (2012). *Histoire du droit des obligations*. 2nd ed., Paris: Economica.

De Wall, Heinrich (2017). "Von der Kanonistik zum evangelischen Kirchenrecht – Traditionen und Diskontinuitäten." *Zeitschrift der Savigny-Stiftung für Rechtgeschichte* Kan. Ab., 134, 262-76.

Diesselhorst, Malte (1962). *Die Lehre des Hugo Grotius vom Versprechen*. Köln: Graz.

Dingel, Irene (1994). "Ablehnung und Aneignung: Die Bewertung der Autorität Martin Luthers in den Auseinandersetzungen um die Konkordienformel." *Zeitschrift für Kirchengeschichte* 105, 35-57.

Dingel, Irene (1996). *Concordia controversa. Die öffentlichen Diskussionen um das lutherische Konkordienwerk am Ende des 16. Jahrhunderts*. Gütersloh: Gütersloher Verlaghaus.

Dingel, Irene, Kolb, Robert, Kuropka, Nicole and Wengert, Timothy J., eds (2012). *Philip Melanchthon. Theologian in Classroom, Confession, and Controversy*. Göttingen: Vandenhoeck & Ruprecht.

Dingel, Irene (2012). "Melanchthon and the Establishment of Confessional Norms." Dingel, Irene, Kolb, Robert, Kuropka, Nicole and Wengert, Timothy J., eds. *Philip Melanchthon, Theologian in Classroom, Confession and Controversy*. Göttingen: Vandenhoeck & Ruprecht, 161-80.

Diósdi, György (1981). *Contract in Roman Law: From the Twelve Tables to the Glossators*. Budapest: Akadémiai Kiado.

Dittrich, Ottmar (1932). *Geschichte der Ethik: Die Systeme der Moral vom Altertum bis zur Gegenwart, vol. 4, Von der Kirchenreformation bis zum Ausgang des Mittelalters: 1. Die Reformatoren und der lutherisch-kirchliche Protestantismus*. Leipzig: Meiner.

Divine, Thomas F., S.J. (1959). *Interest. An Historical & Analytical Study in Economics & Modern Ethics*. Milwaukee: The Marquette University Press.

Doherty, Sean (2014). *Theology and Economic Ethics. Martin Luther and Arthur Rich in Dialogue*. Oxford: Oxford University Press.

Dolezalek, Gero (1992). "The Moral Theologians' Doctrine of Restitution and its Juridification in the Sixteenth and Seventeenth Centuries." *Acta Juridica* 104, 104-14.

Donagan, Alan (1982). "Thomas Aquinas on Human Action." Norman Kretzmann, Anthony Kenny and Jan Pinborg, ed. *The Cambridge History of Later Medieval Philosophy from the Rediscovery of Aristotle to the Disintegration of Scholasticism, 1100-1600*. Cambridge: Cambridge University Press, 642-52.

Donnelly, Dorothy F. and Sherman, Mark A. (1991). *Augustine's* De civitate Dei. *An Annotated Bibliography of Modern Criticism, 1960-1990*. New York- Berlin-Bern-Frankfurt am Main-Paris-Wien: Peter Lang.

Döring, Detlef (2009). "Wirkungen des konfessionellen Denkens auf das juristische Werk Samuel Pufendorfs." Christoph Strohm and Heinrich De Wall, eds. *Konfessionalität und Jurisprudenz in der frühen Neuzeit*. Berlin: Duncker & Humbolt, 415-30.

Döring, Detlef (2012). *Samuel Pufendorf in der Welt des 17. Jahrhunderts, Untersuchungen zur Biographie Pufendorfs und zu seinem Wirken als Politiker und Theologe*. Frankfurt am Main: Klostermann.

Dreitzel, Horst (2001). "Samuel Pufendorf." Helmut Holzhey et al., eds. *Die Philosophie des 17. Jahrhunderts*, vol. 4, *Das Heilige Römische Reich deutscher Nation Nord-und Ostmitteleuropa*. Basel: Schwabe & Co., 757-812.

Drobner, Hubertus (2007). *The Fathers of the Church. A Comprehensive Introduction*, Peabody, Hendrickson Publishers, 2007.

Druwé, Wouter (2018). *Transregional Normativity in Learned Legal Practice. Loans and Credit in Consilia and Decisiones in the Northern and Southern Low Countries (c. 1500-1680)*. Diss., Leuven.

Duhr, Bernhard S.J. (1908). "Der 5% Streit im protestantische Regensburg: Ausweisung vom 5 Predigern." *Zeitschrift für katholische Theologie* XXXII, 608-10.

Dunn, Marylin (2003). *The Emergence of Monasticism: from the Desert Fathers to the Early Middle Ages*. Oxford: Blackwell.

Dunoyer, Emilio (1957). *L'Enchiridion Confessariorium del Navarro*. Pamplona: Gurea.

Dutton, Paul Edward, ed. and trans. (1998). *Charlemagne's Courtier. The Complete Einhard*. Peterborough: Broadview Press.

Dürr, Renate (2006). *Politische Kultur in der Frühen Neuzeit*. Göttingen: Gütersloher Verlagshaus.

Dürr, Renate (2013). "Confession as an Instrument of Church Discipline: A Study of Catholic and Lutheran Confessional Manuals from the 16th and 17th Centuries." Sigrid Müller and Cornelia Schweiger, eds. *Between Creativity and Norm-Making. Tensions in the Later Middle Ages and the Early Modern Era*. Leiden-Boston: Brill, 215-40.

Duve, Thomas (2007). "La teoría de la restitución en Domingo de Soto: Su significación para la historia del derecho privado moderno." Juan Cruz Cruz, ed. *La ley natural como fundamento moral y jurídico ed Domingo de Soto*. Pamplona: Eunsa, 181-98.

Duve, Thomas (2008). *Sonderrecht in der Frühen Neuzeit. Studien zum ius singulare und den privilegia miserabilium personarum, senum und indorum in Alter und Neuer Welt*. Frankfurt a. M.: Klostermann.

Duve, Thomas (2011). "Katholisches Kirchenrecht und Moraltheologie im 16. Jahrhundert: Eine globale normative Ordnung im Schatten schwacher Staatlichtkeit." Stefan Kadelbach and Klaus Günther, eds. *Recht ohne Staat?, Zur Normativität nichtstaatlicher Rechtsetzung*. Frankfurt-New York: Campus, 147-74.

Duve, Thomas, *Global Legal History – A Methodological Approach* in *Oxford Handbooks Online – Law*, Jan. 2017, DOI: 10.1093/oxfordhb/9780199935352.013.25 (accessed 7.12.17).

Duve, Thomas (2017). "Was ist ›Multinormativität‹? – Einführende Bemerkungen." *Rechtsgeschichte, Legal History* 25, 88-101.

Ehmer, Hermann (2002). "Johannes Brenz (1499-1570)." Carter Lindberg, ed. *The Reformation Theologians. An Introduction to Theology in the Early Modern Period*. Malden: Blackwell, 124-39.

Ehrenpreis Stefan and Lotz-Heumann, Ute (2002). *Reformation und konfessionelles Zeitalter*. Darmstadt: Wissenschaftliche Buchgesellschaft.

Elert, Werner (1953). *Morphologie des Luthertums*. vol. II, München: C.H. Bech.

Endemann, Wilhelm (1874-1883). *Studien in der romanisch-kanonistischen Wirtschafts- und Rechtslehre*. 2 vols, Berlin: Guttentag.

Ernst, Wolfgang (2007). "Irrtum. Ein Streifzug durch die Dogmengeschichte." Reinhard Zimmermann, ed. *Störungen der Willensbildung bei Vertragschluss*. Tübingen: Mohr Siebeck, 1-34.

Ernst, Wolfgang (2013). "vor § 433. Der Kauf als Vertragstyp." Mathias Schmoeckel et al., eds. *Historisch-kritischer Kommentar zum BGB*, 3. Tübingen: Mohr Siebeck, 36-58.

Essen, Georg and Jansen, Nils, eds. (2011). *Dogmatisierungsprozesse in Recht und Religion*. Tübingen: Mohr Siebeck.

Estes, James Martin (2007). *Christian Magistrate and Territorial Church. Johannes Brenz and the German Reformation*. Toronto: CRRS Publications.

Evans, G.R. (2001). *Mediaeval Commentaries on the sentences of Peter Lombard*. vol. 1., Leiden-Boston: Brill.

Evans, G.R. (2002). *Law and Theology in the Middle Ages*. New York: Routledge.

Fabre, Pierre-Antoine and Maire, Catherine, eds. (2010). *Les Antijésuites. Discours, figures et lieux de l'antijésuitisme à l'époque moderne*. Rennes: Presses universitaires de Rennes.

Falk, Ulrich (2006). *Consilia. Studien zur Praxis der Rechtsgutachten in der frühen Neuzeit*. Frankfurt am Main: Klostermann.

Falzea, Angelo (2008). *Introduzione alle scienze giuridiche*. Milano: Giuffrè.

Falzea, Angelo (2011). "Complessità giuridica." Pietro Sirena, ed. *Oltre il positivismo giuridico. Scritti in onore di Angelo Falzea*. Napoli: ESI, 3-36.

Fantappiè, Carlo (2003). *Introduzione storica al diritto canonico*. Bologna: Il Mulino.

Fedele, Pio (1937). "Considerazioni sull'efficacia dei patti nudi nel diritto canonico." *Annali dell'Università di Macerata* vol. XI, Padova: CEDAM, 5-90.

Feenstra, Robert (1974). "*Impossibilitas* and *Clausola rebus sic stantibus*. Some aspects of frustration of contract in continental legal history up to Grotius." Alan Watson, ed. *Daube Noster: Essays in Legal History for David Daube*. Edinburgh: Scottish academic press, 77-104.

Feenstra Robert and Ahsmann Margreet (1980). *Contract. Aspecten van de begrippen contract en contractsvrijheid in historisch perspectief*. Deventer: Kluwer.

Feenstra, Robert (1990). "Pact and Contract in the Low Countries from the 16th to the 18th Century." John Barton, ed. *Towards a General Law of Contract*. Berlin: Duncker & Humblot, 196-213.

Feenstra, Robert (2006). "Matthäus Wesenbeck (1531-1586) und das römisch-holländische Recht (mit einer Bibliographie seiner juristischen Schriften)." Heiner Lück and Heinrich de Wall, eds. *Wittenberg. Ein Zentrum europäischer Rechsgeschichte und Rechtskultur*. Böhlau: Köln, 175-243.

Fehler, Timothy G. (1999). *Poor Relief and Protestantism: The Evolution of Social Welfare in Sixteenth-century Emden*. Farnham: Ashgate.

Fendt, Leonhard (1953). "Luthers Reformation der Beichte." *Luther. Mitteilungen der Luthersgeselschaft* 24, 3 121-37.

Fiedrowicz, Michael (2010). *Handbuch der Patristik. Quellentexte zur Theologie der Kirchenväter*. Freiburg im Breisgau: Herder.

Fiori, Roberto (1999) *La definizione della 'locatio conductio'. Giurisprudenza romana e tradizione romanistica*. Napoli: Jovene Editore.

Fischer, Paul (2013). "Bankruptcy in early modern German territories." Thomas Max Safley, ed. *The History of Bankruptcy. Economic, social and cultural implications in early modern Europe*. New York: Routledge, 173-84.

Fletcher Roy and Ni Mhaonaigh, Márie, eds. (2016). *The Introduction of Christianity into the Early Medieval Insular World: Converting the Isles I*. Turnhout: Brepols.

Fliche, Augustin (1924-37). *La Réforme Grégorienne*. 3 vols. Louvain: Spicilegium sacrum Lovaniense.

Flood, David, ed. (1975). *Poverty in the Middle Ages*. Werl: D. Coelde.

Flook, John L. (2016 [1990]). "The Book in Reformation Germany." Jean-François Gilmont, ed. and Maag, Karin, trans. *The Reformation and the Book*. Abigdon Oxon-New York: Routledge, 21-103.

Folgado, Avelino P., o.s.a. (1959). "Los Tratados DE LEGIBUS y DE IUSTITIA ET IURE en los autores españoles del siglo XVI y primera mitad del XVII". *La ciudad de dios, revista agustiniana* v. CLXXII, 275-302.

Foley, Edward (2007). "Franciscan Liturgical Prayer." Timothy J. Johnson, ed. *Franciscans at Prayer*. Leiden, Boston: Brill, 365-412.

Fossier, Arnaud-Vivien (2014). "Le « for de la conscience ». l'invention d'une nouvelle frontiere juridictionnelle (xiiie siecle)." Benoît Garnot, and Bruno Lemesle, ed. *La justice entre droit et conscience du Moyen Âge à nos jours*. Dijon: Éditions universitaires de Dijon, 115-23.

Frank, Günter (1995). *Die theologische Philosophie Philipp Melanchthons (1497-1560)*. Leipzig: St. Benno.

Frank, Günter, ed. (2000). *Der Theologe Melanchthon*. Stuttgart: Thorbecke.

Frank, Günter (2005). "The Reason of Acting: Melanchthon's Concept of Practical Philosophy and the Question of the Unity and Consistency of His Philosophy." Jill Kraye and Risto Saarinen, eds. *Moral Philosophy on the Threshold of Modernity*. Berlin: Springer, 217-233.

Frank, Günter, ed. (2017). *Philipp Melanchthon. Der Reformator zwischen Glauben und Wissen*, Berlin, Boston: De Gruyter.

Frank, Günter and Mundt, Felix, eds. (2012). *Der Philosoph Melanchthon*. Berlin, Boston: De Gruyter.

Franklin, James (2001). *The Science of Conjecture: Evidence and Probability before Pascal*. Baltimore: The John Hopkins University Press.

Frantzen, Allen J. (1983). *The Literature of Penance in Anglo-Saxon England*. New Brunswick, New Jersey: Rutgers University Press.

Frassek, Ralf (2014). "Konflikte und Konfliktlösungen im frühen evangelischen Eherecht im sächsischen Raum." Simona Schellenberger et al., eds. *Eine STARKE FRAUEN geschichte*. 500 Jahre Reformation. Markkleeberg: Sax Verlag, 83-90.

Frey, Christofer (1994 [1989]) *Die Ethik des Protestantismus von der Reformation bis zur Gegenwart*. Gütersloh: Gütersloher Verlaghaus.

Friedeburg, Robert von (1999). *Widerstandsrecht und Konfessionskonflikt. Notwehr und gemeiner Mann im deutsch-britischen Vergleich 1530 bis 1669*. Berlin: Duncker & Humbolt.

Friedeburg, Robert von (2016). *Luther's Legacy: The Thirty Years' War and the Modern Notion of 'State' in the Empire, 1530s-1790s*. Cambridge: Cambridge University Press.

Friedeburg, Robert von (2016). "The Rise of Natural Law in the Early Modern Period." Ulrich L. Lehner, Richard A. Muller and A.G. Roeber, eds. *The Oxford Handbook of Early Modern Theology, 1600-1800*. Oxford: Oxford University Press, 625-41.

Friedmann, Robert (1973). *The Theology of Anabaptism. An Interpretation.* Scottdale, Pennsylvania: Herald Press.

Friedrich, Markus et al., eds. (2017). *Konfession, Politik und Gelehrsamkeit. Der Jenear Theologe Johann Gerhard (1582-1637) im Kontext seiner Zeit.* Stuttgart: Franz Steiner.

Fries, Bruno (1963). *Forum in der Rechtssprache.* München: Hueber.

Fromm, Erich (1977). *Avere o essere.* Transl. Francesco Saba Sardi. Milano: Mondadori.

Gallagher, Lowell (1991). *Medusa's Gaze: Casuistry and Conscience in the Renaissance.* Stanford, Calif: Stanford University Press.

Garrán Martínez, José Maria (2004). *La prohibición de la mendicidad. La controversia entre Domingo de Soto y Juan de Robles en Salamanca (1545).* Salamanca: Ediciones Universidad de Salamanca.

Gasper, Giles E.M. and Logan, Ian, eds. (2012). *Saint Anselm of Canterbury and his Legacy.* Toronto: Pontifical Institute of Mediaeval Studies.

Gass, Wilhelm (1881). *Geschichte der christlichen Ethik.* vol. 2/1, Berlin: Reimer.

Gehrke, Jarrett A. (2014). "The Virtue of Epieikeia: A Study in Luther and his Sources" *Seminar Ridge Review*, 17.1, 68-101.

Geipel, Jochen (1965). *Die Konsiliarpraxis der Eberhard-Karls-Universität und die Behandlung der Eherverletzung in den Tübinger Konsilien.* Stuttgart: Müller & Gräff.

Geisst, Charles R. (2013). *Beggar Thy Neighbor, A History of Usury and Debt.* Philadelphia: University of Pennsylvania Press.

Germann, Michael (2017). "Justus Henning Böhmers Abhandlung über die Gewissensfreiheit. Eine Stichprobe zum Gewissensdiskurs aus der prostestantischen Kirchenrechtslehre zu beginn des 18. Jahrhunderts." Michael Germann and Wim Decock, eds. *Das Gewissen in den Rechtslehren der protestantischen und kaholischen Reformationen. Conscience in the Legal Teachings of the Protestant and Catholic Reformations.* Leipzig: Evangelische Verlagsanstalt, 313-33.

Giard, Luce, ed. (1995). *Les Jésuites à la Renaissance. Système éducatif et production du savoir.* Paris: PUF.

Gilchrist, John T. (1969). *The Church and Economic Activity in the Middle Ages.* New York: Macmillan.

Gilomen, Hans J. (1984). *Der Rentenkauf im Mittelalter*, Habilitationsschrift, Universität Basel, http://www.hist.uzh.ch/fachbereiche/mittelalter/emeriti/gilomen/publikationen/Rentenkauf.pdf (January 05, 2017).

Gilson, Étienne (1959). *Johannes Duns Scotus. Einführung in die Grundlagen seiner Lehre.* Düsseldorf.

Glamann, Kristof (1983). "The Changing Patterns of Trade." E.E. Rich, and C.H. Wilson, eds. *The Cambridge Economic History of Europe Vol. V, The Economic Organization of Early Modern Europe*, Cambridge, London, New York, Melbourne: Cambridge University Press, 185-289.

Goehring, James E. (1999). *Ascetics, Society, and the Desert. Studies in Early Egyptian Monasticism.* Harrisburg: Trinity Press International.

Goering, Joseph (1981). "The Changing Face of the Village Parish: The Thirteenth Century." James Ambrose Raftis, ed. *Pathways to Mediaeval Paesants*, Toronto: Pontifical Institute of Mediaeval Studies.

Goering, Joseph (1992). *William de Montibus (ca. 1140-1213): The School and The Literature of Pastoral Care*, Toronto: Pontifical Institute of Mediaeval Studies.

Goering, Joseph and Payer, Pierre J. (1993). "The 'Summa penitentie Fratrum Predicatorum': A Thirteenth-Century Confessional Formulary." *Mediaeval Studies* 55, 1-50.

Goering, Joseph (2008). "The Internal Forum and the Literature of Penance and Confession." Wilfried Hartmann and Kenneth Pennington, eds. *The History of Medieval Canon Law in the Classical Period, 1140-1234: from Gratian to the decretals of Pope Gregory IX*. Washington D.C.: The Catholic University of America Press, 379-428.

Goering, Joseph (2008). "The Scholastic Turn (1100-1500): Penitential Theology and Law in the Schools." Abigail Firey, ed. *A New History of Penance*. Leiden: Brill, 219-38.

Gómez Camacho, Francisco (1998). *Economia y filosofia moral: la formacion del pensamiento economico europeo en la Escolastica espanola*. Madrid: Sintesis.

Gordley, James (1981). "Equality in Exchange." *California Law Review* 69, n. 6, 1587-1656.

Gordley, James (1991). *The Philosophical Origins of Modern Contract Doctrine*. Oxford: Clarendon University Press.

Gordley, James (2006). *Foundations of Private Law. Property, Tort, Contract, Unjust Enrichment*. Oxford: Oxford University Press.

Gordon, William M. (1970). *Studies in the Transfer of Property by Traditio*. Aberdeen: University of Aberdeen.

Göschel, Karl Friedrich (1842). *Zerstreute Blätter aus den Hand- und Hülfsakten eines Juristen: wissenschaftliches und Geschichtliches aus der Theorie und Praxis oder aus der Lehre und dem Leben des Rechts, 3.Th./2, Zur theologisch-juristischen Biographie und Literatur*. Schleusingen.

Gregory, Brad Stephan (2012), *The Unintended Reformation. How a Religious Revolution Secularized Society*. Cambridge Mass.-London: Harvard University Press.

Grimm, Harold J. (1970). "Luther's Contribution to Sixteenth-Century Organization of Poor Relief." *Archif für Reformationsgeschichte* 61, 222-34.

Grossi, Paolo, "Somme penitenziali, diritto canonico, diritto comune." *Annali della Facoltà giuridica di Macerata* N.S. 1, 95-134.

Grossi, Paolo (1973). "La proprietà nel sistema privatistico della seconda scolastica." *La seconda scolastica della formazione del diritto privato moderno. Incontro di studio. Firenze, 16-19 Ottobre 1972, Atti*. Milano: Giuffrè, 117-222.

Grossi, Paolo (1986). "Sulla 'natura' del contratto (qualche nota sul 'mestiere' di storico del diritto, a proposito di un recente corso di lezioni)." *Quaderni fiorentini* 15, 593-619.

Grosso, Giuseppe (1963). *Il sistema romano dei contratti*. Torino: Giappichelli.

Groupe de la Bussiere (1983). *Practiques de la Confession. Des Pères du désert à Vatican II*. Paris: Cerf.

Grunert, Frank (2000). *Normbegründung und politische Legimität: zur Rechts- und Staatsphilosophie der deutschen Frühaufklärung*. Tübingen: Niemeyer.

Grunert, Frank (2003). "The Reception of Hugo Grotius's De Jure Belli ac Pacis, in the early German Enlightenment." Tim Hochstrasser and Peter Schröder, eds. *Early Modern Natural Law Theories. Contexts and Strategies in the Early Enlightenment*. Berlin: Springer, 89-106.

Guerra Medici, M. Teresa (1993). *Principi e giuristi nella prima età moderna. Antonino e Gaspare Antonio Tesauro magistrati del duca di Savoia*. Napoli: ESI.

Guzmán Brito, Alejandro (2001). "Causa del contrato y causa de la obligación en la dogmática de los juristas romanos, medievales y modernos y en la codificación europea y americana." *Rev. estud. hist.-juríd.* 23, 209-367, http://dx.doi.org/10.4067/S0716-54552001002300006 (November 4, 2018).

Guzmán Brito, Alejandro (2005). *Acto, negocio, contrato y causa en la tradición del derecho europeo e iberoamericano*. Cizur Menor (Navarra): Aranzadi.

Haakonssen, Knud (1996). *Natural Law and Moral Philosophy: From Grotius to the Scottish Enlightenment*. Cambridge: Cambridge University Press.

Haakonssen, Knud (2017). "Early Modern Natural Law Theories." George Duke and Robert P. George, eds., *The Cambridge Companion to Natural Law Jurisprudence*. Cambridge: Cambridge University Press. 76-102.

Häberlein, Mark (2013). "Merchants' Bankruptcies, Economic Development and Social Relations in German Cities During the Long 16th Century." Thomas Max Safley, ed. *The History of Bankruptcy. Economic, Social and Cultural Implications in Early Modern Europe*. New York: Routledge. 19-33.

Hachfeld, Hermann (1867). *Martin Chemnitz nach seinem Leben und Wirken*. Leipzig: Von Breitkopf und Härtel.

Hackett, Jo Ann (2010). *A Basic Introduction to Biblical Hebrew*. Peabody: Hendrickson.

Haemig, Mary Jane (2000). "Communication, Consolation and Discipline: Two Early Lutheran Preachers on Confession." Kathrine Jackson Lualdi and Anne T. Thayer, eds. *Penitence in the Age of Reformations*. Aldershot: Ashgate, 30-48.

Haferkamp, Hans Peter and Repgen, Tilman (2007). *Usus modernus pandectarum Römisches Recht, Deutsches Recht und Naturrecht in der Frühen Neuzeit*. Köln: Böhlau.

Hafner, Felix, Loretan, Adrian and Spenlé, Christoph (2001). *Naturrecht und Menschenrecht. Der Beitrag der Spanischen Spätscholastik zur Entwicklung der Menschenrechte*. Frank Grunert and Kurt Seelmann, eds. *Die Ordnung der Praxis. Neue Studien zur Spanischen Spätscholastik*. Berlin: De Gruyter, 123-53.

Hake, Karsten Alexander (2013). *Juristenfakultäten, Aktenversendung und Reichskammergericht.* Aachen: Shaker Verlag.

Hallebeek, Jan (1996). *The Concept of Unjust Enrichment in Late Scholasticism.* Nijmegen: GNI.

Halpérin, Jean-Louis (2009). "French Legal Science in the 17th and 18th Centuries: To the Limits of the Theory of Law." Enrico Pattaro, Damiano Canale, Paolo Grossi, Hasso Hofmann and Patrick Riley, eds. *A Treatise of Legal Philosophy and General Jurisprudence, Vol. 9: A History of the Philosophy of Law in the Civil Law World, 1600-1900.* Dordrecht: Springer, 43-68.

Haltemann, Jim (2014). "Anabaptists Approaches to Economics." Paul Oslington, ed. *The Oxford Handbook of Christianity and Economics.* Oxford: Oxford University Press, 246-61.

Halvorson, Michael J. (2010). *Heinrich Heshusius and Confessional Polemic in Early Lutheran Orthodoxy.* London-New York: Routledge.

Hamouda, O.F. and Price, B.B. (1997). "The Justice of the Just Price." *The European Journal of the History of Economic Thought* 4, n. 2, 191-216.

Hankins, James (2007). "Humanism, Scholasticism and Renaissance Philosophy." James Hankins, ed. *The Cambridge Companion to Renaissance Philosophy.* Cambridge: Cambridge University Press, 30-48.

Harmless, William S.J. (2004). *Desert Christians. An Introduction to the Literature of Early Monasticism.* Oxford: Oxford University Press.

Härter, Karl (1994). "Disciplinamento sociale e ordinanze di polizia nella prima età moderna." Paolo Prodi, ed. *Disciplina dell'anima, disciplina del corpo e disciplina della società tra medioevo ed età moderna.* Bologna: Il Mulino, 635-58.

Härter, Karl (2000). *Policey und frühneuzeitliche Gesellschaft.* Frankfurt am Main: Klostermann.

Härter, Karl (2010). "Security and "Gute Policey" in Early Modern Europe: Concepts, Laws, and Instruments." *Historical Social Research,* 35, 4, 41-65.

Härter, Karl (2012). "Konfliktregulierung im Umfeld frühneuzeitlicher Strafgerichte. Das Konzept der Infrajustiz in der historischen Kriminalitätsforschung." *Kritische Vierteljahresschrift für Gesetzgebung und Rechtsprechung* 95, 130-44.

Hasselhoff, Görge K. and Mayenburg, David von, eds. (2012). *Die Zwölf Artikel von 1525 und das 'Göttliche Recht' der Bauern – rechtshistorische und theologische Dimensionen.* Würzburg: Erzog.

Hazard, Paul (1934). *La Crise de la conscience europeenne 1680-1715.* 3 vols., Paris: Boivin.

Headley, John M., Hillerbrand, Hans Joachim and Papalas, Anthony J., eds. (2016). *Confessionalization in Europe, 1555-1700: Essays in Honor and Memory of Bodo Nischan.* 2nd ed., Abingdon, Oxon-New York: Routledge.

Heckel, Johannes (1953). *Lex charitatis. Eine juristische Untersuchung über das Recht in der Theologie Martin Luthers.* München: Bayerische Akademie der Wissenschaften.

Heckel, Johannes (1955). "Das Decretum Gratiani und das evangelische Kirchenrecht." *Studia Gratiana* 3, 483-538.

Heckel, Martin (2001). *Deutschland in konfessionellen Zeitalter*. 2nd ed. Göttingen: Vandenhoeck & Ruprecht.

Heckel, Martin (1986). "Reichsrecht und 'Zweite Reformation': Theologisch-juristische Probleme der reformierten Konfessionalisierung." Heinz Schilling, ed. *Die reformierte Konfessionalisierung in Deutschland – Das Problem der 'Zweite Reformation'*. Gütersloh: Gütersloher Verlagshaus. 379-86.

Heckel, Martin (2016). *Martin Luthers Reformation und das Recht: Die Entwicklung der Theologie Luthers und ihre Auswirkung auf das Recht unter den Rahmenbedingungen der Reichsreform und der Territorialstaatsbildung im Kampf mit Rom und den »Schwärmern«*. Tübingen: Mohr Siebeck.

Hecker, Christian (2008). *Lohn- und Preisgerechtigkeit. Historische Rückblicke und aktuelle Perspektiven unter besonderer Berücksichtigung der christlichen Soziallehren*. Marburg: Metropolis-Verlag.

Hecker, Christian (2015). "Wenn aus Kontingenz Notwendigkeit wird. Die neue Welt der Finanzmärkte und die alten Warnungen Martin Luthers." *Zeitschrift für Evangelische Ethik* 59, 3, 191-204.

Heger, Martin (2010). "Recht im „Alten Reich" – Der Usus modernus." *Zeitschrift für das Juristische Studium* 1, 29-39.

Helmholz, Richard (1992). *Canon law in Protestant Lands*. Berlin: Duncker & Humblot.

Helmholz, Richard (2010). *The Spirit of Classical Canon Law*. Athens-London: The University of Georgia Press.

Hendrix, Scott (2002). *Urbanus Rhegius*. Carter Lindberg, ed. *The Reformation Theologians: An Introduction to Theology in the Early Modern Period*. Malden: Blackwell, 109-23.

Hermann, Hans Georg (2016). "Eigennutz und Übervorteilung: kanonistische Sichtweisen auf eine prekäre Optimierungsstrategie im Vertrag." Mathias Schmoeckel, David von Mayenburg, Orazio Condorelli and Franck Roumy, eds. *Der Einfluss der Kanonistik auf die europäische Rechtskultur 5: Das Recht der Wirtschaft*. Köln: Böhlau, 203-33.

Hill, Kat (2015). *Baptism, Brotherhood, and Belief in Reformation Germany: Anabaptism and Lutheranism, 1525-1585*. Oxford: Oxford University Press.

Hinnebusch, William A. (1966). *The History of the Dominican Order. Intellectual and Cultural Life to 1500*. vol. II, Staten Island: Alba House.

Hinz, Werner (1991). *Die Entwicklung des gutgläubigen Fahrniserwerbs in der Epoche des usus modernus und des Naturrechts*. Berlin: Duncker & Humblot.

Hödl, Ludwig (1960). *Die Geschichte der scholastischen Literatur und der Theologie der Schlüsselgewalt*. 1 Teil. Münster: Aschendorffsche Verlagsbuchhandlung.

Höffner, Joseph (1941). *Wirtschaftsethik und Monopole im fünfzehnten und sechzehnten Jahrhundert*. Jena: Fischer.

Hofmeister Pich, Robert ed. (2011). *Anselm of Canterbury (1033-1109) – Philosophical Theology and Ethics*. Turnhout: Brepols.

Holl, Karl (1969 [1898]). *Enthusiasmus und Bußgewalt beim griechischen Mönchtum*. Hildesheim: Olms.

Hollingworth, Miles (2013). *Saint Augustine of Hippo: An Intellectual Biography*. London: Bloomsbury.

Holmes, Peter J., ed. (1981). *Elizabethan Casuistry*. London: Catholic Record Society.

Holmes, Peter J., ed. (2012). *Caroline Casuistry: The Cases of Conscience of Fr Thomas Southwell, SJ*. London: Catholic Record Society.

Holtz, Sabine (1993). *Theologie und Alltag. Lehre und Leben in den Predigten der Tübinger Theologen 1550-1750*. Tübingen: Mohr Siebeck.

Honecker, Martin (1968). *Cura religionis magistratus christiani. Studien zum Kirchenrecht im Luthertum des 17. Jahrhunderts insbesondere bei Johann Gerhard*. München: Claudius.

Honecker, Martin (1990). *Einführung in die theologische Ethik: Grundlagen und Grundbegriffe*. Berlin-New York: De Gruyter.

Honecker, Martin (1992). "Sozialethik des Luthertums." Hans C. Rublack, ed. *Die lutherische Konfessionalisierung in Deutschland (1589-1613)*. Gütersloh: Gerd Mohn, 316-40.

Hopf, Costantin (1946). *Martin Bucer and the English Reformation*. Oxford: Blackwell.

Horn, Johannes von (1802). *Narratio pragmatica conversionum, quas theologia moralis seculo XVIII experta est apud lutheranos, reformatos, catholicos atque sectas christianas minores*. Goettinga: Vandenhoeck & Ruprecht.

Howe, John (2016). *Before the Gregorian Reform: The Latin Church at the Turn of the First Millennium*. Ithaca-London: Cornell University Press.

Hunter, Ian (2007). *The Secularisation of the Confessional State. The Political Thought of Christian Thomasius*. Cambridge: Cambridge University Press.

Hurtubise, Pierre (2005). *La casuistique dans tous ses états: De Martin Azpilcueta à Alphonse de Liguori*. Ottawa: Novalis.

Huschke, Rolf Bernhard (1968). *Melanchthons Lehre vom Ordo politicus. Ein Beitrag zum Verhältnis von Glauben und politischem Handeln bei Melanchthon*. Gütersloh: Mohn.

Hutchinson, E.J. and Maas, Korey D. (2014). "Niels Hemmingsen (1513-1600) and the Development of Lutheran Natural-Law Teaching." *Journal of Markets and Morality* 17 (2), 595-617.

Ibbetson, David (2012). "Comparative Legal History: A Methodology." Anthony Musson and Chantal Stebbings, eds. *Making Legal History: Approaches and Methodologies*. Cambridge: Cambridge University Press, 131-45.

Ickx, Johan (2009). "Ipsa vero officii maioris Penitentiarii institutio non reperitur? La nascita di un tribunale della coscienza." Manlio Sodi and Johan Ickx, eds. *La penitenzieria apostolica e il sacramento della penitenza. Percorsi storici, giuridici, teologici e prospettive pastorali.* Libreria Editrice Vaticana: Città del Vaticano, 19-50.

Ihmels, Jochen (1957). *Das Naturrecht bei Valentin Alberti, Die Lehre des Compendium Iuris Naturae von 1678/96.* Diss., Leipzig.

Ikadatsu, Yasushiro (2002). *Der Paradigmawechsel der Privatrechtstheorie und die Neukonstruktion der Vertragstheorie in seinem Rahmen, Pufendorf, Wolff, Kant und Savigny.* Ebelsbach: Aktiv Druck.

Innes, Matthew (2005). "Charlemagne's Government." Joanna Story, ed. *Charlemagne: Empire and Society.* Manchester-New York: Manchester University Press, 71-89.

Irsigler, Franz (1983). "Luthers Herkunf und Umwelt-Wirtschaft und Gesellschaft der Zeit." Bott, G. (ed.), *Martin Luther und die Reformation in Deutschland,* Frankfurt am Main, Insel, 1983, 17-40.

Irwin, Terence (2007). *The Development of Ethics. A Historical and Critical Study, Vol. I: From Socrates to the Reformation.* Oxford: Oxford University Press.

Isabell, Laurence D. ofm (1973). *The Practice and Meaning of Confession in the Primitive Franciscan Community According to the Writings of Saint Francis of Assisi and Thomas of Celano.* Diss. Assisi: Instituto Theologiae Spiritualis Pontificiae Universitatis Gregorianae.

Isenmann, Eberhard (1986). "Reichsrecht und Reichsverfassung in Konsilien reichsstädtischer Juristen (15.-17. Jahrhundert)." Roman Schnur, ed. *Die Rolle der Juristen bei der Entstehung des modernen Staates.* Berlin: Duncker & Humblot, 545-628.

Isenmann, Eberhard (2008). "Wirtschaftsrecht und Wirtschaftsethik um 1500. Theologische und juristische Konsilien zum Barchenthandel in der Reichsstadt Ulm." Rolf Lieberwirth and Heiner Lück, ed. *Akten des 36. Deutschen Rechtshistorikertages Halle an der Saale.* 10.-14. September 2006, Baden-Baden: Nomos, 195-259.

Isenmann, Eberhard (2014). *Die deutsche Stadt im Mittelalter 1150-1550. Stadtgestalt, Recht, Verfassung, Stadtregiment, Kirche, Gesellschaft, Wirtschaft.* 2nd. ed. Köln-Weimar-Wien: Böhlau.

Jansen, Nils (2013). *Theologie, Philosophie und Jurisprudenz in der spätscholastischen Lehre von der Restitution.* Tübingen: Mohr Siebeck.

Jansen, Nils and Kästle, David, eds. (2014). *Kommentare in Recht und Religion.* Tübingen: Mohr Siebeck.

Janzow, F. Samuel (1978). *Luther's Large Catechism: A Contemporary Translation with Study Questions.* St. Louis: Concordia Publishing House.

Jenkins, Keith (2003 [1991]). *Re-thinking History.* London: Routledge.

Jenkins, Robert C. (1889). *The Life of Valentin Alberti,* London: D. Nutt.

Jerouschek, Günther, Schild, Wolfgang and Gropp Walter, eds. (2000). *Benedict Carpzov: Neue Perspektiven zu einem umstrittenen sächsischen Juristen*. Tübingen: Diskord.

Johnson, Junius (2016). *Patristic and Medieval Atonement Theory. A Guide to Research*. Lanham: Rowman & Littlefield.

Jones, David W. (2004). *Reforming the Morality of Usury: A Study of Differences that Separated the Protestant Reformers*. Lanham: University Press of America.

Jones, Norman (1989). *God and the Moneylenders. Usury and Law in Early Modern England*. Southampton: Blackwell.

Jonsen, Albert R. and Toulmin, Stephen (1988). *The Abuse of Casuistry: A History of Moral Reasoning*. Berkeley: University of California Press.

Jungkuntz, Theodore R. (1977). *Formulators of the Formula of Concord. Four Architects of Lutheran Unity*. Eugene: Wipf and Stock Publishers.

Jünke, Wolfgang A., ed. (1986). *Der zweite Martin der Lutherischen Kirche. Festschrift zum 400. Todestag von Martin Chemnitz*. Braunschweig: Ev.-luth. Stadtkirchenverband und Propstei Braunschweig.

Jütte, Robert (1994). *Poverty and Deviance in Early Modern Europe*. Cambridge: Cambridge University Press.

Kahlert, Helmut (1956). "Luther und Melanchthons Stellung zu den Wirtschaftsfragen ihrer Zeit". *Luther: Mitteilungen der Luthergesellschaft* H. 3, 122-33.

Kantola, Ilkka (1994). *Probability and Moral Uncertainty in Late Medieval and Early Modern Times*. Helsinki: Luther – Agricola Society.

Kaser, Max (1971). *Das römische Privatrecht*. vol. I., 2nd ed., München: Beck.

Kaufmann, Matthias (2011). "Die Willensfreiheit, das moralisch Gute und das Ziel des Menschen bei Duns Scotus, Ockham and Molina." Hubertus Busche, ed. *Departure from Modern Europe. A Handbook of Early Modern Philosophy (1400-1700)*. Hamburg: Felix Meiner, 167-79.

Kaufmann, Matthias (2017). "Willensfreiheit und Gewissen bei Luis de Molina." Michael Germann and Wim Decock, eds. *Das Gewissen in den Rechtslehren der protestantischen und katholischen Reformationen. Conscience in the Legal Teachings of the Protestant and Catholic Reformations*. Leipzig: Evangelische Verlagsanstalt, 72-86.

Kaufmann, Thomas (1997). *Universität und lutherische Konfessionalisierung. Die Rostocker Theologieprofessoren und ihr Beitrag zur theologischen Bildung und kirchlichen Gestaltung im Herzogtum Mecklenburg zwischen 1550 und 1675*. Gütersloh: Gütersloher Verlaghaus.

Kaufmann, Thomas (2006). *Konfession und Kultur. Lutherischen Protestantismus in der zweiten Hälfte des Reformationsjahrhunderts*. Tübingen: Mohr Siebeck.

Kaufmann, Thomas (2017). *Erlöste und Verdammte. Eine Geschichte der Reformation*. 2nd ed. München: C.H. Beck.

Kaye, Joel (1998). *Economy and Nature in the Fourteenth Century: Money, Market Exchange, and the Emergence of Scientific Thought.* Cambridge: Cambridge University Press.

Keenan, James F. (1995). "William Perkins (1558-1602) and the Birth of British Casuistry." James F. Keenan and Thomas A. Shannon, eds. *The Context of Casuistry.* Washington D.C.: Georgetown University Press, 105-30.

Keller, Rudolf (1994). *Die Confessio Augustana im theologischen Wirken des Rostocker Professors David Chyträus (1530-1600).* Göttingen: Vandenhoeck & Ruprecht.

Kelly, Henry A. (2008). "Penitential Theology and Law at the Turn of the Fifteenth Century." Abigail Firey, ed. *A New History of Penance.* Leiden: Brill, 239-318.

Kempis, Karl von (1988). *Andreas Gail (1526-1587). Zum Leben und Werk eines Juristen der frühen Neuzeit.* Frankfurt am Main: Lang.

Kent, Bonnie (1984). *Aristotle and the Franciscans: Gerald Odonis' Commentary on the Nicomachean Ethics.* Diss. New York: Columbia University.

Kent, Bonnie (1995). *Virtues of the Will. The Transformation of Ethics in the Late Thirteenth Century.* Washington: The Catholic University of America Press.

Kerr, Fergus G. (2009). *Thomas Aquinas: A Very Short Introduction.* Oxford: Oxford University Press.

Kerridge, Eric (2002). *Usury, Interest, and the Reformation.* Aldershot: Ashgate.

Kinder, Ernst (1952). "Beichte und Absolution nach den lutherischen Bekenntenisschriften." *Theologische Literaturzeitung* 77,2, 543-50.

Kirby, Torrance (2013). "Public Forum and Forum of the Conscience: John Calvin's Theological Groundwork of the Modern Public Sphere." Torrance Kirby, ed. *Persuasion and Conversion: Essays on Religion, Politics, and the Public Sphere in Early Modern England.* Leiden-Boston: Brill, 36-51.

Kirk, Kenneth (1999 [1927]). *Conscience and Its Problems. An Introduction to Casuistry.* Cambridge: James & Co.

Kittsteiner, Heinz D. (1991). *Die Entstehung des modernen Gewissen.* Frankfurt am Main-Leipzig: Insel Verlag.

Klaasen, Walter (1981). *Anabaptism in Outline: Selected Primary Sources.* Waterloo ont.: Herald Press.

Klinck, Dennis R. (2010). *Conscience, Equity and the Court of Chancery in Early Modern England.* Aldershot-Burlington USA-Singapore-Sydney: Ashgate.

Klingenberg, Eberhard (1977). *Das israelitische Zinsverbot in Torah, Mišnah und Talmud.* Mainz: Akademie der Wissenschaften und der Literatur.

Klugkist, Engelbert (1967). "Die Aktenversendung an Juristenfakultäten." *Juristenzeitung* 22, 155-8.

Knebel, Sven K. (2000). *Wille, Würfel und Wahrscheinlichkeit, Das System der moralischen Notwendigkeit in der Jesuitenscholastik.* Hamburg: Meiner.

Knebel, Sven K. (2005). "Casuistry and the Early Modern Paradigm Shift in the Notion of Charity." Jill Kraye and Risto Saarinen, eds. *Moral Philosophy on the Threshold of Modernity*. Dordrecht: Springer, 115-40.

Knobler, Abby Phyllis (1992). *Luther and the Legal Concept of the Poor in the Sixteenth-Century German Church Ordinances*. Ann Arbor, MI: UMI Press.

Koch, Ernst (2000). *Das konfessionelle Zeitalter-Katholizismus, Luthertum, Calvinismus (1563-1675)*. Leipzig: Evangelische Verlagsanstalt.

Kohle, Armin and Kusche, Beate (2015). "Die Wittenberger Theologische Fakultät in ihrer Anfangszeit-Beobachtungen zu Strukturen, Personal und Profil". Herman Selderhuis and Ernst-Joachim Waschke, eds. *Reformation und Rationalität*. Göttingen: Vandenhoeck & Ruprecht, 27-42.

Kolb, Robert (2000). "Nikolaus Gallus critique of Philip Melanchthon's teaching on the freedom of the will." *Archiv für Reformationsgeschichte* 91, 87-110.

Kolb, Robert (2002). "Martin Chemnitz (1522-1586)." Carter Lindberg, ed. *The Reformation Theologians. An Introduction to Theology in the Early Modern Period*. Malden: Blackwell, 140-53.

Kolb, Robert (2006). "Lutheran Theology in Seventeenth Century Germany." *Lutheran Quarterly* vol. XX, 429-56.

Kolb, Robert, Dingel, Irene and Batka, L'ubomír, eds. (2014). *The Oxford Handbook of Martin Luther's Theology*. Oxford: Oxford University Press.

Kottje, Raymund (1987). "Busspraxis und Bussritus, in Segni e riti nella Chiesa alto-medioevale occidentale." *Settimane di studio del Centro Italiano di Studi sull'Alto Medioevo* 33.1, Spoleto: Centro Italiano di Studi sull'alto Medioevo, 369-95.

Koyama, Mark (2010). "Evading the 'Taint of Usury': The usury prohibition as a barrier to entry." *Explorations in Economic History* 47, 420-42.

Kreiker, Sebastian (1997). *Armut, Schule, Obrigkeit. Armenversorgung und Schulwesen in der evangelischen Kirchenordnungen des 16. Jahrhunderts*. Bielefeld: Verlag für Regionalgeschichte.

Kunkel, Wolfgang and Schmelzeisen, Gustav Klemens, eds. (1968). *Polizei- und Landesordnungen*. Köln: Böhlau.

Kuropka, Nicole (2002). *Philipp Melanchthon: Wissenschaft und Gesellschaft*. Tübingen: Mohr Siebeck.

Kuropka, Nicole (2012). "Philip Melanchthon and Aristotle." Irene Dingel, Robert Kolb, Nicole Kuropka and Timothy J. Wengert, eds. *Philip Melanchthon, Theologian in Classroom, Confession and Controversy*. Göttingen: Vandenhoeck & Ruprecht, 17-28.

Kusukawa, Sachiko (1995). *The Transformation of Natural Philosophy: The Case of Philip Melanchthon*. Cambridge: Cambridge University Press.

Kuttner, Stephan (1953). "Zur Entstehungsgeschichte der <<Summa de casibus poenitentiae>> des hl. Raymund von Penyafort." *Zeitschrift der Savigny-Stiftung für Rechtsgeschichte* Kan. Ab., 70, 419-34.

Kuttner, Stephan (1988). "Research in Gratian: Acta and Agenda." Peter Linehan, ed. *Proceedings of the Seventh International Congress of Medieval Canon Law*. Vatican City: Biblioteca Apostolica Vaticana, 3-36, Repr. Kuttner, Stephan (1990). *Studies in the History of Medieval Canon Law*. Aldershot: Variorum.

Ladner, Gerhart B. (1967). *The Idea of Reform: its Impact on Christian Thought and Action in the Age of the Fathers*. Cambridge (Mass): Harvard University Press.

Lambert, David (2013). "The Making of Authority. Patterns of Augustine's reception, 430-c.700". Karla Pollmann, ed. *The Oxford Guide to the Historical Reception of Augustine*. Vol. 1 Oxford: Oxford University Press, 15-23.

Lambert, Malcolm D. (1961). *Franciscan Poverty. The Doctrine of the Absolute Poverty of Christ and the Apostles in the Franciscan Order, 1210-1323*. London: SPCK.

Lamprecht, Dietmar (1980). *Urbanus Rhegius: der vergessene Reformator der Lüneburger Heide; eine Erinnerung*. Hermannsburg: Missionsbuchhandlung.

Landau, Peter (1999). "Methoden des kanonischen Rechts in der Frühen Neuzeit zwischen Humanismus und Naturrecht." *Zeitschrift für neure Rechtsgeschichte* 21, 7-28.

Landau, Peter (2003). "Pacta sunt servanda. Zu den kanonistischen Grundlagen der Privatautonomie." Mario Ascheri, Friedrich Ebel et al., eds. *"Ins Wasser geworfen und Ozeane durchquert": Feschrift für K.W. Nörr*. Köln-Weimar-Wien: Böhlau, 457-74.

Landi, Andrea (2004). *Ad evitandas usuras. Ricerche sul contratto di censo nell'*Usus Modernus Pandectarum. Roma: Fondazione Sergio Mochi Onory.

Lange, Tyler (2016). *Excommunication for Debt in Late Medieval France*. Cambridge: Cambridge University Press.

Langholm, Odd (1979). *Price and Value in the Aristotelian Tradition*. Bergen: Universitetsforlaget.

Langholm, Odd (1984). *The Aristotelian Analysis of Usury*. Bergen-Oslo-Stavanger-Tromsø: Universitetsforlaget As.

Langholm, Odd (1992). *Economics in the Medieval Schools. Wealth, Exchange, Value, Money and Usury according to the Paris Theological Tradition. 1200-1350*. Leiden-New York-Köln: Brill.

Langholm, Odd (1998). *The Legacy of Scholasticism in Economic Thought: Antecedents of Choice and Power*. Cambridge-New York-Melbourne: Cambridge University Press.

Langholm, Odd (2003) *The Merchant in the Confessional. Trade and Price in the Pre-Reformation Penitential Handbooks, Studies in Medieval and Reformation Thought*. Leiden-Boston: Brill.

Langholm, Odd (2009). "Martin Luther's Doctrine on Trade and Price in Its Literary Context." *History of Political Economy* 41:1, 89-107.

Lapp, Michael (2012). "Denn es ist geld ein ungewis, wanckelbar ding". Die Wirtschaftsethik Martin Luthers anhand seiner Schriften gegen den Wucher." *Luther: Zeitschrift der Luther-Gesellschaft* 83(2), 91-107.

Larson, Atria L. (2014). *Master of Penance: Gratian and the Development of Penitential Thought and Law in the Twelfth Century*. Washington D.C.: The Catholic University of America Press.

Larson, Atria L. (2016). *Gratian's Tractatus de Poenitentia*. Washington D.C.: The Catholic University of America Press.

Lavenia, Vincenzo (2004). *L'infamia e il perdono: tributi, pene e confessione nella teologia morale della prima età moderna*. Il Mulino: Bologna.

Lavenia, Vincenzo (2009). "Fraus et Cautela Théologie morale et fiscalité." Serge Boarini, ed. *La casuistique classique: genèse, formes, devenir*. Saint-Étienne: Publications de l'Université de Saint-Étienne, 43-57.

Lawrence, C.H. (1984). *Medieval Monasticism*. New York: Longman Inc.

Lawrence, C.H. (2013 [1994]). *The Friars. The Impact of the Mendicant Orders on Medieval Society*. London: I.B. Tauris.

Lea, Henry Charles (1896). *A History of Auricular Confession and Indulgences in the Latin Church*. vol. 1, Philadelphia: Lea Brothers.

Legendre, Pierre (1980). "L'inscription du droit canon dans la théologie: Remarques sur la Seconde Scolastique." *Proceedings of the V International Congress of Medieval Canon Law*. Vatican City: Biblioteca Apostolica Vaticana, 443-54.

Le Goff, Jacques (1986). *La bourse et la vie. Économie et religion au Moyen Age*. Paris: Hachette.

Le Goff, Marcel (1905). *Du Moulin et le prêt à intérêt: le légiste, son influence*. Genève: Mégariotis.

Leinsle, Ulrich G. (1988). "Die Scholastik der Neuzeit bis zur Aufklärung." Emerich Coreth, Walter M. Neidl and Georg Pfligersdorffer, eds. *Christliche Philosophie im katholischen Denken des 19. und 20. Jahrhunderts*. vol. 2, Graz-Wien-Köln: Styria, 54-69.

Leinsle, Ulrich G. (2010). *Introduction to Scholastic Theology*. Washington D.C.: The Catholic University of America Press.

Leites, Edmund, ed. (1988). *Conscience and Casuistry in Early Modern Europe*. Cambridge: Cambridge University Press.

Leone, Marialucrezia (2008). "The Theologian and the Contracts: Henry of Ghent and the emptio-venditio reddituum." *Recherches de Théologie et Philosophie Médiévales* 75/1, 137-60.

Levering, Matthew W. (2013). *The Theology of Augustine: An Introductory Guide to his Most Important Works*. Grand Rapids: Baker Academic.

Lévy, Jean-Philippe (1939). "Un palliatif à la prohibition de l'usure: le contractus trinus ou triplex." *Revue historique du droit* 63, 423-33.

Liebmann, Maximilian (1980). *Urbanus Rhegius und die Anfänge der Reformation: Beiträge zu seinem Leben, seiner Lehre und seinem Wirken bis zum Augsburger Reichstag von 1530 mit einer Bibliographie seiner Schriften*. Münster: Aschendorff.

Liermann, Hans (1955). "Das kanonische Recht als Gegenstand des gelehrten Unterrichts an den protestantischen Universitäten in den ersten Jahrunderten nach der Reformation." *Studia Gratiana* vol. 3, 541-66.

Lindberg, Carter (1993). *Beyond Charity. Reformation Initiatives for the Poor*. Minneapolis: Fortress Press.

Lindberg, Carter (1996). *The European Reformations*. Cambridge, Mass.: Blackwell.

Lindsley, Arthur W. (1982). *Conscience and Casuistry in the English Puritan Concept of Reformation*. Diss., University of Pittsburg.

Lines, David A. (2002). *Aristotle's Ethics in the Italian Renaissance (Ca. 1300-1650). The Universities and the Problem of Moral Education*. Leiden-Boston-Köln: Brill.

Lipp, Martin (2006). "Das privatrechtliche Wirken Benedikt (II) Carpzovs im Kontext der europäischen Zivilrechtswissenschaft." Heiner Lück and Henrich de Wall, eds. *Wittenberg. Ein Zentrum europäischer Rechsgeschichte und Rechtskultur*. Köln: Böhlau, 245-73.

Lockwood O' Donovan, Joan (2001). "The Theological Economics of Medieval Usury Theory." *Studies in Christian Ethics* 14 (1), 48-64.

Lohr, Charles H. (1988). "The Medieval Interpretation of Aristotle." Norman Kretzmann, Anthony Kenny Jan Pinborg and Eleonore Stump, Kenny, eds. *The Cambridge History of Later Medieval Philosophy: From the Rediscovery of Aristotle to the Disintegration of Scholasticism, 1100-1600*. Cambridge: Cambridge University Press, 80-98.

Lohse, Bernhard (1968). "Die Privatbeichte bei Luther." *Kerigma und Dogma* 14, 207-28.

Lohse, Bernhard (1999). "Martin Luther's Theology: Its Historical and Systematic Development." Edinburgh: T &T Clarck.

Lombardo, Nicholas E. (2013). *The Father's Will: Christ's Crucifixion and the Goodness of God*. Oxford: Oxford University Press.

Loy, Friedrich (1925). *Der Regensburger Wucherstreit: ein Beitrag zum Kampf des Luthertums gegen den Kapitalismus*. Erlangen: Junge.

Lück, Heiner (1991). "Ein Niederländer in Wittenberg. Der Jurist Matthäus Wesenbeck (1531-1586)." *Zentrum für Niederlande Studie* Jahrbuch 2, 199-209.

Luig, Klaus (1987). "Einleitung zur Sektion 2: Usus modernus und Dogmengeschichte des Privatrechts." Dieter Simon, ed. *Akten des 26. Deutschen Rechtshistorikertages, Frankfurt am Main 22. bis 26 September 1986*. Frankfurt am Main: Klostermann, 233-35.

Luig, Klaus (1991). "Samuel Stryk (1640-1710) und der *Usus modernus pandectarum*." Michael Stolleis, ed. *Die Bedeutung der Wörter. Studien zur europäischen Rechtsgeschichte; Festschrift für Sten Gagnér zum 70. Geburtstag*. München: Beck, 219-35.

Luthardt, Christoph E. (1893). *Geschichte der christlichen Ethik, Zweite Hälfte: Geschichte der christlichen Ethik seit der Reformation*. Leipzig: Dörffling & Franke.

Lutz, Heinrich (1979). *Reformation und Gegenreformation*. München-Wien: Oldenburg.

Mager, Inge (1969). *Georg Calixts theologische Ethik und ihre Nachwirkungen*. Göttingen: Vandenhoeck & Ruprecht.

Maher, Michael SJ (2000). "Confession and Consolation: The Society of Jesus and its Promotion of the General Confession." Katharine Jackson Lualdi and Anne T. Thayer, eds. *Penitence in the Age of Reformations*. Aldershot: Ashgate, 184-200.

Maihold, Harald (2005). *Strafe für fremde Schuld? Die Systematisierung des Strafbegriffs in der Spanischen Spätscholastik und Naturrechtslehre*. Wien-Köln-Weimar: Böhlau.

Maihold, Harald (2014). "God's Wrath and Charity Criminal Law in (Counter-) Reforming Discourse of Redemption and Retribution." Wim Decock, Jordan J. Ballor, Michael Germann and Laurent Waelkens, eds. *Law and Religion. The Legal Teachings of the Protestant and Catholic Reformations*. Göttingen: Vandenhoeck & Ruprecht, 149-173.

Maihold, Harald (2017). "'Himmel und Erde'. Die Abgrenzung von *forum internum* und *forum externum* in der frühen Neuzeit." Michael Germann and Wim Decock eds. *Das Gewissen in den Rechtslehren der protestantischen und katolischen Reformationen. Conscience in the Legal Teachings of the Protestant and Catholic Reformations*. Leipzig: Evangelische Verlagsanstalt. 51-71.

Mäkinen, Virpi (2001). *Property Rights in the Late Medieval Discussion on Franciscan Poverty*. Leuven: Peeters.

Mäkinen, Virpi, ed. (2006). *Lutheran Reformation and the Law*. Leiden: Brill.

Mäkinen, Virpi (2006). "Rights and Duties in Late Scholastic Discussion on Extreme Necessity." Virpi Mäkinen and Petter Korkman, *Transformations in Medieval and Early-Modern Rights Discourse*. Dordrecht: Springer.

Mäkinen, Virpi and Raunio, Antti (2006). "Right and Dominion in Luther's Thought and Its Medieval Background." Virpi Mäkinen, ed. *Lutheran Reformation and the Law*. Leiden-Boston: Brill, 63-92.

Malinowski, Bronislaw (1935). *Coral Gardens and Their Magic: A Study of the Methods of Thilling the Soil and of Agricoltural Rites in the Trobriand Islands*, vol. 2: *The Language of Magic and Gardening*. London: George Allen & Unwin.

Mann, Jesse D. (1990). "Unstudied manuscript of the Summa de Poenitentia of Raymynd de Pennaforte." *Manuscripta* 34, 45-9.

Marangon, Paolo (1978). "Il rapporto culturale tra Università e ordini mendicanti nella Padova del Duecento." *Il Santo* 18, II, 129-32.

Marenborn, John (1997). *The Philosophy of Peter Abelard*. Cambridge: Cambridge University Press.

Martin, Roderick H. (2008). *The Reformation of Conscience: Rhetoric in the Lutheran Casuistry of Friedrich Balduin (1575-1627)*. Diss., University of Virginia.

Maryks, Robert A. (2014). *A Companion to Ignatius of Loyola. Life, Writings, Spirituality, Influence*. Leiden-Boston: Brill.

Massironi, Andrea (2012). *Nell'officina dell'interprete. La qualificazione del contratto nel diritto comune (secoli XIV-XVI)*. Milano: Giuffrè.

Mattes, Mark (2014). "Luther on Justification as Forensic and Effective." Kolb, Robert, Dingel, Irene and Batka, L'ubomír, eds. *The Oxford Handbook of Martin Luther's Theology*. Oxford: Oxford University Press, 264-73.

Matthias, Markus (2004). *Theologie und Konfession. Der Beitrag von Ägidius Hunnius (1550-1603) zur Entstehung einer lutherischen Religionskultur*. Leipzig: Evangelische Verlagsanstalt.

Matz, Wolfgang (2001). *Der befreite Mensch. Die Willenslehre in der Theologie Philipp Melanchthons*. Göttingen: Vandenhoeck & Ruprecht.

Mayer-Maly, Theo (1975). *Der Konsens als Grundlage des Vertrages*. Heinz Hübner, Ernst Klingmüller and Andreas Wacke, eds. *Festschrift für Erwin Seidl zum 70. Geburstag*. Köln: P. Hanstein, 118-29.

Mayes, Benjamin T.G. (2011). *Counsel and Conscience. Lutheran Casuistry and Moral Reasoning after the Reformation*. Göttingen: Vandenhoeck & Ruprecht.

McConnell, Michael W., Cochran Jr., Robert F. and Carmella Angela C., eds. (2001). *Christian Perspectives on Legal Thought*. New Haven & London: Yale University Press.

McDurmon, Joel (2012). "Reassessing Jacob Strauss and the Mosaic Code." *HTS Teologiese Studies/Theological Studies* 68(1), Art. #1253, 4 pages. http://dx.doi.org/10.4102/hts.v68i1.1253 (February 4, 2018).

McGovern, John F. (1972). "The Rise of New Economic Attitudes in Canon and Civil Law, A.D. 1200-1500." *The Jurist* 32, 44-55.

McKitterick, Rosamond (2005). "The Carolingian Renaissance of Culture and Learning." Joanna Story, ed. *Charlemagne: Empire and Society*. Manchester-New York: Manchester University Press, 151-66.

McLaughlin, Terence P. (1939). "The Teaching of the Canonists on Usury." *Medieval Studies* 1, 81-147.

McNeill, John T., Gamer, Helena M. (1979 [1938]). *Medieval Handbooks of Penance. A Translation of the Principal Libri Poenitentiales and Selections from Related Documents*. New York: Columbia University Press.

Meens Rob (2014). *Penance in Medieval Europe: 600-1200*. Cambridge: Cambridge University Press.

Meens, Rob (2014). "Penitential Varieties." John H. Arnold, ed. *The Oxford Handbook of Medieval Christianity*. Oxford: Oxford University Press, 254-70.

Melillo, Generoso (1994). *Contrahere, pacisci, transigere. Contributi allo studio del negozio bilaterale romano*. Napoli: Liguori.

Mertens, Bernd (1996). *Im Kampf gegen die Monopole*. Tübingen: Mohr Siebeck.

Meyer, Elizabeth A. (2004). *Legitimacy and Law in the Roman World: Tabulae in Roman Belief and Practice*. Cambridge: Cambridge University press.

Michaud-Quantin, Pierre (1962). *Sommes de casuistique et manuels de confession au Moyen Âge (xiie-xvie siècles)*. Louvain: Nauwelaerts.

Miller, Richard B. (1995). "Moral Sources, Ordinary Life and Truth Telling in Jeremy Taylor's Casuistry." James F. Keenan, Thomas A. Shannon, *The Context of Casuistry*. Washington: Georgetown University Press, 131-58.

Mills, Ludo J.R. (1992). *Angelic Monks and Earthly Men. Monasticism and its Meaning to Medieval Society*. Woodbridge: The Boydell Press.

Minnucci, Giovanni (2011). "Foro della coscienza e foro esterno nel pensiero giuridico della prima età moderna." Gerhard Dilcher and Diego Quaglioni, eds. *Gli inizi del diritto pubblico, vol. 3: verso la costruzione del diritto pubblico tra medioevo e modernità*. Bologna: Il Mulino, 55-81.

Minnucci, Giovanni (2016). Silete theologi in munere alieno. *Alberico Gentili tra diritto, teologia e religione*. Milano: Monduzzi.

Moccia, Luigi (1994). "Promessa e contratto (Spunti storico-comparativi)." *Rivista di diritto civile* 27, I, 818-52.

Monsalve, Fabio (2014). "Late Spanish Doctors on Usury, and the Evolving Scholastic Tradition." *Journal of the History of Economic Thought* 36, n. 2, 215-35.

Moore, Robert I. (2000). *The First European Revolution, c. 970-1215*. Oxford: Blackwell.

Mörke, Olaf (2005). *Die Reformation. Voraussetzungen und Durchsetzung*. München: Oldenbourg.

Morris, Colin (1972). *The discovery of the individual. 1050-1200*. London: SPCK.

Mörsdorf, Klaus (1957). "Der Rechtscharakter der iuridisdictio fori interni." *Münchener theologische Zeitschrift* 8, 161-73.

Mortimer, Robert C. (1939). *The Origins of Private Penance in the Western Church*. Oxford: Clarendon Press.

Mostaza Rodríguez, Antonio (1968). "Forum internum-Forum externum. En torno a la naturaleza juridica del fuero interno." *Revista española de derecho canonico* 23, 253-331; 24, 339-64.

Mulchaney, Marian Michèle (1998). *First the Bow is Bent in Study ... Dominican Education before 1350*. Toronto: Pontifical Institute of Mediaeval Studies.

Mullaney, Thomas U. (1950). *Suarez on Human Freedom*. Baltimore: Carroll Press.

Muller, Richard A. (2006). *Post-Reformation Reformed Dogmatics*, vol. I-II, Grand Rapids MI: Baker Academic.

Munro, John H. (2003). "The Medieval Origins of the Financial Revolution: Usury, Rentes, and Negotiability." *The International History Review* 25, 3, 505-62.

Munro, John H. (2013). "Rentes and the European 'Financial Revolution'." in Gerard Caprio, ed. *Handbook of Key Global Financial Markets, Institutions and Infrastructure*. London-Waltham-San Diego: Elsevier, 235-49.

Muzzarelli, Maria Giuseppina, ed. (1980). *Una componente della mentalità occidentale: i Penitenziali nell'alto medioevo*. Bologna: Pàtron Editore.

Muzzarelli, Maria Giuseppina (2001). *Il denaro e la salvezza: l'invenzione del Monte di Pietà*. Bologna: Il Mulino.

Nanz, Klaus Peter (1985). *Die Entstehung des allgemeinen Vertragsbegriffs im 16. bis 18. Jahrhundert*. München: Schweitzer.

Navarretta, Emanuela (2014). "L'evoluzione dell'autonomia contrattuale tra ideologie e principi." *Quaderni fiorentini* 43, I, 589-647.

Nehlsen- von Stryk, Karin (1988). "Die Monopolgutachten des rechtsgelehrten Humanisten Conrad Peutinger aus dem frühen 16. Jahrhundert. Ein Beitrag zum frühneuzeitlichen Wirtschaftrecht." *Zeitschrift für neuere Rechtsgeschichte* 10, 1-18.

Nelson, Benjamin N. (1949). *The Idea of Usury. From Tribal Brotherhood to Universal Otherhood*. Princeton: Princeton University Press.

Neumann, Max (1865). *Geschichte des Wuchers in Deutschland bis zur Begründung der heutigen Zinsengesetze (1654)*. Halle: Verlag der Buchhandlung des Waisenhauses.

Neuser, Wilhelm H. (1987). *Bibliographie der Confessio Augustana und Apologie 1530-1580*. Leiden-Boston: Brill.

Newhauser, Richard (2005). *In the Garden of Evil: The Vices and Culture in the Middle Ages*. Toronto: Pontifical Institute of Mediaeval Studies.

Newhauser Richard, ed. (2007). *The Seven Deadly Sins. From Communities to Individuals*. Leiden-Boston: Brill.

Newhauser, Richard G. and Susan J. Ridyard, eds. (2012). *Sin in Medieval and Early Modern Culture: The Tradition of the Seven Deadly Sins*. York: Woodbridge.

Nieden, Marcel (2006). *Die Erfindung des Theologen: Wittenberger Anweisungen zum Theologiestudium im Zeitalter von Reformation und Konfessionalisierung*. Tübingen: Mohr.

Noonan, John T., Jr. (1957). *The Scholastic Analysis of Usury*. Cambridge Mass.: Harvard University Press.

Nörr, Knut Wolfgang (1993). "Recht und Religion: über drei Schnittstellen im Recht der mittelalterlichen Kirche." *Zeitschrift der Savigny-Stiftung für Rechtsgeschichte* Kan. Ab. 79, 1, 1-15.

Noth, Gottfried (1930) *Grundlinien der Theologie des Martin Chemnitz*. Erlagen.

Novotný, Daniel D. (2013). *Ens rationis from Suárez to Caramuel: A Study in Scholasticism of the Baroque Era*. New York: Fordham University Press.

Nüssel, Friederike (1996). *Bund und Versöhnung. Zur Begründnung der Dogmatik bei Johann Franz Buddeus*. Göttingen: Vandenhoeck & Ruprecht.

Oaxley, Thomas P. (1923). *English Penitential Discipline and Anglo-Saxon law in their Joint Influence*. New York: Columbia University Press.

Oakley, Thomas P. (1932). "The Cooperation of Medieval Penance and Secular Law." *Speculum* 7, 515-24.

Oaxley, Thomas P. (1939). "Les commutations et les redemptions dans les pénitentiels du continent." *Revue historique de droit francais et ètranger* (4 Ser. 18).

Oberman, Heiko A. (1977). *Werden und Wertung der Reformation. Vom Wegestreit zum Glaubenskampf.* Tübingen: Mohr.

O'Daly, Gerard (1999). *Augustine's City of God. A Reader's Guide.* Clarendon Press: Oxford.

Oestmann, Peter (2013). "§§ 535-580a. Mietvertrag". Mathias Schmoeckel et al., eds. *Historisch-kritischer Kommentar zum BGB*, 3. Tübingen: Mohr Siebeck, 464-594.

O'Malley, John W. (1993). *The First Jesuits.* Cambridge Mass.-London: Harvard University Press.

O'Reilly, Francisco (2006). *Duda y opinion, La consciencia moral en Soto y Medina.* Pamplona: Universidad de Navarra.

Orrego-Sanchez, Santiago (2004). *La actualidad del ser en la Primera Escuela de Salamanca. Con lecciones inéditas de Vitoria, Soto y Cano.* Pamplona: Ediciones Universidad de Navarra.

Orrego-Sanchez, Santiago (2008). "The 16th Century School of Salamanca as a Context of Synthesis Between the Middle Ages and the Renaissance in Theological and Philosophical Matters." Guido Giglioni et al., eds. (2008). *Continuities and Disruptions between the Middle Ages and the Renaissance: Proceedings of the colloquium held at the Warburg Institute, 15-16 June 2007.* Louvain-la-Neuve: FIDEM, 113-38.

Osterhorn, Ernst Dietrich (1962). *Die Naturrechtslehre Valentin Albertis. Ein Beitrag zum Rechtsdenken der lutherischen Orthodoxie des 17. Jahrhunderts.* Diss. Freiburg im Breisgau.

Osti, Giuseppe (1912). "La clausola "rebus sic stantibus" nel suo sviluppo storico." *Rivista di diritto civile*, 1-58.

Otte, Gerhard (1971). *Dialektik und Jurisprudenz: Untersuchungen zur Methode der Glossatoren.* Frankfurt am Main: Klostermann.

Otte, Gerhard (1973). "Der Probabilismus: eine Theorie auf der Grenze zwischen Theologie und Jurisprudenz." Paolo Grossi, ed. *La seconda scolastica nella formazione del diritto privato moderno.* Milano: Giuffrè, 283-302.

Otto, Eckart (1996). "Gerechtigkeit und Erbamen im Recht des Alten Testaments und seiner christlichen Rezeption." Eckard Otto, *Kontinuum und Proprium: Studien zur Sozial-und Rechtsgeschichte des Alten Orients und des Alten Testaments.* Wiesbaden: Harrassowitz, 342-57.

Oyer, John (1977). "The influence of Jacob Strauss on the Anabaptists. A problem in historical methodology." Marc Lienhard, ed. *The Origins and Characteristics of Anabaptism.* The Hague: Springer, 1977, 62-82.

Packull, Werner O. and Dipple, Geoffrey L., eds. (1999). *Radical Reformation Studies, Essays presented to J.M. Stayer.* Aldershot-Brookfield USA-Singapore-Sydney: Ashgate.

Padoa Schioppa, Antonio (2007). *Storia del diritto in Europa. Dal medioevo all'età contemporanea.* Bologna: Il Mulino.

Pagden, Anthony (2011). "The School of Salamanca." George Klosko, ed. *The Oxford Handbook of the History of Political Philosophy*. Oxford: Oxford University Press, 246-57.

Palaia, Roberto, ed. (2013). *Coscienza, nella filosofia della prima modernità*. Firenze: Olschki.

Palladini, Fiammetta (1978). *Discussioni seicentesche su Samuele Pufendorf. Scritti latini:1663-1700*. Bologna: Il Mulino.

Palladini, Fiammetta and Hartung, Gerald, eds. (1996). *Samuel Pufendorf und die europäische Frühaufklärung: Werk und Einfluss eines deutschen Bürgers der Gelehrtenrepublik nach 300 Jahren (1694-1994)*. Berlin: Akademie.

Pansters, Krijn (2012). *Franciscan Virtue. Spiritual Growth and the Virtues in Franciscan Literature and Instruction of the Thirteenth Century*. Leiden- Boston: Brill.

Pavur, Claude, ed. and trans. (2005). *The Ratio Studiorum: The Official Plan for Jesuit Education*. St. Louis: The Institute of Jesuit Sources.

Pawlas, Andreas (2000). *Die lutherische Beruf- und Wirtschaftsethik. Eine Einführung*. Neukirchen-Vluyn: Neukirchener.

Pawlas, Andreas (2013). "Luther zu Geld und Zins. Mit einem Vorwort über Lutherische Erwägungen zu Geld und Zins." *Uppsala University Coin Cabinet Working Papers, Uppsala*, Uppsala Universitet, 4-36 http://uu.diva-portal.org/smash/get/diva2:676716/FULLTEXT01.pdf (June 27, 2016).

Pawlas, Andreas (2014). "Die Wirtschaft des Menschen zwischen Fluch und Segen. Ökonomische Kritik bei Luther und Calvin." *Paradoxie der Freiheit. Zur Relevanz von Luthers ökonomischer Kritik und Calvins Wirtschaftsmoral für das Verhältnis von Kirche, Staat und Wirtschaft*, epd-Dokumentation 21, 12-33.

Pawlas, Andreas (2015). "Did Calvin Have a Better Understanding of Modern Economics as Luther? Max Weber's Ideas to the Test." *Research in World Economy* 6, n. 1, 36-57.

Payer, Pierre J. (1984). "The Humanism of the Penitentials and the Continuity of the Penitential Tradition." *Mediaeval Studies*, 46, 340-54.

Payer, Pierre J. (2009). *Sex and the New Medieval Literature of Confession, 1150-1300*. Toronto: Pontifical Institute of Mediaeval Studies.

Pelt, Anton F.L. (1843). *Theologische Encyklopädie als System: im Zusammenhange mit der Geschichte der theologischen Wissenschaft und ihrer einzelnen Zweige entwickelt*. Hamburg-Gotha: Perthes.

Pelt, L. (1848). "Die christliche Ethik in der lutherischen Kirche vor Calixt." Johann C.L. Gieseler, ed. *Theologische Studien und Kritiken: Beitr. zur Theologie u. Religionswissenschaft* (ThStKr 21), Hamburg, 271-319.

Pena González, Miguel A. (2009). *La Escuela de Salamanca. De la Monarquía hispánica al Orbe católico*. Madrid: Biblioteca de Autores Cristianos.

Pennington, Kenneth (1984). *Popes and Bishops. The Papal Monarchy in the Twelfth and Thirteenth Centuries*. Philadelphia PA: University of Pennsylvania Press.

Pennington, Kenneth (1993). *The Prince and the Law, 1200-1600: Sovereignty and Rights in the Western Legal Tradition*. Berkeley CA: University of California Press.

Pennington, Kenneth (2015). "Protestant Ecclesiastical Law and the Ius Commune." *Rivista internazionale di diritto comune* 26, 9-36.

Pesch, Otto H. (1985). *Theologie der Rechtfertigung bei Martin Luther und Thomas von Aquin: Versuch eines systematisch-theologischen Dialogs*. Mainz: Grünewald-Verlag.

Petersen, Peter (1921). *Geschichte der Aristotelischen Philosophie im Protestantischen Deutschland*. Leipzig: F. Meiner.

Petronio, Ugo, (1990). "Sinallagma e analisi strutturale dei contratti all'origine del sistema contrattuale moderno." John Barton, ed. *Towards a General Law of Contract*. Berlin: Duncker & Humblot, 215-47.

Petzoldt, Martin (1989). "Konfessionalisierung als Identitätssuche." Helmut Baier, ed. *Konfessionalisierung vom 16.19. Jahrhundert: Kirche und Traditionspflege*. Neustadt an der Aisch: Degener, 67-86.

Peukert, Helge (2010). "Martin Luther. A First Modern Economist." Jürgen G. Backhaus, ed. *The Reformation as a Precondition for Modern Capitalism*. Münster: Lit, 13-64.

Pierce, Rosamond (1975). "The 'Frankish' Penitentials." *Studies in Church History* 11, 31-9.

Pifferri, Michele (2006). *Generalia delictorum. Il Tractatus criminalis di Tiberio Deciani e la "parte generale" di diritto penale*. Milano: Giuffrè.

Pincherle, Alberto (1955). "Graziano e Lutero." *Studia Gratiana* 3, 451-82.

Pink, Thomas (2007). "Action Will and Law in Late Scholasticism". Kraye, J., Saarinen, R. (eds.), *Moral Philosophy on the Threshold of Modernity*, Dordrecht, Springer, 2007, 31-51.

Piron, Sylvain (1998). "Marchands et confesseurs, Le Traité des contrats d'Olivi dans son contexte (Narbonne, fin XIIIe-début XIVe siècle)". *L'Argent au Moyen Age, XXVIIIe Congrès de la SHMESP (Clermont-Ferrand, 1997)*. Paris: Publications de la Sorbonne, 289-308.

Piron Sylvain (2005). "Le devoir de gratitude. Émergence et vogue de la notion d'antidora au XIIIe siècle." Diego Quaglioni, Giacomo Todeschini and Gian Maria Varanini, eds. *Credito e usura fra teologia, diritto e amministrazione. Linguaggi a confronto (sec. XII-XVI)*. Convegno internazionale a Trento, 3-5 settembre 2001. Roma: Ecole Française de Rome, 73-101.

Piron, Sylvain (2012). *Pierre de Jean Olivi, Traité de contrats*. Paris: Les Belles Lettres.

Plasger, Georg (1993). *Die Not-wendigkeit der Gerechtigkeit: eine Interpretation zu Cur Deus homo von Anselm von Canterbury*. Münster: Aschendorff.

Pohl, Walter (2010). "Introduction: Ego Trouble?." Richard Corradini et al., eds. *Ego Trouble. Authors and their Identities in the Early Middle Ages*. Vienna: Austrian Academy of Sciences, 9-21.

Porter, Jean (1999). *Natural and Divine Law. Reclaiming the Tradition for Christian Ethics*. Grand Rapids, MI.- Cambridge, U.K.: Eerdmans.

Poschmann, Bernhard (1923). *Kirchenbusse und correptio secreta bei Augustinus.* Braunsberg: Druck der Ermländischen Zeitungs- und Verlagsdruckerei.

Poschmann, Bernhard (1928). *Die abendländische Kirchenbusse im Ausgang des christlichen Altertums.* München: Kösel & Friedrich Pustet.

Poschmann, Bernhard (1930). *Die abendländische Kirchenbuße im frühen Mittelalter.* Breslau: Müller & Seiffert.

Poschmann, Bernhard (1951). *Busse und Letzte Olung.* Freiburg: Verlag Herder.

Potts, Timothy C. (1980). *Conscience in Medieval Philosophy.* Cambridge: Cambridge University Press.

Preus, Jacob A.O. (1994). *The Second Martin: The Life and Theology of Martin Chemnitz.* St. Louis: Concordia Publishing House.

Preus, Robert D. (1970). *The Theology of Post-Reformation Lutheranism. A Study of Theological Prolegomena.* London: Concordia Publishing House.

Prien, Hans Jürgen (1992). *Luthers Wirtschaftsethik.* Göttingen: Vandenhoeck & Ruprecht.

Prodi, Paolo (2000). *Una storia della giustizia: del pluralismo dei fori al moderno dualismo tra coscienza e diritto.* Bologna: Il Mulino.

Prodi, Paolo (2009). *Settimo non rubare. Furto e mercato nella storia dell'Occidente.* Bologna: Il Mulino.

Prodi, Paolo (2012). *Cristianesimo e potere.* Bologna: Il Mulino.

Prosperi, Adriano (1996). "La confessione e il foro della coscienza." Paolo Prodi and Wolfgang Reinhard, eds. *Il concilio di Trento e il moderno.* Bologna: Il Mulino, 225-54.

Prosperi, Adriano (2009 [1996]). *Tribunali della coscienza. Inquisitori, confessori, missionari.* Torino: Einaudi.

Quaglioni, Diego, Todeschini, Giacomo and Varanini, Gian Maria, eds. (2005). *Credito e usura fra teologia, diritto e amministrazione. Linguaggi a confronto* (*sec. XII-XVI*), Convegno internazionale a Trento, 3-5 settembre 2001. Roma: Ecole Française de Rome.

Rambaud-Buhot, Jacqueline (1965). "Le leges de l'ancien droit: Gratien." Gabriel Le Bras et al., eds. *L'Age classique 1140-1378, vol. I, Sources et théorie du droit.* Paris: Sirey, 47-129.

Ramp, Ernst (1949). *Das Zinsproblem. Eine historische Untersuchung*, Zürich: Zwingli Verlag.

Raunio, Antti (2001). *Summe des christlichen Lebens: die Goldene Regel als Gesetz der Liebe in der Theologie Martin Luthers von 1510-1527.* Mainz: Von Zabern.

Raunio, Antti (2006). "Divine and Natural Law in Luther and Melanchthon." Virpi Mäkinen, ed. *Lutheran Reformation and the Law.* Leiden-Boston: Brill, 21-62.

Raunio, Antti (2017). "Natural Law in the Lutheran Tradition." Norman Doe, ed. *Christianity and Natural Law: An Introduction.* Cambridge: Cambridge University Press, 77-97.

Reali, Nicola (2017). *Lutero e il diritto, certezza della fede e istituzioni ecclesiali*. Venezia: Marcianum Press.

Reibstein, Ernst (1955). *Johannes Althusius als Fortsetzer der Schule von Salamanca. Untersuchungen zur Ideengeschichte des Rechtsstaates und zur altprotestantischen Naturrechtslehre*. Karlsruhe: Müller.

Reinhardt, Nicole (2016). *Voices of Conscience. Royal Confessors and Political Counsel in Seventeenth Century Spain and France*. Oxford: Oxford University Press.

Repgen, Tilman (2001). *Die soziale Aufgabe des Privatrechts*. Tübingen: Mohr Siebeck.

Rester Todd (2014). "Roman Canon Law in Protestant Reformed Theologians as Both Touchstone and Foil." Wim Decock, Jordan J. Ballor, Michael Germann, and Laurent Waelkens, eds. *Law and Religion: The Legal Teachings of the Protestant and Catholic Reformations*. Göttingen: Vandenhoeck & Ruprecht, 174-85.

Reulos, Michel (1954). "Le Décret de Gratien chez les humanistes, les gallicans et les réformés français du XVI siècle." *Studia Gratiana* 2, 677-96.

Rexroth, Frank (2013). "Die scholastische Wissenschaft in den Meistererzählungen der europäischen Geschichte." Klaus Ridder and Steffen Patzold, eds. *Die Aktualität der Vormoderne. Epochenentwürfe zwischen Alterität und Kontinuität*. Berlin: De Gruyter, 111-134.

Reynolds, Roger E. (1987). "Rites of Separation and Reconciliation in the Early Middle Ages." *Segni e riti nella Chiesa altomedioevale occidentale. Settimane di studio del Centro Italiano di Studi sull'Alto Medioevo*, 33,1. Spoleto: Centro Italiano di Studi sull'alto Medioevo, 405-33.

Rice, Eugene F. Jr. and Grafton, Anthony (1994). *The Foundation of Early Modern Europe, 1460-1559*. New York: Norton.

Rieth, Ricardo (2014). "Luther's Treatment of Economic Life." Robert Kolb, Irene Dingel, and L'Ubomír Batka, eds. *The Oxford Handbook of Martin Luther's Theology*. Oxford: Oxford University Press, 383-96.

Riley, Patrick (2009). "Leibniz on Justice as "The Charity of Wise". Patrick Riley, ed., *A Treatise of Legal Philosophy and General Jurisprudence, Vol. 10: The Philosophers' Philosophy of Law from the Seventeenth Century to Our Days*. Berlin: Springer, 77-106.

Rittgers, Ronald K. (2000). "Private Confession and Religious Authority in Reformation Nürnberg." in Kathrine Jackson Lualdi and Anne T. Thayer, eds. *Penitence in the Age of Reformations*. Aldershot: Ashgate, 2000, 49-70.

Rittgers, Ronald K. (2004). *The Reformation of the Keys. Confession, Conscience, and Authority in Sixteenth-Century Germany*. Cambridge Mass.: Harvard University Press.

Rittgers, Ronald K. (2008). "Embracing the "True Relic" of Christ: Suffering, Penance, and Private Confession in the Thought of Martin Luther." Abigail Firey, ed. *A New History of Penance*. Leiden-Boston: Brill, 377-95.

Rittgers, Ronald K. (2017). "Confession (Private) and the Confessional." Timothy J. Wengert, ed. *Dictionary of Luther and the Lutheran Traditions*. Grand Rapids MI: Baker.

Roberti, Melchiorre (1935). "L'influenza cristiana nello svolgimento storico dei patti nudi." Melchiorre Roberti, *Cristianesimo e diritto romano*. Milano: Vita e pensiero, 87-169.

Robinson Rössner, Philipp (2016). "The Crisis of the Reformation." *Le crisi finanziarie. Gestione, implicazioni sociali e conseguenze nell'età preindustriale. The Financial Crises. Their Management, Their Social Implications and Their Consequences in Pre-Industrial Times. Selezione di ricerche, Selection of Essays*. Firenze: Firenze University Press, 19-48.

Rodriquez Penelos, Horacio (2007). "Contribución de Domingo de Soto a la gestación del pensiamiento económico hispanoamericano." Juan Cruz Cruz, ed. *La ley natural como fundamento moral y jurídico ed Domingo de Soto*. Pamplona: Eunsa, 223-40.

Roest, Bert (2000). *A History of Franciscan Education (c.1210-1517)*. Köln- Leiden-Boston: Brill.

Roest, Bert (2015). *Franciscan Learning, Preaching and Mission, c. 1220-1650. Cum scientia sit donum Dei, armatura ad defendendam sanctam fidem catholicam* ... Leiden-Boston: Brill.

Rosemann, Philipp W., ed. (2009-15) *Mediaeval Commentaries on the sentences of Peter Lombard*. vol. 2 and 3, Leiden: Brill.

Ross, Richard J. (2008). "Puritan Godly Discipline in Comparative Perspective. Legal Pluralism and the Sources of 'Intensity'." *American Historical Review* 113, 975-1002.

Ross, Richard J. (2015). "Binding in Conscience: Early Modern English Protestants and Spanish Tomists on Law and the Fate of the Soul." *Law and History Review* 33, 803-37.

Roth, Erich (1952). *Die Privatbeichte und Schlüsselgewalt in der Theologie der Reformatoren*. Gütersloh: Bertelsmann.

Roth, John D. and Stayer, James M., eds. (2007). *A Companion to Anabaptism and Spiritualism, 1521-1700*. Leiden: Brill.

Roussier, Jules (1933). *Le fondement de l'obligation contractuelle dans le droit classique de l'Eglise*. Paris: Domat-Montchrestien.

Rummel, Erika (1995). *The Humanistic-Scholastic Debate in the Renaissance and Reformation*. Cambridge Mass.-London: Harvard University Press.

Rummel, Michael (1991). *Die 'clausola rebus sic stantibus'. Eine dogmengeschichtliche Untersuchung unter Berücksichtigung der Zeit von der Rezeption im 14. Jahrhundert bis zum jüngeren Usus Modernus in der ersten Hälfte des 18. Jahrhunderts*. Baden Baden: Nomos.

Rusconi, Roberto (2010). *L'ordine dei peccati. La confessione tra Medioevo ed età moderna*. Bologna: Il Mulino.

Russell, James C. (1994). *The Germanization of Early Medieval Christianity: A Sociohistorical Approach to Religious Transformation*. Oxford: Oxford University Press.

Saether, Arild (2017). *Natural Law and the Origin of Political Economy. Samuel Pufendorf and the History of Economics*. Abington-New York: Routledge.

Safley, Thomas Max (2009). "Business Failure and Civil Scandal in Early Modern Europe." *The Business History Review* 83,1, 35-60.

Safley, Thomas Max, ed. (2011). *A Companion to Multiconfessionalism in the Early Modern World*. Leiden-Boston: Brill.

Santarelli, Umberto (1984). *La categoria dei contratti irregolari: lezioni di storia del diritto*. Torino: Giappichelli.

Savelli, Rodolfo (1993). "Diritto romano e teologia riformata: Du Moulin di fronte al problema dell'interesse del denaro." *Materiali per una storia della cultura giuridica* XXIII, 291-324.

Savelli, Rodolfo (1997). "Derecho romano y teología reformada, Du Moulin frente al problema del interés del dinero." Carlos Petit, ed. *Del 'Ius mercatorum' al derecho mercantil*. Madrid: Marcial Pons, 257-90.

Savelli, Rodolfo (2001). "Da Venezia a Napoli: diffusione e censura delle opere di Du Moulin nel cinquecento italiano." Cristina Stango, ed. *Censura ecclesiastica e cultura politica in Italia tra Cinquecento e Seicento: VI Giornata Luigi Firpo; atti del convegno, 5 marzo 1999*. Firenze: Olschki, 101-54.

Scattola, Merio (1999). *Das Naturrecht vor dem Naturrecht. Zur Geschichte des >ius naturae< im 16. Jahrhundert*. Tübingen: Max Niemeyer Verlag.

Scattola, Merio (2009). "Scientia iuris and ius naturae: The Jurisprudence of the Holy Roman Empire in the Seventeenth and Eighteenth Centuries." Enrico Pattaro, Damiano Canale, Paolo Grossi, Hasso Hofmann and Patrick Riley, eds. *A Treatise of Legal Philosophy and General Jurisprudence, Vol. 9: A History of the Philosophy of Law in the Civil Law World, 1600-1900*. Berlin: Springer, 1-41.

Scattola, Merio (2015). "Gewissen und Gerechtigkeit in den Beichtbüchern der Frühen Neuzeit." *Journal of Early Modern Christianity* 2015 (2), 117-58.

Scattola, Merio (2017). "Natural Law Part II: The Protestant and Philosophy Traditions". Hendrik Lagerlund and Benjamin Hill, eds. *The Routledge Companion to Sixteenth Century Philosophy*. New York: Routledge, 580-613.

Schäfer, Rudolf (1915). "Die Geltung des kanonischen Recht in der evangelischen Kirche von Luther bis zum Gegenwart." *Zeitschrift für Rechtsgeschichte*, Kan. Abt. 36, 181-202.

Schaff, Philip et al., eds. (1896). *Nicene and Post-Nicene Fathers: Second Series*. vol. 10. Revised and edited for New Advent by Kevin Knight http://www.newadvent.org/fathers/34013.htm (December 5, 2017).

Schaff, Philip, ed. (1889). *Saint Chrysostom: Homilies on the Epistles of Paul to the Corinthians, Nicene and Post-Nicene Fathers.* vol. 12. http://www.ccel.org/ccel/schaff/npnf112.html (December 5, 2017).

Schermaier, Martin J. (2000). *Die Bestimmung des wesentlichen Irrtums von den Glossatoren bis zum BGB.* Wien-Köln-Weimar: Böhlau.

Schild, Wolfgang, ed. (1997). *Benedikt Carpzov 1595-1666, Werk und Wirken; Gesammelte Aufsätze, Vorträge und Dissertationen zu Carpzov aus drei Jahrhunderten.* Goldbach: Keip.

Schilling, Heinz (1992). *Religion, Political Culture and The Emergence of Early Modern Society. Essays in German and Dutch History.* Leiden-New York- Köln: Brill.

Schilling, Heinz and Tóth, István György (2006), "From Empire to Family Circles: Religious and Cultural Borderlines in the Age of Confessionalization." Heinz Schilling and István György Tóth, eds. *Religion and Cultural Exchange in Europe, 1400-1700.* Cambridge: Cambridge University Press, 25-48.

Schmelzeisen, Gustav K. (1955). *Polizeiordnungen und Privatrecht.* Münster-Köln: Böhlau, 475-500.

Schmelzeisen, Gustav K. (1978). "Zinsvertrag und Rentenkauf." *Zeitschrift der Savigny-Stiftung für Rechtsgeschichte* Germ. Ab. 95, 229-36.

Schmitz, Herm J. (1958 [1883-98]). *Die Bussbücher und die Bussdisciplin der Kirche.* vol. I-II, Graz: Akademische Druck, U. Verlagsanstalt.

Schmoeckel, Mathias (2000). "Rechtsgeschichte im 21 Jahrhundert, Ein Diskussionsbeitrag zur Standortbestimmung." *Forum Historiae Iuris,* http://www.forhistiur.de/2000-05-schmoeckel/ (December 13, 2018).

Schmoeckel, Mathias (2004). "Der Entwurf eines Strafrechts der Gegenreformation. Prova, pena e penitenza nel sistema posttridentino." Marco Cavina, eds. *Tiberio Deciani (1509-1582). Alle origini del pensiero giuridico moderno.* Udine: Forum, 207-34.

Schmoeckel, Mathias (2008). "Erkenntnis durch ratio und conscientia: Die Begründung der modernen Wissenschflichkeit des Rechts durch Melanchthons Naturrechtslehre." Görge K. Hasselhoff and Michael Meyer-Blanck, eds. *Religion und Rationalität.* Würzburg: Ergon, 179-220.

Schmoeckel, Mathias (2012). "Der Bauernkrieg und Melanchthons Kehre." Görge K. Hasselhoff and David von Mayenburg, eds. *Die Zwölf Artikel von 1525 und das "Göttliche Recht" der Bauern – rechtshistorische und theologische Dimensionen.* Würzburg: Ergon, 179-202.

Schmoeckel, Mathias (2014). "Das kanonische Zinsverbot und die Konfessionalisierung." Wim Decock, Jordan J. Ballor, Michael Germann and Laurent Waelkens, eds *Law and Religion: The Legal Teachings of the Protestant and Catholic Reformations.* Göttingen: Vandenhoeck & Ruprecht, 186-212.

Schmoeckel, Mathias (2014). *Das Recht des Reformation. Die epistemologische Revolution der Wissenschaft und die Spaltung der Rechtsordnung in der Frühen Neuzeit*. Tübingen: Mohr Siebeck.

Schmoeckel, Mathias (2014). "Der Pastor als Richter? Der Einfluss der lutherischen Reformation auf die untere kirchliche Gerichtsbarkeit." Max Engammare and Alexandre Vauautgaerden, eds. *L'intime du droit à la Reinassance. Actes du cinquantenaire de la FISIER*. Genève: Droz, 307-35.

Schmoeckel, Mathias (2016). "Zur Bedeutung der Reformation." *Zeitschrift der Savigny-Stiftung für Rechtsgeschichte*, Kan. Ab.,102 (2016), 317-58.

Schmoeckel, Mathias (2017). "Ein Denker des Ausgleichs. Die Rechtslehre des Johann Gerhard." Markus Friedrich, Sascha Salatowsky and Luise Schorn-Schütte, eds. *Konfession, Politik und Gelehrsamkeit. Der Jenear Theologe Johann Gerhard (1582-1637) im Kontext seiner Zeit*. Stuttgart: Franz Steiner, 20-35.

Schmoeckel, Mathias (2018). "Melanchthons Konzeption der Verträge. Archäologie der Privatautonomie." *Zeitschrift für Rechtsgeschichte* Kan. Abt. 104, 304-45.

Schmoller, Gustav (1860). "Zur Geschichte der national-ökonomischen Ansichten in Deutschland während der Reformations-Periode." *Zeitschrift für die gesamte Staatswissenschaft / Journal of Institutional and Theoretical Economics* 1-16 (3/4), 461-716.

Schnapper, Bernard (1957). *Les rentes au XVIe siècle. Histoire d'un instrument de crédit*. École pratique des hautes études – VIe section. Centre de recherches historiques. Affaires et gens d'affaires XII. Paris: S.E.V.P.E.N.

Schnapper, Bernard (1965). "Les rentes chez les théologiens et les canonistes du XIIIe au XVIe siècle." *Études d'historie du droit canonique dédiées à Gabriel Le Bras*. Paris: Sirey, 965-95.

Schneider, Bernd C. (2001). *Ius Reformandi. Die Entwicklung eines Staatkirchenrechts von seinen Anfängen bis zum Ende des Alten Reiches*. Tübingen: Mohr Siebeck.

Schneider, Hans-Peter (1967). *Justitia Universalis. Quellenstudien zur Geschichte des Christlichen Naturrechts bei Gottfried Wilhelm Leibniz*. Frankfurt am main: Klostermann.

Schneider, Hans-Peter (2001) "Christliches Naturrecht." Helmut Holzhey et al., eds. *Die Philosophie des 17. Jahrhunderts, vol. 4, Das Heilige Römische Reich deutscher Nation Nord-und Ostmitteleuropa*. Basel: Schwabe & Co., 813-35.

Schneider, Hans-Peter (2006). "Die Lehre vom christlichen Naturrecht bei Caspar Ziegler," Heiner Lück and Heinrich de Wall, eds. *Wittenberg. Ein Zentrum europäischer Rechsgeschichte und Rechtskultur*. Köln: Böhlau, 273-91.

Schorn-Schütte, Luise (1992). "Lutherische Konfessionalisierung? Das Beispiel Brauchweig-Wolfenbüttel (1589-1613)." Hans C. Rublack, ed. *Die lutherische Konfessionalisierung in Deutschland (1589-1613)*. Gütersloh: Gerd Mohn, 163-94.

Schrage, Eltjo (2003) "Traditionibus et usucapionibus, non nudis pactis dominia rerum transferuntur Die Wahl zwischen dem Konsens- und dem Traditionsprinzip in der Geschichte." Mario Ascheri, Friedrich Ebel et al., eds. *"Ins Wasser geworfen und Ozeane durchquert": Feschrift für K.W. Nörr*. Köln-Weimar-Wien: Böhlau, 913-58.

Schrage, Eltjo (2014). "Luther und das Kirchenrecht". Paola Maffei and Gian Maria Varanini, eds. Honos alit artes. *Studi per il settantesimo compleanno di Mario Ascheri. Il cammino delle idee dal medioevo all'antico regime. Diritto e cultura nell'esperienza europea*. Firenze: Firenze University Press, 407-17.

Schröder, Jan (1979). *Wissenschaftstheorie und Lehre der "praktischen Jurisprudenz"*. Frankfurt am Main: Klostermann.

Schüßler, Rudolf (2003). *Moral im Zweifel, vol. I: Die scholastische Theorie des Entscheidens unter moralischer Unsicherheit*. Paderborn: Mentis.

Schüßler, Rudolf (2006). *Moral im Zweifel, vol. II: Die Herausforderung des Probabilismus*. Paderborn: Mentis.

Schüßler, Rudolf (2006). "Moral self-ownership and 'ius possessionis' in late scholastics." Virpi Mäkinen and Petter Korkman, eds. *Transformations in Medieval and Early-Modern Rights Discourse*. Dordrecht: Springer, 149-72.

Schüßler, Rudolf (2011). "Johan Gerson, Moral Certainty and the Renaissance of Ancient Scepticism." Harald E. Braun and Edward Vallance, eds. *The Reinassance Conscience*. Oxford: Wiley-Blackwell, 11-28.

Schwartz, Daniel (2014). "Probabilism Reconsidered: Deference to Experts, Types of Uncertainty, and Medicines." *Journal of the History of Ideas* 75, 373-93.

Schwarz, Hans ed. (1994). *Reformation und Reichsstadt. Protestantisches Leben in Regensburg*. Regensburg: Universitätsverlag.

Scott Dixon, C., Friest, Dagmar and Greengrass, Mark, eds. (2009). *Living with Religious Diversity in Early Modern Europe*. Aldershot: Ashgate.

Scott, Tom (2016). *The Early Reformation in Germany. Between Secular Impact and Radical Vision*. Abingdon: Routledge.

Selderhuis, Herman J. (2017). "Calvin's views on Conscience and Law." Michael Germann and Wim Decock, eds. *Das Gewissen in den Rechtslehren der protestantischen und katholischen Reformationen. Conscience in the Legal Teachings of the Protestant and Catholic Reformations*. Leipzig: Evangelische Verlagsanstalt, 33-52.

Selzner, Cyril (2009). "Les forges des philistins, La problématique d'une casuistique réformée en Angleterre de William Perkins à Jeremy Taylor." Serge Boarini, ed. *La casuistique classique: genèse, formes, devenir*. Saint-Étienne: Publications de l'Université de Saint-Étienne, 73-86.

Şenocak, Neslihan (2012). *The Poor and the Perfect. The Rise of Learning in the Franciscan Order, 1209-1310*. Ithaca: Cornell University Press.

Şenocak, Neslihan (2013). "The Making of Franciscan Poverty." *Revue Mabillon* 24, 5-26.

Seuffert, Lothar von (1881). *Zur Geschichte der obligatorischen Verträge*. Nördlingen: Verlag der C.H. Beck'schen Buchhandlung.

Shore, Paul (2016). "Theology and the Development of the European Confessional State." Ulrich L. Lehner, Richard A. Muller and A.G. Roeber, eds. *The Oxford Handbook of Early Modern Theology, 1600-1800*. Oxford: Oxford University Press, 43-57.

Sidey, Thomas K. (1918). "The Government of Charlemagne as Influenced by Augustine's "City of God". *The Classical Journal* 14, n. 2, 119-27.

Siems, Harald (1992). *Handel und Wucher im Spiegel frühmittelalterlicher Rechtsquellen*. Hahn: Hannover.

Singer, Irving (1984). *The Nature of Love, vol. 1, Plato to Luther*. 2nd ed. Chicago: The University of Chicago Press.

Singleton, John D. (2011). "Money Is a Sterile Thing": Martin Luther on the Immorality of Usury Reconsidered." *History of Political Economy* 43 issue 4, 683-98.

Skinner, Quentin (1978). *The Foundation of Modern Political Thought, vol. 2, The Age of the Reformation*. Cambridge: Cambridge University Press.

Smalley, Beryl (1952). *The Study of the Bible in the Middle Ages*. Oxford: Blackwell.

Snyder, C. Arnold (2002). *Anabaptist History and Theology: An Introduction*. 3rd ed. Kitchener: Pandora.

Sohngen, Gottlieb (1962). *Grundfragen einer Rechtstheologie*. München: Pustet.

Söllner, Alfred (1960). "Die causa im Kondiktionen- und Vertragsrecht des Mittelalters bei den Glossatoren, Kommentatoren und Kanonisten." *Zeitschrift der Savigny Stiftung, Rom. Abt.* 77, 182-269.

Söllner, Alfred (1977). "Die Literatur zum Gemein und partikularen Recht in Deutschland, Österreich, den Niederlanden und der Schweiz." Helmut Coing, ed. *Handbuch der Quellen und Literatur der nueren europäischen Privatrechtsgeschichte, II/1*. München: C.H. Beck, 501-16.

Somerville, Johann (1988). "The 'New Art of Lying': Equivocation, Mental Reservation and Casuistry." Edmund Leites, ed. *Conscience and Casuistry in Early Modern Europe*. Cambridge: Cambridge University Press, 159-84.

Somma, Alessandro (2000). *Autonomia privata e struttura del consenso contrattuale*. Milano: Giuffrè.

Sparn, Walter (1992). "Die Krise der Frömmigkeit und ihr theologischer Reflex im nachreformatorischen Luthertum." Hans C. Rublack, ed. *Die lutherische Konfessionalisierung in Deutschland (1589-1613)*. Gütersloh: Gerd Mohn, 54-82.

Sparn, Walter (2001). "Die Schulphilosophie in den lutherischen Territorien." Helmut Holzhey et al., eds. *Die Philosophie des 17. Jahrhunderts*, vol. 4, *Das Heilige Römische Reich deutscher Nation Nord-und Ostmitteleuropa*. Basel: Schwabe & Co., 475-606.

Sparn, Walter (2015). "Naturrecht und Verfassungsfrage im frühneuzeitlichen Luthertum – am Beispiel religiöser Toleranz." Robert von Friedeburg and Mathias Schmoeckel, eds. *Recht, Konfession und Verfassung im 17. Jahrhundert. West-und mitteleuropäische Entwicklungen*. Berlin: Duncker & Humblot, 129-49.

Spicciani, Amleto (1990). *Capitale e interesse tra mercatura e povertà nei teologi e canonisti dei secoli XIII-XV*. Jouvence: Roma.

Spies, François (1928). *De l'observation des simples conventions en droit canonique*. Paris: Recueil Sirey.

Stäudlin, Carl Friedrich (1808). *Geschichte der christlichen Moral seit dem Wiederaufleben der Wissenschaften*. Göttingen: Röwer.

Steiger, Johann A. (1997). *Johann Gerhard (1582-1637). Studien zu Theologie und Frömmigkeit des Kirchenvaters der lutherischen Orthodoxie*. Stuttgart-Bad Cannstatt: frommann-holzboog.

Steiger, Johann A. (2003). "Kirchenordnung, Visitation und Alltag. Johann Gerhard (1582-1637) als Visitator und kirchenordnender Theologe." *Zeitschrift für Religions- und Geistesgeschichte* 55/3, 227-52.

Steiger, Johann A. (2003). "Johann Gerhard. Ein Kirchenvater der lutherischen Orthodoxie." Peter Walter and Martin H. Jung, eds. *Theologen des 17. und 18. Jahrhunderts. Konfessionelles Zeitalter – Pietismus-Aufklärung*. Darmstadt: Wissenschaftlische Buchgesellschaft, 54-69.

Steinmetz, Max (1967). "Die Konzeption der deutschen Universitäten im Zeitälter von Humanismus und Reformation." *Les universités européennes du XIV au XVIII siècle: Aspects et problèmes: Actes du Colloque International à l'occasion du VI Centenarie de L'universitè Jagellone de Craovie, 6-8 mai 1964*. Droz: Geneve, 114-27.

Stintzing, Roderich von, Landsberg, Ernst (1880). *Geschichte der deutschen Rechtswissenschaft*. Vol. I. München: Oldenbourg.

Stintzing, Roderich von and Landsberg, Ernst (1884). *Geschischte der deutschen Rechtswissenschaft*. Vol. II. München: Oldenbourg.

Stoll, Abraham (2017). *Conscience in Early Modern Literature*. Cambridge: Cambridge University Press.

Stolleis, Michael (1993). "'Konfessionalisierung' oder 'Säkularisierung' bei der Entstehung des frühmodernen Staates." *Ius Commune* 20, 1-23.

Stolleis, Michael (2012). *Geschichte des öffentlichen Rechts in Deutschland. Erster Band 1600-1800*. 2nd ed. München: CH Beck.

Stolleis, Michael (2013). *History of Social Law in Germany*. Berlin: Springer.

Stolleis, Michael, Härter, Karl and Schilling, Lothar, eds. (1996) *Policey im Europa der Frühen Neuzeit*. Frankfurt am Main: Klostermann.

Stolzenburg, A.F. (1926). *Die Theologie des Joh. Franc. Buddeus und des Chr. Matth. Pfaff*. Berlin.

Stone, M.W.F. (2000). "The Adoption and Rejection of Aristotelian Moral Philosophy in Reformed 'Casuistry'" Jill Kraye and M.W.F. Stone, eds. *Humanism and Early Modern Philosophy*. London: Routledge, 59-90.

Stone, M.W.F. (2003). "Scrupolosity and Conscience. Probabilism in Early Modern Scholastic Ethics." Harald Braun and Edward Wallace, eds. *Contexts of Conscience in Early Modern Europe, 1500-1700*. Basingstoke: Palgrave Macmillan, 1-16.

Stone, M.W.F. (2006). "Scholastic Schools and Early Modern Philosophy." Donald Rutherford, ed. *The Cambridge Companion to Early Modern Philosophy*. Cambridge: Cambridge University Press, 299-327.

Stöve, Eckehart (2002). *Natürliches Recht und Heilige Schrift. Zu einem vergessen Aspekt in Martin Luthers Hermeneutik*. Irene Dingel, Volker Leppin and Christoph Strohm, eds. *Recht und Reformation. Festschrift für Gottfried Seebas*. Gütersloh: Gütersloher Verlagshaus, 11-26.

Sträter, Udo, ed. (1999). *Melanchthonbild und Melanchthonrezeption in der Lutherischen Orthodoxie und im Pietismus. Referate des dritten Wittenberger Symposiums zur Erforschung der Lutherischen Orthodoxie*. Wittenberg: Hans Luft.

Strohm, Christoph (1996). *Ethik im frühen Calvinismus: Humanistische Einflüsse, philosophische, juristische und theologische Argumentationen sowie mentalitätsgeschichtliche Aspekte am Beispiel des Calvin-Schülers Lambertus Danaeus*. Berlin: De Gruyter.

Strohm, Christoph (2000). "Die Voraussetzungen reformatorischer Naturrechtslehre in der humanistischen Jurisprudenz." *Zeitschrift der Savigny-Stiftung für Rechtsgeschichte* Kan. Ab. 86, 398-413.

Strohm, Christoph (2000), *Zugänge zum Naturrecht bei Melanchthon*, in Frank, G. (ed.), *Der Theologe Melanchthon*, Stuttgart: Thorbecke, 339-56.

Strohm, Christoph, ed. (2002). *Martin Bucer und das Recht. Beiträge zum internationalen Symposium vom 1. bis 3 März 2001 in der Johannes a Lasco Bibliothek Emden*. Genève: Droz.

Strohm, Christoph (2008). *Calvinismus und Recht. Weltanschaulich-konfessionelle Aspekte im Werk reformierter Juristen in der Frühen Neuzeit*. Tübingen: Mohr Siebeck.

Strohm, Christoph (2016). "Religion und Recht in der Frühen Neuzeit." *Zeitschrift der Savigny-Stiftung für Rechtsgeschichte Kan. Ab.* 102, 283-316.

Strohm, Christoph, ed. (2017). *Reformation und Recht. Ein Beitrag zur Kontroverse um die Kulturwirkungen der Reformation*. Tübingen: Mohr Siebeck.

Strohm, Christoph (2017). "Die produktive Kraft konfessioneller Konkurrenz für die Rechtsentwicklung." Christoph Strohm, ed. *Reformation und Recht. Ein Beitrag zur Kontroverse um die Kulturwirkungen der Reformation*. Tübingen: Mohr Siebeck, 131-72.

Strohm, Theodor (1983). "Luthers Wirtschafts- und Sozialethik." *Leben und Werk Martin Luthers von 1526 bis 1546. Festgabe zu seinem Geburstag*. vol. 1, Göttingen: Vandenhoeck&Ruprecht, 205-23.

Strubbe, Egied I. (1970). "Jacobus Curtius Brugensis, hellenist en jurist uit de zestiende eeuw." *Anamnheie. Gedenkboek E.A. Leemans*. Brugge.

Stump, Phillip H. (2000). "The Influence of G. Ladner's The Idea of Reform." Thomas M. Izbicki and Christopher M. Bellitto, eds. *Reform and Renewal in the Middle Ages and the Renaissance: Studies in Honor of Louis Pascoe, S.J.*. Leiden: Brill.

Suda, Max J. (2006). *Die Ethik Martin Luthers*. Göttingen: Vandenhoeck & Ruprecht.

Svesson, Manfred (2008). "Phillip Melanchthon and the Reception of Aristotelian Natural Law Theory in the European Reformation." Alejandro Néstor García, Mario Šilar and José M. Torralba, eds. *Natural Law. Historical, Systematic and Juridical Approaches*. Newcastle upon Tyne: Cambridge Scholars Publishing, 109-26.

Swatos, William H., Jr. and Lutz Kaelber, eds. (2016). *The Protestant Ethic Turns 100: Essays on the Centenary of the Weber Thesis*. Abingdon, Oxon: Routledge.

Talamanca, Mario (1990). "La tipicità dei contratti romani fra 'conventio' e 'stipulatio' fino a Labeone." Francesco Milazzo, ed., *Contractus e Pactum. Tipicità e libertà negoziale nell'esperienza tardo-repubblicana. Atti del convegno di diritto romano e della presentazione della nuova riproduzione della* littera fiorentina. Napoli: ESI, 35-108.

Tamm, Ditlev (1989). "Nolo falcem in alienam messem mittere. Der Dänische Teologe Niels Hemmingsen (1513-1600) aus juristischer Sicht." Ditlev Tamm, ed. *Med lov skal land bygges og andre rethistoriske afhandliger*. Kopenhagen: Danske Bylag, 175-84.

Tanner, Norman P. (1990). *Decrees of the Ecumenical Councils*. vol. 1, Washington: Georgetown University Press.

Tawney, Richard H. (1933). *Religion and the Rise of Capitalism: A Historical Study*. London: Murray.

Teetaert, Amédée (1926). *La confession aux laiques dans l'église latine depuis le VIII*[e] *jusqu'au XIV*[e] *siècle*. Wetteren: De Meester.

Teetaert, Amédée (1928). "La doctrine pénitentielle de St. Raymond de Penyafort." *Analecta sacra Tarraconensia* 4, 121-82.

Teetaert, Amédée (1928). "La Summa de Poenitentia de Saint Raimond de Penyafort." *Ephemerides Theologicae Lovaniensis* 5, 49-72.

Teetaert, Amédée (1929). *Summa de matrimonio s. Raymundi de Penyafort*. Roma: Jus pontificium.

Tentler, Thomas N. (1977). *Sin and Confession in the Eve of the Reformation*, Princeton: Princeton University Press.

Testuzza, Maria Sole (2016). "Ius corporis, quasi ius de corpore disponendi". *Il* Tractatus de potestate in se ipsum *di Baltasar Gómez de Amescúa*. Milano: Giuffrè.

Theiner, Johann (1970). *Die Entwicklung der Moraltheologie zur eigenständigen Disziplin*. Regensburg: Pustet.

Thier, Andreas (2011). *Legal History*, Ewould Hondius and Christoph Grigoleit, eds. *Unexpected Circumstances in European Contract Law*. Cambridge: Cambridge University Press, 15-32.

Thireau, Jean-Louis (1980). *Charles du Moulin (1500-1566) Étude sur les sources, la méthode, les idées politiques et économiques d'un juriste de la Renaissance*. Genève: Droz.

Throness, Laurie (2016). *A Protestant Purgatory: Theological Origins of the Penitentiary Act, 1779*. 2nd ed. Abigdon, Oxon, New York: Routledge.

Thüringer, Walter and Mundhenk, Christine (2003). *Melanchthons Briefwechsel.* vol. 5, Stuttgart, Bad Cannstatt: frommann-holzboog.

Tierney, Briean (2001). *The Idea of Natural Rights. Studies on Natural Rights, Natural Law, and Church Law 1150-1625.* Grand Rapids MI: Eerdmans.

Toaff, Ariel (2004). "Jews, Franciscans, and the First monti di Pieta in Italy (1462-1500)." Steven J. McMichael and Susan E. Myers, eds. *Friars and Jews in the Middle Ages and Renaissance.* Leiden: Brill, 239-54.

Todescan, Franco (1983-2001). *Le radici teologiche del giusnaturalismo laico.* 3 vols., Milano: Giuffrè.

Todescan, Franco (2007). "Il problema del diritto naturale fra Seconda scolastica e giusnaturalismo laico secentesco. Una introduzione bibliografica." Fausto Arici and Franco Todescan, eds. *Iustus ordo e ordine della natura, Sacra doctrina e saperi politici fra XVI e XVIII secolo.* Padova: CEDAM, 1-61.

Todescan, Franco (2013). "Jus gentium medium est intra jus naturale et jus civile: la "double face" du droit des gens dans la scolastique espagnole du 16ème siècle." Pierre Maria Dupuy et al., eds. *The Roots of International Law / Les fondements du droit international. Liber Amicorum Peter Haggenmacher.* Leiden, Boston: Brill, 121-80.

Todescan, Franco (1973). *Lex, natura, beatitudo, Il problema della legge nella scolastica Spagnola del sec. XVI.* Padova: CEDAM.

Todeschini, Giacomo (2002). *I mercanti e il tempio, la società cristiana e il circolo virtuoso della ricchezza fra Medioevo ed età moderna.* Bologna: Il Mulino.

Todeschini, Giacomo (2004). *Ricchezza francescana. Dalla povertà volontaria alla società di mercato.* Bologna: Il Mulino.

Todeschini, Giacomo (2005). "La riflessione etica sulle attività economiche." Roberto Greci et al., eds. *Economie urbane ed etica economica nell'Italia medievale.* Roma-Bari:Laterza, 151-228.

Toivanen, Juhana (2016). "Voluntarist Anthropology in Peter of John Olivi's De contractibus." *Franciscan Studies* 74, 41-65.

Tortajada, Ramon (1993). "La renaissance de la scolastique, la Réforme et les théories du droit naturel." Alain Béraud and Gilbert Faccarello, eds. *Nouvelle histoire de la pensée économique Vol.1. Des scolastiques aux classiques.* Paris: La Découverte, 71-91.

Trentman, Jonh A. (1982). "Scholasticism in the Seventeenth Century." Norman Kretzmann, Anthony Kenny et al., eds. *The Cambridge History of Later Medieval Philosophy. From the Rediscovery of Aristotle to the Disintegration of Scholasticism 1100-1600.* Cambridge: Cambridge University Press, 818-37.

Trusen, Winfried (1971). "Forum internum und gelehrtes Recht im Spätmittelalter. Summae confessorum und Traktate als Wegbereiter der Rezeption." *Zeitschrift der Savigny-Stiftung für Rechtsgeschichte Kan. Ab.* 57, 83-126.

Trusen, Winfried (1990). “Zur bedeutung des geistlichen Forum internum und externum für die spätmittelalterliche Gesellschaft.” *Zeitschrift der Savigny-Stiftung für Rechtsgeschichte Kan. Ab.* 76, 254-85.

Trusen, Winfried (1997). *Gelehrtes Recht im Mittelalter und in der frühen Neuzeit.* Goldbach: Keip.

Tuck, Richard (1995). *Natural Rights Theories. Their Origin and Development.* Cambridge: Cambridge University Press.

Tully, James (1988). “Governing conduct.” Edmund Leites, ed. *Conscience and Casuistry in Early Modern Europe.* Cambridge: Cambridge University Press, 12-71.

Turner, Cuthbert H. (1899). *Ecclesiae occidentalis monumenta iuris antiquissima.* vol. 1, Oxford: Clarendon.

Turrini, Miriam (1991). *La coscienza e le leggi. Morale e diritto nei testi per la confessione della prima Età moderna.* Bologna: Il Mulino.

Tutino, Stefania (2017). *Uncertainty in Post-Reformation Catholicism: A History of Probabilism.* Oxford: Oxford University Press.

Uhl, Ernst (1932). *Die Sozialethik Johann Gerhards.* München: Kaiser.

Vaage, Leif Eric and Wimbush, Vincent L., eds. (1999). *Asceticism and the New Testament.* London and New York: Routledge.

Van Houdt, Toon (1995). “Money, Time and Labour. Leonard Lessius and the Ethics of Lending and Interest Taking.” *Ethical Perspectives,* 2.1, 11-27.

Van Houdt, Toon (2006). “Implicit intention and the conceptual shift from interesse to interest. An underestimated chapter from the history of scholastic economic thought.” *Lias,* 33.1, 37-58.

Van Roey, Ernest (1902). “Le contractus germanicus ou les controverses sur le 5% au XVI[e] siecle en Allemagne.” *Revue d'Histoire Ecclesiastique,* 39, 901-46.

Varkemaa, Jussi (2005). “Justification through Being: Conrad Summenhart on Natural Rights” Jill Kraye and Risto Saarinen, eds. *Moral Philosophy on the Threshold of Modernity.* Dordrecht: Springer, 181-93.

Varkemaa, Jussi (2012). *Conrad Summenhart's Theory of Individual Rights.* Leiden-Boston: Brill.

Veraja, Fabiano (1960). *Le origini della controversia teologica sul contratto di censo nel XIII secolo.* Roma: Edizioni di Storia e Letteratura.

Vercruysse, Jos (1983). “Schlüsselgewalt und Beichte bei Luther.” Helmar Junghans, ed. *Leben und Werk Martin Luthers von 1526 bis 1546: Festgabe zu seinem 500. Geburtstag.* Göttingen: Vandenhoeck & Ruprecht, 153-69.

Vereecke, Louis (1979-80). *Storia della teologia morale moderna.* vol. 3. Roma: Accademia Alfonsiana, Istituto superiore di teologia morale, Pontificia università lateranense.

Vereecke, Louis (1986). *De Guillaume D'Ockham à Saint Alphonse de Liguori: études d'histoire de la théologie morale moderne 1300-1787.* Roma: Collegium S. Alfonsi de Urbe.

Vidu, Adonis (2014). *Atonement, Law, and Justice: The Cross in Historical and Cultural Contexts*, Grand Rapids: Baker Academic, 2014.

Viladrich, Pedro-Juan (1998). *El consentimiento matrimonial*. Pamplona: Eunsa.

Villey, Michel (1973). "La promotion de la loi et du droit subjectif dans la Seconde Scolastique." Paolo Grossi, ed. *La seconda scolastica nella formazione del diritto privato moderno*. Milano: Giuffrè, 53-72.

Villey, Michel (2003 [1968]). *La formation de la pensee juridique moderne*. Paris: PUF.

Vismara, Paola (2004). *Oltre l'usura: la Chiesa moderna e il prestito a interesse*, Soveria Mannelli: Rubbettino.

Vogel, Cyrille (1978). *Typologie des sources du moyen âge occidental / Les "Libri paenitentiales"*. Turnhout: Brepols.

Vogel, Cyrille (2007). *Le pécheur et la penitence au moyen-age*. Paris: Cerf.

Voigt-Goy, Christopher (2014). *Potestates und ministerium publicum. Eine Studie zur Amtstheologie im Mittelalter und bei Martin Luther*. Tübingen: Mohr Siebeck.

Volante, Raffaele (2001). *Il sistema contrattuale del diritto comune classico*. Milano: Giuffrè.

Waelkens, Laurent (2005). ""Libertas ecclesiae" herbekeken." Jaak Ockeley et al., eds. *Recht in Geschiedenis. Een bundel bijdragen over rechtsgeschiedenis van de Middeleeuwen tot de hedendaagse tijd aangeboden aan Prof. dr. Fernand Vanhemelryck*. Leuven: Davidsfond, 497-504.

Waelkens, Laurent (2015). *Amne Adverso. Roman Legal Heritage in European Culture*. Leuven: Leuven University Press.

Waelkens, Laurent (2017). "The forum internum and its External Features in the legal history of Early Modern Times." Germann, Michael and Decock, Wim, eds. *Das Gewissen in den Rechtslehren der protestantischen und katholischen Reformationen. Conscience in the Legal Teachings of the Protestant and Catholic Reformations*. Leipzig: Evangelische Verlagsanstalt, 17-32.

Walker, Daniel P. (1964). *The Decline of Hell. Seventeenth-Century Discussions of Eternal Torment*. London: Routledge.

Wallach, Luitpold (1959). *Alcuin and Charlemagne: Studies in Carolingian History and Literature*. Ithaca, NY: Cornell University Press.

Wallmann, Johannes (1961). *Der Theologiebegriff bei Johann Gerhard und Georg Calixt*. Tübingen: Mohr Siebeck.

Wallmann, Johannes (1977). "Zwischen Reformation und Humanismus. Eigenart und Wirkungen Helmstedter Theologie unter besonderer Berücksichtigung Georg Calixts." *Zeitschrift für Theologie und Kirche* 74, 348-70.

Wallmann, Johannes (1995). "Die Eigenart der Strassburger lutherischen Orthodoxie im 17. Jahrhundert." Johannes Wallmann, ed. *Theologie und Frömmigkeit im Zeitalter des Barock*. Tübingen: Mohr Siebeck, 87-123.

Wasserschleben, Hermann F.W. (1958 [1851]). *Die Bussordnungen der abendlaendischen Kirche*. Graz: Akademische Druck- U. Verlagsanstalt.

Watkins, Oscar D. (1961). *A History of Penance*, vol. 1-2, New York: Burt Franklin.

Weber, Gottfried (1962). *Grundlagen und Normen politischer Ethik bei Melanchthon*. München: Kaiser.

Wei, John C. (2016). *Gratian the Theologian*. Washington D.C.: The Catholic University of America Press.

Weingart, Richard E. (1970). *The Logic of Divine Love: A Critical Analysis of the Soteriology of Peter Abelard*. Oxford: Clarendon Press.

Weinzierl, Karl (1936). *Die Restitutionslehre der Frühscholastik*. München: Heuber.

Weinzierl, Karl (1939). *Die Restitutionslehre der Hochscholastik bis zum hl. Thomas von Aquin*. München: Heuber.

Wijffels, Alain (2014). "Law and Religion in Early-Modern Europe: Some Tentative Conclusions." Wim Decock, Jordan J. Ballor, Michael Germann and Laurent Waelkens, eds. *Law and Religion. The Legal Teachings of the Protestant and Catholic Reformations*. Göttingen: Vandenhoeck & Ruprecht, 266-75.

Weismann, Christoph (1990). *Die Katechismen des Johannes Brenz*, 1, *Die Entstehung-, Text- und Wirkungsgeschichte*. Berlin, New York: De Gruyter.

Wengert, Timothy J. (1998). *Human Freedom, Christian Righteousness: Philip Melanchthon's Exegetical Dispute with Erasmus of Rotterdam*. New York: Oxford University Press.

Wesenberg, Gerhard and Wesener, Gunter (1969). *Neuere deutsche Privatrechtsgeschichte im Rahmen der europäischen Rechtsentwicklung*. Schauenburg: Lahr.

Westermayer, Anton (1843). *Die Reformation überhaupt und ihre Einführung in Regensburg insbesondere*. Regensburg: Manz, 1843.

Westphal, Siegrid (2017). "Gerhards Tätigkeit als Superintendent und seine Visitationspraxis." Markus Friedrich, Sascha Salatowsky and Luise Schorn-Schütte, eds. *Konfession, Politik und Gelehrsamkeit. Der Jenear Theologe Johann Gerhard (1582-1637) im Kontext seiner Zeit*, Stuttgart: Franz Steiner, 51-68.

Wette, Wilhelm, M. Leberecht de (1833). *Lehrbuch der christlichen Sittenlehre und der Geschichte derselben*, Berlin: Reimer.

Wetzel, James, ed. (2012). *Augustine's City of God. A critical guide*. Cambridge: Cambridge University Press.

Whitman, James Q. (2008). *The Origins of Reasonable Doubt: Theological Roots of the Criminal Trial*. New Haven and London: Yale University Press.

Wiegand, Wolfgang (1974). *Plus petitio*. Berlin: Schweitzer.

Wiegand, Wolfgang (1987). "Die privatrechtlichen Rechtsquellen des usus modernus". Dieter Simon, ed. *Akten des 26. Deutschen Rechtshistorikertages*, Frankfurt: V. Klostermann, 237-52.

Wieland, Josef (1991). "»Wucher muß sein, aber wehe den Wucherern«. Einige Überlegungen zu Martin Luthers Konzeption des Ökonomischen." *Zeitschrift für Evangelische Ethik* 35, 268-84.

Wieland, Josef (2014). "Luthers Ökonomiekritik und ihre Ausläufer in der Wirtschaftsethik der Gegenwart." *Paradoxie der Freiheit. Zur Relevanz von Luthers ökonomischer Kritik und Calvins Wirtschaftsmoral für das Verhältnis von Kirche, Staat und Wirtschaft*, epd-Dokumentation 21/2014, 4-11.

Wiesenmüller, Herbert (1968). *Die Wirtschaftsethik Thomas von Aquins, Luthers und Calvins und das deutsche Unternehmertum des Vor- und Frühkapitalismus*. diss, Erlagen, 1968.

Williams, George H. (1962). *The Radical Reformation*. Philadelphia: The Westminster Press.

Williams, Ronald J. and Beckman, John C. (2007). *Williams' Hebrew Syntax*. 3rd Edition, Toronto, Buffalo and London: University of Toronto Press.

Willoweit, Dietmar (1974). "*Dominium* und *Proprietas*: Zur Entwicklung des Eigentumsbegriffs in der mittelalterlichen und neuzeitlichen Rechtswissentschaft." *Historisches Jahrbuch* 94, 131-56.

Wilson, Arthur J. and Kim, Geetae (2015). "Put-call parity, the triple contract and approaches to usury in medieval contracting." *Financial History Review* 22 (2), 205-33.

Wimbush, Vincent L. and Valantasis, Richard, eds. (1995). *Asceticism*. New York: Oxford University Press.

Winroth, Anders (2000). *The Making of Gratian's Decretum*. Cambridge: Cambridge University Press.

Witchel, Lawrence (2009). *Casuistry in 17th Century England, English Protestant Casuistry, Conscience and Oath-Taking*. Saarbrücken: VDM Verlag Dr. Müller.

Witte, John Jr. (2000). "Canon Law in Lutheran Germany: A Surprising Case of Legal Transplantation." Michael Hoeflich, ed. *Lex et Romanitas: Essays for Alan Watson*. Berkeley: Robbins Collection, School of Law, 181-224.

Witte, John Jr. (2002). *Law and Protestantism: The Legal Teachings of the Lutheran Reformation*. Cambridge: Cambridge University Press.

Witte, John Jr. (2014). "'The Law Written on the Heart': Natural Law and Equity in Early Lutheran Thought." Wim Decock, Jordan J. Ballor, Michael Germann, and Laurent Waelkens, eds *Law and Religion. The Legal Teachings of the Protestant and Catholic Reformations*, Göttingen: Vandenhoeck & Ruprecht, 231-65.

Witte, John Jr. (2016). "From Gospel to Law: The Lutheran Reformation and its Impact on Legal Culture." Thomas A. Howard, Mark A. Noll, eds. *Protestantism After 500 Years*. Oxford: Oxford University Press, 52-74.

Wittreck, Fabian (2002). *Geld als Instrument der Gerechtigkeit. Die Geldrechtslehre des Hl. Thomas von Aquin in ihrem interkulturellen Kontext*. Paderborn, München, Wien, Zürich: Ferdinand Schöningh.

Wolter, Udo (1975). *Ius canonicum in iure civili.* Bohlau: Koln, 1975.

Wood, Diana (2002). *Medieval Economic Thought.* Cambridge: Cambridge University Press.

Wood, Thomas (1952). *English Casuistical Divinity During the Seventeenth Century, with Special Reference to Jeremy Taylor.* London: SPCK.

Wright, William J. (1988). *Capitalism the State, and the Lutheran Reformation: Sixteenth-Century Hesse,* Athens: Ohio University Press.

Wright, William J. (1996). "The Nature of Early Capitalism." Bob Scribner, ed. *Germany. A New Social and Economic History,* vol. I, 1450-1630, London: Arnold, 181-208.

Wright, William J. (2004). "*Mandatum Dei* and *lex naturae* in Luther's Lectures on Genesis" *Lutherjahrbuch* 71, 233 ff.

Wright, William J. (2010). *Martin Luther's Understanding of God's Two Kingdoms: A Response to Skepticism.* Grand Rapids, Mi.: Baker Academic.

Wurm, Johann P. (1997). *Johannes Eck und der oberdeutsche Zinsstreit 1513-1515.* München: Aschendorff.

Wuttke, Adolf (1861). *Handbuch der christlichen Sittenlehre.* vol. 1, Berlin: Fb&c Limited.

Wykes, Michael (2003). "Devaluing the Scholastics: Calvin's Ethics of Usury." *Calvin Theological Journal* 38, 27-51.

Young, Frances (2004). "The Interpretation of Scripture" G.R. Evans, ed. *The First Christian Theologians.* Oxford: Blackwell, 24-38.

Zendri, Christian (2005). "L'usura nella dottrina dei giuristi umanisti: Martin de Azpilcueta (1492-1586)." Diego Quaglioni, Giacomo Todeschini, Gian Maria Varanini, eds. *Credito e usura fra teologia, diritto e amministrazione. Linguaggi a confronto (sec. XII-XVI).* Convegno internazionale a Trento, 3-5 settembre 2001. Roma: Ecole Française de Rome, 265-90.

Ziebritzki, Henning (2000). "Tugend und Affekt: Ansatz, Aufriß und Problematik von Melanchthons Tugendethik, dargestellt anhand der "Ethicae doctrinae elementa" von 1550." Günter Frank, ed. *Der Theologe Melanchthon.* Stuttgart: Thorbecke, 357-73.

Ziegler, Josef G. (1956). *Die Ehelehre der Poenitentialsummen von 1200-1350.* Regensburg: Pustet.

Zimmermann, Reinhard (1990). *The Law of Obligations: Roman Foundations of the Civilian Tradition.* Oxford: Oxford University Press, 1990.

Zschoch, Hellmut (1995). *Reformatorische Existenz und konfessionelle Identität. Urbanus Rhegius als evangelischer Theologe in den Jahren 1520 bis 1530.* Tübingen: Mohr Siebeck.

Zwierlein, Cornel A. (2017). "'Konfessionalisierung' europäisch, global als epistemischer Prozess. Zu den Folgen der Reformation und zur Methodendiskussion." Christoph Strohm, ed. *Reformation und Recht. Ein Beitrag zur Kontroverse um die Kulturwirkungen der Reformation.* Tübingen: Mohr Siebeck, 1-52.